Mano del Desierto (Hand in the Desert) by Sculptor Mario Irarrázabal

MOON HANDBOOKS®
CHILE

FIRST EDITION

WAYNE BERNHARDSON

Mariana.

M_Raymond13@hotmail.com (chilian Guide singer).

AVALON
TRAVEL

Moon Handbooks: Chile
First Edition

Wayne Bernhardson

Published by
Avalon Travel Publishing
1400 65th St., Suite 250
Emeryville, CA 94608, USA

Text © 2002 by Wayne Bernhardson.
Illustrations and maps © 2002
by Avalon Travel Publishing, Inc.
All rights reserved.
Photos and some illustrations are used by permission
and are the property of their original copyright owners.

ISBN: 1-56691-405-1
ISSN: 1540-3394

Editors: Karen Gaynor Bleske, Rebecca K. Browning
Series Manager: Erin Van Rheenen
Graphics Coordinators: Susan Mira Snyder, Erika Howsare
Production Coordinator: Alvaro Villanueva
Layout: Carey Wilson
Cover Designer: Kari Gim
Interior Designers: Amber Pirker, Alvaro Villanueva, Kelly Pendragon
Map Editors: Naomi Adler Dancis, Olivia Solís
Cartographers: Kat Kalamaras, Mike Morgenfeld
Proofreader: Erika Howsare
Indexer: Rachel Kuhn

Front cover photo: © Wayne Bernhardson

Distributed by Publishers Group West

Printed in China through Colorcraft Ltd., Hong Kong

Please send all comments, corrections,
additions, amendments, and critiques to:

Moon Handbooks: Chile
AVALON TRAVEL PUBLISHING
1400 65th St., Suite 250
Emeryville, CA 94608, USA
email: atpfeedback@avalonpub.com
www.moon.com

Printing History
1st edition—November 2002
5 4 3 2 1

Although every effort was made to ensure that the information was correct at the time of going to press, the author and publisher do not assume and hereby disclaim any liability to any party for any loss or damage caused by errors, omissions, or any potential travel disruption due to labor or financial difficulty, whether such errors or omissions result from negligence, accident, or any other cause.

ABOUT THE AUTHOR
Wayne Bernhardson

In the course of researching *Moon Handbooks: Chile,* Wayne Bernhardson totaled two 4WD vehicles on the Carretera Austral, but still managed to walk away from the wreckage and finish the book on deadline. He prefers to attribute responsibility to a blowout and a blind curve. Besides, given the 150,000 or so miles he has accumulated on the highways and backroads of Chile, Argentina, Uruguay, and Paraguay over the past ten-plus years, he's unconcerned about getting behind the wheel again—except in Buenos Aires, where he prefers the sidewalk and the subway.

After writing best-selling guidebooks to Chile, Argentina, Buenos Aires, Santiago de Chile, and Baja California, Wayne defected from Lonely Planet to write for Moon Handbooks. He first traveled to Chile in 1979, during the Pinochet dictatorship, wrote his M.A. thesis on llama and alpaca herding in the Norte Grande's Parque Nacional Lauca, and has returned repeatedly to broaden and deepen his knowledge and appreciation of the country.

Wayne overqualified himself for guidebook writing by earning a Ph.D. in Geography at the University of California Berkeley, before forsaking academia for a life on the road that many university faculty envy. He is also the author of *Moon Handbooks: Guatemala.*

Wayne has written for publications including *Trips, National Geographic Traveler,* the *San Francisco Chronicle,* and the American Geographical Society's *Focus,* and often gives slide lectures on destinations he covers in his books. He lives in Oakland, California, with his wife María Laura Massolo, his daughter Clio Bernhardson-Massolo, their Alaskan malamute, Gardel (named after the iconic Argentine tango singer), and their recently adopted Akita, Sandro (named after a contemporary Argentine pop singer also known as "El Maestro"). Wayne can be reached directly by email at knoblauch@earthlink.net or through www.guidebookwriters.com.

To the memory of
Bernard Nietschmann

Contents

Maps

HANDBOOK DIVISIONS

PERU

BOLIVIA

PACIFIC OCEAN

Iquique

NORTE GRANDE

Antofagasta

THE CHILEAN PACIFIC ISLANDS

Hanga Roa

Rapa Nui (Easter Island)

Archipiélago Juan Fernández

Copiapó

NORTE CHICO

La Serena

Valparaíso

Santiago

Rancagua

SANTIAGO AND VICINITY

THE CHILEAN HEARTLAND

Talca

Concepción

Temuco

SUR CHICO

ARGENTINA

Puerto Montt

Coyhaique

PATAGONIA AND TIERRA DEL FUEGO

ATLANTIC OCEAN

Punta Arenas

© AVALON TRAVEL PUBLISHING, INC.

MAP SYMBOLS

≡≡≡ Divided Highway	◉ Region Capital	⚐ Park/Monument
═══ Primary Road	○ City/Town	▲ Mountain
─── Secondary Road	★ Point of Interest	✕✕ Airport
------- Unpaved Road		✲ Ski Park
.... Ferry	• Accommodation	✦ Unique Natural Feature
≡≡≡ Pedestrian Street	▼ Restaurant/Bar	▬ Building
⦀⦀⦀⦀ Stairs	▪ Other Location	⊬⊬ Ascensor

Abbreviations and Acronyms

a/c—air conditioning
cm—centimeters
Codeff—Consejo de Defensa de la Flora y Fauna (Council for the Defense of Flora and Fauna
Conaf—Corporación Nacional Forestal (National Forestry Corporation)
Conama—Comisión Nacional del Medio Ambiente (National Environmental Commission)
d—double
IVA—Impuesto de Valor Agregado
km—kilometers
mm—millimeters
pp—per person
s—single
t—triple
tel.—telephone

Keeping Current

Since this book went to press, hotels have opened and closed, restaurants have changed hands, and roads have been repaired or fallen into disrepair. Prices also rise and fall (but mostly rise); therefore, all prices in this book should be regarded as approximations and are not guaranteed by the publisher or the author.

If you have any noteworthy experiences (good or bad) with establishments listed in this book, please pass them on. If something is out of place on a map, tell us. If the best restaurant in town is not included, we'd like to know. All contributions will be deeply appreciated. Please address your letters to:

Wayne Bernhardson
Moon Handbooks: Chile
Avalon Travel Publishing
1400 65th St., Suite 250
Emeryville, CA 94608, USA
email: atpfeedback@avalonpub.com

Aerocontinente

In June of 2002, in a continuing tug-of-war with the Peruvian-owned budget carrier Aerocontinente, the Chilean government suspended the airline's authorization to operate within the country. Aerocontinente declared bankruptcy and closed all operations in Chile as this book went to print.

Introduction

In the memorable phrase of Chilean author Benjamín Subercaseaux, Chile embodies *una loca geografía*, an expression that literally translates as "a crazy geography" but more correctly signifies "a geographical extravaganza." Its vast northern deserts, Mediterranean heartland, deep mountain lakes and soaring volcanoes, bountiful temperate rain forests, and sub-Antarctic Patagonian wildlands, not to mention its seemingly endless shoreline and remote Pacific islands, all occur within a land area only a little larger than the state of Texas.

Chile's awesome landscapes include three UNESCO World Biosphere Reserves, plus two World Heritage Sites and another that's a strong candidate to become one. Dotted with archaeological sites, the northern deserts and their uplands were outliers of the central Andean civilizations. Central Chile is legendary wine country, with a smattering of colonial monuments despite the effects of earthquakes and modernization, and also home to one of South America's liveliest and most progressive capital cities. The southern lake district often reminds visitors of North America's Pacific Northwest or parts of the European Alps, while the icefields of Patagonia are some of the world's wildest remaining country. Easter Island (Rapa Nui), in the distant western Pacific, is an iconic destination for its megalithic monuments.

the Andean crest, east of Santiago

© WAYNE BERNHARDSON

Yet, for many years, relatively few braved travel to a country that suffered one of the most brutal and arbitrary military dictatorships on a continent that was infamous for them. In the decade-plus since the return to constitutional government, though, travel has steadily increased to what might be the safest single country in the hemisphere—whether Western or Southern.

About a million of Chile's roughly 15 million citizens are Mapuche Indians, comprising one of South America's most tenacious and outspoken indigenous populations—all the more so since the return to democracy. Most of the rest are mestizos, descendants of Spaniards and the indigenous population, but Chile also has definite European characteristics thanks to a steady, if not large, influx of immigrants and a tendency to look toward the Old World for trends in culture and the arts. Despite recent difficulties, it has South America's most stable economy, with uninterrupted growth for more than a decade.

By North American or European standards, Chile remains an affordable destination. About eight hours by jet from Miami, 10 hours from New York, or 14 hours from Los Angeles, Chile is suitable for short-term visitors focused on special interests in specific regions, but large and diverse enough that travelers with more time will find plenty to see and do along the entire length of the country. Among the many possibilities are hiking, climbing, mountain biking, whitewater rafting and kayaking, and surfing.

© AVALON TRAVEL PUBLISHING, INC.

The fact that the southern spring, summer, and fall months correspond to some of the Northern Hemisphere's coldest months, where most foreign travelers live, adds to Chile's appeal. Still, it remains a year-round destination where winter skiing and desert exploration are possible. Since Chile's in the same standard time zone as New York and Washington—though daylight saving time sometimes throws a small spanner in the works—even jet lag is not an issue.

INTRODUCTION

The Land

Chile's diverse geography, stretching from the desert tropics to the sub-Antarctic and rising from sea level to alpine and altiplano areas well above 4,000 meters, contains nearly every kind of South American environment *except* tropical rain forest.

GEOGRAPHY

With an area of about 800,000 square km, slightly larger than Texas and roughly twice the size of California, Chile is one of South America's smallest countries—only Ecuador, Uruguay, and Paraguay are smaller. This statistic is misleading, though, as it stretches more than 4,300 km from the tropical latitudes of the tripartite border with Peru and Bolivia, at about 17°30' S, to almost exactly 56° S at the famous Cabo de Hornos (Cape Horn), the traditional point of demarcation between the Atlantic and Pacific Oceans.

On the other hand, Chile is a narrow country, never wider than about 285 km between the Pacific and the Andean crest. The Andes themselves run the length of the country; from Santiago north, elevations often exceed 4,000 meters and the highest summits reach well above 6,000; to the south, the cordillera is generally lower but, if anything, even more spectacular.

One of the most seismically active countries in the world, Chile lies at the juncture of the Nazca and South American plates. Positioned along the so-called Pacific "ring of fire," it also has numerous active volcanoes—some of them *very* active—and many active earthquake faults. In 1906, only a few months after earthquake and fire rocked and scorched San Francisco, its Chilean counterpart Valparaíso suffered a similar disaster. The 1960 earthquake centered near the southern city of Valdivia brought a tsunami that devastated coastal areas from Concepción to Chiloé, and it left many thousands homeless. Seismic safety has improved, but earthquakes are not going to disappear.

Mountains

Chile's most imposing physiographic feature is the longitudinal Andean range that extends from its northern borders with Peru and Bolivia to the southern region of Patagonia, where it gradually disappears beneath the Pacific Ocean. The highest point is the 6,885-meter summit of Ojos del Salado, east of the city of Copiapó, but much of the northern Andes and altiplano (high steppe) exceeds 4,000 meters. Throughout most of the country, there is a lower coastal range to the west, but even this reaches upward of 2,000 meters in some areas.

Rivers

From the Andes, a multitude of transverse rivers flow generally west toward the Pacific; in the desert north, they rarely reach the sea, but even in these arid zones they often provide ample irrigation water. From Santiago south, several of them carry enough flow for good to world-class white-water rafting and kayaking, and some of them still irrigate the fields of the Mediterranean Valle Central.

© WAYNE BERNHARDSON

Upper Cajón del Maipo

INTRODUCTION

REGIONS OF CHILE

Physiographically, Chile divides into several more or less discrete vernacular regions, which coincide fairly conveniently with the boundaries of its division into 13 separate administrative regions; all of the latter are ordinally numbered, from north to south, except for the Región Metropolitana (Metropolitan Region) of Santiago.

Norte Grande

So arid that not a single plant grows on many thousands of square kilometers of its surface, the Atacama desert is the outstanding feature of the Norte Grande (Great North), which consists of Region I (Tarapacá) and Region II (Antofagasta). From the Peruvian border south almost to Chañaral, only the Río Loa consistently reaches the Pacific, sustained by rainfall from the Andean precordillera (foothills) and altiplano (high steppe), and meltwater from the highest summits.

While other rivers reach the sea only intermittently, diversions from high-altitude lakes and rivers, along with fossil water from Pleistocene aquifers, have permitted irrigated agriculture and the growth of coastal cities such as Arica, Iquique, and Antofagasta. In the precordillera, Aymara farmers grow potatoes and other native crops; in the altiplano they herd llamas and alpacas.

Ever since colonial times, mining has been the backbone of the economy, though the commodities have changed from gold and silver to nitrates and nowadays copper. While rainfall is almost unheard of on the coast, the cool Peru or Humboldt Current that flows northward moderates the desert temperature to a comfortable level, often obscuring the coastal headlands in fog known as *camanchaca* or *garúa*. Thanks to the upwelling of nutrients from the depths of the Pacific, this is also one of the world's most productive fishing grounds.

Norte Chico

A transitional zone between the barren Norte Grande and the Mediterranean-like heartland, the Norte Chico (Lesser North) consists of Region III (Atacama) and Region IV (Coquimbo). Rainfall is intermittent, increasing from north to south and west to east, but sufficient to support desert scrub, scattered forest cover, and sporadic but spectacular explosions of wildflowers. Some transverse river valleys support irrigated vineyards for *pisco*, Chile's traditional grape brandy; historically, mining is a common but relatively small-scale activity.

The Chilean Heartland

Also known as Middle Chile, the heartland includes the capital city of Santiago, its suburbs and agricultural hinterland, and the central Pacific coast with its ports of Valparaíso, San Antonio, and Talcahuano. Politically, in addition to Santiago's Región Metropolitana, it includes Region V (Valparaíso), Region VI (O'Higgins), Region VII (Maule), and Region VIII (Biobío).

The country's most densely populated region, it is also the most productive in terms of agriculture and industry. More than a third of the population lives in Gran Santiago (Greater Santiago) and almost three-quarters in the entire heartland. The immensely fertile Valle Central, blessed with a mild Mediterranean climate and long growing season, supplies fresh produce for the entire country while still managing to export off-season fruits and quality wines to North America, Europe, Japan, and elsewhere. Nearly all the rain falls in the winter, between May and August, but snowmelt from the Andes allows irrigation.

Minerals from the central Andes, most notably copper, are a major part of the regional economy; much of the cordillera, though, is a grossly undervisited and underappreciated recreational area, and not just during the ski season. Most manufacturing and commerce takes place in Santiago and, to a lesser degree, in the southerly city of Concepción.

Sur Chico

Beyond the Río Biobío, the Sur Chico (Little South) consists of Region IX (La Araucanía) and Region X (Los Lagos). For more than three centuries, this was a zone of conflict where Araucanian (Mapuche) Indians kept both Spanish and Chilean forces and settlers off guard, before finally bowing to Chilean sovereignty in the late 19th century. While marginalized economically, the Mapuche play an increasingly visible role in national politics through their persistent land claims.

Densely forested—though plantations of imported pines and eucalyptus have replaced native *Araucarias* and southern beeches in many areas—the Sur Chico is home to numerous national parks. Its climate is marine west coast, like that of the U.S. Pacific Northwest and British Columbia, with mild temperatures but rainfall spread evenly throughout the year; at higher elevations, through, the winter snowpack can be substantial.

Most of the region's population is urban, but the rural economy supports everything from peasant subsistence plots to extensive cultivation of wheat and grazing of dairy cattle in what, one could argue, is Chile's milk bucket. Traditionally, its southern lake district is the country's conventional holiday playground, with its lakes, rivers, and forests, but recreation-oriented travel, including hiking, climbing, and rafting and kayaking, has grown rapidly over the past decade. The region includes the stormy archipelago of Chiloé, which retains a distinct identity as the cradle of Chilean folklore.

Patagonia and Tierra del Fuego

Chilean Patagonia, south of Chiloé and west of the Andes, is part of an enormous, thinly populated region more often identified with Argentina. The Chilean sector consists of Region XI (Aisén) and Region XII (Magallanes); the latter includes Chile's part of the Tierra del Fuego archipelago and also the country's internationally unrecognized Antarctic claim. Comprising about 30 percent of the national territory (not counting Antarctica), it holds only about 2 percent of the population—most of that concentrated in only two cities, Coyhaique (Aisén) and Punta Arenas (Magallanes).

While Argentine Patagonia is mostly desert steppe, Chilean Patagonia consists of jagged mountains and islands set among inland seas that bear the brunt of Pacific storms; copious quantities of rain and snow feed surging rivers and the sprawling glaciers of the Campo de Hielo Sur, the southern continental ice field. In much of the region, nearly pristine woodlands still cover the mountainsides, though some areas have seen substantial deforestation.

Across the Strait of Magellan from Punta Arenas, Chile and Argentina share the sub-Antarctic Isla Grande de Tierra del Fuego; across the Beagle Channel, Puerto Williams is the last major settlement north of Antarctica. The region's biggest draw, though, is the granitic spires of Parque Nacional Torres del Paine.

The Chilean Pacific Islands

In the vastness of the Pacific, Chile possesses several small islands, but the only two inhabited are the Juan Fernández archipelago, 670 kilometers west of Valparaíso, and Polynesian Easter Island or Rapa Nui, 3,700 kilometers west of the city of Copiapó. Both are volcanic; only Rapa Nui was occupied before the arrival of Europeans. Politically, both belong to Region V (Valparaíso), but they differ so much from the rest of the region as to merit a separate chapter in this book.

The largest and most important rivers are the Biobío, whose lower stretches are navigable but whose upper basin, once a magnet for whitewater daredevils, now lies mostly submerged beneath hydroelectric reservoirs; the Futaleufú, still providing recreational thrills but also threatened with major dam projects; and the remote Baker, which carries the largest flow of any Chilean river.

Lakes

Chile is famous for its southern lake district, where Pleistocene glaciers have left a legacy of indigo bodies of water. Even in the desert north, however, there are surprises such as Parque Nacional Lauca's Lago Chungará, which is home to a wealth of bird life including flamingos and giant coots. The remote Aisén region has countless large lakes barely touched by fishermen—not to mention its inland seas.

CLIMATE

Because Chile stretches from the desert tropics, where solar intensity and length of day vary little over the year, to far southern latitudes where blustery maritime conditions are the rule and seasonal variations can be dramatic, it's difficult to generalize about climate. Moreover, altitude plays a major role in all regions of the country.

As a rule, the Norte Grande is rainless but, due to cool Pacific currents and coastal fogs, it rarely suffers oppressive heat. Rainfall increases from west to east, where the precordillera and altiplano experience a summer rainy season (December to March or April), paradoxically known as the *invierno altiplánico* (altiplano winter) or *invierno boliviano* (Bolivian winter, for the direction from which the storms come). Brief, violent afternoon thundershowers are common at this time of year, often making secondary roads impassable.

While arid, the Norte Chico experiences a brief winter rainy season that, after rare downpours, brings an explosion of vivid wildflowers to the desert floor. Its arid altiplano gets brutally cold in winter.

The Chilean heartland has a pronounced Mediterranean climate, with wet winters and dry summers; the rainy season runs roughly from May to October, the dry season from November to April. The city of Los Ángeles, about 500 km south of Santiago, marks the beginning of the transition to a marine west coast climate with cool temperatures and evenly distributed rainfall throughout the year.

Its receding glaciers particularly sensitive to warming, Chilean Patagonia is a living laboratory for climate change studies. While it's the wettest and coolest part of the country, its inclemency is often overstated—despite its geographical position at the southern tip of the continent, it is not Antarctica. Eastern parts of both Aisén and Magallanes are even arid steppe, with low rainfall but frequent high winds, especially in summer.

Flora and Fauna

With latitudinal limits comparable to those between Havana and Hudson's Bay, and elevations ranging from oceanic to alpine, one would expect Chile to possess a diversity of flora and fauna. While this is true to a degree, it's also a little misleading as, for example, tropical northern Chile is a desert rather than rainforest, and the southern rainforests contain large stands of single species. Still, in its biogeographical isolation west of the high Andes and south of the arid Atacama desert, it does boast flora and fauna that will be novel to many foreign visitors, especially those from the Northern Hemisphere.

CONSERVATION ORGANIZATIONS

Chile's primary government environmental organization, in charge of national parks and other protected areas, is the Corporación Nacional Forestal (Conaf), which provides information and also sells maps, books, and pamphlets at its main offices, Avenida Bulnes 291, Santiago, tel. 2/3900282, 2/3900125, website: www.conaf.cl. It also has offices in every regional capital and

some other cities, and visitor centers and/or ranger stations at nearly all its units.

In the decade-plus since the return to democracy, nonprofit environmental advocacy organizations have proliferated—so much so that it's possible to suggest that their abundance has diluted their influence. Many of them focus on forest preservation, arguably the country's most hot-button issue.

Renace, Seminario 774, Ñuñoa, Santiago, website: www.renace.cl, renace@rdc.cl, is a loose alliance of Chilean environmental organizations. The highly professional Fundación Terram, Huelén 95, 3rd floor, Providencia, Santiago, tel. 2/2640682, fax 2/2642514, website: www.terram.cl, info@terram.cl, emphasizes sustainable development issues.

The best known forest preservation organization is Defensores del Bosque Chileno (Defenders of the Chilean Forest), Diagonal Oriente 2/2041914, Ñuñoa, Santiago, website: www.elbosquechileno.cl, bosquech@entelchile.net. Once again headed by founder Adriana Hoffman, a botanist who served for nearly two years as the Lagos administration's major environmental official, its focus is native forest preservation and restoration.

Chile's oldest environmental organization is the Comité de la Defensa de Flora y Fauna (Committee for the Defense of Flora and Fauna, or Codeff), Luis Uribe 2620, Ñuñoa, Santiago, website: www.codeff.cl, secretaria@codeff.cl. Since 1968, it has primarily focused on practical projects to preserve and restore native plants and animals, often in cooperation with government agencies such as the Corporación Nacional Forestal, or Conaf (National Forestry Corporation).

VEGETATION ZONES

Floral associations are strongly correlated with latitude and altitude.

Coastal Deserts

Much if not most of far northern Chile seems utterly desolate, with no vegetation whatsoever. However, in the transverse river valleys that descend from the Andes to the coast, even if water reaches the ocean only during major altiplano floods, subsurface aquifers support a desert scrub and are even sufficient for irrigated agriculture.

One exception to the sterility of the desert lowlands is the Pampa del Tamarugal, a densely forested plain east of the city of Iquique. These woodlands of *tamarugo (Prosopis chilensis),* a relative of the common mesquite, are mostly plantations, but they represent the restoration of a native species that flourished on fossil water from the Andes before their deforestation for the colonial silver mining industry.

Precordillera

As rainfall increases with altitude and distance from the coast, the hillsides eventually sprout stands of the appropriately named candelabra cactus, *Browningia candelaris.* Eventually, the cacti yield to several species of low-growing shrubs known collectively as *tola* but also scattered stands of stunted *queñoa (Polylepis tarapacana),* one of the world's highest-altitude trees.

Altiplano

The altiplano, also often known as the *puna,* consists mostly of patchy perennial grasses interspersed with *tola,* though there are a few signature species such as the rock-hard *llareta (Laretia compacta),* a shrub so densely branched that it appears, from a

© WAYNE BERNHARDSON

Chilean coastline

distance, to be a spreading moss. While the altiplano is mostly arid, it contains a limited extent of
well-watered marshlands known collectively as
bofedales or *ciénagas,* which provide year-round
pasture for domestic llamas, alpacas, and sheep. In
some cases, by an ingenious system of canals, indigenous pastoralists have actually expanded the
area covered by *bofedales.*

Valdivian Cloud Forest
In scattered parts of the Norte Chico, drip from
the *camanchaca* (dense fog) supports a remarkably
verdant forest flora whose closest geographical
counterpart occurs mostly in the well-watered
Sur Chico. The best place to see this phenomenon is Parque Nacional Bosque de Fray Jorge,
west of the city of Ovalle.

Mediterranean Scrub
From the Norte Chico through most of the
Chilean heartland, the native flora consist mostly of sclerophyllous (glossy-leaved) shrubs that
evolved to survive long dry summers. Their
Northern Hemisphere analogue is the chaparral of both northern and southern California.

Some species of southern beech (*Nothofagus*
spp) appear at higher elevations in the coast range
of the heartland. The native palm *Jubaea chilensis,* once common in the region, is slowly declining, if not quite disappearing, because of
overexploitation for economic ends.

Broadleaf and Coniferous Forest
South of the Río Biobío, various species of broad-
leaved southern beech (*Nothofagus* spp), both
evergreen and deciduous, are the most abundant
trees. However, several notable conifers grow
here, particularly the *paraguas* (umbrella) or monkey puzzle tree *Araucaria araucana,* so called because its crown resembles an umbrella and its
limbs seem to take the shape of a monkey's curled
tail. The long-lived *alerce* or *lawen (Fitzroya cupressoides)* is an endangered species because of its
high timber value, though most stands of the
tree are now protected. Both the *Araucaria* and
the *alerce* are national monuments.

Note that all Chileans except specialists refer
indiscriminately to conifers as *pinos* (pines), even
though there are no true pines (of the genus
Pinus) in the Southern Hemisphere except as or-
namentals in gardens or timber species in forest
plantations.

Temperate Rain Forest
In western Chilean Patagonia, heavy rainfall supports dense and verdant coastal and upland forests
of mostly *Nothofagus* spp, though there are many
other broadleaf trees and even the occasional
conifer such as the *ciprés del los Guaitecas (Pilgerodendron uviferum,* Guaytecas cypress). In
some areas, though, this forest has suffered severe
depredations at the hands of corporations and
colonists.

Patagonian Steppe
On the eastern plains of Magallanes, Tierra del
Fuego, and even parts of Aisén, in the rain shadow of the Andes, decreased rainfall supports extensive grasslands where the winds blow almost
ceaselessly. In some areas, thorn scrub such as
the fruit-bearing *calafate (Berberis buxifolia),* a
barberry, is abundant. From the late 19th century,
sheep grazing for wool had a tremendous detri-
mental impact on these natural pastures.

The Pacific Islands
While greatly transformed because of the introduction of nonnative plants, the Juan Fernández archipelago remains such a repository of
floral diversity that it is a UNESCO World Biosphere Reserve. Easter Island, or Rapa Nui, however, has a seriously impoverished flora partly
because of its deforestation for rollers to move
the massive stone monuments for which it is so
famous. The native tree *toromiro (Sophora
toromiro,)* for instance, no longer exists in its natural environment; efforts to reintroduce it from
mainland botanical gardens have not yet been
successful.

FAUNA
As with the flora, Chile's fauna is largely correlated with altitude. In a biogeographical sense, the
entire country is a sort of island, as the high
Andes separate it from most of the rest of the

continent, while the northern deserts form a barrier against the easy southward migration of plants and animals.

Marine, Coastal, and Aquatic Fauna

Paralleling most of Chile's lengthy coastline, the Peru Chile Trench reaches depths in excess of 8,000 meters; upwelling nutrients and the north-flowing Peru or Humboldt Current makes this one of the world's richest fishing grounds. Chile has always depended on the sea to sustain its economy—even in pre-Colombian times, when northern coastal peoples exchanged fish, shell-fish, and guano for the agricultural products of the precordillera and altiplano. In the south, peoples such as the Yámana and Kawasqar lived largely on maritime resources.

Fish and Shellfish: Seafood, of course, is what lends character to Chilean cuisine—it's so distinctive that one North American foodie wrote that he felt he was observing the marine life of another planet. Tasty fish such as the *cojinova* (*Seriolella* spp), *congrio* (conger eel, *Genypterus* spp), *corvina* (*Cilus gilberti*), *palometa* (*Parona signata*), and others crowd menus from the simplest *picadas* (family eateries) to Santiago's sophisticated bistros.

It's the shellfish, though, that are truly remarkable, from the relatively commonplace *ostión* (scallop, *Argopecten purpuratus* or *Chlamys patagonica*) and *calamar* (squid, *Loligo gahi* or *Ilex argentinus*) to the *loco* (abalone, *Concholepas concholepas*), *erizo* (sea urchin, *Loxechinus albus*), and *picoroco* (giant barnacle, *megabalanus psittacus*). This, though, is only an incomplete sample of the extraordinary sea life off the Chilean coastline, which also includes many varieties of crabs.

(For more information on Chilean seafood, see the Food and Drink entry in the On the Road chapter.)

Marine Mammals: In the Norte Grande, the indigenous Chango fished from rafts made from the hides of the southern sea lion (*Otaria flavescens*), commonly found from the Peruvian border all the way to Tierra del Fuego. The southern elephant seal (*Mirounga leonina*) and southern fur seal (*Arctocephalus australis*) are both on Appendix II of the Endangered Species List

(CITES), classified as threatened or regionally endangered. The Juan Fernández fur seal (*Arctocephalus philippi*) is a narrow endemic found only on its namesake archipelago.

Several other marine mammals found in Chilean waters are on CITES Appendix I, in danger of immediate extinction without remedial action, including beaked whales (*Berardius* or *Mesoplodon* spp), the blue whale (*Balaenoptera musculus*), fin whale (*Balaenoptera physalus*), humpback whale (*Megaptera novaeangliae*), chungungo or sea otter (*Lutra felina*), Minke whale (*Balaenoptera acutorostrata*), pygmy right whale (*Caperea marginata*), sei whale (*Balaenoptera borealis*), and southern right whale (*Eubalaena australis*). The bottlenosed dolphin (*Turciops truncatus*) and its relatives are common sights.

Terrestrial and Freshwater Fauna

Chile is relatively poor in terms of land fauna, especially large mammals.

Mammals: Carnivores are fairly numerous but the only large one is the widely distributed but secretive puma (*Felis concolor*). Other wild felines include the smaller Andean cat (*Felis jacobita*) and the jaguarundi (*Felis yagouarundi*), both endangered species. Two species of otters are also endangered, the long-tailed otter (*Lutra platensis*) and the southern river otter (*Lutra provocax*). There are no wolves but several species of foxes live here, including the threatened Argentine gray fox (*Dusicyon griseus*).

Wild grazing mammals include the vicuña (*Vicugna vicugna*), an endangered relative of the domestic llama (*Lama glama*) and alpaca (*Lama pacos*) that occurs only in the northern altiplano. Their more widely distributed cousin, the wild guanaco (*Lama guanicoe*), is most abundant on the Patagonian steppe but also found in parts of the Andes. Domestic livestock such as cattle, horses, burros, and goats are of course very common.

The South Andean *huemul* (*Hippocamelus bisulcus*), a cervid that appears on Chile's coat-of-arms, is the subject of a joint conservation effort between Chile and Argentina. In the mid-19th century, there were 22,000 in both countries, but at present only about 1,000 survive in each country south of the Río Biobío because

INTRODUCTION

Andean vizcacha, Parque Nacional Lauca

Reptiles and Amphibians: Chile is not quite snake-free, but they are rare and there is no venomous species. Even lizards are a rare sight, but in the Norte Grande look for *Tropidurus tarapacensis,* which, when running on its back legs, looks like a miniature *Tyrannosaurus rex.*

Freshwater Fish and Crustaceans: Crustaceans are particularly uncommon, though the Salar de Atacama is home to the tiny salt *artemia.*

of habitat destruction, contagious livestock diseases, and unregulated hunting.

The North Andean *huemul (Hippocamelus antisensis)* is closely related but found only in the Norte Grande. The *pudú (Pudu pudu)* is a miniature deer found in the Sur Chico well into Chilean Patagonia.

The northern altiplano is home to two noteworthy rodent species, the Andean vizcacha *(Lagidium vizcacha)* and its smaller nocturnal cousin the chinchilla *(Chinchilla lanigera).* The former inhabits large rookeries and it's fairly easy to spot.

Birds

What it lacks in other wildlife, Chile more than compensates in birds, especially in the Norte Grande and the steppe and oceans of southern Patagonia. For visitors and especially dedicated birders from the Northern Hemisphere, the great majority are new additions to their life lists. For recommended birding guides, see the booklist appendix.

In the altiplano east of Arica, for instance, Parque Nacional Lauca, a UNESCO World Biosphere Reserve, and its vicinity are home to more than 150 bird species, about a third of all species registered in the entire country. Among them are the signature Andean condor *(Vultur gryphus),* the ostrichlike *ñandú* or *suri (Pterocnemia pennata),* Andean flamingo

© WAYNE BERNHARDSON/2

Magellanic penguins

(Phoenicoparrus andinus), Chilean flamingo *(Phoenicopterus ruber chilensis),* James flamingo *(Phoenicoparrus jamesi),* the peregrine falcon *(Falco peregrinus),* the *tagua gigante* or giant coot *(Fulica gigantea),* and the Andean gull *(Larus serranus),* not to mention many species of waterfowl.

Some 240 bird species inhabit the Magellanic region, including the wandering albatross *(Diomedea exulans),* with its awesome four-meter wingspan, the black-necked swan *(Cygnus melanocoryphus),* Coscoroba swan *(Coscoroba coscoroba),* flightless steamer duck *(Tachyeres pteneres),* kelp gull *(Larus dominicanus),* and several species of penguins, most commonly the Magellanic or jackass penguin *(Spheniscus magellanicus),* whose close relative the Humboldt penguin *(Spheniscus humboldtii)* is an endangered species that ranges far to the north. The greater rhea *(Rhea americana albescens),* also commonly known as *ñandú,* also roams the Patagonian steppes.

Invertebrates

For purely practical purposes, visitors should pay attention to pests and dangers such as mosquitoes, flies, and ticks, which can be serious disease vectors, even though maladies such as malaria and dengue are almost unheard of—the mosquito vector for dengue has been found on Easter Island (Rapa Nui), and the disease itself has recently been detected.

The reduvid or assassin bug, which bears trypanosomiasis (Chagas' disease), is present in Chile, though it is hardly cause for hysteria. (For more information, see the Health and Safety entry in the On the Road chapter.)

The Cultural Landscape

While Chile's natural landscapes, flora, and fauna are fascinating and enchanting, the country also has a cultural landscape, one transformed by human agency over the millennia. Few parts of the country are truly pristine, but their landscapes are no less interesting for all that.

As outliers of the great Andean civilizations, the Norte Grande and Norte Chico, and even parts of the heartland, still show tangible evidence of those times. While their monuments are not so grand as those of Peru and Bolivia, many *pukarás* (fortresses), *pircas* (walls), and pre-Columbian roads survive, along with geoglyphs that cover entire hillsides along ancient trade routes.

In the southern heartland, the Sur Chico, and Patagonia, shifting cultivators and nomadic pre-Columbian peoples left less conspicuous landmarks, but there are some aboriginal rock art sites, and one of the most important early man sites on the continent is at Monte Verde, near Puerto Montt.

AGRICULTURE AND THE LANDSCAPE

In some areas, such as the precordillera of Region I (Tarapacá), local communities have retained control of their better lands and constructed durable terrace systems that have conserved soil and maintained productivity. Native crops such as quinoa *(Chenopodium quinoa)* are still grown in some areas.

While the marshy *bofedales* may appear to be natural habitat—they do support abundant wildfowl—contemporary Aymara llama and alpaca herders continue to expand the area covered by these valuable grasslands with ingenious irrigation canals that are not obvious except on close inspection.

The pre-Columbian peoples of the south were shifting cultivators and, as such, their impact on the landscape is less obvious. Because they cut the forest and used fire to clear the fields before planting, their impact was significant, but long fallow periods allowed the woodlands to recover. Much of what seems to be virgin forest may in fact be secondary growth.

The arrival of the Spaniards, of course, led to major transformations. At first content to collect tribute from the indigenous population, they became landholders as that population declined from various causes, mostly important introduced diseases. Their large rural estates, known as haciendas or *fundos,* consisted of relatively small areas of intensively cultivated land surrounded by large areas on which grazed cattle, horses, and other European livestock. In Patagonia, the sheep *estancia,* an extensive unit producing wool for export to Europe and North America, was the dominant agricultural institution.

SETTLEMENT LANDSCAPES

After the Spaniards took control of Chile, as in the rest of their American dominions, they instituted an overt policy of *congregación* or *reducción,* which meant concentrating native populations in villages or towns for the purpose of political control and religious evangelization. For most of Chile's indigenous peoples, who lived in dispersed settlements near their fields or their animals, this was an inconvenience at best, and it contributed to land disputes both within indigenous communities and between indigenous communities and Spaniards.

Still, in many areas, the need to be close to one's fields or animals has reinforced a dispersed rural settlement pattern—in the altiplano, for instance, some apparently deserted villages have become primarily ceremonial sites where people gather for the festival of their patron saint. The standard house is often an adobe, usually with a thatched or tiled roof, and small windows to conserve heat; the prevalence of earthquakes, though, has encouraged reinforced concrete block construction, and galvanized roofing has become more common.

Some unique vernacular architecture survives in the southern regions. In parts of Mapuche country, indigenous peoples still inhabit traditional *rucas,* or plank houses with thatched roofs traditionally erected with community labor rather than by individual families. On the island of Chiloé, some neighborhoods of *palafitos* (fishermen's houses on stilts or pilings) have managed to withstand earthquakes and tsunamis. In Patagonia, dating from the 19th century, so-called "Magellanic" houses often affect a Victorian style, with wooden framing but covered by metal cladding and topped by corrugated metal roofs.

Cities, of course, differ greatly from the countryside. Traditionally, as in Santiago de Chile, colonial houses fronted directly on the street or sidewalk, with an interior patio or garden for family use; any setback was almost unheard of. This pattern has largely continued to the present, though building materials have mostly changed from adobe to concrete. It is also true, however, that many wealthier Chileans have built houses with large gardens, on the North American suburban model, in a frenzy of conspicuous consumption—but still surrounded by high fences and state-of-the-art security.

Northern mining towns such as Iquique, which boomed with nitrates in the late 19th and early 20th centuries, are notable for their Georgian-style gingerbread architecture, but the most distinctive urban architecture belongs to the spontaneous, organic city of Valparaíso, which has adapted itself admirably to the contours of its hilly terrain.

Environmental Issues

Chile faces a multitude of serious environmental issues, both urban and rural, none of which is likely to be solved any time soon. Among them are air, water, and noise pollution, garbage disposal, wildland conservation, and soil degradation. Hardly any of these, of course, is easily separated from the others, but for purposes of discussion they appear below under these categories.

The Chilean government's major environmental agency is the Comisión Nacional del Medio Ambiente (Conama), which reports directly to the president. In October 2001, however, Conama director Adriana Hoffmann, whose impeccable credentials included the founding of the nonprofit Defensores del Bosque Chileno (Defenders of the Chilean Forest), resigned partly because she thought that, during the economic slowdown, the Lagos administration was paying less attention to environmental issues. She had also lost support within the environmental community for her unwillingness or inability to influence the president on some key issues.

According to a study by the nonprofit Fundación Terram, the mining, fishing, and forestry industries are Chile's most serious environmental culprits. By considering externalities such as air and water pollution, for instance, it calculated that mining's environmental damage in a given year totaled roughly half the sector's contribution to Gross Domestic Product. Overfishing reduced the value of that sector's resource to about half of its output between 1990 and 1998, while timber companies diminished the value of Chile's woodlands by US$900 million, equivalent to more than 5 percent of the sector's GDP.

AIR POLLUTION

One of Chile's most intractable problems is air pollution, particularly in Santiago and most of the Región Metropolitana. In 2001, the prestigious journal *Science* ranked the capital as the second most polluted city in the Americas, after only Mexico City.

Santiago's geography, similar to that of Los Angeles (California), does not help; it lies in a basin between the coastal range and an even higher Andean crest that blocks the dispersal of pollutants from smokestack industries, automobile emissions (unleaded fuel is not yet universal), diesel exhaust from aging city buses, and dust from the many unpaved streets and roads outside the central city. Rain quickly washes some pollutants out of the atmosphere, but the long dry summer and the particularly stagnant autumn air leaves heavy haze over the city for much of the year.

Successive governments have had limited success in reducing polluting gases. Except in the summer, there is a weekday vehicle restriction of vehicles without catalytic converters according to the last digit of their license plates, but when the Lagos administration placed very limited restrictions on vehicles with catalytic converters on days of truly extreme smog, rightist politicians and automobile owners protested vociferously.

Another political obstacle is that Gran Santiago (Greater Santiago) consists of 32 distinct boroughs, each governed by a mayor and administration whose constituents have very distinct ideas of what causes pollution and how to remedy it. Residents of the eastern suburbs, often wealthy professionals, argue that their state-of-the-art vehicles pollute less than the dirty diesel buses used by working-class commuters. While this argument has some truth to it, it overlooks the congestion created by large numbers of private vehicles, which increases the time that internal combustion engines spend idling.

Newer natural gas-powered buses are in the works, to be financed by small fare increases over time, but the politically powerful private bus companies continue to resist major changes. Other anti-pollution measures include downtown bus-only lanes on the Alameda, the city's major thoroughfare, and some other streets, and higher quality, lower sulfur diesel fuel.

The countryside, alas, is not free of air pollution problems. Agricultural burning is widespread and forest fires are also common in summer, especially in the heartland's dry Mediterranean climate. In mining areas such as Chuquicamata, in the Norte Grande, clouds of toxic tailings billow across the desert with the Pacific westerlies.

A different sort of air pollution is the deterioration of the Antarctic ozone layer, which has exposed both humans and livestock in far southern Chile to ultraviolet radiation in summer. Though ozone depletion from aerosols is a global problem over which Chileans have relatively little control, they suffer the consequences of the growing ozone hole.

WATER POLLUTION

Most municipalities have sewerage systems, but wastewater treatment is inconsistent, so that rivers, lakes and oceans themselves can become open sewers—according to one study, 350 factories dump untreated waste into the sea. Recently enacted legislation requires Santiago to become the first Latin American capital to treat all its wastewater, with 16 new treatment plants at a cost of US$781 million.

More than half of the country's industry is in Santiago, and additional legislation requires private factories to draft wastewater management plans and implement them within five years at a cost of US$1.7 billion.

Nonmetropolitan industries such as agriculture, forestry, and mining also contribute to the contamination of Chilean streams and seas. Among the worst offenders are commercial fruit growers, many of whom rely on far more chemical fertilizers and pesticides than necessary to augment their booming exports.

Salmon farming, a booming and increasingly concentrated industry (10 of 40 registered companies control more than half the production) cause problems with runoff in the Sur Chico and Patagonia. Farms of Lago Llanquihue, Lago Puyehue, Lago Ranco, Lago Rupanco, and other areas discharge 15 to 20 times the acceptable level of contaminants such as growth chemicals, antibiotics, and salmon feces. Moreover, salmon often escape to colonize streams and seas at the expense of native fish, and some farmers have

been accused of killing sea lions that prey on the caged fish.

NOISE POLLUTION

Just as Santiago's fleet of antique diesel buses contributes to air pollution, so it raises the decibel level, especially in downtown's highrise canyons. Other contributors include cars and motorcycles with inadequate mufflers, jet skis on some of the Sur Chico's otherwise placid lakes, and public performances of amplified evangelical music.

SOLID WASTE

Poor solid waste management also contributes to air pollution and consequent health problems, not to mention the aesthetics of the matter—at Lampa, on Santiago's northern outskirts, productive farmland is disappearing beneath unregulated dumping. Chile also has many informal rubbish dumps.

According to Conama, which is preparing new standards for solid waste disposal, more than two-thirds of the country's 246 dumps lack the necessary sanitary permits, and only 4.5 percent of them have presented reports to the Environmental Impact System (SEIA). A new major sanitary landfill has been proposed on the outskirts of Gran Santiago, but all the proposed sites—Til-Til, Pudahuel, San Bernardo, Puente Alto and Maipú—have raised objections.

Despite the disposal problems, city streets are relatively clean even if, in the course of Chile's rush toward "development," the country has grown into an unfortunate reliance on disposable beverage containers and other undesirable sorts of packaging.

DEFORESTATION AND SOIL CONSERVATION

According to Conaf, the country possesses 13.4 million hectares of native forest, 3.9 million of which enjoy government protection as part of the Sistema Nacional de Áreas Silvestres Protegidas (Snaspe, or National System of Protected Wild Areas). The remaining 9.5 million hectares are in private hands, 80 percent of whom are small or medium-sized landowners. Most of these forests are in southern Chile.

Native forest conservation is a hot-button issue for many Chilean activists, who have led determined and successful opposition to schemes such as the Cascada Chile wood chip project in Region X (Los Lagos), which was canceled in early 2001, and a similar effort by the U.S.-based Trillium Corporation in Region XII (Magallanes).

According to the industry-oriented Corporación de Madera (Corma), 90 percent of the wood that arrives in Chilean factories comes from forest plantations and only 10 percent from native forests. This figure is misleading, however, in the sense that plantations of eucalyptus and Monterey pine have substituted for heavily logged native woodlands. More-over, of the 10 million cubic meters of wood used annually for heating and cooking in Chilean households, 70 percent comes from native forests.

Some foreign environmental organizations, such as the Sierra Club, question potential free trade agreements as they believe Chile's environmental legislation, particularly that on native forests, to be weak. A proposed Ley de Bosques Nativos (Native Forest Law) would, however, offer economic incentives for owners of native forest properties, promoting sustainable harvest with subsidies of almost US$500 per hectare, and would discourage plantations of nonnatives. A preliminary commission includes government authorities, members of Corma, and the environmental NGOs (nongovernmental organizations) Fundación Terram and Codeff.

History

On the periphery of the continent's pre-Columbian civilizations, Chile cannot match their renown and colossal monuments, but its history has an epic intensity all its own. Integrating that past with the present is a challenge and it's hard for many analysts to avoid polemic.

PREHISTORY

Human occupation of the Americas, unlike that of Africa, Europe, and Asia, is relatively recent. The earliest immigrants reached North America from East Asia more than 12,500 years ago, when sea levels fell during the last major period of continental glaciation and united the two continents via a land bridge across the Bering Strait. Some researchers believe this migration, interrupted by various interglacials during which rising sea levels submerged the crossing, began tens of thousands of years earlier. Nevertheless, by the time the bridge last closed about 10,000 years ago, the entire Western Hemisphere was populated, at least thinly, with bands of hunter-gatherers in environments that varied from barren, torrid deserts to sopping rainforests to frigid uplands and everything in between.

Evidence of Paleo-Indian hunter-gatherers is relatively scarce in Chile, but one of the continent's oldest confirmed archaeological sites is at Monte Verde, just north of Puerto Montt. Radiocarbon dating at Monte Verde has given a figure of 13,000 years at a site that, according to University of Kentucky archaeologist Tom Dillehay, has some of the continent's earliest evidence of architecture, as well as use of wild potatoes and other native tubers. The most geographically proximate Early Man sites—later than Monte Verde—are 900 km or more to the north, and Dillehay's research, while generally accepted, has earned some criticism for its early dates.

As important as hunting was to the first Americans, gathering wild foods probably contributed more to the diet. As population gradually reached the saturation point under hunter-gatherer technology, they began to rely on so-called incipient agriculture, one of whose hearths was the Peruvian highlands. In the process of gathering, incipient agriculturalists had acquired knowledge of the annual cycles of seed plants, and selected, scattered, and harvested them in a lengthy domestication process. In fact, the earliest domesticated plants could have been root crops such as manioc in the Amazon lowlands, but as these are perishable tubers rather than durable seeds, there is little archaeological evidence to support this supposition.

In any event, starting about 6000 B.C., beans (*Phaseolus* spp), squash (*Cucurbita* spp), and potatoes (*Solanum* spp) became the staples of an agricultural complex that, as population grew, supported a settled village life and, eventually, the great Andean civilizations. When the Spaniards finally arrived, according to one scholar, they found "the richest assemblage of food plants in the western hemisphere." Domestic animals were few, however—only the dog (sometimes raised for food), the guinea pig (definitely raised for food), and the llama and alpaca (both raised for food and fiber, with the llama also serving as a pack animal).

Slower to develop than the Andean region, at least partly because of late demographic saturation under the available technology, mainland southern Chilean society remained semisedentary and more egalitarian until only a short time before the Spanish invasion. In Patagonia, some indigenous peoples sustained a hunter-gatherer way of life even into the 20th century.

PRE-COLUMBIAN CIVILIZATION AND CULTURES

In Pre-Columbian times, then, what is now Chile comprised a diversity of native peoples who varied from small isolated bands of hunter-gatherers to semiurbanized outliers of Tiwanaku (in present-day Bolivia) and Inka Cuzco (in present-day Peru).

Inhabiting the westward-sloping precordillera and the altiplano of what is now the Norte Grande, politically subordinate to the Inka, the Aymara were part of a long-established exchange system between peoples occupying different ecological niches. The coastal Chango, for instance, moved products such as fish and guano up the transverse river valleys in return for agricultural and livestock products such as maize, *chuño* (freeze-dried potatoes), and *ch'arki* (freeze-dried meat) and wool, the latter two from the llama and alpaca. Llamas, of course, carried the goods from

sea level to the *puna;* their depictions on enormous hillside geoglyphs mark their routes.

South of the Río Loa, the Atacameño practiced a nearly identical subsistence, but both they and the more southerly Diaguita operated on a looser tether from the demands of the demanding Inka state and its tributary obligations. South of the Chilean heartland, where the Inka had an equally tenuous control over the sedentary Picunche, other Araucanian peoples—the semisedentary Mapuche and the closely related Pehuenche, Huilliche, and Puelche, as well as the Cunco—withstood both the Inka expansion and, for more than three centuries, the Spanish invasion. Among the reasons they survived were their mobility, as shifting cultivators, and their decentralized political structure—not easily conquered or co-opted by the bureaucratic Inka.

In Patagonia, hunting, fishing, and gathering were the primary means of subsistence for peoples such as the Chonos, Tehuelche, Kawasqar (Alacaluf), Yámana (Yahgan), and Selkn'am (Ona), who proved unconquerable until sheep occupied their hunting grounds and introduced European diseases nearly obliterated them.

Inka Empire and Its Collapse

At the time of the Spanish invasion, the Inka ruled an administratively centralized but geographically unwieldy empire; their hold was especially tenuous on the southern Araucanian (Mapuche) frontier, just as it would be for the Spaniards in only a few years. Though Inka political achievements were impressive, their realm also stretching into present-day Colombia in the north, it's important to recognize that they were relative latecomers in the pre-Columbian Andes, only consolidating their power about A.D. 1438. Building on earlier Andean advances in mathematics, astronomy, and other sciences, they were a literate and administratively sophisticated society, but their hierarchical organization, like that of the modern Soviet Union, was ultimately unsustainable.

Toward the end of the 15th century, then, just before the Spanish invasion of the New World, the Inka empire was no monolith, but rather a diverse empire ruling a mosaic of peoples who resisted domination, especially on its most remote frontiers. Because of internal divisions after the premature deaths of the Inka ruler Huayna Capac and his immediate heir, there developed a struggle between potential successors Atahualpa and Huáscar. The fact that the Inka empire was a house divided against itself helps explain why a relatively small contingent of Spanish invaders could overcome vastly superior numbers, but it's only part of the story.

THE SPANISH INVASION AND COLONIAL CHILE

Christopher Columbus's so-called "discovery" of the "New World" was, of course, one of the signal events of human history. While he may have bungled his way into fame—according to geographer Carl Sauer, "The geography in the mind of Columbus was a mixture of fact, fancy and credulity"—the incompetently audacious Genoan sailor excited the interest and imagination of Spaniards and others who, within barely half a century, brought virtually all of what is now known as Latin America under at least nominal control.

Europeans had roamed the Caribbean for more than three decades after Columbus's initial voyage, but the impulse to conquest in South America came from Mexico and especially Panama, which Francisco Pizarro and his brothers used as a base to take Peru. From there, in 1535, Pizarro's partner and rival Diego de Almagro made the first attempt to take Chile, but his poorly organized expedition ended in grisly failure as most of his personnel, retainers, and even livestock died. Four years later, after defeating an uprising by Almagro, Pizarro designated Pedro de Valdivia to

Chilean coat-of-arms

undertake the conquest of Chile and, by 1541, Valdivia had founded Santiago.

In short order, he also founded La Serena, Concepción, Valparaíso, Villarrica, and his namesake city Valdivia before finally meeting his match, his own former Araucanian slave Lautaro, at the Battle of Tucapel. Before his death—according to some accounts, Valdivia pleaded for his life by offering unimaginable wealth to his captors before being killed with a blow to the head—he had laid the groundwork for the country that was to become Chile.

The Spanish Imposition

From the beginning, the Spanish presence in the Americas had contradictory goals. Most of the Spaniards who conquered the wealthy civilizations of Mexico, Peru, and points between and beyond did so with the goal of getting rich. But others were Christian idealists who sought to save the souls of the millions of Indians they found there (putting aside for the moment the fact that these millions already had their own elaborate religious beliefs).

Consequently, the Spanish Crown obliged its invading forces to read a statement known as the *requerimiento,* which offered their opposition the option to accept papal and Spanish authority over their lands in lieu of military subjugation. Whether or not they accepted, the result was the same—they became subject to a Spanish colonial system that, if less overtly violent than military conquest, was overwhelmingly stacked against them.

Many prisoners of war became Spanish slaves and were shipped elsewhere throughout the Americas. Others who remained were obliged to provide labor for individual Spaniards through

banknote with portrait of Pedro de Valdivia, conqueror of Chile

the *repartimiento,* an ostensibly paid system of manpower not always easily distinguishable from slavery. The *repartimiento,* in turn, is not always easy to distinguish from the *encomienda,* a grant of Indian labor and tribute within a given geographical area. In principle, the Spanish *encomendero,* or holder of such a grant, was to provide reciprocal instruction in the Spanish language and catechization in the Catholic Church, but the distant Spanish administration could rarely enforce these requirements. The *encomienda,* it should be emphasized, was *not* a land grant, though many *encomenderos* also became large landholders.

Spanish institutions were most easily imposed in those areas that had been under Inka influence, as a long history of hierarchical government made it possible for the Spaniards to place themselves at the top of the pyramid. Subjects accustomed to paying tribute to the representative of the Inka now paid it to the *encomendero,* the representative of the Spanish Crown. This was different, however, with the unsubjugated Araucanians of the south.

The Demographic Collapse and Its Consequences

One of the perpetual mysteries of the invasion, at least on its face, was how so few Spaniards could dominate such large indigenous populations in so little time. Spanish weapons were not markedly superior to those of the native populations—it took much longer to reload a harquebus than a bow, for example, and the bow and arrow were probably more accurate. The presence of cavalry gave the Spaniards a tactical edge in open terrain, but this was only occasionally decisive. Certainly the Spaniards took advantage of factionalism within South American societies, but that was not the entire story either. The Spaniards' greatest allies may have been microbes.

From the time the Bering Strait land bridge closed, the Americas had been geographically isolated from Europe and Asia. Diseases that had evolved and spread in the Old World, such as smallpox, measles, plague, and typhus, no longer took a catastrophic toll there, but when the Spaniards inadvertently brought them to the New World they encountered immunologically defenseless human populations and spread like the plague in 14th-century Europe. One exhaustively researched and statistically sophisticated study, by the late historian Woodrow Borah and his physiologist colleague Sherburne Cook, concluded that introduced European diseases reduced the population of highland Mexico from 25.2 million in 1518 to just a little over one million in 1605.

Similar disasters occurred throughout the Americas, though in general the effect was heaviest in the humid tropical lowlands, the ideal incubator for deadly contagion. In the cooler, drier highlands, disease did not spread so quickly nor so thoroughly, but it was still overwhelming. In some parts of South America, it even preceded direct contact with the Spaniards—the death of Huayna Capac himself may have been the result of European smallpox spread indirectly. For this reason, historian Murdo Macleod has called introduced diseases "the shock troops of the conquest."

The demographic collapse had a significant influence on the development of Chilean society, especially in the Norte Grande (politically part of Peru and Bolivia until the late 19th century) and the central heartland. While the population was large, *encomiendas* were a valuable source of wealth for those who held them (including, by the way, the Catholic Church). As the population plummeted, however, *encomiendas* lost their value, since dead Indians paid no tribute.

At the same time, the *encomienda* also came under political, legal, and judicial assault, as pro-Indian clergy such as the Mexico-based Dominican Bartolomé de las Casas (himself a reformed *encomendero*) argued strenuously for reform of the institution in Spain. The result was Charles V's so-called "New Laws" of 1542, which theoretically dissolved *encomiendas* on the death of the *encomendero*. While enforcement, which depended on local representatives of the Crown and the Church, was lax, the *encomienda's* days were numbered.

In the absence of large Indian populations to exploit, Spaniards took economic refuge in large rural estates, or haciendas, but struggled to find labor to work them. Over time, however, unattached Spanish men formed unions—formal and informal—with indigenous women, and their resulting mestizo offspring (of mixed heritage) brought a demographic rebound.

As long as the indigenous or mestizo peasant population was small, land conflicts were few;

> *Historian Murdo Macleod has called introduced diseases "the shock troops of the conquest."*

as numbers recovered, though, the concentrations of *latifundia* (large landholdings) contrasted dramatically with the *minifundia* (smallholdings) of peasant cultivators who toiled to have enough to eat, especially as average farm size declined with subdivision by succeeding generations. This had profound implications for the country's future, as it divided the country into groups of haves and have-nots, based on their access to land—a situation that would contribute to the upheavals of the late 20th century.

South of the heartland, of course, the situation was different, as the mobile Araucanians, assisted by their rapid adoption of the Spanish-introduced horse, staved off the Spaniards and then the Chileans for more than three centuries. In fact, the area south of the Río Biobío was widely known as a separate country called "Arauco." In far-off Patagonia, the situation was even more tenuous, as tentative Spanish colonization efforts failed disastrously because of poor planning and extreme environmental conditions.

The Dissolution of Colonial Chile

In colonial times, Chile was an *audiencia,* an administrative subdivision of the Viceroyalty of Peru; Spain had three other viceroyalties, in New Spain (Mexico), Nueva Granada (Colombia), and the Río de la Plata (present-day Argentina). The Audiencia of Chile was larger than the current republic, encompassing territory including the trans-Andean Cuyo region of modern Argentina and much of present-day Argentine Patagonia. Its capital was Santiago del Nuevo Extremo, now commonly known as Santiago de Chile.

Appointed by the Spanish Crown, all major officials of the viceroyalty governed from the capital city, and economic power was also concentrated there. Even Santiago, however, formally depended on distant Madrid for legitimacy. Outside the capital, though, isolated by geographical barriers, provincial bosses created their own power bases. When Napoleon

© WAYNE BERNHARDSON

bell tower and shrine at Parinacota

invaded Spain, in the early 19th century, the glue that held its colonial possessions together began to dissolve, leading to independence in several steps.

Contributing to this tendency was a changing sense of identity among the people of Chile. In the early generations, of course, people identified themselves as Spaniards, but over time so-called criollos (American-born Spaniards) began to differentiate themselves from *peninsulares* (European-born Spaniards). It bears mention that while the mestizos and even the remaining indigenous population may have identified more closely with Chile than Spain, it was the criollo intelligentsia who found the Spanish yoke most oppressive, and to whom the notion of independence had the greatest appeal.

The South American independence movements commenced on the periphery, with figures such as Argentina's José de San Martín, Venezuela's Simón Bolívar and, of course, Chile's Bernardo O'Higgins, the Chillán-born illegiti-mate son of the Irish Viceroy of Peru, Ambrosio O'Higgins. Chile marks its independence from 1810, when a local junta took over government in the name of Fernando VII of Spain, but it was nearly eight years more before a formal declaration. As Bolívar and San Martín converged on Lima for final victory over the Spaniards, O'Higgins remained in Santiago to consolidate Chile's self-determination.

REPUBLICAN CHILE

As heir to the *intendencias* of Santiago and Concepción, administrative subdivisions of the Viceroyalty of Peru, newly independent Chile was far smaller than it is now, comprising only the area from about Copiapó in the north to Concepción, on the north bank of the Río Biobío, in the south. A few other outlier settlements, such as the city of Valdivia and the archipelago of Chiloé, lay in areas nominally under Chilean control, but the Araucanian (Mapuche) Indians still ruled the countryside.

To some degree, though, this worked to Chile's advantage. Unlike its sprawling neighbor Argentina, where provincial warlords conducted a series of civil wars with a weak central government, the compact Chilean polity and its more or less homogenous population proved relatively easy to govern. Nevertheless, despite Chile's reputation for liberal democracy, nearly all of the 19th century leaders (and many of the 20th as well) were military men.

O'Higgins himself was the first of these, but he enjoyed a short honeymoon as his own authoritarian tendencies and opposition from the powerful landholding oligarchy undercut his position. After his resignation and exile in 1823, there were several years of instability before the wealthy merchant Diego Portales emerged as the power behind the executive under a constitution that he himself wrote. It was a measure of Portales's astuteness that his constitution, which created a unitary state with Roman Catholicism as the official religion and limited direct political participation to a narrow electorate of literate adult male property owners, survived his death in a military mutiny in 1837.

By the time Chile adopted a new constitution, in 1925, Portales's document had been in force for nearly a century.

Chile's stability was assisted by favorable economic developments. In the 1830s, the discovery of a bonanza silver mine at Chañarcillo, southeast of Copiapó, ignited the mining industry and helped make the country solvent. Shortly thereafter, the California Gold Rush kindled demand for Chilean wheat, making Valparaíso one of the premier ports on the Pacific coast of the Americas. Simultaneously, as a country with a long coastline, Chile developed a navy to project its power elsewhere on the continent.

The Guerra del Pacífico and Territorial Consolidation

In the 50 years before the last quarter of the 19th century, Chile's population had roughly tripled to about 2.5 million, its economy had grown, and its commercial influence expanded beyond its borders. In 1879, after Chilean nitrate mining interests complained of unfair taxation at the hands of Bolivian authorities in the vicinity of Antofagasta—then part of Bolivia—Chilean forces occupied the port city, sparking the Guerra del Pacífico (War of the Pacific).

Despite Bolivia's secret strategic alliance with Peru, which then became public, within four years Chile's well-organized and disciplined forces had not only claimed otherwise landlocked Bolivia's only outlet to the Pacific. They had also taken Peru's southern provinces of Tacna, Arica, and Tarapacá, and even occupied the Peruvian capital of Lima for more than two years. Eventually the Chileans returned Tacna, but they kept nitrate-rich Tarapacá and the port of Arica, where they granted Bolivia transit rights on a railroad to the Pacific.

Like the silver strikes at Chañarcillo, nitrate shipments from the docks of Antofagasta,

> *While the mestizos and even the remaining indigenous population may have identified more closely with Chile than Spain, it was the criollo intelligentsia (American-born Spaniards) who found the Spanish yoke most oppressive, and to whom the notion of independence had the greatest appeal.*

Iquique, and other ports that no longer exist brought enormous amounts of revenue into the Chilean exchequer and made certain individuals fabulously wealthy—mansions such as Santiago's Palacio Alhambra, Valparaíso's Palacio Baburizza, and Iquique's Palacio Astoreca all date from this period. At the same time, the proliferation of mining company towns in the wastes of the Norte Grande created a militant working class whose significance would not become completely apparent until the following century. One omen, though, was a march on Iquique by nitrate strikers, hundreds of whom—men, women and children—died when the army fired on their refuge in the Escuela Santa María.

While disposing of Peru and Bolivia in the north, Chile also managed to turn its attention south to the troublesome Araucanian frontier in the south and, soon thereafter, into the southern oceans. In 1881, treaty agreements with the Mapuche paved the way for European, mostly German, immigration south of the Biobío, and in 1888 the country participated in the classic age of imperialism by annexing Easter Island, a volcanic speck in the vast Pacific, 3,700 km to the west.

At the same time, Chile had consolidated its hold on its Patagonian territories. Theoretically, much of what is now far southern Argentina was once Chilean territory, but the growth of the city of Punta Arenas with the California Gold Rush and the subsequent wool boom contributed to the country's newfound prosperity. The glitch in this trajectory was the brief but bloody civil war of 1891, which began as the reformist President José Manuel Balmaceda attempted to spread the benefits of that prosperity to the population at large. Balmaceda's suicide ended the era of presidential supremacy, but it did nothing to eliminate the gaps between haves and have-nots.

The Modern Republic and Its Demise

The early years of the 20th century looked bright as nitrate income filled the state coffers, foreign freighters called at the busy harbors of Valparaíso and other cities, and the nascent copper industry advanced with North American investment. Soon, though, synthetic nitrates superseded Chile's northern ores, the opening of the Panama Canal reduced traffic around the Horn, and World War I reduced commerce with Chile's traditional British and German trading partners. Through succeeding decades, copper came to dominate the economy, as it does to the present.

As the Norte Grande's nitrate towns closed, Chilean industry was unable to absorb the increasing number of immigrants to the cities. In the countryside, the persistence of large but underused rural estates pushed the landless into the cities, even as visionary but ultimately ineffectual leaders such as President Arturo Alessandri Palma attempted to improve their lot through improvements in education, health care, and working conditions. Increasingly well represented in government, the democratic left took a more interventionist role in industry and agriculture through the state development corporation Corfo, but it could never overcome the entrenched power of the landed elite.

The electorate, meanwhile, fragmented into an alphabet soup of political parties in which the centrist Democracia Cristiana (DC) and its allies held the balance of power between a reactionary right that coalesced around the Partido Nacional (PN) and a multiplicity of leftist parties, of whom the relatively moderate Partido Comunista (PC, Communist Party) and the more radical Partido Socialista (Socialist Party, PS) were the most important. Organizations such as the Movimiento de Izquierda Revolucionario (Revolutionary Leftist Movement, MIR) advocated overthrow of the state and made common cause with labor activists, Mapuche militants, and other rural land reform crusaders.

The election of DC reformist President Eduardo Frei Montalva in 1964 was a hopeful sign, but his six-year term was unsuccessful in defusing the increasing polarization that resulted in the election, by a small plurality, of Socialist President Salvador Allende Gossens, in 1970. In his fifth presidential candidacy, heading a leftist coalition known as the Unidad Popular (Popular Unity, UP), Allende became famous as the world's first freely elected Marxist head of state.

Allende, the Unidad Popular, and the *Golpe de Estado*

Universally despised by the political right, widely distrusted by the Christian Democratic center, and viewed suspiciously at best by U.S. President Richard Nixon and his adviser Henry Kissinger, Allende faced the overwhelming task of redistributing Chile's wealth by constitutional means (Allende's conspicuously friendly relations with Cuba and his public friendship with Cuban strongman Fidel Castro did not improve his stock with Nixon and Kissinger). The government nationalized the critical copper industry and began a land reform program that enraged the right but failed to satisfy the left, which pressured for immediate and more radical measures, by force if necessary.

In this confrontational milieu, political violence from both left and right increased, and the government's policy of printing money to cover its costs and obligations brought triple-digit inflation. Conservative truckers paralyzed the economy with a transport strike, and finally, on September 11, 1973, the army's previously obscure General Augusto Pinochet Ugarte let loose a ferocious *golpe de estado* (coup d'etat) that marked the onset of one of the most durable military dictatorships ever on a continent that has been notorious for such regimes.

Under orders from Pinochet and his colleagues in the navy, air force, and Carabineros (national police), soldiers stormed Santiago's La Moneda presidential palace as planes bombed and strafed the historic building where Allende and his supporters made their last stand. Finally, according to Allende's personal physician Patricio Guijón, the president killed himself with a machine gun given him by Fidel Castro (Castro claimed—but how would he know?—that Allende died defending the rights of the common people with a gun in his hand). Like Balmaceda in 1891, Allende ended his life to make a statement rather than go into exile.

The immediate aftermath of the coup was nightmarish, as the police and military rounded up thousands of Allende partisans and sympathizers, incarcerating them in locales such as Santiago's Estadio Nacional (National Stadium) and clandestine torture centers. At least 3,000 died, many more were tortured, and the term "disappeared" came into widespread international use to describe known opponents of the military whose remains were never found. Army General Sergio Arellano Stark conducted a tour of northern Chilean cities to identify leftist figures for execution in what became known as the "Caravan of Death."

Pinochet emerged from the coup as the strongman of a four-member junta that also included the heads of the navy, air force, and Carabineros. While terrorizing Chileans at large, his agents also conducted a state-sponsored terrorist campaign that used car bombs to assassinate exiles such as constitutionalist General Carlos Prats in Buenos Aires (1974) and former diplomat Orlando Letelier in Washington D.C. (1976), and they seriously injured Christian Democrat politician Bernardo Leighton in a shooting in Italy (1975).

The Pinochet Dictatorship

While the Pinochet dictatorship was a murderous police state, it was more than just that. Compared with neighboring Argentina, which experienced a bloodless 1976 coup with a bloody aftermath that went on for years afterward, the Pinochet regime did its worst at the beginning. While suspending civil liberties, banning political parties, and enforcing measures such as a *toque de queda* (curfew) that required citizens to be off the street by 11 P.M. well into the 1980s, it also undertook a coherent, if controversial, economic program that transformed the way many Chileans live and work.

Inspired by the "Chicago School" of economists, the regime instituted the most radical free market transformation experiment ever implemented. It auctioned off state enterprises to balance the budget, drastically reduced regulatory functions, promoted private health and pension plans in competition with the state-run system, and encouraged foreign investment with favorable

legislation. Despite some glitches—high inflation persisted for several years, an unanticipated devaluation reduced salaries to a pittance, and continued low copper prices slowed recovery—nontraditional exports such as off-season temperate fruits helped diversify the economy. By 1980, the recovery was impressive enough that Pinochet could hold—and win—a plebiscite that established a new constitution and confirmed his "presidency" until 1989. Many voters, however, abstained from the plebiscite, whose options were a simple "yes" or "no."

Confident of public support, Pinochet permitted political parties to operate openly again in 1987. Under his customized constitution, drafted by rightist lawyer Jaime Guzmán, Pinochet held another plebiscite to extend his period in office until 1997. In this instance, though, the increasing space for public dialogue encouraged an alliance of centrist and center-left parties that became known as the Concertación para la Democracia (Consensus for Democracy) to oppose him.

The turning point in the so-called "No" campaign occurred when Socialist Ricardo Lagos, in a television appearance on April 25, 1988, stared down the dictator with a *dedazo* (pointing finger) and a verbal challenge: "You promise the country another eight years of torture, disappearances, and human rights violations." Despite widespread expectations that Lagos (now Chile's president) would be arrested, the regime's failure to respond emboldened the Concertación, and the electorate rejected the extension of Pinochet's term by a healthy majority.

Rejuvenating Democracy

In 1989, Christian Democrat Patricio Aylwin easily won a four-year transitional presidency as candidate of the Concertación. Nevertheless, certain provisions of the Pinochet-Guzmán constitution—congressional elections that required doubling the opposition vote to take both seats in a district, designated senators from the armed forces, Pinochet's continuance as head of the army until 1997, and his subsequent senatorship as a former "president of the republic"—all perpetuated a dictatorial legacy.

SEE YOU IN COURT

Even though the Pinochet dictatorship ended more than a decade ago, repercussions from those years are likely to continue as unresolved issues work their way through the courts in Chile, Argentina, and elsewhere. A Buenos Aires judge, for instance, has asked for the extradition of General Pinochet and others, including General Manuel Contreras, U.S. citizen Michael Townley, and Townley's ex-wife Mariana Callejas, for the car bomb assassination of exiled General Carlos Prats and his wife in 1974.

Recently, according to the U.S. TV news program *60 Minutes,* the family of Chilean constitutionalist General René Schneider, killed in a botched October 1970 kidnapping attempt that hoped to evoke a military coup and prevent Salvador Allende from taking office, has filed suit against former U.S. national security adviser Henry Kissinger. The suit alleges that Kissinger's involvement with Chilean coup plotters led to Schneider's death, though Kissinger asserts he had ceased contact with them.

Even the big fish may be back in the aquarium. In January 2002, Chilean Supreme Court President Mario Garrido Montt surprisingly agreed, on a technicality, to review the previous July's Appeals Court ruling (also on a technicality) that temporarily suspended "Caravan of Death" charges against Pinochet for health reasons.

agreement and argued that only Chilean courts could deal with crimes alleged to have occurred in Chile, Pinochet suffered a series of legal reverses in British courts. The general's ordeal—if one can describe house arrest in a suburban London mansion by such a word—ended in March of 2000, when British Home Secretary Jack Straw released him on grounds of ill health.

Though Pinochet went home, he was not quite home free. Unexpectedly, the Chilean justice system and Santiago judge Juan Guzmán in particular undertook an aggressive investigation of human rights complaints that resulted in the loss of Pinochet's senatorial immunity and his indictment in the Caravan of Death and numerous other cases. Unfortunately, a Chilean appeals court ruled, in a divided decision, that the general's ostensibly deteriorating health prevented his mounting a defense and it suspended the proceedings, even though the Chilean criminal code stipulates that only dementia and insanity can justify such a suspension. While Guzmán could theoretically resume the investigation if Pinochet's health improved, the advanced age of the general (born 1915) makes a dramatic recovery unlikely—not to mention inconvenient.

CONTEMPORARY CHILE

Even if Pinochet has escaped final judgment, the fact of his 16-month detention in London, followed by indictment in Chilean courts, released political dialogue from the straitjacket it had worn since 1973. One measure of this new openness was the election to the presidency, in early 2000, of Pinochet critic Ricardo Lagos—the first Socialist to occupy the office since Salvador Allende. Current military leaders, for their part, appear embarrassed by the revelations of the past few years and seem more than willing to resume an apolitical role, subservient to civilian power.

In 1993 presidential elections, Christian Democrat Eduardo Frei Ruiz-Tagle, son of the late President Eduardo Frei Montalva, won a six-year presidential term. Both presidents only tweaked with the economic model they inherited, as Chile experienced strong and steady growth, while arguing for constitutional reforms that would abolish its antidemocratic aspects.

Events overtook this moderate reformism in October 1998, when Scotland Yard officials arrested General Pinochet for human rights violations at the behest of Spanish judge Báltazar Garzón as Garzón investigated deaths and disappearances of Spanish citizens after the 1973 coup. Despite public support from the Frei government, which felt it had to honor its part of the transition

Another positive indicator was a public apology by conservative legislator María Pía Guzmán for having been aware of and ignoring human rights abuses committed during the dictatorship—though she drew fire from her unreconstructed colleagues on the right. Leftist commentator Tomás Moulián, in response, called

the offices of phone company Torre Telefónica CTC, in the shape of a cell phone

© WAYNE BERNHARDSON

Guzmán's apology an example to Chilean society and asked for understanding for those who were in similar circumstances during the military regime. Moulián also denounced those who continue to deny such abuses as a "Taliban" unwilling to give up their holy war against the left.

Nevertheless, most Chileans appear to have moved on. According to editor Patricio Fernández of the iconoclastic newspaper *The Clinic:*

> *[T]he day they indicted the former unconstitutional president [Pinochet], after the surprise of it all, no one really gave a hoot. With the exception of those who lost family members during the military government, or those who are political fanatics, or their accomplices, or three or four strange devils who went out to shout in the streets—the rest of us took the news in stride.*

Still, in Fernández's words:

> *We are left uncomfortable knowing that the Chilean state would much more forcefully prosecute a chicken thief than it would someone responsible for thousands of atrocities.*

Government and Politics

Traditionally, Chilean politics is highly centralized, the ongoing legacy of Diego Portales in a country whose sprawling capital holds more than a third of the country's population. The 1980 constitution, written by Pinochet's favorite lawyer Jaime Guzmán, changed this only marginally, moving the legislature to the port city of Valparaíso. The central government appoints governors and other officials of the 13 regions, but municipalities or *comunas* elect their own mayors and councilors.

ORGANIZATION

Chile's national government consists of separate and legally independent executive, legislative, and judicial branches. The popularly elected president works out of Santiago's La Moneda presidential palace but no longer resides in the building.

The bicameral Congreso Nacional (National Congress) consists of a 46-member Senado (Senate) and a 120-member Cámara de Diputados, both based in Valparaíso. Only 38 senators are elected, however, as eight are "institutional," including former heads of the armed forces and ex-presidents, a still controversial legacy of the Pinochet years. Public sentiment is strongly in favor of abolishing the institutional senators, whose very presence makes obtaining the two-thirds majority vote necessary for passing a constitutional amendment exceptionally difficult to achieve, but as of early 2002 even the right-wing UDI (confident of its increasing electoral strength) appeared willing to consider reforms.

The 21-member Corte Suprema, the Santiago-based Supreme Court, is the highest judicial authority.

POLITICAL PARTIES

Chile has many political parties, but Guzmán's carefully and cleverly crafted electoral system (see below) rewards coalitions that pool their votes rather than parties that stand alone. There are two major coalitions: the center-left Concertación para la Democracia (Consensus for Democracy) and the center-right Alianza por Chile (Alliance for Chile). Even within these coalitions, there are ideological and practical tensions that often obstruct their efficient collaboration.

The Concertación, which has won the presidency in every election since the return to democracy, consists of the centrist Democracia Cristiana (DC, Christian Democrats), the more leftist Partido Socialista (PS, Socialist Party, far less radical than it was under Salvador Allende) and Partido por la Democracia (PPD, Party for Democracy), and the Partido Radical Socialista Demócrata (PRSD, Radical Socialist Democratic Party), but there is considerable ideological overlap among all four parties.

The Alianza por Chile consists of the center-right Renovación Nacional (RN, National Renovation) and the far-right Unión Demócratica Independiente (UDI, Independent Democratic Union). While again there is ideological overlap between these parties, the cohesive and fast-growing UDI, founded by Jaime Guzmán, is most closely identified with the military dictatorship. It has also managed to make inroads into poorer neighborhoods with a populist approach.

In addition to the main alliances, there is an assortment of less influential parties, including the Partido Comunista (PC, Communist Party), the Partido Humanista (Humanist Party), and the Partido Liberal (Liberal Party), none of which has any congressional representation.

ELECTIONS

Chile's constitution establishes a six-year term for a popularly elected president, who is not eligible for immediate reelection, though he or she may run again after a six-year hiatus. If no candidate obtains a majority, there is a runoff between the top two finishers.

In a January 2000 presidential runoff, the Concertación's candidate, Socialist Ricardo Lagos,

demonstration by families of disappeared persons

© WAYNE BERNHARDSON

narrowly but clearly defeated the Alianza's Joaquín Lavín after falling just short of a majority in a multicandidate race the month before. Lavín, who presents an agreeable moderate image that has been lacking in the UDI, is by consensus the presidential frontrunner for the 2006 elections, but it's premature even to grant him the nomination; look for a challenge from the RN's Sebastián Piñera, a technocrat who broke early with the Pinochet dictatorship. Lavín's operative (some would say controller) Pablo Longueira is such a hardline Pinochet supporter that opponents have characterized him as a Chilean Taliban.

Under the Pinochet-Guzmán constitution of 1980, the Congreso has a binomial electoral system by which each district (60 for deputies and 19 for senators) elects two officials, but a list or coalition must double its rivals' votes to take both seats. In practice, this has distorted representation in favor of the conservative Alianza, whose total vote has always been smaller than that of the Concertación, though the difference is narrowing. The Congreso renews the 120-strong Chamber of Deputies and half the 38 elected members of the Senate every four years. Voting is obligatory for those registered, but registering to vote is not.

In the congressional elections of December 2001, the Concertación retained a reduced majority in the Cámara de Diputados, with 63 seats to 57, but lost its majority in the Senate, where the Alianza por Chile gained a single seat to tie the Concertación at 24 seats each (the tie exists only because Senator-for-Life Pinochet is unable to occupy his seat without risking resumed prosecution). The biggest single winner was the UDI, which increased its vote percentage over the previous congressional election from 17 to about 25 percent, making it the country's single largest party. On balance, the Concertación drew about 48 percent of the vote and the Alianza about 44 percent, with 5 percent going to the Communists (who have no representation in the Congreso) and the rest to fringe parties.

BUREAUCRACY

Unlike most other Latin American countries, Chile has a reputation for relative cleanliness and honesty in public administration—regularly, the country receives the region's highest rating from the anticorruption organization Transparency International.

For the year 2000, using standards of general corruption in the political arena, bribery in the public sector, irregular payment practices, and obstacles to business, Transparency gave Chile a 7.5 rating on a 10-point scale, making it the 18th-cleanest of the 91 states evaluated in the study. The next closest Latin American country was Uruguay, which received a 5.1 rating; the United States, by way of comparison, received an only slightly higher rating of 7.8. In a business survey by Price Waterhouse Cooper, Chile ranked second after Singapore in terms of transparency.

The government institutions most travelers are likely to come into contact with are immigration, customs, and police, all of which are trustworthy as institutions. There are, however, instances of renegade cops who rob, steal, and intimidate, especially in lower-class neighborhoods.

THE MILITARY

Only a few years ago, it would have been impossible to write about Chilean politics without emphasizing the role of the military, whose impunity was the single greatest menace to domestic tranquility despite its background role. After Pinochet's arrest in London, his subsequent (suspended) prosecution in Santiago, the public revelations of human rights abuses under the dictatorship, and the imprisonment of individuals such as former intelligence officer Manuel Contreras, the current military leadership has kept its distance from the former regime, though many retired officers remain unrepentant.

Under the constitution, the heads of the army, navy, air force, and Carabineros form a large part of the Consejo Nacional de Seguridad (Cosena, or National Security Council), which can suspend civil liberties and declare martial law; in addition, the president may not dismiss the heads of the armed forces, and he must choose a replacement for retiring service heads from a list provided by the services themselves. Despite these provisions, as of mid-2001 it seemed likely that constitutional reforms would make the military commanders-in-chief subject to civilian authority and remove them from a voting role in the Cosena.

The army has also begun to reduce its ranks, as its commander-in-chief General Ricardo Izurieta confirmed the dismissal of 2,000 soldiers by the end of 2001 and a reduction of the number of generals from 41 to 38. Still, the army has nearly 50,000 members in active service, almost half of them youthful conscripts carrying out their obligatory military service (which, however, is not universal). The remainder include 4,500 officers and 16,000 noncommissioned officers.

The navy contingent of 25,000 includes about 5,200 marines; its hardware consists of 29 vessels, only six of which are combat ships, plus three Talcahuano-based submarines. The 12,500-strong air force (FaCh) has bases at Iquique, Antofagasta, Santiago, Puerto Montt, and Punta Arenas, and on Antarctica's King George Island.

There are about 30,000 Carabineros, or paramilitary police.

Educational changes in the military are tentatively encouraging. The class of 2001 at the army's Escuela Militar (War College) will study human rights and international humanitarian law, a first in Chile's history. Cadets will also pursue civilian courses parallel to their military studies and graduate with a major in military science and a minor in humanities or science, which will be equally recognized in civilian careers. In addition, the navy, the most conservative branch of the forces, will finally admit women in 2003, but only as doctors and lawyers.

The military continues to enjoy substantial privileges, however. Chile devotes a higher percentage of its GDP than any other Latin American country to military spending, which the law stipulates cannot fall below 1989 levels nor drop in real terms, and the law guarantees it 10 percent of the profits from Codelco's state copper sales.

Economy

While far from the largest economy in Latin America, Chile is one of the most stable and dynamic in the region. For the last decade and a half, its economic performance has been one of almost uninterrupted growth, though the dramatic 7.6 percent average growth rate for the decade that ended in 1998 has fallen into the 3 to 4 percent range. For the year 2000, the estimated GDP was US$70.1 billion, with a per capita figure of about US$4,620, though this disguises considerable income disparities. Inflation for the year 2001 was only 2.6 percent, the second-lowest since Chile began compiling a consumer price index in 1939.

According to the Banco Central (Central Bank), foreign debt is a matter of some concern, as it grew by 7.8 percent in 2000 to a total of US$36.8 billion. This, however, was lower than the 16 percent increases recorded in 1997 and 1998, it was relatively small in relation to Chile's GDP (which has grown 85 percent in the last decade), and only about US$5 billion was publicly held. Toward the end of 2001, as neighboring Argentina headed

for default on its own foreign debt, the Chilean peso faltered but then recovered steadily as it became apparent that the better-managed Chilean economy was unlikely to collapse.

The World Economic Forum's competitiveness evaluation rated Chile among the region's best economies. In addition to a global No. 27 rating, Chile ranked No. 29 in growth potential, No. 21 in macroeconomics and institutions, and No. 28 in business environment, but only No. 42 in technology. Telecommunications, nevertheless, are state-of-the-art and reasonably priced, so that even many Chileans of limited means have access to telephones. The same is less true for Internet connections, as investment in a computer is beyond the reach of many households.

In a similar survey by the International Institute for Management Development, Chile finished first among Latin American economies and 24th in the global rankings—ahead of several European countries, including France and Italy. Rankings depend on nearly 300 separate criteria,

SALVAGING CHILE'S RIVERS

Over the past decade, the only environmental issue to rival forest preservation has been Chile's wild rivers, and the struggle over water rights and development will likely continue well into the future. This complex matter encompasses indigenous rights, energy use, air and water pollution, and economic development, and there's no easy answer.

Chile is poor in fossil-fuel resources, obtaining only about 10 percent of its own crude petroleum consumption and a small amount of coal from domestic sources in the southern region of Magallanes. Both industry and transportation rely on imported fuels, and the capital of Santiago in particular has paid the price with some of the world's most polluted urban skies.

For both economic and environmental reasons, Chile would like to increase its supply of relatively clean hydroelectricity by building dams to hold the spring snowmelt from its numerous transverse rivers. In the course of constructing a series of dams on the Río Biobío, though, the Spanish-Chilean utility Endesa ran afoul of a few determined Pehuenche Indian families who, backed by the Ley Indígena (Indigenous Law) of 1992, vowed that "The only way we will be taken away from here, is once we are dead." In their opposition to the Ralco dam, one of half a dozen planned for the area, the Pehuenche were backed by conservationists and recreationists who saw the Biobío as one of the world's top streamside habitats and white-water rivers, even after construction of Endesa's Pangue dam a few years ago.

The Biobío is not the only threatened Chilean river. Many rafters and kayakers consider the Futaleufú, in southern Region X near the Argentine border, the world's greatest white-water challenge, but Endesa and other energy companies have options on its water rights, despite its isolation. Near the town of Puerto Aisén, in Region XI, the Canadian multinational Noranda has ambitious plans for an aluminum plant that would require hydroelectric dams on three regional rivers to support an industry with high energy requirements and a bad environmental reputation.

Environmental advocates argue that sustainable activities, such as rafting and kayaking, fly-fishing, and even salmon farming (a bogeyman to some conservationists) are more appropriate uses. To promote their cause, Chilean conservation organizations such as the Grupo de Acción Biobío (Biobío Action Group) have made common cause with overseas affiliates such as the International Rivers Network, 1847 Berkeley Way, Berkeley, CA 94703, tel. 510/848-1155, fax 510/848-1008, website: www.irn.org, info@irn.org; and FutaFriends, P.O. Box 1942, Bozeman, MT 59771, tel. 406/586-3460, website: www.futafriends.org, info@futafriends.org.

In the long run, though, narrow economics may win out. In early 2002, former Pehuenche stalwart Berta Quintreman signed a preliminary agreement to sell her disputed lands on the Biobío for a reported several hundred thousand dollars, far more than Endesa paid to other families who moved. Reportedly, the contract has an escape clause, but the precedent is not encouraging.

---

including technological infrastructure and development, government efficiency, educational quality, and workforce productivity.

Perhaps the economy's most obvious weakness is its continuing dependence on mining in general and copper in particular. It is also vulnerable to energy weaknesses: the country gets less than 10 percent of its petroleum consumption from domestic sources, and fuel prices rose by 37 percent in peso terms in 2001; it also depends on erratic rainfall to fill its hydroelectric reservoirs, which produce 60 percent of the energy in the Central Interconnected Power System (SIC), which delivers electricity to 93 percent of the population. South-central Chile's heavy rainfall and extensive rivers make hydroelectricity the country's cheapest energy source, but at considerable environmental cost.

Despite its macroeconomic achievements, contemporary Chile is not without critics. Journalist María Monckeberg's polemical new book, *El Saqueo de Los Grupos Económicos al Estado de*

Chile (The Plundering of the Chilean State by Economic Groups), published in 2001, takes a muckraking approach toward the dictatorship's privatizations, suggesting that the regime's political supporters benefited disproportionately from its economic policies. According to Monckeberg, Pinochet's cronies:

> *appropriated the big state-owned companies at a time when there were no freedoms, no real parliament, no unions and not a single newspaper that realized what was going on or was free to print it. Given those circumstances, the bottom line is they were free to do whatever they wanted.*

EMPLOYMENT, UNEMPLOYMENT, AND UNDEREMPLOYMENT

In the International Institute for Management Development's 2001 survey, Chile displayed many strengths, but the quality of its labor force was a mixed bag, as Chileans worked the longest hours on average of any country in the world, but per-hour productivity was low. According to a survey by Swiss bank UBS of working hours in 60 cities worldwide, the average Santiago resident worked 2,244 hours in 2000—equivalent to six hours per day for 365 consecutive days (Chile has no legal limits on work hours per week).

Santiago's number-one ranking put it well above the Latin American average of 2,048 work-hours per year. On the other hand, the production level of the average U.S. worker is equivalent to US$36.29 per hour, while the Chilean average is US$5.50 per hour.

In the last quarter of 2001, according to the Instituto Nacional de Estadística (INE, National Statistics Institute), Chile's unemployment figures hovered around 9.7 percent. It was higher in some regions, however, exceeding 11 percent in Region I (Tarapacá), Region III (Atacama), and Region VIII (Biobío). Even in the Metropolitan Region of Santiago, normally the most economically robust part of the country, it exceeded 9 percent. These figures can be misleading, however, as unemployment is substantially higher among young people.

It is also misleading in the sense that the standard for calculating unemployment is whether an individual worked at all; if someone spends even an hour in casual labor, he or she counts among the employed. Many individuals also labor as street vendors who hawk ice cream, newspapers, and music cassettes, but their earnings are low and they often run afoul of the police. Likewise, there is seasonal work in agriculture, so unemployment figures tend to fall in the spring and rise again after the autumn harvest.

AGRICULTURE

Chile's agriculture is as diverse as its geography—from peasant cultivation of native grains and tubers on the precordillera terraces of the Norte Grande to the dairy farms of the Sur Chico, the potato fields of Chiloé, the sprawling wool *estancias* of Magallanes and Tierra del Fuego, and even the Polynesian horticultural complex of Easter Island (Rapa Nui). In the narrowest economic sense, though, the most valuable and productive lands are those of the Mediterranean-like heartland.

Pedro de Valdivia himself painted Middle Chile as "the most abounding land in pastures and fields, and for yielding every kind of livestock and plant imaginable." With its fertile alluvial soils, mild temperatures, and lengthy growing season, it yielded more than enough to support the Spaniards—in fact, as the population was so small in the early decades and even into republican times, the land was widely underused despite its suitability for wine grapes, temperate fruits, and abundant grains. It first attracted global attention when Chilean wheat fed the '49ers who scrambled over the Great Plains and sailed around the Horn en route to the California gold fields.

Today, Chile's US$1.6 billion fresh fruit export industry provides half the off-season wintertime fruit consumed in Northern Hemisphere countries, but it's facing sharply increased competition from other Southern Hemisphere producers such as Argentina, New Zealand, and South Africa.

Some Chilean growers are attempting to maintain their leadership in the field by reducing dependency on agricultural chemicals and meeting Good Agricultural Practices (GAP) standards for environmental friendliness and safety; since September 2000, 215 growers, 37 export firms, and 91 packinghouses have committed themselves to this voluntary program. This would represent about 80 percent of exported Chilean fruit.

Chile has produced wine ever since colonial times, but only the influx of French varieties in the 19th century gave it commercial significance, and the great export boom in Chilean wines has occurred in the past decade or so. Commercial vines are grown from Region III (Atacama) in the north, where the crop primarily consists of *pisco* grapes, to Region IX (Araucanía) in the south, where production is precarious, but the prime wine district runs from Region V (Valparaíso) through Region VII (Maule).

The United States is the largest export market for Chilean wines and, though fine wine exports have grown substantially in recent years, some experts are concerned that Chilean production is unsustainably dependent on chemicals. Chile has declined to participate in the Treaty on Standardized Wine-Making Practices, signed by the United States, Australia, New Zealand, and Canada, but European and North American producers are nevertheless establishing Chilean operations.

One interesting development in Chilean agriculture is a plan to establish organic agricultural standards for all of Region XI (Aisén), which would ease the export of products such as beef to the European Community. This could also apply to fruit-growing in the small but productive "banana belt" around Lago General Carrera, and even to fish farming.

INDUSTRY

If tropical Latin American nations have been "banana republics," Chile for most of the 20th century was a "copper republic," and mining remains its major foreign exchange earner. In the year 2000, copper revenues of US$7.3 billion accounted for 40 percent of all exports. Falling copper prices, from US$.82 per pound in 2000 to only US$.60 at the end of 2001, make the sector and the economy vulnerable.

Its share of total exports has dropped by half since the early 1970s but has remained stable since the early 1990s. While Chile has been in the vanguard of privatization of state-owned companies, even the Pinochet dictatorship did not dare privatize Codelco, the powerful state copper corporation—likely because the law designates 10 percent of all copper profits to the military. Private mining companies now outproduce Codelco, however.

Mining as a whole accounts for more than 11 percent of Chilean GDP; other minerals include iron ore, nitrates, precious metals, lithium, and molybdenum. The greatest mines are in the Norte Grande, where Chuquicamata is the world's largest open pit mine but several others of more recent vintage are making substantial progress. The El Teniente mine east of Rancagua is the world's largest subsurface mine.

Other industrial activities include mineral refining and metal manufacturing, food and fish processing, forest products industries including paper and wood (see below), and textiles. In addition to Santiago, the major industrial centers are the Concepción-Talcahuano and Valparaíso-Viña del Mar conurbations.

FORESTRY

After mining, the single most important export contributor is forestry, expected to total about US$2.1 million in the year 2001, a figure roughly equivalent to 11 percent of exports. This is down about 10 percent, however, from a banner year in 1999. Most exports consist of wood pulp, though finished furniture is increasing.

The forestry sector is a controversial one for environmental reasons, as overexploitation of native forests and their subsequent replacement by plantations of exotics such as Monterey pine and eucalyptus have created biological deserts. It is also controversial for social and political reasons, as forestry companies have occupied ancestral lands of the Mapuche Indians, who are increasingly vocal in seeking their return.

LANDS FOR THE MAPUCHE

In the decade-plus since the end of Chile's military dictatorship, Mapuche communities have become increasingly assertive in seeking the return of ancestral lands. During the Pinochet regime, in the area south of the Biobío, Chilean and foreign forestry companies purchased and planted former Mapuche lands with fast-growing exotics such as eucalyptus and Monterey pine, but since the center-left Concertación gained the presidency in 1990, it has acquired more than 120,000 hectares for the Mapuche.

The government of President Ricardo Lagos hopes to return another 150,000 hectares, roughly the amount held by the Mapuche in 1973, before its term expires in 2006. In January 2001, it even created a Comisión de Verdad y Nuevo Trato para los Pueblos Indígenas (Indigenous People's Historic Truth and Reform Commission), headed by former President Patricio Aylwin, with representatives from Mapuche, the Aymara, Easter Islanders, and Atacameños, as well as government officials, religious leaders, and academics.

Not everyone was satisfied, however. The commission excluded groups such as the militant Coordinador Arauco-Malleco, a direct-action splinter that rejects all negotiations with forestry companies,

and the Consejo Todas las Tierras (All Lands Council). Some Mapuche leaders, such as *lonko* Juana Calfunao Paillalef, called for creation of an autonomous Mapuche parliament. A handful of violent incidents led the previous administration of President Eduardo Frei Ruiz-Tagle to speculate on a new Chiapas smoldering in the south.

According to Lagos, though, only about 50 of 2,200 Mapuche communities are in conflict with the government, though about 60 different Mapuche organizations in Santiago were prepared to join protests in Arauco, including a march from Tirúa to the Region VIII capital of Concepción. One of the demands of the urban Mapuche was the creation of a Mapuche municipality in the Metropolitan Region.

Worried about the decline in forestry investment, the government managed to persuade Forestal Mininco, one of the targets of Mapuche protest, to provide job training and economic assistance for surrounding communities. This, however, is unlikely to placate those dissatisfied with shortcomings in health, educational, and what they consider the inferior quality of the lands so far returned to the aboriginal peoples of the south.

FISHING AND FISH FARMING

Thanks to the productive north-flowing Humboldt or Peru Current that parallels the coast, Chile has become one of the world's leading fisheries countries. Northern cities such as Iquique and Antofagasta are major producers of fishmeal, but a more recent development is salmon farming in the cool ocean inlets and lakes from the southern Sur Chico south through Aisén and into Magallanes.

According to the Asociación de Productores de Salmón y Trucha (Association of Salmon and Trout Producers), the total volume of Chile's salmon exports for the year 2000 was 206,000 tons, valued at US$973 million. Of those exports, Japan took 53.7 percent (110,600 tons, valued at US$477 million), while the United States took 31.6 percent (65,000 tons, US$358

million). Other Latin American countries amounted to only 6.4 percent (13,100 tons), European countries 5.5 percent (11,300 tons) and others 3 percent (6,300 tons).

This flourishing industry and its profits, however, have largely developed at the expense of environmental quality. Salmon feces, waste feed, and antibiotics have contaminated previously pristine lakes and waterways, and escaped fish have flourished at the expense of native stock. Some salmon farmers have also been responsible for killing sea lions who find easy dinner pickings around the floating cages.

RICH AND POOR

The gap between rich and poor, once an issue of the landed and the landless, is more complex today. The issue has not totally disappeared, especially among the Mapuche of the southern heartland and northern Sur Chico who hope to reclaim ancestral lands from forestry companies and *fundos,* but in general the notion of agrarian reform and land redistribution is a matter of the past.

More important is the difference between hereditary wealth and a nouveau riche plutocracy on the one hand, and a struggling working class on the other. The gap between rich and poor remains one of Chile's most intractable problems despite the country's macroeconomic successes—in 1998, according to the Economist Intelligence Unit, the wealthiest 20 percent of Chileans received 61 percent of all income, while the top 10 percent received 46 percent of all income. The lowest 20 percent, by contrast, earned only 3.5 percent of total income. The income ratio of the highest to lowest 20 percent was 17 to 1.

According to Planning Minister Alejandra Krauss, three million or about 20 percent of all

© WAYNE BERNHARDSON

reeling in sea urchins on a fishing pier in Pisagua

Chileans live in poverty, earning less than US$66 per month. About 850,000 live in abject poverty, on less than US$33 per month. While these figures are an improvement from the last years of the Pinochet dictatorship, when the poverty figure was 40 percent, the rate is falling more slowly at present. Further statistics indicate that a third of Chilean children live in poverty.

By contrast, two Chileans made the most recent *Forbes* list of the world's richest people: Andronico Luksic and Eliodoro Matte shared 387th place with estimated fortunes of US$1.3 billion. Luksic owns a majority stake in the giant CCU brewery, Banco Edwards, Banco de Chile, the manufacturer Madeco, the Carrera hotel group, and Latin America's biggest mining group, while Matte owns forestry company CMPC and the Bicecorp financial conglomerate. In 1996, five Chileans made the list: Luksic, Matte, fisheries magnate Anacleto Angelini, Ricardo Claro (owner of the Santa Rita winery, glass manufacturer Cristalerías Chile, and the CSAV shipping company), and Jose Said (owner of soft drinks distributor Embotelladora Andina and Santiago's enormous Parque Arauco shopping mall).

To put this into context, it would take a Chilean earning the national minimum wage (US$175 per month) 571,428 years to equal Luksic and Matte's fortune, and a little under three million years to displace Microsoft's Bill Gates from the top of the list. White-collar crime (fraud and tax evasion) by the rich are also common, by some estimates as high as 7 percent of GDP. Failure to provide benefits and overtime to employees is endemic and Chilean wages are, in any event, low compared to price levels for many items.

The gap between rich and poor has geographical as well as social dimensions—during the 1990s boom, the most flourishing regions, with growth rates in the 10 percent range, were northern Region I (Tarapacá), Region II (Antofagasta), Region III (Atacama), and the Metropolitan Region of Santiago (which, incidentally, accounts for 40 percent of the country's GDP). By contrast, the southern Region XII (Magallanes) grew by less than 2 percent, though it also has the lowest poverty rates at 10.9 percent; Aisén (Region XI) has the highest at 32.1 percent. Even the apparent prosperity of the north is a bit misleading, since capital-intensive mining has been responsible for most of the growth.

Rural poverty is decreasing, however. According to the governmental Instituto de Desarrollo Agropecuario (INDAP, National Agricultural Development Institute), more than half the rural population lived below the poverty line in 1990 and more than 20 percent had no form of income. Today the figures are 26.7 percent and 8.7 percent, respectively.

EDUCATION

Literacy is formally high, upward of 95 percent, but many more Chileans may be functionally illiterate, unable to understand instructions, prescriptions, warning labels, and even classified advertisements. Education is free through high school and compulsory to age 12, but 1.2 million of the five million labor force have not completed their secondary education. Many schoolchildren lack complementary educational resources, such as books and computers, at home, and scores on international math and science tests are relatively low.

While university education is generally of high quality, it traditionally generates a surfeit of high-status degrees in fields such as law or intellectually stimulating but less clearly practical subjects such as sociology, and not enough in hands-on fields such as engineering and computer science. At the same time, there is little respect for technical or vocational skills, even when those jobs pay more than white-collar positions or office work. Many workers lack initiative and require supervision to go beyond narrowly prescribed duties.

TOURISM

Tourism is a growing factor in the economy, employing more than 200,000 Chileans. According to Sernatur, the state agency in charge of the sector, the number of foreign visitors increased 6.8 percent in 2000, to a total of 1,742,666. Total tourism revenues for the year were about US$2.8 billion, representing about 4 percent of GDP.

Most visitors, however, come from other South American countries, mainly Argentina (856,675 in 2000), Peru (155,060), Bolivia (110,284), and Brazil (72,789). From outside the continent, the greatest numbers came from the United States (133,998), Germany (43,918), Spain (36,271), France (32,713), the United Kingdom (28,544), and Italy (20,015). Over the previous year, these figures represent increases of 15 percent from the United Kingdom, 12.2 percent from Canada, 8 percent from the United States and 5 percent from France.

The 350,000 American and European travelers who came to Chile accounted for only 20 percent of the visitors to the country, but they spent nearly US$500 million, or about half the total tourism income. North American visitors spent an average of US$78 daily and Europeans spent an average of US$65, while Argentines, for example, spent only US$30 per day. Overseas visitors also stay longer—the average European spent about two weeks in the country, while guests from other South American countries stayed only about nine days. In the aftermath of the 2001 terrorist attacks on the United States, Chile appears to have benefited from increased European tourist traffic, but North American numbers have stagnated.

Compared with other countries, however, Chile spends little on promotion; in 2001, the total was about US$2.6 million, only about US$700,000 of that from government, according to the Santiago-based Corporación de Promoción Turística. Argentina, by contrast, spent about US$13 million and New Zealand US$45 million. There are few tourist offices outside the country—in Miami and Madrid only.

Chile is proposing an entry tax hike to generate up to US$15 million to promote tourism from the United States and Europe, in the hope that doubling visitors from those regions will triple income. One great advantage, in addition to Chile's natural and cultural attractions, is that it may well be the safest country in the hemisphere, but it would also be fair to add that it has a low international profile except for the hangover from unfortunate publicity such as the Pinochet controversy.

Population and People

According to initial returns from the 2002 census, Chile's population is estimated at about 15 million. It is growing at a modest rate of approximately 1.3 percent per annum, at which it would take more than 53 years to double. Similar to rates in many Western European countries, this is one of the continent's most stable figures; consequently the population is getting older—by 2009, the population under age 15 and over 65 will be about equal.

Birth rates are decreasing, infant mortality decreasing, and life expectancy increasing (the average is now 75 years, 72 for males and 78 for females). The Instituto Nacional de Estadística (INE, National Statistics Institute) calculates that by the year 2020 more than 3 million of the predicted 18.7 million Chileans will be more than 60 years old. This, of course, will require significant changes in health care.

Up to another million Chileans live outside their homeland's borders. Other countries with substantial Chilean populations include Argentina (338,000), the United States (106,000), Brazil (54,000), Venezuela (45,000), Canada (33,000), and Spain (26,000). On the other hand, one recent estimate says that more than 66,000 Peruvians live in Chile.

POPULATION GEOGRAPHY

The population distribution is complex, both regionally and in urban-rural terms. About 86 percent of all Chileans live in cities or towns, roughly a third of them in Santiago, its suburbs, and the rest of the Metropolitan Region. Santiago's population is at least 10 times greater than Valparaíso/Viña del Mar or Concepción/Talcahuano, the country's next largest urban areas.

At the other extreme, about 50,000 people, less than half a percent of the population, live in the remote Aisén region, which comprises about a third of the country's territory. In the desert north, there is a handful of large cities, such as Antofagasta, Iquique, and Arica, but rural settlements are few and small; in much of the heartland and the Sur Chico, rural population density is relatively high.

Indigenous Peoples

Chile's population is largely mestizo, of mixed Spanish and indigenous heritage, but roughly a

WHAT'S IN A NAME?

Like many other Latin Americans, Chileans customarily use double surnames to identify themselves; a child takes both the paternal and maternal surnames, in that order. In the case of Salvador Allende Gossens, for example, Allende comes from the father's side, while Gossens comes from the mother. Normally, Salvador would go by the surname Allende, but he would sign legal documents as Allende Gossens.

Marriage complicates the issue somewhat. After marrying Salvador Allende, Hortensia Bussi Soto became Hortensia Bussi de Allende. Their daughter Isabel (not the novelist, but a current Socialist legislator), in turn, goes by the surnames Allende Bussi. Hortensia's own surname would be lost in the succeeding generation.

There are exceptions even to these rules, especially when elite families want to retain conspicuous evidence of their heritage—the late President Eduardo Frei Montalva (1964–70) married María Ruiz-Tagle Jiménez, whose hyphenated first surname dates well back into Chilean history. The children of their son, former President Eduardo Frei Ruiz-Tagle (1994–2000), will lose the prestigious Ruiz-Tagle surname, however.

For visitors to Chile, aside from knowing which surname to use when dealing with locals, this has a more practical application—don't be surprised to hear Chilean officials, at immigration offices or elsewhere, use your middle name on the assumption that it's really your father's surname.

© WAYNE BERNHARDSON

Aymara women in Parinacota

million Mapuche inhabit the area south of the Biobío—not to mention Santiago boroughs such as Cerro Navia, La Pintana, El Bosque, Pudahuel, and Peñalolén, where some community leaders are concerned that the younger generations are losing contact with their heritage.

The Mapuche constitute about 90 percent of Chile's total indigenous population. About 5 percent are Aymara in Region I (Tarapacá), with much smaller numbers of Kolla (Quechua) and Atacameños in Region II (Antofagasta), Rapanui on their namesake island, and remnants of Kawasqar (Alacaluf) and Yámana (Yahgan) in the southern fjords and rainforests of Region XI (Aisén) and Region XII (Magallanes).

Eighty percent of the indigenous population lives in cities and towns, only 20 percent in the countryside, but urban indigenous populations are getting less assistance in buying property than those who remain on the land. Still, some feel optimistic about developments in the country—in the words of one Aymara woman, because of

an increasingly sympathetic government, "it's a good time to be an indigenous person in Chile."

Ethnic Minorities

The surnames of Chile's nonindigenous populations suggest a potpourri of nationalities—Spanish, Basque, Italian, German, Anglo, and many others—but they do not form such obvious ethnic communities as, say, Italian Americans in New York or Irish Americans in Boston.

Chile has a small community of Jews in Santiago and Viña del Mar, and a somewhat larger population of Palestinian origin; the two appear to live without animosity. In the Norte Grande, once part of Peru, there exists a small but increasingly vocal Afro-Chilean minority; living primarily in the rural communities of Azapa, Lluta, and Camarones, they have formed an organization called Oro Negro (Black Gold) and are trying to determine the number of Chileans with African ancestry.

Language Groups

Spanish is the dominant language, but English is widely spoken in business circles and the tourist industry. The next most widely spoken is Mapundungun, the vernacular of the Mapuche, followed by Aymara, Kolla, Rapanui, Yámana, and Kawasqar.

Several languages have disappeared since the arrival of the Europeans: Chango, Atacameño, Diaguita, Selk'nam, and Chono. Both Yámana and Kawasqar have only a handful of native speakers and may disappear; there are, however, projects to preserve Kawasqar and Yámana, including the creation of alphabets and dictionaries and studies of their grammar.

Rapanui, meanwhile, is at risk because of the island's curious demographic history, which has caused it to be mixed with Tahitian, French, English, and Spanish (which is now universal). Only about 800 people speak the language fluently, but a committee is working on a dictionary and also promoting language use among island youth.

RELIGION

Once almost exclusively Roman Catholic, Chile's religious landscape has become a complex mosaic.

Orthodox Roman Catholicism, of course, was the religion of the conquerors and is still the most widespread faith, though there are conservative and liberal, even radical, factions. Evangelical Protestantism has made tremendous inroads in many sectors of the population in recent decades. A small Jewish community practices in Santiago, while the Mapuche, Aymara, and other indigenous peoples practice their own, sometimes syncretic, rituals.

The Indigenous Heritage

The Spaniards effectively destroyed the institutional religion of the great Andean civilizations, but they were unable to eradicate the deeper pantheistic belief systems that persist to the present in the northern altiplano. Certain Aymara individuals, for instance, are still acknowledged as *yatiri* (healer or diviner), and many natural features such as mountain peaks are considered *wak'a* (shrines or spirits), and even meteorological events such as lightning may have a spiritual significance. Possessing and chewing coca leaves (though technically illegal in Chile) and sacrificing llamas are not unusual. An unself-conscious syncretism is also routine: blatantly phallic statuary, for instance, adorns the perimeter walls of the classic colonial church at the altiplano hamlet of Parinacota.

Mapuche religious practices differ considerably from those of the Aymara, as they are more clearly oriented toward a supreme being, though the antiquity of this belief is uncertain. Shamanism is also widespread, however, and the *machi* combine the roles of seer and healer. Since the 18th century, women have ordinarily been *machis,* but male transvestites are not unheard of; the *machis* also participate in public rituals.

Roman Catholicism

Ever since Pedro de Valdivia arrived in the Río Mapocho valley, Roman Catholicism has played an influential role in Chilean history. The Church has also left its imprint on the cultural landscape—despite the ravages of earthquakes, colonial churches have left a lasting imprint in Santiago de Chile and other cities and towns, along with chapels in the altiplano. The unique churches and chapels of Chiloé have made the archipelago a UNESCO World Heritage Site.

Starting with the famous Dominican Bartolomé de las Casas in Mexico, factions in the Church have wrestled with the contradictions between its official mission of recruiting and saving souls and its duty to alleviate the misery of those who have experienced secular injustice and persecution. Chile is no exception–figures such as the contemporary priest Miguel Hasbun have been outright apologists for the Pinochet regime but others, such as the Church's Vicaría de la Solidaridad, lobbied against its excesses and for return to democracy. Some more militant clergy worked in the slums under the influence of "liberation theology," and some lost their lives in the aftermath of the Pinochet coup.

While most observers laud the Church's tireless work on behalf on human rights, it is doctrinally one of the most conservative in Latin America. Though Catholicism has not been the official state religion since 1925, for instance, its intense lobbying has prevented Chile from enacting a divorce law. This has exposed it to charges of hypocrisy, as it often tolerates "annulments" of longstanding marriages for technical reasons.

As elsewhere in Latin America, the Chilean Church has had problems in staffing its widespread dominion, and many sizeable towns lack resident priests. This is one of many factors that have contributed to the rise of evangelical Protestantism in the country.

In both geographical and theological areas, folk beliefs overlap into the official. One of these is the great pilgrimage site at La Tirana, in the pampa east of the Norte Grande city of Iquique, where legend says an Inka princess who had resisted the Spaniards but also taken a Spanish captive as her lover was executed by her followers for accepting his spiritual beliefs.

Protestantism

Protestantism in Chile dates from the 19th century, when European merchants established themselves in Valparaíso, Santiago, and other Chilean cities after independence. The first "nonconformist" cemetery was in the Norte Chico port of Caldera, and other cities soon had their "Cementerios de

Disidentes," but it would be fair to say that most Chileans looked upon Anglicans, Lutherans, and other conventional Protestant denominations with an air of distrust and even disdain for many decades. This has changed enough, however, that the Protestant affiliation of Ricardo Lagos was not an issue in the 1999–2000 presidential election.

Evangelical Protestantism: Evangelical Protestantism boomed in the late 20th century as the Catholic Church neglected many isolated rural communities, and it skyrocketed as desperate people sought spiritual solace in the turmoil of the 1970s and 1980s.

Among evangelical Protestantism's strengths are its spontaneity, absence of hierarchy, and opposition to alcoholism, a scourge of many communities. It takes years of arduous study to become a Catholic priest, but evangelism is a free market and almost anybody with the charisma and intensity to attract enough followers can be a successful street or storefront preacher. That said, the evangelicals get lots of financial support from overseas and political support from within.

Many evangelicals are reformed alcoholics, while spouses and family members of alcoholics, while the Catholic Church has often taken a very laissez-faire attitude toward a problem that has divided families and communities for centuries. The particularly aggressive Church of Jesus Christ of Latter Day Saints is a controversial presence and Mormon churches were, until a few years ago, targets of repeated bombings.

Evangelical Protestantism is especially strong among low-income communities and in rural areas, where the official Catholic presence is weak. A study by the Universidad Católica admits that about 14 percent of Chileans are evangelicals, but this rises to 21 percent among low-income populations. Among upper-income Chileans, about 82 percent are Catholic and only 6 percent evangelical.

Other Religions

The Chilean constitution guarantees freedom of religion, and adherents of non-Christian faiths are no longer rare, if not exactly widespread or numerous. Among those represented are Judaism, Islam, the Baha'i faith, Sikhism, and Buddhism.

LANGUAGE

Spanish is Chile's official language and the language of commerce. In the tourist sector, it's not unusual to find English speakers, but it's better to obtain a working knowledge of Spanish than to rely absolutely on finding them. Even if your linguistic skills are limited, making an effort earns a lot of goodwill.

While Spanish is nearly universal, many indigenous Chileans are bilingual or even multilingual.

Language Study

There are significant opportunities for studying Spanish in Chile. The major centers for language study are in Santiago, but there are also possibilities in Iquique, Talca, Los Ángeles, and Coyhaique. (For more information, see the appropriate geographical entries.)

CONDUCT AND CUSTOMS

Proper conduct and respect for local mores require special attention from travelers unaccustomed to traveling among indigenous peoples. When greeting Chileans, it is always good form to offer the appropriate polite greeting *buenos días* (good morning), *buenas tardes* (good afternoon), or *buenas noches* (good evening or good night), depending on the time of day.

In terms of general conduct, both women and men should dress conservatively and inconspicuously when visiting churches, chapels, and sacred sites. This, again, is an issue of respect for local customs.

Photographic Etiquette

It is highly inappropriate to take an in-your-face approach to photographing indigenous peoples, particularly the Mapuche, however irresistible the temptation. If the inclusion of people is incidental to, say, a landscape, this is usually not a problem, but where a person is the primary subject of the photograph it is best, if you manage Spanish or have another language in common, to try to establish a relationship before asking permission to photograph. If you have negotiated a crafts market purchase, for instance, there will almost certainly be no problem, but when in doubt ask, and respect your subject's decision.

If photographing an individual with his or her consent, it is appropriate to offer to send him or her a copy of the photo; in some areas, people believe that all cameras are Polaroids (*cámaras instantáneas*) and may expect to see the results immediately.

Women Travelers

Like many other parts of Latin America, Chilean society has strong *machista* (male chauvinist) elements. Though nearly everybody visits and leaves Chile without experiencing any unpleasantness, women are certainly not exempt from harassment and, rarely, violence.

If you do receive unwanted attention, the best strategy is to ignore it, and the odds are that the problem will go away on his own. If not, the next best option is to return to your hotel, a restaurant, or some other public place where harassment will be more conspicuous and you're likely to find support. Some women have suggested wearing a bogus wedding ring, but it's possible truly persistent suitors might see this as a challenge.

Gay and Lesbian Travelers

Publicly, at least, homosexuality is taboo in Chile, though there are a substantial number of openly gay entertainment venues in Santiago and in resort towns such as Viña del Mar. When in doubt, though, discretion is advisable. (For more information, see the Special Interests entry in the On the Road chapter.)

On the Road

Chile's highlights are plentiful, but only a handful of them, such as Parque Nacional Torres del Paine and Rapa Nui (Easter Island) enjoy a high international profile—the former is a UNESCO World Biosphere Reserve, the latter a World Heritage Site. It's a pity—but perhaps a plus for those who prefer to avoid the crowds—that most of its other natural and cultural attractions get little attention.

In the Norte Grande, for instance, Parque Nacional Lauca is an equally important World Biosphere Reserve that blends high Andean scenery with abundant wildlife and ruins and descendants of the continent's great pre-Columbian civilizations. The Atacama Desert village of San Pedro de Atacama retains much of its indigenous and colonial ambience even as it swarms with overseas tourists who explore its polychrome Valle de la Luna and the geysers at El Tatio. East of the port of Iquique, spectacular pre-Columbian geoglyphs adorn the desert hillsides and atmospheric ghost towns recall the nitrate mining boom of a century ago.

While most beachgoers might choose the Caribbean, the city of La Serena has miles of long sandy beaches and its nearby Elqui valley is the place to sample *pisco,* Chile's powerful grape brandy and watch the stars—some claim UFOs—under the Southern Hemisphere's clearest skies. The more southerly and traditional beach resort of Viña del Mar may be overrated, but the winding alleyways and dis-

PTO. MONTT 594
TEMUCO 968
SANTIAGO 1639
COPIAPO 2444
ARICA 3704
CON TRANSBORDO
EN CHAITEN

Settlements along the Carretera Austral are few and far between.

tinctive architecture of the nearby port of Valparaíso offer one of the continent's greatest urban experiences.

If Viña del Mar is overrated, the capital city of Santiago is an underrated metropolis of quality museums, lively neighborhoods and nightlife, and worth a trip just for the food; in winter, major ski resorts are less than an hour from downtown. Increasingly accessible to tourist traffic, vineyards in the vicinity complement Santiago's gastronomic progressivism.

Almost unknown to non-Chileans, the wild Andean backcountry east of the city of Talca would draw hordes of visitors if it were so close to a comparable midsize town in North America or Europe. Farther south, in the Sur Chico, towns such as Pucón and Puerto Varas are gateways to the popular Andean lake region and Chile's most popular national parks, but even here the backcountry gets relatively few hikers and trekkers, especially outside the January–February peak season.

Archipelagic Chile, to the south, starts with the Chiloé group, with its scenic inlets and especially its vernacular architecture, which have earned it World Heritage Site status. The Carretera Austral, a discontinuous longitudinal highway linked to the mainland by ferries, snakes southward through the mountainous and well-watered Aisén region, paralleled by a spectacularly scenic and sheltered ferry route that reaches Puerto Natales, the gateway to Torres del Paine. An even more spectacular fjordland lies beneath the ice caps of Tierra del Fuego, southeast of the Gold Rush city of Punta Arenas.

And for the ultimate escape, don't forget the Juan Fernández archipelago, another World Biosphere Reserve that also gave literature the story of Robinson Crusoe, the planet's most famous castaway.

Outdoor Recreation

Chile offers exciting options for hiking, climbing, and mountain-biking in the Andes, bird-watching in the high lakes of the northern altiplano, the shoreline and wetlands of the Pacific Ocean, and the fjords of the southern rainforests. From Santiago south to Aisén, rafting and kayaking on Chile's various transverse rivers vary from suitable for novices to world-class. The long Pacific shoreline provides a multitude of breaks for surfers.

(For suggestions as to possible operators, see the Organized Tours entry below.)

PROTECTED AREAS

While Chile has an impressive roster of national parks, reserves, and monuments, covering a remarkably large area, it has been criticized for not doing more to conserve environmentally significant areas close to population centers, especially when conservation conflicts with established economic interests such as forestry and mining.

The main conservation agency is the Corporación Nacional Forestal (Conaf, or National Forestry Corporation), which manages the Sistema Nacional de Áreas Silvestres Protegidas (Snaspe, or National Protected Areas System). Within Snaspe, Chile has three principal categories of protected areas: *parques nacionales* (national parks), *reservas nacionales* (national reserves), and *monumentos naturales* (natural monuments). In addition, Chilean law allows the establishment of *reservas naturales privadas* or *santuarios de la naturaleza,* private nature reserves of which there are only a few as yet.

Conaf defines each of its 31 *parques nacionales* as "a generally extensive area where there exist either unique or biologically representative environments, not significantly affected by human intervention and capable of self-sustainability, whose flora and fauna or geological formations are of special educational, scientific or recreational interest." Its management objectives are to preserve samples of these environments, their cultural and scenic characteristics, the continuity of natural processes, and promote activities associated with education, research, and recreation.

Chile has 15 *monumentos naturales,* defined as a smaller area "characterized by the presence of native flora and fauna, or the existence of geologically relevant sites of scenic, cultural or scientific interest." Its management objectives are similar to those of national parks, on a scale commensurate with its resources.

The 48 *reservas nacionales,* according to Conaf, are areas "whose natural resources require special attention because of their susceptibility to degradation or importance to the welfare of nearby communities." The primary management objectives are soil and watershed conservation, the preservation of endangered wild flora and fauna, and the application of appropriate technologies to those ends.

The following paragraphs summarize Snaspe's most important units by vernacular region but omit some of the less accessible ones (for details, see individual geographical entries). They also include privately owned protected areas, some of which are, again, covered in detail by individual geographical entries.

Norte Grande

The Norte Grande's greatest and most accessible protected area is **Parque Nacional Lauca,** a UNESCO World Biosphere Reserve of snow-topped volcanic cones, cobalt blue lakes teeming with wildfowl, and high-altitude grasslands that pasture the endangered vicuña, along with the llamas and alpacas of Aymara herders. Also featuring charming indigenous villages with colonial churches and chapels, 137,883-hectare Lauca is contiguous to the equally interesting 209,131-hectare **Reserva Nacional Las Vicuñas** and the 11,298-hectare **Monumento Natural Salar de Surire,** both of which once formed part of the park but now have separate management plans.

In the pampa east of the coastal city of Iquique, the 100,650-hectare **Reserva Nacional Pampa del Tamarugal** protects plantations of the native *tamarugo,* a relative of the North American mesquite, which covered large parts of the region before its near extinction for mining. To its east, hugging the Bolivian border, the 174,744-hectare **Parque Nacional Volcán Isluga** resembles Lauca in its landscapes, flora, and fauna, but it has even more impressive cultural and historical resources; new roads and improved transportation have made it more accessible.

North of the city of Antofagasta, the 31-hectare **Monumento Natural La Portada** is an offshore stack with a natural arch that is the symbol of the city. In the vicinity of the colonial village of San Pedro de Atacama, the 73,896-hectare **Reserva Nacional Los Flamencos** comprises several discrete sectors of environments that vary from blinding salt flats to ashen volcanic summits, all with remarkable scenery and a surprising abundance of wildlife.

North of the city of Calama, the recently created **Reserva Nacional Alto Loa** is yet difficult to reach. Southeast of Antofagasta, the 268,670-hectare **Parque Nacional Llullaillaco** is not open to the public at present because of the presence of land mines along the Argentine border. (The area was mined when the two countries nearly went to war in the late 1970s, and removal has proved slower than both would like.)

Norte Chico

Though it overlaps the Norte Grande's Region II (Antofagasta), the 43,769-hectare **Parque Nacional Pan de Azúcar** is a coastal unit most easily accessible from the Norte Chico town of Chañaral and best known for its offshore Humboldt penguin colonies. Northwest of La Serena, the 859-hectare **Reserva Nacional Pingüino de Humboldt** consists of three offshore islands with even more penguins, many other birds, and marine mammals.

Northeast of the regional capital of Copiapó, the 118,162-hectare **Parque Nacional Nevado Tres Cruces** consists of three separate sectors of arid uplands, occasionally punctuated with high shallow lakes crowded with waterfowl, near the Argentine border.

Northwest of the city of Vallenar, toward the coast, the 45,708-hectare **Parque Nacional Llanos de Challe** is notable for its flora, especially during *desierto florido* (flowering desert) events after rare heavy rains.

In the coast range west of the city of Ovalle, the 9,959-hectare **Parque Nacional Bosque de Fray Jorge** preserves the last substantial segment of endemic Valdivian rainforest in an otherwise arid zone. East of Ovalle, the 128-hectare **Monumento Natural Bosques Petrificados** is the remains of a petrified forest that also contains archaeological sites.

East of Illapel, the 4,229-hectare **Reserva Nacional Las Chinchillas** guards the habitat of the small rodent species that was nearly extinguished for its fur in the early 20th century.

Santiago and the Heartland

In the coast range northeast of Viña del Mar, the 8,000-hectare **Parque Nacional La Campana** is a compact gem of native forest and high peaks that offer spectacular views toward the Andean crest and along the coastline. To the northwest, near the stylish seaside village of Zapallar, the 4.5-hectare **Monumento Natural Isla Cachagua** is a small offshore seabird sanctuary.

Southeast of Viña, the 9,260-hectare **Reserva Nacional Laguna Peñuelas** consists of rolling forest that surrounds the water supply for Viña and the port city of Valparaíso.

Almost directly east of Santiago, the **Santuario de la Naturaleza Yerba Loca** is a municipal but Conaf-administered precordillera forest preserve, with fine hiking trails. Southeast of the capital, the 10,185-hectare **Reserva Nacional Río Clarillo** is a native forest preserve on a tributary of the Río Maipo, but it has fewer trails. To its east, in the upper reaches of the Cajón del Maipo, the 3,009-hectare **Monumento Natural El Morado** is a small but accessible glacial valley with outstanding hiking.

In the Andes east of the regional capital of Rancagua, the 36,882-hectare **Reserva Nacional Río de los Cipreses** is an underappreciated scenic area of coniferous forest. Reached from the cities of Curicó and Talca are two similar and nearly contiguous Andean units: the 5,026-hectare **Reserva Nacional Radal Siete Tazas**, renowned for its staircase of seven scenic waterfalls and pools on the Río Claro, and the 12,163-hectare **Reserva Nacional Altos del Lircay,** with extraordinary high-country hiking.

In the cordillera east of Los Ángeles, the 11,880-hectare **Parque Nacional Laguna del Laja** is a starkly attractive volcanic upland with its large namesake lake and scattered groves of native forest, especially along the Río Laja as it descends from the cordillera. West of Angol, the 6,832-hectare **Parque Nacional Nahuelbuta** protects the only extensive forests of *Araucarias* (monkey puzzle trees) in the coast range. Southwest of Angol, the 82-hectare **Monumento Natural Contulmo** is a verdant forest corridor hugging the paved highway to Cañete.

Sur Chico

Within the city limits of the regional capital of Temuco, the 90-hectare **Monumento Natural Cerro Ñielol** is a historic site and also home to Chile's national flower, the *copihue*. Northeast of Temuco, the 6,474-hectare **Parque Nacional Tolhuaca** is a well-kept secret along the banks of the Río Malleco. Directly east of Temuco, the 60,833-hectare **Parque Nacional Conguillío** is famous for its *Araucaria* forests and its diverse volcanic landforms, including the 3,125-meter cone of Volcán Llaima. Only a short distance to its northeast, there's fine hiking at 13,730-hectare **Reserva Nacional Malalcahuello** and the contiguous 13,775-hectare **Reserva Nacional Las Nalcas.**

In the vicinity of Pucón, southeast of Temuco, are two popular hikers' parks: the densely forested 12,500-hectare **Parque Nacional Huerquehue** and the 63,000-hectare **Parque Nacional Villarrica,** famed for its namesake smoldering snow-capped cone, 2,840 meters above sea level and Chile's most active volcano.

East of Osorno, the 106,772-hectare **Parque Nacional Puyehue** is locally popular for its hot springs, but the barren volcanic backcountry is truly unique. To the south, east of Puerto Varas, the 231,000-hectare **Parque Nacional Vicente Pérez Rosales** is the gateway to Argentina via Lago Todos los Santos and a bus-boat shuttle to Bariloche.

Southeast of Puerto Montt are two well-forested units, the 39,255-hectare **Parque Nacional Alerce Andino,** so called for its endangered false larch trees, and 48,232-hectare **Parque Nacional Hornopirén,** a wilderness with little access except by foot. On the western shore of the Isla Grande de Chiloé is the rainy, thickly forested 43,507-hectare **Parque Nacional Chiloé.**

Patagonia and Tierra del Fuego

At the northern gateway to the Carretera Austral, north of the town of Chaitén, the private **Parque Natural Pumalín** is a 317,000-hectare unit of verdant temperate rainforest. Southwest of Chaitén, near the Argentine border, the 12,065-hectare **Reserva Nacional Futaleufú** takes its name from the wild white-water river that flows west.

Near the hamlet of Puerto Puyuhuapi, the 154,093-hectare **Parque Nacional Queulat** is wonderland of temperate rainforest, hanging glaciers, ribbonlike waterfalls, and trout-filled streams and lakes. West of the regional capital of Coyhaique, 41,634-hectare **Reserva Nacional Río Simpson** is an equally lush but lower-altitude unit that also appeals to fishermen. Just north of the city, the 2,676-hectare **Reserva Nacional Coyhaique** is wild high country only a few minutes from the plaza. Southeast of the city, toward the Argentine border, the 181-hectare **Monumento Natural Dos Lagunas** is a small protected wetland. Southwest of Coyhaique, accessible only by air taxi or by ferry from Puerto Chacabuco, the Campo de Hielo Norte (Northern Continental Ice Sheet) meets the sea at the 1,742,000-hectare **Parque Nacional Laguna San Rafael.** Immediately to its south, the even larger 3,525,901-hectare **Parque Nacional Bernardo O'Higgins** stretches well into Region XII (Magallanes).

South of Coyhaique via an excellent paved road, the towering glacial summits of 179,550-hectare **Reserva Nacional Cerro Castillo** are a popular hikers' destination. Across Lago General Carrera and south of Chile Chico, 161,100-hectare **Reserva Nacional Lago Jeinemeni** is popular with fly fishermen, as is the 6,925-hectare **Reserva Nacional Lago Cochrane,** east of the town of Cochrane. At the southern terminus of the Carretera Austral, the municipality of Villa O'Higgins has established its own **Reserva Natural Shöen,** a counterpart to Pumalín.

Contiguous with Parque Nacional Bernardo O'Higgins, the 181,414-hectare **Parque Nacional Torres del Paine** is far more famous for its soaring granite towers. To its south, the 189-hectare **Monumento Natural Cueva del Milodón** was once inhabited by the late Pleistocene ground sloth and, later, by early humans. To the southeast, along the Argentine border, the 5,030-hectare **Parque Nacional Pali Aike** is also a major archaeological site for its cave dwellings and home to wildlife such as the wild guanaco.

Several reserves are in the vicinity of the city of Punta Arenas, including two scenic forest reserves: the 13,500-hectare **Reserva Nacional Magallanes** in the hills only a short distance west of town and the 18,000-hectare **Reserva Nacional Laguna Parillar,** which also features wetlands. The 97-hectare **Monumento Natural Los Pingüinos** consists of Isla Magdalena, a huge Magellanic penguin colony in the Strait of Magellan. Across the Strait, just north of the town of Porvenir, the 25-hectare **Monumento Natural Laguna de los Cisnes** is a seasonal wetland.

Several huge units occupy nearly the entirety of archipelagic Magallanes: the 1,097,975-hectare **Reserva Nacional Las Guaitecas,** 2,313,875-hectare **Reserva Nacional Alacalufes,** the 1,460,000-hectare **Parque Nacional Alberto de Agostini,** and the 63,903-hectare **Parque Nacional Cabo de Hornos.**

Argentine National Parks: Two Argentine national parks fall within the coverage of this guidebook: the 600,000-hectare **Parque Nacional Los Glaciares,** with the awesome Moreno glacier, plus snow- and ice-covered pinnacles to match or surpass Torres del Paine; and the 63,000-hectare **Parque Nacional Tierra del Fuego,** ranging from the wildlife-rich Beagle Channel coastline through Patagonian forests to the needles of the Andean uplands.

The Chilean Pacific Islands

About 670 km west of Valparaíso the 9,571-hectare **Parque Nacional Archipiélago Juan Fernández** is a World Biosphere Reserve comprising most of three islands filled with rare endemic flora. The 7,130-hectare **Parque Nacional Rapa Nui** is primarily an archaeological park occupying most of Easter Island (Rapa Nui), 3,700 km west of the Chilean mainland.

HIKING

Chile has plenty of ideal hiking terrain, but only a few parks and reserves have truly integrated

hiker on Selkirk's lookout,
Isla Robinson Crusoe

and well-maintained trail systems. Instituto Geográfico Militar maps at a scale of 1:50,000 are available for most of the country, but for the most part don't expect to find trails with clearly signposted junctions—multiple tracks are the rule. If necessary, try to contract a local guide.

The best areas for hiking and backpacking are the mountains east of Santiago and near Viña del Mar, the Andes east of the heartland city of Talca, the lakes district of the Sur Chico, and Patagonia. The season is longer farther north, stretching from September into May or even longer in some areas. Patagonia can be inclement at any time of year, but the season at popular Torres del Paine is consistently lengthening.

CLIMBING

Chile's thousands of miles of cordillera make it a climber's paradise, if not yet a mecca. Volcanoes are a particular attraction—from the Peruvian border in the north to the remoteness of the southern Aisén region, Chile is part of the Pacific "ring of fire"—but there is snow, ice, and rock climbing on all kinds of surfaces. Summer is the season for most climbers, but far northern peaks such as Parque Nacional Lauca's Volcán Parinacota may be better outside the summer rainy season, when thunderstorms can be a serious hazard.

The most frequently climbed volcano, near the resort town of Pucón, is 2,840-meter Volcán Villarrica, which is also one of the most active; it's a day excursion that's sometimes canceled when Conaf determines that the crater is a little too lively. A local guide is imperative. Volcán Osorno, near the town of Puerto Varas, is also commercially climbed but is more technical.

Capable independent climbers can tackle many summits on their own, but peaks in the vicinity of international borders require clearance from the Chilean Foreign Ministry's Dirección de Fronteras y Límites (Difrol), Bandera 52, 4th floor, Santiago, tel. 2/6714110, fax 2/6971909, difrol3@minrel.cl. To get this permission, which may be done from overseas before arrival, each participant must present complete name, passport number, nationality, date of birth, residence address, profession, date of arrival and departure from the country, and a detailed itinerary. Issuance of permission usually takes two to three days, and it must be presented to the nearest Carabineros police station before participants actually undertake the climb.

For general information on climbing in Chile, including suggestions on dealing with the bureaucracy, contact the Federación de Andinismo, Almirante Simpson 77, Providencia, Santiago, tel. 2/2220888, fax 2/6359089, website: www.feach.cl, contacto@feach.cl. See also the bilingual Chile Climbing Page website: www.escalando.cl.

There are now several options for climbing instruction, including climbing walls and classes, in the vicinity of Santiago; the Cajón del Maipo southeast of the city is a particular hot spot. Climbing Planet, Avenida Condell 703, Providencia, tel. 2/6346391, website: www.climbingplanet.cl, has the biggest facility in town. For technical climbers, Geo Expediciones has a climbing wall at its Centro de Escalada, Camino al

THE CHILEAN PATH TO CONSERVATION

One of Latin America's most far-sighted conservation projects ever is the Lagos administration's *Sendero de Chile* (Chilean Trail), a 6,000-kilometer foot-, bicycle-, and horse path linking the altiplano of the Norte Grande with the sub-Antarctic tundra of southern Patagonia. Intended for both environmental and recreational purposes, its initial segments opened in 2001, but the ambitious goal is to finish the entire project by 2010, the bicentennial of Chilean independence.

Comparable to the United States's Pacific Crest Trail in the terrain it covers, but more akin to the older Appalachian Trail in that authorities hope to encourage community input for maintenance, the Sendero de Chile will pass through a representative sample of precordillera and upper Andean ecosystems. There is even the unprecedented possibility of cooperation with Argentina where the route passes through the vicinity of the Campo de Hielo Sur, the southern Patagonian ice sheet that was once the object of a bitter border dispute between the two countries.

Conama, the state environmental agency entrusted with the project, will permit no motorized transport whatsoever on the two-meter-wide dirt and gravel trail. Mostly following the An-

dean foothills, the route will have detours to important natural, cultural, or even commercial features such as archaeological sites, wineries, and crafts markets.

Conama hopes the trail will attract both urban day-trippers and Chilean and international outdoor enthusiasts who want to hike some or all of its length. Along the route there will be rustic cabins and campsites, built in styles appropriate to the local environment, as well as mileage markers and informational panels on flora and fauna. Because one goal of the project is to encourage local development, there will be special emphasis on local place names and cultural monuments.

President Ricardo Lagos himself inaugurated the first kilometer at Parque Nacional Conguillío in early 2001; before the end of the year, another 24 kilometers were to be officially added, with overlooks, parking areas, and interpretive panels. It's not really starting from scratch, though, as parts of it will link preexisting trails in national parks, reserves, and monuments. Some segments, though, will pass through private land, and private companies and individuals will become involved. You can follow its progress on the website: www.senderodechile.cl.

Volcán 07910, tel. 2/8424776, website: www.geo-expediciones.cl, geoexpediciones@yahoo.com. Farther up the Cajón del Maipo, Cascada Expediciones, Camino al Volcán 17710, Guayacán, tel. 2/8611777, fax 2/8612222, website: www.cascada-expediciones.com, info@cascada-expediciones.com, also offers climbing.

CYCLING AND MOUNTAIN BIKING

Both long-distance riders and recreational mountain bikers will find Chile's spectacular landscapes appealing and rugged terrain challenging. Because many Chilean roads have dirt or gravel surfaces, and because paved roads are often so narrow that riding on the shoulder is essential, a mountain bike is the best alternative. Riders without their own bikes will find them readily

available in tourist towns such as Pucón, Puerto Varas, and the like, but their condition varies widely—check brakes, tires, and everything else before renting.

In some parts of the country, cycling may be a seasonal activity, though in the Atacama Desert the weather is suitable all year (though water is scarce). If touring, it's wise to carry rain gear, a tent, and supplementary camping gear, especially since some of the most enjoyable riding areas have almost no services.

Possible touring routes are numerous, but one of the finest is the Carretera Austral, a discontinuous 1,100-km penetration road from Puerto Montt that is now complete to the southern outpost of Villa O'Higgins. Still requiring several ferry crossings, it passes through some of the country's, if not the continent's, most spectacular wild terrain; increasing numbers of cyclists, some of them through riders from Alaska to Tierra del Fuego, are braving the changeable weather on a road that, except for a few paved segments around the regional capital of Coyhaique, is mostly gravel. A sturdy mountain bike is imperative, along with a knowledge of bicycle repairs and a rugged tent—services are few and far between. Feasible as early as October, it's probably best from December to April.

Ruta 5, the Carretera Panamericana (Panamerican Highway) that runs from the Peruvian border to the tip of the Isla Grande Chiloé, is a common route for long-distance cyclists; from La Serena south, it is now a four-lane toll highway with wide shoulders, but there are more interesting alternatives. One of these is the desert coastal highway from Iquique south to Antofagasta, though this increasingly popular highway is narrow in places and carries heavy truck traffic. One of the most interesting routes is the high road that follows the old railroad line from La Ligua north to Ovalle (for details, see the sidebar in the Norte Chico chapter).

While the Panamericana is at present the only continuous road that links the entire mainland, plans are to complete a parallel coastal route despite the questionable economic utility of many sections. Another parallel route is the Sendero de Chile, intended to link the Andean uplands for pedestrians, bicycles, and horseback riders only. Much of this will use existing roads and trails including, in the north, former Inka roads.

HORSEBACK RIDING

Recreational horseback riding is fairly common even in localities near the capital, such as the Cajón del Maipo. Several operators lead extended treks into remote parts of the Norte Chico, the Andean cordillera east of Talca, the Cochamó area near Puerto Varas, and Parque Nacional Torres del Paine. (For details, see the Organized Tours listing below and/or the appropriate geographical entry.)

SKIING

Since the seasons are reversed in southern South America, the Andean slopes reach their peak in August. Chile has 15 international and regional ski resorts, from the famous Portillo, near the Argentine border northeast of Santiago, to the truly obscure Reserva Nacional Magallanes near Punta Arenas in the south. For current snowpack statistics, updated every Friday, check the English-language Chile Information Project's travel website: www.chiptravel.cl; the most upscale resorts now have snow-making equipment.

Portillo, Chile's most famous ski area, is about two hours northwest of Santiago, but three major sites are up the canyon of the Río Mapocho, less than an hour from the capital—making it possible to stay cheaply in the city while spending the day on the slopes. The next best resort is Termas de Chillán, east of the heartland city of Chillán, but Parque Nacional Villarrica (near the town of Pucón) and Antillanca in Parque Nacional Puyehue (near the city of Osorno) are also good choices. The upscale resorts have snow-making equipment.

(For more detail, see individual geographical entries and the Organized Tour listings below.)

BIRDING

It might lack tropical rainforests, with their extraordinary biological diversity, but Chile's "geographical extravaganza" accounts for a remarkably large variety of birds and, for visitors from the Northern Hemisphere, it's a chance to add lots of new species to their life lists. The finest birding areas are the northern altiplano, particularly Parque Nacional Lauca; the Pacific littoral and its coastal wetlands; and the southern Patagonian region. The village of Putre, on the approach to Lauca, and Hostería Las Torres in Parque Nacional Torres del Paine have reliable operators with English-speaking personnel (see also the Organized Tour entry below).

PARAGLIDING

A relatively recent arrival, *parapente* is most popular in the Norte Grande city of Iquique, whose steep coast range is ideal for takeoffs into the thermals on which a skilled glider can stay aloft for hours. There is also paragliding in the Cajón del Maipo, southeast of Santiago.

ON THE ROAD

WATER SPORTS

Chileans have always flocked to the country's Pacific beaches and southern lakes, but have only recently begun to enjoy active water sports such as surfing, sea kayaking, and white-water rafting and kayaking.

White-Water Rafting and Kayaking

Chile's best water sports option is its variety of white-water rafting experiences, many of them close to major population centers. From Santiago south, descending the steep gradient from the high Andes to Chile's central valley toward the Pacific, numerous transverse rivers have cut through the foothills en route to the Pacific. The happy result is an abundance of Class III to IV rapids for rafters and kayakers on rivers including the Maipo near Santiago, the Tinguiririca near San Fernando, the Claro and several others in the vicinity of Talca, the Fuy near Panguipulli, the Petrohué near Puerto Varas, and the Baker south of Coyhaique. The Class V classic Biobío near Los Ángeles is fast disappearing beneath a series of hydroelectric dams, but the even more powerful Futaleufú, in a remote area near the southern Argentine border, has become a magnet for river recreationists from around the world.

The powerful Futaleufú, in a remote area near the southern Argentine border, has become a magnet for river recreationists from around the world.

Chile's southern rivers are usually runnable from the spring runoff in October to early days of April, but the Maipo near Santiago is feasible even in winter.

(For information on rafting and kayaking operators, see the Organized Tours listing below, as well as the appropriate geographical entries.)

Diving

Diving is less common in Chile than one might expect, since the long, straight Pacific coastline drops off abruptly into the deeps, the water is usually cold, and there are no coral islands or significant reefs there. It is possible, however, in Reserva Nacional Pingüino de Humboldt, the Juan Fernández archipelago, and on Rapa Nui (Easter Island).

Sea Kayaking

The village of Dalcahue, on the Isla Grande de Chiloé, is the main center for commercial sea kayaking, though there are many other suitable locations, among them Puerto Natales and the spectacular Cordillera Darwin on Tierra del Fuego.

Surfing

The good news is, with a coastline the length of Chile's and a relatively small population of dedicated surfers, there's little competition for waves except at beach towns such as Pichilemu, which is close to the heartland's major population centers. Even there, except on weekends, the competition's not that abundant. The bad news is, except around the Norte Grande beach resorts of Iquique and Arica, the cold Pacific currents make wet suits essential even in midsummer. Heavy rip currents and late-breaking waves make some areas hazardous.

In and around central Chile, the summer months from January to March are the peak for surfers, but winter storms bring the best waves in the desert north. Champion Chilean surfers come from Iquique and Arica, but there are also hotbeds of interest around La Serena, the coastline north of Viña del Mar, Buchupureo, Pullay, and even as far south as Valdivia—with a truly well-insulated wet suit. Chilean surfers themselves tend toward body boards rather than long boards.

Fishing

Chile is a major commercial fishing power, but it's also a popular destination for fly-fishing enthusiasts eager to test their skill on lakes, rivers, and fjords from the Sur Chico almost to Magallanes. The most popular area is the Aisén region, along the Carretera Austral and lateral roads, where there are plenty of specialized fishing lodges as well as resorts that include fly-fishing among their offerings.

Spectator Sports

As in most of the rest of Latin America, *fútbol* (soccer) is by far the most popular spectator sport. As of April 2002, Chile placed 42nd in the FIFA world soccer rankings and had failed to make the 2002 World Cup in Japan and South Korea. Strikers Marcelo Salas, nicknamed El Matador, and Iván Zamorano (Bam-Bam) have been stars in Europe.

Ténis (tennis) also has adherents and par-ticipants. Left-handed Marcelo Ríos is among the world's top players, while Nicolás Massú is also a fixture on the international tournament circuit.

Thoroughbred horse-racing (including betting) is a popular pastime. Santiago has two major *hipódromos* (racetracks), plus many smaller cities have their own venues. Rodeo racing is an entirely different animal, so to speak.

Arts and Entertainment

FINE ARTS

Chile's contributions to the fine arts are remarkable for a country of its size. In literature, in particular, the results have been extraordinary—with a pair of Nobel Prize poets. Chileans have also had an impact on art, architecture, cinema, music, and other fields.

Literature

Chile is famous for its poets, and the progenitor of them all was the conquistador Alonso de Ercilla (1533–94), who paid his indigenous adversaries tribute in his 16th-century epic *La Araucana*. The first Chilean-born poet of note was Pedro de Oña (1570–1643), whose *Arauco Domado* (Arauco Tamed) extols the Spaniards' martial achievements, particularly those of García Hurtado de Mendoza, whom Ercilla had disparaged.

The dean of modern Chilean poets was Vicente Huidobro (1893–1948), who lived many years in Paris among his French contemporaries, such as Rimbaud, Verlaine, and Mallarmé. The country's most famous literary figure, though, was the flamboyant, politically committed poet Pablo Neruda (1904–73), who earned the 1971 Nobel Prize for a body of work including *Las Alturas de Macchu Picchu* (The Heights of Machu Picchu, first published in 1948) and *Canto General* (1950). Neruda's work is widely available in English translation (the minimalist poet Nicanor Parra, a brother of the late folksinger Violeta Parra, bills himself as the "anti-Neruda" for his spare imagery).

Despite her 1945 Nobel Prize, the works of Gabriela Mistral (1889–1957), Chile's other Nobel Prize poet, are less widely known, perhaps because she left Chile at the age of 30 and rarely returned, possibly because she was a woman, and maybe even for (a)political reasons—the Communist writer Volodia Teitelboim left her out of his and Eduardo Anguita's *Antología de la Poesía Chilena* (Anthology of Chilean Poetry, 1953). Recently, however, the Santiago-based Editorial Andrés Bello published her five collections under the title *Poesías Completas de Gabriela Mistral* (Complete Poetry of Gabriela Mistral, 2001). Her work is less readily available than Neruda's in translation, but look for Langston Hughes's *Selected Poems of Gabriela Mistral* (Indiana University Press, 1957).

The Chilean novel didn't really find its voice until the late 20th century, though Alberto Blest Gana's 19th-century work merits attention for its literary competence and historical interest. Though not a novelist, the Venezuelan polymath Andrés Bello influenced Chilean intellectual life through his essays and his transformation of the country's educational system.

The most famous contemporary Chilean writer is unquestionably novelist Isabel Allende (born 1942), a niece of the late president. Though she now lives in Marin County, California, she

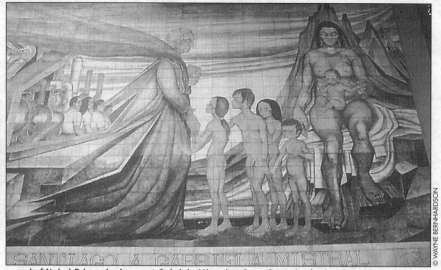

mural of Nobel Prize-winning poet Gabriela Mistral at Cerro Santa Lucía, Santiago

continues to write on Chilean (and Californian-Chilean) themes (for suggested readings, see the Booklist appendix).

Known for his pessimism, novelist José Donoso (1924–96) left a legacy of stories such as *The Obscene Bird of Night* (1970), about a failed writer going mad, and *Curfew* (1988), the disheartening tale of a returned exile to Pinochet's Chile.

Antonio Skármeta (born 1940) is a novelist who acquired a certain fame as the author of *Burning Patience* (New York: Random House, 1987), which served as a *very* rough template, cleansed of its political content, for director Michael Radford's Oscar-winning film *Il Postino* (1995); Neruda was a key character in the story. In the Spanish-speaking world, the portly Skármeta is also a critic known as the host of the surprisingly popular literary program *El Show de los Libros*—more than a step above Oprah.

Marco Antonio de la Parra (born 1952) is a playwright and novelist whose *The Secret Holy War of Santiago de Chile* (New York: Interlink, 1994) uses Chile's capital city as the backdrop for a "magical realist" interpretation of the last years of the Pinochet dictatorship. Alberto Fuguet (born 1964) is a California-raised Chilean novelist whose *Bad Vibes* (New York: St. Martin's, 1997) tells a tale of disaffected affluent youth whose families profited economically from the dictatorship.

Roberto Ampuero's place-oriented mystery novels explore locales such as Valparaíso and San Pedro de Atacama, but unfortunately none of his Cayetano Brulé novels has yet appeared in English (though some have been translated into German). Interestingly enough, Ampuero's nonmystery *Nuestros Años Olivos Verdes* (Our Olive Green Years) is a fictional exploration of the failures of the Revolution in his detective protagonist's Cuban homeland. Ampuero's unadorned style makes his books a good choice for neophytes easing their way into Spanish-language literature.

Buenos Aires–born novelist, playwright, and essayist Ariel Dorfman (born 1942) spent much of his youth in the United States and Chile (where he was a strong supporter of the Unidad Popular and harsh critic of the United States) before escaping to exile after the coup of 1973. He has gradually reconciled his hybrid intellectual heritage—he writes and speaks fluently in both languages and lives half the year in North Carolina—without compromising his political ideals. The famous director Roman Polanski made an

English-language film version (1994) of Dorfman's play *Death and the Maiden,* starring Ben Kingsley and Sigourney Weaver.

Visual Arts

The earliest Chilean art was, of course, ecclesiastical, and it's evident in museums such as the Museo de Arte Colonial in Santiago's Iglesia San Francisco, the city's oldest surviving church. With the arrival of independence, the tendency was toward pompous portraits of military men such as O'Higgins and their contemporaries who played key roles in the war against Spain, and most provincial museums contain dreary works of this sort. Nevertheless, there is more adventurous contemporary work in collections such as those in Santiago's Museo de Bellas Artes (Fine Arts Museum) with its frequent rotating exhibits, the capital's fine new Museo de Artes Visuales (Museum of Visual Arts), Castro's Museo de Arte Moderno (Modern Art Museum), and Providencia's Museo Parque de las Esculturas (Sculpture Park Museum), outdoors on the banks of the Mapocho. One of the most historically noteworthy sites is the Chillán's Escuela México, whose library walls are adorned by murals by the famous David Alfaro Siqueiros and his contemporary Xavier Guerrero.

Northern European influences began to appear in Chilean painting with landscapes such as those of 19th-century Englishman Thomas Somerscales (1842–1927), who spent 23 years in Valparaíso and vicinity. The country's most influential living painter is the now elderly surrealist Roberto Matta (born 1911), who has lived mostly in Paris but also in Mexico and New York. He is also a sculptor and engraver. The versatile Mario Irarrázaval (born 1940) erected the famous roadside sculpture *Mano del Desierto* (Hand in the Desert) on the Panamericana south of Antofagasta; he is also the sculptor of the *Tabernáculo* (Tabernacle) at the Templo Votivo de Maipú, a pilgrimage site in northwestern Santiago, and the painter of *El Juicio* (The Judgment), a harsh portrayal of military "justice."

Chilean photography is not widely known, but one noteworthy figure is Marcos Chamudes, who emigrated to the United States, joined the U.S. Army in World War II, and photographed the war in Europe before returning to Chile for the rest of his life.

Architecture

Indigenous architecture survives in the adobe houses of the Aymara of the northern altiplano and the thatched *rucas* of the Mapuche in the south. Spanish culture, of course, has left an enduring imprint on both official and vernacular architecture, as buildings with thick adobe walls and tiled roofs are common with all social classes in the heartland; in response to repeated earthquakes, these generally were larger structures of lower proportions.

In older cities and towns, there is generally no setback from the street; houses usually have a central patio surrounded by the various rooms. In rural areas, houses are similar but more isolated from their neighbors. In newer subdivisions, however, single-family houses fronted by lawns are becoming more common.

Regional variations are significant. Norte Grande cities such as Iquique and Antofagasta, which grew most dramatically during the nitrate era of the late 19th and early 20th centuries, are distinguished by their Georgian and Victorian buildings, with second-story balconies. These are built of Douglas fir imported from California and Oregon (Douglas fir is widely but inaccurately known as *pino oregón,* or Oregon pine).

In Sur Chico settlements such as Puerto Varas, 19th-century German immigration has left a

*The archipelago of Chiloé has become a UNESCO World Heritage Site for its remarkable assortment of shingled churches and chapels—the diversity of shingle designs is truly extraordinary—but its remaining **palafitos** (houses on stilts or pilings) are a treasure of vernacular architecture.*

ON THE ROAD

legacy of shingled houses that seemingly might have come straight from Bavaria. The archipelago of Chiloé has become a UNESCO World Heritage Site for its remarkable assortment of shingled churches and chapels—the diversity of shingle designs is truly extraordinary—but its remaining *palafitos* (houses on stilts or pilings) are a treasure of vernacular architecture.

Southernmost Chile, especially the city of Punta Arenas, is notable for the mansions erected during the wool boom of the late 19th and early 20th centuries but also for its more modest wooden-framed, metal-clad "Magellanic" houses. Some of the best of these are in the town of Porvenir, on the Chilean side of the Isla Grande de Tierra del Fuego, but many also remain in Argentine Tierra del Fuego.

Contemporary Chilean architecture, mostly in Santiago, tends toward the functional and utilitarian rather than the decorative. At its worst, it's a clutter of shopping malls, though there are some distinguished buildings. Many dignified French-style buildings remain from the 19th century, however.

Music

Globally, the most famous Chilean musical figures are folk artists such as Violeta Parra, her children Angel and Isabel, Patricio Manns, Víctor Jara, and other contributors to the *Nueva Canción Chilena* (New Chilean Song Movement) of the 1950s and 1960s, known for its committed leftist politics and *peñas* (cultural centers). Both Violeta Parra (1917–67) and Jara (1932–73) met unhappy ends; Parra committed suicide, and Jara died at the hands of the military.

In addition to singer-songwriters, Chile has several folk-oriented bands whose work adapted Andean music and instrumentation, such as the *zampoña* (panpipes), *charango* (a stringed instrument vaguely resembling the mandolin), and others, along with the traditional guitars. Among them are Inti-Illimani, Quilapayún, and Illapu.

In the popular music field, the Mexico-based Chilean band La Ley won a 2001 Grammy for best alternative Latin rock album and has toured the United States, playing at the legendary Fillmore Auditorium in San Francisco. The mas-

sively popular rock band Los Prisioneros, founded during the Pinochet dictatorship and expressing the frustration of Chilean youth in those times, disbanded in the aftermath of its greatest popularity but has recently reformed for public appearances. Though based in France, Los Jaivas tour Chile every summer with their blend of Chilean folk themes, Pink Floydish technological prowess, and a rapport with their public that would be the envy of many performers.

A handful of classical musicians have earned a worldwide reputation. Chillán-born Claudio Arrau (1903–91) was Chile's best-known classical pianist, an artistic descendant of Franz Liszt through Liszt's student Martin Krause. Oscar Gacitúa (1926–2001), who committed suicide by throwing himself in front of the Santiago Metro, was a disciple of Arrau's who had earned an honorable mention at the Warsaw Chopin competition in 1955.

Punta Arenas tenor Tito Beltrán (born 1965), a Swedish resident for a decade and a half and widely considered one of the world's dozen best opera singers in his range, has sung alongside Luciano Pavarotti. Sergio Ortega (born 1938), who composed the anthem for Salvador Allende's Unidad Popular, adapted Pablo Neruda's verses to opera in *Muerte y Fulgor de Joaquín Murieta*, the tale of the legendary (but probably fictional) Chilean outlaw in Gold Rush California.

Cinema

Chileans have played a greater role in global cinema than most people realize, though it's best not to exaggerate. It has its origins, surprisingly enough, in the tiny Tierra del Fuego town of Porvenir, where German-born José Bohr made an early movie before eventually finding an erratic career in Hollywood. Many but not nearly all recent Chilean films are available on video.

With state support in the late 1960s and early 1970s, talented but noncommercial filmmakers such as Alejandro Jodorowsky (born 1930), Miguel Littín (born 1942), and Raúl Ruiz (born 1941) did some truly audacious work, most notably Jodorowsky's esoteric Mexican western *El Topo* (The Mole, 1971). Littín's crime melodrama *El Chacal de Nahueltoro* (The Jackal of

Nahueltoro, 1968) was a Chilean hit, but he's best known for *Alsino and the Condor* (1983), filmed in exile in Nicaragua, which earned an Academy Award nomination for Best Foreign Film. His most recent effort is *Tierra del Fuego* (2000), characterized by the director as an "existentialist western."

The France-based Ruiz has directed many films, but only the psychological whodunit *Shattered Image* (1998), starring William Baldwin and Anne Parillaud, has appeared in English. Ruiz dared to take on Marcel Proust in *Time Regained* (1999), based on the last volume of Proust's *Remembrance of Things Past,* which starred Catherine Deneuve, John Malkovich, and Vicente Pérez.

Documentary filmmaker Patricio Guzmán (born 1941) earned a certain fame for his three-part *La Batalla de Chile* (The Battle of Chile, 1975–79) on the Unidad Popular and its overthrow by the Pinochet dictatorship. More recently, he has produced *The Pinochet Case* (2001), another documentary about the dictator's arrest and subsequent events.

Chilean-born but Spanish-bred, Alejandro Amenábar wrote and directed *The Others* (2001), a subtle haunted-house story with a twist. The youthful (born 1973), multitalented Amenábar also wrote the film's musical score. Another young filmmaker is Gustavo Graef-Marino (born 1965), whose *Johnny Cien Pesos* (1993) is a character-driven Santiago crime story based on true events. He also filmed the Hollywood action movie *Diplomatic Siege* (1999).

Other recent films to look for include Andrés Wood's (born 1963) *Historias de Fútbol* (Soccer Stories, 1997); Cristián Galaz's *El Chacotero Sentimental* (The Sentimental Teaser, 1999), about a sympathetic radio talk show host; and Orlando Lubbert's (born 1945) *Taxi para Tres* (Taxi for Three, 2001), an action comedy with social undertones set in a poor Santiago neighborhood that earned a "Concha de Oro" best-picture award at Spain's San Sebastián film festival.

Theater

Santiago has a theater scene as lively as any on the continent, but even in the regions live theater has an audience. Conventional theater plays venues such as Santiago's Teatro Municipal and Providencia's Teatro de la Universidad de Chile, but there's a thriving alternative theater scene in other parts of downtown Santiago, Barrio Bellavista, parts of Providencia, and even otherwise staid, middle-class Ñuñoa.

One of the most popular plays in recent years is *La Negra Ester,* a prostitute's story written by Roberto Parra (1921–95), a musician brother of Violeta and Nicanor Parra. Since its debut in 1988, more than three million theatergoers have seen the play in various venues.

Among Chile's other prominent playwrights are Ariel Dorfman and Marco de Antonio de la Parra (for more detail on them, see the Literature entry above and the Booklist appendix).

Dance

Chile's national dance is the *cueca,* an innocently suggestive cock-and-hen courtship ritual that's a staple of mid-September's patriotic holidays and many rural festivals. While tango is an Argentine import, it has devoted adherents in Santiago, Valparaíso, and some other cities.

Performances of classical and modern dance, such as ballet, take place at formal venues such as Santiago's Teatro Municipal or Providencia's Teatro de la Universidad de Chile.

ARTS AND CRAFTS

Certain crafts are similar and nearly universal throughout the country: basketry, carvings of both stone and wood, copperware, lapiz lazuli jewelry and statuary, and cotton and woolen weavings. There are also regional specialties.

In the Norte Grande, especially in the altiplano, Aymara weavers produce llama and alpaca caps, sweaters, and other clothing items, but much of this material is also imported from Peru and Bolivia. Throughout the heartland and well into the south, *huaso* horsegear is unique—look for the elaborately carved stirrups in particular. Mapuche silverwork can be exquisite. Carvers on the Chiloé archipelago produce model *dalcas* (dugouts), *palafitos* (houses on pilings), and dolls, while weavers in the entire Sur Chico and into Patagonia create sweaters and caps (from sheep's wool rather than llama or alpaca).

The Polynesian people of Easter Island (Rapa Nui) produce souvenir *moai* of both wood and stone, modeled after the massive pre-Columbian stone statues but also in the style of later indigenous carvings. While there is plenty of ready-made stuff to buy, it's also possible to order a custom *moai* of a larger size; since this may take several days, you should do it soon after arrival.

ENTERTAINMENT

Chileans are night people, and visitors to Santiago and many provincial cities will be astonished that even the harshest military dictatorship could ever impose an 11 P.M. curfew.

Discos and Bars

Santiago's Bellavista and Providencia neighborhoods have the largest numbers of places to dance and drink; Latin salsa, *cumbia,* and merengue are the styles of choice. Santiago has some cavernous dance clubs with state-of-the-art sound systems and recorded techno music, but the more interesting venues are smaller clubs with live folk, rock, and even jazz.

Cinemas

Santiago is the only Chilean city that still has a real downtown cinema district, but even there many theaters have consolidated into multiplexes that specialize in first-run Hollywood fare; there are also suburban-style multiplexes in sprawling shopping centers such as Las Condes' Parque Arauco. In some provincial cities, the central cinemas have closed but multiplexes have also opened in suburban areas. Santiago is the only city with a substantial art house or repertory circuit, but cultural centers and universities in regional capitals often reprise classics or show less commercial movies.

Most imported films appear in the original language, with Spanish subtitles. The major exceptions are animated and children's films, which are invariably dubbed into Spanish.

FESTIVALS

The year's first major event is **Semana Santa** (Holy Week), culminating in **Pascua** (Easter Sunday), but it's a relatively sober and earnest observation compared with, say, its far more colorful counterpart in Guatemala. From Maundy Thursday through Sunday, though, it's a major travel time, when prices rise for accommoda-

the bar at Taberna Barracuda, Iquique

© WAYNE BERNHARDSON

tions and demand can be high—reservations may be advisable.

Chileans celebrate September's patriotic holidays, their major secular celebrations, with parades, military marches, and gatherings in public parks.

November 2's **Día de Todos los Santos,** also known as **Día de los Muertos** (Day of the Dead), is when Chileans recall their departed, visiting their graves and leaving them elaborate flower arrangements, among other tributes. Though far less spectacular than its Mexican counterpart, it's still an impressive occasion.

Several unofficial festivals take place throughout the year, most of which appear under the appropriate geographical entry. One worth special attention is mid-July's weeklong **Festival de la Virgen del Carmen,** when tens of thousands of celebrants converge on the tiny Norte Grande town of La Tirana for the most important popular religion fiesta in the entire country. Another colorful event is December 26's **Fiesta de la Virgen de Andacollo** in the Norte Chico, though it's more strictly official than La Tirana.

SHOPPING

Chile may lack the colorful indigenous highland markets of its Andean neighbors Peru and Bolivia, but it compensates with artisanal *ferias* in both urban and rural areas, especially in summer. Santiago's Barrio Bellavista is one of the best bets in the cities, but Valparaíso and Viña del Mar also have good selections. Valparaíso's Plaza O'Higgins has the country's best antiques market, on Sundays.

Mapuche communities and resorts in the Sur Chico do have good selections of indigenous crafts, and the towns of Angelmó (Puerto Montt), and Dalcahue and Castro (both on the Isla Grande de Chiloé) have waterfront markets that are both picturesque and practical. Bargaining is less common and aggressive than it is in the Central Andean highlands, but it's not completely inappropriate; just don't make insultingly low offers. In souvenir shops and other businesses with an obvious overhead, such as those at suburban shopping malls, bargaining is inappropriate.

CHILEAN HOLIDAYS

Government offices and most businesses close on national holidays, more than half of which are religious observations. Traditionally, many Chileans take "sandwich holidays" between actual holidays and the weekend, but the government is attempting to eliminate the practice by moving some holidays to the nearest Monday.

January 1: **Año Nuevo** (New Year's Day)

March/April (moveable): **Semana Santa** (Easter Week)

May 1: **Día del Trabajo** (International Labor Day)

May 21: **Glorias Navales** (naval Battle of Iquique)

May 30: **Corpus Christi**

June 29: **Día de San Pedro y San Pablo** (Saint Peter and Saint Paul's Day)

August 15: **Asunción de la Virgen** (Assumption)

September 18: **Día de la Independencia Nacional** (Independence Day)

September 19: **Día del Ejército** (Armed Forces Day)

October 12: **Día de la Raza** (Columbus Day)

November 2: **Todo los Santos** (All Saints' Day)

December 8: **Inmaculada Concepción** (Immaculate Conception)

December 25: **Navidad** (Christmas Day)

Accommodations

Chilean accommodations vary from camping to barebones guest houses to modest hotels to elegant colonial inns and deluxe hot springs resorts in the countryside, and five-star luxury highrise hotels in Santiago and some other locales. In the main tourist centers, there are alternatives for every budget, but in some remote areas everyone may have to settle for shoestring sleeping quarters.

Sernatur, the national tourism service, publishes a useful, annually updated accommodations brochure with approximate prices for accommodations; often, but not always, it excludes budget options and even omits some midrange and high-end places. Prices, for that matter, are often negotiable, especially outside the January–February peak. Travelers should not take hotel ratings too seriously as they often represent an ideal rather than a reality, and some one- or two-star places are better than others that theoretically rank higher.

Note that prices often rise in January and February—Chileans and Argentines (who statistically speaking are the most numerous foreign visitors) usually take their vacations after the school year ends in December—and during holiday periods such as Semana Santa (Holy Week) and Chilean patriotic holidays (mid-September).

Note also that midrange to top-end Chilean hotels levy 18 percent in Impuesto de Valor Agregado or IVA (Value Added Tax or VAT), but they will discount that to bona fide tourists with the appropriate documentation—passport and tourist card. Foreign residents of Chile are *not* eligible for this discount. At the same time, the discount can be smaller than expected if the hotel exchange rate is unfavorable.

Note also that while rates for accommodations in this book are quoted for both single and double occupancy, they are grouped in price categories according to the cost for double occupancy. The categories are as follows:

US$10 or Less
US$10–25
US$25–50
US$50–100
US$100–150
US$150–200
More than US$200

CAMPING

Organized camping is a common alternative in Chile, especially in the southern mainland lake district, but it's a popular choice for families on economical vacations throughout the country. In wilder, more remote areas such as Aisén and Magallanes, it's possible to camp just about anywhere for free, though there are restrictions in the most popular sites, such as Parque Nacional Torres del Paine. Note that many Chilean campgrounds charge per site (for up to five or six people) rather than per person, which can make camping less appealing economically for single people or couples, who can often stay equally cheaply at pretty good budget accommodations.

HOSTELS

While Chile has only one specifically dedicated Hostelling International facility, in Santiago's Barrio Brasil, there are several affiliates throughout the country that give discounts to HI members. With a few exceptions, they are usually not dramatically cheaper than some more conventional budget options, but they do offer the opportunity to get together with like-minded travelers.

For up-to-the-minute information on official Chilean hostels, contact Hostelling International Santiago, Cienfuegos 151, Santiago Centro, tel. 2/6718532, fax 2/6728880, website: www.hostelling.cl, histgoch@entelchile.net, or the Asociación Chilena de Albergues Turísticos Juveniles, Hernando de Aguirre 201, Oficina 602, Providencia, Santiago, tel. 2/2333220, fax 2/2322555, hostelling@hostelling.cl.

BUDGET ACCOMMODATIONS

Budget accommodations, which can be as cheap as US$5 pp and rarely a bit less, go by a variety of names that may be misleading as to their quality—they can vary from dingy fleabags with mattresses that sag like hammocks to simple but cheerful and tidy places with firm new beds. Some will even have parking, except in densely built areas such as central Santiago.

Among the budget lodgings are *hospedajes,* which are generally family-run accommodations with a few spare rooms, *pensiones,* and *casas de huéspedes,* all terms that may be used relatively interchangeably. All may often have long-term residents as well as overnight guests. *Residenciales* are generally buildings constructed with short-stay accommodations in mind, but they may also have semipermanent inhabitants. An *hostería* is generally a step up and often refers to a country hotel with a restaurant. All of these places may even go by the term *hotel,* though usually that belongs to a more formal category.

That said, there are also some exceptionally good values in all these categories. Many will have shared bath and toilet *(baño general* or *baño compartido),* or offer a choice between shared and private bath *baño privado;* bathtubs are rare. In some cases, they will have ceiling fans and even cable TV, but there is often an extra charge for cable and almost always a surcharge for air-conditioning.

Travelers intending to stay at budget accommodations should bring their own towels and, if traveling in the colder parts of the country, perhaps even their own sleeping bags. Many but by no means all include breakfast in their rates; ask to be certain.

Showers

At the very bottom end of the price range, a very few accommodations may lack hot water. On rare occasions, where there is hot water, it will come from an electric in-line heater that's capable of rendering a startling shock to unsuspecting users—*never* touch the fixture or the shower head while in the shower. Generally, these showers work best with relatively low water flows; as the flow increases, heating the volume of water becomes more difficult.

There has been improvement in electric in-line showers in recent years, both with respect to safety and heating efficiency, but most of the better budget lodgings do have gas-powered water heaters. Erratic water pressure sometimes makes it difficult to regulate the temperature.

Most Chilean showers, however, use natural gas in a *calefón,* which heats the water as it passes through the gas-run water heater. Opening the tap normally triggers the *calefón,* presuming the *piloto* (pilot) is lit, but some budget-conscious accommodations light the pilot only when someone wants to take a shower. Before getting in the shower, be sure the pilot is lit.

MIDRANGE ACCOMMODATIONS

Midrange hotels generally offer larger, more comfortable, and better furnished rooms, almost always with private bath, than even the best budget places. Ceiling fans, cable TV, and even a/c are common, but they may not have on-site parking. Some have restaurants. Rates can range anywhere from US$30 up to US$100 d; some are better values than their high-end counterparts.

HIGH-END ACCOMMODATIONS

Some of the best options in this category are country inns and hot springs resorts, offering traditional hospitality and ambience with style unmatchable at other high-end places. Prices may be upward of US$100, often substantially upward.

Luxury hotels with top-flight service, which can range well upward of US$100 per night, are few outside the capital and major resort areas such as Viña del Mar. In the capital, these will usually offer amenities such as restaurants, swimming pools, gym facilities, office space, Internet connections, and conference rooms; outside the capital, these are mostly resort hotels and will lack the business facilities. Invariably they will offer secure parking.

M

ON THE ROAD

Food and Drink

Chile's long rich coastline and productive farmland provide seafood, meat, fresh fruit, and vegetables in abundance. While the everyday Chilean diet may have some shortcomings, in most areas visitors will have no difficulty finding appealing food and drink.

According to historian John C. Super, whatever the negative consequences of the Spanish invasion, it actually improved a diet that was, by some accounts, nutritionally deficient (often protein-poor) in late pre-Columbian times. In Super's opinion:

> *The combination of European and American foods created diversified, nutritionally rich diets. Crop yields were higher than those in Europe, and longer or staggered growing seasons made fresh food available during much of the year. The potential for one of the best diets in the history of the world was evident soon after discovery of the New World. For Europeans, the introduction of livestock and wheat was an essential step in creating that diet.*

When the Europeans first set foot in South America, the staples of the Andes were beans, squash, and a variety of potatoes and other tubers, but the diet was low in animal protein—only the llama, alpaca, guinea pig, and wild game were readily available, and these not in all areas. The cultivation of tubers stretched into high latitudes such as archipelagic Chiloé, one of the areas of greatest diversity for potatoes. This, of course, spread across the Atlantic, but so did nonstaples such as chiles and avocados. Spanish introductions such as wheat and barley, which yielded only a four to one harvest ratio in Europe, reached at least two to three times that in the Americas.

The Spanish introductions blended with the indigenous base to create many of the edibles found on Chilean tables today. The abundance of seafood, combined with the increase of European livestock and the high productivity of European fruits such as apples, apricots, grapes, pears, and many others, resulted in a diverse food production and consumption system which, however, is changing today.

A government survey recently reported that the Chilean diet at large is deteriorating and obesity growing because of increased intake of fats and cholesterol, partly because of fast food and a more sedentary lifestyle; there is particular concern over young schoolchildren and pregnant women. Consumption of red meat has grown among lower classes even though it has decreased among the affluent. On the other hand, it's a third lower than in neighboring Argentina, and chicken, pork, and turkey consumption are increasing more rapidly than that of beef. Lamb and mutton are stable, but despite Chile's coastline and wealth of marine resources, seafood consumption is lower than in Europe.

The consumption of cereals and vegetables has decreased in all classes; that of vegetables in particular is about half internationally recommended quantities. While Chileans' consumption of mayonnaise, alcohol, and soft drinks have all tripled, on the plus side they are also eating greater quantities of fresh fruit. Fortunately, plenty of good food is available even if Chileans don't always avail themselves of all their options.

WHERE TO EAT

Places to eat vary from hole-in-the-wall *comedores* or *cocinerías* (both roughly translatable as "eateries") with no formal menu to elegant *restaurantes* in Santiago and major tourist centers. About the only hard and fast rule in looking at places to eat is to avoid those in which single men—or groups of men—sit and drink beer.

There is, however, an elaborate but inconsistent terminology and, though *restaurante* generally refers to places where there is sit-down service, it can cover a seemingly infinite range of possibilities. *Fuente de soda,* literally meaning "soda fountain," really signifies a place with a generally modest menu that lacks a liquor license. *Cafeterías* provide

WARINGS

Many Chileans glop high-fat *mayonesa* (mayonnaise) on almost anything, including sandwiches, salads, and seafood. If you don't like mayonnaise, ask whether your dish comes with it; even if you like the stuff yourself, you may prefer to ask for a side dish and apply it in the desired quantity. Similarly, fresh-fruit drinks are often oversugared; if the fruit alone is sweet enough for your taste, request it *sin azúcar, por favor.*

Note also that the preferred terms for waiters are *garzón* and *mesero.* The term *mozo,* widely used and totally innocuous in neighboring Argentina, is an insult in Chile.

plain meals, usually without table service, but the misleadingly named *salón de té* (literally "teahouse") can be more like a European-style café, sometimes with sidewalk seating. *Hosterías* are generally country-style restaurants serving large numbers of customers on weekend or holiday outings; if they're open on weekdays, crowds will usually be smaller. Note that *hostería* can also mean a type of accommodation, though such places will usually have restaurants as well.

The most common term for menu is *la carta; el menú* is almost equally common but can also mean a fixed-price lunch or dinner. The bill is *la cuenta.*

One option worth watching for is the *picada,* generally a small family-run eatery that begins informally, often with just a couple of tables in a spare room facing the street, but can develop into something more elaborate. In some beachfront towns north of Viña del Mar, for instance, seafood *picadas* offer excellent food at modest prices.

In places other than simple *comedores* or *cocinerías,* a 10 percent tip is the norm. At *comedores,* tips are generally unexpected, but that doesn't mean they're unwelcome or inappropriate.

WHAT TO EAT

For those who read Spanish and enjoy cooking, the *Gran Libro de la Cocina Chilena* (Santiago:

Editorial Bibliográfica, 1990) contains more than 500 pages of recipes for drinks, appetizers, soups, salads, meats, poultry, pasta, seafood, and many other specialties from the Chilean kitchen.

Cereals

Maíz (maize or corn) is a main ingredient in many Chilean dishes, including the tasty traditional casserole of chicken, ground beef, olives, and other ingredients known as *pastel de choclo.* Maize leaves often serve as a wrapping for traditional dishes such as *humitas,* the Chilean equivalent of Mexican tamales.

Trigo (wheat), a Spanish introduction, is primarily for *pan* (bread), but it is also common in the form of pasta. *Arroz* (rice) is a common *agregado* (side dish).

Fruits

As its seasons are reversed from those of the Northern Hemisphere, temperate Chile produces many of the same fruits, often available as delicious fresh juices. Items such as *manzana* (apple), *pera* (pear), *naranja* (orange), *ciruela* (plum), *sandía* (watermelon), *membrillo* (quince), *durazno* (peach), *frambuesa* (raspberry), and *frutilla* (strawberry) will be familiar to almost everyone.

Also widely available, though mostly through import, are tropical and subtropical fruits such as banana, chirimoya, and *piña* (pineapple). Less commonly consumed locally, but often exported, are nontraditional temperate fruits such as *arándano* (blueberry) and kiwi.

The *palta* (avocado), a Central American domesticate known as *aguacate* in its area of origin, appears frequently in Chilean dishes, especially in sandwiches.

Legumes, Vegetables, and Tubers

Salads are generally safe in Chile, but short-term visitors with tender stomachs may want to verify whether the greens have been washed with purified water. The traditional *ensalada chilena* (Chilean salad) of tomato and onion, sometimes garnished with cilantro, is one of the best items on the salad menu.

Porotos (beans) are traditionally the main protein source in the working class diet, but all

Chileans eat them. Other legumes include *porotos verdes* (green beans), *arvejas* (peas), *lentejas* (lentils), and *habas* (fava beans).

In many varieties, *zapallo* (squash) remains part of the traditional diet, as does the *tomate* (tomato). Many Old World vegetables are also widely consumed, including *acelga* (chard), berenjena (eggplant), *coliflor* (cauliflower), *lechuga* (lettuce), and *repollo* (cabbage). Despite the country's name, *chiles* (peppers) are relatively uncommon, and most Chilean cuisine is fairly bland despite the presence of chile-based *ají* or *pebre* at virtually every meal.

Native to the Andes, *papas* (potatoes) grow in well-drained soils at higher elevations or relatively high latitudes such as Chiloé; *papas fritas* (French fries) are virtually universal, but spuds also appear as *purée* (mashed potatoes) and in many other forms. Other common tubers include *zanahorias* (carrots) and *rábanos* (radishes).

Vegetarianism

Note that while vegetarian restaurants are relatively few except in Santiago, the ingredients for quality vegetarian meals are easy to obtain, and many eateries prepare dishes such as pasta and salads, which are easily adapted into a vegetarian format. Before ordering pasta dishes, clarify whether it comes with a meat sauce—*carne* means beef in the Southern Cone, and waiters or waitresses may consider chicken, pork, and similar items as part of another category—sometimes called *carne blanca* (literally, white meat). Faced with a reticent cook, you can always claim *alergia* (allergy).

Meats and Poultry

Before the Spaniards, South America's only domesticated animals were the *cuy* (guinea pig), the llama and alpaca, and the dog, which was sometimes used for food. The Spaniards enriched the American diet with their domestic animals, including cattle, sheep, pigs, and poultry, including chicken and ducks.

Carne, often modified as *carne de vacuno,* or *bife* (beef) is the most common menu item in a variety of cuts. The widest selection is usually available in the *parrillada* or *asado,* a mixed grill

that includes prime cuts but also offal such as *chunchules* (small intestines), *morcilla* (blood sausage), and *riñones* (kidneys). *Asado* can also mean a simple roast.

Cordero (lamb), often roasted on a spit over an open fire, is a fairly common item in the Sur Chico and Chilean Patagonia. *Cerdo* (pork) appears in many forms, from *chuletas* (chops) to *tocino* (bacon) and *chicharrones* (rinds).

Ave (poultry) most often means *pollo* (chicken), which sometimes appears on menus as *gallina* (literally, hen). *Pavo* (turkey) is becoming more common. Eggs are *huevos.*

Fish and Seafood

Seafood, among the most abundant sources of animal protein in pre-Columbian times, includes both *pescado* (fish) and *mariscos* (shellfish and crustaceans), of which Chile has an abundance. The most common fish are *congrio* (conger eel, covering a variety of species), *corvina* (sea bass), *lenguado* (sole or flounder), *merluza* (hake); *salmón* (salmon) normally comes from fish farms on the inlets, fjords, and freshwater lakes of the Sur Chico and Aisén.

Note that the cheapest restaurants often ruin perfectly good-quality fish by preparing it *frito* (overpoweringly deep fried), but on request almost all will prepare it *a la plancha* (grilled, usually with a bit of butter) or *al vapor* (steamed). Higher-priced restaurants will add elaborate sauces, often with shellfish.

Chilean cuisine really distinguishes itself in its *mariscos.* Most visitors will recognize the relatively commonplace *almejas* (clams), *calamares* (squid), *camarones* (shrimp), *cangrejo* or *jaiva* (crab), *centolla* (king crab), *cholgas* and *choritos* (different varieties of mussels), *machas* (razor clams), *ostiones* (scallops), *ostras* (oysters), and *pulpo* (octopus), whose quality can be extraordinary. Less familiar will be items such as the *choro zapato* ("shoe mussel," so called because of its enormous size); *erizos* (sea urchins, definitely an acquired taste and frequently exported to Japan); the oddly named *locos* (giant abalone, literally "crazies"); *picoroco* (giant barnacle); and *piure* (resembling a dirty sponge, according to food writer Robb Walsh). Many of these have

lobster on Isla Robinson Crusoe

duction) is more common. *Arroz con leche* (rice pudding) and *flan* (egg custard) are better choices in most places except the Sur Chico, Patagonia, and scattered places elsewhere in the country, where German immigrants have left a legacy of kuchen (pastries such as apple strudel and raspberry tarts).

MEALS AND MEALTIMES

Chile's cuisine is relatively uniform throughout the country, except in Santiago, where diverse ethnic and international cuisine is abundant, and in resort areas such as Viña del Mar.

By North American and European standards, Chileans are late risers and late eaters. Even in hotels, you'll often find it difficult to get breakfast before 8 A.M. Lunch, commonly referred to as *almuerzo* but also as *colación* usually starts around 2 P.M., *cena* (dinner) around 9 P.M. or later—sometimes much later. Chileans bide their time between lunch and dinner with a late afternoon *onces* (elevenses, equivalent to afternoon tea) that consists of a sandwich or some sort of pastry or dessert; it can be very substantial.

Breakfast

Most Chileans eat only a light breakfast of tea and *pan tostado* (toast), with perhaps eggs on the side. Eggs may be either *fritos* (fried) or *revueltos* (scrambled), or occasionally *duros* (hardboiled).

North American breakfast foods such as cornflakes have also made inroads in Chile. *Avena* (oatmeal) is common in wintertime.

Lunch

Lunch is often the main meal of the day, usually including an *entrada* (appetizer), followed by a *plato de fondo* (entrée), accompanied by an *agregado* (side dish) and a *bebida* (soft drink) or *agua mineral* (mineral water) and followed by *postre* (dessert).

Upscale Santiago restaurants sometimes offer fixed-price lunches that make it possible to eat well and stylishly without busting the budget, but elsewhere this is usually not the case. It's also possible to find fast-food items such as *hamburguesas* (hamburgers), sandwiches, pizza, and pasta.

closed seasons, when they may not be taken, so be aware.

Seafood often appears on the menu in the form of **ceviche,** raw fish or shellfish heavily marinated in lime juice and spiced with cilantro. In the rivers of Patagonia, trout is a common item. On the Juan Fernández archipelago and Easter Island, *langosta* (literally lobster, though really a crayfish) is a frequent but not inexpensive menu item.

Among seafood specialties worth looking for are *chupes* (thick, buttery stews) of *congrio, jaiva,* and *locos,* and *curanto,* a kitchen-sink stew that can include fish, shellfish, beef, chicken, lamb, pork, potato, and vegetables.

Desserts

Helado (ice cream) is popular almost everywhere, but the quality is usually only so-so except in the capital and major beach resorts, where *elaboración artesanal* (small-scale pro-

ON THE ROAD

Onces

Onces, the third meal of the typical Chilean day, can vary from a late-afternoon sandwich to the equivalent of afternoon tea, with elaborate cakes and cookies, and it is often a social occasion as well. Presumably intended to tide people over until their relatively late dinnertime, it often becomes larger and more elaborate than that would imply.

Dinner

Dinner resembles lunch, but in formal restaurants it may be much more elaborate (and expensive); it can be a major social occasion. Chileans dine late–9 P.M. is early, and arriving earlier will likely earn "What are you doing here?" stares from waiters.

INTERNATIONAL AND ETHNIC FOOD

Santiago, one of the continent's underappreciated gastronomic centers, has the greatest variety of international food, though some tourist-oriented areas also have good selections. Italian and Chinese are probably the most common foreign cuisines—*chifa* is a common term for inexpensive Chinese restaurants in the Norte Grande—but French, German, and Spanish food is also plentiful. Brazilian, Mexican, and Middle Eastern cuisines are less common; some popular world food cuisines, such as Thai, are only now making inroads.

BUYING GROCERIES

Virtually every city, town, village, and hamlet in Chile has a central market where it's possible to buy fresh produce. Even in these locales that don't have central markets, there are almost always small shops where groceries are available.

In larger cities, North American-style supermarkets carry a wide selection of processed foods but a lesser variety (and quality) of fresh produce than is available in produce markets.

BEVERAGES

Coffee, Tea, and Chocolate

Chilean coffee is a disappointment for most caffeine addicts—powdered Nescafé is the norm, and espresso is a rare commodity except in the capital. *Café negro* is Nescafé mixed with hot water; *café con leche* (coffee with milk) is usually Nescafé dissolved in warm milk.

Té negro (black tea) usually comes in bags and is insipid by most standards. Those wanting tea with milk in the British manner should ask for tea first and milk later; for most Chileans, *té con leche* is a tea bag steeped in hot water with *leche en polvo* (powdered milk). Herbal teas, from the nearly universal *té de manzanilla* (chamomile) and *rosa mosqueta* (rose hips) to Chilean specialties such as *llantén* (plantain), *cedrón* (lemon verbena), *paico* (saltwort), *boldo,* and many others, are often better alternatives. In the far south, some Chileans follow the Argentine custom of taking *yerba mate,* the so-called "Paraguayan tea."

It's possible to get a good cup of *chocolate* (hot chocolate) in Santiago and much of the southern lake district, where Swiss-German influence is most significant. Elsewhere, it will be powdered chocolate mixed with hot water.

Water, Juices, and Soft Drinks

Chilean tap water is potable almost everywhere; ask for *agua de la llave.* For ice, request it *con hielo.* Visitors on brief vacations where a stomach upset can be disastrous might consider bottled water, which is widely available. Ask for *agua pura* or *agua mineral;* for carbonated water, add *con gas.* Sometimes these are known by brand names such as Cachantún.

Gaseosas (in the plural) are sweetened, bottled soft drinks (including most of the major transnational brands); Chile has the second-largest individual consumption of soft drinks in the world, 94.7 liters per person per annum. The Chilean market is estimated at US$1 billion per annum, and the only country in the world that consumes more is Mexico.

Licuados are fruit-based drinks mixed with water or blended with *leche* (milk). Unless you have an insatiable sweet tooth, always ask to have them prepared without sugar (*sin azúcar, por favor*). Fresh-squeezed *jugos* (fruit juices) are exceptionally good; but again, watch the sugar. This is usually not a problem with orange juice, but it is with others.

Alcoholic Drinks

While Chile is famous for its wines, Chileans themselves are leaning more toward beer. The most widely available Chilean beers are Cristal, Becker, and similar lagers, which are palatable but unexceptional. They taste best as *chopp,* direct from the tap, rather than from bottles or cans.

Chile, of course, is one of the world's major wine producers, and exports have boomed since the end of the dictatorship, during which many people boycotted Chilean products. In early 2001, though, the industry's prestige received a blow when *New York Times* wine writer Frank J. Prial trashed Chilean wines in general as "second rate," the majority of cabernets "insipid," and chardonnays as "flabby and lacking in tannin."

While exports to the United States have increased 30-fold in recent years, Prial said that Chilean vintners have sacrificed quality to quantity, and that even the better high-end Chilean wines were overpriced. Nevertheless, Chile's total area under cultivation has grown from 50,000 to 85,000 hectares in the past few years, and production will likely increase to a billion liters by 2004, half of it to be exported.

Chilean wine lists only rarely indicate the source region or the vintage, so when dining you may have to ask to see the bottle itself. Only the best restaurants have a wide wine selection, usually in full bottles though sometimes it's possible to get a *media botella* (half bottle) or, increasingly frequently but expensively, wine by the glass. At some places it's possible to order *vino individual* or *botellín,* a small bottle that's usually a little more than a single glass, but these are rarely premium wines.

Wine tourism is developing rapidly, though it's still not so spontaneous as in locales such as California's Napa Valley—with a few exceptions, it's necessary to call ahead for reservations or book a tour. There are nascent "Rutas del Vino" (Wine Routes) in the Aconcagua, Casablanca, Colchagua, and Maule valleys; for details, see the website vinasdechile.com.

Chile is also, along with Peru, the major producer of the potent variety of grape brandy known as *pisco,* the base of the legendary pisco sour. The Norte Chico valleys of Copiapó, Huasco, and Elqui are the major producing areas, and *pisco* has also spawned a small tourist industry.

Another popular aperitif is the *vaina,* a concoction of port, cognac, cocoa, and egg white that some Chileans consider a "woman's drink."

Getting There

Most overseas visitors arrive by air, though many also arrive overland from Argentina, Bolivia, and Peru. Almost all of the latter arrive by bus or private vehicle; the only international rail service at present is from Bolivia, though the short line from Arica to Tacna (Peru) may resume after repairs from the damage it suffered during floods in early 2001.

BY AIR

Most air passengers arrive at Santiago's Aeropuerto Internacional Arturo Merino Benitez (SCL), one of the most modern and well-monitored in the world; according to Chile's Dirección General de Aeronáutica Civil (DGAC, Civil Aeronautics Commission), it is so secure that it may become a regional security checkpoint for flights to the United States. All metal detectors and X-ray scanning machines were purchased since 2001, and its scanner can examine up to 4,000 pieces of luggage per hour.

Six million passengers traveled through the airport in the year 2000, and its infrastructure can support up to nine million. New technology will allow for increased air traffic without disrupting flight activity.

Most major international airlines fly out of the capital, while airports at Arica, Iquique, Antofagasta, La Serena, Temuco, Puerto Montt, and Punta Arenas have a handful of flights to neighboring countries only. (For addresses and telephone of airlines in Santiago, see the list in this chapter; for the others, see the appropriate geographical entries.)

From the United States and Canada

From these North American countries, the main gateways to Chile are Miami, Atlanta, New York, Dallas, and Los Angeles. Since the events of September 11, 2001, schedules are in flux, but Miami still has the greatest number of flights, with American Airlines, LanChile (which also flies from New York), and United (which also flies from Orlando). The Peruvian airline Aero-Continente has undercut the major carriers' fares—charging as little as US$500 for a 30-day round-trip to Santiago via Lima—but it seems unlikely it will be able to do so for very long; for a time, the line's viability was even in question.

The only other line operating from the southeastern United States is Delta, which flies daily from Atlanta to Santiago. American Airlines flies nonstop from Dallas, which enables travelers from the Midwest, Rocky Mountain states, and even the Pacific coast to avoid the longer Miami and Atlanta routes. West Coast carriers from Los Angeles include LanChile, United, and American, but only LanChile goes via Lima (Peru), the shortest route; American goes via Dallas and United via Miami. LanChile now has a code-share arrangement with Alaska Airlines from Vancouver, B.C., via Los Angeles.

Several other carriers serve Santiago and some other Chilean destinations via more roundabout routes. These include Aerolíneas Argentinas (from Miami, New York, and Los Angeles via Buenos Aires); Avianca (from Miami and New York via Bogotá and occasionally Buenos Aires); Copa (from Miami, Orlando, Newark, Houston, and Los Angeles via Panama); Grupo Taca (from Miami via Lima, and from New Orleans, New York, Los Angeles, and San Francisco via San José, Costa Rica); Lloyd Aéreo Boliviano (from Miami via Panama and Santa Cruz de la Sierra to either Santiago or Iquique, or from Miami via Manaus and Santa Cruz de la Sierra to Santiago or Iquique); TAM Mercosur (from Miami via São Paulo and Asunción to Santiago or Iquique); Varig (from Miami, New York, and Los Angeles via São Paulo).

For the cheapest fares, avoid the Christmas–New Year's period, when many Chileans return home for the holidays and flights are invariably full. Chilean patriotic holidays in mid-September are also very busy. Going and returning just before or after holiday periods will produce much better deals, as will shoulder-season travel in the southern spring or autumn. Standard coach fares range from about US$1,200 on the East Coast to US$2,000 from the Pacific Coast, but consolidators can often find bargains that cut up to 40 percent off the price, especially outside the southern summer peak.

From Mexico, Central America, and the Caribbean

Mexico City is the region's main gateway, served by Aeroméxico (which also flies from Cancún), Copa (via Panama), Grupo Taca (via Costa Rica), LanChile (which also flies out of Cancún), Mexicana, and Varig (via Cancún or Bogotá and São Paulo).

From Central America, Grupo Taca's main gateway is San José, Costa Rica, but it also flies out of Guatemala City. There are more flights from Panama, however, with AeroContinente, and Copa (with connections from Cancún, the Dominican Republic, Jamaica, Puerto Rico, and Costa Rica).

From the Caribbean, Cubana flies from Havana via Lima, while LanChile flies nonstop from Havana after arrival from Miami and Cancún, and nonstop from the Dominican Republic after arrival from Miami. TAME flies weekly from Havana via Guayaquil and Quito, but this entails an overnight stay in Quito. Copa flies from Havana via Panama.

From Europe

Most flights from Europe pass through São Paulo, Brazil, or Buenos Aires, but there are a handful of nonstops. The main gateways are London, Frankfurt, and Madrid.

Iberia has two nonstops daily from Madrid, while LanChile flies daily from Frankfurt via Madrid. Pluna flies from Madrid via São Paulo five times weekly via Montevideo, and once via Montevideo only. Spanair flies four times weekly from Barcelona via Madrid and Buenos Aires.

British Airways flies six times weekly to Santiago via Buenos Aires. Lufthansa flies daily from Frankfurt via Buenos Aires, while SAS flies three times weekly from Stockholm and Copenhagen via São Paulo; on other days, it links up with Lufthansa or Spanair.

Varig flies via São Paulo from Madrid; from Milan via São Paulo and also via Rome, Rio de Janeiro, and São Paulo; nine times weekly from London via São Paulo, three times weekly from Munich via São Paulo, and Sunday only from Frankfurt via São Paulo.

Alitalia flies four times weekly from Rome and three times weekly from Milan; all flights pass through Buenos Aires. Air France flies three times weekly from Paris via Buenos Aires.

From Asia, Africa, and the Pacific

From Australia, the simplest route to Chile is via Papeete, Tahiti, where LanChile flies two or three times weekly via Easter Island (Rapa Nui), where stopovers are permitted, to Santiago. Qantas flies weekly from Sydney via Auckland to Papeete, where its partner Polynesian Airlines does the final segment to Santiago. Qantas also flies twice weekly to Buenos Aires via Auckland, but then it's necessary to find an onward flight from Buenos Aires to Santiago.

South African Airlines flies five times weekly from Johannesburg via São Paulo, while Malaysia Airlines flies twice weekly from Kuala Lumpur via South Africa and Buenos Aires. Varig flies daily from either Tokyo or Nagoya via Los Angeles.

Within South America

Santiago has connections to neighboring countries of Peru, Bolivia, and Argentina, and elsewhere on the continent.

From Neighboring Countries: LanChile, the Peruvian budget carrier AeroContinente, and Grupo Taca all compete on the Lima-Santiago route.

Lloyd Aéreo Boliviano flies from Santa Cruz de la Sierra and La Paz to Santiago via Iquique a total of five times weekly. LanChile flies daily from La Paz to Santiago via Arica and Iquique.

LanChile flies several times daily from Buenos Aires, twice daily from Córdoba, and twice daily from Mendoza. Aerolíneas Argentinas also flies several times daily from Buenos Aires, while AeroContinente once or twice daily from Buenos Aires, and four times weekly from Mendoza.

The Argentine airline Southern Winds has only recently begun flights from Santiago to Mendoza and Buenos Aires, where it lands at close-in Aeroparque rather than the remote international airport at Ezeiza. Southern Winds also plans to fly from Temuco to Buenos Aires via the Argentine Patagonian city of Neuquén.

Note that the Buenos Aires–Santiago route is a highly competitive one because many European carriers lose most of their passengers at Buenos Aires and, consequently, sell the empty seats at bargain prices.

From Other South American Countries: Except for the Guianas, Santiago has service from all other South American capitals, including the Falkland Islands. LanChile has service to all of them, often continuing to North America or Europe. Other carriers include Avianca from Bogotá, Colombia; Grupo Taca from Caracas, Venezuela, via Lima; TAME from Quito and Guayaquil, Ecuador; TAM Mercosur from Asunción, Paraguay, with an additional three flights weekly to Iquique; Varig from Brazil; and Pluna from Montevideo, Uruguay. Note that there is only one flight weekly from the Falklands to Punta Arenas, continuing to Santiago.

BY LAND

Chile has a few border crossings with Peru and Bolivia, and quite a few with Argentina. Only a handful of these have scheduled transportation: the Peruvian crossing from Tacna; the Bolivian crossings from La Paz to Arica via Parque Nacional Lauca, from Oruro to Iquique via Colchane; the rail and road crossing from Uyuni to Calama via Ollagüe, and the long and legendary overland 4WD excursion from Uyuni to San Pedro de Atacama via Laguna Verde.

From Argentina, there are buses from Salta and Jujuy to San Pedro de Atacama and Calama via the Paso de Jama, which is already smoothly paved on the Chilean side and should be completed on the Argentine side before the next edition of this book. The busiest crossing, though, is the Los Libertadores tunnel between Mendoza and Santiago. Buses cross in summer only from Malargüe to Talca over the 2,553-meter Paso del Maule (also known as the Paso Pehuenche).

In the Sur Chico there are buses from Neuquén to Temuco over the 1,884-meter Paso de Pino Hachado via Curacautín and Lonquimay; the alternative 1,298-meter Paso de Icalma is slightly to the south. There are also a regular bus service from San Martín de los Andes to Temuco via the Paso de Mamuil Malal (Paso Tromen to Argentines); a bus-boat combination from San Martín de los Andes to Panguipulli via the 659-meter Paso Huahum and Lago Pirehueico; a paved highway from Bariloche to Osorno via the Paso de Cardenal Samoré that's the second-busiest crossing between the two countries; and the scenic bus-boat shuttle from Bariloche to Puerto Varas and Puerto Montt.

Patagonia has many crossings, but the roads are often bad and only a few have public transportation. Those served by scheduled transport include the mostly gravel road from Esquel (local buses only) to Futaleufú, where there are connections to Chaitén; Comodoro Rivadavia to Coyhaique on a mostly paved road via Río Mayo on comfortable long-distance coaches; Los Antiguos to Chile Chico (shuttles with onward connections in either direction); El Calafate to Puerto Natales via Río Turbio on a steadily improving but mostly gravel route; Río Gallegos to Punta Arenas via an almost entirely paved highway with one brutal stretch on the Argentine side; and Ushuaia and Río Grande to Punta Arenas.

In addition, many border crossings are suitable for private motor vehicles and mountain bikes, and a few by foot. (For information on these see below as well as the appropriate geographical entries.)

Bus and *Taxi Colectivo*

International bus service is available from the neighboring republics, Argentina, Bolivia, and Peru, and also from more distant destinations such as Uruguay, Brazil, Paraguay, Ecuador, and Colombia. (For carrier and itinerary details, see individual geographical entries.)

Both international and domestic bus services normally have comfortable reclining seats (with every passenger guaranteed a seat), clean toilets, a/c, and meals and refreshments served on board, at least on the longest trips. If not, they make regular meal stops. Between Santiago and Mendoza, there are *taxi colectivos,* shared taxis that are slightly more expensive but faster than full-sized buses.

Train

In March of 2001, floods on the Río Lluta washed out bridges and rails along the line that connects the northern city of Arica with the Peruvian city of Tacna. Since there are many faster, cheaper buses and shared taxis on this route, its lingering closure is only an inconvenience for trainspotters. The former passenger line from Arica to the Bolivian border at Charaña, a freight-only line for several years, also suffered considerable damage in the floods, but word was that it would reopen for passenger service to La Paz.

The only other international passenger line connects the Chilean city of Calama with the Bolivian border at Ollagüe, where passengers have to change trains coming from or going to the Bolivian city of Uyuni. The freight line from the Argentine city of Salta to the Chilean border at Socompa, with connections to the Chilean rail graveyard of Baquedano, will carry truly determined passengers with plenty of time, patience, and grit.

Car, Motorcycle, and Bicycle

Overland travel from North America or elsewhere is problematic because Panama's Darien Gap to Colombia is impassable for motor vehicles, very difficult and potentially dangerous even for those on foot, and passes through areas controlled by drug smugglers, guerrillas, and/or brutal Colombian paramilitaries. Fortunately, with its minimal bureaucracy, Chile is probably the best country on the continent for shipping a vehicle; the author has twice retrieved vehicles from Chilean customs in less than two hours. Even with the expense of shipping, anyone traveling at least three to four months in South America will probably find it competitive with, or cheaper than, renting a vehicle for the same amount of time.

To find a shipper, check the Yellow Pages of your local phone directory under Automobile Transporters, who are normally freight consolidators rather than the company that owns the ship, which will charge higher rates for containers. Since many more people ship vehicles to Europe than to South America, it may take patience to find the right shipper; one recommended North American consolidator is McClary, Swift & Co., 360 Swift Ave., South San Francisco, CA 94080, tel. 650/872-2121, website: home.netcom.com/~mc-swift/home.html, swift@unitedshipping.com, which has agents at many U.S. ports.

The recommended and most probable ports of entry are San Antonio, southwest of Santiago, and Valparaíso, northwest of the capital. It does pay to be there within a couple of days of the vehicle's arrival, or storage charges can mount up. Leave the gas tank as nearly empty as possible (for safety's sake) and leave no valuables, including tools, in the vehicle.

To arrange a shipment from San Antonio or Valparaíso, contact the Santiago consolidator Ultramar, Moneda 970, 18th floor, Santiago Centro, tel. 2/6301817, fax 2/6986552, italia@ultramar.cl. For a trustworthy customs broker to handle the paperwork, contact the office of Juan Alarcón Rojas, Fidel Oteíza 1921, 12th floor, Providencia, Santiago, tel. 2/2252780, fax 2/2045302, alrcon@entelchile.net.

Bicycles, of course, can be partially dismantled, packaged, and easily shipped aboard airplanes, sometimes for no additional charge.

Vehicle Documents and Driver's License: Most South American countries, including Chile, Argentina, Uruguay, and Brazil, have dispensed with the cumbersome *Carnet de Passage en Douanes* that required depositing a large bond to import a motor vehicle. Officials at the port of arrival issue a 90- to 180-day *Título de Importación Temporal de Vehículos* on presentation of the vehicle title, registration, bill of lading, and your passport. There are some small but relatively insignificant port charges (unless the vehicle has been stored more than a few days).

It is not possible for the vehicle owner to leave the country without the vehicle except by transferring responsibility for it to a legal Chilean resident. It is not possible to sell a used vehicle in Chile except in the Zona Franca (duty-free zone) of either Iquique or Punta Arenas, where vehicles are so abundant that prices are depressed.

Before traveling to Chile, obtain an International or Interamerican Driving Permit (travelers intending to visit Uruguay should note that that country officially recognizes only the latter, though in practice it appears more flexible). These permits are available through the American Automobile Association (AAA) or its counterpart in your home country, and are normally valid for one calendar year from date of issue.

BY WATER

Cruise ships and private yachts can and do call at Chilean ports, but scheduled international water transport is rare. The scenic crossing from the Argentine city of Bariloche to Chile's Puerto Varas and Puerto Montt involves shuttling over several lakes on tourist boats whose ports are linked by buses. The Chilean fjords cruise with Terra Australis (see Organized Tours, below) does allow passengers to board in Punta Arenas and disembark in Ushuaia, on Argentine Tierra del Fuego, or vice versa. Launch shuttles from Ushuaia across the Beagle Channel to the newly declared port of entry at Puerto Navarino, on Chile's Isla Navarino, may soon commence.

Getting Around

Chilean air services are well-developed along the length of the country, though connecting the desert north with the humid south will always involve changing planes in the capital. Bus is the primary means of overland transport, as the once extensive rail network now reaches only from Santiago to the southern cities of Temuco and Concepción, and from Calama to Ollagüe, on the Bolivian border route to Uyuni. There is also commuter rail service from Santiago to points south as far as San Fernando.

AIR

Besides the airports mentioned above, additional domestic airports with commercial flights are at Calama, Copiapó, El Salvador, Los Ángeles, Chillán, Pucón, Valdivia, Osorno, Chaitén, and Balmaceda (Coyhaique). Smaller airfields are also in Santiago for flights to the Juan Fernández archipelago, and in Coyhaique for flights to Laguna San Rafael (for details, see the appropriate geographical entries).

LanChile is the 800-pound gorilla of Chilean civil aviation, dominating the domestic market through its independently operated subsidiary LanExpress, which replaced the former Ladeco in September of 2001. In addition to its fleet of Boeing 767s, it has acquired six new Airbus A320s for domestic service. The planes are fairly spacious for a country whose longest domestic flight is only about three hours.

No competitor has had much luck challenging LanChile's supremacy, especially as the company is professionally managed and has deeper pockets than its rivals; in early 2001, Avant Airlines (founded by the exceptionally well-managed Tur-Bus company) was the latest to go under. The Peruvian airline AeroContinente, which competes with LanChile on some international routes, was briefly forced to suspend operations after what some observers considered politically motivated allegations of drug money laundering in 2001. After being cleared and reopening, it reduced its Chilean domestic operations from

Santiago to the northern cities of Antofagasta, Iquique, and Arica, and the southern cities of Puerto Montt and Punta Arenas.

Chilean domestic airfares are generally reasonable, but buying tickets a few days ahead of time can often result in substantial discounts. For international visitors arriving on LanChile, that airline has recently renewed its "Visit Chile" pass, which can result in substantial savings; travelers can buy three flight coupons for US$250, and additional coupons for US$60 each. Coupons are valid for travel to 14 Chilean cities, including Arica, Iquique, Calama, Antofagasta, El Salvador, Copiapó, La Serena, Concepción, Temuco, Valdivia, Osorno, Puerto Montt, Balmaceda (Coyhaique), and Punta Arenas.

Chile's flagship airline has recently inaugurated **LanChile Vacations,** toll-free tel. 877/219-0345 in the United States, website: www lanchilevacations.com, with a variety of individually crafted itineraries in its home country and other destinations that it serves.

For student discounts on both international and domestic flights, try the Student Flight Center, Hernando de Aguirre 201, Oficina 401, Providencia, Santiago, tel. 2/3350395, fax 2/3350394, studentflightcenter@sertur.cl.

BUS

Buses along the principal longitudinal highways, and those connecting other main cities and resorts, are frequent and almost invariably spacious and comfortable, even luxurious. A few on backroads routes are only a little better than Central American "chicken buses," and they may be infrequent, but distances are relatively short.

So-called Pullman buses have reclining seats, and for short to medium runs, say up to six or seven hours, they're more than adequate. Seats are guaranteed. For truly long distances, some travelers prefer *semi-cama* or *salón cama* service, which provides greater leg room in seats that recline almost horizontally. Fares are very reasonable by international standards—the longest route in the

© WAYNE BERNHARDSON

Hito Cajones border crossing from Bolivia to San Pedro de Atacama

country, the 26-hour marathon from Santiago to the border town of Arica, costs only about US$60 in *salón cama,* including onboard and/or roadside meal service.

Most cities have a central *terminal de buses* (bus terminal) or *terminal rodoviario,* but in some towns there are multiple terminals for long-distance, regional, and rural services, or for individual companies. Some companies also have separate ticket offices in more central locations than the terminals themselves—in Santiago, for instance, some companies have outlets at Metro stations.

Bus services are so frequent that reservations are rarely necessary except for a few infrequently traveled routes and some international services, or during holiday periods such as mid-September's independence celebrations, the Semana Santa (Holy Week) and Christmas/New Year's periods, and occasionally during the January/February summer vacation season.

According to Chilean transport regulations, bus tickets may be returned for 85 percent of their face value up to four hours before departure time. Exchanges are possible free of charge.

TRAIN

Once the primary means of interurban transportation, domestic rail service is now limited to the longitudinal line that runs from Santiago to Temuco, with a spur to Concepción, and a relic narrow-gauge short line that runs from the heartland city of Talca to the port of Constitución. Many tourists, however, enjoy, the wood-paneled, German-built 1920s sleepers on the Temuco line; nearly all those patronizing the dining cars are foreigners.

Trains are cheap if slow. Ordinary fares to Temuco are only US$7.50–12, and sleepers from US$23–29 for the 12.5-hour journey (the train averages only about 50 km per hour). Train tickets may be returned for 90 percent of their face value up to one week before departure, or for 50 percent between six to 24 hours before departure.

Tentatively, the state-run Empresa de Ferrocarriles del Estado (EFE) has slated the rail network for a modernization program that would increase speeds about 40 percent and perhaps fund a extension of the southern longitudinal line to its former terminus at Puerto Montt. At present, commuter trains serve on the longitudinal line as far as Rancagua and San Fernando, but plans were in the works to open a new commuter line on the 70 km between Santiago and the southwestern town of Melipilla soon, and to the northerly town of Tiltil by 2004.

Also under consideration was a high-speed line to Valparaíso, at a cost of US$800 million, to cut travel time from the capital to 50 minutes at speeds of up to 180 km per hour. Valparaíso and Viña del Mar have their own Metro rail system, Merval, used by up to eight million passengers per year.

HITCHHIKING

Chile and Argentina, where private cars are more abundant than in most other South American countries, are probably the best two countries on the continent for hitchhiking. In some rural areas, where buses are few, hitching a lift in a truck or pickup truck is sometimes the only alternative. Unlike the Andean countries of Peru and Bolivia, drivers normally do not expect to be paid.

Hitching has the advantage of flexibility, but it can also be unpredictable; carry food, water, and appropriate clothing for the climate and season. Hitching is fairly common—many young Chileans hit the Panamericana north and south in summer, so there's plenty of competition—but it can also be unsafe. Single women, in particular, should pay attention to security matters.

CAR AND MOTORCYCLE

The longitudinal Panamericana or Ruta 5, which stretches from the Peruvian border to Puerto Montt and the Isla Grande de Chiloé, is Chile's main transport artery, though the shorter and more scenic coastal Ruta 1 has superseded it between Iquique and Antofagasta. The Panamericana is smoothly paved for its entire length; from La Serena south to Puerto Montt, it either is or soon will be a four-lane divided highway for its entire length. Even so, despite the presence of call boxes, rest areas, and *peajes* (toll booths), there are occasionally loose livestock, pedestri-

ans crossing at unsuitable places, and even vendors hawking a range of items from sweets and ice cream to fresh produce and cheese to dressed kid goat, ready for barbecue.

Many more roads are paved or smoothly graded, though Ruta 7, the legendary Carretera Austral (Southern Highway) in the Aisén region is often narrow, mostly gravel, and occasionally precarious (the author has wrecked two 4WD vehicles on it, with extenuating circumstances). Heavy truck traffic can make all these routes dangerous, but most Chileans are courteous and cautious drivers despite occasional incidents of road rage in Santiago. Watch, however, for Argentine license plates, as many trans-Andean visitors drive far more aggressively.

Congested Santiago can be a traffic madhouse, and the routes out of the capital can be difficult for drivers without local experience. It's better to park the car, preferably in a guarded lot, and use public transport. Avoid leaving conspicuous valuables in the car.

In both the city and the countryside, watch for *lomas de burro* (speed bumps), also colloquially known as *pacos acostados* (sleeping policemen). Night driving is not advisable in some rural areas, as domestic livestock and inebriated campesinos may roam freely.

Police checkpoints are far less common than they were under the Pinochet dictatorship, but always stop when the Carabineros, the national police force, signal you to do so; this is usually a routine document check. Note that the Carabineros have been trained to refuse bribes, so don't even think about offering one, which can get you in serious trouble; if you have committed an *infracción* (traffic violation), the best thing to do is reason with them, and it is possible that you will get off unless your offense is truly flagrant or particularly dangerous. Note also that the slang term *paco* for a policeman is widely considered an insult—never use it to a cop's face.

Speed limits on most highways are generally around 100 km/hour, but authorities are considering raising the maximum to 120 km/hour on those segments of the Panamericana that are four-lane divided roads. Carabineros with radar guns are common sights along all highways.

In remote areas where gas stations are few, such as Aisén or the altiplano east of Arica and Iquique, carry additional fuel. Note that members of the American Automobile Association (AAA), Britain's Automobile Association (AA), and similar foreign automobile clubs are often eligible for limited roadside assistance and towing through the Automóvil Club de Chile (Acchi), whose main office is at Avenida Vitacura 8620, Vitacura, Santiago, tel. 2/2125702, website: www.acchi.cl. It has affiliates in most Chilean cities.

Expenses

Operating a gasoline-powered vehicle in Chile is more expensive than in the United States but still substantially cheaper than in Europe, even though Chile now imports about 90 percent of its oil. The cost of *benzina* (gasoline) is about US$.50 per liter (roughly US$1.90 per U.S. gallon) in Santiago; prices generally increase with distance from the capital, and reach US$.80 per liter (US$3 per gallon) or upward in remote parts of Aisén. These prices, however, are subject to fluctuations in the exchange rate and international crude oil prices.

Unleaded fuel is available everywhere, but many older vehicles still use leaded. There is no price difference between lower octane leaded *(con plomo)* and unleaded *(sin plomo)* fuels; higher octane unleaded is only slightly more expensive. Diesel *(gasoil)* fuel, though, is about a third cheaper than gasoline. Note that gasoline is significantly *more* expensive in Argentina except in Patagonia south of the town of El Bolsón, where it is subsidized and consequently cheaper than in Chile.

If importing a car as a tourist, be sure to obtain Chilean insurance, which is available in major cities. *Seguro mínimo,* a cheap no fault policy with limited personal injury coverage, is obligatory but inadequate for any serious accident.

Repairs are cheap in terms of labor but can be expensive in terms of parts, nearly all of which must be imported. Fortunately, Chilean mechanics are skilled at rehabilitating virtually any salvageable part.

Car and Motorcycle Rental

Rental cars are widely available in Santiago and other major cities and tourist centers, but they're not cheap; rates start around US$25 per day or US$150 per week for economical vehicles such as the Fiat Uno and around US$75 per day or US$450 per week or up for twin cab pickup trucks. Even more expensive are 4WD vehicles, commonly referred to as *doble tracción* or *cuatro por cuatro* (the latter usually written "4X4"). On the other hand, if they're shared among a group, they can be fairly reasonable.

Local agencies are usually cheaper than major international franchises, and monthly rates can be relative bargains. All car rentals pay 18 percent IVA. Note that taking a Chilean vehicle into Argentina involves additional paperwork and a surcharge, as well as supplementary insurance. Returning a vehicle to an office other than the one you rented from, which is impossible with the cheapest local companies, usually means a hefty surcharge.

To rent a vehicle, you must have a valid driver's license, a credit card, and be at least 25 years of age. Rental insurance does not completely cover you against losses—there is almost always a deductible of several hundred dollars or more in case of serious damage, total destruction, or theft of the vehicle.

In Santiago, camping vehicles, from pickup trucks with shells to fully equipped motor homes, are available through Holiday Rent, Suecia 734, Providencia, tel. 2/2582000, fax 2/2324975, website: www.chile-travel.com/holiday.htm, holiday@firstpremium.cl.

Buying a Vehicle

If you are visiting Chile and other parts of South America for several months, buying a vehicle is worth consideration. With relatively slow economic growth since 1999, Chileans have not been making big ticket purchases, so there are plenty of good used vehicles in stock, even if you can't quite name your price. Santiago has the largest selection; be circumspect about buying a vehicle in Region I (Tarapacá) or Region XII (Magallanes), where *zona franca* duty-free regulations limit purchases of many vehicles to permanent residents. Only a vehicle that is legally *liberado* may be sold in and taken outside those regions.

To buy a car, you need a RUT (Rol Unico Tributario) Chilean tax ID number, which takes only a few minutes at any office of the Servicio de Impuestos Internos (SII, Internal Revenue Service); you need not be a legal resident of the country. The SII issues a provisional RUT, valid for any purpose, and sends the permanent card to an address that you designate; this requires, of course, having an address in the country.

Before buying the vehicle, request a *Certificado de Inscripción y Anotaciones Vigentes* from any office of the Registro Civil (Civil Registry); this document, which costs only a couple of dollars, will alert you to title problems if any, as well as any legal issues (such as accident settlements) pending. To be licensed, the vehicle also needs an up-to-date *revisión técnica* (safety and emissions test).

Registering the sale itself is relatively straightforward at any office of the Registro Civil, involving a notarized *compraventa* (bill of sale, about US$15); an official *Giro y Pago del Impuesto a la Transferencia de Vehículos Motorizados* (Proof of Payment of Motor Vehicle Transfer Tax, made at a local bank, variable depending on the value of the vehicle but modest for a used car); and a *Solicitud Registro Nacional de Vehículos Motorizados* (Application to the National Registry of Motorized Vehicles, about US$25). The Registro then issues a provisional title and mails the permanent title, usually within a month, to the address on your RUT.

Theoretically, the *compraventa* and other documents entitle you to take the vehicle out of the country, but since the purchase of a Chilean vehicle by foreigners is still a little unusual, it may be worth making a special request to accelerate the issuance of the permanent title, which requires a brief letter to the head of the Registro. Personnel at the office can help with this.

BICYCLE

For the physically fit, or those intending to become physically fit, cycling is an ideal way to see the country. Because so many roads are unpaved in the most scenic areas, a *todo terreno* (mountain bike) is a much better choice than a touring bike. Cyclists should have a knowledge of basic mechanics, though the increasing availability of mountain bikes within the country means that

parts and mechanics are easier to find than they once were. In an emergency, it's easy to put a bicycle on board a bus.

Some cyclists visiting Chile dislike the busy Panamericana, much of which is also relatively uninteresting, but its completion as a four-lane divided highway with broad paved shoulders should make it safer, at least. There are many alternative roads, however, and some really exciting ones, such as the rarely used route that follows the former rail line in the Norte Chico (see the special topic Taking the High Road in the Norte Chico chapter).

FERRY

From Puerto Montt south through the Aisén and Magallanes regions, lacustrine and maritime transportation fills gaps in the highway network. This is even true in parts of the Sur Chico, where ferries on finger lakes such as Lago Pirehueico and Lago Todos los Santos (passengers only) form part of trans-Andean routes to Argentina.

Navimag and Transmarchilay operate ferries from Puerto Montt to Chaitén and Puerto Chacabuco, while Catamaranes del Sur runs high-speed passenger catamarans to Chaitén, Castro (Chiloé), and back to Puerto Montt in summer only. Both Navimag and Transmarchilay continue to the icefields of Parque Nacional Laguna San Rafael, a route also traveled by the tourist cruise ship *Skorpios* and the luxury passenger catamaran *Patagonia Connection*. (For details on the former two, see the entry for Parque Nacional Laguna San Rafael in the Patagonia chapter; for the latter two, see the Organized Tours entry below.)

Navimag's ferries *Puerto Edén* and *Magallanes* connect Puerto Montt with Puerto Natales, a three-day journey through the scenic fjords of Aisén and northern Magallanes; the former calls at its namesake village en route, while the latter stops at Puerto Chacabuco. (For details, see the appropriate geographical entries, the Organized Tours entry below, and the special topic Chile's Inside Passage in the Sur Chico chapter.)

Transmarchilay also runs a shuttle ferry across the mouth of the Reloncaví estuary, from La Arena to Puelche, about 45 km southeast of Puerto Montt. The village of Hornopirén, 60 km farther southeast, is the port for Transmarchilay's summer-only ferry to Caleta Gonzalo, the gateway to Chaitén and the Carretera Austral.

Transmarchilay and Cruz del Sur ferries connect Pargua, on the mainland Sur Chico, with Chacao, on the Isla Grande de Chiloé. Ferries also travel from Quellón, at the south end of the Isla Grande, to Chaitén and occasionally to Puerto Chacabuco. (For details, see the appropriate geographical entry.)

Naviera Sotramin sails the *Pilchero* from the Aisén village of Puerto Ingeniero Ibáñez, on the north shore of Lago General Carrera, to the border town of Chile Chico on the south shore; while Chile Chico is also accessible by a road around the lake, the ferry is both faster and cheaper.

In Magallanes, there's a daily ferry from Punta Arenas across the Strait of Magellan to Porvenir, on the Chilean side of the Isla Grande de Tierra del Fuego; a more frequent shuttle ferry crosses the Strait from Primera Angostura, northwest of Punta Arenas.

Transmarchilay's Santiago representative is Turismo El Colono, Avenida Providencia 2653, Local 24, Providencia, tel. 2/2341464, fax 2/2344899, turismo@elcolono.cl. Navimag's Santiago offices are at Avenida El Bosque Norte 0440, 11th floor, Las Condes, tel. 2/4423110, fax 2/2035173, website: www.australis.com, info@australis.com.

Catamaranes del Sur is in Santiago at Isidora Goyenechea 3250, Oficina 802, Las Condes, tel. 2/3377127, fax 2/2329736, website: www.catamaranesdelsur.cl, catamaranes@central.detroit.cl.

LOCAL TRANSPORTATION

Even as automobiles clog the streets of Santiago and other cities, most Chileans still rely on public transportation to get around.

Metro and Metrobús

Well into its third decade, carrying upward of 200 million passengers per year, Santiago's privately operated Metro looks almost as good as the day it opened in 1975, and it is steadily improving its coverage of the sprawling capital. Government expects ridership to nearly double as the system ex-

© WAYNE BERNHARDSON

ON THE ROAD

entrance to Baquedano Metro station, Providencia

pands over the next several years (for details of its three lines, see the Santiago chapter).

In early 2001, the Metro imposed a nearly 50 percent price increase that shocked its patrons, but even those new fares are cheaper than those of the *micros* (city buses) that carry most of the capital's passenger traffic, and they are very reasonable by international standards.

The Metro runs from 6:30 A.M.–10:30 P.M. Peak "normal" hours are now 7:15–9 A.M. and 6–7:30 P.M., while all other hours, including weekends, are *económico*. Normal fares are about US$.50, while *económico* fares are about US$.40; the multitrip discount *boleto inteligente* or *boleto valor* costs US$4.50 and can pay for up to a dozen trips, depending on the time of day.

Integrated with the Metro, Metrobuses are blue feeder buses that link various neighborhoods with the Metro and cost about US$.65 per trip. A new combined Metro and Metrobús ticket makes the combination cheaper and may eventually be extended to other buses.

Train

The state-run Ferrocarriles del Estado operates a longitudinal commuter line south to the cities of Rancagua and San Fernando. The Metro de Valparaíso (Merval) links the port city, the nearby resort town of Viña del Mar, and nearby suburbs; within a few years, it is due to go underground.

Bus

Santiago, all other large cities, and even most small towns have local bus systems that cover the farthest extent of urban areas. City buses are usually known as *micros,* but smaller ones carrying only about 20–25 passengers are often referred to as *liebres* (literally, hares).

Bus routes can and do change, but most buses are numbered and have obvious placards indicating the major streets along their routes. If in doubt, ask the driver, as identically numbered buses sometimes follow slightly different routes. Fares are about US$.40–.45 in Santiago, occasionally a little cheaper elsewhere. In Santiago, authorities have mandated the installation of automatic ticket machines to spare the driver the distraction of making change, but some bus companies (which are private) have rebelled at the cost of installing the machines and continue to operate as before.

Taxi

Taxis are moderately priced in Santiago but more expensive in resorts and other towns. Painted black with yellow roofs, all of them have meters; fares start around Ch$150 (US$.25) to *bajar la bandera* (literally, drop the flag), then cost Ch$70–80 (US$.12–.14) per 100 meters.

In Santiago, there's also a system of radio taxis, and hotels and restaurants will usually call these cabs for their guests. Slightly cheaper than metered taxis, radio taxis offered fixed fares that are agreed upon in advance. These vehicles look like ordinary automobiles, with no obvious identifying characteristics except that they are invariably new and have large antennae.

Taxi Colectivo

One of the great conveniences in Chilean public transport is the *taxi colectivo,* which operates like a city bus on a fixed route. Only slightly more expensive than a city bus, a *taxi colectivo* is usually faster and often more comfortable. *Taxi colectivos* are identifiable by the illuminated plastic signs on top of their roofs, which show major destinations along the route.

Airport Buses and Shuttles

Santiago enjoys inexpensive service to the airport—US$1.50–2 pp—but getting to the bus stop can be a nuisance for those with more than a little luggage. Most but not all regional airports also have bus service; if not, a shuttle or taxi is necessary.

In Santiago and several other cities, there are inexpensive door-to-door shuttles (US$3.50–7 pp, depending on the distance from the airport, that are ideal if you have substantial amounts of baggage. In general, it's best to arrange this the day before your flight, but they can often accommodate passengers on short notice. (For details and phone numbers, see the appropriate geographical entry.)

ORGANIZED TOURS

Because of Chile's complex travel logistics, organized tours can be a useful option for visitors with limited time, and many reputable U.S. and Chilean operators offer and even coordinate tours. Sometimes these take in sights in neighboring countries, usually Argentina but sometimes Peru or Bolivia. Within each category, the companies below are listed in alphabetical order.

U.S.-Based Operators

Primarily but not exclusively for cyclists, **Backroads,** 801 Cedar St., Berkeley, CA 94710, tel. 800/462-2848 or 510/527-1555, fax 510/527-1444; website: www.backroads.com, offers an 11-day "Chile & Argentina Mountain Biking" excursion in the Chilean and Argentine lake district around Puerto Varas, and Argentina's Bariloche and San Martín de los Andes for US$3,798 pp. Its nine-day "Patagonian Hiking" trip stays at luxury lodgings in Parque Nacional Torres del Paine and Argentina's Parque Nacional Los Glaciares; rates are US$5,298 pp. The 11-day

"Chile & Argentina Hiking" takes in Puerto Varas and vicinity along with Argentina's Parque Nacional Nahuel Huapi for US$3,798 pp.

Bio Bio Expeditions, P.O. Box 2028, Truckee, CA 96160, tel. 800/246-7238, fax 530/550-9670, website: www.bbxrafting.com, larsalvarez@compuserve.com, offers weeklong trips from Puerto Montt to its base camp on the Futaleufú for kayaking and multisport trips in the US$2,300 pp range.

Earth River Expeditions, 180 Towpath Rd., Accord, NY 12404, tel. 800/643-2784 or 845/626-2665, fax 845/626-4423, website: www.earthriver.com, earthriv@ulster.net, offers 10-day rafting and multisport trips on and around the Río Futaleufú for US$2,700–2,900 from Puerto Montt. It has its own deluxe camp on the river.

The **Earthwatch Institute,** 3 Clocktower Pl., Maynard, MA 01754, tel. 800/776-0188, fax 978/461-2332, website: www.earthwatch.org, arranges a variety of volunteer programs in which participants pay for the privilege of assisting university faculty and independent researchers in archaeological, environmental, or similar projects. Among the projects in Chile have been archaeological digs at Pisagua, river otters on the Río Toltén, and owls in the Cape Horn area.

¡Ecole! Adventures International, P.O. Box 2453, Redway, CA 95560, tel. 800/447-1483; tel./fax 707/923-3001, website: asis.com/ecole/index/html, staff@ecole-adventure.com, arranges hiking and fishing trips in the vicinity of Pucón and the upper Biobío drainage through its Chilean affiliate Hostería ¡Ecole! and excursions to more remote areas such as the Fiordo de Cahuelmó (part of Douglas Tompkins' Parque Natural Pumalín) in Region X.

Encounter Patagonia, 5209 Saratoga Ave., Chevy Chase, MD 20815, tel. 888/280-7036, website: www.encounterpatagonia.com, info@encounterpatagonia.com, does a diverse 13-day "Patagonia Auténtica" program that includes climbing, hiking, fly-fishing, white-water rafting, ranch visits, and rodeos for US$2,950. For US$3,850, the 15-day "Patagonia Cultura" package is a more upscale mix of hot springs and spas, the catamaran to Laguna San Rafael, and sea

kayaking, with some overlap with the previous trip. The 15-day "Chile Completo" (US$3,340) takes in Santiago and its landmarks, including a winery visit, trekking in Torres del Paine, whitewater rafting on the Río Petrohué, and various other excursions in the lake district. It also arranges specialist activity-oriented trips—skiing, rafting, fly-fishing, and extreme mountaineering.

Former U.S. Olympian Chris Spelius's **Expediciones Chile,** P.O. Box 1640, Bryson City, NC 28713, tel. 888/488-9082, tel./fax 847/400-0790, website: www.kayakchile.com, office@kayakchile.com, was a pioneer on the Futaleufú and has its own sprawling and secluded but cozy Campo Tres Monjas on the south bank of the river. While it specializes in kayaking on the Fu, it also offers rafting and multisport trips including hiking and horseback riding. Weeklong stays at Tres Monjas go for US$1,395 pp with plenty of time and instruction on the river; this includes transportation from Chaitén.

Far Horizons Archaeological and Cultural Trips, P.O. Box 91900, Albuquerque, NM 87199, tel. 800/552-4575, website: www.farhorizon.com, journey@farhorizon.com, offers trips to Rapa Nui (Easter Island) and the Atacama Desert. Tour leaders are top academics in their fields, such as linguist Steven Roger Fischer, who deciphered Rapa Nui's *rongorongo* tablets. Nine-day trips to Easter Island cost US$4,295 pp double occupancy, not including international airfares, while a weeklong Atacama extension costs US$2,295 pp double occupancy.

Mountain Travel Sobek, 6420 Fairmount Ave., El Cerrito, CA 94530, tel. 888/687-6235, fax 510/525-7710, website: www.mtsobek.com, info@mtsobek.com, does a 17-day "Trekking the Paine Circuit" for US$4,270, and a 10-day "Futaleufú Adventure Sampler," which includes rafting, mountain biking, and hiking, for US$2,655 pp. Its 17-day "Hiker's Patagonia" begins in Santiago but flies almost immediately to Punta Arenas and Parque Nacional Torres del Paine, later crossing the border to Argentina's Parque Nacional Los Glaciares and finishing with a free day in Buenos Aires. The cost is US$4,475 pp, international airfare not included. For US$5,290, it offers a 17-day "Patagonia Explorer" that includes some of the same sights as "Hiker's Patagonia" plus the weeklong *Terra Australis* cruise through the fjords of Tierra del Fuego. Mountain Travel Sobek also has contact numbers in Europe, tel. 44/1494/448901, sales@ mtsobekeu.com, and in Australia, tel. 61/2/9327-0666, toll-free tel. 300/130218, info@classicsafaricompany.com.au.

Nature Expeditions International, 7860 Peters Rd., Suite F-103, Plantation, FL 33324, tel. 800/869-0639 or 954/693-8852, fax 954/693-8854, website: www.naturexp.com, naturexp@aol.com, operates upscale "soft adventure" and culture-oriented tours to the Southern Cone countries of Chile and Argentina, among other destinations. A 16-day Chilean trip taking in Santiago, Viña del Mar, Lago Llanquihue, Chiloé, Termas de Puyuhuapi, Torres del Paine, and Punta Arenas costs US$3,925 to US$4,940, depending whether it includes an optional side trip to Laguna San Rafael. It also offers extensions to Easter Island (Rapa Nui) and the Atacama, and combined trips that take in parts of Argentina as well.

Powderquest Tours, 7108 Pinetree Rd., Richmond, VA 23229, tel. 888/565-7158 or 804/285-4961, fax 240/209-4312, website: www.powderquest.com, info@powderquest.com, runs five or six nine- to 13-day ski tours annually. Resorts visited include Portillo, Valle Nevado, and Termas de Chillán on the Chilean side, and Las Leñas on the Argentine side.

Affiliated with the Smithsonian Institution, **Smithsonian Odyssey Tours,** 222 Berkeley St., Boston, MA 02116, tel. 800/258-5885, website: www.sagaholidays.com, offers a 17-night cruise from Rio de Janeiro (Brazil) to Valparaíso via Montevideo (Uruguay), Buenos Aires (Argentina), Stanley (Falkland Islands), Punta Arenas, and Puerto Montt, with transfer to Santiago for the flight home. Fares start at US$4,999 pp, airfare included from Boston, New York, Philadelphia, or Washington D.C. An airfare surcharge applies from other U.S. cities.

Smithsonian Study Tours, 1100 Jefferson Dr. SW, Suite 3077, Washington, D.C. 20560, tel. 877/338-8687, website: www.smithsonianstudytours.org, offers a 14-day package including Santiago, Puerto Varas and vicinity, Punta Arenas, Puerto Natales, and Torres del Paine. The fare is US$5,995 pp including round-trip airfare from Miami; excluding airfare, the cost is US$4,925.

University of California Research Expeditions, 1 Shields Ave., Davis, CA 95616, tel. 530/757-3529, fax 530/757-3537, website: www.urep.ucdavis.edu, conducts research expeditions in which participants pay to aid in research projects, covering their own expenses. Chilean projects have included vertebrate zoology in Parque Nacional Bosque de Fray Jorge.

Wilderness Travel, 1102 Ninth St., Berkeley, CA 94710, tel. 510/558-2488 or 800/368-2794, fax 510/558-2849, offers a variety of trips focused primarily on Patagonia, including the 11-day "In Patagonia" excursion that focuses mostly on Argentina but does visit Torres del Paine, for US$4,595–5,095 pp depending on the number of clients; a 15-day "To the Ends of the Earth" sea kayaking expedition to Tierra del Fuego's Cordillera Darwin for US$4,395–4,895 pp; and a 16-day "Peaks of Patagonia" that takes in Torres del Paine and Argentina's Moreno Glacier and Fitzroy areas for US$3,595–3,995 pp.

Wildland Adventures, 3516 N.E. 155th St., Seattle, WA 98155, tel. 800/345-4453, fax 206/363-6615, website: www.wildland.com, info@wildland.com, operates small group tours (two to eight people) through locally based guides. Among its offerings are an eight-day "Paine Sojourn" for US$2,195 pp; a nine-day "Paine Base Camp Trek" for US$1,945 pp; and a 13-day "Chile Adventure: Land of Contrasts" that samples the northern altiplano, the Atacama, the southern mainland lakes, and Torres del Paine for US$3,495 pp. In Argentina, its "Best of Patagonia" takes in the Moreno Glacier and other sights via Buenos Aires for US$2,890 pp.

Chilean-Based Operators

All the following operators are permanently based in Chile, though not all are Chilean. When phoning or sending a fax to any of the numbers below, use the Chilean country code 56 as a prefix.

AlSur Expediciones, Del Salvador 100, Puerto Varas, tel./fax 65/232300, alsur@telsur.cl, operates tours and activities in the Sur Chico and specializes in Parque Pumalín, the large private nature reserve in continental Chiloé.

Based in summer only at the town of Dalcahue on the Isla Grande de Chiloé, **Altué Sea Kayaking** has extensive itineraries around the eastern shore of the archipelago. For reservations, its Santiago contact is Altué Active Travel, Encomenderos 83, Las Condes, Santiago, tel. 2/2332964, fax 2/2336799, website: www.seakayakchile.com, altue@seakayakchile.com.

Atacama Desert Expeditions, Casilla (P.O. Box) 10, San Pedro de Atacama, tel. 55/851140, fax 55/851037, website: www.adex.cl, atacamadesert@adex.cl, organizes all-inclusive excursions to San Pedro with accommodations at its outstanding Terrantai Lodge. Rates start at US$634/990 s/d for three-day, two-night packages and reach US$1,452/2,036 for six-day, five-night options.

United States- and Peruvian-run **Austral Adventures,** Arturo Prat 176-B, Ancud, Chiloé, tel./fax 65/625977, website: www.austral-adventures.com, tours@austral-adventures.com, offers custom boat tours of the archipelago from Ancud south to Laguna San Rafael, as well as land-based programs on the Isla Grande. Half-day tours in the vicinity of Ancud start around US$40, while weeklong expeditions to Parque Pumalín or Laguna San Rafael cost around US$1,600 pp, including gourmet meals. The website gives a very complete overview of the alternatives.

Azimut 360, Arzobispo Casanova 3, Providencia, Santiago, tel. 2/7358034, fax 2/7772375, website: www.azimut.cl, arranges a wide variety of excursions throughout the country that vary from the routine to the rugged, including ascents of summits such as Ojos del Salado. Its specialty, though, is the Carretera Austral and vicinity, where it has its own guesthouse on Lago General Carrera, near Puerto Guadal. It also maintains a summer office at San Pedro Atacama.

Big Foot Adventure Patagonia, Bories 206, Puerto Natales, tel. 61/414611, fax 61/414276, website: www.bigfootpatagonia.com, explore @bigfootpatagonia.com, operates recreation-oriented trips to Patagonia, overwhelmingly but not exclusively in Parque Nacional Torres del Paine, where it has concessions for activities

such as ice hiking and mountaineering. It offers a diverse set of packages ranging from six days and five nights for US$690 to US$1,040 pp, to 14 days and 13 nights for US$1,790 to US$2,500 pp, depending on the number of passengers.

Putre-based but U.S.-run **Birding Altoandino,** voicemail tel. 58/300013, fax 58/222735, website: www.birdingaltoandino.com, beknapton@hotmail.com, conducts birding, botany, and even archaeological tours of the Norte Grande, with special options available for those who cannot or prefer not to deal with very high elevations. Operator Barbara Knapton has an exceptional library of books on Andean natural history at her Putre house.

In the Sur Chico, **Campo Aventura,** San Bernardo 318, Puerto Varas, tel./fax 65/232910, website: www. campo-aventura.com, outsider@telsur.cl, offers four-day, three-night horseback explorations of the spectacularly scenic Cochamó backcountry southeast of Puerto Varas, for US$349 pp. English, German, French, Spanish, and Luxemburgisch are spoken. Longer trips are available for the truly motivated.

German-run **Casa Chueca,** tel. 71/1970096, tel./fax 71/1970097, cellular 09/4190625 or 09/8371440, website: www.trekkingchile.com, casachueca@hotmail.com, operates a number of backcountry trips in the vicinity of Talca and Curicó, an area that gets far fewer visitors than it deserves.

Based in the Cajón del Maipo southeast of Santiago, **Cascada Expediciones,** Camino al Volcán 17710, Guayacán, San José de Maipo, tel. 2/8611777, fax 2/8612222, website: www.cascada-expediciones.com, info@cascada-expediciones.com, offers a variety of activity-oriented excursions from the city and, during the summer seasons, trips farther afield to destinations such as Pucón, Futaleufú, and Torres del Paine.

Chile Birding, Magallanes 960, 2nd floor, Punta Arenas, tel./fax 61/226054, website: www.chilebirding.com, birding@chileaustral.com, offers a variety of birding tours throughout the country, but its specialty is southern Patagonia, specifically Magallanes.

From October to April, **Cruceros Australis,** Avenida Bosque Norte 0440, 11th floor, Santiago, tel. 2/4423110, fax 2/2035173, website: www.australis.com, offers three-, four-, and seven-day cruises through the fjords of southern Tierra del Fuego and Cape Horn on its luxury liner *Mare Australis.* Low-season (October and April) rates range US$681–1,207 pp for three-day, US$785–1,393 for four-day, and US$1,152–1,857 pp for weeklong trips. Midseason (November to mid-December and all of March) rates range US$858–1,528 pp for three-day, US$990–1,764 for four-day, and US$1,452–2,352 pp for weeklong trips. High-season (mid-December to March) rates range US$1,078–1,931 pp for three-day, US$1,244–2,299 for four-day, and US$1,659–2,871 pp for weeklong trips.

From September through May, **Cruceros Marítimos Skorpios,** Augusto Leguía 118, Las Condes, Santiago, tel. 2/2311030, fax 2/2322269, website: www.skorpios.cl, skoinfo@skorpios.cl, conducts four-day, three-night cruises from Puerto Chacabuco in Region XI (Aisén) to Parque Nacional Laguna San Rafael. Rates range from US$410 pp in low season to US$777 pp in high season (mid-December to mid-March), depending on the quality of the cabin. Some cruises include a side trip to hot springs in the Quitralco fjord.

Explora Hotels, Américo Vespucio Sur 80, 5th floor, Las Condes, Santiago, tel. 2/2066060, fax 2/2284655, website: www.explora.com, reservexplora@explora-chile.cl, offers very expensive and all-inclusive packages, from three days to a week, in San Pedro de Atacama and Parque Nacional Torres del Paine. The former has attracted considerable criticism for its impact on the community and local environment, but the latter is a remarkable achievement.

Based in the Norte Chico east of the town of Ovalle, German-operated **Hacienda Los Andes,** Correo Hurtado, tel. 53/198-2106, website: www.haciendalosandes.com, info@haciendalosandes.com, runs a variety of horseback and other excursions through a truly off-the-beaten-track part of the Andes. Rates for day trips run mostly between US$65–80 pp, overnight excursions US$135–252 pp; these include transfers from either Ovalle or Vicuña. Four-day, three-night

backcountry trips cost US$371 pp. B&B accommodations in colonial-style rooms are also available from US$27 pp.

At La Serena's **Intijalsu,** tel. 09/548-8318, website: www.geocities.com/intijalsu, intijalsu@yahoo.com, professional astronomers practice their sideline of archaeoastronomical excursions in the Norte Chico, using mobile equipment to get to the best viewing sites depending on up-to-the-minute atmospheric conditions.

Crucero's Australis's sister company **Navimag,** Avenida El Bosque Norte 0440, 11th floor, Santiago, tel. 2/4423120, fax 2/2035025, website: www.navimag.com, sails the fjords of Region XI (Aisén) from Puerto Montt to Puerto Chacabuco and Laguna San Rafael, and from Puerto Montt to Puerto Natales in Magallanes (Region XII). While these are not cruises in the traditional sense of the word, they are more than just utilitarian transportation as they pass through the spectacular fjordlands of archipelagic Chile. (For details and fares, see its website or the special topic Chile's Inside Passage in the Sur Chico chapter.)

Patagonia Connection, Fidel Oteíza 1951, Oficina 1006, Providencia, Santiago, tel. 2/2256489, fax 2/2748111, website: www.patagonia-connection.com, offers four-day three-night to six-day five-night packages based at its Termas de Puyuhuapi hot springs resort in Region XI (Aisén), including a full-day catamaran excursion to Parque Nacional Laguna San Rafael. Low-season rates, depending on the type of accommodations, start around US$850–1,760 pp for the shorter tours and US$1,130–2,280 pp for the longer tours. In high season, the shorter tours cost US$1,270–2,300 pp and the longer tours US$1,620–3,130 pp.

Based at Puerto Williams, German-run **Sea & Ice & Mountains Adventures Unlimited,** tel./fax 61/621150 or 61/621227, website: www. simltd. com, sim@entelchile.net, does yacht tours through Tierra del Fuego and Cape Horn in the summer.

Motorcycle touring specialist **Yanko Motor Tour** (YMT), Casilla 1097, 7-1/2 Norte 230, Talca, tel. 71/213094, website: www.mototour.com, yanko@mototour.com, offers a variety of two-week to one-month tours throughout northern Chile and Patagonia, starting around US$3,500.

Information and Services

Chilean embassies usually have a tourist representative in their delegation—the Chilean Embassy in the United States, for instance, has a Tourism Section at 1732 Massachusetts Ave. NW, Washington, D.C. 20036, tel. 202/785-1746, 202/530-4109, or 202/530-4108, fax 202/887-5579, ofitur@embassyofchile.org.

Chile's Corporación de Promoción Turística, a public-private partnership, has also recently opened a Miami tourist information office through LanChile, tel. 800/244-5366, infochile@chiletourdesk.com. See also LanChile's website: www.lanchile.com.

United States-based AmeriSpan, P.O. Box 40513, Philadelphia, PA 19106-0513, tel. 215/985-4522 or 800/879-6640, fax 215/985-4524, provides information on travel in Chile and elsewhere in Latin America, and specifically on the region's language schools. It also maintains a useful website: www.amerispan.com.

In Canada, Chile has a tourist information office at 56 Sparks St., Suite 801, Ottawa, Ontario K1P 5I4, tel. 613/235-4402.

VISAS AND OFFICIALDOM

Entry requirements are mostly straightforward. Argentines, Brazilians, Uruguayans, and Paraguayans need only national identity cards, but every other nationality needs a passport. Citizens of the United States and Canada, along with those of the European Community, Switzerland, Norway, Israel, Mexico, Australia, and New Zealand need passports but not advance visas.

Nationalities that *must* obtain advance visas include Indians, Jamaicans, Koreans, Poles, Russians, and Thais. (See the accompanying chart for addresses and telephones of the most important overseas Chilean embassies and consulates.)

Chile routinely grants 90-day entry permits to foreign visitors, in the form of a tourist card that must be surrendered on departure from the country. Formally, visitors must have a return or onward ticket, but the author has entered Chile dozens of times over many years, at the international airport and at some of the most remote border posts, without ever having been asked for a return or onward ticket.

Ninety-day extensions can take several days and cost roughly US$100, plus two color photos, at the Departamento de Extranjería, Moneda 1342, Santiago Centro, tel. 2/6725320, or in regional capitals. Visitors close to the Argentine, Peruvian, or Bolivian borders may find it quicker and cheaper to dash across the line and return. For lost tourist cards, it's necessary to request a replacement from the Policía Internacional, General Borgoño 1052, Independencia, Santiago, tel. 2/7371292, or from offices in regional capitals.

Always carry identification, since the Carabineros (national police) can request it at any moment, though they rarely do so without some reason. Passports are also necessary for routine transactions such as checking into hotels and cashing traveler's checks.

Lost or Stolen Passports

Visitors who suffer a lost or stolen passport must obtain a replacement at their own embassy or consulate. After obtaining a replacement passport, it's necessary to visit the Policia Internacional (see above) to replace the tourist card.

Taxes

Chile's international departure tax recently rose to US$26, but this is normally included in the price of the ticket. A frequent unpleasant surprise, however, is the hefty *arrival* tax that Chile's Ministerio de Relaciones Exteriores (Foreign Ministry) has imposed on nationals of certain countries: US$15 for Mexicans, US$34 for Australians, US$55 for Canadians, and US$61 for citizens of the United States. These are one-time fees, valid for the life of the user's passport, and collected only at airports.

CHILEAN EMBASSIES AND CONSULATES ABROAD

Chile has embassies and consulates throughout much of the world; those listed below should be most useful to intending visitors. Some sites have a tourist information office at a separate address (for details of these, see the Information and Services entry).

Argentina
San Martín 439, 9th floor, Buenos Aires, tel. 11/4394-6371

Australia
10 Culgoa Circuit, O'Malley, ACT 2606, tel. 2/6286-2430
Consulates:
80 Collins St., Level 43, Melbourne, Victoria 3000, tel. 3/9654-4982
44 Market St., Level 18, Sydney, NSW 2000, tel. 2/9299-2533

Bolivia
Avenida Hernando Siles 5873, Barrio Obrajes, La Paz, tel. 2/2785269

Brazil
Praia do Flamengo 344, 7th floor, Flamengo, Rio de Janeiro, tel. 21/2552-5349
Avenida Paulista 1009, 10th floor, São Paulo, tel. 11/3284-2148

Canada
50 O'Connor St., Suite 1413, Ottawa, Ontario K1P 6L2, tel. 613/235-4402
Consulates:
2 Bloor St. W, Suite 1801, Toronto, Ontario M4W 3E2, tel. 416/924-0106
1010 Sherbrooke St. W, Suite 710, Montréal, Québec H3A 2R7, tel. 514/499-0405
1250-1185 W. Georgia St., Vancouver, British Columbia V6E 4E6, tel. 604/681-9162

France
64 Blvd. de la Tour Maubourg, Paris, tel. 1/4705-4661

Germany
Mohrenstraße 63, Berlin, tel. 30/726-2035
Consulate:
Humboldtstraße 94, Frankfurt-am-Main, tel. 69/550194

Netherlands
Stadhouderskade 2,5° 1054 Es, Amsterdam, tel. 20/612-0086

New Zealand
7th floor, Willis CorroonHouse, 1-3 Welleston St., Wellington, tel. 4/471-6270

Paraguay
Emilio Nudelman 351, Asunción, tel. 21/600671

Peru
Javier Prado Oeste 790, San Isidro, Lima, tel. 1/221-2187

Switzerland
Eigerplatz 5, 12 Stock, Bern, tel. 31/371-7050

United Kingdom
12 Devonshire St., London W1N 2DS, tel. 20/7580-1023

Uruguay
Andes 1365, 1st floor, Montevideo, tel. 2/902-6316

United States of America
1736 Massachusetts Ave. NW, Washington, DC 20036, tel. 202/785-3159
Consulates:
866 United Nations Plaza, Suite 601, New York, NY 10017, tel. 212/355-0612
79 Milk St., Suite 600, Boston, MA 02109, tel. 617/426-1678
Public Ledger Building, 6th and Chestnut Sts., Suite 1030, Philadelphia, PA 19142, tel. 215/829-9520
800 Brickell Ave., Suite 1230, Miami, FL 33131, tel. 305/373-8623
Edificio American Airlines, Suite 800, 1509 López Landrón, Santurce, San Juan, PR 00911, tel. 809/725-6365
875 N. Michigan Ave., Suite 3352, Chicago, IL 60611, tel. 312/654-8780
1360 Post Oak Blvd., Suite 2330, Houston, TX 77056, tel. 713/621-5853
870 Market St., Suite 1062, San Francisco, CA 94105, tel. 415/982-7662
1900 Avenue of the Stars, Suite 2450, Los Angeles, CA 90067, tel. 310/785-0047

The not unreasonable rationale behind these fees, officially described as a *gasto administrativo de reciprocidad* (administrative reciprocity charge) is that the governments of those countries require Chilean citizens to pay the same amounts simply to apply for a visa (with no guarantee of being issued one). At the same time, the misunderstandings provoked when unsuspecting arriving visitors from those countries are diverted to a special line to pay the additional fee generates ill will for Chile.

A domestic airport departure tax of US$8 is normally included in the price of the ticket. At land borders, immigration officials sometimes collect a token fee for agricultural inspections.

Customs

Visitors to Chile may import personal effects, including clothing, jewelry, medicine, sporting gear, camping equipment and accessories, photographic and video equipment, personal computers and the like, and wheelchairs for disabled individuals, as well as 500 grams of tobacco, three liters of wine or alcoholic beverages (adults only), and small quantities of perfume.

Customs inspections are usually routine, but at Santiago's international airport and some land borders, incoming checked baggage must pass through X-rays; do not put photographic film in your bag en route from Mendoza, Argentina, to Santiago, for instance. At the Peruvian and Bolivian borders, inspectors pay special attention to illegal drugs; at the international airport, there are drug-sniffing beagles.

Travelers bound from Region I (Tarapacá) and Region XII (Magallanes) will undergo internal customs checks because those regions have *zona franca* duty free status. At many borders, the Servicio Agrícola Ganadero (SAG, Agriculture and Livestock Service) conducts agricultural inspections—fresh food will be confiscated—and sometimes levies a small charge for doing so. At some remote border posts, the Carabineros (national police) handle all border formalities, from immigration to customs to agricultural inspections.

Border Crossings

Chile has a handful of border crossings from Peru and Bolivia, and many from Argentina, but only a few of them have regular public transportation (for details, see the Getting There entry above). Some crossings are seasonal, especially in the high Andes and Patagonia, and others have limited opening hours.

Bad weather can close many of the passes across the Andes from Bolivia and Argentina at times, but many stay open all year. In addition to the Peruvian crossing from Tacna to Arica, all-year crossings include the Bolivian routes from La Paz to Arica, from Oruro to Iquique, Uyuni to Calama, and Uyuni to San Pedro de Atacama.

From Argentina, all-year routes include Salta and Jujuy to San Pedro de Atacama and Calama; the Los Libertadores tunnel between Mendoza and Santiago; the San Martín de los Andes to Temuco route via Paso de Mamuil Malal (Paso Tromen to Argentines); the Bariloche-Osorno highway; and the bus-boat shuttle from Bariloche to Puerto Varas.

There are many Patagonian crossings. Those open all year include the road from Esquel (local buses only) to Futaleufú and Chaitén; Comodoro Rivadavia to Coyhaique via Río Mayo; Los Antiguos to Chile Chico; El Calafate to Puerto Natales via Río Turbio; Río Gallegos to Punta Arenas; and Ushuaia and Río Grande to Punta Arenas.

Police

Chile's Carabineros are probably the most professional force on the continent, with a reputation for integrity and a low tolerance for bribery and similar corruption (Argentine motorists, accustomed to bribing the cops for traffic violations in their own country, have had their vehicles confiscated for trying to do so in Chile). Known popularly but scornfully as *pacos* by some Chileans, the Carabineros are normally polite and helpful in public, but they can be stern with lawbreakers—or individuals they suspect of being lawbreakers.

Chile's figure of 240 police officers per million inhabitants is below the world average of 286, but somehow there always seems to be a policeman within sight.

ON THE ROAD

SPECIAL INTERESTS

Work

Remunerative work is theoretically hard to come by for foreigners who are not temporary or permanent residents, but many people work informally on tourist visas. Among the options are teaching English or another foreign language, work in the tourist industry, or casual labor in bars or restaurants. The problem with such jobs is that they either require some time to build up a clientele (in the case of teaching), are seasonal (in the case of tourism), or poorly paid (in the case of restaurants, except in a handful of places where tips are high).

According to the Chilean Interior Ministry, 12,000 of 150,000 foreign workers in Chile are undocumented, though this number seems low. In the year 2000, Interior granted 18,000 residence permits, more than triple the previous year, but many workers are unskilled Bolivians and Peruvians.

Legal residence, which permits eligibility for a greater number of better-paying jobs, usually requires local or foreign sponsorship, a substantial investment, marriage to a Chilean spouse or other permanent resident, or a reliable retirement income. There are three types of working visas: a temporary visa issued to professionals and trained technicians, whose qualifications must be evaluated by an appropriate Chilean institution; a contract-specific visa with a specific employer, valid up to two years and primarily for low-skilled workers, who must have a return ticket to country of origin; and a visa for exchange students seeking part-time work. In theory, temporary working visas can lead to residence, but some workers have continued on them for several years, as the Interior Ministry bureaucracy turns slowly.

Study

Most people who undertake study programs in Chile are Spanish-language students in Santiago, though there are also programs in Iquique, Pucón, and Coyhaique. While theoretically a student visa is obligatory, in practice virtually everyone arrives and registers on a tourist visa. (For more information on Spanish language programs, see the appropriate geographical entries.)

Several U.S. universities also have undergraduate exchange programs with the Universidad de Chile, the Universidad Católica, and other Chilean universities; for more information, contact your own university's overseas programs department.

Travel with Children

In most ways, Chile is a child-friendly country. In fact, since many Chileans have and enjoy large extended families, they may feel little in common with people in their late 20s and older who do *not* have children, and traveling with kids can open doors.

There are also practical advantages to traveling with children. On buses, for instance, small children who do not occupy a separate seat do not pay, and budget hotels often make no additional charge for kids.

Women

Like other Latin American societies, Chile has a strong *machista* (chauvinist) element. Chilean women are traditionally mothers, homemakers, and children's caregivers, while men are providers and decision-makers, though this is changing rapidly. Domestic violence is a serious problem, especially among the lower classes, but it is not unique to them.

Many Chilean men view foreign women as sexually available, and this can lead to harassment problems. Harassment is usually verbal, but it can turn ugly. It is best to ignore such comments, which are obvious by tone of voice even if you don't understand them; dressing and acting conservatively can go a long way in helping avoid problems.

Despite problems, women have begun to acquire political prominence. Soledad Alvear is the foreign minister for President Ricardo Lagos, and several other women occupy important posts, including former Health and current Defense Minister Michelle Bachelet, Education Minister Mariana Aylwin, and Planning Minister Alejandra Krauss. Longtime activist Gladys

Marín was the Communist party candidate for president in 1999 (during the campaign, though, a TV interviewer remarked that Marín had the best legs of any of the candidates—to which she responded with her most *simpática* smile).

Gays and Lesbians

While there may be no legal prohibition on homosexual behavior, in a country where machismo is the rule, public homosexual behavior can be risky and police harassment is possible. Things are definitely better, however, than during the authoritarian presidency of General Carlos Ibáñez del Campo (1924–31), when government agents rounded up homosexuals and threw them into the sea with concrete weights on their feet. Playwright Andrés Pérez turned this period into a play titled *La Huida,* recently produced in Santiago.

Santiago has an active gay scene centered around the neighborhood of Barrio Bellavista, and there are enclaves elsewhere, most notably in Viña del Mar. Tempo Travel is the country's only gay travel agency, reached through the portal www.gaychile.com or www.tempotravel.cl.

Disabled

For people with disabilities, Chile can a problematic country. The narrow, uneven sidewalks in the cities, and fast-moving traffic, and the rugged terrain in the countryside are unkind to people with disabilities, especially those who need wheelchairs. Valparaíso, with its picturesque hill neighborhoods and winding pathways and staircases, can be a nightmare for those using wheelchairs.

Public transportation can rarely accommodate passengers with disabilities, though Santiago's newer Metro stations have elevators. Santiago also has specially equipped taxis with Tixi Service, tel. 800/223097 toll-free.

Few older buildings are specifically equipped for people with disabilities, but the prevalence or earthquakes means they are low and can often accommodate them. Newer hotels are often highrises, and disabled access is obligatory.

Health and Safety

As a mostly midlatitude country, Chile presents relatively few unusual health problems—even in the north, which lies within tropical latitudes, there is no malaria or similar tropical diseases thanks to the arid climate.

A good general source on foreign health matters is Dr. Richard Dawood's *Travelers' Health* (New York, Random House, 1994), a small encyclopedia on the topic. Dr. Stuart R. Rose's *International Travel Health Guide* (Northampton, MA: Travel Medicine Inc., 2000) is annually updated and regionally focused. Try also the fifth edition of Dirk G. Schroeder's *Staying Healthy in Asia, Africa, and Latin America* (Avalon Travel Publishing, 2000).

For up-to-date information on health issues in Chile and elsewhere in the Southern Cone, see the U.S. Centers for Disease Control (CDC) Temperate South America regional page on its website: www.cdc.gov/travel/temsam.htm, covering Chile, Argentina, Uruguay, and the Falkland Islands. Another good source is the United Kingdom's Department of Health, website: www.doh.gov.uk/traveladvice/index.htm, which provides a chart of recommended prophylaxis by country.

BEFORE YOU GO

Theoretically, no vaccinations are obligatory for entry to Chile, but if you are coming from a tropical country where yellow fever is endemic, authorities could ask for a vaccination certificate.

Traveling to Chile or elsewhere without adequate medical insurance is risky. Before leaving your home country, obtain medical insurance that includes evacuation in case of serious emergency. Foreign health insurance may not be accepted in Chile, so you may be required to pay out of your own pocket for later reimbursement. Often, however, private medical providers in Chile accept international credit cards in return for services.

Numerous carriers provide medical and evacuation coverage; an extensive list, including Internet links, is available at the U.S. State Department's website: www.travel.state.gov/medical.html.

GENERAL HEALTH MAINTENANCE

Common-sense precautions can reduce the possibility of illness considerably. Washing the hands frequently with soap and water, and drinking only bottled, boiled, or carbonated water will all help diminish the likelihood of contagion for short-term visitors—though Chilean tap water is potable almost everywhere.

Where purified water is impossible to obtain, such as back-country streams where there may be livestock or problems with human waste, pass drinking water through a one-micron filter and further purify it with iodine drops or tablets (but avoid prolonged consumption of iodine-purified water). Nonpasteurized dairy products, such as goat cheese, can be problematic and are best avoided.

FOOD- OR WATER-BORNE DISEASES

While relatively few visitors to Chile run into problems of this sort, contaminated food and drink are not unheard of. In many cases, it's simply exposure to different sorts of bugs to which your body soon becomes accustomed, but if symptoms persist the problem may be more serious.

Traveler's Diarrhea

Often colloquially known as *turista* in Latin America, the classic traveler's diarrhea (TD) usually lasts only a few days and almost always less than a week. Besides "the runs," symptoms include nausea, vomiting, bloating, and general weakness. The usual cause is the notorious *Escherichia coli* bacterium from contaminated food or water; in some cases *E. coli* infections can be fatal.

Fluids, including fruit juices, and small amounts of bland foods, such as freshly cooked rice or soda crackers, may help relieve symptoms and help sufferers regain strength. Dehydration is a serious problem, especially for children, who may need to be treated with an oral rehydration solution (ORS) of carbohydrates and salt.

Over-the-counter remedies such as Pepto-Bismol, Lomotil, and Immodium may relieve symptoms but can also cause problems. Prescription drugs such as doxycyline and trimethoprim/sulfamethoxazole can also shorten the cycle. These may not, however, be suitable for children, and it's better for everyone to avoid them if at all possible.

Continuing and worsening symptoms, including bloody stools, may mean dysentery, a much more serious ailment that requires a physician's attention.

Dysentery

Bacterial dysentery, which resembles a more intense form of TD, responds well to antibiotics, but amoebic dysentery is far more serious, sometimes leading to intestinal perforation, peritonitis, and liver abscesses. Like diarrhea, its symptoms include soft and even bloody stools, but some people may be asymptomatic even as they pass on *Entamoeba hystolica* through unsanitary toilet and food preparation practices. Metronidazole, known by the brand names Flagyl or Protostat, is an effective treatment, but a physician's diagnosis is advisable.

Cholera

Resulting from poor hygiene, inadequate sewage disposal, and contaminated food, contemporary cholera is less devastating than its historic antecedents, which produced rapid dehydration, watery diarrhea, and imminent death without almost equally rapid rehydration. While today's cholera strains are highly infectious, most carriers do not even come down with symptoms. Existing vaccinations are ineffective, so international health authorities now recommend against them.

Treatment can only relieve symptoms. On average, about 5 percent of victims die, but those who recover are immune. It is not a common problem in Chile, but it's not unheard of either.

Hepatitis A

Usually passed by fecal-oral contact under conditions of poor hygiene and overcrowding, hepatitis A is a virus. The traditional gamma globulin prophylaxis has limited efficacy and wears off in only a few months. New hepatitis A vaccines, however, are more effective and last longer.

Typhoid

Typhoid is a serious disease common under unsanitary conditions, but the recommended vaccination is an effective prophylaxis.

INSECT-BORNE DISEASES

Chile is malaria-free, but a few other insect-borne diseases may be present if not exactly prevalent.

Chagas' Disease

Also known as South American trypanosomiasis, Chagas' disease is most common in Brazil but affects about 18 million people between Mexico and Argentina; 50,000 people die from it every year. Not a tropical disease per se, it has a discontinuous distribution—Panama and Costa Rica, for instance, are Chagas-free.

Since it is spread by the bite of the conenose or assassin bug, which lives in adobe structures and feeds at night, avoid such structures; if it's impossible to do so, sleep away from the walls. Insect repellents carrying DEET offer some protection. Chickens, dogs, and opossums may carry the disease.

Chagas' initial form is a swollen bite that may be accompanied by fever, which soon subsides. In the long run, though, it may cause heart damage leading to sudden death, intestinal constipation, and difficulty in swallowing; there is no cure. Charles Darwin may have been a chronic Chagas sufferer.

Dengue

Like malaria, dengue is a mosquito-borne disease of the lowland tropics, but it's less common than malaria and only rarely fatal. Often debilitating in the short term, its symptoms include fever, headache, severe joint pain, and skin rashes, but most people recover fairly quickly though there is no treatment. Uncommon but often fatal, the more severe dengue hemorrhagic fever sometimes occurs in children, particularly those who have suffered from the disease previously.

Mainland Chile has not recorded any cases of dengue, but the arrival of dengue's white-spotted mosquito vector *Aëdes aegypti* on Easter Island (Rapa Nui)—an apparent arrival from tropical French Polynesia—has caused an outbreak of cases there. This mosquito bites during the daytime, making the usual malarial recommendation for long sleeves and long trousers harder to live up to—if you must wear shorts and short sleeves, make sure you're covered with insect repellent.

HANTAVIRUS

Since 1993, in Chile there have been nearly 200 cases of hantavirus, an uncommon but very deadly disease contracted by breathing, touching, or ingesting feces or urine of the long-tailed rat; about 70 of the victims have died. Primarily a rural phenomenon and most prevalent in the south, the virus thrives in enclosed areas; when exposed to sunlight or fresh air, it normally loses its potency. Avoid places frequented by rodents, particularly abandoned buildings, but note that there have been apparent cases in which hikers and farm workers have contracted the disease in open spaces.

There have also been hantavirus cases in similar areas of neighboring Argentina.

RABIES

Rabies, a virus transmitted through bites or scratches by domestic animals (such as dogs and cats) and wild mammals (such as bats), is a concern; many domestic animals in Chile go unvaccinated. Human prophylactic vaccination is possible but may be incompatible with malaria medication.

Untreated rabies can cause an agonizingly painful death. In case of an animal bite or scratch, immediately clean the affected area with soap and running water, and then with antiseptic substances such as iodine or 40 percent-plus alcohol. If possible, try to capture the animal for diagnosis, but not at the risk of further bites; in areas where rabies is endemic, painful post-exposure vaccination may be unavoidable.

SNAKEBITE

Herpetophobes can travel without concern. Chile has no poisonous snakes—except perhaps in zoos—and only a few nonpoisonous ones. Neighboring Argentina does have poisonous snakes, but not in the areas covered by this book.

SEXUALLY TRANSMITTED DISEASES

While life-threatening AIDS is by far the most hazardous of sexually transmitted diseases (STDs) and certainly gets the most press, other STDs are far more prevalent and also serious if left untreated. All are spread by unprotected sexual conduct; the use of latex condoms by males can greatly reduce the possibility of contracting sexually transmitted diseases but not necessarily eliminate it.

Most STDs, including gonorrhea, chlamydia, and syphilis, are treatable with antibiotics, but some strains have developed a rapid immunity to penicillin and alternative treatments. If taking antibiotics, be sure to complete the prescribed course, since an interrupted treatment may not kill the infection and could even help it develop immunity.

The most common of STDs is **gonorrhea,** characterized by a burning sensation during urination and penile or vaginal discharge; it may cause infertility. **Chlamydia** has milder symptoms but similar complications. **Syphilis,** the only major disease that apparently spread to Europe from its American origins in the aftermath of the Spanish invasion, begins with ulcer and rash symptoms that soon disappear; long-term complications, however, can include cardiovascular problems and even mental derangement.

Herpes, a virus that causes small but irritating ulcers in the genital area, has no effective treatment. It is likely to recur, easily spread when active, and can contribute to cervical cancer. **Hepatitis B,** though not exclusively a sexually transmitted disease, can spread through the mixing of bodily fluids such as saliva, semen, and menstrual and vaginal secretions. It can also spread through insufficiently sanitary medical procedures, inadequately sterilized or shared syringes, during body piercing, and similar circumstances. Like Hepatitits A, it can lead to liver damage but is more serious; vaccination is advisable for high-risk individuals, but it is expensive.

HIV/AIDS

As in most countries, HIV/AIDS is an issue of increasing concern. According to Chile's Health Ministry, there are at least 8,000 full-blown AIDS cases and 30,000 HIV-infected individuals, but concerns are that the figure may be substantially higher—many carriers are probably unaware they are infected. The Ministry suggests that by 2005 about 5,000 Chileans will die of AIDS, and that by 2010 the projected mortality figure of 174.5 per 1,000 citizens would make it the country's leading cause of death. A report from the United Nations World Health Organization (WHO) is more conservative, suggesting that 15,300 Chileans were living with AIDS or HIV in 2000; of these, 81.3 percent were men, 17 percent women, and 1.7 percent children.

HIV/AIDS is not exclusively a sexually transmitted disease (intravenous drug users can get it by sharing needles), but unprotected sexual activity is a common means of transmission; the use of latex condoms can reduce the possibility of infection. While many consider it a homosexual disease, female prostitutes may also be infected.

Despite the problem and the current administration's open-mindedness, many would still prefer to turn a blind eye. Pressure from the Bishop of Valparaíso Gonzalo Duarte de Cortázar, for instance, forced health workers to stop handing out free condoms at Viña del Mar in summer on the grounds that it gave the impression that Viña was a "city of promiscuous people."

Vivo Positivo is an advocacy organization for AIDS and HIV victims at Ernesto Pinto Lagarrigue 131, on the Recoleta side of Barrio Bellavista, Santiago, tel. 2/7325081, website: www .vivopositivo.cl, cornavih@interactiva.cl. The Health Ministry has a toll-free AIDS hotline, Fonosida, tel. 800/202120.

ALTITUDE SICKNESS

At the highest elevations, above about 3,000 meters in the northern altiplano and the central Andes, *apunamiento* or *soroche* can be an annoyance and even a danger, of particular concern to older people with respiratory problems. Even among young, robust individuals, a quick rise from sea level to the altiplano, in the space of a couple of hours, can cause intense headaches, vertigo, either drowsiness or insomnia, shortness of breath, and other symptoms. Combined with hypothermia, it can easily be life-threatening.

For most people, rest and relaxation will help relieve these symptoms as the body gradually adapts to the reduced oxygen at higher altitudes; aspirin or a comparable painkiller will combat headache. Should symptoms persist or worsen, moving to a lower elevation will usually have the desired effect. Be aware that some individuals have died at elevations above 4,000 meters; it is better to stay at an intermediate altitude than to climb to these very high elevations from sea level on the same day. Do not overeat, avoid or limit alcohol consumption, and drink extra fluids.

Stephen Bezruchka's *Altitude Illness, Prevention & Treatment* (Seattle: The Mountaineers, 1994) deals with the topic in great detail; the fifth edition of James A. Wilkerson's edited collection *Medicine for Mountaineering & Other Wilderness Activities* (Seattle: The Mountaineers, 2001) discusses other potential problems as well.

SUNBURN

Most of Chile lies within temperature latitudes comparable to those in the Northern Hemisphere, but sunburn is nevertheless a potentially serious problem. In the northernmost tropical and subtropical deserts, nearly vertical solar rays are far more intense; in the oxygen-poor air of the altiplano, sunburn can combine with altitude sickness to be life-threatening. Wearing a baseball cap or similar head covering is advisable; at lower altitudes, long-sleeved cotton shirts and long trousers can help protect your skin. If you dress for the beach, use a heavy sunblock.

In southernmost Chile, where aerosols have damaged the ozone layer over Magallanes, ultraviolet radiation has caused skin problems for people and even for livestock such as cattle and sheep. Again, wear head coverings and a heavy sunblock.

HYPOTHERMIA

Hypothermia is a dangerously quick loss of body heat, most common in cold and damp weather at high altitudes or high latitudes—be particularly careful in areas with major temperature variations between day and night. Symptoms include shivering, disorientation, loss of motor functions, skin numbness, and physical exhaustion. The best remedy is warmth, shelter, and food; unlike cottons, woolen clothing retains warmth even when wet. Avoid falling asleep if at all possible; in truly hazardous conditions, it's possible you will not regain consciousness. Carry high-energy snacks and drinking water.

SMOKING

Tobacco use is more prevalent in Chile than in the United States but less so than in Europe. It is absolutely prohibited on public transportation, including airplanes, long-distance buses, the subway, and city buses (though in some neighborhoods you might see the odd smoker light up in the back). Many, though by no means all, restaurants have nonsmoking areas, and Chileans are generally considerate and observant of these (unlike in Argentina, which is a free-for-all). Totally nonsmoking restaurants are few.

LOCAL DOCTORS

Top-quality medical services are available in Santiago and other major cities, though simple clinics may have to do in the smallest settlements. Foreign embassies sometimes maintain lists of English-speaking doctors, who may have overseas training and are numerous in the capital and other large cities.

Public facilities, such as Santiago's Posta Central, are often understaffed and underfunded; it's better to patronize private clinics rather than demand services that, in any event, are geared toward poorer people with no alternatives. That said, public staff will try to do their best in an emergency.

PHARMACIES

Pharmacies serve an important role in public health, but they also carry certain risks. Pharmacists will often provide drugs on the basis of symptoms that they may not completely comprehend, especially if there is a language barrier; while the cumulative societal impact may be positive, individual recommendations may be erroneous.

Note that many medications available by prescription only in North America or Europe may be sold over the counter in Chilean pharmacies. Travelers should be cautious about self-medication even when drugs are available; check expiration dates, as many expired drugs are never cleared off the shelf.

In large cities and some smaller towns, pharmacies remain open all night for emergency prescription service on a rotating basis. The *farmacia de turno* and its address will usually be posted in the window of other pharmacies, or advertised in the newspaper.

CRIME

Even though many Chileans believe assaults, rapes, homicide, and crimes against property are increasing, Chile is a safe country by almost any standard. According to one United Nations study, Chile has one of the world's lowest robbery rates, only slightly more than Jordan (Bahamas has the highest rate).

Still, certain precautions almost go without saying—most crimes are crimes of opportunity. Never leave luggage unattended, store valuables in the hotel safe, keep close watch on your belongings at sidewalk cafés, and carry a photocopy of your passport with the date of entry into the country. Do not carry large amounts of cash (money belts or leg pouches are good alternatives for hiding cash), do leave valuable jewelry at home, and do keep conspicuous items such as photo and video cameras out of sight as much as possible. Do not presume that any area is totally secure.

If you should be accosted by anyone with a firearm or other potentially lethal weapon, do not resist. While guns are uncommon—knives are the weapon of choice—and truly violent crime is unusual, the consequences of a misjudgment can be lethal.

Money

While traveling in Chile, it makes sense to have a variety of money alternatives. Traveler's checks are the safest way to carry money, since they're refundable in case of loss or theft, but banks keep limited hours and in some remote areas they're simply nonexistent. In these cases, it makes sense to carry cash.

International credit cards are widely accepted, and foreign ATM cards work everywhere except at the Banco del Estado de Chile. Because ATMs are open 24 hours, many visitors prefer this alternative in both Chile and Argentina, though the above comment on scarcity of banks in rural areas still holds. Note that because of the current economic instability in Argentina, and recent regulations that limit cash withdrawals for Argentines, Argentine ATMs can be iffy; carrying cash makes sense there. Cashing traveler's checks in Argentina is a nightmarish experience even when stability reigns.

It also makes sense to carry an emergency cash reserve in U.S. dollars, preferably hidden in an inconspicuous leg pouch or money belt (not the bulky kind that fits around the waist, which thieves or robbers easily recognize, but a zippered leather belt that looks like any other).

CURRENCY

Chile's unit of currency is the peso (Ch$). Coins with denominations of Ch$5, Ch$10, and Ch$50 all display profiles of Chilean liberator Bernardo O'Higgins. Ch$100 coins issued by the former dictatorship, with the inscription "Libertad" (Freedom) breaking chains and the coup date of September 11, 1973, are still in circulation, but newer coins are gradually replacing them. The most recent contains an image of a Mapuche woman. The Ch$500 coin honors the late Cardinal Raúl Henríquez Silva, one of the country's most beloved religious figures.

Banknotes come in values of Ch$500 (with a portrait of Pedro de Valdivia), Ch$1,000 (Ignacio Carrera Pinto), Ch$2,000 (Manuel Rodríguez), Ch$5,000 (Gabriela Mistral), Ch$10,000 (Arturo Prat), and Ch$20,000 (Andrés Bello).

EXCHANGE RATES

During the main period of research, from December 2000 through December 2001, rates for the U.S. dollar, the benchmark foreign currency, ranged between about Ch$580 and Ch$710 but stabilized around US$660 toward the end of that period. Rates tend to be highest in Santiago and lower in the regions, but this is not so meaningful as it used to be, for reasons explained in the following paragraphs.

For the most up-to-date exchange rates, consult the business section of your daily newspaper or an online currency converter such as www.oanda.com. There is no black market.

In Chile, the best source for trends in the exchange rate is the financial daily *Estrategia*.

CHANGING MONEY

Money can be changed at banks and *casas de cambio* (exchange houses), though not every bank cashes traveler's checks. ATMs, abundant and becoming universal except in a few remote areas, match the best bank rates and are accessible all day every day. Note, however, that ATMs operated by Banco del Estado, the only option in many small towns, are incompatible with foreign ATM cards.

Before heading out into the countryside, where many smaller villages do not even have banks, be sure to change enough money to get you to the next major town. Likewise, in the countryside, carry plenty of smaller bills—for a small shopkeeper with limited resources, changing a Ch$5,000 note may be impossible.

TRAVELER'S CHECKS AND REFUNDS

Traveler's checks are still the safest means of carrying money, though the bureaucracy of changing them at banks can be exasperating. Banks and *cambios* also pay slightly less for traveler's checks than for cash, in lieu of a separate commission.

For assistance in replacing lost or stolen American Express checks, contact its local representative, Turismo Cocha, Avenida Bosque Norte 0430, Las Condes, Santiago, tel. 2/4641242. The Thomas Cook affiliate is Turismo Tajamar, Orrego Luco 023, Providencia, Santiago, tel. 2/2315112.

BANK TRANSFERS

Many Chilean exchange houses are affiliated with Western Union, making it relatively straightforward to send money from overseas. For a list of Western Union affiliates in Chile, see its website at www.westernunion.com.

In an emergency, it is possible to forward money to U.S. citizens via the U.S. embassy in Chile by establishing a Department of State trust account through its Overseas Citizens Services, Washington, D.C. 20520, tel. 202/647-5225; there is a US$20 service charge for setting up the account. It is possible to arrange this as a wire or overnight mail transfer through Western Union, tel. 800/325-6000; for details see the Department of State's website: www.travel.state.gov.

CREDIT CARDS

As usual, credit cards are widely accepted in the capital and major tourist centers but less so in the remote countryside. The mostly reliably used are Visa and MasterCard, though American Express is possible in some areas. Many banks will provide cash advances on either Visa or MasterCard, though Visa is more common.

Services such as hotels, restaurants, and car rental agencies rarely, but occasionally, impose a *recargo* (surcharge) on credit card purchases; ask before paying.

For lost or stolen credit cards there are local contacts for Visa and MasterCard, tel. 2/6317003; Diner's Club, tel. 2/2320000; and American Express, tel. 800/201022 toll-free.

COSTS

By global standards, travel in Chile is moderately priced, but much depends on the traveler's expectations and where in the country he or she goes. Chile has suitable services for everyone, from bare-bones budget backpackers to pampered international business travelers.

The countryside is cheaper than the cities, and truly disciplined travelers in rural areas can find it possible to get away with as little as US$15 or less per day by staying in the cheapest basic accommodations, buying groceries and cooking for themselves, or eating market food. Public transportation is moderately priced, especially given the long distances on some routes, but the fact that Chile imports nearly all its oil makes the sector vulnerable to fluctuations.

In the capital, the cities, and main tourist areas, however, costs are higher for a wider range of services. Budget travelers will find hotel rooms under US$10 pp scarce, though there are some excellent values for only a little more money. Hotels and resorts of international stature, such as the Hyatt and Sheraton chains and their local equivalents, charge corresponding prices. Likewise, meals are a couple dollars or even less at the simplest *comedores,* but restaurants with sophisticated international cuisine can charge a lot more; even the latter, however, often serve moderately priced lunchtime specials.

TAXES

Chile imposes an 18 percent *impuesto de valor agregado* (IVA, value added tax or VAT) on all goods and services, though this is normally included in the advertised price; if in doubt, ask for clarification (*¿Incluye los impuestos?*). Most midrange to upscale hotels, however, legally discount IVA for foreign visitors who receive a *factura de exportación* (export receipt) along with their hotel bill (for details, see the Accommodations entry above).

TIPPING

In restaurants with table service, a 10 percent gratuity is customary, but in smaller family-run *comedores* the practice is rare. Taxi drivers are customarily not tipped, but rounding off the fare to the next highest convenient number is appropriate. Where there is no meter, this is not an issue.

BARGAINING

Bargaining is not the way of life in Chile that it is in some other Latin American countries, but in crafts markets the vendor may start at a higher price than he or she expects to receive—avoid insultingly low offers, or such a high offer that the vendor will think you a fool. Depending on your language and bargaining skills, you should be able to achieve a compromise that satisfies everybody.

STUDENT DISCOUNTS

Student discounts are relatively few, and prices are so low for most services that it's rarely worth arguing the point. In the case of foreign travel, however, students may be eligible for discount international airfares (see the Getting There and Getting Around entries for details).

Communications and Media

POSTAL SERVICES

Since the privatization of Correos de Chile, the Chilean post office, service is more reliable than in the past. Domestic services are generally cheap, international services more expensive. Major international couriers, such as DHL, provide fast, reliable services at premium prices.

General delivery at Chilean post offices is *lista de correos,* quite literally a list arranged in alphabetical order. Because Chileans use both paternal and maternal surnames, postal employees may confuse foreign middle names with paternal surnames—thus a letter to Ricardo Lagos Escobar would be found under "L," while one to "Albert Arnold Gore, Jr." might be found under the letter "A" rather than "G."

Note that, in Spanish-language street addresses, the number follows rather than precedes the name; instead of "1343 Washington Ave.," for example, a comparable Chilean address would read "Avenida Bilbao 272." Chileans and other Spanish speakers normally omit the word *calle* (street) from addresses; where an English speaker might write "499 Jones St.," a Chilean would simply use "Carrera 272," for example. It

is not unusual for street addresses to lack a number, as indicated by *s/n* (*sin número,* without a number).

TELEPHONE AND FAX

Chile's country code is 56; there are a number of area codes for individual cities and, in some cases, entire regions. All telephone numbers in the Región Metropolitana have seven digits, while those in the other regions generally have six, but in some rural areas they have seven digits beginning with 1.

Cellular phones all have seven digits, prefixed by 09. In addition, certain toll-free and other specialty numbers have six digits with a three-digit prefix.

According to *The Economist,* Chile has about 22 fixed-line telephones per 100 people, and about the same number of mobile phones. The fixed-line figure is equal to or greater than all other countries in Latin America, except for Uruguay; the mobile phone figure is the region's highest.

These figures may overstate the abundance of mobile phone usage. Since such usage functions on a caller-pays basis, many Chileans use them primarily for receiving calls, rather than paying

high mobile phone charges. Cheaper fixed lines carry far more traffic.

Public telephones are abundant; some of them operate with coins only, but most also accept magnetic phone cards or rechargeable account cards. The basic local phone rate is Ch$100 (about US$.15) for five minutes or so; domestic long-distance is not that much more expensive. Magnetic cards, in values of Ch$1,000, Ch$2,000, Ch$3,000, and Ch$5,000 are convenient for in-country calls but less useful for more expensive overseas calls.

For long-distance and overseas calls, and fax services, it's simplest to use *centros de llamados* (call centers), which are abundant in both Santiago and the regions. Prices can be very competitive, and they now tend to be much cheaper than placing *cobro revertido* (collect) or *tarjeta de crédito* (credit card) calls to the United States or any other country.

Entel and CTC Telefónica Chile, the two major long-distance companies, both have toll-free numbers for international collect and credit card calls, however. Entel numbers include Australia, tel. 800/360150; Belgium, tel. 800/ 360121; Canada, tel. 800/360280; France, tel. 800/360110; Germany, tel. 123/003491; Israel, tel. 123/0039721; Italy, tel. 800/360099; Netherlands, tel. 123/003311; Spain, tel. 800/360055; U.K. (British Telecom), tel. 800/360066; USA (AT&T), tel. 800/800311; USA (MCI), tel. 800/360180; and USA (Sprint), tel. 800/360777. For other countries' numbers, dial 800/123123.

CTC Telefónica contact numbers include the following: Australia, tel. 800/800-287; Canada, tel. 800/800226; France, tel. 800/800372; Germany, tel. 800/800049; Italy, tel. 800/800039; Spain, tel. 800/207334; U.K. (British Telecom), 800/800044; USA (AT&T), tel. 800/800288;

phone card

USA (MCI), tel. 800/207300; and USA (Sprint), tel. 800/800777. For other countries, contact CTC Telefónica at tel. 800/200300.

INTERNET ACCESS

In the last few years, public Internet access has become both abundant and cheap—rarely does it cost more than about US$2 per hour, and it is often even cheaper. Many *centros de llamados* offer access, but there are also numerous Internet cafés in Santiago and other cities, and especially in university neighborhoods. Some Internet service providers, most notably AOL and Compuserve, have local dial-up numbers in Chile. In this book, email addresses are listed after websites.

NEWSPAPERS AND MAGAZINES

Chile may have emerged from dictatorship, but freedom of expression still has its limits. A recent study by the Universidad de Chile has criticized the concentration of print media, in particular, in the hands of large consortia such as Agustín Edwards' El Mercurio group, which owns its influential namesake daily *El Mercurio* along with the daily tabloids *La Segunda* and *Las Ultimas Noticias,* and the Consorcio Periodistico de Chile (Copesa), which owns the tabloids *La Tercera, La Hora,* and the particularly sensationalist *La Cuarta*.

The study noted not just the business aspects of the oligopoly—though the El Mercurio group earns about 70 percent of the roughly US$640 million advertising revenue for print media—but also the "ideological monopoly" of the country's most conservative elements. The Copesa group, in particular, consists of a daily newspaper and three magazines controlled by former officials of the Pinochet regime. Ironically enough,

THE RISING STAR OF DON FRANCISCO

Chile's biggest TV star and one of the Spanish-speaking world's most famous entertainers, Mario Kreutzberger is better known as "Don Francisco," his stage name as host of the Miami-based variety show *Sábado Gigante*. A four-hour marathon of audience participation contests and singalongs, comedy and interviews, *Sábado Gigante* (Giant Saturday) holds a spot in the Guinness Book of Records as the world's longest-running TV show never to offer a rerun—since its inception in Santiago in 1962, it has never repeated itself. According to the host network Univisión, 100 million viewers in more than 30 countries watch it every week.

Born in 1940, the son of German Jewish refugees who settled in Talca before eventually moving to Santiago, the young but audacious Don Francisco talked his way into a pilot show on the Universidad Católica's Canal 13. To almost everyone's surprise—perhaps even his own—it quickly acquired a devoted following even in an unfavorable Saturday-morning time slot. In its Chilean prime, the program was a nine-hour test of the host's stamina; since its move to Miami in 1986, it's a long program even in its attenuated four-hour version.

Not simply a self-promoter, Don Francisco has also dedicated himself to charitable causes, particularly early December's annual Teletón (Telethon) for handicapped children. A fixture on Chilean television since 1978, inspired by Jerry Lewis, the Teletón brings together Chilean and other Latin American celebrities for 27 hours of televised entertainment to raise money for the cause. The Teletón also kicks off the Christmas season, as Chilean businesses either place Don Francisco on their billboards or make donations to use its symbol on their propaganda. All Chilean stations broadcast the event, widely considered a symbol of unity within the country. Since its inception, it has collected more than US$120 million in donations.

For his efforts on *Sábado Gigante,* the Teletón, and contributions to Unicef, in 2001 Don Francisco became the first South American to appear on Hollywood Boulevard's Walk of Fame (the only others of Latin origin include the legendary Mexican actor Mario Moreno (Cantinflas), Spanish pop singer Julio Iglesias, Spanish tenor Plácido Domingo, and Cuban salsa singer Celia Cruz).

Don Francisco does not lack critics, though. Many consider the pan-Hispanic *Sábado Gigante* a vulgar pageant of homogenized mass culture with no clear distinction between content and product promotion. And though Don Francisco insists "we never got involved in politics," Chilean writer Pedro Lemebel declared during an interview on the TVN discussion program *De Pe a Pa* that Don Francisco often lunched with the notorious retired general and convicted human rights violator Manuel Contreras. On the other hand, one of Don Francisco's closest friends is a Chilean judge responsible for sentencing Contreras to prison and lifting General Pinochet's congressional immunity.

To appreciate the Don Francisco experience in person, pay a visit to Barrio Brasil's *Estudio Gigante,* Catedral 1850, tel. 2/6971727, but don't be tempted by the abundant, moderately priced buffet lunches or dinners—they look good, but they're really glorified cafeteria food. Instead, have a glass of Chilean chardonnay or a pisco sour at the bar, and enjoy the good-hearted Chileans enjoying themselves.

Estudio Gigante also shows that Don Francisco is true to his convictions—wide ramps ease the way into the building, in one of the oldest parts of town, and it has some of the few toilets easily accessible for wheelchairs outside Santiago's international airport.

Pinochet's political departure in 1990 made times harder for critical journalists, since they had lost their easiest editorial target.

Pinochet's arrest and subsequent legal troubles, however, opened up a whole new space for irreverently satirical papers such as *The Clinic,* whose bimonthly circulation of 40,000 is a remarkable success story (the paper named itself for the London clinic at which the former dictator was detained). If *The Clinic* might be called Chile's Yippie left, the magazine *El Rocinante* represents its more traditional and solemn intellectual left. For an English-language summary of the Chilean daily press, plus occasional original reporting, look at the Internet-only *Santiago Times* (www.chip.cl); the weekly print tabloid *News Review* is largely business-oriented and relatively bland.

A major restraint on freedom of expression for Chilean journalists disappeared when, in early 2001, Congress repealed a clause of the Pinochet-era National Security Law that permitted imprisonment for anyone who would "defame, injure, or slander members of the high courts." The immediate impact of this was to end legal proceedings against Alejandra Matus, whose *Libro Negro de la Justicia Chilena* (Black Book of Chilean Justice) detailed judicial complicity in human rights abuses of the 1970s and 1980s. When Chilean Supreme Court justice Servan-

do Jordán invoked Article 6b of the law against Matus in May 1999, also prohibiting distribution of the book, the result was that Matus had to ask political asylum in Miami, embarrassing the administration of former President Eduardo Frei Ruiz-Tagle. With approval of a new press law, Matus was able to return to the country in July 2001, though the book remained at least temporarily embargoed for procedural reasons—though it was still visibly on sale by informal street vendors. A judge finally lifted the ban later in the year.

RADIO AND TELEVISION

In contrast with the print media, radio and TV journalism are more pluralistic, at least in terms of ownership, as private media with foreign capital have competed with local sources since the early 1990s. That said, the state-run Television Nacional (TVN) and the Universidad Católica's Canal 13 (Channel 13) are still the most important broadcast outlets. International cable TV, widely available throughout the country and even in some very moderately priced hotels, provides a more cosmopolitan perspective.

There are also many radio stations on both AM and FM bands, but radio tends to be more an entertainment than a journalistic outlet.

Maps and Tourist Information

MAPS

Offices of the Servicio Nacional de Turismo (Sernatur, or National Tourism Service) in Santiago and in regional capitals, and municipal tourist offices throughout the country, distribute free, serviceable, and often very good, country and city maps. Better maps are available for a price and, for activities such as backcountry hiking, they're often essential.

For preliminary planning, the American Automobile Association (AAA) publishes a general South American road map that's free to members; offices are all across the United States. The author of this book wrote the text and did much of the

field research for the *Chile & Easter Island Travel Atlas* (Lonely Planet, 1997), but subsequent highway development has rendered it obsolete except as a general reference.

International Travel Maps and Books (ITMB), 530 W. Broadway, Vancouver BC, V5Z 1E9, tel. 604/879-3621, fax 604/879-4521, website: www.itmb.com, itmb@itmb.com, publishes a series of maps that cover all or parts of Chile at a variety of scales, including *Southern South America* (1:2,800,000), Argentina (1:4,000,000), Tierra del Fuego (1:700,000), Easter Island (1:30,000), and Santiago (1:12,500).

It's worth mentioning that the Santiago map, while accurate enough on the streets, has numerous transcription errors. The most complete map of the capital is Publiguías' *Plano de Santiago,* updated annually and available at many kiosks in the city; moderately priced, it includes an index of streets in even the most remote *comunas.* The annually updated three-volume Turistel guidebook series (Spanish only) contains the most current road maps at the back of its *Norte* (North), *Centro* (Center), and *Sur* volumes, along with numerous useful city maps which, unfortunately, lack scales.

JLM Cartografía, General del Canto 105, Oficina 1506, tel./fax 2/2364808, Providencia, Santiago, jmatassi@interactiva.cl, publishes a series of regional and local maps at varying scale (even within the same map) in both Spanish and imperfect but generally serviceable English. Some cover parts of neighboring countries. Titles include *Sudamérica* (South America); *Chile/Santiago; Altiplano: Chile-Bolivia-Peru; San Pedro de Atacama; Playas de Chile/Valles Centrales* (Chilean Beaches and Central Valley); *Andes Centrales/Cajón del Maipo* (Central Andes and Cajón del Maipo); *Isla de Pascua* (Easter Island); *Araucanía, Maule a Toltén* (Araucanía, from Maule to Toltén); *Pucón/San Martín de los Andes; Lagos Andinos, Temuco a Bariloche* (Andean Lakes, from Temuco to Bariloche); *Ruta de los Jesuitas, Puerto Montt a Bariloche* (Trail of the Jesuits, from Puerto Montt to Bariloche); *Chiloé/Patagonia, Costa a Costa* (Chiloé and Patagonia, from Coast to Coast); *Camino Austral/Patagonia Chilena; Torres del Paine; Patagonia Sur/Tierra del Fuego* (Southern Patagonia and Tierra del Fuego); *Tierra del Fuego;* and *Antártica/Polo Sur* (Antarctica and the South Pole).

The Instituto Geográfico Militar (IGM), Dieciocho 369, Santiago Centro, tel. 2/4606800, fax 2/4608924, website: www.igm.cl, informaciones@igm.cl, publishes detailed topographic maps covering the entire country at a scale of 1:50,000; some of these, however, are "proprietary" as they adjoin what the armed forces consider to be sensitive border areas. They are also expensive at about US$10 and up, but the Instituto also sells a variety of city maps, road atlases, and books that are useful to the everyday visitor, and the staff are professional and efficient.

Hours are Monday 9 A.M.–5:30 P.M., Tuesday through Friday 9 A.M.–5:50 P.M.

TOURIST OFFICES

Sernatur, the national tourism service, maintains public information offices in Santiago and all regional capitals, and also in Chillán, Valdivia, and Puerto Natales. Most are normally open weekdays only, but in summer and in some localities they are open weekends. (For details, see the appropriate geographical entries.)

In addition to Sernatur's offices, many cities and towns have their own municipal tourist offices, especially in southern lake district resorts such as Villarrica, Pucón, and Puerto Varas, which keep long summer hours but are limited the rest of the year. Many smaller towns have offices in summer only (January and February). (Again, for details, see the appropriate geographical entries.)

LIBRARIES

Chile's most important library is downtown Santiago's Biblioteca Nacional (National Library), housed in a massive neoclassical structure that also includes the Archivo Nacional (National Archive). Chile also has public and private university libraries; some of the latter, created during a politically motivated transformation of Chile's higher education system by the Pinochet regime, have ironically enough saved some of Chile's literary and academic heritage in their libraries by buying collections that might otherwise have been sold overseas.

Most cities and towns have public libraries with resources that range from meager to plentiful, depending on their tax base, but a central government initiative was due to provide every community library with Internet access within the next few years.

BOOKSTORES

Santiago and some other cities have fine general-interest bookstores, as well as specialist shops that deal with academic and rare books, and others with English-language materials (for details, see the appropriate geographical entries). In addition, there are used bookshops and informal book exchanges in main tourist centers, such as San Pedro de Atacama, Pucón, and Puerto Montt.

MAGAZINES AND NEWSLETTERS

For travelers who read Spanish, the three-volume, annually updated *Turistel* guidebook series, published by Turiscom, is useful for its maps of even the smallest villages and notable for flashy graphics that occasionally help explain topics such as architectural detail and copper processing. It is even more notable for its omissions—politics is so taboo that, from reading it, one would not even be aware that Chile endured a dictatorship 1973–90, much less know who was in charge.

Several freebies are tourist-oriented, including *Santiago Alive,* a bilingual monthly that is primarily promotional; *Traveling Chile,* a glossy bilingual tourist-oriented magazine that comes out bimonthly; and the Spanish-only *SCL Magazine,* the international airport's official magazine. All of these have useful maps and listings.

What to Take

LUGGAGE

What sort of luggage you bring depends on what sort of trip you're planning, for how long, and where you're planning to go. For shoestring travelers planning months in Chile and neighboring countries, for instance, a spacious but lightweight backpack is the best choice; a small daypack for local excursions is also a good idea.

Even for nonbackpackers, light luggage is advisable, even though traveling on airplanes, shuttles, and taxis can be logistically simpler than buses alone—door-to-door service is the rule. Even then, a small daypack for excursions is convenient.

Small but sturdy lightweight locks are advisable for all sorts of luggage, if only to discourage temptation.

CLOTHING

Because of Chile's great altitudinal and latitudinal variation, from sea level to more than 4,000 meters above sea level and from the desert tropics to the sub-Antarctic, the necessary clothing can vary from light cottons to heavy woolens. Much also depends on the season and the activity; obviously, if you're skiing at Portillo in July, your requirements are different than if you're beach-

combing at La Serena in January. A good rule of thumb is to bring appropriately seasonal clothing for comparable latitudes and altitudes in the Northern Hemisphere—though nowhere in North America or Europe, except their highest summits, matches Andean altitudes that are readily reached by car in Chile.

Certain items are de rigueur. Both hikers and city walkers should have a wide-brimmed hat for protection from the sun. In the Sur Chico, an umbrella is useful at any time of the year, but Patagonian squalls can shred your *paraguas* in a second—heavier raingear is desirable.

CAMPING GEAR

Good-quality camping gear is more readily available for sale than it used to be, and renting equipment is possible in outdoorsy resort towns such as Pucón and Puerto Natales. Bring a lightweight tent with a rain fly for shedding the showers and, at the highest altitudes, keeping out the cold. A three-season sleeping bag should be sufficient for most weather—unless you're camping or bivouacking on the Patagonian ice sheets or the massive volcanoes of the altiplano.

For those hiking through either the highlands or the lowland forests, lightweight rain gear is also a good idea, along with fabric hiking boots that dry out quickly. Pack a wide-brimmed hat for protection from both sun and rain.

Since fresh water is in short supply in some places—many volcanic areas have no surface streams, especially in the dry season—sturdy plastic water bottles, a water filter, and even iodine drops or tablets are indispensable—*Giardia* can be a problem in some heavily hiked areas. Also carry insect repellent, not just for mosquitoes but also for the large biting *tábanos* (horseflies) of the Sur Chico.

ODDS AND ENDS

Since public toilets often lack toilet paper, travelers should always carry some, even though it's readily available within the country. Many budget hotels have thin walls and squeaky floors, so earplugs are a good idea.

Leg pouches and money belts are good options for securing cash, traveler's checks, and important documents. A compact pair of binoculars is a good idea for birders and others who enjoy wildlife and the landscape.

Film and Photography

Color print film is widely available, color slide film somewhat less so. It tends to be cheaper in North America or Europe, so it's best to bring as much as possible. If buying film in Chile, check the expiration date to make sure it's current, especially in out-of-the-way places. In the capital and larger tourist centers, competent print film processing is readily available and moderately priced, but it's better to hold slide film until your return to your home country if possible (but store it under cool, dark, and dry conditions).

Environmental conditions can affect the quality of your photographs and the type of film you should use. At high altitudes, bright sun can wash out photographs; it's best to use a relatively slow film, around ASA 64 or 100, and a polarizing filter to reduce glare. A polarizing filter also improves contrast, dramatizing the sky and clouds, but can result in a dark foreground if you're not careful.

Photographing the southern temperate rainforests presents special problems, as sunlight does not penetrate the dense canopy easily. A haze or UV filter is still a good idea, but a high-speed film, at least ASA 200 or preferably ASA 400, is advisable under low-light conditions. Alternatively, a tripod makes it easier to photograph in poor light, but moving subjects such as birds or other wildlife may be blurred.

ETIQUETTE

Most Chileans are not exactly camera-shy, but travelers should still be circumspect when photographing indigenous people in particular. While some do not object, others consider it an invasion of their privacy.

Generally, if a person's presence in a photograph is incidental, as in a townscape, it's probably unnecessary to ask permission. If in doubt, though, ask; if rejected, don't insist. If you're buying something from a market vendor, he or she will almost certainly agree to a photographic request.

Weights and Measures

TIME

Chile is three hours behind GMT for most of the year, but it does observe daylight saving time (summer time), though dates for the changeover vary from year to year. When the U.S. Eastern Time Zone is on daylight saving time, during the Northern Hemisphere summer, and Chile is on standard time, the hour is identical in New York and Santiago.

All of continental Chile goes on daylight saving time despite latitudes that range from about 18° to 56° S, and this causes some anomalies. In summer, northern cities such as Arica, where the length of day is relatively equal throughout the year, do not see daylight until almost 8 A.M.; at this time of the year, they are two hours ahead of nearby Peru. In the far south, by contrast, midsummer daylight can last until nearly 11 P.M. or later. Argentina does not observe daylight saving time, so there is no time difference between the two countries in summer.

Easter Island (Rapa Nui) is two hours behind the continent.

ELECTRICITY

Throughout the country, nearly all outlets are 220 volts, 50 cycles, so converters are necessary for North American appliances such as computers, electric razors, and so on. Plugs are two rounded prongs. Electrical supply stores on Santiago's Calle San Pablo, north of the Plaza de Armas, sell plug adapters but adequately powered converters are harder to find, and it's better to bring one from overseas.

MEASUREMENTS

The metric system is official, but this doesn't completely eliminate the variety of vernacular measures that Chileans use in everyday life. In rural areas, people often use the *legua* (league) of about five km as a measure of distance, and the *quintal* of 46 kilos is also widely used, especially in wholesale markets and statistics.

At airports, the Chilean military invariably measures altitude in feet above sea level. Tire pressure is often measured in pounds per square inch.

Santiago and Vicinity

Introduction

For most visitors to Chile, the sprawling megalopolis of Santiago de Chile, and the Mediterranean hillsides and snow-covered Andean crest of its hinterland, are their first impression of the country. Santiago may lack the high international profile of Buenos Aires, but many of its attractions can match or some say even surpass those of the Argentine capital. And few world capitals can match the skiing, hiking, climbing, and white-water rafting and kayaking that are barely an hour beyond the city limits.

Five million people, more than a third of all Chileans, live in Gran Santiago (Greater Santiago), the sprawling capital city at the foot of the Andes. The locus of Chile's political and economic power, it has, like most other capitals in the region, grown inexorably at the expense of the regions, but internally its growth has been uneven—while some of its 32 *comunas* or boroughs have become prosperous and even wealthy, others are poor or even desperately poor. The residential segregation by class is particularly striking, even if the standards of poverty are less extreme than in cities such as La Paz, Lima, or Mexico City.

Parque de las Esculturas, on the banks of the Río Mapocho

That said, there is no question that, since the return to constitutional government and the economic boom of the 1990s, conditions have improved in many neighborhoods. Both individuals and businesses, for instance, have restored or rehabbed houses and buildings in once rundown Barrio Brasil, where entrepreneurs have also replaced unsalvageable structures with tasteful apartment blocks. The city has also experienced a gastronomic boom in neighborhoods such as Barrio Bellavista, the center of its nightlife, and international commerce flourishes in boroughs such as Providencia and Las Condes.

Santiaguinos have paid a price for their affluence. A million automobiles are now in the city, at least 15 times more than it had four decades ago; clogging the narrow colonial streets, idling behind sooty diesel buses, they contribute to one of the world's worst urban smog problems. Industry adds its share as well.

Still, according to one survey of about 250 major cities worldwide, Santiago is the continent's third most livable city, behind only Montevideo and Buenos Aires, though it ranks only 80th on the entire list. Another survey, by the respected magazine *América Economía,* ranked Santiago above even Buenos Aires in its blend of cultural life, entertainment, personal security, and efficiency.

Most points of interest are in downtown Santiago, the city's colonial nucleus, surrounding boroughs such as Recoleta, Independencia, Quinta Normal, and Estación Central, and eastern suburban boroughs such as Providencia, Las Condes, and Ñuñoa.

LAND AND CLIMATE

The megacity of Santiago is really many cities, consisting of 32 different *comunas* or boroughs, all of which have separate municipal governments. The national government, though, controls services that overlap municipal boundaries, such as transportation.

Between the high Andes and the lower coast range, Gran Santiago sprawls from north of the Río Mapocho to south of the Río Maipo; the meandering Mapocho eventually joins the Maipo

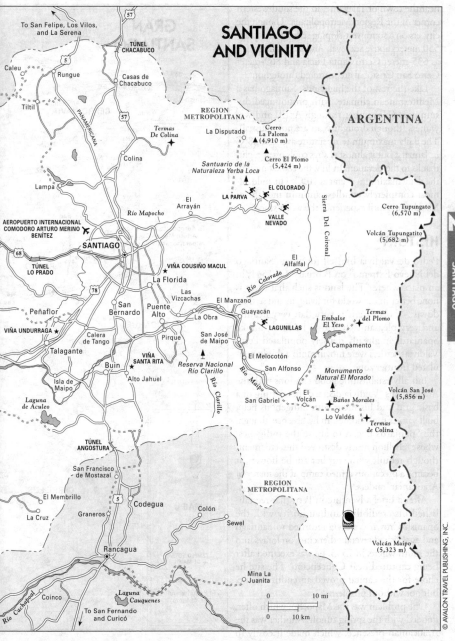

SANTIAGO AND VICINITY

near the town of Talagante, in the southwestern corner of the Región Metropolitana. Though the city sits on a southwest-sloping sedimentary plain 550 meters above sea level, Andean outliers such as 635-meter Cerro Santa Lucía and 869-meter Cerro San Cristóbal are scattered throughout.

Like the rest of the highlands, Santiago has a Mediterranean climate, with pronounced dry summers (November through April) and wet winters (though drought years are not unusual). The daily maximum temperature averages 28°C in January, but it almost always cools off at night, thanks to the elevation. In July, the coolest month, the daily maximum averages 10°C. The mild, almost completely windless autumn months of March and April experience the worst smog.

HISTORY

Pedro de Valdivia himself founded "Santiago del Nuevo Extremo" on February 12, 1541, in an place where "The land is such that there is none better in the world for living in and settling down . . . because it is very flat, very healthy and very pleasant." It had to be since, unlike Spaniards in already densely populated Peru, Valdivia's settlers were moving into a thinly populated frontier zone.

Initially establishing good relations with the Araucanians, Valdivia decreed the platting of a basic grid and his men, with indigenous help, built some simple houses. In his absence, though, the Spaniards began to abuse the indigenes, whose rebellion nearly destroyed the settlement; though rebuilt with sturdier adobe houses, it became a precarious armed camp at the mercy of Araucanian raiders.

After a brief adventure in Peru that reestablished his credibility and authority with the Spanish Crown, Valdivia returned to Santiago and established several other cities on forays into the south where, in 1553, he was executed after being captured near Concepción. The site he chose for the capital proved an enduring one, but not without problems.

One problem was the Mapocho, which often flooded with the spring runoff. Another was the Araucanian presence, which made it costly to

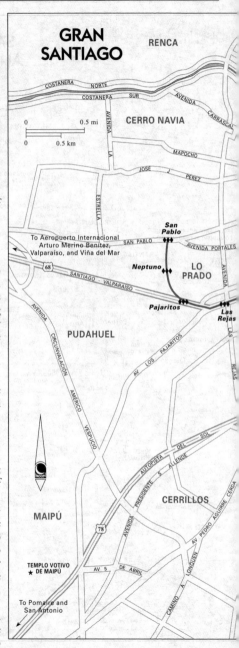

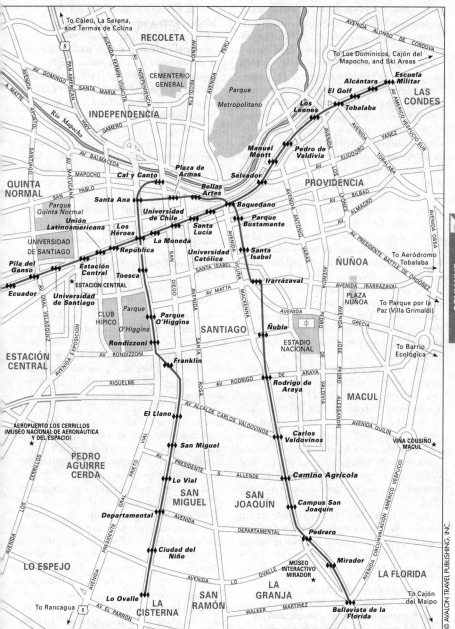

SANTIAGO

maintain—after the initial Araucanian assault, according to historian John A. Crow, "the meager garrison of Santiago held body and soul together on a starvation diet, working, thinking, living only for the future." Between 1600 and 1606, the governing Viceroyalty of Lima had to quadruple Chile's military budget just to maintain its presence. Nearly all the city's Spanish residents were soldiers, former soldiers, and their families; by the end of the 16th century, according to Chilean historian Eduardo Solar Correa, Santiago's "appearance was sad and miserable: narrow streets, dusty in summer and impassable with mud in winter, low-lying houses of clay and adobe, whose meager and only half-finished rooms were lighted at night by a tallow candle."

The abundance of Spanish soldiers and the absence of Spanish women left an evident and enduring legacy on the nascent colony. Many Spanish soldiers formed both fleeting and permanent unions with indigenous women, their mestizo children forming the foundation of a new society, but one in which class distinctions became critically important. Landed proprietors, successors to the *encomenderos,* dominated Santiago society, though their economic and power base was in the countryside.

With the 18th century, though, came material improvements such as construction of a cathedral, creation of the Casa de la Moneda (colonial mint) to spur economic activity, *tajamares* (dikes) to contain the floods of the Mapocho, and improved roads to link the city to the countryside and to the port of Valparaíso. Cultural life also improved with establishment of the Universidad de San Felipe (founded in 1758 as a law school), later to become the Universidad de Chile.

By the time Chile became an independent country, Santiago was a modest city that made mixed impressions. On her first visit to the capital, in 1822, the Englishwoman Maria Graham remarked that:

The disposition of the houses, though pleasant enough to the inhabitants, is ugly without, and gives a mean, dull air to the streets, which are wide and well paved, having a footpath flagged with slabs of granite and porphyry; and through most of them a small stream is constantly running, which, with a little more attention from the police, might make it the cleanest city in the world: it is not very dirty; and when I recollect Rio de Janeiro and Bahia, I am ready to call it absolutely clean.

Mrs. Graham, of course, reflected the perspective of Santiago's elite and the British community, so her experience hardly reflects the lives of the laborers and peasants (there were country estates in areas now utterly urban) who lived beyond those enclaves. Darwin, more than a decade later, enjoyed the city but found it equally nondescript:

it is not so fine or so large as Buenos Ayres, but it is built after the same model.

Frequent earthquakes often destroyed landmark buildings and encouraged utilitarian rather than elaborate construction.

Post-independence Santiago, however, was poised for a boom. The California Gold Rush of the mid-19th century created a huge market for Chilean wheat, wine, and other produce, and the beneficiaries were a landed elite who were able to build splendid city mansions, furnish them extravagantly with imported luxury items, and support exclusive institutions such as the Club Hípico (Racing Club). By the 1870s, the progressive Mayor Benjamín Vicuña Mackenna was transforming areas such as Cerro Santa Lucía into magnificent public parks, but at a cost—displacing some of the city's less fortunate residents from convenient central areas.

At the same time, the city was progressing culturally, thanks largely to the efforts of the Venezuelan-born scholar Andrés Bello, who almost single-handedly reformed the moribund Universidad de San Felipe into the present-day Universidad de Chile and taught many of the country's 19th-century leaders. Figures such as the exiled Argentine politician and educator Domingo Faustino Sarmiento, later his country's president, also enriched the intellectual life of a city whose population exceeded 100,000 by mid-century.

Conflict with Peru and Bolivia in the War of the Pacific (1879–84) changed the city and the country dramatically over the next several decades, in ways that were not immediately apparent. Chilean interests grew wealthy with control of the nitrate-rich Atacama Desert, financing a new round of conspicuous consumption by mining magnates and bringing revenue to the government treasury. At the same time, lack of land forced small farmers to the city, just as the failure of the nitrate mines in the early 1900s drove a militant labor force to the capital. For a time, industrialization absorbed the excess labor, but continued rural chaos exacerbated urban immigration and resulted in spontaneous peripheral squatter settlements known as *callampas* (mushrooms). These exploded with activism during the years of the Unidad Popular, but in the aftermath of the 1973 coup they had to bide their time as wealthy eastern suburbs such as Las Condes literally reached for the skies in high-rise apartments and office blocks.

The dictatorship's economic policies—largely intact despite more than a decade of constitutional government—also encouraged suburban sprawl and private automobile ownership that have aggravated traffic congestion and air pollution. The fact that more than a third of Chile's 15 million inhabitants live in Gran Santiago is an indicator that these problems are not going to disappear soon, but it's only fair to add that some central city neighborhoods, such as Barrio Brasil, are undergoing an urban renaissance and becoming increasingly livable.

ORIENTATION

Santiago's compact colonial core lies south of the Mapocho, north of the east-west thoroughfare Avenida del Libertador General Bernardo O'Higgins (popularly known as the "Alameda"), and east of the Vía Norte Sur, the downtown segment of the Carretera Panamericana. The center of the grid is the rectangular Plaza de Armas, the locus of Spanish colonial power and site of major public buildings such as the cathedral. Most of those colonial buildings are long gone from the plaza, but several others survive in the vicinity. During the past two decades, municipal authorities have converted several narrow downtown streets—Puente, Ahumada, Huérfanos, Estado, and others—into *paseos* or *peatonales* (pedestrian malls).

Santiago Centro consists of several informal barrios or neighborhoods with their own distinctive character. Around Plaza de la Constitución, southwest of the Plaza de Armas, the Barrio Cívico contains most of government offices; farther west, across the Vía Norte Sur, the once dilapidated Barrio Brasil is undergoing a residential renaissance. South of the Alameda, the winding streets of Barrio París Londres break the grid pattern, as do those of Barrio Lastarria, east of Cerro Santa Lucía.

Beyond Santiago Centro, several other *comunas* have points of interest, both sights and services. The most important are the easterly suburbs of Providencia and Las Condes, but others include Estación Central, Quinta Normal, Independencia, Recoleta, Vitacura, and Ñuñoa. Some of these boast their own distinctive neighborhoods: north of the Mapocho, the restaurant and nightlife mecca of Barrio Bellavista lies half in Recoleta, half in Providencia. Providencia's traditional point of identification, though, is Plaza Baquedano, universally known as Plaza Italia, where the eastbound Alameda becomes Avenida Providencia.

Las Condes and Vitacura are increasingly affluent eastward extensions of affluent Providencia, while the more southeasterly Ñuñoa is middle-class without being dull. Independencia, Quinta Normal, and Estación Central have fewer points of tourist interest and services, except for the presence of major museums and parks and a handful of important services such as long-distance bus terminals.

Santiago Sights

Downtown Santiago has the greatest density of sights in the city, clustered in or around the Plaza de Armas, Plaza de la Constitución, Cerro Santa Lucía, Barrio Lastarria, and Barrio Brasil, with a handful scattered elsewhere. Note that the municipal tourist authority, with separate offices at the Casa Colorada near the Plaza de Armas and on Cerro Santa Lucía, offers a variety of free walking tours that include admission to some of the city's best museums; check for the most current itineraries.

Sights in others *comunas* tend to be more spread out.

PLAZA DE ARMAS AND VICINITY

The Plaza de Armas, Santiago's colonial heart, is the center of a *zona típica* national monument whose boundaries were originally platted by Pedro de Valdivia's surveyor Pedro de Gamboa. Until 1821, when the central market moved north to the banks of the Mapocho, the plaza was also the city's commercial center.

On its west side, the plaza's oldest surviving landmark is the **Catedral Metropolitana,** begun in 1748 but, because of setbacks including earthquakes and fires, not formally completed until around 1830; this early bishopric attained cathedral status in 1840. Italian architect Joaquín Toesca, who assumed direction of the project in 1780, was responsible for its neoclassical facade and other elements that gave a hodgepodge project a stately unity, modified into a Tuscan style by Ignacio Cremonesi at the end of the 19th century.

Secular authority occupied the north side of the plaza—indeed, it belonged entirely to Pedro de Valdivia until his death at the battle of Tucapel in 1553. Its oldest structure is the **Municipalidad de Santiago** (1785). Immediately to its west, the **Palacio de la Real Audiencia** (1804) houses the Museo Histórico Nacional (see below); at the corner of Paseo Puente, the French-style **Correo Central** (1882) occupies the site of the demolished Casa del Gobernador del Reino de Chile, where the colonial and early republican governments resided until 1846.

Commerce monopolized the plaza's south side; after the central market moved, the handsome 19th-century arcade known as the **Portal Fernández Concha** replaced it, though its current hot dog and sandwich stands make it a less prestigious address than it once was. Half a block east, at Merced 860, the **Casa Colorada** (1769) houses the municipal tourist office and the city museum (see below).

One block west of the plaza, occupying an entire block bounded by Bandera, Catedral, Morandé, and Compañía, the current **Ministerio de Relaciones Exteriores** (Foreign Ministry) was the Congreso de la República until the 1973 coup. The building suffered a whole series of setbacks, however, from its inception under President Manuel Montt in the 1850s: death of an architect, shortages of funds, and a fire that destroyed the adjacent Iglesia de la Compañía (today the building's gardens). Finally finished in 1876, a great part of it was destroyed by fire in 1895; by 1901, it was rebuilt and reinaugurated in its present neoclassical style. After the 1973 coup, it suffered earthquake damage in 1985, but it has since had a seismic upgrade and there is talk of relocating the legislature from Valparaíso.

Immediately north of the ex-Congreso, at Catedral 1183, the Foreign Ministry trains both Chilean and foreign diplomats at its Academia Diplomática (Diplomatic Academy) in the Renaissance-style **Palacio Edwards** (1888). Designed by architect Juan Eduardo Feherman for Anglo-Chilean banker and publisher Agustín Edwards, who died the year after its completion, it passed through the hands of several heirs, a real estate agency, and a political party before its acquisition by the state, which restored it in the late 1960s.

One block from the southwest corner of the plaza, at Bandera 361, the **Palacio de la Real Aduana** (Royal Customs House) now accommodates the Museo Chileno de Arte Precolombino (Chilean Museum of Pre-Columbian Art; see separate entry below). Immediately across the street and south of the former Congreso, but facing Compañía, stand the neoclassical **Tribunales de Justicia** (Law Courts, 1912–30). Another block west, at Compañía 1340, Chañarcillo mining tycoon Francisco Ignacio Ossa Mercado inhabited the **Palacio La Alhambra** (1862), a Moorish-style structure that now serves as an art gallery and cultural center.

Half a block north of the plaza, on Paseo Puente, the French-style **Cuerpo de Bomberos** (completed in 1893) bears a broad resemblance to the post office. One block north of the plaza, built of massive blocks, the **Templo de Santo Domingo** (begun in 1747, but not finished until 1808) stands at 21 de Mayo and Monjitas; two blocks north, on a lot once known as the "Dominicans' trash dump," stands the **Mercado Central,** the landmark central market that's also a major tourist attraction for its moderately priced seafood restaurants. (See below for more detail.)

From 1913 until 1987, trains to Valparaíso, northern Chile, and Mendoza (Argentina) used Eiffel-influenced architect Emilio Jecquier's monumental **Estación Mapocho;** closed in 1987 and reopened as a cultural center after a competition during Patricio Aylwin's presidency, it hosts major events such as Santiago's annual book fair. In the nearby Cal y Canto Metro station, parts of the foundations of the colonial **Puente Cal y Canto** bridge across the Mapocho have been exposed to view.

Northeast of the Templo de Santo Domingo stand two remaining colonial residences. The mid-18th century **Posada del Corregidor,** Esmeralda 749, is an adobe structure with colonial features such as a corner pillar and balconies but no interior patios. Despite its name, no Spanish colonial official ever worked or lived within; for nearly a century after 1830, it went by the ironic nickname "Filarmónica" because of the dance hall that operated within its walls. At Santo Domingo and MacIver stands the **Casa Manso de Velasco** (1730), named for José Manso de Velasco, governor of Chile (1737–44) and later Viceroy of Peru.

Museo Histórico Nacional (Palacio de la Real Audiencia)

After 1609, the Real Audiencia served as Chile's colonial supreme court, but earthquakes destroyed its quarters in both 1647 and 1730. Architect Juan José de Goycolea y Zañartu designed the current neoclassical building, which opened in 1808, but its clocktower owes its presence to the late 19th-century Francophile Mayor Benjamín Vicuña Mackenna.

Only three years later, during the wars of independence, the first Congreso Nacional met here, but royalist General Manuel Osorio reestablished Spanish authority and restored the Real Audiencia 1814–17. After the battle of Chacabuco in February of that year, the Cabildo of Santiago met here to make Argentine General José de San Martín the head of state, but San Martín declined in favor of Bernardo O'Higgins. The building served as the seat of government until President Manuel Bulnes moved executive offices to the Casa de la Moneda, after which it served successively as the Intendencia de Santiago (1847–1929) and as part of the post office until 1978, when it became a museum.

Having undergone a professional makeover, the once-moribund museum deserves a visit. Thematically, its collections encompass Mapuche silverwork, colonial and republican furniture and art, material folklore, numismatics, textiles, weapons, and photography. Chronologically, its numerous exhibits trace the development of Chile from its indigenous roots through the Spanish invasion, the subsequent establishment of church and state, colonial times and the collapse of the Spanish empire, the early republic and its 19th-century territorial expansion, the oligarchy that ruled parliament, and the failed efforts at reform that resulted in the coup of 1973—when the story abruptly ends.

Also hosting occasional special exhibits, the museum is at Plaza de Armas 951, tel. 2/6330462. Hours are 10 A.M.–5:30 P.M. daily except Monday; admission costs US$1 except for Sunday, when it's free. A specialized library is open 10 A.M.–1:30 P.M. and 3–5:30 P.M. weekdays except Monday.

SANTIAGO

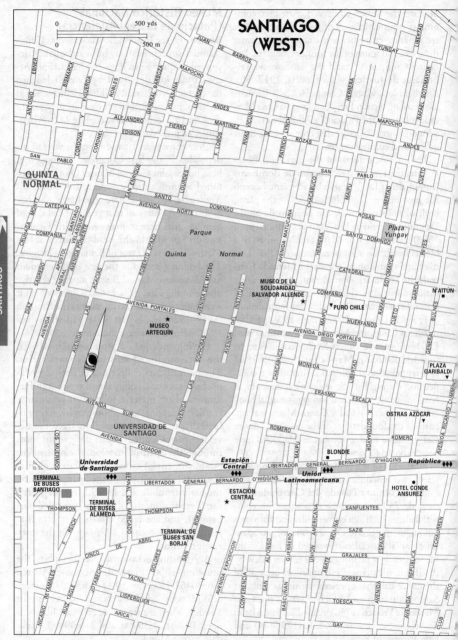

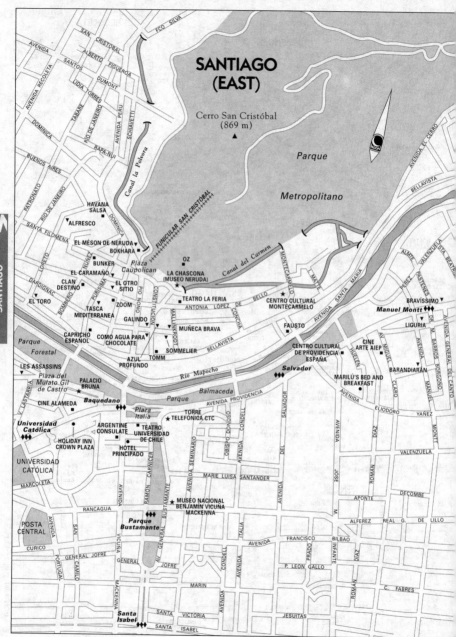

SANTIAGO
(EAST)

Cerro San Cristóbal
(869 m)

Parque

Metropolitano

Parque

Parque
Forestal

Museo de Santiago

Possibly Santiago's best-preserved colonial house, the Casa Colorada was home to Mateo de Toro y Zambrano, who became Chile's interim governor, at age 83, after the resignation of the colonial governor in 1810 (Toro y Zambrano died the following year). Named for its reddish paint, it hosted both José de San Martín and Bernardo O'Higgins after the battle of Chacabuco (1817), and the famous mercenary Lord Cochrane later lived here. For many years, various businesses occupied the building, and only after 1977 did restoration begin with its expropriation by municipal authorities.

While the Casa Colorada's style is true to colonial times, only the two-story facade facing Merced is truly original, distinguished by its forged iron balconies. Behind the Casa Colorada, during the construction of a parking garage, archaeologists discovered a new site with pre-Hispanic artifacts, bone fragments, clay vessels, and even a colonial sewage system, but the private property development has taken precedence.

The museum itself makes an outstanding effort at chronicling the city's development from its pre-Hispanic origins in the Mapocho valley through its founding by Pedro de Valdivia, the evolution of colonial society and the political events that resulted in independence, and its transformation into a modern city under the leadership of Benjamín Vicuña Mackenna. It is particularly vivid in the models of historic buildings and dioramas of events such as the fire that destroyed the Iglesia de la Compañía in 1863.

The Museo de Santiago, Merced 860, tel. 2/6330723, is open 10 A.M.–6 P.M. weekdays except Monday, 10 A.M.–5 P.M. Saturday, and 11 A.M.–2 P.M. Sunday and holidays. Admission costs US$1. The municipal tourist office has its main public branch here as well.

Museo Chileno de Arte Precolombino

Chilean architect and collector Sergio Larraín García-Moreno donated more than 50 years' worth of acquisitions to a private family foundation to create this exceptional museum in the former Real Casa de Aduana (Royal Customs House), a neoclassical late colonial structure only a block west of the Plaza de Armas.

After Chilean independence, only a few years after the building's completion in 1805, it became the Biblioteca Nacional (National Library) and then the Tribunales de Justicia (Law Courts) until a 1968 fire destroyed most of its interior and archives. The two-story structure has twin patios separated by a broad staircase that climbs to the second-floor exhibition halls.

The permanent collections from Mesoamerica (Mexico and Central America) and the Central and Southern Andes are large and impressive; there are smaller displays on the Caribbean, the Amazon, and on Andean textiles. Particularly impressive are the carved wooden *chemamull,* larger-than-life-sized funerary statues that one might call the "*moai* of the Mapuche." The museum also possesses Aguateca's Stele 6, from a Late Classic Maya site in Guatemala's Petén lowlands that's suffered more than its share of depredations.

Operated by the founder's heirs' Fundación Familia Larraín Echenique, the Museo Chileno de Arte Precolombino, Bandera 361, tel. 2/6887348, is open 10 A.M.–6 P.M. Tuesday to Saturday, 10 A.M.–2 P.M. Sunday and holidays; it closes during Semana Santa (Holy Week) and on May 1, September 18, Christmas, and New Year's Eve. Admission costs US$2.50, but it is free for students and children, and for everyone on Sunday.

Mercado Central

In 1817, Bernardo O'Higgins himself shifted the disorderly market on the south side of the Plaza de Armas to an area once known as "the Dominican garbage dump" on the south bank of the Mapocho, just a few blocks to the north. When the informal market installations on the newly designated Plaza de Abasto burned to the ground in 1864, municipal authorities hired Manuel Aldunate to create more permanent facilities, but the current structure (1872) is largely the work of Fermín Vivaceta.

Shop additions fronting on the street have concealed the original facade except where the building faces the river, on Ismael Valdés Vergara; there are entrances, however, on San Pablo, Paseo Puente, and 21 de Mayo. From the interior, the handsome wrought-iron superstructure, embellished with the recurring lone star from the Chilean flag, provides an airy setting for merchants to display their fresh fruit, vegetables, and seafood—in the words of food and travel writer Robb Walsh:

a display of fishes and shellfish so vast and unfamiliar that I felt I was observing the marine life of another planet.

Lunching and people-watching at tables set among the piles of produce has become a popular tourist pastime, but many Santiaguinos enjoy the market just as much as foreigners. Note, however, that the smallish restaurants on the periphery are cheaper and nearly as good as the two or three that have the monopoly on the prime sites beneath the high ceilings.

BARRIO CÍVICO AND VICINITY

Straddling the Alameda, several blocks southwest of the Plaza de Armas, the Barrio Cívico is the country's political and administrative center. Facing the **Plaza de la República,** the recently repainted, late-colonial Palacio de la Moneda (see below) is the locus of presidential authority, though the chief executive no longer resides in the building. At 10 A.M. on even-numbered days, the Carabineros' presidential guard holds a changing-of-the-guard ceremony on the plaza.

In a development that rankles General Pinochet's diehard supporters, a dignified statue of former President Salvador Allende now stands at the plaza's southeast corner, with a plaque inscribed with words from his last radio address: "I have faith in Chile and her destiny," September 11, 1973.

Several major public buildings occupy the vicinity. On the west side of Plaza de la Constitución, at Teatinos 120, the sturdily elegant doors of the **Ministerio de Hacienda** (1933) seemingly signify the solidity of the Chilean treasury. **Codelco,** arguably the government's single most powerful agency for its control of the copper industry, has its headquarters at Paseo Huérfanos 1276.

At Moneda and Morandé, the **Intendencia de Santiago** (1914–16) features an attractive corner entrance and a spectacular interior cupola. Today, ironically enough, it houses regional government offices in a building that was the headquarters of *El Diario Ilustrado,* a newspaper founded by the Partido Conservador (Conservative Party)—and a persistent critic of various administrations to occupy the Moneda. The government of Carlos Ibáñez del Campo acquired it in 1928, barely a decade after its completion.

One block east of the plaza, Augustine nuns owned the entire block bounded by Bandera, Ahumada, Moneda, and Alameda until the early 20th century, when they subdivided some of Santiago's most valuable real estate, keeping only the mid-19th-century **Iglesia de las Agustinas** (restored in 1994), which fronts on Moneda itself and replaced earlier temples destroyed by earthquakes. Mammon supplanted Jehovah with construction of the flatiron-style **Bolsa de Comercio** (1917), La Bolsa 84, designed by French architect Emilio Jecquier and begun in 1914, but delayed when World War I disrupted the arrival of materials from New York. Immediately to its south, fronting on the Alameda but reached by a cobbled Y-pattern passageway, Alberto Cruz Montt designed the members-only **Club de la Unión** (1925) to give the stockbrokers a place to schmooze on their lunch hours.

Immediately south of the Moneda, **Plaza de la Libertad** looks across the Alameda to the **Altar de la Patria,** whose eternal flame tops the sepulcher of Chilean liberator General Bernardo O'Higgins. One block west, at Alameda and Amunátegui, the 128-meter **Torre Entel** (1976) communications tower is a more contemporary landmark.

Palacio de la Moneda

Never intended as the seat of government, the neoclassical Palacio de la Moneda only became the presidential palace in 1846, when Manuel Bulnes moved his residence and executive offices to the former colonial mint. The Moneda made global headlines in 1973, when the Chilean air force strafed and bombed it in General Pinochet's coup against constitutional President Salvador Allende who, faced with surrender, shot himself to death before he could be taken prisoner.

© WAYNE BERNHARDSON

Palacio de la Moneda, Barrio Civico

Around 1730, in the midst of an economic depression, the Cabildo de Santiago requested the Spanish crown to establish a local mint but Madrid, itself short of resources, designated Spanish businessman Francisco García Huidobro as treasurer of a mint at Huérfanos and Morandé—perhaps one of the earliest privatizations on record. Its first gold coin bore the image of King Fernando VI.

After García Huidobro's death, the mint moved to a former Jesuit school alongside the Iglesia de la Compañía, but when that proved inadequate, Governor Agustín Jáuregui proposed a purpose-built mint in 1780 under the direction of Italian architect Joaquín Toesca. Begun in 1784, its cement came from Hacienda Polpaico (north of Santiago and still a functioning factory today), sand from the Río Maipo, colored stone from a quarry on Cerro San Cristóbal, and oak and cypress from Chile's own Valdivian forests. Details such as forged iron came from Spain. Toesca, unfortunately, died six years before its completion in 1805.

> *The Moneda made global headlines in 1973, when the Chilean air force strafed and bombed it in General Pinochet's coup against constitutional President Salvador Allende who, faced with surrender, shot himself to death before he could be taken prisoner.*

After the air attacks of 1973, the Pinochet dictatorship restored the building to Toesca's original dignified design by 1981, but the building is no longer the presidential residence. Ricardo Lagos, the first Socialist president to be elected since Allende, has opened the building's main passageway to the public for one-way traffic from the main entrance on Plaza de la Constitución to the exit on Plaza de la Libertad, from 10 A.M.–6 P.M. weekdays only. While the orange trees on its interior Patio de los Naranjos have withered, visitors on a walk-through can enjoy sculptures such as Roberto Matta's *El Toromiro* (named for a tree now extinct on its native Easter Island) and Hernán Puelma's *El Astrónomo* (The Astronomer).

For a longer guided tour of the interior, visit the Dirección Administrativa del Palacio de la Moneda at its office beneath Plaza de la Constitución, entered from Morandé, tel. 2/6714103. Theoretically, it takes nearly three weeks to arrange such visits, but an in-person request can accelerate the process. Intending visitors must show their passports and fill out a short *Solicitud de Visita Palacio de la Moneda* (Request to Visit the Moneda Palace).

CERRO SANTA LUCÍA AND VICINITY

East of Paseo Ahumada and north of the Alameda, the promontory that the Mapuche called Cerro Welén was the place where Pedro de Valdivia held out against the indigenous forces that threatened to expel the Spaniards from the valley of the Río Mapocho. Nearly three centuries later, in 1822, Maria Graham marveled at the view:

From Santa Lucía we discovered the whole plain of Santiago to the Cuesta de Prado, the plain of Maypu stretching even to the horizon, the snowy Cordillera, and beneath our feet the city, its garden, churches and its magnificent bridge all lit up by the rays of the setting sun . . . what pen or pencil can impart a thousandth part of the sublime beauty of sunset on the Andes?

In the winter of 1834, Darwin seconded Mrs. Graham's opinion in a more matter-of-fact manner:

It is an inexhaustible source of pleasure to climb Cerro Santa Lucía, a small hill that rises up in the center of the city, from which the view is truly impressive and unique.

It took Benjamín Vicuña Mackenna to bring Santa Lucía's potential to fruition, as his efforts—along with donations from wealthy citizens and

© WAYNE BERNHARDSON

view of the Andean front range from Cerro Santa Lucía

convict labor—transformed a barren quarry into an urban beauty spot with more than 60 hectares of gardens, fountains, and statuary. Vicuña Mackenna's own tomb is the **Capilla La Ermita**, a tiny chapel just beneath the 629-meter summit, 69 meters above the streets below.

From the summit, approached by any number of meandering footpaths and reached by a final steep climb to a tiny parapet, there are stupendous views of the Andes to the east—at least on a rare clear day—as well as panoramic views of the city and Cerro San Cristóbal. A lower but broader terrace offers less panoramic but almost equally impressive views toward Providencia and the Andes.

Royalist forces built **Fuerte Hidalgo** (1816), toward the north end of the park, to defend the city from Chilean revolutionary forces. On its lower northeastern slope, along Victoria Subercaseaux, the recently created **Jardín Japonés** (Japanese Garden) is a noteworthy addition; along the Alameda, look for the inscription of Pedro de Valdivia's letter to the king and the tile mural of Nobel Prize poet Gabriela Mistral.

Fenced except around its lowest periphery and steepest slope, Cerro Santa Lucía has two main entrances: from the Alameda just east of Plaza Vicuña Mackenna, where twin staircases climb around the fountains of **Plaza Neptuno,** and by a cobbled road from the east end of Agustinas. There is also a modern glass *ascensor* or elevator, at the east end of Huérfanos, that is often out of service for lack of personnel (authorities apparently do not trust the citizenry to press buttons on their own). In an exaggerated attempt to improve security, they now require all visitors to sign in (as if muggers would do so), but the park is not really a dangerous place.

Hours are 9 A.M.–8 P.M. daily, but the best introduction to the park is a guided tour (English and Spanish) that starts from its municipal tourist office branch at 11 A.M. every Thursday and visits most of the main sights. These include Vicuña Mackenna's tomb and the still-functioning gun emplacement (several years ago, authorities halted the customary weekday noon cannon shot because of neighbors' complaints, but broader public pressure restored the tradition at a lower decibel level).

Between Cerro Santa Lucía and Paseo Ahuma-

da are several landmarks of mostly republican vintage. The most imposing is the magnificent classicist **Biblioteca Nacional** (National Library, 1914–27) on the Alameda between MacIver and Miraflores; built on the site of a former nunnery, it also houses the **Archivo Nacional** (National Archive). Two blocks north, the ornate **Teatro Municipal** (Municipal Theater, 1857) was the work of a team of architects headed by the Frenchman Francisco Brunet des Baines; despite a series of fires and earthquakes, it retains most of its original neoclassical features. High-culture figures who have performed here include Sarah Bernhardt, Igor Stravinsky, Plácido Domingo, Anna Pavlova, and the Chilean classical pianist Claudio Arrau.

One block west, at Agustinas and Estado, the once baroque **Templo de San Agustín** (1784) fell on hard times during the early republican years, its convent even used as military barracks, until architect Fermín Vivaceta salvaged it with a more contemporary facade, which survives to the present, in 1863.

BARRIO PARÍS LONDRES AND VICINITY

South of the Alameda, Santiago Centro's major landmark is the early colonial **Iglesia y Convento de San Francisco** (1618), Alameda 834, Chile's oldest colonial building and one of the few structures of its vintage to survive the capital's repeated fires and earthquakes; the church's former convent is also home to the incompletely named **Museo de Arte Colonial,** a collection of entirely ecclesiastical colonial art (see below).

Until the early 1920s, the Franciscan congregation controlled much of this area, but a financial crisis and the pressures of Santiago's expansion forced it to sell 30,000 square meters of land to developer Walter Lihn. Lihn demolished the Franciscan school, refectory, second cloister, several patios, and its gardens, but architects Roberto Araya and Ernesto Holzmann broke the city's rigid grid pattern to create an intimate neighborhood of meandering cobbled streets on the medievalist principles of Austrian architect Camilo Sitte.

Betraying the neighborhood's legacy, the house at **Londres 38** was a detention and torture center during the Pinochet dictatorship. Two blocks west of Iglesia San Francisco, the **Casa Central de la Universidad de Chile** (1863–72), the main campus of the state university, stretches along the Alameda. Several blocks south, Ricardo Larraín Bravo designed the **Basílica Los Sacramentinos,** Arturo Prat 471, after Paris's Eglise de Sacre Coeur. The 1985 earthquake caused damage that still awaits repair.

Iglesia y Convento de San Francisco

Pedro de Valdivia himself established the Ermita del Socorro to house the image of the Virgen del Socorro that he brought along to Chile—and to which he credited the Spaniards' survival from Mapuche attacks. In 1554, in exchange for 12 city lots, the Franciscan order built a church to house the image, but an earthquake destroyed the original church in 1583. After finishing the present church—today the country's oldest surviving colonial building—in 1618, they built a pair of cloisters for their monks and gradually added patios, gardens, a refectory, and other structures. The original towers toppled as a result of earthquakes in 1643 and 1751, but Fermín Vivaceta's 19th-century clock tower has managed to withstand every shock since. The church's interior is notable for its Mudéjar details and carved cypress doors.

For nearly 4.5 centuries, the Franciscans have kept faith with Valdivia by continuing to host the Virgen del Socorro. In addition, their **Museo de Arte Colonial** boasts a collection of 42 separate canvases, representing the life of St. Francis of Assisi, from the Cuzco school of the second half of the 17th century. A later wall-sized painting chronicles the lineage of the Franciscans and their patrons.

The Museo de Arte Colonial, Londres 4, tel. 2/6398737, is open 10 A.M.–1:30 P.M. and 3–6 P.M. Tuesday to Saturday, 10 A.M.–2 P.M. Sunday and holidays. Admission is US$1 for adults, US$.50 for children.

BARRIO LASTARRIA AND VICINITY

East of Cerro Santa Lucía, comprising most of the triangle also bounded by Parque Forestal on the north and the Alameda on the south, Barrio Lastarria is a neighborhood of narrow streets and cul-de-sacs that's also home to several intimate restaurants and bars.

The barrio's main axis is its namesake street José Victorino Lastarria, where the **Plaza del Mulato Gil de Castro** is an adaptive reuse that combined several early 20th-century buildings into a commercial/cultural cluster that features two noteworthy museums: the **Museo Arqueológico de Santiago** and the eye-catching new **Museo de Artes Visuales.** The block of Lastarria between Rosal and Merced has been converted into an attractive new pedestrian mall, but neighborhood residents resisted any further street closures because of concern the area would become a Bellavista-style nightlife scene.

One long block east, originally built for a nitrate baron at Merced and Estados Unidos, the Italian Renaissance **Palacio Bruna** (1916–21) soon became the U.S. ambassador's residence; it later served as the consulate, until the Colossus of the North built its pharaonic new embassy in Las Condes.

To the immediate north, the Mapocho's banks and floodplain were home to slums and rubbish dumps until the early 20th century, when Mayor Enrique Cousiño redeveloped it as the **Parque Forestal,** which stretches from the Estación Mapocho on the west to the Pío Nono bridge on the east. Shaded with mature trees and dotted with statues and fountains, it's a verdant refuge from the midday summer heat.

Toward the west, directly north of Cerro Santa Lucía, stands the Palacio de Bellas Artes, the city's traditional fine arts museum. South of the Plaza del Mulato Gil, at Lastarria 124, the neoclassical **Iglesia de la Vera Cruz** (1858) is the neighborhood church and a national monument designed by French architect Brunet des Baines.

On the north side of the Alameda, east of Lastarria proper, the modern **Edificio Diego Portales** served as the Pinochet dictatorship's seat of government when the air force's bombing and strafing left the Palacio de la Moneda unusable for eight years; it now serves as offices and an events center. Just across the Alameda, toward downtown, is the central campus of the **Universidad**

Católica (1913), which has several other locales in Gran Santiago.

Museo Arqueológico de Santiago

With its excellent but almost unchanging exhibits on Chile's indigenous peoples from colonial times to the present, Santiago's deceptively named archaeological museum—"ethnohistorical" would be more accurate—is worthwhile for first-time visitors only. The presentation is professional, even if the accompanying text seems annoyingly patronizing to the peoples whose past it presumes to chronicle.

The Museo Arqueológico, within the Plaza del Mulato Gil de Castro complex at Lastarria 321, tel. 2/6383502, is open 10:30 A.M.–2 P.M. daily except Sunday, 3:30–7 P.M. weekdays only. Admission is free.

Museo de Artes Visuales

With a permanent collection of 650 pieces by 250 different contemporary Chilean artists, among them Roberto Matta and Alfredo Jaar, Santiago's new visual arts museum opened in early 2001. About 140 of these pieces, in media as diverse as engravings, paintings, photographs, and sculptures, are on display at any one time in half a dozen spacious rooms with high ceilings and polished wooden floors. Flawless lighting accentuates each piece's individual qualities.

Architect Cristián Undurraga's design incorporates 1,400 square meters of display space. The English translations are better than at some Chilean museums, but a reliance on cognates makes some of them a bit vague. Museum directors also anticipate occasional special exhibitions.

Privately owned and financed, the Museo de Artes Visuales, Lastarria 305 in the Plaza del Mulato Gil complex, tel. 2/6649397, is open 10:30 A.M.–6:30 P.M. daily except Monday. Admission costs US$1.50 for adults, half that for children 8–to 12. Children under eight get in free. There is also a good museum shop.

Palacio de Bellas Artes

Built for the centennial of Chile's independence and fashioned after Paris's Petit Palais, Santiago's neoclassical fine arts museum is the pride of Parque Forestal. Its collections vary from colonial and religious art to nearly contemporary figurative and abstract works by artists such as José Gil de Castro, Pedro Lira, and the still-living Roberto Matta and Roser Bru. It also has a sample of French, Italian, and Dutch painting, and frequent prestigious special exhibits.

While Bellas Artes is a traditional museum, it has managed to adapt to the contemporary art world. A new website (www.mnba.cl) is to make the works of 2,000 Chilean artists accessible to the world in a "museum without walls."

The Museo de Bellas Artes, José Miguel de La Barra s/n, tel. 2/6330655, is open 11 A.M.–8 P.M. Tuesday to Saturday, 11 A.M.–7 P.M. Sunday and holidays from December through March; the rest of the year, hours are 10 A.M.–7 P.M. Tuesday to Saturday, 10 A.M.–6 P.M. Sunday and holidays. Admission costs US$1, but it is free on Sunday; children pay half.

BARRIO BRASIL AND VICINITY

West of the Vía Norte Sur, Barrio Brasil was a prestigious early 20th-century residential area that fell upon hard times with the modernization of Providencia and Las Condes, but it has made a major comeback in the past several years without losing its character. The best way to approach the barrio is the new Huérfanos pedestrian suspension bridge that crosses the Vía Norte Sur to an area where recently constituted private universities—in some ways a controversial legacy of the Pinochet years—have rehabbed buildings, salvaged libraries, built collections, and introduced a youthful vigor. It's also a good area for moderately priced accommodations and restaurants.

The barrio's focus is its lovingly landscaped namesake **Plaza Brasil,** bounded by Avenida Brasil, Compañía, Maturana, and Huérfanos. Its most impressive single landmark may be the neo-Gothic **Basílica del Salvador** (1892), Huérfanos 1781, if only because it's still standing after the 1985 earthquake (see below for more detail). Many other buildings are of interest, but the hands-down most idiosyncratic is the **Club Colo Colo** (1926), Cienfuegos 41, an erstwhile private residence whose grinning gargoyles and smiling skulls, jutting from its facade, never fail to attract attention. It now houses the business offices of Chile's most famous soccer team.

On Santiago Centro's western edge, beyond Barrio Brasil proper, the Parque Quinta Normal is a welcome respite from a densely built area and is also home to several museums. The area's other main attraction is the recently relocated **Museo de la Solidaridad Salvador Allende,** a modern art collection and cultural center that occupies the former **Escuela Normal No. 1 de Niñas** (Girls' Normal School), a national monument at Herrera 360.

Basílica del Salvador

After the Jesuit Iglesia de la Compañía burned to the ground in 1863, Archbishop Rafael Valdivieso decreed what became one of the city's longest ongoing construction projects—it took seven years to lay the cornerstone, three more to start building in earnest, and 19 more before its formal inauguration in 1892. Now a national monument, the massive church could hold 5,000 worshippers in an area 89 meters long, 37 meters wide, and 30 meters high.

Elevated to basílica status in 1938 by Pius XI, the neo-Gothic structure also contains murals by Aristódemo Lattanza Borghini, bronzes by Virginio Arias, and altars and altarpieces by Onofre Jarpa. Large sections of the building tumbled in the 7.8 earthquake of March 1985, however, and reinforced concrete columns have replaced some of the finely decorated originals. Rigid metal buttresses support some of the exterior walls as well, and restoring the basílica will be a long and expensive process–presuming no further earthquakes. Its main entrance is at Huérfanos 1781.

Parque Quinta Normal

At the western edge of Santiago Centro, Parque Quinta Normal is a traditional open space whose 40 or so hectares constituted the city's first de facto botanical garden, sporting both native and exotic tree species. It also provides Santiaguinos with playgrounds, soccer fields, tennis courts, skating rinks, and pools, along with a cluster of museums.

The park's most notable museum is the **Museo Nacional de Historia Natural** (Natural History Museum), a research facility that also has public exhibits on archaeology, ethnography, physical anthropology, mineralogy, paleontology, botany, and zoology. Dating from 1830, when the Chilean government contracted the French naturalist Claude Gay to make an inventory of the country's natural resources, the Museo de Historia Natural, tel. 2/6814095, is open 10 A.M.–5:30 P.M. Tuesday to Saturday all year; Sunday hours are 11 A.M.–6:30 P.M. September to March, noon–5:30 P.M. the rest of the year. Admission costs US$1 for adults, US$.50 for kids, but is free on Sunday and holidays, though it's closed January 1, Easter Sunday, May 1, September 18–19, November 1, and December 25.

A private concessionaire operates three additional museums. The interactive **Museo de Ciencia y Tecnología** (Mucytec), tel. 2/6816022, is open 10 A.M.–5:30 P.M. Tuesday to Friday and 11 A.M.–6 P.M. weekends and holidays. Admission costs US$1 for adults, slightly less for children.

Trainspotters will enjoy the **Museo Parque Ferroviario,** tel. 2/6814627, with more than a baker's dozen of antique locomotives, additional railcars, and an audiovisual salon. It's open 10 A.M.–5:30 P.M. Tuesday to Friday all year; weekend and holiday hours are 11 A.M.–7 P.M. in summer, 11 A.M.–5:30 P.M. the rest of the year. Admission costs US$1.20 for adults, half that for children.

The **Museo Infantil,** tel. 2/6818808, is more oriented toward groups of schoolchildren and requires reservations. It's open 9:30 A.M.–5 P.M. weekdays only; admission costs US$1.

Parque Quinta Normal's main entrance is on Matucana at the west end of Compañía, but there are additional gateways on Avenida Portales, Santo Domingo, and Apostól Santiago; the nearest Metro station is Estación Central. Grounds are open 8 A.M.–8:30 P.M. daily except Monday.

Museo de la Solidaridad Salvador Allende

Created in 1971 with donations from artists throughout the Americas and Europe who identified with Chile's Marxist experiment, this contemporary art museum contains more than 1,500 works from the 1950s through the 1980s. Among the artists represented are Roberto Matta, Joan Miró, Alexander Calder, Diego Rivera, and other famous figures.

Despite the artists' personal leftist sympathies, few of those works are explicitly political, though the initial collection spent 17 years of military dictatorship in anonymous storage. After the return to representative government, the founders came out of hiding to form the Fundación Salvador Allende, and the collections made their debut in Parque Forestal's Museo de Bellas Artes.

Since then, the museum has acquired permanent quarters in the former Escuela Normal No. 1 de Niñas (Girls' Normal School), a national monument at Herrera 360, tel. 2/6817542, near Parque Quinta Normal. It's open 10 A.M.–7 P.M. daily except Monday; admission is free. The Fundación Salvador Allende also operates the Centro Cultural Salvador Allende.

OTHER SANTIAGO CENTRO SIGHTS

While most downtown sights are fairly central, a handful are scattered elsewhere.

Palacio Cousiño

South of the Alameda, 19th-century Calle Dieciocho was once an aristocratic area of Parisian-style mansions, long before the oligarchy moved to the eastern suburbs. One of its keystone families was the Cousiños, originally Portuguese immigrants who made their money in wine and mining.

Funds for the Palacio Cousiño, completed in 1878, came from the estate of Luis Cousiño, an art collector whose wealth derived from his father Matías's Chañarcillo silver fortune (Luis Cousiño died unexpectedly in 1873, at age 38, but his widow Isidora Goyenechea was the force behind the house's construction). Architect Paul Lauthoud, also responsible for the Museo de Historia Natural in Parque Quinta Normal, designed the three-story house with marble staircases, a music hall, winter garden, and even a one-person elevator, the country's first.

Decorative touches included baroque cabinets made for the Russian czar Nicholas II and freestanding Ming vases. Spanish landscape architect Miguel Arana Bórica fashioned extensive formal gardens, but the city's subsequent development has steamrolled most of them. The Palacio Cousiño remained in family hands until 1941, when the city bought it for a museum but also used it as a guesthouse for high-profile visitors such as Charles DeGaulle, Marshal Tito, and Golda Meir. A fire destroyed the third-floor interior and prevented Queen Elizabeth II of England from spending the night on her state visit in 1968.

The *palacio* is at Dieciocho 438, tel. 2/6985063, near the Toesca Metro station. Hours are 9:30 A.M.–1:30 P.M. daily except Monday and 2:30–5 P.M. Tuesday to Friday only. Admission, including guided tours in Spanish or English, costs US$2.25 for adults, US$.75 for children. Photographers and videographers may shoot the gardens and exterior of the Palacio Cousiño, but not the interior.

Parque O'Higgins

As Mayor Benjamín Vicuña Mackenna used his influence as a public official to transform Cerro Santa Lucía into a stunning city park, Luis Cousiño used private resources to turn barren southwestern Santiago into a pastoral showcase— but at a price. What is today Parque O'Higgins had its origins as "La Pampilla," an area of truck gardens and military parade ground where, in mid-September, Chileans of all social classes gathered to celebrate their patriotic holidays.

Cousiño admired Europe's great public parks and, after acquiring 90-plus hectares in 1870, proposed donating it to the city. He hired Spanish landscaper Miguel Arana Bórica to turn the wasteland into an urban woodland, but Cousiño died in 1873, well before its completion. When the 80 Chilean laborers hired for the project had to go to war in the north, 140 Peruvian prisoners of the conflict took their places.

Vicuña Mackenna named the final product after its late benefactor, but the improvements created an unspoken but very real social segregation in a place that once belonged to all

Chileans. It reached its peak around the centenary of Chilean independence, in 1910, when the procession of elegant horse-drawn carriages led one observer to remark that:

Not in London's Hyde Park, New York's Central Park, nor Buenos Aires' Palermo would you find better presented teams than those that parade through Parque Cousiño.

The park's development stimulated construction of graceful mansions in what became a garden barrio, but the arrival of the automobile contributed to an eastward movement into the open spaces of Providencia and Ñuñoa in the years before and after World War II. As the elite moved out, the area declined economically—and the park along with it—but it was once again accessible to working-class Chileans whose forebears had celebrated their country's holidays here.

In the early 1970s, the park's name was changed in favor of Chile's independence hero, it was fenced, and new developments ate into its green spaces—the park has shrunk from an original 91.7 hectares to only 76.7. Parts of it are still rundown, but it remains a favorite weekend outing for local families who can't get out of the capital.

Harking back to the days of La Pampilla, but dating from the 1970s, the park's **El Pueblito** village recreates a vision (if stereotyped) of 19th-century agrarian Chile, as do the menus of its inexpensive *picadas*. It also has three museums: the folkloric **Museo del Huaso,** tel. 2/5550054, which pays homage to Chile's traditional horsemen, is open 8:30 A.M.–5 P.M. weekdays, 10 A.M.–2 P.M. weekends. The others, both open 10 A.M.–8 P.M. daily, are the **Museo Acuario** (Municipal Aquarium), tel. 2/5565680, and the **Museo de Insectas y Caracoles** (Museum of Insects and Snails), also tel. 2/5565680.

Also on the park grounds, the children's theme park **Fantasilandia,** tel. 2/6893035, keeps summer hours of 2–8 P.M. except Monday and 11 A.M.–8 P.M. weekends and holidays. The rest of the year, it's open 11 A.M.–8 P.M. weekends and holidays only. General admission, including unlimited rides, is US$7 pp, but children shorter than 140 centimeters get a small discount.

Just west of the Vía Norte Sur, Parque O'Higgins is a short walk from its namesake Metro station, on Línea 2.

Club Hípico

Immediately west of Parque O'Higgins, the more exclusive of Santiago's two major racetracks dates from 1870, when it marked a major social change—discarding the Chilean custom of linear racing, riders would now steer their mounts around an oval track. Like an outing in Parque Cousiño, horse racing became a privilege of the elite rather than a pastime of the peasantry.

Today much of that has changed—the windows accept bets from anyone with cash to place them—but the elegance of architect Josué Smith Solar's Francophile design, based upon the Bois de Boulogne's Longchamps track, has survived. A fire destroyed the original club and grandstands in 1892, but Smith's replacement (1918), surrounded by Guillermo Renée's French Baroque gardens, accentuated the views across the track to the Andean front range.

Races at Club Hípico, Avenida Blanco Encalada 2540, tel. 2/6939600, usually take place Monday and Thursday, but there are also occasional Sunday events. It is walking distance from the Unión Latinoamericana and República Metro stations.

ESTACIÓN CENTRAL

West of Santiago Centro, the *comuna* of Estación Central is partly residential and partly industrial, most notable as a transit point because the city's train and bus stations are here. The *comuna* takes its name from the **Estación Central** (1897), Alameda 3322, the late 19th-century train station built in Paris on a design by the famous Gustav Eiffel. Shipped in pieces across the Atlantic, it was first proposed in 1885 by then-Senator Benjamín Vicuña Mackenna.

Directly across from the station, the **Planetario de la Universidad de Santiago,** Alameda 3349, tel. 2/6812171, is part of the campus of the Universidad de Santiago. While light-polluted Santiago is not the best place in the country to view the night skies (see the Norte Chico and Norte Grande chapters for alternatives) the audiovisual shows at the Planetario can simulate Chile's astronomical sophistication. These take place daily at 3:30 P.M. and cost about US$3 for adults, US$2 for children ages 3–10; there are also special entertainment-oriented shows such as tributes to Pink Floyd and similar rock groups.

Directly across the street from Parque Quinta Normal, the **Museo Artequín,** Avenida Portales 3530, tel. 2/6818687, is an interactive art museum that deals exclusively in reproductions of (mostly) European art; the building itself, built for the Paris Exhibition of 1889, then dismantled and shipped across the Pacific to be erected here, is really more interesting than the family-oriented exhibits themselves. It's open 9 A.M.–5 P.M. Tuesday to Friday, 11 A.M.–6 P.M. weekends and holidays. Admission is free, but donations are accepted.

PROVIDENCIA AND VICINITY

At the eastern end of the Alameda, **Plaza Italia** (formally known as Plaza Baquedano) is one of the main hubs of activity in the entire city. It also marks the western boundary of the *comuna* of Providencia, the westernmost of the affluent eastern suburbs that also include Las Condes, Vitacura, and Ñuñoa. While this is a mostly staid, middle-class to upper middle-class area and home to modern shopping malls that look like something straight out of the San Fernando Valley, it has Bohemian enclaves such as Barrio Bellavista (the city's main restaurant and nightlife area) and barhopper neighborhoods such as Avenida Suecia. Except in compact Bellavista, points of interest in this area are generally more spread out than in Santiago Centro, but two Metro lines and many bus lines make public transportation convenient.

From Plaza Italia, the northbound Puente Pío Nono (Pío Nono Bridge) crosses the Mapocho to Barrio Bellavista (see below for more detail). The area's single most conspicuous landmark, at Avenida Providencia 111, is the 31-story **Torre Telefónica CTC,** the company headquarters in the form of a 140-meter cell phone! While the

company's architectural aesthetic may be open to question, its **Sala de Arte Telefónica,** tel. 2/6812873, is open 10 A.M.–8 P.M. daily with rotating exhibits of notable Chilean and foreign artists. Admission is free.

South of Plaza Italia, Avenida Vicuña Mackenna is the dividing line between the *comunas* of Santiago Centro, on the one hand, and Providencia and Ñuñoa, on the other. On the Providencia side, the **Museo Nacional Benjamín Vicuña Mackenna,** Avenida Vicuña Mackenna 94, tel. 2/2229642, honors the mayor responsible for the capital's modernization in the 1870s; he was also a prolific historian and journalist, and diplomat and world traveler. Also equipped with a 10,000-volume research library, the museum is open 9:30 A.M.–1 P.M. and 2–6 P.M. daily except Sunday and Monday; admission costs US$1 for adults, half that for children and seniors.

Also in Providencia, on the north bank of the Mapocho between the Padre Letelier and Pedro de Valdivia bridges, the open-air **Parque de las Esculturas,** Avenida Santa María 2201, tel. 2/3407303, showcases abstract works on the order of Federico Assler's *Conjunto Escultórico* (Sculpture Group), Sergio Castillo's *Erupción* (Eruption), Marta Colvin's *Madre Tierra* (Mother Earth), José Vicente Gajardo's *Sol y Luna* (Sun and Moon), and Osvaldo Peña's *Verde y Viento* (Green and Wind). Open 10 A.M.–7 P.M. daily, it also has a small semiunderground gallery with rotating exhibitions.

The Municipalidad de Providencia offers free open-air bus tours of the *comuna,* visiting the Museo Nacional Benjamín Vicuña Mackenna, Neruda's La Chascona house in Barrio Bellavista, the Parque Metropolitana, and other sights. These leave from Plaza Centenario, Pedro de Valdivia 963, at 10 A.M. in January and February only. For more information, phone tel. 2/3407373 or see the website: www.providencia.cl.

Barrio Bellavista and Vicinity

At the foot of massive Cerro San Cristóbal, compact Bellavista is a walker's delight. In the daytime, Santiaguinos cross the Pío Nono bridge to

North of the Mapocho, the first major landmarks are **Parque Gómez Rojas,** with a weekend crafts market that stretches up the west side of Avenida Pío Nono, and the **Facultad de Derecho de la Universidad de Chile** (law school) to the east. On weekends, **Avenida Pío Nono** itself is a frenetic blend of crafts market, cheap sidewalk restaurants, and beer joints that, while not so bad as that might sound, is less appealing than the barrio's perpendicular and parallel side streets.

To get a notion of Bellavista's best, pass some time on a bench at **Plazuela Camilo Mori,** a small triangular plaza at the corner of Antonia López de Bello and Constitución. Walking north, turn into the cul-de-sac at Márquez de la Plata 0192, where poet Pablo Neruda lived at the house he called La Chascona and which is now the Museo Neruda (see below for more detail). A short walk to the northwest is **Plaza Caupolicán,** the main entry point to Santiago's hillside and hilltop Parque Metropolitano.

On the Recoleta side, at the north end of Avenida La Paz, famous figures from Chile's past, as well as many ordinary Chileans, are among the two million who repose in the **Cementerio General** (General Cemetery), whose imposing frontispiece dates from 1897.

La Chascona (Museo Neruda)

Modest enough from the street side of its cul-de-sac location, Pablo Neruda's hillside house is by no means extravagant—in fact, it may be the most conventional of his three houses (the other two, also open for visits, are in Valparaíso and the central coast community of Isla Negra). Opposite the house, at the end of the block, a small amphitheater tucked into the slope beneath Chucre Manzur is an ideal complement to this national monument, restored since its sacking by the military in 1973 (Neruda, a committed leftist supporter of Salvador Allende, died only about a month after the 1973 coup).

The Fundación Neruda, Márquez de La Plata 0192, tel. 2/7378712, offers guided tours of La Chascona on a drop-in basis, from 10 A.M.–1 P.M. and 3–6 P.M. daily except Monday. Lasting about an hour, tours cost US$2.50 for adults, US$1.25 for children.

contemporary high-rise office buildings in Providencia

© WAYNE BERNHARDSON

stroll its leafy streets, parks, and plazas and enjoy modest lunch specials at some of the city's most innovative restaurants, while at night they crowd the same places for elaborate dinners before a night on the town at its bars, discos, salsa clubs, theaters, and other diversions. Daytime visitors, by the way, may not even realize that this is the nightlife center of the city—most dance clubs, for instance, do not *open* until 1 A.M. or so, and few of them have prominent signs.

While most visitors see Bellavista as a single discrete neighborhood, there is a clear division—Avenida Pío Nono—between the two *comunas* that comprise the barrio, rough-edged Recoleta to the west and the more fashionable Providencia to the east. This is more a matter of style than substance, as security-obsessed Providencia makes more conspicuous efforts to prevent auto burglaries and other petty crime in what is, for the most part, a safe neighborhood. Especially on weekends, crowds are on the street day or night—well into the wee hours.

SANTIAGO

Parque Metropolitano

When Benjamín Vicuña Mackenna envisioned the beautification of Santiago in the 1870s, he thought of Cerro San Cristóbal as well as Cerro Santa Lucía, but he lacked the means to implement his plans on the much larger hill. The idea did not surface again until around 1909, when Mayor Pablo Urzúa began a modest afforestation program, but widespread support developed shortly thereafter under the administration of Ramón Subercaseaux, who expropriated property and built roads and canals. Despite the infrastructural improvements, it did not officially become the 722-hectare Parque Metropolitano until 1966.

From Plaza Caupolicán, the **Funicular San Cristóbal,** built with support from Santiago's Italian community 1922–25, gains 240 meters in elevation en route to its upper terminal at **Terraza Bellavista;** its grade is almost exactly 45 degrees. At the midway point, there's a stop at the city's improved **Jardín Zoológico** (zoo), tel. 2/7776666, which opened about the same time as the funicular. Now emphasizing native fauna such as puma, *pudú, ñandú,* and the like, it's open 10 A.M.–6 P.M. daily except Monday; admission costs US$3 for adults, US$1 for children.

Above Terraza Bellavista, a 14-meter statue of the Virgin Mary with an armspan of 10 meters, atop an eight-meter pedestal, towers over the amphitheater of the **Santuario Inmaculada Concepción,** which owes its own conception to the 50th anniversary of the papal declaration of that particular dogma. Workers placed the cornerstone for the Paris-built statue, designed by the Italian sculptor Jacometti and based on a similar work in Rome's Plaza de España, in 1904. After the 1906 earthquake, though, they altered plans to anchor the 36,000-plus kilogram monument to the bedrock, and it was finally inaugurated in 1908.

From the nearby **Estación Cumbre,** a modern two-km **Teleférico** (cable gondola) connects the summit sector with Providencia's Avenida Pedro de Valdivia Norte, an alternative route to and from the park. About two-thirds of the way, passengers can descend at **Estación Tupahue** to visit the **Piscina Tupahue** (swimming pool), the **Casa de la Cultura Anájuac** (art museum, open 9 A.M.–5 P.M. daily but with free concerts Sunday

at noon), the **Enoteca** (a wine museum with a restaurant), and the **Jardín Botánico Mapulemu** (an erstwhile quarry reclaimed as a botanical garden). The even larger **Piscina Antilén** is also within walking distance.

The funicular operates 1–8:30 P.M. Monday, and 10 A.M.–8:30 P.M. the rest of the week; the *teleférico* operates 2:30–8 P.M. weekdays, 10:30 A.M.–8 P.M. weekends and holidays. Both have slightly reduced winter hours. The funicular-*teleférico* combination costs about US$2.50 for adults, US$1.50 for children. The funicular alone costs US$1 to Estación Cumbre, US$1.50 for a round-trip, again with discounts for children; the *teleférico* costs US$2 round-trip, US$1 for children. Buses from Plaza Caupolicán also make the loop to Avenida Pedro de Valdivia Norte.

Cementerio General

Among the cemetery's Gothic, Greek, Moorish, and Egyptian-style sepulchers, all but two of the country's presidents are interred—Bernardo O'Higgins's remains rest in the Altar de la Patria on the Alameda and Gabriel González Videla was buried in his native La Serena. Other notable figures include diplomat Orlando Letelier (killed by a car bomb in Washington, D.C., by military intelligence agents under orders from Pinochet's henchman General Manuel Contreras), Venezuelan-born scholar and educator Andrés Bello, and cultural icon folksinger and songwriter Violeta Parra. Nobel Prize poets Gabriela Mistral and Pablo Neruda were both interred here as well, but Mistral's body was moved to her Elqui valley birthplace and Neruda's to his Isla Negra coastal residence.

Salvador Allende moved in the other direction—after 17 years in Viña del Mar, he regained his freedom to travel to a monumental memorial here with the end of the Pinochet dictatorship. Another indicator of change is sculptor Francisco Gazitua's *Rostros* (Faces), a memorial to the regime's detained and executed victims.

LAS CONDES AND VITACURA

On Américo Vespucio just north of Avenida Apoquindo, where Línea 1 of the Metro ends in Las

Condes, high fences and lack of cover on the expansive lawns should discourage any assault on the **Escuela Militar** (Army War College); the building is impressive enough from a distance, but a closer inspection shows cracked walls and weeds wedging apart the patios. Its **Museo Histórico de la Escuela Militar** (see below for more detail) tells Chilean history from, euphemistically speaking, a consistent point of view.

In colonial times, Las Condes was bucolic farmland. One of few survivals from that time, the late colonial **Iglesia y Convento San Vicente Ferrer de los Dominicos,** at Avenida Apoquindo 9085 where the avenue dead-ends at Padre Hurtado, sits on lands that Pedro de Valdivia himself seized from Mapuche cacique Apoquindo for Valdivia's mistress Inés de Suárez. Willed to the Dominican order by a subsequent owner, the property deteriorated during more than a century of litigation, but the Dominicans managed to add its twin Byzantine domes in 1847.

Alongside the church, **Los Graneros del Alba** is Santiago's biggest crafts market and also popular for its country cuisine and impromptu entertainment. Popularly known as "Los Dominicos," it's open 10 A.M.–7:30 P.M. daily all year. Several buses out the Alameda, Avenida Providencia, and Avenida Apoquindo go directly to the church and market; the quickest alternative is Línea 1 of the Metro Escuela Militar and then either the bus or a taxi (about US$3.50) out Avenida Apoquindo.

Vitacura's **Museo Ralli,** Alonso de Sotomayor 4110, tel. 2/2064224, is one of several transnational museums dedicated to contemporary Latin American art; it has other locales in Uruguay, Spain, and Israel. Completely noncommercial—lacking even a museum shop—it showcases painting and sculpture from many American countries, with a handful of items from well-known Europeans such as Salvador Dalí, in more than 3,000 square meters in a modern building in a quiet residential neighborhood. Open 10:30 A.M.–4 P.M. daily except Monday and Thursday, charging no admission fee, it's well-served by public transportation—any bus out Avenida Vitacura will drop you at the corner of Candelaria Goyenechea, where it's just one block to the north.

Also in Vitacura, the misleadingly named **Museo de Artes Decorativas Lo Matta** (Museum of Decorative Arts), Avenida Presidente Kennedy 9350, tel. 2/2124633, has a third-rate assortment of contemporary landscapes. The property itself, a national monument that's the last remnant of a 16th-century land grant to Francisco de Riberos, features an 18th-century adobe and surrounding gardens that passed through many hands, including the family of Antonio Martínez de Matta y Casamiglia from whom it takes its name, before being acquired by the Municipalidad de Vitacura in 1967. While the regular collections barely merit a detour, the building and gardens deserve a look, and the Corporación Cultural de Vitacura also hosts special exhibitions and open-air concerts here. The museum itself is open 9 A.M.–6 P.M. weekdays, 9 A.M.–2 P.M. Saturday; admission is free.

Museo Histórico de la Escuela Militar

As an exercise in self-congratulatory triumphalism, the Museo del Escuela Militar (War College Museum) has to be considered a success, but the army's one-sided account of its 19th-century adventures on the southern Mapuche frontier and its victory over Bolivia and Peru in the War of the Pacific (1879–83) may interest sociologists more than historians. Surprisingly little deals directly with the 1973 coup, except for what appear to be death masks of the original military junta (General Pinochet is the only one left alive, as Admiral José Toribio Merino and Carabineros General César Mendoza died in 1996, and air force General Gustavo Leigh in 1999).

Both sociologists and historians, though, will find interest in the museum's **Sala Presidente Augusto Pinochet,** an entire room filled with awards, honors, and medals to the former dictator. Astonishingly, Dade County and the City of Miami actually presented him keys to the city. Another honor, from New York City's Hispanic International Research Institute, reads as follows:

Premio Internacional de la Libertad [International Freedom Prize], granted to His Excellency the Chief of State of the Chilean Republic General August

Pinochet Ugarte and his heroic people for having restored freedom, progress and security in their beautiful homeland, a heartfelt testimony to those who with Your Excellency consecrate their life to a Chilean renaissance.

Granted September 28, 1974, by the Hispanic International Research Institute of New York City, by Hispanic American Division Chairman Carlos G. Carrillo, José A. López Ivalo, Chairman of the Hispanic Division, and Colonel Orville L. Rogers RT, International Chairman.

Besides these unsettlingly explicit glorifications of a man who escaped prosecution only because of his age, alleged infirmity, and intense lobbying by Chile's political right, there is a large library of the general's Napoleon memorabilia in Spanish, English, and French (Pinochet's father was French). There are several busts of Napoleon in the room. The museum, Los Militares 4500, tel. 2/2083701, is open 3–6 P.M. weekdays by appointment only.

ÑUÑOA

South of Providencia and east of Santiago Centro, middle-class Ñuñoa has few landmarks but the vigorous cultural life on and around **Plaza Ñuñoa,** thanks partly to nearby campuses of the Universidad Católica and the Universidad de Chile, has made it a growing attraction, with good but unpretentious restaurants, bars, and dance clubs, for Santiaguinos.

With the Andean front range in the distance, Ñuñoa's one unforgettable landmark is the **Estadio Nacional** (National Stadium), at Avenida Grecia and Campo de Deportes. Famous for the 1962 World Cup, it became infamous as an impromptu prison camp. In the days and weeks after the 1973 coup, 7,000 Allende sympathizers (and suspected sympathizers) were incarcerated, many tortured, and more than a few executed (including folksinger Victor Jara, and U.S. citizens Charles Horman and Frank Teruggi). Today, the stadium is once again the site of the country's most important soccer matches.

Frequent buses to Plaza Ñuñoa leave from Plaza Italia (Plaza Baquedano), while Metrobús makes a direct connection from Estación Salvador on Línea 1 of the Metro. The Estadio Nacional is reasonable walking distance from Línea 5's Ñuble station.

OUTER *COMUNAS*

Most of Gran Santiago's outer *comunas* have few points of interest, but some of them are very worthwhile. They are mostly toward the southeastern part of the city.

Museo Nacional de Aeronáutica y del Espacio

At Aeropuerto Los Cerrillos, Santiago's former international and domestic airport, the air and space museum's hangar harbors a hodgepodge of historic planes such as DC-3s and covers Chile's tiny role in space—Apollo 14 carried the Chilean flag to the moon in 1971. The Museo Nacional de Aeronáutica y del Espacio, at Avenida Pedro Aguirre Cerda 5000 in the *comuna* of Cerrillos, tel. 2/5570344, is open 10 A.M.–6 P.M. daily except Monday.

Templo Votivo de Maipú

After victory over the Spaniards at the battle of Maipú in 1818, Bernardo O'Higgins himself proposed construction of a tributary temple to the Virgen del Carmen, Chile's patron saint. Begun shortly thereafter, the original temple went unfinished until 1887, then suffered such serious damage in the earthquakes of 1906 and 1927 that this new modernist—some might say brutalist—church was constructed of reinforced concrete. Architect Juan Martínez Gutiérrez began the project in 1944, dropping out 20 years later, and not until 1974 was it complete.

Still, the Templo Votivo draws big crowds of the faithful, especially around July 16, date of the Fiesta de la Virgen del Carmen. Standing ruins of the earlier church are fenced off; the adjacent **Museo del Carmen,** tel. 2/9429669, displays patriotic and ecclesiastical artifacts.

The temple, Avenida 5 de Abril s/n, Maipú, is open 8:30 A.M.–8 P.M. daily, while the museum is open 9 A.M.–1 P.M. Tuesday through Friday, 10 A.M.–1 P.M. Saturday, Sunday, and holidays, and

3–8 P.M. Sunday and holidays only. Any bus with the placard "Templo" goes directly to the site; *taxi colectivos* leave from the corner of Alameda and Amunátegui.

Viña Cousiño Macul

In the southeastern *comuna* of Peñalolén, Cousiño Macul is one of Chile's oldest wineries, in the same family since 1856, when Matías Cousiño bought vineyards that had already been producing for nearly three centuries. Its *bodegas* (cellars) and Museo del Vino (Wine Museum) are open for free guided tours at 11 A.M. daily except Sunday by reservation only, though it's likely drop-ins would be accepted if space were available. Reserve wines are available for tasting at about US$2 per glass in an attractive bar cum sales room; the house produces cabernet, merlot, chardonnay, sauvignon blanc, and riesling.

Viña Cousiño Macul is at Avenida Quilín 7100, tel. 2/2841011, fax 2/2841509, website: www.cousinomacul.cl, vtaparticular@cousino-macul.cl. Bus No. 210 from the Alameda goes within walking distance of the grounds.

Parque por la Paz

The most subtly eloquent memorial to the victims of the Pinochet dictatorship, Peñalolén's Parque por la Paz (Park for Peace) occupies the grounds of the former Villa Grimaldi, an isolated mansion that served as the principal incarceration and torture center for the Directorio de Inteligencia Nacional (DINA), General Manuel Contreras's ruthless and vicious intelligence service. Before it closed, more than 200 political prisoners died here, and many more were interrogated and tortured.

In the regime's final days, the military bulldozed nearly all the buildings to destroy the evidence, but the nonprofit Fundación Parque por la Paz has transformed the property into a place of pilgrimage that honors and remembers the victims without ever stooping to overt political posturing. It has locked shut the original streetside gates, by which prisoners entered the grounds, with a declaration that it is "never to be opened again."

Parque por la Paz, in the 8300 block of José Arrieta, is open 11 A.M.–8:30 P.M. daily except Monday; there is no admission charge. Several

THE TRANSFORMATION OF VILLA GRIMALDI

During the 17-year dictatorship of General Pinochet, when more than 3,000 people were murdered or disappeared and as many as 400,000 others detained and tortured, no single site evoked more fear than Villa Grimaldi, its largest detention and torture center.

Before the 1973 coup, Villa Grimaldi, in a then-isolated neighborhood in the geographically peripheral *comuna* of Peñalolén, was a retreat popular with leftists and intellectuals. Appropriated by the dictatorship, between 1973 and 1980 it saw the deaths and disappearance of well over 200 people—though no bodies have been found there—and more than 5,000 detentions.

Villa Grimaldi also served as a training center for General Manuel Contreras's infamous Directorio de Inteligencia Nacional (Dina, National Intelligence Directorate) and its successor, the Centro de Inteligencia Nacional (CNI, National Intelligence Center). It was also the Chilean headquarters for Operación Cóndor, a covert alliance with the so-

called "security forces" of military dictatorships in Argentina, Uruguay, and Brazil.

When it became apparent that General Pinochet had lost his bid to extend his "presidency" for another eight years, military authorities tried to eradicate all evidence of Villa Grimaldi's violent past and sold the property. Outraged community members, though, successfully lobbied the incoming administration of Christian Democrat President Patricio Aylwin to buy back the land and turn it into a contemplative memorial.

A recent book titled *Grito mi Silencio* (I Shout My Silence; Santiago: Librería Pax, 2001), written under the pen name Rodrigo by a Spanish-Chilean businessman who was inexplicably detained after an innocent inquiry about some family property, recounts the conditions at Villa Grimaldi. Just as inexplicably released, the detainee waited 25 years before he could feel comfortable enough to tell his story, even though he was not tortured, and his book has caused a minor sensation.

bus lines pass nearby: No. 242 from Avenida Providencia, No. 337 from Estación Central and the Alameda, and No. 433 from Plaza Italia.

Barrio Ecológico

In upper Peñalolén, Santiago's single most non-conformist community occupies a conflictive area alongside middle-class suburban subdivisions and working-class squatter settlements where the militant leftist Movimiento Izquierdista Revolucionario (MIR) is loath to let the police even enter. Nevertheless, the residents of the self-consciously environmentally correct community have fashioned a neighborhood where campesinos once toiled to eke out low yields from barren soils.

In the 1960s, as Chilean peasants clamored for land, President Eduardo Frei Montalva's cautious redistribution program had hesitated to tackle the powerful landowners of the fertile lowlands, preferring to acquire less desirable areas such as Peñalolén where landowners were more amenable to a buyout. After most peasant farmers failed, naïve but sincere back-to-the-land types supplanted them, living—camping, really—without utilities, but gradually planting trees and gardens and creating their own spontaneous architecture. Eventually, municipal authorities accepted the barrio as a permanent buffer against suburban sprawl, and it now enjoys running water, electricity, and telephone service—but not paved streets. The houses themselves, while atypical, have acquired an air of greater permanence, and many individuals from the arts and literary communities now live here.

Bus route No. 318, from Estación Mapocho via Calle Santa Lucía and Diagonal Paraguay, goes directly to the Barrio Ecológico—in fact, it's the place where the buses turn around and return to Santiago Centro. An ideal walking area, it has a small handicrafts market (best on weekends) and good but simple eateries.

Museo Interactivo Mirador

South of Peñalolén, in the *comuna* of La Granja, the Museo Interactivo Mirador is a visual and tactile environment, where everything is meant to be touched and manipulated—primarily for kids, though many adults seem to enjoy it as well. With very little textual explanation, it relies on seeing and doing.

It's good in the physical sciences, including water and its properties, plate tectonics, but also in the psychology of perception. The building itself is a two-story concrete block with an open floor plan and curved lath ceilings where, unfortunately, some pigeons appear to have taken up residence. The museum has many good things about it, but it appears to underestimate reading. An imaginative historical exhibit is on hats and hatmaking. One unique exhibit lets you choose your daily diet as in a cafeteria line and then provides nutritional information on the menu you have chosen.

Avenida Punta Arenas 6711, tel. 2/2943955, is the official address, but the actual entrance and ticket booth are on Sebastopol, a couple of hundred meters west from Punta Arenas. Admission costs US$4.50 for adults, US$3 for children, but coupons offering free children's admission with a paying adult are not hard to find—from the toll booth at the airport. Use the Mirador Azul Metro station.

Santiago Practicalities

ACCOMMODATIONS

Nearly all of Santiago's budget to moderately priced accommodations are in and around Santiago Centro, while most luxury hotels are in Providencia and Las Condes, but a variety of places in all categories are scattered throughout most of the city. At the bottom end of the scale, taxes are not an issue, but midrange and top-end hotels discount IVA for foreign visitors. Many of the upper-range hotels are representatives of international chains.

Unless otherwise indicated, the hotels below are in Santiago Centro, with some of them more narrowly defined by their barrio. Many hotels in other *comunas* are primarily business-oriented, but that doesn't mean they're unwilling to take ordinary travelers or tourists.

US$10–25

Youthful Israelis just out of their military service look for traveling companions at **Hotel Indiana,** in a rundown but relatively safe area at Rosas 1343, tel. 2/6714251, where accommodations start around US$6 pp. Close to Metro República, Barrio Brasil's simple but friendly **Residencial Vicky,** Moneda 2055, tel. 2/6960787, charges just US$6 pp.

Not far from Hotel Indiana, in what was the heart of the backpacker zone before demolition of the Terminal de Buses Norte, **Hotel Caribe,** San Martín 851, tel. 2/6966681, now stands pretty much alone but is only a few blocks from Metro Cal y Canto. For US$7 pp, it still provides good service, including cheap breakfasts and other meals, free storage for luggage, friendly management, and Internet access, but other more conveniently located places are just as good for only a little more money. Light sleepers may notice the doorbell and squeaky tile floors at all hours—avoid the forward rooms.

Run by a Catholic charity that provides reliable student and traveler housing throughout the country, the labyrinthine **Casa Kolping,** also in Barrio Brasil at Avenida Ricardo Cumming 102,

tel. 2/6991192 or 2/6988171, fax 2/6990451, is a bit worn but spacious. Rates are US$7 pp for hostel-style bunks, US$15 d with shared bath, and US$14/22 s/d with private bath. Breakfast (US$1.50) and other meals are available.

Used mostly by groups and a steady influx of independent foreign travelers, the well-managed **Hostelling International,** Cienfuegos 151, tel. 2/6718532, fax 2/6728880, histgoch@entelchile.net, charges US$10 pp for dorm-style accommodations (four to six beds per room). The cafeteria has inexpensive meals (in the US$2–3 range for lunch or dinner); the hostel also has cheap, efficient laundry service and plenty of spacious common areas.

In the winding cobbled streets south of the Alameda, **Residencial Londres,** Londres 54, tel. 2/6339192, fax 2/6382215, is the Hilton or Hyatt of Santiago's backpacker or budget hotels, but with more charm than the international chains. It's still a bargain for US$11 pp with shared bath—such a bargain that reservations have become almost imperative. Breakfast is extra.

Some of the best values are in Barrio Brasil, starting with **Residencial del Norte,** Catedral 2207, tel. 2/6951876, fax 2/6969251, which costs US$9 pp with shared bath and a very simple breakfast; if it has a shortcoming, it's the creaking floors and walls of this old building (most noticeable when somebody returns at 2 or 3 A.M.) and the street noise from passing buses.

US$25–50

Hostal Río Amazonas, in a quirky 19th-century adobe at Rosas 2234, tel./fax 2/6719013, tel. 2/6984092, website: www.altiro.com/amazonas, amazona@entelchile.net, charges US$22/35 s/d for large rooms with breakfast and private bath, some of them with sleeping lofts. A couple of cheaper rooms have shared bath, and Internet access costs US$2 per hour.

The modest eight-room **Hotel Europa,** Amunátegui 449, tel. 2/6952448, fax 2/6971378, charges US$30/35 s/d. At the north end of Cerro Santa Lucía, the otherwise enjoyable and underrated **Hotel Foresta,** Subercaseaux 353, tel. 2/6396262, fax 2/6322996, has suffered from traffic noise, but the recent undergrounding of a nearby avenue should help. Rates are US$30/40 with breakfast.

Well-located on the east side of Cerro Santa Lucía, within easy walking distance of many good restaurants in Barrio Lastarria, **Hotel Montecarlo,** Subercaseaux 209, tel. 2/6392945, fax 2/6335577, charges US$35/40 s/d for what might charitably be called compact rooms, with breakfast and private bath. While decent enough, it's not so good a value as the Foresta.

Barrio Brasil's cozy **Hotel Los Arcos,** Agustinas 2173, tel. 2/6990998, deserves consideration for US$20 pp (without breakfast). A few blocks west, **Hotel Turismo Japón,** Almirante Barroso 160, tel. 2/6984500, attracts a steady foreign clientele for US$35/45 with breakfast, thanks partly to its convenient location, attractive grounds, and book exchange.

Marilú's Bed & Breakfast, in a good Providencia location at Rafael Cañas 246, tel. 2/2355302, fax 2/2643318, website: www.bedandbreakfast.cl, banbchile@yahoo.com, occupies the first and third floors of an apartment building close to Metro Salvador. Rates are around US$25 pp for rooms that vary in size, some with shared and some with private bath; there is no smoking indoors. The common rooms have TV, with tea and coffee available all day, and the management can handle both English and French.

One of downtown's best midrange values, **Hotel Santa Lucía,** Huérfanos 779, 4th floor, tel. 2/6398201, fax 2/6331844, charges US$41/50 s/d for rooms with breakfast and standard amenities such as cable TV, refrigerator/bar, and telephone.

US$50–100

At recommended **Hotel Conde Ansurez,** Avenida República 25, tel./fax 2/6960807, ansurez@cepri.cl, note that one side of the 44-room building fronts the busy, noisy Alameda, and ask for a room at the back. Rates for modest rooms with private bath and buffet breakfast are US$45/54 s/d.

In a neighborhood that's both central and attractive, and easy walking distance from Metro Universidad de Chile, **Hotel Vegas,** Londres 49, tel. 2/6322498, fax 2/6325084, charges US$48/55 s/d; despite the lack of a/c, it manages to stay cool in summer. New in Barrio Brasil is the promising **Hotel Plaza Verde,** Huérfanos 2293, tel. 2/6887693, fax 2/6887688, plazaverde@terra.cl, which charges US$55/65 s/d.

Completely restored to its glory days and beyond, overlooking the gardens of the former Congreso Nacional, the business-oriented **Hotel España,** Morandé 510, tel. 2/6966066, website: www.hotelespania.com, hotelespania@entelchile.net, has spacious cheerful rooms with modernized baths, exceptional natural light on the fourth floor in particular, plus cable TV, modem lines, and electronic strong boxes with guest-controlled combinations. Rates are US$50/55 s/d for standard rooms, US$60/65 s/d for superior rooms, both with breakfast, but there are a couple of bargain rooms for US$30/35 s/d that are smaller but still very fine. The street is busy during the daytime, but quiet at night.

On the border between Providencia and Santiago Centro, the traditional **Hotel Principado,** Avenida Vicuña Mackenna 30, tel. 2/2228142, fax 2/2226065, hprincip@ctc-mundo.net, charges US$60/70 s/d with breakfast. In contrast to Providencia's elegant but often corporate accommodations, **Hostal Thayer,** Luis Thayer Ojeda 746, tel. 2/2339703, fax 2/2337022, is an intimate boutique-style hotel with contemporary conveniences for US$65/75 s/d with breakfast.

Despite its inauspicious location half a block east of the busy Vía Norte-Sur, **Hotel Majestic,** Santo Domingo 1526, tel. 2/6958366, fax 2/6974051, hotelmajestic@entelchile.net, has an outstanding reputation for US$70/80 s/d with a buffet breakfast; it has double-paned windows to keep out the noise, and a swimming pool. Only two blocks from Metro Santa Ana, its restaurant features Indian specialties such as curry and tandoori.

Rates at downtown's rehabbed **Hotel Tupahue,** a massive 209-room hotel one block east of the Plaza de Armas at San Antonio 477, tel. 2/6383810, fax 2/6392899, hotel@tupahue.cl, are US$74/84 s/d with a buffet breakfast.

Providencia's renovated **Hotel Bonaparte,** Mar del Plata 2171, tel. 2/2740621, fax 2/2048907, hotel.bonaparte@entelchile.net, charges US$80/88 s/d except in summer, when rates are US$70 s or d, and on weekends, when they're US$60 s or d. For business visitors, it offers services equivalent to many more expensive hotels at a substantially lower price, partly because the neighborhood, though attractive enough, is a little less accessible to the Metro. It also has recreational facilities including a swimming pool and gymnasium, and spacious gardens where native trees are due to replace the eucalyptus.

On the eastern outskirts of town, in the *comuna* of Vitacura, the unique **Hotel Acacias de Vitacura,** El Manantial 1781, tel. 2/2118601, fax 2/2127858, acacias@ctcreuna.cl, is a family-run four-star hotel whose gardens and foyer feature an astonishing assortment of antique machinery and artifacts from around the world. The building itself lacks character, but the rooms are comfortable, the service impeccable, the recreational facilities outstanding, and it's convenient to summer hiking and winter skiing in the Cajón del Mapocho. Rates are US$83/92 s/d including a buffet breakfast, with a family suite available for US$184.

Over the past 30 years, high-rise apartments have replaced many of the handsome French-style buildings that once graced the streets of Providencia, but one survivor is the 23-room **Hotel Orly,** whose ornate facade and mansard roof stand out at Avenida Pedro de Valdivia 027, tel. 2/2318947, fax 2/2520051, h.orly@ctcinternet.cl. Rates are US$84/95 s/d for midsize rooms with breakfast and assiduous service.

By Las Condes standards, the 33-room **Hotel Montebianco,** nestled into a neighborhood of high-rises at Isidora Goyenechea 2911, tel. 2/2325034, fax 2/2330420, montebia@entelchile.net, is a bargain at US$77/99 s/d with buffet breakfast, a/c, and other amenities. Convenient to the Metro and the Bosque Norte restaurant cluster, this modern minor gem offers more personalized atmosphere than the area's international megahotels can provide.

Rates at the modern **Hotel Galerías,** near the busy Alameda at San Antonio 65, tel. 2/3611911, fax 2/6330821, galerias@entelchile.net, start at US$80/100 s/d with breakfast and a welcome drink. Befitting its name, it hosts frequent art exhibits and has recreational facilities including a swimming pool.

In trendy Barrio Lastarria, around the corner from Plaza Mulato Gil de Castro, the 30-room **Hostal del Parque,** Merced 294, tel. 2/6392694, fax 2/6392754, is a minor jewel that costs US$99/100 s/d with breakfast for rooms equipped with kitchenettes, and it offers free airport transfers.

US$100–150

The Best Western affiliate **Hotel Director,** Avenida Vitacura 3600 in Las Condes, tel. 2/2071580, fax 2/2287503, dire1000@netline.cl, offers chain reliability, offering huge rooms for US$105 s or d with a buffet breakfast. Rates at the 80-room **Hotel Torremayor,** Avenida Ricardo Lyon 322, tel. 2/2342000, fax 2/2343779, reservas@hoteltorremayor.cl, start at US$100/140 s/d, with buffet breakfast, for well-equipped quarters.

Rates at **Hotel Plaza San Francisco,** Alameda 816, tel. 2/6393832, fax 2/6397826, fcohotel@entelchile.net, start at US$145 s or d for "standard" rooms during the summer off-season—this is a business-oriented place—but most of the year they range from US$159 to US$185. There are substantially more expensive luxury suites.

Now boasting nearly 300 rooms, half of them nonsmoking, the **Hotel Intercontinental Santiago,** Luz 2920, tel. 2/2342200, fax 2/2517814, santiago@interconti.com, is one of Las Condes' best-located hotels, easy walking distance to the Bosque Norte restaurant zone and Línea 1 of the Metro. The rooms themselves are large and the service admirable; rates start at US$145 s or d.

US$150–200

Overlooking the river from the base of Cerro San Cristóbal, with garden space unavailable to downtown luxury hotels, Providencia's **Sheraton San Cristóbal,** Avenida Santa María 1742, tel. 2/2335000, fax 2/2341729, sheraton@chilepac.net, charges US$160 s or d for stylishly decorated rooms with a substantial buffet breakfast included.

Melding modern conveniences with traditional style, the business-oriented **Hotel Fundador,**

Paseo Serrano 34, tel./fax 2/6322566, hotelfundador@hotelfundador.cl, charges rack rates of US$150/170 but, with discounts sometimes half that, it's one of the best values in town. It's also part of one of Santiago Centro's most distinctive neighborhoods, the Barrio París-Londres, with its curving streets.

In Las Condes, rates at the stylish high-rise **Hotel Regal Pacific,** Avenida Apoquindo 5680, tel. 2/2294000, fax 2/2294005, regalpac@entelchile.net, start at US$175/180 s/d. Facilities at this business-oriented hotel include conference and meeting rooms, two restaurants, a health club, and the like.

Las Condes's skyscraping **Marriott Hotel,** Avenida Kennedy 5741, tel. 2/4262000, fax 2/4262001, is one of the newest additions to Santiago's hotel scene and also one of the city's tallest buildings. Rates start at US$198 s or d, but it's possible to spend much more.

Las Condes's **Radisson Royal Santiago Hotel,** Avenida Vitacura 2610, tel. 2/2036000, fax 2/3373111, radisson@iusanet.cl, charges around US$200 s or d for luxury accommodations catering primarily to business travelers—each room comes with its own cell phone, for instance, and it occupies part of Santiago's World Trade Center. There are also, of course, amenities such as a rooftop pool, gymnasium, and jacuzzis, and views of the nearby Andes to the east.

More than US$200

Also in Las Condes, the 310-room high-rise **Hotel Hyatt Regency Santiago,** Avenida Kennedy 4601, tel. 2/2181234, fax 2/2182279, hyattscl@chilepac.net, made *Condé Nast Traveler*'s 2001 list of top 10 Latin hotels, in part for the lofty atrium, topped by a glass dome, that lets natural light stream into the building. Rates start at US$210 s or d for midsize to capacious rooms, some of which offer spectacular Andean views, in a business-oriented environment that also has recreational facilities including a gymnasium, tennis courts, and a swimming pool. Its Anakena restaurant is one of the best in town.

In Providencia, the **Hotel Santiago Park Plaza,** Ricardo Lyon 207, tel. 2/2336363, fax 2/2336668, pplaza@netline.cl, is a business-ori-

ented hotel whose antique-studded foyer belies the modernity of its wired rooms and recreational facilities, including a glassed-in rooftop pool. Rates are US$230 s or d.

In the grand hotel tradition, on the west side of Plaza de la Constitución, the 307-room **Hotel Carrera,** Teatinos 180, tel. 2/6982011, fax 2/67-21083, hotel.carrera@chilnet.cl, has made *Condé Nast*'s list several times. Rack rates are US$260/280 s/d with breakfast for a classic that has evolved into modernity without sacrificing tradition.

Rates at the business-oriented international chain **Holiday Inn Crowne Plaza,** Alameda 136, tel. 2/6381042, fax 2/6336015, start at US$319 s or d. Virtually self-contained, it features recreational facilities including a gymnasium and swimming pool, shops, and even its own post office.

FOOD

Santiago's diverse and innovative gastronomy is becoming one of the city's (and Chile's) main attractions, but on a global level it's still an underappreciated secret. The distribution of restaurants generally mirrors that of hotels, with cheaper eateries downtown and the bulk of upscale restaurants in Providencia and Las Condes—though Barrio Bellavista, across the Río Mapocho, offers the city's most original dining and congenial ambience. Nevertheless, there are good values in all parts of town.

Santiago Centro

For morning espresso, try standup bars such as **Café Caribe,** Ahumada 120; **Café Haití,** Ahumada 140; or **Café Cousiño,** Matías Cousiño 107. Note, however, that while these places have the best and cheapest coffee in town, their clientele are *overwhelmingly* male because of the scantily clad waitresses. For more variety, and a place to sit for muffins, croissants, juice, and coffee, there's **Au Bon Pain,** Miraflores 235, tel. 2/6321688, a North American chain.

For pretty good lunches at moderate prices—around US$5—try the chain **Bavaria,** Avenida Bulnes 178, tel. 2/6983723. For whimsical decor, traditional Chilean food, and even more reasonable prices (about US$3–4 for most lunches), there's **La Chimenea,** Príncipe de Gales 90, tel. 2/6970131; in the same location since 1952, it also sponsors theme-based film programs, free of charge, Saturday at 8 P.M.

On the south side of the Plaza de Armas, **Chez Henry,** Portal Fernández Concha 962, tel. 2/6966612, is a classic that was once among Santiago's best; with the gastronomic boom, it's lost some of its luster, but it still merits consideration for seafood and Chilean specialties such as *pastel de choclo,* at midrange prices of US$6–10. **Bar Nacional 1,** Bandera 317, tel. 2/6953368, serves similar food in more modest surroundings.

In Barrio Lastarria, near Cerro Santa Lucía, **R,** José Victorino Lastarria 297, tel. 2/6649844, has outstanding pasta dishes starting around US$6, as well as fish and chicken entrées, and fine desserts. The service is attentive, and there is limited open-air seating. Nearby **Don Victorino,** José Victorino Lastarria 138, tel. 2/6395263, serves a fine fixed-price lunch for about US$6 with choice of three entrées, in attractive surroundings. **Les Assassins,** Merced 297-B, tel. 2/6384280, does the same with French cuisine, but it's a tiny venue that gets very crowded around lunchtime.

Kintaro Monjitas 450, tel. 2/6382448, is one of Santiago's cheapest sushi options, with large fresh fish and shrimp plates—mostly more than a single individual can consume in a sitting—in the US$9 range. Sashimi and rice-based plates such as *donburi* are also on the menu. Not quite so good or diverse, but significantly cheaper, is **Izakaya Yoko,** Merced 456, tel. 2/6321954.

Le Due Torri, San Antonio 258, tel. 2/63-33799, is the established standard for Italian food, though there are more imaginative places in Barrio Brasil and Providencia.

In the five-star Hotel San Francisco, **Bristol,** Alameda 816, tel. 2/6393832, provides prix-fixe lunches and dinners that include an appetizer, main dish, and a dessert buffet for US$25; extensive wine tasting is also part of the package.

Barrio Brasil

Several years after its opening, **Las Vacas Gordas,** Cienfuegos 280, tel. 2/6971066, has managed to maintain both high standards with high volume and low prices, but it's crowded at nearly all hours except Sunday night—when it's closed. The fare is primarily *parrillada,* but pasta and fish are also on the menu. One drawback is the high decibel level, but the service is exceptional for such a busy place.

Open for lunch and dinner, **El Puente de Chabuca,** Brasil 75, tel. 2/6967962, serves moderately priced Peruvian food in a classic Barrio Brasil building, and it also has live music on weekends.

For a diverse selection of Mexican tacos complemented by enchiladas, quesadillas, *sincronizadas,* and similar *antojitos* at bargain prices, try **Charro de Oro,** Avenida Ricardo Cumming 342-A, tel. 2/6972695. Some of the fillings are a little spicy for the Chilean palate, but those who have eaten Mexican food elsewhere will probably not be bothered. Its main drawback is the erratic hours, though it's ostensibly open for lunch and dinner daily except Sunday, and to 3 A.M. Friday and Saturday.

The barrio's best Mexican option, though, is **Plaza Garibaldi,** Moneda 2319, tel. 2/6994278, which continues to draw diners who once wouldn't be seen dead in this part of town. Brightly decorated, operated by a Chilean woman who lived many years in exile in Mexico City and once cooked for Salvador Allende's widow Hortensia Bussi, its diverse and rapidly evolving menu merits a visit even for those who live in areas where Mexican food is common. Entrées are mostly in the US$6–10 range, and the margaritas and Mexican beers are first-rate.

Several seafood restaurants are on Calle Bulnes (not to be confused with Avenida Bulnes). **Caleta Bulnes,** Bulnes 86, tel. 2/6988151, has good seafood—US$5 for a tasty *chupe de locos*—and is open Sunday night when most other restaurants in the barrio are closed. Across the street, **Marisquería Tongoy,** Bulnes 91, tel. 2/6971144, in the same range, is a traditional seafood choice so popular that it has another branch just down the block at Bulnes 72, tel. 2/6814329. Service is fast, and the downstairs at the main branch is nonsmoking.

Ocean Pacific's, Avenida Ricardo Cumming 221, tel. 2/6972413, is another very decent traditional seafood restaurant with moderate prices. **Ostras Azócar,** Bulnes 37, tel. 2/6816109 or 2/6822293, is equally traditional but serves a more affluent clientele.

While Barrio Brasil has many decent restaurants, there's nothing else quite like **Puro Chile,** Maipú 363, tel. 2/6819355, which uses the freshest local ingredients to create diverse Latin American cuisine, served in surroundings so wildly imaginative that it looks like a Barrio Bellavista transplant. Entrées run US$7–9.

Barrio Bellavista

North of the Mapocho via the Pío Nono bridge, Barrio Bellavista is Santiago's gourmet ghetto, with dozens of first-rate restaurants virtually side-by-side—but not on Pío Nono itself, where most of the options are only a little better than greasy spoons. The bulk of the choices are east of Pío Nono, on the Providencia side of the barrio, but there are still many outstanding possibilities on the Recoleta side, to the west.

Surviving in the midst of rampant gentrification by serving outstanding sandwiches and simple but well-prepared Chilean dishes to a Bohemian clientele, **Galindo,** Dardignac 098, tel. 2/7770116, is one of the oldest eateries on the Providencia side of Bellavista. Even more casual is **El Caramaño,** Purísima 257, tel. 2/7377043, so absent of decor—lacking even a street sign—that you need to bang on the door to get in, lending it a slumming sort of "members only" atmosphere.

Most of the remaining inexpensive options in Bellavista are not very good, but there are a couple of exceptions: **Pizzas Gloria,** Dardignac 0188, tel. 2/7359968, for Italo-Argentine pizza and pasta in a no-frills setting, and **Café de la Dulcería Las Palmas,** Antonia López de Bello 0190, tel. 2/7774586, for fresh juices, sandwiches, and desserts in more appealing surroundings.

While other more fashionable locales may be superseding it in the neighborhood, **Ají Verde,** Constitución 284, tel. 2/7353329, continues to produce midrange to upscale versions of such

typical Chilean dishes as *pastel de choclo,* shellfish, and *parrillada.* Entrées start around US$6, in agreeable surroundings with flawless service.

Picoroco, Ernesto Pinto Lagarrigue 123, tel. 2/7354549, is a traditional seafood restaurant with an extensive menu and professional service; entrées are in the US$5–10 range. It also serves beef and chicken dishes and is open Sunday afternoons when many other Bellavista restaurants are closed. The nearby **La Casona de Lima,** Ernesto Pinto Lagarrigue 195, tel. 2/7320428, is one of several Peruvian restaurants in the vicinity—not quite so good but considerably less expensive than most of its competition, with entrées in the US$6 range.

Exploiting Santiago's current fad for Peruvian food, the chain import **Alfresco** has opened an outlet in a rehabbed warehouse at Loreto 509, tel. 2/7379340. Fortunately, it doesn't have the feel of a chain, but it'll have to rely on moderate prices—around US$6–7 for most entrées—to challenge its established counterparts in the barrio.

One of Santiago's best in any category, the Peruvian **El Otro Sitio,** Antonia López de Bello 53, tel. 2/7773059, is expensive but worth the splurge for a special occasion.

Under the same management as El Otro Sitio, **Todo Fresco,** Antonia López de Bello 61, tel. 2/7350988, has fresh seafood, fine service, and airy decor, but it manages to be distractingly noisy even with a handful of patrons. Entrées are mostly in the US$7–10 range except for *centolla* (king crab) which, when available, costs at least double those prices.

Dining at **Azul Profundo,** Constitución 111, tel. 2/7380288, must be the closest possible experience to eating at Pablo Neruda's—its whimsical decor, including its signature deep blue exterior, a bowsprit above the door, and all sorts of maritime memorabilia within, feel as if it could have come straight from the poet's beloved Isla Negra residence. Seafood, of course, is the house specialty, and it's put as much effort into its kitchen as its character; though not cheap, with entrées in the US$10 and up range, it's worth a splurge.

Serving unconventional—at least for Santiago—Japanese and Vietnamese specialties, **Etniko,** Constitución 172, tel. 2/7320119, is more of a scene than a restaurant, but its popularity is un-

© WAYNE BERNHARDSON

Avenida Pío Nono, Barrio Bellavista

SANTIAGO

deniable and the food is better than just palatable. One block east, **Muñeca Brava,** Mallinkrodt 170, tel. 2/7321338, looks like a scene—or scenes from the films that its elaborate cinematic decor evokes—but the menu, especially the seafood, is consistently excellent. Entrées start in the US$8–10 range.

Meridiano, Dardignac 0185, tel. 2/7380006, is a stylish venue where diners stir-fry their own *tabla* of fresh beef, chicken, fish, or shellfish, or some mixture of them, on gas-heated grills in the center of each table. Surrounded by an array of condiments and intended for two people, each *tabla* is probably large enough to satisfy a third without difficulty. Prices start around US$10 pp for the simplest beef and chicken, but rise upward of US$15 for combos of albacore, scallops, and the like. Salads, desserts, and drinks can raise the tab substantially.

Kilomètre 11069, Dardignac 0145, tel. 2/7770410, is a combination French restaurant and wine bar that's exactly that distance from Paris. Standard French entrées are in the US$8–10 range, but the wines are the big attraction. Unlike most barrio restaurants, the Franco-Chilean **Sommelier,** Dardignac 0163, tel. 2/7320034, is a subdued, self-consciously sophisticated locale with a menu of rich but not overpowering continental dishes. Entrées cost around US$12 and up, but the service sometimes lags behind the food.

For Spanish food, **La Tasca Mediterránea** is a lively and cheaper bookstore/café-type venue at Purísima 161, tel. 2/7353901. The somewhat more upscale **El Mesón Nerudiano** at Dominica 35, tel. 2/7371542, also has live jazz on weekends. **Santos Pecadores,** opposite Tasca Mediterránea at Purísima 156, tel. 2/7355690, serves both dinner and dessert crepes with an aphrodisiac theme in the US$4–5 range, but the kitchen, astonishingly, is faster than the bar.

Looking like a set from the movie based on its namesake novel by Mexican writer Laura Esquivel, **Como Agua Para Chocolate,** Constitución 88, tel. 2/7778740, is one of Bellavista's many smart new restaurants. Mexican-Caribbean style entrées start around US$8–10; try the *reineta a la plancha* (grilled fish) with coconut sauce. There's also an elaborate dessert menu, and a large wine list that includes the exceptional late harvest dessert wine.

On the Recoleta side of the barrio are several Middle Eastern restaurants, such as **Omar Khayyam,** Avenida Perú 570, tel. 2/7774129.

It's stretching things a bit to call it Bellavista—it's really in Recoleta's Patronato garment district—but Argentine-run **El Toro,** Loreto 33, tel. 09/4196307, has attracted a loyal following for its crepes, moderately priced lunches, and nonconformist sidewalk atmosphere.

One of Bellavista's best new places is **Off the Record,** Antonia Lopez de Bello 0155, tel. 2/7777710, a bar/restaurant whose wood-paneled walls sport photos of figures from the Chilean arts community. Excellent meat, seafood, and pasta entrées, and combinations thereof, cost in the US$6–10 range, with wines by the glass for about US$2.50. Politically conscious, it also has a website, www.offtherecord-cultura.cl., and is open Monday to Saturday 9 A.M.–1 A.M., Sunday 6–9 P.M. only.

Among all Bellavista's exclusive and inventive eateries, Italian *cucina* might seem the odd man out, but **Il Siciliano,** Dardignac 0102, tel. 2/7372265, has managed to surmount the stodginess of its upscale competitors elsewhere in town. Three-course lunches, around US$9–10 pp, are the best bet; dinners are substantially more expensive.

Providencia

For croissant sandwiches, muffins, *pain au chocolat,* and espresso, the North American franchise **Au Bon Pain,** Avenida Providencia 1936, tel. 2/2336912, is as good or better than any other place in this part of town, though there are better options in Las Condes.

Liguria, Avenida Providencia 1373, tel. 2/2357914, is a traditional hangout that offers plain but reliable Chilean food at moderate prices, usually around US$5. **Eladio,** a fifth-floor patio restaurant at Avenida 11 de Septiembre 2250, tel. 2/2314224, specializes in beef but has a varied menu that will satisfy almost anyone at moderate prices, with entrées mostly in the US$3.50–7.50 range, and good cheap pisco sours—barely a dollar each.

Within a surprisingly secluded setback of bookstores and other specialty shops on an otherwise hectic avenue, the **Phone Box Pub,** Avenida Providencia 1670, tel. 2/2359972, is a pub grub kind of place with a shady grape arbor and lunches in the US$6–8 range, plus plenty of imported beers on tap and in the bottle. In the same complex is the vegetarian **Café del Patio,** Providencia 1670, Local 8-A, tel./2361251.

El Huerto, Orrego Luco 054, tel. 2/2332690, is one of the continent's landmark vegetarian restaurants, with dishes so appetizing that even dedicated carnivores don't seem to notice the lack of meat. Its adjoining café **La Huerta** has a limited menu but lower prices—try the filling fresh fruit bowl with yogurt, granola, and honey for about US$4.

For authentic regional Mexican cuisine, it's hard to beat the embassy-sponsored **Casa de la Cultura de México,** Bucarest 162, tel. 2/3343848. The *antojitos* plates, such as *taquitos* and quesadillas, are outstanding, cheap (around US$5), and filling, while more elaborate regional dishes are dearer but still reasonable for the quality. It also serves some of the best margaritas in town.

A good but generally cheaper Mexican option is **Dos Cuates,** Avenida Manuel Montt 235, tel. 2/2647376, which features live mariachi Thursday and Friday evenings and Saturday afternoon.

In an old but spacious and appealing Providencia house with high ceilings and painted in exuberant primary colors, **Barandiarán,** Manuel Montt 315, tel. 2/2366854, prepares a variety of tangy appetizers and ceviches, spicy Peruvian entrées in the US$8–10 range, and a diverse dessert menu. The corvina with mango sauce rates special mention, but the lamb dishes are a bit heavy on the cilantro.

It's no longer a secret—go early for dinner or call ahead for reservations at **Puerto Perú,** Avenida Condell 1298, tel. 2/3639886, a once-modest Peruvian place that put the neighborhood south of Avenida Providencia, near the border with Ñuñoa, on the gastronomic map. Prices are still lower than at Bellavista's best, but the difference in quality is negligible.

Despite the untimely closure of Buenos Aires import **Freddo,** Providencia still has several of the city's best ice creameries: **Bravíssimo**, Avenida Providencia 1406, tel. 2/2352511; **Sebastián,** Andrés de Fuenzalida 26, tel. 2/2319968; and **La Escarcha,** Avenida Providencia 1762.

Las Condes and Vitacura

For Sunday brunch, and fine lunches, the hands-down best choice is **Café Melba,** Don Carlos 2898, tel. 2/2324546, fax 2/2463650, just around the corner from the British Embassy on Avenida Bosque Norte. There's sidewalk seating, and the omelettes, fresh juices, and similar breakfast fare are unmatchable in their category. Half an hour's Internet access comes with every purchase over about US$1, and more time is available for free if it's not busy.

Though its more limited menu is obvious from its name, a good and slightly cheaper alternative is the nearby **New York Bagel Bakery,** Roger de Flor 2894, tel. 2/2463060.

Bohemia, offering sidewalk dining at Avenida Bosque Norte 0139, tel. 2/3311214, is a pizza and pasta place with Peruvian-style pisco sours but also items such as stuffed chicken breast, but the kitchen is a little slow. **PubLicity,** nearby at Avenida El Bosque Norte 0155, tel. 2/2466414, has similar fare, but the best pub-style food is at the lively **Flannery's Irish Geo Pub,** Encomenderos 83, tel. 2/2336675, which offers a variety of lunchtime specials in the US$4–7 range, along with Guinness and other imported beers on tap.

The flashy Italian venue **Da Renato,** Avenida Isidora Goyenechea 3471, tel. 2/2316196, specializes in entrées such as fettuccini, *panzotti,* and veal marsala in the US$10 range, with elaborate desserts and an extensive wine list. **Gioia,** Isidora Goyenechea 3456, tel. 2/33-53610, serves an elaborate Italian menu in surroundings equivalent to a Mediterranean villa. Most pasta and seafood entrées are in the US$10–12 range.

Le Due Torri, Isidora Goyenechea 2908, tel. 2/2313427, is an offshoot of downtown's reputable Italian favorite. **Da Dino,** Avenida Apoquindo 4228, tel. 2/2081344, has one of the city's finest and most diverse pizza menus.

Hereford Grill, Avenida El Bosque Norte 0355, tel. 2/2319117, is the main *parrilla* in this part of town, and it's relatively expensive. Noncarnivores should look to the midrange **El Naturista,** nearby at Avenida Vitacura 2751, tel. 2/2365147.

The Hyatt Regency Santiago's highly regarded **Anakena,** Avenida Kennedy 4601, tel. 2/3633177, has one of a handful of Thai menus in town. Popular with the diplomatic corps, **Shoogun,** Enrique Foster Norte 172, tel. 2/2311604, is an upscale Japanese venue.

La Cocina de Javier, Alonso de Córdova 4309, tel. 2/2456317 or 2/2061329, fills up fast even on weeknights, partly because chef Javier Pascual Sáenz has his own cooking show on TV Nacional but mostly because the fish (particularly the trout) and seafood (particularly the corvinas) are first-rate. Entrées are in the US$10 and up range, the portions are modest but tasty, the desserts good and reasonably priced, but the house wines are mediocre.

One of Santiago's prestige restaurants is **El Madroñal,** Avenida Vitacura 2911, tel. 2/23-36312—the walls are adorned with photographs of celebrities who have dined here, including former U.S. President Bill Clinton and his wife, current U.S. Senator Hillary Clinton, former Chilean President Eduardo Frei Ruiz-Tagle, Chilean TV personality Mario Kreutzberger (popularly known as Don Francisco), and the great Peruvian novelist Mario Vargas Llosa. The place of honor, though, is reserved for General Pinochet—people in this neighborhood feel no need to apologize for supporting the dictator. The menu is diverse, but the seafood is the best choice for entrées such as corvina with octopus sauce, alongside items such as fish soup including corvina, shrimp, and scallops for US$8, and abalone appetizers for US$9.

ENTERTAINMENT AND EVENTS

Just as it's the center of Santiago's restaurant scene, Barrio Bellavista is the focus of the city's nightlife—in a neighborhood where most clubs don't *open* until midnight or 1 A.M., and hardly anybody goes before 2 A.M., it's almost impossible to believe that, during the Pinochet dictatorship, there was an 11 P.M. *curfew* in the city.

Additional pockets of nightspots are in and around Santiago Centro, along Providencia's Avenida Suecia and side streets, and in and around Plaza Ñuñoa, in the largely middle-class borough

SANTIAGO

of the same name. Note that many bars and dance clubs, especially gay venues, have no obvious public signs except during opening hours.

Bars

Barrio Lastarria's **Bar Berri,** Rosal 321, tel. 2/6384734, is a quiet neighborhood bar that also serves fine fixed-price lunches.

Barrio Brasil's **N'aitún,** Avenida Ricardo Cumming 453, tel. 2/6718410, is a throwback to the Allende years: an activist bookstore that has an upstairs bar with basic food—sandwiches and snacks—along with folk-oriented music and political theater.

Bellavista's **La Casa en el Aire,** Antonia López de Bello 0125, tel. 2/7356680, website: www.casaenelaire.cl, is a direct descendent of the *peñas* of the 1960s and 1970s, with folkloric music, storytelling, films, and the like in a distinctly alternative milieu; for the most current events listing, see the website. Besides the original Bellavista locale, there's a branch at Santa Isabel 0411, Providencia, tel. 2/2228789.

La Cámara Negra, Antonia Lopez de Bello 0126, tel. 2/7776763, offers live jazz on weekends. Also in Bellavista, **Altazor,** Antonia López de Bello 0189, tel. 2/7779651, is a folk music venue, like the traditional **Peña Nano Parra,** Ernesto Pinto Lagarrigue 80, tel. 2/7356093.

Finding rock bands in small venues is not easy, but try **Clan Destino,** on the Recoleta side of Bellavista, Antonia López de Bello 146, tel. 2/7771346. The consistently best locale for rock music is Ñuñoa's **La Batuta,** directly on Plaza Ñuñoa at Jorge Washington 52, tel. 2/2747096.

As unlikely as it seems, one of Chile's most popular bands is the homegrown reggae group Gondwana; when it's not in town, Santiago's wannabe dreads hang out to hear Bob Marley at Bellavista's **Jammin' Club,** Antonia López de Bello 49.

Providencia's Avenida Suecia and cross streets are home to a swarm of slick theme-oriented bars that tend toward kitsch, but the drinks are good, often imaginative, and a bargain during happy hours that, on weeknights, can last until midnight. Among them are Australian-run **Boomerang,** General Holley 2285, tel.

2/3345081, which has managed to survive and even sustain its popularity in a highly competitive environment; the roughly comparable **Brannigan's,** Avenida Suecia 035, tel. 2/2325172; **Old Boston Pub,** General Holley 2291, tel. 2/2315169; **Wall Street,** General Holley 99, tel. 2/2325548; and **Mister Ed,** Avenida Suecia 0152, tel. 2/2312624. Many of these places are also popular locales for lunch and *onces,* though the food is only ordinary.

Despite its relative isolation in Las Condes's uptown business district, the one-of-a-kind **Los Andes,** Avenida Apoquindo 3012, tel. 2/2311911, is an increasingly trendy brewpub (while Chilean draft beer is not bad, it's usually factory batch stuff).

Discos and Dance Clubs

Blondie, Alameda 2879, tel. 2/6817793, is a four-floor dance club, featuring a variety of musical styles and occasional live acts, that can accommodate up to 2,000 people at a time—two-thirds of those on the main floor.

Bellavista's **Oz,** Chucre Manzur 6, tel. 2/7377066, is a techno disco and events center in a cavernous ex-warehouse on the southern slope of Cerro San Cristóbal; open Thursday, Friday, and Saturday 11:30 P.M.–4:30 A.M., it collects US$12 pp cover. **Zoom,** Antonia López de Bello 56, tel. 2/7351167, has both live and recorded music for dancing, while **Tomm,** Bellavista 098, tel. 2/7779985, emphasizes live acts.

Salsa is booming on the Recoleta side of Barrio Bellavista, thanks to the Habana Vieja ambience at **Havana Salsa,** Dominica 142, tel. 2/7371737, but canned music is the rule; only **Salsoteca Maestra Vida,** Pío Nono 380, tel. 2/7357416, has live bands, and not every night.

Nightclubs

Several venerable venues hold stage and floor shows, often but not always featuring clichéd versions of aspects of Chilean culture such as the *cueca,* along with typical cuisine such as *pastel de choclo* and *cazuela de ave.* The most interesting of these is **Confitería Las Torres,** Alameda 1570, tel. 2/6986220, a magnificent building exuding 19th-century ambience out of the woodwork and that hosts live tango shows on weekends. If you can't make Buenos Aires' Café Tortoni, this is the next best option.

The garish **Los Adobes de Argomedo,** south of the Alameda at Argomedo 411, tel. 2/2222104, is a popular stop for foreign tour groups on the farewell dinners, but it gets plenty of Chilean business as well. The floor show is participatory—get ready to *cueca.*

In the same Barrio Brasil location since 1939, **Los Buenos Muchachos,** Avenida Ricardo Cumming 1031, tel. 2/6980112, seats up to 1,000 people for lunch or dinner and show, with its own orchestra and floor show and occasional special guest performances.

Gay and Lesbian Venues

The Recoleta side of Barrio Bellavista is home to most of Santiago's gay clubs, but there are a few scattered elsewhere around town. The most discreet of the bunch is **Capricho Español,** Purísima 65, tel. 2/7777674, whose patrons often meet for a quiet drink and/or dinner before a night on the town. **Vox Populi,** Ernesto Pinto Lagarrigue 364, tel. 2/7380562, is also a casual café-style spot.

Venues such as the gigantic **Bunker,** which holds up to 1,000 partygoers on Thursday, Friday, and Saturday nights at Bombero Núñez 159, tel. 2/7773760, appeal to those who can afford the US$10-plus cover charge. **Bokhara,** Pío Nono 430, tel. 2/7321050, is a lively scene that looks bigger than it is, as plenty of hangers-on crowd around the entrance without actually entering. **Fausto,** a bit less central at Avenida Santa María 0832, tel. 2/7771041, draws a mixed-aged crowd on separate levels linked by a broad staircase that encourages interaction. **Queen,** on the south side of the Mapocho at Coronel Bueras 128, tel. 2/6398703, does drag shows with a modest cover charge.

Lesbians are welcome at all of these places, but they also have their own options, such as **Máscara's,** Purísima 129, tel. 2/7374123.

Cultural Centers

The **Instituto Chileno-Norteamericano de Cultura,** Moneda 1467, tel. 2/6963215, sponsors art exhibits and similar cultural events and has an English-language library, as does the **Instituto Chileno-Británico,** Santa Lucía 124, tel. 2/6382156. The most elaborate and active foreign cultural center, however, is Providencia's

CINEMAS

Santiago's traditional cinema district is downtown along Paseo Huérfanos and nearby streets, where many former large theaters have been modified into multiscreen facilities. Elsewhere in town, newer custom-built multiplexes are the rule.

Foreign films generally appear in the original language with Spanish subtitles. Most theaters offer half-price discounts Wednesdays only.

Gran Palace, Huérfanos 1176, tel. 2/6960082

Cine Hoyts, Huérfanos 735, tel. 2/6641861

Cine Huelén, Huérfanos 779, tel. 2/6331603

Cine Las Condes, Apoquindo and Noruega, Las Condes, tel. 2/2208816

Cine Lido, Huérfanos 680, tel. 2/6330797

Cine Lo Castillo, Candelaria Goyenechea 3820, Vitacura, tel. 2/2421342

Teatro Oriente, Pedro de Valdivia 099, Providencia, tel. 2/2317151

Showcase Cinemas Parque Arauco, Avenida Kennedy 5413, Local 250, Las Condes, tel. 2/2247707

Art Houses
Independent films generally show at smaller venues scattered around town. Wednesday discounts are also available.

Cine Alameda, Alameda 139, tel. 2/6392479

Cine Arte Aiep, Miguel Claro 177, Providencia, tel. 2/2649698

Cine Arte Vitacura, Embajador Doussignane 1767, Vitacura, tel. 2/2192384

Centro de Extensión de la Universidad Católica, Alameda 390, tel. 2/6351994

Cine El Biógrafo, Lastarria 181, tel. 2/6334435

Cine Normandie, Tarapacá 1181, tel 2/6972979

Cine Tobalaba, Avenida Providencia 2563, Providencia, tel. 2/2316630

Centro Cultural de España, Avenida Providencia 927, tel. 2/2351105, which has events nearly every night.

Cinema

Several multiscreen cinemas, both in Santiago Centro and outlying *comunas,* show current films, often in English with Spanish subtitles. Children's films and animated features such as Disney productions, however, usually appear in Spanish. (For locations and phone numbers, see the accompanying chart.)

Performing Arts

Santiago has many live theater and music venues, with a range of offerings from serious classical and contemporary drama to vulgar burlesque, and from traditional folk to rock and classical; the best place to find current offerings is the entertainment section of the daily *El Mercurio.*

The landmark **Teatro Municipal,** Agustinas 794, tel. 2/3690282, is the city's most prestigious performing arts venue, hosting classical music, opera, and occasional popular musicals. Only opening performances are truly formal, however, and Santiaguinos sometimes show up in surprisingly casual clothes; during opera performances, the theater projects a Spanish translation of the libretto above the stage so that it's easier to follow the plot (if you read Spanish).

Musicians rave about the sound quality at the **Teatro Universidad de Chile,** Avenida Providencia 043, tel. 2/6345295, best known for ballet and classical music, but which even hosts the occasional rock event.

The Centro Cultural Estación Mapocho, occupying the restored former northern railway station at Balmaceda 1301, houses two important playhouses: the **Teatro Casa Amarilla,** tel. 2/6720347, and the **Teatro Estación Mapocho,** tel. 2/7356046. Other Santiago Centro locales include the **Teatro Nacional Chileno,** Morandé 25, tel. 2/6717850; the Universidad de Chile's **Sala Agustín Sire,** Morandé 750, tel. 2/6965142; and the smallish **Teatro La Comedia,** Merced 349, tel. 2/6391523. South of the Alameda, the capacious **Teatro Monumental,** San Diego 850, tel. 2/6922000, showcases rock and pop music.

Smaller repertory groups play Barrio Bellavista venues such as **Teatro Bellavista,** Dardignac 0110, tel. 2/7356264; **Teatro El Conventillo,** Bellavista 173, tel. 2/7774164; **Teatro Galpón,** Chucre Manzur 9-B, tel. 2/7375786; and **Teatro La Feria,** Crucero Exeter 0250, tel. 2/7377371. Possibly the most unusual venue is the **Teatro del Puente,** Parque Forestal s/n, tel. 2/7324883, literally built on a bridge across the Mapocho.

Festivals

March's **Feria Internacional del Aire y del Espacio,** which takes place at Aeropuerto Los Cerrillos, the former domestic principal domestic airport in the *comuna* of Maipú, draws big crowds interested in general aviation but is also a showcase for international weapons manufacturers.

September's patriotic holidays are an excuse for parties and parades, but the month can also be contentious—September 11, the date of Pinochet's coup, usually sees disturbances around Providencia's Avenida 11 de Septiembre. September 18, **Día de la Independencia** (Independence Day) sees cheerful barbecues in the parks, but September 19's **Día del Ejército** (Armed Forces Day) is less universally beloved.

Note that, while **Halloween** (October 31) is not really a Chilean holiday, in nonconformist Bellavista it's one of the biggest nights of the year. Chileans honor their dead on **Día de los Muertos** (Day of the Dead), November 2.

At the Estación Mapocho, November's 10-day **Feria de Libro** (Book Festival) draws both Chilean writers and internationally recognized authors, such as Argentina's Federico Andahazi, in what has become a major event.

On the north bank of the Mapocho, Providencia's Centro Cultural Montecarmelo, Bellavista 594, tel. 2/7770882, hosts an annual **Fiesta de Cerámica** (Ceramics Festival) during the two weeks before Christmas.

SPORTS AND RECREATION

Santiago and environs offer a surprising number of alternatives for both personal recreation and spectator sports (for details, see the geographical entries under Vicinity of Santiago, below).

Soccer

Like other Latin Americans, Chileans are passionate about soccer. Most major matches take place in Ñuñoa's **Estadio Nacional,** the single biggest venue in town, built for the 1960 World Cup and then used, 13 years later, for incarcerating, torturing, and executing political prisoners in the aftermath of the Pinochet coup.

SHOPPING

Santiago may not be one of the world's great shopping meccas, but good-quality handicrafts and antiques from around the country are widely available. Many visitors, of course, take home Chilean wines.

Books

The **Feria Chilena del Libro** chain has several branches, but the largest is downtown at Huérfanos 623, tel. 2/6396758. Nearby, within the Biblioteca Nacional, **Ediciones Lom,** Moneda 650, tel. 2/3605321, has the best selection of current titles on Chilean history and culture; it has an additional branch at the ex-Estación Mapocho.

For academic and antiquarian tastes, try downtown's **Librería Luis Rivano,** San Diego 119, Local 7, or especially Providencia's **Librería Chile Ilustrado,** Avenida Providencia 1652, tel. 2/2358145. At the same address, **Books** has a selection of used English-language paperbacks at fairly high prices.

Vitacura's outstanding **Librería Eduardo Albers,** Avenida Vitacura 5648, tel. 2/2185371, has a fine selection of guidebooks (including this one) and other general-interest books in English and German.

Music

For CDs or tapes of present and past Chilean music, try the chain **Feria del Disco,** Ahumada 286, tel. 2/6715290.

Handicrafts

Downtown's best souvenir shops are **Chile Típico,** Moneda 1025, Local 149, tel. 2/6965504, and **Huimpalay,** Huérfanos 1162, tel.

2/6721395, but they charge premium prices. Cerro Santa Lucía's **Centro de Exposición de Arte Indígena,** in the semisubterranean Grutas del Cerro Welén at Alameda 499, tel. 2/6641352, has the best choice of Mapuche, Aymara, and Rapanui crafts; it's open daily except Sunday 10 A.M.–6 P.M. Directly across the Alameda is the open-air **Centro Artesanal Santa Lucía.**

Bellavista is the destination for lapis lazuli jewelry, at locales such as **Lapiz Lazuli House,** Bellavista 014, tel. 2/7321419 (numerous alternatives are in the vicinity). **Chile Vivo,** Dardignac 15, tel. 2/7353959, displays a large selection of handicrafts—from basketry to lapis lazuli, leather, silverwork, and wood carvings. For items from the countryside, try the **Cooperativa Almacén Campesina,** Purísima 303, tel. 2/7372117.

Antiques

The best antique shops are concentrated in the vicinity of Cerro Santa Lucía, such as **Antigüedades Haddad,** José Miguel de la Barra 496, tel. 2/6392157, and in Bellavista, **Arte del Mundo,** Dardignac 67, tel. 2/7352507.

Wine

If visiting wineries isn't on your agenda but buying wine is, several representative outlets are in Las Condes: **Vinópolis,** Avenida El Bosque Norte 038, tel. 2/2323814; the **Vinoteca,** Isidora Goyenechea 3520, tel. 2/3341987; and **The Wine House,** Avenida Vitacura 3446, tel. 2/2073533, fax 2/2070581, winehous@entelchile.net.

SERVICES

Like accommodations and restaurants, most of the major tourist services are concentrated in Santiago Centro, Providencia, and Las Condes, though a few important addresses are elsewhere in the city.

Money

ATMs are so abundant that exchange houses have become virtual dinosaurs except for changing traveler's checks or leftover cash. Most exchange houses are downtown on Agustinas, between Bandera and Ahumada, but there are others in Providencia and at the airport (where rates are substantially lower).

For replacing lost or stolen traveler's checks, contact the AmEx or Thomas Cook representatives (see the entry for Travel Agencies, below).

Postal

The Correo Central (main post office), Plaza de Armas 983, is open 8 A.M.–10 P.M. weekdays, 8 A.M.–6 P.M. Saturday. In addition to *poste restante* (general delivery), it has a philatelic office. Many branch offices are scattered around town.

For international courier service, the most reliable office is Federal Express, Avenida Providencia 1951, tel. 2/2315250.

Telephone and Internet

Santiago has many long-distance *centros de llamados,* such as Entelchile at Paseo Huérfanos 1133, Chilesat at Avenida 11 de Septiembre 1949 in Providencia, and Telefónica CTC at Metro stations and elsewhere. The metropolitan region's area code is 2.

The number of Internet outlets has increased rapidly and prices have fallen to around US$2 per hour or even less. One of the most central is Dazoc@, opposite the Bellas Artes Metro station at Monjitas 448, tel. 2/6339377.

Barrio Brasil has several outlets in a university area within a block or so of Hostelling International: Via@net, Moneda 1946, tel. 2/6972568, open 9 A.M.–midnight daily; Cyber Café Punto-Com, Cienfuegos 161; and Webtrade, tel. 2/6991574, Agustinas 1838, Local 4.

In Barrio Bellavista, ChileInternet, Antonia Lopez de Bello 45, tel. 2/7320669, sometimes misses its opening hours of 10 A.M. (weekdays) and noon (weekends). It's open until midnight every night.

Providencia's Café Phonet, General Holley 2312, has equally inexpensive Internet connections and international telephone service. It's open 9 A.M.–11 P.M.; its Las Condes branch at San Sebastián 2815 stays open into the early hours.

Providencia's Dity Office, Fidel Oteíza 1930, tel. 2/2692610, is an efficient business-oriented place, but it's a bit more expensive than most.

Immigration

The Departamento de Extranjería, Moneda 1342, Santiago Centro, tel. 2/6725320, is open for tourist visa extensions 8:30 A.M.–3:30 P.M. daily (remember that the hefty fee, about US$100, can as easily pay for a trip across the Argentine border). Replacing a lost tourist card requires a trip to the Policía Internacional, General Borgoño 1052, Independencia, tel. 2/7371292, just across the Mapocho from the old railroad station. Hours are 8:30 A.M.–12:30 P.M. and 3–7 P.M. weekdays.

Laundry

Convenient laundries are in most parts of town, including Santiago Centro's Lavandería Autoservicio, Monjitas 507, tel. 2/6321772; Barrio Brasil's Lavandería Lolos, Moneda 2296, tel. 2/6995376; and Providencia's Laverap, Avenida Providencia 1645.

Travel Agencies

One of Chile's biggest travel agencies, Las Condes' Turismo Cocha, Avenida El Bosque Norte 0430, tel. 2/2301000, fax 2/2035110, is the AmEx representative, offering a variety of services. Turismo Tajamar, Orrego Luco 023, tel. 2/2329595, Providencia, is the Thomas Cook affiliate.

The Student Flight Center, Hernando de Aguirre 201, Oficina 401, Providencia, tel. 2/3350395, fax 2/3350394, stflictr@ctc-mundo. net, offers big discounts to those with just about any sort of student identification; it can also help the general public.

(For operators and excursions in the vicinity of Santiago, see the separate entry below.)

Camera Repair and Service

For simple camera repairs and service, try Von Stowasser, Santa Magdalena 16, Providencia, tel. 2/2315559. For more complex needs, visit Harry Müller Thierfelder, Ahumada 312, Oficina 312, Santiago Centro, tel. 2/6983596, or Photo Service, Avenida Suecia 84, 8th floor, Oficina 81, Providencia, tel. 2/3354460.

Medical

The Posta Central is a state-run emergency clinic at Avenida Portugal 125, Santiago Centro, tel. 2/6341650; the private Clínica Universidad

Católica is nearby at Lira 40, tel. 2/6334122. The Clínica Alemana, Avenida Vitacura 5951, Vitacura, tel. 2129700, is highly regarded.

INFORMATION

Santiago is home to Chile's central tourism agency but also to municipal authorities and some private information sources.

Tourist Offices

Sernatur, the national tourist service, has its headquarters at Avenida Providencia 1550, tel. 2/7318300, info@sernatur.cl. Open 9:30 A.M.–8 P.M. weekdays, 9:30 A.M.–6 P.M. weekends, it has competent English-speaking personnel who distribute maps and information on city attractions and services and brochures on the rest of the country. It also has an international airport office, tel. 2/6019320, open 8:15 A.M.–9:30 P.M. daily.

The municipal Oficina de Turismo, half a block east of the Plaza de Armas at Merced 860, tel. 2/6327785, tur-ims@entelchile.net, shares space with the colonial Casa Colorada; a satellite office is on Cerro Santa Lucía, tel. 2/6644206. Both are open 10 A.M.–6 P.M. Monday through Thursday, 10 A.M.–5 P.M. Friday. A municipal tourist kiosk is also at the intersection of the Huérfanos and Ahumada pedestrian malls.

Motorists

The Automóvil Club de Chile (Acchi), Fidel Oteíza 1960, Providencia, tel. 2/2253790, has reciprocal agreements with overseas automobile clubs such as the AAA (in the United States) and the AA (in Britain).

National Parks

The Corporación Nacional Forestal (Conaf), south of the Alameda at Avenida Bulnes 291,

---

FOREIGN EMBASSIES AND CONSULATES IN SANTIAGO

All major European and South American states, plus many others, have diplomatic representation in Santiago. The bordering countries of Argentina, Bolivia, and Peru have consulates in several other cities; their addresses appear in the appropriate geographical entry.

Argentina, Vicuña Mackenna 41, tel. 2/2228977

Australia, Gertrudis Echeñique 420, Las Condes, tel. 2/2285065

Bolivia, Avenida Santa María 2796, Providencia, tel. 2/2328180

Brazil, MacIver 225, 15th floor, tel. 2/6398867

Canada, Nueva Tajamar 481, 12th floor, Las Condes, tel. 2/3629660

France, Condell 65, Providencia, tel. 2/2251030

Germany, Las Hualtatas 55677, Vitacura, tel. 2/4632500, fax 2/4632525

Israel, San Sebastián 2812, 5th floor, Las Condes, tel. 2/7500500

Italy, Román Díaz 1270, Providencia, tel. 2/2259212

Mexico, Félix de Amesti 128, Las Condes, tel. 2/2066132

Netherlands, Las Violetas 2368, Providencia, tel. 2/2236825

New Zealand, El Golf 99, Oficina 703, Las Condes, tel. 2/2909802

Paraguay, Huérfanos 886, Oficina 514, tel. 2/6394640

Peru, Padre Mariano 10, Oficina 309, Providencia, tel. 2/2354600

Spain, Avenida 11 de Septiembre 2353, 9th floor, Providencia, tel. 2/2334070

Sweden, Avenida 11 de Septiembre 2353, 4th floor, Providencia, tel. 2/2312733

Switzerland, Américo Vespucio Sur 100, 14th floor, tel. 2/2634211

United Kingdom, Avenida El Bosque Norte 0125, 3rd floor, Las Condes, tel. 2/2313737

Uruguay, Pedro de Valdivia 711, Providencia, tel. 2/2238398

United States of America, Avenida Costanera Andrés Bello 2800, Las Condes, tel. 2/2322600

tel. 2/3900282 or 2/3900125, provides information on national parks, reserves, and natural monuments; it also sells decent but inexpensive maps of protected areas that are often not available in the regions, as well as books and pamphlets. It's open 9 A.M.–1 P.M. and 2–4:30 P.M. weekdays only.

Maps

Though it no longer comes in a compact and relatively durable paperback book format, Telefónica CTC's *Plano de Santiago* is indispensable for its full-color coverage and detailed index of city streets. The format now resembles a Sunday newspaper supplement, on flimsy newsprint.

JLM Cartografía's *Santiago* covers most of the city well, but it lacks a scale; it also includes a country map at a scale of 1:3,000,000. Widely available overseas, ITM's *Santiago de Chile,* at a scale of 1:12,500, is good for getting around and has a street index, but it has numerous misspellings.

Libraries

The Biblioteca Nacional (National Library) is at Alameda 651, tel. 2/3605200.

Newspapers

Santiago's most venerable newspaper is the conservative daily *El Mercurio,* but it partially compensates for its editorial bias with broad international, business, cultural, and entertainment coverage. The tabloid *La Nación* is the official government daily, but its editorial line has a more diverse and independent feel than *Mercurio. La Tercera* and *La Cuarta* are both conservative dailies—the former has some credibility, but the latter focuses on sensationalist crime and sex stories.

LANGUAGE SCHOOLS

Perhaps because Chilean Spanish is so distinctive and Santiago is distant from the language study centers of Mexico and Central America, it lacks the critical mass of language schools that some other Latin American capitals have. Still, there are several possibilities in the city; most work with small groups of students but offer one-on-one classes for higher fees. Most of them offer housing or can help arrange housing with a Chilean family.

Near Cerro Santa Lucía, the **Instituto Chileno-Suizo de Idiomas,** José Victorino Lastarria 93, 2nd floor, tel. 2/6385414, website: www.chilenosuizo.tie.cl, chilenosuizo@tie.cl, charges from US$156 for weeklong courses (20 hours' instruction) to US$780 for monthlong courses (100 hours). Private one-on-one classes cost US$15 per hour.

Providencia's **Natalis Language Center,** Vicuña Mackenna 6, 7th floor, tel./fax 2/2228721, website: www.natalislang.com, info@natalis.com, charges US$150 pp for weeklong courses (25 hours) with small groups; discounts are available for longer courses.

Bellavista's **Escuela Violeta Parra,** Ernesto Pinto Lagarrigue 362-A, Recoleta, tel. 2/7358240, fax 2/2298246, website: www.tandemsantiago.cl, vioparra@entelchile.net, is particularly strong on field excursions that tie in with its political and social commitment. Rates start at US$135 weekly for four hours' daily instruction.

The **Centro de Idiomas Bellavista,** Crucero Exeter 0325, Providencia, tel. 2/7357651, website: www.cib.in.cl, fdo@cib.cl, charges US$285 pp for three-week courses (five hours' instruction daily) for groups up to four people; besides arranging accommodations with Chilean families, it has its own guesthouse, charging US$14 pp per day.

TRANSPORTATION

The only means of arriving in Santiago are by air or overland. There is international air service from most South American capitals and some provincial cities, and from Europe, North America and the Caribbean, and across the Pacific. Domestic air service is available from Arica, near the Peruvian border, to Punta Arenas, in the far south, and to Easter Island (Rapa Nui) and the Juan Fernández archipelago.

International and domestic overland passengers arrive by bus from Peru, Argentina, and many destinations throughout the country. Regular passenger train service connects Santiago with the southern cities of Temuco and Concepción.

INTERNATIONAL AIRLINES IN SANTIAGO

This list includes only airlines that fly to and from Santiago, though several other foreign airlines also have local representatives. Unless otherwise noted, the offices are in Santiago Centro.

Aerolíneas Argentinas, Moneda 756, tel. 2/6393922

Aerocontinente, Marchant Pereira 353, Providencia, tel. 2/2042424

Aeroméxico, Ebro 2738, Las Condes, tel. 2/2345851

Air France, Alcántara 44, 6th floor, Las Condes, tel. 2/2909330

Air New Zealand, Avenida 11 de Septiembre 1881, Oficina 713, Providencia, tel. 2/3769039

Alitalia, Avenida Bosque Norte 0107, Oficina 21, tel. 2/3788230

American Airlines, Huérfanos 1199, tel. 2/6790000

Avianca, Santa Magdalena 116, Local 101, Providencia, tel. 2/2706620

British Airways, Isidora Goyenechea 2934, Oficina 302, Las Condes, tel. 2/3308600

Copa, Fidel Oteíza 1921, Oficina 703, Providencia, tel. 2/2002100

Cubana de Aviación, Fidel Oteíza 1971, Oficina 201, Providencia, tel. 2/2741819

Delta, Isidora Goyenechea 2939, Oficina 401, Las Condes, tel. 2/2801600

Grupo Taca, Barros Borgoño 105, 2nd floor, Providencia, tel. 2/2355500

Iberia, Bandera 206, 8th floor, tel. 2/8701010

LanChile, Agustinas 640, tel. 2/6323442

Lloyd Aéreo Boliviano (LAB), Moneda 1170, tel. 2/6888680

Lufthansa, Moneda 970, 16th floor, tel. 2/6301655

Mexicana, Avenida 11 de Septiembre 2329, Providencia, tel. 2/2329057

Pluna, Avenida El Bosque Norte 0177, 9th floor, Las Condes, tel. 2/7078000

Qantas, Isidora Goyenechea 2934, Oficina 301, Las Condes, tel. 2/2329562

SAS/Spanair, Mardoqueo Fernández 128, Oficina 502, Providencia, tel. 2/2333585

Saeta, Santa Magdalena 75, Oficina 209, Providencia, tel. 2/3344427

South African, Zurich 221, Oficina 11, Las Condes, tel. 2/5205880

Transportes Aéreos Mercosur (TAM), Santa Magdalena 94, Providencia, tel. 2/3811337

TAME (Ecuador), Moneda 970, 16th floor, tel. 2/6301681

United Airlines, Tenderini 171, tel. 2/6320279; Avenida El Bosque Norte 0177, 19th floor, Las Condes, tel. 2/3370000

Varig, Avenida El Bosque Norte 0177, Oficina 903, Las Condes, tel. 2/7078000

Air

Serving all international and nearly all domestic flights, the modern Aeropuerto Internacional Arturo Merino Benítez is 26 km west of Santiago Centro in the *comuna* of Pudahuel, tel. 2/6019001 or 2/6019709; there are separate international and domestic terminals alongside each other.

Flights to and from the Juan Fernández archipelago use the former principal domestic Aeropuerto Cerrillos, Avenida Pedro Aguirre Cerda in the southwestern part of the city, and Aeródromo Tobalaba, Avenida Larraín 7941 in the southeastern *comuna* of La Reina. (For information on these flights, see the Chilean Pacific Islands chapter.)

LanExpress, the domestic service of LanChile, Agustinas 640, tel. 2/6323442, flies northbound to La Serena, Antofagasta, Calama, Iquique, and Arica, and southbound to Concepción, Temuco, Valdivia, Puerto Montt, Balmaceda, and Punta Arenas. LanChile's international flights to Tahiti stop at Easter Island before continuing across the Pacific (for details on this route, see the Chilean Pacific Islands chapter).

Aerocontinente, Marchant Pereira 357, tel. 2/2424242, flies northbound to Antofagasta (US$75–159), Iquique (US$84–159) and Arica

TERRAPUERTO LOS HÉROES

Carriers serving northern and southern destinations from Terrapuerto Los Héroes, Tucapel Jiménez 21, tel. 2/4200099, heroebus@entelchile.net, include the following.

Buses Ahumada, tel. 2/6969798, to the central coast and south to Puerto Montt and intermediates

Buses Fénix, tel. 2/6969321, to Arica and intermediates

Buses Libac, tel. 2/6985974, to the Norte Chico

Cruz del Sur, tel. 2/6969324, to Los Lagos and Chiloé

Flota Barrios, tel. 2/6969311, to Valparaíso/Viña del Mar and north to Arica and intermediates

Pullman del Sur, tel. 2/6731967, to Puerto Montt and intermediates

Tas Choapa, tel. 2/6969326, north to Antofagasta and intermediates and south to Puerto Montt and intermediates

(US$89–165), and southbound to Puerto Montt (US$62–125) and Punta Arenas (US$95–159).

(For more information on international carriers and destinations, see the accompanying chart and the On the Road chapter.)

Bus

Santiago's four major bus terminals are on or near the Alameda; some companies have offices at more than one of these. Most northbound long-distance carriers use Terminal San Borja, San Borja 184, tel. 2/7760645, most easily reached through the market alongside the Estación Central, the central railroad station. Some northbound carriers also use Terrapuerto Los Héroes, Tucapel Jiménez 21, tel. 2/4200099, where some long-distance buses from Terminal Santiago (see below) pick up additional passengers.

Tur-Bus, its discount subsidiary Cóndor Bus, and Pullman Bus use the Terminal de Buses Alameda, Alameda 3750, tel. 2/3761755, for a wide variety of destinations; the closest Metro station is Universidad de Santiago. Most southbound carriers use the nearby Terminal Santiago (also known as Terminal de Buses Sur), Alameda 3848, tel. 2/3761750.

In addition, several carriers maintain ticket outlets at the Torres de Tajamar complex, Avenida Providencia 1100: Buses Jac, tel. 2/2352484; Fénix Pullman Norte, tel. 2/2359707; Libac, tel. 2/2352520; Los Corsarios, tel. 2/2354810; Pullman Bus, tel. 2/2358142; Tas Choapa, tel. 2/2352405; and Tur-Bus, tel. 2/2362595.

Domestic Destinations and Fares: Fares can fluctuate both seasonally and among companies, so comparison pricing is advisable. Note also that the correlation between distance and price is imperfect—some longer trips can be cheaper because competition is greater to certain destinations.

Sample destinations, fares, and journey times include Valparaíso or Viña del Mar (US$4, two hours); La Serena (US$13–20, seven hours); Copiapó (US$17–28, 11 hours); Antofagasta (US$33–42, 19 hours); Calama (US$41, 22 hours); Iquique (US$40–50, 26 hours); Arica (US$48–60, 28 hours); Chillán (US$11, six hours); Concepción (US$9–12, eight hours); Temuco (US$10–16, eight hours); Villarrica (US$12–20, 10 hours); Valdivia (US$15, 11 hours); Osorno (US$18, 14 hours); Puerto Montt (US$20, 16 hours); and Castro (US$18–22, 19 hours).

International Destinations and Fares: Most international carriers use Terminal Santiago, but the

TERMINAL DE BUSES ALAMEDA

The following carriers use the Terminal de Buses Alameda, Alameda 3750, tel. 2/3761755.

Cóndor Bus, tel. 2/7796724, to Valparaíso/Viña del Mar

Pullman Bus, tel. 2/7792036, to Valparaíso/Viña del Mar and northbound to Arica and intermediate points

Tur-Bus, tel. 2/2707500, to Valparaíso/Viña del Mar, northbound to Arica and intermediates, and southbound to Puerto Montt and intermediates

TERMINAL SAN BORJA

The following carriers serve coastal and northern destinations from Terminal San Borja, San Borja 184, tel. 2/7760645, website: www.paseoestacion.cl.

Buses Al Sur, tel. 2/7786637, to Rancagua

Buses Carmelita, tel. 2/7787579, to Arica and intermediates

Buses Combarbalá, tel. 2/7787362, to the Norte Chico and its interior

Buses Evans, tel. 2/7787361, to Arica and intermediates

Buses Fénix, tel. 2/7787074, to Arica and intermediates

Buses Golondrina, tel. 2/7787082, to Calera, Olmué, and Limache (Parque Nacional Las Campanas)

Buses Lit, tel. 2/7786857, to the Norte Chico

Buses Ruta 57, tel. 2/7794224, to Los Andes and San Felipe

Buses Tas Choapa, tel. 2/7786827, to the Norte Chico

Cóndor Bus, tel. 2/7787089, Valparaíso and Viña del Mar, the Norte Chico, and Puerto Montt and intermediates

Covalle Bus, tel. 2/7787576, to La Serena

Elqui Bus Palacios, tel. 2/7787045, to the Norte Chico

Expreso Norte/Vía Choapa, tel. 2/7787570, to the Norte Chico

Flota Barrios, tel. 2/7787363, to Valparaíso/Viña del Mar and north to Arica and intermediates

Libac, tel. 2/7787071, to Copiapó and intermediates

Los Corsarios, tel. 2/7787087, to the Norte Chico and Antofagasta

Pullman Bus, tel. 2/7787086, to Arica and intermediates

Pullman Fichtur, tel. 2/7787070, to Arica and intermediates

Ramos Cholele, tel. 2/7787551, to Iquique and Arica

Tur-Bus, tel. 2/7787336, Panamericana destinations north to Arica and south to Puerto Montt

handful that use Terminal los Héroes are specifically mentioned below. Note that for Mendoza-bound passengers, in addition to buses there are faster but only slightly more expensive *taxi colectivos*.

The Argentine city of Mendoza (US$15–20, seven hours), just across the Andes via the Libertadores tunnel, is the most frequent foreign destination; Mendoza's massive bus terminal has frequent onward connections throughout Argentina and to Brazil, Uruguay, and Paraguay. Mendoza-bound carriers include Andesmar, tel. 2/7762416; Buses Fénix, tel. 2/7767928; Cata, tel. 2/7793660; Covalle Bus, tel. 2/7787576; El Rápido Internacional, tel. 2/7790316; Transportes Automotores Cuyo (TAC), tel. 2/7796920; and Tur-Bus, tel. 2/7644716.

From Terminal Santiago, there are also *taxi colectivos* to Mendoza with Coitram, tel. 2/7761891, and Nevada, tel. 2/7764116, which are only slightly more expensive (around US$20).

From Terminal Los Héroes, Tas Choapa, tel. 2/6969326, serves Mendoza and Córdoba (US$40, 15 hours) via the Libertadores crossing, and Bariloche (US$36, 21 hours) via Osorno. Cruz del Sur, tel. 2/7790607, also goes to Bariloche via Osorno.

Buses Ahumada, also at Terminal Los Héroes, tel. 2/6969798, goes to Mendoza and Buenos Aires (US$52, 18 hours). Nar-Bus, tel. 2/7781235, goes to Junín de los Andes, San Martín de los Andes, and Neuquén via Temuco.

Pullman Bus, tel. 2/7795243, goes to Asunción, Paraguay (US$78, 30 hours) twice weekly. EGAS, tel. 2/7793536, goes to Montevideo, Uruguay (US$90, 28 hours) with onward connections to Brazil.

Pluma, tel. 2/7796054, goes weekly to Rio de Janeiro, Brazil (US$100, 52 hours), a direct service that does not allow stopovers in Argentina. Chile Bus, tel. 2/7765557, goes four times weekly to São Paulo (US$95, 50 hours) and to Rio de Janeiro; it also goes to La Paz, Bolivia,

TERMINAL DE BUSES SANTIAGO

Carriers that use the Terminal de Buses Santiago, Alameda 3848, tel. 2/3761750, serving southern and some northern destinations, appear in the list below. (For international services from the same terminal, see the separate entry in the main text.)

Buses Ahumada, tel. 2/7782703, to the central coast and Sur Chico

Andimar, tel. 2/7793810, to San Fernando (Ruta del Vino), Pichilemu, and Constitución

Bus Norte, tel. 2/7795433, to Sur Chico and Punta Arenas

Buses al Sur, tel. 2/3761750, to Rancagua and Talca

Buses Jac, tel. 2/7761582, to Temuco, Villarrica, and Pucón

Cóndor Bus, tel. 2/7793721, Valparaíso/Viña del Mar and Puerto Montt and intermediates

Cruz del Sur, tel. 2/7790607, to Los Lagos and Chiloé

Igi Llaima, tel. 2/7791751, to Sur Chico

Inter Sur, tel. 2/7796312, to Sur Chico

Buses Lit, tel. 2/7795710, to La Serena and vicinity

Panguisur, tel. 2/7781278, to Panguipulli and Los Lagos

Buses Tas Choapa, tel. 2/7794925, Puerto Montt and intermediates

Tur-Bus, tel. 2/7763690, Panamericana destinations between Arica and Puerto Montt

Buses Vía Tur, tel. 2/4508246, to Chillán, Concepción, and Puerto Montt and intermediates

---

via the Norte Grande, but this requires a change of buses in Iquique.

Ormeño, tel. 2/7793443, goes to Lima, Peru (US$100, 50 hours) twice weekly, continuing to Quito, Bogotá, and Caracas—certified by the *Guinness Book of Records* as the world's longest bus route.

Train

From the Estación Central, Alameda 3322, tel. 2/3768500, Ferrocarriles del Estado has an 8 P.M. train nightly to Temuco and intermediates, a 10:30 P.M. train nightly to Concepción and intermediates, and 8:30 A.M., 2:30 P.M., and 6:30 P.M. trains to Chillán; there is an additional 7:15 P.M. Friday train to Chillán. Tickets are also on sale at two Metro stations: Universidad de Chile, Local 10, tel. 2/6883284, and Escuela Militar, Galería Sur, tel. 2/2282983.

While trains may be few, fares are low. Sample destinations and fares, depending on the type of seat, include Curicó (US$2.60–3), Talca (US$3–5), Chillán (US$4.50–7.50), Saltos del Laja (US$5.50–9), Victoria (US$7–11), and Temuco (US$7.50–12).

The night trains also include classic sleeper cars whose *cama baja* (lower berths) cost about US$23 to Concepción, US$29 to Temuco; *cama alta* (upper berths) cost US$17 to Concepción, US$23 to Temuco.

GETTING AROUND

Santiago has plenty of public transport at reasonable cost, with a particularly outstanding Metro. A big help in finding your way around the city is Sernatur's free *Plano de Santiago*.

Airport Transport

The Metro's Línea 1 has an end-of-the-line station at Pudahuel, but it goes nowhere close to the airport; fortunately, there are several other convenient options, from inexpensive buses to moderately priced shuttles and more expensive taxis (not that expensive if shared by several people).

The cheapest option (US$1.50 pp) is Centropuerto, tel. 2/6958058, which has about 40 buses daily between 5:55 A.M. and 10:30 P.M.; return buses leave the international terminal 6:40 A.M.–11:30 P.M. Buses leave from Plazoleta Los Héroes, just off the eastbound lanes of the Alameda outside the Los Héroes Metro station.

On weekdays, Tur-Bus, Moneda 1529, tel. 2/6717380, goes to the airport every 15 minutes 6:30 A.M.–8:30 P.M., then every half hour until 10 P.M.; weekend schedules are every half hour 5:30 A.M.–10:30 P.M. Weekday return times are every 15 minutes 6 A.M.–11:15 P.M., weekends every half hour. From the Terminal de Buses Alameda, Tur-Bus goes to the airport every half hour 6:30 A.M.–9 P.M., returning 7:20 A.M.–8:20 P.M. Fares are US$1.75 pp.

For shuttle services, it's better to call a day in advance. Transvip, tel. 2/6773000, provides door-to-door service for the entire city, starting around US$5 to Santiago Centro; Providencia, Las Condes, and other eastern *comunas* are slightly more expensive. With frequent departures to and from the airport, this is the best option for travelers with heavy luggage or those who ar-

METROARTE

One of the quickest and cheapest ways to gain an appreciation of contemporary Chilean art is to spend at least part of a day riding the Metro. Since beginning its "MetroArte" program in 1993, the system has decorated many stations, all but one of them on Línea 1, with massive murals and sculptures, not to mention display cases with historical dioramas and other cultural items.

At **Estación Universidad de Chile,** Mario Toral's epic two-part, 1,200-square-meter *Memoria Visual de una Nación* (Visual Memory of a Nation) is perhaps the most remarkable of all MetroArte works in that it deals with controversial and conflictive episodes in Chilean history, including the 1907 massacre of nitrate workers at Iquique and the air force bombing of the Palacio de la Moneda in 1973. In the same station, Hernán Miranda's relatively small (24 square meters) oil *Interior Urbano* (Urban Interior) is a reflection on psychological isolation in the city.

At the sprawling **Estación Baquedano** transfer station, there are five separate works. Osvaldo Peña's *El Puente* (The Bridge) portrays a human figure, carved from native cypress, crossing a 15-meter bridge of iron and *coigüe,* another native wood. Hernán Miranda's *Ojo en Azul* (Blue Eye) is a digital painting on synthetic fabric. Samy Benmayor's playful *Declaración de Amor* (Declaration of Love), a take on the fable of Cupid that reflects his affection for the city, consists of brightly painted cast-iron figures mounted on a concrete wall. Francisco Smythe's *Vía Láctea* (Milky Way) is an abstract jumble of color and light, covering 286 square meters. Matías Pinto D'Aguiar's *La Bajada* (The Descent) depicts several horses descending to the platform.

At **Estación Pedro de Valdivia,** Juan Santiago Tapia's *El Cielo* (The Sky) covers the entire vaulted ceiling above the station platforms with colored glass to mimic the night sky. Enrique Zamudio's *La Ciudad* (The City) consists of four separate murals with enameled silkscreen portrayals of some of Santiago's best-known landmarks. Osvaldo Peña's cast-iron sculpture *El Viaje* depicts a typical Santiago commuter.

At **Estación Santa Lucía,** a donation from the city of Lisbon, Rogerio Ribeiro's *Azulejos para Santiago* (Tiles for Santiago) comprises 44,000 separate tiles, covering 600 square meters in four separate panels, each with a distinct historical theme: the sea, the land, the voyage, and discovery.

At **Estación Los Leones,** covering 480 square meters, Ramón Vergara Grez's ceramic mural *Geometría Andina* (Andean Geometry) is a colorful mosaic profile of the Andes. At **Estación Los Héroes,** Pablo McClure's abstract oil *Constelación II* (Constellation II) covers 380 square meters.

At **Estación República,** the youth collective Niños de Integra fashioned the brightly painted ceramic surface of *La República de los Niños* (The Children's Republic). At **Estación Parque Bustamante,** on Línea 5, Pablo Rivera's copper-plated abstract sculpture *El Sitio de las Cosas* (The Place of Things) consists of polyurethane injected into fiberglass.

In addition to these permanent works, the Metro reserves space in its **Galería Cal y Canto,** at its namesake station, for up-and-coming artists through its *Arte Joven en el Metro* (Young Art in the Metro) program. It also offers rotating exhibitions in the **Esplanada Cultural** at Estación Baquedano, a **Sala Patrimonial** (Historical Hall) at Estación Plaza de Armas, and a space for the most prestigious established artists at **Estación Bellas Artes.**

rive late at night. Delfos, tel. 2/2266020, has similar services.

Hotels can help arrange taxi or radio-taxi service, which can be cost-effective if shared by several people.

Metro

Carrying 200 million passengers per annum, Santiago's quiet, clean, and efficient Metro would be the pride of many European cities. Three interconnected lines cover most points of interest; most visitors will find Línea 1, which runs beneath the Alameda, Avenida Providencia, and Avenida Apoquindo, between Pudahuel to the west and Escuela Militar to the east, the most important of the three. Línea 2 connects the northern Cal y Canto station, near the former Estación Mapocho, with the southern *comuna* of Lo Ovalle. Línea 5 (there is no Línea 3 or 4 as yet) connects Santa Ana with the southeastern *comuna* of La Florida. There are three transfer stations: Los Héroes between Línea 1 and Línea

2, Baquedano between Línea 1 and Línea 5, and Santa Ana between Línea 2 and Línea 5.

While the Metro is somewhat faster than city buses running between comparable destinations, its major drawback is a lack of seats, and not just because it's crowded—many cars appear to have been designed with very few places to sit. It operates 6:30 A.M.–10:30 P.M. daily except Sunday and holidays, when hours are 8 A.M.–10:30 P.M.

Fares depend on the time of the trip. During *hora normal,* 7:15–9 A.M. and 6–7:30 P.M. weekdays, a single trip costs US$.50; the rest of the day and on weekends, the *hora económica* fare is about US$.40. However, those who buy a *boleto inteligente* or *boleto valor* (multitrip ticket) pay about 10–15 percent less in either category, and more than one person may use the same ticket by passing it back across the turnstile (this is not illegal). When the entire value is used up, the machine swallows the ticket.

Metrobús: Metrobús is a system of feeder lines from the outer suburbs into the Metro system and back. There are Metrobús connections at Escuela Militar, Pedro de Valdivia, Salvador, Las Rejas, Puente Cal y Canto, Lo Ovalle, La Florida, Bellavista, and Pedrero. Fares are more expensive than ordinary city buses, about US$.70.

Bus

City buses are numerous, cheap (about US$.40), and run all day and all night to virtually every part of town, but many are run-down and spew black clouds of diesel into Santiago's already smoggy skies. Along the Alameda are dedicated bus lanes and fixed stops, intended to speed up traffic, but in most of the rest of the city the buses contribute to traffic congestion. After the Metro closes, it's the main means of getting around town.

Destinations are marked on window signs and at fixed stops, but frequent changes can make this more complex than it sounds. Regional authorities are trying to force private bus owners to adopt automatic fare machines, but most drivers still make change. Inspectors often ask for tickets, so don't toss yours on the floor.

city bus

© WAYNE BERNHARDSON

Train

From the Estación Central, Metrotrén runs 19 trains daily to Rancagua (US$1.50) between 6:15 A.M. and 10:45 P.M. Ten of these continue to San Fernando, the last of which leaves at 10 P.M.

Taxi

Black with yellow roofs, regular taxis charge about US$.40 to start the meter and US$.10 more for every subsequent 200 meters. A system of radio taxis with fixed fares operates within certain zones; among the choices are Radio Taxi Arauco, tel. 2/2461114, and Radio Taxi Alameda, tel. 2/7764730.

Taxi Colectivos

Designated by illuminated roof signs, *taxi colectivos* are route taxis that carry up to four or five passengers on fixed itineraries. Slightly more expensive than regular buses, they cover many of the same routes but are usually quicker.

Car Rental

All of the major international agencies as well as several locally-owned operators offer rental cars in Santiago, both at the airport and in town. (For addresses and telephones, see the accompanying chart.)

CAR RENTAL AGENCIES IN SANTIAGO

Santiago's numerous car rental agencies, both international franchises and local companies (the latter generally cheaper), are scattered throughout the city. Most airport rentals are franchises. Note that demand is high for economy cars, so reserve well in advance for the best rates.

Alameda, Avenida Libertador Bernardo O'Higgins 4332, Estación Central, tel. 2/7790609 or 2/7798545, website: www.alamedarentacar.cl, alamed@alamedarentacar.cl

Alamo, Avenida 11 de Septiembre 2155, Oficina 1204, Providencia, tel. 2/2334343, fax 2/2334766

Ansa, Eliodoro Yáñez 1198, Providencia, tel. 2/2510256

Atal, Avenida Costanera Andrés Bello 1051, Providencia, tel. 2/2359222, fax 2/2360636

Automóvil Club de Chile (Acchi), Avenida Vitacura 8620, Vitacura, tel. 2/2125702 or 2/2746261, fax 2/2295295

Avis, Avenida Santa María 1742, Providencia, tel. 2/2747621, fax 2/6019757

Econorent, Avenida Manquehue Sur 600, Las Condes, tel. 2/2208292, fax 2/2241175

Chilean, Bellavista 0185, Providencia, tel./fax 2/7379650

First, Rancagua 0514, Providencia, tel. 2/2256328

Hertz, Avenida Costanera Andrés Bello 1469, Providencia, tel. 2/2359666, fax 2/2360252

Lacroce, Seminario 298, Providencia, tel. 2/6651325, fax 2/6651321, website: www.lacroce.cl, lacroce.car.rental@entelchile.net

Lys, Miraflores 541, tel. 2/6337600, fax 2/6399332, rent@lys.cl

United, Padre Mariano 420, Providencia, tel. 2/2361483

Vicinity of Santiago

An extraordinary number of interesting sights are near Santiago, suitable both for day trips and overnights. Among the many activities are winery tours, winter skiing and summer hiking, horseback riding, and white-water rafting and kayaking.

Chip Travel, Avenida Santa María 227, Oficina 12, tel. 2/7775376, website: www.chip.cl, vchip@rdc.cl, is the only operator to offer alternative "Human Rights Legacy" tours that take in Parque por la Paz" (Villa Grimaldi), the Cementerio General, the Fundación Pinochet, and the Escuela Militar. In addition, it offers more traditional historical and cultural tours, winery excursions to Maipo, Cachapoal, and Colchagua valleys, trips to Pablo Neruda's Isla Negra house, and rural Caleu. Rates, with fluent English-speaking personnel, start at US$30 pp for half-day excursions and US$55 pp for full-day excursions.

Turismo Chileandino, Avenida Providencia 2237, 4th floor, Providencia, tel. 2/3358520 or 09/6997851, does wine tours to Cousiño Macul (US$26) in Santiago proper, Concha y Toro (US$29) in Pirque, and Veramonte in the Casablanca valley (US$38).

Activities-oriented operators include **Cascada Expediciones,** which has recently opened new quarters in the Cajón del Maipo at Camino al Volcán 17710, Guayacán, San José de Maipo, tel. 2/8611777, fax 2/8612222, website: www.cascada-expediciones.com, info@cascada-expediciones.com. Try also **Altué Active Travel,** Encomenderos 83, Las Condes, Santiago, tel. 2/2321103, though its day excursions are substantially more expensive.

CALEU

In a secluded coast range valley on the border between the Metropolitan Region and Region V (Valparaíso), northwest of Santiago, the village of Caleu has attained a certain rustic chic among the Santiago elite—including President Ricardo Lagos, who owns a weekend house here (Lagos, for what it's worth, is an apartment-dweller in the capital). Perhaps because it's avoided the more garish aspects of Chile's economic transformation, Caleu is widely regarded as symbolic of a simpler past, with its modest artisans' market and November's equally modest Feria Artesanal y Gastronómico (Crafts and Food Fair).

There's not a lot to do in Caleu except relaxing, walking, riding, and birding in the nearby mountains (Parque Nacional La Campana is just across the regional border to the west, via the serpentine road over the pass known as Cuesta la Dormida). **La Cabaña de Steve,** tel. 09/5394862, can sleep up to five people on orchard grounds with a small swimming pool for about US$40.

Caleu is about 75 km northwest of Santiago via Ruta 5 (the Panamericana), the town of Tiltil, and a northbound lateral off the road over the Cuesta la Dormida. An alternative route leaves the Panamericana at Rungue and heads directly east to Caleu. The only regular public transportation is daily with Buses Colina, Avenida La Paz 350, Independencia, tel. 2/7374572, which leaves at 3:45 P.M. daily (US$2, 1.5 hours).

Chip Travel, Avenida Santa María 227, Oficina 12, Recoleta, tel. 2/7775376, website: www.chip.cl, offers day tours of Caleu and vicinity, including transportation, snack, lunch, and hiking, for US$75 pp for a minimum of three people; larger groups pay less per person. Horseback riding costs an additional US$25 pp.

TERMAS DE COLINA

About 45 km north of Santiago, in the Andean foothills but close enough for a day trip, Termas de Colina is a woodsy hot springs resort in a dead-end canyon just outside the town of Colina. Its mineral waters reach a natural temperature of 31°C, warm enough for a comfortable soak but not exactly hot-tub level.

Hotel Termas de Colina, Camino Las Termas s/n, tel. 2/8440990, charges US$80/120 s/d with full board for spacious rooms with balcony views of the surrounding sierra. Nonguests can use the pool, thermal baths, sauna, or jacuzzi for US$6 pp. Camping is US$5 pp.

Buses Colina, Avenida La Paz 350, Independencia, tel. 2/7374572, goes every 10 minutes or so to the town of Colina (US$.70, one hour), but it's necessary to hire a taxi for the last several km to the Termas.

CAJÓN DEL MAPOCHO

From the eastern *comuna* of Lo Barnechea, a narrow paved road climbs gradually up the canyon of the Río Mapocho, past the entrance to the massive La Disputada copper mine, and then snakes its way up dozens of switchbacks before branching into separate routes to Santiago's three most popular, and easily accessible, ski areas. On this winding road with numbered curves, some people suffer motion sickness—so much so that some even take medication.

Note that, during ski season, there are road restrictions on weekends and holidays: traffic goes uphill only 8 A.M.–2 P.M., downhill only 4–8 P.M., and both directions at all other hours. Carabineros en route may require chains beyond a certain point.

Santuario de la Naturaleza Yerba Loca

Just before the road begins its final ascent to the major ski resorts, it passes the entrance to Yerba Loca, one of Santiago's best hiking and mountain biking options—even in winter much of this scenic high mountain area remains below the snow line. Donated to the *comuna* of Las Condes by former *fundo* owner Hans von Kiesling and now under Conaf management, this national monument gets far fewer visitors than it deserves.

Geography and Climate: In the Andean front range 27 km east of Santiago, the sanctuary comprises 39,029 mountainous hectares between the parallel Andean ridges of El Plomo-La Parva to the east and Yerba Loca to the west; the Estero de la Yerba Loca is a U-shaped fluvioglacial valley between the two that drains south into the Mapocho. Elevations range from about 1,500 meters on the Mapocho itself to 4,910 meters on the summit of Cerro La Paloma.

Yerba Loca's climate is Mediterranean, with long dry summers and short wet winters that include snow at the highest elevations. Because of its higher elevation, seasonal and diurnal temperature variations are greater than in Santiago proper.

Flora and Fauna: Yerba Loca's vegetation consists of spiny shrubs and sclerophyllous (glossy-leaved) trees at lower elevations, with sparse bunch grasses at higher altitudes. The remaining native fauna include mostly rodents, but there are also many birds, including predators such as the peregrine falcon *(Falco peregrinus)* and carancho *(Phalcoboenus megalopteris)*, the striking *bandurria* or buff-necked ibis *(Theristicus caudatus)*, and even the occasional scavenging Andean condor.

Sights and Recreation: From the ranger station at Curva 15, the former vehicle road is now an excellent 4.2-km trail that takes about 1.5 hours to **Villa Paulina,** the former *fundo* headquarters and site of a Conaf campground. Mountain bikers leave their cars at the park entrance and ride to Paulina and beyond.

Continuing north from Paulina, the **Sendero al Glaciar** is a 30-km round-trip to an icefield at the foot of Cerro La Paloma; the shorter **Sendero Interpretativo La Leonera** is a 45-minute nature trail.

Practicalities: Conaf's campground, or at least part of it, occupies an aging pear orchard where it's possible to collect fresh fruit in the fall. There are good picnic tables and clean flush toilets, but no hot water.

Conaf's Guardería at Curva 15 collects a US$2 admission charge.

Ski Resorts

At the upper end of the Cajón del Mapocho, barely an hour from Santiago in the area known as Tres Valles, there are three major ski resorts: El Colorado, La Parva, and Valle Nevado. Where the road forks, the left fork goes to El Colorado and La Parva, while the right fork goes to Valle Nevado.

While Chilean ski areas enjoy high elevations, the start of the rainy (and snowy) season can be erratic in this Mediterranean climate, though it generally runs from June to early October. For this reason, Chilean resorts now have snow-making equipment to help augment the natural snowfall at the beginning of the season; for current snow conditions, see the online English-language news service *Santiago Times* (website: www.chip.cl).

Full equipment rentals—boots, skis, poles—cost around US$15 per day, but high-performance equipment garners at least a 50 percent premium. Snowboards cost about US$20 per day. Both lift tickets and rental equipment are marginally cheaper when purchased from Skitotal in Las Condes.

Skitotal, Avenida Apoquindo 4900, Local 42-46, Las Condes, tel. 2/2460156, website: www.skitotal.cl, skitotal@skitotal.cl, also runs inexpensive shuttles to El Colorado (US$9), La Parva (US$9), and Valle Nevado (US$10). Departures are around 8:15 A.M. daily, returning around 5 P.M. from each site. Skitotal can also arrange budget lodging, from US$38 pp with bed and breakfast.

Note that some skiers have remarked that, unlike forested areas in most of Europe and North America, the barren Chilean landscape makes depth perception difficult.

El Colorado: Just 39 km east of Santiago, with a maximum elevation of 3,333 meters, El Colorado has 18 lifts from a base elevation of 2,750 meters and a maximum elevation of 3,333 meters. Weekend and holiday lift tickets are around US$25 per day; weekday tickets run about US$20. There are discounts for children and seniors; seniors get the best deal at El Colorado, for just US$5 per day.

The **Colorado Apart Hotel,** tel. 2/6720168, fax 2/6720267, skiandes@entelchile.net, offers apartments for two at US$139 in high season. At the Swiss-style **Hotel Posada de Farellones,** tel. 2/2013704, fax 2/2487071, rates are US$65 d with shared bath, US$85 with two single beds, and US$109 with double bed. Rates include breakfast, dinner, and lift transportation.

For additional information in Santiago, contact **Centro de Ski El Colorado,** Avenida Apoquindo 4900, Local 47-48, Las Condes, tel. 2/2463344, fax 2/2064078, website: www.elcolorado.cl, ski@elcolorado.cl; this is a major departure point for minibuses from Santiago.

La Parva: Only a short distance north of El Colorado, La Parva's skiable runs range from 2,662 to 3,630 meters above sea level—nearly a 1,000-meter vertical drop. Lift tickets cost about the same as at El Colorado, US$25 on weekends and US$20 on weekdays.

Accommodations are available on a weekly basis at **Apart Hotel Condominio Nueva La Parva,** tel. 2/2121363, fax 2/2208510, roparva@netline.cl, for about US$2,600 for up to six people. For general information, contact **Centro de Ski La Parva,** La Concepción 266, Oficina 301, tel. 2/2641466, fax 2/2641569, Providencia, website: www.laparva.cl.

Valle Nevado: Highest of the three resorts, 14 km beyond the Farellones junction, Valle Nevado reaches 3,670 meters above sea level, though its base is 2,860. There are 37 km of trails, even more for those who can afford to indulge in helicopter dropoffs that aren't accessible by the lifts.

Valle Nevado is a full-service resort, with multiple hotels, restaurants, cinema, bars, day care, and many other amenities. For nonguests, weekend and holiday lift tickets cost around US$27; weekday tickets run about US$22.

Valle Nevado has three luxury hotels: **Hotel Valle Nevado** (US$207/324 s/d to US$537/762 with half board per night, varying between low and high season), **Hotel Tres Puntas** (US$124/196 to US$298/434), and **Hotel Puerta del Sol** (US$167/302 to US$420/748).

Among the restaurants, **Don Giovanni** has reasonably priced pizza with thin crust and a fair amount of toppings, including scallops and artichoke, but the buffet is expensive. Its **Slalom** is the fast-food outlet, but don't buy the hot chocolate—cross instead to Hotel Puerto del Sol's tiny **Palais D'Or** chocolate shop, where the chocolate is half the price and twice as good.

For more information, contact **Valle Nevado,** Gertrudis Echeñique 441, Las Condes, tel. 2/206-0027, fax 2/2080695, website: www.vallenevado.com, info@vallenevado.com. Valle Nevado has toll-free numbers in the United States, tel. 800/669-0554, and Canada, tel. 888/301-3248.

VIÑA UNDURRAGA

One of the traditional big names in Chilean wine, Viña Undurraga is 34 km southwest of

Santiago in the lower Maipo valley between Peñaflor and Talagante. The vineyards here produce mostly cabernet sauvignon and chardonnay; the cellars and bottling plant, along with grounds designed by 19th-century French landscape architect Pierre Dubois, are open for free guided tours weekdays 10 A.M.–4 P.M. For reservations, contact Viña Undurraga, tel. 2/81-72346.

From Santiago's Terminal San Borja, San Borja 184, Buses Peñaflor, tel. 2/7761025, has regular bus service.

POMAIRE

About 70 km southwest of the capital via Ruta 68, the dusty village of Pomaire produces many of the clay pots that contain *cazuela de ave, paila marina,* and *pastel de choclo* in homes and restaurants throughout the country. Foot-powered potters' wheels and wood-heated kilns are still the rule, but electrical equipment is supplanting some of the traditional technology. Before attempting to haul any of this fragile material home, get it well and tightly packed.

Pomaire is busiest on weekends, when excursionists from Santiago crowd the streets and pack eateries such as **Los Naranjos,** Rolando Bravo 44-A, tel. 2/8311791, and **San Antonio,** San Antonio 298, tel. 2/8312168. Traditional hearty Chilean dishes are, of course, the standard—no Santiago pseudosophisticates here.

From Santiago's Terminal San Borja, San Borja 184, Buses Melipilla, tel. 2/7763881, has frequent bus service to Pomaire, continuing to Melipilla.

CAJÓN DEL MAIPO

Barely an hour southeast of downtown Santiago, the Río Maipo has cut a deep canyon through more than 70 km of the Andean foothills before it meanders onto the plains near the town of Pirque. Once the border of the Kollasuyu, the southernmost limit of the Inka empire, the Cajón del Maipo (Canyon of the Maipo) is one of urban Santiago's great escapes, barely an hour from the Plaza de Armas.

Starting with fine wineries at Pirque and Santa Rita, the canyon just gets better as it climbs toward, but doesn't quite reach, the Andean crest. While parts of the main road are cluttered with *cabañas,* campgrounds, and restaurants, it still provides access to plenty of high and wild country—not to mention the river itself. Paved as far as San Gabriel, it and a parallel road from Pirque are good enough for touring bikes, but other routes are suitable for mountain bikers, and hikers and horseback riders can explore the trails of Monumento Natural El Morado and the private nature reserve Cascada de las Animas.

The Class III-IV Río Maipo provides plenty of thrills for rafters and kayakers even though diversions for irrigation works and even more from sand and gravel quarrying have taken their toll. At the end of the day, there are several rustic hot springs suitable for a soak. While the area gets crowded in summer and on weekends and holidays, especially from December to March, the rest of the year it's fairly sedate.

Transportation to the Cajón del Maipo is good and getting better—though perhaps not so interesting as when, half a century ago, a military train carried passengers from Puente Alto to El Volcán. From the Parque O'Higgins Metro station, Buses Cajón del Maipo, tel. 2/6972520 or 2/8611518, ascends as far as Baños Morales; from the end of Metro Línea 5, at La Florida, Metrobús No. 72 goes as far as San José de Maipo. *Taxi colectivos* also shuttle up and down the canyon from Pirque.

Viña Santa Rita

Bernardo O'Higgins and 120 of his troops hid from the Spaniards in the catacombs at Hacienda Santa Rita, a distinguished winery that named its main line of wines—120—after the event. Today, its main house is a hotel, the former colonial house (a national monument) is a restaurant, and the grounds and cellars (also a national monument) are open for tours (US$5 pp with tasting additional) five times daily from Tuesday to Friday. On weekends and holidays, tours are free with lunch. For obligatory reservations, contact Viña Santa Rita, tel. 2/3622520, rrivas@santarita.cl.

© WAYNE BERNHARDSON

Cajón del Maipo, southeast of Santiago

The winery's 16-room **Hotel Casa Real,** tel. 2/3622535, website: www.santarita.com, rrivas@santarita.cl, is also open by reservation only; rates are US$190 d. Its restaurant, **La Casa de Doña Paula,** tel. 2/3622520, is open 12:30–3:30 P.M. daily.

Though it's not quite in the Cajón del Maipo proper, Viña Santa Rita, Camino Padre Hurtado 0695, Alto Jahuel, is part of the Maipo drainage, east of Buin and southwest of Pirque. From the Lo Ovalle station, terminus of Línea 2 of the Metro, Metrobús No. 56 goes right past the entrance.

Pirque

On the south bank of the Maipo, 30 km from Santiago, Pirque is a tranquil community that has resisted the cookie-cutter suburbanization that mars much of the rest of southeastern Santiago. Its major attraction is Viña Concha y Toro, one of Chile's largest and oldest wineries, but it also boasts a weekend crafts fair and is the starting point for a scenic but narrow paved road

that climbs the canyon before rejoining the main road via a bridge at El Toyo.

Viña Concha y Toro, Victoria Subercaseaux 210, tel. 2/8217069, website: www.conchaytoro.com, rspublica@conchaytoro.com, offers guided English-language tours with tasting (US$4 pp) of its vineyards, estate grounds, cellars, and museum at 11:30 A.M. and 3 P.M. weekdays, 10 A.M. and noon Saturday. Spanish-language tours take place 10:30 A.M. and 4 P.M. weekdays, 11 A.M. Saturday, but there's a good chance a bilingual guide may be able to handle English-speakers on these tours as well. While reservations are desirable, it's often possible to join an existing group that might include—who knows?—figures such as Mick Jagger, Bono, Helmut Kohl, Nicaraguan poet Ernesto Cardenal, and others who have toured the winery.

After the winery tour, look for lunch at any number of eateries along Ramón Subercaseaux, the main road up the south bank of the Maipo. Among the local favorites are the **Café Wailea,** Ramón Subercaseaux 2900, tel. 2/8546333, for short orders, and the expansive **La Vaquita Echá,** Ramón Subercaseaux 3355, tel. 2/8546025, which can seat up to 500 people indoors and outdoors for Chilean country specialties such as *pastel de choclo* and *cazuela de ave.*

The easiest route to Pirque is Línea 5 of the Metro to Bellavista de la Florida and then Metrobús No. 70 or a *taxi colectivo* from Paradero 14, just outside the station. Metrobús No. 80 also goes here from the Pedrero Metro station.

Reserva Nacional Río Clarillo

In the precordillera southeast of Pirque, Río Clarillo is a 10,185-hectare unit of glossy-leaved Mediterranean scrub woodland, plus denser gallery forest along the course of its namesake river, a tributary of the Maipo. While Conaf does not allow camping here, it does permit picnicking and hiking.

Two short nature trails have interpretive panels: the 1.2-km **Sendero Interpretativo Quebrada Jorquera** and the 1.7-km **Sendero Interpretativo Aliven Mahuida,** a more biologically diverse path. Conaf collects a US$4 admission charge except on summer weekends, when it rises to US$6 pp.

Reserva Nacional Río Clarillo is 45 km southeast of Santiago and 18 km from Pirque. From the end of Metro Línea 5, at Bellavista de la Florida, Metrobús No. 74 goes to El Principal, about two km from the reserve entrance.

Las Vizcachas

At the western approach to the main road up the north side of the Cajón del Maipo, just beyond the Carabineros police post at Las Vizcachas, note the informal shrine for the folk saint **Difunta Correa,** strongly identified with the Argentine province of San Juan but with a distinctly binational twist here. According to legend, the young mother Deolinda Correa died of thirst in the desert in the 19th century, but her baby survived at her breast; her need for water explains the bottles left by her devotees.

In addition to this unique shrine, uncommon but not unheard of in Chile, Las Vizcachas also has a weekend **Autocine** (drive-in theater), perhaps the only one in the country—Joe Bob sez check it out. On the south side of the highway, a bit farther on, **Vinícola Cavas del Maipo,** tel. 09/3303811, website: www.cavasdelmaipo.co.cl, cavasdelmaipo@entelchile.net, offers guided winery tours; it's open 8 A.M.–5:45 P.M. daily except Sunday.

For technical climbers, **Geo Expediciones** has a climbing wall at its Centro de Escalada, Camino al Volcán 07910, tel. 2/8424776, website: www.geoexpediciones.cl, geoexpediciones@yahoo.com. It also organizes hiking, mountain biking, horseback riding, rafting, and paragliding excursions.

La Obra

A short distance east of Las Vizcachas, 790 meters above sea level, La Obra was a stop on the military railroad that once climbed from Puente Alto to El Volcán; its **Estación La Obra** is a national monument. **Hostería y Restaurant El Tucán,** directly on the highway at La Obra 675, tel. 2/8711089, website: www.eltucan.cl, reservas@eltucan.cl, offers accommodations for US$20 pp without breakfast, and it is a popular dining spot that appeals to the masses—seating up to 200 people.

Just east of La Obra, the rise known as Cuesta las Chilcas was the site of the Frente Patriótico

Manuel Rodríguez's 1986 assassination attempt on General Pinochet as he returned to Santiago from his country house at El Melocotón. Five of Pinochet's bodyguards died in a hail of bullets and a rocket launcher attack, but his chauffeur's skilled driving saved the dictator's life. Pinochet's admirers have commemorated the event with a monument honoring his bodyguards.

El Manzano

With sunny outdoor seating overlooking the river, **Trattoria Calypso,** Camino al Volcán 5247, tel. 2/8711498, is an outstanding Italian restaurant that makes a great stop on the way up the Cajón del Maipo. The menu, of course, concentrates on pasta, but with greater variety than in many Italian restaurants in Santiago proper, and the restaurant offers an exceptional dessert menu. Befitting its weekend business, it's open Thursday through Sunday, 1–8:30 P.M. only. Figure about US$7–10 for most entrées.

Guayacán

At a bend in the river, a few kilometers north of San José de Maipo, **Casa Bosque** has the most extravagant decor of any Cajón del Maipo restaurant—the twisted trunks of polished cypress that hold it up seem more like something from Grimm's most nightmarish tales or an early Disney misadventure. Unfortunately, the putatively simple menu based on beef, plus a few chicken and pork dishes, doesn't match what might, with more courtesy than accuracy, be called imaginative architecture. Most entrées are in the US$7–10 range, but the chicken salad (US$3) puts the rest of the menu to shame. The background music is irritating. Casa Bosque, Camino El Volcán 16829, tel. 2/8711570, is worth seeing for the spectacle; if you can't stop here, have a gander at its website: www.casabosque.cl.

The adventure travel operator **Cascada Expediciones** has new quarters here at Camino al Volcán 17710, tel. 2/8611777, fax 2/8612222, website: www.cascada-expediciones.com, info@cascada-expediciones.com. Its main base of operations, though, is at Cascada de las Animas in San Alfonso.

rafting and kayaking on Río Maipo

San José de Maipo

The canyon's largest town, 967 meters above sea level, San José has a leafy Plaza de Armas focused on its **Iglesia y Casa Parroquial,** a national monument dating from late colonial times. Its former **Estación de Ferrocarril,** also a national monument, was a stop on the military railroad from Puente Alto to El Volcán.

Lagunillas

From a turnoff just south of San José, a winding dirt road leads 19 km northeast to Lagunillas, a scenic but no-frills ski area rather than a high-powered resort such as Valle Nevado or Portillo. At the final approach, there's an oddball sculpture that may have been intended as Jesus Christ—three or four meters high—but could just as easily be a Rasta (someone has even scribbled "legalize it" on one of its legs).

In ski season, day tours from Santiago cost US$32 pp, while lift tickets cost just US$12 weekdays, US$18 on weekends. For details, and information on accommodations, contact the

Club Andino, tel. 2/3583529, website: www.geocities.com/centroandino/refugio.htm, lagu-nillas@softhome.net.

El Melocotón

About five km south of San José de Maipo, El Melocotón is most famous—or notorious—as the site of General Pinochet's riverfront home (the first kayakers to descend the Maipo, in the 1970s, found automatic rifles pointed at them from the shore). It briefly made the news again in 2001 when it was discovered that a former member of the FPMR had rented a house only a few hundred meters from the general's residence.

San Alfonso

San Alfonso, about six km southeast of El Melocotón and 1,106 meters above sea level, made news in 1997 when local residents successfully forced relocation of a natural gas pipeline from Argentina by establishing a private nature reserve at Cascada de las Animas, just south of the highway by a tree-lined dirt road. A short distance up this road from the signed turnoff, look for the scale miniature railway circling the house and gardens of José Sagall ("Pepe Tren"), as well as his assortment of full-scale antique railcars. About 100 meters farther, the former **Estación San Alfonso** is a national monument as part of the military short line that also hauled passengers to their weekend getaways from the capital.

Santuario de la Naturaleza Cascada de las Animas: In the midst of a multiyear struggle to divert a natural gas pipeline from Argentina, the Andean precordillera of the Astorga family's former *fundo* Cascada de la Ánimas became one of Chile's first private nature reserves in 1995. Only two years later, though, did the owners manage to definitively defeat the pipeline.

In practice, the official designation hasn't made much difference, but it allows the family to continue, without disruption, the activities-oriented recreation that has made the 3,600-hectare property a prime destination for hikers, riders, and especially white-water rafters and kayakers. The Maipo is a class III-IV river that's suitable for novices but can be wild enough for more experienced white-water lovers, especially during the spring runoff. Elevations range from about 1,100 meters along the river to 3,050 meters on the highest summit.

Many Santiaguino families come here for camping and swimming (US$4 pp for adults, US$2.50 for children) at Cascada's large outdoor pool on the more developed north side of the river. Most other activities take place on the south side of the Cajón del Maipo, where the **Sendero Cascada de las Ánimas** is a short guided hike to its namesake waterfall. More foreigners than Chileans undertake the two- to three-hour guided climb to the summit of **Cerro Pangal.** While horseback riders will enjoy this scenic terrain, much of it is very steep and novice riders should be particularly cautious.

Cascada also offers longer two- to three-day rides into the back country, and even across the Andes into Argentina in summer only.

Hostería Posada Los Ciervos, Camino el Volcán 31411, tel./fax 2/8611581, is an aging, somewhat ramshackle place that still manages to exude personality for US$20 pp with private bath and breakfast, US$33 pp with full board. Its restaurant has good desserts.

Camping y Cabañas Cascada de las Ánimas, tel. 2/8611303, fax 2/8611833, charges US$6 pp for camping for adults, US$3 for children; *cabañas* that sleep up to four people cost US$56, while larger *cabañas* sleeping up to 10 cost US$89. It also has a very good, moderately priced riverview restaurant with open-air deck seating.

Monumento Natural El Morado

Beyond San Gabriel, where the Río Yeso joins the Maipo and the paved road ends, it's 23 km farther to one of the canyon's finest excursions, a taste of the high Andes at Monumento Natural El Morado. Only 92 km from downtown Santiago, it overlooks the valley of the Río Volcán, a Maipo tributary that joins the main river a few kilometers south of San Gabriel.

Despite its modest size—only 3,009 hectares—El Morado gets hikers into the high country fast, with easy access to Andean lakes and glaciers. Though it's a feasible day trip from the capital, the camping and accommodations in the vicinity make it a good overnight option as well.

the Andean crest

Geography and Climate: At altitudes ranging from about 1,750 meters in the valley of the Río Morales to 5,060 meters on the summit of Cerro El Morado, this is an alpine environment shaped by flowing ice and running water. It is also shaped by tectonic forces—over 100 million years, the rising Andes have carried maritime fossils upward of 3,500 meters at Cerro Rubillar.

El Morado's climate is Mediterranean, with a pronounced dry summer and temperatures ranging up to 25°C, but upward of two meters of snow can accumulate in its cold winters. Because of the altitude, nights are cool even in summer.

Flora and Fauna: Vegetation covers only about 20 percent of the park's otherwise rocky and icy surface, mostly in the form of Andean steppe. There are few shrubs and almost no trees, but where water accumulates there is a more diverse plant life.

Mammals are few, though foxes and skunks are occasionally seen, along with hares introduced from Europe. Waterfowl inhabit parts of the marshes, hummingbirds flit amongst the

Andean scrub, and the occasional raptor or condor soars overhead.

Sights and Recreation: From the visitor center at the **Baños Morales** hot springs, the **Sendero El Ventisquero** is a six-km trail that climbs steeply at the outset before leveling off at **Aguas Panimávida,** a series of small thermal springs. It continues to Laguna El Morado, a small lake at 2,400 meters, and on to the tongue of the **Ventisquero San Francisco.** From here, all further travel is cross-country.

Visitors disinclined to walk can rent horses for around US$5 per hour at Baños Morales.

Practicalities: Conaf has a small rustic campground at Laguna El Morado; at Baños Morales, there is the inexpensive **Camping del Valle** and simple accommodations as well in summer.

The area's best alternative, though, is across the valley at the **Refugio Alemán,** Camino El Volcán s/n, tel. 2/2028761, terrainc@entelchile.net. Also known as Refugio Lo Valdés, this popular poplar-studded hillside hotel is not a luxury lodging, but it has had a loyal public for both accommodations and food since the 1930s. Room with full board costs US$53 pp; children to age seven pay half, while those two or under stay free. There are also B&B and half-board packages, and budget backpacker space in the attic (sleeping bag essential). Nonguests can also take breakfast, lunch, dinner, or *onces* at the restaurant.

Conaf rangers collect an admission charge of US$1 for adults, US$.50 for children, at the **Centro de Información** at the park entrance.

Weekend buses leave from the Parque O'Higgins Metro at 7:15 A.M., returning at 6 P.M., with Buses Cajón del Maipo, tel. 2/6972520; the fare is US$3 pp each way. Make reservations for T-Arrpué, tel. 2/2117165, which leaves from Plaza Italia.

Baños Colina

At the end of the road, 12 km from Baños Morales and 2,500 meters above sea level, barren Baños Colina is a no-frills hot springs with rocky, exposed campsites charging about US$4 pp. Summer pack trips across the Andes to Argentina start here (only organized tour companies such as Cascada Expediciones can easily handle the logistics), but there are opportunities for shorter rides in the vicinity.

Transportation is not so easy here, but several companies offer weekend transportation for about US$12 pp including access to the baths, including **Expediciones Manzur,** tel. 2/6435651, which leaves from Plaza Italia; **Buses Cordillera,** tel. 2/7773881, from the corner of Alameda and San Ysidro; and **Alicia Miranda,** tel. 2/7372844, from the corner of Alameda and Santa Rosa. These buses generally leave around 7:30 A.M. and return at 5 P.M. It's possible to stay overnight and return the following day, and if demand is high there may be weekday trips as well.

The Chilean Heartland

Chile's Mediterranean heartland, also referred to by geographers as Middle Chile, roughly comprises the area from the Río Aconcagua in the north to the Río Biobío drainage in the south, the point where the rainfall regime begins its transition from the dry summer/wet winter profile to the more evenly distributed precipitation associated with a marine west coast climate. Politically, it consists of Santiago's Región Metropolitana (covered in the previous chapter), Region V (Valparaíso), Region VI (O'Higgins), Region VII (Maule), and Region VIII (Biobío). In addition,

this chapter also includes a couple of localities in Region IX (Araucanía) that are most easily accessible from the Panamericana in Region VIII.

Nearly three-quarters of all Chileans live in the densely populated heartland (including the capital), and the great majority of economic activity—both industrial and agricultural—takes place here. The ports of Valparaíso, San Antonio, and Talcahuano link the cities of the central valley and the copper mines of the cordillera to the rest of the world, while the Los Libertadores tunnel connects them to the Argentine city of

Congreso Nacional, El Almendral, Valparaíso

THE CHILEAN HEARTLAND

PACIFIC OCEAN

HEARTLAND

Papudo
La Ligua
To Los Vilos and La Serena
REGION V (VALPARAÍSO)
Parque Provincial Aconcagua
RN 7
Zapallar
Monumento Natural Isla Cachagua
San Felipe
To Mendoza →
Quintero
Parque Provincial Volcán Tupungato
60
Los Andes
Viña del Mar
60
62
P.N. La Campana
ARGENTINA
Valparaíso
Colina
Santuario de la Naturaleza Yerba Loca
ISLA NEGRA ★
68
SANTIAGO
Monumento Natural El Morado
Cartagena
78
Talagante
San Bernardo
San Antonio
Melipilla
R.N. Río Clarillo
66
CHAPA VERDE
Rancagua
SEWELL
Termas de Cauquenes
Lago Rapel
5
R.N. Río de los Cipreses
Volcán El Palomo (4,860 m)
Pichilemu
San Fernando
To San Rafael and Mendoza
Santa Cruz
REGION VI (O'HIGGINS)
Bucalemu
Volcán Tinguiririca (4,280 m)
Curicó
Paso de Vergara (2,502 m)
REGION VII (MAULE)
LAS LEÑAS
Constitución
Talca
R.N. Radal Siete Tazas
RN 40
R.N. Atlos de Lircay
Volcán Descabezado Grande (3,830 m)
San Javier
Bardas Blancas
R.N. Los Ruiles
115
RP 224
R.N. Federico Albert
Linares
Volcán San Pedro (3,621 m)
Chanco
5
Cauquenes
128
Parral
Cobquecura
Ninhue
San Carlos
ARGENTINA
Tomé
Chillán
Nevados de Chillán (3,212 m)
Talcahuano
152
Penco
Barrancas
San Pedro
Concepción
REGION VIII (BIOBÍO)
Termas de Chillán
Coronel
Río Biobío
Andacollo
Chos Malal
Lota
P.N. Laguna del Laja
5
RP 6
Los Angeles
Volcán Antuco (2,895 m)
150
Curanilahue
Lebu
180
Mulchén
Capahue
Churriaca
P.N. Nahuelbuta
Angol
Collipulli
Loncopué
RN 40
Purén
To Temuco
Victoria
REGION IX (LA ARAUCANÍA)
To Zapala
Monumento Natural Contulmo

Cordillera de los Andes

0   30 mi
0   30 km

© AVALON TRAVEL PUBLISHING, INC.

Mendoza. The coastline attracts tourists from throughout central Chile and the neighboring republic.

In terms of physical geography, the heartland features a rugged Pacific coastline at the foot of coastal mountains that reach upward of 2,000 meters in some areas. East of the coast range, millions of years of runoff from the soaring Andes have deposited fertile sediments in the long but narrow central valley—really a structural depression rather than a single watershed—making it Chile's most productive agricultural region, suitable for grains, orchards, and vineyards. The Andes themselves, dissected by several transverse rivers, rise stunningly behind the central valley, which is barely 70 km across at its widest point.

A legacy of colonial times, large rural landholdings occupied nearly all the best arable land well into the 20th

> *East of the coast range, millions of years of runoff from the soaring Andes have deposited fertile sediments in the long but narrow central valley, making it Chile's most productive agricultural region, suitable for grains, orchards, and vineyards. The Andes themselves rise stunningly behind the central valley.*

century, despite surprisingly frequent changes of ownership. As population pressure grew on the low-productivity lands outside the *fundos,* so did the political pressure on the *fundos,* as the landless and their advocates clamored for agrarian reform. Both the Christian Democrat and Socialist governments of the 1960s and early 1970s made solid but controversial advances in reform, but the Pinochet coup of 1973 abruptly reversed these efforts.

Since then, the region has become an export-oriented fruit basket, taking advantage of Northern Hemisphere demand for off-season commodities such as apples, apricots, blueberries, cherries, grapes, peaches, pears, and raspberries. Unfortunately, despite the traditional high quality of Chilean fruit, many growers overapply petrochemical fertilizers and pesticides.

The Central Coast

From the port of Valparaíso and its twin city Viña del Mar, north to Papudo and south to Cartagena, Chile's Mediterranean coastline is the traditional destination for domestic holidaymakers and for Argentine visitors from across the Andes. Though travelers from overseas often find the rocky headlands of its Mediterranean shoreline beautiful but many beaches crowded and the water cold, Valparaíso itself is a marvel of vernacular architecture and spontaneous urban growth, and the mountainous backcountry of Parque Nacional La Campana is a delight at any time of year. Poet Pablo Neruda enjoyed both the city and the coastline, making homes in both Valparaíso and at Isla Negra to the south.

Separated from Santiago and the central valley by the coastal cordillera, the seashore enjoys a mild year-round climate, but the cool Humboldt Current often deters bathers from

staying too long in the water. The *camanchaca,* which often obscures the sun until early afternoon, is a further deterrent to beachgoers, but the cool waters don't seem to deter surfers who bring proper wet suits.

VALPARAÍSO

Like San Francisco, Chile's historic Pacific port is a child of the California Gold Rush, as it became a major seaport on the passage around the Horn. Also like San Francisco, it has so many hills that a walking tour of its streets, steps, and winding footpaths can be as productive a cardiovascular workout as a lengthy session on the StairMaster. For those who tire of walking, a series of 15 funiculars—the functional equivalent of San Francisco's cable cars—lift Porteños, as Valparaíso residents are known,

HEARTLAND

VALPARAÍSO

★ MUSEO NAVAL
Y MARÍTIMO

SUB. ARTILLERÍA

To Playa
Ancha

B a h í a

AVENIDA CARAMPANGUE

ASCENSOR
ARTILLERÍA

Plaza
Aduana

BUSTAMANTE

MARQUEZ

VALDIVIA

d e

SANTO
DOMINGO

LOS PORTEÑOS
NO. 2

**CERRO
SANTO
DOMINGO**

IGLESIA
MATRIZ

MERCADO
CENTRAL

MATRIZ

SERRANO

COCHRANE

BLANCO

CLAVE

Plaza
Echaurren

BOTE
SALVAVIDAS

MUELLE
PRATT

V a l p a r a í s o

SAN FRANCISCO

ASCENSOR
CORDILLERA

SEE DETAIL

ESTACIÓN
PUERTO

Plaza
Sotomayor

AVENIDA

BLANCO

ERRAZURIZ

CANOVAS

**CERRO
CORDILLERA**

TOMAS RAMOS

PRAT

COCHRANE

AVENIDA

ASCENSOR
SAN AGUSTÍN

URRIOLA

ESMERALDA

ROSS

ALEGRE

ROLAND
BAR

ESTACIÓN
BELLAVISTA

ADUANILLA

MONTE

PAPUDO

Plaza
Blanco

BELLAVISTA

MIRANDA

SAN ENRIQUE

TEMPLEMAN

BEETHOVEN

MELGAREJO

PIDETO

**CERRO
ALEGRE**

**CERRO
CONCEPCIÓN**

O'HIGGINS

BLANCO

N. MARIMBO

RAMIREZ

MOLINA

AVENIDA BRASIL

CM. CINTURA

**CERRO
PANTEÓN**

ELEUTERIO

AVENIDA BRASI

EYZAGUIRRE

ALMIRANTE MONTT

ASCENSOR
REINA VICTORIA

CUMMING

HOTEL PUERTA
DEL ALCALÁ

HOTEL PUERTO
PRINCIPAL

YUNGAY

CEMENTERIO
CATÓLICO

SALVADOR

DONOSO

Plaza Simón
Bolívar

MUNICH HOSPITAL

BAMBÚ

HOTEL PRAT

IGLESIA
CATEDRAL

ELIAS

EMILE
DUBOIS

Plaza
Victoria

INDEPENDENCIA

EDWARDS

ATAHUALPA

CEMENTERIO
DE DISIDENTES

PALACIO
LYON ★

**CERRO
LA CÁRCEL**

CLUB NAVAL ★

MERCADO
ARTESANAL
PERMANENT

AV. ALEMANIA

CUMMING

FUNDACIÓN
VALPARAÍSO

ASCENSOR
ESPIRITU SANTO

CARRERA

Plaza
Bísmarck

CARLOS NEWMAN

AVENIDA

ECUADOR

MUSEO A
CIELO ABIERTO

SALA HERBERT
JONCKERS

MANZANO

YERBAS

**CERRO
BELLAVISTA**

AVENIDA ALEMANIA

GENERAL MACKENNA

BUENAS

ASCENSOR
FLORIDA

PEREZ

CARLOS LYON

BETINA

PLACILLA

R. FERRARI

ASCENSOR
MARIPOSA

JENOFONTE

LO VENEGAS

AVENIDA SAN JUAN DE DIOS

GUILLERMO RIVERA

HECTOR CALVO

MEJIA

AMALIA ASTORGA

Plaza
Yungay

AV. BAQUEDANO

**CERRO
MARIPOSA**

0   400 yds

0   400 m

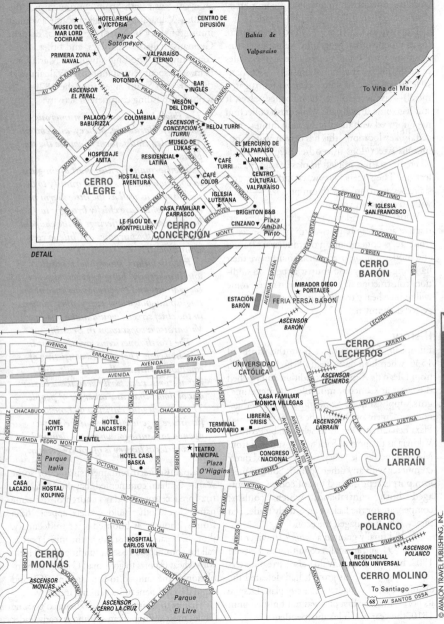

DETAIL

MUSEO DEL MAR LORD COCHRANE

HOTEL REINA VICTORIA

Plaza Sotomayor

CENTRO DE DIFUSIÓN

Bahía de Valparaíso

PRIMERA ZONA NAVAL

VALPARAÍSO ETERNO

AV TOMAS RAMOS

ASCENSOR EL PERAL

LA ROTONDA

BLANCO

COCHRANE

PRAT

BAR INGLÉS

MESÓN DEL LORD

To Viña del Mar

PALACIO BABURIZZA

LA COLOMBINA

ASCENSOR CONCEPCIÓN (TURRI)

RELOJ TURRI

EL MERCURIO DE VALPARAÍSO

HIGUERA

ALEGRE

MIRAMAR

MUSEO DE LUKAS

LANCHILE

HOSPEDAJE ANITA

RESIDENCIAL LATINA

CAFÉ TURRI

CENTRO CULTURAL VALPARAÍSO

CERRO ALEGRE

HOSTAL CASA AVENTURA

CAFÉ COLOR

IGLESIA LUTERANA

MONTE

SAN ENRIQUE

TEMPLEMAN

PILCOMAYO

ABTAO

PAPUDO

URRIOLA

CASA FAMILIAR CARRASCO

BEETHOVEN

BRIGHTON B&B

LE FILOU DE MONTPELLIER

CERRO CONCEPCIÓN

CINZANO

Plaza Aníbal Pinto

MONTT

AVENIDA

ERRAZURIZ

GOMEZ CARREÑO

P ATKINSON

AVENIDA DIEGO PORTALES

NELSON

O'BRIEN

CERRO BARÓN

ESTACIÓN BARÓN

MIRADOR DIEGO PORTALES

FERIA PERSA BARÓN

SEPTIMIO

CASTRO

SEPTIMIO

IGLESIA SAN FRANCISCO

TOCORNAL

GONZALEZ

VEGA

ASCENSOR BARÓN

LECHEROS

CERRO LECHEROS

ARRATIA

AVENIDA ESPAÑA

AVENIDA

ERRAZURIZ

AVENIDA

BRASIL

AVENIDA

BRASIL

UNIVERSIDAD CATÓLICA

ASCENSOR LECHEROS

EDUARDO JENNER

EUSEBIO LILLO

FREIRE

CRUZ

YUNGAY

URUGUAY

RAWSON

CASA FAMILIAR MÓNICA VILLEGAS

HINOS CLARK

SANTA JUSTINA

CHACABUCO

CINE HOYTS

GENERAL

FRANCA

SAN IGNACIO

CHACABUCO

SIMON

LIBRERÍA CRISIS

ASCENSOR LARRAÍN

CERRO LARRAÍN

RODRIGUEZ

AVENIDA PEDRO MONTT

ENTEL

HOTEL LANCASTER

TERMINAL RODOVIARIO

CONGRESO NACIONAL

AVENIDA ARGENTINA

Parque Italia

HOTEL CASA BASKA

MORRIS

BOLIVAR

TEATRO MUNICIPAL

Plaza O'Higgins

AVENIDA ARGENTINA

CASA LACAZIO

HOSTAL KOLPING

VICTORIA

INDEPENDENCIA

E. DEFORMES

VICTORIA

ROSS

SARMIENTO

CERRO POLANCO

LATORRE

AVENIDA

COLON

URUGUAY

RETAMO

BARROSO

JUANA

RANCAGUA

CERRO MONJAS

GARIBALDI

HOSPITAL CARLOS VAN BUREN

VAN BUREN

ALMTE. SIMPSON

ASCENSOR POLANCO

RESIDENCIAL EL RINCÓN UNIVERSAL

CERRO MOLINO

ASCENSOR MONJAS

BAQUEDANO

ASCENSOR CERRO LA CRUZ

BLAS CUEVAS

HONTANEDA

POCURO

Parque El Litre

CANCIANI

To Santiago

68 AV SANTOS OSSA

HEARTLAND

© AVALON TRAVEL PUBLISHING, INC.

from the downtown financial and commercial districts to their hillside neighborhoods.

Proposed as a UNESCO World Heritage Site for its unique urban geography, Valparaíso is undergoing a real-estate renaissance as the values of its distinctive traditional houses—Victorian-style structures clad with *calamina* (corrugated metal)—rise as steeply as the hills themselves. It still has some drawbacks: while trash collection has improved with the placement of dumpsters at certain key locations, this has driven Valpo's numerous street dogs into other neighborhoods where the trash is still left in plastic bags for collection. The streets, alleyways, sidewalks, and staircases are dappled with canine *soretes*—watch your step or wash your feet.

Valparaíso's rundown port, the city's least attractive area despite its two km of prime ocean frontage, is undergoing an overdue privatization and modernization of its docks to improve their handling capacity and tourist appeal. In addition, construction of a new southern access route will reduce heavy truck traffic through the congested downtown.

History

European Valparaíso dates from the winter of 1536, when Juan de Saavedra, who had split off from Diego de Almagro's expedition and reached the coast at Concón, miraculously met Almagro's supply ship *El Santiaguillo* at the indigenous settlement of Quintil, the site of present-day Plaza Echaurren. Despite its selection by Pedro de Valdivia as the port of Santiago, it suffered from Madrid's mercantile policy, which restricted direct commerce with any other Spanish South American port except Lima. This, of course, encouraged both contraband, which couldn't compensate for the lack of an orderly trade, and piracy, which damaged the economy.

Madrid finally granted a *cabildo* (town council) in 1791 and formal recognition as a city in 1802, but by that time Valparaíso's irregular terrain and spontaneous growth had defeated the Spanish ideal of a quadrangular city plan. Despite its port status, the first pier was not finished until 1810, the year of Chile's independence.

While independence was more a process than an event—war with Spain continued into the 1820s—Valparaíso eventually became a vibrant immigrant city of North Americans, British, Germans, Italians, Yugoslavs, and other ethnic communities. The Englishwoman Maria Graham, who spent several months in Valparaíso as the war with Spain raged into the 1820s, described its bustling commercial activity:

> *The English shops are more numerous than any. Hardware, pottery, and cotton and woolen cloths, form of course the staple articles. . . .*
>
> *The Germans furnish most of the glass in common use. It is of bad quality to be sure, but it, as well as the little German mirrors, which are chiefly brought to hang up as votive offerings in the chapels, answers all the purposes of Chileno consumption. . . .*
>
> *English tailors, shoemakers, saddlers and inn-keepers, hang out their signs in every street, and the preponderance of the English language over every other spoken in the chief streets, would make one fancy Valparaíso a coast town in Britain.*
>
> *The North Americans greatly assist in this, however. Their goods, consisting of common furniture, flour, biscuit, and naval stores, necessarily keep them busier out of doors than any other set of people. The more elegant Parisian or London furniture is generally despatched unopened to Santiago, where the demand for articles of luxury is of course greater.*

Valparaíso itself remained simple for some years—Graham commented that the Iglesia Matriz (predecessor of today's church of the same name) "like all other buildings here, appears mean from without. " It boomed after midcentury, though, because of its status as the initial port of call for commercial vessels rounding Cape Horn, with wheat exports to gold-mad California, completion of the railroad to Santiago in 1863, and rapid development of its banking industry.

Thanks to its immigrants, Valparaíso became Chile's most cosmopolitan city and an early leader in modern infrastructure such as tramways, electricity, and gas. Like San Francisco, the Americas' other great cosmopolitan Pacific port, Valparaíso suffered a devastating 1906 earthquake. The opening of the Panama Canal was an even more crippling blow—it became a terminal rather than an intermediate port, as European shipping could avoid the slower and more dangerous route around the Horn. The collapse of nitrate exports due to the development of synthetic substitutes, followed by the Great Depression of the 1930s, nearly paralyzed the economy until after the end of World War II, when copper exports recovered.

Even with the recovery of the Chilean economy after the 1970s, Valparaíso has lost its primary port status to San Antonio, southeast of and rather closer to Santiago, over easier terrain. It has, however, gained political influence with the transfer of the Chilean Congress under Pinochet's custom constitution (Pinochet is a Valparaíso native), though there are strong sentiments, and many practical reasons, for moving the Congress back to Santiago.

Traditionally, Valparaíso has played second fiddle to nearby Viña del Mar in the tourist trade, but growing appreciation of its role in Chilean history and its pending application for UNESCO World Heritage Site status have spawned interest in its unique urban environment. With the opening of ever more tourist hotels, B&Bs and restaurants, Valpo is fast becoming a viable alternative to Viña.

Orientation

For nonnatives of Valparaíso, 120 km northwest of Santiago via Ruta 68, orientation can be a challenge. Along the curving shoreline of the Bahía de Valparaíso, built largely on fill, the relatively regular downtown area consists of long east-west streets and avenues, crossed by short, mostly north-south, streets and alleyways.

Northwest of Cerro Concepción, marked by the Reloj Turri clocktower and the *Mercurio de Valparaíso* newspaper headquarters, this narrow coastal strip is generally known as the Barrio Puerto; to the east, the wider level area is known as El Almendral. Merval, the regional rapid transit system, parallels the shoreline.

In the spontaneously gridless hills neighborhoods, though, all bets are off. A free but basic map, available at the tourist office, is essential, but a more detailed version such as the one in Turistel's *Centro* volume is a good idea. Even the best map, though, can't cover every winding medieval staircase and passageway.

> *Even the best map can't cover every winding medieval staircase and passageway in the spontaneously gridless hills neighborhoods.*

Barrio Puerto

Modern Valparaíso's maritime orientation is palpable in the Barrio Puerto, where the main public buildings cluster around recently remodeled **Plaza Sotomayor,** now vehicle-free after construction of an underground parking garage; while it's clearly an improvement over the previous parking lot, the plaza's barrenness is still disconcerting.

At the upper end of the plaza, the former Intendencia Regional (1910), built to seat the provincial government, is now the **Primera Zona Naval,** the national naval headquarters that symbolizes the navy's influence. Built to replace an earlier structure with shaky foundations, this impressive, French-inspired, five-story building, with an area of 8,000 square meters, was the work of architect Ernesto Urquieta; his design won a contest for a building that served as the provincial governor's residence and a summer house for presidents.

On the harbor side of the plaza the **Monumento a los Héroes de Iquique** is the crypt for Arturo Prat, Ignacio Serrano, and other fatalities of the *Esmeralda*'s ill-advised assault on the Peruvian ironclad *Huáscar* in Iquique harbor during the War of the Pacific. After the bodies were saved from a common grave and then shifted to a parish church that burned down, the Chilean government sponsored a contest to build the monument in Valparaíso; French architect Diogene Ulysse Mayllard was responsible for the general design and French sculptor Denis Pierre

Iglesia Luterana, Cerro Concepción

Puech for the statuary (according to an unverified account, the judges rejected Rodin's sculpture *La Defensa,* now at Viña del Mar's Palacio Carrasco). The Chilean Virginio Arias, who supervised the work, sculpted the bas reliefs.

At the foot of the plaza, **Muelle Prat** is the passenger pier; there are maritime excursions with the motor yacht *Maite* (US$14), tel. 09/3244352, and the catamaran *Spirit of Valparaíso* (US$10), tel. 09/6600924. The pier is also home to a so-so crafts market, a branch of the municipal tourist office, and a replica of the *Carabela Santiaguillo,* the vessel that first brought the Spaniards to Valparaíso (only 18 meters long and five meters wide, it seems almost miraculous that it survived a winter voyage from Lima). Facing each other across the plaza are the current **Aduana Nacional** (customs house) and the **Estación Puerto,** the terminus for suburban commuter trains (note the colorful murals).

Marking the approximate border between the Puerto Barrio and El Almendral, the **Reloj Turri** clocktower, at the narrow end of a flatiron building at Prat and Carreño, is directly across from Ascensor Concepción. One long block east, at Esmeralda and Ross, the neoclassical headquarters of **El Mercurio de Valparaíso** (1903) belongs to Chile's most venerable newspaper (first published in 1827).

El Almendral

East of Cerro Concepción, also bounded by the port, Avenida Argentina, and Avenida Colón, El Almendral is the commercial as opposed to the administrative heart of Valparaíso. When Maria Graham lived here in the 1820s, though, it was "full of olive groves, and of almond gardens, whence it has its name."

El Almendral still has fewer conspicuous architectural landmarks than the Barrio Puerto, but its several plazas—**Plaza Simón Bolívar, Plaza de la Victoria, Parque Italia** and **Plaza O'Higgins** (home to Chile's finest antiques market)—are the axes of Valparaíso's street life.

At the west end of the barrio, at Salvador Donoso 1337, the ornate, almost rococo **Palacio Ross** (1888) was home to one of Valparaíso's elite families before they moved to Viña del Mar; it later became (and still is) the **Club Alemán,** social center for one of the city's most important ethnic communities.

At Condell 1546, near Huito, the neoclassical **Palacio Lyon** (1881) holds both the **Museo de Historia Natural** (Natural History Museum) and the **Galería de Arte Municipal** (Municipal Art Gallery; see separate entries below). Two blocks north, on Avenida Brasil, the **Arco Británico** honors the port's British colony.

At the southwest corner of Plaza de la Victoria, the **Club Naval** (1895) shows French influence. At Avenida Brasil and Avenida Argentina, architect Ernesto Urquieta (of ex-Intendencia fame) also designed the **Universidad Católica.**

On Avenida Pedro Montt, between Barroso and Avenida Argentina, rises Valparaíso's most conspicuous single monument, the pharaonic **Congreso Nacional**(1990); Pinochet's custom constitution dictated the move of the national legislature from Santiago to Valparaíso, though there is frequent talk of moving it back to the capital.

THE *ASCENSORES* OF VALPARAÍSO

Nothing else distinguishes Valparaíso so much as its hillside *ascensores* or elevators, once 33 in number but now down to 14 or so (not including the private one on the grounds of the Hospital Van Buren). Such a part of the city are they that the Fundación Valparaíso uses the slogan "Un ascensor es un barrio" (An elevator is a neighborhood).

In fact, only Ascensor Polanco is an elevator in the strictest sense of the word—the rest are funiculars. They date from the late 19th century; as the port, commercial, and financial districts quickly occupied the city's limited level terrain, residential neighborhoods climbed and spread up the canyons and over the nearby hillsides.

English, German, French, Yugoslav, and other immigrants who had made their fortunes in business, finance, and mining built mansions

© WAYNE BERNHARDSON

Ascensor Artillería

and houses in the hills, but the precipitous topography and complicated street plan created access problems. The elegantly simple solution was the construction of the *ascensores,* which carried residents quickly and directly to their neighborhoods.

As Valparaíso advances toward World Heritage Site status, the remaining *ascensores* are one of the attractions that make the city unique. Authorities hope that improving the surrounding areas with better sidewalks, ornamentation, lighting, and landscaping will encourage a vigorous street life in areas that, until recently, were marginal neighborhoods, and restore the city's shine.

Below is a list of the existing *ascensores* with their main characteristics. All charge small fares, usually less than US$.20; some are privately operated, while others are public. For more detail, those who can read Spanish should see Juan Cameron's *Ascensores Porteños* (Viña del Mar/Santiago: Ediciones Altazor, 1998).

Ascensor Villaseca

Now out of order, the most westerly of Valparaíso's *ascensores* climbs from an almost hidden lower station on Avenida Antonio Varas to an upper station on Pedro León Gallo, on Cerro Playa Ancha. The 155-meter line has a 23-degree gradient. It dates from 1907.

Ascensor Artillería

From Plaza Aduana, also known as Plaza Wheelwright, Ascensor Artillería extends for 175 meters with a 30-degree gradient. One of the most popular tourist funiculars, it carries passengers 50 meters above the port to Cerro Playa Ancha, with panoramic views from Paseo 21 de Mayo toward Viña del Mar; the Museo Naval (Naval Museum) is nearby. It dates from 1894.

Ascensor Cordillera

Known also as Ascensor Serrano, for the street that its lower station faces, Ascensor Cordillera is one of Valpo's shortest funiculars, climbing just 60 meters

(continued on next page)

HEARTLAND

THE *ASCENSORES* OF VALPARAÍSO (cont'd)

up the side of its namesake hill to Plaza Eleuterio Ramírez, easy walking distance from the Museo Lord Cochrane. Dating from 1887, it has a gradient of 32 degrees.

Ascensor San Agustín
Now out of order, San Agustín is on the northwest side of Cerro Cordillera. It dates from 1913 and has a total length of 51 meters, with a gradient of 36 degrees.

Ascensor El Peral
From a nearly hidden entrance just off the Plaza de Justicia, but easily found by a conspicuous sign, Ascensor El Peral climbs 52 meters at a 48-degree gradient to Cerro Alegre's Paseo Yugoslavo and the Palacio Baburizza. This is one of the best walking areas in the hills, easily linking up to Cerro Concepción and its namesake *ascensor*. It dates from 1902.

Ascensor Concepción (Turri)
Dating from 1883, Valparaíso's oldest funicular is also one of the city's most popular, climbing 69 meters at a 45-degree gradient to Paseo Gervasoni, home to a popular hillside restaurant and the starting point for walking tours of Concepción and Cerro Alegre. Its lower station entrance is opposite the Reloj Turri clocktower, from which it takes its popular name Ascensor Turri.

Ascensor Reina Victoria
One of the city's most entertaining funiculars, Cerro Concepción's Ascensor Reina Victoria (1902) climbs 40 meters of rails at a 57-degree gradient in cars that hold only seven passengers. Reached from Plaza Aníbal Pinto via Cumming and Quebrada Elías, it has its upper station at Paseo Dimalow, another good starting point for walking tours of Cerro Concepción and Cerro Alegre.

Ascensor Espíritu Santo
Immediately southwest of El Almendral's Plaza Victoria, Espíritu Santo is the best approach to rapidly rejuvenating Cerro Bellavista, home to the open-air Museo al Cielo Abierto and the late Pablo Neruda's Valparaíso residence, now a museum and cultural center. Dating from 1911, it's officially known as Ascensor del Cerro Bellavista; it climbs 66 meters, at a gradient of nearly 45 degrees, to its upper terminus at Paseo Rudolph.

Ascensor Florida
At the south end of Carrera, also in El Almendral, Ascensor Florida is an alternative route to Cerro Bellavista and to Neruda's La Sebastiana house,

Hills of Valparaíso

Valparaíso is a walker's city, so long as those walkers are willing to test their legs and lungs on its steep staircases and narrow alleyways—even if they may prefer to use the *ascensores* whenever possible. The following paragraphs detail the main hill neighborhoods from west to east (unofficial estimates put the total number of hills at about 45).

While the most prominent landmarks are mentioned here, there is much more to see, as the city's typical constructions, with *calamina* siding and remarkable if unexpected architectural flourishes, seemingly occupy every square inch of declivitous lots that would be considered unbuildable almost anywhere else in the world.

For a good introductory walking tour of Valparaíso's central hill neighborhoods at a rea-

sonable price (US$4, two hours), contact Christian Güntert at Cerro Concepción's Hostal Casa Aventura, Pasaje Gálvez 11, tel. 32/755763, casatur@ctcinternet.cl.

Cerro Artillería: At the base of Cerro Artillería, the **Plaza Aduana** (alternatively known as Plaza Wheelwright) is the site of the former **Aduana de Valparaíso** (customs house, 1854), a national monument since superseded by a newer building on Plaza Sotomayor. The **Ascensor Artillería** climbs to **Paseo 21 de Mayo,** a harborview terrace that's home to the Museo Naval y Marítimo (1893), the naval and maritime museum (see separate entry below).

Cerro Santo Domingo: Several blocks north of Plaza Sotomayor, at the foot of Cerro Santo Domingo, **Plaza Echaurren** is the likely spot of

via Calle Ferrari. Built in 1906, with a length of 138 meters, it has a relatively gentle gradient—by Valparaíso standards—of only 19 degrees.

Ascensor Mariposa

Climbing Cerro Mariposa from the hidden Paseo Barbosa, in El Almendral southwest of Parque Italia, Ascensor Mariposa is the longest of all Valparaíso's funiculars, extending 177 meters at a gradient of 25 degrees. Built in 1904, its upper station is at Teniente Pinto, only a couple of blocks from Avenida Alemania, a sort of ring road with bus service back to downtown Valpo.

Ascensor Las Monjas

At the foot of Cerro Monja, on Subida Baquedano just west of Avenida Francia, El Almendral's Ascensor Las Monjas covers 110 meters at a gradient of 30 degrees. Dating from 1912, it stands almost directly opposite its now-abandoned twin, **Ascensor Cerro La Cruz,** on the other side of Avenida Francia.

Ascensor Barón

Offering some of the best views of any of the city's funiculars, Ascensor Barón (1906) overlooks the east end of the waterfront, immediately behind the Fersa Persa flea market. It ascends a gradient of

nearly 60 degrees over its 98-meter length before arriving at Paseo Diego Portales for panoramas of the entire harbor; this is the best approach to the landmark Iglesia San Francisco.

Ascensor Lecheros

At the east end of Pasaje Quillota, reached from Avenida Argentina, the 98-meter Ascensor Lecheros climbs a gradient of 58 degrees before reaching its upper station, where a walkway links it to Calle Miguel de Cervantes. It dates from 1906, but it underwent a major restoration in the mid-1990s.

Ascensor Larraín

East of Avenida Argentina, Ascensor Larraín is a short (60-meter) line with a 35-degree gradient that leads to its namesake hill; from the upper station, a wooden walkway leads to Calle Hermanos Clark. It dates from 1909.

Ascensor Polanco

The only true elevator of them all, at the southeast end of town and reached by a 140-meter tunnel from Calle Simpson, Ascensor Polanco climbs absolutely vertically for 60 meters, though there's an intermediate station at Carvallo, 34 meters above the base. Dating from 1916, it carries only eight passengers.

HEARTLAND

Saavedra's original landing in 1536. Almost immediately west, overlooking the **Plaza Matriz,** the **Iglesia la Matriz del Salvador** (1842) is one of a series of successors to the original colonial chapel built in 1559. Designed by parish priest José Antonio Riobó, the basilica-style construction is a national historical monument and the heart of Valparaíso's oldest barrio; itself a *zona típica* national monument, the neighborhood has a reputation for petty crime, but Sunday mornings are safe enough, as Porteño faithful gather for Mass and most of the delinquents are sleeping off their Saturday night debaucheries.

Cerro Cordillera: From the top of Calle Hurtado, midway between Plaza Echaurren and Plaza Sotomayor, the **Ascensor Cordillera** (1887) climbs to **Plaza Eleuterio Ramírez,** a short stroll from the

Museo del Mar Lord Cochrane, which occupies a colonial-style house built by Juan Mouat in 1841 (see separate entry below). This was also the location of Chile's first astronomical observatory.

Cerro Alegre: From the **Plaza de Justicia,** immediately behind Plaza Sotomayor and the Primera Zona Naval, **Ascensor El Peral** (1902) is the access point to Cerro Alegre, a neighborhood that was picturesque enough to serve as a backdrop for a Chilean TV soap opera a few years back.

From El Peral's upper exit, **Paseo Yugoeslavo** leads directly to the **Palacio Baburizza,** a former mansion housing the city's Museo de Bellas Artes (Fine Arts Museum; see separate entry below). Immediately adjacent is the Universidad de Playa Ancha's **Facultad de Artes,** a haven for Porteño art students.

Almost directly to the south, toward Cerro Concepción, the passageway steps known as **Pasaje Bavestrello** pass directly through the middle of an apartment building, a nearly perfect integration of public and private space; on occasion, locals project movies onto the apartment walls. Calle Urriola marks the border between Cerro Alegre and Cerro Concepción.

Cerro Concepción: The city's first funicular, **Ascensor Concepción** (1883) climbs from a nearly hidden entrance at the upper end of Carreño, just off Prat, to scenic Paseo Gervasoni. Among the sights in this *zona típica* are the Museo de Lukas, memorializing Porteño cartoonist and caricaturist Renzo Pecchenino, directly on Gervasoni (see entry below); Chile's second Protestant church, the **Iglesia Anglicana San Pablo** (1858), Pilcomayo 566 (classical organ concerts take place every Sunday at 12:30 P.M.); and the Gothic-style **Iglesia Luterana** (1897), at Beethoven and Abtao. **Paseo Atkinson** and **Paseo Dimalow** are typical hillside promenades, the latter linking with **Ascensor Reina Victoria** (1902), an easy route to or from Plaza Aníbal Pinto.

Cerro Panteón: Reached by a series of steep streets and staircases, but no *ascensores,* Cerro Panteón is home to three ridgetop cemeteries, of which the most interesting is the **Cementerio de Disidentes,** where Valparaíso's non-Catholic immigrant communities found their final resting place. Immediately east is **Cerro Cárcel,** site of the former city prison.

POLISHING THE PEARL

Valparaíso is Chile's most unusual city, but much of its distinctive architecture declined with the city's economy after the opening of the Panama Canal undercut its once-thriving port. The end of the nitrate era was another blow—the houses and mansions of its hill neighborhoods deteriorated as there was no money to maintain them. Fortunately, there wasn't enough money to tear them down either, and much of that heritage remains on the steep slopes behind the port.

In its heyday, Valparaíso sported the nickname *La Perla del Pacífico* (Pearl of the Pacific), as much for its incomparable setting and vernacular distinction as for any genuine glitter. Over the past decade or so, though, municipal officials and private organizations have begun to appreciate what Valparaíso has to offer and are making a genuine effort to salvage what remains.

One of the leaders in this effort is the Fundación Valparaíso, a nonprofit that is heading the campaign to make the city a UNESCO World Heritage Site. Already, with help from the World Monuments Fund, it has restored and adapted a magnificent building on Cerro Bellavista as its headquarters, and it is attempting to identify and restore the facades of buildings dating from 1914 or earlier—before the Panama Canal. The *fundación* is able to help restore rusted *calamina* (metal siding) in the original style, insulate the buildings while the *calamina* is off, repair roofs, and provide scaffolding and donated paint. It is hoping for a spinoff effect with other neighbors to improve their properties, even though those properties may be more recent.

Cities seeking World Heritage Site status, such as Venice, Rome, Prague, Saint Petersburg, Istanbul, Cuzco, and Cartagena (Colombia), are chosen for their historical, cultural, architectural, and urban merits. While such comparisons might not seem obvious to those unfamiliar with Valparaíso, its historic status in the golden age of Pacific trade around Cape Horn, its spontaneous growth and eclectic architecture, and its immigrant ethnic diversity combine to make a strong case for its inclusion.

The Fundación Valparaíso, along with its other activities, is attempting to reclaim public space for community use, tourism, and cultural purposes. It is also helping restore the Museo al Cielo Abierto, participating with the state arts agency Fondart in promoting the annual Festival de Cine de Valparaíso (Valparaíso Film Festival), and opening its own space to the public with a new bookstore café, with literary events, and with an international restaurant.

To visit the Fundación Valparaíso, take Ascensor Espíritu Santo to the stop and walk to its headquarters, painted a cheerful yellow with a blue mansard and extraordinary details at Héctor Calvo 205, tel. 32/593156. It also has a website: www.fundacionvalparaiso.cl.

Cerro Bellavista: At the upper end of Huito, reached by **Ascensor Espíritu Santo** but also by streets and staircases, Cerro Bellavista is the site of the **Museo al Cielo Abierto** (Open Sky Museum), a series of colorful, mostly abstract, murals in strategic sites by more than a dozen well-known Chilean artists, including Roberto Matta, Nemesio Antúnez, and Roser Bru.

Cerro Bellavista is also the focus of city renovation efforts by the **Fundación Valparaíso,** which has renovated an abandoned and dilapidated house into its "campus" at Héctor Calvo 205. Families in several historical houses here have taken advantage of the Fundación's technical and financial assistance to restore the facades of their homes.

On Bellavista's uppermost reaches, poet Pablo Neruda bought La Sebastiana, one of his three outlandish houses—the other two are in Santiago and at Isla Negra, south of Valparaíso. Like the other two, La Sebastiana is open to the public (see separate entry below).

Cerro Barón: One of Valpo's more easterly neighborhoods, Cerro Barón is home to one of its most literally conspicuous landmarks: for ships at sea, the towering **Iglesia San Francisco** (1845), a national historical monument at Blanco Viel and Zañartu, was their first glimpse of the city (the port's historical nickname "Pancho," a diminutive of Francisco, also derives from the church). Overlooking Avenida España, to the northwest, the imposing **Universidad Técnica Federico Santa María** (1931) overlooks Avenida España from Cerro Los Placeres.

From the Feria Persa Barón, a working-class flea market at the north end of Avenida Argentina, the **Ascensor Barón** (1906) (the city's first electric funicular) climbs to the **Mirador Diego Portales,** a scenic overlook that's the best starting point for exploring the neighborhood.

Museums

All the museums mentioned briefly above are described in more detail here.

Museo Naval y Marítimo: Housed in the former Escuela Naval (naval academy) on Cerro Artillería's Paseo 21 de Mayo, this misleadingly labeled museum is far more naval than maritime—it focuses on famous military figures such as Bernardo O'Higgins, the mercenary Lord Thomas Cochrane, and Admiral Manuel Blanco Encalada, and promotes nationalistic explanations of events such as the War of the Pacific (including its foolhardy hero Arturo Prat). It also pays exaggerated homage to the authoritarian Diego Portales, a behind-the-scenes political operative who promoted Chilean seapower in early independence times, but contains next to nothing on early exploration and discovery, and even less on the contemporary significance of maritime resources in the Chilean economy.

Beautifully maintained, with an immaculately landscaped central patio, the museum, tel. 32/251845, *anexo* 7930, is open 10 A.M.–6 P.M. daily except Monday; admission costs about US$1 for adults, US$.50 for children. From Plaza Aduana (Plaza Wheelwright), Ascensor Artillería climbs almost to the entrance.

Museo del Mar Lord Cochrane: In a colonial-style structure dating from 1842, this misleadingly named museum has little to do with Lord Cochrane (one of the most colorful figures of the South American wars of independence) but much to do with ships in bottles—the Club de Modelismo Naval de Valparaíso exhibits its best work here. There are also occasional special exhibitions and events, and the views from the terrace alone are worth the trip.

Reached by Ascensor Cordillera from Calle Serrano, near its intersection with Plaza Sotomayor, the Museo del Mar, Merlet 195, tel. 32/213124, is open Tuesday to Sunday 10 A.M.–6 P.M. Admission is free.

Museo de Bellas Artes (Palacio Baburizza): Designed by architects Arnaldo Barison and Renato Schiavon, this sprawling Art Nouveau chalet (1916) bears the name of Croatian-born nitrate baron Pascual Baburizza, who began his career selling meat and fish in the *oficinas* around Iquique, and who lived here until his death in 1946; the city acquired the building, now a national monument, in 1971.

Fortunate enough to cash out of the nitrate industry before its crash, Baburizza donated more than 90 19th- and 20th-century paintings to the municipal art collections, among them historic

Porteño landscapes by Thomas Somerscales and Alfredo Helsby, but there is little contemporary work on exhibit.

At Paseo Yugoeslavo 166, Cerro Alegre, the museum, tel. 32/252332, has been undergoing a prolonged renovation, with its collections in storage; the building itself, with remarkable details in its woodwork, wrought iron, and central turret, is a true artifact of its era. Presuming the restoration ever ends, its theoretical hours are 10 A.M.–6 P.M. daily, but the grounds are accessible even if the building itself is closed. Admission is free.

Museo de Lukas: On Cerro Concepción, this unique museum is the legacy of Renzo Pecchenino, an Italian-born artist and honorary Porteño who worked in several different media—cartoons and caricatures of his adopted country and sketches of the cityscape of Valparaíso. Published in newspapers such as *El Mercurio de Valparaíso,* he went by the pseudonym "Lukas." Some of his cartoons are displayed on brief videos.

At Paseo Gervasoni 448, easily reached by Ascensor Concepción, the Museo de Lukas, tel. 32/221344, is open daily except Monday, 11 A.M.–8 P.M.; admission costs US$1.

Museo de Historia Natural: In the resplendent Palacio Lyon, Valparaíso's natural history museum does much of what the Museo Naval y Marítimo has apparently abdicated, emphasizing the future of the oceans from an ecologically conscious—rather than simply strategic—point of view. It also depicts, admirably, the diversity of pre-Columbian Chile and its culture through dioramas, but the natural history specimens are a routine and disappointing effort at taxidermy.

The Museo de Historia Natural, Condell 1546, tel. 32/257441, is open Tuesday to Saturday 10 A.M.–1 P.M. and 2–6 P.M., Sunday and holidays 10 A.M. to 2 P.M. only. Admission costs US$1, US$.50 for children and retired people, but is free Wednesday and Sunday.

Galería de Arte Municipal: In the basement of the Palacio Lyon, but with a separate entrance at Condell 1550, the municipal art gallery features rotating fine-arts exhibitions. Hours at the Galería de Arte, tel. 32/220062, are 10 A.M.–7 P.M. daily except Sunday; admission is free.

La Sebastiana: With his love for the sea, Pablo Neruda could hardly resist a residence in Valparaíso, and he bought this five-story house in 1961. He also loved the city's informality and spontaneity:

> *Valparaíso grabbed me, she subjected me to her will, to her absurdity:*
> *Valparaíso is a mess, a cluster of crazy houses.*

The Fundación Neruda opened La Sebastiana to the public in 1992, and in at least one sense it's the best of his three houses—unlike Santiago's La Chascona and Isla Negra, with their relatively regimented guided tours, visitors can roam through the house more or less at will. Like La Chascona and Isla Negra, it displays a whimsical assortment of artifacts collected by the poet on his global travels. In addition to the house, the Fundación operates a café, cultural center, and a souvenir shop.

La Sebastiana, Ferrari 692, tel. 32/256606, is open Tuesday to Friday 10:30 A.M.–2:10 P.M. and 3:30–6 P.M., weekends and holidays 10:30 A.M.–6 P.M. In the summer months of January and February, hours are 10:30 A.M.–6:50 P.M. daily except Monday. If either Monday or Tuesday is a holiday, closing day can change. Admission costs US$2.50, but children, students, and retired people pay half on weekdays.

The most direct route to La Sebastiana is to walk up Cerro Bellavista and follow the signs from the Museo de Aire Libre; alternatively, take a *taxi colectivo* from Plazuela Ecuador or the Verde Mar bus "O," from Plaza Sotomayor to the 6900 block of Avenida Alemania, from which the house is a short walk.

Accommodations

Nearby Viña del Mar still has many more alternatives for accommodations, but options in Valparaíso are increasing and, in many cases, more interesting. The tourist office maintains a list of inexpensive *casas de familia,* several of them in scenic hill neighborhoods; there are also several good new hotels, though nothing in the luxury category. **US$10–25:** Only a few doors from the bus terminal, **Casa Familiar Eliana Castillo,** Avenida

Pedro Montt 2881, tel. 32/253583, charges US$6 pp. At the west end of town on Cerro Playa Ancha, rates at **Villa Kunterbunt,** Avenida Quebrada Verde 192, tel. 32/288873, are US$7 pp without breakfast; the owners speak English and German as well as Spanish. City buses 1, 2, 5, 6, 17, 111, and N all stop nearby.

Barely a block from the terminal, **Casa Familiar Mónica Villegas,** Avenida Argentina 322-B, tel. 32/215673, charges US$9 with breakfast, but fronts on a busy avenue.

On Cerro Alegre, for US$9 pp, **Hostal Casa Aventura,** Pasaje Gálvez 11, tel. 32/755963, casatur@ctcinternet.cl, has rooms with high ceilings, burnished wooden floors, and one, two, or three beds, as well as two shared baths, and kitchen facilities. Rates also include an outstanding breakfast, with bread, fresh cheese, and fresh fruit; its major drawback, despite the hills location, is that it faces busy Calle Urriola, which gets lots of downshifting cars, buses, and trucks.

Nearby on Cerro Concepción, renovated **Residencial Latina,** Papudo 462, tel. 32/494622, clatina@vtr.net, deserves serious consideration for US$10 pp with breakfast; it was to open its patio to guests. Also on Cerro Concepción, **Casa Familiar Juan Carrasco,** Abtao 668, tel./fax 32/210737, is one of Valpo's finest values for US$12 pp with breakfast in a four-story house, furnished with antiques and capped by a rooftop terrace with sensational panoramas of the harbor and coastline. Reached via Ascensor Concepción (Turri), with a affable family atmosphere, it's an exceptional choice.

In the historic center, facing Plaza Sotomayor, the aging **Hotel Reina Victoria,** Plaza Sotomayor 190, tel. 32/212203, charges US$15/20 s/d with shared bath and breakfast, but fourth-floor walk-up singles cost only US$10.

At **Residencial El Rincón Universal,** Avenida Argentina 825, tel. 32/235184, rooms with private bath and breakfast, plus access to laundry service, cable TV, and Internet, cost US$13 pp. On Cerro Alegre, highly regarded **Hospedaje Anita,** Higueras 107, tel. 32/239327, has only three rooms—phone ahead. Rates are US$12 pp.

US$25–50: Facing Plaza Victoria, recommended **Hostal Kolping,** Francisco Valdés Vergara 622, tel.

32/216306, fax 32/230352, charges US$15/23 s/d with shared bath, US$23/27 s/d with private bath, including breakfast. Another good new choice is the deco-style **Hotel Puerto Principal,** Huito 361, tel./fax 32/745629, hotel@ecosa.cl, for US$20/27 s/d with private bath.

The rather ordinary **Hotel Prat,** Condell 1443, tel. 32/253081, fax 32/213368, costs US$25 s or d with breakfast; a better choice is **Hotel Lancaster,** Chacabuco 2362, tel. 32/217391, fax 32/230216, for US$23/35. **Hostal Casa Baska,** Victoria 2449, tel. 32/234036, fax 32/219915, is well worth US$24/33 s/d.

Capturing traditional Valparaíso style in new accommodations built from salvaged materials, Cerro Concepción's **Brighton B&B,** Paseo Atkinson 151, tel./fax 32/223513, overlooks Plaza Aníbal Pinto. Rooms cost US$20 pp, though those with harbor views command a substantial surcharge; nonguests can savor the view during lunch or dinner at its terrace restaurant.

Recently constructed **Hotel Puerta del Alcalá,** Pirámide 524, tel. 32/227478, fax 32/745642, is a welcome addition to Valpo's accommodations scene. Rates are US$44 s or d.

Food

Valparaíso's dining scene is improving, but few places can match the upscale elegance of Viña del Mar's best. Most are traditional seafood restaurants, the cheapest of which are the second-floor *marisquerías* at the **Mercado Central** (Central Market), bounded by Cochrane, Valdivia, Blanco, and San Martín. Across from the market, **Los Porteños No. 2,** Valdivia 169, tel. 32/252511, is a good and slightly more expensive alternative.

Valparaíso Eterno, Señoret 150, 2nd floor, tel. 32/255605, has more Porteño personality than any other downtown dining spot, and it is reasonably priced, with lunches around US$5. Successor to an earlier landmark that burned to the ground, the **Roland Bar,** Avenida Errázuriz 1152, tel. 32/235123, is comparable but less colorful. Alternatively, **Bambú,** Pudeto 450, tel. 32/234216, serves vegetarian specials.

Other good but traditional and broadly similar seafood alternatives include moderately priced **Mesón del Lord,** Cochrane 859, tel.

terrace restaurant at Brighton B&B

32/231096; the more expensive **Bar Inglés,** Cochrane 851 but with a separate entrance at Blanco 870, tel. 32/214625; **La Rotonda,** Prat 701, tel. 32/217746; and **Bote Salvavidas,** Muelle Prat s/n, tel. 32/251477.

It can seem moribund on weeknights, but **Cinzano,** Plaza Aníbal Pinto 1182, tel. 32/213043, serves good traditional Chilean food at moderate prices, along with cheap mixed drinks and a good selection of beers. From Thursday to Sunday, it has live tango music; on nights when there's no live music, the selection of recorded material is excellent. Another tango venue is **La Puerta del Sol,** Avenida Pedro Montt 2037.

On Cerro Concepción, at the east end of Paseo Gervasoni near the exit of Ascensor Concepción, **Café Turri,** Templeman 147, tel. 32/252091, has seafood to match its fine views and outdoor dining on warm days. Figure US$8–10 for the average entrée. In the same neighborhood, French-run **Le Filou de Montpellier,** Avenida

Pedro Montt 382, has well-prepared but inexpensive (about US$4) lunches—the chocolate flan dessert comes recommended.

On Cerro Alegre, reached by Ascensor El Peral, **La Colombina,** Paseo Yugoeslavo 15, tel. 32/236254, has fine food and an even finer panoramic dining room. Entrées cost around US$9–10, with prices steadily rising; it's open Tuesday to Saturday noon–4 P.M. and 8 P.M.–noon, Sunday noon–6 P.M. It also has a pub open 9 P.M.–2:30 A.M. Thursday to Saturday.

On Cerro Bellavista, the Fundación Valparaíso's **El Gato Tuerto,** Héctor Calvo 205, is part of the nonprofit's effort to reinvigorate the city. It also has a bookstore/café. Toward Viña del Mar, on Cerro Esperanza above Avenida España, **Portofino,** Bellamar 301, tel. 32/621464, is widely considered one of Valpo's finest restaurants.

Entertainment

Bars: Valparaíso has an increasingly active nightlife, largely focused on Avenida Ecuador, where there are more than 20 bars of various kinds, with little to choose between them.

Named for the first murderer to be executed in Chile, **Emile Dubois,** Ecuador 144, tel. 32/21-3486, is a relatively sedate and friendly wine bar in a neighborhood full of popular but generally more boisterous drinking establishments. Among the latter are **Liverpool,** Ecuador 130, tel. 32/610109, and **Mr. Egg,** Ecuador 50, tel. 32/257534.

On Cerro Concepción, **Café Color,** Papudo 526, tel. 32/746136, is more a teahouse but has the ambience of a classic neighborhood bar, its walls covered with photographs of people and paintings and postcards of Valpo. Stocking a selection of menus from restaurants around town, it's a good place to go to decide where to eat if the simple sandwich fare here isn't enough for you; lively without being noisy, it's small and intimate, with *simpático* staff.

Cinema: Within the Centro Cultural Valparaíso, the **Centro Cine,** Esmeralda 1083, tel. 32/21-6953, is a repertory house. The five-screen **Cine Hoyts,** Pedro Montt 2111, tel. 32/594709, is a more strictly commercial cinema.

Theater: The **Teatro Municipal,** Avenida Uruguay 410, tel. 32/214654, is the main performing arts venue. The **Sala Herbert Jonckers,** Avenida Colón 1712, tel. 32/221680, has similar offerings.

Spectator Sports: Valparaíso's first-division soccer team, Santiago Wanderers, has offices at Independencia 2061, tel. 32/217210 or 32/594555; its home stadium is the Estadio Municipal at Playa Ancha.

Events

Hundreds of thousands of Chileans converge on the port city to see the massive fireworks display at **Año Nuevo** (New Year's Eve). April 17 marks the **Fundación de la Ciudad,** the city's official founding in 1791.

The annual **Festival Cinematográfico de Valparaíso** (Valparaíso Film Festival) takes place in August.

Shopping

Valparaíso is home to a horde of crafts, flea, and antiques markets. The most commercial is Muelle Prat's **Feria de Artesanías,** at the foot of Plaza Sotomayor, but the **Mercado Artesanal Permanente,** at the corner of Avenida Pedro Montt and Las Heras, has a better crafts selection.

Valparaíso has two main flea markets, one on **Plaza Radomiro Tomic,** the median strip dividing the lanes of Avenida Argentina, which includes mostly cheap manufactured goods but also some indigenous crafts, and the more structured **Feria Persa Barón,** where Avenida Argentina becomes Avenida España toward Viña del Mar.

On Plaza O'Higgins, on weekends and holidays, the **Feria de Antigüedades y Libros La Merced** is an extraordinary but expensive antiques and book market comparable—except for the lack of tango—to the famous Feria de San Telmo in Buenos Aires's Plaza Dorrego. **Casa Lacazio,** Independencia 1976, tel. 32/255111, is a permanent antiques outlet.

Services

Money: Banco de Chile has an ATM at Condell 1481. For exchange houses, try Inter Cambio on Plaza Sotomayor or Cambio Exprinter, Prat 895.
Postal: Correos de Chile is at Plaza Sotomayor 233.

Telephone and Internet: Telefónica CTC is at Esmeralda 1054, Avenida Pedro Montt 2023, and at the Terminal Rodoviario. Entel is at Condell 1495 and at Avenida Pedro Montt and the corner of Cruz. Valparaíso's area code is 32.

Servinet, Cochrane 625, is a tiny Internet café—three computers only. Café Riquet, Plaza Aníbal Pinto 1199, tel. 32/213171, is a traditional Porteño favorite that's moved into the cyber age.
Laundry: On Cerro Alegre, Lavanda Café, Avenida Pedro Montt 454, does your laundry and steams your espresso.
Medical: Hospital Carlos van Buren is at Avenida Colón 2454, tel. 32/254074.

Information

Tourist Offices: The municipal Departamento de Turismo, Condell 1490, tel. 32/939108, is open 8:30 A.M.–2 P.M. and 3:30–5:30 P.M. weekdays. On the waterfront Muelle Prat pier, at the foot of Plaza Sotomayor, its Centro de Difusión, tel. 32/236322, is open 10 A.M.–7 P.M. daily in summer, but the rest of the year it's open 10 A.M.–2 P.M. and 3–6 P.M. only; it provides maps and brochures, usually has English-speaking staff, and shows video presentations on the city. A satellite office at the Terminal Rodoviario (bus station), at Avenida Pedro Montt and Rawson, tel. 32/213246, is open 10 A.M.–2 P.M. and 3–7 P.M. daily in summer, but it is closed Monday the rest of the year.
Consulates: Several neighboring and overseas countries have consulates in Valparaíso: Argentina at Blanco 890, Oficina 204, tel. 32/258165; Germany at Blanco 1215, 11th floor, tel. 32/256749; Peru at Avenida Errázuriz 1178, Oficina 71, tel. 32/253403, fax 32/217289, conpeval@entelchile.net; and Great Britain at Blanco 1199, 5th floor, tel. 32/213063, con.britanico@entelchile.net.
Bookstores: Librería Crisis, Avenida Pedro Montt 2871, tel. 32/218504, offers a good stock of used books on Chilean history and literature. For local maps and local guidebooks, try Librería Ivens, Plaza Aníbal Pinto 339.

Transportation

Transportation in and out of Valparaíso is essentially bus transportation; though LanChile and

LanExpress, Esmeralda 1048, tel. 32/251441, fax 32/233374, sell tickets and confirm reservations, Santiago is the nearest commercial airport.

Unless otherwise indicated, all buses depart from Valparaíso's aging Terminal Rodoviario at Avenida Pedro Montt 2800, corner of Rawson, tel. 32/213246. Regional, long-distance, and international services from Valparaíso and Viña del Mar are almost identical, so most details appear here and only those which differ (such as some telephone numbers) appear in the listing for Viña's much newer Terminal Rodoviario. Some northbound long-distance buses link up with departures from Santiago, which can mean waiting at the junction with the Panamericana for a transfer.

Regional Buses: Buses La Porteña, with its own terminal at Molina 366, tel. 32/216568, serves coastal and interior destinations in northern Region V, including La Ligua (US$2.50), Pichidangui (US$3.50), and Los Vilos (US$4), at 6:50 and 10:40 A.M., and at 3 and 5:10 P.M. daily. In the main terminal, Cóndor Bus, tel. 32/212927, goes to La Ligua daily at 4:20 P.M.

Sol del Pacífico, tel. 32/213776 and 32/2-81026, serves Quintero (US$1), running every 10 minutes, and other northern Region V beaches, including Papudo, continuing to La Ligua and Cabildo (US$3), every 45 minutes or so until 6:10 P.M.

Hourly between 5:20 A.M. and 6:50 P.M., Buses Dhino's, tel. 32/221298, goes to Los Andes via Limache, Quillota, and San Felipe. Buses JM, tel. 32/256581, goes every 30 minutes to Los Andes (US$3.50) between 6:45 A.M. and 9:15 P.M.; Pullman Bus, tel. 32/253125, goes hourly between 6:30 A.M. and 9 P.M.

Pullman Bus Lago Peñuelas, tel. 32/224025, goes to southern Region V beach towns including Algarrobo and nearby Isla Negra (US$2), site of Pablo Neruda's most famous house, every quarter hour between 6:20 A.M. and 10 P.M.

Buses to Santiago: To the capital (US$3–4, two hours), the most frequent connections are with Tur-Bus, tel. 32/212028; buses leave every 15 minutes between 5:20 A.M. and 10:30 P.M. Tur-Bus's more economical subsidiary Cóndor Bus, tel. 32/212927, leaves every half hour between 6 A.M. and 9 P.M.

Sol del Pacífico, tel. 32/213776, leaves hourly between 6:50 A.M. and 9:30 P.M., while Pullman Lit, tel. 32/237290, goes every two hours between 8:10 A.M. and 7:10 P.M. Sol del Sur, tel. 32/252211, has half a dozen buses daily between 9:20 A.M. and 4:50 P.M.

Interregional Buses: In addition to its Santiago schedules, Tur-Bus also runs northbound routes on the Panamericana to Arica and intermediates and southbound to Puerto Montt and intermediates. Other companies on the Panamericana Norte include Buses Zambrano, tel. 32/258986; Pullman Bus, tel. 32/220595; Flota Barrios, tel. 32/253674; and Fénix Pullman Norte, tel. 32/2-57993. Transportes Inca Bus/Lasval, tel. 32/2-14915, goes to the Norte Chico cities of Ovalle and La Serena.

Southbound carriers on the Panamericana, to Puerto Montt and intermediates, include Buses Norte, tel. 32/258322; and Tas Choapa, tel. 32/252921. Buses Lit, tel. 32/237200; Intersur, tel. 32/212297; Sol del Pacífico, tel. 32/213776 or 32/281026; and Sol del Sur, tel. 32/252211, go as far as Talca and Chillán before turning west toward Concepción.

Sample northbound destinations, with approximate times and fares, include La Serena (US$11, six hours), Copiapó (US$25, 10 hours), Antofagasta (US$32, 18 hours), Iquique (US$35, 24 hours) and Arica (US$42, 27 hours); southbound destinations include Talca (US$9, six hours), Chillán (US$13, 7.5 hours), Concepción (US$15, nine hours), Temuco (US$17, 12 hours), Osorno (US$20, 14 hours), and Puerto Montt (US$24, 16 hours).

International Buses: International buses to Argentina, Uruguay, and Brazil bypass Santiago, but most pass through Viña del Mar. Nearly all leave early, between 8 and 8:30 A.M., and stop in Mendoza (US$15, seven hours); the exception to early departures is Buses Ahumada, tel. 32/216663, which has service to Buenos Aires (US$46), at noon and 9 P.M. daily. Other Buenos Aires carriers include El Rápido, tel. 32/685474, and Buses TAC, tel. 32/257587.

Other Argentina-bound carriers include Fénix Pullman Norte, tel. 32/681785, to Mendoza only, and Tas Choapa, tel. 32/252921, daily to

Mendoza, San Juan, and Córdoba (US$30). Buses Pluma, tel. 32/258322, goes Tuesday, Friday, and Sunday to Mendoza and Rosario (US$36) and to the Brazilian cities of Florianópolis (US$78), São Paulo (US$81), and Rio de Janeiro (US$84).

Buses Géminis, tel. 32/258322, goes Monday, Wednesday, and Friday to Oruro and La Paz, Bolivia (US$60), via Iquique.

Getting Around

Easily the most interesting and entertaining way to get around town is on foot and via the funiculars, detailed above, but there are other mechanized alternatives as well.

Bus and *Taxi Colectivo:* Numerous local buses and *taxi colectivos* connect Valparaíso with Viña del Mar, only a few kilometers north. They also thread in and around the hill neighborhoods, necessarily via very indirect routes.

Train: From the Estación Puerto, Avenida Errázuriz 711, tel. 32/212453, the Metro Regional de Valparaíso (Merval) is a suburban commuter line that goes to Valpo's own Estación Barón and to Viña del Mar, El Salto, Quilpué, Villa Alemana, Peñablanca, and Limache. The maximum fare is less than US$1.

VICINITY OF VALPARAÍSO

East and south of Valparaíso are several options for excursions, including the wineries of the Casablanca valley and Pablo Neruda's beachfront home at Isla Negra (see below, under The South Central Coast). For moderately priced excursions around both Valpo and Viña, contact Christian Güntert at **Hostal Casa Aventura,** Pasaje Gálvez 11, tel. 32/755963, casatur@ctcinternet.cl.

Reserva Nacional Lago Peñuelas

About 25 km southeast of Valparaíso, fronting directly on Ruta 68 at Km 95, misleadingly named Lago Peñuelas is really a reservoir, built at the end of the 19th century, that serves as Valparaíso's and Viña del Mar's water supply. Surrounded by both native sclerophyllous (glossy-leaved) woodland and plantations of eucalyptus and other exotic species, the reservoir is open weekends and holidays only to the public for fishing and picnicking, from 9 A.M.–5:30 P.M., with a small admission charge.

In total, the reserve covers 9,260 hectares and supports substantial populations of waterfowl, other birds, and terrestrial fauna native to the region. Buses between Santiago and the coastal cities can drop visitors directly at the entrance, on the north side of Ruta 68.

Lo Vásquez (Santuario de la Inmaculada Concepción)

Ruta 68 between Santiago and Valparaíso is one of Chile's busiest highways, but every December 8 motor vehicle traffic miraculously vanishes as up to half a million faithful congregate at the **Santuario de la Inmaculada Concepción,** 32 km southeast of Valparaíso and 68 km northwest of Santiago.

After the original chapel was destroyed by the 1906 Valparaíso earthquake, it took more than 30 years to build the present church, which dates from 1940. The 4000-square-meter amphitheater, which can seat 1,158 people and accommodate another 1,800 in standing room, will soon be roofed at a cost of US$600,000, and further improvements will double its capacity.

Authorities divert Valparaíso- and Viña-bound traffic north through Ruta 5 and Ruta 60 to Quillota, as pedestrian pilgrims literally take over the highway, most walking and some even crawling the final five or six km to one of official Catholicism's holiest Chilean shrines. Many start days earlier from Santiago and even farther away, sleeping outdoors en route before arriving to attend open-air Masses, which take place from 6 P.M. the afternoon of the 7th until 8 P.M. the following evening of the 8th; the festivities close with a procession led by the bishop of Valparaíso.

Throughout the event, hawkers sell prodigious quantities of food and souvenirs—though there are almost permanent eateries and the sanctuary has its own souvenir shop—and pilgrims deposit up to 20 tons of trash. At other times, they leave small monetary offerings in hopes of avoiding traffic accidents or perhaps speeding tickets, as the Carabineros patrol this stretch of highway zealously, sometimes catching speeding legislators en route to Valparaíso.

Casablanca (Ruta del Vino)

Midway between Valparaíso and Santiago, the Casablanca valley is one of Chile's fastest-growing wine regions, best known for its whites and, recently, for champagne geared toward the domestic Chilean market. Only a couple of wineries are open to the public at present, but this number is likely to increase; since the ones below are almost directly on the highway, transportation is not a problem.

At Km 72, on the south side of Ruta 68, the international Seagram's company has opened its modern **Viña Elaboradora de Champagne Cuvée Mumm,** tel. 32/741703, for tours, which include a video introduction followed by a visit to the cellars, weekdays at 9:30 and 10:30 A.M., noon, and at 2, 3:30, and 5 P.M., Saturday at 9:30 and 10:30 A.M. only. After the tour, there is free tasting at its well-designed *sala de ventas* (bar and shop); Chilean palates prefer fruity sparkling wines, flavored with pineapple, strawberry, peach, and melon, but some drier varieties are also in stock. Note that, while schedules can be tight and reservations advisable in summer, the rest of the year it may be possible to drop in.

On the north side of the highway and west of the Zapata tunnel, at Km 66, **Viña Vera-monte,** tel. 32/742421, salaventa@veramonte.cl, is a project of the Chilean-run Franciscan Vineyards in California's Napa Valley. It's open 9:30 A.M.–6:30 P.M. daily except Sunday for visits to its cellars, bottling plant, and wine shop.

On the Algarrobo highway, five km south of Ruta 68, **Viña La Providencia** has a *sala de ventas* selling its specialty chardonnay but also fresh cheese, chocolate, butter, honey, and various types of marmalade.

The South Central Coast

There is no direct road south from Valparaíso, but the paved road west-southwest from the Casablanca valley passes through a series of popular beachfront towns. Regular bus service from Valparaíso is with Pullman Bus Lago Peñuelas, and from Santiago with several companies.

Algarrobo: Home to many Santiaguino summer houses, Algarrobo hosts the **Regata Mil Millas Náuticas** for yachties every February; the postcolonial adobe **Iglesia de la Candelaria** (1837) is a national historical monument.

Hotel Pacífico, Avenida Carlos Alessandri 1930, tel. 35/482818, charges US$25 pp with full board off-season, but rather more in summer.

Isla Negra: About 10 km south of Algarrobo, Isla Negra—which is not an island—has become famous for the **Casa de Pablo Neruda,** the poet's favorite beachfront house and burial site. Built to entertain his friends and hold his eclectic and whimsical collections of nautical memorabilia, including bowsprits, ships-in-bottles, and wood carvings, the house has been open to the public for more than a decade. The Fundación Neruda, which administers the site, recently added a room originally planned by Neruda, but never completed, to house his huge assortment of sea snails, clam shells, and narwhal spikes.

Unfortunately, because Isla Negra is Neruda's most popular house, the half-hour guided tours are so rushed that the guides sometimes find themselves talking over each other. No photography is permitted in the house itself, but after the tour is over, visitors may remain on the grounds and photograph the exterior.

In summer, reservations are essential at Isla Negra, tel. 35/461284, which is open Tuesday to Sunday, 10 A.M.–8 P.M. The rest of the year, when hours are 10 A.M.–2 P.M. and 3–6 P.M. Tuesday to Friday and 10 A.M.–8 P.M. weekends and holidays, it's easier to join a tour on a drop-in basis. Admission, including the tour, costs US$3.50 for adults, half that for children and retired people, but tours in English or French cost about US$1 pp more.

Most people come to Isla Negra for the day, but the accommodations at **Casa Azul,** Avenida Santa Lucía s/n, tel. 35/461154, have drawn praise from several travelers. Rates are US$9 pp with breakfast. The Fundación Neruda's own **El Rincón del Poeta,** tel. 35/461774, has good seafood lunches for about US$6.

Cartagena: About 25 km south of Isla Negra, the town of Cartagena was an elite beach resort from the 1870s but became a mass domestic tourist destination in the early 1920s, when the railroad from Santiago to the port of San Antonio was extended north. As Cartagena was only 120 km from Santiago (about 60 km closer than Viña del Mar because the rail route to Viña was so roundabout), it became immensely popular with working-class day-trippers from the capital.

Sort of a mini-Valparaíso in its vernacular architectural style, though its topography is not quite so extreme, Cartagena was the home of poet Vicente Huidobro, a Picasso contemporary who fought in the Spanish Civil War; both the **Tumba de Vicente Huidobro** (his gravesite) and the **Estación de Ferrocarril,** the former train station, are national historical monuments.

Several hotels lie along Avenida Playa Chica, the shoreline road; **Hotel Playa,** Avenida Playa Chica 98, tel. 35/450370, charges US$10/18 s/d with private bath.

VIÑA DEL MAR

Famous for the white-sand beaches that stretch from Caleta Abarca north through the suburbs of Reñaca and Concón, fabled Viña del Mar is also known as the Ciudad Jardín (Garden City) for its Mediterranean cityscapes—one of its signature symbols is the Reloj de Flores, the "Clock of Flowers" at the Avenida Marina approach from Valparaíso.

In the immediate post-independence times, though, what is now Viña was *puro campo,* a bucolic countryside that was part of the Carrera family's Hacienda Las Siete Hermanas. Among Chile's founding families, the Carreras sold the hacienda to the Alvarez-Vergara family who, as the Santiago-Valparaíso railroad increased land values, sold off parts of the property to wealthy Valparaíso businessmen, marking a transition from semirurality to elegant residential suburb and beach resort.

Throughout the latter half of the 20th century, though, Viña became a more democratic destination and even began to pull Argentine tourists from across the Andes—despite the fact that its constant fogs, cool sea breezes, and cold Pacific

Fabled Viña del Mar is known as the Ciudad Jardín (Garden City) for its Mediterranean cityscapes—one of its signature symbols is the Reloj de Flores, the "Clock of Flowers."

currents can make entering the water without a warm wet suit a forbidding experience. Once Chile's prestige beach resort, Viña has lost ground to competitors such as La Serena—whose seaside climate is only slightly milder—but still gets plenty of weekend and summer beachgoers from metropolitan Santiago.

Orientation

Viña del Mar is 120 km northeast of Santiago via Ruta 68 and about 10 km north of Valparaíso via Avenida España, which hugs the coastline. The Estero Marga Marga, a potentially stunning riverbank asset that's been turned into a disgraceful backhoe parking lot crossed by a series of parallel bridges, divides the city in two: to the south, between the estuary and the railroad tracks, the commercial district is centered on Plaza Vergara, with many of the city's traditional mansions beyond the tracks, including the fabled grounds of the Quinta Vergara; to the north, Avenida Libertad crosses the river to a more regular residential grid, where most streets and avenues bear numbers rather than names. They are further distinguished by direction, Norte (north), Oriente (east) or Poniente (west); at the district's western edge, paralleling the beach, Avenida San Martín and surrounding site streets are home to most of Viña's better restaurants and nightlife venues.

Several blocks of Avenida Valparaíso, Viña's main commercial thoroughfare, have been repaved and retiled into an attractive pedestrian mall. Terraces of luxury condos cover the beachfront hillsides of Reñaca, politically part of Viña del Mar but with its own distinct identity, as surely as rice paddies climb the mountainsides of Southeast Asia.

Viña is less spontaneously engaging than Valparaíso—there are fewer real surprises as you walk around town—but there is a scattering of historical monuments and museums. One entertaining way of orienting yourself to town is to hire one of Plaza Vergara's elegant *victorias* (horse-drawn carriages), for about US$15 per hour.

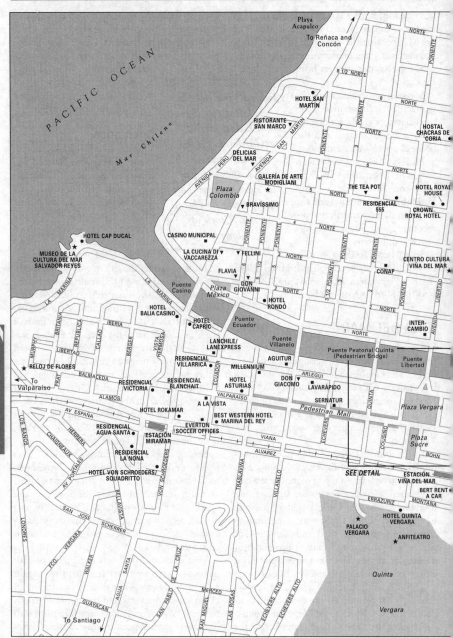

PACIFIC OCEAN

Mar Chileno

Playa
Acapulco
To Reñaca and
Concón

HOTEL SAN
MARTIN

RISTORANTE
SAN MARCO

DÉLICIAS
DEL MAR

HOTEL CAP DUCAL

MUSEO DE LA
CULTURA DEL MAR
SALVADOR REYES

GALERÍA DE ARTE
MODIGLIANI

Plaza
Colombia

BRAVÍSSIMO

HOSTAL
CHACRAS DE
CORIA

THE TEA POT

HOTEL ROYAL
HOUSE

RESIDENCIAL
555

CROWN
ROYAL HOTEL

CASINO MUNICIPAL

LA CUCINA DI
VACCAREZZA

FELLINI

CENTRO CULTURA
VIÑA DEL MAR

CONAF

FLAVIA

DON
GIOVANNI

HOTEL
RONDÓ

Plaza
México

Puente
Casino

HOTEL
BALIA CASINO

HOTEL
CAPRIC

Puente
Ecuador

LANCHILE/
LANEXPRESS

Puente
Villanelo

Puente Peatonal Quinta
(Pedestrian Bridge)

Puente
Libertad

RELOJ DE FLORES

To
Valparaíso

RESIDENCIAL
VILLARRICA

RESIDENCIAL
VICTORIA

RESIDENCIAL
BLANCHAIT

MILLENNIUM

AGUITUR

HOTEL
ASTURIAS

DON
GIACOMO

ARLEGUI

LAVARÁPIDO

SERNATUR

Plaza Vergara

A LA VISTA

HOTEL ROKAMAR

BEST WESTERN HOTEL
MARINA DEL REY

Pedestrian Mall

RESIDENCIAL
AGUA SANTA

EVERTON
SOCCER OFFICES

ESTACIÓN
MIRAMAR

VIANA

Plaza
Sucre

BOHN

RESIDENCIAL
LA NOÑA

ALVAREZ

HOTEL VON SCHROEDERS/
SQUADRITTO

SEE DETAIL

ESTACIÓN
VIÑA DEL MAR

BERT RENT
A CAR

ERRAZURIZ

MONTANA

HOTEL QUINTA
VERGARA

PALACIO
VERGARA

ANFITEATRO

To Santiago

Quinta

Vergara

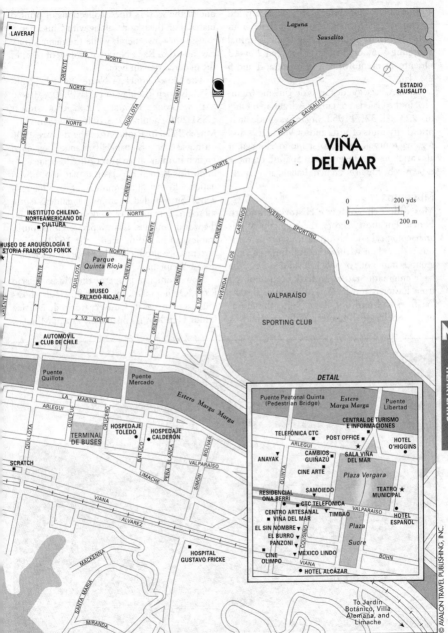

VIÑA
DEL MAR

0   200 yds

0   200 m

Laguna
Sausalito

ESTADIO
SAUSALITO

VALPARAÍSO

SPORTING CLUB

LAVERAP

NORTE

NORTE

NORTE

NORTE

NORTE

NORTE

INSTITUTO CHILENO-
NORTEAMERICANO DE
CULTURA

MUSEO DE ARQUEOLOGÍA E
STORIA FRANCISCO FONCK

Parque
Quinta Rioja

MUSEO
PALACIO RIOJA

2 1/2 NORTE

AUTOMÓVIL
CLUB DE CHILE

Puente
Quillota

Puente
Mercado

Estero Marga Marga

LA   MARINA

ARLEGUI

HOSPEDAJE
TOLEDO

HOSPEDAJE
CALDERÓN

TERMINAL
DE BUSES

VALPARAÍSO

SCRATCH

LIMACHE

VIANA

ALVAREZ

MACKENNA

HOSPITAL
GUSTAVO FRICKE

SANTA MARÍA

MIRANDA

DETAIL

Puente Peatonal Quinta
(Pedestrian Bridge)

Estero
Marga Marga

Puente
Libertad

TELEFÓNICA CTC

CENTRAL DE TURISMO
E INFORMACIONES

POST OFFICE

HOTEL
O'HIGGINS

ARLEGUI

ANAYAK

CAMBIOS
GUIÑAZÚ

CINE ARTE

SALA VIÑA
DEL MAR

Plaza Vergara

RESIDENCIAL
ONA BERRI

SAMOIEDO

CTC TELEFÓNICA

CENTRO ARTESANAL
VIÑA DEL MAR

TIMBAO

EL SIN NOMBRE

EL BURRO
PANZONI

CINE
OLIMPO

MÉXICO LINDO

VIANA

HOTEL ALCÁZAR

TEATRO
MUNICIPAL

VALPARAÍSO

HOTEL
ESPAÑOL

Plaza

Sucre

BOHN

To Jardín
Botánico, Villa
Alemana, and
Limache

HEARTLAND

© AVALON TRAVEL PUBLISHING, INC.

Alternatively, for about US$5 pp, slightly less for children, the Sernatur-sponsored Trolley Tour is 1.5-hour city tours, leaving from Terminal Shopping Viña on 15 Norte between 2 and 3 Oriente, at the north end of town, at 3 and 5 P.M. daily.

Viña's Asociación de Guías de Turismo (Aguitur), in the Galería Fontana at Arlegui 364, Oficina 223, tel. 32/711052, organizes moderately priced city tours of Viña and/or Valparaíso, and regional tours along the coast and to Santiago. It also arranges private guides in Spanish or, more expensively, English, French, Italian, and Greek.

Museums

Museo de Arqueología e Historia Francisco Fonck: For most visitors, the highlight of this archaeological and historical museum is without rather than within the building—on the grounds stands one of only half a dozen *moai,* the large enigmatic statues, to have been removed from Easter Island (Rapa Nui), Chile's distant Pacific island territory. Rapa Nui is the museum's specialty (its Biblioteca William Mulloy is one of the world's finest collections of printed material on the island), along with Chilean natural history in general; while the main library has moved to Rapa Nui itself, copies of most of the material remain here.

The Museo Fonck, 4 Norte 784, tel. 32/68-6753, is open Tuesday to Friday 9:30 A.M. to 6 P.M., weekends 10 A.M.–2 P.M. Admission is US$1.20 for adults, US$.20 for children.

Museo Palacio Rioja: After the massive 1906 earthquake, Spanish banker Fernando Rioja hired French immigrant architect Alfredo Azancot to build this French neoclassical mansion, now a national historical monument, as his Viña residence. Surrounded by sprawling gardens (since substantially reduced) of exotic trees from around the world, embellished with pools, tennis courts, stables, and a riding arena, the 1620-square-meter palace also included a private theater, now used as a cinema.

Now municipal property, the Museo Palacio Rioja, Quillota 214, tel. 32/689665, also hosts musical events at its **Conservatorio de Música Izidor Handler.** It's open daily except Monday,

Museo Fonck with Easter Island moai

© WAYNE BERNHARDSON

10 A.M.–1 P.M. and 3–7 P.M.; admission costs US$.50 for adults, US$.20 for children.

Palacio Carrasco (Centro Cultural Viña del Mar): In 1912, nine years after buying a full block of land fronting on Avenida Libertad, nitrate magnate Emilio Carrasco Alliende hired Alfred Azancot, designer of the Palacio Rioja, to build this two-story structure, whose facade features a portico with three Norman arches, topped by a mansard roof.

Carrasco died in 1923, before actually moving in, and the following year his heirs sold the building. In 1930, Viña Mayor Manuel Ossa Sainete acquired it for the city and it served as city hall until 1971, despite quake damage in 1965. After further quake damage in 1971, it was condemned in 1975, but fortunately it escaped demolition; since 1977, this national historical monument has housed the Centro Cultural de Viña del Mar. The grounds include Rodin's sculpture *La Defensa,* supposedly rejected in a competition for Valparaíso's Plaza de los Héroes de Iquique.

The Centro Cultural Viña del Mar, Avenida Libertad 250, tel. 32/269708, hosts exhibitions of painting and sculpture. It's open weekdays 9:30 A.M.–1 P.M. and 2–6:30 P.M., Saturday 10 A.M.–1 P.M. only. Admission is free except for special summer exhibitions, when there's a modest charge.

Museo de la Cultura del Mar Salvador Reyes (Castillo Wulff): Displaying the furniture, paintings, engravings, nautical possessions, and documents that belonged to novelist, storyteller, and journalist Salvador Reyes (1899–1970), this extravagant structure dates from 1906, when Valparaíso businessman Gustavo Adolfo Wülff Mowle of Valparaíso indulged himself by building atop a rocky headland at the mouth of the Marga Marga. In 1920, Wulff added its signature tower and a section of transparent floor to see the waves breaking on the rocks below.

After Wulff's death in 1946, the castle passed through several different hands, including the city of Viña and the Chilean navy, before finally coming under control of the national Dirección de Bibliotecas, Archivos y Museos, which incorporated the Reyes collections in 1990. On Avenida Marina near the outlet of the Marga Marga, the museum, tel. 32/625427, is open Tuesday to Friday 10 A.M.–1 P.M. and 2:30–5:45 P.M., weekends and holidays 10 A.M.–2 P.M. only. Admission costs US$1 for adults, half that for children, but is free weekends and holidays.

Quinta Vergara

Originally part of the colonial Hacienda Las Siete Hermanas, Viña's famous public park and performing arts venue passed through the hands of the Carreras, one of Chile's founding families, before being sold to Portuguese businessman Francisco Alvarez, whose granddaughter Mercedes married José Francisco Vergara, the founder of Viña.

Spectacularly landscaped, thanks to the Alvarez family's propensity to import exotic tree species from their extensive overseas travels, the grounds of the Quinta Vergara feature the Venetian-style **Palacio Vergara** (1908), which replaced the original house destroyed in the 1906 earthquake; within the *palacio,* Viña's **Museo Municipal de Bellas Artes** (fine arts museum), tel. 32/680618, is open daily except Monday 10 A.M.–2 P.M. and 3–6 P.M. Adult admission costs about US$.50, while cost for kids is US$.20.

The Quinta's 15,000-spectator **Anfiteatro** (amphitheater) is the principal venue for the annual Festival Internacional de la Canción (International Song Festival), as well as other concert events throughout the year. There is no admission charge to the grounds, entered from the south end of Calle Quinta and open 7 A.M.–6 P.M. (7 P.M. in summer) daily.

Jardín Botánico Nacional

At the east end of town, Chile's national botanical garden owes its existence to Croatian nitrate entrepreneur Pascual Baburizza, who acquired Fundo El Olivar in the early 20th century and donated it to the Compañia del Salitre with the stipulation that, on the dissolution of the company, it would pass into the hands of the city of Viña for public use. While it has been a public recreational area for most of its existence, in the past two decades Conaf and the Instituto de Desarollo Agropecuario (Indap, the governmental Agrarian Development Institute) have paid greater attention to its research and educational missions.

It has since come under control of a private foundation with continued state assistance. Unfortunately, in a recent controversy, heavy machinery for highway improvements on the north bank of the Marga Marga has damaged the grounds despite protests from Conaf, Indap, and Corema, the regional environmental protection agency.

From downtown Viña's Calle Viana, on the south side of the Marga Marga, eastbound Bus No. 20 reaches the end of the line at a bridge that is about a 10-minute walk from the *jardín,* tel. 32/672566. The grounds are open 9 A.M.–7 P.M. daily from September to March; the rest of the year, hours are 10 A.M.–6 P.M. Admission costs about US$1 pp, half that for retired people, and a bit less for children.

Accommodations

Despite Viña's historical reputation as an elite beach resort, there are plenty of economical alternatives south of the Marga Marga. When the Argentine economy is weak, as it has been in recent years, weak demand can depress hotel prices—consider looking at more upscale options.

US$10–25: Viña's Hostelling International affiliate is **Hotel Asturias,** Avenida Valparaíso 299, tel. 32/711565, fax 32/698590, hotelasturi@entelchile.net, which has dorm-style accommodations for US$9 pp and singles for US$15. In summer, when it gets crowded, the hostel overflow goes to **Hotel Capric,** Von Schroeders 39, tel. 32/978295, also for US$9 pp.

Just east of the new bus terminal, facing each other on a quiet block, are **Hospedaje Calderón,** Batuco 147, tel. 32/970456, and **Hospedaje Toledo,** Batuco 160, tel. 32/881496. Both are homey accommodations that maintain prices around US$10–12 pp throughout the year, but singles can be hard to come by in summer.

Residencial Agua Santa, Agua Santa 36, tel. 32/901531, costs US$9 pp with shared bath and breakfast. Just up the block, **Residencial La Nona,** Agua Santa 48, tel. 32/663825, charges US$10 pp with shared bath, US$12 pp with private bath, both with breakfast. **Residencial Villarrica,** Arlegui 172, tel. 32/881484, charges US$13/20 s/d.

Residencial Victoria, Avenida Valparaíso 40, tel. 32/977370, charges US$10 pp with shared bath, US$14 pp with private bath. A few doors east, **Residencial Blanchait,** Avenida Valparaíso 82-A, tel. 32/974949, fax 32/978395, costs US$14/22 s/d with shared bath.

US$25–50: In addition to its dorm-style hostel facilities, improved **Hotel Capric,** Von Schroeders 39, tel. 32/978295, has rooms with private bath for US$15/22 s/d—really a better value. Downtown **Residencial Ona Berri,** Avenida Valparaíso 618, tel. 32/688187, fax 32/686875, costs US$12 pp with shared bath, but only slightly more with private bath.

Just north of the Quinta Vergara, **Residencial El Navegante,** in a stylish house on a quiet block at Alcalde Prieto Nieto 0332, tel. 32/482648, is an exceptional value for US$12 pp with shared bath, US$20 d with private bath, both with breakfast.

Recommended **Hotel Asturias,** Avenida Valparaíso 299, tel. 32/711565, fax 32/698590, costs US$23/37 s/d. **Hotel Rokamar,** south of the tracks at Viana 107, tel./fax 32/690019, charges US$27/32 s/d.

In the largely residential area across the Marga Marga, **Hotel Royal House,** 5 Norte 683, tel. 32/681922, charges US$24/30 s/d for rooms with private bath and cable TV, but it is close to busy Avenida Libertad. A few doors west, at the **Crown Royal Hotel,** a reddish stucco structure at 5 Norte 655, tel. 32/664161, crown@entelchile.net, rates of US$25/31 s/d include a buffet breakfast.

Another block west, the highly regarded, intimate (nine-room) **Residencial 555,** 5 Norte 555, tel./fax 32/972240, charges US$22/30 s/d with shared bath, US$30/35 with private bath. Rates at **Hostal Chacras de Coria,** 7 Norte 669, tel. 32/901419, are US$30/36 with breakfast.

Near the Casino bridge, the upgraded **Hotel Balia Casino,** Von Schroeders 36, tel. 32/978310, fax 32/680724, hotelbaliacasino@elhostal.cl, charges US$30/35 with many conveniences, including breakfast and unlimited Internet access. Alongside the Teatro Municipal, **Hotel Español,** a classic French-style construction at Plaza Vergara 191, tel. 32/685145, fax

32/691472, hotelesespanol@elhostal.cl, costs US$35/45 s/d.

US$50–100: Well-regarded **Hotel Rondó,** north of the river at 1 Norte 157, tel./fax 32/883144, rondo@aclaris.cl, costs US$40/52 with breakfast. Adjacent to the grounds of Viña's famous performing arts venue—a disadvantage during the weeklong summer song festival—**Hotel Quinta Vergara,** Errázuriz 690, tel. 32/685073, fax 32/691978, charges US$40/54 with breakfast.

In a surprisingly quiet location south of the railroad line, gracefully aging but less than luxurious **Hotel Von Schroeders,** Von Schroeders 392, tel. 32/626063, has gorgeous natural wood paneling and wainscoting and high ceilings; on the other hand, the furniture is worn and, though most everything works well, its biggest drawback is the mesh spring beds, some of which sag uncomfortably. Rates are US$48/54 s/d with breakfast, private bath, and cable TV; its restaurant Squadritto is worth a lunch or dinner stop even for nonguests.

For US$53/70 s/d with breakfast, the highrise **Hotel San Martín,** Avenida San Martín 667, tel. 32/689191, fax 32/689195, hotel-san-martin@entelchile.net, offers beachfront convenience but an impersonal style.

Affiliated with the Best Western chain, **Hotel Marina del Rey,** Ecuador 299, tel. 32/710071, fax 32/978571, costs US$72 s or d. Rates at the full-service **Hotel Alcázar,** Alvarez 646, tel. 32/685112, fax 32/884245, reservas@alcazar.cl, are US$68/83 with breakfast.

US$100–150: For about US$90/110, the unique **Hotel Cap Ducal,** Avenida Marina 51, tel. 32/626655, fax 32/665471, exploits its nautical theme to the max, with the sound of the surf literally outside the window.

Showing its age despite its dignified appearance, the classic **Hotel O'Higgins,** Plaza Vergara s/n, tel. 32/882016, fax 32/883587, has rates starting around US$91/103, but suites are much dearer.

Food

Viña probably has a denser concentration of fine restaurants than Valparaíso, but there are many good values in town as well. For breakfast, snacks,

and *onces,* there is a variety of options at cafés such as **Anayak,** Quinta 134, tel. 32/680093, and **Samoiedo,** Avenida Valparaíso 637, tel. 32/684610. **The Tea Pot,** 5 Norte 475, tel. 32/687761, serves 50 varieties of teas plus a wide selection of sandwiches and desserts.

On the Pasaje Cousiño *peatonal* near Plaza Vergara, in addition to the daily crafts market, there's a diverse assortment of modest ethnic restaurants, open primarily for lunch: **Panzoni,** Cousiño 12-B, tel. 32/682134, for tasty Italian and Middle Eastern specialties; **México Lindo,** Cousiño 136, 2nd floor, tel. 32/714144, for Tex-Mex; and **El Sin Nombre,** Cousiño s/n, tel. 32/881204, for Chilean food.

Squadritto, part of Hotel Von Schroeders at Von Schroeders 392, tel. 32/626063, has an outstanding nightly dinner special for about US$10 that includes a wide choice of Italian or Chilean appetizers, entrées, and desserts. The substantially more expensive **Fellini,** 3 Norte 88, tel. 32/9-75742, is better but perhaps not *that* much better (though the cannelloni with chicken and almonds and the pesto salmon for about US$8 are exceptional). Portions are large and the service is exemplary, but it suffers from a high decibel level.

Other Italian choices, all of them tending toward the upscale and pretty good, include **Don Giacomo**, Villanelo 135, 2nd floor, tel. 32/6-88889; **Don Giovanni,** 2 Norte 112, tel. 32/9-77891; **Flavia,** 6 Poniente 121, tel. 32/686358; **La Cucina di Vaccarezza,** Avenida San Martín 180, tel. 32/975790; and **Ristorante San Marco,** San Martín 597, tel. 32/975304.

Delicias del Mar, Avenida San Martín 459, tel. 32/901837, is a fine Basque seafood restaurant with entrées in the US$10 range and an owner who, to judge from the decor, might be stalking Marilyn Monroe were she still alive. Unlike many Chilean restaurants, it firmly discourages cell phones, and the service is exemplary.

For Mexican food a bit more complex than the standard *antojitos* such as enchiladas and burritos, there's popular **Cuernavaca,** 2 Norte 190, tel. 32/906374, but the noise factor is considerable here.

Viña has two fine ice creameries: **Bravíssimo,** Avenida San Martín 302, tel. 32/681862, is a chain, while **Timbao,** Avenida Valparaíso 670, is more strictly artisanal.

Entertainment

Viña del Mar is one of Chile's entertainment and events hotbeds.

Pubs: El Burro, Pasaje Cousiño 12-D, draws crowds on weekends. **Café Journal,** Agua Santa 2, tel. 32/666654, is a taste of Bohemian Valparaíso in Viña, so successful at both food and entertainment that it's planning expansion.

Discotheques: Scratch, Bohn 970, tel. 32/978219, is a longtime local favorite. **Millennium,** Arlegui 302, 2nd floor, is an alternative.

Galleries: The **Sala Viña del Mar,** Arlegui 683, tel. 32/680633, offers visual arts exhibitions. The **Galería de Arte Modigliani,** 5 Norte 168, tel. 32/684991, displays local and regional paintings and sculpture.

Cinema: Viña has several movie theaters, including the downtown **Cine Olimpo,** a two-screener at Quinta 294, tel. 32/711607, and the eight-screen **Cinemark,** 15 Norte 961, Local 224, tel. 32/993391, at the north end of town. The **Cine Arte,** Plaza Vergara 142, tel. 32/882798, is a repertory house. The **Instituto Chileno-Norteamericano,** 2 Oriente 385, tel. 32/686191, shows occasional films as well.

Theater: The **Teatro Municipal,** Plaza Vergara s/n, tel. 32/681739, hosts live theater, concerts, and occasional films.

Spectator Sports: Everton, Viña's soccer team, has its offices at Viana 161, tel. 32/689504; it holds its matches at Estadio Sausalito, Avenida Sausalito s/n, tel. 32/978250. The **Valparaíso Sporting Club,** Avenida Los Castaños 404, tel. 32/689393, is the site for horse racing.

Gambling: Stylistically it's not Las Vegas—¡gracias a Dios!—but Viña's **Casino Municipal,** on the north shore of the Marga Marga at Avenida San Martín 199, tel. 32/500700, is still the place where risk addicts can fritter away their finances on bingo, cards, roulette, slots, and other money-losing diversions (those with an elementary knowledge of statistics and probability can limit themselves to dinner, drinks, and live entertainment). Amazingly, the construction of this 1930s landmark took only nine months.

Open from 6 P.M. into the wee hours, the casino charges a US$5 cover for those visiting the main floor (formal attire is the rule). For bingo and the slots (known in Spanish as *tragamonedas,* "coin-swallowers"), hours start at noon or 2 P.M.

Events

For two weeks in January, sponsored by the Cámara Chilena del Libro (Chilean Book Chamber), Viña's **Feria del Libro** attracts literary figures such as novelist Alberto Fuguet, playwright-novelist Marco Antonio de la Parra, and essayist Pedro Lemebel. Regionally oriented, it includes live readings, interviews, theater and music performances, and children's shows.

Viña's single biggest event, though, is February's **Festival Internacional de la Canción,** where nearly 100,000 ticketholders crowd the Quinta Vergara to hear Spanish-speaking acts from around the Americas and the Mediterranean, plus a handful of big-name but over-the-hill performers from North America—Creedence Clearwater *sans* John Fogerty, for example—or Northern Europe. Since it's partly a competitive event, the week's highlight is the best song award, which usually seems to go to the most pedestrian tune by the dreariest diva or a cheerless crooner. Nevertheless, the festival fills TV screens throughout the country and the Latin American TV network Univisión broadcasts part of the event overseas.

During mid-September's **Fiestas Patrias,** the Estadio Sausalito is the site of an informal Chilean food festival with folkloric music.

Shopping

The crafts booths along **Pasaje Cousiño** hawk the usual routine jewelry, but the leather and copper goods are more interesting. The larger **Centro Artesanal Viña del Mar,** Quinta 220, is also worth a visit.

Services

Money: Banco de Chile has an ATM at Avenida Valparaíso 667, but there are many more. Exchange houses include Cambios Guiñazú, Arlegui 686, and Inter-Cambio, 1 Norte 655-B.

Postal: Correos de Chile is at Plaza Latorre 32, near the municipal tourist office.

Telephone and Internet: Telefónica is at Valparaíso 628, and on Arlegui between Quinta and Plaza Vergara. The area code is 32, the same as Valparaíso's.

Café Cytel, Avenida Valparaíso 651, has international telephone service and inexpensive Internet connections from 9 A.M.–11 P.M. daily. Other Internet options include A La Vista, Avenida Valparaíso 196, and Etniacom, Avenida Valparaíso 323, 2nd floor, tel. 32/711841.

Laundry: Viña has two convenient laundries: Lavarápido, Arlegui 440, tel. 32/688331, and Laverap, Libertad 902.

Medical: Hospital Gustavo Fricke, Alvarez 1532, tel. 32/680041, is south of the tracks and several blocks east of the main Merval train station.

Information

Tourist Offices: Viña's municipal Central de Turismo e Informaciones is at Avenida Marina s/n, tel. 32/269330, directly opposite the tiny triangular Plaza Latorre near the Libertad bridge. Hours are 9 A.M.–8 P.M. weekdays, 10 A.M.–8 P.M. Saturday, and 10 A.M.–7 P.M. Sunday and holidays. Its monthly newsletter *Todo Viña* is an exhaustive calendar of events and entertainment in Viña, Valparaíso, and suburbs; it also offers a free city map.

There is also an Oficina de Informaciones at the Terminal Rodoviario, at Avenida Valparaíso 1055, tel. 32/752093, open 8 A.M.–8 P.M. daily.

Sernatur's regional office is at Valparaíso 507, 3rd floor, tel. 32/882285, fax 32/684117, sernaturvalpso@entelchile.net; it's open weekdays 8:30 A.M.–5:30 P.M.

Motorists: The Automóvil Club de Chile (Acchi) is at 1 Norte 901, tel. 32/689505.

National Parks: The regional office of Conaf, 3 Norte 541, tel. 32/970108, has information on Parque Nacional La Campana, Reserva Nacional Lago Peñuelas, and other protected areas.

Transportation

Like Valparaíso, Viña del Mar relies exclusively on bus transportation to and from the city.

Air: LanChile/LanExpress is at Ecuador 80, tel. 32/690365, but there are no commercial flights out of Viña's Aeropuerto Torquemada.

Bus: Viña's bright new Terminal Rodoviario, Avenida Valparaíso 1055, tel. 32/752000, is about 300 meters east of Plaza Vergara. Carriers and services are almost identical to those from Valparaíso; all northbound and international buses from Valpo stop in Viña (see the Valparaíso entry for additional details).

Tur-Bus, tel. 32/882661, goes to Santiago every 10 minutes between 5:50 A.M. and 10 P.M. Other Santiago carriers include Cóndor Bus, tel. 32/882345; Pullman Bus, tel. 32/680424; Pullman Lit, tel. 32/690783; Sol del Pacífico, tel. 32/883156; and Sol del Sur, tel. 32/687277.

Getting Around

Train: Merval trains between Valparaíso and Limache make several Viña stops, at Estación Miramar, Plaza Vergara, and El Salto. Over the next few years, a new 5.5-km underground with four new stations, at a cost of US$300 million, will replace the present system.

Bus and *Taxi Colectivo:* From Arlegui, west of Plaza Vergara, local buses marked "Aduana" or "Puerto" connect Viña with Valpo, as do *taxi colectivos.*

Car Rental: Bert, Alvarez 762, tel. 32/685515, is the most economical. Mach Viña is at Viana 33, tel. 32/694236.

VICINITY OF VIÑA DEL MAR

From Viña north, a string of beach towns corresponding to various social classes lies scattered among the headlands (see Northern Beach Resorts, below). To the interior, the towns of Limache and Olmué are gateways to Parque Nacional La Campana, one of the region's underappreciated gems; a northern park access point from the Panamericana is near the town of Hijuelas.

In January, Olmué hosts the **Festival del Huaso de Olmué,** honoring the Chilean counterpart to the Argentine gaucho. The largest folk festival in the country, it is a far less commercial event than February's international song competition in Viña.

Parque Nacional La Campana

Rising above the fertile coastal plain of Quillota, Parque Nacional La Campana comprises 8,000 hectares of sheer-sided scrubland, scattered "oak" forests, and the greatest remaining concentration of the rare Chilean palm. A UNESCO World Biosphere Reserve since 1984, the former Jesuit hacienda of San Isidro is the place where the forests of temperate southern Chile reach their northernmost extent, overlapping the desert vegetation of the Norte Chico.

Noteworthy for a network of integrated hiking trails that cross ridges and scale summits with spectacular views from the Pacific Ocean to the Andean summit of Aconcagua (across the border in Argentina), it is also a historic site. Trekking toward the Andes from Valparaíso in the winter of 1834, Charles Darwin detoured to climb the summit of Cerro La Campana, an experience that he detailed in *The Voyage of the Beagle*:

> *The evening was fine, and the atmosphere so clear, that the masts of the vessels at anchor in the bay of Valparaíso, although no less than twenty-six geographical miles distant, could be distinguished clearly as little black streaks. A ship doubling the point under sail, appeared as a bright white speck. . . .*

> *The setting of the sun was glorious; the valleys being black, whilst the snowy peaks of the Andes yet retained a ruby tint. . . .*

> *We spent the day on the summit, and I never enjoyed one more thoroughly. Chile, bounded by the Andes and the Pacific, was seen as in a map. The pleasure from the scenery, in itself beautiful, was heightened by the many reflections which arose from the mere view of the Campana range with its lesser parallel ones, and of the broad valley of Quillota directly intersecting them. . . .*

Geography and Climate: In the coastal range east of Viña del Mar, Parque Nacional La Campana consists of three sectors: the adjacent Sector Granizo and Sector Cajón Grande are about 45 km east of Viña via Ruta 62 through Villa Alemana, Limache, and Olmué, while Sector Omoa is about 110 km northwest of Santiago via the Panamericana.

Elevations range from about 400 meters near the park entrances to 2,222 meters at the summit of Cerro El Roble, the park's highest point; the rugged topography can be challenging even

palm forest in Parque Nacional La Campana

© WAYNE BERNHARDSON

THE CHILEAN PALM

Also known as the *palma de coquitos* because its tiny fruits resembled coconuts, the Chilean palm *Jubaea chilensis* was once abundant in the Chilean heartland—Darwin found them "excessively numerous in some parts of Chile." Indiscriminate cutting for its sap, which yields what Chileans calls *miel de palma* (palm honey), reduced this abundance; the ruined ovens scattered around La Campana's Sector Ocoa, used to boil down the sap into treacle, are evidence of the palm honey trade. Each mature tree could yield up to 200 liters of sweetener.

In Darwin's words:

The palms themselves are, for their family, ugly trees. Their stem is very large, and of a curious form, being thicker in the middle than at the base or top.

In fact, their diameter can exceed a meter and a half, and they can reach a height of 25 meters. They are slow-growing, though; around age 60, when their height is usually less than 10 meters, they yield their first fruit. Thanks to a planting program begun by the Hacienda Las Palmas de Cocalán in the 1940s and continued by Conaf after La Campana became a national park in 1967, there are now about 100,000 specimens in Sector Ocoa.

for very fit hikers. Like coastal Southern California, La Campana enjoys a mild Mediterranean climate, cooled by the maritime influences of the Pacific Ocean. While the annual precipitation is only about 800 mm, nearly all of it falls between May and September; the dry summer and autumn are fire season. Winter can bring snowfall to the summits, but even in summer a sweater or light jacket is a good idea at upper elevations.

Flora and Fauna: La Campana has more than 300 different plant species forming several different associations. In the relatively well-watered ravines, between about 300 and 1,000 meters above sea level, there are gallery forests of species such as *patagua (Crinodendron patagua), lingue*

(Persea meyeniana), and *belloto (Beilschmedia miersii).* On south-facing slopes, up to about 1,000 meters, sclerophyllous (glossy-leaved) forests of *peumo (Cryptocarpa alba), boldo (Peumus boldus),* and *quillay (Quillaja saponaria)* tolerate the annual summer drought.

At higher altitudes, above 800 meters, deciduous forests of *roble de Santiago* (*Nothofagus obliqua,* referred to by Chileans as an "oak") constitute the most northerly species of this "false beech" genus. There are also communities of Chilean palm *(Jubaea chilensis),* punctuated with occasional cacti, and open thorn forests of *Acacia caven* and smaller shrubs.

In addition, on north-facing slopes, shrub communities known as *matorrales* resemble the chaparral of California, relying on natural fires to renew themselves at regular intervals. Above 1,500 meters, similar but more widely spaced communities occupy relatively thin soils. Scattered throughout the park are clusters of cacti, mostly *cardón (Puya berteroniana)* and *quisco (Echinopsis chilensis).*

Guanacos once roamed the park, but today's fauna are less conspicuous and far smaller—foxes, vizcachas, skunks, and tinier rodents, along with more than 50 species of birds, most notably quail, pheasant, owls, and hummingbirds.

Sights and Recreation: Most of the sights are accessible by a variety of trails that crisscross the park or loop through it. Near the Granizo entrance, the **Sendero La Canasta** provides a good introduction to the forest, looping past several labeled trees and shrubs in the course of half an hour's walk (the identifications on this new nature trail, though, do not place the information in an ecological context).

More gratifying, if far more strenuous, is the seven-km **Sendero Andinista,** from the Granizo entrance to the 1,880-meter summit of Cerro La Campana, where hikers can enjoy the same views that entranced Darwin. While the distance itself may not seem great and the climb is not technical, the elevation gain of 1,507 meters means an average grade of almost 22 percent. For most people, it's a full-day excursion, far more exhausting than Patagonia's famous Torres del Paine. Note that the hard-baked trail can be slippery even when dry, and wear suitable shoes.

Fortunately, most of the hike passes through shady forest and three cool springs with potable water: **Primera Aguada,** 580 meters above sea level, about an hour along the trail; **Segunda Aguada,** about the midway point, where camping is possible; and **La Mina,** the drive-in campground at the abandoned mine site, where the trail continues to the summit (in dry weather, with a high-clearance vehicle, it's possible to reach La Mina by road).

Beyond the mine site, the trail becomes narrower and even steeper; here, at 1,500 meters above sea level, the Sociedad Científica de Valparaíso and the city's British community placed a commemorative plaque on the 101st anniversary of Darwin's ascent (which he reached on August 17, 1834, having camped below the summit on the previous day). Another plaque, dedicated by the Club Montañés de Valparaíso, remembers climbers who died when a earthquake triggered a landslide in 1868.

Sector Ocoa, at the northern approach to La Campana, is its largest sector, about 5,440 hectares. From Casino, two km beyond the entrance station, the **Sendero El Amasijo** climbs gradually up the palm-filled gorge of the Estero Rabuco to the saddle known as the Portezuelo de Granizo, where it bifurcates: the southern **Sendero Los Robles** descends to Sector Cajón Grande, while the **Sendero Los Peumos** heads west to Sector Granizo. Either route is a feasible day trip, but it's also possible to camp in the Estero Rabuco. Carry plenty of water since, except for a spring just below the Portezuelo de Granizo, livestock have made the streams unpotable.

Also at Sector Ocoa, the **Sendero La Cascada** is a four-hour round-trip to an attractive waterfall; there are several other shorter trails in the area.
Accommodations and Food: Within the park, camping is the only option. Organized camping for up to six people costs US$10 at Conaf's **Sector Granizo** (23 sites), **Sector Cajón Grande** (22 sites), and **Sector Ocoa** (16 sites). Backcountry camping is possible, but only with Conaf permission in an area that is steep, rocky, and fire-prone.

Outside the park boundaries, in Olmué, **Hostería Aire Puro,** Avenida Granizo 7672, tel./fax 33/441381, rents *cabañas* for US$30 d with breakfast; reservations are advisable. The dining room is attractive and the service attentive, but the food is erratic.

Olmué's **Hostería Copihue,** Diego Portales 2203, tel. 33/441544, hcopihue@chilesat.net, is an upscale resort with pool, tennis courts, and other luxuries; rates are US$54/90 s/d with full board in low season, but US$80/130 s/d in high season.

Information: At each park entrance, Conaf rangers collect a US$2 admission fee (retired people and children pay half). The Granizo ranger station occasionally has maps, for a small charge, and usually has books on flora, fauna, and other conservation topics.

There is an outstanding website on Parque Nacional La Campana (www.parquelacampana.cl) in both Spanish and imperfect but reasonably good English. Visitors specifically interested in flora can buy Rodrigo Villaseñor Castro's inexpensive (Spanish-only) *Guía para el Reconocimiento de las Especies Arbóreas y Arbustivas en el Parque Nacional La Campana* (1998), a joint publication of Conaf and Valparaíso's Universidad de Playa Ancha.

Transportation: La Campana is readily accessible from Viña del Mar, less so from Santiago. From 1 Norte in Viña, Ciferal Express, tel. 32/345247, goes to within a short distance of the Granizo and Cajón Grande entrances every half hour. Merval trains go as far as Limache, where Agdabus goes every 20 minutes to Olmué.

From Santiago, any northbound bus along the Panamericana can drop passengers at Hijuelas, where an ill-marked gravel road heads south just before the main highway bridge over the Río Aconcagua. There is no regular public transportation on this gravel road, which is 12 km from the Ocoa entrance.

Christian Güntert of Valparaíso's Hostal Casa Aventura, Pasaje Gálvez 12, tel. 32/755763, casatur@ctcinternet.cl., offers full-day guided treks in the park for US$20 pp for a minimum of four people, crossing from Ocoa to Cajón Grande;

occasionally, groups choose the summit of La Campana.

From October to April, Santiago's Altué Active Travel, Encomenderos 83, Las Condes, tel. 2/2321103, fax 2/2336799, altue@chileout-doors.com, offers full-day excursions for US$155 pp for a minimum of two people, climbing Cerro La Campana and including lunch and transportation. Larger parties pay less per person.

Northern Beach Resorts

From the Viña suburb of Concón to Papudo, the northern coastal towns offer visitors the same general sorts of attractions, but they are not quite cookie-cutter beach resorts—in fact, in terms of clientele, there is considerable diversity among them.

Concón: Contiguous to Viña but politically separate, Concón has been a holiday destination since the construction of a coastal highway and the first beach houses in 1917. From Reñaca, Avenida Borgoño follows the coastline past **Playa Amarilla,** the preferred beach for swimmers and sunbathers; **Playa Negra** is a favorite with bodyboarders. Concón has its own Oficina de Informaciones Turísticas, tel. 32/818291, at the roundabout near the Río Aconcagua.

Concón's greatest attraction, though, is the gaggle of seafood *picadas* at Caleta Higuerillas, near the Club de Yates, and at Playa La Boca, near the outlet of the Río Aconcagua. At Caleta Higuerillas, reached via a staircase from Avenida Borgoño, **La Picá Horizonte,** San Pedro 120, tel. 32/903665, is an established favorite, but **Picá los Delfines,** San Pedro 130, tel. 32/814919, and other nearby places are by no means inferior.

At Playa La Boca, one of the most popular resort choices is **La Perla del Pacífico,** Avenida Borgoño 25007, tel. 32/812330. **La Picá de Emeterio,** Avenida Borgoño 25069, tel. 32/811352, is cheaper but only so-so, despite attentive service.

Quintero: About 16 km north of the Río Aconcagua, a paved road heads west to Quintero, a working-class isthmian beach town that once was Lord Cochrane's hacienda (Maria Graham was Cochrane's guest during the earthquake

of 1822). Before turning inland to Quillota and La Campana, Darwin rode here to see:

> *the great beds of shells, which stand some yards above the level of the sea, and are burnt for lime.*

A few kilometers south of Quintero, the hamlet of **Ritoque** is the place where surfing started in Chile.

In a state of advanced but apparently arrested decay, the architecturally distinctive **Hotel Mona-co,** 21 de Mayo 1500, tel. 32/930939, is economical for US$6 pp with shared bath, US$15 pp with private bath. At **Residencial Victoria,** Vicuña Mackenna 1460, tel. 32/930208, charges are US$9 pp with shared bath. The utilitarian **Residencial Brazilian,** 21 de Mayo 1336, tel./fax 32/930590, costs US$20/33 s/d with breakfast.

Like Concón, Quintero has a score or more of seafood *picadas,* lining 21 de Mayo, for inexpensive family-style dining.

Las Ventanas: Across Bahía Quintero, in what otherwise appears to be an industrial sacrifice area with a major power plant, the **Estero de Puchuncaví** is a wetland reserve that appears to be a environmental mitigation project. Just to its north, at the tiny fishing port of Las Ventanas, salvage crews have been pulling scrap metal off a grounded LPG tanker that's been sitting on the beach for decades. Despite the coal-fired power plant nearby, this is one of the primo surfing spots on the north coast.

Horcón: About five km north of Las Ventanas, on its namesake harbor and off the main highway, the community of Horcón is a combination fishing port and artisan and artists' colony that has a holdover reputation as a hippie hideaway. Its single main street dead-ends at the small but sheltered beach, where fishermen sell their catch directly to waterfront *picadas.*

Just to the south, **Playa Cau Cau** is a onetime nude beach that has gentrified but is now a more conventional destination for sunbathers, surfers, and swimmers. The only remaining nude beach is **Playa La Luna,** immediately to the south.

Maitencillo: At Maitencillo, 12 km north of Horcón, rocky outcrops along Avenida del Mar separate the long sandy beaches of **Playa Aguas**

Blancas and **Playa Larga,** among the region's best. Maitencillo's dominant tourist institution, though, is the sprawling **Marbella Resort,** Km 35 Carretera Concón-Zapallar, tel. 32/772020, fax 32/772030, resorts@chilesat.net.

Occupying most of the broad hilltop above Avenida del Mar, Marbella is an all-inclusive resort with a conference center, restaurants, and bars, with recreational facilities that include swimming pools and tennis courts, an 18-hole golf course, a nine-hole par three, and polo grounds (Chile has few public golf courses, but guests can play here).

For everything it offers, the rates are not excessive, starting at US$120 s or d with a buffet breakfast for garden-view rooms; seaview rooms cost US$195 s or d. There are also more expensive suites, and a variety of weekend and week-long packages that are more reasonably priced.

Marbella's Santiago contact address is Cruz del Sur 133, 5th floor, Las Condes, tel. 2/2065454, fax 2/2283198. Marbella also has a website: www.marbella.cl.

Cachagua: Filled with weekend and vacation houses for Santiaguinos, 10 km north of Maitencillo, Cachagua is an upscale village where kids ride docile horses and plump burros over hard-packed sandy roads. There are no accommodations, but the beachfront restaurant **Entre Olas,** reached via a staircase at the south end of Avenida Los Eucaliptos, is a good lunch alternative.

Opposite the west end of the beach, Humboldt penguins and other seabirds breed at Conaf's **Monumento Natural Isla Cachagua,** separated from the mainland by a 100-meter channel. Measuring only 300 by 150 meters, the nearly barren granitic island harbors a breeding population of 1,000 to 2,000 penguins, roughly 10 percent of the global population and 15 percent of the Chilean population. There are also numerous pelicans, cormorants, oystercatchers, Dominican gulls, and other bird species, while sea lions and otters frolic offshore, the otters subsisting on the abundant shellfish. While divers take some sea urchins and other shellfish, the human disturbance is minimal.

Zapallar: Three km north of Cachagua and 80 km from Viña, curving tree-lined streets nearly block the view of the ocean at Zapallar, originally part of Francisco Javier Ovalle's Hacienda

Catapilco. After inheriting the property in 1884 and making a tour of European beach resorts, his son Olegario began to give away lots to his friends on the condition that they build houses within two years, and Zapallar quickly became an elite community for monied Santiaguinos.

The 1906 earthquake destroyed many of the early buildings, but the inhabitants of Zapallar rebuilt with a vengeance, creating some of the largest and most elegant properties on the coast. Now a *zona típica* national monument, Zapallar is an eclectic mix of colonial-style *casas,* neo-Gothic mansions, and fashionably rustic villas, on large lots with extensive gardens. The **Rambla,** a broad footpath, follows the coastline.

Many of the town's founding families still own properties here. Among the notable mansions are those of Manuel Vicuña Subercaseaux (1912) and Carlos Aldunate Solar (1915), both designed by Josué Smith Solar; the extravagant castle of painter Alvaro Casanova; and the Bavarian-style Casa Hildesheim of María Luisa MacClure.

Rates at the 44-room luxury **Hotel Isla Seca,** Camino Costero s/n, tel. 33/741224, fax 33/7-41228, are US$137 s or d with breakfast, but ask for IVA discounts.

The beachfront **César,** Rambla s/n, tel. 33/741507, is an upscale seafood restaurant with outdoor as well as indoor seating.

Papudo: Seven km north of Zapallar, the sheltered harbor of Papudo is a more egalitarian destination than its snobbish southern neighbor. Its natural assets sparked an extravagant enthusiasm from Pedro de Valdivia who, in a letter to Spanish King Carlos V in 1545, wrote:

> *Among all the new world's lands, the port of Papudo has a greater abundance of good things than any other, it is like God's paradise; it has a mild climate, great and rugged mountains, fertile expanses covered with cattle, herds of horses, abundant grains, delicious fruits, inexhaustible amounts of fish, crabs, and shellfish, saturated with milk and rennet and wines, and rich with honey, timber, salt and other minerals and products that make life worthwhile.*

Fertile Papudo was the port for colonial Hacienda La Ligua, but it became part of Fernando Irarrázaval Mackenna's Hacienda Pullalli in the mid-19th century and shortly thereafter an official port. After 1898, with the arrival of the railway, it took off as a beach resort, its landmark Gran Hotel (since destroyed by fire) designed by architect Josué Smith. After 1927, it became a separate municipality from La Ligua, forsaking its port status for the tourist trade.

Sights: The main highway, known in town as Avenida Irarrázaval, parallels the central **Playa Chica** and the more extensive **Playa Larga,** which stretches northeast. At Avenida Irarrázaval and Avenida Latorre, the main remaining landmark is the neocolonial **Iglesia Nuestra Señora de las Mercedes** (1918), a national monument, which features a baroque facade by architect Alberto Cruz Montt, also designer of Santiago's Banco Central y Club de la Unión.

Beyond the Club de Yates, at the west end of Playa Chica, brown pelicans hang out on rocky outcrops where the town has created an informally landscaped **Camino del Conquistador** footpath to trace the steps of Pedro de Valdivia. There are more formal beachfront promenades along Avenida Irarrázaval.

Accommodations and Food: Though the rooms are a little cramped, family-run **Residencial La Plaza,** Chorrillos 119, tel. 33/791391, maintains year-round rates of US$9 pp with private bath and breakfast. Made of mismatched materials, **Hotel Carandé,** Chorrillos 89, tel. 33/791105, fax 33/791118, may be overpriced at 30/35 s/d in summer, but for US$15 pp with breakfast in the off-season, it's not bad. Rooms are heated, the service is decent, and the hot water abundant and easy to regulate (there are only two cable channels, however).

Playa Chica's **Gran Azul,** Avenida Irarrázaval 86, tel. 33/791584, prepares fine fish and seafood, with attentive service, at moderate prices (US$5–7 for entrées); in a dining room with high ceilings and natural wood beams, large windows face the sea and surf.

La Ligua: About 15 km inland from Papudo and just east of the Panamericana, the farming town of La Ligua is famous for its *dulces de la Ligua*—on both sides of the highway, platoons of handkerchief-waving, white-coated vendors flag down passing vehicles to sell their varied cakes, cookies, meringues, and other sweets typical of the area. About 20 companies employ more than 300 people in their manufacture, and another 2,000 depend indirectly on the trade.

La Ligua is also known for its textiles and, at 1997's annual **Feria del Tejido** (Weavers' Festival), the world's largest vest made the Guinness Book of Records. More normal sizes are available in stores and at the artisans' market on the Plaza de Armas.

For northbound motorists, La Ligua is the starting point for an adventurous but not difficult backcountry alternative through the Andean foothills via the abandoned railroad line, now a dirt-and-gravel road, to Ovalle (for more details, see the special topic Taking the High Road through the Norte Chico in the Norte Chico chapter).

Sights: Occupying the erstwhile abattoir, the **Museo de La Ligua** traces local prehistory from the early Molle and Animas cultures through the Aymara, Mapuche, and Diaguita/Inka who successively dominated the area. It also deals with issues of cultural change during colonial times through institutions such as the *encomienda,* the 19th-century mining industry, and urban development in the 20th century.

Six blocks north of the Plaza de Armas, the Museo de La Ligua, Pedro Polanco 698, tel. 33/712143, is Tuesday to Friday 9 A.M.–1 P.M. and 3:30–7 P.M., Saturday 10 A.M.–2 P.M. only; admission costs US$.40.

Accommodations and Food: La Ligua has inexpensive but pleasing lodgings at **Residencial Regine I,** Esmeralda 27, tel. 33/711192, for about US$6 pp; for US$12, its sister **Residencial Regine II,** a particularly fine choice at Condell 360, tel. 33/711196, has rooms with private bath. **Hotel Anchimallén,** a block west of the Plaza de Armas at Ortiz de Rosas 694, tel. 33/711683, fax 33/711696, charges US$30/40 s/d with breakfast and private bath.

Lihuén, Ortiz de Rosas 303, tel. 33/711143, offers snacks, sandwiches, and homemade ice cream. **Costa Brava,** on Ortiz de Rozas half a block west of the Plaza de Armas, is a new seafood locale.

Services: Banco de Chile has an ATM at Ortiz de Rosas 485. There's a Centro de Llamados on the west side of the Plaza de Armas; La Ligua's area code is 33.

Information: La Ligua has an Oficina de Información Turística at the Plaza de Armas, at Ortiz de Rozas and Uribe, tel. 33/711036, *anexo* 140.

Transportation: Terminal La Ligua, on Papudo between Pedro Polanco and Uribe, tel. 33/7-11101, is just a block south of the Plaza de Armas; it has some of the brightest, cleanest toilets of any bus station in the country. Tur-Bus, Pullman Bus, Cóndor Bus, and Sol del Pacífico have services running north and south on the Panamericana, and down the coast to Viña del Mar.

The Aconcagua Valley

East of Quillota and north of metropolitan Santiago, but politically part of Region V, the Río Aconcagua's main attraction is the legendary ski resort of Portillo, near the Argentine border. The lower part of the valley, though, is home to colonial towns with a growing wine industry and its own nascent Ruta del Vino.

SAN FELIPE

Encircled by mountains, at an altitude of 630 meters, San Felipe El Real (population about 65,000) is the political and commercial center of a valley that exports grapes and wine thanks to its favorable microclimate. Founded in 1740 by José Manso de Velasco, later to be Viceroy of Peru, its central core retains a colonial ambience; in addition to its attractive Plaza de Armas, it has several smaller *plazuelas* that supply greenery and open space to the otherwise densely built downtown.

Orientation

San Felipe is 94 km north of Santiago via Ruta 57, the northbound highway to Argentina, and a secondary paved highway that passes through Rinconada. It's a little farther, about 117 km, via the Panamericana and Ruta 60, the international highway from Concón to the Argentine border.

Sights

The centerpiece of San Felipe's shady **Plaza de Armas** is a multileveled fountain that bears a strong resemblance to the rocky Andes visible in the distance to the east. Embellished with stat-

uary, the plaza has a permanent artisans' market and a small tourist information kiosk.

The city has several historical monuments, including the **Catedral de San Felipe** on the north side of the Plaza de Armas, and the **Iglesia y Claustro del Buen Pastor** on Avenida Yungay between Avenida O'Higgins and San Martín (next to the bus terminal), and the colonial **Casa Mardones,** Avenida Yungay 10.

The **Teatro Municipal,** on the west side of the plaza, keeps a solid calendar of cultural events, from films to jazz and art exhibits. There is a local **Museo Histórico de Aconcagua** at Avenida Riquelme 60.

Accommodations and Food

Friendly **Hotel Reinares,** Carlos Condell 75, tel./fax 34/510359, charges US$8 pp for utilitarian rooms with shared bath, US$11 pp with private bath, and has a large and popular restaurant.

Boxy and architecturally undistinguished **Hotel San Felipe,** Merced 204, tel. 34/510508, fax 34/513356, has comfortable carpeted rooms with cable TV, central heating, and private bath for US$25/29 s/d. Its restaurant, **Alterra,** serves Italian food.

The inviting **Los Faroles de Portus,** Portus 156, tel. 34/519952, serves good traditional Chilean food for as little as US$2, with a two-person *parrillada* for only about US$7.

Club Social San Felipe, in the historic Casona Mardones at Avenida Yungay 10, tel. 34/510402, is an upscale Francophile restaurant. Half a block east of the Plaza de Armas, the **Centro Arabe,** Prat 124, serves Middle Eastern dishes.

Services

Telephone and Internet: Telefónica CTC, on the east side of the Plaza de Armas, has long-distance service. There are two Internet alternatives: Vipnet, Salinas 352, tel. 34/519741, and Cybercentro Fastnet, San Martín 149, which is open 10 A.M.–10 P.M. daily except Sunday and holidays, when it's open 4–10 P.M. only.

Travel Agencies: Bio Turismo, Bernardo Cruz 1258, tel. 34/515672 or 34/505254, website: www.bioturismo.cl, marcela@bioturismo.cl, specializes in thematic Aconcagua valley excursions, from wine to history to health resorts and even religion (several pilgrimage sites are in the vicinity).

Transportation

San Felipe's Terminal de Buses is on Avenida Yungay between Freire and San Martín. There are frequent buses to Santiago, and along Ruta 60 west to Viña del Mar and east toward Los Andes and the Argentine border.

VICINITY OF SAN FELIPE

Thanks to its colonial surroundings and wineries, San Felipe is attracting more interest from travelers.

Curimón

Franciscan missionaries arrived at Curimón, about seven km east of present-day San Felipe, at the end of 17th century, and they began to construct a church and convent at the beginning of the 18th, but the massive quake of 1730 destroyed them both. The rebuilt **Iglesia de Curimón San Felipe,** dating from 1733, has 1.2-meter-thick adobe walls and, thanks to 19th-century remodeling, a three-arched portico topped by a two-tiered bell tower. In 1740, José Manso de Velasco signed the founding papers for San Felipe here, and José de San Martín's Ejército de los Andes (Army of the Andes) lodged here in 1817 before the decisive defeat of the Spanish royalists at Chacabuco.

An adjacent museum, featuring Franciscan relics, is open daily except Monday, 9 A.M.–1 P.M. and 1:30–8 P.M. in summer, 9 A.M.–1 P.M. and 3:30–7 P.M. the rest of the year.

Ruta del Vino Aconcagua

Five wineries in the Aconcagua valley are open to visitors. Three require reservations: **Viña Errázuriz,** tel. 2/2036688 in Santiago, wine.export@errazuriz.cl, west of San Felipe; **Viña San Esteban,** tel. 34/481050, sanesteban@entelchile.net, website: www.sanestebanwines.cl, just north of Los Andes; and **Viña Mendoza,** tel. 34/536648, f.mendoza@atn.cl, a few kilometers east of San Felipe. Two others are open on a drop-in basis: **Vinícola Almendral,** tel. 34/536734, a few kilometers east of San Felipe; and **Viña Sánchez de Loria,** tel. 34/591054, west of San Felipe on Ruta 60.

At Rinconada, south of San Felipe, there is a new **Museo del Vino,** tel. 34/401121, in a traditional tile-roofed adobe, open daily except Monday. For general information on the route, contact Claudia Silva, tel. 34/509031 or 09/7743125.

LOS ANDES

Los Andes, the main overland port of entry into Chile (though the actual border post is far to the east), is a crossroads where international Ruta 60 from Viña del Mar and Concón meets Ruta 57 from Santiago. Founded in late colonial times (1791) by Ambrosio O'Higgins, father of the Chilean liberator, its central core retains something of that earlier atmosphere. Like Los Andes, it's also the center of a fruit- and wine-growing area.

Orientation

Los Andes is 80 km north of Santiago via Ruta 57, and 133 km east of Viña del Mar via Ruta 60. The two main highways traditionally meet at Avenida Santa Teresa, from the south, and Avenida Argentina, from the west, though there is now a bypass from Santiago that allows motorists to avoid Los Andes.

Sights

In the precise center of the city's colonial core, an area seven blocks square that constitutes a *zona típica* national monument, the shady **Plaza de Armas** remains the focus of urban life. On the

HEARTLAND

north side of the plaza, the neoclassical **Gobernación Provincial** (1888-91), a national monument, was the provincial governor's residence until 1964; today a number of government offices cluster around its central patio, but the arched portal beneath its facade is a popular gathering place. Half a block east of the plaza, at Esmeralda 246, Nobel Prize poet Gabriela Mistral taught at the erstwhile **Colegio de Niñas** (Girls' School) for several years in the early 20th century.

Emphasizing local cultures, the **Museo Arqueológico de Los Andes,** Avenida Santa Teresa 398, tel. 34/420115, displays collections of funerary items, stone tools, pottery, and petroglyphs from Molle times (around A.D. 1–800) through the Aconcagua culture (about A.D. 800–1500) and the brief Inka presence (A.D. 1450 to the Spanish takeover). Horse gear and household goods date from more recent times, and there are also some Mapuche items. The English translations are far better than in most small provincial museums. Hours are 10 A.M.–6:30 P.M. daily except Monday; admission costs US$1.

Across the avenue, the 19th-century **Museo Antiguo Monasterio del Espíritu Santo,** Avenida Santa Teresa 389, tel. 34/421765, was once the Convento Carmelitas Descalzas del Espíritu Santo de los Andes, a cloister for Carmelite nuns. The Chilean Santa Teresa de los Andes, beatified in 1993, lived at this national monument, rebuilt in the 1920s, and many of the faithful undertake pilgrimages here. The museum also honors Laura Vicuña, a Santiago-born girl whose widowed mother took an Argentine lover, to keep the family together, after they fled across the Andes to avoid political persecution; according to legend, Laura's deteriorating health was an attempt to persuade her mother to change her ways.

At the north end of Avenida Santa Teresa, the waiting room of the former **Estación Ferrocarril Transandino,** the railroad line that ran erratically to the Argentine city of Mendoza between 1910 and 1984, contains Gregorio de la Fuente's mural *A la Hermandad Chileno-Argentina* (To Chilean-Argentine Brotherhood). Railroad historian Ian Thomson referred to the line, frequently damaged by avalanches and rockslides, "as a marvel to engineers, a disaster to accountants."

Accommodations

Two blocks north of the plaza, the simple **Residencial Susi,** Santa Rosa 151, tel. 34/428600, costs just US$4 per person. Half a block east of the plaza, the poorly lit but acceptable **Hotel Central,** Esmeralda 278, tel. 34/421275, costs US$7 pp with shared bath, US$15 pp with private bath.

Rates at **Hotel Don Ambrosio,** Freire 472, tel./fax 34/425496, are US$20/28 s/d. **Hotel Plaza,** Rodríguez 370, tel. 34/421169, fax 34/426029, charges US$32/34 s/d with breakfast for cozy rooms with cable TV, some with small patios, and parking. Note that it also has a pedestrian entrance directly on the Plaza de Armas, at Esmeralda 353.

Food

Several reasonable Chilean eateries line Avenida Santa Teresa, among them **Lomo House,** Avenida Santa Teresa 194, tel. 34/422422, which serves huge sandwiches at low prices, plus lunch or dinner entrées in the US$5 range, with attentive service. **El Guatón,** Avenida Santa Teresa 240, tel. 34/423596, serves traditional items such as *pastel de choclo.*

Downtown **Mülhausen,** Esmeralda 251, has fixed-price meals for about US$4. Across the street, **Círculo Italiano,** Esmeralda 246, serves Italian meals on the site of the former Escuela de Niñas. Half a block east of the museum, the **Centro Español,** O'Higgins 674, is a local classic.

Chocolatería Marcam, Avenida Santa Teresa 108, tel. 34/427712, makes fine homemade ice cream and other desserts.

Services

Money: Banco de Chile has an ATM at Maipú 350, on the east side of the Plaza de Armas.

Postal: Correos de Chile is at the corner of Santa Rosa and Esmeralda.

Telephone: Entel is at Esmeralda 423; the area code is 34.

Medical: Hospital San Juan de Dios is at Avenida Argentina and Avenida Hermanos Clark, tel. 34/421121 or 34/421666.

Information

In summer, the municipal Quiosco Turístico, Avenida Santa Teresa 333, tel. 34/421121, is

open 10 A.M.–2 P.M. and 4–8 P.M., weekends 10
A.M.–6 P.M.

Transportation

Now one of the country's better bus stations, the
Rodoviario Internacional Los Andes occupies
the former Estación Ferrocarril Transandino, at
the north end of Avenida Santa Teresa. Pullman
Bus, tel. 34/421262, has the most frequent schedules. Mendoza-bound international buses from
Santiago or Viña may stop here, but reservations
are a good idea—these are often full.

PORTILLO

For more than half a century, Portillo has been
Chile's prestige ski resort and, while first-rate ski
centers closer to Santiago have been expanding,
Portillo has retained its reputation for quality dry
powder and steep slopes that have yielded downhill
speed records—in 1987, Michael Prufer reached
217.68 km per hour. Its 23 different runs vary
from beginner and intermediate to advanced and
expert, the longest of which is 3.2 kilometers. Altitudes range from 2,590 to 3,322 meters, and it
gets an average of six meters of snow every winter.

Accommodations and Food

With a capacity for 500 skiers, **Hotel Portillo**
hosts weeklong packages only, starting at US$840
pp in low season, rising as high as US$2,250 pp
in peak season; prices include four meals daily,
but not taxes (nonresidents are exempt from the
18 percent IVA). Perks include a cinema, day-care
facilities, gymnasium, game rooms, a discotheque,
and live music; extras include a ski school, sauna
and massage, Internet access, and a beauty salon.
It overlooks the spectacular **Laguna del Inca,** a
cobalt blue alpine lake.

For budget travelers, Portillo's **Inca Lodge**
and **Octagon Lodge** offer ski weeks, with bunk-
style accommodations starting around US$500
to US$610 pp; both have four bunks to a room,
but the latter offers private rather than com-
munal baths.

For nonguests, lift tickets cost around US$27
daily; meals are available at the hotel restaurant,
which has superb views of Laguna del Inca. Moderately priced accommodation is also available
in the city of Los Andes, below the snow line, 69
km to the west.

There are now efforts to promote Portillo
as a year-round destination and, in summer,

© WAYNE BERNHARDSON

Laguna del Inca at Portillo ski resort

the resort rents *cabañas* for US$77/110 s/d, with breakfast.

Transportation

Almost directly on the international border via Ruta 60 from Los Andes, Portillo is 164 km from Santiago and about 200 km from Viña del Mar.

For transportation from either the airport or the capital, contact the Centro de Ski Portillo in Santiago at Renato Sánchez 4270, Las Condes, tel. 2/2630606, fax 2/2630595, info@skiportillo.com (Metro: Escuela Militar). Its very complete website is www.skiportillo.com; in the United States there's a toll-free number, tel. 800/829-5325.

The Southern Heartland

Besides Region V (Valparaíso), the southern heartland consists of Region VI (Rancagua), Region VII (Maule), and Region VIII (Biobío). This is wine country, with a great and growing density of vineyards, but its coastline will appeal to surfers in particular. Its real secret, though, is the Andean backcountry—if the cordillera from Rancagua south past Curicó, Talca, and Chillán were in North America or Europe, it would swarm with hikers in its mountain meadows and forests every summer. Instead, it gets only a handful of outdoor recreationists compared with the mainland lake district to the south, not to mention Torres del Paine.

RANCAGUA

Rancagua dates from 1743, when colonial governor José Manso de Velasco established the city as Villa Santa Cruz de Triana, on lands relinquished by Tomás Guaglén, the last Picunche cacique. It was here, in October of 1814, that the army of Bernardo O'Higgins suffered the Desastre de Rancagua (Disaster of Rancagua), resulting in the exile of many of its leaders to the Juan Fernández archipelago and delaying independence by several more years.

Colonial Rancagua was ranch and farming country, and it's still an agricultural service center and home to Chile's annual rodeo championships. As the capital of Region VI, it has important administrative functions and several historical sites, but the main motor of the economy is the El Teniente copper mine, in the Andes to the east. For most visitors, the city itself may be a brief stop or a day trip rather than an overnight, but its nearby Andean attractions—the mining

town of Sewell, the luxury hot springs of Termas de Cauquenes, and the wild high country of Reserva Nacional Río de los Cipreses—are among the most underappreciated places in the country.

Orientation

Rancagua is 87 km south of Santiago via the Panamericana, which bypasses the city to the east. The Plaza de los Héroes is the focus of its original grid, eight blocks square, but many services are west of Avenida San Martín, one of the boundaries of that grid. Between Plaza de los Héroes and Avenida San Martín, Calle Independencia, the central business cluster, is a pedestrian mall.

Sights

Rancagua's historic center is the **Plaza Los Héroes,** though no colonial buildings remain here. Its main landmarks are the neoclassical **Gobernación Provincial** (1889), a national monument, and the **Iglesia Catedral** (1861) at the south end of the plaza. On and around the plaza are several monuments: a banal equestrian statue of Bernardo O'Higgins, a hideously stylized stone sculpture of the city's founder (and later Viceroy of Peru) José Manso de Velasco, and an eye-catching image of Picunche chief Tomás Guaglén carved from a tree trunk.

One block north, at Estado and Cuevas, O'Higgins and his troops occupied the late 18th-century **Iglesia de la Merced** during the battle of Rancagua. From the tower of this tile-roofed adobe, O'Higgins watched hopefully for the arrival of reinforcements, but two-thirds of his forces died here.

At opposite corners of Estado and Ibieta, two late colonial houses, both national monuments, together form the **Museo Regional,** tel. 72/221254. The more distinctive is the **Casa del Pilar de Esquina,** Estado 684, with exhibits on local prehistory, mining, and agriculture. Named for the corner pillar often used as an architectural flourish in colonial times and owned by independence hero Fernando Errázuriz Aldunate, who initiated the constitution of 1833 in his capacity as acting president, it's open weekdays except Monday, 10 A.M.–6 P.M., weekends and holidays 9 A.M.–1 P.M. only. Admission is US$1 for adults, US$.50 for children, but it's free for everyone Tuesday.

The **Casa de Calixto Rodríguez,** Estado 685, tel. 72/221254, is filled with period furniture and colonial religious art, as well as an almost equally devotional tribute to O'Higgins's role in Chilean independence. Hours and admission fees are the same as the Casa del Pilar de Esquina.

One block south, at Avenida Millán and Avenida Cachapoal, the **Casa Patronal del Ex Fundo El Puente** was the landowner's residence that housed royalist Colonel Mariano de Osorio during the Battle of Rancagua (Osorio's victory earned him the viceroy's appointment as governor of Chile, a position whose power he wielded ruthlessly). Also a national monument and now the city's Casa de la Cultura, it occasionally exhibits paintings and photographs.

Accommodations

Accommodations are few, and relatively expensive compared with those in other Chilean cities of comparable size; for the annual March rodeo, prices can rise substantially. The best value is **Hostal Yaimán,** Bueras 655, tel. 72/230742, for US$12 pp without breakfast, but **Hotel España,** Avenida San Martín 367, tel. 72/230141, fax 72/234196, is a good alternative for US$19/27 s/d with private bath and breakfast.

Modest **Hotel Rancagua,** Avenida San Martín 85, tel. 72/232633, fax 72/241155, costs US$-27/40 s/d. **Hotel Aguila Real,** Avenida Brasil 1045, tel. 72/222047, fax 72/223002, charges US$30/45.

Rates at **Hotel Turismo Santiago,** Avenida Brasil 1036, tel. 72/230860, fax 72/230822,

start at US$32/48 including cable TV and breakfast. The best in town is the established **Hotel Camino del Rey,** Estado 275, tel. 72/239765, fax 72/232314, for US$45/64.

Food

Bavaria, Avenida San Martín 255, tel. 72/2-41241, is the local representative of the reliable nationwide chain, best for breakfasts and sandwiches. **Reina Victoria,** Independencia 667, has moderately priced lunches and fine ice cream. Carnivores can try **Torito,** Zañartu 323, a decent *parrilla* with an attractive dining room.

Rancagua has two Cantonese-style restaurants: **La Perla Oriental,** Cuevas 714, tel. 72/235447, and **Chung Hwa,** Cuevas 559.

Easily the city's most sophisticated restaurant, **Guy,** Astorga 319, tel. 72/226053, serves rich French-style cuisine with Chilean ingredients—try the *reineta con salsa de centolla* (white fish with crab sauce) for US$9 including a side order. Most other plates are in the US$8–10 range, but there's also a daily four-course lunch for US$9. The desserts (around US$3.50) are rich, imaginative, and the portions are large—try the mango parfait.

For cheaper but by no means inferior desserts, the Santiago ice creamery **Bravíssimo** has a Rancagua branch at Astorga 307, tel. 72/230596.

Entertainment

Varadero, at the corner of Ocarrol and Avenida Santa María, is a salsa venue. The **Retro Bar,** Avenida San Martín 226, tel. 72/243556, has drinks and recorded music.

Events

In mid- to late March, Rancagua hosts the **Campeonato Nacional de Rodeo** (national rodeo championships) at the Medialuna de Rancagua, the rodeo ring on Avenida España, the northward extension of Avenida San Martín.

Services

Money: Forex, Astorga 367, tel. 72/244499, is the only exchange house. Banco Sudamericano has an ATM at Independencia 696, corner of Bueras.

Telephone and Internet: Correos de Chile is on Campos between Cuevas and Independencia. Entel has long-distance offices at Independencia 468; the area code is 72.

Enlace Digital, set at the back of a gallery of shops at Independencia and Astorga, offers Internet access.

Laundry: Lava Express is at Avenida San Martín 270, tel. 72/241738.

Medical: The Hospital Regional is at Avenida O'Higgins 611, tel. 72/239555.

Information

Tourist Office: Sernatur, Germán Riesco 277, 1st floor, tel. 72/230413, fax 72/232297, sernatur_rancag@entelchile.net, is open 8:30 A.M.–5:15 P.M. weekdays only.

Motorists: Acchi, the Automóvil Club de Chile, is at Ibieta 09, tel. 72/239930.

National Parks: Conaf is at Cuevas 480, tel. 72/297505.

Transportation

Bus: Mostly rural and regional bus companies use the Terminal Rodoviario at Doctor Salinas 1165, just north of the Mercado Central. The long-distance exception is Via Tur, tel. 72/234502, which goes to Los Ángeles, Puerto Montt, and intermediates. Andimar, tel. 72/237818, goes to coastal destinations such as Pichilemu.

Tur-Bus, Ocarrol 1175, tel. 72/241117, has frequent service to Santiago (US$2, 1.5 hours) and extensive long-distance routes. Other Santiago-bound buses leave from the Terminal de Buses al Sur, Ocarrol 1039, tel. 72/230340.

Train: From the Estación de Ferrocarril, on Avenida Viña del Mar between Ocarrol and Ignacio Carrera Pinto, tel. 72/225239, Metrotrén runs 19 commuter trains daily to Santiago (US$1.50, one hour-plus), between 6:05 A.M. and 10:15 P.M. Long-distance passenger trains to Temuco and Concepción also stop here.

VICINITY OF RANCAGUA

The Andean backcountry east of Rancagua, little visited even by Santiaguinos, offers some exceptional excursions.

Termas de Cauquenes

Ever since the Jesuits first established themselves at the foothills hot springs Termas de Cauquenes in the 17th century, it's pulled in prestigious passengers such as Bernardo O'Higgins, José de San Martín, and Charles Darwin. In their day, though, it wasn't the luxurious resort it is now—in 1834, Darwin described it as "a square of miserable little hovels, each with a single table and bench."

In 1876, though, nitrate magnate Apolinario Soto of Copiapó modernized the facilities, creating a Vichy-style pavilion with tubs of Carrara marble, and Termas de Cauquenes has retained its elite image ever since. Temperatures in the pools range between 42° and 48°C.

Hotel Termas de Cauquenes, tel./fax 72/899010, fax 72/899011 in Rancagua, tel. 2/6381610, fax 2/6322365 in Santiago, charges US$77/146 s/d with full board; it also has pools and tubs, modern conference facilities, and a fine—though some consider it overpriced—riverview restaurant. The rooms are more than comfortable and the grounds are beautifully landscaped.

Both the restaurant and the pools are open to nonguests. An hour's soak in individual tubs costs US$4 pp, while those with Jacuzzi cost US$7.

On the south bank of Río Cachapoal, 760 km above sea level, Termas de Cauquenes is 31 km from Rancagua via the paved highway east to Coya and a six-km gravel road to the south. From Andén 13 of Rancagua's Terminal Rodoviario, Buses Coya (US$1.50) goes daily to Cauquenes at 9:30 A.M. and 1:30 P.M., returning at 11 A.M. and 5:15 P.M.

El Teniente (Sewell)

Part of state-run Codelco, El Teniente is the world's largest underground mine; in 1999, its more than 1,500 km of tunnels yielded 346,283 metric tons of copper ore. It dates from 1904, when the U.S.-based Braden Copper Company began operations; after its acquisition by the Kennecott Copper Company and the outbreak of World War I, production increased rapidly and the company became enormously wealthy. Widespread resentment of its dominant role pressured the state and, by 1967, the government had acquired majority shareholdings; in 1971, the Unidad Popular government of Salvador Allende expropriated El Teniente and the entire copper industry.

Until the late 1960s, when President Eduardo Frei Montalva's Operación Valle began to transfer all its 14,000 workers and their families to Rancagua, El Teniente's residential community of Sewell (named for Braden's first president) was a classic 20th-century company town. Parts have been dismantled or demolished, such as the so-called Barrio Americano where North American technicians lived with their families, but many structures, such as the hospital, the Escuela Industrial (Industrial School) and the Club Social, remain intact.

Supported by the Fundación Cardoén and in conjunction with the 30th anniversary of the nationalization of copper, Codelco has proposed Sewell for UNESCO World Heritage status, intending to develop a cultural and tourism project emphasizing the historic, economic, and social significance of copper mining in the region. The *fundación*—linked to arms merchant Carlos Cardoén—will provide museum expertise, while Codelco will provide resources and personnel.

Sewell, 2,600 meters above sea level and 55 km northeast of Rancagua, is open to the public for organized tours only, as Codelco plans to work with travel agents and tour operators to offers tours of the ghost town. For more information, contact Francisco Ayala at the Consorcio Turismo Sewell, tel. 2/6982270 in Santiago.

Centro de Esqui Chapa Verde

One of the perks of Codelco's presence is the Chapa Verde ski area, part of the El Teniente complex. Open to the general public in the winter, 3,100 meters above sea level, the 1,200-hectare area has four lifts and 22 separate runs, rated from beginner to expert. There is limited night skiing on an illuminated run.

Adult lift tickets cost US$16 weekdays, US$20 weekends; children pay half. There is also a ski school (US$8 for group lessons, US$20 for in-dividual lessons), rental equipment (US$18 per day), a café, and a restaurant. The Chapa Verde road is not a public highway; visitors must take Codelco buses (US$6 return) from the Hipermercado Independencia in Rancagua, Avenida Manuel Ramírez 665, tel. 72/294255. Departures are at 9 A.M. weekdays, or between 8 and 9:30 A.M. weekends.

Reserva Nacional Río de los Cipreses

Rarely visited except by locals, the forested foothills, rushing rivers, hanging valleys, and volcanic summits of Reserva Nacional de Los Cipreses are grossly underappreciated.

> *Rarely visited except by locals, the forested foothills, rushing rivers, hanging valleys, and volcanic summits of Reserva Nacional de Los Cipreses are grossly underappreciated.*

Orientation: Fifty km southeast of Rancagua via the paved road to Coya and a gravel road that passes through Termas de Cauquenes, Los Cipreses is a 36,882-hectare unit ranging from 900-meter foothills to the 4,850-meter summit of Volcán El Palomo.

Flora and Fauna: Los Cipreses's flora include not just the endangered native conifer *Austrocedrus chilensis* from which it takes its name, but also stands of *hualo (Nothofagus glauca), olivillo (Aextoxicum punctatum), peumo (Cryptocarpa alba)* and other native tree species. The endangered *flor de la araña* (literally, spider's flower, *Arachnitis uniflora*), is an endangered bloom that bears an eye-catching resemblance to a daddy longlegs.

The fauna includes guanaco, fox, vizcacha, Andean condors, owls, parrots, small reptiles, and the controversial puma, a recent reintroduction that local farmers assume attacks their livestock.

Sights and Recreation: Several sites near park headquarters have petroglyphs; Conaf can provide directions. Near the Ranchillos campground, the **Sendero de Excursion Los Peumos** is a short nature trail that also passes near small mines that once existed in the reserve.

One longer trail, suitable for at least an overnight backpack, climbs the Río de los Cipreses valley to a basic Conaf *refugio* at Urriola, about 20 km from the end of the road; the road itself is gated past Ranchillos, and motorists must get Conaf permission to continue to the trailhead (hikers or cyclists can easily bypass the gate).

Practicalities: Conaf's **Camping Ranchillos,** six km south of the park headquarters, is the only alternative, but it's a good one. Sites with picnic tables, barbecues, water, and some shade cost US$7. There is also a swimming pool. Bring all food from Rancagua—there is nothing for sale here.

At the park entrance, Conaf's **Centro de Visitantes** displays a scale model of the reserve, along with material on flora and fauna, including full skeletons of guanacos and foxes, taxidermy specimens of birds and reptiles, and display cases of insects. It also has highly motivated and helpful personnel.

Public transportation goes only as Termas de Cauquenes (see above); it's another 15 km to the park entrance. Conaf's Rancagua office may be able to offer suggestions.

SAN FERNANDO

About an hour south of Rancagua, 142 km from Santiago and west of the Panamericana, the smallish agricultural service center of San Fernando is the gateway to the wineries of the Colchagua valley. Colonial landowner Juan Jiménez de León donated the lands for its founding, in the mid-18th century.

Sights

Several of San Fernando's landmarks are national monuments. On the north side of the Plaza de Armas, at Argomedo and Valdivia, the two-story, neoclassical **Liceo de Hombres Neandro Schilling** (boys' school) dates from 1846. Three blocks south, at Valdivia and Manuel Rodríguez, the **Iglesia de San Francisco** (1891) has a clock tower with an unusual onion-shaped dome.

Several blocks northwest of the plaza, adjacent to the hospital, is the **Capilla San Juan de Dios** (1889), Negrete s/n, a brick building with elaborate filigree cornices, unfortunately damaged by the 1985 earthquake. Two blocks north, the **Casa Patronal del Fundo de Nilcunlauta,** at

Jiménez and Avenida Manso de Velasco, belonged to Juan Jiménez de León; now a museum, tel. 72/717326, it's open Tuesday to Saturday 10 A.M.–12:30 P.M. and 3–6:30 P.M., Sunday 10 A.M.–1 P.M. and 4–6 P.M. Admission costs US$2 for adults, US$1 for children.

Accommodations and Food

San Fernando's best value is **Hotel Diego Portales,** Avenida Bernardo O'Higgins 701, tel. 72/714696, where rates are US$12 pp with private bath but without breakfast. There's nothing much more elaborate, but try **Hotel Marcano,** Manuel Rodríguez 968, tel. 72/714759, fax 72/713943, where rates start around US$21/32 with private bath and breakfast; there are a few cheaper rooms with shared bath.

Transportation

Bus: The Terminal de Buses is at Avenida Manso de Velasco and Rancagua, four blocks east of the Plaza de Armas. Tur-Bus, tel. 72/712923, has extensive schedules north- and southbound on the Panamericana, while regional services connect the city with destinations west, including Santa Cruz (for the wine route) and Pichilemu (on the Pacific).

Train: The Estación de Ferrocarril is three blocks south of the bus terminal, at the east end of Quechereguas. Metrotrén runs 10 commuter trains daily to Santiago, from 6 A.M.–9:30 P.M. EFE trains between Santiago and Temuco and Concepción also stop here.

VICINITY OF SAN FERNANDO

Rural San Fernando has no eye-popping attractions, but Hacienda Los Lingues is one of South America's elite—though not totally elitist—resorts, and those exploring the countryside will find some absorbing surprises in addition to the wineries.

Hacienda Los Lingues

Short of time travel, the easiest way to grasp the sum and substance of life on a colonial hacienda—at least from the landowner's point of view—is to visit or, preferably, spend a night or more at Hacienda Los Lingues. Founded in the 16th century, though the present buildings date from the 17th, it's the best-preserved unit of its kind in the area, and perhaps the best in the country. It is also the only Chilean affiliate of the international Relais & Chateaux group of luxury accommodations, and one of few on the entire continent.

Decorated almost exclusively with antiques, the 10 rooms at Hacienda Los Lingues retain their colonial style but also have contemporary comforts such as private baths—but not TV. Set among sprawling but manicured gardens in the midst of a working farm, it also has a colonial chapel, a rodeo ring, and breeding stables. The Claro family, which owns the property, still resides here; it took years for Germán Claro Lyon, who manages the resort, to convince his parents to open it to tourists.

In addition to accommodations, Los Lingues offers activities such as tennis and swimming, hiking, mountain-biking, riding, and fly-fishing. Those who can't afford the luxury accommodations can book a day tour (US$46) which includes a tour of the main house, lunch (but not wine), pool access, and a rodeo at the farm's *medialuna* (rodeo ring). Most of the grounds, though, are closed to everyone except hotel guests.

In Santiago, Hacienda Los Lingues has offices at Avenida Providencia 1100, Torre C de Tajamar, Oficina 205, Providencia, tel. 2/2355446 or 2/2352458, fax 2/2357604, website: www. loslingues.cl, loslingues@entelchile.net. Rates are US$198 s or d for lodging only, US$ 217/236 s/d with breakfast, US$279/360 s/d with half board, and US$325/452 with full board. Suites are available starting at US$420 pp for accommodations only, ranging up to US$674 pp with full board.

Hacienda Los Lingues is about 20 km north of San Fernando and 32 km south of Rancagua, a short distance east of the Panamericana by a well-marked gravel road; north-south buses can drop you at the junction, where it's possible to find a cab to the hacienda. Los Lingues also provides round-trip transportation from Santiago for US$220 for up to six people, or from the international airport for US$320 for up to 11 people.

San Vicente de Tagua Tagua and Vicinity

At the town of **Pelequén,** about 20 km north of San Fernando on the Panamericana, the outstanding landmark is the shining copper dome of the **Iglesia y Santuario de Santa Rosa de Lima,** site of an annual festival for its patron saint every August 30th. From here, a paved two-lane road heads west along the valley of the Estero Zamorano, a tributary of the Río Cachapoal, to the town of San Vicente de Tagua Tagua.

Regional authorities are promoting this area as the Ruta Huasa, a repository of peasant tradition. In the cultural landscape, the object of interest is the succession of traditional *azudas* (waterwheels), which lift water from the river and divert it through wooden *canaletas* (flumes or chutes) to the fields.

Located mostly in the vicinity of **Larmahue,** these Muslim-style structures date from colonial times. Measuring six to eight meters in diameter, fitted with 16 to 32 wooden spokes of poplar, roble, *raulí,* or eucalyptus, they need frequent repairs but are cheaper to operate than gasoline-powered pumps. Of the several dozen in the area, 17 of the older ones are national monuments.

At San Vicente itself, **Hostería San Vicente de Tagua Tagua,** Diego Portales 222, tel. 72/5-71336, fax 72/572062, has accommodations for US$30/42 with breakfast.

Ruta del Vino de Colchagua

West of San Fernando, the Ruta del Vino de Colchagua is one of several emerging Chilean wine routes, and it's one of the best organized. Working out of a common office in the town of Santa Cruz, four wineries comprise the main route, which require reservations, preferably with 48 hours' notice; another two are open for tours on either a drop-in basis or short notice. The area is best known for its reds; one winery, MontGras, is attempting to cultivate Carménère, a variety that survived here after disappearing in France because of a 19th-century agricultural plague.

Starting around 10:30 A.M., full-day tours visit two of four wineries in the vicinity of Santa Cruz—**Viña Bisquertt, Viña MontGras, Viña Santa Laura,** and **Viña Viu Manent** (try the

HEARTLAND

Malbec). Rates vary depending on the number of guests—US$70 pp for two, US$55 pp for three to five, US$45 pp for six to 10. In addition to lunch at Santa Cruz's **Club Social** or one of the vineyards, tours visit either Santa Cruz's Museo de Colchagua or the Casa de Huique, north of town (see below).

To reserve excursions, contact the Ruta del Vino de Colchagua, Plaza de Armas 140, Oficina 6, Santa Cruz, tel./fax 72/823199, rv@uva.cl. The office is staffed daily except Sunday, 9 A.M.–1 P.M. and 3–6 P.M. Both English- and French-speaking guides are available on request.

In addition, Santa Cruz's **Viña La Posada,** Rafael Casanova 570, tel. 72/822589, laposada@entelchile.net, is open 8 A.M.–6 P.M. weekdays on a drop-in basis; weekends and holidays, reservations are obligatory for tours and tasting, which cost US$2 pp. In Nancagua, midway between San Fernando and Santa Cruz, **Viña Pueblo Antiguo,** Florencio Valdés 236, tel. 72/858296, puebloantiguo@hotmail.com, keeps similar schedules. Both wineries offer lunch for about US$10, while La Posada also has accommodations for US$70 d with breakfast.

Most tours of the Colchagua valley take in the **Museo de Colchagua,** an exceptional historical museum. The largest nonpublic museum in the country, it was built by arms merchant Carlos Cardoén to display his collections of paleontological specimens, pre-Columbian art, and historical materials, including a remarkable assortment of antique carriages and farm machinery. Its professional organization matches or surpasses that of Santiago's Museo Precolombino.

Open 10 A.M.–7 P.M. daily except Monday, the Museo de Colchagua, Errázuriz 145, tel. 72/821050, charges US$3 admission, but only US$2 for retired individuals and US$1 for children. Ruta del Vino tours usually include the admission price.

Donated to the Chilean army by the Sánchez Errázuriz family in 1976, **Casa de Huique,** the hacienda house of San José del Carmen de El Huique, dates from 1828, though the hacienda itself was created in the 17th century. Having spent more than 200 years in the same family, it one of the best preserved of its kind in the country; it is also one of the largest, its facade measuring 250 meters across.

One of Huique's owners, Federico Errázuriz Echaurren, served as president of Chile from 1896 to 1901. The house itself is richly decorated with period art and furniture, as well as family heirlooms and photographs.

Open Wednesday to Sunday 11 A.M.–5:30 P.M., Casa de Huique, tel. 72/933083, is 19 km north of Santa Cruz. It charges US$1.50 admission, half that for retired people and children.

Practicalities: For those who prefer not to travel from Santiago early in the morning, Santa Cruz has decent accommodations at **Hotel Alcázar,** Besoaín 285, tel./fax 72/822465, for US$13 pp with shared bath and breakfast, US$21/35 s/d with private bath. Cardoen's new **Hotel Santa Cruz Plaza,** Plaza de Armas 286, tel. 72/821010, fax 72/823445, reservas@hscp.cl, charges US$67/77.

The **Club Social de Santa Cruz,** Plaza de Armas 178, tel. 72/822529, is the traditional dining favorite for winery tours.

From the Terminal de Buses Santiago, Alameda 3750 in the capital, Santa Cruz is a three-hour bus trip with Andimar or Nilahue. An alternative would be to take Metrotrén to San Fernando and a local bus for the last 37 km to Santa Cruz.

PICHILEMU AND VICINITY

In the early 20th century, the Pacific beach town of Pichilemu was an aristocratic destination thanks to Agustín Ross Edwards, who bought Fundo Petrén in 1885 with the idea of turning it into a commercial port; after his project failed, despite using his parliamentary seat to promote it, he settled for a beach resort with European pretensions.

Pichilemu owes its current celebrity, though, to the left break at Punta de Lobos, six km south of town, where the **Campeonato Nacional de Surf** (national surfing championships) take place every summer. The water is notoriously chilly, though, and a good wet suit is imperative.

Other good surf spots include the point break at La Puntilla, right in town, though spectators will find the breaks a little far offshore to see well without binoculars; the smaller point break at Infiernillo just to its south; and Cahuil, 15 km south of town at the mouth of Estero Nilahue. At Bucalemu, 37 km south via Cahuil and a barge across the Nilahue, General Pinochet was briefly under house arrest in his vacation home.

Orientation

Pichilemu is 126 km west of San Fernando via Santa Cruz. At the north end of town, Playa Terrazas is a long sandy beach, but the curving coast toward the south is studded with rocky outcrops. Unlike most Chilean cities, Pichilemu's grid is irregular in spots, though the Avenida Costanera follows the shoreline.

Sights

Directly on Playa Terrazas, the restored **Parque Ross,** with broad lawns, a pool, and walkways lined with palms, is Pichilemu's de facto Plaza de Armas and a national monument. Across the street, Ross built the **Edificio Casino** (1906), consisting of a pair of two-story pavilions topped by a mansard level that lodged the staff; after losing its casino license to Viña del Mar in 1932, it served as a hotel.

At the north end of town, the former **Estación de Ferrocarriles** (railroad station, 1925), a national monument, is now a cultural center.

Accommodations and Food

Inland from the beach, **Camping Pequeño Bosque,** Santa Teresa s/n, tel. 72/841601, charges US$11 for up to four people for wooded sites with picnic tables and electric light, with access to clean toilets and hot showers.

Among regular accommodations, the simple **Residencial Las Salinas,** Aníbal Pinto 51, tel. 72/841071, costs US$7 pp with shared bath, US$11 pp with private bath, both with breakfast. Surfer-friendly **Hotel Chile España,** Avenida Ortúzar 255, tel./fax 72/841270, charges US$12 pp with shared bath, US$15 with private bath, both with breakfast; rates with full board are US$19 with shared bath, US$25 with private bath.

At the south end of town, **Cabañas Dunamar,** Playa Hermosa s/n, tel./fax 72/841576, has rea-sonably priced accommodations for US$30 d. Its beachfront restaurant is also a good lunch or dinner choice—a full meal with *pastel de jaiva,* empanadas, wine, and dessert costs only about US$6.

Information

Pichilemu's municipal Oficina de Información Turística is at Angel Gaete 365, tel. 72/841017.

Transportation

Buses Andimar, Avenida Ortúzar 483, tel. 72/841081, links Pichilemu with Santiago via San Fernando.

CURICÓ

Like many other central valley cities, San José de Buena Vista de Curicó owes its origins to a military base intended to protect settlers on the colonial frontier. Founded in 1743, along with Rancagua and San Fernando, by José Antonio Manso de Velasco, the town center was moved a few years later when the original site proved prone to flooding from the Río Guaiquillo.

In some ways a model garden city—or at least known as one for its magnificently landscaped Plaza de Armas—Curicó has recently undertaken a major street-tree planting program. The surrounding area is known for its wineries and for Reserva Nacional Radal Siete Tazas, a small but interesting park in the Andean foothills.

Orientation

Curicó is 195 km south of Santiago via the Panamericana. Like many colonial Chilean cities, its core is a rectangle seven blocks square, centered on the Plaza de Armas.

Sights

Curicó's **Plaza de Armas** and its surroundings are a *zona típica* national monument. After the city became a provincial capital in 1865, local authorities began to beautify what had been a parking lot for horses, planting Canary Island palms around the perimeter and placing a pool known as *Las Tres Gracias* (The Three Graces) at its center; on occasion, black-necked swans paddle around the fountain.

Several modern sculptures embellish the plaza, also shaded by *Araucarias,* robles, *boldos,* and *tilos,* along with other native and exotic trees; one dead trunk has been carved into a representation of the Mapuche hero Lautaro. The **Quiosco Cívico,** a forged-iron bandshell modeled after one a Curicó mayor saw in Santiago, dates from 1905.

On the west side of the plaza, at Merced and Yungay, the earthquake-damaged **Iglesia Matriz** is undergoing restoration. Six blocks east and one block south of the Plaza de Armas, opposite Plaza Luis Cruz, the soaring brick neo-Gothic **Iglesia San Francisco** is also a national monument.

Accommodations

Residencial Colonial Manuel Rodríguez 461, tel. 75/314103, is the cheapest at US$6 pp with shared bath, though it fills up fast at that price. Traditional budget favorite **Hotel Prat,** Peña 427, tel. 75/311069, charges US$7 pp with shared bath, US$12 pp with private bath. Just across the street, but not quite so appealing, **Residencial Rahue,** Peña 410, tel. 75/312194, also costs US$7 with shared bath.

Room sizes vary at family-run, somewhat ramshackle **Residencial Ensueño,** across the street at Manuel Rodríguez 460, tel. 75/312648, but the beds are comfortable, and there's plenty of hot water and good water pressure. If other guests aren't quiet, the sounds carries, but they switch the TV off early. Rates are US$7 pp with shared bath and breakfast, US$25 d with private bath and cable TV.

Better than its worn exterior would suggest, **Hotel Comercio,** Yungay 730, tel. 75/312443, fax 75/317001, has smallish but tidy rooms with shared bath and breakfast for US$22/33. Larger rooms with private bath cost US$33/49 s/d.

In primo condition, though the rooms are on the small side, **Hotel Palmas Express,** Membrillar 728, tel. 75/320066, fax 75/321425, villa-el-descanso@entelchile.net, offers cable TV, a/c, parking, and a buffet breakfast for US$46/56.

Despite its name, **Hotel Turismo,** Arturo Prat 301, tel. 75/310552, fax 75/310823, is more accurately the business traveler's favorite, though

tourists will feel just as much at home in its large rooms and spacious, stylish common areas. Rack rates are US$60/68, but ask for IVA discounts.

Food

Unfortunately, Curicó's restaurant scene is pretty bleak, but the **Casino de Bomberos,** Membrillar 690, is a reliable choice in most Chilean cities. The nationwide chain **Bavaria,** Yungay 615, tel. 75/319972, is also palatable but unexceptional.

The **Societá Mutuo Soccorro Italia,** tel. 75/310482, isn't quite what it sounds—there's nothing obviously Italian on the menu—but it has cheap lunches. The forlorn-looking **Fogón Chileno,** Estado 531, serves beef.

There are two Cantonese choices: **Whai Hau,** Yungay 853, tel. 75/326526, and **Nueva Era,** Argomedo 84, tel. 75/310480. The dining room at **Hotel Turismo,** Arturo Prat 301, is only so-so despite attractive surroundings.

Entertainment and Events

Curicó is a quiet provincial town, but the local branch of the **Centro Cultural Universidad de Talca,** Merced 437, shows movies and stages concerts, as does the **Centro Cultural Universidad Católica,** Prat 220.

Curicó's biggest annual event is late March's **Festival de la Vendimia** (wine harvest festival), which has grown since Catalan winemaker Miguel Torres began operations here in 1986.

Services

Money: Forex, Carmen 497, is the only exchange house. Banco de Crédito has an ATM at Merced 315, Banco Santander at Estado 336.

Postal: Correos de Chile is at Carmen 556, on the east side of the Plaza de Armas.

Telephone and Internet: Telefónica is at Avenida Camilo Henríquez 412, Entel at Peña 650. Curicó's area code is 75.

For Internet access, try C&M Computación, at the corner of Carmen and Argomedo, for about US$1.50 per hour; it's open 11 A.M.–11 P.M. daily except Sunday.

Medical: The Hospital de Curicó is on Chacabuco between Avenida San Martín and Buen Pastor, tel. 75/310252.

Information

Tourist Office: In summer, Sernatur sometimes opens a kiosk at the Edificio Servicios Públicos at the corner of Carmen and Merced, on the east side of the Plaza de Armas; hours are 9 A.M.–6:30 P.M. weekdays only.

Motorists: The Automóvil Club de Chile (Acchi) is at Chacabuco 759, tel. 75/311156.

Transportation

Bus: Most long-distance carriers now have their own offices; fares to Santiago (2.5 hours) are about US$4.50. Companies include Pullman del Sur, four blocks north of the plaza on Avenida Camilo Henríquez between Carmen and Membrillar, tel. 75/310387; Buses Lit, four blocks south and three blocks west of the plaza, on Avenida Manso de Velasco at the corner of Buen Pastor, tel. 75/315648; and Tur-Bus, near the Panamericana at Manso de Velasco 0106, tel. 75/312115.

A few long-distance carriers, plus regional and local buses, operate out of the Terminal de Buses Rurales. Those serving Santiago include Andimar, tel. 75/312000, which also goes to Santa Cruz, Pichilemu, and Termas del Flaco; Buses Díaz, tel. 75/311905, which also goes to the coastal town of Llico; Buses Ilomar, tel. 75/310358 or 75/317105, which also goes to the coastal resort of Iloca; and Davitur. Buses Bravo, tel. 75/312193, serves Lago Vichuquén and Iloca, while Talmocur goes to Molina and Talca, the regional capital.

Transportation to Reserva Nacional Radal Siete Tazas leaves from nearby Molina (for details, see the separate entry for the reserve, below).

Train: EFE trains between Santiago and Temuco, and Santiago and Concepción, stop at the Estación de Ferrocarril, Maipú 657, tel. 75/310028, four blocks west of the Plaza de Armas.

VICINITY OF CURICÓ

There is more of interest surrounding Curicó than in Curicó itself. For horseback excursions into Reserva Nacional Radal Siete Tazas and other parts of the Andean backcountry east of Curicó and Talca, contact Jean Pierre Gibert C. at **Rutarriera Chile** in Santiago, tel. 2/5549139, 2/6890937, or 09/4326017, rutarrie@netexpress.cl.

vineyards near Curicó

© WAYNE BERNHARDSON

HEARTLAND

Vinícola Miguel Torres

Just a few kilometers south of Curicó, Vinícola Miguel Torres is a Spanish vintner that began buying properties in Chile in the late 1970s. With wines that vary from cabernet sauvignon and rosé to chardonnay, sauvignon blanc, and riesling, as well as champagne, it is also one of Chile's largest wineries. Its modern Curicó bodegas are open on a drop-in basis for free hour-long tours that begin with a video that emphasizes the company's operations in Spain and California, followed by a visit to the local facilities and free tasting.

Vinícola Miguel Torres, at Km 195 of the Panamericana, tel. 75/310455, mailadmin@migueltorres.cl, is open 9 A.M.–7 P.M. weekdays and 10 A.M.–2 P.M. Saturday; from December to April, it's also open 10 A.M.–2 P.M. Sunday From the corner of Avenida Camilo Henríquez and Manuel Rodríguez in Curicó, Molina-bound *taxi colectivos* will drop passengers almost at the entrance.

Reserva Nacional Laguna Torca

Just a short distance inland from the Pacific, 108 km west of Curicó, Laguna Torca is a 606-hectare wetland reserve where the water level, in particularly heavy winters, rises to form an even larger body of water with nearby Lago Vichuquén. It is most notable for waterfowl, including black-necked and coscoroba swans, but there are many other species.

Conaf collects a US$1.50 admission charge for adults, but only US$.40 for children, at its Centro de Información Ambiental. It charges US$11 for campsites at a eucalyptus plantation about one km from Laguna Torca proper.

From Curicó, Buses Díaz goes to Llico, within reasonable walking distance of Laguna Torca.

Reserva Nacional Radal Siete Tazas

In the Andean precordillera southeast of Curicó, the Río Claro plunges steeply over basalt bedrock into a series of pools known as the Siete Tazas (Seven Teacups), a feature that has given its name to this 5,026-hectare reserve. When the water is high with spring snowmelt, skilled kayakers have made this one of their favorite stops in the coun-

try, but the reserve itself gets relatively few foreign visitors. Even when Chileans crowd it in summer and on weekends, areas off the main road are almost people-free.

Ecologically, distributions of drought-tolerant plants from Mediterranean northern Chile overlap the evergreen forests of southern Chile at Radal Siete Tazas. Ranging from 600 to 2,156 meters above sea level, the park does not reach the high Andean summits to the east.

Nonkayakers can view the **Siete Tazas** via a short trail off the main road; a slightly longer footpath leads to an overlook to the **Salto de la Leona,** a tributary falls that plummets more than 50 meters into the Claro.

Longer hikes up the **Valle del Indio** and **Cerro El Fraile** are also possible, but the lengthy trek north across the Claro to Reserva Nacional Altos del Lircay requires a guide—multiple tracks make route-finding difficult for those who don't know the area (for more information, see the separate entry for Altos del Lircay).

Accommodations and Food: At Radal and Parque Inglés, there are rudimentary campgrounds with basic services; the former is community-run, the latter administered by Conaf. Sites at the private **Camping Los Robles,** tel. 71/225858 or 09/3458371, cost US$14 for up to six people.

Near Parque Inglés, **Hostería Flor de la Canela,** tel. 75/491613, offers accommodations from December to March for US$30 pp with shared bath, US$38 with private bath, both with full board. Basic supplies are available, but there's a better selection in Curicó or Molina.

Information: Conaf collects a US$1.70 entrance fee (US$.40 for kids) at its Centro de Información at Parque Inglés, the entrance to the park. It also offers Saturday nature talks.

Transportation: The Parque Inglés entrance to the park is 50 km east of Molina via an unsurfaced road. From Molina, Buses Hernández, Maipú 1723, tel. 75/491607 or 75/491179, goes as far as Parque Inglés (US$2) eight times each weekday between 7:30 A.M. and 7 P.M.; on Saturday, the earliest departure is at 7 A.M. On Sunday there is a reduced schedule, with five departures between 7:30 A.M. and 9:30 P.M.

TALCA

Tomás Marín de Poveda founded Talca in 1690 but, after a major earthquake, José Manso de Velasco refounded it in 1742 under the name Villa San Agustín de Talca. Bernardo O'Higgins signed Chile's declaration of independence here and, while it has settled into the comfortable roles of political capital (of Region VII, Maule) and service center, it does not lack a cultural component—especially since the founding of the Universidad de Talca in 1981, the arts have flourished here.

Orientation

Wedged between the Río Claro to the west and the Panamericana to the east, Talca is 257 km south of Santiago. Unlike most Chilean cities, its streets are numbered rather than named, but the central core still has a regular colonial grid.

Sights

In 1818, Bernardo O'Higgins signed Chile's declaration of independence at the **Museo O'Higginiano y de Bellas Artes,** built in 1762 by Portuguese merchant Juan Albano Pereira y Márquez; Pereira and his wife, Bartolina de la Cruz, were in fact O'Higgins's godparents, and O'Higgins spent part of his youth in the house, a national historical monument. Unfortunately, the exhibits on O'Higgins here are marginal. More substantial are the archaeological and numismatic exhibits, the five rooms of Chilean art from colonial times to the 20th century, and materials on the origins of local journalism.

From October to March, the museum, 1 Norte 875, tel. 71/227330, is open Tuesday to Friday 10 A.M.–7 P.M., weekends and holidays 10 A.M.–2 P.M.; the rest of the year, Tuesday to Friday hours are 10 A.M.–6 P.M., but weekend and holiday hours are the same. Admission is free.

In the fire station, the **Museo Bomberil Benito Riquelme,** 2 Sur 1172, displays old photographs and antique fire-fighting gear. Admission is free, but it keeps no regular hours.

Accommodations

Talca lacks much quality budget accommodation, but some of the midrange choices are outstanding values. In addition to the places mentioned below, consider Casa Chueca, which has a separate listing as it is in many ways a destination in itself (see Vicinity of Talca).

US$10–25: Hostal del Maule, 2 Sur 1381, tel. 71/220995, is one of Talca's better bargains at US$12/17 s/d but without breakfast. A block north of the train station, **Hostal Victoria,** 1 Sur 1737, tel. 71/212074, costs US$12 pp.

US$25–50: Centrally located, a block north of the plaza, **Hostal Balcones del Maule,** 2 Norte 830, tel. 71/230503, charges US$15/26. Despite its location on a busy street, **Hotel Amalfi,** 2 Sur 1265, tel. 71/239292, fax 71/233389, has a cloistered interior garden; rates are US$16/28 s/d with shared bath, US$25/36 with private bath, but without breakfast.

Rates at **Hotel Cordillera,** 2 Sur 1360, tel./fax 71/221817, are US$16/28 s/d with shared bath and breakfast, while rooms with private bath and TV cost US$25/40, also with breakfast.

For US$35 s or d without breakfast, **Hostal del Puente,** 1 Sur 411, tel. 71/220930, fax 71/2-25448, enjoys a quiet location on a dead-end street where the only steady noise is the flow of the Estero Piduco, a tributary of the Río Claro. It also has agreeable English-speaking management.

Others in this range include **Hotel Napoli,** 2 Sur 1314, tel. 71/227373, for US$33/49 with breakfast, and **Hotel Inca del Oro,** 1 Sur 1026, tel. 71/239608, fax 71/239603, for US$37/50, also with breakfast.

US$50–100: Hotel Marcos Gamero, 1 Oriente 1070, tel. 71/223100, fax 71/224400, charges US$45/59. On the west side of the Plaza de Armas, the old but still stylish **Hotel Plaza,** 1

Poniente 1141, tel. 71/226150, fax 71/230864, costs US$44/66 with breakfast. One block west, the newer and also stylish **Hotel Terrabella,** 1 Sur 641, tel./fax 71/226555, charges US$55/65.

Food

For truly cheap eats, there are the several *cocinerías* in the **Mercado Central,** bounded by 1 Norte, 1 Sur, 4 Oriente, and 5 Oriente. For many years now, the unassuming **Picada José Barrera,** 1 Sur 530, tel. 71/224120, has offered the best cheap lunches in town, in the US$2–3 range, in pleasant surroundings with good service. **Lomitón,** 1 Sur 1134, tel. 71/210333, is a fast-food sandwich place; **Bavaria,** 1 Sur 1330, tel. 71/227088, has similar sandwich fare and some more elaborate dishes.

El Gobelino, 1 Sur 770, tel. 71/233980, serves fixed-price Chilean lunches in the US$3 range—good enough, but unexceptional. Alongside the fire station, the **Casino de Bomberos,** 2 Sur 1160, tel. 71/212903, is a reliable choice in almost every Chilean city.

The **Casino Caja de Empleados Particulares,** on 1 Oriente between 1 and 2 Norte, is another bargain lunch spot. **Varoli,** 3 Oriente 1189, tel. 71/224097, serves passable pizza.

Always one of Talca's better traditional choices, **El Alero de Gastón,** 2 Norte 858, tel. 71/233785, has even improved over recent years, with meat dishes cooked precisely to order, fine pisco sours, and impeccable service. There's a shady patio for outdoors dining in summer.

Other options include the more formal **Centro Español,** 3 Oriente 1109, tel. 71/224664, and **Ibiza,** 1 Sur 1168. Highly regarded, upscale **Rubén Tapia** is at 2 Oriente 1339, tel. 71/237875.

Entertainment

The local bar scene includes the newly popular **Wild West Pub,** on 5 Oriente between 3 and 4 Sur, and the leftish **Varadero,** directly across the street.

Run by the Universidad de Talca, the **Centro de Extensión Pedro Olmos Muñoz,** 2 Norte 685, sponsors films, lectures, and art exhibitions. The **Centro Cultural de Talca,** on 1 Oriente

between 1 and 2 Norte, is also a venue for art exhibits, and for live theater and concerts.

For commercial movies, try the **Cine Plaza,** 1 Sur 770, tel. 71/232310, or the **Cine Star 2,** 1 Sur 1278. During the March to December university year, the **Centro de Extensión de la Universidad Católica,** 2 Sur 1525, tel. 71/226303, offers retrospectives and non-Hollywood films.

Services

Money: The only exchange houses are Marcelo Cancino Cortés, 1 Sur 898, Oficina 15, and Forex, 1 Sur 1133. Banco de Crédito has an ATM at 1 Sur 732, on the south side of the Plaza de Armas; Banco Santiago has one at 1 Sur 853, a block east of the plaza.

Postal: Correos de Chile is on 1 Oriente, on the east side of the Plaza de Armas.

Telephone and Internet: Entel is at 1 Sur 908. Talca's area code is 71. Net.works, 7 Oriente 1180, tel. 71/214226, has fast and cheap Internet connections, only about US$1 per hour, but dueling MP3 downloads can make it noisy.

Medical: The Hospital Regional is at 1 Norte 1990, just east of the railway tracks, tel. 71/209100.

Information

Tourist Office: Sernatur, 1 Poniente 1281, tel. 71/233669, fax 71/226940, sernatur_talca@entelchile.net, has some English-speaking staff; it's open 8:30 A.M.–4:30 P.M. weekdays.

Motorists: The Automóvil Club de Chile (Acchi) is nearby at 1 Poniente 1267, tel. 71/232774.

National Parks: Conaf's Patrimonio Silvestre office, which specializes in protected areas, is at the corner of 2 Poniente and 3 Sur, tel. 71/228029.

Transportation

Talca has no air services, but buses are frequent and it's a stop on the EFE railroad line between Santiago, on the one hand, and Temuco and Concepción on the other. It also has Chile's last operating short-line passenger railroad, to the coastal resort of Constitución.

Bus: Talca's Rodoviario Municipal, 2 Sur 1920, tel. 71/243270, is east of the railroad tracks.

Long-distance carriers on the Panamericana include Tur-Bus, tel. 71/245704; Buses Lit, tel. 71/242048; Tas Choapa, tel. 71/243334; Intersur, tel. 71/245920; Buses Jac (Santiago to Temuco and intermediates); and Sol del Pacífico, tel. 71/244199 (between Valparaíso/Viña del Mar to Concepción and intermediates). Buses Vilches, tel. 71/243366, has three buses daily, at 7:15 A.M. and at 1 and 4:50 P.M., to Vilches Alto and Reserva Nacional Altos del Lircay.

Pullman Contimar, tel. 71/244197, goes frequently to and from the coastal town of Constitución (US$2, two hours), as does Pullman del Sur, tel. 71/244039.

Buses Biotal, tel. 71/223727, represents Linares-based Transporte Pehuenche, tel. 73/212322, whose summer minibuses pick up passengers in Talca en route to the Argentine cities of Malargüe (US$40) and San Rafael (US$60), via the Paso Pehuenche in the upper Maule drainage, southeast of Talca.

Sample destinations and fares include Chillán (US$3.50, two hours), Rancagua (US$4, 2.5 hours), Santiago (US$5, four hours), Los Ángeles or Concepción (US$7.50, 3.5 hours), Temuco (US$8.50, six hours), Valdivia (US$10, eight hours), Osorno (US$12.50, nine hours) and Puerto Montt (US$14, 10 hours).

Train: Trains between Santiago and Temuco or Concepción stop at Talca's Estación de Ferrocarril, 11 Oriente 1100, tel. 71/226254, at the east end of Avenida 2 Sur.

The daily train to the port/beach resort of Constitución, leaving at 7:30 A.M. daily, costs US$2 and takes 2.5 hours. (For details of this entertaining service, see the special topic The Ferrocarril Constitución.)

VICINITY OF TALCA

From the coast to the cordillera, the countryside around Talca has abundant recreational opportunities, even more than Curicó. San Clemente's **Turismo Siete Ríos,** Huamachuco s/n, 1 Norte 1652, tel. 71/210611 or 09/7950372, tour7rios@mixmail.com, does rafting descents of several area rivers, including the Claro, Lircay-Corel, Lontué, upper and lower Maule, and Achibueno, along with kayaking and horseback riding. Rates are very reasonable, ranging from as little as US$10 pp for an hour-plus on the lower Maule to US$60 pp for a day on the upper Maule (with a four-person minimum). It also does hiking and climbing excursions in the parks and reserves of the cordillera.

Huilquilemu

Across the Panamericana from Talca, the former *fundo* of Huilquilemu is one of Chile's single most impressive big houses, with its long corridors, thick adobe walls, multiple patios, wooden ceilings, and extensive gardens of native and exotic trees. Under the administration of the Universidad Católica, it boasts a religious art museum, an assortment of historic farm equipment, an elegant library honoring regional writers including Neruda and Pablo de Rokha, and a spectacular display of folk art from throughout the Americas. The sprawling, forested gardens include specimens of sequoias, deodar cedars, and palms.

Huilquilemu, tel. 71/242474, is 10 km east of Talca on the San Clemente road; hours are daily except Monday 10 A.M.–1 P.M. and 2:30–6:30 P.M.; adult admission costs US$.65, while children pay US$.20. Any San Clemente-bound micro from Talca's Rodoviario Municipal passes the site. Its restaurant **Mesón de Rugendas** is open only on weekends.

Casa Chueca

In a quiet location on the south bank of the Río Lircay, just across the Panamericana from Talca, German-Austrian Casa Chueca is a fashionably decorated colonial-style guesthouse with all the essential comforts—firm beds, hot showers, clean toilets, a library, and even a small gym—and none of the inessential—in particular, it lacks TV. Set among sprawling lawns with a large swimming pool, it's become a destination in itself for weekenders from Santiago and vagabonds along the Panamericana.

The accommodations themselves are impeccable, with spacious rooms for US$20 pp with an abundant breakfast. There is also backpackers' accommodation for US$10 pp, in equally spacious and comfortable rooms with private bath, but with half a dozen bunks. Mainly vegetarian

© WAYNE BERNHARDSON

Centro Cultural Huilquilemu, Talca

lunches and dinners cost US$2–4, and mixed drinks and wine are equally reasonable.

In addition to accommodations, Casa Chueca offers well-guided excursions into the Andean backcountry of Altos del Lircay, Radal Siete Tazas, and the upper Río Maule toward the Argentine border, all areas greatly underappreciated by Chileans and foreigners alike. The owners and staff are also generous with information to independent travelers and speak Spanish, English, German, Swedish, French, and Portuguese.

To reach Casa Chueca from Talca's bus terminal, take the local Taxutal A micro to the end of the line at the Toro Bayo restaurant, about a 10-minute ride, and walk another 20 minutes along the dirt road. Casa Chueca will also provide the first transfer free from Toro Bayo—contact Casa Chueca, tel. 71/1970096, tel./fax 71/1970097, cellular 09/4-190625 or 09/8371440, website: www.trekking-chile.com, casachueca@hotmail.com. Bicycles are available for going to town.

Ruta del Vino del Maule

Like other heartland wine areas, the Maule valley has a rapidly developing tourist circuit, with nine wineries open to the public, from Talca south toward San Javier and west toward Constitu-ción. Only two, however, are open on a drop-in basis; the rest require advance arrangements.

Directly east of the Panamericana, at the 2.4 Km point just past the ProTerra home improvement store, a gravel road leads south for 3.5 km to **Viña Domaine Oriental,** acquired in 1989 from the Donoso family by French-Tahitian interests who renamed the property and began to focus on cabernet sauvignon, merlot, chardonnay, and carménère for export; the winery is also planting cabernet franc, malbec, and césar. Tours with tasting (US$1.50) are available weekdays 8 A.M.–6 P.M. weekdays; contact Viña Domaine Oriental, Fundo La Oriental, Talca, tel. 71/2-42506, website: www.domaineoriental.cl, courrier@domaineoriental.cl.

South of Talca, where the Panamericana crosses the canyon of the Río Maule, it parallels the **Puente Ferroviario Maule** (1885), a 442-meter iron railroad bridge that still carries trains to Chillán, Concepción, and Temuco. Another two km south is San Javier's modern **Viña Balduzzi,** Avenida Balmaceda 1189, tel. 73/322138, website: www.balduzzi.cl, balduzzi@entelchile.net, which produces mostly chardonnay, sauvignon blanc, late harvest, and cabernet sauvignon. It's open daily except Sunday 9 A.M.–6 P.M. for guided visits; there are many buses from Talca's Rodoviario Municipal.

To arrange a more extensive itinerary, contact the Ruta del Vino del Maule, Sargento Aldea 2491, San Javier, tel. 73/323945, tel./fax 73/323657, website: www.chilewineroute.com, wineroute@entelchile.net.

Reserva Nacional Altos del Lircay

In the precordillera southeast of Talca, Altos del Lircay is another of Chile's hidden secrets, a forested wilderness of 12,163 hectares with multiple options for backcountry hiking and camping in canyons, valleys, and summits that range from 600 to 2,448 meters above sea level. It has warm, dry summers, but substantial snowfall can accumulate in winter.

Flora and Fauna: Closely resembling the forests of nearby Radal Siete Tazas, Lircay's woodlands consist of species toward the northern limits of their range, such as the southern beech *coigüe (Nothofagus dombeyi),* overlapping central Andean species such as *lingue (Persea lingue), boldo,* and *peumo.* They have abundant bird life, including the burrowing parrot, black woodpecker, thrush, and California quail (an introduced species). The largest mammal is the puma, a reintroduction under a joint program between Conaf and the Talca branch of the conservation organization Codeff.

Sights: Lircay's aboriginal population ground their grains at the **Piedras Tacitas,** a series of creekside mortars reached by a short signed trail from Conaf's Centro de Información Ambiental. On the north side of the former logging road that leads east from the park entrance, the **Mirador del Indio** offers views of the Lircay valley; it's possible to hike across the Lircay drainage to the Río Claro and Reserva Nacional Radal Siete Tazas but, because there are multiple tracks through the area, a local guide is almost obligatory.

Two km east of Mirador del Indio, a signed trail climbs north and then east to **El Enladrillado,** a sprawling tableland where weathering has uncovered columns of hexagonal basalt formed millions of years ago beneath the earth's surface. This tiring hike, which Conaf suggests should take two days, is possible in a day, but

carry adequate water and high-energy snacks. The views of the Río Claro valley, 3,830-meter Volcán Descabezado Grande, and the Andean ridge along the Argentine border are among the best in the country.

More ambitious hikers can consider a five-day trek on the **Sendero Valle del Venado** to the summit of Descabezado Grande and back; for details on current conditions and further suggestions, contact Casa Chueca in Talca.

Accommodations and Food: Conaf has a multi-site campground near the entrance to the reserve, charging US$13, but there are also several private campgrounds along the dusty road just before the entrance. A few small shops are nearby, but supplies are cheaper and more abundant in Talca.

Information: At the park entrance, Conaf collects an admission charge of US$1.70 for adults, US$.40 for children. Its Centro de Información Ambiental contains exhibits on natural and cultural history.

Reasonably priced rental horses are available just outside the park entrance. When off-duty, Conaf ranger Leonardo Cáceres, tel. 09/8923625, leads hikes across the Río Lircay to Radal Siete Tazas.

Transportation: Altos del Lircay is 66 km southeast of Talca via paved Ruta 115 and a 26-km unpaved side road that billows with dust in the dry summer and splatters mud in winter, when the last few kilometers can be difficult. From Talca's Terminal Rodoviario, Buses Vilches, tel. 71/235327, goes to the Administración (park office) at 7:15 A.M. and at 1 and 4:50 P.M., returning at 7:15 and 9:15 A.M., noon, and at 6:15 P.M. There are usually additional buses in summer; the fare is US$1.50.

CONSTITUCIÓN

West of Talca, at the mouth of the Maule, the town of Constitución lives on paper pulp, port traffic, and weekenders who take launch excursions on the estuary. It has a handful of handsome colonial houses with tiled roofs, but for some visitors the main reason for coming here is getting here—the picturesque railroad from Talca is the last operating line of its kind in the country.

Sights

The admirably landscaped **Plaza de Armas** features a distinctive wrought-iron bandshell that dates from 1923; on its south side, the **Iglesia Parroquial San José** wears a neoclassical facade. The **Edificios Públicos** (Civic Center) on the west side of the plaza includes the 1950s-style **Teatro Municipal** (Municipal Theater).

At the west end of town, the 90-meter summit of **Cerro Mutrún** should offer views over the town, out to sea, and south toward the Celulosa Arauco (Celco) pulp mill. Fast-growing pines have blocked the view toward the mill, but your nose knows where it is.

Accommodations

Though old and worn, **Hotel Pradenas,** Cruz 353, tel. 71/671213, retains some character for US$10 pp with breakfast and shared bath.

Only the exterior retains its colonial integrity at **Hotel Colonial,** Portales 85, tel. 71/671215, fax 71/671335, whose carpeted, heated, utilitarian rooms are adequate for US$36/40 s/d with

breakfast and private bath. Telephone service, cable TV, and parking are also included.

Constitución's best, the **Hostería Constitución,** Echeverría 460, tel. 71/671450, fax 71/673735, charges US$62/67 s/d with breakfast and cable TV for garden rooms, US$75/80 s/d for spacious riverview rooms with balconies.

Food

Otto Schop, Oñederra 601, at the southeast corner of the Plaza de Armas, has good sandwiches and other short orders. **Paola,** a block north of the plaza at O'Higgins 596, tel. 09/4181503, has good fish and desserts at moderate prices, but mediocre pisco sours; on Friday and Saturday, people bring their own tango cassettes for dancing.

Services

On the north side of the Plaza de Armas, both Banco de Chile and Banco Santiago have ATMs.

Entel, on the Plaza de Armas at Cruz and Freire, has both long-distance telephone services and Internet access. Constitución's area code is 71, the same as Talca's.

Transportation

Easily the most entertaining way to Constitución is the morning train from Talca (see the special topic The Ferrocarril Constitución for details). Still, it's advisable to take a bus or *taxi colectivo* back to Talca—though a little farther, it's faster and takes a different route.

The train and bus station are alongside each other on Rozas between Echeverría and Bulnes, several blocks northeast of the Plaza de Armas. Along with several other companies, Pullman Contimar, tel. 71/672929, connects Constitución with Talca (US$2, two hours).

CHILLÁN

Beset by natural disasters throughout its history, modern Chillán lacks even the limited colonial character of heartland cities such as Talca. But the birthplace of Chilean liberator Bernardo O'Higgins compensates with museums, its renowned Mexican murals—reason enough for

© WAYNE BERNHARDSON

Plaza de Armas, Constitución

stopping in the city—and the most vibrant fruit-and-vegetable market in the entire country. In addition to O'Higgins, Chillán is the birthplace of internationally known concert pianist Claudio Arrau.

History

Initially established as a Spanish fortress in 1565, Chillán dates officially from 1580, when Chilean governor Martín Ruiz de Gamboa decreed the founding of the city of San Bartolomé de Gamboa. Almost destroyed by fire in 1655 and earthquake in 1751, it was rebuilt at what is now Chillán Viejo, a few kilometers southwest, but moved to its current site after yet another quake, in 1835. In 1939, though, a truly cataclysmic upheaval leveled most of the city and, as rebuilding proceeded on the same site with updated seismic safety standards, it has few structures of any antiquity. Chillán Viejo, ironically, survives to this day.

Orientation

Chillán is 407 km south of Santiago and 270 km north of Temuco by the Panamericana, which bypasses the city to the west. Between the Río Ñuble to the north and the Río Chillán to the south, its unstable alluvial soils have probably contributed to its repeated natural disasters.

Bounded by Libertad, 18 de Septiembre, Constitución, and Arauco, Plaza Bernardo O'Higgins marks the city center, though there are several satellite plazas. The divided, tree-lined Avenidas Ecuador, Brasil, Collín, and Argentina circumscribe the central core, an area 12 blocks square. Three blocks west of the plaza, Avenida O'Higgins provides access to the northbound Panamericana (toward Santiago) and the southbound Panamericana (toward Los Ángeles and Temuco) via Chillán Viejo.

Sights

Produce from throughout the region converges on the **Feria de Chillán,** a vigorous fruit-and-vegetable market that fills the entire Plaza de la Merced, southeast of the Plaza de Armas, and overflows onto nearby streets. Also boasting an impressive assortment of handicrafts, it's open every day, but most active on Saturday.

THE FERROCARRIL CONSTITUCIÓN

Chile's last operating short-line passenger spur, the Ferrocarril Constitución owes its shaky existence primarily to state subsidies. Departing Talca early every morning, it's the only Chilean rail line with no parallel highway, as it pauses at many settlements and whistlestops that have no other regular public transport—Colín, Corinto, Curtiduría, González Bastías, Toconey, Pichamán, Forel, Huinganes, and Maquehue—before finally shuddering to a stop at Constitución.

For most of the route, on a one-meter narrow-gauge track, the 1961-vintage FerroStaal railbus (the first car is also the locomotive) follows the north bank of the Río Maule. There are several bridges and one tunnel; just before arrival at Constitución, the line crosses to the south bank of the broad Maule estuary.

Most of the passengers are peasants with no other mode of transport; flat-brimmed sombreros, rather than nylon baseball caps, are the headgear of choice. Conversation runs from "look at that pasture" and "look at those melons" to "how are the grapes this year?" as you pass the fields near Talca and proceed between the peaks of the coast range.

As the train approaches Constitución station, plantations of Monterey pine cover the hillsides—at least where they haven't been clearcut—betraying the importance of the city's main employer, the Celulosa Arauco y Constitucion (Celco) pulp mill. Soon enough, the scent gives it away.

© WAYNE BERNHARDSON

mural by Mexican muralist David Siqueiros, Escuela de Mexico, Chillán

Chillán's **Museo Franciscano,** part of its eponymous church on Plaza General Lagos, honors the contributions of colonial Franciscan missionaries who used Chillán as a base to evangelize the Mapuche to the south (even after Chilean independence, this was the northern limit of the area commonly known as "La Frontera," much of it under effective indigenous control). At the corner of Sargento Aldea and Vega de Saldías, the museum, tel. 42/237606, is open Tuesday to Saturday 9 A.M.–1 P.M. and 3–6 P.M., Sunday 1–2 P.M. only.

One of few structures of any antiquity, the **Capilla del Hospital San Juan de Dios** (1874) is the remaining chapel of the former main hospital; on Avenida O'Higgins, a few blocks south of Avenida Collín, Chillán's only national historical monument is rapidly deteriorating.

Though it lacks official landmark status, the **Escuela México,** on Avenida O'Higgins between Gamero and Vega de Saldías, probably gets more attention than any other local attraction because of its famous frescos by the Mexican muralist David Alfaro Siqueiros and his countryman Xavier Guerrero. The school itself was part of a relief effort by Mexican President Lázaro Cárdenas's government after the cataclysmic 1939 earthquake.

Siqueiros was outspokenly political and, like other Mexican muralists and many other artists of his time, a Communist. His library murals, collectively titled *Muerte al Invasor* (Death to the Invader), reveal his commitment to the rebel and the underdog. Dedicated to Mexico, the north wall depicts individuals such as Aztec emperor Cuauhtémoc, revolutionary priest Miguel Hidalgo, President Benito Juárez (a Zapotec Indian), 20th-century revolutionary Emiliano Zapata, and President Cárdenas himself—not to mention Spanish conquistador Hernán Cortés. Devoted to Chile, the southern wall features Mapuche leaders Caupolicán, Lautaro, and Galvarino (the latter's bleeding hands amputated on the orders of Pedro de Valdivia, also depicted here), independence hero Bernardo O'Higgins, and reformist President José Manuel Balmaceda, who committed suicide after defeat in the civil war of the 1890s.

Less obviously political, Guerrero's *Hermanos Mexicanos* (Mexican Brothers) fill the library's stairwells with muscular figures symbolizing their country's dedication to the relief effort. Unfortunately, both sets of murals are in serious need of restoration. Though the Escuela México, at Avenida O'Higgins 250, is still a public school, the library is open to the public 10 A.M.–12:45

P.M. and 3–6:30 P.M. weekdays; on weekends and holidays, hours are 10 A.M.–6 P.M. Admission is free.

Accommodations

Chillán has a good selection of budget and midrange accommodations, but not much in the upper tier. Only a few include breakfast in their rates.

US$10–25: For US$7 pp with shared bath, the simple **Hostal Canadá,** Avenida Libertad 269, tel. 42/221263, is friendly enough but the rooms are a little dark. Others in the same category include homey, well-established **Hospedaje Sonia Segui,** Itata 288, tel. 42/214879, and **Residencial Su Casa,** Cocharcas 555, tel. 42/2-23931. The **Claris Hotel,** 18 de Septiembre 357, tel. 42/221980, charges US$7/16 with shared bath, US$13/19 with private bath, but without breakfast.

US$25–50: Though past its peak, **Hotel Libertador,** Avenida Libertad 85, tel. 42/223255, still offers decent value at US$11/21 s/d with shared bath, US$18/25 s/d with private bath. **Hotel Floresta,** 18 de Septiembre 278, tel. 42/222253, charges US$20/26 s/d with private bath and breakfast. So-so **Hotel Martín Ruiz de Gamboa,** O'Higgins 497, tel. 42/221013, costs US$14/21 s/d with shared bath, US$24/27 with private bath.

Hotel Javiera Carrera, Carrera 481, tel./fax 221175, tel. 42/244360, hotel.javiera.carrera@terra.cl, has smallish rooms and even claustrophobic showers, but also remarkably attentive staff for an inexpensive hotel. Rack rates are US$21/26 s/d with breakfast, but try negotiating a discount; in winter, space heaters are available.

Though it gets some short-stay trade, the motel-style **Hotel Los Cardenales** Bulnes 34, tel. 42/224251, also manages to attract families to its spotless rooms, with cable TV and private bath, for US$20/28 s/d.

At a busy intersection at the southeast corner of the plaza, **Hotel Cordillera,** Arauco 619, tel. 42/215211, fax 42/211198, cordihot@chilesat.net, charges a very reasonable US$26/31 s/d. **Hotel Quinchamalí,** El Roble 634, tel. 42/223381, fax 42/227365, charges US$27/43 s/d, while rates at

Hotel Rucamanqui, Herminda Martín 590, tel. 42/222704, fax 42/212072, are US$28/42 s/d.

Rates at traditional favorite **Gran Hotel Isabel Riquelme,** Arauco 600, tel. 42/213663, fax 42/211541, start at US$38/47. **Hotel Paso Nevado,** Avenida Libertad 219, tel. 42/237788, fax 42/237666, charges US$38/51.

US$50–100: Rates at **Hotel de la Avenida,** Avenida O'Higgins 398, tel. 42/230256, are reasonable at US$33/59 s/d, but the owner's arbitrary exchange rate for the U.S. dollar pretty much wipes out the IVA discount for what could be a better deal.

Hotel Las Terrazas, Constitución 664, 5th floor, tel. 42/227000, fax 42/227001, is in a category of its own at US$67/74, and it is in fact a very fine place.

Food

Café París, Arauco 666, tel. 42/223881, is an outstanding breakfast choice and one of few places in the provinces where caffeine junkies can find an espresso. Across the street, the **Fuente Alemana,** Arauco 661, tel. 42/212720, specializes in sandwiches and desserts. Another good dessert option is the ice cream at **Friatto,** Isabel Riquelme 621, tel. 42/222878.

For inexpensive traditional Chilean food, including some of the country's finest *pastel de choclo* in summer and outstanding *pastel de papas* (potato pie) at almost any time of year, the best bet is any of the several simple *cocinerías* in the **Mercado Central,** a rejuvenated landmark on Maipón between 5 de Abril and Isabel Riquelme. If the market's closed, the **Casino Cuerpo de Bomberos,** at El Roble and 18 de Septiembre, is a good alternative.

Two restaurants with different menus occupy the same space at Rosas 392: the pizzería **Ficus,** tel. 42/212176, and the beef-oriented **La Parrillada de Córdoba,** tel. 42/233522. Entrées start in the US$5 range. **Jai Yang,** Avenida Libertad 250, tel. 42/225429, serves Chinese specialties.

There are only a handful of upscale restaurants, among them the traditional **Centro Español,** in dignified surroundings at Arauco 555, tel. 42/216212, and **Kuranepe,** north of the bus station at O'Higgins 0420, tel. 42/221409.

Entertainment

Performing arts events, as well as film showings, take place at the **Teatro Municipal,** 18 de Septiembre 590, tel. 42/231048, *anexo* 334. It's also has a gallery for special exhibits, open 9 A.M.–2 P.M. and 3–6 P.M. weekdays.

Cine El Roble, El Roble 770, tel. 42/239022, is a twin-screen cinema in the Plaza El Roble shopping mall. **Cine O'Higgins** is at Avenida Libertad 210, tel. 42/214687.

Services

Money: The main exchange house is Schüler Cambios, Constitución 608, open 9 A.M.–1 P.M. and 3:30–7 P.M. weekdays, 10 A.M.–6 P.M. Saturday and 11 A.M.–1:30 P.M. Sunday. There are ATMs at Banco de Crédito, on the north side of the Plaza de Armas at Avenida Libertad 677, and at Banco Concepción, Constitución 550, on the south side of the plaza.

Postal: Correos de Chile is at Libertad 505.

Telephone and Internet: Telefónica CTC is at Arauco 625 and at the long-distance bus terminal. Entel is at Arauco 623. Chillán's area code is 42.

Planet Cybercafé Arauco 683, 2nd floor, tel. 42/222797, provides Internet access seven days a week. So does Gateway Informática, Avenida Libertad 360-B, tel. 42/238865.

Laundry: Lava Matic is at Prat 357-B.

Medical: Hospital Herminda Martín is at Avenida Francisco Ramírez s/n, tel. 42/212345, six blocks east of the plaza.

Information

Tourist Office: The local Sernatur office, at 18 de Septiembre 455, tel./fax 42/223272, is open 8:30 A.M.–7:30 P.M. weekdays; from mid-December to the end of February, it's also open 10 A.M.–2 P.M. weekends. There's also a small information kiosk at the main bus terminal.

Motorists: The Automóvil Club de Chile (Acchi) is at O'Higgins 677, tel. 42/216410.

Transportation

Bus: Chillán has several bus terminals. For long-distance services, the main facility is the Terminal María Teresa at Avenida O'Higgins 010, just north of Avenida Ecuador, tel. 42/272149. A few companies also use the dingy Terminal de Buses Interregionales at Constitución 01, tel. 42/221014, and several others have ticket offices in the immediate vicinity.

Tur-Bus, tel. 42/272163 at Terminal María Teresa, tel. 42/212502 at the Interregionales, has numerous buses to Santiago, Puerto Montt, and intermediates along the Panamericana, and to Concepción. Tas Choapa, at the Interregionales, tel. 42/223062, also goes to Santiago, Puerto Montt, and intermediates, and directly to Valparaíso/Viña del Mar.

Sol del Sur and Sol del Pacífico, at Terminal Santa Teresa, also go to Santiago, Viña, and Valparaíso, as does Buses Lit at the Interregionales, tel. 42/222960. Línea Azul, at the Interregionales, tel. 42/211192, has frequent service to Concepción, plus two departures daily for Santiago. Other carriers along the Panamericana, from Terminal María Teresa include Buses Jac, between Temuco and Santiago, tel. 42/273581; Via Tur, to Santiago, Temuco, and Valdivia; and Inter Sur, tel. 42/258699, to Santiago.

Buses Jota Be, at Terminal María Teresa, tel. 42/272157, has at least seven buses daily to Salto del Laja and Los Ángeles, some continuing to Angol. Biotal, also at Terminal María Teresa, tel. 42/272162, goes to Los Ángeles, Concepción, and Talca. Cinta Azul, Constitución 85, tel. 42/212505, and at Terminal María Teresa, tel. 42/272158, goes to Concepción and Santiago.

Linea Azul, tel. 42/211192 at the Interregionales, goes twice daily to Termas de Chillán in summer, but the rest of the year goes only on weekends. For other rural and regional services, the Terminal Paseo La Merced is on Sargento Aldea, between Maipón and Arturo Prat, tel. 42/223606. REM Bus, tel. 42/224087, goes as far as Las Trancas, on the road to Termas de Chillán.

Typical destinations, fares, and times include Concepción or Los Ángeles (US$2.50, 1.5 hours), Angol or Talca (US$5, three hours), Temuco (US$7, five hours), Valdivia (US$8, six hours), Osorno (US$10, 7.5 hours), Puerto Montt (US$13, nine hours), Santiago (US$11, six hours), and Valparaíso/Viña del Mar (US$13, eight hours).

Train: EFE trains between Santiago and Temuco (two daily) and Santiago and Concepción (one daily) use the Estación de Ferrocarril on Avenida Brasil, tel. 42/222424, at the west end of Avenida Libertad.

Getting Around

For rental cars, try Jorge Ibáñez Méndez, 18 de Septiembre 380, tel. 42/212243.

VICINITY OF CHILLÁN

Parque Monumental Bernardo O'Higgins

In Chillán Viejo, only a few kilometers southwest of modern Chillán, the outstanding element in this park and museum complex is an impressive tiled mural—60 meters long—depicting scenes from the liberator's life. What works in an artistic context, though, doesn't work in the colonial-style **Centro Histórico y Cultural** itself, where the romanticized perspective is misleading—even if illegitimate, the viceroy's son was no rustic.

From December to March, the *centro,* tel. 42/223536, is open 8 A.M.–8 P.M. daily; the rest of the year, it's open 8 A.M.–6 P.M. Admission is free.

Termas de Chillán

Southeast of Chillán, campgrounds, *cabañas,* and country-style restaurants line much of the paved highway to **Valle Las Trancas,** where a gravel road continues through southern beech forests for the last few kilometers to Termas de Chillán, the only southern Chilean ski resort that can match Portillo and Valle Nevado in terms of luxury accommodations and snowfall—while not so far above sea level as its northern counterparts, it enjoys a climate with generally higher precipitation.

Beneath the slopes of the 3,122-meter Volcán Chillán, at a base elevation of 1,600 meters, Termas de Chillán's ski season extends from mid-June to mid-October. It is also a summer destination, though, thanks to its luxury lodgings and hot springs.

Termas de Chillán's 28 separate ski runs range from 90 to 700 meters in vertical drop, and from 400 to 2,500 meters in length. For nonguests, lift tickets cost US$26 pp. Day-use admission to Termas de Chillán's heated pools, open all year, costs US$17 pp for adults, US$13 for children; a full-day program including lunch costs US$35.

Accommodations and Food: For those who can't afford to stay at the extravagant Hotel Termas de Chillán or its slightly cheaper neighbor Pirigallo (see below), **Albergue Las Trancas,** tel. 42/243211 or 42/244628, website: www.valle-lastrancas.cl, j.bocaz@ctcinternetl.cl, has rooms with one to six beds starting at US$10 pp in low season and rising to only US$15 pp in ski season. Affiliated with Hostelling International, it's a bargain in this resort area, especially for a hostelry with natural wood decor throughout and a homey fireplace in its restaurant and bar.

Hotel Parador Jamón, Pan y Vino, at Km 74 in Las Trancas, tel./fax 42/242316, offers hotel and *cabaña* accommodations set among sprawling lawns surrounding a swimming pool and a wading pool. Rates are US$67 d. It also has good food.

Also at Las Trancas, in a quiet woodsy setting just off the main highway at Km 72, **Hotel Robledal,** tel. 42/214407, website: www.hotelrobledal.cl, hotelrobledal@hotmail.com, has fine midsized rooms in a building that, despite its prefab exterior, is stylish enough inside. Rates start at US$60 pp with half board in ski season, rather less in summer; the restaurant has very fine desserts, in particular.

In ski season, weekly accommodations at Termas de Chillán's luxury **Nuevo Hotel Pirigallo** start at US$600 pp, double occupancy with half board, reaching US$1,095 with half board; rates include lift tickets and other amenities. Weekly four-to-a-room bunk accommodations start at US$499–890 pp with half board, including lift tickets. At the even more sumptuous **Gran Hotel Termas de Chillán,** rates start at US$820–1565 pp.

In summer, hotel rates at the Pirigallo start at US$76 with full board, though bunk accommodations go for US$60 pp; the Gran Hotel starts at US$96 pp with breakfast. Centro de Ski Termas de Chillán has regional offices at Avenida Libertad 1042, Chillán, tel. 42/223887, fax 42/223576, ventachi@termachillan.cl; the Santiago offices are at Avenida Providencia 2237, Oficina P-41,

HEARTLAND

To Aeropuerto Internacional Carriel Sur and Talcahuano

LAS HERAS
CARRERAS
MAIPU
LOS
ANGOL
LINCOYAN
RENGO
CAUPOLICAN
ANIBAL
PINTO
COLO-COLO
CASTELLON
TUCAPEL

HOTEL CRUZ DEL SUR
TUR-BUS
CENTRO ITALIANO
SEE DETAIL

MERCADO CENTRAL
FREIRE
Plaza Independencia
SALA ANDES

ARTURO PRAT
IGNACIO SERRANO
MAIPU
FREIRE
ARANA
BARROS
O'HIGGINS

HOTEL CONCEPCIÓN
JULIO'S PIZZA
ITALIAN CONSULATE
CONAF
CHUNG-HWA
HOTEL EL DORADO
BANCO DE CRÉDITO/ATM
INSTITUTO CHILENO-BRITÁNICO
LAVERAP
HOTEL GERMANIA
HOTEL ALONSO DE ERCILLA

EL MEDIO TORO
CHORIPÁN
HOTEL CECIL
MEZCAL
TABLÓN
Plaza España
COMANCHE PUB
SANDUNGA
TREINTA Y TANTOS
EL OTRO PUERTO
EL RANCHO DE JULIO

HOTEL TERRANO
PORTAL CYBER-CAFÉ
ARGENTINE CONSULATE
INSTITUTO CHILENO-NORTEAMERICANO
LIBRERÍA INGLESA
HOTEL DELLA CRUZ
ECONOREN

ESTACIÓN DE FERROCARRIL
SAN MARTIN
HIPOLITO
IGNACIO SERRANO
SALAS
CHACABUCO
COCHRANE
RENGO
CYBERCAFÉ DOBLE CLICK
SALA LESSING
AVIS
COLO-COLO

GERMAN CONSULATE

P. DE VALDIVIA
VICTOR LAMAS
VETERANOS DEL 79
Ecuador
Parque

GALERÍA DE HISTORIA

BIO-BIO
ESMERALDA
To Coronel Lota, Angol, and Temuco
Cerro Caracol

RANCAGUA

GABRIELA MISTRAL

MOON

Río Biobío

DETAIL

FREIRE
FERIA ARTESANAL
RENGO
CAUPOLICAN
COLO-COLO

CHELA'S
HOTEL EL ARAUCANO/INTER-SANTIAGO
HOTEL RITZ
HOTEL BÍO BÍO

HOTEL ALBORADA
AFEX
CAFÉ HAITÍ
CENTRO ESPAÑOL
HOTEL SAN SEBASTIÁN
BARROS ARANA
CINE ROMANO

RESIDENCIAL METRO
ENTEL
LANCHILE/LANEXPRESS
FERROCARRILES DEL ESTADO
HOTEL MAQUEHUE
ANIBAL
PINTO
POST OFFICE
RINCÓN MARINO

IGLESIA CATEDRAL
Plaza Independencia
SERNATUR

RESIDENCIAL O'HIGGINS
FUENTE ALEMANA
O'HIGGINS
CINE CONCEPCIÓN

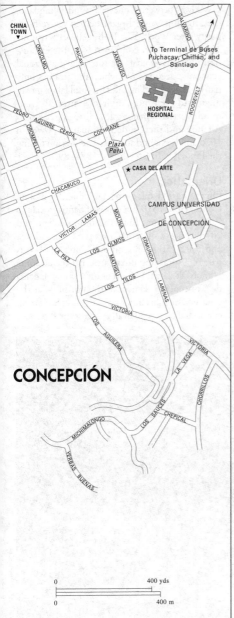

CHINA TOWN ▼

CONCEPCIÓN

HOSPITAL REGIONAL

To Terminal de Buses Puchacay, Chillán, and Santiago

Plaza Perú

★ CASA DEL ARTE

CAMPUS UNIVERSIDAD DE CONCEPCIÓN

0   400 yds
0   400 m

Providencia, tel. 2/2331313, fax 2/2315963, ventanac@termachillan.cl. Termas de Chillán also has a website: www.termaschillan.cl.

Transportation: Termas de Chillán is 82 km east of the city of Chillán. In summer only, the resort offers its own transportation for US$25 pp from the city. Linea Azul, at Chillán's Terminal de Buses Interregionales, tel. 42/211192, goes twice daily to Termas de Chillán in summer, but the rest of the year goes only on weekends.

CONCEPCIÓN

For much of its history, the capital of Region VIII (Biobío) has been Chile's industrial powerhouse, thanks to its navigable river, convenient coal resources, the Huachipato steel plant, and sheltered port of Talcahuano. Fishing and forestry contribute to the regional economy, and it is also a major educational center with 30,000 university students, but the economy has suffered in recent years with the closure of coal mining at nearby Lota. A hoped-for tourism boom has not yet taken hold.

Concepción's estimated population for 1998 was about 225,000, but with contiguous Talcahuano and San Pedro (across the Biobío), the metropolitan area exceeds half a million.

History

For more than three centuries from its founding in 1550, Concepción was a frontier city in a war zone. What Mapuche raiders could not destroy in the Guerra del Arauco, plate tectonics did—after major earthquakes and tsunamis in 1730 and 1751, the city moved to the Valle de la Mocha from its original site at Penco, about 12 km to the north (residents of Concepción are still known as *penquistas*).

Spaniards first saw the area in 1544, when Juan Bautista de Pastene and Jerónimo de Alderete sailed up the Biobío on the *San Pedro*. Pedro de Valdivia made it here in 1550, founding Concepción de María Purísima del Nuevo Extremo at the southeast corner of the Bahia de Concepción, a sheltered harbor formed by the Península de Tumbes.

HEARTLAND

The move to the Valle de la Mocha did not end the city's vulnerability to earthquakes, as its tiled adobe construction failed to meet seismic safety standards. When Darwin visited the city after a tsunami in 1835, he found:

> *the whole coast being strewed over with timber and furniture as if a thousand ships had been wrecked. Besides chairs, tables, book-shelves etc in great numbers, there were several roofs of cottages, which had been transported almost whole. The store-houses at Talcahuano had been burst open, and great bags of cotton, yerba, and other valuable merchandise were scattered on the shore.*

Concepción remained remote from the rest of Chile until the railroad reached the city in 1872, and by that time it had developed its own industrial base and identity, thanks partly to the presence of undersea lignite seams at nearby Lota. When the Mapuche wars finally ended in the 1880s, the railroad bridged the Biobío and the city became a gateway to the southern lake district.

Midway between Concepción and Talcahuano, the Huachipato steel plant helped revive prosperity after World War II, but the catastrophic 1960 earthquake, combined with the exhaustion of the Lota coal deposits, began a gradual economic decline from which the area has only partly recovered. The militant local labor movement and even more militant university community played a major role in bringing Salvador Allende and the Unidad Popular to power in 1970 and brought down heavy repression during the Pinochet dictatorship of 1973–89.

Orientation

On the north bank of the navigable Río Biobío, Concepción is 519 km south of Santiago via the Panamericana and Ruta 152 from Chillán, and 287 km north of Temuco via the Panamericana and Ruta 180 from Collipulli and Angol. It is part of a sprawling urban area that includes the port of Talcahuano, 15 km northwest on the Bahía de Concepción; Penco, to the northeast at the other end of Bahía de Concepción; and San Pedro, connected by several bridges across the Biobío.

section of Gregorio de la Fuente's mural "Latidos y Rutas de Concepción"

Plaza Independencia is the focus of Concepción's central grid, which trends northeast-southwest rather than north-south. Southeast of the plaza, Parque Ecuador and the 256-meter summit of Cerro Caracol mark the edge of the downtown area, while the riverfront to the southwest is the subject of ambitious redevelopment plans.

Sights

Concepción's repeated earthquakes have leveled nearly all its colonial remains—the last remaining one is the **Muro de la Merced,** a crumbling convent wall on Castellón between Maipú and Freire that's a national monument.

Surrounded by architecturally drab but seismically sensible buildings such as the **Catedral de la Santísima Concepción, Plaza Independencia** is still the heart of the city. Its centerpiece is the **Pileta de la Plaza,** a fountain originally planned in 1750 but unfinished until 1856. Lavishly landscaped, the plaza serves as a stage for mimes, musicians, and other street performers; the Barros Arana and Aníbal Pinto *peatonales* encourage foot traffic through the area.

Southwest of Plaza Independencia, where Barros Arana intersects Arturo Prat, the **Barrio Estación** is an area of trendy bars and restaurants around **Plaza España,** but whether its character will survive redevelopment is an open question. A new railroad station was due to replace the crumbling **Estación de Ferrocarril** (1941-43), notable for the columns on its facade, the work of modernist architect Luis Herreros. Its waiting room features Gregorio de la Fuente's spectacular mural *Latidos y Rutas de Concepción,* depicting scenes from pre-Hispanic regional history, the Araucanian wars, Chilean rural society, the mining industry, and its manufacturing offshoots. They also show the natural disasters—earthquakes, fires, and tsunamis—that have devastated the city throughout its history.

Northeast of downtown, in the vicinity of **Plaza Perú,** the **Barrio Universitario** enjoys a vigorous cultural and student life. On the campus of the Universidad de Concepción, at the corner of Chacabuco and Eduardo Larenas, the university's **Casa del Arte** art museum, tel. 41/204290, features Mexican muralist Jorge González Camarena's *La Presencia de América Latina,* along with smaller galleries of portraits and landscapes. It's open Tuesday to Friday 10 A.M.–6 P.M., Saturday 10 A.M.–4 P.M., and Sunday 10 A.M.–1 P.M. Admission is free.

Four blocks southeast of Plaza Independencia, **Parque Ecuador** stretches for nine blocks along Avenida Víctor Lamas; immediately behind it, the woodsy summit of Cerro Caracol offers views of the city. At the park's southwestern edge, at the corner of Lincoyán, the **Galería de la Historia** relates regional history through Rodolfo Gutiérrez's dioramas of pre-Columbian Mapuche subsistence and their post-Columbian guerrilla resistance, the garrison origins of Spanish colonial society at nearby Penco, negotiations between the indigenous nation and the invaders, Spanish soldier-poet Alonso de Ercilla, the catastrophic 1939 earthquake, and the city's 20th-century industrial development. Unchanged since its debut in the mid-1980s, the gallery, tel. 41/231830, is open weekdays 3–6:30 P.M., Tuesday through Friday 10 A.M.–1:30 P.M., and weekends 10 A.M.–2 P.M. and 3–7 P.M. Admission is free.

Accommodations

Concepción is short on budget accommodations, midrange places are fairly numerous but without any great bargains, and there are relatively few luxury options.

US$10–25: There are a few downtown *residenciales* at reasonable rates, such as **Residencial Metro,** in a vintage building at Barros Arana 464, tel. 41/225305, which charges US$8/14 s/d with breakfast. The aging **Residencial O'Higgins,** O'Higgins 457, tel. 41/228303, charges US$9 pp with breakfast. **Residencial Central,** Rengo 673, tel. 41/227309, costs US$11/20 s/d.

Improving along with the neighborhood, across from the railroad station, the 1938 landmark **Hotel Cecil,** Barros Arana 9, tel. 41/230677, santamariaclaramuntja001@chilnet.cl, charges US$17/25 s/d with private bath and breakfast.

US$25–50: At simple but renovated **Hotel Ritz,** near Plaza Independencia on the *peatonal* at Barros Arana 721, tel. 41/226696, fax 41/243249, ritz@ctcinternet.cl, rates are US$24/32 s/d with breakfast and private bath. Rates start from

US$26/35 s/d at **Hotel Maquehue,** Barros Arana 786, tel. 41/238348, fax 41/238350. **Hotel San Sebastián,** Rengo 463, tel./fax 41/243412, charges US$26/37 s/d.

On the pedestrian mall at Barros Arana 751, **Hotel Bío Bío,** tel./fax 41/228018, hotelbiobio001@chilnet.cl, occupies the upstairs interior of a gallery building; this means that some rooms of this older hotel are darkish, but they're also protected from street noise. Rates are US$25/32 for medium-sized "B" rooms with shared bath and breakfast, but "A" rooms with private bath are only slightly more expensive at US$30/41, even less with occasional discounts. There's one bargain single for US$21.

Hotel Germania, Aníbal Pinto 295, tel. 41/222555, fax 41/222550, charges US$41 s or d, while **Hotel El Dorado,** Barros Arana 348, tel. 41/229400, fax 41/231018, costs US$45/48 s/d. Cheerful but cramped **Hotel della Cruz,** Aníbal Pinto 240, tel./fax 41/240016, costs US$40/50 with breakfast, private bath, and convenient parking.

US$50–100: Downtown **Hotel El Araucano,** Caupolicán 521, tel. 41/740606, fax 41/740690, carrera.araucano@chilnet.cl, charges from US$47 s or d, and has nonsmoking rooms; rates include an airport pickup. Rates at **Hotel Alborada,** Barros Arana 457, tel./fax 41/242144, halborada@entelchile.net, start at US$50/60 s/d with a buffet breakfast.

Hotel Concepción, Serrano 512, tel. 41/2-28851, fax 41/230948, hotelconcepci001@chilnet.cl, costs US$37/53 s/d with breakfast. **Hotel Cruz del Sur,** Freire 889, tel. 41/230944, fax 41/235655, hotelcruzdels001@chilnet.cl, costs US$39/55 with breakfast.

Only a short stroll from the plaza, the modern **Hotel Alonso de Ercilla,** tel. 41/227984, fax 41/230053, website: www.hotelalonsodeercilla.co.cl, halonsoe@entelchile.net, charges US$45/63 s/d for comfortable but otherwise unimpressive rooms with private bath, breakfast, cable TV, covered parking, and good service. Smaller "B" singles cost about US$38.

Rates at business-oriented **Hotel Terrano,** O'Higgins 340, tel./fax 41/240078, hotelterrano001@chilnet.cl, start at US$59/71 with breakfast and amenities including telephone and cable TV, gym and sauna.

Food

For typical Chilean food such as *pastel de papas* and *pastel de choclo,* at bargain basement prices, try the sit-down *cocinerías* at the cavernous (3,600-square-meter) **Mercado Central,** fronting on Caupolicán, two blocks west of Plaza Independencia.

Only slightly more formal, the **Casino de Bomberos,** Salas 347, tel. 41/227535, is a reliable choice throughout the country. **Chela's,** Barros Arana 405, tel. 41/243367, also serves Chilean dishes such as *pastel de choclo,* as well as sandwiches and desserts.

The **Fuente Alemana,** O'Higgins 513, tel. 41/228307, is comparable to Chela's, but with a wider selection of kuchen and cold beer on tap. **Café Haití,** Caupolicán 511, Local 7, tel. 41/2-30755, also serves sandwiches, but it's the best choice for espresso drinks.

Concepción's Spanish and Italian communities have downtown club restaurants at the **Centro Español,** Barros Arana 675, tel. 41/230685, and the **Centro Italiano,** tel. 41/230724, Barros Arana 935, 2nd floor. Peruvian food isn't quite the rage in Concepción that it is in Santiago, but there is **El Otro Puerto,** Arturo Prat 430.

Julio's Pizza, Barros Arana 337, tel. 41/2-28207, can't match the Argentine pizza it claims to emulate, but the pasta, in the US$6 range, is above average. Under the same ownership, **El Rancho de Julio,** O'Higgins 36, tel. 41/239976, comes closer to the Argentine experience in ambience and quality—the beef dishes are well worth a try if pricier than at most of its competitors. **Rincón Marino,** Colo Colo 486, tel. 41/230311, is a seafood locale where beef, though available, is secondary.

There's a pair of long-lived downtown *chifas:* **Chung-Hwa,** Barros Arana 262, tel. 41/229539, and **China Town,** Barros Arana 1115, tel. 41/233218.

Entertainment

Bars: Until redevelopment overwhelms it, one hopes at least a few years down the line, the Barrio Estación around Plaza España should continue to be Concepción's liveliest neighborhood. **30 y Tantos,** Arturo Prat 402, tel. 41/251516, is lively even on weeknights, with informal, eclectic decor—note the Three Stooges photo gallery—and recorded music. There are also 21 varieties of fried empanadas, the only item on the food menu, for US$1.50 each.

Also on the southeast side of the Plaza España are **Sandunga,** Prat 438, tel. 41/240232, and the **Comanche Pub,** Prat 442, tel. 41/238429. On the opposite side of the plaza, northwest of Barros Arana, are **Tablón,** Prat 528; **Mezcal,** Prat 532; **Choripán,** Prat 546; and **El Medio Toro,** Prat 592, tel. 41/247365, which serves pizza and has live rock music.

Cinema: The downtown movie theater **Cine Concepción,** O'Higgins 650, tel. 41/227193, also hosts live performances. **Cine Romano** is at Barros Arana 780, tel. 41/227364.

Several binational cultural centers still sometimes show films: the **Instituto Chileno-Norteamericano,** Caupolicán 315, tel. 41/225506; the **Instituto Chileno-Británico,** San Martín 531, tel. 41/242300; the **Instituto Chileno-Alemán,** Chacabuco 840, tel. 41/229287; and the **Instituto Chileno-Español,** San Martín 450, 2nd floor, tel. 41/244573.

Performing Arts: The downtown **Teatro Concepción,** O'Higgins 650, tel. 41/227193, hosts live theater and music as well as movies. Other venues include the **Sala Andes,** Tucapel 374, tel. 41/227264; the Instituto Chileno-Alemán's **Sala Lessing,** Chacabuco 840, tel. 41/229287, and the **Casa del Arte** at Chacabuco and Larenas in the Barrio Universitario, tel. 41/234985.

Spectator Sports: Concepción's professional soccer team offices are at Colo Colo 486, tel. 41/242684. Games are held at **Estadio Collao,** on Avenida General Bonilla near the Terminal de Buses Collao (Puchacay).

Events

Lasting two weeks in mid-January, Parque Ecuador's **Feria Internacional de Arte Popular** (International People's Art Festival) has drawn artists and artisans from as far away as Russia, Egypt, and Senegal. In early October, the week-

long **Fiesta de la Primavera** (Festival of Spring) celebrates the city's founding in 1550.

Shopping

For handicrafts, from basketry and ceramics to woolen goods and leather, try the **Mercado Central,** fronting on Caupolicán between Maipú and Freire, or the **Feria Artesanal** at Freire 757.

Services

Money: Downtown exchange houses include Afex at Barros Arana 565, Local 57, and Inter-Santiago, Caupolicán 521, Local 58. Several downtown banks have ATMs, such as Banco de Crédito at O'Higgins 399.

Postal: Correos de Chile is at O'Higgins 799.

Telephone and Internet: Entel is at Barros Arana 541, Local 2. Concepción's area code is 41.

Concepción has several Internet outlets, mostly north and east of the Plaza de Armas, charging in the US$1.50–2 range per hour. They include Portal Cyber-Café, San Martín 420, tel. 41/523817, and Ciberc@fe Doble Click, Chacabuco 707, tel. 41/210458.

Laundry: Laverap is at Caupolicán 334.

Medical: The Hospital Regional is at San Martín and Avenida Roosevelt, tel. 41/237445, eight blocks northeast of Plaza Independencia.

Information

Tourist Office: Sernatur has its upgraded regional office at Aníbal Pinto 460, tel. 41/227976, serna08@entelchile.net. In summer, it's open 8:30 A.M.–8 P.M. daily; otherwise, hours are 8:30 A.M.–1 P.M. and 3–5:30 P.M. weekdays only.

Consulates: Concepción has several foreign consulates, most notably neighboring Argentina at San Martín 472, 5th floor, Departamento 52, tel. 41/230257. Germany is at Chacabuco 556, tel. 242591; Italy at Barros Arana 243, 2nd floor, tel. 41/229506; and Spain at Barros Arana 675, tel. 41/224249.

Motorists: The Automóvil Club de Chile (Acchi), Freire 1867, tel. 41/311968, can help with information.

Bookstores: Librería Inglesa, in the Edificio Los Arrayanes on San Martín between Rengo and Caupolicán, sells English-language titles. Other bookshops include Librería Manantial, O'Higgins 680, tel. 41/223614.

National Parks: Conaf is at Barros Arana 215, tel. 41/220094, though Region VIII has few parks or reserves—the closest are the very small Monumento Natural Contulmo and Parque Nacional Nahuelbuta, the latter administered out of Temuco though part of it is in Region VIII.

Transportation

Air: Aeropuerto Internacional Carriel Sur is five km northwest of downtown on the road to Talcahuano.

LanChile/LanExpress is at Barros Arana 600, tel. 41/248824; it averages three to four flights per day to Santiago. It also flies Friday and Sunday to Temuco and Puerto Montt, twice daily to Valdivia, and daily except Friday and Saturday to Puerto Montt.

Aerocontinente, Barros Arana 544, tel. 41/523200, flies daily except Saturday to Santiago (US$59–99) and to Temuco.

Bus: Most long-distance buses use the Terminal de Buses Collao, Tegualda 860, tel. 41/316666, near the soccer stadium on Avenida General Bonilla (Ruta 148), the toll road to Chillán; unless otherwise detailed, buses leave from this terminal, which is also known as Terminal Puchacay. Some carriers use the Terminal Chillancito at Camilo Henríquez 2565, tel. 41/315036, the northward extension of Bulnes. All companies except for Tur-Bus have closed their downtown ticket offices.

Tur-Bus has a downtown ticket office at Tucapel 530, tel. 41/237409; it is also at Terminal Chillancito, tel. 41/315555, and at Terminal Collao, tel. 41/316989. Tur-Bus has 16 daily departures for Santiago, five to Valparaíso/Viña del Mar, and it also goes southbound on the Panamericana to Temuco (six daily), Valdivia (five daily), and Puerto Montt (six daily).

Other Santiago carriers include Sol del Pacífico, tel. 41/314366 (nine daily); Estrella del Sur, tel. 41/321383 (five daily via Talca); Sol del Sur, tel. 41/313841 (three daily); Buses Lit, tel. 41/313652 (two daily); and Tas Choapa, tel. 41/312639 (two daily). Sol del Pacífico's Santiago buses all continue to Valparaíso/Viña; two others, at 7:30 A.M. and 4 P.M., bypass Santiago.

Igi Llaima, tel. 41/312498, goes seven times daily to Temuco and Puerto Montt, while Cruz del Sur, tel. 41/314372, goes five times. Igi Llaima and Cruz del Sur also go to Valdivia.

Buses Biobío, tel. 41/310764, has 15 buses daily to Temuco via Los Ángeles and 13 to Angol; Jota Be, tel. 41/312652, has 19 buses daily to Los Ángeles, Igi Llaima another 10. Línea Azul, tel. 41/311126, goes to Chillán every 20 minutes from 6:40 A.M.–9:40 P.M.

Destinations, fares, and times include Chillán or Los Ángeles (US$2.50–3, 1.5 hours), Angol (US$3–4, two hours), Talca (US$6, four hours), Temuco (US$6–7, four hours), Valdivia (US$9–11, six hours), Puerto Montt (US$13– 16, seven hours), Santiago (US$9–12, seven hours), and Valparaíso/Viña del Mar (US$12– 14, nine hours).

In addition to the long-distance terminals, there are two for regional buses. From the Terminal Costa Azul, Las Heras 530, tel. 41/237562, northbound buses go to the beach towns of Tomé, Dichato, and Cobquecura. From Terminal Jota Ewert, at Lincoyán and Manuel Rodríguez, tel. 41/229212, southbound buses go to the Costa del Carbón cities of Arauco, Lebu, Cañete, Tirúa, and Contulmo.

Train: For the time being, EFE trains to Chillán and Santiago leave from the aging Estación de Ferrocarril, on Arturo Prat at the end of Barros Arana, tel. 41/227777, but it was due to move northwest as the present building is redeveloped for regional government offices. EFE also has a Venta de Pasajes (ticket office) at Aníbal Pinto 478, Local 3, tel. 41/225286. Trains leave nightly at 10 P.M. Fares are US$13 *salón,* US$22 *cama alta,* and US$27 *cama baja.*

Getting Around

To the Airport: Airport Service, tel. 41/239371, provides door-to-door service to Carriel Sur for about US$3.50 pp.

To the Bus Terminal: From downtown Concepción, both buses and *taxi colectivos* go to Terminal Collao (Puchacay) via Calle San Martín; to Terminal Chillancito, they leave from the corner of Maipú and Rengo.

Car Rental: Econorent is at Castellón 134, tel. 41/225377, fax 41/245550, ecorent@chilesat.net;

it also has an airport office, tel. 41/481212. The Automóvil Club de Chile (Acchi) is at Freire 1867, tel. 41/317111, while Avis is at Chacabuco 726, tel. 41/235837.

VICINITY OF CONCEPCIÓN

Concepción is not a hotbed of tourism, but most nearby attractions are accessible by public transportation.

Altaluz Turismo, San Martín 586, 2nd floor, tel. 41/217727 or 09/8345763, does offer tours in and around the city. **South Expediciones,** Gesswein 44, tel. 09/7197690, operates adventure travel excursions like river rafting, mountain biking, and horseback riding.

Talcahuano

Only 15 km northwest of Concepción, Talcahuano is the city's main port and the site of the Segunda Zona Naval, one of Chile's largest naval bases. For Chilean nationalists, it's the site of the **Museo Huáscar,** a floating museum dedicated to naval icon Arturo Prat.

In his assault in Iquique harbor on May 21, 1879, Prat died on board the *Huáscar,* a British-built ironclad, captured from the Peruvian navy at the battle of Angamos less than three weeks later. Today, anchored in Talcahuano harbor, *Huáscar* is the mummy of maritime museums, a monument on which naval conscripts, under their officers' stifling supervision, bestow the same attention that Soviet morticians did on Lenin's cadaver.

From Calle San Martín in downtown Concepción, buses with "Base Naval" placards go to the Puerta los Leones gate at the end of Avenida Villaroel. You leave your passport at the gate; small launches shuttle from the jetty to the ship. Photographing the *Huáscar* is permitted, but not other naval ships or the base itself. The museum, tel. 41/505016, is open 9:30 A.M.–12:30 P.M. and 1:30–7:30 P.M. daily except Monday. Admission is US$1 for adults, US$.65 for children.

Museo Fundo Hualpén (Parque Pedro del Río Zañartu)

At the mouth of the Biobío, 18 km west of Concepción, businessman, farmer, whaler, nitrate baron, and writer Pedro del Río Zañartu (1840–1918) inhabited this late 19th-century mansion, set among extensive grounds planted with native and foreign trees and crisscrossed by numerous footpaths (Del Río stipulated in his will that no tree be removed, only pruned).

A chronic globetrotter, Del Río circled the world four times before his death, when he left his travel mementos—not to mention Hualpén and its grounds—to the city of Concepción. Opened to the public as a museum in 1938, it remains partly as it did when Del Río lived here, with information on his voyages and family history, plus bedrooms, a dining room, and a music conservatory with period furniture. Visibly warping because of deferred maintenance, the house encloses a central patio, but a sunny east- and north-facing gallery runs around part of the exterior.

In addition, several exhibit rooms show off his eclectic assortment of artifacts from Europe, the Near East, ancient Egypt (including a mummy), the Far East, Chile, and Easter Island, along with 18th-century weapons, religious icons, and materials on American ethnology, history, and folklore. The grounds extend to the coast, where there's a small island and several guano-covered rocks.

Museo Hualpén, tel. 41/225916, is open daily except Monday 10 A.M.–1 P.M. and 2–7 P.M. in summer, 9 A.M.–1 P.M. and 2–6 P.M. the rest of the year. Museum and park admission are free, but vehicles pay US$2.50 for parking.
Food: At the mouth of the river, the **Casino Club de Caza y Pesca,** tel. 09/4420921 or 09/8282737, offers ample, simply prepared fish dishes in the US$5 range. The club, too, is part of Del Río's legacy—the area was to be left open for hunting and fishing, though there can't be much game left on the periphery of an urban area of more than half a million people.
Transportation: No regular public transportation reaches Hualpén, though city buses from downtown Concepción to Avenida Las Golondrinas go within a few kilometers of the entrance. A cab is probably the best alternative.

Lota

Across the Biobío from Concepción, the lignite seams of Lota have given their cachet to the Costa del Carbón (Coast of Coal), a string of towns that once relied on this surprisingly rare fossil fuel for their livelihood (in the entire Southern Cone, the only other coal deposits are at Peket, near Punta Arenas, and Río Turbio, in the Argentine province of Santa Cruz). Today, undergoing a difficult transition from an entrenched mining culture, this is one of Chile's most economically depressed areas—unemployment exceeds 20 percent, and nearly half live below the poverty line.

Nevertheless, the coast is a popular weekend destination for working-class beachgoers. For foreign visitors, the towns of Coronel and Lota, with their company town architecture, the sloping coal shafts of Mina Chiflón, the Central Chivilingo hydroelectric plant, and the remarkable Parque de Lota are the major points of interest. Lota has its own informative website: www.lotasorprendente.cl.

Parque de Lota Isidora Cousiño: In the mid-19th century at Lota, 30 km south of Concepción, mining magnate Matías Cousiño began to transform a 14-hectare headland into a lavish garden that his daughter-in-law Isidora Goyenechea would finally complete after the deaths of both her father-in-law and his son Luis Cousiño. British landscapers designed the flowered and wooded grounds, still flourishing almost alongside mounds of coal slag, and studded them with neoclassical statues of figures such as Neptune, Venus, and Diana the Huntress, plus, incongruously, the Mapuche warrior Caupolicán. The tomb of Matías Cousiño's son (and Luis's brother) Carlos Cousiño is also here.

One of the biggest attractions in the vicinity of Concepción, Parque Cousiño, Avenida del Parque s/n, tel. 41/871549, fchlota@chilesat.net, is open 9 A.M.–8 P.M. daily. Now operated by the private Fundación Chile, it charges US$2.50 pp admission for adults, US$1.50 for kids. Guides in 19th-century dress, known as Isidoras after the matriarch of the founding family, lead tours around the park.

Mina Chiflón Carlos: Adjacent to Parque de Lota, Mina Chiflón Carlos offers the opportunity to descend into the pits beneath the sea as local miners once did. Guided by former miners themselves, visits (US$6 pp) take place 9 A.M.–8 P.M. daily from November to March, 9 A.M.–6 P.M. the rest of the year. For more information, contact Mina Chiflón Carlos, El Morro, Barrio Arturo, tel. 41/871565 or 41/871008.

Central Chivilingo

About 12 km south of Lota, a gravel road climbs east up the valley of the Río Chivilingo to Chile's earliest hydroelectric plant (1897), a national monument reported to have been designed by Thomas Alva Edison. Built by the Compañía Explotadora de Lota y Coronel, successor to the Sociedad Cousiño e Hijos, it featured two Pelton wheels with 250-kw alternators; a 10-km line transmitted the power to Lota, where various substations redistributed it to various installations, including the rails that ran beneath the sea. The station also provided power to the city of Lota until 1975, when it became too expensive to operate.

Sturdy enough to withstand the massive 1960 earthquake, Central Chivilingo is also the site of the interactive **Museo Big Bang,** specifically designed as a tourist attraction (admission US$1.50 pp). There is also a 100-site campground here; rates run about US$12 per site.

Cañete

About 97 km south of Lota via Ruta 150, Cañete is the site of the improved **Museo Mapuche de Cañete Juan Antonio Ríos Morales,** which provides a good cartographic introduction to the region's indigenous geography, along with displays on subsistence activities, mortuary customs, and silverwork and other art. Directly on the highway, the museum, tel. 41/611093, is open Tuesday to Friday 9:30 A.M.–12:30 P.M. and 2–6:30 P.M., Saturday 10 A.M.–12:30 P.M. and 2–6:30 P.M., and Sunday 1:30–6:30 P.M. Admission costs US$1 for adults, US$.50 for kids or retired people.

Monumento Natural Contulmo

One of Conaf's smallest protected areas, 38 km southeast of Cañete, the native forest of Contulmo occupies 82 hectares of a rugged southerly spur of the Cordillera de Nahuelbuta, directly contiguous to the paved highway to Angol. Barely half a kilometer across at its widest, it still boasts a 3.2-km loop trail through verdant moist forest (the park gets nearly two meters rainfall per annum), punctuated with tree ferns whose individual fronds reach two meters or more in height. Contulmo has an information center and a picnic ground, but no camping; there is an admission fee of US$1.50 pp for adults, US$.50 for children.

LOS ÁNGELES

A farm-and-factory town with few attractions in its own right, the city of Los Ángeles is strategically located for access to the coast range, the upper Biobío, and Parque Nacional Laguna del Laja, in the Andes to the east. It was also strategically located when, in 1739, it was founded as a military outpost against the Mapuche.

Less than a decade later, in 1748, it received official recognition from Chilean governor José Antonio Manso de Velasco as Villa de Nuestra Señora de Los Ángeles de la Alta Frontera del Reino de Chile. The city began to prosper in 1875 with arrival of the railroad, but it has a distinct contemporary aspect, as the major public buildings date from the 1940s.

Orientation

Los Ángeles is a medium-sized town with a compact commercial center, 517 km south of Santiago and 110 km south of Chillán via the Panamericana; it is 162 km north of Temuco, also via the Panamericana.

Most major public buildings are on and around the Plaza de Armas, which was undergoing renovation and which is bounded by Lautaro, Valdivia, Caupolicán, and Colón. Most businesses and services are on or near Colón, from the plaza north.

Sights

The municipal **Museo de la Alta Frontera** is mediocre but for an exceptional assortment of traditional Mapuche silverwork—unfortunately, it lacks space to display all 600 pieces in the collection, and the lack of accompanying text makes it seem more like a jewelry store before the price tags have been affixed.

At Colón 195, 2nd floor, the museum, tel. 43/409400, is open 8 A.M.–1 P.M. and 2:30–8 P.M. weekdays, 8 A.M.–1 P.M. and 5–8 P.M. Saturday, and 10 A.M.–1 P.M. and 5–8 P.M. Sunday. Admission is free.

Accommodations

The deco-style **Hotel de Turismo Winner,** Rengo 138, tel. 43/343040, charges US$9 pp for sensory deprivation cells, US$12 for slightly larger rooms with far better natural light, both with shared bath; rates for substantially larger rooms with private bath are US$26 s or d.

Hotel Residencial Diego de Almagro, Almagro 393, tel./fax 43/310927, offers simple economy rooms for US$9 pp with shared bath; those with private bath go for US$20/33 s/d, but the staff seem lethargic and it's nothing special, only adequate.

Under new ownership, **Hotel Océano,** Colo Colo 327, tel. 43/322432, charges US$12 pp with shared bath and breakfast, US$17/25 s/d with private bath. **Hotel de Villena,** Lautaro 579, tel. 43/321643, charges US$15/20 with private bath and breakfast.

On the west side of the Plaza de Armas, **Gran Hotel Muso,** Valdivia 222, tel. 43/313183, charges US$43/57. Just off the plaza, **Hotel Mariscal Alcázar,** Lautaro 385, tel. 43/311725, has older but spacious "A" rooms with private bath (including tubs) and breakfast for US$43/54; smaller but newer VIP rooms, facing the interior garden, go for US$49/63.

Food

Café Prymos, Colón 400, tel. 43/323731, serves exceptional breakfasts and sandwiches and also has outstanding ice cream. The **Casino Cuerpo de Bomberos,** two blocks south of the plaza at O'Higgins 119, is almost always a good bet for reasonable lunches and dinners.

The chain restaurant **Bavaria,** Colón 357, tel. 43/315531, serves sandwiches and standard Chilean dishes. **Cafeteros,** Colo Colo 458, is for serious coffee drinkers, the only reliable place for espresso.

Julio's Pizza, Colón 452, tel. 43/314530, serves pasta as well. The **Centro Español,** Colón

482, tel. 43/311669, is a traditional club-style restaurant. Likewise, the **Club de la Unión,** Colón 261, tel. 43/322218, has prix-fixe lunches and dinners for US$5.

El Alero, Colo Colo 235, tel. 43/312899, is a *parrilla,* while **Su Rodeo,** Colo Colo 555, is a new Chilean venue. **Donde Anitamaría,** Colón 782, tel. 43/315812, specializes in seafood.

Entertainment

The **Cine Star,** on Colo Colo between Valdivia and Colón, is the local movie house. The *parrilla* **Dónde Ramón,** on Colón between Janequeo and Lincoyán, is also a *peña.*

Services

Money: Afex, Caupolicán 350, is the only exchange house. Banco de Chile has an ATM at Colón 299, Banco BHIF at Colón 492.

Postal: Correos de Chile is on Caupolicán, on the south side of the Plaza de Armas.

Telephone and Internet: Telefónica long-distance offices are at the bus terminal. Entel is at Colo Colo 489, Local 1, and at Avenida Alemania 320, where it also offers Internet access. Los Ángeles's area code is 43.

Laundry: Lavaseco Las Novedades is at Lautaro 551, tel. 43/321098.

Medical: The Hospital Regional is at Avenida Ricardo Vicuña 147, tel. 43/321456 or 43/409720.

Information

Tourist Office: The Municipalidad operates an Oficina de Información Turística, tel. 43/340161, on the second floor of the museum at the corner of Caupolicán and Colón, open weekdays only. Neither it nor the private office on Caupolicán, alongside the post office on the south side of the plaza, is particularly well-prepared.

Motorists: The Automóvil Club de Chile (Acchi) is at Caupolicán 201, tel. 43/314209.

National Parks: Conaf is at José Manso de Velasco 275, tel. 43/322126.

Transportation

Most long-distance buses depart from the modern Terminal Santa María, Avenida Sor Vicente 2051, northeast of downtown via Avenida Villagrán. Tur-Bus, though, has its own terminal at Avenida Sor Vicenta 2061, tel. 43/315610, for Santiago, Chiloé, and intermediates. Its affiliate Cóndor Bus is slightly cheaper.

Other carriers with north-south services along the Panamericana include Biotal, tel. 43/317357; Cruz del Sur, tel. 43/317630; Intersur; Buses Jac, tel. 43/317469, which also goes to Villarrica and Pucón; Sol del Pacífico, to Santiago and Valparaíso; Tas Choapa, tel. 43/322266; and Unión del Sur, tel. 43/363045.

Buses Jota Be, tel. 43/363037, has numerous buses to Angol, the gateway to Parque Nacional Nahuelbuta, and to Chillán. There are frequent services between Los Ángeles and Concepción with Buses Biobío, tel. 43/363044, which also goes to Angol, Curacautín, and Temuco; Igi Llaima, tel. 43/321666; and Los Alces.

From Terminal Santa Rita, at Villagrán and Rengo, ERS goes to Antuco, near the entrance to Parque Nacional Laguna del Laja, seven times daily on weekends, three times each weekday. Other rural services leave from the Terminal Vega Techada, at the corner of Villagrán and Tucapel.

Sample destinations, fares, and times include Angol (US$1.50, one hour), Chillán (US$2.50, 1.5 hours), Temuco (US$4, four hours), Puerto Montt (US$10, eight hours), and Santiago (US$10, eight hours).

Getting Around

First Rent-a-Car is at Caupolicán 350, tel. 43/313812, in the Inter-Bruna travel agency. Oregón Rent a Car is at Colón 431, Oficina 201, tel. 43/314218.

VICINITY OF LOS ÁNGELES

Los Ángeles is centrally located for excursions to several protected areas, including Parque Nacional Laguna del Laja and Parque Nacional Nahuelbuta (though the latter is closer to Angol). The waterfall at Salto del Laja is a traditional Chilean holiday destination, while a couple of rural accommodations are destinations in themselves.

German-run El Rincón (see below) does tours in and around the area.

El Rincón

On two hectares of secluded riverside property 15 km north of Los Ángeles, El Rincón is not so much a place to stay as a destination in itself, where guests remain several days to relax among densely wooded grounds with vegetable and flower gardens. At night the only sound is the wind in the trees, but on some weekends roaring dirt bikes break the peace in a nearby quarry that they have appropriated for their "sport."

B&B costs US$17 pp in four cozy double rooms with private bath and natural wood in the main accommodations; there is one single with private bath. In a separate house, there are rooms with shared bath for US$14 pp with an abundant breakfast. Breakfast, lunch (US$10 pp), and dinner (also US$10 pp) all take place on the patio or in the dining room of the main house, where there's a large German-language library and a smaller book exchange (mostly in English). The food is both diverse and filling, and the wine is reasonably priced.

El Rincón, tel. 09/4415019, fax 43/317168, elrincon@cvmail.cl, has its own marked exit at Km 494 of the Panamericana north of Los Ángeles. It is a couple of kilometers farther east via a gravel road and a private dirt road, but owners Winfried and Elke Lohmar will pick up passengers at the highway, or in Los Ángeles, by arrangement. English, Spanish, and German are spoken.

The Lohmars also arrange horseback riding for US$4.50 per hour, with lessons available for US$8 per hour; Spanish lessons cost US$350 weekly pp, minimum two people, with room and full board; there is a US$120 single supplement. They also offer full-day excursions to Parque Nacional Laguna del Laja, Parque Nacional Nahuelbuta, and Concepción and vicinity. Ask for copies of their excellent informational brochures on the geology of Laguna del Laja and Nahuelbuta, available in Spanish, English, and German.

Salto del Laja

With its kitschy clutter of campgrounds, *cabañas*, hotels, and souvenir stands, the 50-meter waterfall of Salto del Laja is Chile's miniature counterpart to Niagara Falls. After descending from the Andes, the Río Laja drops more than 50 meters over a broad escarpment before flowing on toward its confluence with the Biobío at La Laja, 40 km to the west. Like Niagara, though, Salto del Laja is also vulnerable to irregular releases from reservoirs in its upper drainage, and power needs may or may not coincide with tourists' desire to view the spectacle. In dry years, the flow can slow to a trickle.

One positive development is the relocation of the Panamericana, now a four-lane divided toll road, to the west. No longer do long-distance buses, overloaded 18-wheelers, and speeding SUVs clog the former Panamericana, a two-lane road that bridges the river—though walking in the middle of it is still inadvisable.

At the falls themselves, B&B accommodations options include **Hotel Los Manantiales,** tel./fax 43/314275, for US$32/40 s/d, and **Hostería Salto del Laja,** tel. 43/321706, fax 43/313996, for US$58/70. Both also have campgrounds, and Hotel Los Manantiales has official Hostelling International accommodations for US$10 pp.

Fundo Curanilahue

Part of a growing trend toward rural tourism, this Anglo-Chilean *fundo* is a 500-hectare unit that specializes in wheat and sugar beets, but it also raises beef and dairy cattle, and alfalfa to feed them. While it's not a dude ranch in the North American sense—guests are not expected to participate in farm activities—it does offer garden *cabañas* with fireplaces and private bath, and diverse recreational options both on and off the *fundo.*

From mid-November to mid-March, accommodations cost US$150 pp with full board, including wine, aperitifs, beer, and soft drinks; the rest of the year, rates are US$130 pp. Most of the food comes from the *fundo's* own organic gardens. Also included in the basic rates are horseback riding through plantations of pine and eucalyptus, swimming in the heated pool, access to tennis, laundry service, and motorboat excursions up the Río Laja.

In addition, Curanilahue also arranges excursions into the Andean backcountry and the coast range, including day trips to Parque Nacional Laguna del Laja, Parque Nacional Nahuelbuta, or

Termas de Chillán (US$100 per group), and the Laja Golf Club or the Chillán market (US$50). Transfers to or from the Concepción airport cost US$50, to or from Temuco airport US$100.

Reached by a turnoff from the Panamericana a few kilometers north of Salto del Laja and a gravel road that leads east from the Carabineros police station through the hamlet of Chillancito, Fundo Curanilahue is open all year, but reservations are essential. For more information, contact John or Louisa Jackson at Fundo Curanilahue, Casilla 1165, Los Ángeles, tel. 43/1972819, fax 43/1-972829, ljackson@curanilahue.com, jackson-may@entelchile.net. There is also a website: www.curanilahue.com.

PARQUE NACIONAL LAGUNA DEL LAJA

Barren can be beautiful and the volcanic landscape of Laguna del Laja is the proof. The park's centerpiece Volcán Antuco is actually a volcano within a volcano, rising from the caldera that exploded cataclysmically about 6,000 years ago. Though its last eruption was nearly 90 years ago, Antuco was once one of Chile's most active volcanoes, with 11 separate episodes in the 19th century—when Darwin visited Concepción a couple of weeks after the calamitous earthquake and tsunami of 1835, he observed that locals had, in their own way, inferred a cause-and-effect relationship between that event and Antuco's relative silence:

> *The lower orders in Talcahuano thought that the earthquake was caused by some old Indian women, who two years ago being offended stopped the volcano of Antuco. This silly belief is curious, because it shows that experience has taught them to observe, that there exists a relation between the suppressed action of the volcanoes, and the trembling of the ground. It was necessary to apply the witchcraft to the point where their perception of cause and effect failed.*

Whatever its role in this and other earthquakes, over the past 130,000 years Antuco's avalanches and its basaltic lava flows helped form Laguna del

waterfalls on the Río Laja, Parque Nacional Laguna del Laja

Laja and have, at various times, raised and lowered its surface level. There is still weak fumarole activity in the crater, but no indication of a major eruption any time in the near future.

The highway from Los Ángeles to Laguna del Laja now continues to the border at 2,062-meter Paso Pichachén and the Argentine town of Chos Malal, but it is open in summer only. Parts of the route can be tricky for vehicles with low clearance during the spring runoff—in one spot, the road goes right through the channel of the Río de los Pinos.

Geography and Climate

In the upper Río Laja basin, 96 km east of Los Ángeles, the 11,600-hectare park takes its name from Laguna del Laja, a natural lake transformed by hydroelectric development. It ranges in altitude from 976 meters in its western precordillera to 2,985 meters on Antuco's conical summit. To the southwest, but beyond the park boundaries, the glacial Sierra Velluda reaches even greater heights.

In winter, enough snow accumulates to support a ski season from June to October. Summer is dry, especially late in the season on the Antuco circuit, so hikers must carry plenty of water.

Flora and Fauna

The slopes of Volcán Antuco and the shores of Laguna del Laja are almost completely barren except for some pioneer grasses and shrubs, but coniferous forests of mountain cypress (*Austrocedrus chilensis*) and monkey puzzle tree (*Araucaria araucana*) cover parts of the well-watered precordillera. The most conspicuous fauna are the nearly 50 bird species, most notably the Andean condor, but there are also vizcachas, pumas, and some smaller cats.

Sights

At Sector Chacay, from a parking area just off the main road near Conaf's Centro de Información Ambiental, a short hike leads to **Salto Chilcas,** which topples in multiple falls over a basalt flow into Río Laja gorge; reached by a spur off the main trail, the **Salto de Torbellino** is a smaller and shorter but thunderous cascade from a tributary creek. When the sun is out, Torbellino usually sports a rainbow.

For more ambitious hikers, a three-day **Volcán Antuco** circuit from Chacay offers views of the Laguna del Laja, the Sierra Velluda, and the opportunity to climb the summit itself. The last part of the circuit returns along the road back to Chacay, so it may be possible to catch a lift back to the park entrance or even Los Ángeles.

Accommodations and Food

Within the park proper, the only option is Conaf's **Camping y Cabañas Lagunillas,** tel. 43/322126 in Los Ángeles. Wooded campsites here cost US$8.50 with running water, hot showers, and electricity, while three-bedroom A-frame *cabañas* with kitchen facilities cost US$42 for up to six people.

In wintertime, for skiers, Concepción's Dirección General de Deportes y Recreación operates the 50-bed **Refugio Digeder** at the Volcán Antuco ski area. Besides hostel accommodations, it offers meals and rental equipment. For reservations, contact Digeder, O'Higgins 740, Oficina 23, Concepción, tel. 41/226797.

At Abanico, only five km from the park entrance and 12 km from the lake, the simple but appealing **Hostería El Bosque,** tel. 43/372719, delivers more than its modest prices—US$6 pp for lodging only, US$12 with half board, US$15 with full board—would suggest. On attractive grounds, with hospitable owners and a small swimming pool, it's one of the region's best values. In fact, it's a better choice than the nearby and more expensive—US$14 pp—eight-room **Hotel Malalcura,** tel. 43/372720, fax 43/312768, which does boast both larger grounds and a larger pool.

For food, the ski area's **Casino Club de Ski Los Ángeles,** open all year, is marginal at best. Supplies are cheaper and more diverse in Los Ángeles than in either Antuco or El Abanico.

Information

Conaf's Centro de Información Ambiental at Chacay, 11 km east of Abanico, is rarely open. Conaf does, however, collect a US$1.50 admission fee pp at the park gates, five km east of Abanico.

Transportation

From Los Ángeles' Terminal Santa Rita, at Rengo and Villagrán, ERS buses go five times daily to El Abanico (US$1.70, 1.5 hours) via Antuco. Departure times are 11:30 A.M. and 1:30, 2:45, 5:30 and 7:15 P.M. daily except Sunday, when departures are at 11:30 A.M. and 1:30 and 7:15 P.M. only.

From El Abanico, there's no public transportation for the five km uphill to the park entrance; the park office is six km farther.

ANGOL

A veritable frontier fortress, Angol de los Confines suffered devastation at least six times during the three-century Guerra del Arauco before outlasting the tenacious Mapuche in the late 19th century. Now known for its annual folklore festival and kitschy knicknacks created by local ceramicists, it's the main access point for the coast range's Parque Nacional Nahuelbuta, with extensive *Araucaria* (monkey puzzle) forests.

Orientation

Between the Panamericana and the Cordillera de Nahuelbuta, Angol belongs politically to Region IX (Araucanía), but is most easily accessible from Los Ángeles, 60 km to the northeast; it is 608 km south of Santiago.

Angol's colonial core, centered on the lavishly landscaped Plaza de Armas, lies west of the Río Vergara, while the newer part of the city has sprawled to the east.

Sights

On the Plaza de Armas, the central fountain and its four marble sculptures, imported from Italy and representing Europe, Asia, Africa, and America, are a national historical monument. Several blocks to the northeast, at Covadonga and Vergara, the **Iglesia y Convento San Buenaventura** (1863) is the region's oldest church.

Five km east of Angol, 19th-century Anglo-Chilean landscaper Manuel Bunster created El Vergel, a horticultural nursery that, after Methodist missionaries took it over in the 1920s, became the **Escuela Agrícola El Vergel,** an agricultural school. Its **Museo Dillman S. Bullock** takes its name from Michigan Methodist Dillman S. Bullock (1878–1971), who willed his natural history and archaeological collections to the Angol school.

Bullock first visited the area in 1902 and, after serving as U.S. agricultural attaché in Buenos Aires, returned to take charge of El Vergel in 1924; he was one of the first foreigners to study the Mapuche systematically, learning their language. Bullock also proposed creation of Parque Nacional Nahuelbuta as early as 1929 (it finally happened in 1939) and worked tenaciously to preserve the region's *Araucaria* forests. He was also an enthusiastic ornithologist.

Among Bullock's greatest contributions was to study the Vergel I and II complexes of the pre-Mapuche Kofkeche, between the Biobío and the Río Toltén, south of Temuco. His Vergel discoveries, designated as a national monument, suggested a dispersed settlement pattern, primarily agricultural but with some hunting and gathering; from about A.D. 1200, there are dramatic improvements in burial patterns, with bodies interred in ceramic urns rather than surrounded by clusters of stones.

From Angol's Plaza de Armas, *taxi colectivo* No. 2 drops passengers at the gate to El Vergel's grounds, which are open 9 A.M.–7 P.M. daily; admission is free. Admission to the museum, tel. 45/441675 (same as the school), which is open 9 A.M.–1 P.M. and 3–7 P.M. daily, is US$.75 for adults, US$.35 for children.

Accommodations

Residencial Olimpia, northwest of the plaza at Caupolicán 625, tel. 45/711162, is the cheapest alternative at US$10 pp with shared bath. Just east of town, on the grounds of the Escuela Agrícola El Vergel (see above), the slowly declining **Hostal El Vergel,** tel. 45/712103, charges US$12 pp with shared bath, US$30 d with private bath, but it's probably the quietest option.

Hotel Millaray, 1.5 blocks west of the plaza at Prat 420, tel. 45/711570, costs US$15/25 s/d with shared, US$23/32 with private bath, both with breakfast. Northwest of the plaza, the **Hotel Club Social,** Caupolicán 498, tel. 45/711103, fax 45/712269, charges US$27/33 s/d with private bath; it boasts a pool, a bar, and a restaurant.

Food

Lomitón, at Lautaro and Bunster, is a fast-food *sandwichería*. **El Vergel,** at the agricultural college's hotel, does less with its abundant fresh produce than it could or should. **El Rancho de Julio,** east of the river at Avenida O'Higgins 1151, tel. 45/714407, serves Argentine-style *parrillada*.

Other options include the restaurant at the **Club Social,** Caupolicán 498, tel. 45/711103, and **Las Totoras,** Ilabaca 806, tel. 45/712275. For pizza, try **Pizzería Sparlatto,** Caupolicán 418, tel. 45/716272.

Events

Since the early 1980s, Angol has hosted Brotes de Chile, a folkloric song festival with cash prizes that also features dance, traditional Chilean food, and artisanal crafts. It takes place the second week of January.

Services

Money: Banco de Chile has an ATM at Lautaro 2, west of the plaza. For cash or traveler's checks, try Nahuel Tour, Pedro Aguirre Cerda 307, tel. 45/715457, or Turismo Christopher, Ilabaca 421, tel. 45/715156.

Postal: Correos de Chile is at Chorrillos and Lautaro, at the northeast corner of the plaza.

Telephone and Internet: Entel has long-distance offices at Lautaro 317, just west of the Plaza de Armas. Angol's area code is 45.

The Telecentro de Angol, in the Biblioteca Pública Municipal (Public Library), Lautaro 501, provides public Internet access weekdays 9 A.M.–1 P.M. and 2:45–7 P.M.

Information

Tourist Office: Just east of the bridge over the Río Vergara, Angol's motivated Oficina Municipal de Turismo, in the Edificio Cema Chile at Avenida Bernardo O'Higgins s/n, tel. 45/711930, fax 45/711714, is open 9 A.M.–1 P.M. and 3–7 P.M. weekdays all year, plus 9 A.M.–1 P.M. Saturday in summer only.

National Parks: Conaf, Prat 191, 2nd floor, tel. 45/712191, should have the latest on transportation to Parque Nacional Nahuelbuta.

Transportation

Angol's Terminal Rodoviario is at Caupolicán 200, a block north of the plaza, tel. 45/711854. Tur-Bus, tel. 711655, has the most departures for Santiago (US$12, eight hours). Buses Biobío, tel. 45/7-11777, has frequent service to Temuco (US$3, two hours) and Concepción (US$2, 2.5 hours). Igi Llaima, tel. 45/711920, goes to Los Ángeles and Concepción and to Santiago (nightly).

For rural and regional carriers, the Terminal Rural is at Ilabaca 422, three blocks east of the plaza, tel. 45/712021. Buses Thiele, tel. 45/7-11100, goes to the Costa del Carbón via Contulmo, Cañete, and Lebú (US$3.50), and to Concepción via Nacimiento and Santa Juana. Buses Jota Be, tel. 45/712262, has frequent buses to Los Ángeles (US$2) via Renaico.

(For bus schedules and tours to Parque Nacional Nahuelbuta, see the separate entry for the park below.)

PARQUE NACIONAL NAHUELBUTA

In the coast range west of Angol, 6,832-hectare Nahuelbuta is the last major coast range sanctuary for the *Araucaria* (monkey puzzle) tree, a rare conifer also known as the *paragua* (umbrella) for the shape of its crown (the Mapuche refer to it as *pehuén* or *pewen*). Dramatically undervisited, except on summer weekends, the park features a series of medium-length loop trails through the forest; from the highest summits, reaching almost 1,600 meters, several Andean volcanoes are visible to the east and south.

Geography and Climate

At the northern edge of Region IX (La Araucanía), in the province of Malleco, the igneous Cordillera de Nahuelbuta comprises a mostly rolling plain, about 950 meters above sea level, but also cut by steep ravines and punctuated by craggy summits such as 1,530-meter Cerro Alto Nahuelbuta.

Nahuelbuta is open all year, though the steeper segments of the dirt road can get muddy and even impassable when it rains. Summers are mild and nearly rainless, but higher elevations can get a dusting of snow in winter. Nearly all the rainfall, about 1,000 mm per annum, falls from May to September.

Flora and Fauna

In addition to *Araucaria araucana,* whose largest specimens measure 50 meters in height and two meters in diameter, dense woodlands of *coigüe* (*Nothofagus dombeyi,* southern beech) cover the steeper hillsides of Nahuelbuta.

In Nahuelbuta's dense forests, rare and endangered mammals like the *pudú* (*Pudu pudu,* the dwarf Chilean deer), *zorro chilote* (*Pseudalopex fulvipes,* Chiloé fox), and puma are present but rarely seen. The endangered peregrine falcon is the rarest of the bird species.

Sights and Recreation

Camping and hiking are the main activities at Nahuelbuta. From the park Administración at Pehuenco, a twisting four-km footpath climbs through *Araucaria* woodlands to 1,379-meter **Piedra del Aguila,** a granodiorite pinnacle with awesome panoramas of the snow-topped Andean volcanoes from Antuco in the north to Villarrica, Lanín, and sometimes as far as Osorno in the south (Nahuelbuta occupies a transitional zone between the clear and almost cloudless Mediterranean climate to the north and the frequently drizzly marine west coast climate to the south). To the west, the Pacific stretches to infinity. Rather than returning by the same route, follow the trail that zigzags south into the valley of the Estero Cabrería from the west side of Piedra del Aguila; just beyond the main stream crossing, the trail becomes a road that leads back to Pehuenco.

From the campground at Coimallín, a much shorter footpath through much flatter terrain reaches the 1,450-meter summit of **Cerro Anay,** which offers comparable vistas. The park's highest point, 1,530-meter **Cerro Alto Nahuelbuta,** is once again open to hikers after being closed for a puma reintroduction project several years ago.

Accommodations and Food

Nahuelbuta has two drive-in campgrounds. The more developed of the two, **Camping Pehuenco,** has 11 secluded sites near the park administration; all have picnic tables, flush toilets, and (cold) showers. Rates are US$9 for up to six people. Five km north of Pehuenco, **Camping Coimallín** has a half dozen sites with basic infrastructure—pit toilets, no running water. Rates are the same.

There are no concessionaires in Nahuelbuta, so buy supplies in Angol or elsewhere before coming here.

Information

At Los Portones, the eastern entrance to the park, 35 km from Angol, Conaf rangers collect an admission charge of US$3 for adults, US$1 for children; it's open 8 A.M.–1 P.M. and 4–8 P.M. daily. At Pehuenco, five km farther west, Conaf's Centro de Informaciones Ecológicas includes a small museum where rangers sometimes provide slide shows or video shows on park ecology. It keeps the same hours, but in spring and summer only.

Transportation

Buses Angol, Ilabaca s/n, tel. 45/712021, goes to Vegas Blancas (US$2), seven km west of the Los Portones entrance, Monday, Wednesday, and Friday at 6:45 A.M. and 4 P.M.; return times are 9 A.M. and 5:45 P.M. On Tuesday, Thursday, and Saturday, Buses Nahuelbuta, at Ilabaca and Caupolicán, goes to Vegas Blancas on the same schedule.

On summer Sundays, Buses Angol also offers park tours for US$13 pp, departing the Terminal Rural at 6:45 A.M.

Norte Grande

From the Peruvian border south to Taltal, the Atacama Desert of Chile's "Great North" is perhaps the world's greatest wasteland, a territory where precipitation is so scarce that, for several hundred kilometers, the landscape is utterly barren except when the runoff from infrequent Andean rains moistens its dry watercourses. The cool Humboldt or Peru Current, though, flows north along the Chilean coastline, moderating the tropical temperatures and producing the *camanchaca,* the dense fog that condenses at higher elevations in the coastal mountains.

Despite its superficial desolation, the Norte Grande's attractions are many and often startlingly spectacular: the Victorian architecture of 19th-century ports such as Iquique; the giant pre-Columbian geoglyphs that cover otherwise barren hillsides; nitrate ghost towns that only decades ago were thriving communities; scattered Andean hamlets, their colonial chapels surrounded by stone-faced agricultural terraces; and the immense high plains, punctuated by snow-capped volcanic cones, where indigenous herders still tend their flocks of llamas and alpacas in areas now protected as national parks.

Broadly speaking, the Norte Grande's environments comprise three major ecological zones—the coast (and its transverse agricultural valleys), the precordillera, and the altiplano. As rainfall increases from east to west, so does plant cover, from isolated cacti to scattered shrubs and discontinuous grasslands. Most rainfall occurs in the summer

village of Parinacota, Parque Nacional Lauca

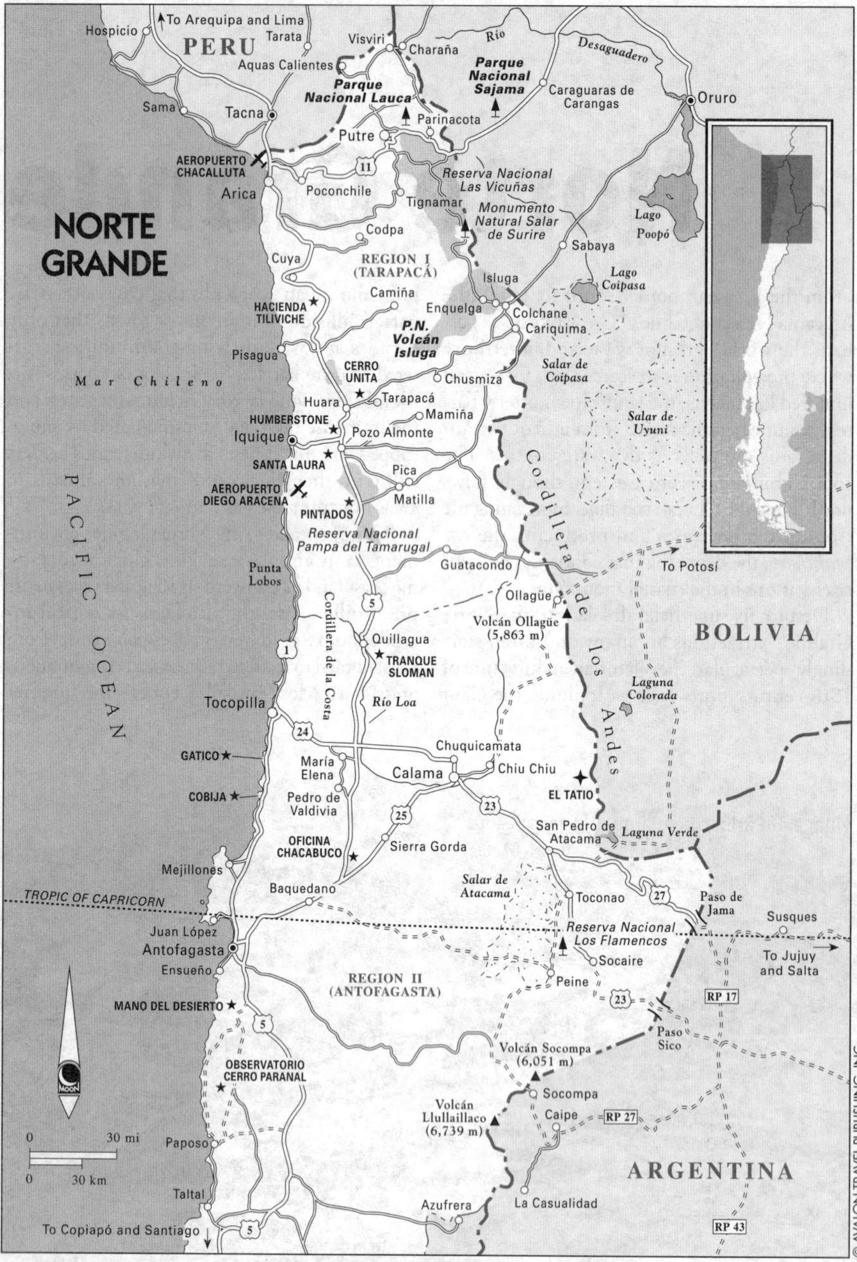

NORTE GRANDE

PERU

Hospicio
To Arequipa and Lima
Tarata
Visviri
Charaña
Río
Desaguadero
Aquas Calientes
Parque Nacional Lauca
Parque Nacional Sajama
Caraguaras de Carangas
Oruro
Sama
Tacna
Putre
Parinacota
AEROPUERTO CHACALLUTA
Arica
Poconchile
Reserva Nacional Las Vicuñas
Lago Poopó
Codpa
Tignamar
Monumento Natural Salar de Surire
Cuya
REGION I (TARAPACÁ)
Isluga
Sabaya
Lago Coipasa
HACIENDA TILIVICHE
Camiña
Enquelga
Colchane
Cariquima
Mar Chileno
Pisagua
P.N. Volcán Isluga
Salar de Coipasa
CERRO UNITA
Chusmiza
Salar de Uyuni
Huara
Tarapacá
Mamiña
HUMBERSTONE
Pozo Almonte
Iquique
SANTA LAURA
Pica
AEROPUERTO DIEGO ARACENA
Matilla
PINTADOS
Reserva Nacional Pampa del Tamarugal
Guatacondo
To Potosí
Punta Lobos
Cordillera de la Costa
5
Ollagüe
Volcán Ollagüe (5,863 m)
BOLIVIA
Quillagua
TRANQUE SLOMAN
Laguna Colorada
1
Río Loa
Tocopilla
24
Chuquicamata
GATICO
María Elena
Calama
Chiu Chiu
EL TATIO
Laguna Verde
COBIJA
Pedro de Valdivia
25
San Pedro de Atacama
OFICINA CHACABUCO
Sierra Gorda
23
Mejillones
Baquedano
Salar de Atacama
Toconao
27
Paso de Jama
Susques
TROPIC OF CAPRICORN
Juan López
Antofagasta
Reserva Nacional Los Flamencos
To Jujuy and Salta
Ensueño
Socaire
REGION II (ANTOFAGASTA)
Peine
23
RP 17
MANO DEL DESIERTO
5
Paso Sico
OBSERVATORIO CERRO PARANAL
Volcán Socompa (6,051 m)
Socompa
RP 27
Volcán Llullaillaco (6,739 m)
Caipe
Paposo
RP 27
ARGENTINA
Taltal
Azufrera
La Casualidad
RP 43
To Copiapó and Santiago
5

0   30 mi
0   30 km

NORTE GRANDE

Cordillera de los Andes

PACIFIC OCEAN

© AVALON TRAVEL PUBLISHING, INC.

months of December, January and February, known colloquially as the *invierno boliviano* (Bolivian winter) or *invierno altiplánico* (altiplano winter), when the plant cover increases.

Because of its aridity, the Norte Grande is an archaeological wonderland. The dry climate has preserved prehistory on the valley slopes, whose geoglyphs depict the passing of llama trains en route to and from the highlands, and in the *tambos* (way stations) and *pukarás* (fortresses) whose ruins dot the ancient routes. In some areas, hikers may even come across mummies desiccated by

the dry air and tanned by centuries of tropical sunshine.

In early 2001, a particularly heavy rainy season did considerable damage in the region, cutting both roads and rail lines, but conditions quickly returned to normal. Major infrastructure improvements are planned for the highlands, including a so-called Camino del Inca linking destinations and settlements from Visviri, near the Peruvian and Bolivian borders, through the altiplano to San Pedro de Atacama (the region's real Inka road from Cuzco ran through the precordillera).

History

Around 10,000 B.C., the first hunter-gatherers occupied the central Andean highlands; eventually, several thousand years later, they found their way down the transverse river valleys to the arid Pacific littoral, where they prospered on the abundant fish stocks and swapped guano for maize with their kinfolk in the precordillera, where irrigated agriculture was possible, and for meat and wool from the altiplano, where llamas and alpacas grazed the high-altitude Andean steppe.

In the valleys and the precordillera, farmers also cultivated native crops such as the potato and quinoa, a nutritious grain that has begun to earn a niche in today's international markets. While northern Chile was beyond the nucleus of the great central Andean civilizations, both Tiwanaku (after about A.D. 800) and the Inkas of Cuzco (from about A.D. 1450) left lasting imprints throughout the region.

Precisely because of its extreme aridity, the Atacama has been a source of wealth since pre-Columbian times, and remains so today—its mineral wealth was undisguised by vegetative

*The Norte Grande is an archaeological wonderland. The dry climate has preserved prehistory on the valley slopes, whose geoglyphs depict the passing of llama trains en route to and from the highlands, and in the **tambos** (way stations) and **pukarás** (fortresses) whose ruins dot the ancient routes.*

growth. When the Spaniards invaded the Americas in the 16th century, of course they sought gold and silver, but with few exceptions, their expectations were unrealistic (the Huantajaya silver mine, east of present-day Iquique, was one of these exceptions). Still, the real wealth of the Americas was the surprisingly numerous indigenous populations, who provided labor and tribute to the Spaniards until ecologically exotic diseases such as smallpox decimated their numbers.

From the mid-19th century, when the region was under Peruvian and Bolivian sovereignty, the strip mining of mineral nitrates—nicknamed *oro blanco* (white gold)—brought unheard-of wealth and precipitated the War of the Pacific (1879–84), in which Chile expanded its continental territory by nearly a third.

After the Chilean victory, workers from central Chile streamed into the underpopulated region, and their presence resulted in Chile's first organized labor movement despite growing pains—among them the massacre of more than several hundred peacefully protesting nitrate workers in Iquique in 1907.

NORTE GRANDE

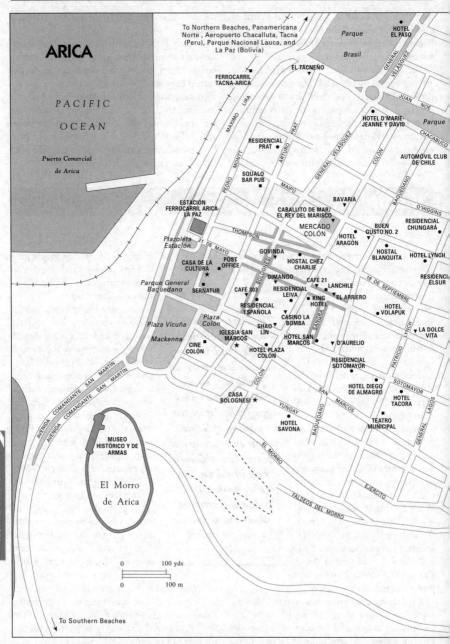

ARICA

PACIFIC OCEAN

Puerto Comercial de Arica

To Northern Beaches, Panamericana Norte, Aeropuerto Chacalluta, Tacna (Peru), Parque Nacional Lauca, and La Paz (Bolivia)

Parque Brasil

HOTEL EL PASO

EL TACNEÑO

FERROCARRIL TACNA-ARICA

HOTEL D'MARIE-JEANNE Y DAVID

Parque

RESIDENCIAL PRAT

AUTOMÓVIL CLUB DE CHILE

SQUALO BAR PUB

BAVARIA

ESTACIÓN FERROCARRIL ARICA-LA PAZ

CABALLITO DE MAR/ EL REY DEL MARISCO

MERCADO COLÓN

BUEN GUSTO NO. 2

RESIDENCIAL CHUNGARÁ

Plazoleta Estación

HOTEL ARAGÓN

HOSTAL BLANQUITA

HOTEL LYNCH

CASA DE LA CULTURA

POST OFFICE

GOVINDA

HOSTAL CHEZ CHARLIE

Parque General Baquedano

SERNATUR

CAFÉ 303

DIMANGO

CAFÉ 21

RESIDENCIAL ELSUR

LANCHILE

Plaza Colón

RESIDENCIAL LEIVA

EL ARRIERO

HOTEL VOLAPUK

Plaza Vicuña Mackenna

RESIDENCIAL ESPAÑOLA

KING HOTEL

CASINO LA BOMBA

SHAO LIN

LA DOLCE VITA

CINE COLÓN

IGLESIA SAN MARCOS

HOTEL SAN MARCOS

D'AURELIO

HOTEL PLAZA COLÓN

RESIDENCIAL SOTOMAYOR

CASA BOLOGNESI

HOTEL DIEGO DE ALMAGRO

HOTEL TACORA

HOTEL SAVONA

TEATRO MUNICIPAL

MUSEO HISTÓRICO Y DE ARMAS

El Morro de Arica

0   100 yds
0   100 m

To Southern Beaches

NORTE GRANDE

© AVALON TRAVEL PUBLISHING, INC.

Mineral nitrates made Chile wealthy until, after World War I, synthetic nitrates supplanted them in European and North American agriculture. When nitrates failed, though, copper stepped in to fill the economic vacuum and has retained its economic dominance to the present. Chuquicamata's open-pit mine, near Calama, is the world's largest; other large copper diggings include Cerro Colorado and Collahuasi, both east of Iquique; El Abra and Radomiro Tomic, both near Calama; and Zaldívar and Escondida, both east of Antofagasta.

Tarapacá Region

For most Chileans, the appeal of Tarapacá is the long sandy beaches of Arica and Iquique and shopping sprees at Iquique's Zona Franca (Zofri) duty-free zone. While the coastline is attractive enough, and the water is warmer than it is farther south, regional authorities have finally admitted that international travelers in search of sun and surf are likelier to visit the Caribbean, and they have decided to emphasize the region's other attractions.

They have plenty to work with: Iquique's classic Victorian architecture; Humberstone's weathering nitrate installations; the archaeological sites of the Azapa and Lluta valleys, and scattered Inka inns and fortresses; Putre's pre-Columbian farm terraces in the precordillera; colonial churches and chapels; and wildlife-rich Parque Nacional Lauca's lakes and steppes. Culturally, too, the north is different—its indigenous population, primarily Aymara, more closely resembles that of southern Peru or the Bolivian highlands. With improved roads, these attractions are more accessible than ever.

ARICA

For most foreign visitors, Arica is the gateway to the country (for arrivals from Peru) and to the altiplano (an excellent paved highway leads east toward several national parks and the Bolivian border). It is also an historic city, though,

NORTE GRANDE

once the port for the legendary silver mine at Potosí in present-day Bolivia and later the stage for dramatic battles between Peruvian and Chilean forces during the War of the Pacific.

Over the past decade or more, Arica has not shared in the prosperity that the Zona Franca free port status brought the city of Iquique; under pressure from local authorities, the Chilean state granted tax breaks and other incentives under the "Ley Arica" of 1995 to help bring the economy out of the doldrums, but progress has been limited. In early 2001, the state decided to provide US$15 million to improve port infrastructure and attract investors, despite conservative criticism of apparent competition with private industry.

Orientation

At the foot of the historic Morro, Arica's central core is a compact grid that roughly parallels the southwest-to-northeast shoreline (the port area is built entirely on fill). Streets perpendicular to the Costanera, such as Maipú, 18 de Septiembre, and 21 de Mayo, are one-way thoroughfares that carry most of the traffic, though 21 de Mayo is a *peatonal* between Prat and Baquedano.

From the foot of the Morro, where Plaza Colón marks the old shoreline, Avenida Comandante San Martín rounds the headlands and several popular beaches before ending abruptly nine km to the south. To the northeast, the Tacna-Arica railway line and Avenida General Velásquez head toward the Panamericana Norte, Aeropuerto Chacalluta, and the Peruvian border.

Sights

For an overview of the city, climb the imposing **El Morro de Arica,** a natural feature and national monument whose 110-meter summit offers expansive views north toward the Peruvian border and south toward the beaches. Atop the summit, its **Museo Histórico y de Armas** recalls the bloody confrontation between Chilean and Peruvian forces on June 7, 1880; in taking the high ground, Chile lost nearly 500 troops, while the Peruvians lost 1,250, including commanding officer Colonel Francisco Bolognesi.

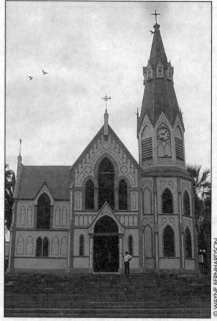

© WAYNE BERNHARDSON

Gustave Eiffel's Iglesia San Marcos de Arica

More recently, in the interest of better relations between the two countries, the 11-meter **Cristo de la Concordia,** by the late Chilean sculptor Raúl Valdivieso, extends a symbolic embrace toward Peru. From the south end of Colón, a sandy trail switchbacks up the Morro, which is also accessible by a paved road from the east end of Sotomayor. The museum, tel. 58/254091, is open 8 A.M.–10 P.M. daily in summer, 8 A.M.–8 P.M. daily the rest of the year; admission costs US$.60.

Beneath the Morro's northern face, fronting on Avenida Comandante San Martín, a cluster of verdant public parks and palm-shaded plazas adjoin each other: **Plaza Vicuña Mackenna, Parque General Baquedano,** the **Plazoleta Estación,** and **Plaza Colón.** Many architectural landmarks stand nearby.

On Plazoleta Estación, a German Esslingen locomotive (1924) faces the **Estación Ferrocarril Arica-La Paz** (1913) from which, for most of a century, it and other Bolivia-bound trains chugged across the high Andes. Until recently, the occasional tourist train still followed the route as far as Chacalluta and occasionally into the altiplano, but heavy floods in early 2001 damaged the tracks and bridges, and services were suspended.

The celebrated Parisian engineer Alexandre Gustave Eiffel, best known for his tower in the French capital, designed numerous prefabricated wrought-iron structures for Peru and other Latin American countries in the late 19th century; several of his constructions, all of them national monuments, are among the few remaining buildings from Arica's Peruvian period. Paint is peeling badly on Plaza Colón's neo-Gothic **Iglesia San Marcos** (1875), initially planned for Lima's beach resort of Ancón but assembled here after an earthquake destroyed its predecessor (Eiffel's church survived the tsunami of 1877 on the existing foundations). Brick walls cover an iron superstructure at the well-restored **Aduana de Arica** (customs house, 1874), which now serves as the municipal Casa de la Cultura, tel. 58/206366; it sponsors special exhibitions in its second-floor gallery, with access by a spiral staircase.

At Colón and Yungay, at the eastern foot of the Morro, the **Casa Bolognesi** was Peru's military headquarters during the War of the Pacific and later served as the Peruvian consulate. Below the Morro's western face, along the Costanera, the former guano island of **Isla de Alacrán** was fortified against pirates during colonial times and still contains some ruins from those times. United with the mainland by fill since 1967, it is now home to the local yacht club.

Beach Activities

Arica is one of few Chilean beach towns where the cold Humboldt Current does not preclude or discourage swimming, surfing, and the like. Some beaches, though, have dangerous rip currents.

Beaches suitable for swimming include, south of the Morro along Avenida Comandante San Martín, **Playa El Laucho, Playa La Lisera,** and **Playa Corazones. Isla Alacrán, La Capilla,** and **Playa Brava** offer outstanding surfing. North of downtown, **Playa Chinchorro** is fine for both swimming and surfing, while **Playa Las Machas** is too rough for most swimmers but suitable for experienced surfers. In wet years such as 2001, the

Río San José and Río Lluta may deposit large amounts of debris that spoil the northerly beaches, at least temporarily.

Arica's surfing culture has spawned a handful of surf shops, including Huntington Surf Shop, 21 de Mayo 493, and Solari Surf Shop, 21 de Mayo 160.

Accommodations

Arica offers a wide variety of accommodations in all categories. The best budget accommodations are in the area southeast of the 21 de Mayo *peatonal* and Colon, mostly along Sotomayor between Baquedano and Arturo Gallo.

US$10–25: Several longstanding budget alternatives are nothing special, but suitable in pinch. Easily the cheapest is barebones **Residencial El Sur,** Maipú 516, tel. 58/252457, for US$3 pp.

Showing its age, but in a good area, **Residencial Sotomayor,** Sotomayor 442, tel. 58/252336, charges US$5 pp. Rates at **Residencial Española,** on the *peatonal* at Bolognesi 340, tel. 58/231703, are US$6/10 s/d. For US$6 pp, **Hostal Blanquita,** Maipú 472, tel. 58/232064, is one of the better alternatives in its range.

In a quiet neighborhood, **Residencial Stagnaro,** Gallo 294, tel. 58/231254, fax 58/256687, is good value for US$7 pp with breakfast and shared bath. Less well located, but with good clean rooms, especially toward the back, **Residencial Chungará,** Patricio Lynch 675, tel. 58/231677, charges the same.

Nearly faultless in its facilities, **Residencial América,** Sotomayor 430, tel. 58/254148, website: www.resamerica.terra.cl, america@terra.cl, suffers from a haughty management style. Still, the rates of US$7 pp with shared bath, US$14 pp with private bath, are more than reasonable.

Belgian-run **Hostal Chez Charlie,** upstairs at Thompson 236, tel./fax 58/250007, latinor@entelchile.net, charges US$7 pp for well-lighted, comfortable rooms with shared bath; breakfast is extra at the downstairs restaurant. Doubles with private bath were under construction and will go for US$20.

At **Residencial Leiva,** Colón 347, tel. 58/232008, rooms with shared bath cost US$8/ 14 s/d, while those with private bath and TV cost US\$14/17; though it's not generally noisy, the upstairs is definitely quieter.

For US\$10/17 s/d with private bath and breakfast, **Hostal Jardín del Sol,** Sotomayor 848, tel. 58/232795, offers quiet accommodations and an ample patio for socializing. Across the street, well-kept, amiable **Residencial Caracas,** Sotomayor 867, tel./fax 58/253688, charges US\$10/17 for comfortable rooms with private bath, TV and breakfast.

Though its location is less appealing than some other options, **Residencial Prat,** Arturo Prat 545, tel. 58/251292, is an excellent choice for US\$17/21, for immaculate rooms with private bath and cable TV. The rather ordinary **Hotel Tacora,** Sotomayor 540, tel./fax 58/2-51240, charges US\$17/22.

Twenty years ago **Hotel Lynch,** Patricio Lynch 589, tel. 58/251959, fax 58/231581, was one of the city's best; while still decent, it's no longer in the top echelon, though the rates of US\$17/20 are good value.

US\$25–50: Though it adjoins a busy street and the grounds are a little barren, the Franco-Chilean **Hotel D'Marie-Jeanne y David,** Avenida General Velásquez 792, tel./fax 58/258231, offers excellent value with comfortable, spotless rooms with private bath and breakfast for US\$17/30 s/d.

Despite its central but less than ideal location overlooking a noisy block, rooms at **Hotel Aragón,** Maipú 344, tel./fax 58/252088, jaragon@ctcinternet.cl, are good value for US\$23/32 with private bath and breakfast.

Central **Hotel King,** Colón 376, tel. 58/232094/5, fax 58/25112, hotelking@chilnet.cl, is a worn but very clean and friendly 1950s-style hotel. Rates are US\$26/36 s/d with private bath, telephone, cable TV, and breakfast. Slightly less central **Hotel San Marcos,** Sotomayor 367, tel. 58/232970, fax 58/251815, hotelsmarcos@entelchile.net, charges US\$30/35 s/d.

Rejuvenated after several years in decline, **Hotel Plaza Colón,** San Marcos 261, tel. 58/254424, fax 58/231244, hotelplazacolon@entelchile.net, is once again worth consideration. Rates are US\$30/42 for rooms that are a bit less sizable than they claim, but all come with private bath, cable TV, telephone, and frigobar.

While parts of the building look past their peak, **Hotel Solar de Almagro,** Sotomayor 490, tel. 58/224444, fax 58/221248, has the largest rooms in town for US\$30/42. Despite thick double-paned glass, the cheaper rooms at the front were noisy until the closure of the lively bar across the street.

Perhaps Arica's best value, on a quiet street but still easy walking distance from everywhere, **Hotel Savona,** Yungay 380, tel. 58/232319, fax 58/231606, boasts friendly service, soothing gardens, and comfortable rooms with private bath, cable TV, and breakfast for US\$33/46 s/d.

US\$50–100: Most of Arica's *hoteles de categoría* are outside the crowded center—both along the beaches and in the Azapa valley. The exception is the modernized and greatly improved **Hotel Volapuk** (ex-Hotel Central), 21 de Mayo 431, tel. 58/252575, fax 58/251168, volapuk@ctcreuna.cl. Affiliated with the Best Western chain, it charges US\$56/84 for well-equipped but relatively small rooms—some too small for the beds that nearly fill them. There is one bargain single for US\$30.

At Azapa, probably the quietest choice except for the odd howling dog in what is still more a rural than a suburban area, the **Azapa Inn,** Guillermo Sánchez 660, tel. 58/244537, fax 58/244517, nrodrig@entelchile.net, costs US\$60/72. Its gardens are a marvel, and it has a swimming pool and a good restaurant.

South of downtown, **Hotel Arica,** Avenida Comandante San Martín 599, tel. 58/254540, fax 58/231133, resarica@entelchile.net, fronts on the crescent beach at Playa el Laucho. Rates are US\$75/90 s/d for beachfront rooms supplemented by amenities such as swimming pools and tennis courts.

Snuggling between the expansive grounds of Parque Brasil and the campus of the Universidad de Tarapacá, just north of downtown, **Hotel El Paso,** General Velásquez 1109, tel. 58/231041, fax 58/231965, reservas@hotelelpaso.cl, charges US\$75/91.

Food

For breakfast, sandwiches, and fresh fruit drinks (ask them to hold the sugar, though), perpetually crowded but tobacco-free **Buen Gusto No.**

2, Baquedano 559, has been a personal favorite for more than 20 years. It has bar-style seating only. A popular meeting place for foreigners and money changers, **Café 21,** at the corner of 21 de Mayo and Colón, tel. 58/231680, has sidewalk seating.

Promising **Pizzería Dolce Vita,** 21 de Mayo 501, tel. 58/232007, may be Arica's best pizzería; for about US$5, "individual" pizzas are large enough to satisfy two people unless they're starving. They need to turn down the music, though, and someone should fling a brick through the TV.

Midrange **La Ciboulette,** Thompson 238, offers good lasagna and other Italian dishes among a more cosmopolitan menu. **D'Aurelio,** Baquedano 369, tel. 58/321471, is a more formal choice for Italian dining, but prices are still moderate.

Within a few blocks of each other, Arica has a pair of popular *parrillas:* **El Arriero,** 21 de Mayo 385, tel. 58/232636, and **Los Aleros de 21,** 21 de Mayo 736, tel. 58/252899. The former (closed Monday) is casual, the latter more formal, but both have good meats.

At Colón and Maipú, the **Mercado Colón** fish and produce market also holds several good seafood restaurants, including the midrange **Caballito del Mar,** tel. 58/241569, downstairs, and the pricier **El Rey del Marisco,** tel. 58/229232, upstairs. Inexpensive **El Tacneño,** at the corner of Prat and Chacabuco, is one of Arica's surprisingly few Peruvian alternatives, also offering seafood.

Fire stations may offer reliable food throughout Chile, but Arica's **Casino La Bomba,** Colón 357, tel. 58/232983, is one of the best of its kind, serving a variety of Chilean dishes at modest prices, especially its lunchtime specials. In a country where seasonings are generally bland, its *ají* is one of Chile's spiciest fresh condiments. Midrange **Bavaria,** Colón 613, tel. 58/251679, maintains the standards of its affiliates elsewhere in the country.

Chifa Shao-Lin, Sotomayor 275, tel. 58/2-31311, serves very good Chinese dishes in the US$3.50–6 range, with excellent service and, unusually for many Chilean restaurants in its category, no TV or loud music. Hare Krishnas run **Govinda,** Bolognesi 430, tel. 58/231028, where vegetarian fare is the rule.

DiMango, 21 de Mayo 244, tel. 58/224575, offers fine ice cream, but the best ice creamery in town, loaded with imaginative tropical fruit flavors, is **La Fontana,** Bolognesi 320, tel. 58/254680.

On the outskirts of town, in the Poblado Artesanal market near the Panamericana Sur and the road to Azapa, **El Tambo,** Hualles 2825, tel. 58/241757, serves Chilean dishes such as *pastel de choclo* at modest prices.

Entertainment and Events

Arica has a gaggle of downtown pubs and similar hangouts, such as **Barabbás,** 18 de Septiembre 520; **Café 303,** Bolognesi 303; and **Le Mans,** Patricio Lynch 770, tel. 58/257176, a wine bar/restaurant with a 1960s musical ambience. **Squalo Bar Pub,** Prat 527, has surfer appeal, while **France Tropicale,** upstairs at Baquedano 371, tel. 58/257217, has a South Seas ambience.

For current movies, go to **Cine Colón,** 7 de Junio 190, tel. 58/231165. The **Teatro Municipal,** at Baquedano and Sotomayor, is the municipal performing arts venue.

Carnaval is not the momentous occasion here that it is in Brazil, but late February's **Carnaval Ginga** stresses the syncretism between indigenous Andean and imported European customs in a parade down Avenida Comandante San Martín. More strictly local, June's **Semana Ariqueña** does include the **Concurso Nacional de Cueca,** celebrating Chile's national folkloric dance.

Shopping

Barely wider than a condor's wingspan, the pedestrian **Pasaje Bolognesi,** between Sotomayor and Thompson, features a spirited crafts market nightly. At the corner of Sotomayor and Baquedano, the **Gendarmería de Chile's Taller Artesanal San Marcos** displays prisoners' handiwork from the colossal new penitentiary on the southeastern outskirts of town.

Also on the outskirts of town, near the traffic circle at mouth of the Azapa valley, the **Poblado Artesanal,** Hualles 2825, tel. 58/222683, is an ersatz altiplano village serving as an Andean crafts market. Open 9:30 A.M.–1:30 P.M. and 3:30–8 P.M. daily, it primarily offers ceramics, weavings, and archaeological reproductions from the north of the country, as well as typical food at its restaurant **El Tambo.**

Services

Money: Exchange houses are fewer than they were before the advent of ATMs, but try Turismo Sol y Mar at Colón 610, Oficina 4 for U.S., Argentine, Bolivian, or Peruvian cash, or for U.S. traveler's checks. Among the numerous banks with ATMs are Banco de Crédito, Bolognesi 221, and Banco Santander, 21 de Mayo 403. Street changers cluster around Café 21, at the corner of 21 de Mayo and Colón.

Postal: Correos de Chile is at Prat 305.

Telephone and Internet: For long-distance phone service, go Telefónica CTC at Colón 476 or Entel at 21 de Mayo 372. Arica's area code is 58.

Arica has some of the country's cheapest Internet outlets, around US$1–1.50 per hour. To get to Neonet, 21 de Mayo 231, the best and cheapest operator, you have to pass through a video arcade gauntlet and then upstairs. Internet Center is nearby at 21 de Mayo 175.

Immigration: The Departamento de Extranjería, Angamos 990, tel. 58/250377, is open 8:30 A.M.–12:30 P.M. and 3:30–6 P.M. weekdays. It's possible to obtain a replacement tourist card or renew one here, but a brief trip to Peru or even Bolivia is almost certainly cheaper than Chile's US$100 renewal charge.

Laundry: Lavandería La Moderna is at 18 de Septiembre 457, tel. 58/232006.

Medical: Hospital Dr. Juan Noé is at 18 de Septiembre 1000, tel. 58/229200.

Information

Tourist Office: Sernatur has new quarters at San Marcos 101, tel. 58/252054. Summer hours are 8:30 A.M.–7 P.M. daily, while the rest of the year it's open 8:30 A.M.–5:20 P.M. weekdays only.

Consulates: The Peruvian consulate, San Martín 235, tel. 58/231020, is open 8:30 A.M.–1 P.M. weekdays. Bolivia has a consulate at Patricio Lynch 292, tel. 58/231030, open 9 A.M.–2 P.M. weekdays.

Motorists: The Automóvil Club de Chile (Acchi), Chacabuco 460, tel. 58/252678, fax 58/232780, offers free information and sells maps. Hours are 9 A.M.–1 P.M. and 3–7 P.M. weekdays, 9 A.M.–1 P.M. only Saturday.

National Parks: Conaf, Vicuña Mackenna 820, tel. 58/250207 or 58/250570, is open 8:30 A.M.–5:15 P.M. weekdays. Its own webpage, www.chilesat.net/conaf-tarapaca, is full of information on the region's protected areas.

Transportation

As a border city, Arica has international connections by air (limited), bus, taxi, and train, though train services are suspended until further notice because of the floods of 2001. Domestic air and bus services are abundant.

Air: Due for an overhaul and expansion, Aeropuerto Internacional Chacalluta, tel. 58/211116, is 18 km north of town, near the Peruvian border.

LanChile and LanExpress share offices at 21 de Mayo 345, tel. 58/252600 or 58/251641; LanExpress flies five times daily to Santiago, usually stopping in Iquique. LanChile has a daily flight to La Paz, Bolivia.

Aerocontinente, Baquedano 343, tel. 58/2-58843, flies daily to Iquique and Santiago.

Lloyd Aéreo Boliviano, 21 de Mayo 423, tel. 58/258259 or 58/251919, flies out of Iquique to Bolivia.

Bus and *Taxi Colectivo:* Arica's main Terminal de Buses is northwest of downtown at Diego Portales 948, at the corner of Avenida Santa María, tel. 58/241390. Immediately adjacent to it on Portales, the deceptively named Terminal Internacional, tel. 58/248709, has both domestic and international services, but some international buses leave from the main terminal. Most regional bus companies have separate offices nearer downtown.

On the regional routes, Bus Lluta has six departures daily to Poconchile, between 5:45 A.M. and 8 P.M. from the southwest corner of Chacabuco and Vicuña Mackenna. At the Terminal Internacional, Buses Martínez, tel. 58/220106, and Transportes Humire, tel. 58/260164, go to the altiplano villages of Parinacota (Parque Nacional Lauca) and Visviri (across from the Bolivian border town of Charaña) Tuesday and Friday at 10 A.M. and 10 P.M. Fares are US$5.50 to Parinacota, US$7.50 to Visviri.

Buses La Paloma, Germán Riesco 2071, tel. 58/222710, goes daily at 6:30 A.M. to Putre (US$3.50), and also to the northern precordillera villages of Socoroma (Tuesday and Saturday at 6:30 A.M., US$3) and Belén (Tuesday and Friday at 6:30 A.M.). La Paloma also has Monday and Friday service, at 8 A.M. to the southern precordillera hamlet of Codpa (US$3, four hours). La Paloma's terminal is 12 blocks east of the hospital, but it will also arrange hotel pickups.

Several companies shuttle frequently between Arica and Iquique, including Buses Carmelita, tel. 58/241591; Pullman Santa Rosa, tel. 58/241029; Buses Zambrano, tel. 58/241587; and Cuevas y González, tel. 58/241090. Faster *taxi colectivos* charge about US$10 pp: the main carriers are Tamarugal, tel. 58/222609; Turiscargo, tel. 58/241052; Turis Auto, tel. 58/244776; and Taxi Tur, tel. 58/228284.

Numerous long-distance carriers link Arica with Santiago and intermediate points, including Fénix Pullman Norte, tel. 58/222457; Tas Choapa, tel. 58/222817; Pullman Bus, tel. 58/223837; Flota Barrios, tel. 58/223587; Tur-Bus, tel. 58/222217, which also goes to Calama; and Carmelita and Zambrano. Zambrano also serves Valparaíso and Viña del Mar. Géminis, tel. 58/241647, goes to Calama, Antofagasta, and intermediates.

Fichtur, tel. 58/241972, has cushier but more expensive *semi-cama* and *salón cama* seating to Santiago.

Sample fares and times include Iquique (US$6, four hours), Calama (US$13–18, nine hours), Antofagasta (US$19, 10 hours), Copiapó (US$32, 16 hours), La Serena (US$36, 19 hours) and Santiago (US$48–60, 26 hours).

The quickest way to Tacna, 55 km to the north, is by *taxi colectivo* from the Terminal Internacional with Chile Lintur, tel. 58/255038; San Remo, tel. 58/260509; or San Marcos, tel. 58/260513. Charging about US$3 pp, these international carriers leave whenever they have five passengers.

The Peruvian carrier Tepsa operates daily services to Lima (US$35, 20 hours) at 2 P.M., and to Arequipa Tuesday and Friday at 7 P.M. (US$18). Truly budget-conscious travelers may wish to cross the border by *taxi colectivo* and pay domestic Peruvian rather than international prices.

Overland transportation to Bolivia is far simpler than in the past, thanks to improving diplomatic relations and infrastructure, but heavy summer rains can still cut the paved highway to La Paz (US$14–25, eight hours). Carriers include Litoral, tel. 58/261092, which also has faster minibuses; Chile Bus, tel. 58/222817, which also goes to Oruro; Géminis, tel. 58/241647; Andes Mar, tel. 58/222365; and Trans Salvador, tel. 58/246064, which also goes to Oruro and Cochabamba. Lauca-bound passengers can take these buses, but they will have to pay full fare to Bolivia.

Both Géminis and Tur-Bus provide services across the Andes to Salta, Argentina, but these require changing buses in Calama and are often full—make reservations as far in advance as possible.

Train: Near the port, the Ferrocarril Arica-Tacna, Máximo Lira 889, tel. 58/231115, traditionally crosses the Peruvian border at 3 P.M. Monday, Wednesday, and Friday, but the rains of early 2001 washed out rails and bridges that have not yet been repaired. Resumption is uncertain, but the 1.5-hour trip should cost around US$1.40. Arrive early for immigration paperwork.

Getting Around

Airport Transfers: Several radio taxi companies carry passengers to Aeropuerto Chacalluta for US$4 pp (shared) or US$10 (s). Among them are Radio Taxi Aeropuerto Chacalluta, Patricio Lynch 371, tel. 58/254812; Radio Taxi Arica, Prat 528, tel. 58/250340; and Fono Taxi, 18 de Septiembre 370, tel. 58/254311.

Local Transportation: Buses and faster *taxi colectivos* (the latter distinguished from other cabs by illuminated signs that indicate their routes) link downtown Arica with the bus terminal, the Azapa valley, and other destinations.

Car Rental: Rates at Cactus Rent A Car, Baquedano 635, Local 40, tel. 58/257430 or 09/54-17067, cactusrent@latinmail.com, range from US$36 per day to US$75 per day (4WD), plus tax. Other agencies include Hertz, Baquedano 999, tel. 58/231487; Klasse, General Velásquez

760, Local 25, tel. 58/254498; and American, General Lagos 559, tel. 58/252234.

Bicycles: Rental bikes are available at Residencial Leiva, Colón 347, tel. 58/232008, and **Latinorizons,** Bolognesi 449, tel. 58/250007. Rates are around US$5 per half day, US$8.50 per full day.

VICINITY OF ARICA

The transverse valleys, precordillera, and altiplano in and around Arica all have their attractions. Many of them, such as the Azapa valley and Tacna (Peru), are easily accessible by routine public transportation, but time constraints and awkward logistics can make organized tours a good alternative for some more remote sights.

Note that, while the operators below may also offer tours to more distant destinations such as Parque Nacional Lauca and Parque Nacional Isluga, they will often double up with other agencies in the interest of economy. In some instances, guides may be essentially drivers with limited knowledge and ability to communicate in any language other than Spanish.

Among established Arica operators, listed here alphabetically, are **Aacción Tour,** Bolognesi 301, tel./fax 58/244889, aacion@correoweb.com; **Ecotour Expediciones,** Bolognesi 460, tel. 58/250000; **Geotours,** Bolognesi 421, tel. 58/2-51675, geotour@entelchile.net; Belgian-run **Latinorizons** (French and English spoken), Bolognesi 449, tel./fax 58/250007, latinor@entelchile.net; **Parinacota Expediciones,** Prat 430, Oficina 5, tel./fax 58/256227; and **Turismo Lauca,** Prat 430, Local 10, tel./fax 58/252322.

Valle de Azapa

In pre-Columbian times, the valley of the Río San José, commonly known as Azapa, was one of the main transport routes between the altiplano and the coast, and its barren hillsides still display evidence of the llama pack trains that once plied the canyon. Since colonial times, it has produced premium olives, citrus, and vegetables in an area where cultivable land, and water to irrigate it, is scarce.

A smooth paved road ascends the valley from Arica to beyond the hamlet of Sobraya, where it becomes a gravel surface and gradually peters out as it approaches the precordillera. The old and roughly parallel Azapa road, along with a few secondary loops, provides access to numerous geoglyphs and other archaeological sites in the vicinity.

For a thorough introduction to regional prehistory and an orientation toward the valley's impressive archaeological resources, visit the **Museo Arqueológico San Miguel de Azapa,** Km 12, tel. 58/205555. One of the country's finest museums, it traces the region's cultural evolution from the earliest hunter-gatherers to present-day Aymara agropastoralists through a series of generally chronological exhibits; in the surrounding gardens, its **Parque de Geoglifos** collection of rock art was salvaged from the valley's urban and agricultural development. In addition, it boasts a bank of interactive computer exhibits, a museum shop that sells books and crafts, and it guards the remarkable Chinchorro mummies, the world's oldest and among the most elaborately prepared. Heather Pringle relates the story of these infant mummies, found at the base of Arica's El Morro headland, in her outstanding book *The Mummy Congress* (New York: Hyperion, 2001).

In January and February, the museum is open 9 A.M.–8 P.M. daily, while the rest of the year hours are 10 A.M.–6 P.M. Admission charges are US$1.50 pp, but only US$.50 for children. It also has a superb webpage, www.uta.cl/masma/index.html, that's nearly as good as an in-person visit.

To see the valley's attractions *in situ,* follow the museum's **Circuito Arqueológico del Valle de Azapa,** which visits a dozen of the most notables sites. The most impressive are probably Cerro Sombrero's **Geoglifos Atoca,** representing a llama train and its guide, from about A.D. 1300; the Tiwanaku-influenced **Pukará San Lorenzo,** a 12th-century fortress on the opposite side of the valley from the museum; and the Incaic **Geoglifos Cerro Sagrado,** dating from around A.D. 1400. Nearby are the **Túmulos Alto Ramírez,** a cluster of funeral mounds dating from 1000 B.C. to A.D. 300.

Food: For Ariqueños, Azapa is also a weekend getaway, where they go for Sunday *asados* at spots such as the **Club de Huasos,** Km 3.5, tel. 58/223991; hours are noon–5 P.M., but it sometimes closes for private functions.

If it's not open, try the **Club Italiano** at Km 2. Visitors to the museum may enjoy **La Picá del Muertito,** alongside the cemetery at Km 13, tel. 58/227437.

Transportation: Azapa has no regular bus service, but *taxi colectivos* from Arica's Parque Chacabuco, at the corner of Chacabuco and Baquedano, shuttle up and down the valley from 7 A.M.–10 P.M. daily. Since these *colectivos* use the main road, visiting some of the sites would mean hiking in the hot sun; a good alternative would be a mountain bike, as this part of the valley rises only gradually toward the east.

Panamericana Sur

From Arica south, the Panamericana turns inland, alternately climbing and dipping steeply through spectacular but barren canyons separated by even more barren plateaus. Though the seemingly vertical walls of Quebrada Vitor and the valley of the Río Camarones are the most impressive, there are surprising points of interest in unexpected places.

Presencias Tutelares: From Arica, the Panamericana relentlessly ascends the hillside of the Quebrada de Acha until, leveling out at the summit or Cuesta de Acha 27 km south of the city, it intersects a smooth dirt road that heads east to the precordillera village of Tignamar. At the junction, the state arts council Fondart has funded the creation of the **Presencias Tutelares** (Guardian Spirits, 1996), a cluster of desert sculptures evoking the region's pre-Columbian civilizations. A subsequent addition to the group, Arica sculptor Juan Gustavo Díaz Fleming's *Nacimiento del Inti* (Birth of the Sun), symbolizes the emergence of the burning disk above the eastern horizon.

Camarones: Some 110 km south of Arica, the hamlet of Cuya is an agricultural sanitation checkpoint and wide spot in the road that is also the administrative center for the *comuna* of Camarones, home to one of the few Afro-Chilean communities in the entire country, dating back to Peruvian times. According to Mayor Sonia Salgado:

© WAYNE BERNHARDSON

Presencias Tutelares sculptures, south of Arica

There is evidence that people of African descent have existed in the north of the country ever since that territory was conquered. Our ancestors arrived here together with the conquerors.

Eleven km west of Cuya via a dirt road, at the outlet of the Río Camarones, **Caleta Camarones** is a fishing settlement that is also a fine place to camp and view migratory birds. About 20 km south of Cuya, the restored **Geoglifos de Chiza** blanket the hillsides for several kilometers.

Valle de Lluta

About nine km north of Arica, paved Ruta 11 climbs east up the valley of the Río Lluta to a junction where a paved lateral heads to the village of Molinos, while the main highway zigzags steeply into the precordillera and the altiplano, eventually reaching the Bolivian border near Lago Chungará. For most of the 20th century the railway, which parallels the highway as far as Molinos before heading northeast to Visviri, was the main

NORTE GRANDE

way to Bolivia, but it now hauls freight rather than passengers. Local buses carry passengers only as far as Molinos, but frequent regional and international buses carry passengers up Ruta 11 to Putre, Parque Nacional Lauca, and across the border to the neighboring capital of La Paz.

One of few northern Chilean rivers that regularly reach the sea, the Lluta flooded spectacularly in the summer of 2001, when runoff from the altiplano washed out roads, rails, and bridges all the way to Poconchile, 35 km up the valley. In February, its flow reached 800,000 liters (800 cubic meters) per second—the highest flow in 31 years—and even destroyed the ostensibly sturdy bridge over the Panamericana, briefly isolating Arica from its airport at Chacalluta and from the nearby Peruvian city of Tacna.

Inferior water quality, though, has limited Lluta's agricultural growth to lower value crops and livestock. Like Azapa, though, it was a major pack train route well into the 20th century, and the enormous series of **Geoglifos de Lluta,** easily visible from the highway, embellish its southern hillsides only a few kilometers up the valley. They date from around A.D. 1000–1300.

At Poconchile, 37 km from Arica, the unadorned 17th-century **Iglesia San Jerónimo** is one of Chile's oldest churches, but its antiquity is deceptive, since it was rebuilt in the 19th century and refurbished in the 20th. After the highway leaves the Lluta valley, it switchbacks up **Cuesta El Aguila** before emerging onto a plateau and then entering, at around Km 73, the **Quebrada Cardones.**

Here, between 2,000 and 2,800 meters, grows the *cactus candelabros (Browningia candelaris),* so called because, in specimens taller than about two meters, its trunk divides into multiple branches resembling a candelabra. Interestingly, the upper branches are almost spineless, while the main trunk is almost covered with vicious needles. It grows at what is roughly the western limit of the summer rains, mostly along dry watercourse, but may also benefit from the high *camanchaca* that penetrates from the coast.

Just west of Km 100, one of the route's unlikeliest sights is the antique rail car, acquired from a nitrate *oficina* near Antofagasta, that marks

Pueblo Maillku. Zealously convinced that visitors to the altiplano need to break their journey precisely at this point to adapt to the altitude, Alexis Troncoso and Andrea Chellew are raising their family here and offering delectable fresh bread, soothing *mate de coca* (coca leaf tea), three guest beds at US$4.50 pp, solar-powered hot showers and clean toilets, camping, and excruciatingly sincere convictions.

Almost precisely at Km 100, 3,270 meters above sea level, the 12th-century hilltop fortifications of the **Pukará de Copaquilla** guarded the pre-Columbian agricultural terraces in the upper drainage of the Río San José, immediately below. Altiplano tours usually take a break at the site, restored by the Universidad de Tarapacá in 1979.

At Km 102, the tight-fitting stonework of the **Tambo de Zapahuira** was an Inka posthouse on the road that ran north to Cuzco and south toward San Pedro de Atacama. Ironically, the nearby contemporary crossroads of Zapahuira, where a lateral heads southeast into the precordillera of Belén, serves much the same function, as Bolivian truckers stop for lunch or dinner before continuing toward Arica or heading back to La Paz.

Below a turnoff at Km 116, deep in its namesake valley and surrounded by pre-Columbian terraces, the village of **Socoroma** is known for its 16th-century **Iglesia de San Francisco** and the fresh *tumbo* (Andean passion fruit, *Passiflora mollisima Bailey*) juice at the house of Emilia Humire, who also offers inexpensive lodging. About three km west, the **Pukará de la Calacruz** is an Incaic ruin.

Precordillera de Belén

From the Zapahuira junction, a gravel road built primarily for the modern Chapiquiña hydroelectric plant follows, in part, the precordillera Inka highway that once linked northern Chile with Peru. At Murmuntani, midway to Chapiquiña, a secondary road switchbacks vertiginously up to the altiplano, an alternative route to Parque Nacional Lauca and Reserva Nacional Las Vicuñas.

On the main road, surrounded by terraces where Aymara farmers still cultivate indigenous crops such as quinoa, the villages of Belén and Tignamar Viejo both feature colonial churches, the former's in better condition. There are also several Inka fortifications, all of them national monuments: the **Pukará de Belén** (six km west of the town and the road), the **Pukará de Lupica** (at the hamlet of the same name), and the **Pukará de Saxamar** (at the confluence of the Río Saxamar and the Río Tignamar).

Beyond Tignamar Viejo, to the southwest, the road worsens through a dusty gorge before improving as it emerges onto the broad but equally dusty Pampa de Chaca, eventually intersecting the Panamericana at the Presencias Tutelares (see separate entry above), 21 km south of Arica. An alternative route back to the Panamericana leaves the road across the Pampa de Chaca and heads south to the town of Codpa, a better choice for southbound travelers.

For travelers without their own motor vehicles or mountain bikes (an interesting alternative despite the shortage of drinking water between Tignamar Viejo and the Panamericana), transportation options are limited. Empresa La Paloma, Germán Riesco 2071, tel. 58/222710 in Arica, goes to Belén Tuesday and Friday at 6:30 A.M. (US$3), to Codpa Monday and Friday at 8 A.M. (US$3, four hours), and to Tignamar Tuesday and Friday at 7 A.M. (US$3.50). Covering the distance between Belén and Tignamar or Codpa depends not only on the schedules, but on negotiating at least 13 km with no public transport.

Putre

Gateway to the altiplano, beneath the 5,500-meter massif of the Nevados de Putre, the village of Putre is capital of the thinly populated province of Parinacota and boasts a burgeoning bureaucracy. In a sense, though, this marks a continuity rather than a break with the past—centuries ago, this Aymara settlement was a Spanish colonial *congregación* or *reducción,* created to control the indigenous population through tax, tribute, and religious indoctrination.

Today, many visitors take advantage of Putre's intermediate altitude—3,500 meters above sea level—to acclimatize before tackling oxygen-poor Parque Nacional Lauca and other areas higher than most of the highest summits of North America and Europe. Increasing numbers, though, are spending more time at Putre itself, which has architectural charm, scenic surroundings, and sufficient infrastructure—good simple hotels and restaurants, at least—to support outdoor activities such as hiking and horseback riding. The total solar eclipse of 1994 brought Putre unprecedented attention, thanks to its clear weather and position directly on the eclipse path.

Orientation: Putre is 150 km east-northeast of Arica by paved Ruta 11, the international route to La Paz, and a paved spur that dips into town. The town itself, a relatively regular grid based on the Plaza de Armas and sloping toward the west, is compact enough that finding one's way is easy.

Sights: Facing the Plaza de Armas, the **Iglesia de Putre** (1670) is built mostly of adobe, though its front wall is a stone construction. Numerous other colonial and early republican buildings have maintained their facades, some of them surprisingly ornate, but their interiors have deteriorated.

Affiliated with the Red de Turismo Rural de la Provincia de Parinacota (Rural Tourism Network of the Province of Parinacota), Aymara guide Freddy Torrejón goes to rock art sites such as the **Pictografías de Vilacanari,** a national archaeological monument seven km from town, and he also has a good knowledge of local wildlife, such as guanacos and *huemules,* and of ethnobotany.

For specialty birding and natural history tours of the altiplano and other fauna and flora-rich areas by 4WD vehicle, contact Putre-based Barbara Knapton's **Birding Alto Andino,** Baquedano 299, tel. (voicemail) 58/300013, fax 58/222735, beknapton@hotmail.com. Destinations include Parque Nacional Lauca's Las Cuevas, Parinacota, Laguna Cotacotani, and Lago Chungará; Reserva Nacional Las Vicuñas; Monumento Natural Salar de Surire; Parque Nacional Isluga; and coastal wetlands around Pisagua. Accommodations can include either camping or Conaf *refugios,* as well her own house in Putre, and can start and end in Arica, Iquique, or Putre. For more details, check the website: www.birdingaltoandino.com.

Accommodations and Food: Putre has several modest but better than adequate accommodations and one that's more elaborate. Most of them also serve meals but none has in-room heating (though they usually provide plenty of blankets).

The cheapest is **Residencial Oasis,** Cochrane s/n, charging US$5 pp but lacking hot water; simple meals are also available. Slightly better, charging around US$6 pp, are **Residencial La Paloma,** Baquedano s/n; **Hostal Rosamel,** Baquedano 401; and **Residencial Cali,** Baquedano 399. The latter also has rooms with private bath for US$10 pp. La Paloma and Rosamel both prepare fixed-price meals for tour groups.

Opposite the army base, three blocks west of the plaza, Conaf's **Refugio Putre** serves no meals but offers bunk-style accommodations with kitchen facilities and hot showers for US$10 pp.

At the eastern approach to town, primarily catering to the mining industry but open to the general public, the 112-room **Hostería Las Vicuñas,** tel. 58/224466, fax 58/228654, reiner55@hotmail.com, charges US$55/80 s/d with half-board.

Besides the restaurants and hotels and *residenciales,* the only nightspot in town is **Kuchu Marka,** Baquedano s/n, which has good food and drinks.

Events: For a small Andean village, Putre's annual **Carnaval,** in February or March depending on the date of Easter, is remarkably extroverted and participatory— locals and outsiders alike may find themselves showered with flour and flocked with colorful paper dots known as *chaya.* Music, rather like the brass bands in Arica's Carnaval Ginga, comes from the youthful *tarqueada* and the more venerable *banda;* the celebrations culminate with the burning of an effigy known as the *momo.*

Services and Information: Correos de Chile is directly on the Plaza de Armas, as is Banco del Estado (changing U.S. cash only). Entel, unfortunately, has closed its telephone office, leaving only a single coin telephone for the town's 700 residents—there are no private land lines and cell phones do not work because of the rugged terrain.

Opposite the army base downhill from the plaza, Conaf has an information office open 8:30 A.M.–1 P.M. and 2–5:30 P.M. daily. It can provide information on Parque Nacional Lauca and other protected areas in the altiplano.

Transportation: From Arica, Buses La Paloma, Germán Riesco 2071, tel. 58/222710, goes daily to Putre at 6:30 A.M. (US$3, three hours), returning at 1:30 P.M.

THE ALTIPLANO OF ARICA

Well above 4,000 meters, the highlands beyond Putre consist of sprawling freshwater lakes and well-watered alluvial plains, surrounded by rounded hills and punctuated by soaring volcanic cones and calderas, some of them perpetually snowbound. Aymara shepherds herd llamas, alpacas, and sheep at scattered homesteads. In drier, more southerly areas, shallow salt lakes are home to copious flocks of flamingos and other birds.

Most of the same operators who offer tours in and around Arica also offer altiplano tours; some offer day trips, but many if not most people prefer to spend at least a night acclimatizing at an intermediate destination such as Putre to avoid *soroche;* if going for the day, be certain the operator carries oxygen. Dehydration and sunburn are also serious matters at this altitude—carry plenty of water and use a powerful sunblock. The combination of altitude sickness and the nearly direct tropical rays is particularly dangerous. Do not hesitate to return to lower elevations—unacclimatized tourists have died here.

One of northern Chile's most interesting excursions is the loop from Arica to Putre, Parinacota and Lago Chungará, then south to Reserva Nacional Las Vicuñas, Monumento Natural Salar de Surire, and Parque Nacional Isluga, then back

WARNING

Because of the altiplano's extremely high elevations, often well above 4,000 meters, *soroche* or *apunamiento* (altitude sickness) is a potentially serious matter in the Norte Grande— even young and vigorous individuals have fallen ill. Before heading to the heights, get familiar with the warning signs (refer to the entry on altitude sickness in the On the Road chapter).

to Arica (or Iquique) via Pozo Almonte and the Panamericana. This is possible either for private or rented vehicles, or with an Arica tour operator. During the summer rainy season, however, it may be impossible to continue south of Guallatire even with 4WD.

Parque Nacional Lauca

Near the Bolivian and Peruvian borders, Parque Nacional Lauca is a top-of-the-world experience—flamingos fly above cobalt blue lakes and Aymara shepherds tend flocks of llamas and alpacas more than 4,000 meters above sea level, at the foot of snow-clad volcanic cones at least 2,000 meters higher. The recovery of the endangered wild vicuña, whose wool a Spanish chronicler called "finer than silk," is one of the great conservation successes of contemporary Latin America.

Occupying 137,883 hectares of soaring volcanoes, rolling hills, sprawling lakes, and marshy bogland—the Aymara word *lawq"a* means "swamp grass"—Parque Nacional Lauca has been a UNESCO World Biosphere Reserve since 1981. Between 3,200 and 6,342 meters above sea level, the park is home to abundant wildlife, including 130 bird species and 21 species of mammals including the vicuña, a wild relative of the domestic llama and alpaca.

Lauca's high altitudes make it less suitable for long hikes without acclimatizing at "foothill" villages such as Putre—only about 3,500 meters above sea level. Well-equipped climbers, in top physical condition, can attempt 6,320-meter Volcán Parinacota.

Lauca is accessible all year, but best from September to April; the December to February rainy season brings afternoon thunderstorms. It is far from secure, though. Since 1983, the park has been reduced from its original 520,000 hectares, though it's only fair to say that part of these disaffected areas became Reserva Nacional Las Vicuñas and Monumento Nacional Salar de Surire. Water diversions for hydroelectricity facilities in the precordillera and agriculture in the Azapa valley have desiccated parts of the high-altitude wetlands and, at the same time, mining interests have pressured the government to remove additional areas near Putre, at the northwestern edge of the park.

Ironically, the return to democracy has contributed to these problems. When the park was originally created in 1970, authorities apparently assumed that all the land in the altiplano belonged

Volcán Parinacota

© WAYNE BERNHARDSON

NORTE GRANDE

to the state, when in fact many Aymara held individual titles since Peruvian times. Records in Arica's land registry indicate that altiplano land was freely bought and sold among them, and that some pastoralists also regularized their de facto occupancy with legal documents. In the past few years, Conaf and other government agencies have acknowledged the legitimacy of these claims, but have not yet managed to reconcile indigenous rights with park management plans—an issue that couldn't even come up in the years of the Pinochet dictatorship.

Flora and Fauna: The Lauca altiplano has two principal types of vegetative associations. The first, and more abundant, is the dry Andean steppe, or *puna,* which consists of *Compositae* shrubs and of perennial bunch grasses of the genera *Stipa, Poa, Festuca,* and others; known collectively as *icchu* in Aymara or *paja brava* in Spanish, the latter form a discontinuous cover that increases with the summer rains. The second is the well-watered alluvial depressions known locally as *bofedales, vegas,* or *ciénegas;* here, dense cushion plants completely cover the soil and, with dwarf annuals and perennial grasses, offer permanent grazing for both wild and domestic livestock.

Some of the plant species are unique to the Andean highlands. Though it appears, from a distance, to be a spongy moss, the prostrate *llareta (Azorella compacta)* is a rock-hard shrub whose branches are so densely packed together that the Aymara must use a pick to break open dead plants, which they use for cooking and heating fuel. In the past, the slow-growing *llareta* was depleted in parts of the altiplano because miners collected it for fuel.

The *queñoa (Polylepis tarapacana),* a tree growing up to five meters in height at altitudes up to 4,500 meters or even a bit higher, still grows in scattered forest clusters. Once used for fuel and lumber (despite its often crooked trunk), it grows in cold and shady ravines.

Lauca is an extraordinary destination for birds and birders. The most conspicuous are the Andean condor *(Vultur gryphus);* the flightless, ostrichlike *ñandú* or *suri* (rhea, *Pterocnemia pennata);* and aquatic species such as the Chilean flamingo *(Phoenicopterus chilensis), tagua gigante* (giant coot, *Fulica gigante*), the *guallata* or *piuquén* (Andean goose, *Chloephaga melanoptera*), and the *gaviota andina* (Andean gull, *Larus serranus*). The *perdiz cordillerana de Arica* (Andean tinamou, *Nothoprocta pentlandii*) is a narrow endemic species.

One of the primary reasons for Lauca's creation was protection of the vicuña *(Vicugna vicugna),* the wild camelid that's kin to the domestic llama *(Lama glama)* and alpaca *(Lama pacos),* both herded by the Aymara shepherds who still inhabit, and own, much of the park. Vicuña numbers, only about 1,000 in the 1970s, have increased to more than 16,000 today thanks to park management and the virtual cessation of poaching.

Other mammals include the rarely seen puma *(Felis concolor,* the park's largest predator), the even rarer *taruca* or northern *huemul (Hippocamelus antisensis),* foxes, and the plump vizcacha *(Lagidium viscacia),* a rodent from the chinchilla family that inhabits scattered rookeries. The domestic sheep, a Spanish introduction that survives in part on forage that llamas and alpacas cannot tolerate, is also numerous.

Sights: Nine km east of the park's western entrance, where Ruta 11 emerges from the narrow Quebrada Taipicahue onto the altiplano, 4,300 meters above sea level, **Las Cuevas** is one of the best places to view and photograph both vicuñas and vizcachas. Nearby are a rock shelter inhabited by hunter-gatherers nearly 10,000 years ago, a *chacu* whose narrowing rock walls trapped vicuñas in pre-Columbian times, and rustic thermal baths whose temperature hovers around 31°C. A short distance to the east, the primary colors of a sorethumb sculpture of an Andean *zampoña* (panpipe) mar the view at the **Mirador Llano de Chucuyo,** a Conaf-constructed observation point.

From the observation point, toward the east, are the Llanos de Chucuyo (Plains of Chucuyo) and the well-watered **Ciénegas de Parinacota,** the marshes or *bofedales* of Parinacota, the park's most productive pasturelands and most diverse assemblage of flora. Culturally augmented by a network of irrigation canals, the marshes provide habitat to wild geese, ducks, coots, and other waterfowl. At the village of **Chucuyo,** where several roadside restaurants cater to passing Bolivian truckers, there's a small colonial chapel and a local weavers' cooperative selling locally produced alpaca woolens.

Just beyond Chucuyo, a dirt road follows the edge of the *bofedal* north toward the seemingly dormant village of **Parinacota,** 4,400 meters above sea level, a *zona típica* national monument for its traditional architecture. During festival dates, such as August 30's Fiesta de Santa Rosa de Lima, Aymara throngs crowd in and around the almost abandoned hamlet's 17th-century **Iglesia de Parinacota,** a national architectural monument in its own right. Surrounded by adobe walls, themselves topped by a peculiar combination of ecclesiastical and phallic statuary, the church features a separate two-story bell tower at its southwest corner. Five meters wide and 22 meters long, with two lateral chapels, the building is roofed with *icchu.* Local vendors sell woolens and other crafts, not all of which are locally made, outside the walls.

Interestingly, the church's interior murals, by an indigenous artist from colonial Cuzco, portray Spanish soldiers leading Christ to the cross, alongside a graphically disconcerting *Final Judgment* in which sinners suffer gruesome tortures before being led to the jaws of a fire-breathing dragon (interestingly enough, the inhabitants of Parinacota remain staunchly Catholic, while those of nearby Chucuyo have converted to evangelical Christianity). Legend says that the small but solid table now shackled to the wall once wandered the village in pursuit of spirits.

Once home to a University of Texas high Andean genetics project, Conaf's Refugio Parinacota no longer provides accommodations, but park rangers stationed here can provide information on nearby excursions such as 5,097-meter **Cerro Guane Guane,** an extinct volcano whose summit offers astounding panoramas of the altiplano. The climb takes at least four hours and the last several hundred meters involves a particularly tiresome assault through volcanic ash and sand.

Less strenuously approached, just to the east of Parinacota, **Laguna Cotacotani** is in fact a series of small lakes whose water levels vary according to diversions toward the Central Chapiquiña hydroelectric plant in the precordillera. These di-

versions have also desiccated parts of the *bofedales,* but there are still crested ducks, Andean geese, and other wildlife, including foxes, at the base of the scattered cinder cones and congealed lava flows that surround it.

East of Chucuyo, toward the Bolivian border, **Lago Chungará** is a shallow but biologically thriving lake formed when lava flows dammed the Río Lauca in Holocene times. At 4,517 meters above sea level, covering an area of 21.5 square km to a maximum depth of only 37 meters, Chungará supports abundant populations of migratory birds such as the Andean goose, the Andean gull, several species of ducks, and even flamingos. Giant coots, about the size of domestic turkeys, build floating nests near the shoreline.

To the north of Chungará, Lauca's most imposing natural landmarks are the twin Pallachata volcanoes, known individually as Parinacota (elevation 6,350 meters) and Pomerabe (6,232 meters). Both are climbable for truly well-equipped parties but require permission from the Dirección de Fronteras y Límites (Difrol) in Santiago, since they are directly on the border. Their snowy cones are dormant but, only a short distance south of the highway, Volcán Guallatire (6,061 meters) smolders constantly.

Conaf maintains a ranger station, as well as a campground and *refugio,* at Chungará, where crafts vendors meet tour buses in the early afternoon; as in Parinacota, not all of its items are locally produced. To the east, directly on the border, the **Feria Tambo Quemado,** taking place on alternate Fridays, is where the local Aymara go to exchange goods with their kin from across the line. **Accommodations and Food:** Conaf's **Camping Parinacota,** in its namesake village, has two small but sheltered tent sites for US$9 each. At Lago Chungará, its somewhat more elaborate and considerably more scenic **Camping Chungará** costs the same, but it's also higher and colder; there are also picnic tables here.

Because of objections from Aymara innkeepers who only recently have begun offering accommodations, Conaf's *Refugio Parinacota* may no longer provide lodging (though campers can use the toilets and showers). Conaf's **Refugio Chungará,** though, still does offer beds, for

NORTE GRANDE

THE AMERICAN CAMELS IN CHILE

One of South America's stereotypes is the native highland herder, with his llamas, in Peru and Bolivia. Aymara and Quechua shepherds, with their colorful clothing, are one of the continent's symbols, but the reality behind the symbol, part of Andean life for millennia, is more complex and interesting. Even 500 years' intrusion of Spanish livestock—cattle and sheep—has not completely displaced indigenous pastoralists and their animals, who play a more practical than picturesque role in their countries' economies.

All four New World camels, the wild guanaco and vicuña and their domestic cousins the llama and alpaca, are present in Chile. All of them have distinct ecological requirements, but the guanaco *(Lama guanicoe)* is the most adaptable, thriving in a discontinuous distribution from the Peruvian Andes all the way to Tierra del Fuego, at altitudes ranging from sea level to several thousand meters. Still a common sight in Chilean and Argentine Patagonia, and occasionally even in the Argentine pampas, the guanaco and its *chulengo* young served the indigenous Tehuelche and other native peoples as food and fiber.

Known for its extraordinarily fine wool—so fine that the Inka rulers reserved it for their personal use—the vicuña *(Vicugna vicugna)* occupies a far smaller geographical and altitudinal range, well above 4,000 meters, from south-central Peru to northwestern Argentina. After the Spanish takeover, uncontrolled hunting and poaching endangered the species until, by the early 1970s, Peru, Bolivia, Chile, and Argentina had all instituted vicuña conservation programs; Chile's, based in Parque Nacional Lauca, was perhaps the most effective.

Most often associated with Peru and Bolivia,

herding of the llama *(Lama glama)* and alpaca *(Lama pacos)* is common in the altiplano of the Norte Grande. Traditionally a pack animal—though llama trains are few in Chile—the llama also provides coarse wool and meat, and it can tolerate a wide variety of environmental conditions; the alpaca, primarily raised for its fine thick fleece and secondarily for meat, needs well-watered marshy pastures known as *bofedales.*

In the northernmost Chilean altiplano, where rainfall is highest and the *bofedales* are most abundant, the blend of the herds is nearly 50–50, with the occasional sheep. In the drier pastures farther south, llamas predominate, but there is also a bewildering mix of hybrids: the *huarizo* (offspring of the female alpaca and the male llama), pacovicuña (female alpaca and a male vicuña), *misti* (female llama and male alpaca), *llamovicuña* (male vicuña and female llama), *pacoguanaco* (male alpaca and female guanaco), *llamoguanaco* (male guanaco and female llama), *warilla* (llama-alpaca hybrid with llama characteristics dominant), and *t'aqa* (llama-alpaca hybrid with alpaca characteristics dominant).

As picturesque as Andean pastoralism appears, as an economic system it works like any other. Some of Chile's Aymara herders do very well, with large numbers of animals and substantial clips of wool, while others barely get by and many have left for opportunities in the city or elsewhere. Far from an ideal egalitarian economy, it has concentrated land and animals in the hands of a relative few. And these are the ones who will probably benefit if, as anticipated, earnings from the commercialization of wool from the recovering vicuña brings reinvestment in the altiplano.

US$7 pp. At Parinacota, the best choice is now **Albergue Francisca Morales,** but there are other options as well.

At Chucuyo, directly on Ruta 11, there are several truckers' restaurants, including **Copihue de Oro** and **Restaurant Matilde,** the latter of which also offers inexpensive beds. Limited supplies are available in both Chucuyo and Parinacota, but it's better to bring food from Arica or Putre.

Information: In addition to its *refugio* at Parinacota, Conaf has opened new Centros de Información Turística at Las Cuevas and Lago Chungará. But, because the rangers are often working in the field, there may not always be someone on duty. Unlike many other Chilean parks, because it is on a major international transit route, Lauca does not collect an admission fee.

Transportation: From Arica's Terminal Internacional, Transporte Humire, tel. 58/260164, and Buses Martínez, tel. 58/220106, go to Parinacota and the Bolivian border at Visviri at 10 A.M. and 10 P.M. Tuesday and Friday. Bolivia-bound buses will drop passengers at Chucuyo (the turnoff for Parinacota) and Lago Chungará, but they should expect to pay the full fare to Arica.

Motorists should bring extra gasoline, though it may be available at Putre and Chucuyo at premium prices. Remember that vehicles at these high altitudes consume at least 20–30 percent more fuel than at sea level.

Reserva Nacional Las Vicuñas

Part of Parque Nacional Lauca until, under pressure from mining interests, it was recategorized to permit exploitation of existing tailings from the gold mine at Choquelimpie, 209,131-hectare Reserva Nacional Las Vicuñas gets far fewer visitors than its northern neighbor—most tours and tourists do not stray far from the paved international highway. Less populated than Lauca, it boasts abundant wildlife—similar to that of Lauca—and a string of Aymara hamlets and shepherds' outposts en route to points south.

Sights: East of Las Cuevas and west of Chucuyo, separate gravel roads leading south merge to continue southeast, passing the junction to the Central Chapiquiña hydroelectric plant in the precordillera and continuing past **Choquelimpie,** a colonial gold mine that only recently closed; for a brief period in the late 1980s and early 1990s, tailings were processed under new technology that permitted exploitation of lower-grade deposits.

From Choquelimpie the road, troublesome in very wet weather, heads southeast toward **Ancuta,** which features a small colonial chapel, and the village of **Guallatire,** at the foot of its smoking namesake volcano. The last substantial settlement for several hours, Guallatire has an impressive 17th-century church with a freestanding bell tower and some of the Chilean altiplano's most productive *bofedales.* Motorists must stop at the Carabineros police checkpoint here.

Just south of the village, on the west side of the road, are the ruins of the colonial **Trapiche de Guallatire,** a hydraulic silver mill and smelter. Beyond here, vicuñas and rheas are common sights, but summer rains can make the road south difficult even for skilled motorists with 4WD despite good bridges over the Río Viluvio and the Río Lauca—avoid the slippery yellow clay if at all possible. Only the occasional isolated shepherd's house is around to lend a hand.

Accommodations and Food: Accommodations options are limited. At Tambokollo, two km from the Choquelimpie crossing, Clara Blanco's well-kept **Albergue Tambokollo,** tel. 58/248688 in Arica, is a simple three-bed adobe lodging with clean toilets and hot showers, serves basic meals, and also offers tours to Guallatire, Surire, and other local sights.

In Guallatire, Conaf's **Refugio Guallatire** charges US$9 pp for bunks in a comfortable building. If planning to stay, though, it's good to make advance inquiries at Conaf in Arica or Putre—rangers are not always present.

Transportation: There is no public transportation whatsoever and few private vehicles, but loop tours from Arica do pass through the area. In summer, 4WD may not be sufficient for areas south of Guallatire; the rest of the year, it's not necessary, though high clearance is a good idea.

Monumento Natural Salar de Surire

Home to three species of flamingos, 4,200 meters above sea level, 11,298-hectare Monumento Natural Salar de Surire is an awkward reserve comprising roughly 70 percent of the sprawling, blindingly white salt lake from which it takes its name. Oddly enough, its Aymara name means "place of the rhea" which, though present in the area, attracts less attention than the flamingos, who feed on microorganisms in pools created by the summer rains.

Created in 1983, when commercial mining interests forced the dismantling of Parque Nacional Lauca into three separate units, it does *not* include 4,560 hectares granted to the Sociedad Química Industrial de Borax in 1989, only months before the formal end of the Pinochet dictatorship, for a surface borax mine. Ironically, of Conaf's various land-use categories, *monumentos naturales* presumably receive the highest level of protection.

Still, up to 10,000 birds spend the summer here. Most of them are Chilean flamingos, but the larger Andean flamingo *(Phoenicoparrus andinus)* and the smaller, rarer James flamingo *(Phoenicoparrus jamesii)* are also present. Vicuñas and rheas are also common sights.

Sights: Wildlife, primarily the large flamingo colonies at the **Lagunas Salar de Surire,** is the main attraction. Just outside the door of Conaf's ranger station on the west side of the reserve, there's a large vizcacha rookery that's an ideal hangout for photographers. Rheas are also a common sight here.

Some 16 km southeast of Conaf's ranger station, the **Termas de Polloquere** is a small geyser field with a handful of large pools suitable for swimming.

Accommodations: On the west side of the Salar, Conaf's **Guardería y Refugio Salar de Surire** has comfortable bunks with kitchen facilities, plus solar-powered electricity and hot showers, for US$9 pp; the rangers who run it welcome visitors and can give essential information for those heading south toward Isluga. Tour groups from Arica often stay here, so it's best to inquire in Arica, Putre, or Parinacota about availability.

Camping is possible at Termas de Polloquere, but the location is very exposed.

Transportation: The Salar de Surire is roughly 126 km southeast of Putre via either Las Cuevas (Parque Nacional Lauca) or the less traveled alternative via the Portezuelo de Chapiquiña, and 48 km south of Guallatire. Again, there is no public transport, so renting a vehicle or taking a tour from Arica is pretty much the only option.

Segments of the road to Parque Nacional Isluga and Colchane, 79 km to the south, can be tricky in wet weather; note also that the distances on Turistel's highway map are grossly inaccurate. Beyond the well-marked junction at Polloquere, the road grows faint over **Cerro Capitán,** then becomes clearer toward **Mucomucone,** where there's a disconcerting river crossing that feels like diving into a pool—high clearance is a good idea, though the bottom is firm and 4WD is not essential. The road then passes through the villages of **Enquelga, Isluga,** and finally to the bleak border post of **Colchane**

(for more detail, see the separate entry on Parque Nacional Isluga).

PISAGUA

From its appearance, it's hard to picture that sleepy Pisagua, at the end of a precipitous zigzag road that descends from the coast range, was once one of northern Chile's principal ports. A town whose population numbered several thousands in the early 20th century has only about 200 inhabitants today, though it's slowly reviving with the export of sea urchins and increasing tourist traffic. There are even new houses being built alongside the historical monuments that remain from its nitrate heyday.

In the 1970s, though, Pisagua was a synonym for terror. Its remote location—only one road in or out, through utterly waterless and unrelentingly shadeless terrain—made it a natural prison after the military putsch of 1973 (some prisoners were forced to run barefoot up the hot

Torre Reloj (clock tower) at Pisagua

barren hillsides, as if to teach them how futile any escape attempt would be). After Chile's return to democracy in 1989, investigators found a mass grave at the town's historic cemetery.

The handful of native-born Pisaguans who still live here keep to themselves, having little to do with recent arrivals. While it's a languid backwater during the week, it can fill up with visitors on weekends.

History

Pisagua was a minor port until the exploitation of nitrates at Zapiga, in the coast range, made it a convenient export point. It was the site of a major battle during the War of the Pacific, when Chilean troops came ashore on November 2, 1879, to defeat allied Peruvian and Bolivian forces. Under Chilean rule, it became the country's third major nitrate port, after Antofagasta and Iquique.

At its peak, Pisagua had two daily newspapers, three banks, and seven piers—three belonging to the Nitrate Railways Company, two to nitrate baron John Thomas North, one to the Compañía Salitrera La Aguada, and one to the Chilean state. After the nitrate collapse, it became a penal colony and continued for many years as the terminus of the Longino, the longitudinal railway that connected the north with the south. It languished for many years thereafter, before coming to unwanted notoriety during the Pinochet years.

Sights

Several striking landmarks from Pisagua's nitrate boom are national architectural monuments. Pisagua's gaily painted, 12-meter wooden **Torre Reloj** (clock tower, 1887) stands sentinel on a bedrock outcrop above the town; its clock no longer functions, however. Immediately to its south, built on fill, the two-story **Hospital de Pisagua** (1906–09) began to slip down the hillside not long after its construction, and was finally abandoned in 1958.

Along the shore—overhanging it, really—the **Teatro Municipal** (1897) was an extravagant performing arts facility for a town of Pisagua's size, complete with private boxes, bench seating

for the proles, and an immense stage. While the regional government has contributed significant funds toward its preservation and restoration, the peeling ceiling murals, unfortunately, are in need of immediate attention. The northern half of the building once housed a market, city offices, the Banco de Londres, and, during the dictatorship, many of the female prisoners. For access to the theater, contact Catarina Saldaña at the tourist kiosk, opposite the main entrance (see Information, below).

Half a block east of the plaza, the Georgianstyle **Cárcel Pública de Pisagua** (1909) served as a standard prison for decades and as a political prison during President González Videla's Communist purge of 1947, but after September of 1973 so many prisoners filled its cells—roughly half the size of a modest bedroom—that there was no room for them to sit down. After a German crew filmed these appalling conditions clandestinely, the military shifted half the prisoners into the market building, separating the women upstairs. The administrators' rooms at the front of the building now serve as hotel accommodations, while those toward the back of the building, ironically, sometimes host banquets.

North of the theater, the rails are gone from the **Estación Ferrocarril de Pisagua,** where nitrates and passengers once arrived, and even the station itself is at risk—posted notices beg people not to carry off any of the remaining lumber. On the northern outskirts of town, the **Monolito Centenario** memorializes the Chilean landing of 1879.

Beyond the cemetery, two km north of town, rusting metal and rotting wooden crosses mark gravesites at the **Cementerio Municipal;** nearby, a recent marker memorializes the victims exhumed from a mass grave with the vow:

> *Although footprints may tread this site for a thousand years, they will not cover the blood of those who fell here.*

North of the cemetery, the road climbs the steep headland of Punta Pisagua and drops into **Pisagua Vieja,** the adobe remains of the town's original site (and also the site of a pre-Columbian cemetery). The estuary of the nearby **Quebrada de**

Tana is a wetland breeding site for shorebirds, but the dirt road that used to ascend the Quebrada to Hacienda Tiliviche is no longer passable.

Accommodations and Food

North of the police station at Playa Blanca, Pisagua's free **Camping Municipal** can draw lots of weekend visitors but hardly anybody during the week. It has clean flush toilets and warm-to-hot showers with water funneled from the former Oficina Dolores, on the Panamericana. If it gets too crowded, there are sites without infrastructure at **Playa Blanca,** near the Monolito Centenario.

Minimarket La Cabaña, on the Costanera, has very simple accommodations—with as many as four beds squeezed into a room—for US$5 pp.

Half a block east of the Plaza de Armas, **Hotel Pisagua,** tel. 57/731509 or 09/5108016, is a hotel with a history—and not a happy one, as it occupies the former prison. It's also, however, a de facto museum holding many relics from the Guerra del Pacífico and the nitrate era, and even subtle references to the events of the 1970s through portrait paintings of Pablo Neruda and folksinger Violeta Parra. Rates are US$24 pp with breakfast and dinner in rooms with shared bath and hot showers; guests do not stay in the former cells, but rather in rooms once occupied by prison administrators.

Pisagua has several seafood *picadas,* including **Don Gato,** Prat s/n, and **Acuario.**

Information

Across from the Teatro Municipal, former exile Catarina Saldaña runs Pisagua's unofficial Oficina de Información Turística, tel. 57/731519 or 57/731502. Catarina, who spent 18 years in Quebec, is knowledgeable about the town and its history—even the most controversial points—and speaks French as well as Spanish.

Transportation

Halfway between Arica and Iquique, Pisagua is accessible only by a slowly deteriorating paved road that leads directly west from the Panamericana at a junction 85 km south of Cuya (Camarones) and 47 km north of Huara. There is no regular public transportation from the junction and vehicles along the route are few, but rumors persist that Iquique travel agencies may start service.

IQUIQUE

Sometimes called—only semifacetiously—the "Miami of Chile" for its high-rise beachfront hotels and condos, the port city of Iquique and its Zona Franca (Zofri) duty-free zone were the main motor of import-led growth during the Norte Grande's economic boom of the 1980s. While that boom has slowed, Iquique stands alone as Tarapacá's political capital, major port, and tourist destination, pulling even Argentines and Paraguayans over the Andes for duty-free shopping.

For foreigners, the city's most unusual sight is its late 19th- and early 20th-century architecture, its fire-prone Georgian and Victorian mansions built of so-called *pino oregón* (literally, "Oregon pine"), which is in fact Douglas fir *(Pseudotsuga mienziesii)* shipped from California and the Pacific Northwest during the nitrate boom.

Iquique is also a center for outdoor activities, most notably surfing and parasailing *(parapente),* both of which bring in visitors from North America and Europe. Cruise ships are also beginning to visit here, and the city may soon have direct air connections, to Paris and Frankfurt via São Paulo. As for the Miami connection, well, Iquique does maintain a "sister city" relationship with Dade County.

History

In colonial times and even after independence, the port of Iquique played second fiddle to Arica; it was, remarked Darwin in 1835:

> *most gloomy; the little port, with its few vessels, and small group of wretched houses, seemed overwhelmed and out of proportion to the rest of the scene.*

In short order, nitrates changed everything. Arica enjoyed a direct route to Potosí via the Lluta and Azapa valleys, but several deeply incised canyons separated it from the broad nitrate pampas that extended from behind the coast range, from Pisagua in the north to Taltal in the south.

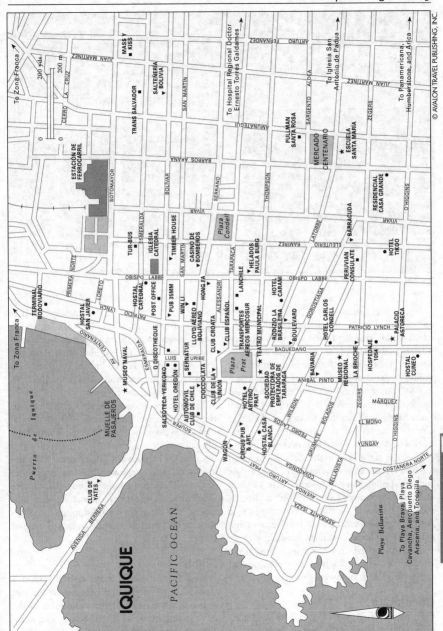

IQUIQUE

PACIFIC OCEAN

Puerto de Iquique

NORTE GRANDE

To Zona Franca

To Zona Franca

© AVALON TRAVEL PUBLISHING, INC.

200 yds.

200 m

MUELLE DE PASAJEROS

CLUB DE YATES

★ MUSEO NAVAL

ESTACIÓN DE FERROCARRIL

TERMINAL RODOVIARIO

HOSTAL SAN JAVIER

TUR-BUS

TRANS SALVADOR

MASS Y KISS

SALTENERÍA BOLIVIA

To Hospital Regional Doctor
Ernesto Torres Galdames

To Iglesia San
Antonio de Padua

To Panamericana,
Humberstone, and Arica

ESCUELA
SANTA MARÍA

MERCADO
CENTENARIO ★

PULLMAN
SANTA ROSA

RESIDENCIAL
CASA GRANDE

HOTEL
TIKO

BARRACUDA

HELADOS
PAULA BURG

Plaza
Condell

IGLESIA
CATEDRAL

TIMBER HOUSE

CASINO DE
BOMBEROS

HOSTAL
CATEDRAL

POST OFFICE

PUB 35MM

WIN FI

HONG FA

LLOYD AÉREO
BOLIVIANO

CLUB CROATA

CLUB ESPAÑOL

LANCHILE

PERUVIAN
CONSULATE

HOTEL
CARLOS
CONDELL

HOSPEDAJE
1054

HOSTAL
CUÑEO

PALACIO
ASTORECA

HOTEL
CARANI

RODIZIO LA
BRASILEIRA

BOULEVARD

TEATRO MUNICIPAL

TRANSPORTES
AÉREOS MERCOSUR

Plaza
Prat

BAVARIA

LA BRIOCHE ★

MUSEO
REGIONAL ★

SOCIEDAD
PROTECTORA DE
EMPLEADOS DE
TARAPACÁ

HOTEL
ARTURO
PRAT

CLUB DE LA
UNIÓN

CIOCCOLATA

SERNATUR

Q DISCOTHEQUE

HOTEL OREGON

SALSOTECA YERIKOKO

AUTOMÓVIL
CLUB DE CHILE

CIRCUS PUB
& ART

HOSTAL CASA
BLANCA

WAGÓN

HOSTAL SAN JAVIER

To Playa Brava Playa
Cavancha, Aeropuerto Diego
Aracena, and Tocopilla

Playa Bellavista

N

Avenida Brasil

AVENIDA ARTURO PRAT

ASPIRANTE ISAZA

COVADONGA

PEDRO LAGOS

GRUMETE BOLADOS

WILSON

ANÍBAL PINTO

BAQUEDANO

PATRICIO LYNCH

OBISPO LABBÉ

GOROSTIAGA

ELEUTERIO RAMÍREZ

LATORRE

O'HIGGINS

VIVAR

ZEGERS

MÁRQUEZ

EL MORRO

YUNGAY

BELLAVISTA

COSTANERA NORTE

SOUPER

ARTURO PRAT

CENTENARIO

PRIMERA NORTE

LORETO

LYNCH

PATRICIO LYNCH

ESMERALDA

OBISPO LABBÉ

LUIS

URIBE

ALESSANDRI

SAN MARTÍN

TARAPACÁ

SERRANO

BOLÍVAR

VIVAR

BARROS ARANA

THOMPSON

SAN MARTÍN

SAN MARTÍN

CERRO LA CRUZ

JUAN MARTÍNEZ

JUAN MARTÍNEZ

AMUNÁTEGUI

ARTURO FERNÁNDEZ

SARGENTO ALDEA

ZEGERS

O'HIGGINS

VIVAR

JUAN MARTÍNEZ

SOTOMAYOR

AVENIDA ABERRA – BERBERA

typical architecture, Calle Baquedano, Iquique

© WAYNE BERNHARDSON

Some nitrate ports, such as Pisagua, stagnated and even died, but Iquique flourished and adapted, as fishing complemented and then replaced nitrates as the basis of the local economy. It was, however, the backdrop for one of the most infamous incidents in Chilean labor history when, in 1907, police and military fired upon and killed hundreds of nitrate strikers holed up in the Escuela Santa María—still standing south of the Mercado Central (the school, unfortunately but unremarkably, is not a national historical monument).

Creation of the Zofri in the mid-1970s spurred a new cycle of immigration into the city. As Iquique's population grew to more than 140,000 and occupied nearly all available space on its narrow coastal shelf, the ridgetop community of Alto Hospicio—which only two decades ago consisted of a handful of farmers who grew vegetables with irrigation water extracted from the *camanchaca*—mushroomed to accommodate tens of thousands of low-wage workers.

Orientation

On a narrow shelf at the foot of a 600-meter escarpment that parallels the Pacific Ocean, Iquique is 1,850 km north of Santiago via the Panamer-

icana and coastal Ruta 1 via Antofagasta. It is 315 km from Arica via paved Ruta 16, which runs east-west to and from a junction near the nitrate ghost town of Humberstone, and the Panamericana; it is 410 km from Calama via Ruta 16, the Panamericana, and paved Ruta 24, the Tocopilla-Calama highway.

Historically, Iquique's center is Plaza Prat, but the city has spread north and, to a greater extent, south along the Pacific beaches. North of the old railroad station, the Barrio Industrial is also home to the commercial Zona Franca, while the areas south and east, toward the towering dunes of Cerro Dragón, are largely residential. On the escarpment above the city, the working-class suburb of Alto Hospicio has mushroomed spontaneously over the surrounding pampa in the past two decades.

Sights

Dating from the nitrate era, central Iquique's characteristic Victorian and Georgian architecture makes it a walker's delight, while most of the city's popular beaches extend south. The Peruvian-era **Torre Reloj** (clock tower, 1877) remains the centerpiece of recently remodeled **Plaza Prat,** surrounded by a cluster of other historic structures, several of them national monuments.

On the south side of the plaza, the **Teatro Municipal** (1890) has been the city's premier performing arts venue for parts of three centuries; immediately alongside it, Iquique's workers literally and figuratively flexed their muscles in building one of the country's first organized labor social clubs, the **Sociedad Protectora de Empleados de Tarapacá** (1913)—only a few years after the 1907 massacre.

Designed by architect Miguel Retornano in a Moorish style, the two-story **Centro Español,** at the northeast corner of the plaza, dates from 1904; home to one of Iquique's best traditional restaurants, it features early 20th-century oils based on *Don Quijote* by Spanish painter Vicente Tordecillas and later scenes from Spanish history by Chilean artist Sixto García. To its immediate north, the **Club Yugoeslavo** also dates from this period.

Originally named Huancavelica, **Calle Baquedano** was renamed for General Manuel Baquedano after the Chilean victory in the War of the Pacific. Along with Plaza Prat, it comprises a *zona típica* national monument for its rows of wooden buildings and houses with airy second-story balconies between Calle Serrano to the north and Calle J. J. Pérez to the south. Some of these buildings are painted with bright contrasting colors, while others have embellished the natural wood with stain and varnish, and they really stand out.

Among the landmarks along Baquedano are the former **Tribunales de Justicia** (1892), now housing the Museo Regional (see below), near the corner of Zegers; the **Palacio Astoreca** (1904), which belonged to a nitrate tycoon who lived there only a short time before his death, at the corner of O'Higgins (see below); and the Chilean army's former headquarters, now the **Museo del Primer Cuerpo del Ejército** at the corner of Riquelme (see below). Just beyond the district is the **Iquique English College,** at Balmaceda and Patricio Lynch.

Iquique has fewer religious landmarks than most other Chilean cities, but a pair of them are noteworthy national monuments: the **Iglesia San Antonio de Padua,** distinguished by its twin bell towers at the corner of Latorre and 21 de Mayo, and its adjacent **Convento Franciscano;** and the **Catedral de la Inmaculada Concepción** (1885) at Obispo Labbé and Bolívar, which replaced an earlier church that burned to the ground. It did not acquire cathedral status until 1929, with the establishment of the bishopric of Iquique.

One block north of the cathedral, at Ramírez and Sotomayor, trains from the Georgian gingerbread **Estación Central** linked Iquique with Santiago as late as the mid-1970s. Along with the adjacent **Casa del Administrador,** a couple of antique locomotives and passenger and dining cars, it is also a national monument.

There's a cluster of historic landmarks on and around the waterfront four blocks north of Plaza Prat. The most significant is the former **Edificio de la Aduana,** which holds the well-kept Museo Naval (naval museum) but is otherwise deteriorating (see below). Immediately to its west, seaborne passengers landed and disembarked at the **Muelle de Pasajeros** (1901), also known as Muelle Prat, a covered pier with concrete steps to accommodate the tides. Harbor tours still leave from here, visiting the **Boya Conmemorativa del Combate de Iquique,** which marks the spot where Chilean naval officer Arturo Prat's corvette *Esmeralda* sank in a confrontation with Peruvian officer Miguel Grau's ironclad *Huáscar* (later captured by the Chileans, the *Huáscar* survives as a museum piece in the naval base at Talcahuano, near Concepción).

Museo Regional

Housed in the former Tribunales, in the Baquedano historic district, the regional museum chronicles the evolution of local cultures, in the context of their basic geography and environment, from early Chinchorro times (4000–2000 B.C.) to the present.

The Chinchorros, a coastal people, used three-log kayaks (of a sort) and rafts made from sea lion pelts for inshore subsistence fishing; some mummies, intentionally deformed skulls, and great numbers of adornments also date from this period. With the rise of agriculture in the valley oases, precordillera, and the Andes, there developed an

NORTE GRANDE

intricate series of contacts between the coast and the interior, which intensified during Tiwanaku times (around A.D. 1000)—geoglyphs and other rock art in the transverse river canyons are the most spectacular proofs of this—and during the Inka conquest (around A.D. 1450). There's an impressive assortment of Tiwanaku and Inka pottery, basketry and textiles, and Inka mummies (probably sacrifices of girls 18 or 19 years old) found at Cerro Esmeralda, near Iquique.

In addition to pre-Columbian Tarapacá, extensive exhibits on the nitrate era offer interpretive presentations on topics such as *fichas,* the tokens used in lieu of cash in nitrate *oficinas, minas,* haciendas, hotels, stores, restaurants, and transportation (*fichas* were outlawed in 1924). There are also a model of the former Oficina La Palma (the current ghost town of Humberstone, east of Iquique) and a full-scale ersatz Aymara village scene from the altiplano.

Summer hours are 9:30 A.M.–1 P.M. and 3–6:30 P.M. weekdays, 10:30 A.M.–1 P.M. and 4–8 P.M. Saturday, and 10 A.M.–1 P.M. Sunday; the rest of the year, weekday hours are 8:30 A.M.–1 P.M. and 3–6:50 P.M., Saturday 10:30 A.M.–1 P.M. The museum is at Baquedano 951, tel. 57/411034; admission costs US$1 pp.

Palacio Astoreca

Built for nitrate baron Juan Higinio Astoreca in 1904, Iquique's most impressive remaining mansion is a Georgian-style edifice whose owner inhabited it for only a few years until his death in 1908. His heirs sold it to the regional government, and from then until 1976 it housed generations of bureaucrats before being restored and opened to the public.

Now sparsely furnished, as it's used primarily as a museum and cultural center with exhibitions by local artists, the Palacio Astoreca is architecturally notable for its 27 capacious and high-ceilinged rooms, embellished with natural wood trim, immense chandeliers, stained glass, and second-story verandas. Constructed mostly of Douglas fir, it's probably the work of Miguel Retornano, designer of the Club Español.

Open 10 A.M.–1 P.M. and 4–7:30 P.M. Tuesday through Friday, 10 A.M.–1:30 P.M. Saturday, and 11 A.M.–2 P.M. Sunday, the *palacio* is at O'Higgins 350, corner of Baquedano, tel. 57/425600. Admission costs US$.60 for adults, US$.30 for children. It also has its own small webpage, http://iqq.cl/palacioastoreca, in passable English.

Museo del Primer Cuerpo del Ejército

In an immaculately maintained building in the historic district, Iquique's military museum reveals more than you probably care to know about military tactics used in War of the Pacific battles at the Morro de Arica, the port of Pisagua, and the nitrate *oficinas* of Dolores and Pampa Germania. While it includes many artifacts of these battles, including heart-wrenching soldiers' letters home, it's really the counterpart of Gettysburg for Civil War zealots.

A courteous military guide does his best to give a thorough explanation—from the Chilean viewpoint—of the issues behind the war. At Baquedano 1396, the museum is open 10 A.M.–3:15 P.M. daily; admission is free.

Edificio de la Aduana (Museo Naval)

Begun in 1871 to replace its predecessor, destroyed by a tsunami in 1869, the former Peruvian customshouse was and still is the port area's major landmark. Its 18th-century colonial design consists of a two-story rectangle with an interior patio surrounded by corridors on each level; reached by a marble staircase, the second floor is covered by a freestanding roof on four gables that extrude from the flat roof and crowned by an octagonal watch tower.

Within the building's meter-thick walls, the naval museum exalts the life and courage—some might say foolishness—of naval Captain Arturo Prat, who died in 1879 while storming the Peruvian ironclad *Huáscar* after it sunk his own *Esmeralda* (whose mast and other artifacts are on display here). Later that same year, though, Chilean forces managed to take Iquique and made the building their headquarters; during the civil war of 1891, the presidential forces of Balmaceda besieged congressional rebels who were holed up here.

Unfortunately, except for the museum, the building is suffering from deferred maintenance and might not survive another tsunami or serious earthquake. Meanwhile, at the corner of Esmeralda and Aníbal Pinto, the Museo Naval is open Tues.–Sat. 10 A.M.–1 P.M. and 3–6 P.M., Sunday and holidays 10 A.M.–1 P.M. only. Admission is free.

Recreation

For most people, Iquique's beaches are its prime recreational attraction, offering swimming, surfing, and sunbathing. The city's ideal geographic and atmospheric conditions have also made it an international destination for *parapente* or paragliding.

Water Sports and Activities: The crescent beach of **Playa Cavancha,** beginning around the intersection of Avenida Balmaceda and Amunátegui and curving south toward its namesake peninsula, is the most popular in the city, thanks largely to its convenience and relatively calm waters. South of Cavancha, paralleling Avenida 11 de Septiembre, **Playa Brava** lives up to its name ("wild beach"), but it's good for sunbathing. A bit farther south, **Playa Huaiquique** is a good surf site and is also the landing point for paragliders who have leapt off the precipice of the coast range east of Cerro Dragón.

Within the city, surfers can also test the breaks at Cavancha's **Sector Saint Tropez,** almost directly at Balmaceda and Amunátegui, and **Playa Bellavista,** near the Intendencia Regional at Avenida Balmaceda and O'Higgins. Outside town, on Ruta 1, there are good breaks at **Punta Gruesa, Punta Aguila,** and **Caleta Loa,** but these would be a full day trip out and back by bus or rental car. The Gringo Surf Shop is at Zegers 734.

From Muelle Prat, there are hourlong tours (US$2.50) past the fishing boats, the buoy where the Esmeralda went down, and the sea lion colony of **Isla de los Lobos;** contact *Lanchas Turísticas Muelle Prat,* tel. 09/3685676. **Nautitour,** tel. 57/421551 or 09/8660119, does more extensive two-hour tours for US$15 pp.

Parapente: Because of its fine, dry weather and late-morning thermals, Iquique is widely considered the best place in South America for paragliding. The city has responded by welcoming paragliders—even to the point of building a takeoff pad on the cliff at the top of the road to Alto Hospicio where, watching the turkey vultures soar when the coastal breeze comes up, participants can judge when to take off. Experienced gliders can conceivably soar for more than 200 km down the coast toward Tocopilla; novices can try short introductory flights in tandem with a guide over the downtown area, offering spectacular views of the city and the dunes of Cerro Dragón before landing at Playa Huaiquique.

French-run **Escuela de Parapente Manutara,** 18 de Septiembre 1512, tel./fax 57/418280, manutarachile@hotmail.com, offers introductory flights for about US$35, three-day courses for US$120. Other operators include the **Escuela de Parapente Altazor,** Serrano 145, Oficina 702, tel. 57/431382, altazor@entelchile.net; **Mane Tour,** Gorostiaga 194, Oficina 2, tel. 09/5811000; **Térmica,** tel. 57/430675 or 09/5-131322; and **Paraventura,** tel. 09/8669281, website: www.parapenteiquique.cl.

Accommodations

Iquique has plentiful accommodations in all categories, but be selective in choosing budget lodgings—the difference in quality is often greater than minor differences in price.

US$10–25: The best of the very cheapest is undoubtedly **Hostal Obispo Labbé,** Obispo Labbé 1272, tel. 57/416181, where simple but spotless rooms with shared bath cost US$6 pp, while freshly painted rooms with private bath and TV cost US$8.50 pp. A good alternative, near Playa Cavancha, is **Hostal América,** Manuel Rodríguez 550, tel. 57/427524, for US$6 pp; though it's been divided up into small rooms, it's been done with a bit more integrity than some other comparably priced places.

From January to mid-March, in a magnificent period house furnished with antiques and embellished with spectacular woodwork, **Hospedaje Baquedano,** Baquedano 1054, tel. 57/423371, offers spacious rooms—not subdivided into cubicles like many others of its sort—for just US$7 pp. It's worth mentioning, though, that the rooms are more sparsely furnished than the common areas, part of which serve as an artists' workshop.

Also part of the historic district, identically priced **Residencial Baquedano,** Baquedano 1315, tel. 57/422990, is open all year. Rates are US$8 pp in small, tidy rooms with shared bath; breakfast is US$1 extra. Near the bus terminal, **Hostal San Javier,** Patricio Lynch 97, tel. 57/427641, is not for claustrophobics—the rooms are almost Lilliputian—but it's seen steady improvement in recent years. Rates are US$10/13 s/d.

Catering primarily but not exclusively to paragliders, French-run **Residencial Manutara,** 18 de Septiembre 1512, tel./fax 57/418280, charges US$10 pp with breakfast and shared bath. It's been slow in developing, but a recent remodel has turned it into an attractive place on a quiet street (some paragliders like to party late, though).

In the historic district, though not really part of it in the architectural sense, **Hostal Cuneo,** Baquedano 1175, tel. 57/428654, is still a good value for US$8 pp with shared bath (only *one* hot shower, however). Next door to a pool hall but otherwise OK, **Hotel Oregón,** San Martín 294, tel. 57/410959, costs US$8.50 pp.

Tidy, friendly **Residencial Casa Grande,** Barros Arana 1071, tel. 57/426846, fax 57/413607, casagrande@entelchile.net, is a fine choice for US$9 pp. For the same price, near Playa Cavancha, the equally friendly and modern **Hostal Beach,** Vivar 1707, tel. 57/429653, has spacious rooms with shared bath.

Across from the cathedral, perennially popular **Hostal Catedral,** Obispo Labbé 233, tel. 57/412184, charges US$8.50 pp with shared bath in patio rooms; it also has rooms with private bath for US$26 s or d.

US$25–50: In a partially modernized older house, **Hostal Casa Blanca,** Gorostiaga 127, tel. 57/420007, fax 57/415586, is clean and comfortable for US$17/26 s/d with private bath, breakfast, telephone, and cable TV; some older rooms are multibedded.

Family-run **Tikoo Hotel,** Ramírez 1051, tel. 57/475031, fax 57/473953, tikoo@ctcinternet.cl, is a real find—an older Iquique house with an attractive new addition in the back. Compact but well-designed rooms with private bath and cable TV cost US$20/30 s/d. **Hotel Costa Norte,** Aníbal Pinto 1150, tel. 57/429449, tel./fax 57/423899, is a new facility offering rooms with private bath, cable TV, telephone, and breakfast for US$25/32 s/d.

In the heart of the historic district, **Hotel Carlos Condell,** Baquedano 964, tel./fax 57/313027, hotel-carlos-condell@123mail.cl, consists of an older sector with spectacular woodwork and a stylish addition toward the back; the elevator is also original, though its exterior has been remodeled. Rates are US$28/42 with standard amenities.

The classic exterior at **Hotel Anakena,** Orella 456, tel./fax 57/510182, paoa@entelchile.net, is deceptive—the modern hotel proper sits behind the historic house, still family-occupied, and the only original area open to the public is the dining room. Rates are US$31/39 s/d with breakfast and private bath.

Hotel Riorsa, Vivar 1542, tel./fax 57/423823, tel. 57/420153, is a modern and friendly but otherwise undistinguished hotel with ample-sized rooms for US$35/45. A reasonable choice in its price range, **Hotel Barros Arana,** Barros Arana 1330, tel. 57/412840, is conventional but reliable. Rates with TV and private bath start around US$38/46.

Hotel Carani, Latorre 426, tel. 57/3999-96/7/9, fax 57/399998, is a modern hotel with numerous amenities, quick service, and a highly professional attitude; rates are US$38/47 s/d.

US$50–100: Iquique's traditional favorite, **Hotel Arturo Prat,** Aníbal Pinto 695, tel. 57/427000, fax 57/429088, website: www.hotelarturoprat.cl, hap@entelchile.net, consists of an older section and a new section with greater amenities but higher prices. Rates are US$48/52 s/d in the older section, US$65/75 in the newer sector. Both include a buffet breakfast.

The upscale high-rise hotels along Playa Cavancha are part of the reason for Iquique's "Miami Beach" image. Among them are **Hostería Cavancha,** Los Rieles 250, tel. 57/431007; charging US$61/74 s/d; **Hotel Chucumata,** Avenida Balmaceda 850, tel. 57/435050, charging US$75/87 s/d; and the **Best Western Hotel Gavina,** Avenida Balmaceda 1497, tel. 57/413030, for US$81/87 s/d.

US$100–150: Another North American chain affiliate, near Playa Brava at the south end of town, the **Holiday Inn Express,** Avenida 11 de Septiembre 1690, tel. 57/433300, costs US$90/104 s/d. At Playa Cavancha, recommended **Hotel Terrado Suites,** Los Rieles 126, tel. 57/488000, charges US$96/110.

Food

La Brioche, Baquedano 882-A, tel. 57/415715, is a good breakfast choice for its espresso and croissants, a good lunch choice for its sandwiches, and a good *onces* choice for its pastries. **Cioccolata,** Aníbal Pinto 487, tel. 57/413010, is a good alternative.

A little different from fire station restaurants elsewhere in the country, the **Compañía Italiana de Bomberos,** Serrano 520, tel. 57/414386, emphasizes its Italian roots. **Bavaria,** Aníbal Pinto 926, tel. 57/427888, is the Iquique branch of the nationwide chain.

For tasty, inexpensive trans-Andean snacks, try **Salteñería Bolivia,** Bolívar 962. *Salteñas* resemble Chilean empanadas but are smaller and spicier, with lighter crusts and a wider variety of fillings.

Like most northern Chilean cities, Iquique has numerous *chifas,* among them **Hong Fa,** Serrano 489, tel. 57/422319, and **Win Li,** San Martín 439, tel. 57/425942. **Rodizio La Brasileira,** Patricio Lynch 758, tel. 57/313909, serves typical Brazilian dishes such as *feijoada,* along with grilled meats.

As the key port for the Norte Grande's fishing industry, Iquique has numerous seafood options, such as the **Club de Yates,** Jorge Barrera s/n, tel. 57/471968, on the water just west of the Muelle de Pasajeros; Playa Cavancha's upscale **El Sombrero,** Los Rieles 704, tel. 57/480296 (closed Mondays); and the more modest **Las Urracas,** Avenida Balmaceda 431, tel. 57/417319.

For cheaper but still excellent seafood, though, try any of the second-floor *cocinerías* in the **Mercado Centenario,** the central market bounded by Barros Arana, Sargento Aldea, Amunátegui, and Latorre.

Several classy restaurants are clustered in historic buildings around Plaza Prat: the **Club Croata,** Plaza Prat 310, tel. 57/416222; the **Club de la Unión,** Plaza Prat 278, 3rd floor, tel. 57/413236; and the resplendent Moorish-styled **Club Español,** Plaza Prat 584, tel. 57/423284, a landmark in its own right. Across the plaza is the almost equally distinctive but more proletarian **Sociedad Protectora de Empleados de Tarapacá,** Thompson 207, which has inexpensive lunches.

Boulevard, Baquedano 790, tel. 57/413695, is an outstanding but expensive French restaurant where entrées range US$7—10 but everything else, including salads and side dishes, is á la carte—making it easy to blow upward of US$30 pp on dinner. The budget-conscious can sample their lunchtime fare for about US$6 prix fixe.

In an archetypically historic Iquique building with magnificent natural woodwork and great decor, **El Viejo Wagón,** Thompson 85, tel. 57/411647, serves regional specialties, mostly fish dishes, such as *papaniagua cañamo,* a fish served in *salsa wacatai,* a sort of sweet-and-sour sauce. Most entrées are in the US$7–9 range but, like Boulevard, á la carte items can make the bill add up. One dining room is decorated in a early cinema motif, another with nitrate relics better than some museums have. Its *pebre* is tastier and spicier than most.

For ice cream, **Helados Paula Burg,** Obispo Labbé 660, is probably the best in town.

Entertainment

Iquique has a pretty active nightlife, with a variety of good bars (some of which have live music and serve pretty good food as well) and dance clubs.

One of Iquique's best choices is lively **Taberna Barracuda,** in a restored building at Gorostiaga 601, tel. 57/427969, which has great Peruvian pisco sours at its burnished wooden bar and an 8–10 P.M. happy hour daily; the kitchen serves excellent Mexican and Peruvian specialties.

Like the Barracuda, the **Timber House,** Bolívar 553, tel. 57/422538, is a bar/restaurant that occupies a traditional Iquique house with great natural woodwork and an architecturally spectacular upper floor that includes a noise-insulated disco.

Other downtown venues worth checking out include the **Circus Pub & Art,** Thompson 123;

Pub 35mm, Bolívar 419; tel. 57/413851, which features live music; **Salsoteca Yerikoko**, Uribe 317, with recorded salsa music; and **Q Discotheque**, Uribe 330.

At the south end of town, the pseudo-Egyptian **Pharo's**, Avenida Costanera 3607, tel. 57/381682, is a dance club that looks as if it had been airlifted in from Las Vegas.

Shopping

For most Chileans, the main shopping destination is the **Zona Franca** (see the special topic Migrating to the Zofri), where it's possible to find reasonably priced cameras, camping equipment, and the like. **Artesanía Tocornal**, Baquedano 1035, tel. 57/410592, sells a sample of crafts and souvenirs from throughout the region.

Services

Money: Downtown banks with ATMs are abundant, but Afex, Serrano 396 Uribe, is the only downtown *cambio* (there are other ATMs and *cambios* at the Zona Franca).

Postal Correos de Chile is at Bolívar 458.

Telephone and Internet: Telefónica CTC is at Ramírez 587 and at the Zona Franca, Módulo 212, 2nd level. Chilesat is at Patricio Lynch 401. The area code is 57.

Entelchile's downtown Centro de Llamados, Obispo Labbé 501, tel. 57/416445, has the fastest Internet connection in town, though it's closed Sundays. More like an Internet café, with longer hours—8 A.M.–2 A.M. or so—C@ctu's Place, Ramírez 1326, tel. 57/510070 or 09/427-0165, feels less institutional.

Laundry: Easy Wash, Bulnes 170, tel. 57/422986, has prompt and efficient services 8:30 A.M.–8 P.M. daily. Lavarápido is at Obispo Labbé 1446, tel. 57/425338, Laverap at San Martín 490, tel. 57/420353, Lavandería Vaporito at Bolívar 505, tel. 57/421652.

Medical: Hospital Regional Doctor Ernesto Torres Galdames is at Avenida Héroes de la Concepción 502, tel. 57/422370, about 10 blocks east of Plaza Condell.

Language School: The Swiss-run Academia de Idiomas del Norte, Ramírez 1345, tel. 57/411827, fax 57/429343, offers intensive Spanish lessons.

Information

Tourist Office: Sernatur now has a permanent office at Aníbal Pinto 486, tel. 57/312238, sernaturiquiq@entelchile.net. Better stocked than it used to be with maps and brochures, it keeps summer hours 9 A.M.–9 P.M. weekdays, 9 A.M.–1

MIGRATING TO THE ZOFRI

Once an attraction in its own right, the **Zona Franca de Iquique**, colloquially known as the Zofri, is the duty-free shopping center that fueled Iquique's economic boom of the 1980s and early 1990s—many Chileans planned Iquique vacations just to take advantage of its bargain prices for consumer goods such as electronics. Some even moved here to be able to buy automobiles at bargain prices (cars purchased in the Zofri may spend no more than 90 days per calendar year outside the region, and the buyer must be a Tarapacá resident).

Today, however, the Zofri is lagging behind upscale shopping malls elsewhere in Iquique and even in other regions, as price differences are not so great as they used to be. Parts of the Zofri look horribly out of date, others smart and modern, but its 1,800 companies still manage to do US$4 billion in business per annum. In 2001, almost half the port of Iquique's total tonnage was sold in the Zofri.

At Avenida Salitrera Victoria s/n, the Zofri, tel. 57/413002, is open 11 A.M.–9 P.M. Mon.–Sat., noon–9 P.M. Sunday; it's easily reached by any northbound *taxi colectivo* from downtown. Among the items on sale are camping gear, musical instruments, electronics (including video and still cameras), auto parts, jewelry and perfume, sporting goods, shoes, and the like. For meals, it has a fairly diverse Plaza de Comidas (food court). It also has a website (www.zofri.cl) in both Spanish and English.

salt flats, Salar de Atacama

P.M. and 4–9 P.M. Saturday and 10 A.M.–1 P.M. Sunday; the rest of the year, hours are 8:30 A.M.–5 P.M. weekdays only.

Consulates: Peru has a consulate at Zegers 570, tel. 57/411466. Bolivia's consulate is at Gorostiaga 215, Departamento E, tel./fax 57/421777.

Motorists: The Automóvil Club de Chile (Acchi), Serrano 154, tel. 57/413206, has both general and motorists' information.

Transportation

Air: Aeropuerto Diego Aracena is 41 km south of Iquique via coastal Ruta 1. Lloyd Aéreo Boliviano, Serrano 442, tel. 57/426750 or 57/427058, flies Monday and Friday to La Paz (US$103), and Wednesday and Sunday to Santa Cruz, Bolivia (US$160).

Aerocontinente, Aníbal Pinto 641, tel. 57/419024, flies Monday, Wednesday, Friday, and Saturday to Santiago, and to Arica.

LanChile, Tarapacá 465, tel. 57/427600 or 57/413038, flies internationally to La Paz, Bo-

livia, daily; domestically LanExpress flies at least three times daily to Arica, and three or four times daily to Santiago. Some southbound flights stop in Antofagasta and La Serena.

Transportes Aéreos Mercosur (TAM), Tarapacá 451, tel. 57/390600, flies Monday, Wednesday, and Friday to Asunción, Paraguay.

Bus: There's talk of a new and badly needed bus terminal, but for now Iquique's down-in-the-mouth Terminal Rodoviario, at Patricio Lynch and Avenida Centenario, tel. 57/426492, will have to do. It does have hot showers, for US$1 pp.

Companies with offices at the Rodoviario include San Andrés; Pullman Bus, tel. 57/429852; Camus, tel. 57/416837; Chile Bus; Evans, tel. 57/413737; Tur-Bus, tel. 57/420634; Flota Barrios, tel. 57/420071; Fénix Pullman Norte, tel. 57/415874; Kenny Bus; Carmelita; and Géminis. Many carriers also pick up passengers at their own separate ticket offices around the Mercado Centenario; where appropriate, their separate addresses, telephones, and destinations appear in the following paragraphs.

Tur-Bus, which probably has the widest choice of routes throughout the country, has remodeled a traditional landmark as its own separate terminal at Esmeralda 594, tel. 57/472984. Tur-Bus also has an additional ticket office at Juan Martínez 788-A, tel. 57/424955.

Domestic northbound services via the Panamericana to Arica are frequent; almost all southbound buses use coastal Ruta 1 to Tocopilla (for Calama and San Pedro de Atacama) and Antofagasta (for Santiago and intermediates). There are also services to Pica with Pullman Santa Angela, Barros Arana 971, tel. 57/423751, and Pullman Santa Rosa, Sargento Aldea 884, tel. 57/428126, but most other interior destinations are served by *taxi colectivos.*

Arica-bound carriers include Pullman Santa Rosa; Buses Carmelita, Sargento Aldea 790, tel. 57/423766, and at Barros Arana 841, tel. 57/4-12237; Cuevas y González, Sargento Aldea 850, tel. 57/412471; Buses San Andrés, Sargento Aldea 798, tel. 57/413953; and Ramos Cholele, Barros Arana 851, tel. 57/411650. (For *taxi colectivo* services to Arica, see below.)

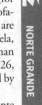

NORTE GRANDE

For Tocopilla and intermediate points, consider Camus, Tur-Bus, and Carmelita. Beyond Tocopilla to Antofagasta, there is service with Kenny Bus, Latorre 944, tel. 57/414159; Flota Barrios; Pullman Santa Rosa; and Tur-Bus. Tur-Bus goes to Calama and on to the Argentine city of Salta.

Buses Zambrano, Sargento Aldea 742, tel. 57/413215, goes to Valparaíso/Viña del Mar and intermediates. Other Valpo-Viña carriers include Pullman Bus, at Juan Martínez and Sargento Aldea, tel. 57/428749; Flota Barrios; and Tur-Bus.

For Santiago and intermediates, try Carmelita, Flota Barrios, Pullman Bus, Ramos Cholele, San Andres, Tur-Bus and Buses Evans, Vivar 955-A, tel. 57/413462.

Typical destinations, fares, and times include Arica (US$6, four hours), Calama (US$12, six hours), Antofagasta (US$14, eight hours), Copiapó (US$27, 15 hours), La Serena (US$30, 18 hours) and Santiago (US$40, 24 hours). *Salón-cama* services cost around US$35 to Chañaral, US$43 to La Serena, and US$50 to Santiago.

International buses include Mass y Kiss, Juan Martínez 182, tel. 57/417106, which goes to the altiplano border town of Colchane (US$8) and continues to Oruro and La Paz. Trans Salvador, Esmeralda 978, also goes to Bolivia.

Tur-Bus's Calama services connect with buses across the Andes to the Argentine city of Salta.

Taxi colectivos to Arica cost about US$12 pp with Tamarugal, Barros Arana 897-B, tel. 57/419288; Taxitur, Sargento Aldea 791, tel. 57/414875; and Turiscargo, Serrano 721, tel. 57/412191. Tamarugal and Taxitur also go to Mamiña (US$4), as does Turismo Mamiña, Latorre 779, tel. 57/420330.

Getting Around

Airport Transportation: Radiotaxi Aeropuerto, Aníbal Pinto 595, provides door-to-door transfers to Aeropuerto Diego Aracena, but cheaper *taxi colectivos* (about US$5 pp) leave from the west side of Plaza Prat.

Car Rental: Rental cars are available from Hertz, Aníbal Pinto 1303, tel. 57/426316; Avis, Manuel Rodríguez 734, tel. 57/472392; Budget, Bolí-

var 615, tel. 57/416332, fax 57/416095; Igsa, Obispo Labbé 1089, tel. 57/429490; and Procar, Serrano 796, tel./fax 57/413470.

VICINITY OF IQUIQUE

Like Arica, Iquique provides urban amenities for travelers and good access to excursions in the coastal range, precordillera, and altiplano. Many of these excursions are possible by public transportation or rental car, but there are also organized options for around US$30 to destinations such as the Quebrada de Tarapacá (including Huara, the Gigante de la Atacama, and possibly Parque Nacional Isluga), the hot springs resorts of Mamiña and/or Pica (including stops at the nitrate ghost towns of Humberstone and Santa Laura, the pilgrimage site of La Tirana, and the colonial village of Matilla), Reserva Nacional Pampa del Tamarugal (including the spectacular geoglyphs at Pintados), and even truly off-the-beaten-track destinations such as the Quebrada de Guatacondo. It's also possible to organize tours to Pisagua (see the separate entry above).

Among Iquique travel agencies offering excursions are **Mane Tour,** Gorostiaga 194, Oficina 2, tel. 57/418715 or 09/5432485, fax 57/473032, manetour@latinmail.com; **Segur,** Serrano 392, Oficinas 1 and 2, tel. 57/410881 or 57/470749, turism@ctcinternet.cl; **Transtours,** Baquedano 982, tel./fax 57/428984; **Surire Tour,** Baquedano 1035, tel. 57/445440, fax 57/411795; and **Turismo Lirima,** Orella 548, tel. 57/390403 or 57/390404. **Civet Adventure,** Bolívar 684, tel./fax 57/428483, offers customized adventure trips to highland destinations.

Ruta 1 Beaches

Since it opened in the early 1990s, paved Ruta 1 has provided better access to beaches as far as Tocopilla and shortened travel times to Antofagasta and other points south. Unfortunately, improved access has come at a price—uncontrolled camping and lack of municipal services beyond Aeropuerto Diego Aracena have resulted in trash accumulation and other environmental problems in what was, until very recently, a nearly pristine coastal area.

MEGA-ART IN THE ATACAMA

Geoglyphs, as art, use the world's largest and greatest canvas (figuratively speaking, of course), the earth's own desert surface. In a sense, they are sculptures on the grandest possible scale—the most famous, Peru's Nazca lines, stretch for several miles across the barren wastes. Chile's Atacama geoglyphs, though more scattered, are equally impressive.

The creators of South America's pre-Columbian geoglyphs took advantage of available resources by two primary techniques that are mirror images of each other. At Nazca, they scraped the desert surface clear of dark stones to create the lines and figures that have become so well known around the world. In Chile, by contrast, the artists gathered and arranged those similar stones, the obverse of what was done at Nazca, to fashion figurative and abstract or geometric designs.

One major difference between the two is, of course, that Nazca's geoglyphs are only visible from the air, while their Chilean counterparts are visible from the ground, though some vantage points are better than others. Culturally, Nazca's geoglyphs bear only a superficial similarity to those of the Norte Grande—Nazca's figures and designs apparently reflect patterns found on pre-Columbian pottery, while the images of felines, fish, llamas, lizards, pelicans, and other figures line pre-Columbian exchange routes.

Those in Chile are far more numerous and widespread, reflecting the exchange of products such as fish, guano, maize, *chuño* (dehydrated potatoes), and *cha'rki* (freeze-dried meat) among kin groups at ecologically distinct elevations; the lengthy llama trains depicted on the hillsides of routes such as the Lluta and Azapa valleys were the means of transportation. Some of the trains include more than 40 animals measuring 75 meters in length. Other routes linked precordillera oases in a north-south axis.

The Chilean figures themselves are tremendously diverse, some measuring as little as a meter in height, but the largest is the so-called "Giant of the Atacama," a Viracocha or Andean creator figure that measures 86 meters in length. Dating the figures has proved difficult, because many are overlays.

The best single site, with the largest and most diverse set of geoglyphs, is probably the Pintados site southeast of Iquique, but sites such as Lluta, Azapa, and Tiliviche all deserve a visit; some, such as Tiliviche, are visible only from a distance, across the canyon on the Panamericana. But bus passengers through any part of the Atacama should keep their eyes peeled for these memorable artistic accomplishments.

At Río Seco, a developing settlement with limited services 95 km south of Iquique, the roadside **Museo Parque** displays pre-Columbian Chango objects and relics from nitrate *oficinas*. At the **Río Loa** border between Region I (Tarapacá) and Region II (Antofagasta), 148 km south of Iquique, there's an internal customs post for merchandise from the Zofri and surfing possibilities at the beach. The Río Loa estuary is the only stream in the Norte Grande where fresh water flows consistently reach the Pacific.

Humberstone

From Iquique, paved Ruta 16 climbs steeply east to the suburb of **Alto Hospicio,** which barely two decades ago was home only to a handful of truck farmers who watered their fields with condensation from the *camanchaca*. Today, on the broad escarpment overlooking Iquique, it's home to working-class families and squatters who can't afford to live in increasingly costly Iquique.

Passing the site of the abandoned colonial silver mine at Huantajaya, northeast of Alto Hospicio, the highway continues to a junction with the Panamericana, where Humberstone and Santa Laura (see below) are two of Chile's few remaining nitrate ghost towns, together forming perhaps the single most popular excursion from Iquique. Both are national monuments, but this protection is largely symbolic.

After a long legal struggle, the Chilean government has handed over control of Humberstone to the Corporación Museo del Salitre, which has a 50-year concession to manage the former company town and its landmark buildings. Until recently, it has been the subject of a

© WAYNE BERNHARDSON

ruins at Oficina Humberstone

struggle between the Andía family, who acquired the property and paid for it by selling scrap metal before falling into bankruptcy, and independent right-wing politician Francisco Errázuriz, who held the mineral rights.

In 2001, Humberstone enjoyed a renaissance in public attention as Televisión Nacional (TVN) filmed part of its miniseries *Pampa Ilusión,* based on life in the *salitreras* circa 1935, in Humberstone. This brought some benefits—TVN tidied the Plaza de Armas, replanting it with bougainvilleas, iceplant, and geraniums, and repainted the sun-bleached facades of several buildings for the shoot. There were also questionable decisions, though—since the plants in the plaza didn't grow fast enough for its purposes, TVN imported plastic plants, hung bogus leaves from dead trees, and even painted the concrete columns of the pergolas to look like brick. Even more stunningly, it built a full-scale facade of its conception of an administrator's residence, since donated to the *comuna* of Pozo Almonte, that burdens this genuine historic site with a Disneylandia millstone.

However ill-advised, the creation of an instant tourist attraction doesn't mean the rest of the site isn't legitimate, and it proves its authenticity

with November's weeklong **Semana del Salitre,** when former residents and employees gather to celebrate what was a community as well as a company town. The event sometimes includes a train from Iquique to Humberstone, as the line is still functional.

History: Founded in 1872 by the Peruvian Nitrate Company, Oficina La Palma was one of Tarapacá's largest nitrate mine within a couple of decades; at its peak, the town had a population of 3,700 and shipped 46,000 quintals of nitrate and 100 quintals of iodine every month. Functioning until 1960 despite a brief stoppage when depression hit the world in the early 1930s, it was one of the last surviving nitrate settlements.

Humberstone's name derives from La Palma's precocious British manager James Humberstone (1850–1939), who arrived in Pisagua at the age of 25 (before the Chilean takeover) and, in the course of a long career, refined the "Shanks system" for obtaining maximum yields from the low-grade caliche (hardpan) of the Atacama's sprawling pampas. After his retirement, the Compañía Salitrera de Tarapacá y Antofagasta renamed the town in his honor and Britain's King Edward VIII honored him with an Order of the British Empire!

Humberstone himself now reposes in the British Cemetery at Hacienda Tiliviche on the Panamericana, north of the Pisagua turnoff.

Sights: More remains of Humberstone's residential core than of the surrounding industrial plant. Around the Plaza de Armas, itself partially transformed by TVN, stand the **Iglesia Jesús Obrero** (its restoration financed by Errázuriz to try to strengthen his claim); the **Teatro Humberstone** (built of Douglas fir, its stage and seating are largely intact; the famous folksinger Violeta Parra once performed here), the **Recova** or market building; the **Pulpería** (company store); and housing for management and workers. The most incongruous sight, a block east of the plaza, is the **Piscina,** an enormous cast-iron swimming pool, now empty but with an intact diving board. There were also tennis and basketball courts.

Most of these buildings date from the 1930s (Humberstone reached its zenith as the Great Depression waned), but the Victorian-style **Casa del Administrador** dates from 1883. West of the residential zone, the former power plant, railyards, and other industrial relics have suffered from depredations by scrap dealers, but there are still locomotives, narrow-gauge rails (the town had a dozen kilometers of track that helped link it to nearby Santa Laura), and dozens of the rail carts that hauled caliche from the fields to the processors. In the distance are stupendous piles of *tortas* (tailings) left after the extraction of the nitrates.

Mornings are the best time to explore Humberstone, before the sun gets too hot, but occasional afternoon breezes can make that time of the day pleasant enough.

Practicalities: There are limited supplies of food—cold drinks, etc.—and a simple restaurant across the highway from the entrance.

A kiosk at the entrance to the ruins sells informational booklets and maps on Humberstone and other nearby sites. There is no entry fee as yet, but donations are accepted.

> *Humberstone and Santa Laura are two of Chile's few remaining nitrate ghost towns, together forming perhaps the single most popular excursion from Iquique.*

From Iquique, any Panamericana-bound bus, as well as buses to precordillera destinations such as Mamiña and Pica and *taxi colectivos* to Pozo Almonte, will drop passengers at Humberstone, which is 45 km east of the regional capital. It's easy enough to flag down a return bus to Iquique as well.

Oficina Santa Laura

Just across Ruta 16, within reasonable walking distance, Humberstone's sister *salitrera* is home to the *in situ* **Museo Santa Laura,** housed in the partially restored **Casa del Administrador.** Several of its rooms have been outfitted with period furniture and other nitrate-era artifacts, but there is lamentably little historical narrative.

While much less remains of Santa Laura than of Humberstone, the site is still well worth a visit. The most impressive structure still standing is the **Planta de Chancado** (ore crusher), with its soaring smokestack, but the building itself suffered serious damage in 1999, when chainsaw vandals cut and sold 31 Douglas fir beams (the thieves were caught by police, however). Craftsmen have restored several of the old horse and mule carts that used to haul ore to the processors, and there are mules and burros in the stable to provide demonstrations.

In late October, folk musicians of the status of Patricio Manns perform at the **Festival Canto a la Pampa** (Pampa Song Festival).

Panamericana Norte

North of Humberstone, the highway has a handful of roadside attractions starting at the town of **Huara,** the junction for the international highway into the altiplano (see separate entry below). Some 33 km from Humberstone, Huara doesn't merit a long stopover, but try to visit its **Farmacia y Droguería Libertad,** Arturo Prat s/n, an old-fashioned apothecary that opened in 1906 but was acquired by the Municipalidad in 1993 as a museum; it's open 10 A.M.–noon and 3–4 P.M.

daily except Sunday, when it's open 10 A.M.–1 P.M. and 4–5 P.M. The nearby church dates from 1890. While there are no accommodations here, you could do worse than to lunch at **La Flor de Huara,** on the west side of the highway.

A few kilometers north of Huara, at Km 1,853 of the Panamericana, the **Geoglifos Ex-Aura,** named for the nitrate *oficina* that once existed here, consist of what appears to be a sun and a human figure.

About 57 km north of Huara and 10 km north of the Pisagua turnoff, **Hacienda Tiliviche** is a British-founded farm nestled in its namesake oasis canyon; the present occupant, Santiago Adán Keith, generally welcomes visitors who want to take a look around, but check in at the *casco* (big house) before doing so. The entrance road is on the south side of the river.

On the north side of the river, readily visible from the highway but reached by crossing from the main house, Tiliviche's **Cementerio de los Ingleses** (British Cemetery), enclosed by a wrought-iron fence, is a national monument dating from 1876. James Humberstone, a legendary figure in the nitrate industry, is among those buried here.

Quebrada de Tarapacá and the Altiplano

From Huara Ruta 55, the international highway to Oruro, Bolivia, passes a number of archaeological and historical sites en route to the bleak border post of Colchane. Though theoretically paved, and despite a couple of smooth new stretches, this scenic road is often potholed and parts are as yet unpaved—it looks better on some maps than it really is. From the altiplano around, though, it's possible to travel the spectacular circuit north toward Parque Nacional Lauca and on or back to Arica through wild and still rarely visited backcountry.

Only 14 km east of Huara, a short distance north of the highway, the isolated hillock of **Cerro Unita** is famous for the 86-meter geoglyph known as **El Gigante de Atacama** (Giant of the Atacama), the world's largest anthropomorphic representation (it is 39 meters wide as well). Dating from about A.D. 900, it probably depicts an indigenous authority of the time but unfortunately, it's becoming hard to distinguish the geoglyph itself from the tire tracks that careless and disrespectful drivers have left here. Everyone cautions against walking on the figure, and that's good advice, but it can't do nearly the damage that uncontrolled jeepers and dirtbikers have.

Nine km east of Cerro Unita, a paved side road descends from the pampa into the Quebrada de Tarapacá, where somnambulant **San Lorenzo de Tarapacá,** an oasis village surrounded by irrigated fields, belies its status as one of colonial Peru's most important local towns and the site of a major battle that took place here during the War of the Pacific. The entire town is a *zona típica* national monument.

Tarapacá's most notable landmark is its **Iglesia San Lorenzo,** a national monument begun in 1717, finished in 1720, and at present undergoing an agonizingly slow restoration; its freestanding *campanario* (bell tower) dates from 1741. At the approach to town, a monument maps the November 27, 1879, Battle of Tarapacá, a bloody but indecisive encounter between Chilean forces under Eleuterio Ramírez (who died here) and a joint Peruvian-Bolivian army.

At **Chusmiza,** 75 km east of Huara and 3,200 meters above sea level, the former hot springs hotel has closed for the foreseeable future, but the bottling plant that produces one of Chile's premium mineral waters remains open. Passing numerous pre-Columbian hillside terraces, some of them still irrigated with alfalfa and even some native crops, the highway climbs out of the precordillera and onto the altiplano, where there are several access points to Parque Nacional Volcán Isluga. It ends at **Colchane,** which, though it's capital of its *comuna,* deserves no more than a brief visit unless the border's closed or you need a bed or food. At 3,750 meters above sea level, on a plain with nothing to stop the wind and weather, it gets cold at night.

Parque Nacional Volcán Isluga

Not quite so high as Parque Nacional Lauca to the north, the 174,744 hectares of Parque Nacional Isluga incorporate environments similar to Lauca's summits, steppes, and marshes, with comparable wildlife, but it also encompasses sev-

Iglesia Santuario, Parque Nacional Volcán Isluga

eral scenic Aymara villages in what is one of their most traditional indigenous strongholds. Its literally high point, though, is 5,218-meter Volcán Isluga, which gave the park its name.

Sights: Six km west of Colchane, the village of **Isluga,** a settlement of about 200 houses that's primarily an Aymara ceremonial center, is a *zona típica* national monument. Its outstanding architectural feature is its spectacular 17th-century **Iglesia Santuario,** perhaps the altiplano's finest single church, bedecked with a traditional tiled roof and complemented by a freestanding bell tower.

Six km west of Isluga, at the village of **Enquelga,** the road crosses the river and follows the south shore of **Laguna Arabilla;** an alternative road west through a series of small villages is frequently cut by the summer rains. The more reliable southerly road continues west to **Latarana,** where it intersects the northbound road to Parque Nacional Lauca, which passes through **Mucomucone** en route to the Salar de Surire (for more information on Surire, see the separate entry above).

Reached by a narrow road from a signed turnoff from Ruta 55, roughly midway between Chusmiza and Colchane, **Termas de Puchuldiza** is a relatively small but active geyser field at 3,800 meters above sea level. In winter, when the condensed steam freezes overnight, it's a fascinating sight, but the rest of the year, it's only mildly interesting, as the scenery is similar elsewhere in the park. Puchuldiza is also accessible by a separate southbound lateral from a junction on the Latarana road, which passes through the village of **Mauque.**

Accommodations and Food: Within the park proper, Conaf's **Refugio Enquelga** is up to its usual standards for US$9 pp, but the nearby **Camping Aguas Calientes,** sited at thermal baths about one km east of town, is dirty.

The only other regular accommodations are at Colchane, outside the park boundaries, where **Residencial Rogelia Castro** charges US$6/10 s/d for lodging and serves breakfast and dinner for an additional US$5 pp. **El Palomo** is the only place to eat.

Information: Colchane's Municipalidad, Avenida Teniente González s/n, tel. 57/794312, will help out with tourist inquiries. Conaf's ranger at Enquelga will provide information on the park.

Transportation: Bolivia-bound buses from Iquique pass through Colchane, which is 180 km northeast of Huara, but there is no regular public transportation into the park proper. Both Arica and Iquique travel agencies offer loop excursions through Isluga and Lauca; it's probably easier to arrange these in Arica.

Panamericana Sur

Between the Humberstone junction and the regional border with Antofagasta, most areas of interest are east of the Panamericana in the precordillera and its canyons. The exception is the Reserva Nacional Pampa de Tamarugal, most of which straddles the highway south of Pozo Almonte, though it has discontinuous sectors north of Huara and in the vicinity of La Tirana.

Pozo Almonte: Just five km south of the Humberstone junction, in the midst of the pampa, bustling Pozo Almonte is the largest town on the Panamericana between Arica and the regional border. Founded in colonial times as a watering hole (*pozo* means "well" in Spanish), it owes its present prosperity to the copper mining boom at Cerro Colorado, 59 northeast of town on the Mamiña road, and at Collahuasi, high in the southeastern Andes near the Bolivian border.

Pozo Almonte's **Museo Histórico Salitrero,** on the south side of the Plaza de Armas, recalls the nitrate days with artifacts and photographs; it's open 9 A.M.–1 P.M. and 4–7:30 P.M. Tues-day through Saturday and charges a negligible admission.

Not many people plan to stay here, but if night falls while you're in town, you could do lots worse than the impeccable **Hotel Estancia Inn,** Comercio 132, tel. 57/752242, which is modern and comfortable for US$16/21, and which also has a restaurant. That said, it's easy to catch buses either north- or southbound on the Panamericana, or *taxi colectivos* to Iquique, Mamiña, La Tirana, or Pica.

La Tirana: About 19 km southeast of Pozo Almonte, along the paved road to Matilla and Pica, the usually placid village of La Tirana nearly bursts with activity between July 12 and 18, when tens of thousands of pilgrims flock to celebrate the annual **Festival de la Virgen del Carmen.** The most important day is July 16, but the entire week is an orgy of frenzied activity from spectators and organized participants who, clad in kaleidoscopic costumes, fill the streets with folkloric music and dance.

The Norte Grande's single most important devotional site, whose permanent population is only about 250, is also a *zona típica* national monument, largely but not exclusively because of its **Santuario de la Tirana.** Fronted by the **Iglesia de la Tirana** (1886), an outlandish structure

THE TALE OF THE TYRANT

Legend tells that Ñusta Huillac, daughter of an Inka priest, had fled with her father from Diego de Almagro's return expedition to Cuzco. Hiding in the Prosopis forests, the princess led guerrilla raids against passing Spaniards, torturing her prisoners and earning her the nickname "La Tirana del Tamarugal" (Tyrant of the Tamarugal).

When, however, Ñusta fell in love with her Portuguese captive Vasco de Almeyda, tried to save him, and accepted Christianity, her followers considered it treason. Condemning both of them to death, they nevertheless granted her wish to place a cross on her grave.

Again according to legend, an 18th-century priest found Ñusta's cross in the midst of the forest, and her cult grew with the construction of an Andean-style temple destroyed by an earthquake in 1866. Today, pilgrims honor her indirectly with dances that post-date the War of the Pacific, when local residents began to honor the Virgen del Carmen de La Tirana, the local version of Chile's patron saint.

La Tirana's cult has spread throughout the country; there are now 200 *cofradías* or brotherhoods, their roots in distant Andean times. Geographically based in Arica, Iquique, Tocopilla, Chuquicamata, and other cities, they converge on La Tirana every July for the annual festivities.

Canadian writer Lake Sagaris, a longtime Chilean resident, recounts the story of Ñusta Huillac, with references to contemporary Chile, in her *Bone and Dream: Into the World's Driest Desert* (Knopf Canada, 2000).

that replaced an earlier counterpart destroyed by earthquakes, this broad but barren ceremonial plaza is the main venue for the July celebrations. The church itself, distinguished by a central dome, twin bell towers, and metal siding, is in deteriorating condition, and there has even been talk of replacing it.

While the July celebrations are the primary attraction, La Tirana also draws plenty of pilgrims during **Pascua de Negros** (January 5–6, Epiphany, when black slaves in colonial times celebrated Christ's birth); **Semana Santa** (Easter), and the **Fiesta de la Oración por Chile** (Chilean Prayer Festival, the last Sunday in September).

On the north side of the plaza, La Tirana's **Museo del Salitre** displays a chaotic collection of objects from the nitrate era. While many of the exhibits are visible from the sidewalk, the entrance is through Almacén El Progreso, the local general store.

La Tirana has no hotels (Pozo Almonte and even Pica are better choices for a room), but pilgrims camp without restriction in the open areas on the east side of town. For food, several simple *comedores* circumfuse the plaza in front of the church.

Mamiña

In the precordillera directly northeast of Pozo Almonte via 73 km of paved two-lane blacktop, the precordillera hot springs resort of Mamiña has long been a popular "hill station" for residents of Iquique, especially on weekends during the winter. Despite Mamiña's tourist orientation, the Aymara presence is still palpable, and the abundant pre-Columbian terraces reinforce its indigenous character. In pre-Columbian times, the town was a fortified way station on the route between the Inka capital of Cuzco and its southern satellites.

Orientation: Though Mamiña's official elevation is 2,700 meters above sea level, its rugged topography makes any such statistic misleading. The compact upper sector of town sits atop an isolated rocky scarp, while the lower sector, site of most of the hot springs hotels, stretches along the Quebrada de Mamiña beneath Cerro Ipla and several other parallel ridges. Winding roads and footpaths link the two sectors.

Sights: Mamiña's **Iglesia de Nuestra Señora del Rosario** dates from the 17th century but has undergone such serious modifications that only the adobe facade is recognizably colonial; the flanking twin bell towers, built of symmetrical stone blocks and topped by blue-painted wood framing, seem oddly incongruous.

Inka influence is apparent in the several *pukarás* in and around the town. The contemporary indigenous presence manifests itself in the **Centro Cultural Kespikala,** in the lower Ipla sector, where Aymara artists and artisans produce and sell their wares; it's also a meeting place for Aymara cultural activists.

Accommodations and Food: While Mamiña offers abundant accommodations, all of them pretty good, at a variety of prices, winter weekends can challenge their capacity. Note that street addresses, while they technically exist, are really pretty meaningless—all are either on the hilltop or in the valley below, on Ipla. House numbers are rare. Where telephones appear, they're Iquique numbers (area code 57), except for cell phones starting with 09—Mamiña has no fixed land lines.

Residencial Cholele, Ipla s/n, offers nothing more or less than good beds, hot showers, and a basic breakfast for US$10 pp. Hilltop **Hotel La Coruña,** Santa Rosa 687, tel. 09/5430370, charges US$17/20 s/d with breakfast, providing additional meals at its attached bar/restaurant.

Hotel Termas Llama Inn, Ipla s/n, tel. 57/419893, has more contemporary style than most other accommodations here; rates are US$33/37 s/d with breakfast and its restaurant, open to nonguests, serves lunch, dinner, and fine desserts. **Hotel Niña de Mis Ojos,** Ipla s/n, tel. 57/420451, costs US$25 pp.

Hotel Los Cardenales, Ipla s/n, tel. 57/438182, offers the most complete services of any accommodations in town: subtropical surroundings (despite the altitude), a covered and heated pool, and Jacuzzis in every room; rates are US$42 pp with full board.

Mamiña's most venerable lodging, the classic but deteriorating **Hotel Refugio del Salitre,** El Tambo s/n, tel. 57/751203, is living in the past with rates of US$50/93 s/d with full board.

Transportation: Buses and *taxi colectivos* from Iquique arrive at and depart from the church plaza (for details, see the Iquique entry).

Pica

Along with Mamiña, the oasis of Pica is the most popular weekend getaway for the residents of Iquique, and it has been since the nitrate boom of the early 20th century. Unlike the canyon country around Mamiña, it occupies a relatively open site on the cusp between the pampa and the precordillera, irrigated by a series of Spanish-built tunnels that reduced evaporation and, in the words of the late geographer Isaiah Bowman, watered its gardens "with scrupulous economy."

Pica was one of Spain's earliest settlements in what is now Chile—both Diego de Almagro and Pedro de Valdivia passed through there, and by 1550 it was the center of an important *encomienda.* Its orchards and vineyards supplied both Arequipa and the silver city of Potosí, in present-day Bolivia, with abundant produce.

When Bowman visited Pica, toward the end of the nitrate era, the Tarapacá Water Company had long since diverted water from Pica to Iquique, affecting the local system for the benefit of the city. Pica's citrus and subtropical fruits—limes, oranges, grapefruits, mangos, and guavas—have maintained their reputation throughout the country, but the last wine harvest took place in 1937.

Orientation: Pica (population about 2,500), 1,325 meters above sea level, is 42 km southeast of La Tirana and 61 km southeast of Pozo Almonte via a smooth paved road. It features an elongated street plan whose main thoroughfare, Avenida Balmaceda, enters town from the west. A parallel thoroughfare two blocks north, Avenida Presidente Ibáñez links the center with the popular pools at the east end of town.

Sights: Pica's **Iglesia San Andrés** (1886), on the south side of the well-landscaped Plaza de Armas, is a national monument that supplanted a colonial structure demolished by earthquakes; its wooden framing is covered by a neoclassical facade of galvanized iron. The **Hospital de Pica,** Balmaceda s/n, is also a national monument.

Most Chileans come to enjoy the natural pools at **Cocha Resbaladero,** at the east end of Avenida Presidente Ibáñez, which collects a small admission charge. In the village of **Matilla,** three km west of Pica, there are two national monuments: its **Iglesia de San Antonio** replaced an earlier church destroyed around the same time as that of Pica, but its freestanding bell tower is original; the **Lagar de Matilla,** built in colonial times, was a working winepress as late as 1937. It was restored by the Universidad de Chile in 1968.

The **Museo de Pica,** Pica's new museum in the same new building as the tourist office and public library, has a professional look but is still a work in progress. Among the exhibits are material on dinosaur tracks at Chacarillas, in an isolated canyon southwest of Pica; the region's early human presence; more recent archaeology, including ceramics, mummies, and burial customs; the nitrate era (including the role of the oasis in feeding the *oficinas*); and the contemporary agricultural economy. Already good, it focuses appropriately on the local and regional, with a fine collection of historical photographs. At Avenida Balmaceda s/n, it's open 9 A.M.–1 P.M. and 4–8 P.M. daily in summer, but weekdays only the rest of the year.

Accommodations: The barren **Camping Miraflores,** the former municipal site at Miraflores 4, tel. 57/741338, charges only US$2 pp; it also has comfortable *cabañas,* sleeping up to six people, with kitchen facilities, for US$40.

Recently reopened **Hotel Palermo**, Prat 233, tel. 57/741129, is the cheapest conventional accommodations at US$6 pp, but it lacks parking. Tobacco-free **Hotel San Andrés,** Balmaceda 197, tel. 57/741319, charges US$8 pp for spacious rooms with good beds and private bath, but it could stand to spruce up them up a bit. **Residencial El Tambo,** Avenida General Ibáñez 68, tel. 57/741041, costs US$7/12 s/d, while **Hostal Los Emilios,** Cochrane 213, tel. 57/7-41126, charges US$8.50 pp.

Friendly, spotless **Hostal Casa Blanca,** Avenida General Ibáñez 75, tel. 57/741410, tel. 57/311992 in Iquique, is an exceptional value for US$10 pp with private bath and breakfast. Though not quite so finished a product as the Casa Blanca, **Hotel Camino del Inca,** Esmeralda 14, tel. 57/741008, has ample rooms with private bath, cable TV, and shady common areas for US$7/17 s/d with breakfast.

At the western approach to town, under the same management as Hotel Palermo, recommended **Hostería O'Higgins,** Avenida Balmaceda 6, tel. 57/741524 or 09/6733566, is good value for US$17/20 s/d without breakfast, but it fills up fast.

Food: La Palmera, opposite the plaza at Balmaceda 115, tel. 57/741444, serves sandwiches, fixed-price meals, and exquisite fruit juices—especially the mango. **La Viña,** General Ibáñez 70, tel. 57/741314, specializes in Chilean cuisine, while **Sou Sang,** Esmeralda 444, serves Chinese dishes.

Los Naranjos, Barbosa 200 at the corner of Esmeralda, tel. 57/741318, is a spotless seven-table *picada* that does a lot with a little, with fine service and imaginative preparation even of routine dishes such as *pollo a la plancha* (grilled chicken)—in this case, marinated in local lime juice. With dinners around US$6 pp with salad, it's also a TV-free zone—unusual for moderately priced restaurants in Chile. One shortcoming is that it sometimes lacks white wine.

Traditionally the town's best restaurant, **El Edén de Pica,** Riquelme 12, tel. 57/741196, displays a diverse Chilean menu of beef, seafood, and even Andean grains such as quinoa, but it keeps an erratic schedule and doesn't always have what's on that menu. Its shady patio, though, offers the best ambience of any restaurant in town.

Information: Pica's Oficina de Información Turística, Balmaceda s/n, tel. 57/741665, in the same building as the Museo de Pica, is open 9 A.M.–1 P.M. and 4–8 P.M. daily in summer, but weekdays only the rest of the year.

Transportation: Pica's Agencia de Buses, two blocks north of the Plaza de Armas on Esmeralda between Barbosa and Maipú, sells tickets for Pullman San Andrés, Pullman Santa Rosa, Pullman Chacón, and Pullman Cpurec. Pullman Santa Rosa also has a separate office at Balmaceda and Barbosa.

There are 13 buses daily to Iquique (US$2.50, two hours) via La Tirana, Pozo Almonte, and Humberstone except on Sunday, when there are only 11. There are also *taxi colectivos.*

Reserva Nacional Pampa del Tamarugal

Before the arrival of the Spaniards, dense forests of *tamarugo (Prosopis tamarugo),* a relative of the widespread North American mesquite, covered much of the arid pampa between the coastal escarpment and the precordillera, from about 20° S latitude to the Río Loa, the present-day boundary between Region I (Tarapacá) and Region II (Antofagasta). Deforested for fuel for the bonanza colonial silver mine at Huantajaya and the post-independence nitrate *oficinas,* this forest has made a remarkable comeback in the last half century, in the face of great obstacles.

Conaf's Reserva Nacional Pampa del Tamarugal preserves the last great extents of *tamarugo* trees, a narrow endemic species. While the forest alone is impressive enough in this desert context, the major attraction is the geoglyphs at Pintados, a national archaeological monument that's one of the continent's most impressive concentrations of pre-Columbian rock art.

Orientation: Reserva Nacional Pampa del Tamarugal consists of 102,264 hectares in three sectors: one north of Huara, one east of La Tirana, and another, the largest and most widely visited, south of Pozo Almonte.

Sights: About 43 km south of Pozo Almonte, at a junction with a paved but potholed road that heads east toward Pica, a westbound gravel road leads past an abandoned nitrate rail station to the **Geoglifos de Cerros Pintados;** here, nearly 1,000 abstract and figurative designs blanket four km of otherwise barren hillsides surrounding the crumbling adobe ruins of a former *oficina.* Many of the figures, which date between A.D. 500 and A.D. 1450, represent humans and animals, including birds, fish, and llamas, that suggest shared beliefs and frequent contacts with the pre-Columbian cultures of highland Peru and Bolivia.

At the old Pintados railroad station, en route to the geoglyphs, there is now a *"memorias salitreras"* stand selling cold drinks and nitrate memorabilia. At the site itself, Conaf has installed a ranger station, erected a gate, built picnic sites and some shaded parking, and instituted a US$1.75 admission fee. Frequently, however, no one is there to collect the charge (this is a mixed blessing, as it

THE WOODLAND IN THE DESERT

The utterly rainless nitrate pampas might seem an improbable place for any forest, but the Pampa del Tamarugal's peculiar geography has provided a favorable environment for *Prosopis tamarugo*. In spite of its saline soils, low humidity, thin cloud cover, and dramatic temperature oscillations between day and night, the pampa is an interior drainage basin where, for tens of thousands of years, the penetration of the flow of transverse river valleys and the westward movement of fresh groundwater created an enormous subterranean aquifer.

With its deep tap root, the *tamarugo* is uniquely adapted to this singular environment. Unfortunately, the colonial and post-colonial mining industry brought about the tree's near-disappearance until the 1950s, when Chile's Corporación de Fomento de la Producción (Chilean Development Corporation, Corfo) instituted a replanting program. The goal was to provide fuel for rural residents and forage for their sheep and goats, who eat the tree's abundant seedpods. While the dense groves straddling the Panamericana are plantations rather than primary forest, they are a remarkable achievement.

That achievement, though, is under threat. Ever since Atacameño times, the pampa's waters had been used for irrigation and, during the nitrate boom, the *oficinas* drew up to 40,000 gallons per day from wells at Dolores (east of Pisagua) and Pozo Almonte. Today, however, wells drilled to satisfy Iquique's urban thirst have lowered the water table from four to 15 meters beneath the surface, making it difficult for existing trees to survive and impossible for seedlings to establish themselves. This is fossil water, and unlikely to be replenished within any period of time meaningful to humans.

---

means walking farther in the hot sun to get to the geoglyphs).

East of the Panamericana, directly opposite the road to Pintados, there's a paved but potholed alternative route to Pica, and a turnoff to **Colonia Agrícola Pintados,** an oasis community that began in the 1960s as a religious colony but developed into a flourishing horticultural settlement. Pumping 80 liters of irrigation water per minute out of the aquifer, it has established markets in Pozo Almonte and Iquique for its carrots, celery, chard, lettuce, tomatoes, maize, onions, peppers, melons, and watermelons.

At Km 1750 of the Panamericana, 57 km south of Pozo Almonte, the town of **Victoria** was a working *oficina* until 1980 but was almost totally dismantled in 1981–82. Now barely a facade along the highway, it could have been another Humberstone; in-

While the forest alone is impressive enough in this desert context, the major attraction is the geoglyphs at Pintados, a national archaeological monument that's one of the continent's most impressive concentrations of pre-Columbian rock art.

stead, it retains only a few storefronts and services, including a restaurant and gas station.

Accommodations and Food: Opposite its Centro de Información, 24 km south of Pozo Almonte, Conaf's **Área de Recreación Refresco** provides *tamarugo*-shaded campsites with picnic tables, clean toilets, and (cold) showers for US$7 per site. Back across the highway, its **Casa de Huéspedes** offers beds for US$9 pp.

At Victoria, 33 km south of Conaf's Centro de Información and directly on the highway, tidy **El Rotito** is a surprisingly good eatery, with shaded parking to boot. Restaurant owner Jaime Armando Godoy Henríquez, who owns most of the rest of the town, has simple accommodations for rent here.

Information: Conaf's **Centro de Información Ambiental,** 24 km south of Pozo Almonte, tel. 57/751055, is open 8:30

A.M.–6 P.M. daily. It has small but informative displays on the pampa environment, particularly the *tamarugo*.

Transportation: Southbound buses on the Panamericana pass near all the major attractions in the Pintados sector and nearby, but it's still a hot dry walk of about seven km in the hot desert sun—carry plenty of water, though the souvenir stand sometimes offers cold drinks. Organized tours from Iquique to Humberstone and Pica often stop at Pintados.

Quebrada de Guatacondo

Foreign visitors anticipating kaleidoscopic desert country like the box canyons of the southwestern United States sometimes find themselves disappointed by the Atacama's mainly monochromatic landscapes, but the isolated Quebrada de Guatacondo, in the southeastern corner of Tarapacá, lives up to expectations.

From a point on the Panamericana, 63 km south of Pintados and 66 km north of the regional border at Quillagua, a broad dusty road crosses 40 km or so of barren pampa, where dust devils swirl across the landscape, before dropping into and then ascending a serpentine canyon to the oasis of Guatacondo. Tours rarely go here, so a rental vehicle, preferably with 4WD, is almost the only possibility.

At Km 40, just before the route begins descending into the Quebrada, the hillside **Geoglifos El Vado** depict a llama pack train. In the canyon itself, at Km 49, the **Petroglifos de Temantica** is a remarkable assortment of engraved stone surfaces reflecting a succession of cultures from Tiwanaku times (A.D. 500–1000), post-Tiwanaku regional development (A.D. 1100–1400), and the relatively brief Inka dominion (A.D. 1450–1530).

Beyond Temantica, the road ascends a dappled sedimentary canyon whose beds have been folded almost vertically over the ages, before arriving at **Guatacondo,** a village so isolated that, in the event of summer rains, it can remain cut off from the rest of the country for months on end. In dry weather, with permission from Carabineros here, it's possible to continue east toward the copper mine at Collahuasi and the paved highway back to Pozo Almonte, but flash floods can make this route—and indeed the entire canyon—dangerous during the summer rainy season.

Antofagasta Region

Mining remains the backbone of Antofagasta's regional economy—it constitutes 98 percent of all its exports—but the Norte Grande's single biggest tourist attraction, the colonial village of San Pedro de Atacama, is its unquestionable highlight. Some regional officials think San Pedro is reaching "carrying capacity" and are attempting to promote off-the-beaten-path alternatives such as Caspana and Toconce, home to new tourist-oriented enterprises, to help spread the wealth around. San Pedro, however, is more easily accessible and central to excursions.

In early 2001, Antofagasta was Chile's fastest-growing region, but it still had high unemployment of 9.4 percent because of immigration from other parts of the country.

ANTOFAGASTA

Antofagasta, a 19th-century city that replaced the colonial port of Cobija with the rise of the nitrate and copper industries, is primarily a service center for the region's mines, though there are several interesting excursions in the vicinity. With 300,000 people straining regional water resources, the city could collapse before the mines run out of ore.

History

Originally known as Peña Blanca, then as La Chimba, Antofagasta was barely a prospectors' base camp when, in 1865, José Santos Ossa discovered mineral nitrates in the Salar del Carmen, only about 20 km east of the city. Together

NORTE GRANDE

ANTOFAGASTA

MUELLE SALITRERO

Puerto Antiguo

To Iquique

RESQUARDO MARÍTIMO

PINACOTECA ANDRÉS SABELLA

MUNICIPAL TOURIST KIOSK

MUSEO REGIONAL

HOTEL ANTOFAGASTA

POST OFFICE

ESTACIÓN DE FERROCARRIL

BUSES GÉMINIS

TERMINAL DE BUSES RURALES

FÉNIX PULLMAN NORTE

Plaza Colón

PULLMAN BUS

TEATRO MUNICIPAL

TUR-BUS

HOTEL NIKYASAN

WASHINGTON

AEROBUS

SERNATUR

DESÉRTICA

CAFÉ BAHÍA

LANCHILE/LANEXPRESS

RESIDENCIAL RIOJANITA

HOTEL PLAZA

FLOTA BARRIOS

CASA DE LA CULTURA

CORSAL

HOTEL SOL DEL HORIZONTE

PUERTO CALICHE

EL ARRIERO

HOTEL DIEGO DE ALMAGRO

HOTEL KIN WONG

SHANGHAI

TEATRO PEDRO DE LA BARRA

CINE NACIONAL

CASINO DE BOMBEROS

LIBRERÍA ANDRÉS BELLO

HELADOS CAPRI

HOSTAL CHILLAN

BONGO

To Calama, San Pedro de Atacama, Arica, and Panamericana Norte

AUTOMÓVIL CLUB DE CHILE

DON POLLO

ROCOMAR HOTEL

HOTEL MARSAL

MERCADO CENTRAL

BAVARIA

HOTEL COSTA MARFIL

PEKIN

CONAF

Puerto de Antofagasta

MUELLE FISCAL

PACIFIC OCEAN

PIZZANTE

HOTEL BRASIL

LAVERAP

BASÍLICA CORAZÓN DE MARÍA

HOTEL CAPRI

HOSPITAL REGIONAL

HOLIDAY INN EXPRESS

CHONG HUA

LA PAMPA PUB

WALLY'S BAR

ARTE BAR CASIOPEA

NOSTRADAMUS

HOTEL TATIO

To Beaches, Puerto Escondida, and Panamericana Sur

EL ARRAYÁN

To Ruinas de Huanchaca

200 yds

200 m

© AVALON TRAVEL PUBLISHING, INC.

NORTE GRANDE

Streets: RAMIREZ, ADAMSON, CARACOLES, LATORRE, PINTO, IQUIQUE, BOLÍVAR, SUCRE, ARTURO PRAT, BALMACEDA, MATTA, RIQUELME, CONDELL, SERRANO, OSSA, 14 DE FEBRERO, SAN MARTÍN, ORELLA, MAIPÚ, BAQUEDANO, URIBE, LATORRE, CONDELL, COPIAPÓ, MATTA, OSSA, 21 DE MAYO, 14 DE FEBRERO, ESMERALDA, CURICÓ, LINARES, AVENIDA, ATACAMA, ARGENTINA, GRECIA, CARRERA, MIGUEL, BERNARDO, JOSÉ, O'HIGGINS, COLUMBO, ACONCAGUA, ORCHARD, SALVADOR REYES, GENERAL VELÁSQUEZ, SAAVEDRA, AVENIDA, MANUEL RODRÍGUEZ, ANDRÉS SABELLA, MAIPÚ, ORELLE, ANTONIO TORO, POUPIN, ARGENTINA, FORT, EDUARDO, ÁLVARE, HERMÓGENES, LORCA, AVELINO, CONTARDO, DÍAZ, GANA, ANGAMOS, VERBAL, MANUEL, AVENIDA, ROJAS

brown pelicans at fish market in Antofagasta

town, but northern and southern access roads link it to the city.

Streets within Antofagasta's central grid, bounded by Avenida Balmaceda, Bolívar, J. S. Ossa, and Uribe, contain most of the city's sights and services. Many better hotels, restaurants, and bars, though, are southwest of downtown, within a few blocks of the waterfront Avenida Grecia.

Sights

Center of Antofagasta's original city plan, a *zona típica* national monument that comprised about 17 blocks, **Plaza Colón** featured, by 1872, a church, banks, and several private businesses—not to mention 35 trees donated by Valparaíso Mayor Francisco Echaurren to help transform the barren cityscape.

The **Torre Reloj** (1912), a Big Ben surrogate built by British community donations in honor of Chile's centenary, is literally the centerpiece of the rejuvenated plaza; built of reinforced concrete, embellished by a tiled facade that interweaves British and Chilean flags, the scale model stands 13.5 meters high, plus a 2.7 meter weathervane.

One block northeast, on Bolívar between Balmaceda and Washington, the restored **Estación Ferrocarril,** a national monument dating from 1887, was the final stop for the Antofagasta–La Paz railway; the second story is a 1900 addition. Passenger service ceased some years ago (though the line still operates between Calama and La Paz), and the building itself is closed to the public.

Almost across the street at the corner of Balmaceda and Bolívar, the former **Aduana de Antofagasta** (customs house, 1866) is a Valparaíso-built prefab with a U-shaped floor plan and Georgian-style balconies, balustrades, moldings, and other features. First assembled in Mejillones, then disassembled and moved here in 1888 because Antofagasta's booming nitrate exports required it, the two-story structure housed Chilean customs until 1966. After its restoration in 1976, the Museo Regional (regional museum; see entry below) moved into the building.

Across Balmaceda, directly on the waterfront and named for a local poet, the art gallery **Pinacoteca Andrés Sabella** occupies what used to be the **Gobernación Marítima** (Port Authority),

with Francisco Puelma and Manuel Antonio de Lama, he formed the Sociedad Explotadora del Desierto de Atacama, which obtained a 15-year concession to exploit, process, and sell its nitrates. It acquired the name Antofagasta in 1870 from Bolivia's President Mariano Melgarejo.

Melgarejo's name stuck, but Bolivian jurisdiction did not, thanks to Chile's triumph in the War of the Pacific. With the ascendancy of nitrates and then copper, Antofagasta's status was assured, despite a brief period when nearby Mejillones threatened to take over—as it does today, with the present Megapuerto project linking the region with the Mercosur countries Brazil, Paraguay, Uruguay, and Argentina.

Orientation

At the foot of the nearly vertical escarpment of the coast range, Antofagasta is 1,350 km north of Santiago via the Panamericana and 490 km south of Iquique via coastal Ruta 1. The Panamericana actually runs through the coast range east of

NORTE GRANDE

© WAYNE BERNHARDSON

Torre Reloj bell tower at Plaza de Armas in Antofagasta

a national monument. The **Pinacoteca Andrés Sabella,** tel. 55/241262, is open Tuesday to Friday 10 A.M.–1 P.M. and 3:30–7 P.M., weekends 11 A.M.–2 P.M. only.

Almost next door, the onetime **Resguardo Marítimo** (port security) dates from 1910. Immediately to its east, freight trains once unloaded their cargos of nitrates on the now rotting **Muelle Salitrero** (1872), a project of the Melbourne Clark Company that's fenced off for safety reasons. Just beyond the *muelle,* on Aníbal Pinto, brown pelicans scramble for scraps at the **Terminal Pesquero** (wholesale fish market), where the budget-conscious can sample fresh shellfish right off the boat.

Across from the Terminal Pesquero, the Sociedad Química de Chile (Soquimich) maintains its **Casa de Administración** (administrative offices), a national monument that was originally the Lautaro Nitrate Company and then became the Anglo Lautaro Nitrate Company before its nationalization in 1968.

South of the plaza, there are fewer architectural landmarks, but the former **Municipalidad de Antofagasta,** Latorre 2535 between Prat and Baquedano, is a national monument that now houses the municipal **Casa de la Cultura.** In 1999, Pope John Paul II declared the Baroque-Byzantine **Iglesia Corazón de María,** at 21 de Mayo and Cochrane, a minor basilica.

Museo Regional de Antofagasta

Gradually expanding to fill Antofagasta's historic customs house, the regional museum emphasizes the region's mineral wealth—the cornerstone of its economy—but also explains its biogeographical diversity and traces the development of regional cultures that adapted to such limiting factors as near total aridity and, in some areas, high elevations and brutally cold temperatures. The museum has moved beyond generally antiquarian topics such as early man and the Inka dominance to tackle subjects such as the nitrate era, its connection to the War of the Pacific, urban development, and contemporary mining. The photographic materials are especially outstanding but some matters, such as the military dictatorship (when the building itself came under threat and one preservationist had to hide in the hills) are still off-limits.

The Museo Regional, Balmaceda 2786 at Bolívar, tel. 55/227016, is open Tuesday to Friday 10 A.M.–1 P.M. and 3:30–6:30 P.M., weekends and holidays 11 A.M.–2 P.M. only. Admission costs US$1 for adults, US$.50 for kids, but it's free Sunday and holidays.

Ruinas de Huanchaca

Starting in 1888, under a British-Bolivian-Chilean consortium that owned the large Pulacayo silver mine near Potosí (Bolivia), construction of this major refinery on the hillslopes above Playa Blanca took four years to complete. The ore itself made a 500-km rail trip to arrive at the plant, which was capable of processing 100 tons of ore per day to produce 20 tons of silver monthly. In addition to the industrial plant itself, the complex included workers' housing, a church, hotel, and shops, but its very expense and falling silver prices resulted in its closure by 1902.

Only the plant's foundations remain, at the south end of Avenida Argentina, but its heights offer spectacular panoramas of the city and coastline. *Taxi colectivo* No. 3 from downtown goes directly to the Minas de Plata.

Museo Geológico Profesor Humberto Fuenzalida V.

On the campus of the Universidad Católica, Antofagasta's geological museum emphasizes the region's mineral resources; on the patio outside lie a number of petrified tree trunks. It's officially at Avenida Angamos 0610, tel. 55/255090 or 55/248198, but that's the campus entrance—follow the signs along the campus road to get there. It's open 9 A.M.–noon and 3–6 P.M. weekdays; admission is free.

Accommodations

Most of Antofagasta's budget and midrange accommodations are mediocre, but there's not much in these price ranges. For the most part, the upscale places offer better value for money.

US$10–25: Residencial Riojanita, Baquedano 464, is probably the best of the cheapest downtown choices for US$6 pp. A better but less accessible choice, south of town at its namesake beach, **Residencial Playa Huáscar** has half a dozen rooms with private bath for US$8 pp; kitchen facilities cost another US$1 pp, and lunch and dinner are also available for around US$3 pp. Owner Hugo Cerda of Expediciones Desértica, Latorre 2732, tel. 55/386877, has negotiated free admission for his guests at nearby pubs and provides one free transfer from downtown. It's also close to beachfront restaurants.

Hotel Brasil, J. S. Ossa 1978, tel. 55/267268, charges US$9/14 s/d for large but otherwise ordinary rooms with shared bath, US$17 d with private bath, both without breakfast. Once-promising **Hotel Capri,** Copiapó 1208, tel. 55/263703, seems to have settled into a subtropical torpor where problems no longer get fixed quickly or correctly, but the rooms are still spacious and reasonably comfortable for US$13/22 s/d with private bath; rates include a marginal breakfast.

Hotel Corán, Sucre 665, tel. 55/269550 or 55/251538, is unremarkable but perfectly ac-

ceptable for US$15/20 s/d. **Hotel Kin Wong,** alongside its namesake Chinese restaurant at Latorre 2418, tel./fax 55/386168, is a new lodgings whose rates of US$17/25 are reasonable enough, but try asking for discounts as well.

US$25–50: In an auspicious location directly opposite the Safe Sex condom shop, **Hostal Chillán,** Sucre 823, tel. 55/227237, has smallish but comfortable rooms with private bath and breakfast for US$14 pp. **Hotel Nikyasan,** Latorre 2743, tel. 55/221297, charges US$16/25 s/d for good upstairs rooms and not-so-good downstairs rooms alike; breakfast is included.

Hotel Costa Marfil, Arturo Prat 950, tel. 55/225569, fax 55/264806, has friendly English-speaking management and rooms with private bath, cable TV, telephone, and breakfast for US$22/30 s/d. There are some cheaper but darker ground-level interior rooms, and the scuffed walls could use some attention.

The **RocoMar Hotel,** Baquedano 810, tel. 55/261139, fax 55/268749, is a good, modern, and well-kept hotel whose rooms, at US$26/33 s/d with breakfast, offer better natural light than most competitors in its range. **Hotel Sol del Horizonte,** Latorre 2450, tel./fax 55/221886, is a respectable choice of recent vintage, but some downstairs rooms are dark; rates are US$28/39 s/d with private bath, cable TV, and telephone.

Some rooms at placid **Marsal Hotel,** Arturo Prat 867, tel. 55/268063, fax 55/221733, marsalhotel@hotmail.com, come with attractive balconies, but other parts show signs of deferred maintenance. Rates are US$32/39 s/d with breakfast.

Ragged around the edges and in special need of recarpeting, **Hotel Nadine,** Baquedano 519, tel. 55/227008, fax 55/265222, has lurid pink rooms with private bath for US$29/42 s/d with breakfast. Well-run **Hotel Ancla Inn,** Baquedano 508, tel. 55/224814, ancla.inn@entelchile.net, has smallish rooms for US$33/43 with breakfast, but it offers plenty of perks, including two pools, a gym, Jacuzzi, and sauna.

Hotel Diego de Almagro, Condell 2624, tel. 55/268331, charges US$33/45 with breakfast. **US$50–100:** Well-regarded **Hotel Tatio,** Avenida Grecia 1000, tel. 55/247561, costs US$48/57 s/d with breakfast. An architecturally utilitarian relic of the Eisenhower era, **Hotel Plaza,** Baquedano 461, tel. 55/269046, fax 55/225498, hplaza@chilesat.net, nevertheless manages to provide service with a smile. Rates of US$55/75 s/d include a buffet breakfast; the rooms have card keys, cable TV, telephone, strongbox, a/c, and other comforts, plus a pool and parking.

For US$95 s or d, **Hotel Holiday Inn Express,** Avenida Grecia 1490, tel. 55/228888, offers multinational chain conventionality. On the waterfront, **Hotel Antofagasta,** Balmaceda 2575, tel. 55/228811, is a traditional business and holiday favorite for US$95/125 s/d.

Food

Low-priced **Bongo,** Baquedano 743, tel. 55/263697, serves perfectly good sandwiches; so does **Café Bahía,** Prat 470, tel. 55/227551, which scores points for coffee as well. Grilled chicken with fries is virtually the entire menu at **Don Pollo,** Ossa 2594, tel. 55/263361.

Like its counterparts in other Chilean cities, the **Casino de Bomberos,** Sucre 763, offers inexpensive set menus at lunchtime. Partially tobacco-free **Pizzanté,** J. M. Carrera 1857, tel. 55/268115, serves a variety of tasty, sizeable pizzas and sandwiches in agreeable surroundings.

Chinese food is popular throughout the north, and Antofagasta is no exception. Among the established choices are **Chong Hua,** García Lorca 1468, tel. 55/251430; **Pekín,** J. S. Ossa 2135, tel. 55/260833; and **Shanghai,** Latorre 2426, tel. 55/262547.

The nationwide chain **Bavaria,** J. S. Ossa 2424, tel. 55/266567, serves everything from sandwiches to *parrillada,* while **El Arriero,** Condell 2644, tel. 55/268759, is a traditional Chilean *parrilla,* with midrange to upscale prices.

The cheapest fresh seafood alternatives are the market stalls at the **Terminal Pesquero,** on Aníbal Pinto near the Muelle Salitrero, and the **Mercado Central,** bounded by J. S. Ossa, Uribe, Matta, and Maipú. For more elaborate seafood, **Puerto Caliche,** Latorre 2462, tel. 55/227878, serves prix-fixe dinners for US$8 with an aperitif, while à la carte entrées range US$5–15.

Occupying an older house with style, **Nostradamus,** Avelino Contardo 908, tel. 55/248299, has a diverse menu emphasizing seafood, with most entrées in the US$5–8 range; it's also a popular gathering place on weekends. Another outstanding seafood choice is **El Arrayán,** Díaz Gana 1314.

Antofagasta's best ice cream is available at **Heladomanía,** in the same building as Hotel Ancla Inn, Baquedano 508. A close second, with other desserts as well, is **Helados Capri,** down the block at Baquedano 632.

Entertainment

As a university town, Antofagasta has reasonably good performing arts alternatives, and the foreign mining presence helps support a fair amount of nightlife.

Bars: Wally's Pub, Antonino Toro 982, tel. 55/223697, is an expat miners' hangout—next to the Servicio Nacional de Geología y Mineralogía (Sernageomin)—where U.S., Canadian, and Australian engineers try to calculate conversions from Celsius to Fahrenheit under the influence of repeated pisco sours.

Others drinking establishments worth a look, in the same general area, include **Arte Bar Casiopea,** Angamos 1207, and **La Pampa Pub,** at Antonino Toro and García Lorca, tel. 55/386564, which is a *peña* with live music.

Cinema: Antofagasta has two movie theaters, the **Cine Nacional,** Sucre 735, tel. 55/269166, and the **Cine Gran Vía,** Angamos 232, tel. 55/241380, south of the stadium.

Theater and Concerts: The principal performing arts venues are **Teatro Pedro de la Barra,** Condell 2495, tel. 55/263400, and the **Teatro Municipal,** Sucre 433, tel. 55/264919.

Spectator Sports: First-division soccer matches take place at the Estadio Regional, at Avenida Angamos and Club Hípico; the local squad is **Club Antofagasta,** J. S. Ossa 2755, tel. 55/221553.

Services

Money: Downtown ATMs such as BankBoston, Arturo Prat 425, are abundant. For cash or traveler's checks, there are Cambio Ancla Inn, Baquedano 508, and Cambio San Marcos, Baquedano 524.

Postal: Correos de Chile is at Washington 2613, facing Plaza Colón.

Telephone and Internet: Telefónica is at Condell 2527 and at Matta 2625. Antofagasta's area code is tel. 55.

Desértica, Latorre 2732, tel. 55/386877, has the best Internet access.

Laundry: Laverap is at 14 de Febrero 1802, tel. 55/251085.

Travel Agency: Intitour, Baquedano 460, tel. 55/266185, fax 55/260882, speaks English with a pronounced Australian accent.

Medical: Antofagasta's Hospital Regional is at Avenida Argentina 1962, tel. 55/269009.

Information

Tourist Office: Sernatur, Prat 384, 1st floor, tel. 55/451818 or 55/451819, is open 8:30 A.M.–1 P.M. and 3–7:30 P.M. weekdays.

In summer, in front of Hotel Antofagasta at Balmaceda and Prat, there's an information kiosk, tel. 55/224834, open 9:30 A.M.–1:30 P.M. and 3–7 P.M. daily except Sunday, when hours are 10:30 A.M.–2 P.M.

Consulates: Two neighboring countries have consulates in Antofagasta: Argentina, Blanco Encalada 1933, tel. 55/220441; and Bolivia, Washington 2675, Oficina 1301, tel. 55/221403.

Motorists: The Automóvil Club de Chile (Acchi) is at Condell 2330, tel. 55/225332.

National Parks: For information on national parks and other protected areas, visit Conaf at Avenida Argentina 2510, tel. 55/227804, asantoro@conaf.cl.

Bookstores: Librería Andrés Bello is a good general-interest bookshop at Condell 2421.

Transportation

Antofagasta has excellent air and overland connections north and south, and overland connections to the interior of the region.

Air: Aeropuerto Cerro Moreno is 25 km north of town on Ruta 1, at the south end of Península Mejillones.

LanChile/LanExpress, Arturo Prat 445, tel. 55/265151, flies north to Iquique and Arica, east to Calama, and south to Copiapó (weekdays only), La Serena, and Santiago.

Aerocontinente, Washington 2552, tel. 55/2-65224, flies Monday, Wednesday, Friday, and Sunday to Calama and Santiago (US$105), and Monday, Wednesday, Friday, and Sunday to Iquique (US$29–39); the Friday and Sunday flights to Iquique continue to Arica (US$48–68).

Bus: Antofagasta lacks any central long-distance bus terminal; the closest approximation is the Terminal de Buses Rurales, Riquelme 513, where several companies have offices. Most other companies, some with fairly elaborate terminals of their own, are clustered to the east of Plaza Colón, in and around San Martín, Latorre, and Condell.

Companies operating out of the Terminal de Buses Rurales include the local carriers Fepstur and Maravilla Bus (to Mejillones); Corsal, on Condell between Bolívar and Sucre, has minibuses to Mejillones.

Also at the Terminal de Buses Rurales, the long-distance carriers Tas Choapa, Fénix Pullman Norte, Buses Iquique, Buses Carmelita, and Pullman Santa Rosa all use Ruta 1 north toward Iquique and have southbound services on the Panamericana. Fepstur also has a separate office at Latorre 2723, while Fénix Pullman Norte has one at San Martín 2717, tel. 55/268896.

Pullman Bus, Latorre 2805, tel. 55/268838, and Tur-Bus, Latorre 2751, tel. 55/266691, both have extensive services northbound, southbound, and east toward Calama and San Pedro de Atacama. Flota Barrios, Condell 2782, tel. 55/268559, has somewhat less ambitious schedules along most of the same routes, as does Géminis, Latorre 3055, tel. 55/251796; Flota Barrios also stops at the nitrate towns of María Elena and Pedro de Valdivia. Iquique/Arica carriers Zambrano, Ramos Cholele, and Camus all share the Géminis terminal.

Typical destination fares and times include Arica (US$18, 10 hours), Iquique (US$15, six hours), Tocopilla (US$6, 2.5 hours), Calama (US$4.50, three hours), Taltal (US$4.50, four hours), Chañaral (US$18, six hours), Copiapó (US$12, eight hours), La Serena (US$17, 12 hours), Valparaíso/Viña del Mar (US$32, 16 hours), and Santiago (US$33, 18 hours).

International services to Jujuy and Salta, Argentina, are available through Tur-Bus Wednesday at 6:15 A.M. and Géminis Sunday at 7 A.M.

Getting Around

Airport Transportation: From the Terminal Pesquero, bus No. 15 goes to the airport for just US$.50, but only every two hours from 7:30 A.M.–10:30 P.M. For US$4 pp, Aerobús, Baquedano 328, tel. 55/262727, offers door-to-door service.

Car Rental: Rental cars are available from Alamo, Avenida Argentina 2779, tel. 55/261864; Avis, Balmaceda 2556, tel. 55/226153; Budget, Baquedano 300, tel. 55/225370, fax 55/452137; First, Bolívar 623, tel. 55/225777; Hertz, Balmaceda 2492, tel. 55/269043; and Automotriz La Portada, Prat 801, tel. 55/263788.

VICINITY OF ANTOFAGASTA

While Antofagasta isn't the obvious choice for excursions that San Pedro de Atacama is, it's still a good base for trips up and down the coast and some destinations on and around the Panamericana.

The most ambitious and imaginative excursion from the city is a full-day tour and transport to San Pedro de Atacama via the railroad museum at Baquedano and then across the southern end of the Salar de Atacama, visiting the villages of Peine and Socaire, the altiplano lakes of Miscanti and Miñiques, and the town of Toconao before arriving in San Pedro de Atacama in time for the sunset at Valle de la Luna.

Antofagasta's **Desértica Expediciones,** Latorre 2732, tel. 55/386877, website: www.desertica.cl, info@desertica.cl, charges US$70 pp for the 12-hour excursion, which leaves at 8 A.M. and includes breakfast and lunch. While the trip is unique, the elevation gain from sea level to above 4,000 meters at Miscanti and Miñiques may cause problems for some individuals.

Caleta Coloso (Mirador Escondida)

At present, the highway south stops a short distance beyond Caleta Coloso, where copper concentrate arrives for processing via a subterranean pipeline from the Escondida mine, 170 km to the east, 3,100 meters above sea level in the Andes. The Mirador Escondida overlook doesn't exactly offer tours, but some pretty sophisticated exhibits explain the copper mining process from 10 A.M.–7 P.M. daily.

At **Dunas de Coloso,** where the new road continues south toward an eventual link with

desert coastline north of Antofagasta

© WAYNE BERNHARDSON

Taltal, Desértica Expediciones (see above) offers sandboard excursions and instruction for US$12—though the climb back up the steep dunes is pretty brutal.

Monumento Natural La Portada

Crowned by Miocene sedimentary strata eroded into a graceful natural arch, Monumento Natural La Portada stands alone on a volcanic platform of Jurassic rocks in the Pacific, opposite a broad sandy beach beneath steeply rising headlands 25 km north of Antofagasta. Unfortunately, because of frequent seismic activity, the headlands are so unstable that it's no longer permitted to descend to the beach of the 31-hectare reserve.

Even so, this symbol of the Norte Grande coastline is probably one of Conaf's most visited units because of its scenery and accessibility. A short distance west of Ruta 1, easily reached by bus No. 15 from Antofagasta's Terminal Pesquero, La Portada also offers a good concentration of seabirds (boobies, gulls, oystercatchers, and pelicans), occasional marine mammals (dolphins, sea lions, and otters) and a decent seafood restaurant at the parking lot. Drivers should lock their cars.

Reserva Marina La Rinconada

Established under fishing laws by Servicio Nacional de Pesca (Sernap), this 332-hectare protected zone is a key habitat for the *ostión del norte* (northern scallop)—*Agropecten purpuratus* has a high genetic diversity and long reproductive season here, from end of spring to middle of autumn. On the south side of the Mejillones peninsula, the reserve is 31 km northwest of Antofagasta on the paved road to the beach town of Juan López.

Juan López

In sheltered waters at the south end of Península Mejillones, at the east end of Bahía Moreno, Juan López is a working-class beach resort that vibrates with street life—and deafening amplified music—in summer and on weekends. To the west, toward the coastal village of Bolsico, Conaf is hoping to create a protected area for the large pelican colonies in a land swap north of Antofagasta, where urban development—even a rubbish dump—is impinging on the former Reserva Nacional La Chimba.

For accommodations or lunch, try **Hostal Restaurant Vitoco** where, however, the live salsa on weekends can be so loud that it sets off car alarms in the street.

In summer, from Juan López, it's possible to approach the offshore stack at Monumento Natural La Portada with the motor launch *Rica Ventura,* daily at 10 A.M., for US$8 pp.

Taxi colectivos link Antofagasta with Juan López in summer and on weekends.

Panamericana Sur

The thinly populated area south of Antofagasta in and around the Panamericana has few conspicuous sights, but visitors with time and transportation will find it worthwhile.

Mano del Desierto: At Km 1,310 of the Panamericana, 51 km south of Antofagasta and 1,100 meters above sea level, Santiago sculptor Mario Irarrázabal erected this enigmatic sculpture of a hand protruding about 12 meters above the barren pampa. Finished in 1992, the hollow structure supports an exterior of *ferrocemento* (literally, "iron cement") only eight centimeters thick. It took two months for three people to build the structure in Santiago and, after it was shipped north, two weeks more to finish the job.

Financed by a group of Antofagasta businessmen—as individuals, rather than as representatives of corporations—the sculpture reflects the artist's intention to give passing motorists "a reason to stop in the middle of nowhere" and "feel the silence and the breeze." Unfortunately, lesser "artists" have felt the need to deface this graceful landmark, on the west side of the highway, with pointless graffiti; the artist himself professes not to be too bothered, but he cleans it off whenever he visits his wife's family in Antofagasta. Irarrázabal has created similar sculptures in Punta del Este (Uruguay), Madrid, and Venice.

Observatorio Cerro Paranal: Only about one km south of the Mano del Desierto, at a poorly marked highway junction, the paved Panamericana swerves southeast, while a wide but phenomenally dusty gravel road heads directly south to the European Space Organization's Cerro

Paranal facility, in an isolated coast range locale, 2,664 meters above sea level.

Opened in March 1999, Paranal's state-of-the-art observatory features four eight-meter Very Large Telescopes (VLTs). Even more distant from light pollution sources than Chile's Norte Chico observatories, it offers ideal conditions for viewing the northern night skies. While not so readily open to the public as the Norte Chico observatories, visits are still possible—contact Esteban Illanes at ESO's Santiago office, Alonso de Córdova 3107, Vitacura, tel. 2/2084254, eillanes@eso.org.

Cerro Paranal is 126 km south of Antofagasta, at the end of a short paved westward lateral off the main road, which continues south and then west through the canyon known as the Quebrada de Despoblado, toward Paposo and Taltal. Note that mining trucks along the route kick up such huge clouds of dust that poor visibility can make driving hazardous.

From Taltal, **Empresa Gali,** San Martín 641, tel./fax 55/611008, 55/611320, or 09/5162925, does day tours to Paranal for US$16 pp.

Sierra del Remiendos: Only 16 km south of the same Panamericana highway junction that leads to Cerro Paranal, a vertiginous gravel road heads southwest through wild desert country to Caleta El Cobre, a now-abandoned copper mine and smelter on the Pacific coast. Eventually, a coastal road will link Caleta El Cobre with Antofagasta, but in the meantime, this is an adventurous alternative through the "Patchwork Sierra" for southbound travelers with their own vehicles (for more details of the road between Caleta El Cobre and Taltal, see the Taltal entry below).

Oficina Alemania: At Km 1,175, about 280 km south of Antofagasta, Oficina Alemania was a key nitrate *oficina* that, unfortunately, was dismantled for scrap only a few years ago. At the turnoff, Héctor Cuadra's Fondart-sponsored sculpture is dedicated to the Shanks-system nitrate workers who, according to Cuadra, "surrendered their lungs" to the nitrate industry.

Taltal

Taltal, the Norte Grande's only sizeable town south of Antofagasta, was much more sizeable when, in the early 20th century, it was one of the region's main nitrate ports, well served by rail to the rest of the pampas. Today, it's an obscure but charming fishing port and beach resort, studded with nitrate-era monuments, far enough off the Panamericana to be off the beaten track but close enough to make an entertaining detour.

History: As a settlement, Taltal dates from about 1850, when mining pioneer José Antonio Moreno first began to exploit its nitrate deposits and ship them from its early port. After a border treaty with Bolivia in 1866, it was Chile's most northerly outpost; by 1877, the government had platted a town and port that grew rapidly with nitrate exploitation here and at nearby Aguas Blancas. After the 1950s, when the last remaining nitrate *oficinas* fizzled, much of the town's infrastructure was dismantled, but government preservation decrees and the bankruptcy of the last remaining enterprises salvaged part of this irreplaceable heritage.

Orientation: Taltal is 325 km from Antofagasta via the Panamericana and a paved northwest lateral that descends the Quebrada de Taltal between the Sierra Vetada and the Sierra de Tipias. It's 170 km north of Chañaral via the Panamericana and the same paved lateral.

Entering town from the southeast, Calle O'Higgins divides Taltal into two: to the southwest, Calle Prat, one block inland from the beach, is the main commercial strip of a regular grid; to the northwest, the former grounds of the former Taltal Railway Company hold most of the local historic monuments.

Sights: Starting operations in 1882, the London-based Taltal Railway Company reached its terminus at Cachinal, 149 km to the east, but it had branch lines to all the *oficinas* in the region. On the east side of O'Higgins, between Esmeralda and Prat, its petroleum-burning **Kinston Meyer Locomotora No. 59** entered service in 1906; along with two railcars filled with historic photographs, it's an *in situ* museum and national monument that keeps irregular hours.

The company's port infrastructure, covering 15 hectares, once included five piers, warehouses, turntables, fuel storage tanks, platforms, and 22 locomotives with 560 cars. The remaining structures include its **Oficinas Generales** (general offices), the **Casa Administrador** (administrator's house), and the 120-meter **Muelle Salitrero** (nitrate pier), now missing many sleepers though its corroded century-old crane still stands. The Municipalidad de Taltal has requested government help in restoring the rotting pier.

In the downtown area, overlooking Plaza Prat, the Gothic-style **Iglesia San Francisco Javier** dates from 1897, while the run-down **Teatro Alhambra** was finished in 1921. One block seaward, between Torreblanca and Ramírez, the waterfront **Plaza Riquelme** is a gathering place behind the **Balneario Municipal** or city beach, but better beaches are north of town.

Half a block northeast of the plaza, Taltal's **Casa de la Cultura Sady Zañartu Bustos,** Prat 642, contains the **Museo Augusto Capdeville,** an archaeological museum.

Accommodations: At **Muelle de Piedra,** two km north of town on the Paposo road, there are inexpensive beach camping sites with shade, toilets, and showers. **Hotel San José,** Ramírez 345, tel. 55/611105, is by no means bad for US$7 pp, but the singles are extremely small—barely room to turn around—though they do have TV.

For US$8.50 pp with shared bath, upstairs rooms with streetside balconies are the best value at amiable **Hotel San Martín,** Juan Martínez 279, tel. 55/611088; downstairs rooms have minimal natural light. Breakfast is extra, but the baths are both spacious and spotless. Doubles with private bath cost US$20.

Hostal del Mar, three blocks southwest of the plaza at Carrera 250, tel. 55/611612costs US$20/25 s/d. Friendly, new, and immaculate, **Hotel Gali,** San Martín 637, 2nd floor, tel. 55/611008, is a very fine choice for US$21 s or d, if you can overlook the lurid red bedspreads.

Despite its pleasing beachfront location, conspicuously deferred maintenance at **Hostería Taltal,** Esmeralda 671, tel. 55/611173, fax 55/611625, suggests that it's passed its peak; in fairness, though, this seems to be more a cosmetic than a practical problem. Rates are US$21/25 s/d with shared bath, US$32/35 s/d with private bath.

Food: For inexpensive breakfasts and sandwiches, there's **Pastelería La Central,** Prat 549, tel. 55/611519, and **Salón de Te Capri,** Ramírez 218, tel. 55/611273.

Taltal has two good, moderately priced seafood restaurants: **Las Brisas,** at the Terminal Pesquero (fish market), Esmeralda s/n; and **Las Anclas,** Juan Martínez 169, near the corner with Esmeralda.

The best choice, though a little more expensive, is **Oficina Salinitas,** Esmeralda 760, run by an owner-chef who clearly enjoys all aspects of running a restaurant, from design and decoration to greeting guests, cooking, and mixing a powerful pisco sour. Seafood entrées such as *ostiones al pil pil* run in the US$6–7 range. Note the maps and photographs on the walls.

Services and Information: For long-distance telephone service, go to Telefónica CTC at Prat 687, or Entel at the corner of Prat and Juan Martínez. Taltal's area code is 55, the same as Antofagasta's.

Correos de Chile, Prat 515, is the local post office.

In a kiosk on Plaza Prat, Taltal's Oficina de Información Turística is open in summer only.

Transportation: Taltal's only remaining bus company, with destinations north and south along the Panamericana and Ruta 1, is Tur-Bus, Prat 631, tel. 55/611426. Destinations, fares, and times include Antofagasta (US$7, 4.5 hours), Tocopilla, US$10, six hours), Calama (US$10, six hours), Iquique (US$25, 14 hours), Arica (US$30, 18 hours), Chañaral (US$8, five hours), La Serena (US$17, 15 hours), and Santiago (US$30, 21 hours).

Vicinity of Taltal

North of Taltal, coastal Ruta 1 is due to reach Antofagasta in a few years, but presently goes only as far as Caleta El Cobre, where a steep, truly remote road turns northwest to intersect the Panamericana about 50 km south of the regional capital.

In early 2001, however, construction improvements slowed because of the discovery of several archaeological sites in the first 10 km north of Taltal. There are an estimated 300 archaeological sites between Taltal and Caleta El Cobre, the oldest of which dates back 6,000 years during hunter-gatherer times; there are also relatively recent Inka sites.

Mano del Desierto (Hand in the Desert) by sculptor Mario Irarrázabal, Ruta Panamericana

© WAYNE BERNHARDSON

The only substantial town along the route, the fish camp of **Paposo** has a newly modernized park and plaza and fishing pier, but not much else—the Conaf station remains closed despite the presence of its **Reserva Nacional Paposo** in the slopes of the coast range.

Beyond Paposo, the northbound road is badly washboarded but there are no washouts; another road turns inland up the Quebrada del Despoblado and intersects a road that leads to the Cerro Paranal observatory. About 85 km north of Paposo, the inland route from Caleta El Blanco is closed but there is no warning sign—be sure to continue to Caleta El Cobre and then turn east toward the Sierra de Remiendos and the Panamericana at the first turn past the abandoned mining camp.

Panamericana Norte

From Antofagasta, the Panamericana trends northeast, crossing the **Hito de Capricornio,** marking the Tropic of Capricorn; after about 70 km, it passes through the rail junction town of Baquedano before turning north again near the ruins of Oficina Chacabuco and continuing to the regional border at Quillagua. While dozens of other abandoned *salitreras* dot both sides of the Panamericana, only Chacabuco and the recently closed or closing mines at Pedro de Valdivia and María Elena have avoided nearly complete dismantling for scrap.

Where the Panamericana turns north, paved Ruta 25 continues to Calama, the gateway to interior destinations such as San Pedro de Atacama, in an area that is Chile's widest geographical point.

Baquedano: At the desert junction of Baquedano, the Ferrocarril a Bolivia (FCAB) between Antofagasta and La Paz crossed the Longino (Longitudinal Railway) that once connected Iquique with Santiago. While the Longino is long since defunct, the FCAB continues to haul freight to Bolivia (passengers can catch a weekly service to La Paz from Calama) and another freight line still reaches the Argentine border at Socompa. The latter carries the occasional passenger through spectacular desert and altiplano landscapes to connect with the legendary Tres a las Nubes (Train to the Clouds) route to the Argentine city of Salta.

For most visitors, though, the more accessible attraction is Baquedano's open-air **Museo Ferroviario,** conserving the Longino's legacy with half a dozen vintage locomotives and numerous antique railcars at a roundhouse that's a national monument.

Visitors interested in crossing the Andes to Salta should contact Ferronor, Sucre 220, 4th floor, tel. 55/224764 or 55/227927, Antofagasta, but be aware that passengers are a lower priority than borax. Antofagasta's Desértica Expediciones is attempting to arrange a regular tourist car on this route.

All buses on the Panamericana have to pass through Baquedano, so it's easy to stop for a look at the station and its surroundings. There are also several basic but decent restaurants for meals and left luggage.

Oficina Chacabuco: Just four km north of the junction between the Panamericana and Ruta

THE FCAB AND THE LONGINO

It may not look like it now but a century ago, before nitrates went bust, Baquedano bustled with both passenger and cargo trains. Rail service on the east-west line between Antofagasta and Bolivia was an outgrowth of early nitrate development, while north-south traffic resulted from the need to link the Chilean heartland with the country's northern deserts.

First proposed in 1866, the international line dates from 1866, when the Bolivian government and private interests first reached agreements for concessions of nitrate, borax, and other mineral ores in what was then the Bolivian province of Cobija. Political instability in Bolivia contributed to disputes over concession areas and sizes, export rights, and railroad right of ways, so Chilean entrepreneurs formed the Compañía Explotadora del Desierto de Atacama in 1868, which was succeeded the following year by Melbourne Clark y Compañía, and then in 1872 by the Compañía de Salitres y Ferrocarril de Antofagasta. After finally getting an authorization to build a rail line from Antofagasta to its offices in Salar de Carmen, east of the city, the latter was soon able to replace its mules and oxcarts with steam locomotives hauling freight cars.

By 1877, the line reached Carmen Alto, near the present-day junction of the Panamericana and the highway to Calama. After taking control of the territory in the War of the Pacific, in 1884 Chile authorized extension of the line to Bolivia. In 1885, the Compañía de Salitres signed a contract with the Compañía Minera Huanchaca de Bolivia for an international line, but after it reached the border at Ollagüe, Minera Huanchaca bought the railroad rights from its partner, sold them to the British Antofagasta and Bolivia Railway Company, and then leased them back. The line finally reached Uyuni in 1889, with a branch line to Pulacayo, site of Huanchaca's silver diggings.

The Longino dates from that same year, when Chilean authorities decided to build a north-south link to several existing private lines between Cabildo, in the Norte Chico, and Iquique (for information on the southernmost sector of this route, see the special topic Taking the High Road

in the Norte Chico chapter). By 1916, it finally formed an unbroken link from La Calera, in the Aconcagua valley northeast of Viña del Mar.

In 1910, the junction received the name of Baquedano, and it continued to enjoy plenty of cargo and passenger movement even as the nitrate boom fizzled after World War I; as late as 1918, it carried a million tons of nitrate in a year, but it survived by transforming itself into a copper railway. Offices and ticket windows of the two lines still stand in the **Estación Baquedano,** a national historical monument, whose **Casa de Máquinas** (1916), built by Ferrocarriles del Estado, is a semicircular building of Douglas fir, divided into 16 *compartimientos* or *cocheras* for each steam locomotive. Half a dozen German and North American locomotives remain, one of them on the station's **Tornamesa** (Turntable), also with a scattering of antique railcars.

A third line that passed through Baquedano, the Ferrocarril Antofagasta-Socompa-Salta, took an astonishing 60 years to complete from the initial proposal of 1888 to its official inauguration in 1948. Though it briefly carried passengers, the 38-hour marathon through the freezing high Andes, which required changing trains at Socompa, discouraged all but the hardiest passengers.

The hardiest passengers can still attempt a crossing to Salta with the private Ferronor company, which bought the FCAB and other constructions in 1950; the FCAB proper still hauls freight from Antofagasta to Bolivia, but it carries passengers from Calama to the Bolivian border only, where it's necessary to change trains.

railroad turntable at Baquedano

NORTE GRANDE

25, the Calama highway, Oficina Chacabuco is second only to Humberstone in terms of preservation among the Atacama's nitrate ghost towns. It also has a more recent and notorious history: in the Pinochet dictatorship's first year, it was a prison camp, though not one of the worst—intervention by the international Red Cross prevented executions. Ironically enough, one of those detained was Salvador Allende's education subsecretary Waldo Sánchez, who only a few months earlier had declared Chacabuco a national monument.

Almost equally ironically, Chacabuco's current caretaker Roberto Zaldívar was himself one of the more than 2,200 people incarcerated in the former workers' housing. While Chacabuco was not so obviously secure as geographically isolated Pisagua, the military surrounded the town with minefields, which have still not been completely removed, to keep the prisoners in. These fields are well-signed, and visitors should take them seriously.

Built by the Lautaro Nitrate Company in 1924, Chacabuco was the last and largest of those using the Shanks system—even as it was under construction, synthetic nitrates were supplanting mineral nitrates, and U.S.-based Guggenheim Brothers was experimenting with a new system to increase nitrate yields from lower quality ores.

At its peak, Chacabuco could produce 15,000 metric tons of nitrate per month, but that peak was brief. Still, technological obsolescence brought about its closure by 1940 and, though it suffered depredations by scrap thieves, it remains one of the best-preserved *oficinas*. The industrial plant included workshops, warehouses, ore crushers, and 54 enormous liquification tanks under a single roof.

Really a city in itself, Chacabuco occupied an area of 36 hectares, its wide streets forming a grid pattern, and reached a maximum population of about 5,000. Its infrastructure included a hospital, theater, hotel, school, market, gymnasium, swimming pool, athletic fields, a tree-lined plaza, and long blocks of workers' housing built of adobe. Beyond the industrial plant, there remain huge piles of low-grade tailings.

Chacabuco's theater, the beneficiary of painstaking restoration work funded by the German Embassy and Santiago's Goethe Institute, is even larger than Humberstone's. Its second and third floors feature a photographic exhibit of Chacabuco in its heyday; note also the well-preserved murals above the stage. Other notable structures include the train station, the general store, the employees' casino, and its tennis courts.

Caretaker Zaldívar has a large but disorganized collection of artifacts from the nitrate era. Admission to the site costs US$1.70 for adults, half that for kids.

Transportation: Chacabuco is only a short distance east of the Panamericana, but since it's four km north of the main highway junction, Calama-bound buses do not pass nearby. All other northbound buses on the Panamericana come within easy walking distance, however.

Pedro de Valdivia: Founded in 1931 by Guggenheim Brothers, the nitrate *oficina* of Pedro de Valdivia was a working company town until its closure in 1996. Because the Guggenheim process of extracting nitrates from the hardpan caliche was so superior to the Shanks system that preceded it, both Pedro de Valdivia and nearby María Elena managed to survive long after Shanks-dependent *oficinas* collapsed.

Officially a *zona típica* national monument since its closure, Pedro de Valdivia is 75 km north of the Calama junction via the Panamericana and a short paved westward lateral.

María Elena: One of Chile's very last working *oficinas,* also founded by Guggenheim Brothers (in 1926), María Elena processed more than a million tons of caliche per year at its peak, in conjunction with Pedro de Valdivia. Today, though, it clings tenuously to life despite its imminent closure. The mine installations belong to the Sociedad Química Chilena (Soquimich), successor to the Guggenheim dynasty, but the town itself is an independent municipality, about 38 km north of Pedro de Valdivia via a paved road that parallels the Panamericana. There is also a paved lateral that leads west from the Panamericana.

On the dusty streets surrounding María Elena's Plaza de Armas, several buildings comprise the **Barrio Cívico,** a *zona típica* national monument. Among them are the former **Escuela Consoli-**

dada (school), the **Pulpería** or general store, the **Mercado** (market), the **Teatro Metro** (Metro Theater), the **Iglesia San Rafael Arcángel, Sindicato N°3** (union headquarters), the **Baños Públicos** (public baths), **Banco del Estado,** and the **Asociación Social y Deportiva** (Social and Sports Association).

Also on the plaza, the **Museo Arqueológico e Histórico,** Ignacio Carrera Pinto s/n, tel. 55/639406, recalls the region's pre-Columbian past and the historic nitrate era. It's open 9 A.M.–1 P.M. and 4–7 P.M. Monday to Saturday, 10 A.M.–1 P.M. and 5–8 P.M. Sunday. Admission is free.

The only place to stay is **Residencial Chacance,** Claudio Vicuña 437, tel. 55/639524; rooms with shared bath cost US$6/9 s/d, while those with private bath cost US$8 pp. The **Club María Elena** is the best dining choice, but there are a couple other simple *comedores.*

Several Antofagasta bus companies, including Camus, Flota Barrios, Kenny Bus, and Pullman Bus, serve María Elena.

Tranque Sloman: Built between 1905 and 1911, this sloping 36-meter-high dam in the canyon of the Río Loa once supplied electricity to several nearby *oficinas,* but nowadays the quarried stone structure merely serves to regulate the release of irrigation water to the fields near Quillagua, about 20 km to the north. Reached by a gravel lateral that leads about three km east from the Panamericana, it is now a national monument that contains a **Casa de Máquina** with three rusting turbines, plus several other constructions.

In 1997, when heavy altiplano rains caused downstream floods, Tranque Sloman was the site of a major fish kill, as the rushing waters apparently stirred up toxic sediments deposited through decades of upstream mining (even naturally, the Río Loa has such high arsenic levels that it must be heavily treated to be potable). The dam's national monument status—not to mention the expense—complicates any cleanup efforts.

Quillagua: Flowing through Quillagua, the Río Loa marks the border between Region I (Tarapacá) and Region II (Antofagasta). Until coastal Ruta 1 opened in the early 1990s, this was always a crowded internal customs check because of merchandise moving back and forth to the duty-

free Zofri, but now it plays second fiddle to the seaside post at the Loa estuary. Nevertheless, it's worth slowing or stopping for the geoglyphs on both sides of the highway about 10 km south of the border.

THE NORTHERN COAST

From Antofagasta, coastal Ruta 1 heads north past the Mejillones peninsula, the copper port of Tocopilla, and several ghost towns and numerous desert beaches before arriving at the estuary of the Río Loa, where there's an internal customs check. Open barely a decade, the paved highway linking Tocopilla with Iquique now carries most of the traffic between Region II and Region I.

Mejillones

Calm Pacific waters lap the long but steep and relatively narrow beaches of sheltered Mejillones, whose shady coastal promenade provides protection from the hot midday sun. Originally founded when the region was part of Bolivia, the town lapsed into subtropical torpor while Antofagasta boomed with nitrate exports, but it still boasts some nitrate-era landmarks. It has long been popular with Antofagastinos as a weekend retreat.

Mejillones' peacefulness is under siege, though. Construction of a multimillion-dollar Megapuerto (megaport) at its east end is supposed to establish the town as the terminus of a transcontinental trade route, oriented toward the Pacific Rim, from Brazil and Paraguay through Argentina and across the Andes to Chile. Nearly all these highways are paved, including the smooth four-lane asphalt road that comes to a dead end about one km before the ocean because objections from Corema, the Regional Environmental Commission, have held up a US$55 million credit from the Inter-American Development Bank (IADB). Still, if all goes according to schedule, the megaport should open by April 2003 and Mejillones may regain its primacy from Antofagasta.

Orientation: Facing its namesake bay and protected from most ocean swells by the Punta Angamos peninsula to the west, Mejillones is about 80 km north of Antofagasta via coastal Ruta 1 and a paved northwestern lateral. Another paved access road connects to Ruta 1 to the northeast.

Avenida Latorre, two blocks south of the beach, is the main thoroughfare, while Avenida San Martín faces the beach. Most services are on or near one or the other.

Sights: Mejillones has no national monuments—but several buildings, all dating from the early 20th century, would be worthy candidates. At the foot of Francisco Pinto, topped by a lighthouse, stands the handsome **Capitanía del Puerto** (port authority). One block south, at Francisco Pinto 110, the **Museo Histórico y Natural,** tel. 55/621289, occupies the former **Aduana de Mejillones,** which replaced an earlier landmark customshouse dismantled and moved to Antofagasta. While the museum posts hours of 10 A.M.–2 P.M. and 3–9 P.M. daily, it rarely keeps them; exhibits include material on marine fauna, historical figures, and local institutions.

The **Locomotora** (locomotive) in the median strip on Manuel Rodríguez, just south of Avenida Latorre, is one of the originals of the Ferrocarril a Bolivia (Mejillones was the terminus of a spur line). Five blocks west, at Avenida Latorre and Avenida Castillo, the soaring **Iglesia Corazón de María** is Mejillones's major ecclesiastical landmark.

At the corner of Avenida Latorre and Las Heras, there's a summer **Mercado Artesanal** (artisans' market).

Accommodations: Though some places shut down in winter, Mejillones offers modest lodgings at **Residencial Elizabeth,** Latorre 440, tel. 55/621568, for around US$6/10 s/d with shared bath, and the slightly more expensive **Residencial Marcela,** General Borgoño 150, tel. 55/621464, which also has rooms with private bath. Quiet, orderly **Hostal Miramar,** San Martín 650, tel. 55/621638, costs US$18 d with shared bath, US$20/30 s/d with private bath.

Scuffed and worn in spots, **Hotel Capitanía,** Avenida San Martín 410, tel./fax 55/621542 or 55/621276, hotelcapitania@entelchile.net, has seaview rooms for US$20/35 s/d with private bath and breakfast, but it's worth haggling a little here. Close to the beach, immaculate rooms with all modern conveniences make **Hotel Costa del Sol,** Manuel Montt 086, tel. 55/621590, fax 55/621646, the best in town at US$49/54 s/d. **Food: Zlatar,** Manuel Rodríguez 125, tel. 55/621580, is a good, moderately priced seafood venue. **Hotel Costa del Sol,** Manuel Montt 086, has a more upscale ambience.

Transportation: There are frequent bus connections to Antofagasta with Corsal Bus, Latorre 735, and Maravilla Bus, Latorre 794. Long-distance carriers include Pullman Bus, Latorre 799, tel. 55/622179; Flota Barrios, Latorre 869, tel. 55/621888; and Tur-Bus, Avenida Latorre 867, tel. 55/621499.

Tocopilla

Once the end of the road, until Ruta 1 opened the coastal trail a decade ago, Tocopilla's dilemma is to get tourists to stop en route north to their sunbathing and shopping sprees at Iquique. To do so, the Municipalidad wants to create artificial beaches and pools at Playa Covadonga, at the south end of town, and relocate traditional vendors and eateries there. There is potentially good surfing in the area, and little competition for waves.

Traditionally, Tocopilla exports the nitrates from María Elena and Pedro de Valdivia (an electric railway carries the cargo to the port), and its massive Central Termoeléctrica powers the copper mine at Chuquicamata, 143 km to the east. Still, unemployment is a serious issue, and a new tax-free regime intended to stimulate mining activity will allow companies to import raw materials and semimanufactured goods for the next few years.

In a offbeat way, Tocopilla is a sports hotbed. About 20 km north of town, just before the Túnel Galleguillos that replaced a long switchback on Ruta 1, the Tocopilla Golf Club is the *literal* Pebble Beach—the "greens" consist of crushed black volcanic rock; most of the rest of the course is one big sand trap. Unfortunately for duffers hoping to challenge these unique conditions, it's not open to the public.

Even more unexpected, though, is Tocopilla's downtown baseball park. The seaside diamond has grand views, but this is true sandlot ball—the entire field is a hard dirt surface—you don't want to dive for balls, and you certainly don't want to crash into the concrete outfield walls. In 2001,

Tocopilla finished second to Iquique in the national championships.

Orientation: On narrow wave-cut terraces above the Pacific, at the foot of the coast range, Tocopilla is 188 km north of Antofagasta and 244 km south of Iquique. It is 143 km west of Chuquicamata via another paved highway, that intersects the north-south Panamericana about midway to Chuqui.

Tocopilla has an elongated city plan in which thoroughfares such as Ruta 1 (known as Arturo Prat through town) and 21 de Mayo (the downtown business street) are crossed by shorter streets that rise fairly steeply from west to east.

Sights: Bounded by 21 de Mayo, Aníbal Pinto, Sucre, and Bolívar, **Plaza Carlos Condell** is the focus of Tocopilla's street life. Other than its industrial installations, Tocopilla's main landmark is its **Torre Reloj,** a wooden clocktower moved from Coya, a former nitrate *oficina* midway between María Elena and Pedro de Valdivia. Within the Municipalidad, on the north side of the plaza, there's a modest **Museo Arqueológico** on the second floor.

Accommodations: For US$4.50 pp with shared bath, **Residencial Royal,** 21 de Mayo 1988, tel. 55/811488, is adequate at best, with soft beds; rooms with private bath are arguably better for US$9/15 s/d. **Residencial Sonia,** Washington 1329, tel. 55/813086, also costs US$4.50 pp with shared bath, as does **Residencial Mary y Pily,** Sucre 1678, tel. 55/819433.

With friendly management but gloomy surroundings that badly need stepped-up maintenance, **Hotel Casablanca,** 21 de Mayo 2054, tel. 55/813222, costs US$10/18 s/d with private bath. The beds, at least, are comfortable.

The hands-down best value is **Hotel Colonial,** 21 de Mayo 1717, tel. 55/811621, fax 55/811940, where rates of US$13/18 include private bath, cable TV, an outstanding breakfast, and service that tops that of many more expensive places.

Modern **Hotel Chungará,** 21 de Mayo 1440, tel. 55/811036, is worth consideration for US$18/21 s/d. **Hotel Vucina,** 21 de Mayo 2069, tel. 55/813088, charges US$18/24 s/d with private bath but without breakfast.

Food: The chain **Bavaria,** Colón 613, tel. 55/251679, is good for breakfast and standard Chilean fare of reliable quality. Though the fare is broadly similar, the **Club de la Unión,** Prat 1354, tel. 55/813198, retains the atmosphere of the bygone nitrate era, with good seafood at modest prices. **Chifa Jok San,** 21 de Mayo 1848, serves Chinese meals.

La Casa de Don Julio, Serrano 1336, at the south end of downtown, passes for haute cuisine in Tocopilla, but it would be considered a decent restaurant just about anywhere in Chile, with pleasant outdoor seating on a quiet block. Seafood dinners cost around US$8.

Entertainment: The surprise in Tocopilla itself is several sidewalk cafés and bars, among them **Piero's Place,** 21 de Mayo 1395; **Tequila Pub,** 21 de Mayo 1330; and **Yanko's Pub,** on Serrano between 21 de Mayo and Sucre.

Services: Correos de Chile is at the corner of 21 de Mayo and Aníbal Pinto.

Entel is at 21 de Mayo 2066; Tocopilla's area code is 55. Ultraweb, 21 de Mayo 1721, has Internet access for about US$1.50 hourly; opening times are 10 A.M.–2 P.M. and 5:30–10:30 P.M. or so.

Tocopilla's Hospital is at Santa Rosa and Matta, tel. 55/821839, a short distance northeast of downtown.

Transportation: Tocopilla has no central bus terminal, but many bus lines pass through town en route between Santiago, Antofagasta, and Iquique. Among them are Buses Camus, 21 de Mayo 1940, tel. 55/813102; Flota Barrios, 21 de Mayo 1720, tel. 55/811861; Tur-Bus, 21 de Mayo 1495, tel. 55/811581; and Pullman Bus, 21 de Mayo 1377, tel. 55/815340.

From the corner of 21 de Mayo and Manuel Rodríguez, *taxi colectivos* connect Tocopilla with Chuquicamata and Calama at 3 and 9 P.M. (US$6, 2.5 hours). Camus also goes to Calama, Monday to Saturday at 7:20 A.M. and 4:50 P.M. with an additional Sunday departure at 7:50 P.M.

Sample destinations and fares include Antofagasta (US$4, 2.5 hours), Calama (US$4, 3.5 hours), Iquique (US$9, 4.5 hours), Chañaral (US$12, 7.5 hours), Copiapó (US$16, 11 hours), La Serena (US$22, 15 hours), and Santiago (US$28, 21 hours).

NORTE GRANDE

Cobija

It's only a set of crumbling adobe ruins today, but in the early 19th century the port of Cobija was the *salida al mar* (outlet to the sea), for which Bolivian governments have clamored ever since losing their maritime frontage to Chile in the War of the Pacific.

About 130 km north of Antofagasta, between Punta Guasilla in the south and Gatico on the north, the shoreline around Cobija constitutes a *zona típica* national monument for its plaza, church, graveyard, and some otherwise mostly unidentifiable structures. Though its population reached 1,500 in the mid-19th century, despite perpetual water shortages, a massive earthquake in 1868 and a tsunami in 1877 delivered the town its death blows. A handful of fishing families subsist here today; the more modern ruins at Gatico, to the north, were once a guesthouse for a nearby mine.

CALAMA

Billing itself as the "land of sun and copper," fast-growing Calama is mainly a crossroads and service center for the mining industry, the foundation of the local economy. One reason it's growing is the closure of nearby Chuquicamata, the world's largest open pit mine, as a residential community—thanks to Codelco's Plan Calama, by 2003 all the miners and their families will have moved from there to here and will commute to Chuqui for work.

Codelco will execute Plan Calama, which anticipates construction of 2,500 houses, on its own land, thereby undercutting property development speculators who bought land on the city's outskirts. This may involve some in-fill, but nothing on the edges of the city.

Many travelers pass through town en route to the famous desert village of San Pedro de Atacama, the main staging post for visits to the altiplano, but Calama does boast nearby sights such as Chuquicamata, the colonial hamlet of Chiu Chiu, and the pre-Columbian Pukará de Lasana, an impressive fortress ruin. It also offers alternatives routes to some destinations more commonly visited from San Pedro, and it is the

starting point for passenger rail service to Oruro, Bolivia.

While tourism takes a back seat to mining, Calama has several good new hotels and some good restaurants, though there's little to see in the city proper—though founded in the 1850s when the area was Bolivian territory, it's really a 20th-century town. Visitors may find it hard to believe, but parts of Calama were under water during the floods of early 2001.

Orientation

Calama is 213 km northeast of Antofagasta via the Panamericana and paved Ruta 25. On the banks of the Río Loa, 2,250 meters above sea level, it has a compact core with a slightly irregular street plan. Calle Ramírez, leading east off the plaza, is a *peatonal* that's a popular meeting place.

Sights

Calama's literal and symbolic center is **Plaza 23 de Marzo,** commemorating the date of its oc-

Plaza 23 de Marzo, Calama

© WAYNE BERNHARDSON

cupation by Chilean troops in the War of the Pacific. It has undergone a complete remodel: the mature pepper trees still extend their shade, but there are also patches of neatly mown grass, newly tiled walkways, new and numerous benches, and tidy trash receptacles. Its bandshell has a copper roof, its church a copper steeple, and a copper plaque memorializes the 34 Calameños executed and disappeared during the infamous Caravan of Death:

Life is not a game and should be taken seriously, so seriously that, even backed against a wall with your hands tied, dying for your ideals so that others may live, you die knowing that nothing is more beautiful, nothing is truer than life itself.

Homage of the Loa community to those who gave their lives for their ideals.

Parque El Loa

On the southern outskirts of town, irrigated by its namesake river, Parque El Loa is a favorite afternoon and weekend retreat for Calameños, with shady picnic grounds, sports fields, and a pair of museums.

The more established museum is the **Museo Arqueológico y Etnológico** (Museum of Archaeology and Ethnology), tel. 55/340112, strong on materials but weak on explanations of the Atacameño peoples and their environment. It's open 10 A.M.–1 P.M. and 3–7:30 P.M. daily except Monday and holidays, when it's closed. The admission charge is minimal.

At the new **Museo de Historia Natural y Cultural del Desierto** (Museum of Natural and Cultural History of the Desert), tel. 55/312311, across the river footbridge from the Museo Arqueológico, there are exhibits on mineralogy, paleontology (especially notable), Andean ecology and environment, Atacameño culture (outstanding), regional history (including one of the better accounts of the War of the Pacific), and mining culture. Comparative clippings from the newspaper *Oasis* report visits by Presidents Salvador Allende (1971) and General Pinochet (de facto, 1975). Hours are daily except Monday,

10 A.M.–1 P.M. and 3:30–7 P.M.; admission costs US$.75.

Accommodations

Calama's accommodations offer some good values in all categories, but selectivity is the rule—there is considerable variation even within individual hotels.

US$10–25: For US$6/10 with shared bath, US$12/17 with private bath, **Residencial Splendid,** Ramírez 1960, tel. 55/341841, is among the best of the cheapest. For only US$7 pp, friendly **Residencial Gran Chile,** Latorre 1474, tel./fax 55/317455, is one of the region's best bargains—all rooms are spotless and spacious, with private bath and cable TV. Its only drawback is the utterly barren exterior, which needs landscaping.

For US$9 pp, **Residencial Cavour,** Sotomayor 1841, tel. 55/317392, is by no means bad, but the stark gray exterior of its corridor of rooms with external bars suggests an unfortunate comparison with a prison cell. For the same price or a little more, depending on the room, friendly **Hostal Camino del Inca,** Bañados Espinoza 1889, tel. 55/349552, offers no frills in its simple but well-maintained quarters.

Another fine budget choice is **Hotel El Loa,** Abaroa 1617, tel. 55/341963, for US$10/17 with shared bath and breakfast.

US$25–50: Past its prime but passable, **Hotel Atenas,** on the *peatonal* at Ramírez 1961, tel. 55/342666, fax 55/315399, has good beds and large baths. Rates are US$12/22 s/d with shared bath, US$20/28 s/d with private bath.

Friendly and newish but not quite immaculate, **Hotel Universo,** Sotomayor 1822, tel. 55/361640, charges US$31/38 s/d including breakfast, private bath, and cable TV. Definitely new and equally friendly, with darkish but comfortable rooms, the **Oasis Hotel,** Vargas 1942, tel. 55/319075, fax 55/316151, charges US$33/41 s/d.

Modernized, with an appalling pistachio color scheme, longtime favorite **Hotel John Kenny,** Avenida Ecuador 1991, tel. 55/341430, costs US$10 pp with shared bath, US$23/41 with private bath.

US$50–100: Easily Calama's most stylish accommodations, in a flawlessly restored building just half a block off the plaza, **Hotel El Mirador,** Sotomayor 2064, tel./fax 55/340329 or 55/310294, charges US$50/60 s/d. The starkly modern **Hotel Olimpo,** Santa María 1673, tel. 55/342367, fax 55/312125, needs greenery; relatively small, utilitarian rooms cost US$51/60 s/d, but IVA discounts are available.

Directly on Plaza 23 de Marzo, **Hotel Quitor,** Ramírez 2116, tel./fax 55/314159 or 55/341716, has been undergoing a major remodel that might eventually justify rates of US$39/63 with breakfast; again, IVA discounts are possible.

Hotel Punakora, Santa María 1640, tel. 55/345539, fax 55/315840, is a modern, spacious, comfortable, and attractive establishment that, astonishingly, can't be bothered to give IVA discounts to foreign visitors. Rates are US$54/61 s/d with breakfast, cable TV, and telephone.

Friendly but a little disorganized as yet, the new **Hotel Paradise in Desert,** Ramírez 1867, tel. 55/341618, fax 55/315479, paradiseindesert@yahoo.com, offers large but kitschy rooms with private bath, Jacuzzi, and other amenities. Rates are US$59/65 s/d.

Modern **Hotel Alfa,** Sotomayor 2016, tel. 55/342496, fax 55/351565, charges US$63/74 s/d, including a buffet breakfast and cable TV, for rooms that differ substantially—if the first room shown seems too small, ask for a larger one.

Hostería Calama, Latorre 1521, tel. 55/310306, has long been a prime top-end choice and is often full despite its size; rates are US$59/76 s/d. At the airport itself, the luxury **Park Hotel Calama**, Camino Aeropuerto 1392, tel. 55/319900, parkcalama@parkplaza.cl, charges US$88/96.

Food

The various *comedores* in the **Mercado Central,** on Latorre between Vargas and Ramírez, are Calama's most economical eateries. **La Paila II,** Vargas 1905, is a popular but inexpensive restaurant that doubles as a pub.

Di Giorgio Ramírez 2099, tel. 55/312353, has massive sandwiches, draft beer, and coffee (including espresso), along with Calama's best ice cream. It's also a good breakfast spot, as is **Bavaria,** Sotomayor 2093, tel. 55/341496, the

Chilean counterpart to Denny's. The **Club Croata,** alternatively known as the **Hrvatski Dom,** Abaroa 1869, tel. 55/342126, serves moderately priced lunches but more expensive dinners.

In new, spacious quarters, traditional favorite **D'Angelo Pizza,** Ramírez 1812, tel. 55/312867, serves a wide variety of excellent pizzas, as well as sandwiches and fresh fruit juices, but the kitchen can be slow at times. **Pizzería D'Alfredo,** Abaroa 1835, tel. 55/319440, is part of a chain whose quality can't quite match that of D'Angelo.

Los Dos Países, an Italo-Chilean restaurant at Santa María 1620, tel. 55/349401, serves pastas including gnocchi, fettuccine, and the like for around US$7, plus an additional US$2 for sauces; since everything else, including appetizers and salads, is à la carte, it can get pricey, but the quality is good.

Highly recommended, with exemplary service, **Las Brasas de Juan Luis,** Balmaceda 1972, tel. 55/344366, is an upscale *parrilla* specializing in beef but also offering fish and shellfish. Entrées are in the US$5–10 range, with appetizers and other items all à la carte.

Calama has several cheapish *chifas,* including **Chi-Kang,** Vivar 2037, tel. 55/341121; the new and promising **Grande Chong Hua,** Latorre 1415; and **Nueva Chong Hua,** Abaroa 2008, tel. 55/313387.

Entertainment and Events: The **Cine Teatro Municipal,** Ramírez 2080, tel. 55/342864, shows recent films, offers live theater and concerts, and hosts art exhibits. Some larger concerts take place at the **Estadio Techado,** one block west.

Cobreloa, Calama's first-division soccer team, plays at the Estadio Municipal, on Avenida Matta east of the train station. Its offices are at Abaroa 1757, tel. 55/341775.

Every March 23, Calama celebrates the city's occupation by Chilean troops during the War of the Pacific.

Services

Money: Banco de Crédito, Sotomayor 2002, has an ATM. There are two exchange houses: Marbumor Money Exchange, Sotomayor 1837, and Moon Valley Money Exchange, on Ramírez between Abaroa and Latorre.

Postal: Correos de Chile is at Vicuña Mackenna 2167.

Telephone and Internet: Calama has several convenient long-distance offices: Chilesat, Abaroa 1928; Entel, Sotomayor 2027; and Telefónica CTC, Abaroa 1756. Calama's area code is 55.

Calama has two Internet outlets only a few doors apart: the Café Ciber at Vargas 2014 and Cybernet at Vargas 2054; the latter is faster, stays open later, and also has long-distance telephone service.

Laundry Lavexpress, Sotomayor 1887, tel. 55/315361, has efficient laundry service.

Medical Hospital Carlos Cisterna is on Avenida Granaderos between Félix Hoyos and Cisterna, tel. 55/342347.

Information

Tourist Office: Calama's municipal Corporación Cultural y Turismo is at Latorre 1689, tel. 55/3-64176, fax 55/345345, calamainfotour@entelchile.net; it's open 9 A.M.–1 P.M. and 3–7 P.M. weekdays, 9 A.M.–1 P.M. only Saturday, closed Sunday and holidays. In addition to providing information, it also conducts walking tours of the city for US$4 pp for a minimum of 10 people (for other tours, see the Vicinity of Calama entry, below).

Consulate: Bolivia has a consulate at Vicuña Mackenna 1984, 2nd floor, tel. 55/341976. It's open 9 A.M.–3 P.M. weekdays only.

Motorists: The Automóvil Club de Chile (Acchi), Avenida Ecuador 1901, tel. 55/342770, is also a good source of information.

Transportation

Air: Aeropuerto El Loa, tel. 55/342348, is on the southern outskirts of town.

LanChile and LanExpress share offices at Latorre 1726, tel. 55/313927; LanExpress flies an average of four times daily to Antofagasta and Santiago; one flight every weekday also stops in Copiapó.

Bus: Calama lacks a central bus terminal, but many of the companies are clustered near the railroad station at the east end of town, and northwest of Plaza 23 de Marzo. There are both regional and long-distance services, and international connections to Bolivia and Argentina.

Buses Frontera, Antofagasta 2041, tel. 55/3-18543, goes nine times daily to San Pedro (US$2.50) and twice to Toconao (US$4). Buses Atacama, Abaroa 2102, tel. 55/314757, goes twice or three times daily to San Pedro.

Several companies cover north- and southbound destinations on the Panamericana, among them Tur-Bus, Ramírez 1802, tel. 55/316699, which also goes to San Pedro de Atacama; Flota Barrios, Ramírez 2298, with an additional ticket office at Sotomayor 1812-A, tel. 55/341497; Pullman Bus, Sotomayor 1802, tel. 55/319665; Géminis, Antofagasta 2239, with a separate ticket office on Sotomayor near Avenida Balmaceda, tel. 55/341993.

Kenny Bus, Vivar 1954, tel. 55/342514, serves Iquique via María Elena and Pozo Almonte, while Buses Camus, Avenida Balmaceda 1802, tel. 55/342800, goes to Tocopilla at 8 A.M. and 4:30 P.M. Monday to Saturday, with an additional 9:30 P.M. departure Sunday.

Sample domestic destinations, times, and fares include Arica (US$13, eight hours), Iquique (US$11, 5.5 hours), Antofagasta (US$4, three hours), Tocopilla (US$4, 3.5 hours), Chañaral (US$18, nine hours), Copiapó (US$17–22, 11 hours), Vallenar (US$20–23, 13 hours), La Serena (US$22–28, 14 hours), and Santiago (US$41, 22 hours).

Since international buses fill up fast, reservations are advisable. Buses Manchego, Alonso de Ercilla 2142, tel. 55/318466, goes to Ollagüe, on the Bolivian border, Wednesday and Sunday at midnight (US$6); a connecting Bolivian bus continues to Uyuni (US$12).

Two companies cross the Andes to Jujuy and Salta, Argentina (US$40 to either city, 12–13 hours), without the necessity of changing buses. Tur-Bus goes Wednesday and Saturday at 9:15 A.M., while Géminis departs Wednesday at 9 A.M., and Thursday and Sunday at 10 A.M.

Taxi Colectivo: Taxi a Tocopilla L. M., Balmaceda 1974, tel. 55/346069, has departures for the coastal city of Tocopilla (US$5) at noon and 6 P.M. daily, passing through the nitrate town of María Elena.

Train: Every Wednesday at 11 P.M., an unheated and uncomfortable train leaves Calama for

Ollagüe, on the Bolivian border (US$12), connecting with Bolivian service to Uyuni and Oruro. For tickets, go to Calama's Estación de Ferrocarril, Avenida Balmaceda 1777, tel. 55/348900; it's open Monday and Tuesday 3–6:30 P.M., Wednesday 8:30 A.M.–1 P.M., 3–6:30 P.M. and 9–11 P.M. Verify whether or not you need a visa at Calama's Bolivian consulate, and take warm clothing—not only is the train unheated, but while changing trains you may have to wait outdoors for Bolivian immigration to open.

Getting Around

Yellow *taxi colectivos* to Chuquicamata leave from a spot on Abaroa just north of Ramírez.

Car Rental: Calama's several car rental agencies include Hertz, Latorre 1510, tel. 55/340018; Avis, Latorre 1498, tel. 55/319797; Comercial Atacama, Abaroa 2201, tel. 55/362447; First Rent A Car, Félix Hoyos 2146, tel. 55/315453; and Alamo, Félix Hoyos 2177, tel. 55/364545.

VICINITY OF CALAMA

Most visitors to the area start their excursions from San Pedro de Atacama, but several Calama agencies also offer their services, including **Turismo Buenaventura,** Sotomayor 1959, 2nd floor, tel. 55/341882; **Tungra Expediciones,** Turi 2089, tel. 55/313081; and **Tour Aventura Valle de la Luna,** Abaroa 1620, tel./fax 55/310720, colle-in@ctc-mundo.net. According to local sources, the latter has been the subject of some complaints.

Besides providing information, Calama's municipal **Corporación Cultural y Turismo** (see above) offers a variety of backcountry tours, though most people usually contract for destinations such as El Tatio (US$9 pp, leaving Calama at 4 A.M.) in San Pedro de Atacama. There's also a half-day circuit to Lasana, Laguna Inca Coya, Chiu Chiu for US$20; a full-day tour to Tatio, Caspana, Laguna Inca Coya, and Chiu Chiu for US$70 with breakfast and lunch; and for the same price, a full-day tour to San Pedro de Atacama, Toconao, the Salar de Atacama, and the Valle de la Luna, including breakfast and a

box lunch. The latter does not include the admission fees to Laguna Chaxa or the museum at San Pedro, and all trips require a minimum of four people.

Chuquicamata

The gaping open pit at Chuquicamata, 16 km north of Calama, is the Grand Canyon of the global copper industry. Managed by Codelco, the state copper company, everything at Chuqui exists on such a massive scale—its towering power shovels, fleet of mammoth diesel trucks, and the virtual mountains of *tortas* (tailings) accumulated over nearly a century of operations—that it could easily be a metaphor for the role of mining in the Chilean economy ever since independence, and for copper through the entire 20th century.

In 1999, the last year for which complete statistics are available, Chuqui's 630,000 tons constituted 47 percent of the country's entire copper production. Copper remains Chile's single largest export and is likely to do so for the foreseeable future, despite diversification efforts.

Chuquicamata itself is a tidy, orderly company town that, for all its controversial role in Chilean history, was also a community with a distinctive working-class culture. All this will end soon, though—the accumulated toxic pollution of more than eight decades of copper extraction and processing has finally forced Codelco to relocate its employees and their families to nearby Calama. By 2003, when the move is completed, "Chuqui" will be merely a work site.

History: While pre-Hispanic peoples worked Chuquicamata's copper deposits for weapons, tools, and other artifacts, it was not until around 1910 that the Guggenheim Brothers first worked the deposit through their Chile Exploration Company. In 1923, the Guggenheims sold their rights to the Anaconda Copper Company of Butte, Montana.

Anaconda controlled Chuqui for nearly half a century, building a city with housing, schools, shopping, medical services, and even entertainment—including a cinema and a full-sized soccer stadium—from scratch. At the same time, the wealthy foreign mining enclave engendered suspicion and resentment among certain sectors of

Chilean society, especially as political radicalism grew in the 1960s. Reformists such as President Eduardo Frei Montalva (1964–70) promoted greater Chilean participation in the industry, but the Socialist government of Salvador Allende (1970–73) successfully nationalized it, with congressional approval.

Even after the Pinochet coup of 1973, the Corporación del Cobre de Chile (Codelco) has kept Chuqui, along with other large copper mines such as El Salvador (Region III, Atacama) and El Teniente (Region VI, O'Higgins) under state control, despite occasional rumors of privatization. Codelco remains the single most important economic player in the entire country.

Sights: In the town proper, the main structures date from Anaconda days, such as the **Estadio Anaconda,** where the Cobreloa soccer team played before moving to Calama; the **Auditorio Sindical,** an immense theater dedicated for labor use and embellished with a mural that recalls the death of several workers during a 1960s strike; and the freestanding **Pala Electromecánica Mundial,** the 26.5-meter, 450-ton power shovel that was the world's largest from its inception in 1949 to its retirement in 1971. Near the offices of Relaciones Públicas (Public Relations), where guided tours of Chuqui begin, a striking statue dignifies the laborers who still risk their lives in the day-to-day operations of the company.

The single most impressive physical feature at Chuquicamata, though, is the enormous **Yacimiento Chuqui,** the terraced oval cavity that measures 4.3 km in length, three km in width, and 750 meters in depth. A railroad once hauled copper ore from its depths, but today massive diesels, riding on tires more than three meters high, carry Chile's most important single commodity to the smelter, which is no longer open to the public.

Tours: Starting at the corner of Avenida J. M. Carrera and Avenida Tocopilla, Relaciones Públicas, tel. 55/328861, conducts free daily tours at 10 A.M. (do not pay Calama travel agencies for spots on the tour); arrive at least an hour early to be certain of a spot—perhaps even earlier during the summer peak.

Visitors must present identification (national ID card or passport); while long trousers and sleeves are no longer obligatory, sensible shoes are—no sandals, in particular. Tours start with a 10-minute Spanish-language video, followed by an English-language version; visitors then board buses for the 1.5-hour excursion. The size of the excavation itself is so great as to be intimidating, though the dust from the trucks often obscures the view.

Transportation: From a stop on Abaroa just north of Ramírez in Calama, yellow *taxi colectivos* leave frequently for Chuquicamata.

Chug Chug

Between Chuquicamata and the Panamericana, the geoglyphs of Chug Chug testify to the antiquity of a caravan route that once linked Chiu Chiu and Calama with Quillagua and the coast—note the human figures, on reed rafts, harpooning fish or sea lions. There are additional human and animal figures, but also abstract designs such as the *rombos escalerados,* rhomboid shapes.

Administered by the *comuna* of María Elena, the geoglyphs of Chug Chug are on the eastern edge of the pampa, 1,200 meters above sea level, about 36 km east of Chuquicamata and 30 km west of the junction with the Panamericana, on the road to Tocopilla.

Alto Loa

North and east of Calama, the rarely visited upper drainage of the Río Loa is home to a scattering of colonial Atacameño villages—though many of their residents reject that broad identity in favor of a more localized one—and a possible future national park, the Reserva Nacional Alto Loa. Unfortunately, except along Ruta 21, which reaches the Bolivian border at Ollagüe, there is no regular public transportation.

Chiu Chiu: At the confluence with the Río Salado, a tributary of the Loa, 33 km east of Calama via paved Ruta 21, the village of Chiu Chiu is famous for its 17th-century **Iglesia de San Francisco;** until the early 20th century, when Calama built its cathedral, Chiu Chiu was the center of ecclesiastical authority in the region.

Chiu Chiu's church is a national monument with buttressed walls, twin bell towers, and a ceiling built of various desert woods held together with leather ties and covered with mud thatch. More than a meter thick, its sturdy adobe walls are originals, but the bell towers are reconstructions of earlier counterparts that collapsed.

Chiu Chiu has accommodations for US$14 pp with private bath and breakfast at **Hotel Tujina,** Esmeralda s/n, tel. 55/342201, which also serves other meals. Try also **Restaurant Muley.**

Pukará de Lasana: North of Chiu Chiu, the pavement ends on Ruta 21, which continues toward Ollagüe, though the parallel route to the El Abra copper mine, which diverges about two km south of Chiu Chiu, is paved for some distance. Either route leads up the Loa valley to the Pukará de Lasana, a well-restored 12th-century defensive fortification that's a national monument.

Ayquina: Nestled in the valley of its namesake river, a tributary of the Loa about 35 km east of Lasana, the village of Ayquina and its surrounding agricultural terraces constitute a *zona típica* national monument. Its colonial **Iglesia de la Virgen de Guadalupe,** dependent on Chiu Chiu, constituted one of the earliest efforts at Catholic evangelization in the region.

Ayquina's **Museo Votivo** is an ethnographic museum that displays ex-voto offerings to its patron saint and displays elaborate and colorful costumes from its 29 folkloric dance groups (the village's September 7–8 festival is the best time to see them in action). The museum is open 10 A.M.–1 P.M. and 3–7:30 P.M. daily except Sunday and holidays.

Vegas de Turi: Directly east of Lasana via a reasonably good gravel road, the Vegas de Turi is a gradually desiccating marshland because of water demands from Calama and the mining industry. It is also, however, the site of the hilltop **Pukará de Turi,** a four-hectare site that was the largest architectural complex ever built during Atacameño times. Dating from about A.D. 900, influenced by immigrants from the Bolivian altiplano, northwestern Argentina and, in its latest stages, Inka Peru, it is also a national monument.

Toconce: At Toconce, a village with only about 50 permanent residents, pre-Columbian terraces climb the slopes to a hilltop site where the colonial **Iglesia San Santiago** overlooks the valley of the Río Toconce, a tributary of the Salado and the Loa. Initially part of the community of Ayquina, Toconce gradually established its own identity though it maintains strong kinship links with the other community.

In the recent past, Toconce had no services whatever, but three young locals have formed Puri Linzor, a travel agency that has built the 10-bed **Albergue Toconce** with hot showers, TV, and kitchen; rates of US$7 pp with breakfast include a tour around the village. Additional meals are also available.

They also rent mountain bikes and conduct tours to more distant destinations such as the archaeological site of Likán and 5,946-meter Volcán Paniri, an Inka religious sanctuary; for more details, contact the Calama tourist office.

Caspana: About midway between Ayquina and Toconce, a winding road drops into the valley of the Río Caspana, whose picturesque namesake village nestles cosily between terraced hillsides; on a promontory above the village stands the colonial **Iglesia de San Lucas,** a national historical monument.

Organized by Maltese anthropologist George Serracino, the **Museo Etnográfico de Caspana** is an exceptional collection for a community of this size; it also sells a selection of locally produced crafts. Open 10 A.M.–1 P.M. and 3–7:30 P.M. daily except Monday and holidays, it charges US$.70 admission.

From Caspana, a southbound road climbs out of the valley and then intersects a zigzag eastbound road over the Cuesta de Chita toward the El Tatio geysers and San Pedro de Atacama. High clearance vehicles only are advisable on this route.

SAN PEDRO DE ATACAMA

On the surface, San Pedro de Atacama is still a serene colonial village where the aboriginal Kunza or Atacameño peoples go about the daily business of farming their fields and tending their flocks, while captivated tourists stroll the adobe-lined streets where conquistador Pedro de Valdivia and his retinue paused on their way south to Santiago.

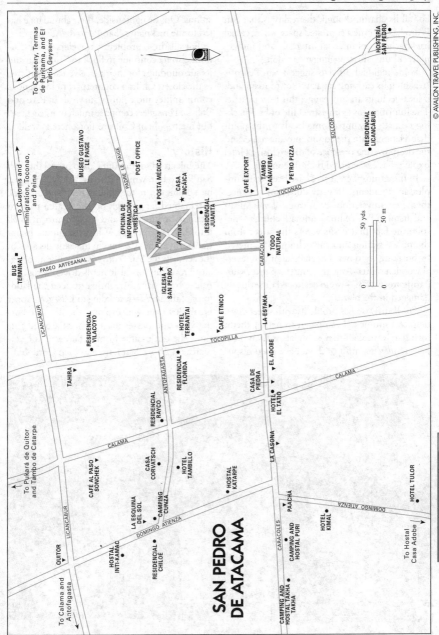

SAN PEDRO
DE ATACAMA

NORTE GRANDE

For all its charm, though, the reality is that San Pedro has become a contested space where casual backpackers, commercial interests, and indigenous cultures are struggling to get along.

Some regional officials suggest San Pedro is "reaching its carrying capacity" for tourism and, if local feelings are any gauge, this may be true. The informal, easygoing street life of backpacking nomads has upset some locals to the point that relations with the community are tense, and the overpowering presence of the exclusive Hotel Explora has exacerbated their discontent.

In this atmosphere, there have been some unpleasant incidents. In early 2001, for instance, there were mysterious twin cases of vandalism and arson in San Pedro's landmark church—despite the fact that it sits across the street from the police station and the delinquents entered by breaking windows. The main altar and several wooden saints—one the church's patron saint dating from 1737—were destroyed or seriously damaged in the blaze.

San Pedro also has problems with street dogs, despite a municipal campaign to neuter them; fortunately, though they seem larger than most *perros callejeros,* most of them have good dispositions. On the lighter side, their abundance has led to the nickname "San Perro de Atacama."

For all these problems, travelers in all economic strata continue to flock to San Pedro and its surroundings for their perceived authenticity, as the closest Chilean counterpart to indigenous communities and colonial survivals in Peru and Bolivia. Foreigners comprise much of its clientele, but metropolitan Chileans flock here as well.

History

The Inka road south from Cuzco passed through San Pedro but, while Pedro de Valdivia stopped here on his way to the Chilean heartland in 1540, it remained far enough off the beaten path to retain its architectural and cultural integrity well into the 20th century. When the nitrate boom transformed the Atacama in the early decades of the century, the San Pedro oasis became an obligatory rest stop for cattle herds driven across the Andes from Salta, Argentina, to feed the labor force of the *oficinas* (according to U.S. geographer Isaiah Bowman, who explored the altiplano borderlands and passes on muleback around this time, the cattle came from as far away as Catamarca, La Rioja, San Luis, and even Córdoba).

Iglesia San Pedro de Atacama

By the 1920s, though, the proliferation of rail transport throughout the Norte Grande, and from Antofagasta across the Andes to Bolivia, had reduced the need for cattle drives that, crossing arid, frigid passes well above 4,000 meters, were even more arduous than those of the legendary Texas cowboys. According to Bowman, "In place of mule transport there is now railroad transport."

Motor roads were an even later development, but mining exploration and tourist imperatives have resulted in improved access not just to San Pedro itself, but also to the polychrome Valle de la Luna (Valley of the Moon), the geysers at El Tatio, the immense salt lakes of the Salar de Atacama and the altiplano, and trans-Andean routes to Argentina and Bolivia.

Orientation

At the north end of the Salar de Atacama, an immense sprawling salt lake that has nearly evaporated, San Pedro de Atacama is 120 km southeast of Calama via paved Ruta 23, which parallels the eastern border of the Salar as it continues south before turning west toward the Argentine border at Paso Sico. An alternative route to Argentina, paved Ruta 23 to Paso Jama and Jujuy, climbs directly east from San Pedro; at about the 45 km point, a short northeastern lateral reaches the new Bolivian border post at Portezuelo del Cajón.

It's not hard to find your way around San Pedro's compact but slightly irregular grid, but street names are only formalities and house numbers are almost nonexistent—the accompanying map is the best means for an initial orientation. Most services are on or around east-west Caracoles, half a block south of the Plaza de Armas.

Sights

All of San Pedro is a *zona típica* national monument, but several landmarks stand out in and around the pepper-shaded Plaza de Armas.

On the east side of the Plaza de Armas, generally acknowledged to be San Pedro's oldest construction, the aged adobe **Casa Incaica** is often, and probably erroneously, claimed to have be-

longed to Pedro de Valdivia. Its interior is not open to the public.

Despite the recent deplorable incidents of vandalism, this 17th-century **Iglesia San Pedro** remains the town's most notable architectural landmark. Constructed with a rectangular floor plan, its thatched roof supported by *algarrobo* beams tied with leather straps, it underwent a major remodel in the mid-18th century. The attached bell tower is an even later addition, from 1890. Breached only by an arched portal, the adobe walls that surround the compound are a reconstruction.

In 1955, long before San Pedro became the tourist magnet it is today, Belgian priest and archaeologist Gustavo Le Paige began to acquire and organize artifacts from the surrounding desert into what has become Chile's foremost archaeological museum, the **Museo Arqueológico Padre Gustavo Le Paige.** By the time of his death in 1980, he had accumulated nearly 400,000 separate pieces, with the help of local villagers and Antofagasta's Universidad Católica del Norte, to help detail the region's cultural evolution and history from the earliest Paleo-Indians, about 11,000 years ago, to the arrival of the Spaniards in the 16th century.

Housed in modern facilities with well-organized display cases in three octagonal pavilions, the museum displays an impressive assortment of stone tools, ceramics, and textiles, details the region's surprisingly diverse natural environments, and replicates pre-Hispanic burial customs; the grounds feature a modest botanical garden. It continues to have one glaring shortcoming—there is nothing on post-conquest Kunza culture, whose once thriving language has become extinct—and despite recent events there is nothing whatsoever on the impact of travel and tourism on San Pedro. While its primary mission may be archaeological, it owes something more to the community that helped build it.

Half a block east on the Plaza de Armas, across from the post office, the Museo Arqueológico, tel. 55/851002, is open 9 A.M.–noon and 2–6 P.M. weekdays, 10 A.M.–noon and 2–6 P.M. weekends and holidays. Admission costs US$1.50 for adults, half that for children.

Accommodations

San Pedro has abundant budget accommodations at reasonable prices, some excellent values in midrange choices, and some real high-enders. During Chilean summer and winter holidays, it can get crowded, with reservations advisable even at budget lodgings.

Up to US$10: The cheapest option is camping. **Camping Cunza,** Antofagasta s/n, tel. 55/8-51183, costs just US$4 pp, but its location alongside a noisy nightspot is a drawback. For about the same price, at the former Pozo 3 site beyond the customs and immigration post three km east of San Pedro, **Camping Alberto Terrazas,** tel. 55/851042, features a swimming pool open to campers and noncampers (though the latter pay US$2 admission.

Back in town, adjacent to each other on Caracoles west of Domingo Atienza, **Camping Puri,** tel. 55/851049, and **Camping Takha Takha,** tel. 55/851038, both cost about US$5 pp for good sites with shade. Both also have hotel-style accommodations (see below), so campers can use the hot showers in the shared baths.

For US$10 per site, the very quiet **Camping Conaf,** at Solcor just beyond the customs post, has shade, clean toilets, and cold showers.

US$10–25: Central enough to be easy walking distance, but distant enough to be quiet, **Hostal Casa Adobe,** Domingo Atienza 582, tel. 55/8-51249, is a new and tidy spot with small and simple but very decent rooms, with firm beds, for US$6 pp.

Several roughly comparable places offer adequate lodging in the US$5–7 pp range: **Residencial Chiloé,** Domingo Atienza s/n; **Residencial Juanita,** Plaza de Armas s/n, tel. 55/851039; and the clapboard **Residencial Vilacoyo,** Tocopilla s/n, tel. 55/851182.

Twenty years ago, **Residencial La Florida,** Tocopilla s/n, tel. 55/851021, was one of a handful of places to stay in the entire town; still living in the past, for US$8 pp, it's suitable if other places are full. Besides offering camping, **Hostal Puri** Caracoles s/n, tel. 55/851049, has rooms with shared bath for about the same price. At adjacent **Hostal Takha Takha,** Caracoles s/n, tel. 55/851038, utilitarian garden rooms with shared bath cost US$9 pp, while more elaborate quarters with private bath cost US$27/34 s/d.

At **Residencial Casa Corvatsch,** Antofagasta s/n, tel. 55/851101, ccorvatsch@entelchile.net, good rooms with shared bath (and closely monitored showers) cost US$8.50 pp; like Camping Cunza, though, it's near that noisy nightspot. Parking is available.

Ordinary but passable **Residencial Don Raúl,** Caracoles s/n, tel. 55/851138, offers simple rooms with shared bath and hot showers for US$9 pp; those with private bath cost US$35 d. Rates at **Residencial Licancábur,** Toconao s/n, tel. 55/851007, are US$9 pp with shared bath, US$42 d with private bath. Once one of San Pedro's better choices, the dorm-style **Residencial Rayco,** Antofagasta s/n, tel. 55/851008, hasn't kept pace with improvements elsewhere, but it's still reasonable for US$10/17 s/d; better rooms with private bath cost US$33 d.

US$25–50: Shady and so small—only four rooms—that it's usually full, **Hostal Inti-Kamac,** Domingo Atienza s/n, tel. 55/851200, is a modest place charging US$26 d with private bath. One of the best values in its range, **Hostal Katarpe,** Domingo Atienza s/n, tel. 55/851033, charges US$30 d. Another good, but rather more expensive option, is **Hotel Tambillo,** Antofagasta 159, tel. 55/851078, for US$39/50.

Several possibilities in this range—**Hostal Takha Takha, Residencial Rayco,** and **Residencial Licancábur**—have cheaper budget rooms and appear under the US$10–25 category.

US$50–100: Some of San Pedro's best values are in this category, such as **Hotel El Tatio,** Caracoles 219, tel./fax 55/851092, hoteleltatio@ usa.net; for US$49/59, it offers satellite TV, phone, pool, laundry, room service, and an independent power supply. With similar services, for US$56/76 s/d, **Hotel Kimal,** Domingo Atienza s/n, tel. 55/851030, also boasts the best restaurant in town.

La Casa de Don Tomás, Tocopilla s/n, tel. 55/851055, fax 55/851175, has comfortable rooms and attractive common areas, with rustically stylish furniture, a pool, and patio, but the exterior is barren and the gardens sparse. Rates are US$56/75 s/d. **Hotel Tulor,** Domingo Atienza

523, tel. 55/851027 or 55/851063, tulor@chile-sat.net, has spacious, comfortable, but not quite deluxe rooms for US$72/86 s/d. It also has a restaurant and a small pool.

US$100–150: San Pedro's traditional top lodgings, **Hostería San Pedro,** Solcor 370, tel. 55/851011, fax 55/851048, hspedro@chile-sat.net, charges US$100/110 s/d with breakfast. In recent years, though, it's faced rugged competition from some less expensive choices and two all-inclusive resort-style options, the Terrantai Lodge and Hotel Explora.

Open primarily for package holidays, the stylish **Terrantai Lodge,** Tocopilla 411, tel. 55/851140, fax 55/851037, atacamadesert@adex.cl, is a compact luxury resort that's done a remarkable job of integrating itself into its village surroundings. All packages include full board, transfers from Calama airport, and specialized tour guides. With tours in English, it is slightly more expensive (for more information and rates, see the Organized Tours entry in the On the Road chapter).

Economically out of sight for most visitors, but a visual sore thumb at the south end of town, Explora's ostentatious **Hotel de Larache** is a water-guzzling extravagance (four swimming pools, dying transplants of *algarrobo* and pepper trees, and other unsuitable landscaping); its impact on San Pedro's culture and environment contrasts dramatically with the company's relatively inconspicuous and award-winning Hotel Salto Chico, in Patagonia's Parque Nacional Torres del Paine. It's only fair to say, though, that visitors have praised the all-inclusive accommodations and especially the excursions. Rates start at US$1,858/2,592 s/d for three days and rise to US$3,534/4,882 s/d for a week's stay. It's open for packages only (for contact details, see the Organized Tours entry in the On the Road chapter).

Food and Entertainment

Several of San Pedro's restaurants double as live music venues at night, and consequently appear here rather than under a separate heading. Note that, because of the local *ley seca* or alcohol control law, restaurants stop serving drinks no later than midnight weekdays and 1 A.M. on week-

ends; depending on recent problems, last call may be even earlier.

Tahira, Tocopilla s/n, tel. 55/851296, serves cheap (US$2 range) but exceptionally well-prepared Chilean meals such as turkey and rice in the US$2 range. More expensive but also worthwhile choices include **Quitor,** Licancábur s/n, tel. 55/851190; **Café al Paso Sonchek,** Calama s/n, a popular breakfast and burger choice; the unexceptional **La Casona,** Caracoles s/n, tel. 55/851004; and **La Esquina del Sol,** Antofagasta s/n, tel. 55/851183, which doubles as a pub at night.

Casa de Piedra, Caracoles s/n, tel. 55/851271, makes fine breakfasts and lunches, such as *pastel de papas,* in the US$3 range and à la carte dishes for US$5–10; service is a little distracted, though. For fresh juices and ice cream, there's no better choice than **Todo Natural,** Caracoles s/n. For sandwiches and espresso, try **Café Export,** Toconao s/n.

Argentine-run **Petro Pizza,** Toconao s/n, serves Buenos Aires-style pizza (closer to the Italian original than its Chilean counterpart) and San Pedro's best hot chocolate (made with steamed milk, the Argentine *submarino* is the equivalent of espresso for coffee drinkers).

As popular for socializing as dining, **La Estaka,** Caracoles s/n, tel. 55/851038, remains one of San Pedro's better choices, but it has done away with nightly specials in favor of a purely à la carte international menu. Consistently popular as a nightspot (more so than as a restaurant in recent years), **Tambo Cañaveral,** Toconao s/n, tel. 55/851060, has been periodically shut down for violating the *ley seca.*

Café Adobe, Caracoles 211, tel. 55/851089, is as much a meeting place—probably the most popular in town—as a dining choice; with wooden tables on a patio surrounding a blazing hearth and murals replicating regional rock art, it's easily the most inviting environment in town. The food, from fine breakfasts through its US$4.50 lunch or dinner specials and à la carte entrées in the US$7–10 range, is a worthy complement to the ambience.

The finest restaurant in town, though, is the Hotel Kimal's **Paachá,** Domingo Atienza s/n, tel. 55/851030, with a diverse international menu—try the roast lamb with rosemary for about US$7. Even shoestring travelers can justify treating themselves here; on top of the fine food, it may also have the best entertainment in town with its live music.

Events

Traditional San Pedro hosts more than a handful of festivals, the most notable of which is June 29's patronal **Fiesta de San Pedro y San Pablo.** In early February, folkloric dances mark the **Fiesta de Nuestra Señora de la Candelaria,** while the Andean **Carnaval** lasts several days in February or March.

In August, the **Limpia de Canales** is the local version of the practice of clearing the irrigation canals, common throughout the Hispanic world, for the coming spring planting. August 30's **Fiesta de Santa Rosa de Lima** celebrates one of the Andean countries' most popular official saints.

Shopping

Between the Plaza de Armas and the bus plaza, San Pedro's **Paseo Artesanal** is a shaded passageway where vendors hawk crafts and souvenirs, many of them imported from Bolivia, such as alpaca woolens and wooden carvings. Individual shops include **Petroglifo** and **La Manada,** both on Caracoles; **La Luna,** Toconao s/n; and **Catalejo,** Tocopilla s/n, which also sells books.

Services

Money: Money Exchange, on Toconao near Solcor, is the only official exchange house, but it discounts traveler's checks considerably. There is some optimism that, when San Pedro acquires 24-hour electricity, there will be a new bank with ATM service.

Postal: Correos de Chile is directly opposite the museum, on Padre Le Paige, half a block east of the Plaza de Armas.

Telephone and Internet: Telefónica CTC is at Caracoles and Vilama, half a block south of the Plaza de Armas; Entel is at the southwest corner of the plaza. San Pedro's area code is 55.

Café Etnico, a coffeehouse and bookstore at Tocopilla 423, has the best Internet access in

town, but it's relatively expensive here compared to other locales in Chile—about US$4 per hour.

Laundry: Laundry Alana, Caracoles s/n near Domingo Atienza, washes clothes.

Medical: San Pedro has no hospital, but the Posta Médica, Toconao s/n, tel. 55/851010, can deal with most routine medical problems. In a real emergency, the nearest hospital is at Calama.

Information

On the east side of the plaza, San Pedro's Oficina de Información Turística, Toconao s/n, is sometimes helpful . Hours are 9:30 A.M.–1 P.M. and 3–7 P.M. weekdays, 9 A.M.–1:30 P.M. weekends.

Transportation

San Pedro lacks a central bus terminal. Though most buses stop at a broad open area on Licancábur just north of the Paseo Artesanal, some companies have separate offices.

Tur-Bus, though it leaves from the Licáncabur site, sells tickets through Turismo Ochoa, Caracoles s/n; it has the only direct services to Antofagasta, at 5:50 P.M. daily, and international services to Jujuy and Salta, Argentina (it's best, however, to buy these tickets in Calama even if you want to board the bus in San Pedro).

Buses Atacama 2000, at the Licancábur site, goes two or three times daily to Calama (US$-1.50), and also to Toconao (US$1) and Peine (US$2) at 2 and 7:40 p.m. daily. Buses Frontera del Norte, tel. 55/851117, goes nine times daily to Calama and twice to Toconao, continuing once to Peine.

Getting Around

Bicycles are a good alternative for nearby sights such as Catarpe, Quitor, and Valle de la Luna, but carry plenty of water; for rentals, try Pangea, Tocopilla s/n, tel. 55/851111.

For horse rentals, visit Rancho Cactus, Toconao s/n, across from Hostería San Pedro.

VICINITY OF SAN PEDRO DE ATACAMA

San Pedro is the primary base for excursions into destinations such as the polychrome Valle de la

Luna (Valley of the Moon), pre-Columbian ruins at Quitor and Catarpe, flamingo breeding sites at high-altitude salt lakes such as Laguna Chaxa and Laguna Miniques, and the world's highest geyser field at El Tatio. In some ways, it's a better option for exploring high altiplano environments than Parque Nacional Lauca, because its elevation (about 2,500 meters above sea level) permits more gradual acclimatization before visiting sites such as El Tatio (at about 4,000 meters).

For several of these destinations, their relative inaccessibility means either booking a tour or hiring a vehicle (preferably with high clearance and/or 4WD). Some agencies are here in summer only, such as Santiago's **Azimut 360,** Caracoles s/n, tel. 55/851469, bose-spa@netline.cl.

Sample prices for tours include Tatio (US$15), Valle de la Luna (US$6), Salar de Atacama (US$13), Altiplano lagoons (US$35, full day), archaeological tour to Quitor, Catarpe, and Tulor (US$10, half day).

Well-established San Pedro agencies include **Atacama Inca Tour,** Toconao s/n, tel. 55/851062; Dutch-run **Cosmo Andino,** Caracoles s/n, tel. 55/851069, fax 55/811156, cosmoandino@entelchile.net, which also boasts Chile's finest foreign-language book exchange; **Desert Adventure,** Tocopilla s/n, tel. 55/851067, desertsp@ctcinternet.cl; **Expediciones Casa Corvatsch,** Tocopilla s/n, tel. 55/851087, website: www.casacorvatsch.cl, ccorvatsch@entelchile.net; **Turismo Labra,** Caracoles s/n, tel. 55/851165; **Turismo Ochoa,** Caracoles s/n, tel. 55/851022; and **Turismo Pachamama,** Toconao s/n, tel. 55/851064, pachamama.tour@entelchile.net.

In a category of its own is Bolivian-run **Turismo Colque,** Caracoles s/n, tel. 55/851109, colquecelvo@entelchile.net, the only San Pedro operator licensed across the border.

Pukará de Quitor

Only three km northwest of San Pedro, the Pukará de Quitor is a 12th-century fortification on the west side of the valley of the Río San Pedro. Originally intended for defense against the Aymara invaders, it consists of about 160 structures spread over 2.5 hectares. At the entrance to the ruins, the eastward view from the newly dedicated **Plaza de Quitor** focuses directly on the summit of Volcán Licancábur, on the Bolivian border.

Relatively easy foot trails zigzag through the ruins—don't attempt to climb the gullied badlands, whose loose rock and soil are serious hazards, especially if no one's around to call for help. Carry water and snacks, as the area is hot and dry.

Tambo de Catarpe

Four km beyond Quitor, on the east side of the river, the erstwhile Inka administrative center of Catarpe really is ruins in the most literal sense of the word—there are barely any walls standing in what was once a large hilltop site. Here, Inka officials ran the tributary system to which all its conquered peoples were subject.

Termas de Puritama

About 30 km northeast of San Pedro, just west of the road to the famous geysers of El Tatio, the volcanic hotsprings of Termas de Puritama now belong to the Explora company and unlimited access comes with their package tours. Reached by a precipitous road that hugs the side of the canyon, its installations have undergone a long overdue refurbishment since the company obtained the concession to run them.

Unfortunately, Puritama is no longer an obligatory stop on the way back from El Tatio because San Pedro tour operators cannot justify the hefty US$8.50 day-use charge. Under pressure, though, Explora has relented to provide free admission to residents of San Pedro, for whom such high fees were a hardship.

Laguna Verde (Bolivia)

For many years, the only secure way to see shimmering blue-green Laguna Verde, just across the Bolivian border from San Pedro, was on a three-day 4WD crossing to the town of Uyuni with a Bolivian tour operator. Chilean operators who dared to cross the line—admittedly illegally—sometimes had their tires shot out and their clients robbed by the Bolivian military.

It's still possible to cross the altiplano to Uyuni but, since the Bolivians opened a new border post at Hito Cajones, directly on the border and less than an hour from San Pedro, it's possible to cross to Laguna Verde for the day without continuing to Uyuni.

In fact, these day trips are part of Turismo Colque's Uyuni crossings. From San Pedro, Colque buses carry both day-trippers and Uyuni-bound passengers to Hito Cajones—one of South America's most isolated international crossings, at least in terms of inaccessibility from the country's heartland—and on to Laguna Blanca, for breakfast at a small hotel.

Day-trippers then are taxied around Laguna Blanca—home to flocks of flamingos—and then to the Laguna Verde overlook to admire its shifting colors before returning to the Laguna Blanca hotel; they then return to San Pedro with westbound passengers from Uyuni.

The day tour to Laguna Verde costs US$16 pp with breakfast; the three-day crossing to Uyuni runs about US$80, including food but not lodging at Laguna Colorada and at Hotel San Juan, near Chiguana.

Geisers del Tatio

Hugging the Bolivian border, 4,321 meters above sea level and 95 km north of San Pedro, the col-lapsed caldera of El Tatio is the world's highest major geyser field and, at dawn, its myriad steaming fumaroles are one of the continent's great natural spectacles. Within the sprawling ancient crater, the deposition of dissolved minerals has created many stunningly delicate individual landforms.

Long suggested as a possible national park, Tatio was the site of an experimental geothermal power project by the state Corporación de Fomento (Corfo) some decades back. Corfo shelved the project, though, because the geysers yielded inconsistent steam, and the saline water clogged the pipes and turbines; still, rusting machinery evidences the effort. There is still a large heated pool in which visitors can enjoy a swim.

In addition to its scenic value, El Tatio is home to impressive concentrations of wildlife—endangered vicuñas graze its pastures and vizcacha scramble among its rookeries. While Conaf would like the area as a park, Corfo insists that new geothermal technology will allow it to install a new plant with no adverse environmental consequences. In addition to Conaf and Corfo, however, the indigenous community of Caspana has taken an interest in Tatio with support from the Corporación Nacional Indígena (Conadi).

swimmers at El Tatio geyser field

© WAYNE BERNHARDSON

Warning: Even though visitors stroll freely among the pools and geysers at El Tatio—there are no formal paths or controls—several serious accidents have taken place when the thin crust failed to hold the weight of walkers. Third-degree burns from waters whose temperature reach 85°C are a serious hazard—err on the side of caution.

Accommodations: Camping is possible at El Tatio, but only with the best equipment—temperatures drop well below zero every night. About two km before the geysers, Corfo has a free but dilapidated *refugio*, which is only slightly warmer than sleeping outside. In either case, bring plenty of food and fuel, as nothing is available on site.

Transportation: Most visitors take tours from San Pedro, occasionally from Calama, but some prefer to hire vehicles (high clearance is imperative, 4WD advisable). To arrive by dawn, when the geysers are most active, it's necessary to leave San Pedro by 4 A.M.; the road is difficult to follow in the dark without trailing tour operators, who do not appreciate the practice. A better option is to drive up the afternoon before, camping or staying at the Corfo *refugio*. From Tatio, it is also possible to cross the Cuesta de Chita to the west, visiting the indigenous villages of Caspana, Ayquina, Toconce, and Chiu Chiu en route to Calama.

Reserva Nacional Los Flamencos

From the salt flats of the Salar de Atacama to the azure lakes of the altiplano, the 73,986-hectare Reserva Nacional Los Flamencos comprises seven scattered sectors in and around San Pedro de Atacama. Its most popular single attraction is the polychrome Valle de la Luna (Valley of the Moon), but the flamingo colonies of Laguna Chaxa and the altiplano are also proving favorites.

At the *ayllu* of Solcor, just a couple km outside town beyond the customs and immigration post, Conaf maintains a Centro de Información Ambiental with very good exhibits on ecology and environment, open 9 A.M.–1 P.M. and 2–6 P.M. daily. Conaf also has a post at the village of Toconao, and a ranger station at Laguna Chaxa.

Valle de la Luna: Every evening at twilight, cars, minivans, and tour buses converge on the Valle de la Luna and its Cordillera de la Sal, where the natural processes of millennia have eroded the sedimentary strata into eerie forms and the slanting sun in the late afternoon highlights their rainbow colors for spectacular sunsets. From the main highway approach to San Pedro, the Valle de la Luna provides only a taste of its polychrome glory—many if not most visitors prefer to climb the dunes at dusk for the best views to the west.

Every San Pedro travel agency offers inexpensive tours—transportation, really, for the most part—to Valle de la Luna, about 15 km west of San Pedro. Some visitors prefer renting mountain bikes, but avoid leaving the main routes—some areas still have landmines left over from the 1970s. Carry food, water, and warm clothing; while the days are warm at this altitude, temperatures drop rapidly after dark.

Laguna Chaxa: On the eastern side of the Salar de Atacama, 61 km south of San Pedro and directly west of the village of Toconao in the Soncor sector of the reserve, Laguna Chaxa is one of three interconnected lagoons where both Chilean and Andean flamingos, as well as Andean gulls, nest in summer. Tours to Toconao and the altiplano lakes east of Socaire usually stop here; Conaf collects an admission charge of US$3 pp.

Salar de Pujsa: About 100 km east of San Pedro, on the paved highway to Paso de Jama and Argentina, 4,500 meters above sea level, the James flamingo pairs up at the 1,900-hectare Salar de Pujsa, though they nest elsewhere in the altiplano.

Salar de Tara: Los Flamencos' largest single sector, 133 km east of San Pedro via the Paso de Jama road, the Salar de Tara comprises 36,674 hectares at an average altitude of 4,300 meters above sea level. It's particularly important bird habitat, with three species of flamingos, Andean gulls, ducks, and other species in its marshlands. The surrounding *puna* grasslands and rookeries support vicuñas, vizcachas, foxes, and armadillos.

Salar de Quisquiro: In the Pampa Loyoques, a short distance before the border, the Salara de Quisquiro was formerly home to breeding colonies of the Chilean flamingo, but no nest has been seen here since 1990—according to Conaf, mining activities, egg collection by locals, and an increasing human presence in general have discouraged breeding colonies here. Still, it continues to serve as a feeding and resting site for the birds.

Laguna Miscanti and Laguna Miniques: From the village of Toconao, 33 km southeast of San Pedro, paved Ruta 23 has reached the picturesque hamlet of **Socaire,** where broad, stone-faced pre-Columbian terraces cover the hillsides. Beyond Socaire, Ruta 23 is still a gravel road to 4,079-meter Paso Sico, an alternative route to Salta, Argentina, whose improvements are lagging behind the Paso de Jama route.

About 15 km beyond Socaire, a short lateral leads to Laguna Miscanti and the smaller Laguna Miniques, 115 km from San Pedro, a flamingo-breeding site that's a frequent destination and lunch stop for tour groups from San Pedro. The lateral eventually rejoins Ruta 23 to the border (if continuing to Argentina, don't forget customs and immigration formalities at San Pedro).

TOCONAO AND VICINITY

On the southeast side of the Salar de Atacama, several interesting destinations are accessible via increasingly good roads with public transportation.

Toconao

The townscape of Toconao, an orchard oasis southeast of San Pedro de Atacama, is like no other in the region—instead of using adobe, its skilled stone carvers have quarried and shaped volcanic bedrock into solid blocks that form the walls of its distinctive houses. Its major landmark, the freestanding **Campanario** (bell tower) in the Plaza de Armas, is a national monument even though, curiously enough, the nearby 18th-century **Iglesia San Lucas** is not.

In the **Quebrada de Jeria,** a well-watered canyon that runs nearly through the middle of town, local growers cultivate almonds, apples, figs, grapes, pears, quinces, and other crops for San Pedro and Calama. Unlike San Pedro, its water quality is so high that, according to Isaiah Bowman's account in the 1920s, it was:

> *celebrated not only for its fruit but for the clearness and purity of its water. About a dozen well-to-do families at San Pedro send peons to Toconao to obtain drinking water, brought in casks on mule back.*

WATCH YOUR STEP: LANDMINES IN THE ALTIPLANO

I n the 1970s, when military dictatorships were the rule in South America, the armies of Chile, Argentina, and Bolivia felt no compunction about mining their borders. Today, while most of their longstanding border disputes have dissipated or disappeared, the legacy of landmines continues, especially in the altiplano of Region II, where the three countries' borders converge.

While Chile has not yet managed to remove mines from the altiplano, in accordance with international treaties, it has managed to mark them and to implement a program to reduce the hazards to tourists who wander the backcountry. The following tips have been adapted from the Primera División de Ejército, the Chilean army's Antofagasta-based First Division.

1. Landmines are powerful explosives; stay out of designated minefields and keep a close watch on children.
2. Be aware that summer rains can shift the location of landmines outside signed boundaries.

3. Wherever possible, stay on the roads, especially at night or when it's snowing.
4. If you find any apparent military artifact in the vicinity of a designated minefield, contact the Carabineros (tel. 133), the Primera División headquarters in Antofagasta (tel. 55/242392), or the Regimiento Ingenieros No. 1, Atacama (Army Corps of Engineers No. 1, Atacama) in Chuquicamata (tel. 55/324376).
5. Similarly, do not take or move any such object. All should be considered active, and specialists will be despatched to deactivate or destroy them.
6. Take *Campo Minado* (Minefield) signs seriously as an indicator of danger—never, under any circumstances, enter a minefield. By keeping your distance, you will guarantee your security.
7. Do not damage or destroy minefield signs or fences, which could expose others to risk.

These pointers are not trivial—tourists have been seriously injured by encounters with landmines.

For just US$5 per person, **Residencial y Restaurant El Valle de Toconao,** Lascar 236, offers clean rooms with new beds, hot water in shared baths, and a verdant patio. Meals are also available.

Buses Frontera goes to San Pedro at 5 and 6 P.M. daily, and to Peine at 8:30 P.M. daily. Buses Atacama 2000, Latorre 164, goes to San Pedro twice daily and once to Peine.

Peine

Some 102 km south of San Pedro, the indigenous village of Peine sits on a elevated scarp just above the southeastern corner of the Salar de Atacama. The village itself is fairly recent, though nearby are three national monuments: the **Tambo Incáico de Peine,** an Inka staging point; the **Pueblo Antiguo de Peine,** the ruins of pre-Columbian Peine; and the **Ruinas de la Capilla de Misiones de Peine Viejo,** a colonial mission chapel.

In an overhang in the canyon adjacent to Peine, only a few minutes' walk from the main drag, the **Pictografías del Alero de Peine** are a cluster of rock art representing at least three distinct styles in local prehistory. The oldest, dating from about 3000–2000 B.C., depict human hunters and their camelid prey in dark ochre, while later figures, between 1200–400 B.C., suggest a transition to a more advanced pastoral society, with elaborate costumes and ritual dances. After a substantial hiatus, more geometrical and abstract designs date from pre-Inka agriculturalists (A.D. 1000–1450).

From Peine, a good westbound road traverses the unrelenting salt crystal landscape of the Salar de Atacama, crossing the Cordillera de Domeyko, to Baquedano, on the Panamericana. It has heavy truck traffic, though, and few landmarks except for the sulfur mine at Lomas Bayas, but for southbound travelers with their own vehicles, it saves time and distance over the return route via San Pedro and Calama. No gasoline is available until Baquedano—fill up in San Pedro.

Peine's only accommodations is a rustic campground. There are no restaurants, but a couple of small stores sell basic supplies.

Peine has two buses daily to San Pedro at 5 P.M., with Buses Atacama 2000 and Buses Frontera.

Norte Chico

One of Chile's least-touristed areas, the Norte Chico has much to offer: stunning, sparsely populated beaches in a nearly rainless climate; such spectacularly clear night skies that international astronomical observatories have flocked here; picturesque villages in remote Andean valleys; and vast, rugged high country along the Argentine border. Its several national parks and reserves are reasonably accessible, and outside the peak summer season visitors are few. One highlight, in rare rainy years, is the *desierto florido*, when evanescent wildflowers carpet the desert floor in color.

North of La Ligua and south from Parque Nacional Pan de Azúcar, Region III (Atacama) and Region IV (Coquimbo) constitute the present-day Norte Chico. Traditionally, though, the regional boundaries are the Río Aconcagua on the south (today part of Region V, Valparaíso) and the drainage of the Río Copiapó, at approximately 27° N. Mining is the traditional backbone of the economy, and irrigated agriculture retains a hold in the region, but tourist development has proliferated in and around the city of La Serena.

railroad bridge on the former Longino (Longitudinal Railway)

NORTE CHICO

To Antofagasta

Taltal
Cifuncho

REGION II
(ANTOFAGASTA)

*Parque
Nacional Pan
de Azúcar*

Diego de
Almagro   El Salvador   *Salar de
Pedernales*

Chañaral

PACIFIC OCEAN

Río Salado   Potrerillos

*Santuario de la
Naturaleza Granito
Orbicular*

REGION III
(ATACAMA)   Paso de San
Francisco
(4,726 m)

Caldera   *P.N. Nevado
Tres Cruces*

Bahía Inglesa   Paipote

Río Copiapó   Copiapó   Cerro Tres Cruces
(6,749 m)   Cerro Ojos del
Salado (6,885 m)

MINA EL TRÁNSITO   Tierra Amarilla

Nantoco   *Laguna del
Negro Francisco*   RP 45

Pabellón

Los Loros   Chaschuil

CHAÑARCILLO   ★ **VIÑA DEL
CERRO**   To Catamarca
and La Rioja

Carrizal Bajo   Las Juntas

P.N. Llanos de Challe

Huasco   *Río Huasco*   Jagüé

Freirina   Vallenar

Alto del
Carmen

*Reserva Nacional
Pingüino de
Humboldt*   Domeyko   San
Félix

Choros   ★ **OBSERVATORIO
LAS CAMPANAS**   Villa Unión

Caleta de Choros   **OBSERVATORIO
LA SILLA**   RN
40

Caleta Los
Hornos   **OBSERVATORIO
COMUNAL CERRO
MAMALLUCA**   **BAÑOS TERMALES
JUNTAS DE EL TORO**

La Serena   **JUNTAS DEL TORO**

Coquimbo   *Río Elqui*

**OBSERVATORIO
CERRO TOLOLO**   Paihuano   Paso del
Agua Negra
(4,765 m)   Rodeo   *Río Bermejo*

Vicuña   41   Monte Grande

Guanaqueros   Pisco Elqui   Pismanta

Tongoy   Andacollo   Cochiguaz   RN
150   Los Flores   San José
de Jáchal

43   **MONUMENTO
NATURAL PICHASCA**

Río Limarí   Ovalle   *Río Jáchal*

**P.N.
Bosque
de Fray
Jorge**   Monte Patria

Embalse La Paloma   RP 436

**TERMAS DE
SOCOS**   REGION IV
(COQUIMBO)   **ARGENTINA**

Combarbalá   RN
40

**RESERVA NACIONAL
LAS CHINCHILLAS**

Río Choapa   Illapel   Mina Los
Pelambres   Calingasta   *Río*

Salamanca   RP 12

Los Vilos   *San Juan*

Pichidangui   Los
Peladeros   Tranquilla   RP 412   San Juan

La Ligua

To Santiago   REGION V
(VALPARAÍSO)   RP 39   To Mendoza

Cordillera de los Andes

N   NORTE CHICO

*Santiago de la
Naturaleza Granito
Orbicular*   31

5   31

0   60 mi
0   60 km

MOON

© AVALON TRAVEL PUBLISHING, INC.

History

Around 11,000 to 15,000 years ago, the Norte Chico's earliest human inhabitants were probably paleo-Indian hunter-gatherers in the upper Huasco valley, near present-day Alto del Carmen. Over the following millennia, the Huentelauquén culture and their successors relied on coastal resources around what are now Chañaral, Huasco, and south to Los Vilos. Only after the beginning of the Christian era, though, were there stable encampments of coastal peoples in and around locales such as Pan de Azúcar, Caldera, Bahía Inglesa, and Puerto Viejo.

First identified in the Elqui valley site of El Molle, the El Molle culture appears in the early centuries of the Christian era and ranges from the Río Salado (Chañaral) and Copiapó valleys south to the Río Choapa. Both farmers and herders, they made the first regional advances in metallurgy and basketry, as well as rock art—Valle del Encanto, near Ovalle, is their best-preserved site.

From about A.D. 900, Diaguita peoples who probably came from Argentina established village-style settlements where they cultivated maize, beans, and squash in the well-watered valleys and grew additional crops such as potatoes and quinoa at higher elevations. They probably also herded llamas, and fished and hunted to add protein to their diet. By the early 15th century, though, the Inka empire began to expand its dominion over the region, linking the Copiapó valley to Cuzco via a highway along the precordillera, and eventually extended its influence into and beyond the Chilean heartland, though its control was weak on the periphery.

Inka domination was short-lived, as the Spanish invasion of Peru quickly spread south. After the Pizarros took Cajamarca, Cuzco, and Quito in the early 1530s, their skeptical partner (and later enemy) Diego de Almagro headed a large but ill-fated expedition of 500 Spaniards and thousands more Indians that crossed the frigid Andean *puna* from Argentina via the 4,726-meter Paso de San Francisco to the Copiapó valley.

En route, Almagro lost men, horses, llamas, and supplies to floods and cold; turning back at the Río Aconcagua, he chose an Andean foothill route rather than risk the brutal high-altitude crossing again. Disappointed in search of gold and silver, he had unknowingly passed within a day's journey of the Chañarcillo silver lode that made 19th-century Copiapó rich. A few years later, Pedro de Valdivia followed Almagro's return path southward, founding the city of La Serena en route to Santiago.

Only after independence, with the discovery of Chañarcillo in 1832, did the Norte Chico gain prominence with impressive technological developments, including one of South America's first railways. While the silver boom lasted only a few decades, copper in the highlands northeast of Copiapó brought a more enduring prosperity—but with great environmental costs. Mining has also proved important in the vicinity of La Serena, but tourism has wrought an urban renaissance in what is becoming the Chilean Riviera. The cultivation of irrigated grapes for export and *pisco* production in the Copiapó, Huasco, and Elqui valleys continues to be important.

Atacama Region

Underappreciated by nationals and foreigners alike, the thinly populated Atacama region has only one major city, the capital of Copiapó, but the ramshackle ports of Caldera and Chañaral—the former also a beachgoers' destination—contain a wealth of 19th-century architecture. Several national parks—Llanos de Challe and Pan de Azúcar on the coast, Nevado Tres Cruces in the *puna*—are attracting more visitors. Nudging the Argentine border, the country's highest peak, 6,885-meter Ojos del Salado, does not belong to any national park but draws growing numbers of climbers.

COPIAPÓ

Founded in 1744 by Francisco Cortés y Cartabio, under the name San Francisco de la Selva de Copiapó, the current regional capital has always been a mining town. The boom that established the city came in the 1830s, when the fortuitous discovery of silver at Chañarcillo, in rugged and remote country almost directly south of the city, brought scads of prospectors, laborers, and speculators to the region—Copiapó's silver heyday was like the California Gold Rush, when ordinary supplies sold for preposterous amounts.

When Darwin visited in 1835, he remarked that:

> *Before the discovery of the famous silver-mines of Chanuncillo [Chañarcillo], Copiapó was in a rapid state of decay, but now it is in a very thriving condition; and the town, which was completely overthrown by an earthquake, has been rebuilt.*

Still, he added, the area's limited agricultural potential—"its produce is sufficient for only three months of the year"—and transport difficulties raised prices to levels that astonished him.

Some of those difficulties were alleviated when, 16 years later, Chile's first railway linked the city to the port of Caldera. While the Chañarcillo deposits gave out in the 1870s, a more diversified mining economy, with copper and iron supplanting silver, has kept the city prosperous—at a cost. The city is a key administrative and service center, and the Universidad de Atacama is the academic equivalent of the famous Colorado School of Mines, but the copper smelter at nearby Paipote (built in 1951) bears the burden for some of the country's worst air and water pollution.

Orientation

Copiapó is 333 km north of La Serena and 801 km north of Santiago via Ruta 5, the Panamericana. Known as Avenida Copayapu as it parallels the Río Copiapó, the Panamericana turns west toward the coastal resort of Caldera and Antofagasta, another 566 km to the north.

While the city itself has sprawled east and west along the river valley, and even up the sides of the hills to the north and south, most points of interest are within a few blocks of Plaza Prat, the city's traditional center. Cerro Chanchoquín, known colloquially as Cerro de la Cruz for the landmark cross placed there by Franciscan father Crisógono Sierra y Velásquez, towers above the city to the northwest. Immediately below, the Alameda Manuel Antonio Matta marks the historic barrio of Copiapó's mining magnates and its pioneer railway.

Sights

Shady **Plaza Prat,** studded with massive pepper trees, is downtown Copiapó's focal point. Its central fountain, with a marble statue honoring the mining industry, is a national monument, as are four other marble statues representing the seasons—ironically enough, in an area that averages only 23 mm of rainfall per annum.

At the western corner of the plaza, Englishman William Rogers built the neoclassical **Iglesia Catedral Nuestra Señora de Rosario** (1851), its elegant portico topped by a three-story bell tower, the latter crowned by a cupola. Also a national monument, the structure itself consists of oak partitions, covered by cane and adobe.

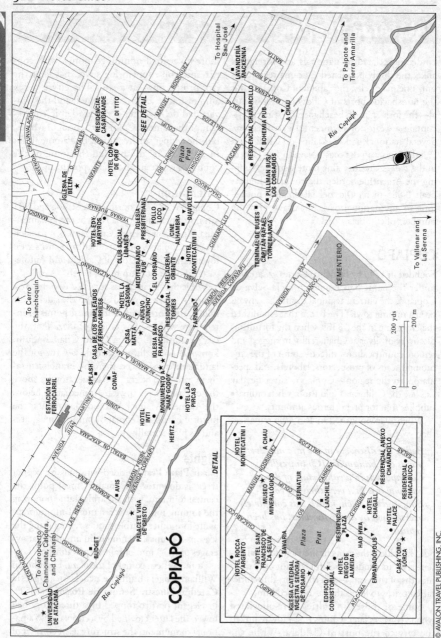

COPIAPÓ

To Hospital San José

To Paipote and Tierra Amarilla

Río Copiapó

LAVANDERÍA MACKENNA

RESIDENCIAL CHAÑARCILLO

BOHEMIA PUB

A CHAU

PULLMAN BUS/ LOS CORSARIOS

To Vallenar and La Serena

CEMENTERIO

TERMINAL DE BUSES CAPITÁN RAFAEL TORREBLANCA

SEE DETAIL

Plaza Prat

DI TITO

RESIDENCIAL CASAGRANDE

HOTEL COPA DE ORO

IGLESIA DE BELÉN

IGLESIA PRESBITERIANA

POLLO LOCO

DIAVOLETTO

HOTEL EDY-MARYROS

CLUB SOCIAL LIBANÉS

MEDITERRÁNEO PUB

EL CORSARIO

CINE ALHAMBRA

HOTEL MONTECATINI II

HELADERÍA ORIENTE

HOTEL LA CASONA

NUEVO QUINCHO

RESIDENCIAL TORRES

FARINSITO

CASA DE LOS EMPLEADOS DE FERROCARRILES

CASA MATTA

IGLESIA SAN FRANCISCO

SPLASH

CONAF

ESTACIÓN DE FERROCARRIL

HOTEL INTI

MONUMENTO JUAN GODOY

HOTEL LAS PIRCAS

HERTZ

AVIS

PALACETE VIÑA DE CRISTO

BUDGET

To Cerro Chanchoquín

To Aeropuerto Chamonate, Caldera, and Chañaral

UNIVERSIDAD DE ATACAMA

Río Copiapó

To MATTA

200 yds
200 m

DETAIL

HOTEL MONTECATINI I

A CHAU

MUSEO MINERALÓGICO

SERNATUR

LANCHILE

RESIDENCIAL ANEXO CHAÑARCILLO

RESIDENCIAL CHACABUCO

HOTEL ROCCA D'ARGENTO

HOTEL SAN FRANCISCO DE LA SELVA

BAVARIA

RESIDENCIAL PLAZA

HAO HWA

HOTEL CHAGALL

HOTEL PALACE

Plaza Prat

IGLESIA CATEDRAL NUESTRA SEÑORA DE ROSARIO

EDIFICIO CONSISTORIAL

HOTEL DIEGO DE ALMEIDA

EMPANADÓPOLIS

CASA TORO LORCA

Kitty-corner from the cathedral, the green-and-gold **Edificio Consistorial,** once a private home and later occupied by the Municipalidad, now hosts art exhibits and performance events as the **Casa de la Cultura Julio Aciares.** Southwest of the plaza, on Atacama between Colipí and Vallejos, the **Casa Toro Lorca** is a national monument from the historic mining era. One short block from the plaza, at the corner of Colipí and Manuel Rodríguez, is the Museo Mineralógico (Mineralogical Museum; see below).

Besides the cathedral, Copiapó boasts several other religious monuments, including the Protestant **Iglesia Presbiteriana** (1890), O'Higgins 391. Three blocks north, near the corner of Infante and Yerbas Buenas, the colonial **Iglesia de Belén,** rebuilt in the mid-19th century, is now the **Santuario Santa Teresa,** dedicated to a Chilean saint from the town of Los Andes, northeast of Santiago.

Several blocks west of the plaza, Chile's Consejo de Monumentos Nacionales has designated the entire neighborhood known as the **Barrio Estación** as a monument in itself. Its main landmarks are the historic **Estación de Ferrocarril** (Railroad Station), the tree-lined avenue known as **Alameda Matta,** and a scattering of other significant buildings, including the **Casa Matta** (home to the Museo Histórico Regional); the onetime **Casa de los Empleados de Ferrocarriles** (built in 1860 as housing for railway employees, now home to Sernageomin, the national mining service), and the **Iglesia San Francisco** (1872), built of Douglas fir and stucco—despite its deceiving appearance of concrete.

On a small plaza facing the Iglesia San Francisco, near the south end of Avenida Matta, the **Monumento a Juan Godoy** honors the muleteer and prospector who stumbled upon the Chañarcillo silver deposits, and mining entrepreneur Apolinario Soto built the Palacete Viña de Cristo (see below) as his personal mansion in 1860, but it passed through several hands before becoming property of the Universidad Técnica del Estado (now the Universidad de Atacama) in 1974.

A short distance west, the former **Escuela de Minas** (School of Mines) is also part of the Universidad de Atacama; the **Locomotora Copiapó,** the Norris Brothers steam locomotive that first linked Caldera to Copiapó, at present resides on the grounds—though there's a remote chance it could be up and running as a tourist train.

Museo Mineralógico

Under the auspices of the Universidad de Atacama, Copiapó's mineral museum possesses a collection of more than 14,000 minerals from around the world, though only about 2,000 are on display at any one time. Among its prize exhibits are a meteorite found in the Atacama, silver ore from Chañarcillo, and the ubiquitous Chilean copper, and there are also some fossils. Everything is magnificently displayed.

At the corner of Colipí and Rodríguez, the museum is open Monday to Saturday mornings 9 A.M.–1 P.M. and weekday afternoons only 3:30–7 P.M. Adults pay US$.50 admission; children's admission is US$.20.

Museo Regional de Atacama

Copiapó's first-rate historical museum focuses on pre-Hispanic cultures and mining (from the truly archaic to the relatively recent Inka-Diaguita, at nearby Viña del Cerro, all the way to contemporary industrial mineral exploitation).

The displays also present key figures in regional history, from conquistador Pedro de Valdivia to prospector Diego de Almeyda, mining magnate Manuel Antonio Matta, essayist José Joaquín Vallejo (better known by his *nom de plume* "Jotabeche"), not to mention illustrious visitors such as Darwin and Vicente Pérez Rosales.

The most imaginative single exhibit is a convincing replica of a mineshaft, complete with miners' artifacts. Built in the 1840s by the influential Mattas, the building is an attraction in its own right, a national monument whose gallery, supported by fluted neoclassical columns, surrounds an interior patio.

The Museo Regional, at Atacama 98, tel. 52/212313, is open Tuesday to Friday 9 A.M.–12:45 P.M. and 3–7:15 P.M., Saturday 10 A.M.–12:45 P.M. and 3–5:45 P.M., and Sunday and holidays 10 A.M.–12:45 P.M. only. Admission costs US$1. The interpretations are generally excellent, but in Spanish only.

Palacete Viña de Cristo

Born in 1808 in San Felipe, north of Santiago, Apolinario Soto moved north with his family as a child. Later, as owner of the Tres Puntas silver mine northwest of the city, near the present-day site of Inca de Oro, he became one of the city's leading citizens.

Completed in 1860, Soto's Georgian-style Palacete Viña de Cristo was the region's most elaborate mansion, fronted by a four-column portico supporting a balcony that, in turn, is covered by a three-gabled roof supported by wrought-iron posts. The main floor held four reception rooms and the second floor seven bedrooms, though most of these are now university offices.

All the building's decorative elements, mostly notably the elaborate wrought iron that resembles that of 18th-century New Orleans, came from the United States. Nearly all the woodwork, including the exquisitely polished staircases, consists of Douglas fir. From the second floor, a spiral staircase leads to a perched *mirador* (overlook) with a 360-degree view.

Unfortunately, the two lateral wings that once flanked the building to form an inverted "U" were demolished in the late 1930s; otherwise the building and its grounds—also much reduced from the days when they held orchards and vineyards—would be even more imposing. These wings held a chapel, a music room, guest bedrooms, and staff facilities, but construction of the Panamericana, which runs directly past the entrance, brought their demise; a further widening also meant an eight-meter displacement of the original wrought-iron fences and gates. Designation as a national monument, which would have saved the original configuration, did not come until 1986.

On the south of the Panamericana (Avenida Copayapu), directly opposite its junction with Rómulo Pena, the Palacete Viña de Cristo is open to the public 8 A.M.–7 P.M. weekdays. Contrary to some guidebook accounts, it has no functioning museum.

Accommodations

Copiapó's budget accommodations are mediocre, with a couple of exceptions, but get better fast in the midrange and upscale categories.

US$10–25: About the cheapest in town, **Residencial Casagrande,** Infante 525, is old, worn, and barely adequate for US$5 pp. Amiable **Residencial Benbow,** Rodríguez 541, tel. 52/217634, also costs just US$5 pp with shared bath, though it's nothing special.

Across the street, **Residencial Rodríguez,** Rodríguez 528, tel. 52/212861, is comparable at US$7/10 s/d, US$12/22 with private bath. Having moved several times in recent years, **Residencial Chacabuco,** Salas 451, tel. 52/213428, charges a modest US$7 pp, but single rooms are few.

Residencial Anexo Chañarcillo, O'Higgins 804, tel. 52/212284, is a ramshackle place that's been turned into more and smaller rooms than it should have been, but that's why it costs only US$7.50 pp with shared bath, US$10 pp with private bath; the staff are friendly and attentive, though, and it's also the only *residencial* in town with onsite parking. Its sister **Residencial Chañarcillo,** Chañarcillo 741, tel. 52/213281, has slightly better rooms for about the same price, which can include parking privileges at the Anexo.

Residencial Torres, Atacama 230, tel. 09/6-247457, costs US$7/12 s/d with shared bath. Well-located **Residencial Plaza,** O'Higgins 670, tel. 52/212671, costs US$8.50/14 s/d with shared bath and is probably the best budget choice. **Residencial Nueva Chañarcillo,** Rodríguez 540, tel. 52/212368, charges US$10/14 with shared bath, US$18/24 with private bath.

Hotel del Sol, Rodríguez 550, tel. 52/215672, rents poor upstairs rooms with shared bath for US$7 pp, but the downstairs rooms with private bath are notably better for US$17.50 pp, with services including breakfast, cable TV, telephone, and parking. The management can be uncompromising on details, however, and indisposed to negotiate.

US$25–50: In primo condition, **Hotel Montecatini I,** Infante 766, tel. 52/211363, fax 52/217021, charges from US$21/29 s/d to US$28/41 but also offers discounts for cash. Offering good value for money, **Hotel Palace,** Atacama 741, tel. 52/212852, charges US$22/32 s/d with private bath for rooms surrounding a shady patio.

Though it's architecturally drab, spic-and-span **Hotel Edy-Maryros,** Yerbas Buenas 593, tel. 52/211408, fax 52/219871, is friendly with outstanding service for US$25/39.

Hotel Copa de Oro, Infante 530, tel./fax 52/216309, is a full-service hotel that is also home to Peruvian Tours, which does excursions into the little-visited Andes east of Copiapó; room rates are US$32/37 s/d. **Hotel Rocca D'Argento,** Maipú 580, tel. 218744, fax 211191, costs US$33/41.

Under the same management as Hotel Montecatini I, **Hotel Montecatini II,** Atacama 374, tel. 52/211516, fax 52/214773, hotelmonte-catin@ole.com, charges US$36/48.

One of Copiapó's best values, **Hotel La Casona,** O'Higgins 150, tel. 52/217277, fax 52/217278, lacasona@entelchile.net, provides comfortable and attractively furnished rooms in a colonial garden setting, starting at US$42/50 s/d. The more modern **Hotel Inti,** Avenida Freire 180, tel. 52/217739, fax 52/217793, has nearly identical rates.

US$50–100: One block from Plaza Prat, **Hotel San Francisco de la Selva,** Los Carrera 525, tel. 52/217013, fax 52/213255, hosanco@entelchile.net, charges US$45/54 for rooms with private bath, cable TV, telephone, and similar amenities. Despite its relatively newness, though, some parts are surprisingly worn; there are a handful of smaller and cheaper rooms.

Half a block from Plaza Prat, **Hotel Chagall,** O'Higgins 760, tel. 52/213775, costs US$57/62. **Hotel Las Pircas,** Avenida Copayapu 095, tel. 52/213220, fax 52/211633, laspirca@chilnet.cl, is a Santa Fe-style motel (in the North American sense of the word) with commodious garden rooms for US$58/67 s/d. The rooms vary in size and quality, however.

Stylish **Hotel Diego de Almeida,** O'Higgins 656, tel. 52/212075, fronts directly on Plaza Prat. Rates range from US$53/98 to US$80/130 s/d.

Food

For about US$1 each, **Empanadópolis,** Colipí 320, tel. 52/240798, produces a far wider variety of empanadas, including tasty scallops and crab,

than most Chilean kitchens; unfortunately, they are deep-fried rather than baked, but they are far better than most other fast-food alternatives.

Pollo Loco, O'Higgins 461, is a fast-food chicken outlet of decent quality. For cheap but tasty lunches, as well as more elaborate fish and seafood, try **Farnisio,** Chañarcillo 272, tel. 52/213880.

Bavaria, Chacabuco 487, tel. 52/217160, is the local rep of the reliable nationwide chain. Offering a diverse Chilean menu, **El Corsario,** Atacama 245, tel. 52/215374, also offers open air dining. The **Club Social Libanés,** Los Carrera 350, tel. 52/212939, offers Middle Eastern specialties, while **Di Tito,** Chacabuco 710, tel. 52/212386, serves pizza and pasta. **Nuevo Quincho,** Atacama 109, tel. 52/214647, is a *parrilla*.

Copiapó has a wide selection of generally high-quality *chifas*—the traditional favorite is **Hao Hwa,** Colipí 340, tel. 52/213261. In spacious and sparkling new quarters, **A Chau,** Chañarcillo 991, tel. 52/249826, serves good Cantonese entrées in the US$5–7 range, with excellent service. The original, less opulent **A Chau** is at Rodríguez 755, tel. 52/212472.

For ice cream, try **Heladería Oriente,** Atacama 278, or **Diavoletto,** Maipú 331, which also features fine sandwiches.

Entertainment

For drinks, there's the **Bohemia Pub,** at Chañarcillo and Vallejos. **Mediterráneo Pub,** on O'Higgins between Yumbel and Yerbas Buenas, is also a dance venue. **Splash,** at Juan Martínez 46 in the Barrio Estación, is a popular discotheque.

For current movies, try the **Cine Alhambra,** Atacama 455, tel. 52/212187.

Events

Beginning the first Sunday of February, the **Festival de Candelaria** is a nine-day event, celebrated with folkloric dances and religious fervor, that pulls up to 50,000 pilgrims from around the region and country. It takes place at the 19th-century Iglesia de la Candelaria, at Los Carrera and Figueroa, about two km east of Plaza Prat.

Día del Minero, honoring the region's miners, takes place August 10. Copiapinos commemorate the **Fundación de la Ciudad** (Founding of the City) on December 8.

Services

As the regional capital, Copiapó has a complete array of services.

Money: Copiapó has no *cambios,* but several banks have ATMs, including Banco de Crédito, Chacabuco 449, and Banco de Chile and Banco Edwards, across from each other at the corner of Colipí and O'Higgins.

Postal: Correos de Chile is in the Intendencia Regional at Los Carrera 691, directly behind the Sernatur office.

Telephone and Internet: For long-distance services, try Telefónica CTC, at the corner of Los Carrera and Chacabuco, on the north side of Plaza Prat, or Entel at Colipí 484, on the east side of the plaza. Copiapó's area code is 52.

Zona Virtual, Colipí 610, tel. 52/243743, provides Internet access for US$2 per hour from 9:30 A.M.–midnight daily. The Biblioteca Regional (Regional Library), on Colipí between Manuel Rodríguez and Los Carrera, offers public access 10 A.M.–1 P.M. Monday through Saturday, 3–7:30 P.M. weekdays.

Laundry: Lavandería Mackenna, Mackenna 430, tel. 52/218775, provides reliable laundry service.

Travel Agencies: Turismo Atacama, Los Carrera 716, tel. 52/212712, and Cobretur, O'Higgins 640, tel. 52/211072, are conventional travel agencies.

Peruvian Tours, in the Hotel Copa de Oro, Infante 530, tel./fax 52/216309, offers city tours as well as excursions to the upper Copiapó valley, Bahía Inglesa, Parque Nacional Pan de Azúcar, and remote backcountry destinations such as Parque Nacional Nevado Tres Cruces and Ojos del Salado.

Other adventure-oriented travel operators include Expediciones Puna Atacama, Arredondo 154, tel./fax 52/211273, m_urbina@entelchile.net; and Maricunga Expediciones, Maipú 580-B, tel. 52/210075, fax 52/211191, simarexp@entelchile.net.

Medical: Hospital San José, at Los Carrera and Vicuña, tel. 52/212023 or 52/218833, is eight blocks southeast of Plaza Prat.

Information

Tourist Office: Sernatur, in a sidewalk office at Los Carrera 691 on the east side of Plaza Prat, tel. 52/231510, fax 52/217248, serna03@entelchile.net, distributes maps and lists of accommodations and has some English-speaking staff. Hours are 8:30 A.M.–7 P.M. weekdays all year, Saturday 10 A.M.–2 P.M. in summer.

National Parks: For information on the region's national parks and reserves, visit Conaf, Juan Martínez 55, tel. 52/239067. It's open weekdays only, 8 A.M.–4:30 P.M.

Transportation

Copiapó has both air and land connections to points north and south.

Air: Copiapó's Aeropuerto Chamonate, tel. 52/214360, is 15 km west of town via the Panamericana.

LanChile and LanExpress share quarters at Colipí 484, Local A-103, tel. 52/213512 or 52/217406, in the Plaza Real shopping center. LanExpress has 18 flights weekly to Santiago, 11 of which stop in La Serena, and also flies daily except Thursday and Saturday to El Salvador (the Chilean copper mining town, not the country).

Bus: Many bus companies have offices, some of them shared, at Copiapó's Terminal de Buses Capitán Rafael Torreblanca, Chacabuco 112, tel. 52/212577, directly on the Panamericana. A few have separate terminals nearby, but unless indicated otherwise, offices are at Terminal Torreblanca.

Several companies operate northbound toward Antofagasta, Iquique, and Arica, including Ramos Cholele, tel. 52/213113, Zambrano, Evans, and Carmelita, all of which share the same office. Carmelita also provides southbound services to La Serena, Coquimbo, Ovalle, and Santiago, as does Buses Fénix, tel. 52/214929, and Libac, tel. 52/213355.

Tas Choapa, Chañarcillo 631, tel. 52/238066, goes to Arica, Santiago, and intermediate points, with southern Chilean connections to Puerto Montt and international connections to Argentina, Uruguay, and Paraguay. Tur-Bus, Chañarcillo 680, tel. 52/238612, has similar domestic routes.

Flota Barrios, tel. 52/213645, serves destinations on the north- and southbound Panamericana, along with Calama, Tocopilla, and Viña del Mar. Pullman Bus, Colipí 109, tel. 52/212977, covers the Panamericana between Arica and Santiago, also reaching Viña and interior Norte Chico destinations such as Illapel, Salamanca, El Salvador, and Potrerillos; it also has a ticket office at the corner of Chacabuco and Chañarcillo. Los Corsarios, also at Colipí 109, serves destinations throughout the Norte Chico.

Pullman Bus, Libac, and Tur-Bus provide costlier *salón cama* services to Santiago and Viña del Mar.

For the beach resorts of Caldera and Bahía Inglesa, try the local carriers Recabarren, Esperanza 557, tel. 52/216991; Casther, at Chacabuco and Esperanza, tel. 52/218889; and Muñoz, tel. 52/213166. Casther and Abarcía, tel. 52/212483, reach upper Copiapó valley destinations, such as Nantoco and Pabellón, Los Loros, Viña del Cerro, and Tranque Lautaro.

Typical destinations and fares include Caldera (US$1.50, one hour), El Salvador (US$5.50, three hours), Taltal (US$10, 4.5 hours), La Serena (US$14, four hours), Santiago (US$17, 11 hours), Antofagasta (US$20, eight hours), Calama (US$25, 11 hours), Iquique (US$30, 14 hours), and Arica (US$35, 16 hours). There are also *salón cama* services to Santiago (US$23–28).

Getting Around

Airport Shuttle: Transfer, tel. 52/231488, carries passengers to and from Aeropuerto Chamonate, 15 km west of Copiapó via the Panamericana, for US$5 pp.

Car Rental: Rental agencies include Hertz, Avenida Copayapu 173, tel. 52/213522; Avis, Rómulo Peña 102, tel. 52/213966; Budget, Ramón Freire 466, tel. 52/218802; Retablo, Los Carrera 955, tel. 52/214427; and Rodaggio, Colipí 127, tel. 52/212153.

Rodaggio, Retablo, and Budget offer the cheapest unlimited mileage rates, around US$30 per day plus 18 percent IVA. High-clearance pickup trucks, though, cost at least US$50 plus IVA, 4WDs at least US$65 plus IVA.

VICINITY OF COPIAPÓ

The fact that Copiapó is not one of Chile's high-profile destinations means there are many off-the-beaten-track alternatives in the desert backcountry and the *puna*.

Valle de Copiapó

Southeast of Copiapó, a paved highway climbs the valley of the Río Copiapó as far as Las Juntas, 97 km away, where it becomes a gravel road that turns northeast toward the Argentine border. Copiapó's Buses Casther, at Chacabuco and Esperanza, tel. 52/218889, carries passengers up the valley.

The route actually begins at Paipote, eight km east, where the **Fundición Hernán Videla Lira** copper smelter is a dubious landmark that, historically, is one of Chile's worst polluters. The ever-observant Darwin, in 1835, noted that:

> *From having firewood, a smelting-furnace had formerly been built here; we found a solitary man in charge of it, whose sole employment was hunting guanacos.*

At the mining and farming village of Tierra Amarilla, 17 km from Copiapó, Spanish architect José Miguel Retornano designed the recently restored, Gothic-style **Iglesia Nuestra Señora de Loreto,** dating from 1898. Immediately to the southwest, a good gravel road climbs to the Sierra de Ojancos and the **Museo de Sitio Mina El Tránsito,** an *in situ* salvage project of a former gold mine that took up much of the slack when the silver deposits at Chañarcillo began to fail. Once a lively community but long since dismantled except for the **Casa del Administrador** (administrator's house, retaining some historic artifacts), a scattering of rusting machinery, and some open shafts, El Tránsito makes an engrossing side trip, also offering views of the modern copper mine at Candelaria to the south. For guided visits of Mina El Tránsito, contact Tierra Amarilla's Casa de la Cultura, tel. 52/320098.

To the south, about 22 km from Copiapó, mining mogul Apolinario Soto had his country house and built a landmark church, both desperately in need of restoration, at **Nantoco.** Soto acquired the property from Francisco Javier Ossa, also a figure in the early mining elite.

Copiapó journalist and politician José Joaquín Vallejo (1811–58), founder of the newspaper *El Copiapino,* resided at **Casa Jotabeche,** on the former Hacienda de Totoralillo at Km 34. Noted for gentle caricatures of his Chilean compatriots and malice toward Argentine rivals such as Domingo Sarmiento, Vallejo was a member of the so-called "Generation of 1842"; he took his pen name, Jotabeche, from the initials of his friend Juan Bautista Cheneau.

The railway from Caldera and Copiapó reached **Pabellón,** a grape-growing area 38 km from Copiapó, in 1854, though it did not open officially until January 1, 1855; by 1859, a spur linked Pabellón to the bonanza silver mine at Chañarcillo, 42 km to the southwest. The main railway line later reached **Los Loros,** 64 km from Copiapó, and its terminus at **San Antonio** in 1867. Modern drip irrigation is transforming this area into a major source of grapes—usually the first of the Chilean harvest—and other export-oriented crops.

Seven km south of San Antonio, a eastbound lateral leads to the archaeological site of **Viña del Cerro,** a national monument where Diaguita and Inka peoples milled copper ore and smelted it in more than two dozen charcoal-fired ovens.

Chañarcillo

Discovered on May 16, 1832, by muleteer and prospector Juan Godoy, the silver mine of Chañarcillo rendered such great wealth that, by 1860, the community that grew up alongside it (by then named for Godoy himself) boasted an impressive infrastructure worthy of many modern Chilean towns—church, school, hospital, theater, and police station. By 1859, it had a railroad spur to Pabellón, and by 1865 it had grown to more than 7,000 inhabitants. Yields fell rapidly after 1870, though, and water in the shafts eventually made further exploitation impossible. Other than a solitary well marked by cluster of trees, all that remains of Juan Godoy are stone foundations, a few adobe walls, and a plundered cemetery.

There are two ways to reach the ruins. The easier one is to follow the Panamericana south to Km 59, where a smooth but dusty road to Mina Bandurrias, an inactive open-pit iron mine, also leads to Chañarcillo. From Pabellón, in the upper Copiapó valley, a rugged dirt road, passable with high clearance and considerable skill but easier with 4WD, follows the abandoned rail spur over the Portezuelo La Viuda ("Widow's Pass") to Chañarcillo. Just before the Portezuelo, a side road climbs precipitously northwest to the abandoned **Mina Tres Marías,** for some of the region's best views.

Parque Nacional Nevado Tres Cruces

Skirting the Argentine border almost directly east of Copiapó, Parque Nacional Nevado Tres Cruces consists of two distinct sectors, totaling about 61,000 hectares about 4,500 meters above sea level. Both sectors protect high-altitude wetlands and surrounding *puna* with abundant wildlife; flamingos feed and other aquatic birds feed and nest in the shallow saline lagoons, while vicuñas and guanacos graze the surrounding grasslands.

The larger, more northerly **Sector Laguna Santa Rosa** consists of 49,000 hectares of which its namesake body of water is a relatively small feature; it also contains about half the sprawling **Salar de Maricunga.** Near the lagoon proper, at the western edge of the sector, Conaf has a very small *refugio* with room to sleep and cook—but no toilet facilities—with a new campground still under consideration.

Its eponymous lagoon comprises a much larger part of the 12,000-hectare **Sector Laguna del Negro Francisco,** about 50 km to the south. While flamingos nest in Brazil, Peru, Bolivia, and Argentina, 6,000 to 8,000 migrate here every summer to feed on plankton and crustaceans in its shallow waters. More than half are Andean flamingos, nearly all the rest Chilean flamingos, while the rare James flamingo is present in smaller numbers. Andean geese and gulls, plus giant and horned coots, are abundant.

At the upper section of Laguna del Negro Francisco, Conaf's spacious **Refugio Laguna del Negro Francisco** once belonged to the Chilean military, who equipped it with electricity, kitchen facilities, snug beds, and toilet facilities, including hot showers. Rates are US$8.50 pp.

Sector Laguna Santa Rosa is 146 km from Copiapó via Ruta 31, the international highway to Argentina, and another dusty road that leads eastward up the Quebrada de Paipote. Ruta 31 continues to the north edge of the Salar de Maricunga, where there's a Chilean immigration and customs post for those continuing to the 4,726-meter Paso San Francisco and the Argentine provinces of La Rioja and Catamarca; all vehicles must stop at immigration and customs, even those not crossing the border.

From Laguna Santa Rosa, Sector Laguna del Negro Francisco is another 85 km south via a road that loops past the former gold mine of Mina Marte and follows the Río Astaburuaga to the lake. From the east end of the intersection with the Mina Marte road, it's possible to continue north through the Salar de Maricunga and the mining town of El Salvador to the Panamericana at Chañaral.

Most visitors arrive by rental car—4WD is advisable but not essential—though Conaf's Copiapó office may be able to offer transportation suggestions. Copiapó adventure travel operators occasionally offer excursions into the area.

Cerro Ojos Del Salado

Though it lies beyond the national park boundaries, 6,885-meter Ojos del Salado is South America's second-highest peak (after Argentina's 6,962-meter Aconcagua) and a favorite climbers' destination. It is also the world's highest active volcano, though the last significant eruptions were in 1937 and 1956. While top physical condition and acclimatization are essential for climbers, it is not a technical ascent except for the last 50 meters to the crater, which requires some rock-climbing skills.

For Ojos del Salado, directly on the border, the best season is October to April. Foreign

> *While flamingos nest in Brazil, Peru, Bolivia, and Argentina, 6,000 to 8,000 migrate here every summer to feed on plankton and crustaceans in the shallow waters of the Laguna del Negro Francisco.*

climbers require permission from Difrol, the Chilean Foreign Ministry's Dirección de Fronteras y Límites (for general requirements, see the On the Road chapter). Once obtained, this permission must be presented to the Carabineros detachment at the north end of the Salar de Maricunga.

Up to a dozen climbers can sleep at the **Refugio Universidad de Atacama** at the 5,100-meter level, while another 24 can occupy the **Refugio César Tejos**, at the 5,750-meter level, which has kitchen facilities and chemical toilets.

CALDERA

As a port, Caldera dates from 1850, when William Wheelwright's Copiapó railway transformed what was a tiny fishing camp into, at least briefly, the second most important port in the country. Shipping silver from the bonanza mine at Chañarcillo, it supplanted Copiapó's original port, Puerto Viejo, 35 km to the south on the Bahía de Copiapó, but faltered as silver deposits diminished. Today it ships copper concentrates from the Candelaria mine near Copiapó and spring grapes and other fruits from the upper Copiapó valley.

It also hosts hordes of beachgoers in January, February, and on weekends. Since the time of the railroad, Copiapinos have grown accustomed to weekends at the beach, and Caldera survived the collapse of Chañarcillo to become the region's most important *balneario;* completion of the Panamericana in the early 1950s made it more accessible for visitors from the north and south.

In the past decade or so, the broader, cleaner beaches at nearby Bahía Inglesa have superseded those at Caldera, but Caldera, with its historic architecture and active summer street life, remains the more interesting of the two. In the off-season, it feels more like a ghost town, and prices drop considerably, but fewer services are available.

THE CALDERA-COPIAPÓ RAILWAY

Frequently but erroneously claimed to be South America's first railway, the Caldera-Copiapó line opened in December of 1851 under the eye of Chile's President Manuel Bulnes. Officially known as the Compañía del Ferrocarril de Copiapó, it was really only the third on the continent—the Demerara Railway Company of British Guyana opened a route from Georgetown to the suburb of Plaisance in 1848, while Peru linked its port of Callao with the capital city of Lima via a 14-km line in 1851.

Still, completion of the 81-km line in less than two years (1849–51) was a remarkable achievement for its time. Later extended to Pabellón (37 km, by 1854, followed by a spur to Chañarcillo) and then to San Antonio (another 39 km, by 1867), it was the pride of the region during the silver boom.

Now resting at the Universidad de Atacama, the original steam locomotive known as *La Copiapó* (1850)—along with first-, second-, and third-class carriages (the differences among them are minimal)—last ran in 1961. For 40 years, the engineer was one Juan O'Donovan, who left Copiapó at 9 A.M. daily, arriving in Caldera at 1 P.M., then departing Caldera at 3 P.M. to arrive in Copiapó at 6:45 P.M.

At present, the line itself hangs on a thread. In 1986, a few years before the end of his dictatorship, General Pinochet signed a decree authorizing removal of the rails, but nature intervened—when rare heavy rains cut the Panamericana, only a rail shuttle kept the areas north and south in contact. Out of necessity, Pinochet signed a second decree annulling the first, but there has been no regular service since.

If local authorities have their way, the rails may sing again. The line has been the subject of a feasibility study to resurrect it as a tourist train, though the expense and limited tourist traffic make the project unlikely.

At the same time, the locomotive has become the subject of controversy as Caldera authorities argue that *La Copiapó* should reside within the recently restored train station (a national monument) at the port, but Copiapinos remain strongly opposed. The engine may never run again, but that doesn't mean it won't generate some steam.

Orientation

On the south shore of its namesake bay, Caldera is 75 km northwest of Copiapó and 92 km south of Chañaral via the Panamericana. Its center is a regular grid, based on the Plaza de Armas, whose streets trend northeast to southwest.

Avenida Diego de Almeyda, the main exit from the Panamericana, changes its name to Avenida Carvallo as it passes through town on the way to Bahía Inglesa, the region's prime beach destination.

Sights

As an historic port and contemporary bathing resort, Caldera is oriented toward the Costanera (waterfront). The central **Muelle de Pasajeros** (passenger pier) and antique **Muelle Fiscal** (government pier), though, are less important than the contemporary **Muelle Mecanizado** (mechanized pier), to the northwest, that ships Mina Candelaria's copper concentrates.

Restoration of Caldera's 19th-century **Estación de Ferrocarril** (railroad station), Chile's oldest, is complete; it now serves partly as a museum but primarily as an events center and exhibition hall. Restoration has probably not completely arrested the termite damage; a section of one wall has been left uncovered, but glassed in, to demonstrate the wattle-and-daub—or lath and plaster—construction style. Unfortunately, there is no exhibit about the station's history, though there are remnants of the rails that once ran here.

Facing the Muelle de Pasajeros, the former 19th-century **Aduana de Caldera** (customshouse) once served as the British consulate and is now the **Centro Cultural Universidad de Atacama**, Gana 100-B, tel. 52/316756. In the basement, its **Museo Histórico de Caldera** is a congeries of photographs, postcards, and just plain junk that really doesn't say much about the town itself. Special exhibits, mostly painting and photography, can be worth a glance. It keeps highly unusual hours—Tuesday through Saturday 4–11 P.M. in summer, 9 A.M.–1 P.M. and 4:30–8 P.M. weekdays the rest of the year. Admission costs US$.35.

Like most Chilean towns, Caldera features a central **Plaza de Armas.** Unlike most Chilean towns, its plaza is not really the focus of local street life, but the **Iglesia San Vicente** (1862), which reaches a height of 36 meters with its Gothic tower, is a distinguished landmark. The less distinguished **Municipalidad** (City Hall) dates from 1855. On summer nights, the **Peatonal Gana,** between the plaza and the Costanera, is the site of a lively summer crafts market.

East toward the Panamericana, along Avenida Diego de Almeyda, forged iron fences enclose the not-so-lively **Cementerio Laico** (1876), the country's oldest non-Catholic cemetery and a national monument. Northern Europeans, primarily Britons and Germans, occupy most of the graves, but *feng shui* must have played a role in siting the elaborate Chinese crypts.

Daily in summer and on weekends the rest of the year, the motor launch *Mizpa I,* tel. 09/8841403, conducts hourlong tours (US$2 pp) of the **Bahía de Caldera,** leaving from the Muelle de Pasajeros (passenger jetty) at the foot of Gana.

Accommodations

Unlike Copiapó, Caldera's prices are highly seasonal, reaching their peak in January and February. The rest of the year, prices moderate considerably, though not much at the very lowest level—where accommodations are pretty dire, in any event.

Residencial Molina, Montt 346, tel. 52/316860, is bottom-of-the-barrel budget accommodation for US$6 pp with shared bath. **Residencial Millaray,** Cousiño 331, tel. 52/315528, is comparable. **Residencial Palermo,** Cifuentes 150, tel. 52/315847, is marginally better for US$11 pp.

Rates at **Hotel Montriri,** Tocornal 371, tel. 52/319055, are US$17/25 s/d for passable, but less than immaculate, rooms—upstairs is better. Friendly **Hotel Costanera,** Wheelwright 543, tel./fax 52/316007, is an excellent midrange choice, charging US$18/32 s/d with for spacious rooms with no frills except breakfast and parking.

Well-maintained despite its unimpressive exterior, **Hotel Montecarlo,** Carvallo 627, tel./fax 52/315388, montecarlohotel@123click.cl, has an occasionally distracted staff and offers no IVA discounts. Rates are US$24/32 s/d.

Hostería Puerta del Sol, Wheelwright 750, tel. 52/315205 or 315507, looks good with its small pool and gardens, but some of the beds are terrible, the hot water can be iffy, and the streetside rooms on Wheelwright get a great deal of foot traffic. Rates are US$24/40 s/d discounting IVA.

Food and Entertainment

Empanadópolis, Carvallo 696, is the Caldera branch of Copiapó's specialty fast-food outlet. Most other places specialize in seafood, such as **Tierras Lejanas,** Edwards 425, a superb *picada* with entrées in the US$4–7 range. Other, more standard seafood choices include **Nuevo Miramar,** Gana 90, tel. 52/315381; **New Charles,** Ossa Cerda 350, tel. 52/315348; **Ramazzi,** Avenida Prat 57, tel. 52/315226; and **Il Piron di Oro,** Cousiño 218, tel. 52/315109.

The **Bartholomeo Pub,** Wheelwright 747, tel. 52/316413, offers an imaginative assortment of Mexican and Asian dishes (including sushi) in the US$5 and up range. **El Teatro,** Gana 12, tel. 52/316768, serves Peruvian food and also offers live music.

La Caleta, at the corner of Ossa Cerda and Wheelwright, is a popular pub with live music in summer.

Services and Information

Postal: Correos de Chile is at Edwards 325.

Telephone: Telefónica CTC Chile, Edwards 360, has long-distance telephone services, while Entel is at the corner of Gallo and Cousiño. Caldera's area code is 52, the same as Copiapó's.

Tourist Office: In January and February, Sernatur maintains a local representative at the municipal Dirección de Relaciones Públicas, tel. 52/316891, in the restored railroad station. Hours are 8:30 A.M.–2 P.M. and 3–5:35 P.M. daily.

The rest of the year, municipal representatives do their best to deal with requests for information. Hours are the same, on weekdays only.

Transportation

Long-distance bus services resemble those to and from Copiapó, an hour to the south, but fewer companies operate here—though some through buses will stop for passengers on the Panamericana. Tur-Bus, Gallo 149, tel. 52/316832, and Pullman Bus, at Gallo and Vallejos, tel. 52/316585, have the most extensive routes. Pullman Carmelita, which also has long-distance services, is at Ossa Varas 710, along with regional carriers Casther, tel. 52/316300, and Recabarren, tel. 52/315034, which both go to Copiapó.

Faster *taxi colectivos* also go to Copiapó, from a spot on Cifuentes just south of Ossa Varas.

VICINITY OF CALDERA

Gruta del Padre Negro

Near the rotunda at the junction of Avenida Carvallo and Canal Beagle at the western end of town, atop a rugged outcrop, Colombian priest Crisógono Sierra y Velásquez built a chapel that, with time and religious murals by painter Luis Cerda, has become a significant pilgrimage site. It's open 9 A.M.–1:30 daily, though it's possible to peek in at the murals at other hours.

Faro Punta Caldera

On a rocky headland five km west of town, Caldera's lighthouse dates from 1875, though it is now solar-powered and fully automated. The building proper is fenced off from the public but, with permission from the Gobernación Marítima (port authority) in Caldera, it's possible to visit.

Bahía Inglesa

From Caldera, a smooth paved highway and a parallel bicycle path connect it to Bahía Inglesa, which takes its name from the British privateers who harbored here in the 17th century. Its sheltered crescent beach, with little surf and relatively shallow waters, make it a favorite family destination, though it can get breezy enough for windsurfers. The *malecón* (waterfront promenade) is the site of a substantial summer crafts market.

Morro Ballena, Avenida el Morro s/n, tel. 09/8863673, offers excursions in and around Bahía Inglesa, including diving trips, and goes as far afield as Reserva Nacional Pingüino de Humboldt, on the border between Region III (Atacama) and Region IV (Coquimbo).

Accommodations: Hotel El Coral, Avenida El Morro 564, tel. 52/315331, charges US$44 s or d for modern, comfortable rooms, some of which have no exterior windows, but this is a bargain by Bahía Inglesa standards. The far more elaborate **Apart Hotel Rocas de Bahía,** Avenida El Morro s/n, tel./fax 52/316005 or 52/316032, rocasdebahia@entelchile.net, is a stylish luxury facility charging US$75/83 s/d with breakfast, US$82/95 with half board, and US$87/107 with full board. Its Santiago contact is at Avenida Pedro de Valdivia 1783, Local A, Providencia, tel. 2/2238670, fax 2/2742509. While obviously not cheap, by international standards it's excellent value for money.

Food: Part of its namesake hotel, **El Coral,** tel. 52/315331, has good seafood starting at US$4 for a fixed-price meal, though à la carte items are significantly dearer. **El Plateao,** on the waterfront at Avenida El Morro 756, specializes in delectable fresh fruit juices, but it also offers snacks and meals.

Transportation: *Taxi colectivos* run constantly between Caldera and Bahía Inglesa, which are only about six km apart.

Santuario de la Naturaleza Granito Orbicular

North of Caldera, occasional sandy beaches interrupt rocky headlands until, at about the 12 km point, the Panamericana passes this small roadside cluster of elliptical and spheroidal curiosities—covering an area of only 375 square meters—that are really more conglomerates than true granites.

CHAÑARAL

The easiest access point to increasingly popular Parque Nacional Pan de Azúcar, the crumbly but picturesque mining port of Chañaral is interesting in its own right for many of the wrong reasons—primarily the natural and man-made disasters this small city experienced during the

20th century. In 1922, a tsunami killed 22 people, in 1940 a major flood and debris flow claimed many more lives, and a 1970 earthquake reached 7.0 on the Richter scale.

Chañaral's biggest disaster, though, is the striking white crescent beach that formerly began at what is now called the Costanera, but that now extends much farther west, as decades of runoff from the economically dominant highland copper mines at Potrerillos and El Salvador have deposited so many thousands of tons of toxic sediments that no one dares use it. The worst pollution, which began around 1920, finally ceased when, in 1988, local residents obtained a court order requiring Codelco to build containment ponds at higher altitudes.

Chañaral actually dates from the early 19th century, when Diego de Almeyda uncovered the Las Ánimas copper deposits. Because of the proximity of (formerly) U.S.-run Anaconda mining company, and the strategic significance of copper, U.S. Marines were stationed in Chañaral during World War II. When the Allende government nationalized copper in the early 1970s, the mines passed to Codelco's administration.

Orientation

Chañaral is 167 km northwest of Copiapó via the Panamericana, which runs east-west as it passes through town. Set among rocky headlands at the foot of the Sierra de las Ánimas, it has a compact center whose main streets more or less follow the contours of the hills, connected to each other by staircases. One of few level streets, the "Costanera" formerly fronted on the beach but now sits several hundred meters inland. One short block south, Merino Jarpa is the main commercial street, while just to the north, the Panamericana follows a route that used to lie beneath the Pacific.

Sights

Chañaral has three national monuments, two of them churches: the Catholic **Iglesia Nuestra Señora del Carmen** (1865), on the east side of the Plaza de Armas, along with its adjacent **Casa Molina** (1904); and the Georgian-style, Protestant **Iglesia Presbiteriana de Chañaral** (1861).

Chañaral's biggest surprise is the **Museo de Historia Natural Rodulfo B. Philippi.** Much more and better than its name alone would suggest, it has an engaged curator and staff who are constantly improving exhibits on entomology, marine biology, and archaeology. Raided by the Chilean military who, in the early 1980s, absconded with large parts of the collections, it still holds a remarkable computerized collection of 700 historic photographs of Chañaral, surrounding localities and mines, including Salvador and Potrerillos, due to be placed onto an Internet website. The museum, at Buin 818, is open 9 A.M.–1 P.M. daily except Sunday; admission costs US$.70.

About two km west of town via the Panamericana, the mechanized pier at Chañaral's dilapidated port of **Barquito** ships both refined copper and copper concentrate that arrives from El Salvador and Potrerillos on ancient railcars (the railway dates from 1871, though the cars aren't quite *that* old). It also imports copper from other Chilean ports for processing at El Salvador.

Accommodations

So-so **Hotel Jiménez,** Merino Jarpa 551, tel. 52/480328, is Chañaral's cheapest at US$7 pp with shared bath, twice that with private bath. Directly across the street, **Hotel Marina,** Merino Jarpa 562, tel. 52/480325, lacks hot water but it's clean, has good beds, and is superior to the Jiménez; it's even a little cheaper at US$5 pp.

The best value in town, though, is modern, well-kept **Hostal Sutivan,** Comercio 365, tel. 52/489123, charging US$13/18 s/d with private bath; it's popular enough that reservations are advisable.

Well-established **Hostería Chañaral,** Müller 268, tel. 52/480050, fax 52/480554, pandeazucar@entelchile.net, has small but comfortable rooms, set among quiet gardens, and friendly service for US$30/37 s/d. It occupies the former site of a 19th-century copper smelter; in fact, parts of the walls came from the smelter.

Food

Besides several standard *comedores* along the Panamericana, where through buses stop for meal breaks, Chañaral has good seafood at **Nuria,**

Yungay 434; **El Rincón Porteño,** Merino Jarpa 567; and the restaurant at Hostería Chañaral. West of town, toward the port of Barquito, **Alicanto,** Panamericana Sur 49, tel. 52/481168, is worth the two-km walk to get there.

Services and Information

Money: Banco de Crédito is at Los Carrera and Maipú, but it has no ATM.

Postal: Correos de Chile is at Comercio and Las Heras.

Telephone: CTC Telefónica Chile is at Merino Jarpa 506, Entel at Merino Jarpa 1197. Chañaral's area code is 52.

Tourist Office: From December through March, the municipal Oficina de Información Turística, Merino Jarpa 539, tel. 09/6463701, is open 8:30 A.M.–1:30 P.M. and 4–10:30 P.M. daily.

Transportation

Many north-south buses pass through on the Panamericana, but several companies have offices in town, including Tur-Bus, Merino Jarpa 858, tel. 52/481012; Flota Barrios, Merino Jarpa 567, tel. 52/480894; and Pullman Bus, Los Baños 200 at Merino Jarpa, tel. 52/480153, which goes to the interior destinations of Diego de Almagro and El Salvador.

Turismo Chango, Panamericana s/n, tel. 52/4-80484 or 52/480668, provides seemingly improvised service to Parque Nacional Pan de Azúcar, though it's officially scheduled at 8:30 A.M. and 3 P.M. daily in summer. It leaves not from its offices, but from a spot opposite the Municipalidad, at Merino Jarpa and Los Baños, though it also makes a run through town looking for passengers.

Getting Around

Rodrigo Zepeda Vecchiola, tel. 52/481092 or 09/5428936, zyv@chilesat.net, at the junction of the Panamericana Norte and Merino Jarpa, rents cars.

PARQUE NACIONAL PAN DE AZÚCAR

Copious marine wildlife, scattered rare flora, and a starkly beautiful desert coastline are the big draws to Parque Nacional Pan de Azúcar, a 43,769-hectare reserve straddling the border between the regions of Copiapó and Antofagasta. Most visitors see only the coastal sections, but those who manage to visit the fog-sodden uplands find a diversity of flora and even the occasional guanaco, at altitudes up to 900 meters.

Pan de Azúcar's humid coastal environment rarely experiences rain as such, but it is often overcast until late morning from the *camanchaca* that rises out of the ocean. Temperatures are mild—the average daytime maximum temperature is 19.3°C, while the nighttime minimum is 12.3°C. Combined with sea breezes, these temperatures can feel even cooler, and a sweater or light jacket is a good idea.

Sights

At sheltered **Caleta Pan de Azúcar,** a traditional fishing camp where families have been able to maintain their livelihood despite the presence of the park, fishermen fillet the day's catch on the rocks, while brown pelicans fight it out over the scraps. The area has a good beach, though the surface is steep.

Other beaches of interest are **Playa Los Piqueros,** a short distance to the south beneath the landmark hill of Cerro Soldado, and **Playa Blanca,** on Caleta Coquimbo, near the park's southern entrance.

The park's most popular excursion is to the offshore **Isla Pan de Azúcar** where, besides 2,000–3,000 Humboldt penguins and numerous brown pelicans, there are olivaceous and red-footed cormorants, blue-footed boobies, Dominican gulls, and other seabirds. There are also otters (rarely seen) and substantial breeding colonies of southern sea lions. In summer and on weekends, there are frequent launch excursions to the island, but these are fewer the rest of the year. Landing is not permitted, but launches can go close enough to see both birds and mammals clearly. (See below for more details.)

Excursions

At Caleta Pan de Azúcar, Rodrigo Carvajal Robles, tel. 09/6411674 or 09/7430011, carvajalrodrigo@hotmail.com, offers one-hour launch excursions along the coast of Isla Pan de Azúcar (landing on the island is not permitted, but there are still good views of penguins and sea lions). Charges are US$6 pp based on a six-person voyage, but with a minimum charge of US$35; smaller groups must pay more per person.

Accommodations and Food

Conaf has ample campsites at **Caleta Pan de Azúcar** and at **Playa Piqueros;** for visitors without their own vehicles, the Pan de Azúcar campground has better access to services. Sites with fire pits, picnic tables, and shade cost US$8.50 per day for up to six people, while those with no frills cost half that. Both types of sites have access to clean, modern toilets and 20 liters of potable water per day, but no showers.

Conaf also rents several *cabañas*, sleeping up to six people with kitchen facilities and solar panel electricity, for US$35 between April and October, US$60 the rest of the year. Demand is particularly high in summer and on weekends, when reservations are desirable; contact Conaf's regional office, Juan Martínez 55, Copiapó, tel. 52/239067.

El Changuito, Caleta Pan de Azúcar's only restaurant, has *dorado* and other fresh fish—but ask for it *a la plancha* or you'll get it fried—and homemade *pan amasado* (kneaded bread). There's also a small grocery, and fresh fish is available directly off the boat.

Information

At Caleta Pan de Azúcar, Conaf's Centro de Información Ambiental is open 8:30 A.M.–12:30 P.M. and 2–6 P.M. daily. Besides slide talks about park ecology, it also features a cactarium for those unable to visit the uplands. At the southern entrance from Chañaral, Conaf rangers usually collect an admission fee of US$7 for foreigners, US$2 for children up to 18 years of age. For Chilean residents, fees are US$2.50 for adults and US$1 for children; foreigners over age 60 may pay Chilean rates. Note that no fee is collected at the eastern entrance.

Transportation

Turismo Chango runs buses to and from Chañaral, 30 km to the south via a smooth gravel road

(see the Chañaral entry for details). It's also possible to hitchhike from Chañaral; you can also hire a taxi in Chañaral (though it's necessary to pay both directions) or rent a car.

Southbound cyclists and even motorists will find it more interesting (and for cyclists, easier) to approach the park from the east, from a poorly marked turnoff at Las Bombas, a wide spot in the road at Km 1,014 on the Panamericana, about 45 km northwest of Chañaral. The good dirt road goes directly down the Quebrada Pan de Azúcar all the way to the coast.

EL SALVADOR AND VICINITY

From Chañaral, a smooth two-lane blacktop road climbs the valley of the Río del Salado east to El Salvador, an orderly Codelco company town 129 km to the east and 2,300 meters above sea level. The famous Brazilian architect Oscar Niemeyer devised its street plan, laid out in the shape of a Roman helmet; the city dates from 1959, when its copper deposits superseded those of nearby **Potrerillos,** which continues to operate a smelter and sulfuric acid plant. The operation was once owned by the Andes Mining Company, a subsidiary of the U.S.-based Anaconda Corporation that dominated Chile's economy for decades, it came under state control in the 1970s.

As an isolated company town, El Salvador has amenities that many larger Chilean cities lack, including an airport, a stadium that's home to a first-division soccer team, a cinema and museum, and sports and social clubs. The presence of Potrerillos means, however, that it is also one of the most polluted places in all of Chile.

From El Salvador and Potrerillos, a good but unpaved road goes east and then south to a customs post at the north end of the **Salar de Maricunga** and then to Parque Nacional Nevado Tres Cruces, where it turns east toward the border crossing, the 4,726-meter Paso San Francisco. From the border, the road continues to the Argentine cities of La Rioja and Catamarca, capitals of their namesake provinces. All vehicles must stop at Chilean customs, even those not crossing the border. Carry extra fuel.

Accommodations and Food

Hostería El Salvador, Avenida Potrerillos 003, tel. 52/475749, costs US$7/13 s/d with shared bath, US$18/30 s/d with private bath, but without breakfast. Catering primarily to mining executives and engineers, **Hotel Camino del Inca,** Avenida El Tofo 330, tel. 52/475252, charges US$56/63 s/d with breakfast.

Cosquín, Avenida 18 de Septiembre 2312, serves workingmen's lunches. For better fare, try Hotel Camino del Inca.

Transportation

Aeropuerto El Salvador is 16 km west of town. LanExpress, Coquimbo 1, tel. 52/475447, flies Monday, Tuesday, Wednesday, Friday, and Sunday to Copiapó, La Serena, and Santiago.

Buses to Chañaral and other points on the Panamericana leave from the Pullman Bus, at Avenida Potrerillos Norte and Avenida O' Higgins, tel. 52/475349.

VALLENAR

In a valley so deep and narrow that the Panamericana passes high above it on a bridge over the Río Huasco, the mining and agricultural service center of Vallenar stretches east toward the Andes and west toward the Pacific Ocean. The Irish-born colonial governor Ambrosio O'Higgins, father of Chilean independence hero Bernardo O'Higgins and later the Viceroy of Peru, chose the site and named the city "Villa de San Ambrosio de Vallenar" for his hometown of Ballenary in County Sligo (though there is some evidence he came from County Meath).

Vallenar is home to one unique Chilean product, the white dessert wine known as *pajarete,* and is also known for local specialties such as olives and river shrimp. From here, it's also possible to head east toward Alto del Carmen, one of Chile's main *pisco* zones, or west toward Huasco and Parque Nacional Llanos de Challe, one of the best places to see the *desierto florido,* or flowering desert.

Orientation

Vallenar is 145 km south of Copiapó and 188 km north of La Serena via the Panamericana. While the Puente Huasco across the valley bypasses the city, eastbound roads descend into the town center at each end of the bridge. At the south end of the bridge, a paved highway heads west toward the fishing port and beach resort of Huasco.

The city itself sits on the north bank of the Río Huasco. Most services are on or near Plaza Ambrosio O'Higgins, the historical center of the city, or on the east-west Avenida Prat.

Sights

Most of Vallenar's buildings are relatively new wooden or modern concrete structures, since a 1922 earthquake destroyed most of its characteristic adobes. One building that survived is the **Iglesia Parroquial San Ambrosio,** distinguished by its shiny copper dome, at the southeast corner of Plaza O'Higgins.

The **Museo del Huasco,** Sargento Aldea 742, contains exhibits on regional mineralogy, paleontology, botany, zoology, archaeology, and history. Its outstanding photo collection includes several of the aftermath of the 1922 earthquake. Hours are 10 A.M.–1 P.M. and 3:30–6 P.M. weekdays only. Admission charges are nominal.

One of the most positive efforts to improve the livability of any Chilean city in the past few years has been Vallenar's reclamation of the **Paseo Ribereño,** a green belt on the north bank of the Río Huasco. With broad lawns, shady trees, basketball and tennis courts, and barbecue pits, it's become one of the most popular hangouts in the city, especially on weekends.

Accommodations

The quality of accommodations at Vallenar is better than at most comparably sized Chilean cities, even at simple budget choices such as **Residencial Oriental,** Serrano 720, tel. 51/613889, where singles with shared bath cost US$7 pp, while rooms with private bath cost US$10/13 s/d. Smallish but spotless rooms at **Hotel Viña del Mar,** Serrano 611, tel. 51/611478, cost US$9 pp with shared bath, US$14/26 s/d with private bath, cable TV, and parking.

Residencial L&M, Serrano 1378, tel./fax 51/611756, is one of the better budget picks in town—friendly, tidy, and constantly being upgraded—for US$12 pp. In an excellent location, friendly **Hostal Real Quillahue,** Plaza O'Higgins s/n, tel. 51/619992, has small but impeccable rooms with private bath, good beds, cable TV, and an ample breakfast for US$15 pp.

Plain but friendly and nearly flawless, **Hostal Vall,** Aconcagua 455, tel. 51/611266, is one of Vallenar's top values for US$17/25 with private bath, cable TV, and parking included.

Clean but worn, **Hostal Camino del Rey,** Ramirez 731, tel. 51/615507 or 51/613184, has plain but spacious rooms, some with antiquated plumbing and electricity, as well as suspect beds. Rates are US$21/32 s/d with private bath, US$14 pp with shared bath. There's a second **Hostal Camino del Rey** at Merced 943, tel. 51/613184.

Despite its unimpressive faux brick exterior, **Hotel Garra de León** Serrano 1052, tel./fax 51/613753, offers spacious, well-decorated and maintained rooms for US$45/54. Clearly the city's best choice, spacious **Hostería Vallenar,** Alonso de Ercilla 848, tel. 51/614370, offers *superior* rooms with private bath (shower only) and breakfast for US$58/67; *lujo* (luxury) rooms with tubs go for US$67/77.

Food

At the **Mercado Municipal,** at the corner of Santiago and Serrano, several *cocinerías* offer cheap but nutritious meals. The **Cuba Café,** Prat 290, serves espresso, difficult to find in provincial cities.

Il Bocatto, Plaza O'Higgins s/n, tel. 51/61-4609, serves moderately priced pizza, sandwiches, and other light meals. The reliable nationwide chain **Bavaria** is at Serrano 802, tel. 51/613504.

The seafood restaurant **El Galeón,** Ramírez 934, tel. 51/614641, also has live music some nights. In the former railroad station, **Don Baucha,** Avenida Matta s/n, is a new branch of a fine seafood restaurant in the port of Huasco.

The **Club Social,** Prat 899, tel. 51/616403, serves a variety of Chilean, international, and seafood dishes, with a US$4.50 special.

Entertainment and Events

Within the Centro Cultural Vallenar, the **Cine Municipal,** Prat 1094, tel. 51/611501, shows current films.

Swimming at the **Piscina Municipal,** across from Hostería Vallenar at the corner of Alonso de Ercilla and Sargento Aldea, costs US$3.50, including a soft drink. On the grounds of the Piscina Municipal, **CubAire** has live salsa on weekends.

January 5's **Fundación de la Ciudad** commemorates the anniversary of Ambrosio O'Higgins's founding of the city in 1789. Another summer event, the **Festival Vallenar Canta,** is a musical celebration toward the end of the month.

Services and Information

Money: Banco de Crédito has an ATM at Prat 1070.

Postal: Correos de Chile is on the north side of Plaza O'Higgins, near the corner with Vallejos.

Telephone and Internet: Entel long-distance offices are at Prat 1040, between Brasil and Colchagua. Vallenar's area code is 51.

Internet access at the Cyber Café, Santiago 422, tel. 51/342850, costs US$2 per hour.

Medical: Contact Hospital Vallenar at Merced and Talca, tel. 51/611202.

Tourist Information: At the south end of the Huasco bridge, on the east side of the Panamericana, there's a kiosk intended for municipal tourist information, but it's only rarely staffed. If it's not open, the next best alternative is the Museo del Huasco (see above).

Transportation

All Vallenar's long-distance bus companies have finally moved from downtown offices to locales in or near the main Terminal de Buses, at Avenida Matta and Prat, across from the old train station. There are frequent services north and south along the Panamericana with Tas Choapa, tel. 51/613822; Flota Barrios, tel. 51/614295; Carmelita, tel. 51/613037; Libac, tel. 51/613755; Fénix Pullman Norte; and Expreso Norte.

Two key companies have their own newer terminals: Tur-Bus, at Prat 32, tel. 51/611738, and Pullman Bus, at the corner of Prat and Atacama, tel. 51/619587 or 51/612461. Both have extensive services in both directions.

For transportation to the village of Freirina and the port and seaside resort of Huasco, and to the village of Alto del Carmen in the upper Huasco valley, try Buses Tal, at the main terminal, tel. 51/612574. Colectivo Via Mar, Serrano 959, provides shared taxi service to Huasco as soon as there are four passengers.

Sample destinations and times include Copiapó (US$4.50, two hours), La Serena (US$5, 2.5 hours), Caldera (US$5, three hours), and Santiago (US$16, nine hours).

VICINITY OF VALLENAR

Huasco
From the south end of the Puente Huasco, a smooth paved highway parallels the river west to the village of **Freirina,** founded in 1752. Its **Iglesia Santa Rosa de Lima,** dating from 1869, is a national monument, as is the neoclassical **Edificio Los Portales** (1870), whose nine-arched portal faces the Plaza de Armas.

From Freirina, the road continues to the beach resort and fishing port of **Huasco,** suitable for either a day trip or an overnight, but it gets crowded on weekends. Most locals head for the **Playa Grande,** which stretches east and north from Avenida Craig, the main commercial street, but the **Playa Chica** is closer to hotels and restaurants.

Accommodations and Food: Ocean-view **Hostal San Fernando,** Pedro de Valdivia 176, tel./fax 51/531726, offers roomy but aging accommodations with shared bath but without breakfast for US$7.50 pp, but a recent addition costs US$20 s or d with private bath. **Hostería Huasco,** Ignacio Carrera Pinto 110, tel. 51/531026, is a slightly pricier alternative, with traditional style, for US$32/38.

For lunch or dinner, try the seafood at **Don Baucha,** Craig 134, tel. 51/531028.

Transportation: Buses and *taxi colectivos* run frequently between Huasco and Vallenar.

Parque Nacional Llanos de Challe
North of Huasco Bajo, a good but unpaved road parallels the coast for 50 km to the dilapidated but increasingly popular beach town of **Carrizal Bajo.** En route it passes through the coastal Sector Punta Los Pozos of Parque Nacional Llanos de Challe, a 45,708-hectare unit whose main attraction is its rare but ephemeral flora. There is a contiguous inland sector of the park directly inland from Carrizal Bajo.

Inundated by campers from Vallenar and land sharks gambling that improvement of the road north to Puerto Viejo and Caldera will drive real estate prices through the roof, Carrizal Bajo has a crumbling church that's slated for restoration. It's infamous for a 1986 incident in which the insurrectionist Frente Patriótico Manuel Rodríguez (FPMR) landed a load of Cuban weapons here and shipped some of them to Viña del Mar. Later that same year, the FPMR assaulted General Pinochet's motorcade in the Cajón del Maipo near Santiago, killing several bodyguards but failing to touch the general.

> *In rare rainy years, Llanos de Challe is the place to observe the desierto florido, when the desert floor erupts with wildflowers.*

In rare rainy years, Llanos de Challe is *the* place to observe the *desierto florido,* when the desert floor erupts with wildflowers. It's not a common event, though—French naturalist Claudio Gay went north in 1831 in search of this fleeting carpet of color, but he had to wait until 1840 to actually observe the phenomenon.

There were major *desierto florido* events in 1983, 1987, 1991, and 1997 (when 96 mm of rain fell in only 15 hours), but erratic rainfall distribution makes finding the best spots a challenge. Even then, the phenomenon is brief as the rain quickly percolates into the sandy soils and the sun soon evaporates standing water on the desert floor. September is usually the best month, but the phenomenon can happen at any time between July and November.

Llanos de Challe's signature species is the *garra de león* ("lion's claw," *Leontochir ovallei*), a fleshy-stemmed creeper whose multiple flowers, either yellow or red, form a single mass. Endemic to parts of the Atacama coast and first collected by Javier Ovalle in 1866, it has been the unfortunate target of seed poachers and introduced to Japan as an ornamental. There are many other wild-flowers, though, as well as numerous cacti, and mammals including guanacos and foxes.

Conaf has been planning to install a camp-ground at Punta Los Pozos, but the project is on the back burner at present. The nearest for-mal accommodations are at Huasco, though many people camp informally at or near Car-rizal Bajo.

There is occasional public transport from Val-lenar to Bajo Carrizal via Huasco. Southbound motorists or cyclists have the option of turning west onto a gravel road at Algarrobal, 52 km north of Vallenar, while northbound travelers can turn northwest at a junction 15 km north of Vallenar.

Alto del Carmen

About 40 km up the valley from Huasco, the mountain town of Alto del Carmen is home to the distillery of its namesake *pisco* but, unfortu-nately, it's not open for tours or tasting. There are passable accommodations, though, at **Residen-cial El Asadón del Valle,** Padre Alonso García s/n, tel. 51/617695, for US$6 pp with shared bath, US$14 d with private bath. It also has a restaurant, or you can try **Quitapena,** at the western approach to town.

While Alto del Carmen may not offer *pisco* tasting, the village of San Félix, another 25 km up the valley of the Río Huasco on a gravel road, holds a **Festival de la Vendimia** (grape harvest festival) in late February.

Coquimbo Region

North of the Chilean heartland, the region of Coquimbo is close enough to Santiago for a long weekend, but it deserves more. Chileans and Ar-gentines flock to the beaches in and around La Serena in the summer, but spring and fall are less crowded and cheaper. Even winter, when southern Chile stays in out of the rain, Co-quimbo often enjoys warm clear days—if cool nights.

Coquimbo has several protected areas, the best of which are Parque Nacional Pingüino de Humboldt, Parque Nacional Bosque de Fray Jorge, and Reserva Nacional Las Chinchillas. Other enticements include the Elqui valley (home to *pisco* and to poet Gabriela Mistral) and the chance to scan the southern constellations on nighttime tours and learn the latest in astronomy from professionals at international observato-ries. Opportunities for outdoor recreation, par-ticularly hiking, mountain biking, and horseback riding, are plentiful.

LA SERENA

Given its chill Pacific waters and the *camancha-ca* that cools the city until it burns off—usually—in midafternoon, it seems surprising that La Serena has displaced Viña del Mar as Chile's

prime beach resort for many international visi-tors—primarily Argentines accustomed to the calm, warm waters of their own Atlantic coast (Viña's waters, of course, are no warmer than La Serena's, but they're closer to Argentina). Still, the Chilean government is banking on Serena's tourist appeal enough to even propose a new air-port at Tongoy, south of the city, to permit the ar-rival of larger jets than the present Aeropuerto La Florida, just east of the city, can handle.

With its museums, university, and other cul-tural resources, La Serena is an appealing base for excursions to regional attractions varying from its numerous beaches to offshore penguin colonies, several astronomical observatories, and the *pisco*-producing Elqui valley. Its colonial as-pect is deceptive—most of the buildings are far newer than their style suggests—but the pedes-trian-friendly core has much to recommend it. With its nearby port of Coquimbo, though, it is one of Chile's largest urban conurbations.

History

Originally founded as Villanueva de la Serena by Pedro de Valdivia's subordinate Juan Bohón some time between late 1543 and early 1545, Chile's second-oldest city soon burned to the ground during an indigenous revolt in which

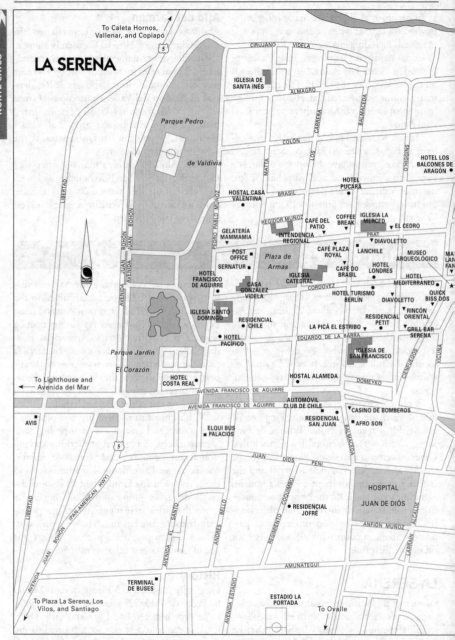

LA SERENA

To Caleta Hornos, Vallenar, and Copiapó

CIRUJANO VIDELA

IGLESIA DE SANTA INÉS

ALMAGRO

BALMACEDA

Parque Pedro de Valdivia

COLÓN

CARRERA

LOS

O'HIGGINS

HOTEL LOS BALCONES DE ARAGÓN

HOTEL PUCARÁ

MATTA

BRASIL

HOSTAL CASA VALENTINA

REGIDOR MUÑOZ

CAFÉ DEL PATIO

COFFEE BREAK

IGLESIA LA MERCED

EL CEDRO

GELATERÍA MAMMAMIA

PEDRO PABLO MUÑOZ

INTENDENCIA REGIONAL

PRAT

DIAVOLETTO

POST OFFICE

SERNATUR

Plaza de Armas

CAFÉ PLAZA ROYAL

LANCHILE

MUSEO ARQUEOLÓGICO

MA LAN FAN

HOTEL FRANCISCO DE AGUIRRE

CASA GONZÁLEZ VIDELA

IGLESIA CATEDRAL

CAFÉ DO BRASIL

HOTEL LONDRES

HOTEL MEDITERRÁNEO

QUICK BISS DOS

CORDOVEZ

HOTEL TURISMO BERLÍN

DIAVOLETTO

RINCÓN ORIENTAL

IGLESIA SANTO DOMINGO

RESIDENCIAL CHILE

LA PICÁ EL ESTRIBO

RESIDENCIAL PETIT

GRILL BAR SERENA

EDUARDO DE LA BARRA

HOTEL PACÍFICO

Parque Jardín El Corazón

IGLESIA DE SAN FRANCISCO

CHENFUEGOS

VICUÑA

To Lighthouse and Avenida del Mar

HOSTAL ALAMEDA

DOMEYKO

HOTEL COSTA REAL

AVENIDA FRANCISCO DE AGUIRRE

AVENIDA FRANCISCO DE AGUIRRE

AUTOMÓVIL CLUB DE CHILE

CASINO DE BOMBEROS

AVIS

ELQUI BUS PALACIOS

RESIDENCIAL SAN JUAN

AFRO SON

BALMACEDA

LIBERTAD

BOHÓN

JUAN DIOS

PENI

AVENIDA JUAN BOHÓN (PAN-AMERICAN HWY.)

COQUIMBO

REGIMIENTO

HOSPITAL JUAN DE DIÓS

RESIDENCIAL JOFRÉ

ANFIÓN MUÑOZ

ALCALDE

LARRAÍN

AVENIDA EL SANTO

ANDRES BELLO

AMUNÁTEGUI

TERMINAL DE BUSES

AVENIDA ESTADIO

ESTADIO LA PORTADA

To Plaza La Serena, Los Vilos, and Santiago

To Ovalle

most of the resident Spaniards, including Bohón, died. Refounded in 1549 later as San Bartolomé de la Serena by Francisco de Aguirre, by the end of the century it had about 100 Spanish citizens and 800 Indians in *encomienda*.

In the 17th century, La Serena suffered repeated raids by the English and French, among them Sir Francis Drake, Bartholomew Sharp, Edward Davis, and George Anson, leading to fortification of the city by the end of the century (Sharp's 1680 attack destroyed the Cabildo, in which many valuable records burned). While the city survived, the recurring attacks contributed to an economic stagnation that persisted until independence, when La Serena evolved into a commercial and administrative center for the Norte Chico, and the port of Coquimbo developed to accommodate the copper industry. In the early 20th century, the exploitation of iron brought an influx of population from elsewhere in the country.

While La Serena has few truly colonial remains, it has colonial character thanks to its original city grid and former President Gabriel González Videla's Plan Serena, which spawned an architectural style known as "colonial renaissance." Part of a larger and less successful scheme to reduce the political and economical dominance of metropolitan Santiago, González Videla's plan left a visible legacy that made the tourist development of the 1980s and 1990s possible.

Orientation

Near the mouth of the Río Elqui, La Serena (population about 142,000) is 474 km north of Santiago via the Panamericana, a four-lane divided toll road the entire way, and 333 km south of Copiapó. Its central core, bounded by the streets Pedro Pablo Muñoz, Amunátegui, Justo Donoso, Castro, and Cirujano Videla, lies south of the Río Elqui and, as a *zona típica*, is officially a national monument. From its junction with the Panamericana, Avenida Francisco de Aguirre leads directly west to the landmark lighthouse, where Avenida del Mar hugs the shoreline to the south, past the city's many beaches—not to mention hotels, restaurants, discos, and pubs.

Sights

Literally the centerpiece of González Videla's Plan Serena, the city's **Plaza de Armas** features subtropical plantings of palms and similar species and a central fountain by sculptor Samuel Román. Its most venerable building, on the east side at the corner of Los Carrera and Cordovez, is the **Iglesia Catedral** (1844), a national monument; the columns that support the roof of this elegant stone edifice are particularly impressive.

Across the plaza, at the corner of Matta and Cordovez, the former president's own **Casa González Videla** (1890) was his home for half a century, from 1927 to 1977. A national monument, it now houses the regional history museum that bears his name. Many nearby buildings, such as the regional government's **Intendencia** and the **Municipalidad,** reflect González Videla's influence, though the nearly indistinguishable **Tribunales** (Law Courts) date from 1938, a few years before his plan took effect.

To the west, between Pedro Pablo Muñoz and the Panamericana, **Parque Pedro de Valdivia** is one of Serena's largest open spaces, but substantial parts of it are suffering from years of deferred maintenance. The exception is the fastidiously landscaped **Parque Jardín El Corazón,** a 2.6-hectare Japanese garden that commemorated the 450th anniversary of the city's founding. Open 10 A.M.–6 P.M. daily except in winter, when it's closed Mondays, the Parque Jardín, tel. 51/224492, charges US$1 admission for adults, US$.50 for children.

Most of Serena's other landmarks are ecclesiastical. At the corner of Balmaceda and Eduardo de la Barra, the colonial **Iglesia de San Francisco,** begun in 1585 and completed in 1627, is a national monument with meter-thick walls and graceful corbelled arches; venerable religious paintings adorn the lateral walls, but its Museo de Arte Religioso continues to be closed for repairs, an apparently permanent situation.

While La Serena has few truly colonial remains, it has colonial character thanks to its original city grid and former President Gabriel González Videla's Plan Serena, which spawned an architectural style known as "colonial renaissance."

Half a block west of the plaza, on Cordovez, the **Iglesia Santo Domingo** dates from 1755, but its hexagonal bell tower is a comparatively recent addition (1912). A national monument, it is also known as the **Iglesia Padres Carmelitas** after the order that now controls it.

Three blocks north of the plaza, at the corner of Almagro and Matta, the **Iglesia de Santa Inés** is yet another national monument. It dates from the 19th century but occupies the site of a 17th-century hermitage.

At the corner of Prat and Balmaceda, fronted by its own *plazuela,* the **Iglesia La Merced** dates from 1709 but has undergone frequent modifications; note the block construction and the unusual porthole window.

At the corner of Cienfuegos and Cantournet, three blocks east of the plaza, the Jesuit-built **Iglesia San Agustín** (1755) came under Augustinian control after the Jesuit expulsion from the Americas in 1767. Recently completed renovations, necessitated by the 1975 earthquake, have left it looking better than ever.

At the east end of Cantournet, on an imposing hilltop site, the neoclassical **Iglesia y Claustro de la Casa de La Providencia** (1872), Justo Donoso 420, was built as an orphanage. One block south and one block west, at the corner of Gandarillas and Manuel Rodríguez, the **Iglesia Las Carmelitas** (1755) is a national monument particularly notable for its magnificently carved doors.

At the corner of Balmaceda and Juan de Dios Peni, the 19th-century **Capilla San Juan de Dios,** part of its namesake hospital, is a stucco-covered adobe that resembles stone blocks, while its impressive doors and columns are made of wood from the *alerce.* Also a national monument, its two-story bell tower, topped by a bulbous cupola, is well worth a look.

Museo Histórico Gabriel González Videla

González Videla was La Serena's native son, and this regional history museum contains extensive personal effects, including photographs of and correspondence between the Chilean president and major international figures such as Argentina's Juan Perón, Brazil's Getulio Vargas, and U.S. President Harry Truman (though some of the letters seem more formulaic than personal).

During his term, from 1946 to 1952, Chile claimed a sector of Antarctica, building icy strongholds known as Base Arturo Prat, Base Bernardo O'Higgins, and then, in 1952, Base González Videla. It also symbolically strengthened its ties to the Pacific when on January 19, 1951, Comandante Roberto Parragué Singer flew the *Manutara* from La Serena to Hanga Roa in 20 hours—the first flight ever from the continent to distant Easter Island. More than symbolically, González Videla's administration granted women the vote in 1948.

The museum overlooks the authoritarian aspects of his presidency, during which he outlawed the Communist party (once his supporters) and even prosecuted the senator and poet Pablo Neruda, who fled to Argentina for a year. Some caustic caricatures do suggest that González Videla was not a great intellect, but one room is devoted to Plan Serena, the cornerstone of the president's project to combat centralism and make provincial cities more livable.

In addition to the material on González Videla, the main floor is also home to the **Pinacoteca Oscar Prager,** a collection of both abstract and figurative Chilean art from the first half of the 20th century. Among the works are portraits and, especially, a large assortment of landscapes by Osvaldo Ramírez Ossandón (1904–90), also known as Mister Rou. The recently opened second floor has exhibits on colonial and contemporary history.

At the southwest corner of the Plaza de Armas, the museum, Matta 495, tel. 51/215082, is a national monument. Open 9 A.M.–1 P.M. and 4–7 P.M. Tues.–Sat., it charges US$1 admission for adults, US$.50 for kids, except Sunday, when it's 10 A.M.–1 P.M. only and admission is free.

Museo Arqueológico

Greatly improved over the past decade, Serena's archaeological museum contains exhibit halls on geology and fossils, agricultural origins and early coastal settlements, and regional cultures. During construction of Embalse Puclaro, a sprawling reservoir behind a large new dam between La Serena and Vicuña, archaeologists salvaged many artifacts that are now on display here.

The local succession includes several distinct cultures that gradually evolved into the Inka-Diaguita hybrid that greeted the first Spaniards. From about 130 B.C. to A.D. 600, distinguished by its ceramics and metallurgy, the El Molle culture occupied the area between present-day Copiapó and the Río Choapa, in the vicinity of Illapel. There is a reproduction of the El Molle site known as Valle del Encanto, near Ovalle.

The successor Las Animas culture, dating roughly from A.D. 700 to A.D. 1000, had a more maritime orientation but also imported traits from the La Aguada complex in the present-day Argentine provinces of La Rioja and Catamarca; it set the stage for the Diaguitas (A.D. 1000–1536), a settled agricultural people with much more elaborate ceramics who came under Inca domination in the 16th century.

One of the museum's prize items, in the Easter Island display, is the 2.5-meter *moai* designated No. 659 by the German priest and archaeologist Sebastián Englert, who spent many years in the Pacific. Donated to La Serena via González Videla, it was initially installed at the Chilean army's Regimiento Arica, then to a public park on Avenida Colo Colo before being shipped to exhibits in Milán, Barcelona, and Burdeos (France). In the process of shipping, it suffered serious damage, but it was repaired and then returned to Serena in 1996.

On a more contemporary note, the museum contains a photographic exhibit of the city's development/evolution, as well as an excellent sample of crafts and souvenirs, including reproductions of Diaguita pottery, lapis lazuli jewelry, and also books. At the corner of Cordovez and Cienfuegos, the museum, tel. 51/224492 or 51/226050, muarse@entelchile.net, is open Tuesday to Friday 9 A.M.–1:30 P.M. and 3–7 P.M., Saturday 10 A.M.–1

P.M. and 4–7 P.M., and Sunday 10 A.M.–1 P.M. only. It has a reciprocal admissions policy with the Museo González Videla—what's valid for one is also valid for the other, on the same day.

The museum also maintains a 15,000-volume library, open 9 A.M.–1 P.M. and 4–7 P.M. Tuesday to Friday only.

Museo Mineralógico Ignacio Domeyko

Beneath a distribution map of the region's mineral deposits, wooden display cases fill one large room with samples of 2,160 minerals native to the region in this simple but orderly mineralogical museum. On the grounds of the Universidad de La Serena, it takes its name from Polish immigrant explorer and scientist Ignacio Domeyko, who explored northern Chile extensively between 1839 and 1844 (an Andean front range that bears his name stretches from the latitude of Copiapó to that of Antofagasta).

At Anfión Muñoz 870, the Museo Mineralógico, tel. 51/204096, is open 9:30 A.M.–12:30 P.M. weekdays. Admission costs US$.50.

Beaches

South of the lighthouse at the west end of Avenida Francisco de Aguirre, Avenida del Mar parallels a string of more than a dozen beaches all the way to Peñuelas, where the road turns back inland toward the Panamericana. Nearly all of these are reasonably safe for activities as various as sunbathing and swimming to surfing and windsurfing, but **Playa Cuatro Esquinas** (appropriately close to the Kamikaze Pub) bears watching for its rip currents.

Accommodations

La Serena has a wide range of accommodations options in all categories; the priciest alternatives are right on the beach.

US$10–25: The Argentine-run **Residencial El Francesito,** Cantournet 1083, tel. 51/217489, offers hostel-style accommodations, in remodeled rooms with new beds and brilliantly modern shared baths, for US$7 pp. There are also kitchen and laundry privileges, cable TV, and a large ping-pong table. Though it's no longer officially associated with Hostelling International, **Residencial Limmat,** Lautaro 914, tel. 51/211373, still draws international travelers to very good hostel-style services for US$7 pp; it also offers rooms with private bath and other services at higher prices (see below).

A labyrinth of small to medium-sized rooms, **Residencial Petit,** Eduardo de la Barra 586, tel. 51/212536, offers a good location, family atmosphere, and rates of US$8 pp with shared bath, plus a small additional charge for breakfast. While perfectly acceptable, some of the downstairs rooms are inescapably dark.

The quiet **Residencial San Juan,** Balmaceda 827, tel. 51/212794, has plain but large rooms, with shared bath and hot water, for US$9 pp. For the same price, friendly, family-run **Residencial Lorena,** Cantournet 950, tel. 51/223380, is a fine choice, though the shower stalls in the shared baths are not for claustrophobics.

New on the scene, but bidding to become one of Serena's most popular lodgings, Chilean-German **Hostal Casa Valentina,** Brasil 271, tel. 51/223142, fampintz@hotmail.com, has cheerful, comfortable, and freshly painted rooms with high ceilings and new beds for US$10 pp including an elaborate breakfast, shared bath with hot showers, and kitchen access. Spanish, English, German, and Italian are spoken, and reasonable laundry service is also available. Unlike many older buildings that now serve as *residenciales,* it has maintained the original configuration of its rooms.

Hostal Croata, Cienfuegos 248, tel./fax 51/224997, hostalcroata@entelchile.net, is the official Hostelling International affiliate and, at US$10 pp for members, not a bad deal.

Half a block south of the plaza, longtime favorite **Residencial Chile,** Matta 561, tel. 51/211694, is quiet and friendly, with good rooms for US$10 pp, but there are better choices for the same price or only a little more. Near the bus terminal, travelers' choice **Residencial Jofré,** Regimiento Coquimbo 964, tel. 51/222335, costs US$10 pp with private bath and breakfast, plus kitchen privileges, but singles are hard to come by. There are also cheaper rooms with shared bath.

Having recently changed hands, **Hostal Alameda,** Avenida Francisco de Aguirre 450, tel.

51/213052 or 51/220028, is tolerable enough, with decent-sized rooms with shared bath for US$11/23 s/d, while those with shared bath cost US$16/25.

Charmingly anachronous **Hotel Pacífico,** Eduardo del la Barra 252, tel. 51/225674, offers some of the best service for the price in town, at US$10/16 s/d with shared bath (the best and newest baths are far in the back), US$16/21 s/d with private bath. Some of the staff in this onetime mansion seem as venerable as the building itself.

Hotel Palmas de Mallorca, Cordovez 750, tel. 51/224072 or 09/5542198, occupies a spacious and attractive older building, all of whose rooms front on the second-floor patio area. For US$18/21 s/d, all rooms offer private bath, color TV, and free parking—the latter a bit unusual for this price in this congested part of town.

In addition to its popular hostel facilities, **Residencial Limmat,** Lautaro 914, tel. 51/211373, offers larger rooms with private bath and cable TV for US$18/23 s/d.

US$25–50: The modernized, immaculate, and amiable **Residencial Suiza,** Cienfuegos 250, tel. 51/216092, costs US$20/30 s/d with private bath and breakfast. Despite a stellar reputation, **Hostal Croata,** Cienfuegos 248, tel./fax 51/2-24997, hostalcroata@entelchile.net, is only so-so for US$32 d—it has no singles.

It won't win any design awards, but **Hotel Pucará,** Balmaceda 319, tel. 51/211966, tel./fax 51/211933, has a wide array of services including private bath, telephone, cable TV, parking, and laundry service. Rates start at US$32/36 with the IVA discount, making it good value for the money.

It's hard to imagine that prices won't rise as travelers discover renovated **Hotel Londres,** Cordovez 550, tel. 51/219066, website: www.hotel-londres.cl, whose spacious, cheerfully decorated rooms cost only US$32/44. Services include Internet access and many other perks.

On a quiet block, **Hotel Brüggen,** Gandarillas 850, tel. 51/210839 or 51/210983, is a little disorganized but the rooms themselves are fine for US$35/44. Smallish but efficiently designed rooms at **Hotel Casablanca,** Vicuña 414, tel. 51/213070, fax 51/212062, costs US$36/43 with breakfast. Some interior rooms lack natural light.

US$50–100: It still looks a little worn from the outside, but the nicely remodeled downstairs rooms at **Hotel Turismo Berlín,** Cordovez 535, tel. 51/222927 or 51/233583, fax 51/223575, are more than agreeable for US$49/63 s/d with breakfast and private bath; for US$21/41, guests in the older upstairs rooms, as worn as the exterior but still passable, can enjoy the hotel's attractive common spaces as much as those paying higher rates. Breakfast and onsite parking are both included.

In an improbable location next to a major supermarket, **Hotel Mediterráneo,** Cienfuegos 509, tel./fax 51/225837, tel. 51/225838, has an unimpressive lobby, but the eight upstairs rooms are quiet, comfortable, and immaculate, with all essential services except parking (available at night only). Rates are US$50/62 with IVA.

Rates are US$63/74 s/d at **Hotel Los Balcones de Aragón,** Cienfuegos 289, tel. 51/2-11982, fax 51/211800, an excellent choice with numerous amenities in a quiet location with parking; if business is slow, it's possible to leverage discounts of 30 percent or so.

La Serena's traditional luxury choice, **Hotel Francisco de Aguirre,** Cordovez 210, tel. 51/2-22991, fax 51/210992, hotelfranciscodeaguirre@entelchile.net, continues to maintain its reputation as one of the city's best; "standard" rooms cost US$62/77, while "superior" units cost US$71/82.

US$100–150: Despite its location at a busy intersection, the stylishly modern **Hotel Costa Real,** Avenida Francisco de Aguirre 170, tel. 51/221010, fax 51/221122, creal@ctcinternet.cl, has curbside appeal and comfortable rooms with all amenities for US$95/115.

Food

For high-quality, low-priced fast food, try **Quick Biss Dos,** Cienfuegos 545, 2nd floor, tel. 51/226300. Moderately priced **Café Plaza Royal,** Prat 461, tel. 51/217166, is a good breakfast, lunch, and snack choice. **Café do Brasil,** Balmaceda 461, tel. 51/221839, has similar fare.

Gelatería Mammamia, Prat 220, tel. 09/8-268241, has the best ice cream in town, though Diavoletto, with branches at Prat 563 and O'Higgins 535, tel. 51/212887, runs a close second; Diavoletto, though, also offers the best and best-priced sandwiches in town. Another spot for breakfast, ice cream, desserts, and coffee is Coffee Break, Prat 490, tel. 51/221673.

The Casino de Bomberos, at Balmaceda and Colo Colo, tel. 51/225047, is a traditional lunch and dinner choice. Fixed-price lunches, as cheap as US$1.50, are a bargain.

Upstairs in the Mercado La Recova, at Cienfuegos and Cantournet, a dozen crowded seafood eateries offer inexpensive lunches, in the US$5 range, that often include a free pisco sour. The quality is above average at places such as Caleta Hornos, tel. 51/221152; Serena; Lidia, tel. 51/214076; and El Galeón.

For US$5, the fixed-price dinners at La Picá El Estribo, Eduardo de la Barra 526, tel. 51/213736, include an aperitif (usually a pisco sour), an appetizer, one of several meticulously prepared and well-presented main-course options along with a side dish, dessert, coffee or tea, and a *bajativo* (after-dinner drink). Portions are large, and lunches are even cheaper and just as good.

Grill-Bar Serena, Eduardo de la Barra 614, tel. 51/211962, serves good seafood at modest prices, especially for lunch; entrées cost around US$4–8. Dónde El Guatón, Brasil 750, tel. 51/211519, is a popular *parrilla* with beef dishes in the US$5–9 range. El Cedro, Prat 568, tel. 51/219501, serves upscale Middle Eastern and Chilean dishes in a relaxing patio setting.

La Serena has several respectable Chinese choices, the best of which is probably Rincón Oriental, O'Higgins 570, with fixed-price lunches in the US$3–4 range and regular entrées from US$5–7. Formosa, Cantournet 844, tel. 51/214407, and Mai Lan Fan, Cordovez 740, tel. 51/214828, are comparable.

Along Avenida del Mar, between the lighthouse and the suburb of Peñuelas, many seaside restaurants offer mostly seafood, with the occasional exception such as the Mexican El Atajo, Avenida del Mar s/n, tel. 51/247391. More typical are Quinta Ola, Avenida del Mar 4000, tel. 51/2-

16066, a popular pub restaurant with good service but a misleading menu—only a handful of the many listed sauces are readily available—and Tololo Beach, Avenida del Mar s/n, tel. 51/242656.

Entertainment

As a beach resort, La Serena has numerous bars and entertainment venues that come and go every summer. Many of these are along Avenida del Mar, while the ones that follow are downtown.

Having recently changed hands, Café del Patio, Prat 470, tel. 51/212634, is open nightly but generally has live music only on weekends, when it stays open into the early hours. Bar VIP, Eduardo de la Barra 465, tel. 51/227641, also features live music. La Barra Bohemia, O'Higgins 624, is a good drinks option.

In the landmark lighthouse at the foot of Avenida Francisco de Aguirre, Pub El Faro, Avenida del Mar s/n, is fast becoming a popular meeting and drinking place and has good sandwiches as well; the interior remodeling is a success, and there are plans to incorporate the exterior patios into the pub.

The least commercial and most typically Chilean option is usually the folk music at Afro Son, Balmaceda 824, tel. 51/229344, within the Centro Latinoamericano de Arte y Cultura.

While La Serena's only downtown cinema recently closed, the multiscreen Cinemark, Huanhualí s/n, tel. 51/213103, is at the Plaza La Serena shopping center, a short distance south of the bus terminal.

Events

La Serena hosts a variety of events, mostly in summer, many of which take place on Plaza González Videla, just north of the former president's house on the west side of the Plaza de Armas. Among the most enduring are January's Encuentro Nacional de Artesanía, a crafts fair; and February's Feria del Libro de La Serena, a book fair that attracts national and international publishers, along with mostly Chilean authors.

Shopping

For the best permanent display of crafts and souvenirs, visit the Mercado la Recova at the corner of Cienfuegos and Cantournet. There's another crafts market at the **Plazuela La Merced,** directly in front of its namesake church at the corner of Prat and Balmaceda, and a big summer crafts market at **Plaza González Videla,** just north of the Casa González Videla, on the west side of the Plaza de Armas.

For regional and national works of art, visit the **Galería Carmen Codoceo,** Prat 424, tel. 51/211186.

Services

Money: La Serena has several *cambios,* including Intercam, Eduardo de la Barra 435-A; Cambios Talinay, Prat 515; and Gira Tour, Prat 689. Numerous banks have ATMs, including Banco Santander, Cordovez 351.

Postal: Correos de Chile is at Matta and Prat, on the west side of the Plaza de Armas.

Telephone and Internet: Long-distance phone offices include Telefónica CTC, Cordovez 446; Entel, Prat 571; and Chilesat, Balmaceda 469. La Serena's area code is 51.

The most popular Internet outlet is Net Café, Cordovez 285, tel. 51/212187, open 10 A.M.–2 P.M. daily; it also has good sandwiches, snacks, coffee, and discounts for Net customers who order them. Compucenter, Cordovez 588, Oficina 403, tel. 51/211594, also offers Internet access but is more impersonal.

Laundry: Lavaseco Universal is at Francisco de Aguirre 447. Lavaseco Nevada, Los Carrera 635, charges US$6 for five kilograms.

Medical: Hospital Juan de Diós, Balmaceda 916, tel. 51/200500, occupies an entire block also bounded by Juan de Diós Peni, Larraín Alcalde, and Anfión Muñoz. Its emergency entrance is at the southeast corner of the grounds, at Larraín Alcalde and Anfión Muñoz.

Information

Tourist Offices: Sernatur, on the west side of the Plaza de Armas at Matta 461, tel./fax 51/225199, serna04@entelchile.net, is open 8:45 A.M.–8 P.M. daily in December, January, and February; the rest of the year, hours are 8:45 A.M.–6:30 P.M. weekdays, 8:30 A.M.–2 P.M. weekends.

At the Terminal de Buses, Amunátegui s/n, the Municipalidad operates an Oficina de Información Turística, tel. 51/206631, open weekdays 9 A.M.–1 P.M. and 3–6 P.M.

At Plaza La Merced, at the corner of Prat and Balmaceda, the private Cámara de Turismo, tel. 51/206631, laserena@munitel.cl, has placed a information booth that's theoretically open daily except Sunday, 10 A.M.–2 P.M. and 5–9 P.M. In practice, it's closed more often than not.

Motorists: The helpful Automóvil Club de Chile (Acchi), Avenida Francisco de Aguirre 455, tel. 51/217583, fax 51/225279, provides motorist information.

National Parks: Conaf's Patrimonio Silvestre office is just west of Aeropuerto La Florida, at Ruta 41 s/n, tel./fax 51/272798 or 51/272799.

Bookstores: La Serena has two fine bookstores: Librerías Universitarias, Cordovez 470, and Librería Andrés Bello, Matta 510.

Transportation

La Serena has northbound and southbound air services, along with long-distance and regional bus and taxi services.

Air: A new international airport may be in the planning stages, but for the moment the airport is close-in Aeropuerto La Florida, tel. 51/225944, on Ruta 41 only a few kilometers east of downtown. Only domestic flights leave from here.

LanChile and LanExpress share offices at Balmaceda 406, tel. 51/225753 or 51/221531, fax 51/219496. There are 30 flights per week to Santiago, daily flights to Antofagasta and Iquique, and daily flights to Copiapó; the Sunday flight to Copiapó continues to El Salvador.

Bus: Most long-distance and regional services leave from Terminal de Buses, at Amunátegui and Avenida El Santo, tel. 51/224573, but several companies also have convenient downtown ticket offices. Elqui valley buses also stop at the Plaza de Abasto, at Colo Colo and Avenida Cisternas.

Regional buses include Buses Serenamar, tel. 51/211735, serving the southerly Panamericana resorts of Guanaqueros and Tongoy (US$1.75), every 20 minutes between 8 A.M. and 8:30 P.M.

Several carriers go to upper Elqui valley destinations, such as Vicuña (US$2, one hour) and

Pisco Elqui (US$2.75, 1.5 hours), but the main one is Via Elqui/Megal Bus, tel. 51/314710, which has eight buses daily to Vicuña, all but one of which continue to Pisco Elqui. Others, which are also long-distance carriers, include Expreso Norte, tel. 51/224857; Fénix Pullman Norte, tel. 51/225555; Buses Tal, Balmaceda 594, tel. 51/226148; and Pullman Bus, O'Higgins 663, tel. 51/225284.

To Ovalle, an hour to the south, the main carriers are Cormar, tel. 51/211707, which has 26 buses daily between 9 A.M. and 10 P.M., and Horvitur, tel. 09/8397044, which operates between 7:15 A.M. and 8 P.M. Other Ovalle carriers include Tas Choapa, O'Higgins 599, tel. 51/225959 or 51/224915; Lasval/Inca Bus, Cienfuegos 698, tel. 51/225627 or 51/214456; Elqui Bus Palacios, Pedro Pablo Muñoz 864-A, tel. 51/224448; and Siktur, tel. 51/216072.

Lasval/Inca Bus and Pullman Bus go several times daily to Los Vilos (US$5) and the upper Choapa valley destinations of Illapel (US$7) and Salamanca (US$8.50). Expreso Norte also goes to Salamanca.

Buses Postal, tel. 51/211707, and Buses J. F., tel. 09/7275830, go several times daily to the pilgrimage center of Andacollo (US$1.50).

Numerous long-distance southbound and northbound Panamericana carriers stop in La Serena en route between Santiago and Arica, including the above-mentioned Tas Choapa; Elqui Bus Palacios; Expreso Norte; Fénix Pullman Norte; Buses Tal; and Pullman Bus. Others are Flota Barrios, tel. 51/213394 or 51/226361; Tur-Bus, Cordovez 309, tel. 51/212007; and Buses Libac, Avenida Francisco de Aguirre 452, tel. 51/226101 or 51/225172. Lasval/Inca Bus, Pullman Bus, and Los Corsarios, O'Higgins 663, tel. 51/225157, all serve Valparaíso and Viña del Mar.

Sample destinations and fares include Santiago (US$13, seven hours), Valparaíso/Viña del Mar (US$13, seven hours), Los Vilos (US$8, three hours), Vallenar (US$5.50, 2.5 hours), Copiapó (US$7.50, four hours), Chañaral (US$8.50, six hours), Antofagasta (US$24, 13 hours), Calama (US$27, 16 hours), Iquique (US$32, 19 hours), and Arica (US$35, 21 hours). For very long distances, *salón cama* buses are available at about a 30 percent premium.

Most international travelers bound for Argentina must change buses in Santiago, but in summer Covalle Bus, Infante 538, tel. 51/2-13127, goes directly to the Argentine cities of Mendoza (US$30, 12 hours) and San Juan (US$40, 14 hours) via the Libertadores tunnel, Tuesday, Thursday, and Sunday. Cata, tel. 51/218744, also goes to Mendoza.

Taxi Colectivos: *Taxi colectivos* leave from Domeyko, a blocklong street between Balmaceda and O'Higgins, just north of and parallel to Colo Colo.

Tacso, Domeyko 524, tel. 51/224517, serves Andacollo, Ovalle, and the Elqui valley destinations of Vicuña and Pisco Elqui. Colectivos Vicuña-La Serena, Domeyko 565, tel. 51/2-24517, also serves the Elqui valley.

Anserco, also at Domeyko 524, tel. 51/217567, goes to Andacollo as well. Fremop, on Domeyko near the corner of O'Higgins, goes to Ovalle.

Getting Around

Car-rental agencies include the Automóvil Club de Chile (Acchi), Avenida Francisco de Aguirre 455, tel. 51/217583, fax 51/225279; Avis, Avenida Francisco de Aguirre 063 (west of the Panamericana), tel. 51/227049; Hertz, Avenida Francisco de Aguirre 0225 (also west of the Panamericana), tel. 51/225471; and Callegari, O'Higgins 672, tel. 51/211688.

VICINITY OF LA SERENA

Several Serena-based travel agencies either offer excursions to regional attractions such as Reserva Nacional Pingüino de Humboldt, the Elqui valley, the Mamalluca municipal observatory, and international observatories such as Cerro Tololo, La Silla, and La Campana; those that don't can book them through other operators. While it's possible to do many of these excursions independently, booking them with an agency can simplify the logistics to areas where public transportation is limited or even nonexistent.

Talinay Adventure Expeditions, Prat 470, tel./fax 51/218658, juan-pe@starmedia.com, does full-day excursions to the Elqui valley and Cochiguaz (US$40), Reserva Nacional Pingüino de Humboldt, and the La Silla or La Campana observatories. It also offers horseback excursions to the upper Elqui settlements of Alcohuaz (US$65 for a day trip) and Cochiguaz (US$190, overnight).

Other well-established agencies include **Turismo San Bartolomé,** Balmaceda 417, Departamento 28, tel. 51/211670, fax 51/221992, sanbartolome@entelchile.net; **Diaguitas Tour,** Matta 518, Local 10, tel. 51/214129, fax 51/217265; and **Ingservtur,** Matta 611, tel. 51/220165, ingservtur@entelchile.net. Note that some agencies may add a surcharge for English-speaking guides—ask before booking.

Typical excursion charges include the La Serena city tour (US$12), the Valle de Elqui (US$30–40), Mamalluca observatory (US$30), Parque Nacional Bosque de Fray Jorge (US$30), Reserva Nacional Pingüino de Humboldt (US$50–70), and the La Silla or La Campana observatories (US$70).

Coquimbo

At the south end of its namesake bay, on a rocky headland, Coquimbo is the region's main port, a 19th-century city that grew slowly with copper exports—in 1852, seven years after its official port designation, it had only about 40 houses of inhabitants to help service the Edwards and Lambert smelter, just north of La Serena, that became its prime economic motor. Within a few years there were eight smelters in the area and the city grid, designed by French architect Jean Herbage in apparent defiance of the rugged topography, began to fill in.

Today the Romeral iron mine north of La Serena, which ships its ore to the mechanized port on the south side of the peninsula, is the dominant economic force.

Coquimbo's major contemporary landmark is the conspicuous 93-meter **Cruz del Tercer Milenio** (Cross of the Third Millennium), which sits atop Cerro El Vigía and offers 360-degree views of the peninsula. Besides three symmetrical columns symbolizing the Holy Trinity, there are a dozen pillars representing Christ's apostles, 10 smaller columns signifying the Ten Commandments, and 2,000 steps standing for the years of Christianity. There is also a prayer chapel that can hold up to 1,500 people.

On Plaza Gabriela Mistral, adjacent to the municipal tourist office, the **Museo de Sitio** is a pre-Diaguita cemetery dating from Las Animas times, about A.D. 900–1000. Excavations in the process of demolishing several buildings to expand the plaza unearthed evidence of a local variant that combined maritime subsistence with herding of llamas and alpacas and sacrificed domestic animals to be buried with their owners. Archaeologists from the museum at La Serena also found sophisticated metallurgy, primarily copper, and ceramics, along with bone tools and projectile points.

From the Terminal Pesquero on Avenida Costanera, hourlong harbor tours on the *Catamarán Mistral* include a visit to an offshore sea lion colony. In summer, there are hourly departures between 11 A.M. and 7 P.M.; the rest of the year, weekday excursions take place at 3 P.M. weekdays and at 1, 3, and 5 P.M. weekends and holidays. Fares are US$2 pp; for more details, contact Turismo Ensenada, tel. 51/315295.

Accommodations and Food: Most people stay in La Serena, but Coquimbo offers respectable lodgings at **Hotel Iberia,** Lastra 400, tel. 51/312141, for about US$12/22 s/d with private bath, breakfast, and TV. **Hotel Lig,** Aldunate 1577, tel. 51/311171, fax 51/313717, charges US$30/45 s/d.

Mai Lan Fan, Avenida Ossandón 1, tel. 51/315615, is the Coquimbo branch of La Serena's popular *chifa.* The waterfront **La Picada,** Avenida Costanera s/n, tel. 51/311214, is the choice for seafood.

Information: Coquimbo's municipal Oficina de Información Turística, on Plaza Gabriela Mistral at Melgarejo and Las Heras, tel. 51/313971, is open 9 A.M.–6 P.M. weekdays only.

Transportation: Coquimbo's Terminal Rodoviario, Varela 1300 between Borgoño and Barriga, tel. 51/326651, has long-distance services similar to La Serena's. There are frequent local buses and *taxi colectivos* between the two cities, and south to Guanaqueros and Tongoy.

South of Coquimbo

South of Coquimbo several small-scale beach resorts dot the Panamericana, though once-sedate **Las Tacas** is a megaproject exception to the rule, ironically described by Roberto Ampuero in his detective novel *El Alemán de Atacama.* Rates at **Apart Hotel Las Tacas,** Ruta 5, Km 445, tel. 51/399100, fax 51/399133, are US$140/160 s/d.

About 35 km southwest of Coquimbo, at the south end of its eponymous bay, **Guanaqueros** is a village of sandy streets and an equally sandy crescent beach, with an Oficina de Información Turística at Avenida Costanera 2847, tel. 51/395048. There are numerous campgrounds and *cabañas.* The waterfront restaurant **El Pequeño,** Avenida Costanera 306, tel. 51/391341, specializes in fish, shellfish, and empanadas.

Straddling an isthmus between a rocky promontory and an estuary floodplain flanked by two sandy beaches, 11 km south of Guanaqueros, the resort of **Tongoy** makes a fine excursion from La Serena—after a swim at the sandy northside Playa Socos, cross the isthmus for lunch at any of the beachfront *marisquerías* at the hard-packed Playa Grande. Its Oficina de Información Turística is at Fundación Norte 37, tel. 51/391860.

For those who choose to stay, Tongoy's basic **Residencial D'Pardo,** Fundición Norte 668, is the best bargain for US$8.50 pp with shared bath. The **Hotel Yachting Club,** Avenida Costanera 20, tel. 51/391154, costs US$45 s or d, while the modernist **Hotelera Gálvez** (ex-Hostería Tongoy), Avenida Costanera 10, tel. 51/391203, charges US$60 s or d; both include breakfast. Visitors jam the numerous *marisquerías* such as **La Picá del Veguita,** Avenida Playa Grande s/n, tel. 51/391475, for seafood, but for variety try **Pizzería Gigino,** Avenida Costanera Norte 134.

Transportation: Frequent buses and *taxi colectivos* from La Serena and Coquimbo continue to Guanaqueros and Tongoy.

Caleta Los Hornos

About 35 km north of La Serena, straddling the Panamericana, the fishing village of Caleta los Hornos is home to several seafood *picadas,* including **Alto Aquí, Brisas Marinas,** and **La Caleta.** It also has a beach camping area with water, toilets, and cold showers.

Reserva Nacional Pingüino de Humboldt

Increasingly popular for its prolific wildlife, which includes both birds and marine mammals, Reserva Nacional Pingüino de Humboldt comprises three islands, two of them—**Isla Damas** and **Isla Choros**—in Region IV and easily accessible from La Serena. The third, **Isla Chañaral,** belongs to Region III (Atacama) and is less frequented, while a fourth island closer to the continent, Isla Gaviotas, is the site of an elaborate and inappropriate real-estate scheme.

Totaling about 860 hectares of land area, surrounded by cobalt Pacific waters, the reserve is home to breeding populations of *Spheniscus humboldti,* also known as the Peruvian penguin. Other nesting seabirds include boobies, cormorants, and gulls, while mammals include bottle-nosed dolphins, sea lions, and even the occasional *chungungo* (sea otter). Humpbacks, blue whales, and orcas have been spotted around Isla Chañaral.

Sights: From Caleta los Hornos, the Panamericana switchbacks up the Cuesta de Buenos Aires, past the abandoned hilltop iron mine at **El Tofo.** At a junction near Trapiche, 77 km from La Serena, a rugged gravel road heads west to olive-growing **Choros,** Chile's most southerly desert oasis. From Choros, a sandy road continues to **Caleta de Choros** where, for US$65, fishermen's launches carry up to seven passengers out to 320-hectare **Isla Choros,** whose rocky shoreline offers glimpses of the abundant bird life (landing is prohibited). En route, pods of curious dolphins dive, surface, and criss-cross beneath and around the boat.

Of the reserve's three islands, only 60-hectare **Isla Damas** is open to landings—though no more than 50 people may visit the island at any one time. A one-km trail links the two principal beaches: the steep, narrow **Playa La Poza** at the landing and the broader, longer, and less visited **Playa Tijeras.**

Information: At Caleta de Choros, 114 km from La Serena, Conaf's Centro de Información Ambiental has exceptional displays on local ecology and environment. It also collects a US$3 admission charge, applicable to everyone except those camping at Isla Damas (see below).

Accommodations and Food: On Isla Damas, Conaf's **Camping Playa La Poza** costs US$20 per site for up to six people, with a maximum stay of two nights; for reservations contact Conaf's Patrimonio Silvestre office in La Serena. The campground has toilets but no fresh water or food (though local fishermen will sell part of the day's catch). Campstoves are obligatory for cooking, and campers must pack out trash.

If there's no room on the island, try **Camping El Memo** at Caleta de Choros, where sites also cost US$20. Some supplies are available at Caleta de Choros but, except for fresh fish, there's a much wider selection at La Serena.

Transportation: By 2003, Caleta de Choros may have regular public transportation from La Serena, 75 km to the south; meanwhile, numerous travel agencies conduct day tours from La Serena. If driving, note that the gravel road from Trapiche to Choros can be hell on tires.

Andacollo

Every December 26, more than 100,000 pilgrims overrun the gold and copper mining center of Andacollo, in a narrow canyon 53 km southeast of La Serena, to pay homage to the Virgen de Andacollo. With the ambience of a colonial Mexican mountain town, Andacollo is, along with Lo Vásquez and La Tirana, one of Chile's major pilgrimage sites.

At 1,050 meters above sea level, Andacollo is cool and breezy much of the time, as the influence of the coastal *camanchaca* often manages to reach this far inland. *Pirquineros,* small-scale gold miners, still grind their ore in more than 30 *trapiches* or artisanal mills in the vicinity; local boys will, for a small tip, lead visitors to view the miners at work.

In the shadow of Andacollo's imposing Basílica, its Plaza Pedro Nolasco Videla features a crafts market distinguished by local stone carvings, but even here, "positive energy" quartz crystals compete with mementos of the Virgen for devotion. A portable information kiosk on the plaza may relocate as the new municipal building is completed.

Except for truly dedicated pilgrims, Andacollo probably makes a better day trip than an overnight, though travelers with their own cars or serious cyclists might consider continuing on the decent gravel road that goes south to the Hurtado valley, where it's possible to make a loop to Vicuña and back to La Serena, or else go west to Ovalle.

Sights: Italian architect Eusebio Celli designed Andacollo's **Templo Grande** or **Basílica,** built of Douglas fir brought from California, in a Roman-Byzantine style. Begun on Christmas Day of 1873 under the direction of Monseñor José Manuel Orrego, it was inaugurated exactly 20 years later by Monseñor Florencio Fontecilla. Sited on the north side of the plaza, it is now a national monument.

Including the plaza outside, the Basílica can hold 10,000 worshippers. It is 70 meters long, with five separate naves, and 30 meters wide for most of its length, though the cross-style floor plan reaches a maximum width of 40 meters. The central arch is 24 meters high, while the twin towers reach 50 meters and the central cupola 45 meters. The foundations are six meters deep, and the walls are adobe but covered by sheets of galvanized iron.

On the west side of the plaza, the smaller **Templo Antiguo** (1789) contains the **Museo de Ofrendas de la Virgen** that holds all the adornments used in ceremonies on December 26. It also holds ex-votos brought by believers in tribute to the Virgen, including model ships built by Coquimbo stevedores, who appear to be her strongest adherents.

Events: Typified by enthusiastic dancers known as *chinos,* who fill the plaza and surrounding streets in procession, the **Fiesta de la Virgen de Andacollo** takes place the day after Christmas. Many pilgrims arrive on foot from La Serena or elsewhere for the fiesta, which dates from the 16th century, when legend says a Spaniard saved her carved image from the destruction of La Serena during an indigenous rebellion, but the present image of the Virgen del Rosario came from Lima in the 17th century.

In addition to the main fiesta, the Virgen also parades through town during the **Fiesta Chica,** the first Sunday in October.

Accommodations and Food: At the south end of Urmeneta, beyond the bus and *taxi colectivo* stops, are half a dozen or more roughly comparable *residenciales,* charging less than US$10 pp. During the annual fiesta, pilgrims camp just about anywhere they feel like it.

La Rueda, Urmeneta 657, tel. 51/431600, has simple but well-prepared meals in the US$4 range, complemented by excellent service.

Transportation: *Taxi colectivos* from La Serena, the fastest and most efficient way of reaching here, cost US$2.50 pp.

VICUÑA

From La Serena, paved Ruta 41 climbs gradually up the Elqui valley, through irrigated fields of citrus, chirimoya, and papaya, to the village of Vicuña, once home to Nobel Prize poetess Gabriela Mistral, and now to Chile's only major municipal observatory and a prominent *pisco* distillery—the upper Elqui valley grows many of the grapes that generate the region's signature alcoholic beverage.

About midway to Vicuña, the road detours through a tunnel with a view of the recently constructed Embalse Puclaro, a 80-meter-high dam whose sprawling reservoir, with a capacity of 200 million cubic meters of water, inundated several villages, parts of the Río Elqui, and the old highway.

Orientation

About 62 km east of La Serena, 623 meters above sea level on the north bank of the Río Elqui, Vicuña consists of a compact grid of streets whose main thoroughfare, Avenida Gabriela Mistral, runs east-west. Ruta 41 from La Serena, which passes south and east of town, continues to the Argentine border at Paso Aguas Negras, where Argentina's Ruta Nacional (RN) 150 continues to the hot springs resort of Pismanta and the provincial capital of San Juan. On the south side of the river, a scenic but dusty road crosses the Portezuelo Tres Cruces to the valley of the Río Hurtado, an alternative route to Ovalle for motorists and mountain bikers.

© WAYNE BERNHARDSON

Torre Bauer

Sights

Most of Vicuña's sights are on or near the densely landscaped **Plaza de Armas,** with its canopy of mature peppers, palms, and other trees, and a large bandshell often used for open-air concerts. On the west side of the plaza, at the corner of Mistral and San Martín, the offbeat **Torre Bauer** (1905) literally towers above the city—its wooden battlements resembling a medieval castle from the ancestral Germany of former Mayor Alfonso Bauer. Immediately to its south is the deco-style **Teatro Municipal.**

Exactly kitty-corner from the Torre Bauer, on the foundations of the earlier Iglesia La Merced, the **Iglesia de la Inmaculada Concepción** (1909) has its own distinctive wooden tower; unfortunately, the plaster has begun to crack and fall from the ceiling murals beneath its arched roof, supported by impressive wooden columns. The church also displays Gabriela Mistral's baptismal font.

SIGHTING THE SOUTHERN CROSS IN THE NORTE CHICO

Thanks to its perpetually cloudless skies, the precordillera of the Norte Chico is home to the greatest concentration of international astronomical observatories below the Equator. Not only professionals, though, have benefited from the cloudless austral atmosphere—in the two years after it opened in December 1998, more than 30,000 visitors flocked to Vicuña's municipal observatory, and alternative opportunities for skywatching continue to increase and improve.

Even without optical assistance, the southern heavens can be spectacular. Besides the legendary Southern Cross and countless other constellations that are novelties to visitors from the Northern Hemisphere, the Small Magellanic Cloud, a galaxy orbiting the Milky Way 200,000 light years from Earth, is one of the most distant astronomical features visible without a telescope.

Local authorities, mindful of the observatories' actual and potential contribution to the regional economy, are making conscious efforts to save the night skies. Street lighting throughout the region, for instance, now uses mercury lighting instead of sodium, and fixtures have been capped to prevent upward light pollution.

Within about two hours of La Serena, there are three major research observatories: the Cerro Tololo International Observatory (CTIO) near Vicuña; the more remote European Southern Observatory (ESO) at La Silla; and the even more remote—if only because the road is unpaved—Las Campanas Observatory, run by the Carnegie Institution.

All the institutions above are open for guided tours, but on Saturdays only, in daytime hours, and reservations are obligatory. Only the Mamalluca facility at Vicuña permits nighttime visits. Sernatur has published a bilingual pocket guide *Guía de Observación de los Cielos Más Claros del Mundo/Observation Guide of the Clearest Sky of the World* to orient visitors to the area. Though it includes a useful map of the southern skies at every season, it's worth mentioning that the Spanish version of the guide is far more coherent than its English translation.

Observatorio Comunal Cerro Mamalluca

Unlike the research observatories, Mamalluca's intention is to give its visitors a direct experience of the night sky through audiovisual presentations, unaided observation, and a look through its 12-inch professional-grade telescope, donated by AURA in appreciation of Vicuña's efforts at reducing light pollution. In its first two years, it has been such a spectacular success that a US$2 million expansion plan is under way, to be completed by 2003.

Unfortunately, Mamalluca's increasing popularity means that it's increasingly difficult to get a spot on the nightly tours, at least during the peak summer season. If at all possible, try to reserve a spot (US$6 per adult, US$2 for children to age 12) before arriving in Vicuña or La Serena, or if necessary go through one of the La Serena travel agencies. Tours take place at 8 and 10 P.M. and midnight; there is a six-person minimum and a 45-person maximum.

Mamalluca, 1,150 meters above sea level, is nine km northeast of downtown Vicuña via a gravel road. Vehicles leave in convoy from the information office in Vicuña: Observatorio Cerro Mamalluca, Avenida Gabriela Mistral 260, Oficina 1, tel. 51/411352, fax 51/411255, website: www.mamalluca.org, observatorio@mamalluca.org.

Observatorio Interamericano Cerro Tololo (Cerro Tololo International Observatory)

For more than three decades, Cerro Tololo's four-meter telescope was the Southern Hemisphere's largest, but larger lenses at Las Campanas and at Cerro Paranal (the latter in Region II, Antofagasta) have since eclipsed it. Still, the CTIO, operated by the Tucson-based Association of Universities for Research in Astronomy (AURA), is probably the most popular of the professional group for its access to La Serena and Vicuña.

Accomplished Chilean guides who are also fluent English speakers lead Saturday tours, which include an audiovisual introduction and a visit to two of the principal telescopes. There is no looking through telescopes on this daytime visit and there

(continued on next page)

SIGHTING THE SOUTHERN CROSS IN THE NORTE CHICO (cont'd)

would not be even at night—computers now download and organize the data that astronomers interpret at their terminals.

Cerro Tololo is 88 km southeast of La Serena via Ruta 41 and a winding gravel road to its sprawling campus just below the 2,200-meter summit. Prospective visitors should make reservations at its hilltop La Serena campus, just east of downtown, at Colina el Pino, tel. 51/205200. On the day of the tour, private vehicles meet at the gate near the well-signed turnoff on Ruta 41, five km east of the Puclaro tunnel, where they ascend the hill in a convoy.

Observatorio La Silla

On the border between Region III (Atacama) and Region IV (Coquimbo), isolated La Silla is 152 km north of La Serena via the Panamericana and a paved lateral that climbs eastward to a spot just beneath the summit of 2,418-meter Cerro Vizcachas.

Because of its isolation, La Silla has not had to deal with light pollution from urban development, and it enjoys more than 300 cloudless days per year. The diameters of its 14 telescopes reach up to 3.6 meters, and there is also a 15-meter radiotelescope. Guided visits, which take place every Saturday except in July and August, require permission from the European Space Organization (ESO), tel. 2/228-5006 in Santiago.

Observatorio Las Campanas

Operated by the U.S.-based Carnegie Institution, Las Campanas now boasts the area's largest telescopes, two 6.5-meter giants installed at a cost of US$75 million. Working in tandem, their power is nearly triple that of the previous 2.5-meter units, and astronomers here hope to sight undiscovered planets in nearby solar systems and to research the chemical composition of the universe.

Las Campanas is directly on the border between Region III and Region IV, via a gravel turnoff from the paved road to La Silla. Like the other research observatories, it is open Saturdays only; for reservations, contact its La Serena campus at Colina El Pino, tel. 51/224680, near the CTIO campus.

Commercial Tours

In addition to tours to the fixed observatories, many La Serena travel agencies offer nighttime excursions to see the southern skies with portable equipment, taking advantage of the clearest weather in the darkest locales, such as the Quebrada de Talca and Andacollo, southeast of the city. Visitors should time their trips within five days on either side of the new moon. Weather, however, can be a factor even in this area, and trips may be canceled if the weather proves too cloudy.

Staffed by professional astronomers with state-of-the-art mobile equipment, La Serena's Intijalsu Tour, tel. 09/548-8318, focuses primarily on group tours; English- and French-speaking guides are available. Specializing in archaeoastronomy (*intijalsu* means "sunset" in Aymara), this is a virtual and mobile office that chooses viewing sites depending on up-to-the-minute atmospheric conditions. It can also be contacted through its website: www.geocities.com/intijalsu/, or by email: intijalsu@yahoo.com.

Besides these landmarks, Vicuña has several monuments and museums detailed in the following paragraphs, as well as the Capel *pisco* distillery (see the special topic on *pisco* distilleries, Pick of the *Pisco*).

Museo Gabriela Mistral

In some ways, Vicuña's Gabriela Mistral museum seems more like a pilgrimage site, where the devout file quietly past images of the saint and her relics. Unlike the flamboyant, gregarious Pablo Neruda, Chile's other Nobel Prize poet, Mistral was subdued, even dour, and this low-key museum reflects her personality as much as Neruda's three extravagant houses in the Chilean heartland did his.

Among Mistral's relics is a full-sized replica of her birthplace at nearby Monte Grande, which, as it contains some original doors and windows, is a designated national monument. Born Lucila Godoy Alcayaga in 1889 of mixed descent—Spanish, indigenous, and perhaps African—she may have created her pseudonym by combining the names of Italian poet and novelist Gabriel D'Annunzio and the French Provençal poet Frédéric Mistral (also a Nobel Prize winner, in 1904); an alternative explanation says she may have combined the name of the archangel Gabriel with that of the cold, dry north wind of Mediterranean France.

Mistral began writing in local newspapers and Chilean magazines and fell under the influence of the famous Nicaraguan poet Rubén Darío, who spent several years in South America. Like Darío, and Neruda for that matter, she occupied a variety of diplomatic posts in places from Los Angeles, Santa Barbara, New York City, and Florida to Cuba, Guatemala, Brazil, Oporto, Madrid, Nice, and Italy. Some Chilean rightists accused her of being a Communist (ironically enough for someone who may have admired D'Annunzio, an ardent Mussolini supporter), but she maintained public neutrality, even seeming apolitical (unlike Neruda, who *was* a Communist and proud of it).

Among the museum's exhibits are a fine photographic biography, a bookstore that includes titles she donated to the library of Vicuña, and a forbidding bust whose grim expression must have intimidated her students, as much as her writing suggested her affection for them. There's a copy of her Nobel Prize check, which she used to buy a house in the United States.

At Gabriela Mistral 759, the museum, tel. 51/411223, mgmistral@entelchile.net, charges US$1 admission; it also contains an art gallery. Summer hours are 10 A.M.–7 P.M. daily except Sunday, when closing time is an hour earlier. From March to September, hours are 10 A.M.–1 P.M. daily, 2:30–5:45 P.M. weekdays, and 3–5:45 P.M. Saturday. From October to December, hours are 10 A.M.–1 P.M. daily, 3–7 P.M. weekdays, and 3–6 P.M. Saturday.

Museo Entomológico e Historia Natural

Proving what a dedicated, enthusiastic amateur can achieve, owner Guido Castillo has done a remarkable job of organizing this extensive collection of mostly South American insects, providing taxonomic details and illustrating their geographical distribution. The museum also contains a selection of regional minerals and fossils and taxidermy specimens with equally useful information.

A pleasant surprise, the museum, Chacabuco 334, tel. 09/3237177, is open 10:30 A.M.–8:30 P.M. or later daily. Admission costs US$.65 for adults, half that for kids.

Museo Histórico de Elqui

An unfortunate exception to the increasingly professionalization and improvement of Chilean museums, Vicuña's historical museum qualifies as a "museum of the kitchen sink," with minerals, fossils, Diaguita ceramics, and a congeries of household objects gleaned from around the valley. One room displays photos of Gabriela Mistral, most of which are on display, under better conditions, in the Mistral museum.

Theoretically open 10 A.M.–5:30 P.M. daily, the museum is at Prat 90, tel. 51/412104. Admission costs US$.65 for adults, US$.35 for students, and US$.25 for kids.

Casa de los Madariaga

Built by an influential landowning family, this historic adobe (1875) is now a private museum with eight rooms of antiques, artifacts, and photographs from the late 19th century. At Gabriela Mistral 783, the house, tel. 51/411220, is open 10 A.M.–7 P.M. daily; admission costs US$.85 for adults, half that for seniors, and children get in free.

Cerro de la Virgen

For views of Vicuña and the Elqui valley, follow the footpath or road up to this pilgrimage site, where an image of the Virgen de Lourdes overlooks the city. Though it's barely an hour on foot to the top, carry water and food.

Accommodations

Vicuña has relatively few places to stay, but quality is good to excellent in all categories. **Residencial Mistral,** Gabriela Mistral 180, tel. 51/411278, charges US$5 pp with shared bath, though breakfast costs an extra US$1.50; other meals are also available at moderate prices. Utilitarian, even spartan, **Hostal Michel,** Gabriela Mistral 573, tel. 51/411060, costs US$7 pp with private bath but also without breakfast.

Set among gardens and orchards, **Residencial La Elquina,** O'Higgins 65, tel. 51/411317, costs US$8.50 pp with shared bath, US$10 pp with private bath, both with breakfast. Some rooms, though, are cluttered with too many beds. In an older colonial house with an appealing patio, run by a friendly family, **Hostal Valle Hermoso,** Gabriela Mistral 706, tel./fax 51/411206, is a bargain at US$10 pp with breakfast. It also has shortcomings, however—the owners have partitioned large rooms into several smaller (though not tiny) ones at the expense of the building's architectural integrity, and some lumpy mattresses could use replacement. Parking is available.

New on the scene, **Hotel Sol del Valle,** Gabriela Mistral 741, tel. 51/411078, charges US$12 pp with breakfast. Furnished with antiques and remodeled with colonial style, but with modern conveniences including swimming pool and parking, **Hotel Halley,** Gabriela Mistral 542, tel./fax 51/412070, is one of the country's best values. Rack rates are US$25/42 but IVA discounts mean an even better deal at US$21/36.

Hostería Yunkai, O'Higgins 72, tel. 51/411195, fax 51/411593, yunkai@latinmail.com, charges US$50 s or d, breakfast included, and also offers kitchen facilities and a pool. At **Hostería Vicuña,** Sargento Aldea 101, tel. 51/411301, fax 51/411144, rates are US$40/53 s/d with breakfast. Besides a quiet garden location at the west end of town, it boasts amenities such as a restaurant, tennis courts, and a swimming pool.

Food

Vicuña has relatively few places to eat but, again, reasonable quality. Besides the places that follow, try the dining room at Hostería de Vicuña.

At the southwest corner of the Plaza de Armas, **Timbao,** San Martín 203, tel. 51/419204, is a good breakfast choice, with fresh juices to die for; dinners and lunches cost around US$4. The rather ordinary **Pizzería Virgo,** Prat 234, tel. 51/411090, is also moderately priced.

The **Club Social de Vicuña,** Gabriela Mistral 445, tel. 51/411853, serves a traditional Chilean menu at above-average prices in comfortable surroundings.

Cabrito (grilled kid goat, US$7) is the house specialty at **Restaurant Halley,** Gabriela Mistral 410, tel. 51/411225, which also offers a good wine selection, good service, and indoor and outdoor seating, the latter shaded by *totora* mats. Other entrées—a cornucopia of poultry, beef, pork, fish and shellfish—range US$3.50–13.

Entertainment and Events

There's little nightlife in Vicuña, but try **Pub Kharma,** Gabriela Mistral 417, tel. 51/419738. In summer, the Municipalidad sponsors live concerts in the Plaza de Armas; the connecting streets may be blocked off and admission charged, but it's possible to hear from nearby.

Vicuña's grape harvest festival, the **Festival de la Vendimia,** takes place every February, climaxing on February 22, the city's anniversary.

Shopping

The new **Pueblo de Artesanos,** on the north side of the Plaza de Armas, is an attractive new retail space for local products, from *pisco* and papaya to honey, jewelry, and leather. Given the area's oddball reputation, there's surprisingly little New Age esoterica (see Cochiguaz, under the Upper Río Elqui, below).

Mami Sabina, Gabriela Mistral 238, also has a selection of local crafts.

Services

Money: Change elsewhere if at all possible—the only choice for money exchange, Banco del Estado, on the south side of the Plaza de Armas at Chacabuco 384, changes cash only and its ATM accepts only its own cards.

Postal: Correos de Chile has an office at the Municipalidad, on Gabriela Mistral just west of San Martín.

Telephone and Internet: Entel's long-distance office is at Gabriela Mistral 351, on the north side of the Plaza de Armas. Telefónica is on the east side of the plaza, on Prat. Vicuña's area code is 51, the same as La Serena's.

Internet access is more expensive, about US$4 per hour, than in La Serena. Try Café Timbao, San Martín 203, which is open until midnight, or Mami Sabina, Gabriela Mistral 238, which closes around 10 P.M.

Medical: Vicuña's Hospital San Juan de Dios is at the corner of Independencia and Prat, tel. 51/411263.

Information

The municipal Oficina de Información Turística, in the Torre Bauer (see above) at San Martín s/n, tel. 51/209125, luis_hernan_vigorena@latinmail.com, is open weekdays 8:30 A.M.–5:30 P.M. all year; in January and February, it's also open 9:30 A.M.–5:30 A.M. weekends.

Transportation

Buses leave from the Terminal Rodoviario de Vicuña, at the corner of Prat and O'Higgins, a block south of the Plaza de Armas. Several companies go to La Serena, including Vía Elqui, which has eight buses daily to Pisco Elqui (US$1.50). Long-distance carriers include Pullman Bus, tel. 51/411466, to Santiago and Valparaíso/Viña del Mar, and Buses Tal, tel. 51/411404, and Expreso Norte, tel. 51/411348,

both to Santiago and intermediates. La Serena has better long-distance connections.

From the Terminal de Taxi Colectivos, also at Prat and O'Higgins but directly across the street from the Rodoviario, shared taxis go up the Elqui valley to Paihuano (US$1.25), Monte Grande (US$1.50), and Pisco Elqui (US$2), and down the valley to La Serena (US$2.50).

THE UPPER RÍO ELQUI

At Rivadavia, 18 km east of Vicuña, two rivers converge to form the Elqui: the Río Turbio enters from the nearly uninhabited northeast, while the Río Claro descends from the south, an area marked by a series of scenic villages along a smooth paved road that goes all the way to Pisco Elqui and continues as a gravel road to Alcohuaz. Just south of Monte Grande, a gravel road climbs southeast up the valley of the Río Cochiguaz, famous (or infamous) for its cultishness.

Pisco producers may be complaining about competition from imported whiskey in the Chilean market, but their newly planted vines continue climbing the slopes of rocky alluvial fans; apricots also grow abundantly in the upper Claro drainage.

The scenery, fresh dry climate, and clear skies are quickly making the upper Elqui watershed an increasingly popular travel destination, but it's also attracted the country's largest concentration of New Age and UFO aficionados—to the frustration and embarrassment of the serious astronomers who work at area observatories.

Paihuano

Paihuano, 30 km from Vicuña and 978 meters above sea level, is a shady riverside service center. Its **Hostería Río Claro,** tel. 51/227362 or 51/451948, just north of town in the Quebrada de Pinto, has excellent value rooms for US$21 s or d, plus four-person *cabañas* for US$44; there's also a pool and a restaurant with full meals in the US$5 range.

Monte Grande

Gabriela Mistral's birthplace, 10 km south of Paihuano, Monte Grande is also home to the hillside

PICK OF THE *PISCO*

Wine tourism may be growing throughout the Chilean heartland, but grapes from the Norte Chico make more *pisco,* the potent grape brandy that's the foundation of the legendary pisco sour. While *pisco* comes from all of the Norte Chico's transverse valleys—Copiapó, Huasco, Elqui, Límarí, and Choapa—the Elqui, from La Serena to the river's upper reaches, offers the best options to get to know Chile's preferred version of spirits.

Pisco derives from muscatel grapes, which thrive in the narrow valleys, where summer harvest temperatures average around 30°C and the limited winter rains rarely exceed 120 mm. After harvest, the grapes are slowly milled and then fermented under strict temperature controls. After being stored as wine for a time, it undergoes a slow distillation process to extract the ethyl alcohol and other chemical components that typify the product. Finally, the liquor is stored in wooden casks just long enough to stabilize it.

Pisco comes in several categories, according to its alcoholic content (proof is expressed in terms of *grados,* or degrees): *selección* (30°); *especial* (35°); *reservado* (40°); and *gran pisco* (42° to 43°, though in some cases as high as 50°). It also comes in a variety of containers, the most distinctive of which is probably Capel's Easter Island souvenir *moai.*

One pisco sour, though, belongs in a category of its own: on February 16, 1999, opposite the Casino at Peñuelas, 800 people mixed 11,172 bottles of *pisco* (7,202 liters) with 96,000 lemons, 1,800 kg of refined sugar, and 3,724 kg of ice in preparing the world's largest ever. The result of their 24 hours' work was 200,000 servings totaling 12,500 liters in 16,000 bottles.

Planta Control, La Serena

One of Chile's major *pisco* sellers, Control is a co-operative dating from 1933, when numerous small producers united to form the Cooperativa Agrícola Control Pisquero de Elquí. Because of perceived pressures from cheap whiskey imports, Capel and its main rival, Pisco Control, are considering a merger.

Control's La Serena plant, Rengifo 140, tel. 51/207800, is open for visits in January and February only. Weekday hours are 9:30 A.M.–1:30 P.M. and 2–7 P.M.; Saturday hours are 10:30 A.M.–1:30 P.M. only.

recent and older *pisco* plantings

© WAYNE BERNHARDSON

Planta Capel, Vicuña

Capel, a cooperative of 1,500 member growers throughout the Norte Chico, is the Elqui's other main *pisco* producer (Capel stands for Cooperativa Agrícola Pisquera Elqui, or Elqui Agro–Pisco Cooperative). More than 80 percent of the Elqui valley's *pisco* grapes, in varying strengths, are distilled and bottled at Vicuña's Capel plant, which offers tours and tasting the entire year. Among the brands produced here are the standard Pisco Capel brand and the premium Los Artesanos de Cochiguaz, known for its woody flavor, in smaller batches. The plant also turns out *pajarete,* a unique dessert wine.

An easy walk from Vicuña, on the Peralillo road on the south side of the river, Planta Capel, tel. 51/411251, offers guided tours 10 A.M.–6 P.M. daily in summer, 10 A.M.–12:30 P.M. and 2:30–6 P.M. the rest of the year. Individual attention is the rule—there is no minimum size for tour groups—and there's an ample sales room. The plant is closed January 1, May 1, September 20, November 8, and December 25.

Lagar Artesanos de Cochiguaz, Monte Grande

Across from Gabriela Mistral's final resting place,

Capel's premium brand offers a brief view of the milling process—the distilling is done in Vicuña rather than here—along with tasting and sales. For most Chileans, though, the highlight is Ruperto, an ostensibly boozing burro who appears in the company's TV commercials—everyone wants to be photographed with him.

The Lagar, tel. 51/1982534, is open 10 A.M.–1 P.M. and 2:30–6 P.M. daily. Like the Vicuña plant, it's closed January 1, May 1, September 20, November 8, and December 25.

Solar de Pisco Tres Erres

In the increasingly trendy village of Pisco Elqui, Tres Erres, tel. 51/1982503, is as much a museum as a distillery, what with its antique machinery and aging bodegas. Tours and tasting take place 10 A.M.–7 P.M. daily in summer; the rest of the year, hours are 10:30 A.M.–1 P.M. and 2–6:30 P.M.

Destilería Los Nichos

Four km south of Pisco Elqui, Los Nichos, tel. 51/451085, is an old-fashioned distillery where all the processing is done by hand in small batches. It's open 11 A.M.–1 P.M. and 3–7 P.M. daily.

Tumba de Gabriela Mistral—though she lived most of her life away from here and much of it outside the country, her will stipulated that:

> *it is my wish that my body be interred in my dear village of Monte Grande in the Elqui valley.*

Monte Grande is also home to the **Museo de Sitio Casa Escuela Gabriela Mistral,** a former public school that served as the local post office for many years until its restoration in 1980–82; with Mistral's tomb and the nearby church, it comprises a *zona típica* national monument, like the central core of La Serena. Though it displays many of the same photos as other regional museums, it does have some original furniture. Open daily except Monday 10 A.M.–1 P.M. and 3–6 P.M., it charges US$.50 admission.

Monte Grande lacks accommodations, but its **Mesón del Fraile,** directly on the highway

through town, tel. 51/451957, is a popular lunch and dinner choice. It is also the site of the Artesanos de Cochiguaz *pisco* plant (for details on visits, see the special topic Pick of the *Pisco*).

Pisco Elqui

High in the Elqui valley, its restored and modernized adobes apparently becoming trophy houses, the picturesque hillside village of Pisco Elqui seems to be metamorphosing into a scale model of Santa Fe (New Mexico). At 1,247 meters above sea level, on the steep southern slope of the Río Claro canyon and two km south of Monte Grande, it boasts the best tourist infrastructure of any village in the area and a variety of activities varying from souvenir hunting in the artisans' market to *pisco* tasting and horseback riding.

Formerly known as La Unión, Pisco Elqui changed names in 1939, at the urging of then-deputy Gabriel González Videla, in the interest of product promotion—and because of fears that the Peruvian city of Pisco, south of Lima, intended to register the word as an international trademark.

Sights and Recreation: Beneath the towering Gothic steeple of the **Capilla Nuestra Señora del Rosario** (1922), the shady **Plaza de Armas** is the site of summer's **Mercado Artesanal.** At the end of the block, the **Solar de Pisco Tres Erres** provides tours and tasting, as does the **Destilería Los Nichos,** four km farther up the valley (for details, see the special topic Pick of the *Pisco*).

Alcohuaz Expediciones, Prat s/n, tel. 51/1982523 or 09/4492473, offers horseback rides into the outback.

Accommodations and Food: Camping El Olivo, O'Higgins s/n, tel. 51/451790, offers camping for US$6 pp, half that for children, on grounds with a swimming pool.

Pisco Elqui's real landmark accommodations is its cheapest, the decrepit but singular **Hostal Don Juan,** Prat s/n, tel./fax 51/451087, which may remind Hitchcock fans of the house behind the Bates Motel. Rates are US$7 pp.

Hotel Gabriela Mistral, Arturo Prat 59, tel. 51/1982525, tel. 2/696-0351 in Santiago, has good facilities for US$14 pp, plus a decent bar/restaurant. For the same price, **Hotel Elqui,** O'Higgins s/n, tel. 51/451083, is probably a little better, as is its restaurant. Both the Mistral and the Elqui have off-season bargain rates.

Just across the street from Hostal Don Juan, **Hostería Los Dátiles** Prat s/n, tel. 51/451121, has half a dozen utilitarian *cabañas* that aren't bad for US$35 s or d, but until the landscaping matures they'll look a little austere. Its bar/restaurant, in an older and more interesting building, is worth a try.

German-run **El Tesoro de Elqui,** Prat s/n, tel. 51/1822609, elqui@bigfoot.com, has acquired a reputation not just for outstanding accommodations but also for exceptional food.

The picturesque hillside village of Pisco Elqui boasts the best tourist infrastructure of any village in the area and a variety of activities varying from souvenir hunting in the artisans' market to pisco tasting and horseback riding.

Rates are US$16/25 s/d with shared bath, US$40 d with private bath. Day use of the pool costs US$4.50 for adults, US$2.50 for kids.

Pisco Elqui's most stylish choice, **Refugio Misterios del Elqui,** Prat s/n, tel. 51/1982544, rents six hillside view *cabañas* in a Mexican motif with fine furnishings for US$79 d, US$97 q. It also has an appealing restaurant, with a French chef and shady balcony seating.

Living up to the area's extraterrestrial reputation, Pisco Elqui now has a bar/restaurant simply called **Saucer. Jugos Naturales,** across from the church, has spectacular fresh fruit juices for less than US$2.

Transportation: Both buses and *taxi colectivos* run regularly up and down the canyon to Vicuña, some of them continuing to La Serena.

Cochiguaz

Cultish Cochiguaz, an enclave of crystals, cosmic energy, and UFO sightings, is less a nucleated geographical community—the name applies to just about anywhere in the constricted canyon of the Río Cochiguaz—than it is a state of mind. Even then, it's not so flagrantly flaky as some other New Age outposts, and there's even a bit of self-effacing humor; the landmark Refugio Alma-Zen, for instance, is a punning Spanish reference to the irony of running a very practical general store (*almacén* in Spanish) and its apparent Buddhist essence—*alma* means "soul"). Still, it's hard to avoid the temptation to say that all the extraterrestrial sightings here may have more than a little to do with all the *pisco* that's produced and consumed in the area.

Accommodations and Food: There's a string of *cabañas* and campgrounds that runs the length of the Cochiguaz canyon to the end of the road at El Colorado. Note that rural electrification has barely begun here; the *cabañas* have solar power or their own generators, but the campgrounds, unlike those elsewhere in Chile, lack lights or any other hookups.

At Km 6, **Cabañas Naturistas El Albaricoque,** tel./fax 51/230087, tel. 51/1984737, rents several smallish but rustically comfortable *departamentos* for US$35 s or d with private bath—an excellent value. Larger *cabañas,* sleeping up to five people, go for US$61. Full board at its vegetarian restaurant costs an additional US$16 pp, half board US$10 pp. It also deals in alternative therapies and meditation workshops.

At Km 11, **Refugio El Alma Zen,** tel. 9605403 from Santiago, tel. 188/2/9605402 from elsewhere in Chile, website: www.valledelelqui.cl, is the most self-consciously kooky choice along the canyon—in addition to *cabañas* with private bath, hot water, kitchen facilities, there's a quartz crystal swimming pool. Rates start at US$41 s or d; you can have your aura cleansed or perform Tibetan rituals to recover your youth for US$4 each, or do aroma tarot for US$17.

A short distance on, **Camping Río Mágico,** tel. 51/412060, charges US$5 pp in somewhat ragged surroundings. At Km 12.5, **Camping Tambo Huara,** tel. 51/773400, is the best value in the valley for US$6 pp in attractively designed campsites set among a combination of native plants and cultivated fruit trees. Like other sites along the road, it has a couple of meditation gardens, but also offers spotless toilets, potable water at every site, and hot showers from 9 A.M.–noon—not to mention a good portable telescope to observe the southern skies.

Just beyond Tambo Huara, at Km 13, **Cabañas Casa del Agua,** tel. 51/411871, casadelagua@ usa.net, has more luxurious *cabañas* and is considerably less cultish. Rates are US$79 s or d. It offers many activities, including fishing, swimming, hiking, mountain biking, and horseback riding.

Near the end of the road, **Camping Cochiguaz,** tel. 51/451154, is the least value though it does have some outstanding features, most notably plenty of river frontage. For US$14 for up to six people, its facilities can't match those of others lower in the canyon, but try dickering. **Transportation:** There is no regular public transport up the canyon of the Río Cochiguaz, but there are fairly frequent pickup trucks and other vehicles that will offer lifts from the turnoff at Monte Grande.

PASO DEL AGUA NEGRA

From Rivadavia, the international Ruta 41 ascends the valley of the Río Turbio northeast and then southeast for 75 km to the Chilean border post of Juntas del Toro, where it's another 92 km southeast to the Argentine border and the 4,765-meter Paso del Agua Negra, where it continues to the spa of Termas de Pismanta and provincial capital of San Juan. From late November until the first April snows close the pass, the border is open 8 A.M.–6 P.M. daily; authorities recently authorized a feasibility study for the creation of a tunnel to open the area to all-year traffic, but this is likely at least a decade away.

From the border post, another gravel road continues 25 km northeast to the **Hostal y Restaurant Baños Termales Juntas del Toro,** a hot springs site recently opened to the public after the closure of the Mina El Indio gold mine, to whom it belonged. Juntas del Toro has a

© WAYNE BERNHARDSON

penitentes (snow formations), Paso del Agua Negra

Vicuña office at Gabriela Mistral 543, tel. 51/4-12672 or 09/3417904.

There is no regular public transportation over the Paso del Agua Negra to San Juan, but there is constant speculation as to whether—or when—it might commence. In the meantime, La Serena's Talinay Expeditions does occasional overnight excursions to Pismanta, the best way to see the barren *puna,* glaciers, and *penitentes,* frozen snow formations that bear a likeness to lines of monks dressed in the conical headgear known as *cucuruchos.*

OVALLE

Capital of the province of Limarí, Ovalle takes its name from José Tomas Ovalle, vice president of the republic at the city's founding in 1831. Though primarily a service center for the area's farmers and fruit growers, it is also the closest city to Parque Nacional Fray Jorge, the hot springs resort of Termas de Socos, and the Molle archaeological site at Valle del Encanto. It's also the gateway to the upper Hurtado valley, an area of growing interest for its access to the Pichasca petrified forest and backcountry horseback excursions.

Orientation

Ovalle is 88 km south of La Serena by the paved two-lane Ruta 43, and 37 km east from the Termas de Socos turnoff on the Panamericana. Its palm-studded Parque Alameda, between Ariztía Oriente and Ariztía Poniente, separates the main city grid to the west from the newer and slightly more irregular area to the east. Most services are to the west, in and around the Plaza de Armas.

Sights

On the east side of the Plaza de Armas, at present undergoing restoration after earthquake damage in 1997, the adobe **Iglesia San Vicente Ferrer** (1849) features a distinctive bell tower and murals on its wooden ceiling.

Across the Alameda, in the former railroad station (built 1926–30) that now houses the **Centro Cultural Guillermo Durruty Alvarez,** the **Museo del Limarí** houses a collection of

1,700 ceramic pieces, primarily Diaguita (some of them Inka-influenced), though there are also earlier Huentelauquén and Molle artifacts. At the corner of Covarrubias and Antofagasta, the museum, tel. 53/620029, is open 9 A.M.–1 P.M. and 3–7 P.M. Tuesday to Friday, 10 A.M.–1 P.M. Saturday, Sunday, and holidays. Admission costs US$1 for adults, half that for children and seniors, but is free on Sundays.

Farther to the east, at Benavente and Maestranza, the **Feria Modelo de Ovalle** is northern Chile's largest fruit and vegetable market. On the site of the former railroad repair yard, it's open Monday, Wednesday, Friday, and Saturday 8 A.M.–4 P.M.

Accommodations

Basic **Residencial Atenas,** Socos 12, tel. 53/620424, will do for a night, but no longer, at US$7/10 s/d with shared bath; there's a US$1 surcharge for hot showers. Almost next door, the slightly more expensive **Residencial Socos,** Socos 22, tel. 53/629856, gets some short-stay trade.

Though slipping a little, **Hotel Roxy,** Libertad 155, tel. 53/620080, is still one of the better values in town for US$11/17 s/d for large rooms with shared bath, while rooms with private bath cost US$14/22. It still boasts a huge patio with a grape arbor and the hot water is abundant, but some of the beds are soft and there's less attention to detail than in the past. Rooms toward the back are quieter.

Not far from the bus terminal, friendly **Hotel Quisco,** Maestranza 161, tel. 53/620351, has clean, comfortable, utilitarian rooms with cable TV for US$20/26 s/d with private bath, but some interior rooms are dark. It also has a bar/restaurant. The deco-style **Gran Hotel,** Vicuña Mackenna 210, tel./fax 53/621084, yagnam@terra.cl, is a bit worn and less grand than its name would imply, but the smallish rooms are respectable value for US$25/36 s/d with breakfast; parking costs US$2 extra.

Frayed but friendly, **Hotel American,** Vicuña Mackenna 169, tel. 53/620159, tel./fax 53/620722, has ground floor rooms with cable TV, private bath, and free parking for US$25/33 s/d, but more spacious upstairs rooms with bathtubs and, for some enigmatic reason, better cable reception, go for US$29/37 s/d. Under the same management, better-maintained but with similar services, **Hotel Turismo Ovalle,** Victoria 295, tel. 53/623258, tel./fax 53/623536, is the best in town, but not dramatically better than some cheaper alternatives; some of the bathrooms are very small. Rates are US$38/49 s/d.

Food

In and around the **Mercado Municipal,** at the corner of Victoria and Independencia, there are several inexpensive eateries. The standard chain **Bavaria** is at Vicuña Mackenna 161-B, tel. 53/630578.

Like most Chilean cities, Ovalle has a good fire station restaurant, the **Casino La Bomba,** Aguirre 364. The **Club Comercial,** Aguirre 244, is comparable.

For Middle Eastern specialties, as well as beef, chicken, and seafood, try the **Club Social Arabe,** Arauco 255, tel. 53/620015, where entrées run US$3.50–7.50. The most distinctive dining experience, though, is **El Quijote,** Arauco 298, tel. 53/620501, a throwback to the days of the Unidad Popular that serves good Chilean meals with its politics.

Entertainment

La Cukaracha, Independencia s/n, is a pub and disco.

On the south side of the Plaza de Armas, **Cine Cervantes,** Vicuña Mackenna 370, tel. 53/6-20267, shows current movies.

Services

Money: Agencia Tres Valles, Libertad 496, tel. 53/629650, will change U.S. dollars. Banco de Crédito, Vicuña Mackenna 440, and Banco Santander, Victoria 322, both have ATMs.

Postal: Correos de Chile is on Vicuña Mackenna, on the south side of the Plaza de Armas.

Telephone and Internet: Telefónica is at Vicuña Mackenna 95, Entel at Vicuña Mackenna 115, and Chilesat at Vicuña Mackenna 232. The Chilesat office has Internet access for US$4 per hour. Ovalle's area code is 53.

Medical: Ovalle's Hospital Dr. Antonio Tirado is at the north end of Ariztía Poniente, tel. 53/620042.

Information

Limtur, a local travel agency at Vicuña Mackenna 370, Oficina 9-A, tel. 53/630057, limtur@itn.cl, operates an Oficina de Información Turística in a kiosk in the Parque Alameda, on Vicuña Mackenna/Benavente between Ariztía Poniente and Ariztía Oriente. The latter's hours, however, can be erratic.

Transportation

Most bus companies have finally moved from their former offices along Avenida Ariztía to the Terrapuerto Limarí, about four blocks east at Maestranza 443. Since Ovalle is less than an hour from La Serena, services are similar, although many Serena-bound buses use the Panamericana rather than pass through Ovalle.

Regional carriers include Buses López to Combarbalá and La Ligua; Expreso Rojas to Combarbalá and La Serena; Buses Serenamar to the beach resort of Tongoy (seven daily between 8 A.M. and 7:30 P.M.); Expreso Norte/Tacc Vía Choapa to La Serena/Coquimbo, Vicuña, Illapel, Salamanca, and Los Vilos; Buses Vía Elqui to La Serena/Coquimbo, Vicuña, and Pisco Elqui; Pullman Ciktur, tel. 53/620737, to La Serena/Coquimbo, Tongoy, and Guanaqueros; Horvitur to La Serena/Coquimbo; and Lasval/Inca Bus, tel. 53/621574 or 53/620886, to interior destinations such as Combarbalá and Chañaral Alto.

Long-distance carriers include Ara to Chañaral; Tur-Bus, tel. 53/623659, north and south along the Panamericana; Tas Choapa, tel. 53/6-26780, to Santiago; Flota Barrios to Panamericana destinations between Santiago and Arica; Pullman Bus, tel. 53/629906, to Santiago, Valparaíso, Arica, and intermediates; Carmelita, tel. 53/626482, to Santiago, Arica, and intermediates; Los Diamantes de Elqui to La Serena and Santiago; Fénix Pullman Norte; tel. 53/621371, to La Serena, Antofagasta, Iquique, and Arica; and Elqui Bus Palacios, tel. 53/626705, to La Serena/Coquimbo and Santiago.

Sample destinations, fares, and times include La Serena/Coquimbo (US$2.50, one hour), Los Vilos (US$7, 2.5 hours), Vallenar (US$7, 2.5 hours), Santiago (US$11–13, five hours), Copiapó (US$9, four hours), Caldera (US$12, five hours), Chañaral (US$14, six hours), Antofagasta (US$23, 14 hours), Iquique (US$32, 18 hours) Arica (US$35, 22 hours). *Semi-cama* service costs US$27 to Antofagasta, US$36 to Iquique, and US$39 to Arica.

Taxi Colectivo: Fremop, Ariztía Oriente 218, tel. 53/626969, has shared taxis to La Serena (US$3, one hour), as does Colectivos Tacso.

VICINITY OF OVALLE

While Ovalle itself has no major attractions, it's a central location for a number of nearby excursions.

Monumento Arqueológico Valle del Encanto

In a granite bedrock canyon midway between Ovalle and the Panamericana, petroglyphs, pictographs, and *piedras tacitas* (mortars) evidence the presence of the El Molle culture that flourished here in the early centuries of what was, in the Old World, the Christian era. Ranging from present-day Copiapó to the Río Choapa, the Molle culture was agropastoral, probably reflecting a variety of influences from San Pedro de Atacama in the north to the Llolleo of central Chile and the Patrén of the south, not to mention trans-Andean influences from as far as present-day Brazil—the *timbeta* or lip disk common in lowland Amazonia has been found here.

The most typically Andean of the artifacts here are engraved, carved, smoked, or painted ceramics, and the remains of camelids. Best seen around midday, when shadows are not a factor, the petroglyphs of Sector 2 represent masks or tiara-like objects typical of the Limarí region.

Under the authority of the Municipalidad de Ovalle, Valle del Encanto is a national monument. Any bus between Ovalle and the Panamericana will drop passengers at the turnoff, which is 19 km from Ovalle and 18 km from Termas de Socos, but the Valle del Encanto itself is five km south via a bumpy gravel road with no public transportation. The Municipalidad has an information booth where it collects an admission charge of US$.50; hours

petroglyphs at Valle del Encanto

© WAYNE BERNHARDSON

are 8:15 A.M.–8 P.M. daily in summer. The rest of the year, it closes at 7 P.M.

Termas de Socos

Precisely at the junction of the Panamericana and the Ruta 45 turnoff to Ovalle, 370 km north of Santiago and 100 km south of La Serena, Termas de Socos is the most upscale hot springs resort north of Santiago—but at the same time, it's an affordable day trip for anyone who wants to soak in the thermal baths (US$6 pp) or swim in the pool (US$6 for adults, US$4 for kids). Jacuzzis, saunas, massages, and similar services are also available; a plant also produces its own bottled mineral water.

Hotel Termas de Socos, tel. 53/681021 or 09/4180293, tel. 2/2363336 in Santiago, charges US$60/110 s/d in its upper pavilion, US$67/120 s/d in its lower pavilion, both with full board. Nonguests can also lunch or dine at the restaurant.

On the same grounds, **Camping Termas de Socos** provides an economical alternative to the hotel, though it's not cheap by the standards of Chilean campgrounds—up to US$7.50 pp.

THE RÍO HURTADO VALLEY

From an overlook about five km north of Ovalle, a good but dusty road climbs the nearly untouristed valley of the Río Hurtado to the village of Hurtado, where a winding northbound road crosses the Portezuelo Tres Cruces to Vicuña. In his *Canto General* (1946), Nobel Prize poet Pablo Neruda described the valley's rugged landscape as an area

> **between rough and irascible hills, bristling with spines, because here the great Andean cactus rises like a cruel candlestick.**

For motorists or cyclists, though, the Hurtado valley could make an excellent backcountry alternative approach to La Serena and the upper Elqui valley. It was also possible that bus service might commence from Hurtado to La Serena.

Monumento Natural Pischasca

About 45 km east of Ovalle, at the village of San Pedro Viejo, a bridge crosses the river to this 128-hectare semidesert reserve, ranging from 711 to 1,072 meters above sea level. Once full of fossil *Araucarias,* it suffered so much pilferage until it acquired legal protection in 1969 that only a handful of specimens are on site. Dinosaur bones have also been found here, however, and the so-called **Casa de Piedra,** a rock shelter, contains some smoke-blemished Molle rock art.

Open 9 A.M.–6 P.M. daily, Pichasca has picnic sites but no campground. Admission costs US$2.50 for adults, US$1 for children.

From Ovalle's Feria Modelo, M&R buses en route to Hurtado pass San Pedro, from where it's a two-km climb along a dusty road to Pichasca.

Hacienda Los Andes

In the upper valley of the Río Hurtado, a mountainous area whose chaparral and cacti resemble parts of southern California and northern Baja California, German operator Clark Stede has opened a facility for backcountry horseback trips that resembles, except for the arid surroundings, his former Campo Aventura near drizzly Puerto Varas. Near the village of Morrillos, Hacienda Los Andes is a highly professional operation that offers access on sure-footed horses to vast areas of steep and rugged terrain barely touched by tourists. It also has ample river frontage for swimming and relaxing at the end of the day.

Rates for a variety of day trips, not all of them on horseback, run mostly US$65–80 pp; overnight excursions run US$135–252 pp; these include transfers from either Ovalle or Vicuña. Four-day, three-night backcountry trips cost US$371 pp. B&B accommodations in colonial-style rooms are also available from US$27 pp; for more details, contact Hacienda Los Andes, Correo Hurtado, tel. 53/198-2106, website: www.haciendalosandes.com, info@haciendalosandes.com.

Hurtado

In the village of Hurtado, nine km up the valley from Hacienda Los Andes, the only *hospedaje* recently closed, but there is still good food and cold beer at **Restaurant Benita,** open noon–10 P.M. or sometimes later.

COMBARBALÁ

About midway between Ovalle and Illapel, the mountain town of Combarbalá dates from 1789. Originally called Villa de San Francisco de Borja de Combarbalá, it owed its founding to gold, silver, and copper deposits, but *pisco* grapes and citrus now dominate the economic landscape. Some 875 meters above sea level, the city is known for jewelry and other crafts made of *combarbalita,* a semiprecious stone of silicon, quartz, clay, and copper and silver oxides that comes in a variety of colors.

Given its location along the old highland rail route, Combarbalá can be part of an adventurous backroads trek by motor vehicle or bicycle between Ovalle and La Ligua (see the special topic Taking the High Road through the Norte Chico for details). The city is 112 km south of Ovalle by a good paved road via Monte Patria, 99 km south of Ovalle by a 32-km paved road to Punitaqui and another 67 km on gravel. It is 73 km from Illapel via a route that is mostly gravel, and 80 km from the Panamericana via a road that is paved as far as Canela Baja.

Accommodations are few; the cheapest is **Residencial Combarbalina,** Libertad 542, for around US$5 pp. Having recently changed hands, **Hostería Beltrán,** Maipú 197, tel. 53/741532 or 53/741533, offers ample and comfortable rooms at reasonable prices—US$21/28 s/d—but now seems a bit disorganized. It also offers meals.

The Terminal de Buses is on the south side of the Plaza de Armas. Several bus lines connect the city with Ovalle, but there is no service south to Illapel.

PARQUE NACIONAL BOSQUE DE FRAY JORGE

In the coastal range known as the Altos de Talinay, the 9,959-hectare Bosque de Fray Jorge consists of a small but dense Valdivian cloud forest, nurtured by the dripping *camanchaca* but nearly encircled by a barren semidesert. At sea level, precipitation is only about 113 cm per year, but above 450 meters or so, within the forest, it ranges between 800 and 1,000 cm.

Because of its unique flora, of which only about 400 hectares remain, Fray Jorge has been a UNESCO World Biosphere Reserve since 1977. First seen by a Franciscan friar in 1672, it is the subject of debate between scientists who believe these shrinking woodlands are the victims of human activities—primarily woodcutting, farming, and fire—and those who see evidence of long-term climatic change.

Flora and Fauna

The signature species of Fray Jorge's forest are *canelo (Drimys winteri), olivillo (Aetoxicon punctatum),* and *petrillo* (myrtle, *Myrceugenia correifolia*), surrounded by mosses, lichens, and ferns. As the death of old trees has left clearings colonized by opportunistic invaders, recent efforts have attempted to cultivate and replant some of these species.

Park mammals include two fox species, sea otters, skunks, and bats; the guanaco was reintroduced in 1995. There are about 80 bird species, including numerous seabirds and, infrequently, the Andean condor, some reptiles including the rare Chilean iguana, and many insects associated with the Valdivian forest, normally found much farther south.

Sights

Fray Jorge's most frequently visited attraction is the **Sendero El Bosque,** a one-km nature trail that circles through the Valdivian headland forest, seven km west of the Arrayancito campground via a steep exposed road. In the morning, the dense *camanchaca* soaks the trees and shrubs (few of which are labeled, let alone explained) until the sun breaks through. The late afternoon return of a solid wall of fog can be a spectacular sight. In the surrounding area, note the scattered forest patches that may be relics of earlier, denser woodlands.

Three km from the Centro de Información at the park entrance, the **Administración,** once the *casco* (big house) of the hacienda, now contains a *vivero* (plant nursery) attempting to restore Fray Jorge's shrinking forests. From here, there's a 15-km hike to the beach at the mouth of the Río Limarí, the park's southern boundary.

Accommodations and Food

Conaf's wooded **Camping El Arrayancito,** three km from the visitor center and seven km from Sector El Bosque, charges US$13 for each of its 13 campsites, all of which have picnic tables, fire pits, and drinking water; the separate men's and women's toilets both have flush toilets and (cold) showers. El Arrayancito also features an abandoned orchard whose abundant pears and figs can supplement your diet, but there are no supplies for sale with the park.

In addition, alongside the Administración, Conaf has built *cabaña* accommodations sleeping up to five people for US$37. For reservations, contact Conaf's La Serena office, tel. 51/272798 or 51/272799.

Information

Access to Fray Jorge is limited to weekends only most of the year; from January to mid-March, however, it's open Friday, Saturday, and Sunday. Hours are also limited—the gate at the park entrance is open 8:30 A.M.–6 P.M. only, though it may be possible to persuade the rangers to allow a later departure.

Just beyond the gate, the Conaf's Centro de Información Ecológica has modest exhibits on the park's unique environment. Rangers collect an admission charge of US$3 per adult, US$1 for children.

Transportation

From a highway junction 15 km north of Termas de Socos via the Panamericana, Fray Jorge is another 22 km west via an exposed, dusty road suitable for cyclists but probably not for pedestrians. While there is no public transportation, travel agencies in both Ovalle and La Serena offer day tours to the park; some may allow you to camp and return another day.

LOS VILOS

Officially founded in 1894, though it was a minor port as early as 1855, the fishing village and seaside resort of Los Vilos is now the proletarian alternative to increasingly trendy La Serena. Nobody knows the true origin of its name, but one popular legend calls it a corruption of Lord Willow, a privateer who supposedly frequented the area. Another attributes the name to an indigenous word meaning "serpent"—though Chile has few snakes of any kind.

Orientation

Los Vilos is 245 km north of Santiago via the Panamericana, and 225 km south of La Serena. From the Panamericana, Avenida Caupolicán leads west across the railroad tracks to the older part of town, a relatively regular grid where most accommodations and services are. Following the shoreline, the Avenida Costanera is now officially Avenida Presidente Salvador Allende Gossens.

Sights and Recreation

For most visitors, the main attractions are the intown **Playa Los Vilos** and the more northerly **Playa Amarilla;** the former gets quite a few bodyboarders as well as swimmers and sunbathers. At the south end of the beach, local fishmongers hawk the day's catch at **Caleta San Pedro,** where there's a gaggle of inexpensive seafood restaurants. At Avenida Caupolicán and Purén, peruse the **Feria Artesanal** for crafts and souvenirs.

From Caleta San Pedro, there are launch excursions to the offshore seabird colonies at **Isla de Huevos** (US$2 pp) and to the more distant **Isla de Lobos,** a large southern sea lion rookery (US$50 for up to six people). A dirt road also leads south of town to Isla de Lobos, which is visible across the water.

North of Playa Amarilla, at Punta Chungo, the 50.9-hectare **Santuario de la Naturaleza Laguna de Conchalí** is a wetlands haven for storks, herons, egrets, and other shorebirds. Ironically, so to speak, it owes its official status to the Los Pelambres copper mine near the Argentine border, which has constructed a mechanized pier and, under pressure, established the reserve to mitigate environmental concerns. In July of 2000, environmental authorities found traces of copper, molybdenum, and other wastes in the area.

Accommodations

The cheapest in town is **Residencial Jamaica,** Los Molles 354, tel. 53/541211, where rooms with shared bath cost US$6 pp; with private bath, rates are US$8.50 pp. **Residencial Yeko's,** Purén 168, charges US$7 pp for decent patio rooms with shared bath, and it recently added hot water. Another good economical choice is **Residencial Vienesa,** Avenida Los Vilos 11, tel. 53/541143, for US$8.50 pp with shared bath, US$10 for those with cable TV. Parking is also available.

Residencial Las Rejas, Avenida Caupolicán 1310, tel. 53/541026, charges US$7 pp with shared bath, US$10 pp with private bath. **Hotel Bellavista,** Rengo 020, tel. 53/541073, is comparably priced, while **Residencial Turismo,** Avenida Caupolicán 437, tel. 53/541176, costs US$8/17 s/d.

Recently reopened to the public after several years leased out to contractors, **Hostería Lord Willow,** Avenida Los Vilos 1444, tel./fax. 53/541037, charges US$27 d with private bath, slightly more for rooms with an ocean view; breakfast costs US$3 extra.

Near the Panamericana is a cluster of roadside motels that are not the usual by-the-hour rentals. Among them are **Hardy's Motel,** Avenida 1 Norte 248, tel. 53/541098, which charges US$28 d; and the woodsy **American Motel,** Panamericana Km 224, tel. 53/541020, fax 53/541163, which costs US$30/40. Rates at downtown **Motel El Pelusa,** Avenida Caupolicán 411, tel. 53/541041, are US$35/40.

Food

Los Vilos is known for hearty, if conventional, seafood restaurants with reasonable prices, such as **El Faro,** Colipí 224, tel. 53/541190; **Las Brisas,** Avenida Costanera s/n, tel. 53/541242; **Dino,** Purén s/n between Avenida Costanera and Avenida Caupolicán; and **Restaurant Costanera,** Purén 80, tel. 53/541010. The dining room at **Hotel Bellavista,** Rengo 020, tel. 53/541073, is also worth a visit.

On the rocks near the end of the Avenida Costanera, **Caleta Las Conchas** is a good seafood choice with indoor and outdoor seating, full meals with impeccable service for around US$5, and plenty of gulls and pelicans hovering for scraps. Los Vilos's most sophisticated dining is at

Alisio, Avenida Caupolicán 298, tel. 53/542173, where a variety of international entrées run around US$9 each.

Events

February's **Semana Vileña** (Vilos Week) is the tourist season's highlight, but June's **Fiesta de San Pedro Pescador** (Festival of Saint Peter) probably has more resonance for locals.

Services and Information

Money: Banco del Estado, Guacolda 098 at the corner of Avenida Caupolicán, is the only bank, but the Shell and Esso gas stations on the nearby Panamericana have ATMs.

Postal: Correos de Chile is at the corner of Lincoyán and Galvarino, at the northeast corner of the Plaza de Armas.

Telephone: Entel is at Caupolicán 474. Los Vilos' area code is 53.

Laundry: Lavandería Victoria is at Guacoldo 140.

Medical: Los Vilos' Hospital San Pedro has totally new facilities at Talcahuano and Arauco, tel. 53/541061.

Tourist Office: At the junction of the Panamericana and Avenida Caupolicán, the Oficina Regional de Informaciones Turísticas, tel. 09/8768129 or 53/2198857, is open 9 A.M.–8 P.M. daily in summer only.

Transportation

At the west end of Avenida Caupolicán, the old railroad station serves as Los Vilos' Terminal de Buses, though some companies have separate offices and even terminals elsewhere on Caupolicán, and others bypass the city on the Panamericana but will pick up northbound or southbound passengers on the side of the highway.

Tur-Bus, tel. 53/541474, covers the Panamericana between Santiago and Arica; its budget line Cóndor Bus has less frequent services. Tacc/Expreso Norte, tel. 53/741046, Los Corsarios, and Lasval all go to Santiago and destinations in the Norte Chico. Intercomunal goes to Viña del Mar/Valparaíso and intermediates.

Pullman Bus, with its own terminal at Caupolicán and Avenida Estación, tel.

53/541197, also has an office at the main terminal; it goes to Santiago, Arica, and intermediates on the Panamericana, and to some interior destinations. Tas Choapa, also in its own terminal at Avenida Caupolicán 784, tel. 53/541032, also keeps an office at the main terminal; it goes to Santiago and the interior provincial cities of Illapel and Salamanca.

ILLAPEL

Founded in 1754 by General Domingo Ortiz de Rozas, under the name Villa de San Rafael de Rozas, the provincial agricultural town of Illapel is most worthwhile for its access to Reserva Nacional Las Chinchillas, at the end of the paved road northeast, which continues to Combarbalá and Monte Patria as a gravel road.

Accommodations and Food

The cheapest accommodations option is friendly **Residencial Aucó,** Constitución 181, tel. 53/523368, where spotless rooms with shared bath and kitchen privileges cost US$8.50 pp; those with private bath go for US$10 pp. For service, knock or ring at the wooden door directly across the street.

The modern, well-kept **Hotel Diaguitas Illapel,** Constitución 276, tel./fax 53/522587, website: www.choapa.cl, hdiaguitas@entelchile.net,

TAKING THE HIGH ROAD THROUGH THE NORTE CHICO

For motorists, bikers, and cyclists really intent on getting off the beaten track, there's no better alternative than the old highland railroad route that, until the opening of the Panamericana in the early 1950s, connected the Chilean heartland with the Norte Chico and the Norte Grande. Passing through five former train tunnels, with countless ups and downs along the isolated Andean foothills between La Ligua and Ovalle, it's one of the country's unappreciated gems for Chileans and foreigners alike.

From the city of La Ligua, in Region V (Valparaíso), a paved road heads east to the town of Cabildo, where the **Túnel las Grupas** continues north toward Petorca; a semaphore regulates the traffic through it, as las Grupas is the only tunnel in a well-populated area. At Pedegua, 10 km north of Cabildo, the paved road continues northeast to Petorca, but the former rail route heads north-northwest as a good gravel road—4WD is unnecessary—toward Salamanca and Illapel.

Perhaps the most scenic segment is **Cuesta las Palmas,** about 20 km north of Pedegua, where the road has been improved to provide better access to the avocado and citrus orchards in the area. At the Region IV (Coquimbo) border, it passes through the **Túnel las Palmas,** surrounded by mature palm trees in the valley.

About 35 km north of Túnel las Palmas, the largest settlement until Illapel is the strangely named **Caimanes**—there are no large aquatic reptiles here—where Diego de Almagro passed in 1536. Just north of Caimanes, in quick succession, the road passes through three tunnels; the longest is the **Túnel las Astas,** dating from 1912, whose ceilings drip with groundwater. Its length makes it the likeliest in which to encounter a vehicle heading the other direction.

At **Limáhuida,** the turnoff for the old road to Salamanca about 30 km north of Caimanes, the last standing station building on the line serves as a small grocery. Along the route, *huasos* in their characteristic flat-brimmed sombreros are a common sight, as are flocks of goats on the dry hillsides, but Salamanca inhabits a lush green valley. From Salamanca, a paved highway heads northwest to the city of Illapel.

From Illapel north toward Combarbalá, evidence of the rail route is rare, though the road through Reserva Nacional Las Chinchillas passes the foundations of the station at **Aucó,** but from here the road diverges—though the embankments are often visible in the distance. From Combarbalá, a paved road goes to Monte Patria and Ovalle, while a slightly shorter alternative uses a gravel road to Punitaqui and paved road to Ovalle.

Look for condors, though—that enduring symbol of the Andes that serves as a reminder that the erstwhile route was, first and foremost, an Inka road.

costs US\$32/42 s/d; most rooms have balconies, there's a pool, and limited parking is available.

So well-maintained it looks as new as the day it opened in 1988, **Hotel Domingo Ortiz de Rozas,** Avenida Ignacio Silva 241, tel. 53/52-2127, tel./fax 53/521349, charges US\$32/46 s/d for tasteful rooms in a quiet garden setting, with off-street parking.

Tap, Constitución 382, tel. 53/522034, is a good but modest snack bar that serves excellent sandwiches. The **Casino de Bomberos** is at Buin and Vicuña Mackenna, while the Chilean chain **Bavaria** is at Constitución 435, tel. 53/523338.

Services and Transportation

Entel has long-distance services at Constitución 301.

Illapel's Terminal de Buses is at San Martín 260, between Independencia and Doroztizaga. Buses Tacc/Expreso Norte, tel. 53/522651, connects Illapel with Los Vilos, as does Pullman Bus, tel. 53/521734.

RESERVA NACIONAL LAS CHINCHILLAS

Native to the central Chilean Andes, in rocky areas covered with the bromeliad known as the *chagual (Puya chilensis), Chinchilla lanigera* is a nocturnal rodent, weighing about 500 grams, which lives on herbs, bushes, and cacti. Its fine gray pelt, highly valued in the international fur trade, led to its overexploitation in the early decades of the 20th century, but the Chilean government established this 4,229-hectare reserve, 15 km northeast of Illapel, to help protect the endangered species. The largest main colonies remaining are here and at La Higuera, near La Serena.

Sights

On the west side of the highway, at El Espinal, Conaf's **Centro de Información Ambiental** displays a sample of traps once used to catch chinchillas. Even more interestingly, it contains a *nocturnato* where half a dozen native rodent species, including the chinchilla (along with a sole marsupial), are on display in cages whose

CHASING CHINCHILLAS

At least from Inka times and probably much earlier, Andean royalty treasured chinchilla stoles for their soft, dense fur, but *Chinchilla brevicaudata* did not feel the brunt of major commercial exploitation until the late 19th century, when massive trapping and exportation began. Between 1898 and 1900, nearly 1.2 million pelts were shipped abroad, with a maximum of 450,000 in 1899; during a nine-year period around the turn of the 20th century, more than 2.5 million pelts passed through Valparaíso. The trade declined after 1910 because of overexploitation, but Chile did not prohibit hunting and trapping until 1929.

Meanwhile, in 1923, U.S. mining engineer Matthew Chapman exported nine live males and three females from Potrerillos, north of Copiapó, to North America, marking the beginning of an international chinchilla fur industry. Today there are about 150,000 breeding domestic chinchillas worldwide. With a state subsidy in 1929, Chile began its own industry, which now comprises about 40 nurseries with 3,000 females.

blue lights convince the animals it's nighttime. The center is open Thursday to Sunday, 8:30 A.M.–4:30 P.M.

At El Espinal, there is also a one-km **Sendero de Interpretación** (nature trail) for hikers. On the east side of the highway, where only the foundations remain of a former railway station, **Aucó** was once a gypsum mining village of 400 people. Only three houses, with no more than 10 people, remain in the virtual ghost town.

Practicalities

At El Espinal, Conaf charges US\$3.50 for campsites with limited shade, and US\$10 pp for comfortable *cabañas* sleeping up to six. For reservations, contact Conaf's Illapel office, tel. 53/523211 or 53/522331.

Park rangers are on duty at the Centro de Información Thursday to Sunday, 8:30 A.M.–4:30 P.M., and also collect a US\$2.50 admission charge. Children under age 15 pay US\$1.

SALAMANCA

About 30 km southeast of Illapel via a paved highway, in the verdant valley of the Río Choapa, Salamanca enjoys a certain fame for its Fiesta Huasa, which takes place during Semana Santa, and a certain notoriety for legends of witches and witchcraft. Landscaped with mature *Araucarias* (watch for falling cones), mimosas, casuarinas, and cypresses, its Plaza de Armas is the pivot of local life.

At the western approach to Salamanca, there are petroglyphs on a granite outcrop at **Cerro Chilinga,** in the hamlet of the same name, reached by a concrete staircase and a short scramble over the granite. Beginning almost directly behind the church, the trail continues to the summit of the hill, where there are ruins of a small pre-Columbian *pirca* (dry stone wall), and a possible Inka cemetery.

Accommodations and Food

One block east of the Plaza de Armas, **Residencial O'Higgins,** O'Higgins 430, tel. 53/551108, provides simple but very good accommodations with shared bath and garden frontage for US$5.50 pp; breakfast costs US$1.50 more. Its rooms are better than the smaller and slightly more expensive (US$7 pp) but clean budget cells at **Hostería Gálvez,** J. J. Pérez 540, tel. 53/551017, fax 53/552340, one block south of the plaza; the Gálvez, however, also offers larger, comfier rooms with private bath and cable TV for US$18, and it is sometimes willing to bargain the price. The O'Higgins cannot match the Gálvez's huge swimming pool (closed when lifeguards are not available), abundantly productive apricot trees, sprawling grape arbor, and loads of free parking.

Four blocks east of the Plaza de Armas, **Hostal Vasco,** Bulnes 120, tel. 53/551119, tel./fax 53/521349, is an immaculate facility offering spacious, comfortable rooms with private bath, breakfast, cable TV, and a pool, from US$26 s or d; even larger rooms with similar amenities are slightly dearer at US$31 or US$35 s or d.

At the southeast corner of the Plaza de Armas, **Restaurant American,** Bulnes 499, serves excellent fish and seafood for around US$6–8, with attentive service—sometimes overpoweringly so. **Bavaria,** Los Carrera 550, tel. 53/551249, is the local branch of the popular Chilean chain.

Transportation

Salamanca has frequent bus service to Illapel and Los Vilos with Pullman Bus at O'Higgins and Montepío, tel. 53/551127, and Tacc Vía Choapa/Expreso Norte at O'Higgins 500, tel. 53/551111, which also goes twice daily to La Serena and has six departures to Santiago. Buses Intercomunal, O'Higgins 510, goes frequently to Los Vilos, Viña del Mar, and Valparaíso.

Sur Chico

South of the Biobío, popularly known as the "lake district" for the scenic finger lakes left by receding Pleistocene glaciers, the Sur Chico has long been the favorite destination for Chilean and Argentine tourists who enjoy its matchless scenery of ice-capped volcanic cones soaring above dense native forests. Only in the past decade-plus have significant numbers of them, along with foreign visitors, begun to venture beyond conventional lakeside resorts into the Andean backcountry for activities such as hiking, horseback riding, and white-water rafting. Many of Chile's national parks and reserves cover large parts of the Andean cordillera.

Politically, the Sur Chico comprises Region IX (La Araucanía) and Region X (Los Lagos), which includes the archipelago of Chiloé and, on the mainland across the Golfo de Ancud and the Golfo de Corcovado, what is colloquially known as continental Chiloé. Because of continental Chiloé's physical isolation from the rest of Region X—only air taxis, slow-moving ferries, and roundabout buses through Argentina link it to Puerto Montt and Quellón—its coverage appears in the chapter on Chilean Patagonia.

Economically diverse cities such as Temuco, Osorno, and Puerto Montt, which rely on forestry, agricultural services, and manufacturing in addition to tourism, are the gateways to the region, but smaller lakeside towns such as Villarrica, Pucón, and Puerto Varas make better bases for excursions. There are several routes across the Andes to Argentina, which has its own southern lake district centered around the city of Bariloche, while Puerto Montt is the hub for air, land, and sea access to Chilean Patagonia.

Volcán Osorno, Lago Llanquihue

History

Human presence in the Sur Chico dates from at least 13,000 years ago, when mobile bands of hunter-gatherers roamed the area around Monte Verde, 35 km west of Puerto Montt on a tributary of the Río Maullín. One of the oldest and most significant archaeological sites on the continent, Monte Verde benefited from ideal conditions for preservation despite the humid climate, as more than a meter of volcanic ash and peat covered the remains of mastodons, shellfish, seeds, fruits, and roots consumed by the dozen or so families who lived there. From the remaining refuse, researchers have learned that these bands hunted and foraged in an area within a radius of about 100 km.

Unlike the central Andean highlands of Peru and Bolivia, the pre-Columbian Sur Chico never developed great cities or monuments—while its people developed agricultural skills, they were shifting cultivators who occupied dispersed settlements and lacked any centralized political authority. In practice, this benefited their resistance to the Inka empire and, later, Spanish invaders; the Mapuche relied not on highly organized armies but on guerrilla tactics to harass their opponents. More egalitarian than hierarchical, their top leadership was interchangeable rather than irreplaceable.

Thus, by the early 1600s, Mapuche resistance had reduced most Spanish settlements south of the Biobío to ashes and ruin. Except for the river port of Valdivia, reestablished in the mid-17th century, this remained a precarious area for Spanish settlers until a series of treaties between the Chilean government and indigenous forces in the 1880s. Many of the cities and towns in the north in this area—Victoria, Curacautín, Lonquimay, Temuco, Cunco, Villarrica, and Pucón—originally constituted a string of fortresses along the Mapuche frontier.

Chile counts more than a million Mapuche among its 15 million citizens. While many have left for the cities, large numbers still remain in the countryside where, in the more liberal political climate after the Pinochet dictatorship, they have become more outspoken in asserting rights to their ancestral lands.

Part of the controversy dates from the officially encouraged immigration that took place after the mid-19th century, when the Chilean government recruited German emigrés to settle in the area around present-day Puerto Montt and Lago Llanquihue. In fact, in the ensuing years, Llanquihue and other lakes to the north became the region's highways, linking towns such as Puerto Varas and Puerto Octay via sail and steamer until the advent of the railroad in the early 20th century.

German immigrants have left a palpable imprint on the region's economy (through commerce and manufacturing), landscape (through dairy farming and other agricultural pursuits), architecture (some of the country's finest European-style houses are here), and food (Germanic goodies known collectively as kuchen are almost universal). Many other nationalities flowed into the region, however, mostly Spaniards and Italians.

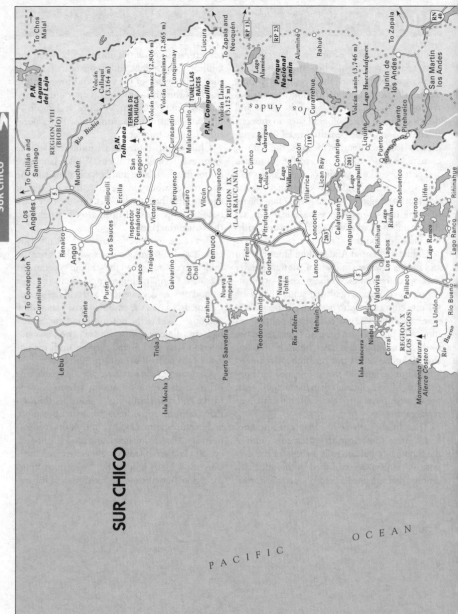

SUR CHICO

SUR CHICO

ARGENTINA

To Neuquén

RN 237

Bariloche

Parque Nacional Nahuel Huapi

RN 231

RN 234

Lago Nahuel Huapi

Puerto Frías

Peulla

El Bolsón

RN 258

Parque Nacional Lago Puelo

Parque Nacional Los Alerces

Esquel

Trevelin

Cordillera de

Parque Nacional Puyehue

Lago Rupanco

P.N. Vicente Pérez Rosales

Cochamó

Lago Puyehue

Las Cascadas

Petrohué

Ralún

Ensenada

P.N. Hornopirén

Hornopirén

Lago Amutui Quimei

Futaleufú

Lago Yelcho

Entre Lagos

215

Osorno

Río Negro

Puerto Octay

Puranque

Frutillar

5

Lago Llanquihue

Puerto Varas

225

Puerto Montt

Lenca

Seno de Reloncaví

Parque

Avacara

Volcán Michinmahuida (2,404 m)

Chaitén

Puerto Cárdenas

Volcán Corcovado (2,300 m)

To Coyhaique

Caleta Gonzalo

Pumalín

Parque Natural Pumalín

Bahía Mansa

Fresia

Los Muermos

Río Maullín

Río Negro

Puranque

Maullín

Carelmapu

Pargua

Calbuco

Chacao

Golfo de Ancud

Islas Chauques

Tenaún

Achao

Isla Talcán

Queilén

Isla Tranqui

Golfo de Corcovado

Ancud

Linao

Quemchi

Mocopulli

Dalcahue

Castro

Rilán

Puqueldón

Chonchi

Chepu

Cucao

Huillinco

Isla Grande de Chiloé

Lago Chaiguato

Quellón

Parque Nacional Chiloé

Río de la Zorra

To Puerto Chacabuco and Puerto Natales

0   30 mi

0   30 km

N

© AVALON TRAVEL PUBLISHING, INC.

Araucanía Region

South of the Chilean heartland, from the Pacific headlands to the monkey puzzle trees on the Andean crest, the Araucanía is the Mapuche heartland. What was a war zone until the 1880s is now, mostly, a tranquil land of native forests beneath smoldering volcanoes whose spring snowmelt feeds the westward-flowing rivers. The initial segment of the Sendero de Chile, a non-motorized trail intended to link the country from the Peruvian border to the tip of Cape Horn by the end of the decade, has been dedicated in Parque Nacional Conguillío.

It's not all peace, love, and understanding, though. Since the end of the Pinochet dictatorship, conflicts between the Mapuche and the forestry companies that occupy much of their ancestral lands has become a burning issue—in some cases, literally so, as there have even been isolated incidents of arson. Some rightist politicians have exaggerated the influence of the more militant Mapuche factions, such as the Consejo de Todas las Tierras (All Lands Council), with alarmist proclamations that the Mexico-based Zapatista movement is spreading to the south (the Zapatistas, while armed and media-savvy, have never provoked any violent confrontation in Chiapas).

Partly in response to Mapuche pressure, forestry companies such as Mininco have attempted to incorporate them into the regional economy, already employing around 800 and planning to add another 300 jobs for timber planting and harvesting in depressed areas such as Galvarino, Lautaro, Ercilla, Lumaco, and Victoria. For some Mapuche, however, only the return of ancestral lands will satisfy their aspirations.

TEMUCO

Its population approaching 250,000, the largest Chilean city south of the Concepción-Talcahuano conurbation is the gateway to the famous Andean lake district, numerous national parks, and many other attractions. As an industrial center that supports and processes agricultural and forest products, metals, and textiles,

its tourist appeal is limited—the city's architecture is largely utilitarian—but it is also a major Mapuche market town. Unfortunately, like Santiago, it has begun to suffer from air pollution problems, especially in winter, as the widespread use of poor-quality wood-burning stoves has contributed to a growing incidence of respiratory infections.

History

As a city, Temuco dates from February 24, 1881, when President Aníbal Pinto sent Interior Minister Manuel Recabarren, veteran General Gregorio Urrutia, engineer Teodoro Schmidt, and the Chilean army to found Fuerte de Temuco (originally Fuerte Recabarren). Later that same year, averting an attack on the fortress, the Chileans reached a treaty agreement and, within 15 years, the railroad had arrived from Angol. Before the turn of the century, colonists had flooded into the region, their farmers displacing the aboriginal inhabitants, and the population exceeded 7,000. The early push from the railroad sustained that growth well into the 20th century, providing easy access to metropolitan markets and technology.

Orientation

On the north margin of the braided Río Cautín, Temuco is 677 km south of Santiago and 339 km north of Puerto Montt via the Panamericana, which enters the city from the northeast and exits at the southwest; known here as Avenida Caupolicán, the highway divides the city into a compact original grid to the east and a slightly more irregular residential area to the west.

Sights

Temuco's focal point is the lushly landscaped Plaza de Armas Aníbal Pinto, whose own showpiece is the massive **Homenaje a la Región de la Araucanía,** a sculpture representing a Mapuche *machi* or female healer, the *Soldado de la Pacificación* (the euphemistically named "Soldier of the Pacification"), a *Colono* ("Early Colonist"), the

SUR CHICO

TEMUCO

AVENIDA A. PINTO

TUCAPEL
JANEQUEO
PATZKE
BILBAO
BALMACEDA

BUSES JGI LLAIMA/NAR-BUS
ESTACIÓN DE FERROCARRIL
TERMINAL DE BUSES RURALES
RESIDENCIAL TEMUCO
MATTA
ZENTENO

HOTEL CASABLANCA
NUEVO HOTEL CHAPELCO
DIEGO PORTALES

AVENIDA SAN MARTIN
Río Cautín
SAN MARTIN

GENERAL CRUZ
GENERAL MACKENNA
ALDUNATE
BULNES
PRAT
V. MACKENNA

CONAF

To Terminal Araucano, Chillán, and Santiago

HOTEL ORIENTE
PAP Y MOL
MERCADO MUNICIPAL
CENTRO ESPAÑOL
HOTEL NICOLÁS
DINO'S
POST OFFICE

CENTRO CULTURAL MUNICIPAL
HOTEL BAYERN
IGLESIA ANGLICANA
Plaza Teodoro Schmidt

HOSPEDAJE MONT
SERNATUR
HOTEL ESPAÑOL
Plaza de Armas Aníbal Pinto

QUINCHO DE LA EMPANADA
LANCHILE
MOSQUITO'S PUB
GIY TURISMO
HOTEL AITUE
HOSTAL ALDUNATE
PUB/RESTAURANT EMPERADOR

HOTEL DE LA FRONTERA

GENERAL MACKENNA

N

0   200 yds
0   200 m

HOTEL TERRAVERDE
PRAT

VICUÑA MACKENNA
LAGOS
LYNCH
MIRAFLORES
LAUTARO
CARRERA
BLANCO

HOSTAL RESIDENCIAL MILLARAY
HOTEL CONTINENTAL
HOTEL ESPELETTE

NUEVO HOTEL DE LA FRONTERA
Plaza Manuel Recabarren

MANUEL MONTT
CLARO SOLAR
BELLO
VARAS
LAS HERAS
CARRERA

O'HIGGINS
HERTZ RENT A CAR

CEMENTERIO
Monumento Natural Cerro Ñielol
Estero Coilaco
Estero Temuco

BALMACEDA
MANUEL RODRÍGUEZ

Plaza Teniente Dagoberto Godoy
HOSPITAL REGIONAL

AVENIDA PRIETO NORTE

(PANAMERICAN) PANAMERICANA
AVENIDA CAUPOLICAN

FREIRE
LEON
GALLO
IMPERIAL
Plaza Las Quilas
PRIETO SUR

CARMINE
STA. LAURA
LA SUERTE
CABO RIQUELME
ARRAYAN
EL BOSQUE

CENTRO DE EXTENSIÓN DE LA UNIVERSIDAD CATÓLICA
DR. CARRILLO
PEDRO DE VALDIVIA

THIERS
PHILLIPI
DINAMARCA
HOLANDESA

MUSEO REGIONAL DE LA ARAUCANÍA
AUTOMOVIL CLUB DE CHILE

SANTA MARGARITA
SAN MARTIN
SAN FEDERICO
O'HIGGINS
GALLO
LEON

To Aeropuerto Maquehue, Valdivia, and Puerto Montt

TRIZANO

HOSTAL FRANCIA 199
FRANCIA
MANUEL RODRÍGUEZ
ESPAÑA
AVENIDA
HOCHSTETTER

TALLER ARTESANAL UNIVERSIDAD CATÓLICA
AVENIDA ALEMANIA
SENADOR ESTÉBANEZ

PIZZERÍA MADONNA
JALISCO
PEPPERONI'S
JAIRO'S
HOSTAL AUSTRIA
CLUB ALEMÁN

AVENIDA
SAN MARTIN
URUGUAY

© AVALON TRAVEL PUBLISHING, INC.

© WAYNE BERNHARDSON

crafts fair, Plaza de Armas, Temuco

conquistador and epic poet Alonso de Ercilla, and the Mapuche *toqui* (leader) Kallfulifán. The gallery beneath the plaza bandshell is the site of frequent rotating cultural exhibits.

Most of the city's other landmarks are scattered, such as the gingerbread-style **Iglesia Anglicana Santa Trinidad,** the century-old Anglican church at the corner of Vicuña Mackenna and Lautaro.

Monumento Natural Cerro Ñielol: Chile's national flower, the *copihue (Lapageria rosea),* shows its autumn blooms in the deciduous lowland forest of Cerro Ñielol, a 90-hectare reserve that rises barely 200 meters above sea level on the north side of Temuco. Several short trails thread among the park's mixed woodlands of roble (*Nothofagus obliqua,* one of many southern beeches in Chile) with either laurel *(Laurelia sempervirens)* or *olivillo (Aextoxican punctatum).*

Cerro Ñielol's forest is also an historical site—under the shade of the so-called **La Patagua del Armisticio,** in 1881, Mapuche leaders finally acceded to the founding of the city. For most of its 65,000 yearly visitors, though, it's a place for weekend picnics and similar recreation, though Conaf also maintains a Centro de Información Ambiental (environmental information center) here. Sernageomin, the national mining service, operates a vulcanological observatory but it's not open to the public.

Reached by strolling north on Prat from the Plaza de Armas for about one km, Cerro Ñielol charges US$1 admission per pedestrian, US$.30 for each child and US$1 per car. Hours are 8:30 A.M.–11 P.M. daily.

Museo Regional de la Araucanía: Created in 1940, Temuco's improving regional museum tackles what might, in a rhetorical sense, sound euphemistic—the "encounter" between the indigenous Mapuche and Spanish-Chilean civilization. In practice, the notion that interactions between these radically distinct cultures were a give-and-take rather than a simple imposition of external authority is a good starting point for reassessing regional history, even if the execution is imperfect.

Housed in the former residence of Carlos Thiers, a German immigrant-style national monument dating from 1924, the museum emphasizes the centrality of the Mapuche and their ancestors in regional history, and it acknowledges the diversity of their various subgroups—the sedentary and shifting agriculturalists of the lowland floodplains and forests, the fisher-gatherer Lafkenche of the Pacific littoral, and the hunter-gatherer Pehuenche of the Andean cordillera.

On the other hand, lapses in rethinking the past persist—the openly expressed perspective on "pacification" in the 300-year war between the two nations is no more appropriate than the U.S. military's attitude during the Vietnam war. Exhibits implicitly credit the Mapuche resistance with fashioning deadly weapons from available materials but neglect their skills as horsemen and tacticians.

Presentations on postwar developments are better. Arrival of the "Ferrocarril de La Frontera" (Frontier Railroad) brought Catholic missionaries and immigrants from northwestern Europe and the Mediterranean. Temuco's urban development, interrupted by the 1960 earthquake, is the subject of maps and photographs. One glaring omission is the marginalization of the contemporary Mapuche.

Unearthed by researchers or donated by local residents, the professionally presented collections comprise more than 3,000 separate items of archaeological, ethnographic, pictorial, photographic, and historical significance. The Mapuche materials, dating from about A.D. 1400–1800, include 19th-century jewelry and textiles. In addition, there is a specialized library on the Mapuche, anthropology, and regional history, plus cartographic coverage of the cities and other communities. All coverage is in Spanish only, however.

The Museo de la Araucanía, Avenida Alemania 084, tel. 45/211108, museoaraucania@terra.cl, is on the west side of the Panamericana, about 10 blocks from the Plaza de Armas. In summer, it's open 9 A.M.–7 P.M. weekdays, 10 A.M.–7 P.M. Saturday, 10 A.M.–5 P.M. Sunday; the rest of the year, hours are 9 A.M.–5:45 P.M. weekdays, 11 A.M.–2 P.M. Sunday only. Admission is US$1 for adults, US$.50 for children, but it is free on Sunday.

Casa de Máquinas de Temuco: With the railroad's arrival from Angol in 1893, Temuco soon became a key rail hub, where long-distance trains changed locomotives; its original *casa de máquinas* (roundhouse) opened in 1920, housed locomotives used on branch lines that ran to Carahue, Cunco, and Cherquenco, and also held repair facilities. By the 1930s, though, these installations were inadequate and the current roundhouse was completed between 1937 and 1941. Temuco was the last Chilean base for steam locomotives; EFE maintained it as a repair and reserve center for them until 1983—there were no permanent diesel facilities here until the 1980s—but it closed soon after.

In the aftermath, the Asociación Chilena de Conservación del Patrimonio Ferroviario (ACCPF, Chilean Association for Conservation of Railroad Patrimony) operated a sporadic tourist train to Lonquimay. It ran only about 30 times in 10 years, though, and the removal of rails from the Túnel Los Raíces southeast of Malalcahuello opened that route to vehicle traffic. EFE officials wanted to tear down the roundhouse and sell off its 14 antique engines and other rolling stock for scrap, but the persistent ACCPF managed to get all of them declared national monuments in what is now an on-site museum of 19 hectares fronting on Avenida Barros Arana, about one km north of the station.

Mercado Municipal: Replacing an earlier market that the city had outgrown, Temuco's municipal bazaar (1928) attracts tourists with its accomplished crafts and typical restaurants that vary from the plain and simple to, if not quite sublime, at least very good. Locals, however, take advantage of abundant fresh produce and utilitarian commodities such as manufactured household goods and clothing.

Two blocks north of the Plaza de Armas, the high-ceilinged landmark fills most of the eastern two-thirds of the block bounded by Diego Portales, Bulnes, Manuel Rodríguez, and Aldunate; it's open Monday to Saturday 8 A.M.–8 P.M. and Sunday and holidays 8 A.M.–3 P.M. in summer; the rest of the year, hours are 8 A.M.–6 P.M. weekdays, same hours on Sunday.

Feria Libre Aníbal Pinto: Comprising more than 700 different stalls, this lively, mainly Mapuche and sometimes disagreeably fragrant produce market fills several blocks along Avenida Aníbal Pinto and Avenida Barros Arana from the Terminal de Buses Rurales south to the EFE railroad station. In July of 2001, members of the indigenous Asociación de Productores de Verduras Nuke Mapu protested their possible eviction from the market, resisting what they claim are the mayor's plans to remodel the entire area to their detriment.

In addition to fruits and vegetables, there are cheap eateries and a selection of Mapuche crafts. Hours are roughly 8 A.M.–5 daily except in summer, when vendors may stick around until 6 P.M. or so.

Accommodations

Temuco's cheapest accommodations are only so-so, but by spending just a little more travelers can get good value. Upper-range choices are generally very good.

US$10–25: Charging US$10 pp with breakfast, kitchen facilities, and laundry service, the local Hostelling International representative is **Residencial Temuco,** a 20-bed hostel at Rodríguez 1341, 2nd floor, tel./fax 45/233721. Since it's small and also serves the wider public, reservations are a good idea; note also that it lacks a street sign.

Central **Hospedaje Montt,** Manuel Montt 965, Departamento 301, tel. 45/211856, costs US$11/17 s/d with shared bath and breakfast.

Rates at **Hostal Aldunate,** in a quiet but still central neighborhood at Aldunate 864, tel./fax 45/231128, are US$11 pp with shared bath, US$13/22 with private bath, both with breakfast. **Hostal Casablanca,** Manuel Montt 1306, tel./fax 45/272677, costs US$8.50 pp with shared bath and breakfast, US$14/25 s/d with private bath, breakfast, and cable TV.

US$25–50: Hostal Residencial Millaray, Claro Solar 471, tel. 45/645720, charges US$7.50 pp with shared bath, but US$20/27 s/d with private bath; both include breakfast. This stylish older building possibly was to change hands, which could mean changes. **Hotel Oriente,** Manuel Rodríguez 1146, tel. 45/233232, costs US$12/20 with shared bath, US$16/29 with private bath and breakfast.

Across the street from the Millaray, **Hotel Espelette,** Claro Solar 492, tel. 45/234805, charges US$12/20 s/d with shared bath, while those with private bath cost US$25/33; both rates include breakfast. Toward the railroad tracks at the east end of downtown, **Nuevo Hotel Chapelco,** General Cruz 401, tel. 45/213473 or 45/404942, costs US$26/31 with private bath and breakfast.

In residential west Temuco, recommended **Hostal Francia 199,** Francia 199, tel. 45/235594, costs US$15/27 s/d with shared bath and breakfast, but only a little more—US$19/33—with private bath. Also west of the Panamericana, **Hostal Austria,** Hochstetter 599, tel./fax 45/247169, offers quiet, comfortable, and spotless accommodations with cable TV and *Gemütlichkeit* for US$16 pp with shared bath and an ample breakfast; rooms with private bath cost only US$3 pp more. There is no indoors smoking. More central, near the Mercado Municipal, **Hotel Nicolás,** General Mackenna 420, tel. 45/210020, fax 45/213468, hotel.nicolas@terra.cl, charges US$33/43 with private bath and TV.

Once the city's most prestigious quarters, the timeless **Hotel Continental,** Varas 709, tel. 45/2-38973, fax 45/233830, hcontine@ctc-mundo.net, is a living monument that boasts a spectacularly anachronistic dining room and an equally classic wooden bar; plaques point out rooms where illustrious tourists such as Presidents Pedro Aguirre Cerda and Salvador Allende, and Nobel Prize poets Gabriela Mistral and Pablo Neruda, have spent the night. Rates start at US$17/25 s/d for rooms with their own washbasins, exterior toilet and shower, and breakfast; rooms that share an adjoining bath go for US$33/36, while those with private bath cost US$39/43.

US$50–100: Well-located near Plaza Teodoro Schmidt, **Hotel Bayern,** Prat 146, tel. 45/276000, fax 45/212291, hotelbayern@tie.cl, charges US$43/50 s/d, with buffet breakfast. **Hotel Aitué,** Antonio Varas 1048, tel. 45/212512, fax 45/2-12608, aituehot@cepri.cl, costs US$43/52.

Hotel de La Frontera, Bulnes 733, tel. 45/200400, fax 45/200402, reservas@hotel-frontera.cl, charges US$50 to US$63 s or d with breakfast; across the street at Bulnes 726, with the same contact information, its sibling **Nuevo Hotel de La Frontera** has greater amenities—swimming pool, gym, and the like—for US$63 to US$83 s or d. The only advantage of the latter, though, is easier access; guests at both are entitled to use them.

US$100 and Up: At the foot of Cerro Ñielol, the five-star **Hotel Terraverde,** Prat 0220, tel. 45/239999, fax 45/239455, resterra@panamericanahoteles.cl, charges US$125 to US$160 s or d.

Food

The truly basic *puestos* (food stalls) in and around the chaotic **Mercado Pinto,** between the Terminal de Buses Rurales and the EFE train station on both sides of its namesake street, are the cheapest choices in town, but the hygiene is open to question at some of them.

Known best as a crafts market and a sight in itself, the downtown **Mercado Municipal,** two blocks north of the Plaza de Armas at Portales and Aldunate, is an even better choice for plain seafood—try **El Caribe,** Puesto 45, tel. 45/213002. Figure about US$4–6 for a good filling meal; the market, however, is primarily a lunch venue, with most eateries closing by 7 P.M.

Dino's, a chain restaurant at Bulnes 360, tel. 45/213660, is for sandwiches and standard Chilean fare. **El Quincho de la Empanada,** Aldunate 698, tel. 45/216307, is a one-of-a-kind specializing in empanadas. **Pap y Mol,** Manuel Rodríguez 1073, is an inexpensive downtown *parrilla.* Among the better downtown choices are the **Centro Español,** Bulnes 483, tel. 45/238664, and the **Centro Arabe,** General Mackenna 462, tel. 45/215080.

More stylish, contemporary dining is available west of the Panamericana, at places such as **Pepperoni's,** Hochstetter 425, tel. 45/261271, a good pizza-and-pasta place where entrées start around US$4 but range up to US$10 depending on the ingredients—shrimp, for instance, is considerably dearer. The service is exemplary, and there's an adequate tobacco-free section. Other good options in the area are the Tex-Mex **Jalisco,** almost next door at Hochstetter 435, tel.

45/243254, which has more of a pub feel; **Jairo's,** Avenida Alemania 0830, tel. 45/248849, for seafood; **Pizzería Madonna,** Avenida Alemania 0660, tel. 45/249191; and the more traditional **Club Alemán,** Senador Estébanez 772, tel. 45/240034.

Entertainment and Events

Temuco isn't exactly a 24-hour city, but there's usually something going on at local cultural facilities or its two universities.

Bars: South-southeast of the Plaza de Armas is a small pub district including **Mosquito's Pub,** Bulnes 778, tel. 45/213920, and **Pub-Restaurant Emperador,** Bulnes 853. There's a great deal of turnover among these places, which also offer short-order meals.

Cinema: The **Showtime Multiplex,** Antonio Varas 846, is the main commercial cinema. The **Sala Universitaria,** Prat 332, tel. 45/325877, shows films during the university year, as does the Universidad Católica's Centro de Extension, west of the Panamericana at Avenida Prieto Norte 371, tel. 45/232760.

Performing Arts: The Centro Cultural Municipal, at the intersection of Avenida Caupolicán (the Panamericana) and Avenida Balmaceda, is a multifacility including the **Teatro Municipal Pablo Neruda,** tel. 45/265868, for performing arts, plus an exhibition hall and the city library.

The **Aula Magna Universidad Católica,** Manuel Montt 256, tel. 45/205421, has an annual event schedule including live theater and films.

Events: The city's biggest single celebration is February's **Aniversario de la Ciudad,** commemorating the city's founding—at that time, it was really a fortress—on February 24, 1881. During the festivities, a high-quality crafts fair nearly fills the Plaza de Armas.

Shopping

Indigenous female artisans sell their work, primarily pottery and textiles, directly to the public at the cooperative **Casa de la Mujer Mapuche,** Prat 283, tel. 45/233886; profits go directly to members in both cash and educational opportunities. There's a bigger selection at the **Mercado Municipal,** at

Diego Portales and Aldunate, which keeps longer hours, but also much more kitsch.

Other crafts alternatives are the **Sala de Exposiciones,** tel. 45/236785, beneath the Plaza de Armas bandshell, and the **Taller Artesanal Universidad Católica** at Avenida Alemania 0422, tel. 45/212081, west of the Panamericana. The latter is open 9 A.M.–1 P.M. and 3–6 P.M. weekdays.

Services

Though it's primarily an administrative and commercial center, Temuco has a full complement of traveler's services as well.

Money: Banco de Crédito has an ATM at Bulnes 615, but there are many other ATMs and also nearby exchange houses: Casa de Cambio Global at Bulnes 655, Local 1; Christopher Money Exchange, Bulnes 667, Local 202; and Intercam, Bulnes 743.

Postal: Correos de Chile is at Diego Portales and Prat.

Telephone and Internet: Entel is at Prat 505, Chilesat at Vicuña Mackenna 557; the former offers inexpensive Internet access. Temuco's area code is 45.

The Escuela de Informática y Comunicaciones, Manuel Montt 334, tel. 45/644812, also provides Internet access for about US$1.50 per hour.

Laundry: Autoservicio Marva is at Manuel Montt 415 and at Manuel Montt 1099.

Medical: The Hospital Regional is at Manuel Montt 115, tel. 45/212525, west of the Panamericana.

Information

Tourist Office: Sernatur, on the north side of the Plaza de Armas at Claro Solar 899, tel. 45/211969, fax 45/215509, serna09@entelchile.net, distributes free city maps and regional leaflets; it often but not always has an English speaker on hand. Summer hours are 8:30 A.M.–7:30 P.M. weekdays, 8:30 A.M.–5 P.M. Saturday, and 10 A.M.–2 P.M. only Sunday and holidays. From March to December, hours are 9 A.M.–1 P.M. and 3–5 P.M. weekdays only.

Motorists: The Automóvil Club de Chile

(Acchi), west of the Panamericana at San Martín 0278, tel. 45/215132, can help motorists.

National Parks: Conaf is at Avenida Bilbao 931, 2nd floor, tel. 45/210407.

Bookstores: Librería Universitaria, Diego Portales 861, is strong on Mapuche ethnography and regional history.

Transportation

Temuco is Araucanía's major transportation hub, with air connections north and south, and even more abundant bus connections north and south along the Panamericana, west toward the coast, and east into the Andes. It is at present the terminus of the railroad from Santiago, a service that may be extended southward in the future.

Air: LanChile and LanExpress are at Bulnes 687, tel. 45/211339; there are about 40 flights weekly to Santiago (US$78 to US$120); one per day stops in Concepción. Southbound, there are three flights daily to Osorno and Friday and Sunday flights to Puerto Montt.

Bus: The chaos of long-distance carriers that once congested downtown streets has been relieved by construction of the new Rodoviario Araucario, Avenida Rudecindo Ortega 01580, tel. 45/255005, at the northern access to the Panamericana. This has not completely concentrated services—the Terminal de Buses Rurales, at Avenida Aníbal Pinto 032, tel. 45/210494, provides regional coverage, and several long-distance companies have ticket offices and even terminals around the axis formed with the perpendicular Avenida Balmaceda. In addition, some buses for Curacautín, Lonquimay, and the upper Biobío leave from Rodoviario Curacautín, Avenida Barros Arana 191.

Among the regional carriers at the Terminal de Buses Rurales are Flota Erbuc, tel. 45/272204, which goes nine times daily to Curacautín, four of them via Lautaro and the other five via Victoria, continuing to Manzanar, Malalcahuello, and Lonquimay; Nar-Bus, tel. 45/407740, which goes to Capitán Pastene (for Parque Nacional Tolhuaca), Cherquenco (for the Llaima sector of Parque Nacional Conguillío), Icalma, five times daily to Cunco, and seven times daily to Melipeuco; and Buses Jac to Villarrica and Pucón, though departures are more frequent from its other office; and Panguisur, which has a dozen buses daily to Panguipulli. Several companies here also go to coastal destinations such as Lago Budi and Puerto Saavedra.

Many carriers connect Temuco with Panamericana destinations between Santiago and Puerto Montt, and to Valdivia. Among them are Pullman Sur and Cruz del Sur, tel. 45/730310, which also serves the Isla Grande de Chiloé; Tas Choapa, Antonio Varas 609, tel. 45/212422, which has a nightly direct service (11:50 P.M.) to Valparaíso/Viña del Mar without transfer in Santiago; Tur-Bus, Claro Solar 598, tel. 45/258361; Buses Lit, tel. 45/403033; Igi Llaima and Nar-Bus, which share attractive new facilities at Miraflores 1535, tel. 45/407777; Bonanza, tel. 45/406204; and Inter Sur, Avenida Balmaceda 1372, tel. 45/234278, in an office shared with Tur-Bus.

Tur-Bus's budget line Cóndor Bus, also at Claro Solar 598, tel. 45/258361, goes to Santiago, Pucón, and intermediates; they also share offices at General Lagos 538, tel. 45/239190. Buses Jac, Avenida Balmaceda 1005, tel. 45/210313, offers nearly constant service to Villarrica and Pucón, with fewer trips to Lican Ray and to Coñaripe (changing buses in Villarrica in off-season), and a daily service to Curarrehue. Panguisur, tel. 45/406200, has three nightly buses to Santiago. Buses Biobío, in its own terminal at Lautaro 853, tel. 45/210599, links Temuco to Angol, Los Ángeles, and Concepción.

Sample domestic destinations, fares, and times include Villarrica (US$3, one hour), Curacautín (US$2.50, 1.5 hours), Panguipulli (US$2.50, two hours), Angol (US$3, two hours), Coñaripe or Curarrehue (US$3.50, 2.5 hours), Ancud (US$10, seven hours), Osorno (US$5, three hours), Puerto Montt (US$7, five hours), Castro (US$12, eight hours), Quellón (US$15, 11 hours), Valdivia or Los Ángeles (US$4, three hours), Chillán (US$7, five hours), Concepción (US$6, 4.5 hours), Talca (US$8.50, six hours), Santiago (US$13 to US$16, eight hours), and Valparaíso/Viña del Mar (US$17, 12 hours). *Salón cama* buses to Santiago cost around US$25 to US$28.

Most Argentina-bound buses use the Paso Mamuil Malal crossing southeast of Pucón (to Junín de los Andes and San Martín de los Andes), but some take the Paso Pino Hachado route, directly east of Temuco via Curacautín and the upper Biobío town of Lonquimay (to Zapala and Neuquén). In addition, there are connections to Bariloche via the Panamericana to Osorno and Ruta 215 east over Paso Cardenal Samoré.

Since the distances are long, the terrain is rugged, and some roads are gravel, some buses across the Andes leave early—some well before daylight. Carriers serving Junín de los Andes and San Martín de los Andes (US$15, six hours) include Buses San Martín Centenario, tel. 45/234017, and Buses Ruta Sur, Miraflores 1151, tel. 45/210079. Igi Llaima and Nar-Bus, in their sparklingly renovated quarters at Miraflores 1535, tel. 45/407707, alternate daily 5 A.M. services to Zapala and Neuquén (US$24, 10 hours).

To Bariloche (US$20, nine hours), the main carriers are Tas Choapa and Cruz del Sur; it's necessary to change in Osorno.

Train: The Estación de Ferrocarriles del Estado is at Avenida Barros Arana s/n, tel. 45/233416, eight blocks northeast of the Plaza de Armas. Nightly EFE trains go north to Santiago (12.5 hours) and intermediate stops at 8:30 and 9:30 P.M. Fares range US$7.50–12 depending on the type of seat; sleepers cost US$23 for upper berths and US$29 for lower berths. Tickets are also available from EFE's downtown ticket office at Bulnes 582, tel. 233522.

Getting Around

City transport is frequent and cheap, with both buses and *taxi colectivos.*

To the Airport: Just six km south of town and west of the Panamericana, Temuco's Aeropuerto Maquehue occupies part of an air force base and is due to move, but may not do so before the next edition of this book. Turismo Gira, Andrés Bello 870, Local 5, tel. 45/406494, arranges airport transfers (around US$4 pp), as do taxis from the northeast corner of the Plaza de Armas.

To the Bus Terminal: From downtown to the Rodoviario, catch Micro No. 2 or No. 7 from Portales and Bulnes, or *taxi colectivo* 11-P or 25-A from the corner of Prat and Claro Solar.

Car Rental: For excursions into the backcountry in and around Temuco, especially the circuit through Parque Nacional Conguillío or the upper Biobío, car rental is the most convenient option. Rental agencies include the Automóvil Club de Chile (Acchi), San Martín 0278, tel. 45/248903; Avis, Vicuña Mackenna 448, tel. 237575, tel. 45/337715 at the airport; First, Antonio Varas 1036, tel. 45/233890, tel. 335793 at the airport; Full Fama's, Andrés Bello 1096, tel./fax 45/215420; Hertz, Las Heras 999, tel. 45/318585, tel. 45/337019 at the airport; and Verschae, Lagos 521, tel. 45/231575.

VICINITY OF TEMUCO

There are worthwhile excursions in every direction from Temuco, but most people focus on the cordillera to the east. Temuco's **Multitour**, Bulnes 307, Oficina 203, tel. 45/237913, fax 45/233536, info@multitour.cjb.net, has English-speaking guides and a good track record for excursions in and around Temuco—primarily toward the Andean national parks and reserves, but also to Mapuche villages to the west.

Parque Nacional Tolhuaca

Native woodlands of *Araucarias* and other species adorn the foothill slopes of Parque Nacional Tolhuaca, where the Río Malleco drains south-southwest into marshy Laguna Malleco before plunging into its lower course toward the coast. Improved access roads have increased visitation, especially in summer and on weekends, but most people stay in the immediate vicinity of Laguna Malleco—the rest of the park is still ideal for camping, hiking, and fishing. (Recent severe forest fires have affected the area around the park; visitors should check the status of the park before they go.)

Geography and Climate: In the Andean precordillera, ranging from 1,000 meters above sea level around Laguna Malleco to 1,821 meters on the summits and ridgelines of Reserva Nacional Malleco to the north, Tolhuaca is a compact 6,374-hectare unit on the north bank of the Río Malleco, which flows northwest toward the town of Collipulli. It has a cool humid climate, with an average annual temperature of 9°C and 2,500–3,000 mm rainfall, but it enjoys mild, relatively dry summers. The park's namesake peak, 2,806-meter Volcán Tolhuaca, is beyond the park boundaries to the southeast.

Flora and Fauna: At higher elevations, Tolhuaca has nearly pure *Araucaria* forests in well-drained soils, but the dense gallery forests along the Río Malleco consist of *coigüe, olivillo,* and other evergreen species, along with deciduous *raulí* and roble. *Quila (Chusquea quila)* forms an impenetrable bamboo undergrowth in some areas. *Junquillos* (reeds) grow in the lakeside sediments, while massive *nalcas (Gunnera chilensis), chilco* (firecracker fuchsia, *Fuchsia magellanica*), ferns, mosses, and other water-loving plants grow on the riverbanks.

Except for waterfowl and coypu in Laguna Malleco, Tolhuaca's fauna are less conspicuous, but there are puma, *pudú* (miniature deer), foxes, and skunks.

Sights and Recreation: As ash and other sediments from the surrounding ridges and peaks sluice into the river and downstream, water-loving reeds are colonizing the shoreline of 76-hectare **Laguna Malleco,** a glacial remnant where Conaf has a loaner rowboat for fishermen and birders. It's an easy walk from the campground, and swimming is possible in several pools en route.

From Laguna Malleco's north shore, the 1,800-meter **Sendero El Salto** winds through thick native forest to **Salto Malleco,** a thunderous 50-meter cascade that plumbs over the rugged basalt into the river's lower drainage. Even more copious foliage surrounds the continuing trail.

Also from Laguna Malleco, **Sendero Prados de Mesacura** switchbacks up the north shore to intersect the **Sendero Lagunillas,** which follows the contour east through nearly waterless *Araucaria* woodlands—the volcanic soil absorbs nearly all the precipitation. From a spot about five km east of Laguna Malleco, toward Termas de Tolhuaca, the eight-km **Sendero Laguna Verde** skirts the southwestern slope of 1,606-meter Cerro Laguna Verde to arrive at its namesake lake, covering 3.6 hectares.

Accommodations and Food: At Laguna Malleco, Conaf's shady **Camping Inalaufquén** has 25 sites with barbecue pits, picnic tables, running water, and clean bathrooms with flush toilets and cold showers. Rates are US$12 per site, but single travelers can try asking for a discount if it's not crowded. For travelers with their own vehicles and more money, Hotel Termas de Tolhuaca is an option (see the separate entry below).

No supplies whatever are available at Laguna Malleco—bring everything you need.

Information: There is no formal visitor center, but Conaf rangers at Laguna Malleco offer daily chats at the outdoor amphitheater. Park admission costs US$3 pp for adults, US$1 for children.

Transportation: There is no direct public transportation to the park, but one bus daily (4 P.M.) goes from Victoria's Terminal de Buses Rurales, 58 km north of Temuco on the Panamericana, to the hamlet of San Gregorio, on a decent gravel road that leads east from the village of Inspector Fernández. This, unfortunately, stops 20 km short of Laguna Malleco, but the road is still a good alternative for hitchhikers, motorists, or mountain bikers.

From Curacautín, 87 km northeast of Temuco via Lautaro or 119 km via Victoria, an improved gravel road reaches the hot springs resort of Termas de Tolhuaca (see separate entry below), 33 km to the north. From Termas de Tolhuaca, what was once a hazardous 4WD road to Laguna Malleco is now passable for ordinary vehicles, at least in summer. *Taxi colectivos* from Curacautín go as far as Termas de Tolhuaca, but it's another nine km to Malleco.

The Upper Cautín and Biobío

From Victoria, 58 km north of Temuco on the Panamericana, a smooth and scenic two-lane highway parallels the former branch railroad that ran from Púa to Curacautín, Lonquimay, and the upper Biobío drainage, a little-visited and underappreciated area north of Parque Nacional Conguillío. Blessed with its own native forests, rushing rivers, and volcanic grandeur, this area is also accessible via a shorter paved alternative that heads northeast from Lautaro (30 km north of Temuco). From the upper Biobío, it's also possible to loop back around on good gravel roads to Melipeuco, the southern gateway to Conguillío, or back to Temuco.

Curacautín: The midsized town of Curacautín dates from 1882, when the Chilean military established Fuerte Ultra Cautín on Pehuenche territory on the banks of the Río Cautín. Today, it's the northern access point to Parque Nacional Conguillío and the gateway to the upper Cautín and upper Biobío. It is 87 km northeast of Temuco via Lautaro or 119 km via the Panamericana and Victoria.

On the highway at the west end of town, homey **Hostal Rayén,** Manuel Rodríguez 104, charges US$9 pp with breakfast and shared bath. **Hotel Turismo**, Tarapacá 140, tel. 45/811116, costs US$10/17 s/d with private bath. Rates at **Hotel Plaza,** on the east side of the Plaza de Armas at Yungay 175, tel. 45/881256, are US$14 pp with private bath and breakfast.

Curacautín has few places to eat, the best of which is probably **La Cabaña,** Yungay 157, next to Hotel Plaza.

Turismo Christopher, Yungay 240, will change foreign currency, but the only ATM belongs to Banco del Estado, which does not work with foreign ATM cards.

CTC Telefónica, at O'Higgins 610-B, has both long-distance service and Internet access (US$2.50 per hour). The area code is 45.

Curacautín's Oficina de Informaciones Turísticas, at the bus terminal on the north side of the Plaza de Armas, is open 10 A.M.–6 P.M. weekdays and 9 A.M.–1:30 A.M. Saturday in summer only.

Curacautín's Terminal Rodoviario is Manuel Rodríguez, just north of the Plaza de Armas and directly on the Lonquimay highway. Erbuc has five buses daily to and from Temuco (US$3) via Victoria and four via Lautaro; there are five to Lonquimay. Erbuc goes to Captrén, the entrance to Parque Nacional Conguillío (US$1) Monday and Friday at 5:45 A.M. and 5:30 P.M.; it's also possible to hire a cab to Conguillío.

Igi Llaima and Nar-Bus pass through Curacautín daily en route to Zapala and Neuquén, Argentina, but make reservations in Temuco to be sure of a seat.

Termas de Tolhuaca: Reached by an improved gravel road that heads north out of Curacautín for 35 km, the once humble hot springs of Termas de Tolhuaca is gradually morphing into a spa, but it is still a pretty good value by international standards and a good alternative for those who want to visit Parque Nacional Tolhuaca but who don't want to camp in the park, which is nine km farther on by road. The resort began in 1898, but today's remodeled facility is a substantial improvement over the rustic Russian-built original.

Accommodations at the 100-bed **Hotel Termas de Tolhuaca** cost US$60 pp with full board and unlimited access to pools and baths; it has its own restaurant. Camping is also possible for US$10 per site for up to six people, there is public access to pools for US$4 pp (US$2 for children), and there are limited supplies on site. For more details or reservations, contact Transporte, Turismo y Agrícola Tolhuaca, Calama 240, Curacautín, tel. 45/881164, fax 45/881211, tolhuaca@ctcreuna.cl. It also has a small but succinct website, www.termasdetolhuaca.co.cl, in both Spanish and serviceable English.

Manzanar: Barely a wide spot in the road, 18 km east of Curacautín and 680 meters above sea level, Manzanar is home to **Hotel Termas de Manzanar,** tel./fax 45/881200, termasmanzanar@indecom.cl, a riverside spa resort set back from the south side of the highway. It offers a variety of accommodations options, from simple rooms with shared bath (US$42/63 s/d for B&B to US$58/89 with full board) to *cabañas* with private bath and Jacuzzi (US$68/104 s/d for B&B, US$83/117 with full board).

For those seeking cheaper alternatives, on the north side of the highway but one km east, the acceptable **Hotel Abarzúa,** tel. 45/870011, charges from US$8 pp with shared bath for B&B, US$25 pp with full board. There are also *cabaña* accommodations with private bath and kitchen facilities for US$38 for up to four people, and orchard campsites with electricity and hot showers for US$12 for up to three people.

Reserva Nacional Malalcahuello: Ten km east of Manzanar, Reserva Nacional Malalcahuello occupies a cool high valley in the shadow of the 2,865-meter Volcán Lonquimay (also known as Volcán Mocho). Thanks to its accessibility—trailheads leave almost from the highway itself—it's an ideal destination for hikers and horseback riders. The reserve shares its name, meaning

"horse corral" in Mapudungun, with the nearby hamlet; its dilapidated ski center, on the southern slope of the volcano, has been superseded by another near the town of Lonquimay.

Combined with the contiguous Reserva Las Nalcas to the north, Malalcahuello comprises 25,000 hectares of wild high country that also serves as a key forestry research center. At altitudes upward of 980 meters, it's substantially colder than areas to the west, and nights can get chilly even in summer.

Higher than Parque Nacional Tolhuaca to the west, Malalcahuello contains an overlapping forest flora of *Araucarias* with deciduous Andean forest with evergreen *coigüe (Nothofagus dombeyi)* and *lenga (Nothofagus pumilio),* and *Araucaria* with *coigüe* mixed with *ñirre.* The fauna resemble those of Tolhuaca, but the Andean condor is a more common sight here, as is the *carpintero negro* (*Campephilus magellanicus,* black woodpecker).

Its flat summit crater filled by a glacier that spills onto the adjoining flanks, symmetrical **Volcán Lonquimay** is the reserve's focal point. Slightly northeast of Malalcahuello proper, it dates from late Pleistocene times, but it has erupted as recently as 1933, almost simultaneously with nearby Volcán Llaima, and lava flows have spilled down its northeastern flanks as late as 1990.

Malalcahuello is the starting point for hikes into the backcountry of Malalcahuello and Las Nalcas, with trails ranging from 2.5 km (to Cerro Cautín) to the summit of Lonquimay. La Suizandina (see below) arranges excursions to Conguillío, Lonquimay, and other local attractions, organizes transportation, and offers information and advice to individuals who wish to undertake them independently. In addition to Spanish, the staff speaks English, German, French, and Italian.

Swiss-run **La Suizandina,** 28 km east of Curacautín, tel. 09/8849541, fax 45/881892, website: www.suizandina.com, is a combination of campground, hostel, *cabaña,* and sparkling new guesthouse just west of Malalcahuello on the north side of the highway. Rates are US$4 pp for camping, US$8–10 pp in well-heated dorm-style accommodations, US$11 pp in not quite so well-heated *cabañas,* and US$22 pp in the more comfortable, centrally heated guesthouse.

Multilingual Tom and Eva Buschor include a Swiss-style breakfast (Tom is a professional baker) and also serve Swiss specialties such as fondue and raclette for lunch or dinner, accompanied by fresh desserts and Chilean wines.

Conaf's ranger station at Malalcahuello is a good source for advice; speakers of English, German, French, and Italian can try Thomas and Eva Buschor at La Suizandina (see above).

Erbuc buses between Temuco and Lonquimay go directly past the gate to Malalcahuello.

Lonquimay: From Malalcahuello, the highway heads southeast to enter the 1930s **Túnel Las Raíces,** where the Púa-Lonquimay railway ran a tourist train as recently as the 1990s. Now open for vehicle traffic, the one-lane, 4.5-km tunnel has sprung leaks that produce meterlong icicles in winter, but it's due for a US$7.1 million upgrade that will include new pavement and roof reinforcement; by the end of the decade, a US$30 million parallel tunnel will permit two-way rather than alternating traffic as at present to facilitate traffic over the Pino Hachado pass to Argentina.

Beyond the tunnel, the highway turns northeast to the village of Lonquimay, in the placid drainage of the upper Biobío, the traditional starting point for descending what was Chile's wildest whitewater river until a series of downstream dams submerged most of the rapids. Parts of the Biobío survive, thanks to an unsettled controversy between the government and a handful of Pehuenche families, but its days are numbered.

Instead of a standard grid, Lonquimay has a peculiar ovoid city plan centered, however, on the usual Plaza de Armas. It has a tourist office at O'Higgins and Carrera Pinto, tel. 45/981911, and restaurants and hotels that traditionally close at the end of February. It also has a sparkling new ski area that may pull the town out of its winter doldrums. From Malalcahuello, a steep eastbound dirt road over Cuesta las Raíces is a shorter alternate route to Lonquimay, which is 900 meters above sea level.

Recently opened, eight km from Lonquimay, **Los Arenales de Lonquimay** is a promising new ski area where the Fondo por Solidaridad e Inversión Social (Fosis, Fund for Solidarity and Social Investment) has created a joint venture

between the Austrian owners and the local Pehuenche population. If all works well, the Pehuenche will build and operate 10 *cabañas,* in the form of traditional *rucas.* Amenities, however, will be suitable for international package tours, including all meals and housekeeping.

Los Arenales at present has two beginner, two intermediate, and four expert runs for skiing and snowboarding, but it anticipates expansion; there are also childcare, a ski school, and a café-restaurant. Lift tickets are cheap at US$11 pp weekdays, US$12 pp weekends and holidays, with ski rentals for US$13 and snowboards for US$20. For more details, contact Los Arenales de Lonquimay, Casilla 5, Lonquimay, tel. 45/891911 for lodging, tel. 09/3132208 for service, esquilosarenales@hotmail.com.

Hospedaje Navidad, Caupolicán 915, tel. 45/891111, charges US$8.50 pp with shared bath and breakfast. **Hostería Hollil Pewenche,** Ignacio Carrera Pinto 110, tel./fax 45/891110, quimque@entelchile.net, costs the same with shared bath but also has rooms with private bath for US$20 pp.

Five Erbuc buses daily connect Lonquimay with Temuco.

Alto Biobío: South of Lonquimay, a gravel road tracks south past Lago Galletué, the official source of the Biobío and part of Conaf's **Reserva Nacional Galletué,** and continues southeast past the border post of Icalma (for the Argentine town of Aluminé); there is no regular public transport across this route. There are numerous simple campgrounds along this main road, which then heads west toward Melipeuco and Parque Nacional Conguillío. From Lonquimay, a newly paved road crosses Conaf's **Reserva Nacional Alto Biobío** via the 1,884-meter Paso Pino Hachado, the route used by buses to the Argentine cities of Zapala and Neuquén.

Melipeuco

In the Río Allipén valley, built precariously on an ancient mudflow 92 km east of Temuco via Cunco and 45 km west of Icalma, the Mapuche agricultural town of Melipeuco is the southern access point to Parque Nacional Conguillío and an alternative route into the upper Biobío loop around Lonquimay. In the 1970s, this was a conflictive area in the agrarian reform movement, and the issue is still alive today.

Melipeuco (population about 3,000) operates a summer-only tourist office on Pedro Aguirre Cerda, across from the YPF gas station. There is a new crafts market here as well.

Accommodations and Food: Melipeuco's cheapest accommodations are **Hospedaje Icalma,** Pedro Aguirre Cerda 729, tel. 45/581108, for US$5 pp with kitchen access; it also arranges excursions into Conguillío. In a quieter location on the banks of the Allipén, recommended **Hospedaje Muñoz,** Aurelio Letelier 80, charges US$8 pp; there is cheaper camping in its orchard.

Rates at the more formal **Hostería Huetelén,** Pedro Aguirre Cerda 1, tel. 45/581005, start at US$33 s or d with private bath. Its restaurant is mediocre, however; try instead the new **Ruminet** at Pedro Aguirre Cerda and Arturo Prat.

Transportation: Nar-Bus has seven buses daily to and from Temuco's Terminal de Buses Rurales (US$2, 1.5 hours). There is no scheduled public transport to Conguillío, but taxis or pickup trucks will take passengers to the visitor center for about US$12–15.

PARQUE NACIONAL CONGUILLÍO

Directly east of Temuco, the smoking crater of 3,125-meter Volcán Llaima is the most eye-catching feature of Parque Nacional Conguillío—since colonial times, Chile's second most active volcano has recorded dozens of violent eruptions and other events, some as recently as 1999. Within its 60,833 hectares, though, this UNESCO biopshere reserve also comprises dozens of lava flows, secondary cones, alpine lakes, river canyons, and the *Araucaria* forest that it was created to protect—the word Conguillío comes from the Mapudungun *kongüijim,* "to enter the *pewen* forest." One of the most popular excursions from Temuco for foreigners and Chileans alike, it justifies a day trip but it deserves more. (Recent severe forest fires have affected the area around the park; visitors should check the status of the park before they go.)

© WAYNE BERNHARDSON

Laguna Conguillío

Geography and Climate

From Temuco, the western limit of Conguillío is only about 80 km away via Cherquenco, but by either Curacautín or Melipeuco it's about 120 km. Altitudes range from around 900 meters in the valley of the Río Truful Truful to 3,125 meters on Llaima's summit. In the northeastern corner of the park, the ruggedly glaciated Sierra Nevada averages above 2,500 meters.

Since most of Conguillío's 2,500 millimeters of precipitation falls as snow between May and September, the mild summer temperatures, averaging around 15°C, make its numerous lakes and streams popular recreational destinations. Even in summer, though, occasional heavy rains can make the road from Curacautín impassable.

Flora and Fauna

Conguillío originally was two separate parks, the other named Los Paraguas after the umbrella shape of the mature *Araucaria* that, at higher elevations above 1,400 meters, mixes with southern beeches such as *coigüe (Nothofagus dombeyi), ñirre (Nothofagus antarctica),* and *lenga (Nothofagus pumilio). Coigüe* is also common at lower elevations, around 900 meters, but mixed with roble *(Nothofagus obliqua);* above 1,200 meters, *raulí (Nothofagus alpina)* succeeds roble.

Traditionally, the Pewenche branch of the Mapuche collected the nuts from the coniferous *Araucaria,* much like indigenous groups who gathered piñon nuts in western North America. The name Pewenche literally means "people of the *pewen,"* the local species of an endemic Southern Hemisphere genus that once enjoyed a greater distribution throughout the Americas.

Given that much of Conguillío's terrain consists of barren volcanic slopes, lava fields, and open woodlands, prime wildlife habitat is scarce and so is wildlife. Birds are most common and resemble those at Tolhuaca or Malalcahuello, but the small reptile *lagartija (Liolaemus tenuis)* manages to flourish in the drier environments.

Sights and Recreation

Towering just west of the park's geographic center, glacier-covered **Volcán Llaima** is a Holocene structure of accumulated lava flows within an eight-km-wide caldera that exploded about 7,200 years ago. It has two active craters, one on the summit and another on its southeastern shoulder.

East of Llaima, the sprawling lava flows of **El Escorial** dammed the Río Truful-Truful to form **Laguna Arco Iris** and **Laguna Verde;** to the north, beneath the Sierra Nevada, **Laguna Conguillío** has a similar origin.

Sector Conguillío: Near Conaf's Centro de Información at the southwest corner of Laguna Conguillío, the **Sendero Araucarias** is a short woodland nature trail suitable for any hiker. For a longer and more challenging excursion that's still a day hike, take the trail from **Playa Linda** at the east end of Laguna Conguillío to the foot of the **Sierra Nevada,** which rewards the hiker with overwhelming views through nearly pure stands of *Araucarias.* This trail continues across the mountains to Termas Río Blanco, but this is a hazardous route on which hikers have died.

At **Laguna Captrén,** at the park's northern entrance, the **Sendero de Chile** is the initial segment of the nonmotorized trail intended to unite the country from the Peruvian border to Tierra del Fuego. At Laguna Arco Iris, to the south, an early settler built the wooden **Casa del Colono** as a homestead cabin. From Laguna Verde, also known as Laguna Quililo, a short wooded footpath goes to the beach at **La Ensenada.**

Conaf's **Sendero Cañadon Truful-Truful,** a 900-meter nature trail, follows the course of the river where erosion has uncovered the rainbow chronology of Llaima's eruptions and ash falls. Along the 800-meter **Sendero Los Vertientes,** subterranean springs emerge from the volcanic terrain.

Sector Los Paraguas: From Sector Los Paraguas, on the west side of the park, well-equipped climbers can scale Llaima; camping is possible in summer, and there is also a *refugio.* An alternative route from Captrén, which has better public transport, is on the north side. Before climbing, ask Conaf permission in Temuco.

Skiers can indulge at Los Paraguas's upgraded **Centro de Ski Las Araucarias,** tel. 45/562313; it has Temuco offices at Bulnes 351, Oficina 47, tel. 45/274141. Lift tickets cost about US$19 per day, while rental gear costs about US$17 pp. Temuco's Club de Esquí Llaima, Las Heras 299, tel. 45/237923, provides classes and rental equipment.

Accommodations and Food

Along the south shore of Laguna Conguillío, Conaf has five campgrounds under private concession: the campground administration is at **Los Ñirres** (44 sites), while there are smaller clusters at **Los Carpinteros** (12 sites), **La Caseta** (12 sites), **El Estero** (10 sites), and **El Hoyón** (10 sites). Rates are US$20 per site for up to five people in summer and during Semana Santa, but Conaf sets aside a handful of sites at El Estero for bicyclists and backpackers for US$5 pp. For more information or reservations in Temuco, contact Alejandro Morales, tel. 45/644388.

Ten km northwest of Laguna Conguillío, Conaf itself still operates the 12 sites at **Laguna Captrén,** which go for US$20 in summer but half that the rest of the year.

Between the park administration and the Los Ñirres campground, built around *pewen* trunks, the older units at **Cabañas Conguillío,** tel./fax 45/272402 in Temuco, reservas@conguillio.cl, are more quaint than practical for US$50 for up to eight people; newer units, for US$85, are a better choice (the older units' days were supposed to be numbered). In the peak summer season, a restaurant and store operate on the lakeshore.

At Laguna Verde, 18 km north of Melipeuco, the new **Cabañas La Baita Conguillío,** tel. 45/236037, fax 45/581075, agytut@terra.cl, charges US$75 for up to eight people.

At Sector Los Paraguas, the **Refugio Escuela Ski,** tel. 45/237923 in Temuco, features bunks for 70 and a restaurant; rates are US$50 pp including lift tickets (the infrastructure is basic) and full board. In summer, operator Oscar Gutiérrez offers climbing and hiking excursions in the vicinity.

At the modern **Centro de Ski Las Araucarias,** tel. 45/562313, dorm beds go for US$11 pp, while six-bed apartments with private bath cost US$80 and more elaborately furnished two-bedroom apartments for US$120. For more details, including transport suggestions, contact the Temuco office at Bulnes 351, Oficina 49, tel. 45/274141.

Information

At Laguna Conguillío, Conaf's Centro de Información Ambiental has good natural-history exhibits and a cozy fireplace; it's open 10 A.M.–1 P.M. and 3–7:30 P.M. daily in January and February, when it organizes children's programs and hiking excursions and provides evening naturalist talks.

Conaf also has ranger stations at the Laguna Captrén and Truful-Truful park entrances.

Transportation

Because public transportation is inconvenient to almost every sector of the park, it's worth considering a car rental, but it's not absolutely essential. Even with a car, the steep, narrow, and sometimes muddy road between Laguna Captrén and the park administration can be difficult to negotiate.

Reaching Curacautín and Melipeuco, the northern and southern gateways to the main park loop, is easy enough by public bus (see the appropriate entries above for details). From Curacautín, Erbuc goes to Laguna Captrén (US$1) Monday and Friday at 5:45 A.M. and 5:30 P.M., but that is the only scheduled transport. From either Curacautín or Melipeuco, it's possible to hire a taxi or pickup truck to Conguillío.

Sector Los Paraguas is the most difficult sector to reach by public transportation. Nar-Bus goes to the village of Cherquenco (US$1.50), but from there it's 17 km farther to the ski lodge at Los Paraguas. An alternative route, requiring a high-clearance vehicle and preferably 4WD, goes from Captrén to Los Paraguas.

Dominating the skyline south of Pucón, the glowing crater of 2,847-meter Volcán Villarrica is a constant reminder that what Spanish conquistador and poet Alonso de Ercilla called its "great neighbor volcano" could, at any moment, obliterate the town in a cataclysm of volcanic bombs, a cloud of ash, or beneath a mudflow triggered by lava and melting snow.

VILLARRICA

Southeast of Temuco, the midsized town of Villarrica marks the beginning of Chile's most traditional resort region, where generations of families have spent their summers on the shores of lakes left by receding Pleistocene glaciers. It also shares its name with Volcán Villarrica, a fuming 2,840-meter cone that's Chile's most active volcano, to the southeast. Much of this area was once wide open country, but a construction boom of hotels and country houses between Villarrica and the neighboring resort of Pucón, to the east, are rapidly eliminating the open spaces.

History

Fiery eruptions from Volcán Villarrica may have deterred some settlers, but the Mapuche resistance to the Spaniards and Chileans was more effective. In 1552, 50 colonists under the command of Gerónimo de Alderete established Santa María

© WAYNE BERNHARDSON

SUR CHICO

Volcán Villarrica

Magdalena de Villarrica, but Mapuche assaults forced its abandonment several times despite speculation about precious metals in the area (the overly optimistic founding name "Villarrica" means "rich town"). After driving out the Spaniards in 1602, the Mapuche enjoyed nearly three centuries of uninterrupted possession until, in 1883, Chilean colonel Gregorio Urrutia reached an agreement with the Mapuche chief Epuléf to regularize the Chilean presence in the area.

Villarrica's declaration as a formal city in 1897 brought an influx of immigrants, many of them German, who gradually transformed the area into a dairy zone and, finally, a durable resort area with an international reputation.

Orientation

Some 87 km southeast of Temuco via the Panamericana and Ruta 199, an international highway to Argentina, Villarrica occupies a favored site at the southwestern corner of Lago Villarrica, at its outlet to the Río Toltén. While it has a regular grid pattern, the focus of local activity is not the Plaza de Armas but rather the lakeshore, along with the main commercial thoroughfare Avenida Pedro de Valdivia, and its perpendicular Camilo Henríquez.

Sights and Recreation

Stone tools, early Mapuche ceramics, and contemporary indigenous jewelry, silver, and leatherwork constitute the collections of the **Museo Histórico y Arqueológico de Villarrica,** Pedro de Valdivia 1050, tel. 45/413445. It's open 9 A.M.–1 P.M. and 3–7:30 P.M. weekdays; admission costs US$0.50.

Directly in front of the museum stands the landmark **Ruca,** a traditional Mapuche dwelling thickly thatched with *junquillo* and *totora* reeds.

The lakefront **Embarcadero,** featuring a cluster of small jetties toward the foot of General Körner, is the starting point for excursions on the water.

Accommodations

Like other lake district resorts, Villarrica's accommodations prices peak in January and February, but Semana Santa, September's Fiestas Patrias, and the ski season can all see higher prices.

US$10–25: In addition to the permanent places listed here, many *hospedajes* are open in summer only—look for signs or ask at the tourist office.

Cyclists in particular flock to the Swiss-run

hostel **La Torre Suiza,** Bilbao 969, tel./fax 45/411213, info@torresuiza.com, an immaculately modernized house with firm comfortable beds, easily regulated hot showers, Internet access, and a tobacco-free interior. Rates are US$5 pp for garden camping, US$8 pp for dorm accommodations, US$20 d with shared bath, and US$24 d with private bath; this includes a European-style breakfast. Owners Béat and Claudia Zbinden also do cycling trips and llama trekking.

The more venerable but less attractive **Hotel Fuentes,** Vicente Reyes 665, tel. 45/411595, goes for about US$8.50 pp with shared bath, US$12 pp with private bath. Rooms are basic and some lack windows, but it's open all year and its bar/restaurant has been a gathering place for quite a while.

US$25–50: Traditionally popular **Hotel Rayhuén,** Pedro Montt 668, tel./fax 45/411571, has cozy rooms for US$20/28 s/d with private bath and breakfast, and it also serves other meals at its restaurant. Rates at recently renovated **Hotel Villa Linda,** Avenida Pedro de Valdivia 678, tel. 45/411392, are US$17 pp with private bath and breakfast. In a quiet residential area near the lake, **Hotel Villarrica,** Körner 255, tel./fax 45/411641, has good values starting at US$27/38 s/d.

Hotel Dieggo's, Gerónimo de Alderete 709, tel. 45/411370, suffers from a busy location, but rates of US$22 pp with breakfast and private bath are not unreasonable. In a far quieter site near the lakeshore, **Hostería Bilbao,** Camilo Henríquez 43, tel. 45/411186, bilbao@7lagos.com, costs US$25/45 s/d.

US$50–100: Rates at the renovated **Hostería Kiel,** Körner 153, tel. 45/411631, fax 45/410925, yachting@villarricanet.com, range from US$35/42 off-season to US$44/58 in summer. Nearby **Hotel El Ciervo,** Körner 241, tel. 45/411215, fax 45/411426, elciervo@villarricanet.com, charges from US$45/61. **Hotel Montebianco,** Pedro de Valdivia 1011, tel. 45/411798, mtc-90@hotmail.com, has made good first impressions for US$46/58, and it has an outstanding restaurant.

Overlooking the lake from the high ground, U.S.-run **Hostería de la Colina,** Las Colinas 115, tel./fax 45/411503, aldrich@entelchile.net, starts at US$40/60 s/d, but the best volcano-view rooms go for US$81/94 s/d. There are attractive gardens and other amenities, including a large English-language library.

Food and Entertainment

Over the past few years, **The Travellers,** Valentín Letelier 753, tel. 45/412830, has earned a comfortable niche with its diverse choice of Chilean, Asian, and Mexican fusion dishes at moderate prices. **El Rey del Marisco,** in a lakeside setting at Valentín Letelier 1030, tel. 45/412093, serves fine but traditional fish and shellfish dishes in the US$6–7 range. Another seafood option is the **Parque Náutico,** Arturo Prat 880, tel. 45/410380.

Hotel Montebianco's **La Vecchia Cucina,** Pedro de Valdivia 1011, tel. 45/411798, offers fine pasta entrées for US$6–7, with slightly cheaper pizzas and fabulous homemade ice cream, all with professional service. Another good alternative, serving continental and Chilean cuisine, is the **Club Social Treffpunkt,** Pedro de Valdivia 640, tel. 45/411081. **El Fogón de Lucho,** Valentín Letelier 893, tel. 45/413841, is a *parrilla.*

For sandwiches and desserts, try **Café Bar 2001,** Camilo Henríquez 379, tel. 45/411470.

Peña La Tranquera, Acevedo 761, is a bar with live folk music.

Shopping

Immediately behind the tourist office, Villarrica's **Feria Artesanal** showcases Mapuche crafts and food in summer, but the rest of the year it's fairly moribund. Permanent crafts outlets include the **Tornería Suiza,** Prat 675, tel. 45/411610, and **Tejidos Ray-Ray,** Anfión Muñoz 386, tel. 45/412006; the latter is strong on woolens.

Services

Money: Turismo Christopher, Pedro de Valdivia 1033, is the only exchange house. There are several ATMs: Banco de Crédito at Gerónimo de Alderete 612, Banco Santander at Pedro de Valdivia 778, and Banco BHIF at Pedro de Valdivia 770.

Postal: Correos de Chile is at Anfión Muñoz 315.

Telephone and Internet: The Centro de Llamados at Camilo Henríquez 544 has both long-distance and Internet service; Entel is at Camilo Henríquez 446, Chilesat at Henríquez 473. Villarrica's area code is 45.

Other Internet options include the Centro de Llamados at Camilo Henríquez 565 and the one at Vicente Reyes 623.

Laundry: Todo Lavado is at General Urrutia 699, Local 7, tel. 45/414452.

Medical: Hospital Villarrica is at San Martín 460, tel. 45/411169.

Information

Well stocked with maps, brochures, and lists of accommodations and prices, Villarrica's municipal Oficina de Turismo is at Pedro de Valdivia 1070, tel. 45/206619, turis@entelchile.net. From January to March, it stays open 8:30 A.M.–11 P.M. daily; the rest of the year, hours are 9 A.M.–1 P.M. and 2:30–6 P.M. weekdays only except in December, when they're 8:30 A.M.–8:30 P.M. daily.

Transportation

Villarrica's Terminal de Buses is at Avenida Pedro de Valdivia 621, though some carriers have individual offices nearby.

Regional: Buses Regional Villarrica, Vicente Reyes 619, tel. 45/411871, has frequent buses to Pucón, where there are connections to other regional destinations such as Curarrehue and Puesco.

Buses Jac, Bilbao 610, tel. 45/411447, shuttles at least every 15 to 30 minutes between Temuco (US$3, one hour) and Pucón (US$.50, half an hour). It also goes to Lican Ray (US$.60) half hourly, to Coñaripe (US$1.50) eight times daily, and nine times daily to Caburgua (US$2) via Pucón.

Long Distance: Northbound services to Santiago and intermediates on the Panamericana are frequent, but some southbound services on the Panamericana require backtracking to Temuco; alternatively, transfer at Freire from any Temuco-bound bus, or at Loncoche from any Valdivia-bound bus.

Many companies go to Santiago, including Buses Jac; Inter Sur, tel. 45/411534; Tur-Bus, Anfión Muñoz 657, tel. 45/411534; and Buses Lit, Anfión Muñoz 640, tel. 45/411555. Jac goes

to Valdivia (US$3.50) five times daily, while Tur-Bus has the only direct service to Puerto Montt.

Fares to Santiago can range from US$10–20, depending on the carrier and seasonal demand, while rates for *salón cama* sleepers can double that. Other sample destinations, fares, and times include Valdivia (US$3.50, three hours), Los Ángeles (US$6, four hours), Concepción (US$7.50, 5.5 hours), and Puerto Montt (US$7, five hours).

International: International services are available to the Argentine cities of Junín de los Andes and San Martín de los Andes; these buses leave from Temuco and add passengers in Villarrica and Pucón. For services to Bariloche, it's necessary to return to Temuco.

Buses San Martín Centenario, Anfión Muñoz 604, tel. 45/411584, alternates daily service to Junín and San Martín with Igi Llaima, at the main terminal, tel. 45/412733.

Getting Around

Automotriz Castillo, Anfión Muñoz 415, tel. 45/411618, hugo77@ctcreuna.cl, is the only car rental alternative.

PUCÓN

At the foot of ominously smoldering Volcán Villarrica, Pucón has gained a name over the past decade as *the* destination for hikers, climbers, mountain bikers, windsurfers, and white-water rafters and kayakers. Still popular with conventional Chilean holidaymakers in the summer peak, it enjoys a longer season than most lake district resorts because hordes of youthful international travelers frequent the area from November to April. It has few sights of its own because almost everything worth seeing or doing is outside town, but at the end of the day everyone swarms to local hotels, restaurants, and bars to party.

That doesn't mean Pucón doesn't have its serious side. Over the past several years, the landmark cooperative Hostería ¡Ecole!, along with the affiliated Fundación Lahuen, has actively promoted forest conservation in the surrounding countryside.

Lago
Villarrica

MUELLE

HOLZAPFEL
BÄCKEREI

C. HOLZAPFEL

GRAN HOTEL
PUCÓN

ANSORENA

CASINO DE
PUCÓN/HOTEL DEL
LAGO

C. HOLZAPFEL

Plaza

PEDRO DE VALDIVIA

ARAUCO

HOTEL
CASABLANCA

GERÓNIMO DE ALDERETE

FRESIA

LA OLLA
CHILENA

PALGUÍN

HOSTERÍA
¡ECOLE!

IL FIORE

COMO
PIZZA

HOTEL LA
POSADA

LINCOYÁN

POST
OFFICE

ARTESANOS
DE PUCÓN

HOTEL CABAÑAS
LA PALMERA

LA TETERA/
HOSTAL LA TETERA

HOTEL
GUDENSCHWAGER

PATAGONIA
CHOCOLATES Y
CAFÉ

BUONATESTA

HOTEL
MUNICH

PUERTO PUCÓN Y
TEQUILLA

GENERAL BASILIO URRUTIA

COPPA
KABANA

GERÓNIMO DE ALDERETE

EN ALTA
MAR

TIJUANA'S

EL FOGÓN

HOTEL
ARAUCARIAS

RESIDENCIAL
LINCOYÁN

LANCHILE

ARABIAN CAFÉ

SUPERMERCADO
ELTIT

HOSTERÍA
MILLARAHUE

KRATER

CAUPOLICÁN

MERCADO
ARTESANAL

AVENIDA LIBERTADOR BERNARDO O'HIGGINS

BRASIL

La
Poza

HOSPEDAJE
SONIA

FRESIA

CÁMARA DE
TURISMO

HOSPEDAJE
IRMA

PJE. CHILE

OFICINA DE
TURISMO

HOSPEDAJE LUCÍA

HOSPITAL
SAN FRANCISCO

ANSORENA

MUELLE

Puerto del Estero

URUGUAY

LINCOYÁN

COSTANERA ROBERTO GEISS

PARAGUAY

PERÚ

0   100 yds
0   100 m

COLOMBIA

HOTEL
INTERLAKEN

LOS
HORNITOS DE
PUCÓN

ECUADOR

To Parque Nacional
Villarrica, Villarrica,
and Temuco

Orientation

Where the Río Pucón enters the lake, 25 km east from the town of Villarrica via Ruta 119, central Pucón occupies a compact grid bounded by the lakeshore to the north and west, Avenida Colo Colo to the east, and the lower slopes of Volcán Villarrica to the south. Its main commercial axis is Avenida Bernardo O'Higgins, which continues as Ruta 119 toward Curarrehue and the Argentine border at Paso Mamuil Malal.

Accommodations

Pucón has abundant budget accommodations, relatively few midrange options, and some opulent upscale choices.

US$10–25: Even in summer, modest accommodations are available for about US$8–10 pp with breakfast or kitchen privileges at established, centrally located *hospedajes* such as **Hostal La Casita,** Palguín 555, tel. 45/444081; **Hospedaje Irma,** Lincoyán 545, tel. 45/442226; and **Hospedaje Lucía,** Lincoyán 565, tel. 45/441271. There are many other options, however.

Over the past decade, comfortable **Hospedaje Sonia,** Lincoyán 485, tel. 45/441269, has become a gathering place for international travelers, offering B&B accommodations for US$10 pp and also arranging its own tours of local highlights. In a quiet site only about 100 meters north of the Tur-Bus terminal, Swiss-run **Hospedaje Travel Pucón,** Blanco Encalada 190, tel. 45/444093, pucontravel@terra.cl, has spacious rooms with both breakfast and kitchen privileges for about the same price. **Residencial Lincoyán,** Lincoyán 323, tel. 45/441144, nefc@entelchile.net, is slightly dearer at about US$12 pp.

US$25–50: More than just a place to stay, **Hostería ¡Ecole!,** General Urrutia 592, tel. 45/441675, fax 45/441660, trek@ecole.mic.cl, has become a destination in itself. Owned and operated by a committed cooperative of Chilean and international environmental activists, it charges US$15 pp for informally stylish B&B-style accommodations with shared bath, with discounts for Hostelling International members. In addition, it has an exceptional but moderately priced and mostly vegetarian restaurant and a book exchange, operates its own excursions in the vicinity of Pucón, and provides information and advice for independent travelers. Undergoing expansion at present, it's so popular that reservations are absolutely essential in summer, and not a bad idea the rest of the year.

Next door to Hostería ¡Ecole!, Swiss-Chilean **Hostal La Tetera,** General Urrutia 580, tel./fax 45/441462, website: www.tetera.cl, info@tetera.cl, charges US$20/30 s/d for stylishly comfortable rooms with good beds, individual reading lights, and shared bath; the walls may be a little thin, but it attracts a quiet clientele and has the best breakfasts in town.

Hostería Milla-Rahue, O'Higgins 460, tel. 45/441610, gudens@cepri.cl, charges US$30 d with breakfast and shared bath. Lakeshore **Hotel Interlaken,** on the western approach to town at Colombia s/n, tel. 45/441276, fax 45/441242, is outstanding value for US$23/45 s/d. **Hostal Casablanca,** Palguín 136, tel. 45/441450, charges US$33/43 with breakfast.

US$50–100: One of the best midrange values is **Hotel Cabañas La Palmera,** Ansorena 221, tel./fax 45/441083, palmera@ceprinet.cl, for US$50/63 s/d. Fronting directly on the lake, classically aging **Hotel Gudenschwager,** Pedro de Valdivia 12, tel./fax 45/441156, gudens@cepri.cl, charges US$63/77 s/d with breakfast.

Having recently added a spa and otherwise modernized, **Hotel Araucarias,** Caupolicán 243, tel. 45/441286, fax 45/441693, hotel@araucarias.cl, costs US$63/89 s/d. The 14-room European-style **Hotel Munich,** Alderete 275, tel. 45/442293, munich@pucon.com, deserves consideration for US$67/75.

US$100–150: Set on ample grounds with a large pool, **Hotel La Posada Plaza,** Pedro de Valdivia 191, tel. 45/441088, fax 45/441762, laposada@unete.com, charges US$92/110.

US$150–200: The mammoth lakefront **Gran Hotel Pucón,** Holzapfel 190, tel./fax 45/441001, info@granhotelpucon.cl, dates from the 1930s, when the state railroad agency Ferrocarriles del Estado decided on Pucón as the next great tourist destination. Enjoying its own black sand beach, it charges rates of US$140/197 s/d. Part of the pharaonic new casino a block to the northwest, the 82-room **Hotel del Lago,** Ansorena 23, tel.

45/291000, sistcasino@entelchile.net, costs US$198/200 s/d.

Two km west of Pucón on the Villarrica road, poised among hillside gardens with immaculate flower beds, pools, and cascades, **Hotel Antumalal,** tel. 45/441011/2, fax 45/441013, antumalal@entelchile.net, prides itself on personal service—on arrival, the staff places a fruit basket in every room and each guest's name on the door. Each of its 20 rooms boasts lake views and a fireplace; there is also a heated pool and a private beach. Rates are US$180/250 s/d with half board in high season (mid-December to March), but the offseason rate of US$120/140 is exceptional.

Food

Food in Pucón varies from simple regional cuisine and fast food—no greasy chain outlets, though—to sophisticated international fare. A good example of both, at the western approach to town, is **Los Hornitos de Pucón,** Caupolicán 710, which specializes in oven-baked takeaway empanadas. **Coppa Kabana,** Urrutia 407, tel. 45/449033, serves sandwiches and plain lunches at reasonable prices.

Even if there's no room to stay at **Hostería ¡Ecole!,** Urrutia 592, tel. 45/441675, don't miss the mostly vegetarian lunches or dinners and the lively tobacco-free atmosphere. For about US$5, this is some of the country's best-value food. For breakfast or *onces,* Swiss-run **La Tetera,** next door at General Urrutia 580, tel. 45/441462, is just as good or perhaps even better.

New on the scene, **La Olla Chilena,** Jerónimo de Alderete 402-B, features freshly prepared and attractively presented versions of Chilean standards such as *pastel de choclo* in the US$5 range, plus a superb and inexpensive (US$1.50) *consomé reina* (chicken soup). The service is warm and friendly. **Club 77,** O'Higgins 635, has similar fare, while **El Fogón,** O'Higgins 480, tel. 45/444904, is a *parrilla.*

One of Pucón's many Italian venues, **El Rincón de la Pasta,** Fresia 284, tel. 45/444258, offers superb and varied pasta dishes, with an equally great variety of sauces, with most entrées in the US$6–8 range. Service is impeccable. The Argentine-style **Pizzería Buonatesta,** Fresia 243, tel. 45/441434, is equally outstanding. Nearly the lakefront are two other Italian venues: **Como Pizza,** Holzapfel 71, tel. 45/441109, and the more formal **Il Fiore,** Holzapfel 83, tel. 45/4-41565, which also serves beef and seafood.

¡Viva Perú!, O'Higgins 761, tel. 45/444285, is a recent arrival that's had almost immediate success, and it injects an overdue diversity into Pucón's restaurant scene, but it can't match Santiago's best Peruvian venues. Entrées fall into the US$6–10 range.

Pucón has a pair of Mexican options: the upscale **Puerto Pucón y Tequila,** Fresia 245, tel. 45/441592, and the more modest **Tijuana's,** Ansorena 303. The **Arabian Café,** Fresia 354, tel. 45/443469, serves Middle Eastern specialties.

At **En Alta Mar,** General Urrutia 315, tel. 45/442294, the seafood is good and fresh, and the pisco sours are excellent, but the quality doesn't quite match the US$8–10 price range for most entrées. The service can be surprisingly absent-minded at what presumes to be one of Pucón's better restaurants.

Patagonia, Fresia 223, tel. 45/443165, serves sandwiches, coffee, juices, and particularly exquisite desserts, including homemade ice cream and crepes, as well as artisanal chocolates. The **Holzapfel Bäckerei,** Holzapfel 524, tel. 45/441334, serves kuchen and similar regional specialties, as well as ice cream. **Friatto,** O'Higgins 136-B, also serves very fine ice cream.

Entertainment and Events
There's not much in the way of formal entertainment venues, but somehow Pucón has plenty to do.

Bars: There's a lot of turnover in bars, but several have managed to last more than a few seasons: **Bar del Pelao,** O'Higgins 624; **La Taverna de Barbazul,** Lincoyán 361; **Krater,** O'Higgins 447, tel. 441339; and **Mama's & Tapas,** O'Higgins 587, tel. 45/449002. All these places serve food as well, but that's not their main appeal.

Casino: Filling an entire city block east of the Plaza de Armas, built primarily for gamblers, the colossal Casino de Pucón, Ansorena 23, tel. 45/441873, is also a performing arts venue and contains a cinema.

Events: Early February's **Triatlón Internacional de Pucón** (Pucón International Triathlon) grows in popularity every year. The **Aniversario de Pucón** celebrates the city's founding on February 27.

Shopping
There's a permanent **Mercado Artesanal** (artisans' market) on Ansorena between O'Higgins and Brasil. **Artesanos de Pucón** is on Alderete between Fresia and Ansorena.

Services
Money: Turismo Christopher, O'Higgins 335, TravelSur, Fresia 285, and Supermercado Eltit, O'Higgins 336, change U.S. and Argentine cash. The latter now has an ATM, as does Banco de Crédito at Fresia 174.

Postal: Correos de Chile is at Fresia 183.

Telephone and Internet: Entel is at Ansorena 299. Pucón's area code is 45.

Imsiscom, in Turismo offices at O'Higgins 575, is one of few Internet providers in the country that offers the option of iMacs, though most of its machines are PCs. Brinck House, Ansorena 243, and several other locales have access as well.

Laundry: Lavaseco Elena, General Urrutia 520-B, charges about US$5 per load, washed, dried, and folded. Lavandería Alemana is at Fresia 224, tel. 45/441106, Lavandería Esperanza at Colo Colo 475, tel. 45/441379.

Medical: Hospital San Francisco is at Uruguay 325, tel. 45/441177.

Information
Tourist Offices: The Municipal Oficina de Turismo is at the corner of Caupolicán and Brasil, tel. 45/443338. In summer, it's open 8:30 A.M.–10 P.M. daily; the rest of the year, hours are 8:30 A.M.–7 P.M. weekdays, 10 A.M.–6 P.M. weekends.

Pucón's private Cámara de Turismo, Brasil 115, tel. 45/441671, is open 8 A.M.–midnight in January and February, 10 A.M.–1 P.M. and 4–9 P.M. the rest of the year. Fishing licenses (US$2) are available here.

National Parks: Conaf is at O'Higgins 1355, tel. 45/441261, just east of town on the road to Curarrehue.

Language Classes

Hostería ¡Ecole!, General Urrutia 592, tel. 45/441675, fax 45/441660, trek@ecole.mic.cl, organizes six-day, five-night intensive Spanish classes (three hours per day) complemented with activities such as hiking and visits to local hot springs. Rates are US$700 pp with half board.

La Casita Spanish School, Palguín 555, tel. 45/441712, offers 15 hours' weekly instruction with B&B accommodations for US$290 pp; there is a maximum of two people per class.

Transportation

Bus is the primary means of getting to and away from Pucón, but there are occasional summer flights from Santiago.

Air: LanChile/LanExpress is at General Urrutia 102, tel. 45/443514, but normally flies out of Temuco.

Bus: Long-distance bus service is an extension of that from Villarrica, so schedules and fares do not appear in detail here. The two main carriers have their own terminals: Tur-Bus, at O'Higgins 910, tel. 45/443328; and Buses Jac at Palguín 605, tel. 45/443693. Intersur and Buses San Martín share the Tur-Bus terminal, while other companies have their own terminals around the eastern end of town.

In addition to its frequent Temuco and Santiago schedules, long-distance Buses Jac serves Valdivia five times daily. Tur-Bus has similar schedules, and also goes nightly to Puerto Montt; other Santiago carriers include Buses Lit, at O'Higgins and Colo Colo, tel. 45/441055; Igi Llaima, at O'Higgins and Colo Colo, and at Colo Colo 465, tel. 45/442061; and Cóndor Bus, Colo Colo 430, tel. 45/443023.

Among regional carriers, Buses Regional Villarrica services to Villarrica, Lican Ray, and Coñaripe leave from the Terminal de Minibuses Vipu Ray, on Brasil between Palguín and Arauco.

Buses Jac has frequent departures from Pucón to Villarrica (US$.60, half an hour), nine buses daily to Caburgua (US$1), 18 daily to Curarrehue, and one to the Argentine border at Puesco. In summer, it also goes to Parque Nacional Huerquehue (US$1.50) at 7:30 A.M. and 11:15 A.M., and 5:30 P.M.; the rest of the year, there are departures Monday, Wednesday, and Friday at 8:30 A.M. and 4 P.M., returning at 10 A.M. and 5 P.M.

Taxibuses Rinconada, Ansorena 299, tel. 45/441905, goes to Huepil, on the road to Termas de Huife, at 12:30 P.M. weekdays, and at 4:15 P.M. to Huife Alto via Termas de Huife and Los Pozones, returning the following morning.

International San Martín Centenario buses to Argentina stop at the Tur-Bus terminal, while Igi Llaima uses its own terminal.

Getting Around

Bicycle Rental: Several of the adventure travel agencies on Avenida O'Higgins also rent mountain bikes (for addresses, see the Vicinity of Pucón entry below).

Car Rental: Pucón Rent A Car is at O'Higgins 1395, tel./fax 45/441922 or 45/443052, kernayel@cepri.cl. Rates range from US$38 per day for a compact to US$57 for a *doble cabina* pickup.

VICINITY OF PUCÓN

As the main axis of adventure travel in southern mainland Chile, Pucón offers a range of activities that include climbing Volcán Villarrica to rafting on the Río Trancura, hiking at Huerquehue, horseback riding, fly-fishing, skiing, and visits to nearby thermal baths. Competition—often cutthroat competition—can keep prices low and temperatures high among its numerous local operators. Occasionally, though, they manage to cooperate in putting groups together, especially outside the summer peak.

Among commercial operators are French-run **Aguaventura,** Palguín 336, tel. 45/444246 or 09/6764771, aguaventura@hotmail.com; **Andén Sport,** O'Higgins 545, tel. 45/441048, fax 45/441236, andentur@chilesat.net; **Expediciones Trancura,** O'Higgins 211-C, tel. 45/441189, fax 45/441959, website: www.trancura.com, turismo@trancura.com; **Politur,** O'Higgins 635, tel./fax 45/441373, turismo@politur.com; **Sol y Nieve Expediciones,** O'Higgins 192, tel./fax 45/441070, solnieve@entelchile.net; **Turismo Florencia,** O'Higgins 480, tel. 45/441472; and **Turismo Punta Arenas,** at O'Higgins and Palguín, tel. 45/449510. **El Pescador Don Ele,** Urrutia 384, specializes in fishing trips and sells gear.

Best known as a place to stay, noncommercial **Hostería ¡Ecole!,** General Urrutia 592, tel. 45/441675, fax 45/441660, organizes groups to visit the Fundación Lahuen's nearby Santuario Cañi forest reserve and other alternative excursions, and it offers suggestions for visitors who prefer to undertake independent excursions. For information in the United States, contact Ecole Adventures International, P.O. Box 2453, Redway, California 95560, tel. 800/447-1483, tel./fax 707/923-3001, website: www.ecole/adventures.com, ecole@asis.com.

Cuevas Volcánicas

On the southern slopes of Volcán Villarrica, but outside the national park, the misleadingly named "volcanic caves" are in fact lava tubes, but this privately run attraction provides a very professional introduction to vulcanism starting with a (Spanish-only) video on volcanic hazards through displays on volcanic geology and seismic technology (from a classic seismograph to modern computer monitors) to a 340-meter descent into the tubes themselves (the darkness at the bottom is absolute).

Reached by a fork off the road to Parque Nacional Villarrica, the Cuevas Volcánicas, tel. 45/442002, are 14.5 km south of the main Villarrica-Pucón highway. Some of the well-trained guides can manage English if necessary; admission and the one-hour tour cost US$10 pp.

Río Trancura

Barely half an hour east of Pucón, the Trancura is not one of Chile's premier white-water rivers—there's plenty of calm water between the rapids—but the Class IV waterfalls make parts of the upper sector a wild ride indeed. Heavy competition has kept prices down to about US$20 pp for the Alto Trancura, half that for the calmer Bajo Trancura. Both are morning or afternoon excursions, but the Alto Trancura means a little longer on the water as well. For booking information, see the list of travel agencies above.

One alternative to rafting is hydrospeeding, a sort of white-water body board experience that's gained some popularity in the past couple of years. A trip down the Trancura Alto costs about US$20.

Kila Leufú

At Palguín Bajo, east of Pucón, Kila Leufú is a working Mapuche farm that offers a variety of horseback riding trips, the opportunity to participate (or not) in farm activities, a *ruca* for socializing, and accommodations, all at reasonable prices. Camping costs US$2.50 pp, comfortable accommodations with shared bath costs US$8 pp with breakfast, and additional meals go for US$4 (lunch) and US$5 (dinner), with vegetarian options.

Kila Leufú is 23 km east of Pucón on the road to Curarrehue, just beyond the Cabedañe bridge and the turnoff to Termas de Palguín. For more details, contact Margo Martínez, tel. 09/7118064, who speaks English, German, and French in addition to Spanish.

From Pucón, Curarrehue-bound Buses Jac services pass by Kila Leufú's front door.

Hot Springs

The entire volcanic cordon of the Sur Chico is dotted with *termas,* but there's a particularly dense concentration in the vicinity of Pucón. Several of them have been turned into retreats or resorts that vary from basic day-use facilities to upscale but not-quite-lavish hotels.

Hotel y Termas Huife: On the Río Liucura northeast of Pucón, Termas de Huife is the area's most upmarket alternative, a modern chalet-style resort with spa facilities in 40°C waters, massage therapy, and rooms for US$93/139 s/d from mid-December through mid-March; the rest of the year, rates are US$81/121. For US$10 in summer, US$8.50 the rest of the year, day-trippers can use the outdoor pools; the resort provides its own transportation from Pucón for US$15 return, but infrequent buses also pass near the resort entrance. Both restaurant and cafeteria meals are available.

Termas Huife is 30 km northeast of Pucón via Paillaco on the road to Parque Nacional Huerquehue. For more details, contact Hotel y Termas Huife, tel./fax 45/441222, huife@ceprinet.cl.

Termas Los Pozones: Just two km beyond Huife, the minimalist Termas Los Pozones is a popular budget alternative; admission to a series of riverside pools ranging from 30° to 40°C costs US$5 in the daytime, US$6 at night, when some Pucón travel agencies run tours. Bring food and other supplies, as there's almost nothing on site. Pucón's Taxibuses Rinconada, Ansorena 299, tel. 45/441905, has one or two buses daily (see the Pucón transportation entry for details).

Termas de Palguín: In 1998, the area's oldest hot springs resort, 30 km southeast of Pucón on its namesake river, suffered a major fire that destroyed its landmark hotel; rebuilt in a less distinctive style on a more modest scale, the current **Hotel Termas de Palguín,** Casilla 1-D, Pucón, tel. 45/441968, charges US$60/100 s/d with full board, year-round. For nonguests, admission to the pools or private tubs costs US$6 pp; there is also a restaurant.

Termas de Panqui: The area's most unconventional thermal baths, 58 km from Pucón via the paved road to Curarrehue and an improved gravel road that heads north, exudes distinctly New Age vibes with its material and spiritual hodgepodge of Mapuche *rucas,* Lakota tepees, yoga, tai chi, meditation, and full-moon retreats in a rustic setting that, admittedly, has a great deal to offer in terms of its natural setting. There are also hot pools, mud baths, and a vegetarian restaurant.

Day use admission to Termas de Panqui costs US$8, while tepee accommodations cost US$11 pp and rather dark hotel rooms US$15 pp; the resort also arranges transportation from Pucón for US$8 pp. For more information, contact Termas de Panqui through Limay Tours, Avenida O'Higgins 555, Oficina 1, Pucón, tel. 45/442039, fax 45/442040, ingeluz@yahoo.com.

Rancho de Caballos
At Palguín Alto, near Termas de Palguín, the German-run Rancho de Caballos offers a series of three-hour to 10-day riding tours of the backcountry in and around Parque Nacional Villarrica for about US$60 pp per day. In addition to tours, Rancho de Caballos, Casilla 142, Pucón, tel./fax 45/441575, wolfgang@imaginativa.cl, provides

simple *cabaña* accommodations for US$10 pp with breakfast.

Santuario Cañi
In a high roadless area about 21 km east of Pucón, the Fundación Lahuen administers 400 hectares of mixed *Araucaria* forest in the Santuario Cañi, Chile's initial private nature reserve. Access is limited to guided hikes under Fundación Lahuen, arranged through the Fundación, at Hostería ¡Ecole!, Urrutia 592, Pucón, tel. 45/441675, fax 45/441660. For information in the United States, contact Ancient Forests International, Box 2453, Redway, California 95560, tel. 800/447-1483, tel./fax 707/923-3001.

Parque Nacional Villarrica
Dominating the skyline south of Pucón, the glowing crater of 2,847-meter Volcán Villarrica is a constant reminder that what Spanish conquistador and poet Alonso de Ercilla called its "great neighbor volcano" could, at any moment, oblit-

entrance to Parque Nacional Villarrica

© WAYNE BERNHARDSON

erate the town in a cataclysm of volcanic bombs, a cloud of ash, or beneath a mudflow triggered by lava and melting snow. Its summit, closely monitored and occasionally closed to climbers, is one of the area's most popular excursions.

More than just the volcano, Parque Nacional Villarrica comprises 63,000 hectares of mostly forested Andean cordillera that stretches from Pucón to the 3,746-meter summit of Volcán Lanín, most of which lies within Argentina's Parque Nacional Lanín (intending climbers must cross the border to the Argentine side). Villarrica's accessibility from Pucón makes it a favorite destination in both summer and winter.

Geography and Climate: Immediately south of Pucón, the park ranges from 600 meters above sea level on the lower slopes to 3,746 meters at Volcán Lanín. Barren lava flows and volcanic ash cover much of its surface, but unaffected areas are lushly forested. The other major summit is 2,360-meter Volcán Quetrupillán, halfway to the Argentine border; from Quetrupillán to the east, there are several alpine lakes accessible by foot.

Summertime temperatures generally range from a minimum of about 9°C to a maximum of around 23°C, while wintertime lows average about 4°C. Most precipitation falls between March and August, when Pacific storms can drop up to two meters of snow, but it can rain at any time of year. The park receives about 2,500 to 3,500 millimeters of rain per annum.

Flora and Fauna: At lower elevations, up to about 1,500 meters, mixed Araucaria and Nothofagus woodlands cover the slopes—the Araucaria reaches the southern limit of its distribution at Volcán Quetrupillán. The mañío (*Podocarpus nubigena*) also makes an appearance here. Native bunch grasses have colonized some volcanic areas.

Among the mammals are puma, pudú, foxes, and skunks, as well as the aquatic coypu. Waterfowl such as coots and ducks inhabit the lakes and other watercourses, while large raptors such as the black-shouldered kite and peregrine falcon are occasionally sighted in the skies.

Volcán Villarrica: Chile's most active volcano, Volcán Villarrica is a cauldron of bubbling lava and venting steam that's erupted dozens of times, including a major 1971 event that expelled 30 million cubic meters of lava in a flow that stretched for 14 km.

A strenuous but nontechnical climb, Villarrica requires crampons, an ice ax, rain and wind gear, high energy snacks, and a guide—except for those who manage to wrangle one of few individual private permits from Conaf. For those who contract a tour with one of Pucón's adventure travel agencies, it involves a crash course in mountaineering; in good weather, the summit is about six hours from the ski area, but bad weather sometimes forces groups to turn back. When the sulfurous crater is especially active, Conaf closes the route.

While the climb itself can be a slog through wet snow, the descent involves bodysledding down the volcano's flanks with only a ice ax for braking. Rates for the trip are about US$30 pp but can be more in peak season.

When winter snows cover the volcano's lower slopes, the Centro de Ski Volcán Villarrica operates four lifts with nine runs ranging from 500 to 1,500 meters in length. Lift tickets cost US$26 per day in peak season, US$20 per day in the shoulder season; for more information, contact the office in the Gran Hotel Pucón, Holzapfel 190, tel. 45/441176 or 45/441901, glibcovker@granhotelpucon.cl.

Sector Quetrupillán: Roughly midway between Volcán Villarrica and Volcán Quetrupillán, a rough summer-only road crosses the park from Termas de Palguín to the hot springs town of Coñaripe. Best suited to 4WD or at least high-clearance vehicles, though some daring (or foolhardy) Chileans attempt it with ordinary passenger vehicles, it passes through scenic Araucaria forest that includes the park's only campground.

From the southern slopes of Volcán Villarrica, a series of hiking trails cross the park to Termas de Palguín and continue to Puesco, where Buses Jac has a daily bus back to Pucón. For details, see Clem Lindenmayer's Trekking in the Patagonian Andes (Lonely Planet, 1998).

Accommodations and Food: The only accommodation is Conaf's Camping Chinay, in Sector Quetrupillán on the park's southern boundary on the steep, narrow road between Termas de Palguín and Coñaripe. Summer rates are US$12 per site for up to five people, in the midst of an Araucaria forest; the rest of the year, sites cost only US$8.50.

At the ski area, rebuilt after a fire in early 2001, the Refugio Villarrica serves cafeteria meals, but skiers stay in Pucón.

Information: On the road to the ski area, eight km from Pucón, Conaf's Guardería Rucapillán is the best source for information; rangers collect a US$1.50 pp admission charge (US$.50 for children) here. There are also ranger stations at Sector Quetrupillán and Sector Puesco.

Transportation: Transportation is limited except for organized tours. To Sector Rucapillán, only a few kilometers south of Pucón, taxis are the only nontour option. Buses Jac has one bus daily from Pucón to Sector Puesco.

Parque Nacional Huerquehue

Fast becoming one of the region's most popular parks, Huerquehue comprises 12,500 hectares of scenic Andean precordillera with alpine lakes, rushing rivers, and waterfalls set among dense native forest.

Geography and Climate: Huerquehue is 35 km northeast of Pucón via the hamlet of Paillaco. Elevations range from about 720 meters above sea level near Lago Tinquilco to 2,000 meters on the summit of Cerro Araucano, but glaciers and rivers have eroded deep canyons. It receives just over 2,000 millimeters of rainfall per annum, most of it between May and September, some of it falling as snow at higher elevations. While temperatures are generally mild, rain can fall at any time of year.

Flora and Fauna: On the park's lower slopes, the dominant forest species is the *coigüe (Nothofagus dombeyi),* while *lenga (Nothofagus pumilio)* gives way gradually to *Araucaria* at higher elevations. Birds, from woodpeckers to thrushes, flit within the forest, while Andean condors sometimes soar among the ridgetops and summits.

Sights and Recreation: Huerquehue is a hiker's park, with a good network of trails beginning at the north end of Lago Tinquilco. From here, the well-watered **Sendero Lago Verde** (Lago Verde Trail) zigzags from the 700-meter trailhead to 1,300 meters at its namesake lake. Light gaps in the *coigüe* woodlands provide glimpses of Vol-

cán Villarrica across the Liucura and Pucón valleys to the south, while the surrounding ridges sport *Araucaria* forests.

From Lago Tinquilco, it's about two hours-plus of steady hiking to **Lago Chico,** where the terrain levels off; at a trail junction beyond Lago Chico, the left fork goes to **Lago Verde,** while the right fork goes to **Lago El Toro** and continues to Conaf's simple **Refugio Renahue,** where camping is also possible. From here an eastbound trail continues to **Termas de Río Blanco,** a thermal springs linked to Cunco, Lago Colico, and the north end of Lago Caburgua by a gravel road.

Accommodations and Food: Conaf's wooded 18-site **Camping Tinquilco,** on the lake's eastern shore near the park gate, charges US$13 per site for up to five people in January and February, but only US$8.50 per site the rest of the year.

Just beyond the park entrance, at the north end of the lake near the Lago Verde trailhead, the Canadian-Chilean rustically chic **Refugio Tinquilco,** tel. 2/7777673, fax 2/7323079 in Santiago, website: www.tinquilco.cl, lanfranco-pato@hotmail.com, charges US$9 for hostel-type bunks (with a US$2 surcharge for sheets, if necessary); it also has rooms with king-sized beds for US$30 d with shared bath, US$39 d with private bath. Set on densely wooded grounds, it also has a private beach and offers meals to guests or nonguests: US$2–4 for breakfast, US$5 for lunch or dinner, or US$10 for full board. More elaborate multicourse dinners with aperitifs and wine are available for US$13.

En route to the park, on quiet grounds west of the Pucón–Lago Caburgua road from a turnoff at Km 18 (follow the signs), the three-room, German-run **Landhaus San Sebastián,** tel. 45/35-2360 or 09/4431786, website: www.pucon.com/landhaus, andreas.barth@terra.cl, can be an ideal escape from Pucón's hyperactivity. In addition to accommodations for US$25/40 s/d (note that there is no single rate in summer, however), it has a restaurant that serves exquisite *onces* and desserts.

Information: At the Lago Tinquilco park entrance, Conaf's Centro de Educación e Intepretación Ambiental is open 10 A.M.–8 P.M. daily in summer. Rangers at the park gate collect a US$3.50 pp admission fee (US$1 for children).

Refugio Tinquilco is also a good source of information for hiking alternatives beyond the main Lago Verde route.

Transportation: Thanks to increasing demand, Buses Jac now offers summer service from Pucón to Huerquehue (US$1.50) at 7:30 A.M. and 11:15 A.M. and 5:30 P.M.; the rest of the year, buses leave Pucón Monday, Wednesday, and Friday at 8:30 A.M. and 4 P.M., returning at 10 A.M. and 5 P.M.

Most Pucón adventure travel agencies also offer excursions to Huerquehue.

LICAN RAY

Surrounded by Mapuche communities, on the north shore of Lago Calafquén, Lican Ray is a small tourist enclave of black volcanic sand beaches that dates only from the 1940s, a time when it was accessible only by steamer from the south shore of the lake. Threatened by inundation from a hydroelectric project, it was ironically "saved" by an earthquake that resulted in a scaled-down dam at Pullinque.

Crowded in summer, Lican Ray is nearly abandoned the rest of the year despite its easy accessibility from nearby Villarrica and Pucón, and it provides an alternative backroads route to more southerly lake district destinations. The biggest attraction is Playa Grande, where swimmers and sunbathers congregate.

Orientation

Lican Ray is 30 km south of Villarrica via a smooth paved two-lane road, which becomes General Urrutia, the principal commercial street, as it enters town. At the northern outskirts of town, a bumpy all-weather road leads west and then south to Panguipulli, while a paved bypass heads southeast to Coñaripe, just across the Region X (Los Lagos) border.

Accommodations and Food

Several simple *hospedajes* charge in the US$8–10 pp range with breakfast, the best of which is probably **Residencial Catriñi,** Catriñi 140, tel. 45/431093. Other budget options include **Residencial Temuco,** Gabriela Mistral 515, tel. 45/431130, and **Hospedaje Los Nietos,** Man-

quel 125, tel. 45/431078 or 09/6423718. Playa Grande's **Hostería Inaltulafquén,** Punulef 510, tel. 45/431115, jdf@uniserve.com, charges US$21 pp with private bath and breakfast. Rates at **Hotel Becker,** Manquel 105, tel. 45/431471, are US$50 d for lakeview rooms with private bath and breakfast.

Lican Ray's landmark restaurant is **The Ñaños,** General Urrutia 105, tel. 45/431021, specializing in Chilean dishes. Other options include **Coyote,** on General Urrutia opposite the Plaza de Armas, and **Los Porteños,** on Huenuman half a block south of the plaza.

Shopping

In summer, the nightly **Feria Artesanal** on Esmeralda, immediately behind the Plaza de Armas, offers items by local artisans. Also in summer only, the **Centro Artesanal Nehuen,** Urrutia 315, contains a more geographically diverse assortment of regional and national crafts.

Services

Money: In summer there is sometimes a mobile ATM on the Plaza de Armas, but the closest exchange house is at Villarrica. Supermercado Jumbito, at Urrutia and Millañanco, half a block west of the plaza, may change U.S. or Argentine cash.

Postal: Correos de Chile is at Urrutia and Marichanquín.

Telephone: Telefónica CTC has a long-distance office on Huenumán south of Urrutia; there's another Centro de Llamados north of Urrutia, on the west side of the plaza. Lican Ray's area code is 45, the same as Villarrica and Pucón.

Laundry: Lavandería Lican Ray is on Huenumán south of Urrutia, opposite the Telefónica CTC office.

Medical: Lican Ray's Posta Médica (first-aid clinic) is on Esmeralda, on the north side of the Plaza de Armas.

Information

At the southeast corner of the Plaza de Armas, the municipal Oficina de Turismo, General Urrutia 310, tel. 45/431201, is open 9 A.M.–11 P.M. daily in summer; otherwise, it's open 9 A.M.–12:30 P.M. and 2:30–6 P.M. weekdays.

Transportation

Tur-Bus, Marichanquín 190, tel. 45/431260, provides direct services to Santiago, as does Buses Jac, at General Urrutia and Marichan-quín, tel. 45/431185. Buses Jac also has regional and rural services providing transportation to Villarrica and nearby Coñaripe, with connections to Panguipulli.

Los Lagos Region

Lago Villarrica may be the port of entry to the Chilean lake district, but its heart is farther south, in Region X, where Lago Todos los Santos is widely considered the single most beautiful body of water in the entire country. Volcán Osorno, an almost perfectly symmetrical cone rising above the east end of Lago Llanquihue, offers some of the most breathtaking views anywhere, but there are dozens of other high volcanic summits, scenic lakes and rivers, and shores and estuaries to fill weeks or months of sight-seeing and activities. Puerto Montt, the de facto terminus of the continental Panamericana, is the gateway to Chilean and even Argentine Patagonia.

Like the Araucanía, Los Lagos has a vigorous tourist industry and infrastructure, but there remains a tension between the beauty of the landscape and resource-based industries such as forestry and fisheries. In 2001, vigorous opposition by Chilean conservationists derailed a plan to turn thousands of hectares of native forest into chips for export, but water pollution from large-scale salmon farming in both freshwater lakes and salt-water estuaries continues to cause concern. Overfishing of valuable native fish and shellfish species such as abalone and giant mussels is also a problem.

VALDIVIA

Founded by Pedro de Valdivia himself, the Ciudad de los Ríos dates from 1552, but a Mapuche uprising at the end of the century razed it to the ground. The Peruvian viceroy sent a 900-man naval contingent to establish fortifications at the mouth of the Río Valdivia and to refound the city in the 17th century, and in the 18th century it established fortifications against European powers and pirates, as well as the restive Mapuche.

From colonial times to the present, Valdivia has exported timber from the region's appropriately named Valdivian forests. It saw substantial Middle European immigration from the mid-19th century to the early 20th century, and its most distinctive architecture dates from this period—though repeated fires and the 1960 earthquake have wiped out many landmarks. Valdivia's principal recreational attraction is the river and its downstream monuments.

Orientation

Where the Río Cau Cau joins the winding Río Calle Calle to form the Río Valdivia, the city of Valdivia is 162 km southwest of Temuco and 35 km west of the Panamericana via Mafil; it is 107 km north of Osorno and 46 km from the Panamericana via Paillaco.

Shaped by the shifting rivers, Valdivia's central core is more irregular than those of most Chilean cities, but most points of interest lie within a roughly triangular zone bounded by the shoreline of the Río Valdivia to the west, the Río Calle Calle from the north to the southeast, and the streets Yerbas Buenas and Beauchef to the south. Eastbound Avenida Ramón Picarte links the city to the Panamericana, while the Puente Pedro de Valdivia leads across the river to the suburb of Isla Teja, site of the Universidad Austral, and the historic Pacific beach towns of Niebla and Corral.

Sights

Along the Costanera Prat north of the Sernatur office, the **Feria Fluvial** is a colorful riverside fish, fruit, and vegetable market that is also the departure point for riverboat floats downstream to Niebla and Corral. Southern sea lions have begun to hang out here, and there have been biting incidents that probably resulted from unwise human provocations—enjoy them from a distance.

Valdivia's massive 1960 earthquake destroyed many landmarks, but there remain two small national monuments of colonial times: the 18th-century **Torreón de los Canelos,** at Yerbas Buenas and General Lagos, which guarded the southern approach along the Río Valdivia, and the **Torreón del Barro,** on the Costanera Prat between José Martí and Condell. In practice, though, these watchtowers served as jail cells, powder magazines, and even windmills. From San Carlos south, beyond the Torreón de los Canelos, Calle General Lagos constitutes a *zona típica* national monument for its typical European-style houses.

Across the river on Isla Teja, the **Museo de Arte Contemporáneo,** Los Laureles s/n, tel. 63/221968, is Valdivia's modern art showcase. It occupies the site and sits on the foundations of the former Cervecería Anwandter, destroyed by the 1960 earthquake, and is open daily except Monday, 10 A.M.–1 P.M. and 3–7 P.M. Admission costs US$.70 for adults, US$.35 for children.

Also on Isla Teja, immediately south of the modern art museum, the **Museo Histórico y Arqueológico Mauricio van de Maele** occupies the Casa Anwandter, a two-story mansion and national monument built by brewer Carlos Andwandter, a German immigrant who arrived around 1850. The museum, Los Laureles 47, tel. 63/212872, displays collections from paleo-Indian times to the historic and contemporary Mapuche and the German colonization, and offers guided tours in Spanish only. Open 10 A.M.–1 P.M. and 4–8 P.M. daily from mid-December to mid-March, it charges US$1.50 admission pp for adults, US$.50 for children; the rest of the year, hours are 10 A.M.–1 P.M. and 2–6 P.M. There are launches across the river to the museum, but it's also accessible via the Pedro de Valdivia bridge.

Also reached by the bridge, Isla Teja's **Parque Saval** is a 30-hectare botanical garden that once belonged to the immigrant Prochelle family and is now a favorite outing for local families; its centerpiece is lily-padded **Laguna de los Lotos.**

Accommodations

Valdivia has relatively few budget alternatives except in summer, when university students va-

cate the city. Sernatur maintains a list of seasonal *hospedajes,* which vary from year to year.

US$10–25: Hostal Villa Beauchef, two blocks south of the terminal at Beauchef 844, tel./fax 63/216044, charges US$8 pp with shared bath and breakfast, US$15/25 s/d with private bath. On the same block with several pubs and restaurants, rates at the handsome **Hostal Esmeralda,** tel. 63/215659, fax 63/254530, are US$17/25 s/d with private bath.

Half a block west of the bus terminal, friendly **Hotel Montserrat,** Picarte 849, tel. 63/256391, costs US$9 pp with shared bath and breakfast, US$12 pp with private bath, breakfast, and cable TV. Rates at **Residencial Germania,** Picarte 873, tel. 63/212405, are US$10 pp in heated rooms with shared bath and breakfast, US$25 d with private bath; it has a restaurant, amiable German-speaking owners, and also serves as Valdivia's Hostelling International affiliate, charging US$8.50 pp for hostellers. **Hostal Casa Grande,** half a block west of the bus terminal at Carlos Anwandter 880, tel./fax 63/202035, costs US$17/25 s/d with private bath.

US$25–50: Hostal Dónde Marcelo, in an excellent location at Janequeo 355, tel./fax 63/2-05295, has rooms with private bath, parking, and cable TV for US$23/28 s/d, but too many beds clutter some rooms, the mattresses are soft, and the breakfast is mediocre. Overlooking the Calle Calle, **Hostal Costanera,** Avenida Prat 579, tel. 63/250042, charges US$15 pp with private bath and breakfast. Next door, **Hostal Prat,** Avenida Prat 595, tel./fax 63/222020, costs US$20/30 s/d with private bath and breakfast.

Rates at **Hostal Anwandter,** Anwandter 601, tel./fax 63/218587, are US$12/18 s/d with shared bath and breakfast, US$18/26 s/d with private bath, breakfast, and cable TV. **Hospedaje Internacional,** García Reyes 660, tel. 63/212015, charges US$10 pp with shared bath and breakfast, US$20/30 s/d with private bath and breakfast.

Well-located **Hostal Torreón,** occupying an older but well-kept building at Pérez Rosales 783, tel. 63/212622, charges US$27/42 s/d. A block north of Plaza de la República, at venerable **Hotel Palace,** Chacabuco 308, tel. 63/213319, fax 63/219133, rates start at US$38/44 with

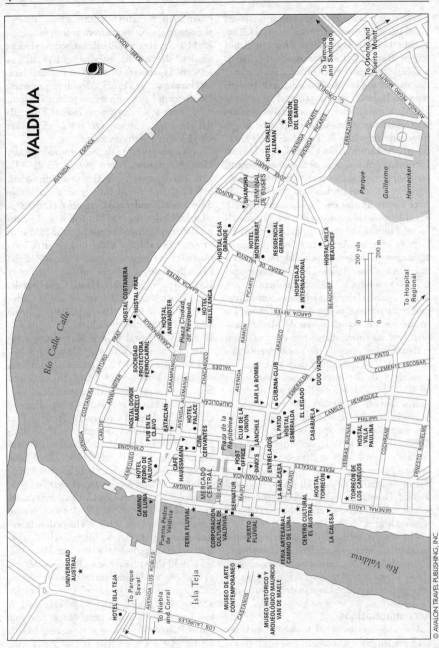

VALDIVIA

Río Calle Calle

ISABEL ROCAS

AVENIDA ESPAÑA

To Osorno and
Puerto Montt

To Temuco
and Santiago

AVENIDA PEDRO MONTT

C. CONDELL

ERRAZURIZ

Parque
Guillermo
Harnecker

JOSE MARTI

AVENIDA PICARTE

AVENIDA PICARTE

TORREÓN
DEL BARRO

HOTEL CHALET
ALEMAN

SHANGHAI

TERMINAL
DE BUSES

HOSTAL CASA
GRANDE

HOTEL
MONTSERRAT

RESIDENCIAL
GERMANIA

HOSPEDAJE
INTERNACIONAL

HOSTAL VILLA
BEAUCHEF

PEDRO DE VALDIVIA

PICARTE

BEAUCHEF

GARCIA REYES

A. MUÑOZ

HOSTAL COSTANERA

HOSTAL PRAT

HOSTAL
ANWANDTER

Plaza Ciudad
de Neuquén

HOTEL
MELILLANCA

GARCIA REYES

PRAT

ARTURO

ANWANDTER

CARAMPANGUE

SOCIEDAD
PROTECTORA
FERROCARRIL

CARAMPANGUE

CHACABUCO

VALDES

RAMON

AVENIDA

ARAUCO

ANIBAL PINTO

CLEMENTE ESCOBAR

HENRIQUEZ

COSTANERA

CARLOS

HOSTAL DONDE
MARCELO

PUB EN EL
CLAVO

BATACLAN

AVENIDA ALEMANIA

AUCOLICAN

BAR LA BOMBA

CUBANA-CLUB

ESMERALDA

QUO VADIS

CAMILO

PHILIPPI

COCHRANE

ERNESTO RIQUELME

To Hospital
Regional

YANEQUEO

O'HIGGINS

HOTEL
PEDRO DE
VALDIVIA

CAFÉ
HAUSSMANN

HOTEL
PALACE

CINE
CERVANTES

Plaza de la
República

CLUB DE LA
UNIÓN

LANCHLE

EL PATIO

HOSTAL
ESMERALDA

EL LEGADO

CASABUELA

YERBAS BUENAS

HOSTAL
VILLA
PAULINA

CAMINO
DE LUNA

MERCADO
CENTRAL

SERNATUR

LIBERTAD

MAIPU

POST
OFFICE

INDEPENDENCIA

DINO'S

LA BAR-CASA

ENTRELAGOS

LAUTARO

PEREZ ROSALES

HOSTAL
TORREÓN

TORREÓN DE
LOS CANELIOS

GENERAL LAGOS

UNIVERSIDAD
AUSTRAL

HOTEL ISLA TEJA

To Parque
Saval

To Niebla
and Corral

AVENIDA LOS ROBLES

LOS LAURELES

CASTAÑOS

Isla Teja

MUSEO DE ARTE
CONTEMPORANEO

MUSEO HISTORICO Y
ARQUEOLOGICO MAURICIO
VAN DE MAELE

Puente Pedro
de Valdivia

FERIA FLUVIAL

CORPORACIÓN
CULTURAL DE
VALDIVIA

PUERTO
FLUVIAL

FERIA ARTESANAL
CAMINO DE LUNA

CENTRO CULTURAL
EL AUSTRAL

LA CALESA

YUNGAY

Río Valdivia

© AVALON TRAVEL PUBLISHING, INC.

0   200 yds

0   200 m

breakfast. On wooded grounds across the river, **Hotel Isla Teja,** Las Encinas 220, tel. 63/215014, fax 63/214911, rooms with private bath start at US$37/45.

US$50–100: Hostal Villa Paulina, in a good residential neighborhood at Yerbas Buenas 389, tel. 63/212445, fax 63/216372, charges US$42/56 with private bath. The well-maintained **Hostal Chalet Alemán,** set back off the busy street at Picarte 1134, tel./fax 63/218810, charges US$37/57.

The modern and central **Hotel Melillanca,** Avenida Alemania 675, tel. 63/212509, fax 63/222740, hmelilla@ctcinternet.cl., costs US$51/72 s/d.

US$100–150: Valdivia's traditional favorite is **Hotel Pedro de Valdivia,** set among extensive grounds near the bridge over the Río Valdivia at Carampangue 190, tel./fax 63/212931, hotelpval@telsur.cl, for US$84/110 s/d with breakfast. Isla Teja's luxury resort **Hotel Puerta del Sur,** Avenida Los Lingues 950, tel. 63/224500, pdl-sur@ctcinternet.cl., charges US$104/116.

Food

In the riverfront **Mercado Central,** bounded by the Costanera, Chacabuco, Yungay, and Libertad, several *marisquerías* serve fish and shellfish at bargain prices. The floating **Camino de Luna,** just north of the Pedro de Valdivia bridge at Prat s/n, tel. 63/213788, is a more formal seafood venue.

Quo Vadis, Esmeralda 693, tel. 63/250714, serves huge portions of Tex-Mex dishes such as burritos for around US$5. **Shanghai,** Anwandter 898, tel. 63/212577, offers Chinese food.

CasAbuela, Camilo Henríquez 746, tel. 63/218807, prepares home-style Chilean dishes such as *humitas* and *pastel de choclo,* with prices in the US$5–7 range. By contrast, **Dino's,** Maipú 191, tel. 63/213061, is a franchise operation but will do in a pinch. **El Patio,** upstairs at Arauco 343, tel. 63/215238, offers both *parrillada* and seafood. The reasonably priced **La Protectora,** Janequeo 491, tel. 63/212715, is a popular beef and seafood locale that belongs to the railroad workers' union.

© WAYNE BERNHARDSON

Mercado Fluvial at Valdivia

Overlooking the Plaza de la República, the traditional **Club de la Unión,** Camilo Henríquez 540, tel. 63/213377, serves fixed-price meals in the US$5 range. Like its counterparts in other Chilean cities, the fire department's **Bar La Bomba,** Caupolicán 594, tel. 63/213317, also has good fixed-price meals.

In a distinctive period house, **La Calesa,** Yungay 735, tel. 63/225467, serves Peruvian specialties (such as a surprisingly spicy *aji de gallina*) in the US$8 range. With side orders and drinks, the bill can really add up, but it's the best splurge in town.

Entrelagos, Pérez Rosales 630, tel. 63/21-8333, is the best choice for tasty desserts, *onces,* and ice cream; its next door branch, **Chocolatería Entrelagos,** Pérez Rosales 622, offers takeaway items. **Café Haussmann,** O'Higgins 394, tel. 63/213878, is also worth a try. On Isla Teja, near the entrance to Parque Saval, the **Universidad Austral** dairy offers ice cream, yogurt, and cheese.

Entertainment and Events

As a university town, Valdivia enjoys an active cultural life and nightlife as well.

Bars: Valdivia has a lively pub scene. Among the options are **Pub en el Clavo,** Avenida Alemania 299, tel. 63/211229, also a live music venue; **Bataclán,** Camilo Henríquez 326, tel. 63/222701, which has live music and a happy hour that lasts almost until midnight; **El Legado,** Esmeralda 657, tel. 63/207546, which features jazz and blues; and the **Cubana Club,** Esmeralda 680, tel. 63/256969. **La Bar-Casa,** San Carlos 169, is a literary bar/café that also has live music.

Cinema: The **Cine Cervantes,** Chacabuco 210, shows current films.

Performing Arts: The **Centro Cultural El Austral,** Yungay 733, tel. 63/213658, is a key performing arts venue. The **Corporación Cultural de Valdivia,** Prat 549, tel. 63/219690, includes the **Sala Ainilebu,** which hosts live theater.

Events: February 9's **Aniversario de la Ciudad** is the biggest local holiday, celebrating the city's founding in 1552, but it's only part of the summer-long **Verano en Valdivia,** which includes many other events.

Shopping

Valdivia has numerous crafts outlets, most notably the **Feria Artesanal Camino de Luna,** located at the corner of Yungay and San Carlos. Other possibilities are the **Galería Artesanal Pehuén,** Arauco 340, tel. 63/251412, and the Mapuche stores **Ruca Indiana,** Camilo Henríquez 758, tel. 63/214946, and **Casa Araucana,** Picarte 841.

Services

Money: Exchange houses include Cambio Arauco at Arauco 331, Local 24, and Cambio La Reconquista at Carampangue 325, which keeps long weekday hours and is also open 10 A.M.–2 P.M. Sunday. Banco Santander has an ATM at Pérez Rosales 585.

Postal: Correos de Chile is at O'Higgins 575, is situated at the southwest corner of Plaza de la República.

Telephone and Internet: There are several long-distance offices: Telefónica del Sur at San Carlos 107, Entel at Pérez Rosales 601, Local 1, and Chilesat at Pérez Rosales 712. Valdivia's area code is 63.

Café Phonet, Libertad 127, is a spacious long-distance office that also has inexpensive Internet access. Public Access Internet is upstairs at Letelier 236, tel. 63/294300.

Laundry: Lavamatic is at Walter Schmidt 305, Lavandería Manantial at Camilo Henríquez 809.

Medical: The Hospital Regional is at Bueras 1003, tel. 63/214066, near Aníbal Pinto at the south end of downtown.

Information

Tourist Offices: Sernatur has riverfront offices at Prat 555, tel. 63/215739, fax 63/213596, serna13a @entelchile.net. It's open 8:30 A.M.–1 P.M. and 2:30–6:48 P.M. weekdays, 10 A.M.–4 P.M. Saturday, and 10 A.M.–2 P.M. Sunday all year, but it stays open through the midday break in summer. The Oficina de Informaciones at the bus terminal, Anfión Muñoz 360, tel. 63/212212, is open 8:30 A.M.–10 P.M. daily.

Bookstores: Libros Chiloé, Caupolicán 410, is a quality bookstore.

Transportation

Valdivia has air and road connections to the rest of Chile, but the railroad no longer runs here.

Air: LanChile/LanExpress is at Maipú 271, tel. 63/258840. There are two flights daily to Santiago, via either Temuco or Concepción.

Bus: The Terminal de Buses is at Anfión Muñoz 360, about eight blocks west of Plaza de la República, tel. 63/212212. There are frequent services along the Panamericana from Santiago to Puerto Montt and intermediate points, and on to Chiloé. Long-distance carriers include Tur-Bus, tel. 63/226010; Tas Choapa, tel. 63/213124; Buses Norte, tel. 63/212800; Igi Llaima, tel. 63/213542; Buses Lit, tel. 63/212835; and Cruz del Sur, tel. 63/213840.

Regionally, Buses Jac, tel. 63/212925, goes to Temuco and to Villarrica and Pucón; it has a downtown ticket office at Arauco 241, tel. 63/224307. Other regional carriers include Buses Pirehueico, tel. 63/218609, to Panguipulli, Bus Futrono, tel. 63/202225, to Futrono, and Buses Cordillera Sur, tel. 63/229533, to other interior lake district destinations.

Internationally, Tas Choapa, Cruz del Sur, Buses Norte, and Andesmar, tel. 63/224665, cross the Argentine border to Bariloche (US$16) via Osorno.

Sample destinations, times, and fares include Panguipulli (US$2.50, 1.5 hours), Temuco or Pucón (US$3, two hours), Puerto Montt (US$4, three hours), Ancud (US$7, five hours), Concepción (US$8, six hours), Talca (US$10, eight hours), and Santiago (US$15, 11 hours).

Getting Around

To the Airport: Aeropuerto Pichoy is 29 km north of Valdivia, on the road to San José de Mariquina, via the Puente Calle Calle. Transfer Valdivia, tel. 63/225553, offers door-to-door service (US$3).

To the Bus Terminal: Buses marked "Plaza" go directly from the bus terminal to Plaza de la República; return buses use Arauco and Picarte. *Taxi colectivos* follow the same routes.

Car Rental: Rental agencies include Autowald, Henríquez 610, tel. 63/212786, and Hertz, Picarte 640, tel. 63/218317.

VICINITY OF VALDIVIA

The most popular excursions follow the course of the Río Valdivia west to its mouth, both by road and by water.

Cervecería Kunstmann

At Km 5 on the paved road to Niebla via Isla Teja, open for guided tours, the Cervecería Kunstmann, tel. 63/292969, is a major brewery that features a **Museo de la Cerveza** (beer museum) and a pub-restaurant. Niebla-bound buses and *taxi colectivos,* leaving from the Pedro de Valdivia bridge, pass by the front door.

The Río Valdivia Fortifications

Downstream from Valdivia, where the Río Valdivia and the Río Tornagaleones empty into the Pacific, the Spanish imperial government built elaborate fortifications at Niebla, Corral, and Isla Mancera in the mid-17th century to protect the refounded city of Valdivia from European privateers and interlopers such as Britain, France, and the Netherlands. In their heyday, these were the largest fortified complex on the Pacific coast of the Americas; they played a major role in Chilean independence when, in 1820, the audacious British mercenary Lord Thomas Cochrane captured them from Spanish forces. Today, all are national monuments.

There are frequent buses from the corner of Chacabuco and Yungay to Corral, which is 17 km from Valdivia, but many visitors prefer to travel downstream by boat from the Puerto Fluvial and return by bus in the afternoon. Among the options are the 90-passenger *Isla del Río,* tel. 63/225244; the 108-passenger *Orion III,* tel. 63/210533; the 130-passenger *Reina Sofía,* tel. 63/207120; the 200-passenger *Río Calle Calle,* tel. 63/202223; the 200-passenger *Catamarán Extasis,* tel. 63/295674; and the 280-passenger *Neptuno,* tel. 63/218952. Departures are fewer outside the peak summer season; the excursions take about 2.5 hours from Valdivia to Corral via Isla Mancera, Amargos, and Niebla. Prices generally range about US$5–10, but some luxury cruises include lunch and even open bar for US$25–50.

Niebla: Combined with the south shore fortifications at Corral and the midriver base at Isla Mancera, the north shore's **Fuerte Niebla** would catch invaders in a three-way crossfire. Nothing remains of the original 1645 structure, but the battlements of the **Castillo de la Pura y Limpia Concepción de Monfort de Lemus** (1671) are the oldest surviving ruins of the entire complex; seven of its 14 cannons are original. The restored commander's house serves as the **Museo de Sitio Fuerte Niebla,** tel. 63/219600; from November to mid-March, it's open 9 A.M.–7 P.M. daily, while the rest of the year hours are 10 A.M.–5:30 P.M. daily except Monday. Admission costs US$1 for adults, US$.50 for children.

The nearby restaurant **Canto del Agua,** Antonio Duce 795, tel. 63/262019, is a fresh fish and shellfish favorite. It is part of **Hostería Reichers,** which has rooms with private bath and kitchenettes for US$35 d.

From Niebla, launches shuttle every half hour across the river to Corral for US$.50 per person. **Corral:** Across the river from Niebla, Corral's original **Castillo San Sebastián de la Cruz** dated from 1645, but the remaining structures are later 17th- and 18th-century structures such as the **Batería de la Argolla** (1764) and the **Batería de la Cortina** (1767), the cannon batteries guarding the harbor. North of Corral, at Punta de Amargos, the **Castillo San Luis de Alba,** built entirely of stone, was considered the equal of Europe's best. From mid-December to mid-March, a costumed demonstration of late colonial Spanish military maneuvers takes place at 4:30 and 6:15 P.M. daily.

Isla Mancera: Isla Mancera's strategic location at the confluence of the Río Valdivia and the Tornagaleones gave it a critical backup position opposite Niebla. Its **Castillo San Pedro de Alcántara** (1645) later served as the military governor's residence; there were several other constructions on the island.

PANGUIPULLI

At the northwest corner of its eponymous lake, tranquil Panguipulli is the gateway to the "Siete Lagos," a relatively little-visited series of lakes

that lie east toward the Argentine border. By a sort of half-truth, it's known as the Ciudad de las Rosas (City of Roses)—with only 8,000 or so inhabitants it's more a small town; it lies 114 km northeast of Valdivia and 49 km from Lanco, the junction with the Panamericana. The area's dominant landmark is 2,415-meter Volcán Choshuenco, at the southeast end of the lake.

Early February's **Semana de las Rosas,** commemorating Panguipulli's founding in 1946, supports the claim of its slogan, however.

Accommodations

Only 200 meters north of the central Plaza Prat, **Camping El Bosque,** tel. 63/311489, has 15 tent sites (no drive-ins), hot showers, and lighting for US$3.50 pp. Otherwise, there are several simple lodgings in the US$10 pp range with shared bath and breakfast, including **Hostal Eva Ray,** Los Ulmos 62, tel. 63/311483; **Hospedaje Berrocal,** Portales 72, tel. 63/311812, also notable for its dinners; and **Hospedaje Monserrat,** O'Higgins 1112, tel. 63/311443.

The slightly more expensive **Hotel Central,** Pedro de Valdivia 115, tel. 63/311331, has rooms with shared bath only, but they are larger and enjoy better natural light than the *hospedajes.* For both comfort and service, **Hostal España,** O'Higgins 790, tel. 63/311166, fax 63/311327, is the best in town for US$23/33 s/d with private bath. Facilities are good enough at the slightly more expensive **Hostería Quetropillán,** Etchegaray 381, tel. 63/311348, but it seems to suffer a persistent attitude problem.

Food

Panguipulli has plenty of good places to eat, even if the variety is limited to standard Chilean specialties, beef, and seafood. **Girasol,** Martínez de Rozas 664, tel. 09/5682927, and the cheerful **Café Central,** Martínez de Rozas 880, tel. 63/311495, are best for sandwiches, snacks, *onces,* and desserts. For full meals, try **El Chapulín,** Martínez de Rozas 639, tel. 63/311560; **Gardylafquen,** Martínez de Rozas 722, tel. 63/311887; or **Rincón Criollo,** Matta 131, tel. 63/311603. There's a spark of ethnic diversity at **El Rincón Italiano,** 11 de Septiembre 326, tel. 63/311921.

Services

Money: Turismo Christopher, Martínez de Rozas 705, is the only exchange house. Banco de Crédito has an ATM in the Supermercado Super, Arturo Prat 54.

Postal: Correos de Chile is on Plaza O'Higgins, a block north of Plaza Prat.

Telephone and Internet: Telefónica del Sur has long-distance offices on Portales between Carrera and Martínez de Rozas. The area code is 63, the same as Valdivia.

Centercom Internet is at Martínez de Rozas 554, tel. 63/311235.

Medical: Hospital Panguipulli is at Cruz Coke s/n, tel. 63/311325.

Information

Panguipulli's Oficina Municipal de Turismo, O'Higgins s/n, tel. 63/312202, turmpangui@telsur.cl, is on the north side of Plaza Arturo Prat. Summer hours, from December to mid-March, are 9 A.M.–9 P.M. daily; the rest of the year, it's open weekdays only, with shorter hours.

Transportation

Panguipulli's Terminal de Buses is at Gabriela Mistral 100, tel. 63/311055. Tur-Bus has a separate terminal at Carrera 784, tel. 63/311377. In addition to Tur-Bus, northbound long-distance carriers on the Panamericana to Temuco and Santiago include Intersur, tel. 63/311309, Igi Llaima, tel. 63/311347, and Panguisur, tel. 63/311502, all at the main terminal. Buses Pirehueico, tel. 63/311497, goes several times daily to Valdivia (2.5 hours) and Puerto Montt, and once to Liquiñe.

Buses San Pedro, tel. 63/311502, circles Lago Calafquén to Coñaripe, with connections to Lican Ray and Villarrica. Buses Hua Hum, tel. 63/311199, goes to Choshuenco, Neltume, and Puerto Fuy, the staging point for the ferry and bus crossing to San Martín de los Andes, Argentina. Buses Lafit also goes to Neltume.

VICINITY OF PANGUIPULLI

East of Panguipulli, the so-called "Siete Lagos" area features a cluster of small towns and hot springs resorts on or near elongated glacial lakes beneath the 2,422-meter summit of Volcán Choshuenco, a glacier-filled crater whose last major eruption took place in 1864. Near Pullingue, paved Ruta 203 becomes a gravel road that turns southeast along the north shore of Lago Panguipulli toward Choshuenco, Neltume, and Puerto Fuy, where a ferry crosses Lago Pirehueico to the Argentine border at Paso Hua Hum for San Martín de los Andes; from the Pullingue junction, graveled Ruta 201 follows the south shore of Lago Calafquén to Coñaripe, Liquiñe, and the Carririñe pass to Junín de los Andes. A gravel road covers the 23 km between Carriringue, on Ruta 201, and the south end of Lago Neltume, on Ruta 203, making it possible to loop through the area.

Coñaripe

It seems placid enough now, but the eastern Lago Calafquén beach community of Coñaripe has seen its share of disruption—not from war or political violence, but from Volcán Villarrica, whose March 1964 eruption triggered a lahar (mud flow) that killed 22 people. It may owe those dazzling black sand beaches to the volcano, but it's paid a price for its proximity.

While Coñaripe is just 37 km east of Panguipulli via Ruta 201, it gets most of its traffic from Villarrica, thanks to the smooth paved road between the two towns. From the corner of the main thoroughfare Beck de Ramberga and Los Olivillos, a scenic but narrow and bumpy road, open in summer only, crosses the Quetrupillán sector of Parque Nacional Villarrica to Termas de Palguín and Pucón. While many Chileans take low-clearance vehicles on this hazardous route, even skilled drivers with high-clearance 4WD vehicles may find it challenging—not least because of others rounding blind curves in the opposite direction.

Accommodations and Food: All of Coñaripe's accommodations range from budget to low midrange, starting with **Hospedaje Iván,** Beck de Ramberga s/n, tel. 63/317227, on the north side of the Plaza de Armas, for US$8.50 pp with breakfast and shared bath. South of the plaza, **Hospedaje Chumay,** Las Tepas 201, tel.

63/317289, charges US$12 pp; its restaurant is probably Coñaripe's best value. Just west of Hospedaje Iván, rates at **Hotel Entre Montañas,** Beck de Ramberga 496, tel. 63/317298, are US$14 pp with shared bath, US$26 pp with private bath, both with breakfast. Lunch and dinner are also available at its restaurant.

Services: Telefónica CTC, at the corner of Beck de Ramberga and Los Alerces, provides long-distance services. Coñaripe's area code is 63.

Information: The municipal Oficina de Información Turística is on the Plaza de Armas at Beck de Ramberga and Las Tepas, tel. 63/317403; hours are 9 A.M.–9 P.M. daily from December through February.

Transportation: Buses Jac, at the corner of Beck de Ramberga and Los Temos, connects Coñaripe with Lican Ray and Villarrica several times daily. Buses San Pedro, at Beck de Ramberga and Los Arrayanes, goes three times daily around the south shore of the lake to Panguipulli (US$1.25, 1.5 hours). Buses Panguipulli also goes to Panguipulli, where there are connections to Valdivia and destinations along the Panamericana. There are also minibuses to the hot springs resort of Liquiñe daily at 1 P.M.

Centro Turístico Termal Coñaripe

About 51 km east of Panguipulli and 15 km southeast of Coñaripe on Ruta 201, the international highway to Junín de los Andes, the luxury Centro Turístico Termal Coñaripe occupies a site at the east end of Lago Pellaifa. Equipped with swimming pools, a spa, tennis courts, footpaths, and bridle trails, not to mention a 120-seat restaurant serving home-grown trout, it charges US$167 d with half board for each of its eight hotel rooms, or US$220 for spacious four-person *cabañas* with full board.

Pools are open to nonguests for US$10 pp (US$5 for children 2–10); access to the indoor pool/spa costs US$10 pp more. Transfers are available from Temuco airport (US$26) or from Villarrica (US$8.50). For more information, contact Centro Turístico Termal Coñaripe, Casilla 603, Lican Ray, tel. 45/431407, 63/317330, or 63/317333, fax 45/411111, info@termasconaripe.com.

Liquiñe and Vicinity

Strung along its namesake river, the Mapuche hamlet of Liquiñe, 31 km southeast of Coñaripe along Ruta 201, is a simple resort whose main hot springs, **Termas de Liquiñe,** inexplicably belong to the Chilean navy but are open to the public all year; rates are US$5 pp for day use. There are several other even more rustic springs in the vicinity, such as **Termas Manquecura,** which has *cabañas* and a restaurant, and **Termas de Punulaf,** which has camping. The gravel highway continues east to Carririñe pass and the Argentine town of Junín de los Andes.

Accommodations and Food: Liquiñe lacks direct dial service and all businesses rely on a single community telephone, tel./fax 63/311060, for message service unless they are so fortunate as to have their own extension. **Hotel La Casona** has basic accommodations in the US$10 pp range with private bath and breakfast, but the best option is **Hotel Termas Río Liquiñe,** tel. 63/311060, *anexo* 2, where *cabañas* with full board and private tubs cost US$53 per person; rooms with Jacuzzis cost US$5 more. For more information, contact the Sociedad Turística Termal Río Liquiñe, Casilla 202, Villarrica, tel. 63/317377.

Transportation: From Villarrica's main terminal, Estrella del Sur has two buses daily to and from Liquiñe. Buses Pirehueico has a daily service to and from Panguipulli.

Choshuenco and Vicinity

At the base of Volcán Choshuenco, 49 km southwest of Panguipulli at the southeast end of Lago Panguipulli, the village of Choshuenco is the main point of access to **Reserva Nacional Mocho-Choshuenco,** a 7,537-hectare unit encircling the volcano. Most visitors, though, come to enjoy its black-sand beach in summer.

Accommodations and Food: Cheapest in town is **Hotel Claris,** San Martín s/n, tel. 63/318245, for US$7 pp with shared bath. **Hotel Choshuenco,** Padre Bernabé s/n, tel. 63/318214, costs US$10 pp for simple rooms with shared bath but without breakfast; all rooms have two single beds. Rates at attractive beachfront **Hotel Rucapillán,** San Martín 85, tel. 63/318220, are

US$18 d with shared bath, US$21 d with private bath, but without breakfast. Both the Rucapillán and the Choshuenco have restaurants.

Transportation: Buses Hua Hum from Panguipulli passes through Choshuenco en route to and from Puerto Fuy.

Puerto Fuy

About 17 km east of Choshuenco, Puerto Fuy isn't exactly the end of the road, but it is the point of departure for the ferry *Mariela*, tel. 63/311334, that sails southeast to Puerto Pirehueico, where the roads continue to the border at Paso Hua Hum. Both the upper and lower Río Fuy are popular with white-water rafters and kayakers.

In January and February, from Puerto Fuy, the two-hour trip departs daily at 7 A.M. and 1 and 6 P.M., returning at 10 A.M. and 3:30 and 8 P.M. In November and December, it operates at 7 A.M. and 2 P.M. daily, returning at 10 A.M. and 5 P.M.; in March and April, the Sunday morning ferry does not run. The rest of the year, departures are at 7 A.M. and 12:30 P.M., returning at 10 A.M. and 3 P.M. except Sunday, when the morning ferry does not run.

Since the *Mariela* can carry a maximum of 21 vehicles, reservations are a good idea at any time of year. Passenger automobiles pay US$21, pickup trucks, jeeps, and vans US$25. Pedestrians pay US$1, motorcyclists US$3.

LAGO RANCO AND VICINITY

Southeast of Valdivia, across the Panamericana, Lago Ranco describes both a large lake, covering 442 square km, encircled by good to not-so-good but improving roads, and a town that bears the name of that lake. Foreign visitors are a rare sight in this Mapuche-dominated area.

Futrono

On Lago Ranco's north shore, Futrono is known for its fishing, crafted artisanal furniture, the fine sand of Playa Galdames, and its Parque Botánico Futronhué, a new woodland park on the lakeshore. Reached by a turnoff from the Panamericana, Futrono is 103 km southeast of

Valdivia; Avenida Balmaceda, the main thoroughfare, leads east to Llifén and Lago Maihue.

The third week of January, the **Semana de Futrono** is a weeklong celebration of the city's founding.

Accommodations and Food: Simple **Hospedaje Futronhué,** Balmaceda 90, tel. 63/481265, charges US$8 pp with shared bath, US$10 pp with private bath. Rates at well-established **Hostería Rincón Arabe,** Manuel Montt s/n, tel. 63/481406, which has lake frontage, a pool, and a Chilean/Middle Eastern restaurant, are US$12 pp with private bath and breakfast. **Hostería Puerto Futrono,** Costanera s/n, tel. 63/481701, charges US$21 pp with private bath and breakfast and also has a restaurant.

Information: The municipal Oficina de Turismo is at O'Higgins and Balmaceda, tel. 63/481389, turiftrn@telsur.cl.

Transportation: Buses Futrono, Buses Pirehueico, and Buses Cordillera Sur all have buses to Valdivia (US$2.50) via Paillaco, where there are north- and southbound connections on the Panamericana. Cordillera Sur buses continue to Llifén and Riñinahue, where there are connections to the town of Lago Ranco.

Llifén

At the east end of the lake via a gravel road, Llifén is a crossroads village where the main road heads south to Riñinahue and then loops west to the town of Lago Ranco, while a lateral heads east to Lago Maihue, a popular fishing area in a more cordilleran zone.

Accommodations at **Hostería Lican,** tel. 63/1971917, fax 63/203005, cost US$9 pp with private bath but without breakfast (though it has a restaurant). At **Hostería Huequecura,** tel. 09/4256276, tel. 63/215732 in Valdivia, rates are US$15 pp for rooms with private bath; it also has a bar/restaurant.

Río Bueno

The gateway to Lago Ranco's southern shore, 30 km north of Osorno and 50 km west of the town of Lago Ranco, Río Bueno is older than most settlements in the area and the site of the colonial **Fortín San José de Alcudía** (1778), which guarded the south bank of the river from the Mapuche. Displaying Mapuche ceramics, German colonial artifacts, and antique weapons, the **Museo Arturo Möller Sandrock,** Pedro Lagos 640, is open Tuesday to Saturday 10 A.M.–noon and 3–6 P.M., Sunday and holidays 10 A.M.–noon only.

Accommodations and Food: Río Bueno has run-of-the-mill accommodations for around US$9 pp at **Hospedaje Río Bueno,** Patricio Lynch 1491, tel. 64/341860, or **Residencial Richmond,** Comercio 755, tel. 64/341363.

Transportation: From Río Bueno, there is regular bus service to the town of Lago Ranco with Obando and Buses Ruta 5.

Lago Ranco

On the southwest shore of the lake, the town of Lago Ranco is an agreeable but nondescript beach resort 50 km east of Río Bueno. The surrounding countryside, including the midlake Isla Huapi, is Mapuche territory. The town celebrates its anniversary during the **Semana Ranquina,** the second week of February.

Sights and Recreation: Local Mapuche ceramics are the strength of the **Museo Arqueológico de Lago Ranco,** Santiago s/n, which is open 8:30 A.M.–1 P.M. and 2:30–7 P.M. daily from mid-December to mid-March. Admission is free.

Visitors can attend late January's Mapuche festival Lepun, which takes place on 850-hectare Isla Huapi, but should leave their cameras on the mainland. Turihott, Valparaíso 111, tel. 63/491201, offers boat excursions to Isla Huapi and car trips around the lake.

Accommodations: Directly on the lake, **Camping Lago Ranco,** tel. 63/491330, has 60 sites with picnic tables for US$10 per tent, and it also has hot showers. The next cheapest alternative is **Hospedaje Los Pinos,** Valparaíso 139, tel. 63/491329, for US$7 pp with shared bath, US$10 pp with private bath. **Hospedaje Alto Pino Tilo,** Concepción 197, tel. 63/491356, costs US$12 pp.

Hostería Phoenix, Viña del Mar 141, tel./fax 63/491226, costs US$11 pp with private bath and breakfast, US$23 pp with full board. Nearby **Hostería Casona Italiana,** Viña del Mar 145, tel. 63/491225, charges US$18 pp with shared bath

and breakfast, but it also has *cabañas* with private bath and breakfast for only a few dollars more.

Information: The municipal Oficina de Turismo, Avenida Concepción s/n, tel. 63/491212, is open 8:30 A.M.–12:30 P.M. and 2:30–6:30 P.M. in summer only.

Transportation: Buses Obando connects Lago Ranco with Río Bueno, for north- and southbound services on the Panamericana, and also goes east to Riñinahue, with connections around the lake. Buses Ruta 5 goes to Osorno via Río Bueno.

OSORNO

More a crossroads than a destination in its own right, Osorno (population about 130,000) relies more on dairying, forestry, and manufacturing than on tourism for its livelihood, but it is a major service center and the gateway to lake district destinations such as Lago Rupanco, Lago Puyehue, Parque Nacional Puyehue, and the Argentine lake district. Osorno dates from 1558, but the Mapuche uprising of 1599 destroyed it and six other cities within five years, even resulting in the death of Spanish governor Oñez de Loyola.

Spanish authorities needed nearly two centuries to refound the city in 1793 with the construction of Fuerte Reina Luisa, a riverside fortification that helped keep out the Mapuche.

Still, though the city survived, it did not flourish until the mid-19th century, as overland communications were too arduous and even hazardous to permit rapid growth of internal markets. This began to change with the arrival of German immigrants in the mid-19th century and accelerated after the definitive "pacification" of the area south of the Biobío in the 1880s, followed by the arrival of the railroad in 1895 and its extension to Puerto Montt by 1911. Around this time, a second wave of immigration brought French Basque, Italian, and Arabic immigration, and Osorno experienced a steady growth throughout most of the century.

Orientation

Osorno is 913 km south of Santiago and 109 km north of Puerto Montt via the Panamericana. Also an east-west crossroads, it is 126 km from the Argentine border at Paso Cardenal Samoré via paved Ruta 215, which is also the gateway to destinations such as Lago Rupanco, Lago Puyehue, and Parque Nacional Puyehue.

Central Osorno, about two km west of the Panamericana, has a slightly irregular grid pattern bordered by the Río Damas to the north, Calles Angulo and Eduvijes to the east, Manuel Rodríguez to the south, and the Río Rahue to the west.

Sights

Despite its colonial origins, Osorno has few really venerable sights—the so-called **Distrito Histórico** west of the Plaza de Armas includes mostly early 20th-century landmarks such as the crumbling **Estación de Ferrocarril** (railroad station, 1912), the restored **Sociedad Molinera de Osorno,** a flour mill now occupied by a pasta factory, and many weathered private residences. A small standout is the ramparts and towers of **Fuerte Reina Luisa** (1793), all that remains of the erstwhile colonial fortress at the foot of Eleuterio Ramírez.

The de facto historic district, though, is on Juan Mackenna between Avenida Matta and Freire, where half a dozen pioneer houses are national monuments: the **Casa Mohr Pérez** at Mackenna 939, the **Casa Enrique Schüller** at Mackenna 1011, the **Casa Sürber** at Mackenna 1027, the **Casa Germán Stückrath** at Mackenna 1047, the **Casa Federico Stückrath** at Mackenna 1069, and the **Casa Conrado Stückrath** at Mackenna 1095.

Osorno's cemeteries chronicle its immigrant history: the **Cementerio Católico** (Catholic cemetery) at Manuel Rodríguez and Eduvijes and the **Cementerio Alemán** on Los Carrera, between Arturo Prat and Angulo.

Museo Histórico Municipal: The municipal historical museum exhibits diverse materials, from Paleoindian archaeology and Mapuche culture to Osorno's colonial founding, its destruction at the hands of the Mapuche and subsequent refounding, the 19th-century city and immigration, and naval hero Eleuterio Ramírez. There are also a natural history room and a new interactive basement display oriented toward children.

The Museo Histórico Municipal, Avenida Matta 809, tel. 64/238615, is open 9:30 A.M. to 5:30 P.M. weekdays all year and 3–6 P.M. Saturday except in summer, when weekend hours are 11 A.M.–7 P.M. Admission is free. Housed in the former Schilling Buschmann residence (1929), a handsome neocolonial building, it is also home to the Casa de la Cultura José Guadalupe Posada.

Accommodations

Osorno has good accommodations alternatives in all categories, though the cheapest places are only so-so.

Less than US$10: Open January to mid-March only, the municipal **Camping Olegario Mohr,** tel. 64/204860, occupies wooded grounds on the banks of the Río Damas just across the Panamericana. Rates are US$8.50 per tent for grassy sites with picnic tables and fire pits; the toilets are clean but there is no hot water and the front gates are locked midnight–8 A.M. Eastbound buses and *taxi colectivos* on Avenida Buschmann pass within a couple of hundred meters of the site.

US$10–25: Several modest but acceptable *hospedajes* east of the bus terminal charge US$7–8 pp with breakfast. Among them are **Hospedaje San Diego,** Los Carrera 1551; **Hospedaje de la Fuente,** Los Carrera 1587, tel. 64/239516; and **Hospedaje Sánchez,** Los Carrera 1595, tel. 64/232560.

Only a block north of the plaza, the slightly more expensive **Hospedaje Weber,** Los Carrera 872, tel. 64/319034, has English-speaking ownership. For about the same price, the best of the cheapest, barely a block west of the bus terminal, may be **Residencial Ortega,** Colón 602, tel. 64/232592. For US$11 pp, another good choice is **Hospedaje Alemana,** Colón 666, tel. 64/250588, but it's often full.

For a significant step up, though, consider **Residencial Hein,** east of the bus terminal at Errázuriz 1757, tel. 64/234116, where rates are US$11/19 s/d with shared bath, US$14/24 s/d with private bath, both with breakfast. Rates at shingled **Residencial Schulz,** two blocks east of the plaza at Freire 530, tel. 64/237211, fax 64/246266, are US$25 d with private bath, but it also offers some slightly cheaper rooms with shared bath.

US$25–50: Opposite the bus terminal, **Hospedaje Millantué,** Errázuriz 1339, tel. 64/233072, fax 64/231080, charges US$17/26 with private bath and breakfast, but it also has a few cheaper rooms with shared bath. In a charming older building four blocks south of the terminal, **Hotel Villa Eduviges,** Eduviges 856, tel./fax 64/235023, hotelvillaeduviges@entelchile.net, costs US$23/35 s/d with private bath and breakfast. Alongside Residencial Schulz, **Hostal Rucaitué,** Freire 546, tel. 64/239922, fax 64/310617, charges US$25/37 s/d with breakfast, TV, and private bath.

Under the same ownership, both charging US$28/38 s/d with private bath and breakfast, the well-regarded **Residencial Bilbao 1,** tel. 64/262200, fax 64/264400, Francisco Bilbao 1019, pazla@telsur.cl, and the **Residencial Bilbao 2,** Juan Mackenna 1205, same telephone, fax 64/262211, are outstanding.

Since its original incarnation in 1930 as the Hotel Burnier, the 65-room **Gran Hotel Osorno,** O'Higgins 615, tel. 64/232171, fax 64/239111, has traditionally been among the town's best. Though it's not quite what it used to be, the deco landmark is still good value for US$31/44 s/d with standard amenities such as private bath, telephone, and cable TV.

US$50–100: A recent addition to Osorno's hotel scene, **Hotel Pumalal,** Bulnes 630, tel./fax 64/242477, invercorsa@telsur.cl, charges US$37/50. Employing friendly, efficient staff, the well-maintained **Hotel Inter Lagos,** Cochrane 515, tel. 64/234695, tel./fax 64/232581, fuenzalida@telsur.cl, offers rooms with cable TV, telephone, central heating, and private bath for US$33/53 s/d with breakfast.

The new **Hotel Lagos del Sur,** O'Higgins 564, tel. 64/245222, fax 64/243696, hotel-lagosdelsur@entelchile.net, charges US$48/63 s/d. Modern carpeted rooms at **Hotel Rayantú,** Patricio Lynch 1462, tel. 64/238114, fax 64/238116, hotelrayantu@entelchile.net, cost US$52/73 s/d with breakfast; amenities include a bar/restaurant and a swimming pool. Rates at the old-style German-run **Hotel Waeger,** Cochrane 816, tel. 64/233721, fax 64/237080, hotelwaeger@telsur.cl, are US$53/75. **Hotel García Hurtado de Mendoza,** Mackenna 1040, tel. 64/237111, fax 64/237113, hotel-ghm@telsur.cl, charges US$69/86.

Food

For real budget meals, nothing's better than the numerous *comedores* in the **Mercado Municipal,** at Prat and Errázuriz, where the seafood is particularly choice (avoid the *fried* fish, though). It's also a good place to buy fresh produce and groceries, as is the **Supermercado Las Brisas,** Mackenna 1150, whose **Kaffeestube,** tel. 64/230262, serves inexpensive sandwiches and lunches.

Upstairs from its namesake bakery, **Pastelería Rhenania,** Ramírez 977, tel. 64/235457, serves sandwiches and pastries, with separate tobacco-free seating. **Dino's,** Ramírez 898, tel. 64/233880, also specializes in sandwiches and light meals, as does its franchise rival **Bavaria,** O'Higgins 743, tel. 64/231302. **Bocatto,** Ramírez 938, tel. 64/238000, has similar offerings but also pizza and probably the best ice cream in town.

The **Club Alemán,** also known as the **Deutscher Verein,** O'Higgins 563, tel. 64/232784, reflects the German community's significance more in name than in menu, which is fairly standard Chilean. The **Club Social,** Juan Mackenna 634, tel. 64/230307, is a labor union restaurant with a good Chilean menu. **Chung Hwa,** Matta 517, tel. 64/233445, serves Cantonese food.

Bell'Italia, Juan Mackenna 1011, tel. 64/26-3100, serves upscale Italian cuisine in stylish surroundings in a house that's a national monument, but fixed-price lunches in the US$6–8 range are a bargain; individual pizzas run about US$4–6. **Del Piero,** Manuel Rodríguez 1081, tel. 64/316767, also serves Italian food.

Entertainment

Osorno ain't Santiago or even Pucón, but it doesn't completely lack things to do at night.

Bars and Clubs: Osorno has an improving bar scene at spots such as **La Pinte,** Freire 677, tel. 64/235944, and **Pub Blue,** Manuel Rodríguez

1039 (ironically enough, next to a Jehovah's Witnesses temple). **Mario's Discotheque** is at Mackenna 555, tel. 64/234978.

Cinema: Show Time, Ramírez 650, tel. 64/23-3890, is a two-screen movie theater.

Performing Arts: The municipal Centro Cultural, Avenida Matta 556, tel. 64/238898, hosts theater and music events, along with rotating art exhibits. Hours are 9 A.M.–1 P.M. and 3–7:30 P.M. daily.

Shopping

Detalles Hecho a Mano, Mackenna 1100, tel. 64/238462, sells regional crafts. **Plazuela Yungay,** at Prat and Ramírez, has an outdoor artisans' market. There are also crafts outlets at the **Mercado Municipal,** Errázuriz 1300.

Services

Money: Osorno's exchange houses include Turismo Frontera at Ramírez 959, Local 11, and Cambiotur at Juan Mackenna 1004. Banco de Chile has an ATM at the corner of Juan Mackenna and Avenida Matta.

Postal: Correos de Chile is at O'Higgins 645, on the west side of the Plaza de Armas.

Telephone and Internet: Entel is at Ramírez 1107, the private Centro de Llamados at Ramírez 816. Osorno's area code is 64.

Gea.com, Vicuña Mackenna 1140, Local 1, provides inexpensive Internet access.

Laundry: Lavandería Limpec, Arturo Prat 678, tel. 64/238966, offers prompt laundry service.

Medical: Osorno's Hospital Base is at Avenida Bühler 1765, the southward extension of Arturo Prat, tel. 64/235571.

Information

Tourist Offices: Sernatur has an office on the ground floor of the Edificio Gobernación Provincial, on the west side of the Plaza de Armas at O'Higgins 667, tel. 64/234104. Hours are 8:30 A.M.–7 P.M. weekdays in summer, when it normally has an English-speaking staff, and 8:30 A.M.–1 P.M. and 2:30–5:30 P.M. daily the rest of the year. Sernatur supports a private information office at the long-distance Terminal de Buses, Errázuriz 1400, tel. 64/234149.

From mid-December through March, at the northwest corner of the Plaza de Armas, the municipal Departamento de Turismo's information kiosk is open 10 A.M.–1:30 P.M. and 2:30–8 P.M. daily except Sunday, when hours are 10 A.M.–2 P.M. only.

Motorists: The Automóvil Club de Chile (Acchi) is at Manuel Bulnes 463, tel. 64/232269.

National Parks: Conaf is at Martínez de Rozas 430, tel. 64/234393.

Transportation

Osorno has limited air connections, but it's a major ground transportation hub for long-distance services along the Panamericana, regional destinations, and across the Andes to Argentina.

Air: LanChile/LanExpress is at Ramírez 802, tel. 64/314900. There are three flights daily to Santiago via Temuco.

Bus: The long-distance Terminal de Buses is at Avenida Errázuriz 1400, tel. 64/234149. Some but not all rural and regional buses use the Terminal de Buses Rurales in the Mercado Municipal, Errázuriz 1300, tel. 64/232073. Services are fairly stable from year to year.

From the regional Terminal de Buses Rurales, three companies go to Entre Lagos, Puyehue, and Aguas Calientes: Buses Puyehue, tel. 64/245026; Expreso Lago Puyehue, tel. 64/243919; and Geosur, tel. 64/230628. Buses Mar, tel. 64/236166, and Maicolpué, tel. 64/234003, go to Bahía Mansa, the only beach resort area easily reachable from Osorno.

At the main terminal, Buses Ruta 5, tel. 64/23-7020, serves Río Bueno, Lago Ranco, and Lago Rupanco. Buses Pirihueico, tel. 64/233050, goes to Panguipulli via Valdivia several times daily.

Transur, tel. 64/234371, in the Igi Llaima offices, goes to the eastern Lago Llanquihue destination of Las Cascadas (US$2). Buses Via Octay, tel. 64/237043, goes frequently to the northern Lago Llanquihue town of Puerto Octay (US$1) and to the western lakeside village of Frutillar. Mini Buses Puerto Octay, at the same office, also goes to Puerto Octay.

Many long-distance carriers connect Osorno with Santiago, Puerto Montt, and intermediates along the Panamericana, among them Bus Norte, tel. 64/233319; Buses Fierro, tel. 64/253775; Buses Lit, tel. 64/234317; Cruz del Sur, tel. 64/232777; Igi Llaima, tel. 64/234371; Tas Choapa, tel. 64/233933; Tur-Bus, tel. 64/234170; Turibús, tel. 64/233633; and Vía Tur, tel. 64/230118. Pullman Sur, tel. 64/232777, goes to Valdivia, Temuco, and Puerto Montt.

Turibús also goes to Punta Arenas (US$40), a marathon trip via Argentina, as does Queilén Bus, while Trans Austral goes to Coyhaique (US$25), also via Argentina. Note that buses to destinations in Chilean Patagonia, such as Coyhaique and Punta Arenas, use Paso Cardenal Samoré, but carry through passengers only— Chilean domestic bus lines are not allowed to drop passengers within Argentina.

Sample destinations, fares, and times include Puerto Montt (US$2.50, 1.5 hours), Temuco (US$4.50, three hours), Ancud (US$5.50, 3.5 hours), Chillán (US$8, seven hours), Concepción (US$10, nine hours), Talca (US$12, 10 hours), Santiago (US$15–18, 14 hours), and Valparaíso/Viña del Mar (US$20, 16 hours).

Most international buses across the Andes to Bariloche (US$17, six hours) and other Argentine destinations use Paso Cardenal Samoré, east of Osorno; the main carriers are Buses Norte, Igi Llaima, Cruz del Sur, and Río de La Plata, tel. 64/233633. Most routes begin in Puerto Montt (see the Puerto Montt Transportation entry for more details).

Tas Choapa and Andesmar, tel. 64/233050, offer connections to Mendoza and Buenos Aires via the Libertadores tunnel northeast of Santiago.

Getting Around

To the Airport: Aeropuerto Carlos Hott Siebert, tel. 64/232529, alternatively known as Cañal Bajo, is seven km east of Osorno via Avenida Buschmann. It's off the city bus routes, but cabs cost only about US$3.

Car Rental: The Automóvil Club de Chile (Acchi), Bulnes 463, tel. 64/232269, and Econorent, Freire 848, tel. 64/235303, have rental cars.

VICINITY OF OSORNO

As a land transport hub, Osorno offers excellent access to some of the most popular summer resort areas in the lakes region. Among them are Lago Puyehue, Termas de Puyehue, and other lesser hot springs resorts in its vicinity, Parque Nacional Puyehue, and the northern and western shores of Lago Llanquihue, including the picturesque towns of Puerto Octay and Frutillar.

Auto Museum Moncopulli

Opened in 1995 and gradually improving its offerings, this private automotive museum contains 36 restored historic vehicles, along with supplementary advertising and marketing materials and other artifacts of the early to mid-20th century, in an 650-square-meter area. It specializes in the now-obscure Studebaker from its beginning as a horsecart manufacturer in South Bend, Indiana, in the 1850s to its first electric automobile in 1902 and the final closure of the plant in 1966. With its futuristic style, the Studebaker was one of the most distinctive automobiles ever produced in the United States, but it never really caught on with the public.

At Km 25 of Ruta 215 east of Osorno, the Auto Museum Moncopulli, tel. 64/237620, also has a pretty good Spanish-only website: www. moncopulli.cl. Hours are generally 10 A.M.–7 P.M. daily except in summer, when closing time is 8:30 P.M. It's closed on Christmas Day and on Wednesday between March and November. Admission costs US$2.50 pp for adults, US$1.50 for retired people and students, and US$.75 for children.

Termas de Puyehue

From modest beginnings in 1908, Termas de Puyehue has become one of Chile's most elegant hot springs resorts, on sprawling wooded grounds near the border of Parque Nacional Puyehue. Housing up to 300 guests in 132 spacious rooms, its stately hotel features a thermal spa with huge swimming pool, offering massage, mud baths, algal treatments, and many other amenities, along with a sophisticated restaurant and bar, a small museum, a library, game rooms, and even an events hall that hosts live classical music concerts. Since 1939, electricity has come from its own small hydroelectric plant.

Hotel Termas de Puyehue, tel. 2/2936000, fax 2/2831010, hotel@puyehue.cl, is at Km 76 of Ruta 215, where the main route continues toward Anticura and the Argentine border, while a paved spur heads to Aguas Calientes, a more modest hot springs, and the Antillanca sector of Parque Nacional Puyehue. High season (January to mid-March) rates start at US$70/80 with breakfast for "standard" forest-view rooms, US$130/150 for "superior" lakeview rooms; half board is available for US$13 more pp, full board for US$24 more pp. The rest of the year, rates start at US$45/65 for standard rooms, US$95/105 for superior rooms.

Termas de Puyehue has Osorno offices at O'Higgins 784, tel. 64/232881. Its Santiago office is at Avenida Vitacura 2898, 2nd level, Las Condes, tel. 2/2342440, fax 2/3332370, ventas@puyehue.cl. It has a fairly thorough website in both Spanish and imperfect but readable English: www.puyehue.cl.

PARQUE NACIONAL PUYEHUE

One of Chile's most visited national parks because of its highly developed hot springs resort at Aguas Calientes and its Antillanca ski area, accessible Puyehue still has plenty of untamed wilderness among its 106,772 hectares of Valdivian rain forest—at least where lava flows and ash from its volcanic vents and summits have not left it as barren as the Atacama.

Geography and Climate

Ranging from the lower valley of the Río Golgol, only about 250 meters above sea level, to 2,240 meters on the summit of Volcán Puyehue, the park is about 80 km east of Osorno and extends all the way to the Argentine border. Volcán Casablanca (1,980 meters) is another major landmark, and the park has abundant creeks, rivers, and lakes that are ideal for fishing.

The annual rainfall, about 5,000 millimeters (much of it falling as snow at higher elevations), supports verdant Valdivian forest. Temperatures are relatively mild at lower elevations, averaging about 14°C in summer and 5°C in winter, with highs in the 25°C range and lows around freezing.

fumaroles on Volcán Puyehue

Flora and Fauna

Puyehue's lush lower Valdivian forest is a mixed woodland of species such as *ulmo (Eucryphia cordifolia),* some specimens of which reach 40 meters or more in height, along with *olivillo (Aextoxicon punctatum), tineo (Weinmannia trichosperma), mañío (Podocarpus nubigena),* and *coigüe (Nothofagus dombeyii).*

Beneath the dense canopy grow smaller trees such as the *arrayán (Myrceugenella apiculata),* a relative of the myrtle, while the solid bamboo *quila (Chusquea quila)* forms impassable thickets in some areas; the endemic *chilco (Fuchsia magellanica,* firecracker fuchsia), along with intensely green ferns and mosses, provides spots of color. The striking *nalca (Gunnera chilensis)* sports umbrella-sized leaves at the end of edible stalks up to two meters in height.

At some higher elevations, though, lava flows and volcanic ash from the 1960 eruption of Volcán Puyehue have left the landscape so barren that grasses and shrubs have only recently begun to colonize the area, despite the substantial rainfall.

Pudú may inhabit the dense forest, but it's difficult to see them or other woodland and riverine species such as foxes, otters, and coypu. About 100 or so bird species flit from tree to tree, along with waterfowl such as the torrent duck *(Merganetta armata* or *pato cortacorriente)* that fishes in the river rapids, and the condors that soar on the thermals overhead.

Sights and Recreation

Puyehue consists of three distinct sectors: Aguas Calientes at its southwestern border, Antillanca at its southeastern border, and Anticura, mostly north of Ruta 215.

Aguas Calientes: From the Termas de Puyehue junction, a paved road leads four km south to Aguas Calientes where, for most visitors, the highlight is its namesake thermal baths, open to hotel guests, campers, and day-trippers alike. Rates are substantially cheaper than at Termas de Puyehue.

Several short nature trails and one longer hike start here. The 1,800-meter **Sendero El Pionero** switchbacks through dense Valdivian forest to a ridgetop with panoramic northern vistas of Lago Puyehue, the forested Río Golgol valley, and the barren cone of Volcán Puyehue. Along its namesake river, the **Sendero Rápidos del Chanleufú** passes through 1,200 meters of gallery forest. The 11-km **Sendero Lago Bertín** climbs steadily to a rustic lakeside *refugio* that may be closed because of hantavirus worries.

Antillanca: From Aguas Calientes, the road becomes a gravel surface that leads another 18 km to the base of Volcán Casablanca, where Antillanca is a popular hotel and ski resort between early June and late October, but in summer it's open for hikers, mountain bikers, fishermen, and general recreationists even though there's no campground in the area. Pool access for nonguests costs US$4 pp, while mountain-bike rental costs US$9–15 per day.

Ranging from 1,050 meters at its base to 1,514 meters above sea level on Cerro Haique, the ski area itself has beginner, intermediate, and expert slopes. For more details, contact the Centro Turístico Deportivo Antillanca at the Club Andino Osorno, Casilla 765, O'Higgins 1073, tel. 64/232297, fax 64/238877, Osorno (see also the listing for Accommodations and Food, below).

Anticura: From Termas de Puyehue, Ruta 215 heads northeast up the Río Golgol valley for 17 km to Anticura before continuing to Chilean customs at Pajaritos and the international border. At Anticura, there is camping along with access to several short trails and some longer ones.

The 950-meter **Sendero Educativo Salto del Indio** is a signed nature trail leading to a waterfall on the Río Golgol; it takes its name from a local legend that says a fugitive Mapuche hid to avoid forced labor in a colonial gold mine. An overnight excursion up the Río Anticura valley leads to **Pampa Frutilla.** Areas east of Pajaritos, the Chilean border post, require Conaf permission to hike or otherwise explore.

From El Caulle, two km west of Anticura, a 16-km trail climbs steeply to the flanks of **Volcán Puyehue,** where Conaf has a well-kept *refugio,* where it's also possible to camp, and continues through a barren volcanic landscape of fumaroles and lava flows to rustic thermal pools; it's possible to camp here also. Note that a private inholder at El Caulle may demand a "toll" for the right to pass through his property en route. It is possible to hike through to Riñinahue, at the south end of Lago Ranco, rather than return to El Caulle.

Volcán Puyehue itself is a flat-topped caldera dating from Holocene times and measuring 2.4 km in diameter; it sits within a larger caldera measuring five km across. The most recent eruptions have come not from the summit caldera, but from vents on its western, southern, and eastern flanks and a small cone on the southern flank.

Accommodations and Food

Some visitors to the area stay at Termas de Puyehue (see separate entry above), but there is a variety of accommodations within the park, from campgrounds to *cabañas* to hotels.

Aguas Calientes: At Aguas Calientes, the 36-site **Camping Chanleufú,** tel. 64/236988 in Osorno, costs US$25 per site for up to four people, while the 20-site **Camping Los Derrumbes** charges US$19 for up to eight people. At the former, fees include access to the thermal baths, but at the latter they do not.

Cabañas Aguas Calientes, tel. 64/374533, fax 64/374529, charges US$103 for up to four people in self-catering *cabañas* for US$103, including access to the baths. It also has a restaurant.

Antillanca: At the ski area, the 73-room **Hotel Antillanca,** Ruta 215, Km 98, tel. 64/235114, fax 64/235672, antillanca@telsur.cl, charges US$58/80 s/d in high season (November to May) for older style "B" rooms, which cost US46/64 s/d in midseason (June and mid-August to October) and US$21–29 s/d in low season (July to mid-August). Newer "A" rooms cost US$86/120 with breakfast in high season, US$63/88 in midseason, and US$34/49 in low season. In Osorno, contact the Centro Turístico Deportivo Antillanca through the Club Andino Osorno, Casilla 765, O'Higgins 1073, tel. 64/232297, fax 64/238877. Transfers from Antillanca to Aguas Calientes cost US$26–31, from Osorno US$54–64.

Anticura: Conaf's eight-site **Camping Catrué,** tel. 64/234393, has basic facilities— running water, picnic tables, fire pits, and pit toilets—for US$10 per site.

Information

At Antillanca, Conaf's Centro de Información Ambiental is open 9 A.M.–6 P.M. daily except in summer, when it's open until 8 P.M. In summer, there are daily slide talks in late afternoon; permanent exhibits focus on natural history (flora and fauna), and on geomorphological topics such as vulcanism. Conaf maintains a smaller information center at Anticura.

Transportation

Ruta 215, now paved all the way to the Argentine border, passes directly through the park. From Osorno's Mercado Municipal, Errázuriz 1300, both buses and *taxi colectivos* serve Termas de Puyehue and Aguas Calientes, with additional service to Anticura and the Chilean border post at Pajaritos (for details, see the Osorno Transportation entry).

In winter, the Club Andino Osorno, O'Higgins 1073, tel. 64/232297, shuttles between Osorno and the ski area at Antillanca.

PUERTO OCTAY

From prosaic 19th-century beginnings as a port at the north of Lago Llanquihue, the apparently idyllic village of Puerto Octay has become one of the most picturesque locales in the entire region, enjoying magnificent views across the lake to Volcán Osorno. Pleasure boats, though, have replaced the steaming freighters that connected Octay with Puerto Varas, and it's become a low-key destination for the summer holidaymakers who arrive by paved road from Osorno, 50 km to the northwest. The German immigrant presence is palpable in its architecture, food, and the checkerboard agricultural landscape of dairy farms and woodlands, and in its apparent middle-class contentment.

Puerto Octay (population about 2,000) also includes Península Centinela, a wooded spit protruding into the lake that's home to several hotels and campgrounds. From the town, it's possible to travel the western shore of the lake to the resort village of Frutillar, or its eastern shore to Ensenada and Parque Nacional Vicente Pérez Rosales, via a road that should soon be completely paved.

> *From prosaic 19th-century beginnings as a port at the north of Lago Llanquihue, the apparently idyllic village of Puerto Octay has become one of the most picturesque locales in the entire region, enjoying magnificent views across the lake to Volcán Osorno. The German immigrant presence is palpable.*

Sights

Puerto Octay dates from 1852, but its architectural heritage of European-style neoclassical and chalet houses dates from the first decade of the 20th century. None of them is a recognized national monument, but at least a dozen private residences and other buildings contribute to its captivating ambience.

One of those buildings is the **Casa de la Cultura Emilio Winkler,** Independencia 591, housing part of the **Museo El Colono,** a well-organized collection of maps, photographs, and other materials on early German colonization. The building is too small, however, to hold an assortment of antique farm equipment that spills out of a barn and onto the grounds of a separate facility at the point where the gravel road to Península Centinela splits off the paved road to Frutillar. It's open 9:30 A.M.–1 P.M. and 3–7 P.M. daily except Sunday, when hours are 11 A.M.–1 P.M. and 3–7 P.M.; from mid-December to mid-March, though, it's closed Monday. Admission costs US$1.

Accommodations

Puerto Octay's accommodations are mostly split between the town proper, which has camping and basic *hospedajes,* and Península Centinela, about two km to the south, which has luxury lodgings but also some more modest alternatives. (See also the Vicinity of Puerto Octay entry below, for the outstanding Zapato Amarillo hostel a short distance north of town.)

Town Center: Camping el Molino, 500 meters south of the Plaza de Armas at Costanera Pichi Juan 124, tel. 64/391375, has lakefront campsites for US$12 for up to five people. Otherwise the options are several *hospedajes* in the US$8–10 pp range: **Hospedaje La Cabaña,** German Wulf 712, tel. 64/391260; **Hospedaje Barrientos,** Independencia 488, tel. 64/391381; and **Hospedaje Costanera,** Pedro Montt 306, tel. 64/391329.

Península Centinela: Andrés Schmoelz leads south out of Puerto Octay proper and dead-ends on Península Centinela after passing campgrounds and other accommodations. **Camping La Baja,** tel. 64/391276, charges US$10 per site. Nearby **Hostería La Baja,** tel. 64/391269, costs US$8.50 pp with breakfast and shared bath, US$20 d with private bath.

At the end of the road, the peninsula's showpiece is the renovated and expanded **Hotel y Cabañas Centinela,** tel./fax 64/391326, hcentinela@surnet.cl, a chalet-type structure which in an earlier heyday hosted guests such as the Prince of Wales (in 1931). Hotel rooms cost

US$56–61 pp with half board in the peak summer season, from mid-December to March; the rest of the year, rates are US$31–35 pp the rest of the year. *Cabañas,* also with half board, cost US$29–48 pp, depending on the *cabaña* and the number of people. Nonguests may also use the restaurant.

Food

Puerto Octay has nothing really out of the ordinary—it's mostly Chilean standbys such as **Restaurant Cabañas,** Pedro Montt 713, tel. 64/391450; **Baviera,** Germán Wulf 582, tel. 64/391460; and **La Naranja,** Independencia 560, tel. 64/391219.

The well-regarded *parrilla* **El Fogón de Anita,** tel. 64/391455, has moved to a location about one km north of town on the Osorno highway. New on the scene is the **Restaurant y Salón de Té Puerto Muñoz Gamero,** Muñoz Gamero 107, tel. 64/391485.

The restaurant at **Hotel Centinela,** on the peninsula, is also open to the public.

Services and Information

Puerto Octay's area code is 64.

The Oficina Municipal de Turismo is a small freestanding office alongside the Municipalidad at Esperanza 555, tel. 64/391491, on the east side of the Plaza de Armas. Hours are 9 A.M.–9 P.M. daily in December through January only.

Transportation

Puerto Octay has no proper bus terminal—buses and minibuses stop on German Wulf just south of the Plaza de Armas. Via Octay, tel. 64/230118, goes to Osorno's main bus terminal several times daily, while Thaebus goes half a dozen times daily to Puerto Montt via Frutillar and Puerto Varas. Four times daily, Arriagada goes south to Las Cascadas, roughly halfway to Ensenada.

VICINITY OF PUERTO OCTAY

Puerto Octay Backpacker Zapato Amarillo

About two km north of town on the Osorno road, the Swiss-run Puerto Octay Backpacker

Zapato Amarillo, tel./fax 64/391575, website: www. zapatoamarillo.8k.com, shiela@telsur.cl, has become a destination in its own right as much as a place to stay. Comfortably stylish hostel-type accommodations on ample grounds, with kitchen facilities but without breakfast, cost US$10–12 pp with breakfast and shared bath from October to April, US$8–10 pp the rest of the year.

In addition to accommodations, though, it offers initial transfers from the town of Puerto Octay, laundry service, rental bikes and canoes, Internet access, information, transfers to La Picada for a hike to Petrohué (US$25 for up to four people), and guided climbs up Volcán Osorno (US$100 for up to four people). Spanish, German, and English are all spoken.

Las Cascadas

Midway to Ensenada, on the eastern shore of Lago Llanquihue, bucolic Las Cascadas sits precariously on a mudflow from looming Volcán Osorno; its primary assets are its black sand beaches and broad vistas of Osorno. Bike touring companies often follow this route south to the village of Ensenada, the gateway to Parque Nacional Vicente Pérez Rosales and junction to Puerto Varas.

Accommodations and Food: The only non-camping budget accommodations, which also serves meals, is **Hostería Irma,** one km south of town toward Ensenada, for US$13 pp. Across the road, **Camping Las Cascadas,** tel. 64/247177 (message only), charges US$10 per site.

About three km south of Las Cascadas, the 18 sites at beachfront **Camping Las Cañitas,** tel. 64/238336, rarcay@ulagos.cl, cost US$17 per site for up to five people. *Cabaña* rentals cost US$44 for up to five people.

Transportation: Bus transportation from Puerto Octay is running more frequent than it used to—four buses per day, at 11 A.M., noon, and 4 and 7 P.M.—instead of just one. As the road to Ensenada is completely paved there may be links farther south as well, but, at the time of this writing, it's another 22 km that involves walking, hitching, or cycling (this is a popular mountain bike route).

FRUTILLAR

Perhaps the most self-consciously perfect example of German colonization in the entire region, the western Lago Llanquihue village of Frutillar is almost a caricature of orderliness–where a sign on the beach says "Deporte, Picnic y Camping Prohibido" (Sports, Picnicking and Camping Prohibited), it almost feels as if it should say "Sport, Picknick und Camping Verboten."

Still, with its almost perfectly preserved European-style houses, Frutillar exudes both style and charm; for a *Dorf* of its size, it also has impressive cultural resources, including a fine museum and one of Chile's most important music festivals. Mirrored in the waters of the lake beyond its sandy beaches, Volcán Osorno rises symmetrically to the east.

Orientation

Frutillar is 63 km south of Osorno and 50 km north of Puerto Montt via the Panamericana. It comprises two separate sectors: the busy commercial area of Frutillar Alto adjoins the Panamericana, while Avenida Carlos Richter leads to the lakeside resort area of Frutillar Bajo, pinched between the sandy lakeshore and a steeply rising hill, about two km east. Avenida Philippi runs north-south along the lakeshore, linked to the parallel Vicente Pérez Rosales by a series of block-long streets; most services and other points of interest face the lake from the west side of Philippi.

Sights

Middle European-style architecture is Frutillar Bajo's trademark, in structures like the 1911 **Iglesia Luterana** (Lutheran church) at Philippi 1000, but the entire lakefront is lined with handsome houses and other buildings.

The highlight, though, is the Universidad Austral's **Museo de la Colonización Alemana,** an indoor-outdoor facility set among immaculate gardens at the base of the hill. Antique farm machinery in mint condition adorns the grounds, while buildings like the **Molino** (a water-powered mill), the **Casa del Herrero** (a working smithery), the **Campanario** (a storage structure with a conical roof supported by a

© WAYNE BERNHARDSON

SUR CHICO

water-driven mill, Museo de la Colonización Alemana

central pillar), and the **Casa del Colono** (a large residence that houses collections of period furniture and household implements) are precise historical reconstructions.

Built partly with aid from the German Federal Republic, the Museo, tel. 65/421143 is on Vicente Pérez Rosales at the east end of Arturo Prat, one short block from the lakeshore. It's open 10 A.M.–2 P.M. and 3–8 P.M. daily from December 15 to March 15 daily; the rest of the year, hours are 10 A.M.–2 P.M. and 3–6 P.M. Admission costs US$2.50 for adults, US$1 for children.

The museum shop sells souvenirs like horseshoes forged in the Casa del Herrero and wood carvings of museum buildings.

Accommodations

Frutillar's accommodations scene is strong at the mid- to upscale range, but budget alternatives are relatively few. All the options below are in Frutillar Bajo, though there are a handful of cheaper *residenciales* in Frutillar Alto.

US$10–25: The otherwise upscale **Hostería Winkler,** Philippi 1155, tel. 65/421388, is also the Hostelling International affiliate, charging US$10 pp with shared bath. In the same range or a little dearer are **Hospedaje Kaiserseehaus,** Philippi 1333, tel. 65/421387, and **Hospedaje Trayén,** Philippi 963, tel. 65/421346, also notable for its restaurant.

US$25–50: A couple of moderately priced places are open in summer only: **Residencial Bruni,** two blocks inland from the lake at Las Piedras 60, tel. 65/421309, and **Hospedaje Michelle,** Antonio Varas 75, tel. 65/421463. **Hotel Klein Salzburg,** Philippi 663, tel. 65/421201, fax 65/421750, costs US$27/47 s/d.

In addition to hostelling accommodations, **Hostería Winkler,** Philippi 1155, tel. 65/421388, has rooms for US$25 pp with private bath and breakfast. **Hotel Frau Holle,** on a hillock with lovely gardens at Antonio Varas 54, tel. 65/421345, frauholle@frutillarsur.cl, charges US$28/50.

$50–100: Frutillar in general is pretty quiet, but at the even quieter north end of town, **Hotel Casona del 32,** Caupolicán 28, tel./fax 65/4-21369, charges US$52/61 s/d. **Hotel Residenz am See,** Philippi 539, tel. 65/421539, fax 65/4-21858, costs US$40 pp with a European-style breakfast and private bath.

The new **Apart Hotel Badenhoff,** Vicente Pérez Rosales 673, tel. 65/421649, has accommodations with kitchen facilities for US$70 d. Rates at renovated **Hotel Ayacara,** Philippi 1215, tel./fax 65/421550, range from US$62/74 to US$76/93 s/d.

Food

Frutillar has several ideal breakfast and *onces* alternatives on the lakefront, starting with the **Salón de Te Trayen,** Philippi 963, but also including the **Andes Café,** Philippi 1057, tel. 65/421845, and **Café del Sur,** Philippi 775, tel. 65/421467. The **Bauernhaus,** Philippi 779, tel. 09/8222489, serves consistently spectacular kuchen and other desserts.

For fixed-price meals for around US$5, the best bet is the **Casino de Bomberos,** Philippi 1065, tel. 65/421588. The traditional **Club Alemán,** San Martín 22, tel. 65/421249, is more formal and more expensive, but not unreasonable. **Parrilla Don Carlos,** on Balmaceda just east of Philippi, tel. 09/6435909, Balmaceda near Philippi, serves Argentine-style beef.

Decorated in a whimsical Hansel/Gretel motif, with numerous dolls on broomsticks hanging from the ceilings, **Selva Negra,** Antonio Varas 24, tel. 65/421164, offers fine food and exceptionally attentive service, with entrées in the US$6–8 range. On occasion, the owner even circulates enthusiastically among the diners, seeking feedback.

In summer, look along the lakeshore for stands with fresh raspberries, raspberry jam, and raspberry kuchen, all specialties of the area.

Events

Frutillar's major annual event is the **Semanas Musicales de Frutillar,** a 10-day extravaganza that has showcased classical, jazz, and ethnic music since 1968. Events take place both during the daytime and at night, when performances are both more formal and more expensive. Reconstruction of the former Hotel Casona del Lago, built on lakeshore landfill between Antonio Varas and Manuel Rodríguez but victim to a devastating fire, will turn the site into a new **Centro de Conciertos y Eventos** (Concert and Events Center), but progress has been slow. The series also includes concerts in other regional cities such as Osorno and Puerto Montt; for current details, see the festival website: www.semanasmusicales.cl.

The town's next most important event is November's **Semana Frutillarina,** celebrating its founding as a lakeport in 1856.

Services

Money: There are no exchange houses, but Banco Santander has an ATM at Philippi 555.
Postal: Correos de Chile is at Pérez Rosales and San Martín.
Telephone and Internet: There's a Centro de Llamados near the corner of Avenida Philippi and Manuel Rodríguez in Frutillar Bajo; Entel is at Carlos Richter 243 in Frutillar Alto. The area code is 65.

Cyber Café Tacitas, Arturo Prat s/n at the corner of Philippi, provides Internet access and rents bicycles.

Laundry: Lavandería Frutillar is at Carlos Richter 335, tel. 65/421555, in Frutillar Alto.
Medical: Hospital de Frutillar is at Las Piedras s/n, tel. 65/421386.

Information

The municipal Oficina de Información Turística is a kiosk at Avenida Philippi s/n, between San Martín and O'Higgins, tel. 65/421198. From December to March, hours are 10 A.M.–9 P.M. daily; the rest of the year, hours are erratic.

Transportation

Bus services arrive and leave from Frutillar Alto; *taxi colectivos* shuttle back and forth to Frutillar Bajo. The two major long-distance carriers are Tur-Bus, Diego Portales 150, tel. 65/421390, and Cruz del Sur, Alessandri 360, tel. 65/421552, both north (Santiago and intermediates) and south (to Puerto Montt) along the Panamericana. Thaebus, at the Alessandri terminal, has half a dozen buses daily to Puerto Octay.

PUERTO VARAS

A little too bourgeois to be Pucón, picturesque Puerto Varas appeals to conventional tourists who come to loll on Lago Llanquihue's beaches, admire its century-old mansions, dine in some of the country's best restaurants, and follow the bus-boat crossing to the famous Argentine resort of Bariloche via Lago Todos los Santos. Increasing numbers of more adventurous travelers, though, also appreciate its access to white-water rafting on the Río Petrohué, the snowclad slopes of Volcán Osorno, the wild backcountry of Cochamó, and other outdoor attractions.

Puerto Varas's architectural heritage, stemming from its German colonization as a 19th-century lake port, gives it its character. Many visitors to the area prefer it to nearby Puerto Montt, and not just as a base for excursions.

Orientation

At the southwestern corner of Lago Llanquihue, Puerto Varas is 89 km south of Osorno, 20 km north of Puerto Montt, and a short distance east of the Panamericana. The boundaries

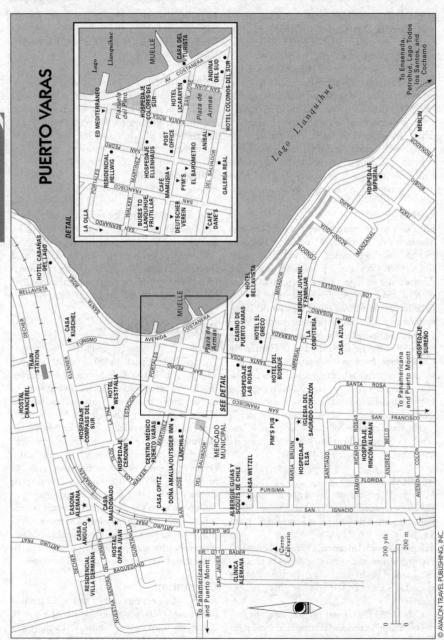

PUERTO VARAS

DETAIL

- ED MEDITERRANEO
- RESIDENCIAL HELLWIG
- HOSPEDAJE COLORES DEL SUR
- Plazuela del Pino
- Lago Llanquihue
- MUELLE
- CASA DEL TURISTA
- AV. COSTANERA
- ANDINA DEL SUD
- HOTEL LICARAYEN
- Plaza de Armas
- POST OFFICE
- HOSPEDAJE ELLENHAUS
- CAFÉ MAMUSIA
- PYM'S
- EL BAROMETRO
- ANIBAL
- HOTEL COLONOS DEL SUR
- GALERIA REAL
- DEUTSCHER VEREIN
- CAFÉ DANE'S
- BUSES TO LLANQUIHUE FRUTILLAR
- LA OLLA

PORTALES · SAN BERNARDO · SAN FRANCISCO · WALKER · SAN PEDRO · MARTINEZ · SANTA ROSA · SAN JUAN · SAN JOSE · DEL SALVADOR · ANIBAL

Lago Llanquihue

To Ensenada, Petrohué, Lago Todos los Santos, and Cochamó

- MERLIN
- TRONADOR
- HOSPEDAJE IMPERIAL
- BIOBIO
- ITATA
- MANZANAR
- ACONCAGUA
- MAIPO
- HOSPEDAJE SUREÑO
- CONDOR
- MIRADOR
- ANGELES
- LOS
- DEL ROSARIO
- ALBERGUE JUVENIL Y FAMILIAR
- HOTEL BELLAVISTA
- CASINO DE PUERTO VARAS
- HOTEL EL GRECO
- LA CONFITERIA
- CASA AZUL
- QUEBRADA
- IMPERIAL
- SANTA ROSA
- HOTEL DEL BOSQUE
- HOSPEDAJE LAS ROSAS
- Plaza de Armas
- MUELLE
- COSTANERA
- AVENIDA
- CASA KUSCHEL
- TURISMO
- BELLAVISTA
- DECHER
- SANTA ROSA
- VINAS
- HOTEL CABAÑAS DEL LAGO
- TRAIN STATION
- HOSTAL CHANCEREL
- HOSPEDAJE COMPASS DEL SUR
- HOTEL WESTFALIA
- KLENNER
- LA PAZ
- ESTACION
- HOSPEDAJE CERONNI
- LOS
- TERRAN
- WALKER
- CASA OPITZ
- CENTRO MÉDICO PUERTO VARAS
- DOÑA AMALIA/OUTSIDER INN
- LANCHILE
- MARTINEZ
- MERCADO MUNICIPAL
- PIM'S PUB
- SAN FRANCISCO
- IGLESIA DEL SAGRADO CORAZON
- MARIA BRUNN
- HOSPEDAJE ELSA
- HOSPEDAJE RINCÓN ALEMAN
- SANTA ROSA
- SAN FRANCISCO
- SANTIAGO
- UNION
- RAMON
- RICARDO ROSAS
- FLORIDA
- ANDRES
- BELLO
- AVENIDA
- COLON
- To Panamericana and Puerto Montt
- ALBERGUE GUIAS Y SCOUTS DE CHILE
- CASA WETZEL
- PURISIMA
- SAN IGNACIO
- CASONA ALEMANA
- CASA MALDONADO
- CASA OPITZ
- DEL SALVADOR
- SAN JOSE
- SAN JUAN
- DR. GIESELER
- CASA ANGULO
- HOSTAL OPAPA JUAN
- DEL CARMEN
- QUINTANILLA
- ARTURO PRAT
- RESIDENCIAL VILLA GERMANA
- NUESTRA SEÑORA
- DECHER
- BAQUEDANO
- SAN JAVIER
- DR. OTTO BADER
- Cerro Calvario
- CLINICA ALEMANA
- To Panamericana and Puerto Montt

SEE DETAIL

200 yds
200 m
0

© AVALON TRAVEL PUBLISHING, INC.

of its compact central grid are the lakeshore to the east, Diego Portales to the north, San Bernardo to the west, and Del Salvador to the south. On all sides except the shoreline, hills rise steeply toward quiet residential neighborhoods that include many places to stay.

From the corner of Del Salvador, the Costanera becomes paved Ruta 225 to the village of Ensenada, the lakeport of Petrohué on Lago Todos los Santos in Parque Nacional Vicente Pérez Rosales, and toward the backcountry of Cochamó.

Sights

Other than the lake and its inspiring views toward Volcán Osorno, Varas's main attraction is its German colonial architecture. The most imposing single structure is the **Iglesia del Sagrado Corazón** (1915), a national monument whose steeple soars above the town from the corner of San Francisco and María Brunn.

Numerous private residences are national monuments; they and many others appear in a map

© WAYNE BERNHARDSON

Iglesia del Sagrado Corazón, Puerto Varas

brochure titled *Paseo Patrimonial* which, despite repeated assurances, has unfortunately not been reprinted, but it's still worth asking about. The monuments, mostly in residential neighborhoods northwest and west of downtown, include the **Casa Kuschel** (1910) at Klenner 299, the **Casona Alemana** (1914) at Nuestra Señora del Carmen 788, **Casa Maldonado** (1915) at Quintanilla 852, **Casa Angulo** (1910) at Miraflores 96, **Casa Opitz** (1913) at Terraplén 861, **Casa Gotschlich** (1932) at Dr. Otto Bader 701-05, and **Casa Yunge** (1932) at San Ignacio 711. A couple of impressive nonmonuments are *hospedajes:* the **Casa Schwerter** (1941–42) at Nuestra Señora del Carmen 873 and the **Casa Hitschfeld** (1930) at Arturo Prat 107.

Accommodations

Puerto Varas has abundant accommodations, some of them very distinctive, in all categories. Some of the cheapest ones are seasonal, but there are always good options.

Up to US$10: In January and February, there are two simple student hostels charging around US$5 pp: the **Albergue Juvenil y Familiar,** in the Liceo Pedro Aguirre Cerda secondary school at Rosario and Imperial, and the **Albergue Guías y Scouts de Chile,** San Ignacio 879, tel. 65/232774. Both offer hot showers and kitchen privileges.

US$10–25: Puerto Varas has several good places in the US$7–10 range with shared bath and breakfast, such as downtown's recommended **Hospedaje Colores del Sur,** upstairs at Santa Rosa 318, tel. 65/338588, and **Hospedaje Ellenhaus,** Walker Martínez 239, tel. 65/233577. Others in the same category include **Hospedaje Sureño,** Colón 179, tel. 65/232648; **Hospedaje Elsa,** María Brun 427, tel. 65/232803; and **Residencial Hellwig,** San Pedro 210, tel. 65/232472. **Hospedaje Imperial,** Mirador 0653, tel. 65/232451, fax 65/232749, is slightly more expensive at US$11 pp.

Watched over by an enormous but almost intimidatingly friendly brindle Brasilian fila named Butch, German-run **Casa Azul,** Manzanal 66, tel. 65/232904, casaazul@telsur.cl, has become a travelers' favorite for rustically stylish and comfortable rooms about 10 minutes' walk from the

Plaza de Armas. Rates are US$12 pp with shared bath (some private) and kitchen access, but the huge fresh fruit and bread breakfast is US$3 extra.

In the same range, but with breakfast included in the price, is **Hospedaje Ceronni,** Estación 262, tel. 65/232016.

US$25–50: Easy walking distance from downtown, but in a quiet barrio opposite the old railway station, **Hospedaje Compass del Sur,** Klenner 467, tel. 65/232044 or 09/7186197, mauro98@telsur.cl, occupies a German colonial-style house with large rooms for US$16 pp with kitchen privileges; breakfast, with muesli and real coffee (not Nescafé), costs US$3.50 extra. There's one bargain single—smallish but comfortable and not claustrophobic—for US$12. Moderately priced laundry service is also available.

Hospedaje Rincón Alemán, San Francisco 1004, tel. 65/232087, charges US$15 pp with private bath and breakfast. In the landmark Casa Schwerter, a national monument, **Residencial Villa Germania,** Nuestra Señora del Carmen 873, tel. 65/233162, charges US$14 pp with shared bath, US$16 with private bath.

Though it's been up for sale, the nearly pristine **Outsider Inn,** San Bernardo 318, tel./fax 65/232910, outsider@telsur.cl, has provided some of Varas's best value for money over the past few years and is still worth considering. Rates are US$17 pp without breakfast.

In the brown shingle Casa Hitschfeld, also a national monument, **Hostal Opapa Juan,** Arturo Prat 107, tel. 65/232234, charges US$25/35 s/d with private bath and breakfast.

It may look remote from downtown, but **Hostal Chancerel,** Decher 400, tel./fax 65/234221, hostalchancerel@latinmail.com, is still only about a 10- to 15-minute walk from the Plaza de Armas. Rates are US$25/37 s/d for spacious rooms with private bath, breakfast, cable TV, and central heating. Other meals and German-style *onces* are also available.

One of Varas's most distinctive accommodations, its natural wood walls covered with work by regional artists, the boutique-style **Hotel El Greco,** Mirador 134, tel. 65/233388, fax 65/233880, website: www.hotelelgreco.com, el-

greco@telsur.cl, is a recycled German-style building that charges modest rates of US$35/44 s/d for its dozen impeccable, moderately sized rooms.

Perched on a hilltop overlooking the town, **Hotel del Bosque,** Santa Rosa 710, tel. 65/2-32897, fax 65/233085, travelsu@chilesat.net, charges US$40/50 s/d with private bath.

US$50–100: Directly on the Costanera, **Hotel Licarayén,** San José 114, tel. 65/232305, fax 65/232955, hasn't quite kept up with competitors in its price range, but it does offer amenities such as a sauna and gym. Rates start at US$58/73 s/d with breakfast.

Under the same management as the more central Hotel Colonos del Sur but in quieter surroundings, **Hotel Westfalia,** La Paz 507, tel. 65/235555, fax 65/235556, westfalia@entelchile.net, has more historic personality than its downtown sibling, with truly grand views from some rooms; it's well worth the rates of US$75 s or d with breakfast, also including access to the sauna at Colonos del Sur.

On the lakeshore just south of the casino, the 38-room **Hotel Bellavista,** Vicente Pérez Rosales 60, tel. 65/232011, fax 65/232013, hotelbellavista@entelchile.net, has outstanding lake views but fewer amenities than some other places in its price category. Summer rates start at US$69/85 s/d, though it's substantially cheaper off-season.

Stretching impressively above the lakeshore, affiliated with the Best Western chain, the hillside **Hotel Cabañas del Lago,** Klenner 195, tel. 65/232291, fax 65/232707, calago@entelchile.net, starts at US$87/99 s/d with breakfast. Besides its impressive views, it has a heated pool.

US$100–150: On the lakeshore, the contemporary **Hotel Colonos del Sur,** Del Salvador 24, tel. 65/233309, fax 65/233394, colonosdelsur@entelchile.net, charges US$93/108 s/d with breakfast for luxury lodgings with a restaurant and bar, café, heated pool, and sauna.

Food

Puerto Varas has some of Chile's best restaurants, and even the run-of-the-mill places are pretty good. **Café Dane's,** Del Salvador 441, tel. 65/2-32371, wins no prizes for decor, but its breakfast, *onces,* and Chilean specialties such as *pastel de* *choclo* are more than a step above most places offering similar fare. **El Barómetro,** San Pedro 418, is a popular meeting place with good sandwiches, desserts, and coffee. **La Confitería,** a bit out of the way at Del Rosario 1010, tel. 65/338188, deserves a detour for its pastries and kuchen.

Mamusia, San José 316, tel. 65/233343, serves good Chilean food, especially *pastel de choclo,* and strong pisco sours, but suffers from erratic service. Most Chilean entrées are US$6–10, but there's a *menú de casa* for US$6. The traditional **Deutscher Verein** (German Club), San José 415, tel. 65/232246, serves fixed-price midday meals. **Aníbal,** at Del Salvador and Santa Rosa, tel. 65/235222, serves pasta and a diverse selection of Argentine pizzas.

For seafood, the Mercado Municipal, Del Salvador 582, holds two reasonable seafood restaurants: **El Mercado** and **El Gordito,** tel. 65/233425. Even better, though, is **La Olla,** San Bernardo 240, tel. 65/234605, whose no-frills decor disguises the quality of its fine seafood in the US$6–10 range; service is also outstanding.

Mediterráneo, at the corner of Diego Portales and the Costanera, does a great stir-fry with a variety of meats and good fish dishes, mostly in the US$7 range. For fine summer afternoons and evenings, it has outdoor deck seating. **Pim's Pub,** San Francisco 712, tel. 65/233998, is a popular meeting place and restaurant, serving Tex-Mex food and margaritas. **Doña Amalia,** San Bernardo 318, is a *parrilla.*

Widely acknowledged as one of Chile's finest restaurants, relocated **Merlín,** Imperial 0605, tel. 65/233105, counts the country's rich and famous among its clientele, but even shoestring travelers should consider a splurge here—prices are not *that* outrageous, though almost everyone spends upward of US$20. German chef Richard Knobloch has become something of a celebrity for adapting fresh local and regional ingredients, particularly seafood and fresh fruit, into a hybrid international cuisine.

Along with Merlín, **Ibis,** Vicente Pérez Rosales 1117, tel. 65/232017, is one of southern Chile's finest dining experiences, with prices to match—appetizers around US$6, most entrées in the US$10 and upward9 range, and desserts US$3–4; with drinks and side orders, it's easy to spend more than US$30 per person. Still, again along with Merlín, it's one of the best splurge choices outside of Santiago for midsized portions of items such as *corvina al cheff,* with shrimp, scallop, and crab sauce; it's one of few places in the country to offer *criadillas*—often known as Rocky Mountain oysters in North America. On the down side, it really doesn't *need* Elton John and the Doobie Brothers.

Pim's, San José 319, has some of southern Chile's best ice cream, but it often runs out of premium flavors. **Vicky Johnson,** Santa Rosa 318, tel. 65/232240, prepares an awesome variety of takeaway truffles for chocoholics.

Entertainment and Events

Puerto Varas has less nightlife than might be expected in a town that gets so much tourist traffic.

Puerto Varas has filled what was until recently an ugly vacant lot with the pharaonic **Casino de Puerto Varas,** occupying an entire block of Del Salvador between the Costanera and San Juan.

Commemorating the city's founding in 1854, the **Aniversario de Puerto Varas** lasts two weeks in late January and early February. Soon thereafter, painters from around the country show their work at the **Concurso de Pintura El Color del Sur.**

Shopping

On the **Plazuela del Pino,** a triangular plaza bounded by the lakefront, Santa Rosa, and Walker Martínez, various *carretas* (carts) offers local crafts and food items.

Services

Money: TravelSur, San José 261, Oficina 4, tel./fax 65/236000, is a general travel agency that also changes money. Banco de Chile has an ATM at Del Salvador 201, Banco de Crédito at Del Salvador 305.

Postal: Correos de Chile is at San Pedro and San José.

Telephone and Internet: Entel, San José 413, provides long-distance telephone services. Puerto Varas's area code is 65.

Cyberservice, Del Salvador 264, Local 6, tel. 65/237911, offers reasonably quick Internet access for about US$2.60 per hour.

Laundry: Lavandería Alba is at Walker Martínez 511, tel. 65/232908.

Medical: Atop Cerro Calvario in southwestern Puerto Varas, the Clínica Alemana is at Dr. Otto Bader 810, tel. 65/232336. The Centro Médico Puerto Varas is at Walker Martínez 576, tel. 65/232792.

Information

Puerto Varas' new Casa del Turista, at the foot of the pier on the Avenida Costanera, tel. 65/23-7272, turismo.puertovaras@munitel.cl, is open 9 A.M.–9 P.M. daily in summer; the rest of the year, hours are 9 A.M.–2 P.M. and 3–6 P.M. In addition to its regular staff, it has a computerized "Turismático" station to consult on the area's attractions and services.

Transportation

Puerto Varas is close enough to the Sur Chico's principal airport, at Puerto Montt, has good regional and long-distance bus connections, and is also on the popular bus-boat route to Argentina.

Air: LanChile/LanExpress has offices at Avenida Gramado 560, tel. 65/234799, but flies out of Puerto Montt (see the Puerto Montt entry for flight details).

Bus: Rather than a single terminal, both regional and long-distance bus companies use their own (sometimes shared) offices within a couple of blocks of the Plaza de Armas. Some long-distance carriers from Puerto Montt pick up northbound passengers here; some regional carriers have no offices but pick up and drop off passengers en route through the city.

Santiago carriers Pullman Sur and Cruz del Sur share offices at San Pedro 210, tel. 65/233008; the latter is also the principal carrier to Chiloé. Cruz del Sur goes Thursday and Sunday to Bariloche (Argentina), while Buses Norte Internacional, at the same offices, goes daily to Bariloche (US$15). Other northbound carriers to Santiago and intermediates include Tur-Bus, Walker Martínez 227-A, tel. 65/233787, and Buses Lit and Intersur, both at Walker Martínez

tourist pier on Lago Llanquihue

© WAYNE BERNHARDSON

227-B, tel. 65/233838. Tas Choapa, across the street at Walker Martínez 230, tel. 65/233831, also goes to Santiago and intermediates.

Santiago fares range from US$15 to US$42, depending on the level of service; the most expensive are nighttime buses with fully reclining seats. Other sample fares include Osorno (US$1.50), Valdivia (US$4), Temuco (US$6), and Concepción (US$16).

Puerto Montt-based Thaebus passes frequently through Puerto Varas, stopping at the corner of San Bernardo and Walker Martínez, en route to and from Frutillar; six of these continue to Puerto Octay (US$1.50). It also goes at 9 A.M. and 2:30 P.M. daily to Petrohué, on Lago Todos los Santos (US$2.50), returning at 11 A.M. and 5 P.M. Expresos Puerto Varas, tel. 65/232253, goes frequently to Puerto Montt; it is commonly known as Mitsubishi for its minibus fleet.

From a stop outside the Galería Real, Del Salvador 257, Buses J. M., tel. 09/6471716, goes to Ensenada and Petrohué at 7:20 and 11 A.M. and

4 P.M. daily except Sunday, when there is no early bus. Buses Interlagos, tel. 65/257015, goes to Ensenada every 15 minutes but continues to Petrohué only if there are enough passengers to justify the trip.

Also from the Galería Real, Buses Josadaro goes to Cochamó and Puelo at 10 A.M., but only to Cochamó at 12:30 and 7:30 P.M. Buses Fierro, tel. 65/253022, goes to Puelo via Cochamó at 1 P.M. Monday to Saturday, at 5:30 P.M. weekdays only, and at 4:30 P.M. Saturday only. It also has daily service to Ralún and Canutillar.

Bus-Boat: Puerto Varas is one of the intermediate points on the bus-boat shuttle from Puerto Montt to Bariloche (Argentina) via Lago Todos los Santos, so it's possible to buy tickets and board the bus to Petrohué here. Most of the year, buses leave Puerto Montt at 8 A.M. daily for Petrohué, returning at 6 P.M.; from April to mid-September, though, they run Wednesday to Sunday only, leaving Puerto Montt at 9 A.M. and returning at 5 P.M. The Puerto Montt operator Andina del Sud has a local office at Del Salvador 72, tel./fax 65/232811.

THE CRUCE DE LAGOS

In the southern lake district, the Cruce de Lagos is a boat-bus-boat shuttle starting in Puerto Montt or Puerto Varas and passing through two national parks before ending in the famous Argentine resort of Bariloche. While it's possible to do this in a day, passively enjoying the mountain scenery, there are hotels and campgrounds at each end of Lago Todos los Santos, on the Chilean side of the border, which provide opportunities for exploratory hikes, though the trail system is not extensive.

The more active can go white-water rafting on the Río Petrohué, canyoning up the steep ravines of Parque Nacional Vicente Pérez Rosales, or even scaling snowcapped Volcán Osorno, a 2,652-meter peak that's a technical challenge.

The Cruce de Lagos is open all year, but best from October to April. It's not necessary to continue beyond Lago Todos los Santos to the Argentine side, but it's worth the effort.

Getting Around

To the Airport: There are no regularly scheduled airport departures, but ETM, tel. 65/294294, will drop off or pick up passengers to and from Varas for US$12 for one person but only US$15 for up to four people. Otherwise it's necessary to make the connection indirectly via Puerto Montt.

Car Rental: TravelSur, San José 261, Oficina 4, tel./fax 65/236000, travelsu@travelsur.com, arranges rental cars.

VICINITY OF PUERTO VARAS

Puerto Varas is the gateway for sights such as Volcán Osorno and Lago Todos los Santos, in Parque Nacional Vicente Pérez Rosales, and the backcountry of Cochamó, and the staging point for adventure activities such as white-water rafting, hiking, climbing, mountain biking, horseback riding, and fishing. Paved Ruta 225 follows the lakeshore east to Ensenada; at a fork two km farther east, the main road goes northwest to Petrohué, while another paved route heads southeast to Ralún, Cochamó, and Puelo.

Among Varas's standard travel agencies are **Andina del Sud,** Del Salvador 72, tel./fax 65/232811, and **TravelSur,** San José 261, Oficina 4, tel./fax 65/236000, travelsu@travelsur.com. Adventure travel operators include **Alsur,** Del Salvador 100, tel./fax 65/232300, alsur@telsur.cl, **Aqua Motion,** San Pedro 422, tel./fax 65/232747, aquamotn@telsur.cl; **Austral Expediciones,** San José 308, 2nd floor, tel. 65/346433; and **Tranco Expediciones,** Santa Rosa 318, tel. 65/311311.

Most of the adventure travel agencies rent mountain bikes and other outdoor sports equipment. **Canoas Tour,** Avenida Costanera s/n just north of the pier, tel. 65/233587, rents kayaks.

Ensenada

At the east end of Lago Llanquihue, 45 km from Puerto Varas, Ensenada occupies a site midway between the perfect cone of 2,660-meter Volcán Osorno, to the northeast, and the serrated caldera of 2,015-meter Volcán Chacabuco, to the southwest. Most services are on or near the junction with the northbound road to Las Cascadas and Puerto Octay.

Accommodations and Food: At Km 43, the 40-site **Camping Playa Trauco,** tel./fax 65/212033, charges US$3–7 pp, depending on proximity to the beach; it has hot showers, a small market, and simple *cabañas* for US$13/17 s/d. One km west, **Hostería Canta Rana,** tel. 65/212010, has good accommodations for US$17 pp and a top-notch but reasonably priced restaurant.

Just north of the Las Cascadas junction, **Hotel Ensenada,** tel. 65/212017 or 65/212028, volcan.hotel.ensenada@entelchile.net, is a century-old classic that oozes character out of the woodwork—all the rooms are spacious, even the third-floor rooms with shared baths, and the common areas are full of museum pieces. Closed from April to September, it charges US$80 d with private bath, US$50 d with shared bath.

In a class by itself, built by tech entrepreneur Michael Darland of Seattle at Km 42, the punning **Yankeeway Lodge** is an over-the-top luxury resort with whimsical (even kitschy) decor targeting big bucks travelers willing to pay up to US$300 pp double occupancy for expedition holidays and US$600 pp for fly fishing—per day. Accommodations include regular hotel rooms and two-unit bungalows (which share walls); the dining room and elaborate kitchen at **Latitude 42** pull in travelers from around the country. For more information, contact Southern Chile Expeditions, Casilla 149, Puerto Varas, tel. 65/212030, fax 65/212031, website: www.southernchileexp.com, reserve@southernchilexp.com.

Transportation: Several buses daily use Ruta 225 between Puerto Varas, Ensenada, and Petrohué; others continue to Ralún, Cochamó, and Puelo. (For more details, see the Puerto Varas Transportation entry.)

From Ensenada, an unpaved road follows the eastern lakeshore for 22 km to Las Cascadas, where it becomes a paved road to Puerto Octay. There is no regular public transportation to Las Cascadas, but there are four buses daily from Las Cascadas to Puerto Octay.

Parque Nacional Vicente Pérez Rosales

Chile's very first national park, created in 1926, is a geographical extravaganza whose dominant features are Volcán Osorno, a symmetrical snow-capped cone that's often called the "Fujiyama of South America," and fjordlike Lagos Todos los Santos, which forms an elongated lacustrine highway toward the Argentine border. It also, though, contains rushing rivers, steep forested canyons, and a scattering of alpine lakes. Like most Chilean parks, Vicente Pérez Rosales has several discrete sectors suitable for various activities.

The 251,000-hectare park takes its name from Vicente Pérez Rosales, an adventurer and explorer whose mid-19th century travels in the region literally cleared the way for European settlement, as he hired the indigenous Huilliche to set fire to the forests near Lago Llanquihue. Pérez Rosales later made a name for himself during the California Gold Rush.

Boat traffic began to cross Lago Todos los Santos as early as 1890, with the first tourists arriving in 1903. Long before Europeans saw the area, though, indigenous peoples had used the southerly Paso de Vuriloche to traverse the Andes, and Jesuit missionaries used a slightly different route south of Volcán Tronador, the area's highest peak.

Geography and Climate: About 50 km northeast of Puerto Varas via Ruta 225, Parque Nacional Vicente Pérez Rosales ranges in altitude from 50 meters above sea level near Ensenada to about 3,460 meters on the summit of Cerro Tronador, a glaciated volcano on the Argentine border that has no recorded historic eruptions. The 2,652-meter summit of Volcán Osorno is its most conspicuous accessible feature; other high peaks include 2,493-meter Volcán Puntiagudo on the park's northern border and 1,710-meter Cerro La Picada, northeast of Volcán Osorno.

Several rivers drain from the cordillera into Lago Todos los Santos, most notably the Río Negro; at 191 meters above sea level, the lake is the source of the Río Petrohué, diverted southward into the Golfo de Reloncaví by lava flows that reached the shores of Lago Llanquihue just north of Ensenada.

© WAYNE BERNHARDSON

Hotel Peulla, Parque Nacional Vicente Pérez Rosales

The park receives about 2,500 mm rainfall per annum at lower elevations but up to 4,000 mm, much of it falling as snow, near the Argentine border. The lake moderates the ambient temperature, which averages about 16°C in summer and 6.5°C in winter, though it gets much colder at altitude. Summertime highs reach about 25°C.

Flora and Fauna: Ecologically, the park's Valdivian rainforest resembles that of other national parks in the region, with dense forests of *coigüe* up to 1,000 meters above sea level, mixed with glossy-leaved *ulmos* and shrubs such as *quila,* as well as ferns and climbing vines. At higher elevations *coigüe* mixes with *lenga;* in a few steep areas grows the rare coniferous *alerce (Fitzroya cuppresoides).*

Within the park are 33 mammal species, among them puma, *pudú,* foxes, and skunks, and 117 bird species, including Chilean torrent ducks, kingfishers, coots, woodpeckers, and hummingbirds. Rainbow and brown trout have been introduced into its lakes and streams, though there are also native trout.

Sector Volcán Osorno: While it hasn't erupted since the mid-19th century, the youthful Holocene crater of 2,652-meter **Volcán Osorno** has active fumaroles and is potentially very dangerous. From the deck of the *Beagle,* Darwin observed its eruption of January 19–20, 1835:

> *At midnight the sentry observed something like a large star, which gradually increased in size until about three o'clock, when it presented a very magnificent spectacle. By the aid of a glass, dark objects, in constant succession, were seen, in the midst of a great glare of red light, to be thrown up and to fall down. The light was sufficient to cast on the water a long bright reflection.*

Adventure travel operators in Puerto Octay and Puerto Varas offer one-day guided climbs of Osorno, ranging from US$100 for up to four people to US$200 pp. This is a much more difficult ascent than Pucón's Volcán Villarrica, requiring either technical skills on snow and ice, or guides with technical skills. Conaf, which regulates climbing here, requires one guide for every three climbers on commercial trips; for independent climbers, it requires proof of experience and presentation of gear before issuing permits.

Sector Petrohué: At the east end of Lago Todos los Santos, the source of its namesake river, Petrohué is most popular as the port for the passenger ferry to Peulla, which leaves in midmorning and returns in early afternoon. Andina del Sud, which operates the Peulla ferry, also runs a daily excursion to **Isla Margarita,** an island that rears its head above the middle of the lake, in January and February only.

Since most of Sector Petrohué lacks an integrated trail network, visiting remote areas requires either hiring a private launch or contracting an activities-oriented tour, but there are a few easily accessible options. From **Playa Larga,** the black sand beach north of Hotel Petrohué, the five-km **Sendero Rincón del Osorno** follows the western shore of the lake. Six km southwest of Petrohué, on the south side of the highway, Conaf charges US$2 admission for the **Sendero Saltos del Petrohué,** a short riverbank trail that follows a series of basalt bedrock rapids and falls too rough for rafting or kayaking; below the falls, Puerto Varas operators start their Class III-IV descents of the **Río Petrohué,** which is suitable for most novice rafters but interesting enough for those with more experience. There are also areas suitable for rock climbing in this area.

Sector Peulla: Where the Río Negro and the Río Peulla empty into Lago Todos los Santos, 20 nautical miles from Petrohué, the hamlet of Peulla earns its livelihood from tourist traffic that patronizes Hotel Peulla and its restaurant, whether overnight, on day excursions from Petrohué, or en route to Bariloche. Chilean customs and immigration is only a short distance east of here.

Day-trippers and through travelers have time enough to walk to **Cascada de Los Novios,** a waterfall just a few minutes from Hotel Peulla. Only overnighters will have time for the eight-km climb of the **Sendero Laguna Margarita.**

Accommodations and Food: Accommodations and food are limited within the park; reservations are advisable at the hotels.

In Sector Volcán Osorno, just below Volcán Osorno's permanent snow line, 1,200 meters above sea level, the **Refugio Teski Ski Club,** tel. 65/212012, charges US$10 for bunks and also serves breakfast (US$4) and lunch and dinner (US$7 each). From a turnoff three km north of the Ensenada junction, the *refugio* is a nine km climb along a gravel road.

In Sector Petrohué, on the south side of the river and reached by rowboat shuttle, the no-frills **Hospedaje Küschel** charges US$10 pp for beds, half that for camping. North of the visitor center, Conaf's 24-site **Camping Playa Petrohué** charges US$17 for up to 10 people.

Rooms at the **Hotel Petrohué,** tel./fax 65/258042 or 09/6540000, reservas@petrohue.com, take the best possible advantage of natural wood grain and color to create a cozy ambience. Rates range from US$58/85 s/d to US$74/105 with breakfast, depending on the room; with half board, prices range from US$68/105 s/d to US$84/125 s/d. Its restaurant, charging US$10–14 for four-course dinners, is open to the general public; otherwise, only limited supplies at high prices are available at Petrohué's only shop.

In Sector Peulla, rates at so-so **Hotel Peulla,** tel. 65/258041, range from US$82/114 to US$98/130 s/d with half board at its restaurant **Tejuela,** which has drawn criticism for both price and quality. There is an unofficial campsite, plus budget accommodations for about US$10 pp in summer only at **Hospedaje Hernández.**

Information: At Petrohué, Conaf's Centro de Visitantes contains exhibits on the park's geography, geology, fauna and flora, and history.

Transportation: Regular bus service connects Petrohué with Puerto Varas and Puerto Montt (for details, see the Puerto Varas Transportation entry, above).

From September to March, Puerto Montt's Andina del Sud, Antonio Varas 437, tel./fax 65/257797, operates daily 8:30 A.M. buses to Ensenada and Petrohué via Puerto Varas, connecting with its own bus-boat crossing to Bariloche (Argentina); return buses leave at 5 P.M. From April to mid-September, buses run Wednesday to Sunday only, leaving Puerto Montt at 10 A.M. but returning at the same hour.

At Petrohué, Andina del Sud has a dockside

kiosk that sells tickets for the three-hour trip to Peulla, where it connects with the bus to the Argentine border at Puerto Frías and a relay of bus-boat links to Bariloche. Tickets to Peulla cost US$20 round-trip for adults, slightly less for children; lunch at Hotel Peulla costs an additional US$10 pp. Andina del Sud offices in Puerto Varas and Puerto Montt also sell tickets.

Cochamó

Two km east of Ensenada, where international Ruta 225 continues to Petrohué, another paved road follows the course of the Río Petrohué southeast for 30 km, where it forks at the north end of the Golfo de Reloncaví. While the right fork heads south to Canutillar, the graveled left fork continues to **Ralún,** where another gravel road forks north to **Cayutué,** on the south arm of Lago Todos los Santos.

The main road, though, continues another 15 km to Cochamó, where the 2,111-meter Volcán Yates, at the south end of the gulf, provides a backdrop for the shingled **Iglesia Parroquial María Inmaculada** and its soaring steeple. The area's big attraction, though, is the yet-untamed grandeur of the upper Río Cochamó, where ribbonlike waterfalls tumble over exfoliated granite domes that rise above the luxuriant rainforest. Still, only small numbers of hikers, dedicated technical climbers, and horseback riders challenge the muddy trail, part of which follows a 19th-century log road that crossed the Andes to Argentina, to the scenic valley of **La Junta** and beyond.

Cochamó is the base for **Campo Aventura,** a horse-trekking company that recently changed hands but continues to offer two- to 10-day horseback trips to its backcountry camp at La Junta, 17 km east and 600 meters above sea level, and beyond. Unfortunately for wilderness enthusiasts, new road construction is slowly but inexorably proceeding up the valley to La Junta, though much of the area is likely to remain roadless for some time and there may be an attempt to declare the log road a national monument, which would be an obstacle to construction of an improved road.

The present road and trail follow the north bank of the river as far as La Junta, where it's nec-

essary to ford the river to Campo Aventura's south bank camp, which has comfortable lodging, camping for US$4 pp, and its own small network of hiking trails. If the river is high, the ford can be dangerous for hikers and, on rare occasions, even riders. For more details, contact Campo Aventura's Puerto Varas office at San Bernardo 318, tel./fax 65/232910, outsider@telsur.cl.

Accommodations and Food: Cochamó proper has two places to stay: the inexpensive but basic **Hospedaje Moreno,** Costanera s/n, tel. 65/250183, *anexo* 256; and **Hotel Cochamó,** Catedral 19, tel. 65/216212.

Horseback tour clients have priority for the three stylish *cabañas* at **Campo Aventura,** five km south of Cochamó proper and 500 meters east of the road to Puelo, on the south side of the bridge over the Río Cochamó; for US$14 pp, they are open to nonclients if there are vacancies. Breakfast costs an additional US$5; seafood and vegetarian lunches and dinners are also available for nonclients.

Open mid-October to mid-April, Campo Aventura has equally stylish if simpler dormitory-style accommodations at La Junta, which have wood-fired hot showers, and a campground as well. Meals, wine, and fresh bread are also available here, but it's best to make advance arrangements for meals in Cochamó.

Transportation: From Puerto Montt, Buses Fierro runs two buses daily from Puerto Montt (US$3), at 12:30 and 5 P.M. weekdays, 12:30 and 4 P.M. Saturday, and 9:30 A.M. and 5 P.M. Sunday and holidays, via Puerto Varas.

PUERTO MONTT

No Chilean city has a more impressive setting than Puerto Montt, where a cordon of forested mountains and snowcapped volcanoes stretches south along the waters of Chile's island-studded "Inside Passage." While the city itself, with a population of less than 100,000, can't match the prosperity and cultural diversity of cities in comparable surroundings, such as Seattle and Vancouver, improvements are under way. Municipal authorities are turning at least part of the waterfront, with its dramatic views, into a park, anchor

formal starting point of the Carretera Austral

businesses such as the Ripley department store are helping make downtown a retail mecca, pedestrian malls are sprouting chic sidewalk cafés, and pubs and bars are proliferating.

As a city whose potential, to this point, is greater than its achievement, the capital of Region X (Los Lagos) remains primarily a gateway to the southern lake district, the archipelago of Chiloé, Chilean Patagonia, and parts of Argentina. As a transport hub where mainland Chile ends and archipelagic Chile begins, it enjoys air, land, or sea connections in all directions but west. Increasing numbers of cruise ships are even calling at its port of Angelmó, from 48 in 2000 to an estimated 100 in 2001, even though there's barely room for them to maneuver in and out of the congested harbor.

History

Puerto Montt dates from 1853, when German colonists landed at the north end of the Seno de Reloncaví in what was then called "Melipulli," a Huilliche word whose definition—"four hills"— aptly described the site of the new settlement. It grew slowly until 1912, when completion of the railroad cut the travel time to Santiago to only 26 hours and it became the jumping-off point for southbound colonists headed for continental Chiloé, Aysén, and Magallanes.

In 1960, a catastrophic earthquake destroyed the port and most of what Jan Morris, only a few years later, called "structures in the Alpine manner, all high-pitched roofs and quaint balconies." Rebuilt in a mostly utilitarian style, Puerto Montt is only now beginning to sport newer buildings of distinction; the earlier style survived to a greater degree in nearby Puerto Varas.

Orientation

Puerto Montt is 1,016 km south of Santiago via the Panamericana, which bypasses the city center en route to archipelago of Chiloé. Like Valparaíso, it occupies a narrow shelf at the foot of a series of hills, but not quite so high as those at Valparaíso. Westbound Avenida Diego Portales becomes Avenida Angelmó, the main approach to the ferry, fishing, and forest products port of Angelmó, which attracts tourists to its permanent crafts fair and seafood restaurants; eastbound, it becomes Avenida Soler Manfredini, the starting point for the discontinuous Carretera Austral, a series of both paved and gravel highways linked,

SUR CHICO

PUERTO MONTT

HOSPITAL BASE

CONAF

HOTEL VIENTO SUR

HOTEL MILLAHUE

COPIAPO

AEROSUR

SERENA

HOTEL EL CANDIL

HOSTAL PANORAMA

RESIDENCIAL MILLANTU

EX-ESTACIÓN DE FERROCARRILES

ILLAPEL

SAN FELIPE

To Pelluco, Hornopirén and Carretera Austral

AVENIDA SOLAR MANFREDINI

AVENIDA ESPAÑA

EGAÑA

QUILLOTA

O'HIGGINS

Plaza de Armas

Manuel Irarrázabal

AVENIDA DIEGO PORTALES

SAN MARTIN

TIMON AUSTRAL

BENGIFO

PUB BIÓGRAFO

RANCAGUA

ANTONIO VARAS

HOTEL LA MIRAGE

PUB SITGES

OCHAGAVIA

G. GALLARDO

Seno de Reloncaví

HOTEL O'GRIMM

IGLESIA DE LOS JESUITAS

VIAL

DR. MARTIN

ALCALDE

SANTA MARIA

REGIÓN

O'HIGGINS

SEMINARIO

EJÉRCITO

PEDRO MONTT

RINCON SUREÑO

SEE DETAIL

DK CORRAL

TALCA

KALABAZA

HOTEL COLINA

APETITO'S

PASTELERÍA NUEVA LISEL

SANDOKAN

CAUQUENES

CHILLAN

BENAVENTE

BALMACEDA

ANIBAL PINTO

URMENETA

TALCAHUANO

AVENIDA DIEGO PORTALES

BAQUEDANO

VALDIVIA

PEREZ ROSALES

MIRA

MUSEO JUAN PABLO II

HOTEL ANTUPIRÉN

RESIDENCIAL BENAVENTE

FREIRE

RODRIGUEZ

ANCUD

JUAN JOSE

MIRAMAR

OTILI

LOTA

RESIDENCIAL EL TALQUINO

RESIDENCIAL LA NAVE

PUEBLITO DE MELIPULLI/ LAHUEN-TUR

TERMINAL DE BUSES

URMENETA

To Panamericana and Santiago

To Angelmó, Isla Tenglo, and Panitao

200 yds

200 m

0

0

DETAIL

BLANCO ENCALADA

RESIDENCIAL URMENETA

GRAN HOTEL DON LUIS

TEATRO DIEGO RIVERA

HOTEL MONTT

AEROCONTINENTE

LANCHILE

BALZAC

CAFÉ EL PASO

O'HIGGINS

OFICINA MUNICIPAL DE TURISMO

CATEDRAL DE PUERTO MONTT

Plaza de Armas

URMENETA

POST OFFICE

SERNATUR

Manuel Irarrázabal

ANTONIO VARAS

ANDINA DEL SUR

HOSPEDAJE PUERTO MONTT

RANCAGUA

CAFÉ REAL

PASTELERÍA ALEMANA

HOTEL VICENTE PÉREZ ROSALES

MUELLE

HOTEL GAMBOA

HELADERÍA LA REINA

G. GALLARDO

DI PIAZZA

DINO'S

MONTT

HOTEL BURG

AMSEL

CATAMARANES DEL SUR

N

© AVALON TRAVEL PUBLISHING, INC.

CHILE'S INSIDE PASSAGE

Even in the darkest days of the 1970s, as Chile chafed under dictatorship and foreign travelers were few, the occasional adventurous visitor found his way south in search of a sailing passage through the archipelagic labyrinth of Chile's southern canals. Nearly uninhabited, the myriad islands south of Chiloé exerted an inexorable magnetism on map mongers, but only a few fast talkers managed their way on board the rustbucket *Río Baker*, the funky freighter that plied the route from Puerto Montt to Puerto Natales, or the ferry *Evangelistas* that replaced it in the last years of the Pinochet regime.

Today, fortunately, it's easier than ever to sail what might be called "the poor man's cruise," a three-day voyage through the western fjords of Aisén and Magallanes. The *Puerto Edén* and the *Magallanes*, the two vessels that shuttle the 900 nautical miles between Puerto Montt and Puerto Natales, are not cruise ships. Rather, they are cargo ferries that also carry passengers in reasonable comfort through some of South America's finest scenery—at least when the weather clears in one of the stormiest regions on earth.

Sailing south from Puerto Montt, on a sunny departure day, there are seemingly infinite views of the volcanic continental cordon of Osorno, Calbuco, Yates, Michinmahuida, and Corcovado. As the ship proceeds south through the waters of the Golfo de Ancud, Golfo de Corcovado, and Canal Moraleda, Michinmahuida's snowfields seem to rotate slowly in the distance until they finally fade from view. To the west, the lighthouse at **Melinka,** a tiny outpost in the Guaitecas archipelago, is the only conspicuous sign of settlement beyond Chiloé.

On entering the Canal Moraleda, the two vessels now take slightly different itineraries. The *Puerto Edén* usually follows its traditional route, south to the Canal Errázuriz and west toward the open Pacific via the Canal Chacabuco. The *Magallanes*, by contrast, pays a visit to **Puerto Chacabuco,** but passengers on the *Puerto Edén* will still see Chacabuco's small-scale fishing fleet, pursued by seabirds, in the Moraleda.

The usual route west to the Pacific is through the Canal Chacabuco, the most southerly option between Isla Humos and Isla FitzRoy, but there are more northerly alternatives such as Canal Darwin between Isla Quemada and Isla Luz; the *Puerto Edén* sometimes takes an even more northerly route via Canal Ninualac, between Isla James and Isla Melchor.

As the ships round Cabo Tres Montes, there are no alternatives to crossing the **Golfo de Penas** (Gulf of Sorrows), as the nautically challenged seek relief through medication before trays start flying around the cafeteria in the rough swells of the open ocean. Most passengers feel literal relief at entering the Canal Messier, passing through **Angostura Inglesa,** a narrows so constricted that, it seems, the queasier passengers might leap off the deck and alight on dry land. Just to the north, the route passes the rusting hulk of the shipwrecked *Capitán Leonidas,* run aground on the Cotopaxi rocks.

The *Magallanes* continues south without a break, but the *Puerto Edén* pauses at its namesake harbor, where Kawasqar (Alacaluf) Indians still board to sell souvenirs or travel themselves to Puerto Natales. South of Puerto Edén, the scenery is enthralling, with emerald forests, countless waterfalls, and glaciers that don't quite reach the sea but still

---

where necessary, by ferries. This highway ends at Villa O'Higgins, 1,240 km to the south in Region XI (Aisén), but most travelers cover at least part of the route via air or ferry from Puerto Montt or Chiloé.

Sights

Puerto Montt's strength is its magnificent geographical setting, but it also has a handful of architectural monuments and other sights. On the south side of **Plaza Manuel Irarrázaval,** built of *alerce* in the style of the Parthenon, the **Catedral de Puerto Montt** (1856) is city's oldest building. Surrounded by woods, the hillside **Torre Campanario del Colegio San Francisco Javier** (1894) rises behind its namesake church, dating from 1872, at the corner of Guillermo Gallardo and Rengifo.

On the waterfront, the **Museo Juan Pablo II** holds collections on natural history, archaeology (including the enormously important Monte Verde early man site 35 km west of Puerto

gleam when the sun breaks through the clouds. As the ship approaches Puerto Natales, the passengers grab their backpacks and prepare to head for the *hospedajes* to make their plans for Torres del Paine and Patagonia.

Practicalities

Because two ferries now cover the route, with Monday and Thursday departures, the frustration that many passengers felt when weather or mechanical difficulties caused delays should diminish. (For contact information, details on booking, and rates, see the Navimag entry under Organized Tours in the On the Road chapter, and the accompanying chart, Navimag Passenger and Vehicle Fares.) The boats run all year, but long summer days mean good visibility even with changeable weather.

New on the route, the *Magallanes,* a Japanese ferry remodeled in Chile, can carry 337 passengers versus the *Puerto Edén's* maximum of 175 or so. The former needs 56 hours between Puerto Montt and Puerto Natales, 66 hours with a stop at Puerto Chacabuco, while the slower *Puerto Edén* needs about 72 hours with a pause at Puerto Edén.

The *Magallanes* is 123 meters long and 21 meters wide, and has a pub, dining room, self-service cafeteria, and spacious upper decks and terraces. Its eight AAA cabins have two bunks each with individual reading lights, private bath, writing desk, chair, locking closet, regulated heat, and an exterior window. Sixteen AA cabins have two upper and two lower bunks and the same amenities. Fourteen A cabins have the same amenities but lack exterior windows. The 132 C berths lack locking closets and have exterior baths. If prone to seasickness, bring medication and take it well before crossing the Golfo de Penas.

On the *Puerto Edén,* most cabins have toilet, sink, shower, and closet, but some have external showers; cabins without portholes are cheaper. *Clase económica* (budget class) is due for improvements, reducing the numbers of bunks and increasing the space for each. There are separate galleys for cabin passengers and *clase económica,* both of which dine in shifts if the boat is full.

The food is still served cafeteria food, but it has improved in quality and increased in quantity—though truly big eaters might consider bringing some of their own snacks. Both bridge and cabin staff are friendly, including the food servers, and prices at the bar are surprisingly moderate. The no-smoking policy, however, is inconsistently enforced.

Navimag carries twice as many foreigners as Chileans on the Puerto Montt–Puerto Natales route, which takes three full days but can still be delayed by bad weather. At the outset of the voyage, there is an orientation and safety talk. Videos and other entertainment do occur on board, including a closing night party.

In the course of the voyage, many people make acquaintances and enduring friendships, and even some marriages have resulted. There's easy access to the bridge, the crew are personable and informative, and it's possible to follow the route on their charts. Some passengers, though, bring their own GPSs and charts, the most comprehensive of which is the British Admiralty's Hydrographer of the Navy Chart No. 561, Cabo Pilar to Golfo Coronado, at a scale of 1:750,000.

Montt) and anthropology, the customs of Chiloé, weapons from the War of the Pacific, ecclesiastical art, 19th-century German colonization, and the history of the city itself, including photographs of the massive 1960 earthquake. For many locals, the high point was the 1987 visit of Pope John Paul II, also documented here, which resulted in the museum's renaming. Directly east of the bus terminal, the museum, Avenida Diego Portales 991, tel. 65/261822, is open 9 A.M.–7 P.M. daily in January and February, 9 A.M.–noon and 2–6 P.M. the rest of the year. Admission costs US\$.40 for adults, US\$.15 for children.

Puerto Montt and **Angelmó**, two km west, have gradually grown together along the waterfront, but the port retains its own identity and attracts more visitors than any other part of town, thanks to its sprawling crafts market and gaggle of *marisquerías,* always jammed with lunch and dinner patrons. Angelmó's most dubious landmark is the mountain of wood chips at the foot of Calle Independencia, a red flag to a Chilean environmental movement that has campaigned, with some success, against the exploitation of the region's native forests—a sign at the port now insists that the chips come from eucalyptus plantations. *Taxi colectivos* out Avenida Diego Portales go directly to the port area, which is also the departure point for southbound ferries.

Accommodations

Puerto Montt has plenty of accommodations, but many of those at the bottom end tend to the unremarkable if not quite dire.

US$10–25: Uphill from the bus terminal, **Residencial El Talquino,** Pérez Rosales 114, tel. 65/253331, fax 65/263363, costs only US$5 pp without breakfast; kitchen privileges cost an extra US$1. Nearer the port, **Hospedaje Rocco,** Pudeto 233, tel. 65/272897, hospedajerocco@entelchile.net, costs US$7.50 pp with breakfast, kitchen facilities, Internet access, and shared bath.

Newish but already a bit worn, **Hostal Aysén,** Avenida Angelmó 1866, tel. 65/272051, charges US$8.50 pp with shared bath and breakfast for sizeable rooms with good beds. Several others fall into the same range: **Residencial Torres del Paine,** Portales 1568, tel. 65/258193; **Hospedaje Emita,** Miraflores 1281, tel. 65/250725; and **Hostal Panorama,** at San Felipe 192 but most easily reached by a hillside staircase from Benavente, tel. 65/277940 (rates here include private bath but not breakfast).

At **Casa Perla** Trigal 312, tel. 65/262104, casaperla@hotmail.com, rooms with shared bath, hot showers, kitchen privileges, and laundry facilities cost US$9 pp; while it's not the most attractive neighborhood, the atmosphere is welcoming, with comfortable common areas including a small library, and the owners speak English. The Hostelling International representative is **Hostal Don Teo,** Andrés Bello 990, 2nd floor, tel. 65/251625, for US$9 pp.

Convenient to the ferry at Angelmó, **Residencial Costanera,** Avenida Angelmó 1528, tel./fax 65/255244, is an older house partitioned into smallish but adequate bedrooms for US$10 pp with breakfast and shared bath. The common spaces are good, and it has plenty of parking—an uncommon attribute for budget

accommodations in Puerto Montt. Uphill from the fish restaurants of Angelmó, homey **Hospedaje Rojas,** Poseidón 103, tel. 65/259654, belongs to an artistic Chilean family; rates are also around US$10 pp.

Once one of Puerto Montt's better budget choices but now showing wear and tear, **Residencial Urmeneta,** Urmeneta 290, 2nd floor, tel. 65/253262, charges US$10/17 s/d with shared bath, US$17/25 with private bath.

US$25–50: Decorated with the paintings of Swiss-Chilean owner Rossy Oelckers, **Hospedaje Suizo,** Independencia 231, tel. 65/252640 or 65/257565, charges US$7–13 pp, depending on the room, but all have shared bath; breakfast costs US$2.50 more. It's straight uphill from the mass of wood chips at the port entrance on Avenida Angelmó.

Hospedaje Puerto Montt, Pedro Montt 180, tel. 65/252276, is friendly and central, but downstairs rooms are darkish with a maximum number of beds packed into each room. With shared bath and an abundant breakfast, rates are US$14 pp for adequate accommodations. For about US$25/28 s/d, **Hotel Colina,** near the waterfront at Talca 81, tel. 65/253502, fax 65/273857, is good value even if its location, and construction, aren't the quietest.

Hotel Gamboa, Pedro Montt 157, tel. 65/252741, is a wonderful old-style hotel with sizable rooms that retain most of their original style, though some of the modern furniture is tacky. Rates are US$12 pp with shared bath, US$14 pp with private bath.

Gradually declining **Residencial Millantú,** Illapel 146, tel./fax 65/263550, charges US$20/30 with private bath and breakfast. So-so **Hotel Montt,** Varas 301, tel. 65/253651, fax 65/253652, charges US$23/33 s/d.

Rates at **Hotel El Candil,** Antonio Varas 177, tel./fax 65/253080, and at well-regarded **Residencial La Nave,** Ancud 103, tel. 65/253740, are US$17 pp with private bath.

Friendly but aging **Hospedaje Benavente,** Benavente 948, tel. 65/253084 or 65/256369, charges US$9 pp with shared bath, US$18 pp with private bath, for adequate rooms, but the Gamboa, among others, is a better option.

Often full during the summer peak season, **Hotel Millahue,** Copiapó 64, tel. 65/253829, fax 65/256317, jacortes@entelchile.net, costs US$23/32 s/d.

The modern **Hotel Le Mirage,** Rancagua 350, tel. 65/255125, fax 65/256302, often fills with groups; rates are US$27/40 s/d with private bath, cable TV, and most other conveniences, but it's worn for its age.

US$50–100: Business-oriented **Hotel Burg,** on the waterfront at Pedro Montt 56, tel. 65/253941, charges US$56/67. **Hotel Antupirén,** Freire 186, tel. 65/313637, fax 313638, is also a business-oriented hotel that's probably overpriced at US$60/70 s/d for fairly small rooms—one might generously call them compact—with buffet breakfast; more spacious rooms with larger beds cost US$70/83 s/d and are probably worth the difference. Service is attentive and efficient.

Hotel O'Grimm, Gallardo 211, tel. 65/25-2845, fax 65/258600, hotel@ogrimm.com, has large rooms with all modern conveniences for US$80/90 s/d, with attentive service. The attractive bar also has a basement pub with occasional live music, but it's acoustically insulated.

The traditional **Hotel Vicente Pérez Rosales,** Antonio Varas 447, tel. 65/252571, fax 65/2-55473, hotelvpr@telsur.cl, charges US$85/99.

US$100–150: A block east of the Plaza de Armas, **Gran Hotel Don Luis,** Quillota 146, tel. 65/259001, fax 65/259005, hdluis@entelchile.net, is a quality choice for US$102/109.

Overlooking the town from a hillside perch, recently remodeled **Hotel Viento Sur,** Ejército 200, tel. 65/258701, fax 65/258700, boasts great views, stylistic integrity, finely finished woodwork, and a restaurant. Popular with foreign tour groups, it charges US$100/110 s/d with breakfast.

Food

With only a couple of exceptions, downtown Puerto Montt restaurants are reasonably priced but run-of-the-mill places such as **Amsel,** Pedro Montt 56, tel. 65/253941; **Apetito's,** Chillán 96, tel. 65/252470; **Dino's,** Antonio Varas 550, tel. 65/252785, with its chain predictability; **Mykonos,** Antonio Varas 326, tel. 65/262627; and **Rincón Sureño,** Talca 84, tel. 65/254597.

Figure about US$3–5 for lunch, somewhat more for dinner.

DiPiazza, Gallardo 118, tel. 65/254174, is only a so-so pizzería, but with moderate prices—individual-sized pizzas start around US$3, and inexpensive pasta plates are also on the menu. The **Club Alemán** or **Deutscher Verein** (German Club), Antonio Varas 264, tel. 65/252551, is a step up in both price and quality. Highly unusual in this part of the world, **Sandokan,** Benavente 670, is a Malaysian restaurant.

Occupying an architectural anachronism, **Balzac,** Urmeneta 305, tel. 65/313251, is probably Puerto Montt's finest seafood restaurant and certainly the best downtown, with service to match, and entrées in the US$6 range–try the *jaiva chardonnay* (crab casserole in white wine sauce) and save room for any of a variety of outstanding desserts.

Any of numerous *palafito marisquerías* (seafood restaurants on stilts, or pilings) clustered at the port of Angelmó are worth trying for fish, shellfish, and *curanto,* but streetside restaurants such as the unpretentious **Asturias,** Avenida Angelmó 2448-C, tel. 65/258496, and the flashier **Marfino,** Avenida Angelmó 1856, tel. 65/259044, deserve consideration. Just uphill from the *palafitos,* where the Chinquehue road turns north at the end of Avenida Angelmó, French-run **Los Piratas,** Pacheco Altamirano 2505, tel. 65/299760, is an attractive place with superb service and prix-fixe seafood specials in the US$6 range, including a glass of wine. À la carte dining ups the ante considerably, though many tempting items appear on a truly diverse menu.

For sandwiches, *onces,* and desserts such as kuchen, try **Pastelería Alemana,** Rancagua 117, tel. 65/254721; **Café Real,** Rancagua 137, tel. 65/253750; **Pastelería Nueva Lisel,** Cauquenes 82; and **Kalabaza,** Antonio Varas 629. **Heladería La Reina,** Urmeneta 508, tel. 65/253979, continues to offer Puerto Montt's finest ice cream.

Entertainment

Pubs: Puerto Montt has a scattering of pubs and bars, including **Pub Sitges,** Rancagua 355, tel. 65/257926; **Café al Passo,** Antonio Varas 350, tel. 65/252947, and the superficially western-themed **OK Corral,** Cauquenes 128, tel. 65/266287. The **Pub Biógrafo,** Rancagua 235, tel. 65/344166, features live music.

Performing Arts: The **Teatro Diego Rivera,** built with Mexican aid and named for the famous muralist, is Puerto Montt's main performing arts venue for theater, dance, and the occasional film. Upstairs in the same building, the **Sala Hardy Wistuba** is a gallery with rotating exhibits of painting, sculpture, and photography. The theater is at Quillota 116, tel. 65/261817; the gallery is open 10 A.M.–1 P.M. daily except Sunday and 3–9 P.M. weekdays only. Admission to exhibitions is free.

Shopping

The artisans' market **Pueblito de Melipulli** is at Diego Portales s/n, tel. 65/263524, directly opposite the bus terminal, but crafts stalls also line both sides of Avenida Angelmó (as well as covering the sidewalks) west of Independencia. Typical items include woolens, copperware, and standard souvenirs.

Timón Austral, Rengifo 430-A, is an antiques dealer.

Services

Puerto Montt has the fullest complement of services south of Temuco.

Money: Exchange houses include Eureka Turismo at Antonio Varas 449, Afex at Diego Portales 516, and La Moneda de Oro at the bus terminal on Diego Portales. Banco de Crédito has an ATM at Antonio Varas 560.

Postal: Correos de Chile is at Rancagua 126.

Telephone and Internet: Chilesat is at Talca 70, while Entel has new quarters at the corner of Pedro Montt and Urmeneta, as well as a small office just outside the Angelmó ferry port. Puerto Montt's area code is 65.

Latin Star Communication Center, Avenida Angelmó 1684, stays open late for Internet access. Try also the Mundo Sur CyberCafé, San Martín 232, tel. 65/295415.

Medical: Puerto Montt's Hospital Regional, Seminario s/n, tel. 65/253992, is northeast of the hilltop Intendencia Regional, reached via O'Higgins and Avenida Décima Región.

Information

Puerto Montt offers a variety of information sources.

Tourist Offices: Puerto Montt's Oficina Municipal de Turismo, a kiosk at Varas and O'Higgins just south of the Plaza de Armas, tel. 65/261700, *anexo* 823, is open 9 A.M.–9 P.M. daily in January and February; the rest of the year, hours are 9 A.M.–1 P.M. and 3–7 P.M. daily except Sunday.

Summer hours at Sernatur, on the west side of the plaza, tel. 65/252626, are 7:30 A.M.–7:30 P.M. weekdays, 9 A.M.–7:30 P.M. weekends; the rest of the year, it's open 8:30 A.M.–5:30 P.M. weekdays only.

Consulates: Neighboring Argentina's consulate, Cauquenes 94, 2nd floor, tel. 65/253996, is open 8 A.M.–1 P.M. weekdays only. Germany has a consulate at Antonio Varas 525, Oficina 306, tel. 65/252920.

National Parks: Conaf's Patrimonio Silvestre unit is at Amunátegui 500, tel. 65/290712.

Bookstore: Sotavento Libros, Diego Portales 580, tel. 65/256650, specializes in local and regional history and literature.

Transportation

Puerto Montt is a major hub for air, land, and sea travel in the Sur Chico.

Air: LanChile/LanExpress, O'Higgins 167, Local 1-B, tel. 65/253315, flies five or six times daily to Santiago (US$138), usually nonstop but sometimes via Temuco or Concepción, or both. It also flies three times daily to Balmaceda/Coyhaique (US$55) and four times daily to Punta Arenas (US$85); one Saturday morning flight continues to the Falkland Islands.

Aerocontinente, O'Higgins 167, Local 2, tel. 65/347777, flies daily to Santiago (US$62–125), and Monday, Tuesday, Friday, and Sunday to Punta Arenas (US$62–79).

Aerosur, Urmeneta 149, tel. 65/252523, normally flies daily except Sunday to Chaitén (US$50), but suspended flights in 2001 after a nonfatality accident damaged the plane beyond repair. Aeromet, Varas 215, tel. 65/299400, also flies daily—more frequently in summer—to Chaitén.

Bus: Puerto Montt's Terminal de Buses is at Avenida Portales and Lota, tel. 65/294533, about one km southwest of the Plaza de Armas. Services are frequent to rural, regional, and most long-distance destinations, as well as to Bariloche, Argentina. Buses to Chilean Patagonia destinations such as Coyhaique and Punta Arenas, which pass through Argentina, are less frequent but fairly reliable.

Among rural and regional carriers, Expreso Puerto Varas has the most frequent service to Puerto Varas (US$.60, 30 minutes), but Thaebus also passes through Varas en route to Frutillar and Puerto Octay.

Buses Fierro, tel. 65/253022, goes to Puerto Varas, Ensenada, Ralún (US$3), Cochamó (US$3.50), and Río Puelo (US$4), weekdays at 12:30 and 5 P.M., Saturday at 12:30 and 4 P.M., and Sunday and holidays at 9:30 A.M. and 5 P.M. Fierro also goes to Lago Chapo (US$3), the northerly access point to Parque Nacional Alerce Andino, several times daily, and to Lenca (US$1.20), the southerly access point to Alerce Andino, and Chaica (US$1.40) five times daily except on weekends, when it goes only twice.

Daily except Sunday, at 8 A.M. and 1:30 and 3 P.M., and Sunday at 3 P.M. and 6:30 P.M., Fierro goes to Hornopirén, also known as Río Negro (US$5, three hours), where daily summer ferries go to Caleta Gonzalo, the gateway to Parque Natural Pumalín and most of the Carretera Austral. Transportation between Caleta Gonzalo and the mainland port of Chaitén, 56 km to the south, is improving, but many more visitors still use the ferry from Puerto Montt or from Quellón, on insular Chiloé, to reach Chaitén.

Long-distance carriers Cruz del Sur, tel. 65/254731, and Transchiloé, tel. 65/254934, go frequently to Ancud, Castro, and other destinations on Chiloé, and to Santiago and intermediates. Buses Pirehueico, tel. 65/252926, goes five times daily to Panguipulli, in northern Region X, and to Valdivia.

Both Buses Lit, tel. 65/254011, and Igi Llaima, tel. 65/254519, go to Concepción and to Santiago and intermediates. Additional Santiago carriers include Buses Norte, tel. 65/254731; Buses Frontera, tel. 65/255052; Pullman Sur, tel.

65/254731; Tas Choapa, tel. 65/254828; Tur-Bus, tel. 65/253329; and Vía Tur, tel. 65/253133. Buses Norte, Tas Choapa, Tur-Bus, and Cóndor Bus, tel. 65/312123, have nightly service to Valparaíso and/or Viña del Mar. Tur-Bus has two direct buses daily to Pucón, while Intersur, tel. 65/259320, has one.

Transportes Turismo Futaleufú goes to Futaleufú (US$28, 11 hours) via Argentina Thursday at 7 A.M.. Several companies operate between Puerto Montt and Punta Arenas (US$42, 30 hours), including Buses Pacheco, Queilén Bus, and Turibús, all of which normally begin in Castro (Chiloé) and pick up passengers here and in Osorno. Buses Trans Austral goes to Coyhaique (US$33) Monday and Thursday via Argentina. Note that these buses are not permitted to drop passengers in Argentina.

Sample destinations, fares, and times include Ancud (US$3.50, two hours), Castro (US$5, three hours), Panguipulli (US$6, six hours), Osorno (US$2, 1.5 hours), Valdivia (US$3.50, 3.5 hours), Temuco (US$5–6, five hours), Concepción (US$9–12, nine hours), Santiago (US$10–17, 16 hours), and Valparaíso/Viña del Mar (US$22, 18 hours).

International Buses Norte, Cruz del Sur, Igi Llaima, and Río de La Plata, tel. 65/253841, cross the Andes to Bariloche, Argentina (US$15, eight hours), via Osorno and the Cardenal Samoré pass.

Andina del Sud, Antonio Varas 437, tel. 65/257797, operates the bus-boat relay to Bariloche (US$120) via Puerto Varas, Ensenada, Petrohué, and Peulla. These leave Puerto Montt in the morning, arriving early evening in Bariloche; in summer they are daily, but the rest of the year Wednesday through Sunday only.

Sea: From Puerto Montt there are passenger and passenger/vehicle ferries or bus-ferry combinations to Chiloé and Chaitén in Region X, Puerto Chacabuco (the port of Coyhaique) in Region XI (Aisén), and Puerto Natales in Region XII (Magallanes). Since these routes follow the relatively sheltered inland sea, seasickness is generally a minor problem except on the open-sea crossing of the Golfo de Penas (literally, Gulf of Sorrows) en route to Puerto Natales. (For sea

NAVIMAG PASSENGER AND VEHICLE FARES

For passengers on the *Magallanes* or *Puerto Edén*, high season runs December to March, shoulder season September through November, and low season April through August. For the most up-to-date information, see Navimag's website: www.australis.com.

In addition to the fares below, reclining seats from Puerto Montt to Puerto Chacabuco cost US$30 pp in high season, US$27 in shoulder or low season.

High Season

AAA Cabins: US$1,513/1,584 s/d Puerto Montt to Puerto Natales; US$1,030/1,080 s/d Puerto Chacabuco to Puerto Natales

AA Cabins: US$398 pp Puerto Montt to Puerto Natales; US$265 pp Puerto Chacabuco to Puerto Natales

A Cabins: US$345 pp Puerto Montt to Puerto Natales; US$230 pp Puerto Chacabuco to Puerto Natales

C Berths: US$250 pp Puerto Montt to Puerto Natales; US$180 pp Puerto Chacabuco to Puerto Natales; US$80 Puerto Montt to Puerto Chacabuco

Shoulder Season

AAA Cabins: US$1,405/1,476 s/d to Puerto Natales; US$1,030/1,080 to Puerto Chacabuco

AA Cabins: US$354 pp Puerto Montt to Puerto Natales; US$250 pp Puerto Chacabuco to Puerto Natales

A Cabins: US$302 pp Puerto Montt to Puerto Natales; US$200 pp Puerto Chacabuco to Puerto Natales

C Berths: US$210 pp Puerto Montt to Puerto Natales; US$150 pp Puerto Chacabuco to Puerto Natales; US$70 Puerto Montt to Puerto Chacabuco

Low Season

AAA Cabins: US$550/600 s/d Puerto Montt to Puerto Natales; US$420/470 s/d Puerto Chacabuco to Puerto Natales; US$140/230 s/d Puerto Montt to Puerto Chacabuco

AA Cabins: US$160 pp Puerto Montt to Puerto Natales; US$110 pp Puerto Chacabuco to Puerto Natales; US$90 Puerto Montt to Puerto Chacabuco

A Cabins: US$125 pp Puerto Montt to Puerto Natales; US$85 pp Puerto Chacabuco to Puerto Natales; US$70 Puerto Montt to Puerto Chacabuco

Rates for vehicles also vary between high season (January through March) and the rest of the year. Unlike passenger rates, these also differ depending on point of origin; northbound rates are lower than southbound rates.

Automobiles and Light Trucks

High-season rates are US$270 Puerto Montt to Puerto Natales, US$200 Puerto Natales to Puerto Montt, US$110 Puerto Natales to Puerto Chacabuco, US$120 Puerto Chacabuco to Puerto Montt. Low-season rates are US$200 Puerto Montt to Puerto Natales, US$170 Puerto Natales to Puerto Montt, US$80 Puerto Natales to Puerto Chacabuco, and US$90 Puerto Chacabuco to Puerto Montt.

Larger Vehicles

High-season rates are US$60 per linear meter Puerto Montt to Puerto Natales, US$50 Puerto Natales to Puerto Montt, US$42 Puerto Chacabuco to Puerto Montt, and US$37 Puerto Natales to Puerto Chacabuco. Low-season rates are US$57 Puerto Montt to Puerto Natales or vice versa, US$34 Puerto Natales to Puerto Chacabuco, or US$40 Puerto Chacabuco to Puerto Montt.

Motorcycles

High-season rates are US$42 Puerto Montt to Puerto Natales, US$33 Puerto Natales to Puerto Chacabuco, US$27 Puerto Chacabuco ot Puerto Montt. Low-season rates are US$30 Puerto Montt to Puerto Natales, US$25 Puerto Natales to Puerto Chacabuco or Puerto Chacabuco to Puerto Montt.

Bicycles

High-season rates are US$25 Puerto Montt to Puerto Natales, US$17 Puerto Chacabuco to Puerto Natales; low-season rates are a flat US$8.50.

routes within these regions, such as excursions to Laguna San Rafael from Puerto Chacabuco, see the appropriate chapter for details.)

Puerto Montt's ferry port, the Terminal de Transbordadores, is at Avenida Angelmó 2187.

To Puerto Chacabuco, Navimag, tel. 65/432300, fax 65/276611, sails the passenger/vehicle ferry *Evangelistas* twice weekly, with extensions to Laguna San Rafael (see the separate Laguna San Rafael entry in the Patagonia chapter for details); to Puerto Natales, it alternates the older *Puerto Edén* and the newer, larger *Magallanes,* with scheduled departures Monday and Thursday evenings. Note that weather can play havoc with these tightly scheduled services, but since there are now two weekly departures this should be less of a problem than in the past.

Evangelistas fares to Puerto Chacabuco range from US$27 pp for reclining seats, to US$117/200 s/d for suites with private bath, all meals included. Cabins with bunks and shared exterior bath cost US$68 pp, while those with shared interior bath cost US$84 pp. Bicycles cost an additional US$8.50, motorcycles US$15, and private vehicles (automobiles or light trucks) US$92; other vehicles pay US$40 per linear meter. (For details on extensions to Laguna San Rafael, see the Chilean Patagonia chapter.)

Navimag's *Alejandrina* sails to Chaitén, Quellón (Chiloé), and Puerto Chacabuco at irregular intervals. Passenger fares to Chaitén range US$17–25. Bicycles pay US$8.50, motorcycles US$25, and automobiles or light trucks US$75.

Addition of the *Magallanes* to Navimag's fleet has reduced some of the pressure on the popular Puerto Montt–Puerto Natales route, though the two ships take slightly different routes—the *Magallanes* stops in Puerto Chacabuco, while the *Puerto Edén* stops at its remote namesake Kawasqar fishing village. Reservations are still advisable in the peak summer season; if in Santiago, visit the Navimag/Terra Australis office there, or else try the Travellers agency in Puerto Montt. Still, it's worth trying for a last-minute berth or cabin. Fares on either ship depend on the season and the quality of the accommodations (see the accompanying chart, Navimag Passenger and Vehicle Fares, for rates).

The recently privatized state ferry agency Transmarchilay is also at the Terminal de Transbordadores, tel. 65/270420, fax 65/270411, turismo@elcolono.cl; its ferries *La Pincoya* and *El Colono* alternate sailings to Chaitén (nine hours) three times weekly, while *El Colono* goes to Puerto Chacabuco (24 hours) Tuesday and Friday. Fares to Chaitén range from US$18 pp for fixed seats to US$25 pp for reclining seats, while those to Chacabuco cost US$37 to US$50. *El Colono* also has cabins with bunks for US$100 pp.

El Colono's Friday voyage boards additional passengers at Puerto Chacabuco en route to Laguna San Rafael (see the separate Parque Nacional Laguna San Rafael entry in the Patagonia chapter for details).

Transmarchilay's vehicle fares to Chaitén are US$85 for automobiles and small trucks less than four meters long, US$92 for vehicles longer than four meters; bicycles cost US$10 and motorcycles US$20. To Puerto Chacabuco, vehicles less than four meters long pay US$127, while longer vehicles pay US$147; bicycles cost US$10, motorcycles US$28.

In January and February, Catamaranes del Sur, Km 13, Chinquehue, tel. 65/482300, fax 65/482308, website: www.catamaranesdelsur.cl, catamaranes@central.detroit.cl, goes daily to Chaitén (four hours), Castro (Chiloé, 2.5 hours), and back to Puerto Montt; the rest of the year, it goes to Chaitén and back Monday, Wednesday, and Friday. Its downtown Puerto Montt office is on Diego Portales near Gallardo.

Cruceros Marítimos Skorpios, Avenida Angelmó 1660, tel. 65/252996, fax 65/275660, operates luxury cruises to Laguna San Rafael beginning in Puerto Montt (for details, see the Parque Nacional Laguna San Rafael entry in the Patagonia chapter).

Getting Around

To the Airport: From the bus terminal, Buses ETM, tel. 65/253133, connects to inbound and outbound flights at Aeropuerto El Tepual, tel. 65/252019, which is 16 km west via the Panamericana and a paved lateral.

Car Rental: For car rentals, try the Automóvil Club de Chile (Acchi), Esmeralda 70, tel.

65/254776; Avis, Benavente 783, tel. 65/25-3307; Budget, Antonio Varas 162, tel. 65/26-0044; Colina, Talca 79, tel. 65/258328; Full Fama's, Portales 506, tel. 65/258060, fax 65/259840; Hertz, Antonio Varas 126, tel. 65/259585; and Travi, Benavente 405, 4th floor, tel. 65/257137. Note that taking a vehicle into Argentina requires notarial permission, which local agencies are best at arranging.

VICINITY OF PUERTO MONTT

From Puerto Montt, travelers can head southwest toward the archipelago of Chiloé, or southeast on the northernmost sector of the Carretera Austral. Only in summer is it possible to commence the full Carretera Austral in this direction, as the ferry link from Hornopirén to Caleta Gonzalo operates in January and February; otherwise, it's necessary to take the ferry from Puerto Montt or Chiloé to Chaitén.

Most travel agencies catering to overseas visitors are in Puerto Varas, but British-run **Travellers,** Avenida Angelmó 2456, tel./fax 65/258555, gochile@entelchile.net, is an experienced resource for the entire region and beyond. In addition to arranging flights, ferry tickets, and rental cars, changing money, and setting up adventure travel excursions with the most reliable local operators, it sells guidebooks and IGM topographic maps, has a large book exchange, and operates an upstairs café and meeting place with a message board.

Parque Provincial Lahuén Nadi

Little native forest remains in the vicinity of Puerto Montt, but substantial stands of *alerce, ulmo, mañío, coigüe,* and other species survive in this 200-hectare park between the city and Aeropuerto El Tepual, despite the steady encroachment of trophy houses surrounded by high fences and guarded by Rottweilers.

On the private Fundo El Rincón, the Conaf-administered park features a small visitor center, a cafeteria, a short nature trail, and one slightly longer hiking trail. Midway between the Panamericana and the airport, a bumpy gravel road leads to the park, about three km to the north; parts of the road can be covered with water when rains are heavy, but the surface is firm gravel and vehicles can pass without 4WD.

Any airport bus can drop you at the junction, which is about a half-hour walk from the park. Admission costs about US$1.70.

Panitao

From Angelmó, a little-used but paved road follows the shoreline southwest past the shipyard and yacht harbor of **Chinquehue,** but then it becomes a gravel road leading to the hamlet of Panitao, where beachfront houses and a hotel are under construction. For the moment, though, the only place to stay is **Camping y Cabañas Anderson,** 20 km from Angelmó on the Bahía de Huequillahue, tel. 65/280813 or 09/6998317, which costs US$3.50 pp for beach camping with hot showers, a fire pit, and organic produce sold on site (though it's best to bring some supplies). A smallish garden *cabaña,* sleeping up to four people, rents for US$20, while a larger one sleeping up to six costs US$50. Both have kitchen facilities and hot water, but no sheets or towels are provided.

Leaving the Puerto Montt bus terminal at 7 A.M. and 12:30, 4, 5, and 8 P.M., Panitao-bound Buses Bohle (US$1) passes the entrance to the camping and *cabañas,* which are a short walk from the highway.

Calbuco

About 30 km southwest of Puerto Montt, a paved lateral off the Panamericana leads 26 km south and across a causeway to the island village of Calbuco, originally settled by Spanish refugees from the destruction of Osorno in the early 17th century. Originally a center for fishing, forestry, and shipbuilding, it now relies more on salmon farming and algae collection but retains a small tourist industry as well.

Residencial Aguas Azules, Avenida Oelckers 159, tel. 65/461427, charges US$10 pp with shared bath, but it also has rooms with private bath for US$33 d. The **Gran Hotel Calbuco,** Los Héroes 502, tel. 65/461833, costs US$31/47 s/d with private bath, central heating, breakfast, and a good restaurant. **Costa Azul,** Vicuña

THE REDWOOD OF THE SOUTH

Like the redwoods of California, the coniferous *alerce (Fitzroya cupressoides)* is long-lived (up to 4,000 years), tall (up to 70 meters, though most mature specimens top out around 40), and an attractive, easily worked, and water- and insect-resistant timber. Spanish shipwrights built vessels from it in colonial times, and some of Chile's historical monuments, most notably the churches of Chiloé that are now a collective UNESCO World Heritage Site, consist of *alerce*. Much of the Sur Chico's vernacular architecture, from the German colonial-style houses of Puerto Varas to the *palafitos* of Chiloé, also use *alerce* lumber.

The *alerce's* natural habitat ranges from coastal Valdivia south to archipelagic and continental Chiloé. Although it grows mostly between 400 and 700 meters above sea level, it also occurs in poorly drained *ñadi* marshlands. The branches of younger specimens touch the ground, but the reddish-barked lower trunks of mature trees are barren.

Known to the Mapuche as the *lawen*, the species is a national monument thanks to the efforts of the conservation organization Codeff, which somehow persuaded the Pinochet dictatorship to protect the remaining *alerce* forests in 1976, a time when any activism was risky. Darwin gave the tree its botanical name, after the famous commanding officer of his equally famous vessel, but he offers only a few descriptive remarks in *The Voyage of the Beagle.*

Mackenna 202, tel. 65/461516, is a waterfront seafood restaurant.

The municipal Oficina de Informaciones is at Avenida Los Héroes s/n, tel. 65/461807.

From Puerto Montt's Terminal de Buses, Buses Bohle, tel. 65/254526, has frequent service to and from Calbuco (US$1–1.50).

Parque Nacional Alerce Andino

Occupying most of the peninsula only a short distance east of Puerto Montt and south of Lago Chapo, adjoining the Carretera Austral, Alerce Andino takes its name from the Andean false larch, which survives both in and around the 39,255-hectare unit. Hiking its woodland trails and camping on the shores of several alpine lakes are its main attractions.

Geography and Climate: Altitudes at Alerce Andino range from sea level just east of La Arena, on the Estuario de Reloncaví, to 1,558 meters above on Cerro Cuadrado, in the most easterly part of the park. While the altitudes are not extreme, the precipitous terrain and dense forest cover make off-trail travel difficult. At higher elevations, there are more than 50 lakes and lakelets of glacial origins.

There are several approaches to the park. From the village of Chamiza, 10 km east of Puerto Montt, a gravel road leads 19 km east to Sector Correntoso and Laguna Sargazo and, a few kilometers beyond, the west end of Sector Lago Chapo. The east end of Lago Chapo is also accessible from the village of Canutillar, reached via a roundabout route through Puerto Varas and Ensenada, while the Carretera Austral passes near the westerly entrance to Sector Chaica, about 32 km southeast of Puerto Montt.

With its maritime west coast climate, Alerce Andino gets up to 4,500 millimeters rainfall per annum at lower elevations and substantial snowfall above 700–800 meters. Temperatures are mild, though, averaging about 7°C in winter and 15°C in summer.

Flora and Fauna: Designated a national monument, the long-lived *alerce (Fitzroya cupressoides)* was the reason for the park's creation in 1982. Ranging from about 400 to 700 meters above sea level, it mixes with other species such as *coigüe, tineo, mañío (Podocarpus nubigena),* and canelo *(Canelo winteri).* Evergreen rain forest of *coigüe, tepa (Laurelia philippiana,* and *ulmo* reaches from sea level up to 900 meters or more, while nearly prostrate *lenga* covers much of the highest areas.

In such dense forest, wildlife is rarely seen, but there are puma, *pudú,* gray fox, skunks, and vizcachas. Bird life includes the Andean condor, the kingfisher, and waterfowl such as the *pato real* (mallard duck) or Chiloé wigeon *(Anas sibilatrix).*

The park's lakes and river sport native trout and introduced species such as rainbow and brown trout.

The most frequently encountered form of wildlife, though, is the large, slow-moving biting fly known as the *tábano,* especially abundant in early summer. Insect repellent, long trousers, and long sleeves are all good precautions, but they're no guarantee of invulnerability.

Sights and Recreation: Footpaths connect the northern and southern sectors of the park, but heavy winters can damage them. From Sector Correntoso, the **Sendero Laguna Fría** climbs 4.5 km up the valley of the Río Sargazo to **Laguna Fría,** where a trail over the drainage divide leads south to **Laguna Chaiquenes,** reached by trail from the southerly **Sector Chaicas.**

For the most up-to-date information on park trails, contact Conaf's Patrimonio Silvestre office in Puerto Montt or the Travellers agency in Angelmó, which arranges trips there but is also helpful to independent hikers and campers.

Accommodations and Food: Within the park, Conaf has campgrounds at Sector Correntoso, at the northern approach to the park, and at the head of the Río Chaica valley. Backcountry camping remains an option, but the trailside *refugios* at Río Pangal, Laguna Sargazo, and Laguna Fría have been neglected.

Outside the park boundaries, the upscale **Alerce Mountain Lodge,** at Km 36 of the Carretera Austral, tel. 65/286969, smontt@telsur.cl, offers package tours of the area, including hiking and horseback riding. Three-day, two-night packages with full board cost US$530/920 s/d; four-day, three-night packages cost US$785/1360; and five-day, four-night packages cost US$1,015/1,760.

Information: Conaf has ranger posts at both Sector Correntoso and Sector Chaica; park admission costs US$1.50.

Transportation: From Monday to Saturday, Buses Fierro has two buses daily, at 12:30 and 5 P.M., from Puerto Montt to Sector Correntoso (US$1), returning at 8:30 A.M. and 3:30 P.M. Sunday departures are at 9 A.M. and 8 P.M., returning at 6:30 P.M. and the following morning. There are also rural buses, from in front of the terminal, at 7:30 A.M., returning at 6 P.M., daily except Sunday.

Fierro also operates five buses each weekday to the Carretera Austral junction at Lenca (US$1.20), where a seven-km gravel road ascends the Río Chaica valley, but there is no public transport along this route.

Hornopirén (Río Negro)

At La Arena, 45 km southeast of Puerto Montt, the mouth of the Estuario de Reloncaví interrupts the graveled Carretera Austral, but frequent ferries cross the water to Puelche and continue to Hornopirén (also known as Río Negro), 48 km farther south. Hornopirén is the access point for its little-visited namesake national park, only a few kilometers to the east; it is also the northern port for the summer vehicle/passenger ferry to Caleta Gonzalo and Parque Natural Pumalín (for more details on these destinations, see the Patagonia chapter).

Sights: Only a short distance west of town, **Parque Nacional Hornopirén** is an almost totally undeveloped 48,232-hectare park surrounded by several volcanoes, including 1,210-meter Apagado, 1,572-meter Hornopirén, and 2,187-meter Yates.

Accommodations and Food: The new **Camping Río Negro Hornopirén,** tel. 65/217215, has eight sites with hot water, fire pits, and electricity for US$13 per day. Aging but charming **Hotel Hornopirén,** Ignacio Carrera Pinto 388, tel. 65/217256, charges US$ 8.50 pp with shared bath and breakfast, and also serves other meals.

Transportation: Buses Fierro, tel. 65/253022 in Puerto Montt, goes to Hornopirén (US$5, four hours) daily except Sunday at 8 A.M. and 1:30 and 3 P.M. Both buses and private vehicles must cross the Estuario de Reloncaví from La Arena to Puelche, where Transmarchilay's *Tehuelche* makes nine crossings daily between 7:30 A.M. and 9 P.M. The half-hour voyage costs US$12 for cars or light trucks, US$6 for motorcycles; passengers pay no additional charge.

In January and February only, Transmarchilay's ferry *Pincoya* sails daily except Monday and Friday to Caleta Gonzalo (five hours) at 3 P.M. Passengers pay US$13 pp, while cyclists pay an extra US$8.50 and motorcyclists US$17. Vehicles shorter than four meters pay US$75, while longer vehicles pay US$90.

Insular Chiloé

The heartland of Chilean folklore, greener than Washington and Oregon, Chiloé is a rain-drenched archipelago whose wild western woodlands are darker than the Black Forest and traversed by trails that lead to secluded ocean beaches with rolling dunes. Its cultural landscape is a mosaic of field and forest, and it is home to some of Chile's most diverse seafood.

About 180 km long and 50 km wide, one of about 40 islands in the group, the Isla Grande is not only Chile's largest island, but it is the second-largest in South America—only Tierra del Fuego (shared between Chile and Argentina) is larger. The sheltered inlets on its more densely populated east coast are ideal for sea kayaking, linking peasant villages with a unique vernacular architecture of elaborately shingled houses—a handful of them *palafitos* on stilts—and churches.

Though it can rain at any time of year, summer is the best time to visit, as the days are long enough at least to hope for a break in the drizzle. On the Pacific side penguins—the ranges of the Humboldt and Magellanic species overlap here—also breed in summer.

> *The heartland of Chilean folklore, greener than Washington and Oregon, Chiloé is a rain-drenched archipelago whose wild western woodlands are darker than the Black Forest and traversed by trails that lead to secluded ocean beaches with rolling dunes.*

what was often called the "last outpost of Christianity." Before their expulsion from the Americas in 1767, the Jesuits encouraged the construction of churches and chapels that were predecessors of the 50-plus scattered around the archipelago today, which have resulted in its designation as a UNESCO World Heritage Site.

Refugees fleeing the mainland Mapuche insurrection of the early 17th century found a haven on Chiloé, creating the first permanent European presence there. Their geographical isolation took political form in a conservatism that made them the Spanish Empire's last holdouts in Chile, which only conquered the fortress of Ancud in 1826.

Economically, isolation meant poverty, though not starvation. Darwin remarked, only a few years after Spain's expulsion, that barter was a way of life:

> *There is no demand for labour, and consequently the lower orders cannot scrape together money sufficient to purchase even the smallest luxuries.*

Emigration for employment elsewhere in the country became a way of life—buses still leave the Isla Grande for Patagonia every day—but developments of the past two decades have improved the economy and reduced isolation. Ferries cross the Canal Chacao to the mainland, a suspension bridge is in the works, and salmon farming, whatever its environmental drawbacks, has brought a measure of prosperity. In summer, the tourist economy also makes a substantial contribution.

HISTORY

Pre-Columbian Chiloé was the province of the Huilliche, the most southerly branch of the Mapuche, who netted and trapped fish, gathered shellfish such as sea urchins, and cultivated maize and especially potatoes in its cool, damp climate. Chiloé's insularity bred a self-reliance that persists to the present, as its residents have ingeniously adapted native materials into technologically simple but useful artifacts.

Spain founded the city of Castro in 1567, but Jesuit missionaries soon established a circuit around

ANCUD

On a sheltered harbor that still enjoys good access to the open Pacific, the late colonial outpost of

Ancud defended Spain's Pacific coastline from foreign powers and privateers so well it even managed to hold out for nearly a decade after Chile's declaration of independence in 1818. Only the Peruvian port of Callao held out longer.

Now Chiloé's largest town, with a population exceeding 20,000, the former fortress was once a major port of entry but arrival of the railroad to Puerto Montt in 1912 undercut Ancud's economic base, and it now relies on fishing for its livelihood. Its high headlands provide exceptional coastal views.

Orientation

On the northern coast of the Isla Grande, facing the Canal de Chacao that divides the archipelago from the mainland, San Carlos de Ancud is 90 km southwest of Puerto Montt, 27 km west of the Pargua-Chacao ferry crossing, and 87 km north of Castro via the Panamericana, which skirts the eastern approach to the city. It occupies a hilly peninsular site whose irregular terrain has generated an equally irregular but compact city plan around the roughly trapezoidal Plaza de Armas.

Sights

At the southwest corner of the Plaza de Armas, the **Museo Azul de las Islas de Chiloé,** alternatively known as the **Museo Aurelio Bórquez Canobra,** is Ancud's regional museum. Informally called the Museo Chilote, it focuses on the archipelago's natural environment and

TO BRIDGE OR NOT TO BRIDGE

Thanks literally to its insularity, Chiloé was the last outpost of Spanish rule in South America—even though Chilean patriots declared independence in 1810, occupied Santiago in 1817, and finally defeated the Spaniards at Maipú a year later, their royalist opponents managed to hold out at Ancud until 1826. Even nine years later, as the *Beagle* anchored at Chacao, Darwin remarked that:

> *The inhabitants were very much astonished at the appearance of men-of-war's boats, and hoped and believed it was the forerunner of a Spanish fleet, coming to recover the island from the patriot government of Chile.*

In their continued isolation, 140,000 inhabitants of Chiloé retain a sense of common identity and cultural tradition that contrasts with continental Chile, even as events threaten to overtake them today.

One of those events is the planned construction of a 2.6-kilometer bridge, by the year 2004, that would shorten the half-hour ferry crossing of the Canal de Chacao to about two minutes in a car or bus. The ferry companies, of course, object, but influential forestry and fish-farming entrepreneurs see the bridge as a way to get their goods to market faster and cheaper.

There's a noncommercial wild card in the mix, though. In 2001, humorless regional authorities forced the closure of a website by the so-called Chiloé Libre (Free Chiloé) movement, ostensibly headed by a mysterious Chilote Marco, that called for the archipelago's independence. Concerned about the bridge's potential impact on Chilote material culture, such as traditional building styles, and the overexploitation of natural resources that improved communications might bring, Chiloé Libre evoked a response out of all proportion by officials suffering from a clear case of irony deficiency.

Region X Governor Julio Muñoz contended that organizations with the stated aims of Libre Chiloé would encourage anarchy, but he finally indicated a willingness to engage in dialogue with the enigmatic group. At the same time, a separate Comité No al Puente (No to the Bridge Committee) has asked for a plebiscite on the bridge, arguing that it was more important to devote the limited financial resources to medical services for the archipelago's smaller islands.

In the meantime, Transmarchilay and Cruz del Sur ferries continue to sail between Pargua and Chacao, charging US$10 for cars, US$11 for light trucks, US$6 for motorcycles, US$2 for bicycles, and US$1 for car or foot passengers. There is no additional charge for bus passengers.

© WAYNE BERNHARDSON

SUR CHICO

artisanal fishing fleet in Ancud

wildlife, regional archaeology, European settlement, ecclesiastical art and architecture, the earthquake of 1960 (which literally shook the island
into the present), and the Castro-Ancud railway
(destroyed by the quake). It includes a vivid relief
map of the archipelago and, on the grounds, a
replica of the city's namesake schooner with
which Juan Williams Rebolledo claimed possession of what is now Chilean Patagonia and Tierra del Fuego in the 1840s. The patios also include
sculptures of folkloric figures such as the sinister,
forest-dwelling Trauco and the siren mermaid
La Pincoya.

Open 10:30 A.M.–7:30 daily in January and
February, 9 A.M.–5:50 P.M. daily the rest of the
year, the Museo Chilote is at Libertad 370, tel.
65/622413. Admission is US$1 for adults,
US$.50 for children.

Guarding the harbor from a promontory just
west of the intersection of Cochrane and San Antonio, the colonial **Fuerte San Antonio** (1770)
was Spain's last Chilean redoubt during the independence struggles—Chilean forces finally lowered the Spanish flag and raised their own in
1826. Its cannon emplacements are still intact.

Accommodations

Ancud has plenty of accommodations—from
camping to mostly midrange choices, with a
handful of not-quite-upscale alternatives.

US$10–25: Surveying the shoreline from its lo-
cation above Playa Gruesa, **Camping Arena
Gruesa,** about 600 meters north of downtown at
Costanera Norte 290, tel. 65/623428, has 60
lighted sites with little privacy but hot showers,
firewood, and other conveniences in a residential
neighborhood, whose major drawbacks are bark-
ing dogs and crowing roosters. Rates are US$12
for up to five people, but individuals or couples
should try asking for a discount.

Ancud's Hostelling International representative
is **Hospedaje Vista al Mar,** Avenida Salvador
Allende 918, tel./fax 65/622617, marcotal-
ca@entelchile.net, charging US$9 pp.

Filled with kitschy decor, friendly **Hospedaje
Alto Bellavista,** Bellavista 449, tel. 65/622384,
charges US$10 pp for reasonably spacious, comfy
rooms with shared bath and an abundant breakfast; parking is limited. For the same price, **Residencial María Carolina,** on spacious grounds in
a quiet residential neighborhood at Almirante

Latorre 558, tel. 65/622458, turismocampesino@yahoo.com, is one of Ancud's better values, but **Residencial Madryn,** Bellavista 491, tel. 65/622128, is even better for US$13/22 s/d with private bath and breakfast.

The bayfront **Hotel Polo Sur** Avenida Salvador Allende 630, tel. 65/622200, costs US$17/24 s/d with private bath and breakfast. **Hostal Chiloé,** O'Higgins 274, tel. 65/622869, is also a good alternative for US$12.50 pp with private bath and a hearty breakfast.

US$25–50: Hotel Lacuy, on a busy one-way street at Pudeto 219, tel. 65/623019, fax 65/62-2235, jyk@entelchile.net, charges US$24/28 with breakfast and private bath, is only a so-so choice. Rates at **Hostería Ahuí,** Avenida Salvador Allende 906, tel./fax 65/622415, are US$18/30 s/d.

Recommended **Hotel Montserrat,** Baquedano 417, tel./fax 65/622957, charges US$27/33 with private bath and breakfast. **Hospedaje Germania,** Pudeto 357, tel./fax 65/622214, has bargain rooms for US$13/19 s/d with shared bath, but those with private bath cost US$35 d.

Rates at traditional favorite **Hotel Lydia,** Pudeto 256, tel. 65/622990, fax 65/622990, are US$13 pp with shared bath; rooms with private bath go for US$33/36 s/d. On the north side of the Plaza de Armas, the modern **Hotel Balai,** Pudeto 169, tel. 65/622966, fax 65/622541, servitur@telsur.cl, charges US$33/37 s/d.

US$50–100: Upscale accommodations are relatively scarce but pretty good, starting with **Hotel Galeón Azul,** Libertad 751, tel. 65/622543, fax 65/622567, for US$54/67 s/d. Easily the best in town, though, with the best views as well, is **Hotel Ancud,** San Antonio 30, tel. 65/622340, fax 65/622350, tel. 2/2349610 in Santiago. Rates are US$75/83.

Food

Most of the menus in most of Ancud's restaurants are similar in content—fish and shellfish—and in price. **Sacho,** Arturo Prat s/n, Local 7 in the Mercado Municipal, has a longstanding reputation for enormous portions of standard Chilean seafood at moderate prices—in the US$4–5 range for most items. Salads are easily large enough for two. Similar fare is available at **El Cangrejo,** Dieciocho 155; **Capri,** Mocopulli 710; and the local favorite **Chiloé,** Pudeto 35.

Slightly more elaborate seafood venues include **La Pincoya,** Prat 61, tel. 65/622613; **Polo Sur,** Avenida Salvador Allende 630, tel. 65/622200; and **Kurantón,** Prat 94, tel. 65/622216, which also serves beef and pizza.

About the only thing out of the ordinary is the **Retro Pub,** Maipú 615, tel. 65/626410, a pub-restaurant that dares to serve pizza and even some Mexican dishes. **Café Lydia,** Pudeto 256, tel. 65/622990, serves sandwiches, desserts, and quality coffee.

Entertainment and Events

Ancud has a small bar scene at the **Chatarra Pub,** Avenida Salvador Allende 580, tel. 65/622178, and the **Retro Pub,** Maipú 615 (see also Food, above).

Performing arts events take place at Ancud's **Teatro Municipal,** Blanco Encalada s/n on the east side of the Plaza de Armas.

Late January's **Semana Ancuditana** (Ancud Week) celebrates the city's founding and the island's folkloric music and dance, and traditional food.

Shopping

Chiloé's crafts offerings include ceramics, wood carvings, and woolens. Local outlets include the **Museo Chilote** (see above), the **Mercado Municipal** on Dieciocho between Libertad and Blanco Encalada, and **Artesanía Francisquita** at Libertad 530.

In January and February only, a small **Feria de Artesanos** occupies the north end of the Plaza de Armas. A new permanent Feria Artesanal was under construction at the corner of Arturo Prat and Pedro Montt, at the rural bus terminal, but progress has been slow.

Services

Money: Ancud has no exchange houses, but Banco de Crédito has an ATM at Ramírez 257. **Postal:** Correos de Chile is at Pudeto and Blanco Encalada.

Telephone and Internet: Entel is at Pudeto 219, with another Centro de Llamados on Ramírez between Chacabuco and Maipú. Ancud's area code is 65.

The Centro Internet is at Avenida Salvador Allende 740, tel. 65/622607. There is another Internet outlet at Aníbal Pinto 446, open 9:30 A.M.–1:30 P.M. and 2:30–10 P.M. daily. Charges are about US$3 per hour.

Laundry: The Clean Center is at Pudeto 45, tel. 65/623838.

Medical: The Hospital de Ancud is at Almirante Latorre 405, tel. 65/622356.

Information

Sernatur, Libertad 665, tel. 65/622800, is the best-equipped office on the island in terms of maps, brochures, and up-to-date accommodations data. It's open 8:30 A.M.–8 P.M. weekdays, 10 A.M.–1:30 P.M. and 3–7:30 P.M. weekends in summer; the rest of the year, hours are 7:30 A.M.–5:30 P.M. weekdays.

Transportation

Ancud's long-distance Terminal de Buses is at Aníbal Pinto and Marcos Vera, about 1.2 km east of downtown. Cruz del Sur, tel. 65/622265, has frequent buses to Puerto Montt, many of which continue to Concepción, and Santiago and intermediates. It also goes frequently to Castro, continuing to Chonchi and Quellón. Transchiloé, tel. 65/622876, serves the same destinations.

Queilén Bus, tel. 65/622140, goes frequently to Castro and Puerto Montt, twice daily to Santiago, and to Punta Arenas Monday, Wednesday, and Friday at 8 A.M. Turibús, tel. 65/622289, goes to Puerto Montt, Concepción, Santiago and intermediates, and Punta Arenas Tuesday, Thursday, and Saturday.

Typical destinations, times, and fares include Castro (US$2, one hour), Chonchi (US$3.50, 1.5 hours), Puerto Montt (US$3.50, two hours), Quellón (US$5, three hours), Temuco (US$10, seven hours), Concepción (US$13–16, 11 hours), Santiago (US$15–20, 15 hours), and Punta Arenas (US$47, 32 hours).

For buses to destinations other than those on or along the Panamericana, the Terminal de Buses Rurales is at Pedro Montt and Arturo Prat, but several companies also have separate offices: Buses

del Río, Colo Colo 318, for Quemchi; Buses Mar Brava, Aníbal Pinto 356, tel. 65/622312, for Península Lacuy; and Buses Chepu, Prat s/n, for Chepu.

VICINITY OF ANCUD

Ancud's U.S.-run **Austral Adventures,** Arturo Prat 176-B, tel./fax 65/625977, tours@austral-adventures.com, conducts local day tours and sea kayak excursions; it specializes, however, in extended explorations of the inner waters of the archipelago and points south on the 15-meter *Cahuella,* built in the traditional style of Chilote fishing boats but with contemporary comforts inside. (For more information, see the Organized Tour entry in the On the Road chapter.)

Isla Puñihuil

About 27 km southwest of Ancud, offshore Isla Puñihuil is home to breeding colonies of both Magellanic and Humboldt penguins. The Fundación Otway, tel. 09/5647866, otwafund@ctcinternet.cl, which administers the site, conducts half-hour Zodiac tours of the colony for US$5 pp once you get there, but there is no public transport.

NORTHEASTERN CHILOÉ

East of the Panamericana and north of the Dalcahue turnoff, several isolated villages are truly off-the-beaten-track destinations, but the government's loosely organized rural tourism network has helped create an infrastructure network that is, in some cases, remarkably good. It is almost invariably hospitable.

Quemchi

On the sheltered east coast of the Isla Grande, Quemchi is a quaint 19th-century village that began as a timber port but now relies on fishing and salmon farming for its livelihood. It is 63 km southeast of Ancud via the Panamericana and a good paved road that leads east from the hamlet of Degán.

The inexpensive **Hospedaje Costanera,** tel. 65/691230, is the only choice in town, but one of the island's real treasures, worth a detour in its own right, is **Hospedaje Tubildad,** tel. 65/691305, a magnificent hillside farmhouse with sea views four km north via a steep but good gravel road. Part of the island's rural tourism network, it's an 80-year-old structure with stunning gardens dotted with Chilote "appropriate technology" such as wooden apple presses, with accommodations in high-ceilinged bedrooms heated by woodstoves or, in a few cases, gas heaters. The downstairs bedrooms are more stylish and better furnished. Run by the gracious Juan and Evangelina Dougnac, who will pick up guests in Quemchi at no extra charge, it costs US$10 pp with shared bath (excellent hot showers) and breakfast; additional meals are also available.

In Quemchi proper, there are a couple of restaurants, including the waterfront **Chijo.**

A small tourist kiosk on the Plaza de Armas provides information in summer only.

From rural bus terminals in both Ancud and Castro there are services to Quemchi.

Tenaún

About 27 km south of Quemchi and 37 km east of Dalcahue via gravel roads, tiny Tenaún is a remote fishing village with an attractive waterfront park, opposite Isla Mechuque. Its 19th-century church, regrettably, seems to be riding a wave—the floors, walls, and columns are all out of plumb, the foundations are sagging precariously, and the next earthquake or tsunami seems likely to knock it to the ground. In the 1920s, locals replaced its *alerce* shingles with galvanized iron cladding. To visit the interior, which has a small ecclesiastical museum, ask for the keys at the house across the street, next to the fire station.

Affiliated with the Red de Agroturismo, the recommended and inexpensive **Hospedaje Vásquez Montaña,** tel. 09/6476750, is just east of the church. Its four rooms, sharing baths with hot water, sleep a maximum of seven people; the proprietors also have their own launch for excursions to Isla Mechuque, which has a church worth visiting.

From Quemchi, it's necessary to drive or hitch to Tenaún, but there are buses from Castro's rural bus terminal.

CASTRO

The Isla Grande's first urban settlement, Castro dates from 1567, when Martín Ruiz de Gamboa made it the base for evangelization of the Huilliche and Chonos peoples of the southern archipelago. Despite the activities of Franciscan, Mercedarian, and Jesuit missionaries, it remained a poor and isolated backwater, subject to earthquakes, tsunamis, fires, and sacking by privateers.

On seeing the city in 1834, barely two decades after Chilean independence, Darwin found it "a most forlorn and deserted place." Even in the early 20th century, Castro had barely 1,000 inhabitants, and its isolation had fostered a townscape still reflected in its remaining *palafitos,* the stilted waterfront houses with their elaborately carved shingles. The 20th century brought greater economic integration within the island, as a narrow-gauge railroad linked Castro with Ancud in 1912, and the rest of the country, as farm exports increased port activity.

The earthquake of 1960 devastated the city, but the advent of salmon farming in the late 1970s began an economic recovery that has continued to this day. Improved ferry connections have brought regular tourist traffic of Chileans and foreigners, the latter mostly Argentines.

Orientation

Castro, 88 km south of Ancud via the paved Panamericana, is a central location for excursions throughout the Isla Grande. Its compact central grid occupies a broad plain above the Estero de Castro, a sheltered ocean inlet, but the Avenida Pedro Montt curves around the shoreline at sea level.

Sights

Castro has a greater number of tourist-oriented sights than any other city on the island, but it's also a fine base for excursions.

Iglesia San Francisco: On the north side of the Plaza de Armas, Castro's landmark church represents both change and continuity in the archipelago's architectural tradition. After fire destroyed its Franciscan-built predecessor in 1902, ecclesiastical authorities broke with tradition in hiring an

THE CHURCHES AND CHAPELS OF CHILOÉ

Chileans have always acknowledged Chiloé's uniqueness, but global recognition finally arrived in 2001, when UNESCO named 14 of the archipelago's churches a World Heritage Site. Recognized collectively by UNESCO, the 14 buildings are prime examples of what Chilean architects call the Escuela Chilota de Arquitectura Religiosa en Madera (Chilote School of Religious Architecture in Wood). These are only a few, however, of the 150 or so churches and chapels on the Isla Grande and offshore islands.

Originally inhabited by Chonos and Huilliche Indians, aboriginal Chiloé quickly converted to Christianity after the Jesuit order succeeded the initial Franciscan and Mercedarian missionaries in 1608. In more than a century and a half, the Jesuit system of itinerant missions, with their skillfully built wooden chapels, literally and figuratively laid the foundation for the archipelago's distinctive architecture. Even after their expulsion from the Americas in 1767 and replacement by Franciscans from Peru, the style they pioneered survived.

Based on timber of *alerce* and cypress, the style owed as much to the locals who erected them as to the missionaries who motivated them. Traditionally, they occupied an esplanade near the shoreline; occasionally this was a plaza, as in Achao and Dalcahue; the size of the esplanade depended on the importance of the individual church's festivals. The buildings themselves were elongated, with gabled roofs and a facade with a tower whose styles reached their peak, so to speak, in the 19th century.

Consisting of two or three tiers, often hexagonal or octagonal to increase their wind resistance, the towers also have nonecclesiastical functions, often serving as reference points for local navigators. Except at Tenaún, whose church has a central tower and two smaller satellites, and at Castro, whose cathedral has twin bell towers, all the churches have single towers at the apex of the roof. All the porticos differ in size, composition, and ornamentation, but usually consist of columns and arches or dintels. Some are almost Gothic in style, as at Dalcahue and Vilupulli.

Normally, the church interior has three naves, separated by columns; only the central nave reaches the rear wall. A beam supports the ceiling. Beautifully enameled figures of locally venerated saints, often imported from Spain, Cuzco, and Quito, but some locally carved, adorn the interior. *Alerce* shingles of various styles, and distinctive doors, arches, and even gable windows—some circular or even, in the case of Tenaún, star-shaped—embellish the exterior.

While the UNESCO designation brings recognition, local, regional, and national officials hope it will also encourage donations toward the estimated US$2 million needed to help restore the churches and promote interest in the archipelago itself. According to Sernatur chief Oscar Santelices, Chiloé's churches are not a historic anachronism, but reflect "the unique nature of the island, its people, and their culture and landscape."

The churches in question, most of them also national architectural monuments, are at Achao, Aldachildo, Castro, Chonchi, Colo, Dalcahue, Detif, Ichuac, Nercón, Quinchao, Rilán, San Juan, Tenaún, and Vilupulli. Many other localities, however, have churches worth seeing.

Iglesia San Francisco, Castro

Italian architect, Eduardo Provasoli, who incorporated both neo-Gothic and classical elements into the twin-tower structure. At the same time, the employment of local master builders and artisans ensured that traditional Chilote elements would survive in the iron-clad wooden structure.

Now a national monument, begun in 1906 but not completed until 1912, the church has changed its colors without surrendering its flamboyance—instead of salmon and violet, its galvanized-iron exterior is now banana yellow with violet towers and dashes of reddish trim. The natural-wood interior is more somber, embellished with traditional Catholic statuary—some of it grisly renderings of the crucifixion.

Museo Regional de Castro: Castro's regional museum, half a block south of the Plaza de Armas, displays Huilliche artifacts and ethnographic materials, "appropriate technology" from the surrounding countryside, accounts on the island's urban development, and greatly improved photographic exhibits. In summer the museum, Esmeralda s/n, tel. 65/635967, is open 9:30 A.M. 8 P.M. daily except Sunday, when hours are 10:30 A.M.–1 P.M. The rest of the year, hours are 9:30 A.M.–1 P.M. and 3–6:30 P.M. daily except Sunday, when it's open 10:30 A.M.–1 P.M. Admission is free, but donations are welcome.

Plazuela El Tren: Now sitting in this newly developed waterfront park on Avenida Pedro Montt, the **Locomotora Ancud-Castro** hauled passengers and freight on the narrow-gauge railroad between 1912 and 1960, when an earthquake and resulting tsunami ended train service on the island. The route followed the present-day Panamericana through Pid Pid and Mocopulli, where it took a parallel route slightly to the northwest through Butalcura, Puntra, Coquiao, and Pupelde before arriving at Ancud.

Museo de Arte Moderno de Chiloé: Occupying airy, well-lighted quarters that once were warehouses, Castro's modern art museum emphasizes up-and-coming Chilean, mostly Chilote painters, sculptors, and multimedia specialists. While it operates on a shoestring, it's well worth a visit. On the grounds of the Parque Municipal at the west end of Galvarino Riveros, the MAM, tel.

65/635454, is open 10 A.M.–7 P.M. daily in summer, when it invites selected artists to show their latest work. In November, December, and March, hours are 11 A.M.– 2 P.M. daily, but it's closed the rest of the year except by appointment. Admission is free, but donations are welcome.

Palafitos: Until the earthquake and tsunami of 1960, shingled houses on stilts lined nearly all the estuaries of the Isla Grande's eastern shore, but only a handful survive today, most notably in Castro and vicinity. Traditionally, Chilote fishermen would tie their vessels to the pilings out their back door, but the houses themselves front on city streets.

Castro has the largest remaining assortment of this unique vernacular architecture, along the Costanera Avenida Pedro Montt at the northern approach to town, at the south end of the Costanera, only two blocks from the Plaza de Armas, and on both sides of the bridge over the Río Gamboa, just southwest of the city center via the Panamericana.

Feria Artesanal: At the south end of the Costanera, Castro's waterfront market integrates tourist appeal—typical woolens, souvenir basketry, and *palafito marisquerías*—with practical items such as food (including edible algae) and fuel (blocks of peat). While Dalcahue's Sunday crafts market gets more hype, this daily market rates nearly as highly.

Accommodations

Accommodations of all sorts are abundant, but there's a notably better selection of top-end places than in Ancud.

US$10–25: In summer the **Albergue Juvenil,** in the Gimnasia Fiscal at Freire 610, tel. 65/632766, offers shoestring accommodations for only about US$3 pp. In addition, there are several suitable *hospedajes* in the US$8–10 range with shared bath, among them **Hospedaje El Molo,** Barros Arana 140, tel. 65/635026; **Hospedaje Mirador,** Barros Arana 127, tel. 65/633795; **Hostal Chilote,** Aldunate 456, tel. 65/635021; and **Residencial La Casona,** Serrano 496, tel. 65/632246.

US$25–50: The waterfront **Hostal Costa Azul,** Lillo 67, tel./fax 65/632440, has some shortcomings, but it's not bad for US$7 pp with shared bath, US$14 pp with private bath, breakfast included. **Hostal O'Higgins,** O'Higgins 831 Interior, tel. 65/632016, charges US$13/20 s/d with shared bath, US$15 pp with private bath, including breakfast.

Hostal Quelcún, San Martín 581, tel./fax 65/632396, quelcun@telsur.cl, just US$7.50 pp with shared bath, but it also has carpeted and centrally heated rooms with private bath and breakfast for US$23/30 s/d. At **Hostal Casablanca,** Los Carrera 308, tel./fax 65/632726, tiny but spotless and comfy singles with breakfast and shared bath cost US$8.50 pp, while rates for larger rooms with private bath are around US$17 pp.

The smallish but tidy rooms at **Hotel Chilhué,** only half a block off the Plaza de Armas at Blanco 278, tel./fax 65/632596, are an outstanding value at US$14/21 s/d with shared bath, US$24/32 s/d with private bath, breakfast included.

One of Castro's best-kept secrets is **Hostal Casa Kolping,** Chacabuco 217, tel. 65/633273, an architecturally noteworthy and immaculately kept hotel in a quiet location south of the plaza. Rates of US$25/40 s/d with private bath and breakfast are reasonable enough in summer; the rest of the year, it's a steal for US$18/25.

Another excellent midrange value is **Hostal Casita Española,** Los Carrera 359, tel. 65/635186, for US$33/40. Decorated in attractive native woods, **Hostal Don Camilo,** Ramírez 566, tel. 65/632180, fax 65/635533, audiex@telsur.cl, charges US$37/40 s/d.

US$50–100: Despite its hideous facade, **Hotel Esmeralda,** Esmeralda 266, tel. 65/637900, fax 65/637910, hesmeralda@telsur.cl, has large modern rooms with breakfast and other amenities, including parking, a restaurant, and a pool hall. Rates are US$20 pp with shared bath, US$42/60 s/d with private bath. **Gran Hotel Alerce Nativo,** O'Higgins 808, tel. 65/632267, fax 65/632309, hotelalerc@telsur.cl, costs US$54/66 with private bath, cable TV, and breakfast.

Highly regarded, architecturally distinctive **Hotel Unicornio Azul,** Pedro Montt 228, tel. 65/622359, dates from 1910; a budget hotel as recently as the 1980s, its steady improvements over the years have driven prices into the US$54/67 range with breakfast. Traditionally, the **Hostería de Castro,** Chacabuco 202, tel. 65/632301, fax 65/635688, hoboston@telsur.cl, rivals it for the honor of being Castro's best hotel; rates are US$59/66 with private bath and breakfast.

Food

For breakfasts, sandwiches, coffee, and desserts, try **Café del Mirador,** Blanco Encalada 388, tel. 65/633958, or **Café La Brújula del Cuerpo,** O'Higgins 308, tel. 65/633229. **La Tavolata,** Balmaceda 245, tel. 65/633882, serves quality pizza at moderate prices.

Most of Castro's best choices are seafood venues, such as **Sacho,** Thompson 213, tel. 65/632079; **Chilos,** Sotomayor and San Martín, tel. 65/635782; **Dónde Eladio,** Lillo 97, tel. 65/635285; and **El Bucanero,** Lillo s/n, tel. 65/637260. Widely acknowledged as one of the city's best, **Octavio,** Avenida Pedro Montt 261, tel. 65/632855, offers waterfront dining with style and fine service at moderate cost with a diverse menu—entrées range from US$4 for chicken to US$12 for king crab. On the minus side, the pisco sours are a little small, and turning off the TV would enhance the dining experience.

Entertainment and Events

The **Centro Cultural de Castro,** Serrano 320, is open 11 A.M.–1 P.M. and 4–9 P.M. daily, but it also serves as a performing arts venue.

The **Casa Salvador Allende,** Gabriela Mistral 357, is a leftist cultural center that holds Saturday night *peñas.*

Late January's **Festival de Huaso Chilote** is an excuse for high-speed horse races at the Parque Municipal. Mid-February's **Festival Costumbrista** is a weekend event with island crafts, folkloric music and dance, traditional foods such as *curanto* and *yoco* (a pork dish), and liquors such as *chicha* (cider).

Services

Money: Castro has two exchange houses, Cambio de Monedas Juan Suárez at Gamboa 411 and Julio Barrientos at Chacabuco 286. Banco de Crédito has an ATM at Gamboa 393.

Postal: Correos de Chile is at O'Higgins 388.
Telephone and Internet: Long-distance telephone providers include Telefónica del Sur at O'Higgins 667 and Entel, which also has Internet access for about US$4 per hour, at O'Higgins 480. The area code is 65.

Cadesof, Gamboa 447, 2nd floor, tel. 65/63-2629, has Internet access 9 A.M.–1 P.M. daily except Sunday, and 3–7 P.M. weekdays.
Laundry: The Clean Center is at Serrano 490.
Medical: The Hospital de Castro is at Freire 852, tel. 65/632445.

Information

Tourist Office: The private Asociación Gremial Hotelera Gastronómica operates a small information booth on the north side of the Plaza de Armas, open 9 A.M.–9 P.M. daily in summer; the rest of the year, hours are 10 A.M.–5 P.M. daily except Sunday, when it's open 10 A.M.–2 P.M. only. It has adequate city maps, an accommodations price list of its member hotels only, and limited information on the vicinity of Castro.
National Parks: Conaf, Gamboa 424, tel. 65/622289 or 65/637266, can provide information on Parque Nacional Chiloé.
Bookstore: El Tren Libros, Thompson 229, tel. 65/633936, has the best selection of books in town.

Transportation

Most transport in and out of Castro is by land, but there is new if limited ferry service to Chaitén.
Bus: Most bus companies work out of the deceptively named Terminal de Buses Rurales, San Martín 667, which is also used by many long-distance carriers. Cruz del Sur has a separate terminal at San Martín 486, tel. 65/632389, also used by Turibús and Transchiloé. Some companies have ticket agents at both locales; unless otherwise indicated, the companies below use the Terminal de Buses Rurales.

Cruz del Sur, tel. 65/632389, operates buses south to Chonchi and Quellón and north to Ancud and Puerto Montt, several of the latter continuing to Santiago and intermediates. Transchiloé, tel. 65/635152, at the Cruz del Sur ter-

minal, has several buses daily north to Ancud and Puerto Montt, and south to Chonchi and Quellón. Regional Sur, tel. 65/632071, also covers the Panamericana between Puerto Montt and Quellón.

Queilén Bus, tel. 65/632173, has numerous buses to Queilén, a handful to Quemchi, and Monday, Wednesday, and Friday service to Punta Arenas. Buses Pacheco, tel. 65/631188, goes to Punta Arenas Wednesday and Saturday. Turibús, tel. 65/632389 at the Cruz del Sur terminal, goes to Punta Arenas Tuesday, Thursday, and Saturday. Trans Austral goes to Coyhaique and Comodoro Rivadavia (Argentina) Thursday and Sunday.

Buses Arroyo, tel. 65/635604, goes two or three times daily to Cucao, the gateway to Parque Nacional Chiloé; Ojeda has additional services on the same route.

Dalcahue Expreso, tel. 65/635164, goes at least half hourly to Dalcahue weekdays, but runs less frequently on weekends. Buses Lemuy and Buses Gallardo, tel. 65/634521, serve Chonchi (US$1.25) and destinations on Isla Lemuy, including Puqueldón.

Sample destinations, fares, and times include Ancud (US$2, one hour), Quellón (US$3, two hours), Puerto Montt (US$5, three hours), Valdivia (US$9, seven hours), Temuco (US$12, eight hours), Concepción (US$15, 12 hours), Santiago (US$18–22, 19 hours), and Punta Arenas (US$45, 36 hours).

Taxi Colectivos: Taxi colectivos to Chonchi leave from the corner of Chacabuco and Esmeralda.
Sea: In January and February only, Catamaranes del Sur, tel. 65/482300 in Puerto Montt, catamaranes@central.detroit.cl, goes to Puerto Montt at 4 P.M. daily (three hours).

VICINITY OF CASTRO

Several companies conduct day trips and longer tours of the area around Castro, including destinations such as Dalcahue, Chonchi, Parque Nacional Chiloé, and offshore islands. Among them are **Turismo Quelcún,** San Martín 581, tel. 65/632396; **Turismo Queilén Bus,** tel. 65/6-32173, at the Terminal de Buses Rurales, San

Martín 667; and **Pehuén Turismo,** Blanco Encalada 299, tel. 65/632361, fax 65/635254, pehuen@chiloeweb.com.

Dalcahue-based in summer, **Altué Sea Kayaking,** tel. 09/4196809, has extensive itineraries around the archipelago's eastern shore. It maintains its Santiago headquarters at Encomenderos 83, Las Condes, tel. 2/2332964, fax 2/2336799, website: www.seakayakchile.com, altue@seakayakchile.com.

Dalcahue's **Turismo Aitué,** Ramón Freire 123, tel. 65/641251, eseron@entelchile.net, arranges boat excursions to offshore islands.

Dalcahue

Artisans from around Chiloé customarily present their wares at Dalcahue's Sunday market, still its biggest attraction, but this modest fishing village is gaining importance as a base for sea kayak excursions among the offshore islands of the archipelago's sheltered eastern shore. Its name derives from the *dalca,* a dugout canoe that might be seen as the predecessor of today's kayaks, and the local shipbuilding industry still has a hold here.

Nothing remains of Dalcahue's *palafitos,* obliterated by the tsunami of 1960, but its 19th-century church is one of the architectural monuments that helped the island gain UNESCO World Heritage Site status. About 20 km northeast of Castro, Dalcahue also has easy access to Isla Quinchao, a worthwhile side trip.

Sights and Recreation: On the north side of the Plaza de Armas, Dalcahue's **Iglesia Parroquial** (1854) replaced an earlier Jesuit chapel. Built of local woods—roble, *ulmo,* cypress, and *alerce*—it features Doric columns and *alerce* shingles but, unfortunately, this national monument is visibly suffering from termites and dry rot. Only the truly devout will appreciate the vestments, books, and newspaper scraps from the Vatican in its **Museo Nuestra Señora de los Dolores Dalcahue.**

Most visitors come to Dalcahue for the **Feria Artesanal,** though the abundance of imported kitsch has undercut the quality basketry, wood carvings, and woolens that used to dominate this lively market. A few doors east, the **Centro Cultural Dalcahue** displays ethnographic materials on the Huilliche, predecessors of today's Chilotes, and run-of-the-mill household goods from the 19th century.

Accommodations and Food: Dalcahue has several simple accommodations charging US$7–10 pp with shared bath, mostly near the waterfront: **Residencial Playa,** Rodríguez 009, tel./fax 65/641397, fernanda@telsur.cl, which is also one of the best places to eat in town; the next-door **Residencial La Feria,** Rodríguez 011; **Residencial San Martín,** San Martín 001, tel./fax 65/641234, omunozb@email.com, which also has a restaurant; and **Pensión Pulemún,** on the main drag through town at Freire 305, tel. 65/651330. Dalcahue's finest, stylishly Chilote despite its modern comforts, is **Hotel La Isla,** Avenida Mocopulli 113, tel. 65/641246, fax 65/641241, which charges US$33/39 s/d.

Overlooking the Feria Artesanal on the waterfront, **Brisas Marinas,** Pedro Montt s/n, has outstanding seafood at moderate prices.

Events: Mid-February's **Semana Dalcahuina** is the town's major festival.

Information: Dalcahue has a small tourist office on the Costanera Pedro Montt, a few doors west of the Feria Artesanal, but it has no fixed schedule.

Transportation: Frequent Dalcahue Expreso buses to and from Castro stop at both the main bus terminal, at Freire and O'Higgins, and also at the Feria Artesanal on the waterfront. There are also *taxi colectivos* to and from Castro.

Ferry service from Dalcahue to Isla Quinchao costs US$7 return for automobiles, but it is free for pedestrians.

Isla Quinchao and Vicinity

Across Canal Dalcahue, a newly paved road follows the center of the elongated Isla Quinchao as far as Achao, where it continues as a gravel road to its southeastern tip. Buses from Castro to Achao use the ferry to cross to the island.

Curaco de Vélez: Ten km south of Dalcahue via the ferry crossing of the Canal de Dalcahue and the paved road, Curaco de Vélez is a village of traditional Chilote houses, some of which were moved to higher ground by oxcart after the 1960

hand thresher at Achao on Isla Quinchao

tsunami. Its contemporary church, on the north side of the Plaza de Armas, replaced an older landmark destroyed by fire in 1971.

The crypt of Galvarino Riveros Cárdenas, a local naval hero of the Guerra del Pacífico, occupies a place of honor on the Plaza de Armas, though Riveros's actual birthplace was in nearby Changuitad, where there's a reconstruction of the building. On the east side of the plaza, Curaco's Centro Cultural has a mediocre museum, but there are several well-restored water mills in the vicinity of town.

Curaco has no accommodation, but there are a couple of seafood restaurants, most notably the beachfront **La Bahía,** downhill from the plaza. **Achao:** About 15 km east of Curaco de Vélez by paved road, accessible Achao has more sights and better services than any other offshore island town in the archipelago. Famous for its February folk festival, it dates from the mid-18th century, when it was home to a Jesuit mission to the Chonos Indians.

Achao's Plaza de Armas occupies a site at the east end of the town's rectangular grid, which reaches only about three blocks inland from the shoreline. Most services are along Calle Serrano, which ends at the **Embarcadero** (fishing jetty), while its sights are in the vicinity of the plaza.

Small but professionally arranged, the new Fondart-sponsored **Museo de Achao** has exhibits of Chilote basketry, weaving, pottery, boat-building, and videos on Chilote culture. At the corner of Delicias and Amunátegui, the museum is open 10:30 A.M.–1 P.M. and 2:30–7 P.M. weekdays only; admission costs US$.50.

The oldest standing church in the archipelago, the **Iglesia Santa María de Achao** dates from 1764; only three years later, its Jesuit builders were expelled from the continent. Built of *alerce* and cypress, covered with *alerce* shingles and firmly fixed with wooden pegs in lieu of nails, this national monument is still suffering from dry rot and termites. It's at Pedro Montt and Zañartu, on the south side of the Plaza de Armas.

Several economical but acceptable accommodations fall into the US$7–10 range with shared bath and breakfast, among them **Hospedaje São Paulo,** Serrano 052, tel. 65/661245, which has a diverse restaurant menu, and **Hospedaje Achao,** Serrano 061, tel. 65/661373. Friendly **Hostal Plaza,** Amunátegui 20, tel. 65/661283, is a very fine choice for US$8.50 pp with private bath and breakfast, if you can ignore the hideous bedspreads.

Best of the bunch, though, is cozy **Hospedaje Sol y Lluvia,** Ricardo Jara 09, tel. 65/661383; rates are US$10 pp with shared bath, US$16 pp with private bath, both with an elaborate breakfast. The beachfront **Hostería La Nave,** Prat s/n, tel. 65/661219, costs US$15 d with shared bath, US$25 d with private bath.

At the foot of the Embarcadero, **Mar y Velas,** Serrano 02, tel. 65/661375, serves fine seafood.

Achao's biggest annual event is early February's **Encuentro Folklórico de las Islas del Archipiélago,** which draws folkloric vocal and instrumental groups from throughout Chiloé. At the same time, the best of Chilote cuisine is on the table at the **Muestra Gastronómica y Artesanal,** where the archipelago's artisans also sell their handiwork.

SUR CHICO

Los Achainos, Amunátegui 20 directly beneath Hostal Plaza, sells some of Chile's best artisanal chocolates.

Banco del Estado, at Miranda and Delicias, is the only money exchange option; it's better to change in Castro, Ancud, or on the mainland.

Correos de Chile is on Serrano between Ricardo Jara and Progreso; there's a long-distance telephone office on Pasaje Freire, between Pedro Montt and Miraflores. The area code is 65.

Achao's hospital is at the corner of Progreso and Riquelme.

Achao's Oficina de Información Turística, at the corner of Serrano and Ricardo Jara, keeps long hours in January and February, but closes the rest of the year.

Achao's Terminal de Buses is at Miraflores and Zañartu, at the east end of town. Buses Arriagada, tel. 65/661500, operates nine or 10 buses daily to Castro via Dalcahue, but there are also *taxi colectivos.*

Isla Llingua: Achao's Oficina de Información Turística, at the corner of Serrano and Ricardo Jara, arranges well-organized two- to three-hour tours (US$5) to offshore Isla Llingua, where local artisans produce what is widely acknowledged as the finest basketry in the archipelago. Llingua is also known for its early 20th-century church and the views from the overlook directly behind the church.

Chonchi

Nicknamed the Ciudad de los Tres Pisos (City of Three Levels) for its sheer hillsides and steep streets, San Carlos de Chonchi was one of the first Jesuit missions on Chiloé, thanks to its strategically central location. Not founded officially until 1767, the year of the Jesuits' expulsion, it managed to keep its own spontaneous street plan and avoid the imposition of the regulation Spanish colonial grid, which would have played havoc with its hilly topography.

While Chonchi briefly prospered with the 19th-century export of coastal cypress, it has largely avoided the growth that has transformed Ancud and Castro into contemporary cities. Even if the 1960 tsunami dashed Chonchi's *palafitos* into toothpicks, the earthquake spared its historic church and many houses along Calle Centenario, an area designated a *zona típica* national monument.

On the shores of Canal Lemuy, 23 km south of Castro, Chonchi is three km east of the Panamericana. Launches and ferries (one of which sank in early 2001) link the town to offshore Isla Lemuy. **Sights and Recreation:** Undergoing restoration since 1995, the shingled neoclassical **Iglesia San Carlos de Chonchi** (1900) has suffered some unfortunate modifications, such as the metal cladding on its bell tower, but it's generally in good repair.

Sloping from the hilltop to the port, **Calle Centenario** features numerous two- and three-story houses with open corridors at street level, glassed-in galleries on the second floor, and spacious interiors on the top floor. The new **Museo de las Tradiciones Chonchinas,** Centenario 116, replicates a typical Chilote kitchen and displays impressive photographs of the 1960 tsunami.

Owner Carl Grady of Hospedaje La Esmeralda (see Accommodations, below), tel. 65/6 71328, grady@telsur.net, conducts boat excursions to a nearby sea lion colony, offshore islands such as Lemuy and Quinchao, and a nearby mussel farm. Grady, who is English, also speaks German and Spanish.

Accommodations and Food: Hospedaje El Mirador, Ciriaco Alvarez 198, tel. 65/671351, is a simple place charging US$6 pp with shared bath, plus US$1 additional for breakfast. Rates with shared bath are similar at **Hospedaje Chonchi,** O'Higgins 379, tel. 65/671288, hospedajechonchi@latinmail.com, which also has rooms with private bath for US$8.50 pp.

Set on spacious grounds with fruit trees and a gazebo, the seaside **Hospedaje La Esmeralda,** Irarrázabal s/n, tel. 65/671328, grady@telsur.cl, charges around US$7.50–8.50 pp with shared bath and breakfast; more spacious rooms with private bath and in-room heating (a good idea in winter) go for about US$11 pp (the room known as "The Bridge" has the best views of the harbor). Other meals—salmon dinners are a tradition—are also available, along with rental bikes, a rowboat and fishing gear, and boat tours of the vicinity.

Hotel Huildín, Centenario 102, tel. 65/671388, fax 65/635030, charges US$10 pp with breakfast and shared bath. The venerable **Posada El Antiguo Chalet,** Irarrázabal s/n, tel./fax 65/671221, charges US$25/30 s/d with shared bath, US$33/43 s/d with private bath.

Chonchi's seafood restaurants include **El Trébol,** Irarrázaval s/n, tel. 65/671203, and **La Quila,** Andrade 183, tel. 65/671389. **Los Tres Pisos,** O'Higgins 359, tel. 65/671433, serves sandwiches, empanadas, and kuchen.

Events: Early February's **Semana Verano Chonchi** is the city's summer festival, featuring folkloric music, dance, and art, along with rural skills such as rodeo.

Shopping: Chonchi is also renowned for its *licor de oro,* a milk-based liqueur that resembles Drambuie.

Services and Information: Correos de Chile is at Sargento Candelaria and Centenario.

The municipal Oficina de Información Turística, at Sargento Candelaria and Centenario, is open 9 A.M.–7 P.M. daily in summer only.

Transportation: Bus lines Cruz del Sur and Transchiloé, which share offices at Pedro Montt 233, tel. 65/671218, have frequent services between Castro and Chonchi. Rural buses and buses to Queilén use the nearby Terminal Municipal. Buses from Castro that are bound for Cucao (Parque Nacional Chiloé) stop here en route; in addition, there are one or more Pepe Vera minibuses to Cucao (US$1.50) from the Terminal Municipal.

Taxi colectivos to Castro (US$1) are frequent.

From the harbor, there are launches to Isla Lemuy's port of Ichuac. From Puerto Huichas, five km south of Chonchi, the ferry *El Caleuche* sails to Chulchuy, with bus connections to Puqueldón, every half hour from 8 A.M.–9 P.M. daily except Sunday, when it's hourly.

PARQUE NACIONAL CHILOÉ

South of Ancud and west of the Panamericana, Chiloé's Pacific coast is an almost roadless area of abrupt headlands, broad sandy beaches, and sprawling dunes at the foot of forested mountains dissected by numerous transverse rivers.

chapel at Cucao, Isla Grande de Chiloé

© WAYNE BERNHARDSON

Much of this landscape, in fact, differs little from Darwin's description in *The Voyage of the Beagle* as he rode west toward Cucao, now the gateway to Parque Nacional Chiloé:

> *At Chonchi we struck across the island, following intricate winding paths, sometimes passing through magnificent forests, and sometimes through pretty cleared spots, abounding with corn and potato crops. This undulating woody country, partially cultivated, reminded me of the wilder parts of England, and therefore had to my eye a most fascinating aspect. At Vilinco [Huillinco], which is situated on the borders of the lake of Cucao, only a few fields were cleared.*

Since its creation in 1982, Parque Nacional Chiloé has protected a representative sample of the Isla Grande's natural habitat and wildlife, while providing recreational access to growing numbers of outdoors enthusiasts, both Chileans and foreigners. At the same time, Conaf administration has been less successful in integrating the area's indigenous Huilliche residents into its future, and matters have changed little from the 19th century when Darwin observed that

> *they are very much secluded from the rest of Chiloé, and have scarcely any sort of commerce.*

Geography and Climate

On the Isla Grande's thinly settled, densely forested Pacific coast, Parque Nacional Chiloé comprises 43,057 hectares in three distinct sectors: 35,207-hectare **Sector Anay,** west of Chonchi near the village of Cucao; 7,800-hectare **Sector Chepu,** southwest of Ancud; and the 50-hectare **Sector Islote Metalqui,** a rugged offshore island.

Altitudes range from sea level to 850 meters in the Cordillera de Piuchén. Annual rainfall in the marine west coast climate varies from about 2,000 millimeters on the coast to 3,000 millimeters at the highest elevations. Temperatures are mild, averaging about 10°C over the course of the year, with few extremes of either heat or cold.

Flora and Fauna

At some lower elevations, mixed evergreen forest of the endemic *coigüe* or *roble de Chiloé (Nothofagus nitida)* covers the valleys and slopes, along with the coniferous *mañío (Podocarpus nubigena)* and climbing vines; in others, enormous ferns cover the soil beneath the *ulmo, arrayán,* and the twisted *tepu (Tepualia stimulis).* Near its northern limit here, the world's most southerly conifer, the *ciprés de los Guaitecas (Pilgirodendron uviferum)* also grows in swampy soils with the *tepu;* the *alerce* reaches the southern limit of its geographical range, at altitudes above 600 meters.

In such dense forest, it's rare to see mammals, though the *pudú* and the Chiloé fox *(Dusicyon fulvipes),* the latter first identified by Darwin, survive here. Both sea otters and sea lions inhabit coastal areas, while the 110 bird species include Magellanic and Humboldt penguins, oystercatchers, and cormorants on the coast; the dense forest is home to the elusive *chucao.*

Sights and Recreation

Cucao is the base for visiting Sector Anay, the park's most accessible and popular area, which has several hiking trails of varying length. Because of the damp climate, wool socks and water-resistant boots are advisable for hikers.

From Conaf's Centro de Visitantes at Chanquín, just across the river from the village, the **Sendero Dunas de Cucao** winds through vestigial forest and traverses a broad field of dunes to arrive at a long white sandy beach, one km to the west. Unfortunately, violent surf, treacherous currents, and frigid Pacific waters make the beach unsuitable for swimming, so the scenery is the main attraction.

Near Conaf's Chanquín campground, the **Sendero Interpretivo El Tepual** makes as many twists and turns as the trunks of *tepu* trees over which it passes. Only 700 meters in length, it passes through boggy, slippery terrain.

North of Cucao, a longer coastal trail goes three km to the Huilliche settlement at **Lago Huelde** and continues to the **Río Cole Cole,** nine km farther, where there is a simple Conaf *refugio* with a fire pit for cooking. Eight km beyond Cole Cole, there's a similar *refugio* at **Río Anay.** Inquire about conditions at these *refugios* before planning to spend the night, and consider a tent as an alternative.

For nonhikers, inexpensive rental horses are available at Cucao, but they're not suitable for forest trails such as El Tepual and, because many of them are untrained for amateur riders, there have been injury accidents.

For organized excursions to more remote parks of the park, on foot, horseback, or via canoe or kayak, contact the Cucao-based Conaf concessionaire Centro de Ecoturismo Parque Nacional Chiloé, tel. 09/6442489, website: www.chiloeweb.com/cucao/index.html, vidasur@telsur.cl.

Accommodations and Food

In and around Cucao, several family-run campgrounds charge around US$2–3 pp, but the only formal campground within the park boundaries is **Camping Chanquín,** under concession to the Centro de Ecoturismo Parque Nacional Chiloé, tel. 09/6442489, about 200 meters beyond

Conaf's visitor center. Designed for privacy, its 20 sites offer running water, firewood, hot showers, and toilets for US$6 pp. At *refugios* or along trails, camping is free.

Noncampers can stay at any of several *hospedajes* at Cucao, all of which may be contacted through Cucao's single public telephone, tel. 65/633040; a handful have cell phones. All charge in the US$7–10 range with breakfast: **Hospedaje Chela, Hospedaje El Paraíso, Hospedaje Pacífico, Hospedaje y Albergue La Pincoya,** and **Albergue y Hospedaje Los Pinos,** and the slightly more expensive **Posada Cucao,** tel. 09/8969855. All of them offer meals as well.

In addition to its Chanquín campground, the **Centro de Ecoturismo Parque Nacional Chiloé,** tel. 09/6442489, vidasur@telsur.cl, also rents handsome *cabañas* for US$35 off-season, US$65 in summer, for up to six people.

At Cucao, in the bus station, **Doña Rosa** offers local fare, while the German-run **Parador Darwin,** just across the bridge, offers a more imaginative menu. Unfortunately, the latter was up for sale, so its survival is open to question.

Cucao has a minimarket, and it's possible to buy fresh fish, potatoes, and the like from local fishermen and farmers, but supplies are more diverse and cheaper in Castro and Chonchi.

Information

About one km west of the concrete bridge over the Río Cucao, rangers collect a US$1.50 admission charge at Chanquín, where Conaf's **Centro de Visitantes** is open 9 A.M.–7:30 P.M. daily. It contains exhibits on the park's flora and fauna, the aboriginal Huilliche, mining history, and regional legends and traditions. The surrounding grounds contain samples of Chilote technology, including a cider press and wooden sleighs used to drag heavy loads over boggy ground.

Transportation

Cucao, the main approach to the park, is 52 km southwest of Castro via the Panamericana and a rugged gravel road, almost always passable but which never seems to improve, and 32 km west of Chonchi. From Castro, there are two to five buses daily, depending on the season, to Cucao,

with Buses Arroyo, tel. 635604, and Ojeda. In summer, from Chonchi, there are also buses to and from Cucao.

Buses Chepu, Arturo Prat s/n in Ancud, goes to Sector Chepu, at the northern end of the park (US$1), daily in summer but only Monday, Wednesday, and Friday the rest of the year.

QUELLÓN

Unlike many settlements on the Isla Grande, the port of Quellón is a 20th-century town that really only came into its own after an alcohol and acetone distillery, using native woods from dense nearby forests, installed itself here in 1905. After the tsunami of 1960, most of its inhabitants moved to high ground away from the port, which is home to a small fishing fleet and, more important for visitors, summer ferry service to Chaitén, in continental Chiloé, and Puerto Chacabuco, in Aisén (Region XI). It is the Chilean terminus of the Panamericana, though an alternative route goes farther south in Argentine Patagonia.

Orientation

On the southeastern coast of the Isla Grande, Quellón is 92 km south of Castro via the Panamericana, which becomes Calle Ladrilleros as it enters town. The townsite rises steeply above the sheltered harbor. Most points of interest and services are on or near the Costanera Pedro Montt, which runs along the shoreline.

Sights

Since its opening a few years ago, the **Museo Inchin Cuivi Ant** has failed to improve promising exhibits dedicated to traditionally improvised Chilote technology such as apple presses, flour mills, and woven living fences, but first-time visitors will still appreciate it, more so if they understand Spanish well enough to read the accompanying panels. On the northern approach to town, the museum, Ladrilleros 225, is open 10 A.M.–1 P.M. and 2–8 P.M. daily in summer only. Admission costs US$1.

Less impressive is the municipal **Museo de Quellón,** at Gómez García and Ercilla, recovering from a flood in early 2001. The **Casa del Profesor,** a cultural center on La Paz between Santos Vargas and Ercilla, showcases local artists.

Accommodations

In summer only, the **Club Deportivo Torino,** La Paz 316, offers floor space with mattresses for US$2 pp. Otherwise, there are several moderately priced options for around US$7–10 pp with shared bath and breakfast, including **Residencial Esteban,** on a quiet block at Aguirre Cerda 353, tel. 65/681438, which has a fine and economical downstairs restaurant; **Hotel El Chico Leo,** Pedro Montt 325, tel. 65/681567, elchicoleo@telsur.cl, which has superb seafood and service; and **Hotel Playa,** Pedro Montt 427, tel. 65/681278, which also has a restaurant.

Hotel Los Suizos, Ladrilleros 399, tel. 65/681787, fax 65/680747, charges US$20/25. The cozy **Hotel La Pincoya,** La Paz 64, tel. 65/681285, costs US$15/23 s/d with shared bath and breakfast; US$22/30 with private bath. Rates at **Hostería Quellón,** Pedro Montt 383, tel. 65/681250, fax 65/681310, marlene@sur-net.cl, start at US$20/33 s/d, while **Hotel Melimoyu,** Pedro Montt 360, tel./fax 65/681310, charges US$33/40 s/d.

Food

In addition to hotel dining rooms, seafood restaurants dot the waterfront, with a handful of venues elsewhere. Among the choices are **Quilineja,** Pedro Montt 363, tel. 681441; **Hostería Romeo Alfa,** Capitán Luis Alcázar 554, which has respectable food but a slow kitchen and even slower service; and **La Quila,** La Paz 385, tel. 681206. **Café Nuevo Amanecer,** 22 de Mayo 344, tel. 682026, serves snacks, sandwiches, and desserts, and becomes a popular hangout in the evening.

Shopping

Quellón's **Feria Artesanal,** an arcade that stretches along Gómez García from the corner of Ladrilleros, displays local crafts.

Services and Information

Services are fewer in Quellón than in Ancud or Castro.

Money: Banco del Estado, at Ladrilleros and Freire, is the only option for either U.S. cash and traveler's checks.

Postal: Correos de Chile is at 22 de Mayo and Ladrilleros.

Telephone and Internet: Telefónica CTC is on the Costanera just west of Gómez García, while Entel is at Ladrilleros 405. Hotel Suizo, Ladrilleros 399, has Internet access.

Medical: The Hospital de Quellón is at Dr. Ahués 305, tel. 681443.

Tourist Office: Quellón's Caseta de Información Turística is two blocks north of the waterfront at Gómez García and Santos Vargas, open 9 A.M.–9 P.M. daily, December to March only.

Transportation

Quellón has bus connections as far north as Puerto Montt and ferry connections to continental Chiloé. Since ferry timetables change seasonally, visitors should double-check schedules.

Bus: Cruz del Sur and Transchiloé, both at Aguirre Cerda 52, tel. 681284, have frequent service to Chonchi, Castro, Ancud, and Puerto Montt. There are also *taxi colectivos* to Castro.

Sea: In January and February, Transmarchilay, Costanera Pedro Montt 471, tel. 681331, sails the ferry *La Pincoya* Wednesday to Chaitén (five hours). Passenger fares to Chaitén range US$13–20, depending on the seat. Vehicle rates range from US$75 (cars less than four meters long) to US$90 (longer than four meters). Bicycles cost US$8.50, motorcycles US$17.

Navimag, Costanera Pedro Montt 457, tel. 68-2207, sails its ferry *Alejandrina* south to Puerto Chacabuco (18 hours); on the return trip, the ship calls at Quellón en route to Chaitén and Puerto Montt. Fares to Chaitén are US$14–20 for passengers, US$8.50 for bicycles, US$18 for motorcycles, and US$67 for cars or light trucks. In summer, some Laguna San Rafael trips stop here.

Patagonia and Tierra del Fuego

Ever since Europeans first saw the extreme southern latitudes of the Americas, Patagonia has held a legendary, even romantic allure. Most accounts, from Darwin's *Voyage of the Beagle* to Bruce Chatwin's contemporary classic *In Patagonia,* deal primarily with sprawling, thinly populated Argentine Patagonia, not the lesser-known narrow strip of Pacific Chile (perhaps even more thinly populated) in the same latitudes.

Chilean Patagonia's exact boundaries are imprecise because, in a sense, the region exists only in the imagination. In Chile, Patagonia has no juridical reality, though nearly everybody would agree that both Region XI (Aisén) and Region XII (Magallanes) are at least part of it. Other more

northerly areas would like to be included, if only to partake of the Patagonian mystique.

Part of the problem in defining Patagonia may stem from the fact that, in neighboring Argentina, it is broadly agreed to be the area south of the Río Colorado, an enormous territory comprising the provinces of Neuquén, Río Negro, Chubut, and Santa Cruz (the Argentine sector of the archipelago of Tierra del Fuego, though it has much in common with those provinces, has its own distinct identity). The most northerly point in Neuquén province is only slightly southeast of the Chilean heartland city of Talca, which is clearly not Patagonia to Chileans. Drawing any line, though, is sure to engender controversy.

© WAYNE BERNHARDSON

penguin burrows on Isla Magdalena

This chapter takes a utilitarian approach to Chilean Patagonia. While Puerto Montt, the de jure starting point for the Carretera Austral Longitudinal (Southern Longitudinal Highway) may be the main gateway, in practice Patagonia is that continental and insular area accessible only by long-distance ferry or airplane, or overland through Argentina. This excludes insular Chiloé, easily reached at present by shuttle ferries and soon to reached by bridge, in Region X (Los Lagos); it includes most of what is referred to as continental Chiloé, south of the town of Hornopirén or Río Negro,

Chilean Patagonia's exact boundaries are imprecise because, in a sense, the region exists only in the imagination.

where a daily summer-only ferry sails to the tiny port of Caleta Gonzalo, the de facto beginning of the Carretera Austral. The chapter also includes both Chilean and Argentine sectors of Tierra del Fuego, and southwestern Santa Cruz province, which is part of a popular circuit that includes Chile's Parque Nacional Torres del Paine.

Note that, throughout Chilean and Argentine Patagonia, overland transportation schedules change from season to season and year to year and may be disrupted by weather, particularly on the Aisén region's Carretera Austral.

Aisén and Continental Chiloé

With the smallest population of any Chilean region, Aisén is a natural wonderland of islands, mountains, fjords, lakes, rivers, and forests that is drawing growing numbers of visitors since completion of the Carretera Austral from Caleta Gonzalo in the north to Villa O'Higgins in the south. The only notable city is the regional capital of Coyhaique, which has a first-rate airport and is a good base for exploring the area, but many visitors begin at the ferry port of Chaitén, in Region X, and work their way south along the Carretera Austral. Other arrive at Puerto Chacabuco, which is now an option for ferry passengers en route to or from Puerto Natales via the fjords of southern Aisén and northern Magallanes.

In addition to the Carretera Austral and its several national parks, Aisén's major attraction is Parque Nacional Laguna San Rafael, accessible only by sea or by air taxi, where the ice meets the sea. In general, the climate resembles that of coastal British Columbia, with the seasons reversed (December, January, and February are summer). Consequently, weather can be wet, windy, and cool at any time of year, especially at higher elevations, so hikers should carry good rain and trekking gear and hope for the best. Summer highs can climb above 25°C around Coyhaique, but cooler temperatures are the rule.

Midsummer days are long, with sunsets around 10 P.M., thanks partly to daylight saving time.

Thanks to tourism, Aisén is increasingly prosperous, but agriculture and extractive industries such as forestry and mining are also important. More recently, the salmon farming industry has brought both wealth and controversy, as its environmental cost has proved greater than some residents believe it's worth.

HISTORY

Europeans first viewed the channels of Aisén in 1553, when Pedro de Valdivia ordered Francisco de Ulloa to explore the Strait of Magellan from the Pacific side. When Ulloa landed on the Taitao peninsula, however, the forerunners of today's Kawasqar (Alacaluf) had been navigating the same waterways for millennia; on the nearby continent, the Tehuelche (Aonikenk) and their predecessors had long stalked the steppes for guanaco and the forest for *huemul.*

Aisén's thinly populated, rugged recesses held limited appeal for the Spaniards. At first, tales of "Trapananda" drew a few fortune hunters in search of the fabulous wealthy but literally fantastic "City of the Caesars" (tales of hidden riches persist to the present, and a small Conaf reserve

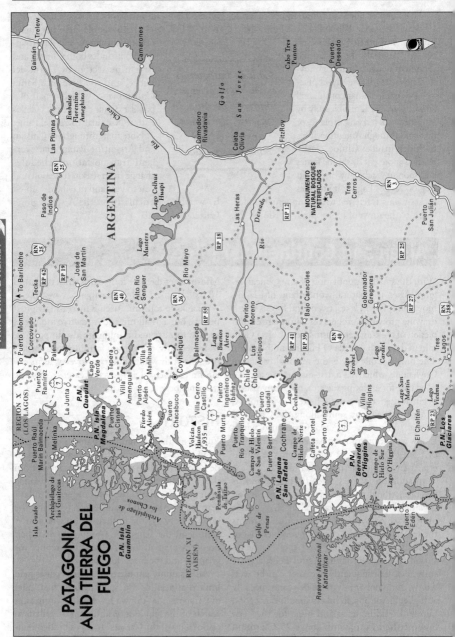

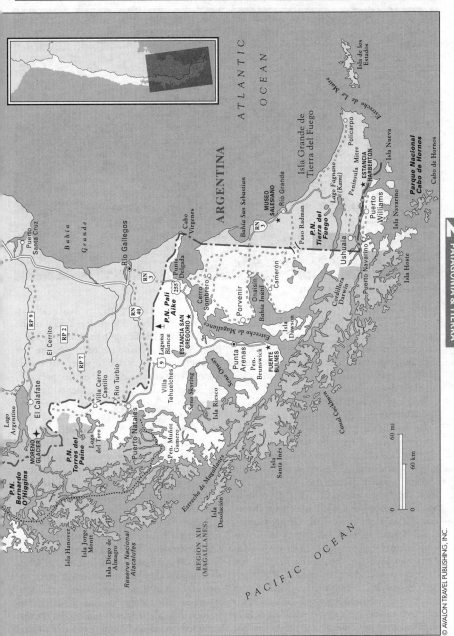

PATAGONIA & TIERRA

© WAYNE BERNHARDSON

Termas de Puyuhuapi hot springs

northeast of Coyhaique even bears the name Trapananda). After the gold fever subsided, the
Spaniards settled in more temperate areas where
they could extract tribute and labor from the indigenous population, a more dependable source
of wealth until introduced diseases reduced their
numbers dramatically.

In the 1670s, both Bartolomé Díaz Gallardo
and Antonio de Vea came upon Laguna San
Rafael and the Campo de Hielo Norte, the northern continental ice sheet, but Jesuit missionaries
working their way south from Chiloé were the region's most dedicated explorers, by both land
and sea, in search of souls until their expulsion
from the Americas in 1767. The list of non-
Spaniards reads like a who's who: John Byron,
grandfather of the famous poet George Gordon
(Lord Byron), suffered a shipwreck in the late
18th century, and Fitzroy and Darwin saw Laguna San Rafael on board the *Beagle* a few
decades later. Under the direction of Admiral
Sir Thomas Baker, commander of the British
navy's South American Squadron, the latter charted much of the area's waters, their work later
supplemented by Chilean naval officer Enrique
Simpson in the 1870s.

Spain made the region's first land grant, an
enormous tract between the Río Yelcho in the
north and the Río Bravo in the south, in 1798,
but Argentine overland explorers were the first
nonindigenous travelers to see much of the area.
Despite concern about the Argentine presence,
which led to territorial disagreements that have
been resolved only within the last few years,
Chile had trouble enough controlling areas south
of the Biobío, let alone remote Aisén. Consequently, it did little to promote settlement until
the early 20th century, when it gave the Sociedad Industrial Aisén (based in Valparaíso) a
huge, long-term concession for sheep ranching
and forest exploitation in the vicinity of what is
now Coyhaique.

News of the concession set off a land rush,
from the Chilean heartland and Argentina's
Chubut province, by settlers who challenged the
Sociedad's state-sanctioned dominance. While
these smallholders held their own against the Sociedad, both of them, along with the Chilean
state, bear responsibility for the large-scale deforestation that followed under a misguided law that
endorsed cutting and burning to establish land
title. Today, when Aisén's hillsides of deciduous

ñirres turn red in the fall, it's a reminder of what the entire region must have looked like six decades ago, before deliberate fires and unintentional wildfires denuded countless slopes and left only pale trunks scattered among pasture grasses, from Mañihuales in the north to Puerto Ibáñez in the south. One unanticipated consequence was that silt carried by the Río Simpson, from erosion triggered by deforestation and grazing, clogged the harbor of region's main port, Puerto Aisén, necessitating its shift to Puerto Chacabuco.

Since the 1970s, the major development in Aisén and continental Chiloé has been construction of the Carretera Austral, parts of which are now being paved, to Villa O'Higgins. With improved relations between Argentina and Chile,

cross-border contacts have also improved, with the side effect of pressures to open up the area to hydroelectric projects on the Río Futaleufú and the Río Baker, both of them also prime recreational resources. While Aisén seems likely to grow, it seems unlikely to attract the large-scale growth, through massive immigration, advocated by some regional politicians.

COYHAIQUE

Originally known as Baquedano, today's regional capital was at first so remote and obscure that letters addressed here often ended up in an Atacama desert mining town of the same name. After a decade of confusion following its founding in

THE DICTATOR'S HIGHWAY?

The Carretera Austral is so crucial to Aisén that Coyhaique's modest museum devotes its largest exhibit to it, and many residents give General Pinochet the credit—one conspicuous photo shows a grandfatherly Pinochet, in civilian dress, beaming at a local schoolboy. A frequent comment is that the military regime was "the last one to pay attention to the region," and one Pinochet partisan claims that "the politicians would never have built this highway. There are no votes here."

But Pinochet may get more credit than he deserves. The original highway studies date from 1968, during the Christian Democrat administration of President Eduardo Frei Montalva, and the project advanced during the Socialist Allende administration of 1970–73. Though work accelerated during the dictatorship, civilian contractors actually did more than the military.

The Carretera's final irony is that the man who finished it, President Ricardo Lagos, is the man who stared down Pinochet in 1988, boldly addressing the dictator through a TV camera: "You promise the country another eight years of torture, disappearances and human rights violations." Lagos's bravery probably turned the tide in a plebiscite that began the end of the military regime. Maps once labeled "Carretera Longitudinal Austral Presidente Pinochet" now simply say "Carretera Longitudinal Austral."

Villa O'Higgins, the hamlet at the end of the road, is governed by the right-wing UDI. Still, the entire town showed up in April 2000 when the newly elected Socialist President Lagos, Pinochet's political nemesis, formally dedicated the Río Bravo–Villa O'Higgins segment, the final piece in the puzzle.

The notoriously timid *huemul*, the emblematic, endangered Andean deer that graces Chile's coat-of-arms along with the Andean condor and the motto "by reason or force," is surprisingly common and even docile along this last segment. In a sense, it's a tangible symbol of change and openness that the highway increasingly represents–not force alone, but reason as well. The highway that began as a military exercise now belongs to everyone, and even the occasional skid off the straight-and-narrow won't change the direction.

While some of the pioneer settlements along the Carretera Austral are acquiring an air of permanence, this is still wild country, where camping is mostly free and easy, with just enough creature comforts for those on bigger budgets. Most Chileans take their vacations in January and February, when prices are at their highest and public transport most frequent. The spring months of October and November and the autumn months of March and April can be good times to travel here, though public transport is less frequent.

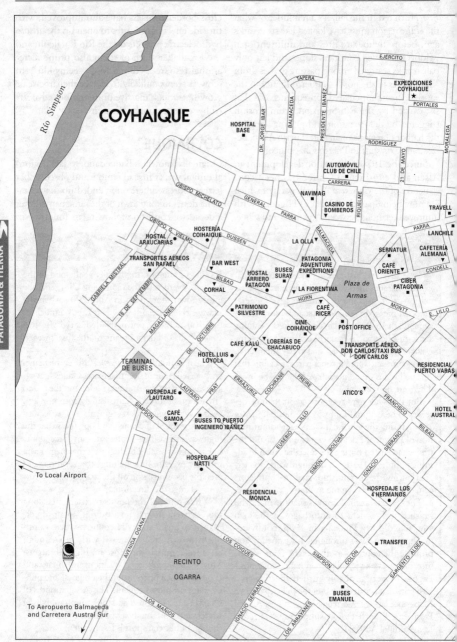

COYHAIQUE

Río Simpson

EJÉRCITO

EXPEDICIONES
COYHAIQUE ★

PORTALES

TAPERA

BALMACEDA

PRESIDENTE IBÁÑEZ

DR. JORGE IBAR

MORALEDA

HOSPITAL
BASE ■

RODRÍGUEZ

21 DE MAYO

OBISPO MICHELATO

AUTOMÓVIL
CLUB DE CHILE ■

CARRERA

GENERAL

PARRA

NAVIMAG ■

CASINO DE
BOMBEROS ▼

RIQUELME

TRAVELL ■

PARRA

OBISPO G. VIELMO

HOSTERÍA
COIHAIQUE ●

DUSSEN

LA OLLA ▼

BALMACEDA

LANCHILE ■

SÉRNATUR ▼

CAFETERÍA
ALEMANA

HOSTAL
ARAUCARIAS ■

GABRIELA MISTRAL

TRANSPORTES AÉREOS
SAN RAFAEL ■

BAR WEST ■

PATAGONIA
ADVENTURE
EXPEDITIONS

CAFÉ
ORIENTE ▼

CONDELL

HOSTAL
ARRIERO
PATAGÓN ■

BUSES
SURAY ■

CIBER
PATAGONIA ■

18 DE SEPTIEMBRE

BILBAO

CORHAL ●

LA FIORENTINA ▼

Plaza de
Armas

MAGALLANES

PATRIMONIO
SILVESTRE ■

HORN

CAFÉ
RICER ▼

MONTT

E. LILLO

CINE
COIHAIQUE ▼

POST OFFICE ■

12 DE OCTUBRE

CAFÉ KALÚ ▼

LOBERÍAS DE
CHACABUCO ▼

TRANSPORTE AÉREO
DON CARLOS/TAXI BUS ■
DON CARLOS

HOTEL LUIS
LOYOLA ●

TERMINAL
DE BUSES ■

LAUTARO

PRAT

ERRAZURIZ

COCHRANE

FREIRE

ATICO'S ▼

FRANCISCO

RESIDENCIAL
PUERTO VARAS ●

HOTEL
AUSTRAL ●

BILBAO

HOSPEDAJE
LAUTARO ■

SIMPSON

CAFÉ
SAMOA ▼

BUSES TO PUERTO
INGENIERO IBÁÑEZ ■

EUSEBIO

LILLO

SIMÓN

BOLÍVAR

SERRANO

HOSPEDAJE
NATTI ■

IGNACIO

HOSPEDAJE LOS
4 HERMANOS ■

RESIDENCIAL
MONICA ■

COLÓN

AVENIDA OGANA

LOS COIGUES

RECINTO
OGARRA

TRANSFER ■

SIMPSON

SARGENTO ALDEA

IGNACIO SERRANO

LOS MAÑIOS

LOS ARRAYANES

BUSES
EMANUEL ■

To Local Airport

MOON

To Aeropuerto Balmaceda
and Carretera Austral Sur

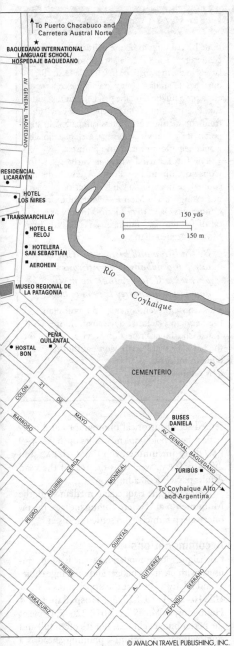

To Puerto Chacabuco and
Carretera Austral Norte

BAQUEDANO INTERNATIONAL
LANGUAGE SCHOOL/
HOSPEDAJE BAQUEDANO

AV. GENERAL BAQUEDANO

RESIDENCIAL
LICARAYÉN

HOTEL
LOS ÑIRES

TRANSMARCHILAY

HOTEL EL
RELOJ

HOTELERA
SAN SEBASTIÁN

AEROHEIN

MUSEO REGIONAL DE
LA PATAGONIA

Río
Coyhaique

0   150 yds
0   150 m

PEÑA
QUILANTAL

HOSTAL
BON

CEMENTERIO

COLON

21

DE

MAYO

BARROSO

AGUIRRE CERDA

MONREAL

BUSES
DANIELA

AV. GENERAL BAQUEDANO

TURIBÚS

PEDRO

To Coyhaique Alto
and Argentina

QUINTAS

FREIRE

LAS

A. GUTIERREZ

ALFONSO SERRANO

ERRAZURIZ

PATAGONIA & TIERRA

1929, the name was changed to Coyhaique, but it did not become the provincial capital until 1973, succeeding Puerto Aisén.

Founded as a service center for the Sociedad Industrial Aisén, its growth spurred by the colonists who flooded the region in its wake, Coyhaique is a mostly modern city whose infrastructure hasn't quite kept up with its growth—in heavy rain, downtown streets drain so poorly and flow of water in the gutters is so broad that the city sets out impromptu pedestrian bridges at some intersections. Still the only substantial city in the entire region, with a population approaching 40,000, it has a complete array of services and is one of the gateways to the Carretera Austral both north and south, and it also offers a route into Argentina.

Orientation

Beneath the basaltic barricade of Cerro Macay, at the confluence of the Río Simpson and the Río Coyhaique, Coyhaique sits roughly at the midpoint of the continental sector of the Carretera Austral, 455 km south of Caleta Gonzalo and 566 km north of Villa O'Higgins. It is 634 km from Puerto Montt via the Carretera Austral.

To the west, a paved highway leads to Puerto Aisén and Puerto Chacabuco, while another paved highway leads southeast to Balmaceda and the Argentine border at Paso Huemules. On the Argentine side, the mostly paved road continues to the Atlantic port of Comodoro Rivadavia, 600 km to the east on what is optimistically called the *Corredor Bioceánico* (Bi-Oceanic Corridor) with Puerto Chacabuco.

Coyhaique's street plan is not for the geometrically challenged, based as it is on a pair of concentric pentagons, the inner of which is the Plaza de Armas. Beyond this, it's more regular and less disorienting, but it still presents problems for anyone unaccustomed to the irregular angles of many streets.

Avenida Baquedano, on the northeast edge of town, connects the paved Puerto Chacabuco road with the gravel road that leads east to the Argentine border at Coyhaique Alto. Avenida Ogana is the main route to Balmaceda and to the southbound Carretera Austral.

THE PHANTOM CAPITAL

For better or worse, wrote the 19th-century Argentine-American naturalist William Henry Hudson in his classic *Idle Days in Patagonia,* Argentine Patagonia's destiny was to remain a desert:

> *During the last twenty years the country has been crossed in various directions, from Atlantic to the Andes, and from the Río Negro to the Straits of Magellan, and has been found all barren.*

Hudson disparaged the delusions of early explorers who believed in an austral El Dorado, adding that:

> *The mysterious illusive city, peopled by whites, which was long believed to exist in the unknown interior, in a valley called Trapananda, is to moderns a myth, a mirage of the mind, as little to the traveler's imagination as the glittering capital of great Manoa, which Alonzo Pizarro and his false friend Orellana failed to discover.*

What, then, would Hudson say of the three Chilean cities that, in the year 2001, were aiming to (dare we say?) "capitalize" on the Patagonian mystique by claiming to be the political and cultural center of a region that crosses borders and exists largely in the imagination? In Chile, at least, "Patagonia" has no juridical reality (even if the concept exerts a powerful hold on the psyche), but that didn't stop Puerto Montt, Punta Arenas, and Coyhaique from conducting public press campaigns in support of their claims to a title that, each one thought, would help promote its tourist industry.

The furor started when, in early 2001, the Consejo Comunal de Punta Arenas, the city council, sent a note to Chile's Interior Ministry protesting Puerto Montt Mayor Rabindranath Quinteros's claim that Puerto Montt was "capital of Patagonia." Punta Arenas Mayor Juan Morano argued that:

> *By tradition and history the title is ours, and nobody's adventurous phrases will change that, no matter how much authority they may have.*

The Consejo even considered a complaint to the Servicio Nacional de Consumidores (National Consumer Protection Service, Sernac) on the rationale that Puerto Montt authorities were lying to tourists.

Morano said that:

Sights

Nearly all visitors to Coyhaique's disorienting pentagonal **Plaza de Armas,** where 10 streets radiate like spokes from a wheel, get lost returning to their hotels. Bewildered travelers can thank the city's founder, Luis Marchant González, a policeman who decided in 1929 that the Carabineros' five-sided badge made an ideal city planning template. It's attractively landscaped, with many mature trees, but the landscaping itself makes it more difficult to spot landmarks for orientation.

Coyhaique's **Museo Regional de la Patagonia,** recently relocated to new quarters in the Casa de la Cultura on Avenida Baquedano between Eusebio Lillo and Prefecto Pradena, documents regional history through a large and well-presented set of historical photographs and early settlers' household implements. It's open 9 A.M.–9 P.M. daily in summer, 8:30 A.M.–1 P.M. and 2:30–6:30 P.M. weekdays the rest of the year. Adults pay US$.60 admission.

Nearby, on the Baquedano median strip, the **Monumento al Ovejero** commemorates the pioneer sheep farmers who settled in Aisén.

Accommodations

Coyhaique's accommodations scene is a little unusual, with plenty of budget and midrange choices and relatively little at the upper end.

US$10–25: For US$7 pp, **Hospedaje Los 4 Hermanos,** Colón 495, tel. 67/232647, is one of the better budget choices, but it's often full and singles are at a premium—phoning ahead is a

> *It's the community itself that determines who is the capital, because people have internalized it—the agreements of politicians and leaders cannot change historic reality, and in the end the people will decide which is the real capital.*

In the meantime, Mayor David Sandoval of Coyhaique and his Consejo Municipal (city council) put in their two cents' worth, and declared their city the capital of this questionable imaginary region.

Coyhaique's argument was that the efforts of its pioneers, the linguistic heritage of the Tehuelche, Chonos, and Kawasqar Indians, and cartography as far back as Magallanes justified their cause. According to Sandoval, "Puerto Montt's pretensions owe more to publicity motivations than to historical and geographical factors." Coyhaique's regional secretary said that the governor had been:

> *Clear in soliciting from the Subsecretaria de Desarollo Regional (Subsecretary of Regional Development) a definition of what constitutes Patagonia; in this sense we consider any argument over the title sterile.*

Sandoval emphasized that:

> *What we are trying to do is to brake the arrogance of Puerto Montt in trying to establish criteria completely unrelated to history and geography. What we want to do is sit down and talk, because tomorrow Argentina could easily pick a city according to the same criteria as capital of Patagonia, or it could be Punta Arenas, and that's not the idea either.*

At the same time, the secretary of Punta Arenas's private Cámara de Turismo (Tourism Bureau) called on locals to defend their city's role as the capital because

> *We should not lose nor let others take away this title, because it could affect our tourist image.*

President Ricardo Lagos, though, took the most sensible approach. He commented that:

> *It's better to project yourselves as a city than to arrogantly claim the idea of capital of Patagonia.*

Hudson, even if he never expected to see cities in the region, would probably agree.

good idea. The comparable **Hospedaje Natti,** Almirante Simpson 417, tel. 67/231047, is a good alternative.

The backpackers' favorite is the Spanish-run hostel **Albergue Las Salamandras,** tel. 67/2-11865, on secluded piney grounds about two km southwest of town on the old airport road. Bunks cost about US$8 pp in an attractive building with large communal spaces, including kitchen privileges, at this Hostelling International affiliate. Camping costs about half that.

So-so **Residencial Puerto Varas,** Serrano 168, tel. 67/233689, hasn't kept pace with some of Coyhaique's better budget places, but it will do in an emergency for US$8.50 pp with breakfast and shared bath; additional meals are available separately.

In a quiet location at the north edge of town, **Hospedaje Baquedano,** Baquedano 20, tel. 67/232520, pguzmanm@entelchile.net, has English-speaking ownership—with traces of Maine and Tennessee in the accent—and comfortable rooms in both the main house and adjacent *cabañas* for US$10 pp.

Hospedaje Lautaro, Lautaro 269, tel./fax 67/238116, charges US$9 pp with shared bath and breakfast for generally decent accommodations, with good common areas and some congenial English-speaking staff. Some rooms, though, are a little cramped and drafty, while others have too many beds.

Residencial Licarayén, J. M. Carrera 33-A, is a motel-style facility charging US$12 pp. **Hostal Arriero Patagón,** Bilbao 260, tel. 67/231596, is a promising new B&B for US$25 d. Try also **Hostal Araucarias,** Obispo Vielmo 71, tel. 67/232707, for about the same price.

US$25–50: Cozier and simply better than most other places in its category, cheerful **Residencial Mónica,** Eusebio Lillo 666, tel. 67/234302, charges US$9 pp with shared bath and breakfast, US$18 pp with private bath. In a few rooms, there are too many beds for the available space.

Hotelera San Sebastián, Baquedano 496, tel. 67/233427, charges US$35/47 with private bath and breakfast. **Hostal Bon,** Serrano 91, tel. 67/231189, charges US$24 pp for plain but comfortable accommodations with breakfast. Rates at **Hotel El Reloj,** Baquedano 444, tel. 67/231108, are US$25 pp with breakfast, identical with **Hotel Austral,** Colón 203, tel. 67/232522.

Hotel Los Ñires, Avenida Baquedano 315, tel./fax 67/232261, losnires@chilesat.net, has inviting rooms with central heating, cable TV, and private bath for $37/50 s/d with breakfast. Large if comfortable beds nearly monopolize the floor space in a few rooms, but the baths are spacious, the hot water abundant, and the water pressure steady.

US$50–100: Hotel Luis Loyola, Prat 455, tel./fax 67/234200, hotel-loyola-coyhaique@chile.net, is a modern, central, and comfortable hotel charging US$47/63 s/d with breakfast. **Hostal Belisario Jara,** Bilbao 662, tel. 67/234250, belisario-jara@entelchile.net, has more personality than most hotels in town, charging US$50/70 s/d off-season, US$70/90 s/d in summer.

US$100–200: On sprawling grounds on the west side of town, Coyhaique's most upscale choice is **Hostería Coihaique,** Magallanes 131, tel. 67/231137, hotelsa@ctcinternet.cl, for US$100/160 s/d.

Food

On the west side of the Plaza de Armas, **Café Ricer,** Horn 48, tel. 67/232920, a longtime favorite with locals and travelers alike, has some of Coyhaique's best food and drink, including Patagonian specialties such as barbecued lamb (about US$10) and even Middle Eastern items such as stuffed grape leaves; humongous sandwiches and snacks are considerably cheaper. Most people eat in the downstairs café, but the slightly more formal upstairs restaurant has better atmosphere, its walls lined with historic photographs of the city and the region. There is live music downstairs on weekends.

La Olla, Prat 176, tel. 67/234700, is one of Coyhaique's better (and more expensive) restaurants, but the budget-conscious can enjoy the moderately priced (around US$5) lunches. The *pollo al ajillo* (garlic chicken) is excellent, but the service can be a bit slow and the pisco sours are a little too sugary for some palates.

With a standard Chilean menu enhanced by the use of top-quality ingredients, the **Casino de Bomberos,** General Parra 365, tel. 67/2-31437, is a traditional favorite, but it's become one of the country's more expensive fire station restaurants. **La Fiorentina,** Prat 230, tel. 67/238899, has good pizza and crisp service at moderate prices.

Loberías de Chacabuco, Prat 386, tel. 67/2-39786, is a seafood venue that seems to be slumming these days, even though it's maintained its quality and kept prices reasonable. **Corhal,** Bilbao 123, tel. 67/233125, remains a good seafood choice. Stick with the beef at **Atico's,** Bilbao 563, tel. 67/234000.

Cafetería Alemana, Condell 119, tel. 67/231731, has a well-deserved reputation for outstanding sandwiches, *onces,* and desserts; down the block is its sister **Café Oriente,** Condell 201, tel. 67/231622. For inexpensive light meals, try **Café Samoa** Prat 653, tel. 67/232864, or **Café Kalú,** Prat 402, tel. 67/233333.

Entertainment

Despite its pioneer-style house, swinging doors, pistols on the wall, and cold beer on tap, **Bar West,** Bilbao 110, tel. 67/210007, serves mediocre pisco sours and plays too much insipid pop music.

Peña Quilantal, Baquedano 791, tel. 67/2-34394, showcases live folkloric music. For dancing, try **Discoteca Corhal,** Bilbao 125, tel. 67/232869.

Cine Coihaique, Cochrane 321, shows occasional recent films.

Shopping

At the **Feria Artesanal de Coihaique,** on the west side of the Plaza de Armas, local horse gear is the main attraction, though there are also wood carvings and woolens. **Manos Azules,** Riquelme 435, tel. 67/230719, is another crafts outlet.

Services

Money: Turismo Prado, 21 de Mayo 417, and Cambios Emperador, Bilbao 222, both exchange cash and traveler's checks.

Banco Santander has an ATM at Condell 184 (Coyhaique is the only town in Aisén where foreign ATM cards work).

Postal: Correos de Chile is at Cochrane 202, near the Plaza de Armas.

Telephone and Internet: Entel, Arturo Prat 340, also has Internet connections. Fono Sur, Horn 51, also has long-distance telephone service. Coyhaique's area code is 67.

Ciber Patagonia, 21 de Mayo 525, tel. 67/2-54700, has both telephone and Internet services. Aysén Net, Prat 470, Local 12, tel. 67/254678, keeps long hours and charges about US$2.50 per hour.

Laundry: Lavandería QL is at Bilbao 160, tel. 67/232266.

Medical: The Hospital Base is at J. M. Carrera 33, tel. 67/231286.

Information

Tourist Office: Sernatur, Bulnes 35, tel. 67/231752, sernatur_coyhai@entelchile.net, is open 8:30 A.M.–9 P.M. weekdays, 11 A.M.–8 P.M. weekends in summer; the rest of the year, hours are 9 A.M.–1 P.M. and 3–7 P.M. weekdays only. It has English-speaking staff and a useful message board.

Motorists: The Automóvil Club de Chile (Acchi) is at J. M Carrera 333, tel. 67/252372.

National Parks: Conaf's Patrimonio Silvestre is at 12 de Octubre 382, tel. 67/212125, fax 67/212130. The private environmental organization Codeff is a block away at 12 de Octubre 288, Oficina 205, tel. 67/234451.

Language Classes

Intensive Spanish classes with room and full board cost US$300 pp weekly at Baquedano International Language School, Baquedano 20, tel. 67/232520, fax 67/231511, pguzmanm@entelchile.net; rates include four hours' instruction daily except Sunday, primarily in summer when the main instructor does not have local teaching obligations.

Transportation

Coyhaique is the transportation hub for the entire region, with flights north and south and bus service along the Carretera Austral to Region X (Los Lagos) and Region XII (Magallanes) via Argentina, and to Argentina itself. Note that buses to Chilean destinations in other regions may not drop passengers in Argentina.

Air: Commercial jets leave from Aeropuerto Balmaceda, a modern airport 50 km southeast of Coyhaique that would be the pride of many large Chilean cities. Small planes still use convenient Aeropuerto Teniente Vidal, only five km southwest of town.

LanChile/LanExpress, Moraleda 402, tel. 67/231188, flies to Puerto Montt (US$54) and Santiago (US$164) three times daily, and Saturday only to Punta Arenas (US$48–89).

Transporte Aéreo Don Carlos, Subteniente Cruz 63, tel./fax 67/231981), flies air taxis to Chile Chico (US$32) daily except Sunday, and to Cochrane (US$58) and Villa O'Higgins (US$86) Monday and Thursday only. Transportes Aéreos San Rafael, 18 de Septiembre 469, tel. 67/232048, fax 67/233408, flies to the remote island settlement of Melinka (US$17) Monday and Thursday, and to Tortel (US$25) Wednesday. In addition to Don Carlos and San Rafael, two other air taxi companies offer charter service to Parque Nacional Laguna San Rafael and elsewhere in the region: Aerohein, Baquedano 500, tel./fax 67/232772, aerohein@entelchile.net, and Patagonia Explorer Aviación, Freire 365, tel. 09/8-172172. (For details on park charters, see the separate Parque Nacional Laguna San Rafael entry.)

Bus: Coyhaique's tatty Terminal de Buses is at Lautaro and Magallanes, but several carriers use their own offices elsewhere in town. Note that services both north and south along the Carretera Austral are most frequent in summer and may be considerably reduced in winter.

To Puerto Aisén (US$1.50) and Puerto Chacabuco (US$2, one hour), there are frequent departures with Buses Suray, Arturo Prat 265, tel. 67/238387, and Buses Don Carlos, Subteniente Cruz 63, tel. 67/231981.

Providing service along the Carretera Austral Norte, Buses São Paulo, at the main terminal, tel. 67/254369, goes north to Mañihuales daily at 1 P.M. via the paved Viviana junction, and to destinations off the Carretera Austral such as Villa Ortega and La Tapera. Buses El Pilchero, also at the main terminal, tel. 67/239218, goes to Villa Amengual, Puerto Cisnes, Puerto Puyuhuapi, La Junta, and Lago Verde Tuesday and Saturday at 8 A.M. Buses Daniela, Baquedano 1122, tel. 67/231701, serves the same route Tuesday and Friday at 10 A.M., and it goes to Chaitén Monday, Wednesday, and Saturday at 8 A.M.

Buses Norte, General Parra 337, tel. 67/232167, goes north to Chaitén and intermediates four times weekly at 8 A.M.; at the same office, Buses Becker goes to Chaitén on alternate days, while B y V Tour goes Monday and Thursday. Buses Basoli, at the same address, goes to Cisnes Wednesday and Saturday at 1 P.M. Buses Emanuel, Simpson 829, tel. 67/231555, goes to Chaitén Tuesday, Friday, and Sunday.

Sample northbound destinations and fares along the Carretera Austral include Mañihuales (US$4), Villa Amengual (US$7), Puerto Cisnes (US$9, six hours) Puerto Puyuhuapi (US$12, six hours), La Junta (US$13), Santa Lucía (US$20), and Chaitén (US$25, 12 hours).

Providing service along the Carretera Austral Sur, minibuses to Puerto Ibáñez (US$6), the ferry port for Chile Chico on the north shore of Lago General Carrera, leave from the corner of Prat and Errázuriz. Among the carriers are Colectivo Puerto Ibáñez, tel. 67/251073; Transportes Ali, tel. 67/250346; and Minibus Don Tito, tel. 67/250280.

At the main terminal, Buses Los Ñadis, tel. 67/254369, goes to Cochrane and intermediates at 10 A.M. Tuesday, Thursday, and Sunday; Acuario 13, also at the terminal, tel. 67/232067, covers the same route Wednesday, Friday, and Saturday, while Buses Don Carlos goes Tuesday and Saturday morning at 8:30 A.M.

Bus Vidal, also at the main terminal, goes to Villa Cerro Castillo, Bahía Murta, and Puerto Río Tranquilo Tuesday and Saturday.

Fares for southbound destinations include Villa Cerro Castillo (US$4), Bahía Murta (US$8), Puerto Río Tranquilo (US$9), Puerto Guadal (US$), Puerto Bertrand (US$13), and Cochrane (US$17).

Interregional buses include Turibús, Baquedano 1171, tel. 67/231333, which goes to Puerto Montt (US$30) Tuesday and Saturday at 5 P.M. for Osorno and Puerto Montt via Argentina. Bus Sur, at the main terminal, tel. 67/211460, goes to Punta Arenas, also via Argentina, Tuesday and Friday (US$42, 20 hours).

International buses include Buses Giobbi, at the main terminal, tel. 67/232067, which has Monday and Saturday buses to Comodoro Rivadavia, Argentina (US$25) at 9:30 A.M. Turibús goes to Comodoro Sunday and Thursday at 11 A.M.

Sea: Coyhaique is obviously not a seaport, but the two ferry companies that sail out of Puerto Chacabuco have offices here: Navimag at Presidente Ibáñez 347, Oficina 1, tel. 67/223306, fax 67/233386, and Transmarchilay at General Parra 86, tel. 67/231971, fax 67/232700.

Turismo Skorpios, which operates luxury cruises from Puerto Chacabuco to Parque Nacional Laguna San Rafael, has a local office at General Parra 21, tel. 67/213755.

Getting Around

To the Airport: Taxis to Aeropuerto Teniente Vidal are cheap enough for about US$4. To the commercial Aeropuerto Balmaceda, about 45 minutes away via a smooth paved highway, there are several door-to-door minivan services for about US$3: Transfer, Lautaro 828, tel. 67/233030; Ildefonso Millalonco, 12 de Octubre 135, tel. 67/236718; and Travell, at Moraleda and General Parra, tel./fax 67/230010.

Car Rental: Even budget travelers often indulge themselves on car rentals in Aisén, since public transport is less frequent than in other parts of Chile and some sights are off the main north-south route. Among Coyhaique's several rental agencies are the Automóvil Club de Chile (Acchi), J. M. Carrera 333, tel. 67/251337,

67/231648, or 09/3184276; **Automotora Traeger,** Baquedano 457, tel. 67/231648, fax 67/231946; **Automundo,** Bilbao 510, tel. 67/231621, fax 67/231794; **Ricer Rent a Car,** Horn 48, tel./fax 67/232920; and **Turismo Prado,** 21 de Mayo 417, tel./fax 67/231271.

VICINITY OF COYHAIQUE

Coyhaique makes a great base for outdoor recreation such as hiking, fishing, and even winter skiing. Fishing probably tops the list, as the season runs from November to May in the region's abundant lakes and rivers.

Among the reliable operators are **Aisén Bridges Travel,** tel./fax 67/233302, lbridges@ aisen.cl, which is on the outskirts of town and is easiest to contact by phone (English spoken); fly-fishing specialists **Expediciones Coyhaique,** Portales 195, tel./fax 67/232300; U.S.-run, Puerto Bertrand-based **Patagonia Adventure Expeditions,** Dusen 357, tel./fax 67/219894, which also offers rafting and kayaking on the Río Simpson; **Patagonia Viva Turismo,** Horn 40, Local 11, tel./fax 67/232920, tel. 67/237950, ricer@hotmail.com; and U.S.-Chilean **Salvaje Corazón,** tel. 67/211488, fax 67/237490, website: www.salvajecorazon.com, cado@salvajecorazon.com, also best contacted by phone (English, Hebrew, Portuguese, and some French also spoken).

Reserva Nacional Coyhaique

Few cities anywhere in the world have so much wild country so near as this mountainous 2,676-hectare reserve, with its top-of-the-world views of Coyhaique, Cerro Macay, and Cerro Castillo to the south, the Río Simpson valley to the west, and even the Patagonian plains stretching away to the east. Local residents enjoy their weekend picnics and barbecues here, only five km north of town, but there's always space away from the crowds and during the week it's almost empty.

Geography and Climate: Altitudes in the reserve range from 400 meters to 1,361 meters on the summit of Cerro Cinchao. More than a meter of rain and snow falls throughout the year, but

summers are mild and fairly dry, with an average temperature of 12°C.

Flora and Fauna: While the reserve is wild and almost undeveloped, it's not exactly pristine. Forests of *coigüe (Nothofagus betuloides)* and *lenga (Nothofagus pumilio)* blanket the hillsides, but plantations of exotic pines and larches have replaced some of the native forest devastated in the 1940s. So close to the city, birds are the most conspicuous wildlife.

Sights and Recreation: The reserve's main sights are literally that—the seemingly infinite panoramas in nearly every direction. It's possible to get different perspectives on those panoramas on nature trails such as the 800-meter **Sendero Laguna Verde,** the four-km **Sendero Laguna Venus,** and the **Sendero Las Piedras,** which leads to the summit of Cerro Cinchao.

Accommodations: Most visitors stay in the city, but Conaf, tel. 67/231065 in Coyhaique, has a rustic six-site campground at **Laguna Verde** and a 10-siter at **Casa Bruja.** Each charges US$6 for up to six people; two of the Laguna Verde sites have roofed shelters. All sites have picnic tables, fresh water, and fire pits; the Casa Bruja site has toilets and hot showers. Bring as much food as necessary for the duration.

Information: At the park entrance, Conaf collects an admission fee of US$1 for adults, US$.30 for children.

Transportation: Three km north of Coyhaique via the paved highway to Puerto Chacabuco, a dirt lateral climbs steeply east to Reserva Nacional Coyhaique. The road itself is passable for most vehicles in summer, but difficult or impossible with rain. It's close enough to the city, though, that anyone in decent physical condition should be able to walk from the highway to the park entrance in about half an hour.

Monumento Natural Dos Lagunas

East of Coyhaique, international Ruta 240 is no longer the main road to the Argentine border at Coyhaique Alto, but it still passes **Laguna El Toro** and **Laguna Escondida,** which shelter grebes, black-necked swans, and other wild waterfowl in this 181-hectare unit on the edge of the Patagonian steppe. Conaf rangers charge US$1 admission for adults, US$.30 for children, and rent six camp-sites for US$6 each for up to six people.

Centro de Ski El Fraile

One of Chile's most obscure ski resorts, the Centro de Ski El Fraile, tel. 67/231690, is 29 km south of Coihaique via the Carretera Austral and an eastbound gravel road. It's a small area, with only two lifts and five runs up to two km long, but the snow quality is good, with options for skiers of all abilities.

Facilities include a café and rental equipment shop. Transportation is available by reservation through Buses Norte, tel. 67/232788, General Parra 337, Coyhaique.

Reserva Nacional Río Simpson

Northwest of Coyhaique, midway to Puerto Chacabuco, paved Ruta 240 passes through the valley of the Río Simpson, flanked by the steep walls and canyons that form this 41,634-hectare forest reserve.

Geography and Climate: Altitudes are only about 100 meters along the river itself, but rise to 1,878 meters in the cordillera. Because the elevations are mostly lower than Reserva Nacional Coyhaique, the weather is milder (averaging around 15–17°C in summer), but it's also wetter, as Pacific storms drop up to 2,500 millimeters of rainfall on their way inland.

Flora and Fauna: Like Reserva Nacional Coyhaique, Río Simpson's forests consist largely of native southern beeches (*Nothofagus* spp.), but the heavy rainfall fosters a verdant undergrowth of ferns, fuchsias, and similar species. *Huemules* are found in the more remote areas, as are puma and *pudú*, along with many birds, including the Andean condor. Bird species, however, diminish in the autumn and winter, returning in the spring.

Sights and Recreation: Opposite the Centro de Visitantes, look for the **Cascada La Virgen,** a waterfall that plunges vertically through intense greenery on the north side of the highway. At the visitor center itself, a trail descends to beach, where both swimming and fishing are possible.

Accommodations: At Km 32 of Ruta 240, five km east of park headquarters, Conaf's eight-site **Camping San Sebastián** now has bath-rooms with hot water. Rates are US$6 for up to six people.

Information: Conaf's Centro de Visitantes, at Km 37 of Ruta 240, boasts a small natural history museum (admission US$.50) and botanical garden. The visitor center was due to move to a new location at Las Chimeneas, at Km 30, but the work had not begun as yet.

Transportation: From Coyhaique, any Suray or Don Carlos bus will drop passengers at the campground, museum, or anywhere along the route.

Puerto Chacabuco

The forests destroyed by fire in the 1940s were more than just embellishments on Aisén's landscape; their dense foliage soften the impact of heavy storms on the hillsides and impeded soil erosion. One side effect of this fire-fed devastation was to increase the sediment load of the Río Simpson and silt up the harbor at Puerto Aisén, forcing authorities to build new port facilities at Puerto Chacabuco, 14 km west.

Now the main maritime gateway to the region, Puerto Chacabuco is also the departure point for trips and cruises to Parque Nacional Laguna San Rafael, and a stop on some voyages between Puerto Montt and Puerto Natales.

Accommodations and Food: Just beyond the port, the so-so **Hotel Moraleda,** O'Higgins 82, tel. 67/351155, is cheap for US$7 pp. The significantly superior **Hotel Loberías de Aisén,** J. M. Carrera 50, tel. 67/351112, fax 67/341188, mercado@mi.terra.cl, charging US$62/85 s/d, is also the best place to eat, and not excessively expensive.

Transportation: Buses shuttle frequently between Puerto Chacabuco and Coyhaique, 82 km to the east via Ruta 240.

Puerto Chacabuco's Terminal de Transbordadores (ferry terminal) is part of the port complex. Both long-distance ferries and excursions to Parque Nacional Laguna San Rafael leave from here (for details of services to and from Laguna San Rafael, see the separate entry below). Frequencies may vary between summer and the rest of the year.

Navimag, tel. 67/351111, fax 67/351192, operates passenger/vehicle ferries between Puerto Montt, Quellón, Puerto Chacabuco, and Puerto

Natales. Its new vessel *Magallanes* now stops here on its weekly runs between Puerto Montt and Puerto Natales and back, making it possible to visit both Aisén and Magallanes (Region XII) without having to backtrack to or from Puerto Montt. Navimag also operates the ferry *Evangelistas* to and from Puerto Montt, with extensions to Laguna San Rafael, and the ferry *Alejandrina* to Quellón, on the Isla Grande de Chiloé, less frequently. (For fares on these routes, see the chart Navimag Passenger and Vehicle Fares and the Quellón entry in the Sur Chico chapter.)

Transmarchilay, tel./fax 67/351144, sails the roll-on, roll-off ferry *El Colono* between Puerto Montt and Puerto Chacabuco. (For fares, see the Transportation entry for Puerto Montt in the Sur Chico chapter.)

Besides Navimag and Transmarchilay, several luxury cruise ships and catamarans visit Laguna San Rafael (see the following entry for details).

PARQUE NACIONAL LAGUNA SAN RAFAEL

Flowing ice meets frigid sea at Parque Nacional Laguna San Rafael, where frozen pinnacles tumble from the crackling western face of Ventisquero San Rafael, a 60-meter-high glacier of the Campo de Hielo Norte, the sprawling northern continental ice field, to become floating icebergs. Misleadingly named Laguna San Rafael itself is really an ocean inlet, though its salinity is relatively low as the icebergs slowly thaw and the receding glacier discharges quantities of fresh water into it.

One of Chile's largest national parks, encompassing 1,742,000 hectares of rugged terrain, Laguna San Rafael is also a UNESCO World Biosphere Reserve for its extraordinary scenery. While remote from any settlement, it's a popular summer excursion for both Chileans and foreigners, and it's accessible throughout the year.

History

For an area so thinly populated and so rarely visited, Laguna San Rafael has an impressive history. The first European to visit was the Spaniard Bartolomé Díaz Gallardo, who crossed the low-lying Istmo de Ofqui (Isthmus of Ofqui) from the Golfo de Penas. Jesuit missionaries visited the area in 1766 and 1767, bestowing its present name, but their order was expelled from the continent soon afterward.

During the voyage of the Beagle, Darwin made observations on Laguna San Rafael, and naval officer Enrique Simpson delivered the first comprehensive report to the Chilean government in 1871. Nearly seven decades later, in 1940, the government started work on a canal across the isthmus to improve communications with the far south but soon gave up the project. In 1959, it declared the area a national park, but as late as the 1980s it entertained proposals to build a road to facilitate cargo transshipments between ships.

Geography and Climate

Laguna San Rafael is about 225 km southwest of Puerto Chacabuco by sea via a series of narrow longitudinal channels but only about 190 km from Coyhaique as the crow flies. To the east rises the rugged Patagonian mainland, while the Archipiélago de Chonos, with its myriad islands, and the Península de Taitao lie to the west.

Altitudes range from sea level to 4,058-meter Monte San Valentín, the southern Andes' highest peak. Temperatures are relatively mild at sea level, averaging about 8°C, with upward of 2,500 millimeters of rainfall per annum; at higher elevations, however, precipitation doubles, temperatures are much colder, and the resulting snowfall feeds 19 major glaciers that form the 300,000-hectare Campo de Hielo Norte. Seemingly endless Pacific storms darken the skies for weeks on end, but when the overcast lifts the views are spectacular.

Flora and Fauna

In areas not covered by ice, up to about 700 meters, grows mixed Valdivian forest so dense that, in Darwin's words:

> *Our faces, hands and shin-bones all bore witness to the maltreatment we received, in attempting to penetrate their forbidding recesses.*

The main tree species are two species of *coigüe*, *Nothofagus dombeyii* and *Nothofagus nitida*, *mañío*

PATAGONIA & TIERRA

macho (Podocarpus nubigena), tepu (Tepualia stimulais), and other species, with a dense understory of shrubs, ferns, mosses, and vines. Above 700 meters, there is almost equally dense forest of *lenga (Nothofagus pumilio)* and *ñirre (Nothofagus antarctica),* with occasional specimens of the coniferous Guaiteca cypress *(Pilgerodendron uviferum).*

Most of the easily visible wildlife congregates around the shoreline, beginning with eye-catching seabirds such as the flightless steamer duck *(Tachyeres pteneres),* Magellanic penguin *(Spheniscus magellanicus),* the soaring black-browed and sooty albatrosses *(Diomedea melanophris* and *Phoebetria palpebrata),* and various species of gulls. Marine mammals include the southern elephant seal *(Mirounga leonina),* southern sea lion *(Otaria flavescens),* and the southern sea otter *(Lutra felina).*

Forest-dwelling animals are harder to see, but mammals such as *pudú* and *huemul* graze the uplands, while foxes and pumas prowl for their prey.

Sights and Recreation

Calving off the face of **Ventisquero San Rafael,** deep indigo icebergs bob and drift in the waters of **Laguna San Rafael,** a nearly circular body of water measuring nine km at its widest and six km at its narrowest, connected to the southern canals by the narrow Río Témpanos. The world's lowest latitude tidewater glacier, Ventisquero San Rafael may not be for much longer, as its retreating face may be a casualty of global warming. Since 1960, it has been in continuous retreat.

Few visitors actually set foot in the park, as most arrive by ferry or catamaran, transferring to smaller craft to approach the glacier's face and navigate among the icebergs. Those who do manage to land and stay a while can hike the **Sendero al Ventisquero,** which leads through seven km of evergreen forest to a glacial overlook.

Accommodations and Food

Conaf's three-site **Camping Laguna Caiquenes,** at park headquarters, charges US$3 per site; no campfires are permitted, however. Its **Casa de**

Huéspedes Laguna Caiquenes offers accommodations with kitchen for US$100, including park admission, for up to six people. For reservations, contact Conaf's Patrimonio Silvestre office at 12 de Octubre 382, Coyhaique, tel. 67/212125, fax 67/212130.

No supplies except fresh water are available, so bring everything from Coyhaique or Puerto Chacabuco. Both ferries and catamarans feed their passengers, the latter usually with an open bar as well.

Information

Conaf's administration and ranger station is on the northeastern shore of Laguna San Rafael. Anyone who literally sets foot in the park pays a US$4 admission fee, but boat passengers do not, as the offshore waters fall under naval rather than Conaf jurisdiction.

Transportation

Still the only practical means of reaching the park, air and sea transportation both have their drawbacks—air travel is expensive and fleeting, while sea travel can be moderately priced but slow, or relatively fast and expensive. From the town of Puerto Río Tranquilo, on the north arm of Lago General Carrera, a new gravel road is advancing slowly toward Bahía Exploradores, only about 65 km north of the glacier, but its completion will not eliminate the need for boat travel, only shorten it.

Air: Light planes only can land at Laguna San Rafael's 775-meter gravel airstrip; several Coyhaique-based companies can carry up to five passengers for US$600–700, remaining only about an hour at the park. Among them are Transporte Aéreo Don Carlos, Subteniente Cruz 63, tel./fax 67/231981; Transportes Aéreos San Rafael, 18 de Septiembre 469, tel. 67/232048, fax 67/233408; Aerohein, Baquedano 500, tel./fax 67/232772, aerohein@entelchile.net; and Patagonia Explorer Aviación, Freire 365, tel. 09/8172172.

Sea: Navimag, Transmarchilay, and several cruise and tour companies offer excursions to Laguna San Rafael in a range of vessels—from slow-moving ferries to high-speed catamarans. For ferries, the overnight voyage can take 12 to 16 hours

EVANGELISTAS FERRY RATES TO PUERTO CHACABUCO AND LAGUNA SAN RAFAEL

For fares from Puerto Montt to Puerto Chacabuco and back on the *Magallanes,* see the chart Navimag Passenger and Vehicle Fares under Puerto Montt in the Sur Chico chapter.

From Puerto Montt to Laguna San Rafael and back to Puerto Montt
AA Cabins: US$577/1,000 s/d
A Berths: US$310 pp
B Berths:US$288 pp
Butacas: US$182

From Puerto Montt to Laguna San Rafael and back to Puerto Chacabuco
AA Cabins: US$500/757 s/d
A Berths: US$280 pp

B Berths: US$258
Butacas: US$167

From Puerto Chacabuco to Laguna San Rafael and back to Puerto Chacabuco
AA Cabins: US$455/682 s/d
A Berths: US$250 pp
B Berths: US$227
Butacas: US$144

Puerto Montt to Puerto Chacabuco and back to Puerto Montt
AA Cabins: US$106/182 s/d
A Berths: US$76
B Berths: US$61
Butacas: US$24

from Puerto Chacabuco, while the catamarans can return the same day. On the other hand, the ferries spend five or six hours at the glacier, while the catamarans have two or three hours at most.

Both Navimag and Transmarchilay cruises begin in Puerto Montt and call in Puerto Chacabuco before continuing to Laguna San Rafael. From Puerto Montt, fares for the five-day, four-night voyage on Navimag's *Evangelistas* range from US$171 pp for reclining seats to bunks (US$260–280) to US$535 pp in three-person cabins with private bath; from Puerto Chacabuco, the comparable round-trip fares are US$135 pp to US$215–235 pp to US$471 pp. For more detail, contact Navimag offices in Santiago, Puerto Montt, Coyhaique, or Puerto Chacabuco, or see its website: www.navimag.com.

Transmarchilay's 230-passenger *El Colono,* departing Puerto Montt at 4 P.M. Friday in summer, calls for additional passengers at Puerto Chacabuco. Fares from Puerto Montt to Laguna San Rafael and back range from US$207 pp for reclining seats to US$460 pp for bunks. More expensive suites with private bath are also available. For more detail, contact Transmarchilay offices in Santiago, Puerto Montt, Coyhaique, or Puerto Chacabuco, or see its website: www.transmarchilay.com.

From Puerto Chacabuco, Patagonia Connection's 70-passenger catamaran *Patagonia Express* sails to Laguna San Rafael every Friday for US$290 pp, including full board and open bar. The outdoor decks can be cold and windy, but the interior seating is cozy and comfortable. For more details, contact Patagonia Connection at tel. 67/325103 in Puerto Puyuhuapi, its Santiago headquarters at Fidel Oteíza 1951, Oficina 1006, Providencia, tel. 2/2256489, fax 2/2748111, or its website: www.patagonia-connection.com.

The 70-passenger *Iceberg Expedition* charges US$286 pp, also including full meals and an open bar; for more details or reservations, contact Geo Turismo, Eusebio Lillo 315, tel. 67/237456 or 67/234098, Coyhaique. For US$5,000, Turismo Rucaray, Teniente Merino 848, tel. 67/332862, fax 67/332725, Puerto Aisén, rucaray@entelchile.net, charters the 10-passenger luxury launch *Patagonia I.*

From September through May, Cruceros Marítimos Skorpios offers four-day, three-night cruises from Puerto Chacabuco every Friday. Rates range from US$430 pp in low season to US$650 pp in high season (mid-December to mid-March), depending on the quality of the cabin; some cruises include a side trip to hot springs in the Quitralco fjord. From Puerto Montt, rates range from US$1,260 to US$2,940 pp for week-long voyages. For more details, contact its offices in Coyhaique or Puerto Montt, its Santiago headquarters at Augusto Leguía 118, Las Condes, Santiago, tel. 2/2311030, fax 2/2322269, or its website: www.skorpios.cl.

THE NORTHERN CARRETERA AUSTRAL

From Coyhaique, the paved Carretera Austral is briefly contiguous with Ruta 240 to Puerto Aisén and Puerto Chacabuco, but after nine km it becomes a gravel road that veers northeast toward Villa Ortega, while Ruta 240 continues west. About 39 km west on Ruta 240, at the Viviana junction, a smooth paved highway turns northeast up the valley of the Río Mañihuales, where it joins the Carretera Austral about 13 km southeast of Villa Mañihuales.

Heavy rains can and do cut the highway north to Chaitén, as happened in March of 2001, when several communities were isolated for days.

Villa Mañihuales

Villa Mañihuales, a pioneer village 76 km north of Coyhaique via the roundabout Viviana junction, is the headquarters for Conaf's **Reserva Nacional Mañihuales,** a 3,596-hectare forest reserve that takes its name from the native *Podocarpus* forest.

Conaf's five-site **Camping Las Lavanderas** charges US$6 for up to six people with facilities including picnic tables and toilets, but cold showers only. **Residencial Mañiguales,** Ibar 280, tel. 67/431403, charges US$7 pp with shared bath; there are a couple of simple eateries.

All buses from Coyhaique pass through Villa Mañihuales en route to northbound Carretera Austral destinations.

Villa Amengual

About 58 km north of Villa Mañihuales, overlooking the Río Cisnes canyon in the shadow of 2,095-meter Cerro Alto Nevado, the pioneer village of Villa Amengual dates only from 1983 and owes its existence to the Carretera Austral. A few kilometers south, an eastbound gravel road climbs

chapel at Villa Amengual on the Carretera Austral

© WAYNE BERNHARDSON

the river valley to the settlement of La Tapera and a rarely used border crossing to Argentina.

Distinguished by its shingled chapel, built in the Chilote immigrant style, Villa Amengual is a popular stop for cyclists, if only because it's one of few places with food and accommodations between Villa Mañihuales and Puerto Puyuhuapi, another 60 km north over rugged terrain. **Residencial El Encanto** has rooms with shared bath for US$7 pp.

Again, all northbound buses pass through here, but some turn west toward Puerto Cisnes from a highway junction only a few kilometers to the north.

Puerto Cisnes

At the mouth of its namesake river, the town of Puerto Cisnes owes its origins to a lumber mill built in the 1920s, but it still serves as a key port for scattered tiny fishing ports in and around the Canal Puyuhuapi; the rarely visited Parque Nacional Isla Magdalena is just across the canal.

Construction of the Carretera Austral partially reoriented it inland and, in recent years, the economy has diversified with salmon farming and tourism, the latter primarily oriented toward fly-fishing. Its population is approaching 2,000.

Puerto Cisnes has several passable accommodations, starting with the reasonably priced **Hospedaje Bellavista,** Séptimo de Línea 112, tel. 67/346408, for US$7 pp with shared bath. **Hostería El Gaucho,** Holmberg 140, tel. 67/346514, is slightly dearer at US$10 pp. **Hostal Michay,** Gabriela Mistral 112, tel. 67/346462, charges US$17 pp. **El Guairao,** Piloto Pardo 58, tel. 67/346473, is considered the best restaurant, but there are other choices on the waterfront.

Transportation: Transportes Terra Austral, Aguada de Dolores s/n, tel. 67/346757, has daily buses at 6 A.M. to Coyhaique (US$12), while Buses Norte Carretera Austral, Aguirre Cerda 048, tel. 67/346693, has a Saturday departure at 1 P.M. For northbound services on the Carretera Austral, it's necessary to wait at the highway junction or backtrack toward Coyhaique.

Parque Nacional Queulat

From the Río Cisnes junction, the steep, narrow Carretera Austral zigzags over the 500-meter Portezuelo Queulat as it enters the 154,093-hectare Parque Nacional Queulat, which rises from the ocean fjords of Canal Puyuhuapi through nearly impenetrable evergreen forests that, except on a handful of well-kept trails, deter all but the most resolute hikers. Beneath snow-capped summits, meltwater cascades off bluish hanging glaciers into frigidly limpid rivers that cut through deep canyons en route to the sea.

Queulat's accessibility has made it a popular destination for those exploring the Carretera Austral, but most see only a sample of its attractions. Many visitors come to enjoy the fishing in particular. (As of early 2002, parts of the park were not yet reopened to the public after a big mud slide near the Ventisquero Colgante; check the status of the park before you go.)

Geography and Climate: Roughly midway between Chaitén and Coihaique, Queulat ranges from sea level on Canal Puyuhuapi to 2,225

meters on the summit of Cerro Alto Nevado. Up to 4,000 millimeters of precipitation, fairly evenly distributed throughout the year, feeds its upper snowfields and glaciers, rushing rivers, and peaceful finger lakes; the more westerly areas are the wettest. The mean annual temperature is around 8°C.

Flora and Fauna: At lower elevations, Queulat's humid climate fosters dense evergreen forests of southern *coigüe (Nothofagus betuloides)* and *tepa (Laurelia philippiana),* which reaches heights of 30 meters or more, with a dense understory of *quila (Chusquea quila),* fuchsia, and ferns. On some slopes, the coniferous Guaiteca cypress *(Pilgerodendron uviferum)* shades massive specimens of the broad-leaved *nalca (Gunnera chilensis),* while at higher altitudes the *coigüe* mixes with *lenga (Nothofagus pumilio).*

Even along the highway, look for the timid *pudú,* no bigger than a border collie, as it emerges from the forest. Foxes, pumas, and Patagonian skunks are also present. The seldom-seen *chucao*

hanging glacier in Parque Nacional Queulat

is a solitary songbird that, legend says, brings good luck if it sings on your right, but bad luck if it sings on your left. The elegant black-necked swan paddles on the fjords and even some lakes.

Sights and Recreation: Many points of interest are on or near the Carretera Austral, but the best base of operations is the **Sector Ventisquero,** where Conaf's Centro de Información, 22 km from Puerto Puyuhuapi via the highway and a short eastbound lateral, is the starting point for several dead-end trails. Even the most sedentary can walk the 200-meter **Sendero El Mirador** to a vista point that looks east up the valley to the **Ventisquero Colgante,** a hanging glacier that conjures images of what California's Yosemite valley must have looked like before the ice melted.

Crossing its eponymous river on a suspension bridge, the 600-meter **Sendero Río Guillermo** arrives at **Laguna Témpanos,** which, despite its name, is iceberg-free. On the turbulent river's north bank, the 3.5-km **Sendero Ventisquero Colgante** climbs unrelentingly to even more breathtaking views of Queulat's hanging glacier. As the afternoon sun warms the atmosphere, chunks of ice tumble onto the rockfalls below.

Just beyond Guardería Pudú, the park's southern entrance, the 1.7-km **Sendero Río de las Cascadas** winds through dripping rainforest until it arrives at a granite amphitheater where ribbons of glacial meltwater mark the river's source. Farther on, where the highway begins to switchback into the famous canyon of the Río Queulat, a short staircase trail approaches the **Salto Río Padre García,** a waterfall named for the Chiloé-based Jesuit missionary who, in 1766–67, may have been the first European to see the area.

Queulat's numerous rivers and lakes, particularly the northern **Lago Risopatrón** and **Lago Rosselot** (part of which comprises a separate reserve near the town of La Junta), are prime destinations for fly-fishing devotees.

Accommodations and Food: Accommodations are decentralized, to say the least, but there are plenty of options from La Junta in the north to the Río Ventisquero and vicinity in the south. (For accommodations in nearby towns, see the separate entries for Puerto Puyuhuapi and La Junta.)

Conaf's inviting **Camping Ventisquero,** near the main trailheads, has 10 relatively barren sites with sheltered cooking areas and immaculate toilets, but if the shower water were any colder the pipes would freeze. Rates are US$12 for up to six people.

On the western shore of Lago Risopatrón, 12 km north of Puerto Puyuhuapi, Conaf's 10-site **Camping Angostura** has similar facilities in a dramatically different setting of humid temperate rainforest with soggy soils. Rates are identical, US$12 for up to six people.

About 17 km south of Puerto Puyuhuapi and five km north of the turnoff to Sector Ventisquero, a garden of technicolor lupines marks **Hospedaje Las Toninas,** a shingled roadside inn where cyclists, campers, and backpackers can stay inexpensively and gorge themselves on enormous plates of fresh crab salad at giveaway prices. Rates are about US$10 pp with breakfast and shared bath; there are also inexpensive campsites.

About half an hour north of Puerto Puyuhuapi on Lago Risopatrón, **Cabañas El Pangue,** Km 240, tel. 67/325128, cpangue@entelchile.net, offers spacious rooms with natural wood, large double beds, and sunken tubs in a woodsy setting. Rates are $95/109 s/d from mid-December to the end of March, but they're a bargain at $54/66 with breakfast the rest of the year. Meals are also available for US$6.50 for breakfast, US$8.30 for special breakfast, US$10.50 for *onces,* US$11–15 for lunch or dinner, US$20 pp for a lamb barbecue outdoors. The management also rents canoes, rowboats, motorboats, and horses, and has a sauna and Jacuzzi.

Information: Conaf has built a new Centro de Información Ambiental at Sector Ventisquero, where rangers can provide guidance on hiking and other activities. Visitors can also consult with Conaf rangers at Guardería Pudú (the park's southern entrance) and Guardería El Pangue (its northern entrance).

Conaf collects a US$2.50 admission charge at Sector Ventisquero only.

Transportation: Buses between Coyhaique, Puerto Puyuhuapi, and Chaitén pass directly through the park on the Carretera Austral, though they drop passengers at least half an hour's walk west of Sector Ventisquero.

Puerto Puyuhuapi

Thanks to its history as a pioneer port established by German immigrants in 1940, Puerto Puyuhuapi has a greater air of permanence than any other settlement on the Carretera Austral between Coyhaique, 225 km to the south, and Chaitén, 195 km to the north. Many of its streets, residents, and businesses still bear names such as Hopperdietzel, Grosse, Ludwig, Rossbach, and Übel.

At the north end of the Seno Ventisquero, a sheltered extension of the larger Canal Puyuhuapi, Puerto Puyuhuapi is now also a gateway to Parque Nacional Queulat and the elite hot springs resort of Termas de Puyuhuapi.

Sights: Since its founding by textile engineer Walter Hopperdietzel in 1940, **Alfombras de Puyuhuapi** has produced handmade woolen carpets, tinted with Swiss dyes, for both internal and export markets. Most of its 20 employees are women weavers from Chiloé, producing items that sell for upward of $1,000, but smaller, more affordable pieces are also on display in its showroom.

Factory tours take place weekdays at 10:30, 11, and 11:30 A.M., and 4, 4:30, and 5 P.M., weekends and holidays at 11:30 A.M. only; admission costs US$1.50 for adults, US$.75 for children. The sales office is open 8:30 A.M.–1 P.M. and 3–7 P.M. daily. For more information, contact Alfombras de Puyuhuapi, Aisén s/n, tel. 67/325131, website: www.puyuhuapi.com, alfombras@puyuhuapi.com.

Accommodations and Food: Puyuhuapi's best budget option is **Hostería Marily,** Avenida Otto Übel s/n, tel. 67/325102; though it has no frills, everything works, the beds are comfortable, and the rates of US$7 pp with breakfast and shared bath, US$10 pp with private bath, are competitive. **Residencial Elizabeth,** Circunvalación s/n, tel. 67/325106, charges US$7.50 pp for B&B and also serves lunch and dinner.

Open December to March only, **Hotel Ludwig,** Avenida Otto Übel 850, tel./fax 67/325220, l.ludwig@entelchile.net, is an eight-room B&B

occupying a landmark house. In December and March, rates are about US$16–24 pp; in January and February, they rise to US$20–30 pp.

Hostería Alemana, Avenida Otto Übel 450, tel. 67/325118, is similar and comparably priced. At the southern outskirts of town is **La Casona de Puyuhuapi,** Carretera Austral s/n, tel. 67/325131, charging US$30 pp.

In addition to hotel dining rooms, there are also salmon dinners and kuchen at inconsistent **Café Rossbach,** Aisén s/n, alongside the carpet factory.

Transportation: Buses Norte Carretera Austral, O'Higgins 39, tel. 67/325130, passes through Puerto Puyuhuapi en route between Coyhaique and Chaitén.

Termas de Puyuhuapi

South of Puerto Puyuhuapi, sumptuous in style but more affordable than it looks, Termas de Puyuhuapi is a secluded spa resort that's not literally an island but, since there's no road and the only access is by launch across the Seno Ventisquero (Ventisquero Sound), it might as well be. Both hotel guests and day visitors can enjoy naturally heated outdoor pools and hiking trails that veer through the forest understory of dense thickets of *quila* (solid bamboo), *chilco* (firecracker fuchsia), colossal tree ferns, and rhubarb-like *nalcas* with leaves the size of umbrellas.

Hotel guests only, though, have access to the modern spa facilities including a gym, heated indoor pool, and massage room that, perched in a tower, enjoys 360-degree views of its scenic surroundings. When the weather lifts, the panorama is the Andean front range of Parque Nacional Queulat where, even at the end of summer, traces of snow linger. More than just traces remain on the enormous hanging glacier that's just out of sight.

Spacious waterfront rooms, stocked with genteel touches such as terrycloth robes and individual umbrellas, look out onto the dock where the catamaran *Patagonia Express* starts its weekly run to Parque Nacional Laguna San Rafael, on the final day of package holidays that range from four days and three nights to six days and five nights. Activities such as hiking, fly-fishing, and excursions along the Carretera Austral are additional.

While the hotel primarily works with multi-day packages, overnight accommodations are possible on a space-available basis, normally Thursday and Friday only. In peak season (Christmas to mid-March), rates start at US$100 s or d with a buffet breakfast; the rest of the year, rates begin at US$90. Spa access costs US$12 pp more. Fixed-price lunches and dinners from the recently remodeled kitchen and dining room, which include salmon from the resort's own hatchery, cost US$22, while deluxe buffet dinners cost US$26.

It sounds exclusive (and it sure ain't proletarian), but Puyuhuapi also lets the riffraff in, at least for day-use of the outdoor pools and baths (US$20 pp for adults, US$10 pp for children). The cafeteria at the pools, open only in daytime, has a cheaper but more limited menu than the hotel restaurant.

Termas de Puyuhuapi's local address is Bahía Dorita s/n, tel. 67/325103. For reservations or information, contact Patagonia Connection's Santiago office at Fidel Oteíza 1951, Oficina 1006, Providencia, tel. 2/2256489, fax 2/2748111, website: www.patagonia-connection.com.

Transportation: Termas de Puyuhuapi provides free transport for its package guests; otherwise, launches from its mainland information center on the Carretera Austral, 14 km south of Puerto Puyuhuapi, charge US$5 pp each way. Scheduled departures from the hotel are at 9:30 A.M., noon, and 2:30 and 6:30 P.M., returning at 10 A.M. and 12:30, 3, and 7:30 P.M., but there are occasional unscheduled crossings as well.

La Junta

At the crossroads town of La Junta, new penetration roads proceed west along the Río Palena to the port of Raúl Marín Balmaceda and east up the Río Figueroa valley toward the Argentine border. La Junta gained a measure of notoriety when, in 2001, municipal authorities erected an unauthorized monolith to General Pinochet—still popular here for building the north-south Carretera Austral.

On a broad plain at the confluence of the two rivers, just south of the regional border between Aisén and Los Lagos, La Junta is the main ac-cess point to **Reserva Nacional Lago Rosselot,** a 12,725-hectare forest unit whose longitudinal finger lake is known for its fishing.

Residencial Valderas, Antonio Varas s/n, tel. 67/314105, charges US$7 pp with shared bath and breakfast, while the more commodious **Hostería Ensueño,** Claro Solar s/n, tel. 67/31-4127, costs US$30 pp. The best choice, though, is the roadside **Hostal Espacio y Tiempo,** Carretera Austral s/n, tel. 67/314141, espacio@entelchile.net, for US$59/84 with breakfast and private bath; it also offers fishing and other excursions in the area.

Like other destinations along the Carretera Austral, La Junta is a regular stop for buses en route between Coyhaique and Chaitén.

Lago Yelcho

About 30 km north of La Junta, where the Carretera Austral bridges the Río Palena, lies the boundary between Region XI (Aisén) and Region X (Los Lagos). Los Lagos's first major attraction is elongated Lago Yelcho, which stretches from Puerto Cárdenas in the north to Puerto Ramírez in the southeast and which formed part of the highway between Chaitén and Futaleufú until completion of the Carretera Austral eliminated the need for ferries. Kayakers, though, can still paddle from Puerto Ramírez to Puerto Cárdenas and even to the Pacific.

At **Villa Santa Lucía,** 70 km north of La Junta and 78 km south of Chaitén, the Carretera Austral continues north but the eastbound lateral Ruta 235 drops steeply to the lakeshore and **Puerto Ramírez,** where **Hostería Verónica,** tel. 65/264431, charges US$10 pp with breakfast and shared bath, US$20 pp with full board. At nearby **Puerto Piedra, Hostal Alexis,** tel. 67/731505 in Chaitén, focuses on cheap all-inclusive fishing holidays for US$100 pp per day, including transfers from Chaitén, but will take individuals guests if there's space available.

At Puerto Ramírez, Ruta 235 continues southeast toward Palena and a minor border crossing to Argentina, while the alternative Ruta 231 proceeds northeast toward the white-water rafting and kayaking capital of Futaleufú and a far more efficient border crossing. (For details, see the separate entries for Futaleufú and Palena below.)

Midway between Villa Santa Lucía and Puerto Cárdenas, on the west side of the Carretera Austral, the north side of the **Puente Ventisquero** (Glacier Bridge) is the starting point for a two-hour hike through soggy evergreen forest to the **Ventisquero Cavi,** a hanging glacier.

Across the highway from the Ventisquero Cavi, the lakeside **Hotel Yelcho en la Patagonia,** tel. 65/731337, specializes in fly-fishing holidays but will also accommodate the general public. Rates are US$59/89 s/d with breakfast in the peak summer season but only US$44/59 the rest of the year; its restaurant is open to the public as well. The Santiago contact is Yelcho en la Patagonia, Alonso Ovalle 612, Oficina 4, Santiago, tel. 2/6326117, fax 2/6384597, website: www.yelcho.cl.

At the north end of the lake, where Lago Yelcho becomes the Río Yelcho, **Puerto Cárdenas** has three simple basic places to stay, all reachable by the same message number, tel. 65/264429: **Hospedaje Lulú, Residencial Los Pinos,** and **Residencial Yelcho.** All are open in summer only. The 250-meter suspension bridge that crosses the river here was the first of its kind in Chile.

Futaleufú

With its reputation for world-class white water—some say it's *the* best—Futaleufú draws outdoor recreationists like a magnet. But what works for this tidy village, its forested mountains, and its namesake river—spectacular natural beauty, cleanliness, and isolation—also works against it. The 1,100 people who live here may be on borrowed time, possibly powerless to fend off Endesa, the powerful Spanish electric utility that wants to build three massive dams where at least three international rafting and kayaking enterprises have elaborate summer camps, and where several Chilean operators spend at least part of the season.

For the time being, though, the "Fu" remains one of the world's most challenging rivers. Both foreign and Chilean operators hope to kindle local and national enthusiasm for preserving the river and its surroundings, and the March 2000 Whitewater Challenge World Championships brought rafters and kayakers from 14 different countries.

Orientation: Only eight km west of the Argentine border, at the confluence of the Río Espolón and the Río Futaleufú, the village is 155 km southeast of Chaitén via the Carretera Austral, Ruta 235 from Villa Santa Lucia, and Ruta 231 from Puerto Ramírez, at the east end of Lago Yelcho.

Futaleufú's plan is a rectangular grid focused, if not exactly centered, on the manicured Plaza de Armas. On the south side of the plaza, Bernardo O'Higgins leads east toward the Argentine border, while Arturo Prat, on the west side, leads south toward westbound Ruta 231.

Recreation: White water is clearly the major attraction, but hiking, climbing, mountain biking, and horseback riding are also attracting attention. Several U.S. rafting/kayaking operators maintain summer camps in the vicinity from October to April (for details, see the Organized Tours entry in the On the Road chapter; Santiago-based operators are also listed there).

The Hostería Río Grande's **Centro de Aventura Futaleufú,** O'Higgins 397, tel. 65/721320, can help drop-ins arrange river trips and other local excursions. Other locally based options are Juan Pablo Cerón's **Rockside Expediciones** at the municipal tourist office, O'Higgins 536; and the **Club de Rafting y Kayak,** Pedro Aguirre Cerda 545, tel. 65/721298.

The Class III Espolón is a good beginner's river, and even parts of the Fu are suitable for those with limited experience, but rapids such as the Class V Terminator can be a challenge even for professionals. According to former U.S. Olympic kayaker Chris Spelius, who runs a camp here:

> *Big water can be forgiving to a certain extent, but this river's so big that it can take a normal human being with a life jacket and hold him under water longer than a normal human being can hold his breath.*

A leisurely float on the Espolón costs about US$30, while a Class III raft descent goes for US$50. For a half-day Class IV descent on the Fu, figure about US$50; a full-day Class IV-V experience costs about US$100.

For hikers, one of the best trails follows the south bank of the Fu, beginning with an undulating oxcart road opposite the Kayak Chile camp about 10 km west of town; ask for directions at Centro de Aventura Futaleufú. The trail continues past peasant homesteads above rapids such as the Terminator before continuing through southern beech forest so dense that, in midafternoon on a sunny day, it's as dark as dusk. It eventually emerges onto a terrace with a couple of new trophy houses; a nearby bridge recrosses the river to the Ruta 231.

Accommodations: Futaleufú has more and better accommodations than any other place of its size (population about 1,000) on or along the Carretera Austral, but with only a couple of exceptions, most are similarly utilitarian.

Just south of town on Ruta 231, before crossing the bridge over the river, **Camping Puerto Espolón** charges US$4 pp for shady sites with grass, clean toilets, and hot showers.

Basic accommodations start at around US$7 pp with shared bath and breakfast at **Residencial Carahue,** O'Higgins 332, tel. 65/721260. Others in the same general category include **Hotel Continental,** Balmaceda 595, tel. 65/721222; **Hospedaje El Campesino,** Prat 107, tel. 65/721275. **Hospedaje Adolfo,** O'Higgins 302, is a step above the rest in price and comfort. **Posada Ely,** Balmaceda 409, tel. 65/721205, charges US$13 pp with private bath and breakfast.

Hostería Río Grande, O'Higgins 397, tel. 65/721320, has rustically styled common areas, a bar/restaurant that's becoming a mecca for rafters and kayakers, and a dozen simple, tastefully decorated twin-bedded rooms. Rates are $26 pp with breakfast. The small TV lounge is full of kayak videos. Outside town, its secluded **Cabañas Aguas Claras,** on the Río Espolón, cost US$120 for up to five people.

The only other upscale choice is **Posada Campesina La Gringa,** set among spacious gardens at Sargento Aldea 456, tel. 65/721260, tel. 2/2359187 in Santiago, which costs US$50/72 s/d with breakfast.

Food: Just like the accommodations, the food is a little bit better in Futaleufú than in most other towns of its size, though Chilean standards such as beef, chicken, and sandwiches are the rule. In addition to the dining room at Hostería Río Grande, recommended choices include **El Encuentro,** O'Higgins 633, tel. 65/721247; **Escorpio,** Gabriela Mistral 255, tel. 65/721228; **Futaleufú,** Pedro Aguirre Cerda 407, tel. 65/721295; and **Hanga Roa,** Pedro Aguirre Cerda 697, tel. 65/721281.

Shopping: For artisanal goods such as horsegear and woolens, visit the nameless shop at Pedro Aguirre Cerda and Manuel Rodríguez, at the northeast corner of the Plaza de Armas.

Services: Banco del Estado, at O'Higgins and Manuel Rodríguez, is the only place to change money.

Telefónica del Sur is at Balmaceda 419. Futaleufú's area code is 65, the same as Puerto Montt's.

Visitors arriving from or departing for Argentina should known that Chilean customs and immigration here is far better organized than at Palena, where Carabineros handle the formalities. The border is open 8 A.M.–8 P.M. daily.

Information: In summer only, the municipal Oficina de Información Turística is at O'Higgins 536, on the south side of the Plaza de Armas. Sernatur operates a summer office at the border post.

Transportation: Buses Codao shuttles passengers to the international border for connections to the Argentine towns of Trevelin and Esquel.

Several companies go to Chaitén (US$10, four hours) at 7:30 A.M. daily, including Transportes Cordillera, Balmaceda 539, tel. 65/721248; Buses Eben Ezer, at the Paquetería Pablo at Balmaceda and Prat, tel. 65/721280; and Turismo Futaleufú, in the Paquetería Pablo at Balmaceda and Prat, tel. 65/721280; the latter also goes to Osorno and Puerto Montt (US$28, 11 hours) Tuesday at 8 A.M. via Argentina.

Chaitén

Between the snowy volcanic cones of Michinmahuida and Corcovado, the modest port of Chaitén is the main gateway to continental Chiloé. Receiving regular ferry traffic from Puerto Montt and from Quellón, at the southern tip

southbound bus on the Carretera Austral

of archipelagic Chiloé, it's the starting point for many trips down the Carretera Austral and the year-round access point for Parque Natural Pumalín, the controversial conservation project of U.S. entrepreneur Douglas Tompkins.

Orientation: Chaitén is 46 km north of Puerto Cárdenas by a segment of the Carretera Austral that is at present being widened and paved, and 56 km south of Caleta Gonzalo, a summer-only ferry port that is also the headquarters of Parque Natural Pumalín. Most services and other points of interest are within a block or two of the Costanera Avenida Corcovado, which runs north-south along the waterfront of the Bahía de Chaitén. The Plaza de Armas is two blocks east, between O'Higgins and Pedro Aguirre Cerda.

The Costanera leads north to Caleta Gonzalo, while Avenida Ignacio Carrera Pinto heads east and then south toward Puerto Cárdenas.

Accommodations: Chaitén has abundant budget accommodations, some of which are pretty good, but relatively little in either midrange or above.

In the US$10–25 range, Israeli travelers favor **Hospedaje Casa de Rita,** at Almirante Riveros and Prat, tel. 65/721502, which offers garden camping for US$2 pp, floor space for US$4 pp,

and rooms with shared bath for US$6 pp. Family-run **Hospedaje Ancud,** Libertad 105, tel. 65/731535, also charges around US$6 pp with shared bath and breakfast and prepares additional meals as well.

Several others charge in the US$8–10 range pp, including **Hospedaje Santana,** Pedro de Valdivia 129, tel. 65/731413, which also offers camping for US$4 pp; **Hospedaje Don Carlos,** Almirante Riveros 53, tel./fax 65/731287; **Hotel Triángulo,** Todesco 2, tel. 65/737312; **Residencial Astoria,** Corcovado 442, tel. 65/731263; and **Hospedaje San Sebastián,** Almirante Riveros 163, tel./fax 65/731225.

Amiable **Hospedaje Jenny,** Corcovado 69, tel./fax 65/731429, charges US$10 pp with shared bath, US$12 pp with private bath, both with breakfast, and features outstanding views. The waterfront **Hostería Llanos,** Corcovado 378, tel. 65/731332, charges US$10 pp with shared bath and breakfast, US$12 pp with private bath.

In the US$25–50 range, **Hostería Puma Verde,** O'Higgins 54, tel./fax 65/731184, pumaverde@telsur.cl, is an older house recycled into a new and intimate, three-room, tobacco-free B&B charging

US$17 pp with breakfast; the dining room also serves meals to nonguests.

Hostería los Coihues, Pedro Aguirre Cerda 398, tel. 65/731461, coihues@telsur.cl, charges US$25/32 pp with breakfast off-season, US$32/40 per person in summer. Summer rates at attractive **Hotel Schilling,** Corcovado 230, tel. 65/731295, are US$38 d with shared bath, US$50 d with private bath, breakfast included. The rest of the year, it charges US$25 d with shared bath, US$37 d with private bath, again with breakfast.

And in the US$50–100 range, **Hotel Mi Casa,** Avenida Norte 206, tel. 65/731285, hotelmicasa@entelchile.net, exudes old-fashioned charm: wallpapered rooms with wood paneling, armoires, twin beds, central heating, and small bathrooms. Rates are $48/67 s/d with a substantial breakfast (bread and cheese, strudel, tea or coffee) in summer; the rest of the year, figure about US$26 pp. Its restaurant is worth consideration for lunch or dinner as well. Note that some beds are soft because they have two mattresses rather than a mattress and box spring—check before taking the room.

Cabañas Brisas del Mar, Corcovado 278, tel. 65/731266, fax 65/731284, charges US$63 d with breakfast and cable TV.

Food: Chaitén has relatively few places to eat beyond the hotel restaurants. Several locales along the waterfront serve seafood, including **Cocinería Marita,** Corcovado 478. In recent years, **Flamengo,** Corcovado 218, has evolved from a budget restaurant to a more upscale venue also specializing in seafood, and it's often packed. **Canasto de Agua,** a little less central at Prat 65, tel. 65/731550, seems not to get the attention it deserves for its outstanding seafood; its bar is one of few real hangouts in town.

Services: Banco del Estado, Libertad 298, changes U.S. cash and traveler's checks, but its ATM does not work with foreign bankcards.

Correos de Chile is at O'Higgins 230, on the north side of the plaza.

Teléfonica del Sur is on the Costanera just north of O'Higgins, and Chilesat is at O'Higgins 53, alongside the bus terminal. Chaitén's area code is 65, the same as Puerto Montt's.

The new Entel office at Pedro Aguirre Cerda 300, on the east side of the Plaza de Armas, has Internet access, as does Chaitur, in the bus terminal at O'Higgins 67.

Lavandería Masol is at Todesco 272, Local B, tel. 65/731566.

The Hospital de Chaitén is at Avenida Ignacio Carrera Pinto 153, tel. 65/731244.

Information: In summer only, the municipal Oficina de Información Turística, on the Costanera at the foot of Todesco, is open 9 A.M. to 1 P.M. daily except Sunday and 3–7 P.M. weekday afternoons.

Chaitur, at the bus terminal at O'Higgins 67, tel. 65/731429, fax 65/731266, nchaitur@hotmail.com, is a good source of information all year, with Spanish-, English- and French-speaking staff. It also sells maps and has a book exchange.

Parque Pumalín has its own Centro de Información at O'Higgins 62, across the street from the bus terminal, tel./fax 65/731341.

Transportation: Chaitén has air connections with Puerto Montt, sea links with Puerto Montt and Chiloé, and roads south to Futaleufú and Coyhaique and north to Caleta Gonzalo.

Aerosur, at Ignacio Carrera Pinto and Almirante Riveros, tel. 65/731228, and Aeromet, Corcovado 243, tel. 65/731844, fly air taxis to and from Puerto Montt (US$50) at least daily in summer, less frequently the rest of the year. Aerosur suspended its services after a nonfatality crash in 2001, but may resume flying in the future.

The main Terminal de Buses is at O'Higgins 67, tel. 65/731429, but some companies are scattered around town though they may stop at the terminal before continuing down the Carretera Austral. The main destinations are Futaleufú and Coyhaique and intermediates, but there are also services north to Caleta Gonzalo (Parque Pumalín).

Services to Coyhaique (US$25, 12 hours) are daily in summer, three times weekly the rest of the year with Buses Norte, Buses Becker, Don Oscar, and Buses Daniela from the main terminal. Departure time is 9 A.M.

B y V Tour, Libertad 432, tel. 65/731390, goes to Coyhaique Thursday and Saturday at 8 A.M. to Coihaique. It also goes to Caleta Gonzalo (US$5) daily at 7 A.M. in summer, less frequently the rest of the year. In summer, Chaitur and other companies go to Caleta Gonzalo (US$6, two hours) daily at 5 P.M. and will make special trips if demand is sufficient.

Buses Emanuel goes to La Junta and Puerto Puyuhuapi (US$12, six hours) daily except Sunday at 3:30 P.M. At 4 P.M. Monday, Wednesday, and Friday, Buses Lago Verde, on Todesco between Corcovado and Portales, goes to Puerto Cárdenas, Villa Santa Lucía, Villa Vanguardia, and La Junta (US$10).

From the main terminal, Buses Eben Ezer goes to Futaleufú (US$10, four hours) at 3:30 P.M. daily in summer, daily except Sunday in winter. Transportes Cordillera goes daily at 3:15 P.M. to Futaleufú.

Buses Palena goes to Palena (US$10, four hours) at 3:30 P.M. Monday, Wednesday, and Friday from the corner of Corcovado and Todesco. In winter, Becker sometimes goes to La Junta, Puerto Cisnes, Lago Verde, and Palena.

Chaitén's ferry dock is a short distance northwest of town via the Costanera.

Navimag, Ignacio Carrera Pinto 188, tel. 65/731570, fax 65/730571, sails the ferry *Alejandrina* to Quellón (Chiloé), Puerto Montt, and Puerto Chacabuco at irregular intervals. Passenger fares to Puerto Montt range US$17–25. Bicycles pay US$8.50, motorcycles US$25, and automobiles or light trucks US$75.

Transmarchilay, Corcovado 266, tel. 65/731272, fax 65/731282, sails to Quellón and to Puerto Montt (nine hours) three times weekly with the ferries *La Pincoya* and *El Colono* to Chaitén (nine hours) three times weekly. Fares to Puerto Montt range from US$18 pp for fixed seats to US$25 pp for reclining seats. Vehicle rates to Chaitén are US$85 for automobiles and small trucks less than four meters long, US$92 for vehicles longer than four meters; bicycles cost US$10 and motorcycles US$20. In summer only, Transmarchilay also sails from Caleta Gonzalo, 56 km north of Chaitén, to the town of Hornopirén.

In January and February, Catamaranes del Sur, Juan Tedesco 188, tel. 65/731199, sails daily to Puerto Montt via Castro (Chiloé, 2.5 hours); the rest of the year, it goes directly to Puerto Montt Monday, Wednesday, and Friday.

Vicinity of Chaitén

English-speaking Nicholas LaPenna at **Chaitur,** at the bus terminal at O'Higgins 67, tel. 65/731429, fax 65/731266, nchaitur@hotmail.com, organizes excursions as far north as Caleta Gonzalo and south to Termas de Amarillo, the Yelcho glacier, and other sites along the Carretera Austral. Chaitur also serves as a general travel agency for Chilean airlines, ferries, and accommodations in the region, including the *cabañas* at Parque Pumalín.

Casa Avión: About 20 km southeast of Chaitén, on the south side of the Carretera Austral, stands one of the region's most offbeat landmarks. In 1974, well before the highway's completion, the Chilean Air Force crashed a DC-3 in the vicinity; unable to fly it out, they salvaged the engine and left the fuselage. Using two oxcarts, farmer Carlos Anabalón hauled it to his roadside property, divided it into three rooms, and lived in the Casa Avión (Airplane House) until the year 2000, when he traded it to a Chaitén policeman for a 4WD Jeep.

Termas El Amarillo: At a highway junction about 25 km southeast of Chaitén, a gravel road turns north for five km to the forested, no-frills hot springs site of Termas El Amarillo. Admission to the outdoor pools costs US$3 pp; it also has walk-in campsites (US$6) and a restaurant.

At the highway junction itself, **Residencial Marcela,** tel. 65/264442, charges US$9/17 s/d with shared bath and breakfast, but it also has *cabañas* with private bath and kitchen for US$33 for up to six people.

Parque Natural Pumalín

In 1991, U.S. businessman Douglas Tompkins and his wife, Kristine McDivitt, cashed out their fortunes from the Esprit and Patagonia clothing empires and began buying large blocks of temperate rainforest to create the area's largest destination—literally—in Parque Pumalín, a 317,000-hectare private nature reserve straddling the highway north of Chaitén. Since then, says the *New York Times,* only Pinochet has had his name in the Chilean press more than Tompkins, who's even received death threats from ultranationalists who accuse him of trying to split the

PATAGONIA & TIERRA

THE SAGA OF PUMALÍN

In the decade-plus since he bought 17,000 hectares of temperate rainforest on Fiordo Reñihué, in continental Chiloé, Californian Douglas Tompkins has become the gringo Chile knows best—or at least the gringo many Chileans think they know best. During that time, as Tompkins acquired a total of about 360,000 hectares in southernmost Region X (Los Lagos), probably not even U.S. President Bill Clinton appeared more often in the Chilean press.

Reported to be Chile's largest landholder, in a country where the *latifundio* has often been anathema, Tompkins is a polarizing figure, but not in the usual sense. Traditionally, objections to large landholdings come from the political left, which fought vociferously against the wealthy *fundos* before the coup of 1973 and advocated redistribution of their properties to landless peasants. The right, by contrast, upheld the status quo and sanctity of private property, and their position seemingly triumphed after 1973.

Tompkins, founder of the Esprit clothing empire, turned conventional Chileans politics on its head. Taking advantage of Chile's uncommon openness toward foreign investors, he used the proceeds from the sale of Esprit to consolidate several large undeveloped properties not for profit but for preservation. While other entrepreneurs were clear-cutting native forest and replanting with fast-growing exotics for the quickest possible profit, Tompkins formed a trust to turn his lands into a de facto national park under a Chilean law that permits creation of private *santuarios de la naturaleza* (nature sanctuaries).

Tompkins anticipated that his Proyecto Pumalín, in a thinly populated and once-inac-cessible area along the Argentine border south of Hornopirén and north of Chaitén, would make him a hero in Chile and it did—among the small but growing Chilean environmental movement for whom forest preservation was a hot-button issue, and who distrusted the growing power of multinational corporations. For them, the millionaire capitalist who believed in philanthropy and biodiversity was a real if improbable hero.

On the other hand, Tompkins's actions aroused the distrust and hostility of conservative sectors that, economically at least, might seem to have much in common with him. He ran afoul, though, of business, military, and religious interests, all with slightly different but overlapping rationales for implacable opposition to the project.

One reason was overt nationalism. Traditionally, Latin American armies place high value on control of their borders, even those of such remote access and difficult terrain as Pumalín, and many civilians supported them. In some cases, nationalist arguments bordered on hysteria; the army argued that any dispute with Tompkins might result in U.S. intervention, while Christian Democrat Senator Sergio Páez called Pumalín a "geopolitical catastrophe" and, preposterously, claimed that if Tompkins's property became a nature sanctuary, the land might eventually be ceded to state of California.

The conservative daily press, ironically and disingenuously, made an argument that pro-Allende radicals might have made in the 1970s: the occupation of so much land by a wealthy foreigner would squeeze economic opportunities for Chilean

country in half. Tompkins also has many Chilean supporters, though, and most criticisms of the park are far less extreme.

Tompkins has allayed many of those concerns by building trails, cabins, campgrounds, and a restaurant and visitor center that have lured visitors from Chaitén to Caleta Gonzalo, a summer ferry port on the Reñihué fjord, and other points along the highway and the park's extensive shoreline. The park still lacks formal legal recognition, however.

Geography and Climate: Pumalín stretches from 42° S in the north, where it's contiguous with Parque Nacional Hornopirén, to nearly 43° S just east of Chaitén in the south. Most visitors, though, see the areas along both sides of the Carretera Austral just north of Chaitén en route to Caleta Gonzalo.

Elevations range from sea level to 2,404 meters on the snowy summit of Volcán Michinmahuida, in the most southerly sector of the park, but even

workers. Owned by the Copec group, which has substantial investments in Chile's forestry sector, *La Tercera* has given the Tompkins story consistently critical front-page coverage. One of Tompkins's fiercest local critics, Chaitén Mayor José Miguel Fritis, apparently turned against him when Tompkins declined to buy what he considered an overpriced property of the mayor's.

The Catholic Church, to which most of Tompkins's critics belong, has its own disagreements with the philanthropist's ideology. In its opinion, Tompkins's "deep ecology" beliefs contradict the church's teaching that humans are superior to other living things, and it disagrees vehemently with what it considers his pro-choice approach to birth control and abortion.

This opposition has been effective at times, blocking Tompkins's purchase of 30,000 hectares from Valparaíso's Universidad Católica in favor of the electric utility Endesa, and consistently delaying the formal establishment of the park. After drawing fire from the Asociación de Productores de Salmón y Truchas (Salmon and Trout Producers' Association) when he complained about water pollution from fish farming, in mid-2001 he threatened to abandon the Pumalín project because of "harassment" from local and national politicians, but he soon reversed his position in what some critics derided as a publicity stunt.

Tompkins has many local and national supporters, though. Both Christian Democrat Deputy Gabriel Ascensio, of Chiloé, and PPD Deputy Leopoldo Sánchez, of Chaitén, favor the park and its tourist potential. PPD Deputy Guido Girardi, one of the country's most outspoken environmentalists, said that opposition to Pumalín was a combination of "extreme nationalism" and lobbying by forestry companies. The Lagos administration has been supportive, and visiting Sernatur chief Oscar Santelices said that:

> *The park is just in the beginnings of what could be a world-class reserve, thanks to the considerable funds invested. In all honesty, this could be the gateway to success for Chilean eco-tourism.*

At the same time, even some of Tompkins's supporters agree his actions have not been so transparent as they might have been—his earliest purchases, in particular, seemed almost surreptitious. As the project has developed, though, public access has improved through hiking trails, campgrounds, *cabañas,* a very good restaurant, and a visitor center, not to mention small-scale sustainable agriculture experiments and other feature to benefit the small local population.

At the moment, Tompkins is still awaiting final government approval to convert Pumalín into a national sanctuary administered by a seven-member, all-Chilean board of directors. It's perhaps an indirect measure of his success, though, that Endesa, which beat him out for the contested Huinay property, felt it had to build its own *cabañas* as a public relations ploy.

For more details on Parque Pumalín, contact the Parque Pumalín, Buin 356, Puerto Montt, tel. 65/250079 or 65/251911, fax 65/255145, website: www.parquepumalin.cl, pumalin@telsur.cl, or the Foundation for Deep Ecology, Building 1062, Fort Cronkhite, Sausalito, CA 94965, tel. 415/229-9339, fax 415/229-9340, website: www.deepecology.org, info@deepecology.org.

these statistics are misleading—the topography rises so steeply in some areas that trails require ladders rather than switchbacks.

Pumalín wouldn't look like it does without rain—lots of rain. While there are no reliable statistics regarding rainfall, probably more than 4,000 millimeters falls every year. At higher elevations, of course, it accumulates as snow.

Flora and Fauna: Pumalín takes its name from the puma *(Felis concolor),* but the principal reason for its creation was to protect the temperate southern rainforest, of which the single most significant species is the *alerce (Fitzroya cupressoides).* There are also several species of southern beech (*Nothofagus* spp.), not to mention the numerous other rainforest species common to southern Chilean environments.

In addition to the puma, the *pudú* inhabits the sopping rainforests, while foxes prowl along the shoreline and other open areas. Southern sea lions inhabit headlands and rookeries, stealing salmon from the fish farms that float offshore beyond the park boundaries—and placing themselves at risk from the powerful companies that bring in much of the region's income.

Hikers here and in other parts of the southern Chilean rainforests should watch for miniature *sanguijuelas* (leeches), which can work their way into boots and trousers (some leeches are used for medical treatments in Chile).

Sights and Recreation: From a trailhead near the café at Caleta Gonzalo, the **Sendero Cascadas** climbs and winds through thick rainforest to a high falls; figure about 1.5 hours each way. At the Centro de Información, it's possible to arrange a tour of the apiaries at **Fundo Pillán,** across the Fiordo de Reñihué, and to obtain fishing licenses (hunting is strictly prohibited).

From a trailhead about 12 km south of Caleta Gonzalo, west of the highway, the **Sendero Laguna Tronador** crosses a *pasarela* (hanging bridge) before ascending a string of slippery stepladders up nearly vertical slopes to the **Mirador Michinmahuida,** a platform where, on clear days, there are astounding views of the volcano's icy summit. The trail continues through nearly pristine forest, dropping gradually to the shores of an amphitheater lake where Tompkins's employees have built a stylish two-site campground with picnic tables, a deck, and an outhouse. It's about 1.5 hours to or from the trailhead.

Only a short distance farther south, on the east side of the highway, **Sendero Los Alerces** crosses the Río Blanco to a large *alerce* grove. Just a little farther, the **Sendero Cascadas Escondidas** leads from its namesake campground to another waterfall.

Accommodations and Food: At Caleta Gonzalo, the walk-in **Camping Río Gonzalo** charges US$1.50 pp for forested sites with fire pits (firewood is for sale), clean toilets, and cold showers. There is a separate large shelter for cooking. Fourteen km south of Caleta Gonzalo, **Auto-Camping Cascadas Escondidas** has four drive-in sites with clean toilets, cold showers, and roofed decks for pitching tents and eating without having to sit on the soggy ground.

Seventeen km south of Caleta Gonzalo,

Camping Lago Negro resembles Cascadas Escondidas, with four sheltered sites. Accessible by an 800-meter footpath, **Camping Punta del Lago** has two lakeside sites. Three km farther south, **Camping Lago Blanco** has similar facilities to Camping Lago Negro.

Tompkins's stylish **Cabañas Caleta Gonzalo,** tel. 65/250079, fax 65/255145 in Puerto Montt, pumalinreservas@telsur.cl, cost US$50/70 s/d. All nine have private bath and hot water but lack kitchen facilities.

The airy **Café Caleta Gonzalo,** open 7:30 A.M.–11:30 P.M. daily, maintains high standards for local cuisine with organic fruit, vegetables, dairy products and meat, and seafood. Four-course lunches or dinners, with fresh bread, fall in the US$7–10 range.

Information: At Caleta Gonzalo, Pumalín's **Centro de Visitantes,** tel. 1712/1964151, distributes brochures, provides information, and displays informational panels with large-scale black-and-white photographs of the park; it also sells books, maps, film, park products such as organic honey and jam, and local crafts items. If it's not open, café personnel can unlock it for you.

Pumalín maintains additional information offices in Chaitén at O'Higgins 62, tel./fax 65/731341; in Puerto Montt at Buin 356, tel. 65/250079, fax 65/255145, pumalin@telsur.cl; and in the United States at The Conservation Land Trust, Building 1062, Fort Cronkhite, Sausalito, CA 94965, tel. 415/229-9339, fax 415/229-9340, pumalin@earthlink.net.

There park also has a detailed website, www.parquepumalin.cl, in Spanish and English. In addition, the park publishes a monthly magazine, *Puma Verde.*

Transportation: In January and February only, Transmarchilay's ferry *Pincoya* sails daily except Monday and Friday to Hornopirén (six hours) at 9 A.M. Passengers pay US$13 pp, while cyclists pay an extra US$8.50 and motorcyclists US$17. Vehicles shorter than four meters pay US$75, while longer vehicles pay US$90.

(For land transportation, see the separate entry for Chaitén, above.)

Because many parts of Pumalín are inaccessible by ordinary public transportation, it's worth considering organized tours by a variety of operators. Alsur, Del Salvador 100, Puerto Varas, tel./fax 65/232300, website: www.alsurexpeditions.com, alsur@telsur.cl, arranges activity-oriented excursions—hiking, sea kayaking, and sailing—throughout the park.

Puerto Montt's Marina del Sur, Camino a Chinquehue Km 4.5, tel. 65/251958, website: www.marinadelsur.cl, mds@marinadelsur.cl, organizes luxury yacht tours in the vicinity. Ancud-based Austral Adventures, Arturo Prat 176-B, tel./fax 65/625977, website: www.austral-adventures.com, tours@austral-adventures.com, offers customized cruises on the 15-meter *Cahuella*.

THE SOUTHERN CARRETERA AUSTRAL

Even more thinly settled than the area north of Coyhaique, southern Aisén is wild country, with few and scattered services; barely 10,000 people live in more than 45,862 square km. The only towns with more than 1,000 inhabitants are Chile Chico, near the Argentine border on the south shore of Lago General Carrera, and Cochrane, directly on the Carretera Austral.

The highway is now paved all the way to Villa Cerro Castillo, 98 km south of Coyhaique. In late 1999, it finally reached its terminus at Villa O'Higgins, though it still requires a ferry shuttle from Puerto Yungay to Río Bravo for the last 100 km.

Reserva Nacional Cerro Castillo

Straddling the Carretera Austral beyond the airport turnoff to Balmaceda, marking the divide between the drainages of the Río Simpson to the north and the Río Ibáñez to the south, Cerro Castillo is a 179,550-hectare unit whose map boundaries look like pieces of a jigsaw puzzle. Its signature landmark is Cerro Castillo itself, whose soaring basaltic battlements, above the tree line, truly resemble a medieval castle.

Geography and Climate: Elevations range from about 500 meters to 2,320 meters on the summit of Cerro Castillo, embellished by three south-facing glaciers. Like most of the rest of the region, it gets substantial rainfall and snow at higher altitudes, but some east-facing areas enjoy a rain shadow effect.

Flora and Fauna: Nearly pure stands of *lenga (Nothofagus pumilio)* dominate the forest landscape up to about 1,200 meters, but there are also *coigüe (Nothofagus betuloides)*, *ñirre (Nothofagus antartica)*, and many shrubs. In rain shadow areas there are steppelike grasslands.

Among the mammals are puma, *huemul (Hippocamelus bisulcus)*, two species of foxes, and skunks. Birds are common, including the soaring Andean condor, various species of owls, the austral blackbird or *tordo (Curaeus curaeus)*, and the austral parakeet or *cachaña (Enicognathus ferrugineus)*.

Sights and Recreation: About eight km south of Laguna Chiguay, the trailhead for **Sendero Las Horquetas** is the starting point for a four-day backpack trip that climbs the valley of Estero la Lima to pass beneath the spires of Cerro Castillo before descending to Villa Cerro Castillo, a small village on the Carretera Austral. For details, see the second edition of Clem Lindenmayer's *Trekking in the Patagonian Andes* (Lonely Planet, 1998).

Accommodations: At the northeastern edge of the reserve, just off the Carretera Austral at Km 67, Conaf's woodsy **Camping Laguna Chiguay** charges US$4 per site. At the south end of the park, there are accommodations at Villa Cerro Castillo, just outside the reserve boundary.

Information: Conaf maintains a ranger station at the Laguna Chiguay campground.

Transportation: All public transportation between Coyhaique, on the one hand, and Puerto Ibáñez and Villa Cerro Castillo on the other hand, pass through the northern sector of the reserve.

Puerto Ingeniero Ibáñez

Before completion of the Carretera Austral, Puerto Ingeniero Ibáñez was a major lacustrine port on the north shore of Lago General Carrera, connecting Coyhaique with Chile Chico, on the south shore, and other ports around the lake. Its current livelihood derives from agriculture, both livestock and tree fruit such as apples and pears.

Since completion of the highway bypass, it's lost some of its economic clout, but the ferry from here to Chile Chico, for an easy border crossing to Argentina, is still quicker than the roundabout road system. It's about 110 km south of Coyhaique via the Carretera Austral and a to-be-paved lateral that bears south about 10 km east of Villa Cerro Castillo. There is also a rugged road crossing from here to Argentina along the north shore of the lake, which is known as Lago Buenos Aires on the other side.

Accommodations and Food: Simple **Residencial Ibáñez,** Dickson 31, tel. 67/423227, charges US$6 pp and also serves meals. Two blocks north, **Residencial Vientos del Sur,** Dickson 282, tel. 67/423208, costs about the same.

Transportation: Several companies operate minibuses to Coyhaique (US$6, three hours)—Colectivo Puerto Ibáñez, Transportes Ali, and Minibus Don Tito.

Naviera Sotramin sails the ferry *Pilchero* to Chile Chico (two hours) daily except Sunday at 10 A.M. Fares are US$3.50 pp for adult passengers, half that for children. Bicycles or motorcycles pay an additional US$7. Passenger vehicles up to five meters long pay US$37, while those longer than five meters pay US$11 per linear meter.

For ferry reservations in Coyhaique, contact Naviera Sotramin, Bolívar 254, tel. 67/234240, fax 67/233515.

Villa Cerro Castillo

Founded in 1966, under the Frei Montalva administration, the former frontier outpost of Villa Cerro Castillo is finally acquiring an air of permanency, though its exposed site makes it one of the bleaker settlements along the Carretera Austral. South of here, 89 km from Coyhaique, the paved segment of the highway ends and the gravel begins.

Hikers who begin the trek through Reserva Nacional Cerro Castillo at Las Horquetas will exit the reserve here. Nivaldo Calderón, at the local school, leads guided visits to nearby rock art sites at **Alero de las Manos,** just south of town.

Accommodations and Food: Cheap enough at US$6 pp with breakfast, **Pensión Andreita** has lots of blankets but lumpy beds and pretty awful food. For the same price, **Hospedaje La Querencia** has firm beds and good food for US$6 pp, but there is only one full bathroom for a maximum of 15 guests (though there are additional toilets). Its restaurant unavoidably gets lots of single men quaffing beers until closing.

The other choice for accommodations is **Hospedaje Torres del Castillo,** next door to La Querencia.

Transportation: All buses between Coyhaique, to the north, and Puerto Río Tranquilo, to the south, pass by the entrance to Villa Cerro Castillo.

Puerto Murta

West of Villa Cerro Castillo, the Carretera Austral climbs above the valley of the Río Ibáñez before veering south to Lago General Carrera and the tiny lakeside town of Puerto Murta, one of the best areas to see fall colors. There are a couple of simple accommodations in the US$6–7 range: **Hostería Lago General Carrera,** Avenida 5 de Abril 647, and **Residencial Patagonia,** Pasaje España 64. Both use the same community telephone, tel. 67/419600.

Puerto Río Tranquilo

Until completion of the Carretera Austral, Puerto Río Tranquilo was a lake port with a weekly supply boat from Puerto Ibáñez, but today it's a slowly but steadily growing settlement at the west end of Lago General Carrera, 25 km south of Puerto Murta. At the north end of town, a new road toward Bahía Exploradores, an inlet of the larger Estero Capquelán, has reached roughly the midway point at Lago Bayo; on completion, it should offer improved access to Parque Nacional Laguna San Rafael.

The area's best excursion goes to **Capilla de Mármol,** a remarkable series of marble grottos on the shoreline of Lago General Carrera, reached by launch from Puerto Río Tranquilo. The trip, which takes about 1.5 hours, costs around US$30 for up to five people, but may not be possible if winds are high. Ask at Residencial Los Pinos (see Accommodations and Food, below) to hire a launch.

Accommodations and Food: Local favorite **Residencial Darka,** two blocks west of the highway at Los Arrayanes 330, has smallish rooms with twin beds and shared bath for US$7 pp. Rates at **Residencial Carretera Austral,** right

Capilla de Mármol (Marble Chapel), Lago General Carrera

on the highway at 1 Sur 223, tel. 67/419500, are US$13 pp, but *cabaña* accommodations work out cheaper at about US$8 pp.

With 10 rooms arranged along each side of a corridor, friendly, family-run **Residencial Los Pinos,** 2 Oriente 41, tel. 67/411576, charges US$25 s or d for spotless accommodations with shared bath and breakfast; rates with private bath are US$33 s or d. Low-season prices are about 10–15 percent cheaper. Its restaurant is good enough, serving fixed-price lunches or dinners for about US$5; the dining room is tobacco-free.
Transportation: Scheduled buses on the Carretera Austral between Coihaique and Cochrane drop and pick up passengers here. Bus Estrella Sur goes to Puerto Guadal Tuesday and Thursday at 5 P.M.

Cruce El Maitén
Cruce El Maitén, about 50 km south of Puerto Río Tranquilo, is not a settlement but rather a crossroads with the eastbound highway to Puerto Guadal and Chile Chico, at the southwest corner of Lago General Carrera.

Almost right at the junction, **Hacienda Tres Lagos,** Km 274, tel./fax 67/411323, is one of the best accommodations options along the Carretera Austral. At the southwestern corner of Lago General Carrera, it provides, in addition to its spacious, well-lighted *cabañas,* sauna, horseback riding, fishing, and excursions to sights on and off the highway. Rates are US$150 s or d with breakfast and sauna access; its restaurant **El Parador Austral,** open to the public, has a superb kitchen. In Santiago, contact Hacienda Tres Lagos at Luis Thayer Ojeda 95, Oficina 302, tel. 2/2311927, fax 2/2316810, website: www.patagoniadream hotel.com, hacienda@terra.cl.

One km north of Hacienda Tres Lagos, at Km 273, **Mallín Colorado** has several log-style *cabañas* starting around US$92 s or d, with similar amenities. For more information, contact Patagonia Pacífica, Marcel Duhaut 2979, Providencia, Santiago, tel. 2/2741807, fax 2/2042785, website: www.patagonia-pacific.cl, chile@patagonia-pacific.cl.

Puerto Guadal
Another of the former lake ports now linked by highway, at the west end of Lago General Carrera, Puerto Guadal is more picturesque than most towns in the area. It lies 13 km east of the El

Maitén junction; from here, a rugged and narrow road leads northeast to Chile Chico and the Argentine border at Los Antiguos.

Accommodations and Food: Puerto Guadal has upgraded its free campground along the lakeshore. Otherwise, the cheapest accommodation is **Hostería Huemules,** Las Magnolias 382, tel. 67/411202, for US$9 pp; it also has a restaurant. **Cabañas Antué,** Los Pinos 456, tel. 67/431215, charges US$40 for up to six people for accommodations with hot showers, full kitchens, and wood stoves for heat; check in at Supermercado Plaza, Las Camelias 147.

On the eastern outskirts of town, the elegantly simple **Terra Luna,** tel. 67/431263, fax 67/431264, website: www.terra-luna.cl, t-luna @netline.cl, enjoys an exceptional woodsy setting overlooking the lakeshore. While it specializes in weeklong activities-oriented packages, it also rents "ministudio" accommodations for US$25 s or d in the off-season, US$35 s or d in summer; rooms in the main lodge go for US$70 s or d off-season, US$120 s or d in summer. Breakfast is included, other meals are extra. Its Santiago contact is Azimut 360, Arzobispo Casanova 3, Providencia, tel. 2/7358034, fax 2/7772375, azimut@reuna.cl.

Café de La Frontera, Los Lirios 399, is the best place to eat in town.

Transportation: Bus Estrella Sur goes Monday and Thursday at 8 A.M. to Coyhaique, and to Puerto Río Tranquilo at 7:30 A.M. Tuesday and Thursday only, returning at 5 P.M. To Chile Chico, there are buses Monday and Friday at 7:30 A.M., returning at 5 P.M.

Several companies now cover the 110 km northeast to Chile Chico (US$7.50, three hours), including Transportes Ale (Tuesday and Friday), Sergio Haro (Thursday and Sunday) and Transportes Seguel (Monday and Friday).

Chile Chico

Settled from Argentina in the early 20th century, on the southern shore of Lago General Carrera, Chile Chico developed in virtually autonomous isolation from the rest of Chile, and connections are still better with Argentina than with most of mainland Chile. One of the easiest border cross-

THE ERUPTION OF VOLCÁN HUDSON

In the vicinity of Lago General Carrera, which continues east across the Argentine border as Lago Buenos Aires, travelers will see the results of the August 1991 eruption of the remote, 1,935-meter Volcán Hudson, northwest of Villa Cerro Castillo. Chile's second-largest 20th-century eruption deposited more than one cubic km of ash in Chile, about two cubic km in Argentine Patagonia, and another two cubic km over the South Atlantic Ocean; in some areas, the accumulated ash fall reached a depth of more than 1.5 meters. Northwesterly winds carried the ash plume southeast to the Falkland Islands and South Georgia, in the South Atlantic, and eventually as far as Australia. Heavy winds, in excess of 100 km per hour, also remobilized already-fallen ash to cover pasture and watercourses, resulting in the deaths of tens of thousands of cattle and sheep.

ings in the region, it also enjoys access to remote protected areas such as Reserva Nacional Jeinimeni, and it is the starting (or finishing) point for the wild rugged highway to or from Puerto Guadal and the Carretera Austral. From Los Antiguos, just across the border, travelers can make connections to the Atlantic coast city of Caleta Olivia, nearby Perito Moreno, and southern Argentine Patagonian destinations such as El Chaltén and El Calafate, which now have reliable bus transportation.

Despite brief mining booms, most recently with the Fachinal gold and silver mine to the west, Chile Chico's enduring economic base has been the production of temperate fruits, thanks to its mild lakeshore microclimate. This has not exactly brought prosperity, however, as even after the completion of the first motor road from Coyhaique to Puerto Ibáñez, in 1952, the town remained remote from any sizable market. Ash deposits from the 1991 eruption of Volcán Hudson depressed agricultural production, which has recovered only in the past few years.

Orientation: Only five km west of the Argentine border, Chile Chico is 122 km northeast of

Cruce El Maitén via the narrow, precipitous road along the south shore of Lago General Carrera. Avenida O'Higgins, one block south of the lakeshore, is the main thoroughfare in both directions; the central grid extends about 10 blocks from east to west, and four blocks from north to south. The Plaza de Armas is in the northwest corner of town.

Museo de la Casa de la Cultura: Much improved in recent years, but still lacking interpretive panels, Chile Chico's museum displays regional painting and sculpture along with paleontological materials, historical artifacts from early colonists, and, connected to the second story by a walkway leading straight to its deck, the restored *Los Andes,* which once ferried passengers and cargo around the lake. The museum, at the corner of O'Higgins and Lautaro, tel. 67/411268, fax 67/411355, is open 10 A.M.–7 P.M. daily except Sunday, from December to March only. Admission is free.

Accommodations: For US$7 pp, **Hospedaje Eben Ezer,** Manuel Rodríguez 302, tel. 67/4-11535, is unexceptional but acceptable. Others in the same category include **Hotel Plaza,** at Balmaceda and O'Higgins, tel. 67/411510, and **Hostal Turismo,** Avenida O'Higgins 750, tel. 67/411030. About one km east of town, **Hospedaje No Me Olvides,** on quiet grounds at Camino Internacional s/n, charges about the same amount.

Hospedaje Don Luis, Balmaceda 175, tel. 67/411384, is the best of the cheapest for US$9 pp without breakfast. For the same price, **Hospedaje Brisas del Lago,** Manuel Rodríguez 443, tel. 67/411204, is a decent alternative.

The Belgian-Chilean **Hostal de la Patagonia,** on the eastern outskirts of town at Camino Internacional s/n, tel./fax 67/411337, is an ivy-covered country inn with large, rustically decorated but cozy rooms for US$17 pp with private bath and breakfast (excellent homemade bread); there's also one tiny single with external bath for US$12. Camping and additional meals are also available. **Hotel Ventura,** Carrera 290, tel. 67/411311, for US$33 d, is possibly the best in town proper since a couple of others in its category closed.

Food: There's nothing really outstanding in Chile Chico, though the dining room at **Hostal de la Patagonia** (see above) is pretty good. **Café Elizabeth y Loly,** on the east side of the Plaza de Armas at González 25, tel. 67/411288, serves reliable breakfasts, sandwiches, and *onces.*

Café Wild West, González 115, tel. 67/411382, serves standard Chilean meals of decent quality. **Pub El Minero,** Carrera 205, tel. 67/411521, serves moderately priced lunches and drinks.

Services: Open 10 A.M.–1 P.M. weekdays only, Banco del Estado, González 112, is slow to change both U.S. cash and traveler's checks (the latter pay high commissions and suffer even worse bureaucracy).

Correos de Chile is at Manuel Rodríguez 121, on the north side of the Plaza de Armas.

There are several long-distance telephone offices: Entel on O'Higgins between Pedro Montt and Lautaro, Fonosol on O'Higgins at Marchant Pereira, and at Café Elizabeth y Loly, González 25. The area code is 67, the same as Coyhaique's.

Hospital Chile Chico is at Lautaro 275, tel. 67/411334.

Information: Chile Chico's Oficina de Información Turística is within the Casa de la Cultura, at O'Higgins and Lautaro. In summer only, it's open Tuesday to Saturday 10 A.M.–1:30 P.M. and 2:30–7:30 P.M., Sunday 10 A.M.–1 P.M. only.

For national parks information, Conaf is at Blest Gana 121, tel. 67/411325.

Transportation: Transporte Aéreo Don Carlos, on González just south of Avenida O'Higgins, tel. 67/411490, flies daily except Sunday to Coyhaique (US$33). Aeródromo Chile Chico, tel. 67/411284, is just east of town, on the road to the Argentine border.

Two bus companies shuttle passengers to the Argentine border at Los Antiguos (US$2, 30 minutes): Transportes Padilla, O'Higgins 424, tel. 67/411224, goes four times daily except on weekends, when it goes once only, and Acotrans, tel. 67/411841, which goes five times daily except Sunday.

Transportes Seguel, also at O'Higgins 424, tel. 67/411443, goes to Puerto Guadal Monday and Friday at 2 P.M. Transportes Ales, Rosa

Amelia 800, tel. 67/411739, goes Tuesday at 10 A.M. to Puerto Guadal (US$9, three hours) and Puerto Río Tranquilo, and Friday at 10 A.M. to Puerto Guadal and Cochrane (US$17, six hours). Sergio Haro, Manuel Rodríguez 30, tel. 67/411251, goes Wednesday and Saturday at 10 A.M. to Puerto Guadal (US$8, three hours) and Cruce El Maitén (US$11), on the Carretera Austral.

Sotramin's vehicle-passenger ferry *El Pilchero* sails weekdays at 5 P.M. and Sunday at noon to Puerto Ingeniero Ibáñez, on the north shore of the lake. (For fares, see the entry for Puerto Ingeniero Ibáñez, above.)

Reserva Nacional Lago Jeinemeni

From Chile Chico, a 4WD-only road parallels the border (not to mention another similar road on the Argentine side) to Reserva Nacional Lago Jeinemeni, a rarely visited protected area of 161,000 hectares. There is little infrastructure except for a campground (US$4); Conaf rangers collect US$1 admission.

Puerto Bertrand

Lago Bertrand, separated from Lago General Carrera by a short narrow channel, is the source of the Río Baker, Chile's largest river in terms of its flow. The village of Puerto Bertrand, beautifully sited on the lake's southeastern shore, is a convenient base for exploring the area, though there are several lodges in the immediate vicinity. It is 11 km south of Cruce El Maitén.

Sights and Recreation: For water sports—rafting, kayaking, and fly-fishing—the **Río Baker** itself is the big draw. Because it has relatively few rocks and play spots, the Baker's Class 2 and 3 rapids draw fewer rafters and kayakers than the rugged Futaleufú, but its fast current, huge flow, large waves, and occasional deep holes make it exciting enough for beginners (a bit farther south of Puerto Bertrand, only a handful of world-class kayakers could survive the Cascada Nef Baker, a thunderous eight-meter waterfall at the Baker's confluence with the Río Nef). A string of fly-fishing lodges lines the highway south of Puerto Bertrand, beneath the glistening backdrop of the northern Patagonian ice field.

From October through April, Bertrand-based, U.S.-run **Patagonia Adventure Expeditions,** tel./fax 67/411330, riobaker@entelchile.net, arranges rafting, kayaking, hiking, climbing, and horseback riding in the vicinity; there is also a specialist fly-fishing guide. Half-day trips down the Baker cost US$25 pp; a more ambitious 212-km, eight- to 12-day descent to the ocean costs US$1,800–2,400 pp. Kayak instruction costs US$100 pp per day, while fly-fishing on the Baker costs US$130 pp for half a day, US$210 for a full day (alternatively, US$180 pp for two people). Its Chilean postal address is Casilla 519, Coyhaique, where it also has a permanent office half a block from the Plaza de Armas (for details, see the Coyhaique entry). Its U.S. contact is 5259 Elk Ridge Rd., Evergreen, CO 80439, tel./fax 303/670-8918.

Accommodations and Food: There are a few accommodations in Puerto Bertrand itself and others in the immediate vicinity, just south of town. Several of them are fishing lodges that cater mostly to weeklong holidays, but if space is available they'll take drop-in guests.

Easily the cheapest option, in town, is the riverside **Camping Municipal,** for only US$3 pp. Several simple places cost in the US$10 pp range with breakfast, among them **Hospedaje Vargas** and **Hospedaje Casa Ester.** The upstairs front room at **Hostería Bertrand,** tel./fax 67/419900, has central heating of a sort—the chimney pipe from the downstairs woodstove passes directly through the middle of the room. Rates are about US$15 pp; its restaurant is also a good place to eat.

Also in town, Argentine-run **Hostería Río Baker,** tel. 67/411447, enjoys a stunning riverside location with great fly-fishing possibilities for $80/120 s/d. It has contact numbers in Buenos Aires, tel. 54/11/48639373 and Mendoza, tel. 54/261/4202196.

Three km south of town, the **Cabañas Rápidos Río Baker,** tel. 67/411199, tel. 67/236867 in Coyhaique, or 09/8215900, website: www.riobaker.cl, aligduran@hotmail.com, charges US$120 for up to six people. Also south of town, on the west side of the highway, the **Patagonia Baker Lodge,** tel. 67/411903, website:

www.patagonia-baker-lodge.cl, rochi@directo.cl, is a new riverside lodge charging US$130 s or d. **Transportation:** Buses between Coyhaique and Cochrane, and between Chile Chico and Cochrane, pass near the entrance to town.

Cruce Paso Roballos

At the confluence of the Río Baker and Río Nef, roughly 15 km south of Puerto Bertrand, the **Cascada Nef Baker** is a thunderous eight-meter waterfall on the property of Dimanc Cárcamo, who charges US$2.50 for cars to enter. The Carretera Austral continues south to Cochrane and Villa O'Higgins, while an eastbound lateral ascends the Río Chacabuco valley to 647-meter Paso Roballos, the region's most southerly border crossing passable to motor vehicles (others farther south are for nonmotorized transport only). Across the border, at the bleak crossroads of Bajo Caracoles (gasoline available), Argentina's dusty Ruta 40 leads south to El Calafate, an alternative approach to Chile's Parque Nacional Torres del Paine.

Cochrane

Once literally the end of the road, the tidy town of Cochrane may still have more horses than automobiles but, says one immigrant:

If you park your horse in front of the bar now, you'll get a ticket for shitting on the sidewalk.

While attractive enough for a frontier settlement, thanks to its neatly landscaped Plaza de Armas and broad paved streets, its main appeal is the surrounding countryside of Reserva Nacional Tamango and Reserva Nacional Cochrane, north and northeast of town.

Cochrane is an obligatory stop for southbound wanderers, partly because it's the last accommodations and food for nearly 300 km and partly because it's home to **Casa Melero,** Patagonia's greatest general store. It's *the* place to buy camping gear, canoes, chainsaws, chocolate, fine wines, fishing gear, and almost anything else you can't find between here and Antarctica. Cochrane also, apparently, was the end of the line for the traveling salesman responsible for the lurid red bedspreads seen in many cheap hotels along the Carretera Austral.

Orientation: Cochrane is 345 km south of Coyhaique and 225 km north of Villa O'Higgins via the Carretera Austral. Its core is a rectangular grid that's only about three blocks from north to south, but about nine blocks from west to east, where the Río Cochrane marks its limit.

highway sign on the Carretera Austral

Note that recent changes mean inconsistencies in street numbering, but the town is small enough that orientation remains fairly simple.

Accommodations: Several places charge in the US$9–10 range pp, including **Residencial Sur Austral,** Prat 281, tel. 67/522150, which also has a restaurant; remodeled **Residencial Paola,** Lago Brown 150; and **Residencial Cochrane,** Dr. Steffens 451, tel. 67/522377. **Residencial El Fogón,** San Valentín 651, tel. 67/522240, charges US$11 pp and has probably the best restaurant in town.

Rates at **Residencial Cero a Cero,** Lago Brown 464, tel. 67/522158, are US$15 pp with private bath. Homey, comfortably furnished **Residencial Rubio,** Teniente Merino 871, tel. 67/522173, has spacious, spotless rooms with twin beds, private bath and breakfast for $24/36 s/d (there are some cheaper rooms with shared bath). It's popular with cycling groups.

On spacious and well-landscaped grounds, **Hotel Wellmann,** Las Golondrinas 36, tel. 67/522171, costs US$23 pp with breakfast. On contrastingly barren grounds in urgent need of landscaping, Spanish-run **Hotel Ultimo Paraíso,** across the street from Residencial Cero a Cero at Lago Brown 455, tel./fax 67/522361, is otherwise exceptional, with eight well-heated, spacious, and attractive rooms with private bath for US$47/58. The restaurant, for guests only, charges US$12 for lunch or dinner.

Food: Part of its namesake *hospedaje,* **El Fogón,** San Valentín 651, is probably Cochrane's best restaurant—while the name implies a *parrilla,* the menu is more diverse than that, with fish, including conger eel, hake, and salmon, and fowl, in the US$7–10 range. Its specialty, though, is the *doble infarto* ("double heart attack") of steak, eggs, onions, and French fries smothered in a pepper cream sauce.

Rogeri, Teniente Merino 502, tel. 67/522264, is a suitable alternative for sandwiches and simple lunches. The dining room at **Residencial Sur Austral,** Prat 281, also deserves consideration.

Services: Banco del Estado, on the east side of the Plaza de Armas at Esmeralda 460, will change cash or traveler's check, but change elsewhere if possible.

Correos de Chile is at Esmeralda 199.

There's a long-distance telephone office at San Valentín and Las Golondrinas. The area code is 67.

Hospital Cochrane is at O'Higgins 755, tel. 67/522131.

Information: From October to March only, the municipal Oficina de Información Turística operates from a kiosk at the southeast corner of the Plaza de Armas; it's open daily except Sunday 10 A.M.–1 P.M. and 2:30–8 P.M.

For information on areas outside town, contact Turismo Rural Río Baker, San Valentín 438, tel. 67/522646, website: www.turismoriobaker.cl, trural@patagoniachile.cl.

For specific information on nearby parks and reserves, visit Conaf at Río Nef 417, tel. 67/522164.

Transportation: Transporte Aéreo Don Carlos, alongside Residencial Sur Austral at Prat 281, tel. 67/522150, flies Monday and Thursday to Coyhaique (US$58). Southbound flights from Coihaique, on the same days, continue to Villa O'Higgins.

Buses Don Carlos, Prat 281, tel. 67/522150, goes to Coyhaique (US$13) Wednesday and Sunday at 8:30 A.M. Buses Los Ñadis, Los Helechos 420, tel. 67/522196, goes to Coyhaique (US$16), Monday, Wednesday, and Saturday at 8:30 A.M., to Villa O'Higgins Thursday at 8 A.M. (US$9), and Puerto Vagabundo (US$6), combining with the launch to Tortel, at 10 A.M. Tuesday, Thursday, and Sunday.

Buses Acuario 13, Río Baker 349, tel. 67/5-22143, goes to Coyhaique Tuesday, Thursday, and Friday at 8:15 A.M., to Villa O'Higgins at 8:15 A.M. Sunday, and to Puerto Vagabundo Tuesday, Thursday, Saturday, and Sunday at 10 A.M.

Transportes Ale, Las Golondrinas 399, tel. 67/522448, goes to Puerto Guadal and Chile Chico Wednesday and Sunday at 10 A.M.

Reserva Nacional Lago Cochrane

Informally but inaccurately known as Reserva Nacional Tamango, Reserva Nacional Lago Cochrane is most notable as home to the endangered *huemul (Hippocamelus bisulcus),* which appears on Chile's coat of arms. On the north

shore of its namesake lake, the 6,925-hectare reserve is only six km northwest of the town of
Cochrane. Admission at the Guardería Húngaro
entrance to the reserve costs US$2 pp.

Launch excursions to see the *huemules,* to the
east end of the lake, cost US$50 for up to six
people. While there is no regular public transportation to the reserve, it's close enough that
hitching is possible and even hiring a taxi is not
prohibitively expensive.

On the north bank of the Río Cochrane,
Conaf's four-site **Camping Las Correntadas**
charges US$10 per site; each site has a picnic
table, wash basin, and fire pit. There is also a
four-person *cabaña* for US$33, which has a bath-
room but no shower.

Accessible only by a 45-minute hike, Conaf's
lakeside **Camping Playa Paleta** also has four
campsites and three *cabañas* with bath but without shower. Prices are the same as at Las Correntadas.

Puerto Vagabundo

Not even a wide spot in the road, Puerto
Vagabundo is nothing more than a dock and a
couple of ancillary buildings at a road-river
junction between the Carretera Austral and the
Río Vagabundo, a tributary of the Río Baker
about 118 km southwest of Cochrane and 15
km north of Puerto Yungay. An extremely basic
A-frame shelter, with a woodstove, keeps the
rain off passengers who are waiting for the
downstream launch to Caleta Tortel, a quaint
fishing village at the mouth of the Baker. A
road along the Baker's south bank to Tortel was
under construction.

Buses running from Cochrane to Vagabundo
link up with the subsidized launch to Tortel,
on which tourists may travel on a space-available
basis. Departures are at 8 A.M. Tuesday, Thursday, and Sunday; for more information, contact Tortel's public telephone at tel. 67/211876.
Alternatively, contact Jorge Arratia, tel.
67/234815, who does charters to Tortel for
US$180 for up to eight passengers, including
side trips to the Jorge Montt and Steffen Glaciers on the Campo de Hielo Norte, the northern
Patagonian ice field.

Caleta Tortel

Caleta Tortel, at the mouth of the Río Baker, is a
uniquely picturesque fishing village whose houses are linked by boardwalks rather than sidewalks—for the moment, at least, water is the
main means of transportation, until completion
of the road from Vagabundos.

For accommodations, contact Sergio Barria,
tel. 67/234815, for nicely designed *cabañas* with
shared bath and kitchen facilities for US$10 pp.
Transportation to Tortel involves either downriver
boat travel from Puerto Vagabundo (see above) or
air taxi service from Coyhaique with Transportes
Aéreos San Rafael, Wednesday, for US$25.

Puerto Yungay

Until 1999 Puerto Yungay, on the north shore of
the Fiordo Mitchell, was the end of the Carretera
Austral, but now it's the port for a flat-bottomed,
four-car ferry to a ramp at Río Bravo, the last
link to Villa O'Higgins, the highway's most
southerly outpost. When the road opened in December of that year, according to Sergeant Eduardo Martínez of the Cuerpo Militar de Trabajo
(CMT, Chile's Army Corps of Engineers), it was
the site of the highway's biggest traffic jam waiting for the ferry:

> *There were so many cars backed up that
> we were working from 7 A.M. until mid-
> night. Some days we couldn't handle all
> of them, so they had to camp and wait
> until the next day.*

The CMT may someday carve a road along
the sheer rock wall of the north side of the fjord,
but it won't be as fast as the ferry to Río Bravo,
where the road to Villa O'Higgins resumes.
There, some visionary (or hallucinatory) politicians envision a further southern link to the famous Parque Nacional Torres del Paine, a project
that could take 20–25 years and still require eight
or nine ferry crossings.

Four *cabañas* formerly belonging to the CMT
were to be donated to the communities of Tortel
and Villa O'Higgins, for use as information centers, accommodations, and cafes. The ferry from
Puerto Yungay now runs on demand during daylight hours; for more information or reservations,

try contacting the Departamento de Vialidad in Cochrane, at the corner of Avenida O'Higgins and Esmeralda, tel. 67/521242.

Villa O'Higgins

For decades, the frontier outpost of Villa O'Higgins was accessible only by air taxi from Coyhaique, or by water from Argentina. It depended on Argentine supplies, and highway construction materials entered via Argentine roads and ferries on Lago O'Higgins (Lago San Martín to Argentines). Now, though, the ferry from Puerto Yungay drops passengers and vehicles at Río Bravo, a boat ramp 100 km northwest of Villa O'Higgins, for the last leg of the trip down the Carretera Austral.

When the new road finally opened, said ex-policeman Arturo Gómez, curious tourists overran the town's 12 square blocks.

> *We were at full capacity, and most of the people here have scarce resources and couldn't arrange things so soon.*

People camped, slept in spare rooms, and rented a handful of *cabañas*. "We didn't evolve step-by-step," said Mayor Alfredo Ronín. "We went from horseback to jet."

Villa O'Higgins is now booming with new construction, and the town of 350 has big plans. The idea, said the mayor, "is to promote the ice, because that's what we've got the most of."

Sights: Directly east of town, a footpath leads to a scenic overlook that's part of the **Reserva Natural Shöen,** Chile's first municipal nature reserve. Hoping to attract adventurous hikers and climbers, local authorities have forged a trail from patching together and signing existing forest paths to a backwoods shelter near the **Ventisquero Mosco** (Mosco Glacier).

Villa O'Higgins lies in the broad valley of the **Río Mayer,** a prime trout stream. Just south of town, a secondary road reaches **Bahía Bahamonde,** where there's a new launch destined to carry tourists up Lago O'Higgins to the **Ventisquero O'Higgins** (O'Higgins Glacier). The town also owns a ferry capable of carrying passengers and vehicles to the Argentine side, but at present it has no authority to do so.

It is possible, however, to make a very difficult border crossing by hiring a launch to the south end of Lago O'Higgins and making a difficult hike through rugged country to Laguna del Desierto, on the Argentine side. From this point there's a road to the village of El Chaltén, in Argentina's Parque Nacional Los Glaciares. Some people have even done this by mountain bike, but that involves carrying the bike and supplies for a good part of the way, and hiring a local guide is a good idea. Consult with Carabineros on border formalities.

Across the valley of the Río Mayer, the steeply rising peaks of the **Campo de Hielo Sur,** the southern Patagonian icecap, may be the next big thing for hikers for whom Torres del Paine has become too tame.

Accommodations and Food: There are many places to camp inexpensively in and around town. Until recently, Villa O'Higgins had only one permanent lodge, the simple but well-kept **Hospedaje Patagonia,** opposite the Plaza de Armas at Río Pascua s/n; for US$12 pp, it has comfortable beds and a decent breakfast. In summer, it serves lunch and dinner as well.

The new **Hospedaje Dónde El Diablo Perdió El Poncho,** tel. 67/216927 for reservations, charges US$13 pp with breakfast, and it also has a bar. About two km south of town, **Cabañas Península la Florida,** tel. 67/232713 for reservations, has comfortable accommodations for up to four people for US$50.

It's hard to get a meal anywhere out of season, though this is likely to change as the influx of tourists increases.

Transportation: Transportes Don Carlos flies to Coyhaique (US$85) Monday and Thursday.

Bus services to and from Cochrane are improving if not exactly frequent. For the moment, Acuario 13 goes to Cochrane at 10 A.M. Monday, while Los Nadis goes at 8 A.M. Friday. The fare is about US$9.

Magallanes Region

Chile's most southerly region has acquired international fame thanks to the Torres del Paine, the magnificent granitic needles that rise above the Patagonian plains. Pacific storms drench the nearly uninhabited western Andean cordillera, feeding alpine and continental glaciers and rushing rivers, but rolling grasslands and seemingly unstoppable winds typify the eastern areas in the Andean rain shadow. Along the Strait of Magellan, the city of Punta Arenas is the center for excursions to a variety of attractions, including easily accessible penguin colonies and the remote fjords of Tierra del Fuego. The region has no direct road connections to the rest of Chile—travelers must arrive by air, sea, and through Argentine Patagonia.

Administratively, Region XII (Magallanes) includes all Chilean territory beyond 49° S—theoretically all the way to the South Pole, as Chile claims a slice of Antarctica between 53° and 90° W longitude. It also takes in the Chilean half of the Isla Grande de Tierra del Fuego, west of about 68°35', and most of archipelagic Tierra del Fuego. For convenience, this section of the chapter also covers the most southeasterly parts of Argentina's Santa Cruz province and the Argentine side of Tierra del Fuego, both of which attract many visitors from the Chilean side.

HISTORY

Some of the oldest archaeological evidence for human habitation on the entire continent comes from Magallanes, from volcanic rock shelters in and near Parque Nacional Pali Aike on the Argentine border. Pleistocene hunter-gatherers once stalked now extinct species such as giant ground sloths and native American horses, but they later adopted more broad-spectrum forms of subsistence that included marine and coastal resources. These peoples were the predecessors of today's few surviving Tehuelche and Kawasqar (Alacaluf) peoples and the nearly extinct Selknam (Ona) and Yámana (Yahgan) who gathered shellfish on the coast and hunted guanaco and rhea with bows and arrows and *boleadoras*.

European familiarity with southernmost South America dates from 1520, when the Portuguese navigator Fernando Magalhaes, in the service of Spain, sailed through the strait that now bears his name (Magallanes in Spanish, Magellan in English). Ranging from three to 25 km in width, the Strait of Magellan became a major maritime thoroughfare en route to the Pacific.

Spain's 16th-century colonization attempts failed miserably, as did the initial Chilean and Argentine efforts, but the city of Punta Arenas finally took hold in 1848—thanks largely to the fortuitous discovery of gold in California only a year later. While gold fever soon subsided, the introduction of sheep brought a wool and mutton boom that benefited from the Franco-Prussian War of the 1870s and led to the creation of enormous *estancias* that dominated the region's political, social, and economic life for nearly a century.

While the livestock industry hangs on, commercial fisheries, the state-run oil industry, and the tourist trade have superseded it in the regional economy. Even these industries, though, have proved vulnerable to fluctuations, declining reserves, and international developments beyond their control, so that Magallanes cannot count on the prosperity that once seemed assured. The Zona Franca free trade zone that once served as the motor of the regional economy, even drawing immigrants from central Chile, has largely stagnated.

PUNTA ARENAS

Patagonia's largest city, Punta Arenas (population about 135,000) is also the regional capital and the traditional port of entry, whether by sea, land, or air. Stretching north-south along the Strait of Magellan, the city boasts an architectural heritage that varies from the Magellanic vernacular of metal-clad houses with steeply pitched roofs to elaborate Francophile mansions erected by the 19th-century wool barons. It is home to several museums and a good base for excursions to historical sites and nearby penguin colonies.

PATAGONIA & TIERRA

Punta Arenas has a diverse economy that depends on fishing, shipping, petroleum, duty-free retail, and tourism. Historically, it's one of the main gateways to Antarctica for both research and tourism, but in recent years the Argentine port of Ushuaia has taken away much of this traffic. Ironically, in a region where there are millions of sheep, it's hard to find woolens here because of the influx of artificial fabrics through the duty-free Zona Franca.

History

After the collapse of Chile's initial Patagonian settlement at Fuerte Bulnes, Governor José Santos Mardones relocated northward to a site on the western shore of the Strait of Magellan, long known to British seamen as "Sandy Point." Soon expanded to include a penal colony, the town adopted that name in Spanish translation.

The Chileans' timing was propitious, as the California Gold Rush of 1849 brought a surge of shipping through the strait that helped keep the new city afloat, even if supplying sealskins, coal, firewood, and lumber did not exactly portend prosperity. A mutiny that resulted in the death of Governor Benjamín Muñoz Gamero did little to improve matters, and traffic fell off in the following years.

What did bring prosperity was Governor Diego Dublé Almeyda's introduction of breeding sheep from the Falkland Islands, their proliferation on the Patagonian plains, and a vigorous immigration policy that brought entrepreneurs such as the Portuguese José Nogueira, the Spaniard José Menéndez, and the Irishman Thomas Fenton—not to mention the polyglot laborers who made their fortunes possible. Together, they transformed the city from a dreary presidio to the booming port of a pastoral empire, with mansions to match those of Buenos Aires, though the maldistribution of wealth and political power remained an intractable issue well into the 20th century.

As the wool economy declined around the end of World War II, petroleum discoveries on Tierra del Fuego and commercial fishing have sustained the city economically. Creation of Zona Franca duty-free zones gave commercial advan-

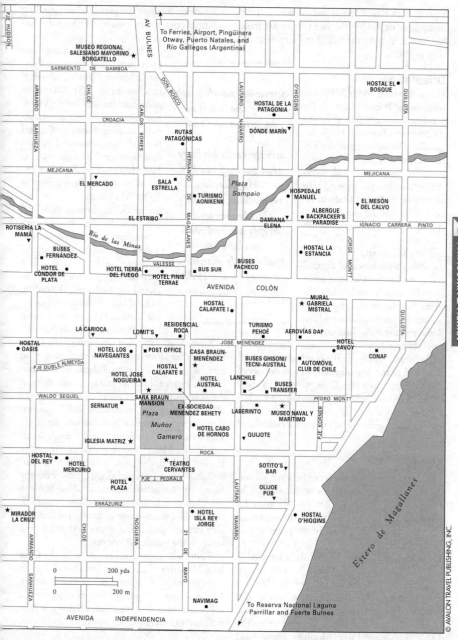

PATAGONIA & TIERRA

tages to both Punta Arenas and the northern city of Iquique in the 1970s, and the tourist trade has increased since the end of military dictatorship in 1989.

Orientation

Punta Arenas is about 2,300 km southeast of Puerto Montt via the Cardenal Samoré pass over the Andes from Osorno, through Argentina. On the western shore of the Strait of Magellan, it occupies a narrow north-south wave-cut terrace, but the ground rises steeply farther west. Only in recent years has the city begun to spread eastward rather than north to south.

Most landmarks and services are within a few blocks of the central Plaza Muñoz Gamero; street names change on each side of the plaza, but the numbering system is continuous. Northbound Ruta 9, the region's major highway, is a smoothly paved road that connects Punta Arenas with Puerto Natales to the northeast, and with Ruta 255 to the Argentine border and the city of Río Gallegos, in Santa Cruz province. A daily vehicle ferry connects Punta with Porvenir, while a gravel road, the most southerly on the South American continent, leads to Fuerte Bulnes and Cabo San Isidro.

Sights

For a panoramic overview of the city's layout, the Strait of Magellan, and the island of Tierra del Fuego in the distance, climb to **Mirador La Cruz,** four blocks west of Plaza Muñoz Gamero via a staircase at the corner of the Fagnano and Señoret.

Plaza Muñoz Gamero: Unlike plazas founded in colonial Chilean cities, Punta Arenas's central plaza was not initially the focus of civic life, but thanks to European immigration and wealth generated by generated by mining, livestock, commerce, and fishing, it became so by the 1880s. Landscaped with Monterey cypress and

Stretching north-south along the Strait of Magellan, the city boasts an architectural heritage that varies from the Magellanic vernacular of metal-clad houses with steeply pitched roofs to elaborate Francophile mansions erected by the 19th-century wool barons.

other exotic conifers, the plaza and surrounding buildings constitute a *zona típica* national monument.

The plaza takes its name from early provincial governor Benjamín Muñoz Gamero, who died in a mutiny in 1851. Among its additional features are the **Victorian kiosk** (1910) that now houses the municipal tourist office and the elaborate sculptural monument sponsored by wool magnate José Menéndez on the 400th anniversary of Magellan's voyage of 1520. Magellan's imposing figure, embellished with a globe and a copy of his log, stand above a Selknam Indian representing Tierra del Fuego, a Tehuelche symbolizing Patagonia, and a mermaid with Chilean and regional coats-of-arms. According to local legend, anyone touching the Tehuelche's now well-worn toe will return to Punta Arenas.

After about 1880, the city's burgeoning elite began to build monuments to their own good fortune, such as the ornate **Palacio Sara Braun** (1895), a national monument in its own right, at the northwest corner of the plaza. Only six years after marrying the Portuguese José Nogueira, Punta's most prosperous businessman, the newly widowed Sara Braun contracted French architect Numa Mayer, who applied contemporary Parisian style in designing a two-story mansard building that contrasted dramatically with the city's earlier utilitarian architecture. Now home to the Club de la Unión and Hotel José Nogueira, the building retains most of its original features, including the west-facing winter garden that now serves as the hotel's bar/restaurant.

Midblock, immediately to the east, the **Casa José Menéndez** belonged to another of Punta's wool barons, while at the plaza's northeast corner, Citibank now occupies the former offices of the influential **Sociedad Menéndez Behety,** at Magallanes 990. Half a block north, at Magallanes

949, the **Casa Braun-Menéndez** (1904) houses the regional museum.

At the southwest corner of the plaza, Punta Arenas's **Iglesia Matriz** (1901) has since earned cathedral status. Immediately to its north, both the **Residencia del Gobernador** (Governors' Residence) and the **Gobernación** date from the same period, filling the rest of the block with offices of the Intendencia Regional, the regional government. On the south side, directly opposite the Victorian tourist kiosk, the former **Palacio Montés** now holds municipal government offices, while the building at the southeast corner, the **Sociedad Braun Blanchard,** belonged to another powerful commercial group (as should be obvious from the names, the first families of Punta Arenas were, commercially at least, an incestuous bunch).

Museo Regional de Magallanes: Like European royalty, the first families of Punta Arenas formed alliances sealed by marriage, and the Casa Braun-Menéndez (1904) is a classic example: the product of a marriage between Mauricio Braun (Sara's brother) and Josefina Menéndez Behety (daughter of José Menéndez and María Behety, daughter of a major wool-growing family in Argentina—though international borders

meant little to wool merchants). Still furnished with the family's belongings, it now serves as the regional museum, replete with pioneer settlers' artifacts and historical photographs.

From November to April, the Casa Braun-Menéndez, Magallanes 949, tel. 61/244216, is open 10:30 A.M.–5 P.M. daily except Sunday, when hours are 10:30 A.M.– 2 P.M.; the rest of the year, hours are 10:30 A.M.–2 P.M. daily except Monday. Admission costs US$1.25 for adults, half that for children, but is free on holidays. Note that, since the Magallanes gate is closed, the grounds are accessible only from Lautaro Navarro, immediately to the east on the opposite side of the property. **More Sights near the Plaza:** Four blocks south of Plaza Muñoz Gamero, at the foot of Avenida Independencia, naval vessels, freighters, cruise ships, Antarctic icebreakers, and yachts from many countries dock at the **Muelle Fiscal Arturo Prat,** the city's major port facility until recently. Open to the public, it is also the point of departure for cruises to the fjords of Tierra del Fuego and to Antarctica.

The late, gifted travel writer Bruce Chatwin found the inspiration for his legendary stories *In Patagonia* through tales of his distant relative Charley Milward, who built and resided at the

PATAGONIA & TIERRA

© WAYNE BERNHARDSON

former Sara Braun mansion in Punta Arenas

Castillo Milward (Milward's Castle), described by Chatwin as "a Victorian parsonage translated to the Strait of Magellan." At Avenida España 959, with "high-pitched gables and gothic windows," the building features a square tower on the street side and an octagonal one at the back.

At the corner of Avenida Colón and O'Higgins, gracing the walls of the former **Liceo de Niñas Sara Braun** (Sara Braun Girls' School), rises a seven-meter **Mural Gabriela Mistral,** honoring the Nobel Prize poet.

Ten blocks north of Plaza Muñoz Gamero, at Avenida Bulnes 029, the **Cementerio Municipal** is home to the extravagant crypts of José Menéndez, José Nogueira, and Sara Braun, but the multinational immigrants who worked for them—English, Scots, Welsh, Croat, German, and Scandinavian—repose in more modest circumstances. A separate monument honors the vanished Selknam (Ona) Indians who once flourished in the strait, and another memorializes German fatalities of the Battle of the Falklands (1914).

Museo Regional Salesiano Mayorino Borgatello: From the 19th century, the Salesian order played a key role in evangelization of southern Patagonia and Tierra del Fuego in both Chile and Argentina. Punta Arenas was their base and, while their rosy view of Christianity's impact on the region's native people may be debatable, there is no doubt figures such as the Italian mountaineer priest Alberto de Agostini (1883–1960) made major contributions to both physical geography and ethnographic knowledge of the region.

Agostini left a substantial collection of ethnographic and geographical photographs, preserved in the museum, which also has a noteworthy library and a small regionally oriented art gallery. Permanent exhibits deal with regional flora and fauna, a handful of early colonial artifacts, ethnography of native peoples, the Salesian missionization of Isla Dawson and other nearby areas, regional cartography, and the local petroleum industry. For Darwinists, there's a scale model of the *Beagle* and, for Chilean patriots, one of the *Ancud,* which sailed from Chiloé to claim the region in 1843.

The Museo Regional Salesiano, Avenida Bulnes 336, tel. 61/221001, musalbor@musalbor.cl, is open daily except Monday 10

A.M.–12:30 P.M. and 3–6 P.M. Admission costs US$2 for adults, US$.20 for children.

Museo Naval y Marítimo: Pleasantly surprising, Punta Arenas' naval and military museum provides perspectives on subjects such as ethnography—in the context of seagoing indigenous peoples in the Strait of Magellan—even while maintaining its military mission as the reason for its existence. It features interactive exhibits, such as a credible warship's bridge, a selection of model ships, and material on the naval history of the southern American oceans.

The most riveting material, though, concerns Chilean pilot Luis Pardo Villalón's 1916 rescue of British explorer Ernest Shackleton's crew at Elephant Island on the Antarctic peninsula. On board the cutter *Yelcho,* with neither heat, electricity, nor radio in foggy and stormy winter weather, Pardo brought the crew back to Punta Arenas in short order; he later served as Chilean consul in Liverpool.

The Museo Naval, Pedro Montt 981, tel. 61/205479, is open Tuesday to Saturday 9:30 A.M.–12:30 P.M. and 2–5 P.M. Admission costs US$1 cents for adults, US$.60 for children.

Museo del Recuerdo: Run by the Instituto de la Patagonia, itself part of the Universidad de Magallanes, the Museo del Recuerdo is a mostly open-air facility displaying pioneer agricultural implements and industrial machinery, reconstructions of a traditional house and shearing shed, and a restored shepherd's trailer house (hauled across the Patagonian plains on wooden wheels). In addition to a modest botanical garden, the institute itself has a library/bookshop with impressive cartographic exhibits.

Admission to the Museo del Recuerdo, Avenida Bulnes 01890, tel. 61/207056, costs US$1.50 for adults, free for children. Weekday hours are 8:30 A.M.–11:30 P.M. and 2:30–6:15 P.M., while Saturday hours are 8:30 A.M.–1 P.M. only. From downtown Punta Arenas, *taxi colectivos* to the Zona Franca (duty-free zone) stop directly opposite the institute's entrance.

Accommodations

Sernatur keeps a complete list of accommodations with up-to-date prices. Note that what, in many parts of Chile, would be called *residenciales* are *hostales* in Punta Arenas.

US$10–25: From November to March only, the **Albergue Backpacker's Paradise,** Ignacio Carrera Pinto 1022, tel. 61/222554, backpackers_paradise_chile@yahoo.com, is a hostel-style facility that jams 30 bunks into only four dormitory rooms, but for US$5 pp, it has its public. On the plus side, it has an adequate living room with cable TV, a kitchen for cooking, and Internet access.

Israeli favorite **Hospedaje Manuel,** O'Higgins 648, tel. 61/220567, fax 61/221295, turmanmi@entelchile.net, charges from US$4 pp in dorm-style rooms to US$7/10 s/d in more spacious quarters.

In January and February only, a better choice is the **Colegio Pierre Fauré,** six blocks south of Plaza Muñoz Gamero at Bellavista 697, tel. 61/226256. Rates are US$2.50 pp for camping in the adjacent garden (or pitching a tent indoors in the gymnasium), US$5 pp for a bed; a simple breakfast costs US$1 more. Toward the north end of town, **Hostal Sonia,** about 10 blocks northwest of the plaza at Pasaje Darwin 175, tel./fax 61/248543, hostalsk@entelchile.net, costs only US$10 pp for Hostelling International members at an otherwise midrange place.

Rutas Patagónicas, Magallanes 535, tel. 61/235220, guiatour_patagonia@hotmail.com, offers backpacker accommodations in an attractive older house that's managed to maintain its original configuration for US$8 pp, but it also offers doubles with private bath for US$17. **Hostal Dinka's House,** Caupolicán 169, tel. 61/226056, tel./fax 244292, fueguino@entelchile.net, charges US$8 pp with breakfast and shared bath, US$12/20 s/d with private bath, but it's often full. Improved **Hostal O'Higgins,** O'Higgins 1205, tel. 61/227999, charges US$9 pp. For the same price, **Residencial Roca,** only a block from the plaza at Magallanes 888, 2nd floor, tel./fax 61/243903, has cable TV, laundry service, and a book exchange.

Rates at **Hostal Oasis,** José Menéndez 485, tel. 61/226849, are US$12/20 s/d with shared bath and breakfast. **Hostal del Rey,** Fagnano 589, Departamento B, tel./fax 61/223924, is a small,

friendly family place with only three doubles and two singles, so it's often full—call ahead. Rates are US$10 pp with an ample breakfast; its major drawback is that the family are heavy smokers.

US$25–50: Well-regarded **Hostal Parediso,** Angamos 1073, tel./fax 61/224212, deserves consideration for US$13/17 s/d with shared bath, US$22/27 with private bath. **Hostal La Estancia,** O'Higgins 765, tel./fax 61/249130, estancia@ctcinternet.cl, charges US$14 pp for spacious rooms with breakfast and telephone.

Hostal El Bosque, O'Higgins 424, tel. 61/221764, fax 61/224637, elbosque@patagonian.com, charges US$18 pp for simple but well-furnished and even homey rooms—every bed has a cozy duvet—with a simple breakfast included. There are basement backpackers' accommodations, also comfortably furnished but darker and more crowded, for around US$10 pp. The spacious dining room has cable TV, and there's a small book exchange.

Hostal Sonia, Pasaje Darwin 175, tel. 61/248543, hostalsk@entelchile.net, has regular rates of US$22/30 s/d with breakfast and private bath. Suitable in a pinch, the so-so **Hostal del Estrecho,** José Menéndez 1048, tel./fax 61/241011, estrecho@chileanpatagonia.com, charges US$17/27 s/d with shared bath, US$32/40 with private bath.

Hostal Turismo Oro Fueguino, Fagnano 356, tel./fax 61/249401, 61/246677, or 09/2183690, fueguino@ctcinternet.cl, occupies a deco-style house with an outlandish interior paint job that somehow holds the place together. Rates are US$33/40 s/d with cable TV, telephone, central heating, breakfast, and private bath; some rooms are windowless but have skylights.

Hostal Calafate I, Lautaro Navarro 850, tel./fax 61/248415, calafate@entelchile.net, is an old-fashioned B&B that offers some modern comforts—most notably cable TV and phones in each room—along with peace and quiet. It falls short in some details, though, and the breakfasts are mediocre. Rates are US$23/32 s/d with shared bath and breakfast, US$37/45 with private bath, and there's free parking.

Despite its misleadingly small streetside facade, the related **Hostal Calafate II,** Magallanes 922, tel./fax 61/241281, is a rambling building with spacious rooms that once held the former Hotel Oviedo; recently remodeled, it charges the same prices as its more traditional counterpart but also keeps a couple of so-called *celdas de castigo* ("prison cells") for backpacker clients for just US$10 pp— a pretty good deal in a well-kept, central facility. Guests at either branch are entitled to half an hour's free Internet access at Hostal Calafate II.

Hostal Rubio, Avenida España 640, tel. 61/226458, charges US$14/20 s/d with shared bath and breakfast, US$26/41 with private bath. **Hostal de la Patagonia,** Croacia 970, tel. 61/249970, tel./fax 61/223670, hostalpatagonia@entelchile.net, costs US$31/50 s/d with private bath and breakfast, but it also has some discount rooms with shared bath.

US$50–100: Hotel Savoy, José Menéndez 1073, tel./fax 61/247979, lacks style—most of the walls have cheap plywood paneling—but the rooms are large and comfortable and the staff is responsive. Rates are US$42/52 s/d. Rates at **Hostal Carpa Manzano,** Lautaro Navarro 336, tel. 61/242296, fax 61/248864, are US$42/54 s/d; the comparable **Hostal de la Avenida,** Avenida Colón 534, tel./fax 61/247532 or 61/249486, is slightly more expensive at US$47/56. Recommended **Hotel Cóndor de Plata,** Avenida Colón 556, tel. 61/247987, fax 61/241149, charges US$45/60 with private bath and breakfast.

Occupying a tastefully modernized older building, **Hotel Mercurio,** Fagnano 595, tel./fax 61/242300, mercurio@chileaustral.com, offers both convenience and charm, with gracious staff to boot. Rates are US$47/61 with private bath and breakfast. Half a block south of Plaza Muñoz Gamero, **Hotel Plaza,** Nogueira 1116, tel. 61/241300, fax 61/248613, hplaza@chileaustral.com, costs US$57/68.

New in 2001, **Hotel Austral,** Pedro Montt 840, tel./fax 61/223322, is a stylishly modern business-oriented hotel whose restaurant and rear rooms look out onto the grounds of the Braun-Menéndez house rather than onto noisy downtown streets. Prices of US$58/75 s/d may rise as the hotel establishes its niche.

US$100–150: Punta Arenas has a good selection of upscale, mostly modern hotels, such as

Hotel Tierra del Fuego, Avenida Colón 716, tel./fax 61/226200, which charges US$98/109 s/d. **Hotel Los Navegantes,** José Menéndez 647, tel. 61/244677, fax 61/247545, hotelnav@chilesat.net, is also a contemporary hotel with standard conveniences in midsized rooms. Rates are US$110/139 s/d.

For US$116/143 s/d, **Hotel Isla Rey Jorge,** 21 de Mayo 1243, tel. 61/222681, fax 61/248220, reyjorge@ctcinternet.cl, is a favorite with foreign tour groups. Traditionally one of the city's best hotels, built by the Sociedad Ganadera Tierra del Fuego, the 1960s high-rise **Hotel Cabo de Hornos,** Plaza Muñoz Gamero 1025, tel./fax 61/242134, rescabo@panamericanahoteles.cl, is gradually recovering from years of decline. Rates start at US$126/149 s/d. **Hotel Finis Terrae,** Avenida Colón 766, tel. 61/228200, fax 61/248124, finister@ctcreuna.cl, charges US$140/160.

Punta Arenas's most distinctive and historic accommodations, **Hotel José Nogueira,** Bories 959, tel. 61/48840, fax 61/248832, nogueira@chileaustral.com, occupies part of the Sara Braun mansion. Room rates are US$141/198 s/d. Its greenhouse restaurant deserves a visit even if you can't afford to stay here.

Food

Los Patiperros, Avenida Colón 782, tel. 61/245298, is a modest but popular café serving full meals in the US$5 range. **Quijote,** Lautaro Navarro 1087, tel. 61/241225, also serves inexpensive lunches, as does the outstanding **Rotisería La Mamá,** Sanhueza 720, tel. 61/225812.

Café Puerto del Estrecho, upstairs in the Casa del Turista at O'Higgins 1401, tel. 61/241022, at the entrance to Muelle Prat, has a variety of espresso-based specialty coffees, such as mocha and amaretto, plus snacks and desserts to accompany them.

Lomit's, José Menéndez 722, tel. 61/243399, is a dependable sandwich chain. By contrast, **La Carioca,** José Menéndez 600, tel. 61/224809, is a one-of-a-kind sandwich outlet that also serves passable pizza, pasta, and draft beer.

Dónde Marín, O'Higgins 504, tel. 61/245291, delivers on its modest pretensions, serving fine if simply prepared fish entrées, including a side order, in the US$5–7 range. The decor is only utilitarian, but the service is professional.

Stick with the meat at **El Estribo,** Ignacio Carrera Pinto 762, tel. 61/244714; its fish dishes are only so-so, but the beef and lamb choices, in the US$4–10 range, are consistently better. The English menu translation is sometimes hilarious, but the service is attentive.

The best new restaurant in town is **Damiana Elena,** O'Higgins 694, tel. 61/222818, where reservations are essential on weekends and advisable even on weeknights. Decorated with antiques, this restored period house serves beef and seafood specialties in the US$4–8 range—very modest prices for the quality it offers—with unobtrusive service. There is limited tobacco-free seating, for which reservations are particularly advisable.

Los Ganaderos, a couple of kilometers north of the plaza at Avenida Bulnes 0977, tel. 61/214597, is a new but classy *parrilla* specializing in succulent Patagonian lamb grilled on a vertical spit—for US$10 *tenedor libre* (all-you-can-eat). There is also a more diverse *parrillada* for two (US$23), and pasta dishes in the US$7 range. Other treats include the regional Patagonian desserts, such as *mousse de calafate* and *mousse de ruibarbo* (rhubarb).

Also specializing in lamb, popular with tour groups, is downtown's **El Mesón del Calvo,** Jorge Montt 687, tel. 61/225015.

Punta Arenas's classic seafood locale is **El Mercado,** open 24 hours at Mejicana 617, 2nd floor, tel. 61/247415; serving a diverse fish and shellfish menu at midrange prices, it affixes a 10 percent surcharge from 1–8 A.M. Another seafood classic is the **Centro Español,** upstairs at Plaza Muñoz Gamero 771, tel. 61/242807; though it never seems to have many clients, it still manages to turn out good food at slightly higher prices than El Mercado.

Other seafood choices, more upscale but not dramatically better, include **Asturias,** Lautaro Navarro 967, tel. 61/243763; **La Casa de Juan,** O'Higgins 1021, tel. 61/223463; **El Beagle,** O'Higgins 1077, tel. 61/243057; and **Sotito's Bar,** O'Higgins 1138, tel. 61/245365.

Entertainment

Except on Sunday, when Punta Arenas is utterly dead, there's usually something to do at night.

Pubs: Laberinto, Pedro Montt 951, tel. 61/223667, and **Olijoe Pub,** at Errázuriz and O'Higgins, are primarily dance clubs. **Makanudo,** El Ovejero 474, tel. 09/6492031, has 7–10 P.M. happy hours Monday to Thursday and live music Friday and Saturday nights from around 1:30 A.M.

Cinema: Punta Arenas has two movie theaters: **Teatro Cervantes,** Plaza Muñoz Gamero 771, tel. 61/223225, and the **Sala Estrella,** Mejicana 777, tel. 61/241262.

Spectator Sports: The **Club Hípico** (municipal racetrack) fronts on Avenida Bulnes between Coronel Mardones and Manantiales, north of downtown. Professional soccer matches take place at the **Estadio Fiscal** (stadium), a few blocks north at Avenida Bulnes and José González.

Shopping

Though it's faltered in recent years, Punta Arenas's major shopping destination is the duty-free **Zona Franca,** four km north of town but easily reached by *taxi colectivo* from Calle Magallanes. Traditionally, consumer electronics were the big attraction, so much so that Santiaguinos flew here for the bargains, but price differentials are not so great as they used to be. If you're traveling by automobile, you should know that prices for replacement tires and similar items are much cheaper here than in Argentina or mainland Chile.

Puerto del Estrecho, O'Higgins 1401, tel. 61/241022, serves as the Sala de Espera (waiting room) for the MV *Mare Australis* cruises to the Chilean fjords but is also a good if fairly pricey souvenir shop; in addition, it has an upstairs café, Internet access, and long-distance telephone service.

For crafts, well-stocked **Artesanías Rama Chile,** Independencia 799, tel. 61/248525, contains items such as wool socks and sweaters and wood carvings of penguins. For media such as metal (copper and bronze) and semiprecious stones (lapis lazuli), visit **Chile Típico,** Ignacio Carrera Pinto 1015, tel. 61/225827. **Tres**

Arroyos, Bories 448, tel. 61/241522, specializes in custom chocolates.

Services

Money: Punta Arenas is one of the easier Chilean cities in which to change both cash and traveler's checks, especially at travel agencies along Lautaro Navarro. Most of these close by midday on Saturday, but Bus Sur, at Magallanes and Colón, will cash traveler's checks then.

Banco Santander has an ATM at Bories 970, half a block north of Plaza Muñoz Gamero.

Postal: Correos de Chile is at Bories 911, just north of Plaza Muñoz Gamero.

Telephone and Internet: Telefónica CTC is at Nogueira 1116, at the southwest corner of Plaza Muñoz Gamero; Entel is at Lautaro Navarro 931. Punta Arenas' area code is 61.

Austro Internet, Croacia 690, tel. 61/229297, is open 9 A.M.–10:30 P.M. weekdays, 10 A.M.–9 P.M. Saturday and 4–9 P.M. Sunday, but it also keeps Sunday morning hours (9 A.M.–1 P.M.) when cruise ships are in port. Cibercafé del Sur, Croacia 1028, tel. 61/235117, stays open 24 hours. Both charge around US$3 per hour.

Laundry: Lavandería Record is at O'Higgins 969, tel. 61/243607.

Medical: Punta Arenas's Hospital Regional is at Arauco and Angamos, tel. 61/244040.

Information

Tourist Offices: Sernatur, Waldo Seguel 689, tel. 61/225385, serna12a@entelchile.net, a couple doors off Plaza Muñoz Gamero, is open 8:15 A.M.–12:45 P.M. and 2:30–6:45 P.M. weekdays only. One of Chile's better regional tourist offices, it has English-speaking personnel, up-to-date information on accommodations and transportation, and a message board.

In summer, the municipal Kiosko de Informaciones on Plaza Muñoz Gamero, tel. 61/200610, is open 8 A.M.–8 P.M. weekdays, 9 A.M.–6 P.M. Saturday, and 9:30 A.M.–2:30 P.M. Sunday. It also has free Internet access for brief periods (longer if no one is waiting).

Consulates: Visitors needing Argentine visas can visit the consulate at 21 de Mayo 1878, tel. 61/261912, open weekdays 10 A.M.–3 P.M. Sev-

headstone of the wool baron José Menéndez in the Cemeterio Municipal

eral other countries have honorary consulates, including Brazil, Arauco 769, tel. 61/241093; Spain, José Menéndez 910, tel. 61/243566; and the United Kingdom, tel. 61/211535.

Motorists: The local branch of the Automóvil Club de Chile (Acchi), O'Higgins 931, tel. 61/243675, also rents cars.

National Parks: Conaf is at José Menéndez 1147, tel. 61/223841.

Bookstore: For books (including some local guidebooks and travel literature in English), maps, and keepsakes, try Southern Patagonia Souvenirs & Books, Bories 404, tel. 61/225973.

Transportation

Punta Arenas has good air connections to mainland Chile, frequent air service to Chilean Tierra del Fuego, infrequent air service to Argentine Tierra del Fuego, and regular weekly service to the Falkland Islands. There are roundabout overland routes to mainland Chile via Argentina, regular bus service to Argentine Tierra del Fuego via a ferry link, direct ferry service to Chilean Tierra del Fuego, and expensive (but extraordinarily scenic) cruise ship service to Ushuaia, in Argentine Tierra del Fuego.

Air: LanChile/LanExpress, Lautaro Navarro 999, tel. 61/241232, flies four times daily to Santiago (US$228), normally via Puerto Montt (US$95), but Saturday only via Balmaceda (US$45). It also flies Saturday to the Falkland Islands (US$295 one way); one Falklands flight monthly stops in the Argentine city of Río Gallegos.

Aerocontinente, Roca 924, tel. 61/220403, flies to Puerto Montt (US$62–79) and Santiago (US$95–159) Tuesday, Thursday, Saturday, and Sunday.

Aerovías DAP, O'Higgins 891, tel. 61/223340, fax 61/221693, ventas@aeroviasdap.cl, flies seven-seater Cessnas to and from Porvenir (US$23), in Chilean Tierra del Fuego, at least daily except Sunday, more often in summer. Daily except Sunday and Monday, it flies 20-seater Twin Otters to and from Puerto Williams on Isla Navarino (US$64 one way). In summer, it also flies Twin Otters to the Argentine Tierra del Fuego cities of Río Grande (US$90) Friday only, and to Ushuaia Monday and Wednesday only (US$100). It also has extensive charter services.

Bus: Punta Arenas has no central bus terminal, though some companies share facilities. Most are within a few blocks of each other north of Plaza Muñoz Gamero.

Several regional carriers go to Puerto Natales (US$4, three hours), including Bus Sur (five buses daily), José Menéndez 565, tel. 61/227145; Buses Fernández (seven daily), Armando Sanhueza 745, tel. 61/242313, which has older but still serviceable vehicles; Buses Pacheco (three daily), Avenida Colón 900, tel. 61/242174, which has smart new buses; and Buses Transfer (three daily), at Pedro Montt 966, tel. 229613, and O'Higgins 1055, tel. 61/243984.

For long-distance service, in addition to its Puerto Natales services, Buses Pacheco goes to Osorno, Puerto Montt, and Castro (US$42, 30–32 hours) Wednesday and Sunday at 8 A.M., via Argentina. Queilén Bus, Armando Sanhueza 745, tel. 61/221812, and Turibús, also at Armando Sanhueza 745, tel. 61/227970, alternate services to Puerto Montt and Castro most mornings at 9:30 A.M.

Besides Puerto Natales, Bus Sur goes to Coyhaique (US$42, 20 hours) Monday and Thursday at 10:30 A.M.

For international service to Río Gallegos (US$12, four hours), Buses Pingüino, Armando Sanhueza 745, tel. 61/221812 or 61/242313, has daily departures at 12:45 P.M. Buses Ghisoni, Lautaro Navarro 975, tel. 61/222078, goes Monday, Wednesday, and Saturday at 11 A.M. and Thursday at 3 P.M. Buses Pacheco goes Tuesday, Friday, and Sunday at 11:30 A.M.

Tecni-Austral, Lautaro Navarro 975, tel. 61/222078, goes direct to Río Grande (US$20, eight hours), in Argentine Tierra del Fuego, daily except Monday at 8:30 A.M.; the Tuesday, Thursday, Saturday, and Sunday buses continue to Ushuaia (US$33, 12 hours). Buses Pacheco goes Monday, Wednesday, and Friday at 7:15 A.M. to Río Grande, with connections to Ushuaia.

Sea: Transbordadora Austral Broom, Avenida Bulnes 05075, tel. 61/218100, tabsa@entelchile.net, sails from Punta Arenas to Porvenir (2.5 hours) at 9 A.M. daily except Sunday, when sailing time is 9:30 A.M. Adult passengers pay US$6 pp except for the drivers, whose own fare is included in the US$37 charge per vehicle (motorcycles pay US$11). Children pay US$2.50 pp. Since the ferry has limited vehicle capacity, reservations are a good idea on the *Melinka,* which leaves from Terminal Tres Puentes, at the north end of town but easily accessible by *taxi colectivo* from the Casa Braun-Menéndez, on Magallanes half a block north of Plaza Muñoz Gamero.

Broom also sails the ferry *Patagonia* to Puerto Williams (38 hours) every Wednesday at 7 P.M. The fare is US$150 for a bunk, US$120 for a seat.

It's neither cheap nor a conventional way of getting to Argentina, but passengers on the luxury MV *Mare Australis,* which sails from Punta Arenas every Saturday for a weeklong cruise of the fjords of Chilean Tierra del Fuego, can disembark in Ushuaia (or board there for that matter). Normally the *Mare Australis* requires reservations well in advance, but a new ship was due to come

SAILING THE FJORDS OF TIERRA DEL FUEGO

PATAGONIA & TIERRA

S hort of Antarctica itself, some of the Southern Hemisphere's most awesome scenery occurs in the Beagle Channel and southern Tierra del Fuego. And as usual, Charles Darwin left one of the most vivid descriptions of the channel named for the famous vessel on which he sailed:

The scenery here becomes even grander than before. The lofty mountains on the north side compose the granitic axis, or backbone of the country, and boldly rise to a height of between three and fourthousand feet, with one peak above six thousand feet. They are covered by a wide mantle of perpetual snow, and numerous cascades pour their waters, through the woods, into the narrow channel below. In many parts, magnificent glaciers extend from the mountain side to the water's edge. It is scarcely possible to imagine anything more beautiful than the beryl-like blue of these glaciers, and especially as contrasted with the dead white of the upper expanse of the snow. The fragments which had fallen from the glacier into the water, were floating away, and the channel with the icebergs presented, for the space of a mile, a miniature likeness of the Polar Sea.

Barely changed since Darwin described it in 1833, the landscape of Tierra del Fuego is still seen by relatively few people, most of them on board the weeklong excursion from Punta Arenas to Ushuaia and back on the *Mare Australis*. Unlike the Navimag ferry from Puerto Montt to Puerto Natales, this is a cruise in the traditional sense—the passengers are waited on hand and foot, and it's not cheap. Yet for the foreseeable future, it remains the only way to see the area short of sailing or hiring your own private yacht, and for that reason it's worth consideration even for those with limited finances.

Until a planned second ship comes onto the route, the *Mare Australis* takes the following route to Ushuaia and back, though itineraries can vary depending on weather conditions in this notoriously changeable climate. After an evening departure from Punta Arenas's Muelle Prat, the *Mare Australis* crosses the Strait of Magellan to enter the **Seno del Almirantazgo** (Admiralty Sound), a westward maritime extension of the freshwater Lago Fagnano trough. Passengers usually go ashore at the sound's lesser inlet **Bahía Parry,** on the north side of the Cordillera Darwin; here, hikers can approach the groaning **Ventisquero Parry** (Parry Glacier), named by Philip Parker King, captain of HMS *Adventure* and hydrographer on the *Beagle* expedition, in honor of Sir William Edward Parry (1790–1855), who made four unsuccessful attempts at the Northwest passage to the Pacific. With its numerous icebergs and low salinity, Bahía Parry has little wildlife.

From Bahía Parry, the ship sails back west, pausing at a small elephant seal colony at **Bahía Ainsworth,** near the **Ventisquero Marinelli,** where there's a short hiking trail through what was once forest until escaped beavers dammed the area into a series of ponds. Farther west, at **Isla Tucker,** there's a small Magellanic penguin colony and it's also possible to see the rare striated caracara, *Phalcoboenus australis.*

After a night's sailing, the ship enters the **Fiordo D'Agostini,** a glacial inlet named for the Italian priest and mountaineer who explored the farthest recesses of the Cordillera Darwin in the early 20th century. When high winds make it impossible to approach the **Glaciar Serrano** (named for Chilean naval Lieutenant Ramón Serrano Montaner, who charted the strait in 1879), an option is the more sheltered **Glaciar D'Agostini,** but even here seracs collapse off the face of the **Glaciar D'Agostini,** touching off a rapid surge of water and ice that runs parallel to a broad gravel beach and, when it subsides, leaves the beach littered with boulders of ice.

Darwin, again, described the dangers of travel in an area that sea kayakers are beginning to explore:

The boats being hauled on shore at our dinner hour, we were admiring from the distance of half a mile a perpendicular cliff of ice, and were wishing that some

*more fragments would fall. At last,
down came a mass with a roaring noise,
and immediately we saw the smooth
outline of a wave traveling toward us.
The men ran down as quickly as they
could to the boats; for the chance of
their being dashed to pieces was evident.
One of the seamen just caught hold of
the bows, as the curling breaker reached
it: he was knocked over and over, but
not hurt; and the boats, though thrice
lifted on high and let fall again, received
no damage. . . .I had previously noted
that some large fragments of rock on the
beach had been lately displaced; but
until seeing this wave, I did not understand the cause.*

Before navigating Canal Cockburn, the ship stops at **Ventisquero Cóndor,** where condors glide low and cormorants nest on the bluffs. Briefly exposed to swells from the open ocean, the vessel turns into the calmer **Canal Ocasión** and eventually enters the north arm of the Beagle Channel, sailing past the so-called **Avenida de los Glaciares,** a series of glaciers named for various European countries, before anchoring at Yendegaia for brief shore-based excursions (for more information, see the separate entry for Estancia Yendegaia).

After leaving Yendegaia, the ships proceeds to **Puerto Williams,** where it spends a few hours before sailing for the Argentine port of Ushuaia. The opening of a Chilean port of entry at Puerto Navarino, directly south of Ushuaia, may expedite immigration formalities and the itineraries, as it will allow the ships to avoid doubling back to Puerto Williams to reenter Chile after leaving Ushuaia (for more information on Ushuaia, see the separate geographical entry).

After reentering Chile, the ship sails south through the Canal Murray (Murray Channel) to disembark at Parque Nacional Cabo de Hornos and, on the return, at the former Anglican mission site at Bahía Wulaia. It then sails westward through the north arm of the Beagle Channel, again passing the Avenida de los Glaciares and entering Fiordo Pía (Pía Fjord), where dozens of waterfalls cascade down sheer metamorphic slopes from the **Glaciar Pía.** A bit farther west, it enters **Fiordo Garibaldi,** at least to the point where the ice is so thick that it can't proceed any farther—even on a comfortable cruise ship, sailing through Tierra del Fuego has the feeling of passing through uncharted waters. After a short backtrack, the most vigorous passengers disembark for a short but strenuous and slippery hike through sopping Magellanic rain forest.

On the last full day, the boat passes through the Angostura Gabriel, a narrows only about 250 meters wide, before entering **Bahía Brooke,** where a nameless river of ice is slowly but inexorably transporting granite boulders down to the sea, and fresh snow avalanches off hanging glaciers. On the final morning, it sails north to **Isla Magdalena** (see the separate entry for Monumento Natural Los Pingüinos) before returning to its home port of Punta Arenas.

Practicalities

Punta Arenas is the home port for cruises to the fjords; check-in takes place at the Casa del Turista at O'Higgins 1401, at the entrance to Muelle Prat, while boarding begins in late afternoon. (For contact information, details on booking, and rates, see the Cruceros Australis entry under Organized Tours in the On the Road chapter.) Some passengers, especially those on the shorter three-or four-day options, begin or end the trip in Ushuaia, in Argentine Tierra del Fuego.

Well-organized without being regimented, the cruise is informal in terms of dress and behavior. As it begins, passengers sign up for meal tables; places are fixed for the duration except at the buffet breakfast, when people tend to straggle in at different times. In general, passengers are grouped according to language, though they often place together people who speak English as a second language. The staff themselves can handle Spanish, English, German, French, and occasionally other languages.

After a welcome drink, usually pisco sour or *vaina* accompanied by mini-empanadas and other finger food, in the bar, there is an introduction of the captain, crew, and staff, a brief folkloric show, and an obligatory safety drill. Except for

(continued on next page)

PATAGONIA & TIERRA

SAILING THE FJORDS OF TIERRA DEL FUEGO (cont'd)

the welcome drink, bar consumption in the bar is extra but not unreasonably priced; drinks at dinner are included. Smoking is prohibited everywhere except on the topmost deck and outdoors.

The cabins themselves are simple but spacious, with either a double or two single beds, built-in reading lights, a writing desk, and a private bath with good hot showers (though it takes a while for the hot water to arrive if you're the first shower of the morning). Each room has a closet with hangers and a small lockbox for valuables. The food is ample and occasionally excellent, though breakfasts are a little monotonous; the wine is superb and the service exceptional. Vegetarian menus are available on request.

Usually this very popular cruise runs full from October to April, except for the last trip before Christmas, which is often only half full; in this case, it may be possible to negotiate a deal in Punta Arenas, getting a private cabin without paying a single supplement, for example. In addition, at this time of year, days are so long that it's possible to enjoy the landscape until after 11 P.M., and there's sufficient light to read by 4 A.M.

For those who tire of the landscape or when the weather is bad, there are on-board activities, including line-dancing (!), PowerPoint slide lectures on flora and fauna, tours of the engine rooms, and demonstrations of culinary artistry with carved cucumbers, peppers, zucchinis, and other vegetables in the shapes of birds and flowers. The farewell dinner is a fairly gala affair, followed by champagne on the topmost deck. As on the *Puerto Edén* ferry from Puerto Montt to Puerto Natales, the crew hands out diplomas on the final night.

At several locations, there are optional shore-based activities as well—at Yendegaia, for instance, there is an horseback tour for US$30. At Puerto Williams, supplementary excursions include a US$30 anthropological bus trip, led by the local museum director, and a US$180 Twin Otter overflight of Cabo de Hornos—the last outlier of South America—for a maximum of 20 passengers. At Ushuaia, the longest port stop on the trip, where many passengers leave and others board, the possibilities for full-day excursions are numerous, but many opt for independent sight-seeing.

---

on line in 2002, increasing capacity substantially. (For more details, see the special topic Sailing the Fjords of Tierra del Fuego.)

Getting Around

To the Airport: Punta Arenas's Aeropuerto Presidente Carlos Ibáñez del Campo is 20 km north of town on Ruta 9, the Puerto Natales highway. Both Transportes Polo Sur, Chiloé 873, tel. 61/243173, and Buses Transfer, Pedro Montt 966, tel. 61/2-29613, offer door-to-door service to the airport for about US$4 pp. Bus companies returning from Puerto Natales will usually drop their passengers at the airport to meet their outgoing flight, but make arrangements before boarding.

Car Rental: Punta Arenas has numerous rental options, including Adel Rent a Car, Pedro Montt 968, Oficina 1, 2nd floor, tel. 61/222207 or 61/2-61497, fax 61/225758, gdreyes@entelchile.net; the Automóvil Club de Chile (Acchi), O'Higgins 931, tel. 61/243675, fax 61/243097; Budget,

O'Higgins 964, tel./fax 61/241696; Emsa, Roca 1044, tel./fax 61/241182; Hertz, O'Higgins 987, tel. 61/248742, fax 61/244729; Internacional, Waldo Seguel 443, tel. 61/228323, fax 61/226334; and Lubag, Magallanes 970, tel./fax 61/242023. **Bicycle:** For rental bikes, contact Claudio Botten, Sarmiento 1132, tel. 61/242107 or 09/6913475.

VICINITY OF PUNTA ARENAS

Punta Arenas' many travel agencies operate a variety of excursions in the vicinity, to nearby destinations such as Reserva Nacional Magallanes, Fuerte Bulnes, the Seno Otway penguin colony, Río Verde, Estancia San Gregorio, and even Parque Nacional Torres del Paine. The most popular half-day excursions, such as Fuerte Bulnes and Otway, cost US$10–15 pp, while longer full-day trips such as Pali Aike can cost up to US$70 pp.

Among the established operators are **Aventour,** José Nogueira 1255, tel. 61/244197, fax 61/2-

43354, aventour@entelchile.net; **Ecotour Patagonia,** Croacia 970, tel. 61/223670, ecopatagonia@entelchile.net; **Transporte Polo Sur,** Chiloé 873, tel. 61/243173; **Turismo Aonikenk,** Magallanes 619, tel. 61/228332; **Turismo Laguna Azul,** José Menéndez 631, tel. 61/225200, fax 61/240275; **Turismo Pali Aike,** Lautaro Navarro 1129, tel./fax 61/223301, paliaike@chilesat.net; **Turismo Viento Sur,** Fagnano 565, tel. 61/2-25167, vientosur@chileaustral.com; and **Turismo Yámana,** Avenida Colón 568, tel. 61/221130, yamana@chileaustral.com.

Reserva Nacional Magallanes

Only eight km west of downtown Punta Arenas, 13,500-hectare Reserva Nacional Magallanes is a combination of Patagonian steppe and southern beech forest which, in good winters, accumulates enough snow for skiing. Despite its proximity to Punta Arenas, official statistics suggest it gets only about 2,800 visitors per year.

From Avenida Independencia, a gravel road that may require chains in winter climbs gradually to a fork whose southern branch leads to the reserve's **Sector Andino,** where the local Club Andino's **Centro de Esquí Cerro Mirador** includes a *refugio* that serves meals, a ski school, and a single well-maintained chairlift. In summer, the **Sendero Mirador** is a two-hour loop hike that winds through the forest and crosses the ski area; there's also a mountain bike circuit.

The northwesterly **Sector Las Minas,** which includes a gated picnic area, charges US$1.50 pp for adult admission but nothing for kids. A longer footpath links up with the trail to the El Mirador summit, which offers panoramas east toward Punta Arenas, the strait, and Tierra del Fuego, and west toward Seno Otway.

Though some Punta Arenas travel agencies offer tours to the reserve, it would also be a good mountain bike excursion.

Pingüinera Seno Otway

Burrowing Magellanic penguins abound along the Atlantic coast of Argentine Patagonia, but they are fewer in Chile. Barely an hour from Punta Arenas, though, the *Spheniscus magellanicus* colony at Seno Otway (Otway Sound) is the closest to any major city on the continent. Under the administration of the nonprofit Fundación Otway, it has grown in a decade from no more than 400 penguins to about 10,000 at present, and it attracts up to 40,000 visitors from October, when the first birds arrive to breed, to April, when the last stragglers head out to sea. The peak season, though, is December through February.

During the season, any number of Punta Arenas operators shuttle visitors to and from the Otway site for about US$10–12 pp, not including the US$3 pp admission charge. Half-day tours take place either in morning (which photographers may prefer) or afternoon. While the site is fenced to keep human visitors out of critical habitat, the birds are relatively tame and easy to photograph; on the down side, this did not prevent stray dogs from killing more than a hundred birds in 2001.

The Fundación Otway, which has a small snack bar at the site, is embroiled in a dispute with the land-owning Kusanovic family, which wants to take over management and build additional tourist facilities.

Otway is about 70 km northwest of Punta Arenas via Ruta 9 and a gravel road that leads west from a signed junction at the Carabineros Kon Aikén checkpoint; the gravel road passes the **Mina Pecket** coal mine before arriving at the *pingüinera*. While the Otway colony is a worthwhile excursion, visitors with flexible schedules and a little more money should consider the larger Isla Magdalena colony in Monumento Natural Los Pingüinos, in the Strait of Magellan (see below).

Monumento Natural Los Pingüinos

From early October, more than 200,000 Magellanic penguins paddle ashore and waddle to burrows that cover nearly all of 97-hectare Isla Magdalena, 20 nautical miles northeast of Punta Arenas, before returning to sea in April. Also the site of a

PINGÜINOS AND PINGÜINERAS

Chilean Patagonia's largest city is close to two breeding colonies of the burrowing Magellanic penguin, *Spheniscus magellanicus*. The Otway Sound colony is about a 45-minute drive from the city, and is interesting enough, but the larger colony on Isla Magdalena, an island in the Strait of Magellan, is two hours away by ferry.

Also known to English speakers as the jackass penguin because its call resembles that of a braying burro, the Magellanic is present from October to April. It is most numerous in January and February, when the chicks hatch in the sandy burrows that the birds have dug beneath the coastal turf. After the chicks have hatched, the parents alternate fishing trips in search of food that they later regurgitate to their young (combined with the scent of bird droppings, this makes any visit to a penguin colony an ol-

factory as well as a visual and auditory experience).

While the birds appear tame, they are wild animals and their sharp beaks can draw blood—maintain a respectful distance for photography. Even though both the Otway and Magdalena colonies have fenced walking routes to restrain tourists, the birds themselves frequently cross these routes.

Besides the countless seabirds and dolphins en route, the Magdalena trip has the added bonus of an historic lighthouse that now serves as a visitor center on an island that's one big warren of penguin burrows. While neither trip is strenuous, any walk in the roaring Patagonian winds can be a workout.

Otway trips leave every day, but Magdalena trips no more than two or three times a week, in January and February, with fewer or no trips outside those months.

landmark century-old lighthouse, Isla Magdalena is the focal point of Monumento Natural Los Pingüinos, one of Conaf's smallest but most interesting reserves.

While the mainland Otway penguin colony gets upward- of 35,000 visitors per year, Isla Magdalena gets only about 4,600 because of its limited accessibility. In the summer, though, the ferry *Melinka* visits the island three times weekly from Punta Arenas. Though more expensive than Otway tours, these excursions also offer the chance to see penguins and dolphins in the water, as well as black-browed albatrosses, cormorants, kelp gulls, skuas, South American terns, and other seabirds in the surrounding skies.

From a floating dock on the east side of the island, a short trail leads along the beach and up the hill to Scottish engineer George Slight's **Faro Magdalena** (1901), a lighthouse whose iron tower rises 13.5 meters above the island's highest point; still functioning, the light has a range of 10 nautical miles. A narrow spiral staircase ascends the tower.

In the building's first five decades, a resident caretaker maintained the acetylene light, but after its automation in 1955 the building was abandoned and vandalized. In 1981, though, the Chilean navy entrusted the building to Conaf; declared a national monument, it has

since become the island's visitor center. It boasts remarkably good exhibits on the island's history (discovery, and early navigation, cartography, and construction of the lighthouse) and natural history in both Spanish and English (though the English text is less complete). The U.S. archaeologist Junius Bird, best known for his work at the mainland site of Pali Aike in the 1930s, also undertook excavations here.

For excursions to Isla Magdalena, contact Turismo Comapa, Avenida Independencia 830, 2nd floor, tel. 241322, tcomapa@entelchile.net. In December, January, and February, after its regular ferry run to Porvenir on Tuesday, Thursday, and Saturday, the *Melinka* makes a passengers-only trip to Isla Magdalena (US$30) from Terminal Tres Puentes; sailing time is 3 P.M. (bring some food—the *Melinka*'s snack bar is pretty dire). Visitors spend about 1.5 hours on the island, returning to Punta Arenas around 9 P.M.

Passengers on the weeklong *Mare Australis* cruise through the fjords of Tierra del Fuego stop at Isla Magdalena on the last morning of the trip.

Fuerte Bulnes

In 1584, Spanish explorer Pedro Sarmiento de Gamboa organized an expedition of 15 ships and 4,000 men to control the Strait of Magellan, but after a series of disasters only three ships with 300 colonists arrived to found **Ciudad del Rey don Felipe,** at Punta Santa Ana south of present-day Punta Arenas. Even worse for the Spaniards, the inhospitable climate and unsuitable soils made agriculture impossible; when the British privateer Thomas Cavendish landed here three years later, in 1587, he found only a handful of survivors and gave it the name Port Famine, which has survived as the Spanish **Puerto del Hambre.**

For many years, the consensus was that starvation alone determined the fate of Puerto Hambre, but Punta Arenas historian Mateo Martinic has suggested that disease, mutual acts of violence, Tehuelche attacks, and a simple sense of anguish or abandonment contributed to its demise. Unfortunately, the military control much of the area, making archaeological excavations that might resolve the question difficult.

The area remained unsettled until 1843, when President Manuel Bulnes ordered the cutter *Ancud* south from Chiloé with tools, construction materials, food, and livestock to take possession for the expansionist Chilean state. The result was **Fuerte Bulnes,** a military outpost that survived only a little longer than the original Spanish settlement before being relocated to Punta Arenas in 1848.

Modern Fuerte Bulnes, on the site of the first Chilean settlement, is a national monument more for its site than for its reconstructions of 19th-century buildings and the defensive walls, of sharpened stakes, that surround them. Among the structures were residences, stables, a blockhouse, a chapel, a jail, and warehouse.

Archaeologists found nearby remnants of Ciudad del Rey don Felipe in 1955, and later excavations turned up human remains, bullets, tombs, and ruins of the church from Puerto Hambre. A relatively recent plaque (1965) celebrates the 125th anniversary of the Pacific Steam Navigation Company's ships *Chile* and *Peru* and their routes around Cape Horn.

Puerto Hambre and Fuerte Bulnes are 58 km south of Punta Arenas via Ruta 9, which is paved about halfway; the rest is bumpy but always passable. There is no regular public transportation, but most Punta Arenas tour operators offer half-day excursions to the area.

Reserva Nacional Laguna Parrillar

About 45 km southwest of Punta Arenas via paved Ruta 9 and a gravel westbound lateral, Laguna Parrillar attracts only about 3,200 visitors per year to its 18,000 hectares of forest and wetland. While it's open to day use only, it has picnic areas and hiking trails to commend it, and it makes a worthwhile excursion from the city.

Río Verde

Some 43 km north of Punta Arenas on Ruta 9, a gravel road loops northwest along the shore of Seno Otway to Seno Skyring and the former Estancia Río Verde, which has seemingly made the transition from a shipshape sheep farm to a model municipality of exquisitely maintained public buildings in the Magellanic style. Note particularly the manicured gardens surrounding the **Escuela Basica,** the local boarding school, which has a small natural history museum.

Ninety km from Punta Arenas and six km south of Río Verde village, **Hostería Río Verde,** tel. 61/311122 or 61/222792, draws big crowds to its Sunday Patagonian lamb barbecues, though it also serves seafood. Accommodations cost US$25 pp with private bath.

The loop road rejoins Ruta 9 at Villa Tehuelches, a wide spot in the road about 90 km. This would make a good alternative route north or south for both motorists and mountain bikers.

Río Rubens

About halfway between Villa Tehuelches and Puerto Natales, Río Rubens is a prime trout stream that flows northeast into Argentina. At Km 183 on Ruta 9, the nearby **Hotel Río Rubens** has resisted the temptation to upgrade itself from a modest rural inn, with a decent restaurant at modest prices, though it has added *cabañas* and camping. Hotel rates are US$12 pp with private bath and breakfast.

Estancia San Gregorio

From a highway junction about 45 km north of Punta Arenas, paved Ruta 225 leads east-northeast to the Argentine border at Monte Aymond, passing the former Estancia San Gregorio, once one of Chilean Patagonia's largest landholdings.

© WAYNE BERNHARDSON

shipwreck at Estancia San Gregorio

Part of the José Menéndez empire, San Gregorio dates from the 1890s, though it reached its peak between 1910 and 1930. Besides wool, it produced frozen mutton, hides, and tallow.

Now run as a cooperative, 120 km from Punta Arenas, San Gregorio is a *zona típica* national monument. It exemplified the Anglo-Scottish model of the Patagonian sheep *estancia,* in which each unit was a self-sufficient hierarchy with a nearly omnipotent administrator at the top. Geographically, it consisted of discrete residential and production sectors: the former included the administrator's house, employee residences, shearers' dormitories, chapel, and the like, while the latter consisted of the shearing shed, warehouses, a smithery, company store, and similarly functional buildings. It had its own railroad and a pier to move the wool clip directly to freighters.

Most of San Gregorio's construction dates from the 1890s, but the **Casa Patronal,** designed by French architect Antoine Beaulier and still occupied by a descendent of the Menéndez dynasty, dates from 1925. The farm featured an extensive system of windbreaks ranging upward of five meters in height, later planted with Monterey cypress for beautification.

While San Gregorio is technically not open to the public, many of its buildings line both sides of the highway to Monte Aymond. Beached on shore are the corroded hulks of the *Ambassador* (a national monument) and the company steamer *Amadeo,* which gave up the ghost in the 1940s.

Kimiri Aike

About 30 km east of San Gregorio, paved Ruta 257 leads southeast to **Punta Delgada,** the port for the ferry crossing to Tierra del Fuego via the Primera Angostura narrows. Depending sometimes on tidal conditions, the ferries *Bahía Azul* and *Patagonia* shuttle across the channel every 1.5 hours between 8:30 A.M. and 11 P.M. Fares are US$2 pp for passengers, US$16 for automobiles. Most buses to Argentine Tierra del Fuego use this route because the longer ferry to Porvenir goes only once daily.

Directly at the highway junction, **Hostería Tehuelche,** tel. 61/221270, was once the *casco* (big house) for the formerly British-run Estancia Kimiri Aike; now, from November to May, it offers satisfactory accommodations for US$25/31 s/d with shared bath. Buses between Punta Arenas and Río Gallegos usually stop here for lunch; breakfast, dinner, and snacks are also available.

Parque Nacional Pali Aike

Hugging the Argentine border north of Kimiri Aike and west of the Monte Aymond border crossing, little-visited Pali Aike is an area of volcanic steppe and rugged lava beds that once supported megafauna such as the ground sloth known as the milodon and the native American horse, both of which disappeared soon after humans first inhabited the area 11,000 years ago.

While Paleo-Indians hunters may have contributed to their extinction, environmental changes after the last major glaciation may also have played a role. In the 1930s, self-taught archaeologist Junius Bird, of New York's American Museum of Natural History, conducted the earliest systematic excavations of Paleo-Indian sites such as Cueva Pali Aike, within the park boundaries, and Cueva Fell, a short distance to the west. These archaeologically rich volcanic shelters (not caves in the strictest sense of the word) are the prime reason Chilean authorities have nominated the area as a UNESCO World Heritage Site.

Findings at Cueva Pali Aike include human remains that have yielded insights on Paleo-Indian funerary customs, while materials from Cueva Fell have helped reveal the transition from relatively simple Paleo-Indian hunting to more complex forms of subsistence. These include sophisticated hunting tools such as the bow and arrow and *boleadoras,* and a greater reliance on coastal and marine resources. There are also indicators of ceremonial artifacts.

Geography and Climate: Part of arid eastern Magallanes, 5,030-hectare Pali Aike consists of rolling steppe grasslands whose porous volcanic soils and slag absorb water quickly. Nearly constant high winds and cool temperatures make it a better summer or autumn excursion.

Flora and Fauna: While the milodon and native horse may have disappeared, the park's grasslands swarm with herds of wild guanaco, and flocks of rheas, upland geese, *bandurria* (ibis), and other birds. Pumas and foxes are the major predators.

Sights and Recreation: Cueva Pali Aike, accessible by road, is a volcanic tube seven meters wide and five meters high at its mouth; it is 17 meters deep but tapers as it advances. In the 1930s,

PATAGONIA & TIERRA

© WAYNE BERNHARDSON

guanacos at Parque Nacional Pali Aike

Bird discovered both human and megafauna remains here.

Tours from Punta Arenas visit Cueva Pali Aike and usually hike the 1.7-km trail through the **Escorial del Diablo** (the appropriately named Devil's Slag Heap, which is hell on hiking boots). The trail ends at the **Crater Morada del Diablo.**

From Cueva Pali Aike, a nine-km footpath leads to **Laguna Ana,** where waterfowl are abundant, and the main road, five km from the park entrance. Mountain bikes should be ideal for this sort of rolling terrain, but it could be even tougher on tires than it is on boots.

Practicalities: A campground is under construction, but there are no tourist services as yet.

At the main park entrance, Conaf has a ranger station; there is no admission charge. A great destination for those seeking solitude, Pali Aike officially gets only about 600 visitors per annum.

Parque Nacional Pali Aike is 196 km northeast of Punta Arenas via Ruta 9, Ruta 255, and a graveled secondary road from the hamlet of Cooperativa Villa O'Higgins, 11 km beyond Kimiri Aike. Just south of the Chilean border post at Monte Aymond, a hard-to-follow dirt road also leads to the park.

There is no public transportation, but Punta Arenas travel agencies can arrange visits. Hiring a car, though, is probably the best alternative, especially if shared among several people.

PUERTO NATALES

In the past 20 years, Puerto Natales has changed from a sleepy wool and fishing port on what seemed the aptly named Seno Última Esperanza—"Last Hope Sound"—to a bustling tourist town whose season has lengthened well beyond the traditional summer months of January and February. Its proximity to the now famous Parque Nacional Torres del Paine, coupled with its status as the southern terminus for the scenic and increasingly popular ferry route from Puerto Montt, has placed it on the international travel map, utterly transforming the local economy.

While Puerto Natales has no knockout attractions in its own right, the town enjoys a magnificent seaside setting, with the snow-capped Cordillera Sarmiento and Campo de Hielo Sur, the southern Patagonian ice cap, visible across the water to the west. For visitors to Paine and other regional sights, it has an abundance of services, including tour operators and rental equipment providers. There are also convenient connections to the Argentine town of El Calafate and that country's Parque Nacional Los Glaciares.

History

Última Esperanza acquired its name because expeditions led by the 16th-century Spaniards Juan Ladrilleros and Pedro Sarmiento de Gamboa failed to find a westbound route to the Pacific here. Puerto Natales proper dates from the early 20th century, a few years after German explorer Hermann Eberhard founded the area's first sheep *estancia* at Puerto Prat. Within a few years, the Sociedad Explotadora de Tierra del Fuego had built a slaughterhouse at nearby Bories to process and pack mutton for the export market. While the livestock economy declined in the second half of the 20th century, the tourist boom has reactivated and diversified the economy.

Orientation

On the eastern shores of Seno Último Esperanza (Last Hope Sound) Puerto Natales is 250 km northwest of Punta Arenas via paved Ruta 9. It is 150 km south of Parque Nacional Torres del Paine, also by Ruta 9, which is paved for 13 km north of the city.

Entering town from the north, Ruta 9 becomes the roughly north-south Costanera Pedro Montt; most services and points of interest are within easy walking distance to the east. The principal commercial streets are east-west Manuel Bulnes and north-south Avenida Baquedano.

Sights

The **Municipalidad,** a gingerbread-style construction dating from 1929 on the east side of the Plaza Arturo Prat, had its construction financed by the Sociedad Explotadora de Tierra del Fuego, which owned large amounts of land in both Chile and Argentina. Immediately to its east, the **Iglesia Parroquial María Auxiliadora** dates from the same era and shares its Magellanic style.

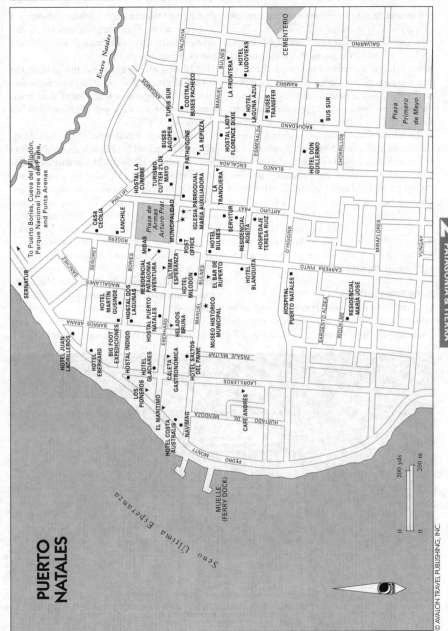

PUERTO
NATALES

PATAGONIA & TIERRA

In the same exterior fashion but with a roomier interior that displays its holdings to advantage, the **Museo Histórico Municipal,** Bulnes 285, tel. 61/411263, muninata@ctcinternet.cl, offers exhibits on natural history, archaeology and the region's aboriginal peoples, European settlement, and the rural economy (including the powerful Sociedad Explotadora de Tierra Fuego), Puerto Natales' own urban evolution, and the local Carabineros, who played a role in the museum's creation. Noteworthy individual artifacts include a Yámana (Yahgan) dugout canoe and Aonikenk (Tehuelche) *boleadoras,* plus historical photographs of Captain Eberhard and the town's development. Summer hours are 8:30 A.M.–12:30 P.M. and 2:30–8 P.M. weekdays, 3–8 P.M. weekends; the rest of the year, hours are 8:30 A.M.–12:30 P.M. and 2:30–6 P.M. weekdays, 3–6 P.M. weekends. Admission costs US$1 for adults, US$.35 for children.

Accommodations

Over the past two decades, Puerto Natales has developed one of the densest offerings of accommodations in the entire country. This is especially true in the budget category, where competition keeps prices low. There are good values in all categories, but plenty of mediocre and ordinary places as well.

US$10 or Less: Residencial Jus-Mar, at the corner of Prat and Esmeralda, has built a fine spacious campground with clearly delineated sites, privacy from the street, electricity, and hot showers for US$3 pp.

Israeli favorite **Residencial María José,** Magallanes 646, tel. 61/412218, is one of Natales's best bargains at US$4 pp. **Hospedaje Magallania,** Tomás Rogers 255, is an informal hostel-style facility with spacious but multibedded rooms, kitchen privileges, a TV room, and *buena onda* (good vibes). Rates are US$5 pp. Others in the same range include **Hospedaje Teresa,** one of the best in its category at Esmeralda 463, tel. 61/410472; **Hospedaje Tierra del Fuego,** Bulnes 23, tel. 61/412138; the rather cramped **Residencial Asturias,** Prat 426, tel. 61/412105; and **Residencial Lago Pingo,** Bulnes 808, tel. 61/413848.

US$10–25: The local Hostelling International affiliate is **Albergue Path@gone,** Eberhard 595, tel.

Municipalidad de Puerto Natales

© WAYNE BERNHARDSON

61/413291, which charges US$7 pp for very good facilities. **Residencial Rosita,** Arturo Prat 367, tel. 61/412259, occupies the upstairs of a crowded family house; the rooms, all with shared bath, are smallish but fairly priced at US$6 pp. For the same price, friendly **Residencial Patagonia Aventura,** Tomás Rogers 179, tel. 61/411028, provides a bit more privacy than its counterparts. Acceptable, but not quite so good, are **Hospedaje Tequendama**, Ladrilleros 141, tel. 61/412951, and **Residencial Sutherland,** Barros Arana 155, tel. 61/410359.

In an older house with considerable character, the homey, hospitable, and well-furnished **Hostal Dos Lagunas,** Barros Arana 104, tel. 61/415733, doslagunas@hotmail.com, is fast becoming a travelers' favorite for US$9 pp with an ample and varied breakfast. Also worth consideration are **Hostal Puerto Natales,** Eberhard 250, tel. 61/411098, for US$10 pp with private bath, and **Hostal La Cumbre,** Eberhard 533, tel. 61/412422, for US$13 pp.

Its decor is tacky—the interior looks more like a house trailer than a house—but cheerful **Hotel Blanquita,** Ignacio Carrera Pinto 409, tel. 61/411674, is spotlessly maintained and often full. Rates with breakfast are US$18/25 s/d with private bath and breakfast, but there are also a couple of singles with shared bath for US$9 pp. **Hotel Natalino,** Eberhard 371, tel. 61/411968, charges US$20/25 s/d with private bath.

Stuck in an off-the-beaten-sidewalk location, **Hostal Don Guillermo**, O'Higgins 657, tel./fax 61/414506, doesn't get the business it deserves, probably because it looks more expensive than it is. Though it lacks private baths, this new, stylish, immaculate, and inviting hostelry is seriously underpriced compared to most other places in town, charging US$12/20 s/d with breakfast, or US$20/25 with cable TV. In all likelihood, it will either go out of business or else jack up prices as demand increases.

US$25–50: Setting local standards for service since its inception many years ago, **Casa Cecilia,** Tomás Rogers 60, tel. 61/411797, redcecilia@entelchile.net, has almost become an attraction in itself—on occasion, nonguests even ask for tours of the hospitable Swiss-Chilean B&B. The rooms are simple, and some are small, but all enjoy central heating, there are kitchen facilities, and a cheerful atrium is a popular gathering place. Rates are US$13/21/27 s/d/t with shared bath, US$25/32 s/d with private bath, including the usual sumptuous breakfast.

Rehabbed **Hostal Indigo,** Ladrilleros 105, tel. 61/413609, fax 61/410169, indigo@entelchile.net, has carved itself a niche as much for its ground-floor pub/restaurant as for its comfortable upstairs accommodations for US$15 pp with breakfast; most but not all rooms have private bath. Climbers can work out on the wall outside.

Cozy and recently upgraded **Hotel Bulnes,** Bulnes 407, tel./fax 61/411307, info@hotelbulnes.com, charges US$25 pp with breakfast for well-heated rooms; there is covered parking. **US$50–100: Hotel Lukovieks,** Ramírez 324, tel./fax 61/412580, charges US$42/58 s/d with private bath and breakfast. Both **Hotel Laguna Azul,** Baquedano 380, tel./fax 61/411207, and **Hotel Milodón,** Bulnes 356, tel. 61/411727, fax 61/411286, are good choices for US$40/65 with similar services. **Hotel Lago Sarmiento,** Bulnes 90, tel./fax 61/411542, costs US$55/70 s/d.

Easily the best value in its range, the architecturally striking **Hotel Lady Florence Dixie,** Manuel Bulnes 659, tel. 61/411158, fax 61/411943, florence@chileanpatagonia.com, has expanded and upgraded what was already a good hotel without becoming a budget-breaker—prices of US$60/75 s/d with breakfast are more than reasonable here.

The newish **Hotel Glaciares,** Eberhard 104, tel./fax 61/411452, is not bad for US$71/86. An even more recent addition to the scene, the handsome **Hotel Saltos del Paine,** Bulnes 156, tel. 61/413607, fax 61/410261, informacion@saltosdelpaine.cl, charges US$75/98 s/d. **US$100–150: Hotel Eberhard,** Costanera Pedro Montt 25, tel. 61/411208, fax 61/411209, hoteleberhard@busesfernandez.com, used to be one of the best in its range; for US$95/104 s/d it's still okay, but others have superseded it. **Hotel Juan Ladrilleros,** Pedro Montt 161, tel. 61/411652, fax 61/412109, ladrilleros@aventouraventuras.com, is about average for US$93/105.

PATAGONIA & TIERRA

It's hard to endorse **Hotel Internacional Alberto de Agostini,** O'Higgins 632, tel. 61/410060, fax 61/410070, hotel.agostini@entelchile.net, very strongly; while the rooms are spacious and have good natural light, the hotel gives off a moribund impression despite its relative newness. Rack rates of US$81/121 are far too high for what it offers, so try bargaining.

Hotel Martín Gusinde, Bories 278, tel. 61/412770, fax 61/412401, hgrey@ctcreuna.cl, is one of the best upscale places for US$116/140 s/d, and a real bargain off-season for US$50/60. Rates at the luxury **Hotel Costa Australis,** Costanera Pedro Montt 262, tel. 61/412000, fax 61/411881, costaus@ctcreuna.cl, range from US$130/147 s/d with a city view to US$164/181 with sea view.

Food

To stock up on supplies for hiking at Puerto Natales, visit **Supermercado La Bombonera,** Bulnes 646.

Known for its seafood, Puerto Natales has plenty of moderately priced eateries and a handful of upscale choices. Relying on their waterfront locations to draw crowds, **El Marítimo,** Pedro Montt 214, and **Los Pioneros,** Pedro Montt 166, tel. 61/410783, are good and popular but not really special. For better atmosphere, try the informal **La Tranquera,** Bulnes 579, tel. 61/411039.

La Caleta Gastronómica, Eberhard 169, is a moderately priced (US$4–7) locale that offers excellent value for money—try the salmon with king crab sauce. Another well-established option is **Café Andrés,** Ladrilleros 381, tel. 61/412380, for cooked-to-order seafood. Underrated **Última Esperanza,** Eberhard 354, tel. 61/411391, deserves more attention than it gets for exceptional food at reasonable prices with outstanding service. **Los Viajeros,** Bulnes 291, tel. 61/411156, is a recent entry in the seafood category.

Evasión, Eberhard 595-B, tel. 61/414605, is a moderately priced café restaurant with daily lunch specials. Comparable choices include **La Frontera,** Bulnes 819, open for lunch only, and **Midas,** Tomás Rogers 169, tel. 61/411045. Basic

Chilean dishes outshine the Italian at **La Repizza,** Blanco Encalada 294, tel. 61/441036. The most diverse food in town may be at **Café Indigo,** part of its namesake accommodations at Ladrilleros 105, tel. 61/413609.

Natales's newest *parrilla,* **El Edén,** Blanco Encalada 345, tel. 61/414120, emphasizes regional dishes—try the *arrollado de cordero,* a stuffed and rolled lamb dish that's remarkably spicy for Chilean food, and rhubarb-*calafate* mousse for dessert. Most entrées are in the US$6–8 range, but the basic *parrillada* for two, at US$9, is a bargain.

Helados Bruna, Natales's best ice creamery, has two locales: Bulnes 585 and Eberhard 217. Rhubarb is the regional specialty.

Entertainment

Puerto Natales's nightlife is limited mostly to low-key bars such as **Café Indigo,** Ladrilleros 105, a Chilean-run but gringo-oriented gathering place with nightly slide shows about Natales and Torres del Paine.

El Bar de Ruperto, Bulnes 371, takes its name from the *pisco*-swilling burro so popular on Chilean TV ads. **Los Canallas del 43** is at Philippi 553.

Shopping

For books, travel literature (some of it in English), maps, and the like, there's a branch of **Southern Patagonia Souvenirs & Books,** Bulnes 688, tel. 61/413017.

Ñandú Artesanía, Eberhard 586, sells maps and books in addition to selection of quality crafts. **World's End,** Blanco Encalada 226, tel. 61/414725, is a Chilean map specialist.

Services

Money: Puerto Natales has several exchange houses: Cambio Mily, Blanco Encalada 266; Cambios Sur, Eberhard 285; and Stop Cambios, Baquedano 380. Banco Santiago has an ATM at Bulnes 598.

Postal: Correos de Chile is at Eberhard 429, at the southeast corner of Plaza Arturo Prat.

Telephone and Internet: Long-distance operators include Telefónica CTC at Blanco Encalada

© WAYNE BERNHARDSON

roadside shrine to Argentine folk saint Difunta Correa, Puerto Natales

and Bulnes, Chile Express at Tomás Rogers 143, and Entel at Baquedano 270. Natales's area code is 61, the same as Punta Arenas.

Internet connections are agonizingly slow here, but there are several outlets for about US$3 per hour: Internet, Bulnes 225, open 8 A.M.–midnight daily; Turismo María José, Bulnes 386; Café Indigo, Ladrilleros 105; and La Repizza, Blanco Encalada 294.

Laundry: Servilaundry is at Bulnes 513, tel. 61/412869. Lavandería Catch is at Bories 218.

Medical: Hospital Puerto Natales is at Ignacio Carrera Pinto 537, tel. 61/411582.

Information

Tourist Offices: Sernatur's local delegation, in a freestanding chalet-style structure at Pedro Montt 19, tel./fax 61/412125, is open 8:30 A.M.–1 P.M. and 2:30–6:30 P.M. weekdays throughout the year; from December to March, it's also open 9 A.M.–1 P.M. weekends. It has helpful personnel, occasionally English-speaking, and fairly thorough information on accommodations, restaurants, and transportation.

National Parks: Conaf has an office at O'Higgins 584, tel. 61/411438.

Transportation

Air: LanChile/LanExpress has an office at Tomás Rogers 78, tel. 61/411236, but has no flights out of Puerto Natales's aerodrome, a few kilometers north of town on the road to Torres del Paine. Punta Arenas–bound buses will leave passengers at that city's Aeropuerto Presidente Carlos Ibáñez del Campo.

Turismo Río Natalis, Bulnes 100, tel. 61/41-5100, is the representative for Aerovías DAP, which flies twice each weekday to El Calafate, in Argentina's Santa Cruz province, from November to March. Puerto Natales has a small but modern airfield just north of town.

LADE, the Argentine air force passenger service, flies from Río Turbio, just over the border from Natales, to Río Gallegos Monday and to El Calafate, Gobernador Gregores, Perito Moreno, and Comodoro Rivadavia on Wednesday. Its Río Turbio address is Avenida Los Mineros 375, tel. 54/2902/491224.

Bus: There is frequent bus service to and from Punta Arenas and Torres del Paine, and regular but less frequent service to the Argentine destinations of Río Turbio, Río Gallegos, and El Calafate.

Carriers serving Punta Arenas (US$4, three hours) include Bus Sur (five buses daily), Baquedano 558, tel. 61/411325; Buses Fernández (seven daily), Eberhard 555, tel. 61/411111; Buses Pacheco (three daily), Baquedano 244, tel. 61/414513; and Buses Transfer (three daily), Baquedano 414, tel. 61/412616.

Buses J B, Prat 258, tel. 61/412824, goes three times daily to Torres del Paine, while Buses Fortaleza, Prat 234, tel. 61/410595, goes twice. Andescape, Eberhard 599, tel. 412877, goes to Paine at 7 A.M. daily, returning at 12:15 P.M., while Turismo Paori, Eberhard 577, tel. 61/411229, goes at 7:30 A.M., returning at 2:30 P.M.

For the Argentine border town of Río Turbio (US$3, one hour), where there are connections to El Calafate and Río Gallegos, try Buses Lagoper, Angamos 640, tel. 61/411831; Buses Cootra, Baquedano 244, tel. 61/412785; Turis Sur, Angamos 658, tel. 61/413353; and Bus Sur.

Turismo Zaahj, Prat 236, tel. 61/412260, goes to El Calafate (US$20, 5.5 hours) Monday, Thursday, and Saturday at 9 A.M. Bus Sur goes at the same hour Monday and Friday, while Bus Sur goes Wednesday and Sunday at 6:30 A.M. Zaahj offers a draining day tour (US$70) to Argentina's Moreno Glacier that's recommended only for those on a very tight schedule who absolutely *must* see this particular ice.

Buses El Pingüino, at the Fernández terminal, Eberhard 555, tel. 61/411111, goes to Río Gallegos Wednesday and Sunday at 11 A.M. (US$18). Bus Sur goes Tuesday and Thursday at 6:30 A.M.

Ferry: Navimag, Pedro Montt 380, tel. 61/411421, fax 61/411642, operates the car/passenger ferries MV *Puerto Edén* and MV *Magallanes* to Puerto Montt; each is on a weekly schedule. The former calls at its namesake village en route north, while the latter stops at Puerto Chacabuco, where it's now possible to continue to Coyhaique and the Carretera Austral. Northbound sailing days are usually Monday and Thursday, but weather and tides can change schedules.

Passengers often spend the night on board before early morning departures, but Navimag also has a Sala de Espera (waiting room) improvised from two shipping containers at the corner of the Pedro Montt and O'Higgins.

Getting Around

Emsa/Avis, Bulnes 632, tel. 61/410775, rents cars, but there's a better selection in Punta Arenas. World's End, Blanco Encalada 226, tel. 61/414725, rents bicycles and motorcycles.

VICINITY OF PUERTO NATALES

Increasing numbers of operators arrange excursions to nearby sites of interest and, of course to Parque Nacional Torres del Paine and even Argentina's Parque Nacional Los Glaciares. Several operators have organized free, one-stop arrangements for Torres del Paine under the umbrella of **Path@gone,** Eberhard 599, tel./fax 61/413290, website: www.chileaustral.com/pathgone, pathgone@chileaustral.com. These include **Andescape,** tel./fax 61/412877 or 61/412592, andescape@ chileaustral.com, which has the concession for the *refugios* and campgrounds in the park; **Onas Aventura Patagonia,** tel./fax 61/412707, onas@chileaustral.com, which also does sea kayaking and trekking; **Fantástico Sur,** Magallanes 960, tel. 61/226653 in Punta Arenas, website: www.lastorres.com, info@lastorres.com; and **Turismo Stipe,** tel. 61/413290, fax 61/413291, turismostipe@entelchile.net.

Others include **Big Foot Expediciones,** Bories 206, tel. 61/414611, fax 61/414276, for sea kayaking, trekking, ice hiking, climbing, mountaineering, and more general excursions as well; and **Servitur,** Prat 353, tel./fax 61/411858. **Baqueano Zamora,** Eberhard 566, tel. 61/413953, baqueano@chileaustral.com, specializes in horseback trips in the park and is also the concessionaire for Posada Río Serrano.

Frigorífico Bories

Only four km north of Puerto Natales, the Sociedad Explotadora de Tierra del Fuego built this state-of-the-art (for its time) meat freezer to prepare excess livestock, primarily sheep, for shipment to Europe. Built of brick masonry between 1912 and 1914, in the Magellanic style, it's the only plant of its kind in a reasonable state of preservation. After its expropriation by the Allende government in 1971, the plant was partially dismantled and finally shut down a few years ago.

Among the remaining structures are the rendering plant, which converted animal fat into tallow, the tannery that prepared hides for shipment, and the main offices, smithery, locomotive repair facilities (Bories had its own short line), freight jetty, power plant, and boilers. The power plant still functions.

Accommodations and food are available here at **Hotel Cisne Cuello Negro;** make reservations through Turismo Pehoé, José Menéndez 918, Punta Arenas, tel. 61/244506, fax 61/248052, pehoe1@ctcreuna.cl. Rack rates are US$70/71 s/d with private bath and restaurant.

Monumento Natural Cueva del Milodón

Northwest of present-day Puerto Natales, on the shores of a small inlet known as Fiordo Eberhard, the giant Pleistocene ground sloth known as the mylodon *(Mylodon darwini)* took shelter in this wave-cut grotto 30 meters high and 80 meters wide at its mouth and 200 meters deep. While the mylodon has been extinct for nearly as long as humans have inhabited the area—11,000 years—the discovery of its remains caused a sensation in Europe, as their state of preservation induced some scientists to believe the animal might still be alive.

German pioneer sheep farmer Hermann Eberhard gets credit for discovering the cave in 1895, but Erland Nordenskjöld (1900) was the first scientist to study the cave, taking sample bones and skin back to Sweden. Its manure has been carbon-dated at roughly 10,400 years before the present, meaning the large herbivore coexisted with humans, but it was most definitely *not* a domesticate. In all probability, though, hunting pressure contributed to its demise (and that of many other Pleistocene megafauna). Oddly enough, no complete skeleton has been found.

The mylodon has gained a spot in the Western imagination, both among scientists and the lay public. United States archaeologist Junius Bird described the animal in his journals, published as *Travel and Archaeology in South Chile* (University of Iowa Press, 1988), edited by John Hyslop of the American Museum of Natural History. Family tales inspired Bruce Chatwin to write his masterpiece *In Patagonia,* which relates far-fetched legends that Paleo-Indians penned the mylodon in the cave and that some animals survived into the 19th century.

Conaf's **Museo de Sitio,** open 8 A.M.–8 P.M. daily, has excellent information on the 192-hectare park, which attracts 41,000 visitors per annum, more than half of them Chilean, but there are no other facilities except for a picnic area. A tacky full-sized statue of the mylodon stands in the cave itself.

Many tours from Puerto Natales take in the sight, but there is no regular public transportation except for Paine-bound buses that pass on Ruta 9, five km to the east. Mountain bike rental could be a good option.

Glaciar Balmaceda (Parque Nacional Bernardo O'Higgins)

Chile's largest national park, covering 3,525,901 hectares of islands and icecaps from near Tortel in Region XI (Aisén) to Última Esperanza in Region XII (Magallanes), has few easy access points, but the Balmaceda glacier at the outlet of the Río Serrano is one of them. From Puerto Natales, it's now a four-hour sail northwest—where Juan Ladrilleros and Pedro de Sarmiento de Gamboa ended their futile quests for a sheltered route to the Pacific—past Puerto Bories, several wool *estancias* reachable only by sea, and nesting colonies of seabirds and breeding colonies of southern sea lions, among U-shaped valleys with glaciers and waterfalls. Andean condors have been sighted in the area.

At the end of the cruise, passengers disembark for an hour or so at **Puerto Toro,** where a half hour's walk through southern beech forest leads to the receding **Glaciar Balmaceda.** Visitors remain about an hour before returning to Natales, unless they take advantage of the option to travel upriver to Torres del Paine, which may be visible in the distance.

Accommodations and Food: There are no formal accommodations in the park proper.

However, across the sound from Puerto Toro, in virtually the quietest location imaginable but for the wind, the nearly new **Hostería Monte Balmaceda,** José Nogueira 1255, Punta Arenas, tel. 61/245664, fax 61/233354, balmaceda @aventouraventuras.com, charges US$110/145 s/d with breakfast.

As it's accessible only by sea, a stay here is usually part of a package including a visit to the park and/or Torres del Paine. As of early 2001–02, however, the place was experiencing financial problems and was not open.

Transportation: Two Puerto Natales operators sail up the sound to the Balmaceda Glacier, usually daily in summer, less frequently the rest of the year. Bad weather and high winds may cause cancellations at any time of year.

Turismo Cutter 21 de Mayo, at Eberhard 554, tel. 61/411978, 21demayo@chileaustral.com, and at Ladrilleros 171, tel./fax 61/411176, operates its eponymous vessel or the yacht *Alberto de Agostini* to the park. Fares are US$60 pp, including an onboard snack. Instead of returning to Puerto Natales, it's possible to continue upriver to Torres del Paine with Puerto Natales's Onas Patagonia, Eberhard 599, tel. 61/414349, tel./fax 61/412707, onas@chileaustral.com. In open Zodiac rafts, supplying all passengers with warm wet weather gear, Onas passes scenic areas not normally seen by visitors to Paine, makes a lunch stop along the Río Serrano, and requires a brief portage around the Serrano rapids before arriving at the Río Serrano campground. The total cost is US$85; the excursion can also be done in the opposite direction.

Cerro Castillo

One of Chile's most thinly populated municipalities, the *comuna* of Torres del Paine has fewer than 500 inhabitants; more than half of them live in Cerro Castillo, 60 km north of Puerto Natales on Ruta 9, alongside the Río Don Guillermo border crossing. Called Cancha Carrera on the Argentine side, this is the most direct route from Parque Nacional Torres del Paine to El Calafate (Argentina) and Parque Nacional Los Glaciares. Formerly seasonal, it is now open all year.

Formerly an *estancia* belonging to the powerful Sociedad Explotadora de Tierra del Fuego, Cerro Castillo has an assortment of services, including a dismal museum at the municipal Departamento de Turismo, Avenida Bernardo O'Higgins s/n, tel. 61/691932, and the only gas station north of Puerto Natales. It also has accommodations at the basic **Residencial Loreto Belén** and more elaborate lodgings at **Hostería El Pionero,** tel. 61/413953, fax 412911 in Puerto Natales, for US$75/90 s/d with private bath and breakfast. Open September to April only, it serves meals to nonguests as well as guests, and it also rents horses.

PARQUE NACIONAL TORRES DEL PAINE

Recently, when a major Pacific Coast shipping company placed a two-page ad in Alaska Airlines' in-flight magazine, the landscape chosen to represent Alaska was . . . Parque Nacional Torres del Paine! While an opportunistic or uninformed photo editor may have been the culprit—interestingly enough for a Southern Hemisphere destination, the image was reversed— the soaring granite spires of Chile's premiere national park have become an international emblem of alpine majesty, well worthy of comparison with Alaska's grandeur.

The soaring granite spires of Chile's premiere national park have become an international emblem of alpine majesty.

But there's more—unlike most of South America's national parks, Torres del Paine has an integrated network of hiking trails suitable for day trips and backpack treks, endangered species such as the wild guanaco in a UNESCO-recognized World Biosphere Reserve, and a range of accommodations options, from rustic campgrounds to cozy trail huts and five-star luxury hotels. Popular enough that some visitors prefer the shoulder seasons of spring (November–December) or fall

(March–April)—the park received more than 71,000 visitors in the year 2000—Torres del Paine has become a major international destination, but it's still wild country.

Nearly everybody visits the park to behold extraordinary natural features such as the **Torres del Paine,** the sheer granite towers that have defied erosion even as the weaker sedimentary strata around them have weathered, and the jagged **Cuernos del Paine,** with their striking interface between igneous and metamorphic rocks. Most hike its trails uneventfully, but all should be aware that, for all its popularity, this is still hazardous terrain. Hikers have disappeared, the rivers run fast and cold, the weather is unpredictable, and there is one documented case of a tourist attacked and killed by a puma.

Orientation

Parque Nacional Torres del Paine is 112 km northwest of Puerto Natales via Ruta 9 through Cerro Castillo; 38 km beyond Castillo, a westbound lateral traces the southern shore of Lago Sarmiento de Gamboa to the park's isolated Lago Verde sector. Three km beyond the Lago Verde junction, another westbound lateral leaves Ruta 9 to follow Lago Sarmiento's north shore to Portería Sarmiento, the park's main gate; it continues southwest for 37 km to the Administración, the park headquarters at the west end of Lago del Toro.

Twelve km east of Portería Sarmiento, another lateral branches northwest and, three km farther on, splits again; the latter leads to Guardería Laguna Azul, in the park's little-visited northern sector, while the latter enters the park at Guardería Laguna Amarga, the most common starting point for the Paine Circuit, and follows the south shore of Lago Nordenskjöld and Lago Pehoé en route to the Administración. Most public transportation takes this route.

Geography and Climate

Parque Nacional Torres del Paine comprises 181,414 hectares of Patagonian steppe, lowland and alpine glacial lakes, glacier-fed torrents and waterfalls, forested uplands, and nearly vertical granite needles. Altitudes range from only about 50 meters above sea level in the vicinity of the lower Río Serrano to 3,050 meters on the summit of Paine Grande, the central massif's tallest peak.

Paine has a cool temperate climate characterized by frequent high winds, especially in spring

PATAGONIA & TIERRA

© WAYNE BERNHARDSON

Cuernos del Paine (Horns of Paine)

and summer. The average summer temperature is about 10.8°C, with maximums reaching around 23°C, while the average minimum in winter is around freezing. Average figures are misleading, however, as the weather is highly changeable. The park lies in the rain shadow of the Campo de Hielo Sur, where westerly storms drop most of their load as snow, so it receives only about 600 millimeters rainfall per annum. Still, snow and hail can fall even in midsummer. Spring is probably the windiest time, while in autumn, March and April, the winds tend to moderate, but days are shorter.

It should go without saying that at higher elevations temperatures are somewhat cooler and snow is likelier to fall. In some areas it's possible to hut-hop between *refugios*, eliminating the need for a tent and sleeping bag but not for warm clothing and impermeable rain gear.

Flora and Fauna

Less diverse than in areas farther north, Paine's vegetation still varies with altitude and distance from the Andes. Bunch grasses of the genera *Festuca* and *Stipa*, known collectively as *coirón*, cover the park's arid southeastern steppes, often interspersed with thorny shrubs such as the *calafate (Berberis buxifolia)*, which produces edible fruit, and *neneo (Anathrophillum desideratum)*. There are also miniature ground-hugging orchids such as the *zapatito (Calceolaria uniflora)* and *capachito (Calceolaria biflora)*.

Approaching the Andes, forests of the deciduous *lenga (Nothofagus pumilio)* blanket the hillsides, along with the evergreen *coigüe* de Magallanes *(Nothofagus betuloides)* and the deciduous *ñirre (Nothofagus antarctica)*. At the highest elevations, there is little vegetation of any kind among the alpine fell fields.

Among Paine's mammals, the most conspicuous is the guanaco *(Lama guanicoe)*, whose numbers—and tameness—have increased dramatically over the past two decades. Many of its young, known as *chulengos*, fall prey to the puma *(Felis concolor)*. A more common predator, or at least a more visible one, is the gray fox *(Dusicyon griseus)*, which lives off the introduced European hare and, outside the park boundaries, off sheep. The endangered *huemul* or Andean deer *(Hippocamelus bisulcus)* is a relatively rare sight.

On the steppes, the fleet but flightless rhea or ñandú *(Pterocnemia pennata)* is the South American counterpart to the ostrich (and is often also called *avestruz*). The monarch of South American birds, of course, is the Andean condor *(Vultur gryphus)*, not a rare sight here. Filtering the lake shallows for plankton, the Chilean flamingo *(Phoenicopterus chilensis)* summers here after breeding in the northern altiplano. The *caiquén* or upland goose *(Chloephaga picta)* grazes the moist grasslands around the lakes, while the black-necked swan *(Cygnus melancoryphus)* paddles peacefully on the surface.

Paine Circuit

More than two decades ago, under a military dictatorship, Chile attracted few foreign visitors, and hiking in Torres del Paine was a solitary experience—on a 10-day trek over the now-famous Paine circuit, the author met only three other hikers, two Americans and a Chilean. Some parts of the route were easy-to-follow stock trails (the park was once an *estancia*), while others, on the east shore of Lago Grey and into the valley of the Río de los Perros in particular, were barely boot-width tracks on steep slopes, or involved scrambling over granite boulders and fording waist-deep glacial meltwater. In the interim, as raging rivers have destroyed bridges at the outlets of Lago Nordenskjöld and Lago Paine, the original trailhead on the north shore on Lago Pehoé no longer exists, and the Laguna Azul exit in the park's northeastern corner is no longer feasible.

At the same time, completion of a trail along the north shore of Lago Nordenskjöld several years back created a new loop and simultaneously provided access to the south side of the Torres del Paine, offering easier access up the Río Ascencio and Valle del Francés in what is often done as the shorter "W" route to Lago Pehoé (see separate entry below for more detail). Where the former circuit crossed the Río Paine and continued along its north bank to the Laguna Azul campground, the new circuit now follows the river's west bank south to Laguna Amarga.

In the interim, trail maintenance and development have improved dramatically, rudimentary and not-so-rudimentary bridges have replaced fallen logs and traversed stream fords, and comfortable concessionaire *refugios* and organized campgrounds have supplanted the lean-tos and *puestos* (outside houses) that once sheltered shepherds on their rounds. Even though it's theoretically possible to complete most of the circuit without a tent or even a sleeping bag, showering and eating at the *refugios,* hikers should not forget that this is still rugged country with unpredictable weather.

Most hikers now tackle the circuit counterclockwise from Guardería Laguna Amarga, where buses from Puerto Natales stop for passengers to pay the park admission fee. An alternative is to continue to Pudeto and take a passenger launch to Refugio Pehoé, or else to the park Administración (which involves a much longer and rather less interesting approach); both of these involve doing the trek clockwise.

At least a week is desirable for the circuit; before beginning, registration with park rangers is obligatory. Camping is permitted only at designated sites, a few of which are free. Buy supplies in Puerto Natales, as only limited goods are available with the park, at premium prices.

Accommodations and Food: For counterclockwise hikers beginning at Laguna Amarga, there is no *refugio* until Lago Dickson (roughly 11 hours), though there is a paying campground at **Campamento Serón** (five hours) and a free one at **Campamento Coirón** (three hours farther).

Under Conaf concession, Puerto Natales's Andescape, Eberhard 599, tel. 61/412877, fax 61/412592, andescape@terra.cl, operates **Refugio Lago Pehóe** (reservations strongly recommended), **Refugio Lago Grey,** and **Refugio Lago Dickson,** plus the **Campamento Río de los Perros.** All these *refugios* closely resemble each other, with 32 bunks charging US$15 pp, with kitchen privileges and hot showers, but without sheets or sleeping bags, which are available for rental but sometimes scarce. Breakfast costs US$5–6, lunch US$7.50, dinner US$10, full board US$22.50. A bunk with full board costs US$37 pp. Campers pay US$4 pp, plus US$1.50 for showers (*refugio* guests, however,

have priority on the hot showers). Tents, sleeping bags, mats, and campstoves are also for rent.

The "W" Variant

From Guardería Laguna Amarga, a narrow undulating road crosses the Río Paine on a narrow bridge to the grounds of **Estancia Cerro Paine,** beneath the 2,640-meter summit of Monte Almirante Nieto. The *estancia* operates a hotel, *refugios,* and campgrounds on its property, and it also shuttles hikers back and forth from Laguna Amarga for US$4 pp.

From Estancia Cerro Paine, a northbound trail parallels the route from Guardería Laguna Amarga, eventually meeting it just south of Campamento Serón. The *estancia* is more notable, though, as the starting point for the "W" route to Lago Pehoé, a scenic and popular option for hikers lacking time for the full circuit. On the western edge of the *estancia* grounds, the trail crosses the Río Ascencio on a footbridge to a junction

Refugio Cuernos, Parque Nacional Torres del Paine

where a northbound lateral climbs the river canyon to Campamento Torres, where a short but very steep trail ascends to a nameless, glacial tarn at the foot of the Torres proper. This is an easy day hike from the *estancia,* though many people prefer to camp or spend the night at the *refugio* (see below for information on accommodations and food).

From the junction, the main trail follows Lago Nordenskjöld's north shore, past another *refugio* and campground, to the free Campamento Italiano at the base of the **Río del Francés** valley. While the main trail continues west toward Lago Pehoé, another northbound lateral climbs steeply up the valley, between the striking metamorphic Cuernos del Paine to the east and the 3,050-meter granite summit of Paine Grande to the west, to the free Campamento Británico.

Accommodations and Food: Technically outside the park boundaries, most of the "W" route along the north shore of Lago Nordenskjöld is under the private control of Punta Arenas' Fantástico Sur, Magallanes 960, tel. 61/226054, fax 61/222641, lastorres@chileaustral.com, which runs the 36-bunk **Refugio Las Torres** on the *estancia*'s main grounds, the 36-bunk **Refugio Chileno** in the upper Río Ascencio valley, and the 28-bunk **Refugio Los Cuernos,** all of which also have campgrounds. Fantástico Sur's *refugios* are more spacious, diverse, and attractive in design than the Conaf *refugios* run by Andescape, and the food is better as well.

Bunks at any of the Fantástico Sur *refugios* cost US$16 pp (US$30 with full board), while camping costs US$4 pp with hot showers. Separately, a continental breakfast costs US$3.50, a U.S.-style breakfast US$5, lunch US$7, or dinner US$9; a full meal package costs US$18. Rental tents, sleeping bags, mats, and stoves are also available.

Other Trails

After heavy runoff destroyed the once-sturdy bridge at the outlet of Lago Paine in the early 1980s, the north shore of the Río Paine became, and has remained, isolated from the rest of the park. A good road, however, still goes from Guardería Laguna Amarga to the east end of La-

guna Azul, where there are a campground and *cabañas,* and the **Sendero Lago Paine,** a four-hour walk to the lake and a simple *refugio.* A trekkers' alternative is the **Sendero Desembocadura,** which leads north from Guardería Laguna Amarga through open country to the west end of Laguna Azul and continues to Lago Paine, but this takes about eight hours. From the north shore of Lago Paine, the **Sendero Lago Dickson** (5.5 hours) leads to the Dickson glacier.

Several easy day hikes are possible in the vicinity of Guardería Lago Pehoé, directly on the road from Laguna Amarga to the Administración. The short **Sendero Salto Grande** leads to the thunderous waterfall, at the outlet of Lago Sarmiento, that was the starting point of the Paine Circuit until unprecedented runoff swept away the iron bridge that crossed to Península Pehoé. From Salto Grande, the **Sendero Mirador Nordenskjöld** is a slightly longer but still easy hike to a vista point on the lakeshore, directly opposite the stunning Cuernos del Paine.

From the Guardería Lago Grey, 18 km northwest of the Administración by road, a short footpath leads to a sandy beach on the south shore of Lago Grey, where icebergs from Glaciar Grey often beach themselves. The longer and less visited **Sendero Lago Pingo** ascends the valley of the Río Pingo to its namesake lake (5.5–six hours); there are two basic *refugios* along the route.

More Recreation

Climbing and Mountaineering: Despite the similarity of terrain, Paine seems to attract fewer groups of climbers than Argentina's neighboring Parque Nacional Los Glaciares, perhaps because fees for climbing permits have been very high here. These fees have fallen considerably, to about US$75 pp, and should not be much of a deterrent to anyone who's come this far to climb mountains this spectacular. Before being granted permission, climbers must present Conaf with current résumés, emergency contact numbers, and authorization from their consulate.

When climbing in sensitive border areas (meaning most of Andean Chile), climbers must also have permission from the Dirección de Fronteras y Límites (Difrol) in Santiago. It's possible to do this through a Chilean consulate overseas or at Difrol's Santiago offices; if you arrive in Puerto Natales without permission, it's possible to request it through the Gobernación Provincial, the regional government offices on the south side of Plaza Arturo Prat, tel. 61/411423, fax 61/411992. The turnaround time is 48 hours. Ask Conaf for more time than you'll need, as each separate trip could require a separate fee.

While climbing and mountaineering activities may be undertaken independently, local concessionaires can provide training and lead groups or individuals with less experience on snow and ice. Puerto Natales's Big Foot Expediciones, for instance, has a base camp at Refugio Grey where it leads full-day traverses of the Ventisquero Grey daily at 9:30 A.M., returning at 5:30 P.M. Except for warm, weatherproof clothing, it provides all equipment. For more detail, contact Big Foot Expediciones, Bories 206, tel. 61/414611, fax 61/414276, explore@bigfootpatagonia.com.

Horseback Riding: The only concessionaire offering horseback trips in Parque Nacional Torres del Paine, Río Serrano–based Baqueano Zamora has a Puerto Natales office at Eberhard 566, tel. 61/413953, baqueano@chileaustral.com. Rates are about US$15 for two hours or US$50 per day (including lunch).

Sea Kayaking: Big Foot Patagonia (see Climbing and Mountaineering, above) arranges guided three-day, two-night ascents of the Río Serrano for US$380.

Accommodations and Food

Park accommodations vary from free trailside campgrounds to first-rate luxury hotels with just about everything in between; in summer, reservations are almost obligatory at hotels and advisable at campgrounds and *refugios*. (For options along the Paine Circuit and other trails, see the separate entries above.)

Camping: River water and pit toilets are the only amenities at Conaf's free **Refugio y Camping Laguna Amarga,** where people wait for the bus to Puerto Natales. At Estancia Cerro Paine, charging US$5 pp, **Camping Las Torres** gets hikers heading up the Río Ascencio valley to the Paine overlook and/or west on the "W" route to

Lago Pehoé, or finishing up the circuit here. Formerly insufficient shower and toilet facilities have improved here.

Also at Las Torres, under concession from Conaf, the **Cascada Eco-Camp** is a dome tent facility designed for minimum impact; on raised platforms, heated by gas stoves, each tent is five meters wide, with wooden floors and two single beds, with towels and bedding including down comforters. Another large tent includes a common living area, dining room, and kitchen; the separate bathrooms have hot showers and composting toilets. It is open, however, only to Cascada clients (for more detail consult its listing under Organized Tours in the On the Road chapter, or see its website: www.cascada-expediciones.com).

On the small peninsula on the eastern shore of its namesake lake, just west of the road to the Administración, the concessionaire-run **Camping Lago Pehoé,** tel. 61/226910 in Punta Arenas, charges US$13 for up to six people; fees include firewood and hot showers. A few kilometers farther south, **Camping Río Serrano** has been closed but should reopen.

In the park's isolated northeastern sector, **Camping Laguna Azul,** tel. 61/411157 in Puerto Natales, charges US$17 per site.

Refugios, Hosterías, and Hotels: Near the Administración, Conaf's **Refugio Lago Toro** charges US$5 pp for bunks (bring your own sleeping bag) plus US$2 for hot showers. The extremely basic **Refugio Pudeto,** on the north shore of Lago Pehoé, is due for a makeover to put it on a par with other park *refugios*.

Posada Río Serrano, tel. 61/413953, is a former *estancia* house adapted into a B&B. Rates are US$66 d with shared bath, US$100 d with private bath, and it has a restaurant/bar as well.

In the park's southeastern Laguna Verde sector, reachable by road along the south shore of Lago Sarmiento or by foot or horseback from the Río Paine, well-regarded **Hostería Mirador del Payne,** tel. 61/410498, charges US$105/128 s/d. Its Punta Arenas representative is Turismo Viento Sur, Fagnano 585, tel./fax 61/228712.

Where Lago Grey becomes the Río Grey, **Hostería Lago Grey** now charges US$173/199 s/d with breakfast, but only US$82/95 off-season;

lunch or dinner costs US$25 pp. For reservations, contact Complejo Turístico Lago Grey, Lautaro Navarro 1065, Punta Arenas, tel. 61/229512, fax 61/225986, hgrey@terra.cl. It also arranges excursions.

On a five-hectare island linked to the mainland by a footbridge, the 25-room **Hostería Pehoé** charges US$145/160 s/d with breakfast. According to several reports, it has improved substantially since the operator won a lawsuit against Conaf and began to reinvest in what had been a rundown facility, with substandard service, in an undeniably spectacular setting. For reservations, contact Turismo Pehoé, José Menéndez 918, Punta Arenas, tel. 61/244506, fax 61/24-8052, pehoe1@ctcreuna.cl.

At Estancia Cerro Paine, **Hostería Las Torres** is one of the park's gems for both its setting, seven km west of Guardería Laguna Amarga beneath Monte Almirante Nieto, and its professionalism. Rates range from US$131/149 to US$163/179 s/d in high season with buffet breakfast, but fall to US$79/89 to US$98/107 from mid-April to the end of September. The restaurant is open to both guests and nonguests. For reservations, contact Hostería Las Torres, Magallanes 960, Punta Arenas, tel. 61/226054, fax 61/222641, info@lastorres.com.

Open for packages only, **Hotel Salto Chico** is a megaluxury resort that, somehow, manages to blend inconspicuously into the landscape while offering some of the grandest views of any hotel in the world. Rates start at US$1,347/2,080 s/d for three nights in the least expensive room, ranging up to US$5,388/6,738 for seven nights in the costliest suite, including transfer to and from Punta Arenas and unlimited excursions within the park. For more information and/or reservations, contact Explora Hotels, Américo Vespucio Sur 80, 5th floor, Las Condes, Santiago, tel. 2/2066060, fax 2/2284655, reservexplora@explora-chile.cl.

Just beyond park boundaries, reached by launch across the Río Serrano, the stylish **Hostería Lago Tyndall**, tel./fax 61/240337 in Punta Arenas, enjoys peace, quiet, and magnificent views for US$105/132 s/d with breakfast. Nearby, the less stylish **Hostería Cabañas del Paine,** tel. 61/220174, fax 61/243354 in Punta Arenas, charges US$90/99 s/d.

Information

Conaf's principal facility is its **Centro de Informaciones Ecológicas,** at the Administración building on the shores of Lago del Toro, which features good natural history exhibits. It's open 8:30 A.M.–8 P.M. daily in summer. Ranger stations at Guardería Laguna Amarga, Portería Lago Sarmiento, Guardería Laguna Azul, Guardería Lago Verde, and Guardería Lago Grey can also provide information.

Entry Fee: For foreigners, Torres del Paine is the most expensive of Chilean national parks—US$11 pp except from May 1 to September 30, when it's only US$6. Rangers at Portería Lago Sarmiento, Guardería Laguna Amarga (where most buses now stop inbound), Guardería Lago Verde, or Guardería Laguna Azul collect the fee and issue receipts.

Books and Maps: The most complete single source on natural history and particularly hiking trails has been Clem Lindenmayer's *Trekking in the Patagonian Andes* (Lonely Planet, 1998), but it was not due for a new edition until mid-2003. The text and coverage of the new fifth edition of Tim Burford's *Chile & Argentina: The Bradt Trekking Guide* (Bradt Publications, 2001) are greatly improved over previous editions, though the maps are only so-so. Climbers should look for Alan Kearney's *Mountaineering in Patagonia* (The Mountaineers, 1998), which includes both historical and practical information on climbing in Torres del Paine and Argentina's Parque Nacional Los Glaciares.

Among the maps, the most regularly updated is JLM Mapas' *Torres del Paine Trekking Map,* at a scale of 1:100,000 with 100-meter contours. Costing about US$6, it's widely available in Punta Arenas and Puerto Natales and less dependably available at Portería Lago Sarmiento and at the park's Centro de Informaciones Ecológicas. Conaf has a very inexpensive map, at a scale of 1:160,000 with erratic contour intervals, that is suitable for orientation but not for trekking.

Gladys Garay N. and Oscar Guineo N. have collaborated in *The Fauna of Torres del Paine*

(1993), a locally produced guide to the park's animal life.

Transportation

Most people choose the bus as the cheapest and quickest way to and from the park, but the trip up Seno Última Esperanza and the Río Serrano by cutter and Zodiac is a viable and entertaining option.

Bus: (For overland transportation details, see the Puerto Natales entry.) All bus companies enter the park at Guardería Laguna Amarga, where many people begin the Paine circuit, before continuing to the Administración at Río Serrano. Roundtrips from Natales are somewhat cheaper, but companies do not accept each others' tickets.

In summer only, there may be direct bus service from Torres del Paine to El Calafate, Argentina, the closest town to that country's Parque Nacional Los Glaciares. Inquire in Puerto Natales or at the park Administración.

River: Transportation up and down the Río Serrano, between the park and Puerto Natales, has become a popular if considerably more expensive alternative than the bus (for details, see the separate entry for Parque Nacional Bernardo O'Higgins and the Balmaceda Glacier). Visitors who want to see only this sector of the river, without continuing to Puerto Natales, can do so as a day trip to Puerto Toro and back.

Getting Around

Buses to and from Puerto Natales will also carry passengers along the main park road, but as their schedules are very similar, there are substantial blocks of time with no public transportation. Hitching is common, but competition is heavy and most Chilean vehicles are full with families. There is a regular shuttle between Guardería Laguna Amarga and Estancia Cerro Paine (Hostería Las Torres).

From October to April, reliable transportation is now available from Refugio Pudeto to Refugio Pehoé (US$15, half an hour) with the catamaran *Hielos Patagónicos,* tel. 61/226054 in Punta Arenas, tel. 61/411380 in Puerto Natales, from October through April. In October and April, there is one departure daily, at noon, from

Pudeto, returning at 12:30 P.M. In November and from mid-March to April, there are departures at noon and 6 P.M., returning at 12:30 and 6:30 P.M. From December through mid-March, there is an additional departure at 9:30 A.M., returning at 10 A.M.

PUERTO EDÉN

Accessible only by sea, the Isla Wellington village of Puerto Edén is the last outpost of the Kawasqar (Alacaluf) Indians, about 15 of whom lead a marginal existence in this soggy but stunningly scenic sector of the southern Chilean channels. Receiving more than 3.5 meters of rainfall per annum, 620 km northwest of Punta Arenas as the crow flies, the settlement of 300 people is also the western gateway to Parque Nacional Bernardo O'Higgins and an obvious choice for truly off-the-beaten-fjord travel—tourist traffic is almost nil.

Part of a project to promote tourism in northernmost Magallanes, Puerto Natales-based Yekchal Turismo, Eberhard 564-A, tel./fax 61/412350 or 61/413591, website: www.patagoniayekchal.co.cl, yekchal@entelchile.net, arranges five-day, four-night to eight-day, seven-night trekking and sailing combinations to Península Exmouth, directly east of Puerto Edén, and Glaciar Pío XI, on the western edge of the Campo de Hielo Sur. For three to five people, the shorter itinerary costs US$600 pp, while the longer costs US$775; for six to nine people, the respective prices are US$375 and US$485. Accommodations are available at **Hospedería Yekchal** for US$11 pp with breakfast; lunch and dinner are also available in the US$4–5 range. The only regular means of transportation to Puerto Edén is its weekly namesake ferry, operated by Navimag, which sails between Puerto Montt and Puerto Natales; Navimag's other ferry, the *Magallanes,* does not call here.

EL CALAFATE AND VICINITY (ARGENTINA)

Over the past decade, improved cross-border communications have meant that many visitors to Puerto Natales and Torres del Paine now visit

PATAGONIA & TIERRA

TRAVEL IN ARGENTINA

Many visitors to Chilean Patagonia also cross the border into Argentine Patagonia and Tierra del Fuego. In fact, anyone traveling overland to Magallanes and Chilean Tierra del Fuego *has* to pass through Argentina, though airplane and ferry passengers can avoid Chile's larger neighbor. Not that they would necessarily want to, as there's plenty to see and do there, and for the most part, it's geographically remote from the country's political upheavals of late 2001 and early 2002.

Because so many travelers to Magallanes visit bordering Santa Cruz province and the Argentine side of Tierra del Fuego, important destinations such as El Calafate, Parque Nacional Los Glaciares, and Ushuaia are covered in detail in this Moon Handbook. Moon has no separate handbook for Argentina at present, but the author has one in the works—look for it soon at your favorite bookseller.

Visas and Officialdom

Very few nationalities need advance visas for Argentina, but requirements can change—if in doubt, check the efficient consulate in Santiago. Otherwise, be aware that there is no Argentine consulate between Puerto Montt and Punta Arenas. Ordinarily, border officials give foreign tourists an automatic 90-day entry permit, but check to be certain—on occasion, they will stamp 30 days for no apparent reason.

The paramilitary Gendarmería (Border Guards) serve as both immigration and customs officials at most Patagonian crossings; at the larger border crossings, most notably San Sebastián (Tierra del Fuego) and Monte Aymond (south of Río Gallegos), the Dirección General de Aduanas (National Customs Service) has a separate presence. Fresh fruit is the biggest taboo, but consumer electronics such as video cameras sometimes attract their attention.

Health

Argentina requires no vaccinations for visitors entering from any country, and public health standards are traditionally the highest on the continent. As in Chile, both Chagas' disease and hantavirus are present, but health risks in Patagonia and Tierra del Fuego are small indeed. There are isolated instances of malaria in humid subtropical northern Argentina.

Money and Prices

Until early 2002, Argentina had followed a rigid "currency basket" policy that fixed the peso at par with the U.S. dollar. Although this had the effect of maintaining relatively high prices, it was also convenient for foreign visitors who could use U.S. dollars in lieu of pesos without concern about exchange rates, and they could even obtain cash dollars from Argentine ATMs.

the Argentine side to see attractions such as the spectacular Moreno Glacier and the El Chaltén sector of Parque Nacional Los Glaciares. Following the Argentine debt default and subsequent devaluation of early 2002, the Argentine peso is no longer at par with the US dollar, and prices have fallen considerably in dollar terms. This has encouraged many formerly reluctant budget travelers, now taking advantage of favorable exchange rates, to visit Argentina.

As in Chile, the summer months and January and February are the peak season, and prices drop considerably in the offseason—though many places also close. Like Puerto Natales and Torres del Paine, the area enjoys a lengthening tourist season.

On the south shore of Lago Argentino, a giant glacial trough fed by melting ice from the Campo

de Hielo Sur, El Calafate is the gateway to Argentina's Parque Nacional Los Glaciares and its spectacular Moreno Glacier. While this town of about 4,000 permanent residents has few points of interests in its own right, it has good and improving services, including hotels and restaurants, and is the main transport hub for southwestern Santa Cruz province. A sparkling new international airport provides direct connections to Buenos Aires and even, in season, to Puerto Natales.

Orientation: While it's only about 50 or 60 km from Torres del Paine as the crow flies, El Calafate is 215 km from the Cerro Castillo border crossing and about 305 km from Puerto Natales via Argentina's Ruta Nacional 40 (RN 40), Ruta Provincial 5 (RP 5), and Ruta Provincial 11 (RP 11), including a small additional distance on the

After a political, foreign debt, and economic crisis that resulted in five presidents in two weeks at the end of 2001, dollar prices have fallen—within a couple of months, the devalued Argentine peso lost nearly two-thirds of its value—but the country's economy is historically unpredictable, with episodes of hyperinflation when prices have risen as much as 50 percent in a month. Keep a close eye on exchange rates and avoid buying too many pesos if the rate is unstable. Prices for Argentine destinations in this book were based on the former one-to-one exchange rate, but as of press time devaluation had reduced price levels by at least half. Though the US dollar is still widely accepted for goods and services, it is usually advantageous to pay in pesos obtained at bank rates.

In general, traveler's checks are difficult to cash, and many banks and exchange houses charge a high commission—as much as 5 or even 10 percent. ATMs and cash dollars remain the best alternative.

Communications

Telephone, Internet, and postal services have been substantially more expensive and less convenient in Argentina than in Chile for many years, but prices may fluctuate with the new exchange regime before it finds a stable level. Argentina's country code is 54; each city or town usually has a separate area code.

Getting Around

Distances in Argentine Patagonia are enormous so, even though roads are improving, some travelers take advantage of flights to cover long distances. This is most important for passengers arriving from Buenos Aires, but some visitors crossing the border from Coyhaique, Chile Chico, or Osorno can make connections to El Calafate or the larger city of Río Gallegos.

Argentine buses are mostly similar to those in Chile—modern, spacious, and fast. Most large towns have a central bus terminal, though Ushuaia does not. There is now regular bus service along dusty Ruta Nacional 40 (RN 40) between El Calafate and Los Antiguos, the Argentine border town opposite Chile Chico; there is also a regular service between El Chaltén, the gateway to the northern sector of Parque Nacional Los Glaciares, and Los Antiguos. These services are relatively expensive compared with Chilean buses, but they are substantially faster and cheaper than other more roundabout routes via the Argentine coastline.

Hitching is difficult along RN 40, as private vehicle traffic is sparse, but more and more cyclists are using this route. So are travelers who rent twin-cabin pickup trucks in Chile en route to Patagonia and back.

Chilean side. It is 320 km northwest of the Santa Cruz provincial capital of Río Gallegos, and 32 km west of northbound RP 40, which leads to the wilder El Chaltén sector of Parque Nacional Los Glaciares and an alternative but little-used overland route back to Chile.

A former stage stop, El Calafate has an elongated city plan that has spread only a few blocks north and south of its main east-west thoroughfare, the pompously named Avenida del Libertador General José de San Martín (for Argentina's independence hero, second only to Venezuela's Simón Bolívar on the continent's pantheon). Nearly all services and points of interest are close to what is colloquially known as "Avenida Libertador" or simply "San Martín."

Sights

After years of apparent abandonment, the **Museo Regional El Calafate,** Avenida Libertador 575, tel. 2902/491924, has finally reopened, but it's hard to say it was worth the wait for the sparse and poorly presented exhibits on paleontology, natural history, geology, and ethnology. The photographic histories of pioneer families show promise, but it would be nice to have some explanation of the labor unrest that led to several shooting deaths on the *estancias* in the 1920s. It's open 10 A.M.–5 P.M. weekdays only.

Just north of town, municipal authorities have transformed a onetime sewage pond into **Reserva Municipal Laguna Nimez,** a freshwater body frequented by more than 100 bird species. Admission costs US$1; it's open 8 A.M.–9 P.M. daily.

Accommodations

El Calafate has a wide variety of accommodations at generally high standards in each category, from camping to five-star comfort. Unless otherwise indicated, prices below are for high season, usually October to April, but specific dates can vary and, if business is slow, rates can be negotiable.

Note that, unlike their Chilean counterparts, Argentine hotels do not discount IVA to foreign visitors. In addition, breakfast is usually (though not always) extra.

US$10 or Less: On the grounds of its namesake *hospedaje*, **Camping Los Dos Pinos,** 9 de Julio 218, tel. 2902/491271, charges US$4 pp for tent sites. At the eastern approach to town, on both sides of Arroyo Calafate, the fenced and forested **Camping Municipal,** José Pantín s/n, tel. 2902/491829, campingmunicipal@cotecal.com.ar, also charges US$4 pp, plus, only in summer, US$4 per tent and US$6 for self-contained camper vehicles. Areas on the east side of the creek are for walk-in campers only. Each site has its own fire pit, and there are good common toilets and hot showers.

US$10–25: Albergue Lago Argentino, a block south of the bus terminal at Campaña del Desierto 1050, tel. 2902/491423, fax 2902/491139, hostellagoargentino@cotecal.com.ar, charges US$6 pp. **Albergue Ahijuna,** Avenida Roca 1316, hospbuenosaires@cotecal.com.ar, costs US$8 pp.

Open September to mid-April, the Hostelling International affiliate **Albergue del Glaciar,** east of Arroyo Calafate at Los Pioneros s/n, tel./fax 2902/491243, info@glaciar.com, charges US$10 for members and US$12 for nonmembers except in September and October, and mid-March to mid-April, when rates are US$8 and US$10 respectively. The hostel has extensive common spaces, including a large lounge, kitchen space, and laundry facilities, provides information, and offers its own excursions to the Moreno Glacier. There is also floor space above the restaurant for US$5 pp.

A couple of good but simple options, charging US$10 pp each with shared bath but without breakfast, are **Hospedaje Alejandra,** Espora 60, tel. 2902/491328, and **Hospedaje Lago Azul,** Perito Moreno 83, tel. 2902/491419. Adolescent boys—not necessarily bad kids, but still adolescents—hang around friendly **Hospedaje Jorgito,** Moyano 943, tel. 2902/491323, which rents multibedded rooms only for US$12 pp with shared bath.

"Think big" seems to be the motto at the new **Calafate Hostel,** Gobernador Moyano 1296, tel. 2902/492450, calafatehostel@cotecal.com.ar, also an HI affiliate openly challenging the more established Albergue Los Glaciares. In a stylish new building with vast common areas, it charges US$12 pp for hostel accommodations with shared bath and balconies, US$40 d for rooms with private bath.

US$25–50: Hospedaje Los Dos Pinos, 9 de Julio 358, tel./fax 2902/491271, losdospinos@cotecal.com.ar, has plain but spacious and immaculate accommodations with in-room heating for US$15 pp. Rates are identical at the so-so **Hospedaje Buenos Aires,** just north of the bus terminal at Ciudad de Buenos Aires 296, tel. 2902/491147, hospbuenosaires@cotecal.com.ar.

Hospedaje del Norte, Los Gauchos 813, tel. 2902/491117, costs US$20/30 s/d with shared bath and breakfast, US$30/36 with private bath, plus US$5 pp for breakfast.

Toward the west end of town, just beyond the EG3 gas station on Avenida Libertador, **Home Garden,** Guillermo Eike 14, tel./fax 2902/493396, hgreginafried@latinmail.com, has friendly family atmosphere with smallish rooms for US$29/42 s/d with private bath and breakfast.

Hospedaje Familiar Las Cabañitas, in a quiet location at Valentín Feilberg 218, tel. 2902/49-1118, lascabanitas@cotecal.com.ar, offers chalet-style accommodations and perhaps the most *simpático* management in town for US$25/36 s/d in low season, US$36/48 in high season. This is a popular choice, and reservations are advisable.

The new and appealing **Hospedaje Sir Thomas,** Espora 257, tel. 2902/492220, fax 2902/491300,hospedajesirthomas@cotecal.com.ar, charges US$20/30 s/d, plus US$5 pp for a continental breakfast or US$8 pp for an American-style breakfast.

US$50–100: Well-regarded **Residencial Los Lagos,** 25 de Mayo 220, tel. 2902/491170, fax 2902/491347, loslagos@cotecal.com.ar, costs US$30 pp in December, January, and February, US$25/40 s/d the rest of the year, with breakfast US$5 more.

Hotel Amado, Avenida Libertador 1072, tel. 2902/491134, familiagomez@cotecal.com.ar, costs US$42/62 s/d in the summer, but only US$28/47 the rest of the year, though breakfast is extra. Appealing **Hotel Cerro Cristal,** Gregores 989, tel. 2902/491088, charges US$40/65 s/d, with breakfast US$4 extra.

The Automóvil Club Argentino (Argentine Automobile Club) operates the **Hostería ACA,** Primero de Mayo 50, tel. 2902/491004, fax 2902/491027, robertolugo@cotecal.com.ar, where rates for members (including those of overseas affiliates) are US$52/69; nonmembers pay US$65/86.

Rates at **Hotel La Loma,** Avenida Roca 849, tel. 2902/491016, lalomahotel@cotecal.com.ar, range from US$40/55 to US$50/80 with breakfast from November to March, but it offers substantial discounts the rest of the year. **Hotel Kapenke,** at Gregores and 9 de Julio, tel. 2902/491093, kapenke@cotecal.com.ar, charges US$60/90 in the summer, US$50/75 off-season.

US$100–200: Recommended **Hostería Kalkén,** Valentín Feilberg 119, tel. 2902/491073, fax 2902/491036, hotelkalken@cotecal.com.ar, charges US$100/110 s/d with an outstanding breakfast from November through March and during Semana Santa; in October, April, and May, rates are US$82/95. **Hotel Michelangelo,** Moyano 1020, tel. 2902/491045, fax 2902/491058, michelangelohotel@cotecal.com.ar, costs US$96/121 s/d with breakfast. **Hotel El Quijote,** Gregores 1191, tel. 2902/491017, fax 2902/491103, elquijote@cotecal.com.ar, costs US$115/140 s/d in peak season, but only US$95/120 in October and April, breakfast included.

The 60-room **Hotel Kosten Aike,** Gobernador Moyano 1243, tel. 2902/492424, fax 2902/49-1538, kostenaike@cotecal.com.ar, is a new and impressive, four-star hotel with every modern convenience, including gym and spa, modem access, and even facilities for the disabled. The prices are equally impressive, ranging from US$120 s or d in low season to US$188 s or d in the summer peak season. In the same category is **Hotel Posada Los Álamos,** Gobernador Moyano 1355, tel. 2902/491144, posadalosalamos@cotecal.com.ar, which charges US$182/188 s/d in peak season, US$135/141 off-season, with breakfast.

Food

Argentine *confiterías* are renowned for *minutas* (short orders), sandwiches, coffee, and the like, and El Calafate has several decent ones. Among them are **Pietro's Café,** Avenida Libertador 1640; **Confitería Casa Blanca,** Avenida Libertador 1202, tel. 2902/491402; **Paso Verlika,** Avenida Libertador 1108, tel. 2902/491009; and **Rick's Café,** Avenida Libertador 1105, tel. 2902/492148.

While famous for its beef, Argentine cuisine also has a strong Italian element. Pizza and pasta are the rule at venues such as **Pizzería Onelli,** Libertador 1197, tel. 2902/491184; **El Hornito,** half a block from the bus terminal at Buenos Aires 155, tel. 2902/491443; and especially **El Rancho,** at Gobernador Moyano and 9 de Julio, tel. 2902/491644, back in action after an unfortunate absence. The most imaginative Italian option is **La Cocina,** Avenida Libertador 1245, tel. 2902/491758, where entrées start around US$8.

Simply decorated, appropriately named **The Family House,** Comandante Espora 18, tel. 2902/492156, is a respectable *parrilla* that also serves pasta dishes in the US$7 and up range, with good service as well. **La Vaca Atada,** Avenida Libertador 1176, tel. 2902/491227, is a popular *parrilla* that also has fine soups and pasta, with most entrées in the US$7–10 range. **Mi Viejo,** Avenida Libertador 1111, tel. 2902/491691, is comparable but a bit more expensive.

The Albergue del Glaciar's **El Témpano Errante,** Los Pioneros s/n, tel. 2902/491243, is worth a detour for its diverse menu and cheerful ambience. **La Posta,** at Bustillo and Moyano, tel. 2902/491144, is the upscale restaurant at Hotel Posada Los Alamos; entrées go for US$15–20 except for pasta dishes, which start around US$10.

Decorated in a Buenos Aires motif, **Tango Sur,** 9 de Julio 265, tel. 2902/491550, has pizzas in the US$4–7 range, with more complex entrées around US$10.

Argentine empanadas differ considerably from their Chilean counterparts in size (smaller), crust (lighter and flakier), and fillings (much more diverse). To sample them in nearly all their variety, visit **Todo Suelto,** a takeaway outlet at Avenida Libertador 1044, tel. 2902/491114.

Astonishingly, El Calafate went nearly 10 years without a quality ice creamery—Argentine *helados* are arguably the best on the continent—but now it has two outstanding ones. **Acuarela,** Avenida Libertador 1177, tel. 2902/491315, and **M&M,** Avenida Libertador 1222, tel. 2902/492422, can both match Buenos Aires' best; for a local treat, try the fresh *calafate* berry flavor at M&M.

Shopping

Downtown Avenida del Libertador is lined with souvenir shops such as **Open Calafate,** Avenida Libertador 996, tel. 2902/491254, which also sells books and maps. For premium homemade chocolates, try **Casa Guerrero,** Avenida Libertador 1246, tel. 2902/491042, or any of several similar locales.

Services

Money: U.S. dollars are readily accepted except for government services such as postage, but changing traveler's checks is difficult and usually entails a high commission. Both Banco de la Provincia de Santa Cruz, Avenida Libertador 1285, and Banco de Tierra del Fuego, 25 de Mayo 40, have ATMs; the latter is more reliable.

Postal: Correo Argentino, Argentina's privatized postal service, is at Avenida Libertador 1133; the postal code is 9405.

Telephone and Internet: The Cooperativa Telefónica de Calafate (Cotecal), Espora 194, also has Internet access; telephone calls are more expensive than in Chile, discount hours are 10 P.M.–8 A.M. only, and there are no collect calls. Open Calafate, Avenida Libertador 996, tel. 2902/491254, provides some competition in both telephone and Internet services.

Argentina's country code is 54; El Calafate's area code is 2902.

Laundry: El Lavadero, Avenida Libertador 1118, tel. 2902/492182, charges US$8 per load.

Medical: The Hospital Municipal Dr. José Formenti is at Avenida Roca 1487, tel. 2902/491001 or 2902/491173.

Information

Tourist Office: At the bus terminal, El Calafate's Ente Municipal Calafate Turismo (Emcatur), tel. 2902/491466, fax 2902/491090, info@calafate .com, maintains a database of hotels and other services and has English-speaking personnel, maps, brochures, and a message board. Hours are 8 A.M.–10 P.M. from November to March, 8 A.M.–8 P.M. the rest of the year.

National Parks: The Administración de Parques Nacionales (APN), at Avenida Libertador 1302, tel. 2902/491755 or 2902/491545, is open 7 A.M.–2 P.M. weekdays only.

Transportation

Air: The glossy new Aeropuerto Internacional El Calafate, tel. 2902/491230, aerocal@cotecal .com.ar, is 23 km east of town, just north of RP 11.

Aerolíneas Argentinas, tel. 0810/22286527, the traditional flagship carrier, flies to Ushuaia and to Trelew and Buenos Aires Monday, Wednesday, Friday, and Sunday.

Líneas Aéreas del Estado (LADE), the passenger arm of the Argentine air force, Avenida Libertador 1080, tel. 2902/491262, ladecalafate @cotecal.com.ar, flies Twin Otters Monday to Río Turbio and Río Gallegos, Wednesday and Thursday to Gobernador Gregores, Perito Moreno, and Comodoro Rivadavia, Wednesday to Río Gallegos, Río Grande, and Ushuaia, and Thursday and Sunday to Río Gallegos.

ARG, Avenida Libertador 1015, tel. 2902/ 491171, flies five times weekly to Buenos Aires: Tuesday and Saturday via Ushuaia, Thursday and Sunday via Puerto Madryn, and Wednesday nonstop.

Southern Winds, 9 de Julio 69, tel. 2902/ 491349, flies Saturday to Bariloche and Buenos

Aires, Sunday to Ushuaia and Río Gallegos, and Sunday and Tuesday to Buenos Aires.

In summer the Chilean carrier Aerovías DAP flies to Puerto Natales (US$50) twice each weekday between November and March. The international departure tax is US$13.

Bus: El Calafate's Terminal de Ómnibus overlooks the town from Avenida Roca 1004; for pedestrians, the easiest approach is a staircase from the corner of Avenida Libertador and 9 de Julio.

In summer, Turismo Zaahj, tel. 2902/491631, goes to Puerto Natales, Chile (US$25, 5.5 hours) Wednesday, Friday, and Sunday at 8:30 A.M. Bus Sur, at the same office, goes Tuesday and Thursday at 8 A.M., while Cootra, tel. 2902/491444, goes Sunday and Thursday at 5 P.M. In winter, these services may be as infrequent as once a week.

Interlagos, tel. 2902/491179, and Quebek Tours, tel. 2902/491843, shuttle between El Calafate and the Santa Cruz provincial capital of Río Gallegos (US$25, four hours), where there are northbound connections to Buenos Aires and intermediates, and southbound connections to Punta Arenas (Chile). These buses will drop passengers at the Río Gallegos airport.

In summer, three companies connect El Calafate with El Chaltén (US$25, five hours), in the Fitzroy sector of Parque Nacional Los Glaciares: Cal Tur, tel. 2902/491842; Chaltén Travel, tel. 2902/49-1833; and Los Glaciares, tel. 2902/491158. Services generally leave between 7:30–8 A.M., but there are sometimes afternoon buses around 5–6 P.M. Winter services may be only once or twice weekly.

Chaltén Travel provides alternate day bus service from El Calafate to Perito Moreno and Los Antiguos (the border crossing for Chile Chico), in Chubut province, along desolate RN 40 (US$68, 13 hours); while this is expensive on the face of it, it's more direct, quicker, and cheaper than alternative routes via coastal RN 3. Passengers from El Chaltén can board the northbound bus from El Calafate at La Leona without returning to El Calafate.

Getting Around

To the Airport: Aerobús, tel. 2902/492492, takes passengers to and from the new international airport for US$5 pp.

Car Rental: The local Hertz representative is Freelander, Paradelo 253, tel. 2902/491446, which also has an office at Avenida Libertador 1025. Localiza is at Avenida Libertador 687, tel. 2902/491398.

Vicinity of El Calafate

Tours and transport to the Moreno Glacier and other nearby attractions are possible with a variety of agencies. Among them are **Turismo Los Glaciares,** Avenida Libertador 924, tel. 2902/491159, losglaciares@cotecal.com.ar; **Solo Patagonia,** Avenida Libertador 963, tel. 2902/491298, fax 2902/491790; **Cal Tur,** Avenida Libertador 1080, tel. 2902/491368, caltur@cotecal.com.ar; and **Interlagos Turismo,** Avenida Libertador 1175, tel. 2902/491175, interlagos@cotecal.com.ar.

Punta Walichu: Seven km west of El Calafate, a northbound dirt road leads for three km to Punta Walichu, a commercialized pre-Columbian rock art grotto on the south shore of Lago Argentino. A small visitor center displays a few fossils and some stone tools and shows a 25-minute video, not to mention spurious replicas of similar sites elsewhere in the province. On the plus side, it's dropped the admission price to US$5 pp.

Punta Walichu, tel. 2902/491059, also has a small library, a souvenir stand, a *confitería,* and bathroom facilities.

Estancia Alice: In recent years, many Argentine *estancias*—but particularly those in Santa Cruz province—have begun an open appeal to the tourist trade, in much the same way as North American cattle ranches did a century or more ago. One of the most convenient, open for day excursions that may include outdoor activities such as birding and horseback riding, as well as exhibitions of sheep herding and shearing, afternoon tea and a barbecued lamb dinner, is Estancia Alice, 20 km west of El Calafate en route to the Moreno Glacier. The latter program costs around US$50 pp.

For details, contact Agroturismo El Galpón, RP 11, Km 22, El Calafate, tel./fax 2902/491793, elgalpon@estanciaalice.com.ar. Its Buenos Aires office is at Avenida Leandro Alem 822, 3rd floor, tel. 11/4312-4473, fax 11/4313-0679.

PATAGONIA & TIERRA

PARQUE NACIONAL LOS GLACIARES

On the eastern slope of the Andes, Parque Nacional Los Glaciares comprises more than 600,000 hectares of flowing ice, interspersed with Magellanic forests, that give birth to frigid rivers and vast lakes along the Chilean border east and north of El Calafate. It is most famous for the Moreno Glacier, which draws thousands of relatively sedentary visitors on day trips from El Calafate and has scientific significance in glaciology and climate studies, but trekkers and climbers favor the relatively remote Fitzroy range in the north. Its wildlife includes the endangered Andean *huemul.*

Geography and Climate

When the Campo de Hielo Sur receded at the end of the Pleistocene, it left behind the two huge glacial troughs that are now Lago Argentino and, to the north, the roughly parallel Lago Viedma. While these lakes are only about 250 meters above sea level, the Andean summits along the Chilean border rise to 3,375 meters on Cerro Fitzroy and nearly as high on pinnacles such as 3,102-meter Cerro Torre, which matches the Torres del Paine for sheer majesty.

Most of these bodies of water lies outside the park boundaries, but the eastern slopes of the Andes still contain their remnants, some of the world's most impressive, and accessible, glaciers. Thirteen major glaciers flow toward the Argentine side, including the benchmark Moreno Glacier; ice covers 30 percent of the park's surface.

Despite the abundance of snow and ice, the Argentine side of the cordillera is substantially drier than the Chilean, receiving only about 400 millimeters precipitation on the eastern steppe, rising to about 900 millimeters at higher elevations to the west, where the terrain is forested. The warmest month is February, with an average maximum temperature of 22°C and a minimum of 9°C, while the coolest month is August, when the maximum averages only 5°C and the minimum -1°C. Like the rest of Patagonia, it receives often ferocious winds, which are strongest in spring and summer.

Cerro Torre, Parque Nacional Los Glaciares

© WAYNE BERNHARDSON

Flora and Fauna

Los Glaciares' flora and fauna resemble those of Torres del Paine. The guanaco grazes the Patagonian steppe, where rainfall is insufficient to support anything other than *coirón* grasses and thorny shrubs like the *calafate (Berberis buxifolia)* that gave the nearby town its name. Foxes and Patagonian skunks are also conspicuous, the flightless rhea or *ñandú* scampers across the open country, the *bandurria* or buff-necked ibis *(Theristicus caudatus)* hunts invertebrates, and flocks of upland geese *(Chloephaga picta)* browse the wetter areas along the lakeshores. The Andean condor soars above the plains and even the highest peaks, but it occasionally lands to feast on carrion.

In the forests, the predominant tree species are the *lenga (Nothofagus pumilio)* and the *coigüe (Nothofagus betuloides,* also known here as *guindo.* The puma still prowls the forest, while the *huemul* and perhaps the *pudú* survive in the vicinity of Lago Viedma. Squawking flocks of austral parakeets *(Enicognathus ferruginaeus)* flit between trees, and the Patagonian woodpecker *(Campephilus magellanicus)* pounds on their trunks. Perching calmly, awaiting nightfall, the austral pygmy owl *(Glaucidium nanum)* is a common sight in the late afternoon.

Along the lakeshores and riverbanks, aquatic birds such as coots and ducks are abundant. The most picturesque is the Patagonian torrent duck *(Merganetta armata),* which dives for prey in the rushing creeks.

Sights and Recreation

In general, the southerly part of the park, east of El Calafate, gets day visitors who come primarily for passive sight-seeing. The northerly sector—a five-hour bus trip from El Calafate—attracts those seeking to spend several days in vigorous exercise, either trekking or the far more demanding and dangerous technical climbing for which the area is famous. Gregory Crouch's *Enduring Patagonia* (Random House, 2001) details one mountaineer's experiences on Fitzroy and Cerro Torre.

Backpackers should note that no campfires are permitted within the park—carrying a campstove is obligatory for cooking.

Glaciar Perito Moreno: Where a low pass in the Andes lets Pacific storms cross the cordillera, countless storms have deposited mountains of snow that, over the millennia, have compressed into the Moreno Glacier, the flowing river of ice that's one of the greatest sights on the continent. Fifteen times during the late 20th century, the advancing glacier blocked the **Brazo Rico** (Rico Arm) of Lago Argentino to form a rising body of water that eventually, when the water's weight became too much for the natural dam, triggered an eruption of ice and water toward the lake's main glacial trough.

That hasn't happened in recent years, but massive icebergs still calve off the glacier's 60-meter face and crash into the **Canal de los Témpanos** (Iceberg Channel) with astonishing frequency. Perched on catwalks and overlooks, many visitors spend entire days either gazing at or, eyes closed, simply listening to this awesome river of ice as it rumbles forward. Descending to lake level is prohibited because of the danger of backwash and

flying chunks of ice. It is possible, however, to contract a full-day "minitrekking" excursion onto the ice for about US$65 pp at El Calafate.

The Moreno glacier is 80 km southwest of El Calafate via RP 11. Organized tours from town leave every day, as does scheduled transportation (see below).

Glaciar Upsala: Even larger than the Moreno Glacier, 50 km long and 10 km wide at its foot, the Upsala Glacier is accessible only by catamaran excursions from Puerto Bandera via Lago Argentino's Brazo Norte (North Arm). The full-day trip, including a side trek to ice-filled **Lago Onelli,** costs about US$55.

Puerto Bandera is 45 km west of Calafate via RP 11 and RP 8. For information and reservations, contact René Fernández Campbell, Avenida Libertador 867, El Calafate, tel. 2902/491155 or 2902/491428, fax 2902/491154, rfcino@cotecal.com.ar.

Lago Roca: Less visited than other parts of the park, the southwesterly sector also known as La Jerónima, along the Brazo Sur (South Arm) of Lago Roca, offers camping and cross-country hiking—there are no formal trails, only routes such as the one up the summit of **Cerro Cristal** from the campground, 55 km from El Calafate.

Sector Fitzroy: In the park's most northerly sector, the Fitzroy Range has sheer vertical spires to match those of the Torres del Paine, but even if you're not one of the world's top 10 technical climbers, the several trails from the village of El Chaltén to the base of summits such as Fitzroy and Cerro Torre make some of the Southern Hemisphere's most satisfying hiking. There are even opportunities for crossing the southern Patagonian icefields, but visitors looking for a more sedate outdoor experience will find a handful of former sheep *estancias,* onetime Patagonian wool producers, that have reinvented themselves as tourist accommodations.

While exposed to fiercely westerly winds and to potential floods from the Río de las Vueltas, El Chaltén has achieved a feeling of permanence in what, only a few years ago, seemed just a bleak assortment of government offices intended to uphold Argentina's presence in a then-disputed border zone (the last of many Chilean-Argentine territorial quarrels, over Lago del Desierto to the north, was finalized only a few years ago).

One reason for El Chaltén's popularity is its easy access to Fitzroy range trailheads–so much so that the village bills itself as "Capital Nacional del Trekking," the national trekking capital. While many of the trails are suitable for overnight backpacks, access is so good that day hikers can cover nearly as much ground.

From a signposted trailhead at the north end of town, just south of the basic Camping Madsen, the **Sendero Laguna Torre** is an 11-km track that gains only about 200 meters in elevation as it winds through southern beech forests to the climbers' base camp for Cerro Torre; figure about three to 3.5 hours. At the lake itself, in clear weather, there are extraordinary views of the 3,102-meter summit of Cerro Torre, crowned by the so-called "mushroom" of snow and ice that technical climbers must surmount. While the Italian Cesare Maestri claimed that he and the Austrian Toni Egger reached the summit in 1959 (Egger died in an avalanche and took the expedition's camera with him), the first undisputed ascent was by the Italian Casimiro Ferrari in 1974.

From the Madsen pack station, the more demanding **Sendero Río Blanco** rises steeply at the outset before leveling out through boggy beech forest and continuing to the Cerro Fitzroy base camp, a total climb of about 350 meters in 10 km. About midway to Río Blanco, a signed lateral leads south to **Laguna Capri,** where there are backcountry campsites but campfires are not permitted.

From Río Blanco, the vertiginous zigzag trail ascends 400 meters in only 2.5 km to **Laguna de los Tres,** a glacial tarn whose name commemorates three members of the French expedition, René Ferlet, Lionel Terray, and Guido Magnone, who reached the summit of Fitzroy in 1952. Truly a top-of-the-world experience, Laguna de los Tres offers some of the finest views in all of Patagonia and probably the rest of the Andes as well.

From the Río Blanco climbers' campground, a northbound trail follows the river's west bank north to **Laguna Piedras Blancas,** whose namesake glacier continually calves icebergs into the lake. The trail continues north to the Río Eléctrico, beyond the park boundaries, where a westbound trail climbs the river to Piedra del Fraile and a possible circuit of the Campo de Hielo Sur, suitable only for experienced snow-and-ice trekkers. At the Río Eléctrico, it's also possible to rejoin the road from El Chaltén to Laguna del Desierto.

From Puerto Bahía Túnel, on the north shore of Lago Viedma, the catamaran *Viedma Discovery* sails to the face of the Viedma Glacier; the cost is US$50 pp plus US$10 pp for transfers to and from the lake, if you don't have your own transportation. Departure time is 9 A.M. from El Chaltén, 9:30 P.M. from Puerto Bahía Túnel.

Lago del Desierto: About 37 km north of El Chaltén by an improved gravel road, elongated Lago del Desierto was such a bone of contention between Chile and Argentina that, many years ago, a Chilean Carabinero even lost his life in a firefight with Argentine soldiers. Despite continuing objections by a handful of extreme Chilean nationalists, the matter is resolved, the border is peaceable, and determined hikers can even cross to Villa O'Higgins (before attempting this, however, clear it with the Argentine Gendarmería (Border Guards) in El Chaltén).

From the south end of the lake, a short trail winds west through dense southern beech forest to a vista point, while a longer route follows the eastern shore to the border, a 20-km trek over relatively easy terrain. From El Chaltén, Chaltén Travel minibuses go to Lago del Desierto at 9:30 A.M. daily, returning at 4:30 P.M., for US$20 round-trip. Hitching is feasible but vehicles are few and often full.

Accommodations

There are limited accommodations and food in the southern sector of the park since most people stay at El Calafate, but El Chaltén has, if not exactly an abundance, at least a reasonable selection. Many places close in winter, but there's always something available.

Note that while El Chaltén now has street names and addresses, they don't really mean very much in a town this size, and people pay little attention to them.

Glaciar Moreno: At the approach to Península Magallanes, 50 km west of El Calafate but 30 km east of the glacier, Camping Río Mitre is a free site. Only seven km east of the glacier, Camping Bahía Escondida charges US$4 pp for sites with running water and fire pits; there are hot showers from 7–10 P.M. only and electricity from 8 P.M.–midnight only. Backpackers can camp free at the Seccional de Guardaparques, the ranger station at the glacier itself, for a maximum of two nights.

Overlooking the glacier itself, Hostería Los Notros, tel. 2902/499510, fax 2902/499511 in El Calafate, has 32 glacier-view rooms open for package tours ranging from US$674 pp for two nights to US$1,359 pp for four nights, including full board and excursions. Its Buenos Aires contact is Hostería Los Notros, Arenales 1457, 7th floor, tel. 11/4814-3934, fax 11/4815-7645, info@losnotros.com, website: www.losnotros.com.

Also at the glacier, the Unidad Turística Ventisquero Moreno operates both a snack bar (sandwiches for US$2.50–4.50, plus coffee and desserts) and a separate restaurant with set meals for US$14–18 pp; there is also an à la carte menu.

Lago Roca: At La Jerónima, Camping Lago Roca, tel. 2902/499500, charges US$6 pp for adults, US$4 pp for children, and also has four-bed *cabañas* for US$48. Hot showers are available, and its *confitería* serves decent meals.

El Chaltén: At the north edge of town, the APN's woodsy Camping Madsen has running water and is free of charge but lacks toilets—dig a latrine—and fires are prohibited. Directly across from the APN office there's another free site, on the banks of the Río Fitzroy, but it's more exposed.

Commercial campgrounds, with services such as hot showers, generally cost US$5–6 pp, plus an additional peso or two for hot showers. Among these are Camping El Relincho, San Martín s/n, tel. 2962/493010, and Camping Ruca Mahuida, Lionel Terray 501, tel. 2962/493018. The latter is best of the bunch and has an exceptional restaurant.

El Chaltén has several hostel-style accommodations, two of which are Hostelling International Affiliates. The only nonaffiliate is the smallish Albergue Los Ñires, Lago del Desierto s/n, tel. 2962/493009, charging US$10 pp, or US$5 pp for camping.

The Dutch-Argentine Albergue Patagonia, San Martín 493, tel. 2962/493019, alpatagonia@infovia.com.ar, has cozy accommodations—four to six beds per room—for US$12 pp (US$10 for HI members or anyone off-season), and also provides cooking facilities, laundry service, meal service, a book exchange, and bike rentals, and organizes excursions. English and Dutch are spoken, and it stays open all year. Its main drawback is that the bathroom facilities, while good enough, are arguably not numerous enough.

The 44-bed Albergue Rancho Grande, San Martín s/n, tel./fax 2962/493005, bigranch@infovia.com.ar, charges US$10 pp for HI members, US$12 for nonmembers, and also offers B&B packages with transportation from El Calafate. For reservations in El Calafate, contact Chaltén Travel, Avenida Libertador 1177, tel. 2902/491833, chaltentravel@cotecal.com.ar.

Family-run Hospedaje La Base, Lago del Desierto 97, tel./fax 2962/493031, charges US$40/50 s/d from mid-December to mid-March, US$30/40 the rest of the year except from June to November, when it's closed.

From December through February, Hotel Lago del Desierto, Lago del Desierto s/n, tel. 2962/493010, charges US$80–90 s or d, but slightly less from October to mid-December and March–April. It also rents six-bed *cabañas* with kitchen facilities for US$90 in summer, US$80 the rest of the year.

It's work in progress—the landscaping really needs attention—but the new Hostería Posada Lunajuim, Trevisan s/n, tel. 2962/493047, posadalunajuim@yahoo.com, has made good first impressions with its attractive common areas (including a bar/restaurant) and with private bath, central heating, and breakfast for US$60/96 s/d in peak season, US$40/65 the rest of the year.

From November through February, the Fitzroy Inn, San Martín 520, tel. 2962/493062, charges US$98/104 s/d with breakfast, US$118/144 with half-board; September–October and March–April, rates are US$75/80 with breakfast, US$95/120 with half board.

On the south shore of Lago Viedma, open November to March only, **Hostería Helsingfors,** San Martín 516, Río Gallegos, tel. 2966/420719, tel./fax 11/4824-6623 or 11/4940-3818 in Buenos Aires, landsur@internet.siscotel.com, was one of the first *estancias* in the area, and also one of the first to open its door to tourists. Room rates are US$200/360 s/d with full board and excursions included. Children under age eight pay half. Helsingfors also offers full board and excursion packages from El Calafate: two-day, one-night packages cost US$225/410 s/d, while US$365/650 s/d. For the most current information, see the Helsingfors website: www.helsingfors.com.ar. Hired in El Calafate, round-trip transportation costs US$440 for up to three passengers, US$690 for four to 11 passengers.

Food
Hikers and climbers can stock up on groceries at **El Chaltén,** Lago del Desierto s/n, **Kiosko Charito,** Güemes s/n, and **El Gringuito,** San Martín s/n. Otherwise, for its size, El Chaltén offers a pretty good choice of places to eat as well.

For snacks and short orders, try **La Senyera del Torre,** Lago del Desierto s/n, tel. 2962/49-3063, which has a publike atmosphere. Nearby, **The Wall,** Lago del Desierto s/n, tel. 2962/493092, is comparable. **Chocolatería Josh Aike,** Lago del Desierto s/n, tel. 2962/493008, is more than it sounds—while the desserts are good enough, the breakfasts and pizzas are also excellent. **Domo Blanco,** Costanera Sur 90, tel. 2962/493036, serves exceptional ice cream but closes in winter.

Open in summer only, **Ruca Mahuida,** Lionel Terray 501, tel. 2962/493018, is one of the most imaginative eateries in town and also sends smokers outside to indulge their habit. **La Casita,** San Martín s/n, tel. 2962/493042, serves a standard Argentine menu—beef, pizza, pasta, and the like—but has its adherents despite its cramped and tobacco-heavy ambience. **Pizzería Patagonicus,** Güemes s/n, tel. 2962/493025, deserves consideration, but the best new place in town is the **Bar de Ahumados,** San Martín s/n, tel. 2962/493019, which is small and popular enough that reservations are a good idea, especially in summer.

Shopping
Viento Oeste, on San Martín s/n just north of Albergue Rancho Grande, tel. 2962/493021,

Moreno Glacier

© WAYNE BERNHARDSON

vientooeste@infovia.com.ar, rents and sells climbing, camping, and wet weather gear.

Services

Telephone and Internet: El Chaltén has an increasing diversity of services, including long-distance phone service, but connections are not yet good enough to support regular Internet connections (though some businesses can download their own email). The area code is 2962. Argentina's country code is 54.

Guides: At El Chaltén, it's possible to arrange a one-day trek and ice climb on Glaciar Torre (US$65) with Fitzroy Expediciones, Lionel Terray 212, tel./fax 2962/493017, fitzroy@infovia.com.ar, which also offers lengthier guided hikes—nine-day expeditions, really—on the Campo de Hielo Sur, the Southern Continental Ice Field.

Information

At the Río Mitre entrance to the park, the main approach for the Moreno Glacier, the Administración de Parques Nacionales (APN) collects a US$5 park admission fee.

At El Chaltén, the APN, tel. 2962/493004, just before the Río Fitzroy bridge at the approach to town, is open 8 A.M.–8 P.M. daily. In addition to offering information, it also issues climbing permits, but there is no admission fee here or at Lago Roca.

Hikers may want to consult Clem Lindenmayer's *Trekking in the Patagonian Andes* (Lonely Planet, 1998), but there is also Miguel A. Alonso's locally available, bilingual *Trekking en Chaltén & Lago del Desierto* (Buenos Aires: Zagier & Urruty, 1998), which covers 18 hikes in the vicinity. Alonso has also written *Lago Argentino & Glaciar Perito Moreno Handbook* (Buenos Aires: Zagier & Urruty, 1997), a more general guide to the park.

Transportation

Glaciar Moreno: The Moreno Glacier is about 80 km west of El Calafate by RP 11; when completely paved, which should happen by the time this book appears, the trip should only take about an hour. Both Interlagos and Quebek, at the El Calafate bus terminal, have scheduled services at 9 A.M. daily (US$30 round-trip), returning in the afternoon. Interlagos also goes to Puerto Banderas at 7:30 A.M. daily (US$20 round-trip), connecting with the catamaran to the Upsala Glacier.

In addition to these regularly scheduled services, guided bus tours are frequent, but both are less frequent in winter (for suggested operators, see the listing under Vicinity of El Calafate in the El Calefate section). El Calafate's Albergue del Glaciar runs its own minivan excursions, leaving about 8:30 A.M. and returning about 5 P.M., for about US$30 pp.

El Chaltén: El Chaltén is 220 km from El Calafate via a roundabout route that follows paved RP 11 east to the Río Bote junction, northbound RN 40 (at present being paved to the east end of Lago Viedma), and inconsistently maintained but always passable RP 23, westbound along the north shore of Lago Viedma.

Several companies connect El Chaltén with El Calafate (US$25 five hours): Cal Tur, tel. 2962/493062; Chaltén Travel, tel. 2962/493005; and Los Glaciares, tel. 2962/493084. Departures are usually in late afternoon, between 5 and 6 P.M. There are several buses daily in summer, but only one or two weekly in winter. Quebek Tour/Taqsa has a weekly direct service to and from Río Gallegos.

With Chaltén Travel, it's possible to travel north on gravel RN 40 to the towns of Perito Moreno and Los Antiguos (the border crossing for Chile Chico), in Chubut province (US$68, 13 hours). These services leave El Calafate on alternate days in summer; passengers from El Chaltén can board the bus at La Leona, on RN 40, without having to return to El Calafate. The rest of the year, there may be only one bus weekly.

An alternative is Daniel Bagnera's Itinerarios y Travesías, Perito Moreno 152, tel. 2962/493088, a single 4WD vehicle with a luggage trailer that sometimes makes a side excursion to the pre-Columbian rock art site of Cueva de las Manos en route to Perito Moreno and Los Antiguos. At US$92, this is more expensive than the bus but still more reasonable than other alternatives in an area little served by public transportation. There is service all year, but only weekly in the winter, almost daily in the summer.

Tierra del Fuego

In his autobiography, pioneer settler Lucas Bridges labeled Tierra del Fuego the "Uttermost Part of the Earth" for its splendid isolation at the southern tip of the southern American continent. Shared between Chile and Argentina, it's a place where fur seals, sea lions, and penguins cavort in the choppy waters of the strait named for the celebrated navigator Ferdinand Magellan, where Darwin sailed on the *Beagle,* and the first '49ers made their way to California. From the seashore, behind the city of Ushuaia, glacial horns rise like sacred steeples nearly 2,000 meters above sea level. The beaches and southern beech forests of Parque Nacional Tierra del Fuego, west of the city, are the terminus of the world's southernmost highway.

Tierra del Fuego is not just an island, but an archipelago, though the Isla Grande de Tierra Fuego is South America's largest island. While parts of the Argentine side of the Isla Grande are urbanized, the Chilean part of the archipelago is thinly populated. Roads are relatively few but improving, and some of them are now paved, especially on the Argentine side; the unpaved roads, though, are hazardous to windshields, which are most cheaply replaced in Punta Arenas.

Two ferry routes go from the mainland to Tierra del Fuego: a shuttle from Punta Delgada, only 45 km south of the Argentine border, across the Primera Angostura narrows to Puerto Espora, and a daily service from Punta Arenas to Porvenir, across one of the widest parts of the strait.

HISTORY

Before their European "discovery" by Magellan in 1520, southern South America's insular extremes were inhabited by dispersed bands of hunter-gatherers such as the Selknam (Ona), Kawasqar (Alacaluf), and Yámana (Yahgan), who lived off maritime and terrestrial resources that they considered abundant—only in the European view was this a land of privation. The archipelago acquired its name from the fires set by the region's so-called "Canoe Indians," the Kawasqar and

Yámana, for heating and cooking; in this soggy region, though, it might have been more accurate to call it Tierra del Humo ("Land of Smoke").

Early navigators dreaded rounding the wild seas of Cape Horn against ferocious westerly winds, and their reports gave their countrymen little reason in settle in or even explore the area. In the early 19th century, Captain Robert Fitzroy of the *Beagle* abducted several Yámana, including the famous Jemmy Button, to England and subjected them to missionary education before returning them to their home on a later voyage. A perplexed Charles Darwin, on the *Beagle* in 1834, commented on the simplicity of their society:

> *The perfect equality among the individuals composing the Fuegian tribes, must for a long time retard their civilization.*

The first to try to bring civilization to the Yámana, rather than the opposite, were Anglican missionaries from the Falkland Islands, some of whose descendents still live in Tierra del Fuego. After abortive attempts that included both Fuegian assaults and the starvation death of British evangelist Allen Gardiner, the Anglican Thomas Bridges settled at present-day Ushuaia, on the Argentine side of the Isla Grande, where he compiled an English-Yahgan dictionary. His son Lucas, who grew up with the Yámana as his playmates, wrote the extraordinary memoir *The Uttermost Part of the Earth,* published a few years before his death in 1950.

In the meantime, both the Chilean and Argentine governments established a presence in the region, and gigantic sheep *estancias* occupied the sprawling grasslands at the expense of native peoples who once hunted guanaco and other game on them. When, as the guanaco slowly disappeared, the desperate Fuegians began to hunt domestic sheep, they often found themselves facing the wrong end of a rifle—though introduced European diseases such as typhoid and measles killed more native people than bullets.

Borders in the archipelago were never clearly defined and the two countries nearly went to war over three small islands in the Beagle Channel in 1979. Positions were uncompromising— one Argentine poster of the period boldly proclaimed that "We will never surrender what is ours!"—but a papal mediation successfully avoided warfare and brought a settlement within a few years despite lingering issues, such as transportation across the channel from Ushuaia to Puerto Williams.

Since then, travel to the uttermost part of the earth has boomed, especially on the Argentine side in the summer. Other important economic factors are the sheep-farming industry and the petroleum industry, on both the Chilean and Argentine sides.

PORVENIR

Chilean Tierra del Fuego's main town, Porvenir sits on a sheltered harbor on the east side of the Strait of Magellan. Local settlement dates from the 1880s, when the area experienced a brief gold rush, but stabilized with the establishment of wool *estancias* around the turn of the 20th century. After the wool boom fizzled in the 1920s, Porvenir settled into an economic torpor that, ironically

enough, has left it a remarkable assortment of corroding metal-clad Magellanic buildings.

Porvenir's inner harbor is a great place to see kelp geese, gulls, cormorants, steamer ducks, and other seabirds, but its main tourist role has been as a gateway to the Argentine sector of the Isla Grande. This may change as small local enterprises begin to provide access to parts of the archipelago that, up to now, have been accessible only through expensive cruises.

Orientation

Only 30 nautical miles east of Punta Arenas, Porvenir occupies a protected site at the east end of Bahía Porvenir, an inlet of the Strait of Magellan. Its port, however, is three km west of the town proper, whose mostly regular grid occupies a sloping south-facing site centered on the Plaza de Armas.

From Porvenir, Ruta 215, a smooth gravel road, leads south and then east along the shore of Bahía Inútil to the Argentine border at San Sebastián, 150 km away; an alternate route leads directly east through the Cordón Baquedano before rejoining Ruta 215 about 55 km to the east. If it's too late to catch the ferry back to Punta Arenas,

© WAYNE BERNHARDSON

Plaza de Armas in Porvenir

another gravel road follows the coast to Puerto Espora, 141 km to the northeast.

Sights

Directly on the water, **Parque Yugoslavo** is a memorial to the earliest gold-seeking immigrants, most of whom were Croatians. It's one of the best spots in town for bird-watching.

Most of the main public buildings surround the neatly landscaped **Plaza de Armas,** two blocks north of Parque Yugoslavo. Among them is the expanded and improved **Museo de Tierra del Fuego Fernando Rusque Cordero,** a regional museum that deals with the island's natural history, indigenous heritage, the early gold rush, the later but longer-lasting wool rush, and even cinematography—German-born local filmmaker José Bohr actually went to Hollywood in 1929 and enjoyed a long if inconsistent career. It has added a skillfully done replica of an early rural store and a good photographic display on local architecture.

The museum takes its name from a Carabineros official who helped found it—and who was no doubt responsible for the permanent exhibit on police uniforms. On the Plaza de Armas, at Zavattaro 402, tel. 61/580098, it's open 9 A.M.–1 P.M. and 2:45–5 P.M. weekdays except Friday, when it closes at 4 P.M.; in January and February only, weekend hours are 11 A.M.–5 P.M. Admission costs US$1.

Accommodations and Food

Friendly **Hostal Patagonia,** Jorge Schythe 230, tel. 61/580371, charges US$8.50 pp for spacious rooms with shared bath and with in-room heat but no other amenities; with private bath, rates are US$12 pp. Rates at **Hotel España,** Croacia 698, tel. 61/580160, are also US$8.50 pp with shared bath, but US$13 pp with private bath. It also has a restaurant.

Hotel Central, Philippi 295, tel. 61/580077, charges US$15/28 s/d with shared bath, US$18/32 with private bath. **Hotel Rosas,** Philippi 296, tel. 61/580088, costs US$22/30 s/d with private bath; its restaurant is one of the best values in a town with, admittedly, only a handful of choices.

Hostería Los Flamencos, Teniente Merino s/n, tel. 61/580049, has undoubtedly seen better days—paint is peeling both inside and outside—but there's also warmth and attentive service from the German-speaking manager. Rates are US$40/49 s/d.

Other than hotel restaurants, the only choices for dining are the basic **Puerto Montt,** Croacia 1199, tel. 61/580207, and the waterfront **Club Social Croata,** a decent choice at Manuel Señoret 542, tel. 61/580053.

Services

Money: Banco del Estado, Philippi 263, is the only option.

Postal: Correos de Chile is at Phillipi 176, at the southwest corner of the Plaza de Armas.

Telephone: The Compañía Chilena de Teléfonos is at Philippi 277. Porvenir's area code is 61, the same as Punta Arenas.

Medical: Hospital Porvenir is at Carlos Wood s/n, between Señoret and Guerrero, tel. 61/580034.

Information

Porvenir's Oficina Municipal de Turismo, in the museum building at Padre Mario Zavattaro 402, tel. 61/580098, *anexo* 305, is open 8:30 A.M.–5 P.M. weekdays except Friday, when it closes at 4 P.M. Weekend hours are 11 A.M.–2 P.M. and 3–5 P.M.

Information is also available at the kiosk on the *costanera* (coast road) between Mardones and Muñoz Gamero.

Transportation

Porvenir has regular but infrequent connections to the mainland and to Argentina.

Air: Aerovías DAP, Manuel Señoret s/n at Muñoz Gamero, tel. 61/580089, operates air-taxi service to Punta Arenas (US$23) at least daily, often more frequently.

Bus: Tecni-Austral, at the corner of Croacia and Muñoz Gamero, goes to Río Grande (Argentina) Tuesday and Sunday at 12:30 P.M., with connections to Ushuaia. Buses Pacheco, leaving from the Club Social Croata at Manuel Señoret 542, goes to Río Grande (US$12, four hours) Tuesday, Thursday, and Saturday at 1 P.M.

wool truck at Porvenir ferry dock

Wednesday at 3 P.M., there's a free municipal bus to Camerón and Timaukel (2.5 hours), in the southwestern corner of the island; another goes to Cerro Sombrero at 5 P.M. the same day from Santos Mardones 330.

There are also buses to Camerón and Timaukel (US$6, 2.5 hours), in the southwestern part of the island, Wednesday at 3 P.M.; these leave from the DAP offices on Señoret. Monday, Wednesday, and Thursday at 5 P.M., there's a bus to Cerro Sombrero (1.5 hours), from Santos Mardones 330.

Sea: Transbordadora Broom, in the same office as DAP at Manuel Señoret s/n, tel. 61/580089, sails the car-passenger ferry *Melinka* to Punta Arenas (2.5 hours) Tuesday, Thursday, and Saturday at 12:30 P.M., Wednesday and Friday at 2 P.M., and Sunday and holidays at 5 P.M. The ferry leaves from Bahía Chilote, about three km west of town. (For fares, see the Punta Arenas entry.)

VICINITY OF PORVENIR

Vicinity is a relative term on Tierra del Fuego, as some fascinating locales are exceptionally difficult—or expensive—to reach. **Cordillera Dar-**

win, Croacia 675, tel. 61/580296 or 09/64-07204, website: www.explorepatagonia.cl, info@explorepatagonia.cl, does brief launch tours around Bahía Chilote, three-day horseback excursions to the Río Cóndor, and a six-day trip to the Cordillera Darwin that is substantially cheaper than the only other possibility, the weeklong luxury cruise on the *Mare Australis* (see the Sailing the Fjords of Tierra del Fuego in the Vicinity of Punta Arenas section).

Monumento Natural Laguna de los Cisnes

International birding groups often make a detour to this 25-hectare saline lake reserve, which sometimes dries out, just north of Porvenir. While it takes its name from the elegant black-necked swan, it is also home to many other species.

Cordón Baquedano

After Chilean naval officer Ramón Serrano Montaner found gold in the rolling hills east of Porvenir in 1879, gold panners from Chile and Croatia flocked to the valley of the Río del Oro, between the Cordón Baquedano and the Sierra Boquerón. Living in sod huts that insulated them from the wind and cold, in hopes of eking out a kilogram per year—though yields were usually smaller—more than 200 worked the placers until they gave out and, by the turn of the century, dredges and steam shovels replaced them. Even then, decreasing yields ended the rush by 1908–09, though a few individuals hang on even today.

From Porvenir, the eastbound road through the Cordón Baquedano passes several of these gold rush sites, some of them with interpretive panels; the literal high point is the **Mirador de la Isla,** an overlook 500 meters above sea level. In many places guanacos, which seem to outnumber sheep, leap gracefully over meter-high fences that stop the sheep cold.

Onaisín

About 100 km east of Porvenir, a major north-south road crosses Ruta 215 at Onaisín, a former Sociedad Explotadora *estancia* whose **Cementerio Inglés** is a national monument. Northbound, the road goes to the petroleum company town of Cerro Sombrero, while southbound it goes to Camerón and Lago Blanco.

Lago Blanco

About 50 km southwest of Onaisín, the road passes through **Camerón,** a well-preserved former *estancia* that is now a municipality, then angles southeast to Lago Blanco, an area known for its fishing and, until recently, a speculative and controversial project for native forest exploitation by the U.S.-based Trillium Corporation. In summer, there's a bumpy border crossing to Río Grande, Argentina, via a dirt road with many livestock gates and a ford of the Río Rasmussen.

On Isla Victoria, in the middle of Lago Blanco, **Lodge de Pesca Isla Victoria,** tel. 61/241197, caters to fly fishermen for US$144/174 s/d.

Estancia Yendegaia

Visited primarily by Chilean cruise ships and private yachts, Estancia Yendegaia conserves 44,000 hectares of native Fuegian forest in the Cordillera Darwin between the Argentine border and Parque Nacional Alberto de Agostini. While the Punta Arenas–based owners hope to establish

Estancia Yendegaia and Cordillera Darwin

a private national park and create an unbroken preservation corridor contiguous with the Beagle Channel, there is government pressure to pave the *estancia*'s airstrip at Caleta María, at the northern end of the property, and to complete a road south from Lago Blanco. The owners, for their part, would rather see the border opened to foot traffic from Argentina's Parque Nacional Tierra del Fuego.

In the meantime, the *estancia* is open to visitors—though access is difficult without chartering a plane or boat or taking an expensive tour such as the *Mare Australis* cruise through the Fuegian fjords. While naval boats between Punta Arenas and Puerto Williams will drop passengers here, these are infrequent enough that getting back could be a problem. For further details and suggestions, contact Ivette Martínez at Turismo Cordillera Darwin, O'Higgins 424, Punta Arenas, tel. 61/221764, fax 61/224637, c_darwin@patagonian.com.

CERRO SOMBRERO

About 70 km north of Onaisín and 43 km south of the Puerto Espora ferry landing, Cerro Sombrero is a company town where employees of Chile's Empresa Nacional de Petróleo (ENAP, National Petroleum Company) live in orderly surroundings with remarkable amenities for a town with only about 150 houses. Dating from the early 1960s, it has an astronomical observatory, a bank, a botanical garden, a cinema, a hospital, recreational facilities including a heated swimming pool, and restaurants. Buses between Río Grande and Punta Arenas take a meal break at **Restaurant El Conti,** just outside town.

PUERTO WILLIAMS

On the north shore of Isla Navarino, across the Beagle Channel from Argentine Tierra del Fuego, Puerto Williams is the so-called "Capital of Antarctica" and gateway to the rugged Los Dientes back-

directional signs in Puerto Williams

country circuit, a difficult five-day hike through rugged soggy terrain. Local residents look forward to establishment of a permanent ferry link to nearby Argentina, but there is much political opposition across the channel because myopic Ushuaia impresarios fear losing business to tiny Williams—however unlikely that possibility.

Founded in the 1950s, formerly known as Puerto Luisa, the town has paved sidewalks but gravel streets. Most of its residents are Chilean naval personnel living in relatively stylish prefabs, but there are also about 60 remaining descendants of the Yámana, of whom only about five speak the language, now a hybrid including many Spanish and English words, among themselves.

Sights

Overlooking the harbor is the **Proa del Escampavía** *Yelcho,* the prow of the famous cutter that, at the command of Luis Pardo Villalón, rescued British Antarctic explorer Edward Shackleton's crew from Elephant Island, on the Antarctic Peninsula, in 1916. A national monument, the bow survived collisions with icebergs to get to its destination; returning to Punta Arenas, the entire ship makes a cameo appearance in original newsreel footage in British director George Butler's *Endurance,* an extraordinary documentary of the Shackleton expedition.

Very professional for a small-town museum, the **Museo Martin Gusinde** has small exhibits on geology, plants with economic uses, and taxidermy, a marker for the former post office, and a sign for the coal mine at Caleta Banner, on nearby Isla Picton, which provisioned the *Yelcho* on its mission to rescue Shackleton's crew. Admission costs US$1.75 pp. Nearby is the **Parque Botánico Omora,** an organized selection of native plants.

Built in Germany for operations on the Rhine, the **MV** *Micalvi* carried supplies for remote settlements before sinking in Puerto Williams's inner harbor in 1962; the upper deck and bridge remain as the yacht club's bar/restaurant.

Accommodations, Food, and Entertainment

Pensión Temuco, Piloto Pardo 224, tel. 61/6-21113, charges US$12.50 pp with shared bath,

© WAYNE BERNHARDSON

US$17 pp with private bath, and also serves meals. Try also the nearby **Residencial Pusaky,** tel. 61/621116.

Refugio Coirón, Ricardo Maragaño 168, tel. 61/621227, coiron@simltd.com, has very good accommodations for US$13 pp with kitchen privileges and shared bath. It's a better choice than the friendly but basic **Hostería Onashaga,** Uspachún 290, tel. 61/621081, which costs US$15 pp for multibedded rooms with shared bath; those with private bath go for US$33 d. Lunch or dinner costs US$3.

South America's southernmost bar/restaurant, the **Club de Yates Micalvi,** occupies the main deck and the bridge of the historic vessel that lies grounded in Puerto Williams's inner harbor.

The **Pingüino Pub** is at the Centro Comercial.

Services

Nearly all of Puerto Williams's services are concentrated around the Centro Comercial, a cluster of storefronts just uphill from the Muelle Guardián Brito, the main passenger pier. These include the post office, several telephone offices, Banco de Chile, the Cema-Chile crafts shop, and Manualidades, which rents mountain bikes.

Transportation

Air: DAP, at the Centro Comercial, flies 20-seat Twin Otters to Punta Arenas (US$64) Tuesday, Thursday, and Saturday from April to October. The rest of the year, flights leave daily except Sunday and Monday. DAP flights are often heavily booked, so make reservations as far in advance as possible.

Sea: Regular connections between Puerto Williams and Ushuaia, on Argentine Tierra del Fuego, continue to be problematical, but hitching a lift across the channel with a yacht is feasible—for a price. For up-to-date information, contact the Gobernación Marítima, tel. 61/621090, the Club de Yates, tel. 61/621041, *anexo* 4250, or Turismo Sim, tel. 61/621150.

In summer, the ferry *Patagonia* sails to Punta Arenas (38 hours) Friday at 7 P.M. Fares are US$150 in a bunk, US$120 for a seat.

VICINITY OF PUERTO WILLIAMS

Operating out of the Centro Comercial, the German-Venezuelan **Sea, Ice & Mountains Adventures Unlimited,** tel. 61/621150, fax 61/621227, website: www.simltd.com, sim@entelchile.net, organizes trekking, climbing, and riding expeditions on Isla Navarino and the Cordillera Darwin, weeklong yacht excursions around the Beagle Channel and to Cape Horn, and even Antarctica. Advance booking is advisable.

The Coastal Road

From Puerto Williams, a coastal road runs 54 km west to the village of Puerto Navarino, now a legal port of entry, and 28 km east to Caleta Eugenia; only two km east of Williams, **Villa Ukika** is the last refuge of the Yámana. From Caleta Eugenia, the road is gradually advancing southeast to **Puerto Toro,** where about 60 boats employ about four people each in search of *centolla,* or king crab.

Cordón de los Dientes

Immediately south of Puerto Williams, **Cordón de los Dientes** is a range of jagged peaks rising more than 1,000 meters above sea level that offers the world's southernmost trekking opportunities. There are, however, few trails through this rugged countryside—anyone undertaking the four- to five-day "circuit" should be experienced in route finding.

RÍO GRANDE (ARGENTINA)

On the Isla Grande's barren, blustery Atlantic shoreline, desolate Río Grande is more a point of transit than a destination in itself, but bus schedules sometimes dictate that travelers pass the night here. Thanks to smoothly paved streets, the huge dust clouds that once blew through this wool and oil town have subsided, services have improved, and there's enough to do that an afternoon spent here need not be a wasted one.

Most visitors who stay in and around Río Grande, though, do so for the fishing. Its population is about 45,000.

Orientation

On the north bank of its namesake river, Río Grande is 79 km southeast of the Chilean border post at San Sebastián and 190 km northeast of Ushuaia via RN 3, which should be entirely paved by the time this book is published. As of writing, however, the mountainous segment between Tolhuin and the Harberton turnoff was still a loose gravel surface on which cracked windshields were an everyday occurrence.

RN 3 bypasses the compact city center, which is reached by southeasterly Avenida San Martín, the main commercial street. Most services are within a few blocks of the axis formed by San Martín and the perpendicular Avenida Manuel Belgrano, which leads east toward the waterfront.

Sights

Río Grande's **Museo de La Ciudad Virginia Choquintel** does a lot with a little, with good materials on natural history, surprisingly sophisticated exhibits on ethnology and aboriginal subsistence, and historic displays on maps and mapmaking, the evolution of communications on the island, and astronomical science. Now occupying the former storehouses of the Asociación Rural de Tierra del Fuego, the Museo de la Ciudad, Alberdi 553, tel. 2964/430647, is open 9 A.M.–5 P.M. weekdays except Monday, and 3–8 P.M. weekends.

Río Grande has few architectural landmarks—or few buildings of any antiquity for that matter—but the **Obras Sanitarias** (1954) waterworks, Lasserre 386 at the northeast corner of the plaza, dates from the Juan Perón era.

Accommodations

Accommodations are fairly scarce, especially inexpensive ones of any quality. Nearly every mid-to upscale place offers a 10 percent discount for payment in cash.

Río Grande has its first backpackers' hostel in the promising **Hotel Argentino,** at the south end of town at San Martín 64, tel. 15/603944, hotelargentino@yahoo.com. It makes special efforts for cyclists, though anyone is welcome, and standards are good from about US$6 pp for BB with shared bath; there are kitchen facilities and

other usable common spaces, and the hostel will provide a free pickup from the bus station.

Perhaps the next-best value in town, family-run **Hospedaje Noal,** Obligado 557, tel. 2964/42-7515, is simple but spotless. Spacious rooms with plenty of closet space, good beds, and shared bath cost US$15 pp—a bargain by Argentine standards. Also a fine choice, though a little more expensive at US$20/30 s/d with private bath, is cozy **Hotel Rawson,** J. M. Estrada 750, tel. 2964/425503, fax 2964/430352. The comparable **Hotel Villa,** San Martín 277, tel. 2964/422312, costs US$25/35 s/d.

Hotel Isla del Mar, close to the bus terminal at Güemes 936, tel. 2964/422883, fax 2964/427283, isladelmar@arnet.com.ar, charges US$44/55 s/d for seaview rooms with breakfast, with cash discounts. Rates at **Hotel Federico Ibarra,** Rosales 357, tel. 2964/430071, are US$63/75 s/d with breakfast, but there's also a cash discount. **Hotel Atlántida,** Avenida Belgrano 582, tel./fax 2964/431914, atlantida@netcombbs.com.ar, charges US$65/80 s/d. The most professional operation in town, **Posada de los Sauces,** Elcano 839, tel. 2964/432895, posadadelossauces@arnet.com.ar, costs US$78/90 with breakfast.

Food

La Nueva Piamontesa, Belgrano 464, tel. 2964/421977, is a longstanding favorite for varied and delicate baked empanadas and the pizzas in its deli, but it's recently added an inexpensive sit-down restaurant as well. Two other places specialize in pizza and pasta: **Café Sonora,** Perito Moreno 705, and **La Colonial,** on Fagnano between Avenida San Martín and Rosales. **Leymi,** 25 de Mayo 1335, tel. 2964/421683, serves fixed-price lunches for about US$5 and has a broad menu of *parrillada,* pasta, and other short orders. **El Rincón de Julio,** Elcano 805, is the place for beef.

Mamá Flora, at the corner of Avenida Belgrano and Rafael Obligado, is a good breakfast choice that also has coffee and exquisite chocolates. The curiously named **Lusso Buffet,** at the corner of Perito Moreno and Espora, is an ice creamery.

Several upscale hotels have their own restaurants.

Entertainment

El Cine 1 & 2, Perito Moreno 211, tel. 2964/433260, shows current films in modern facilities, but it sometimes turns up the volume to excruciating levels—bring or improvise ear plugs, just in case.

Services

Money: Several banks have ATMs, including Banco de Tierra del Fuego at San Martín and 9 de Julio; Bansud at Rosales 241, half a block south of the plaza; and Banca Nazionale del Lavoro, San Martín 194.

Postal: Correo Argentino is on Rivadavia between Moyano and Alberdi, two blocks west of San Martín; the postal code is 9420.

Telephone and Internet: Locutorio Cabo Domingo, Avenida San Martín 458, has long-distance services; the area code is 2964. Argentina's country code is 54. Telefónica, on San Martín just south of 9 de Julio, has Internet access.

Laundry: El Lavadero is at Perito Moreno 221.

Medical: The Hospital Regional is at Ameghino s/n, tel. 2964/422088.

Information

The Instituto Fueguino de Turismo (Infuetur), Belgrano 319, tel. 2964/422887, infuerg@satlink. com, is open 10 A.M.–5 P.M. weekdays only.

Transportation

Air: Readily reached by cab, Aeropuerto Internacional Río Grande is a short distance east of downtown.

Aerolíneas Argentinas, San Martín 607, tel. 2964/422748, flies daily to Aeroparque, Buenos Aires's domestic airport. LAPA, San Martín 641, tel. 2964/432620, also flies daily to Aeroparque; its Tuesday, Thursday, and Saturday flights stop in Río Gallegos.

LADE, Lasserre 447, tel. 2964/421651, flies Tuesday and Thursday mornings to Río Gallegos (US$25). From November to March, Aerovías DAP, 9 de Julio 597, tel. 2964/430249, flies Friday to Punta Arenas, Chile (US$90).

Bus: Río Grande's Terminal de Buses is near the waterfront at Avenida Belgrano 16, tel. 2964/421339, but some companies have offices else-

where in town. Buses Pacheco, tel. 2964/425611, goes to Punta Arenas (US$25, eight hours) Tuesday, Thursday, and Saturday at 11:30 A.M. Tecni-Austral, Moyano 516, tel. 2964/430610, goes to Punta Arenas Monday, Wednesday, and Friday at 11 A.M., to Ushuaia (US$15, four hours) at 7 A.M. and 6 P.M. daily, and to Porvenir, Chile, Tuesday, Thursday, and Saturday at 8 A.M.

Lider, at the main terminal, tel. 2964/420003, goes to Tolhuín (US$8) and Ushuaia (US$15) six times daily except Sunday and holidays, when it goes only four times. Transportes Montiel, also at the main terminal, tel. 2964/420997, goes seven times daily to Ushuaia except Sunday, when it goes four times only.

Getting Around

Ansa International (AI), Ameghino 612, tel. 2964/422657, rents cars and pickup trucks.

VICINITY OF RÍO GRANDE

As the area surrounding Río Grande does not have a well-developed tourist infrastructure, hiring a vehicle is worth consideration.

Reserva Provincial Costa Atlántica de Tierra del Fuego

From Cabo Nombre, at the north end of Bahía San Sebastián, to the mouth of the Río Ewan southeast of Río Grande, the entire shoreline of the Isla Grande is a major bird sanctuary because of the abundance of plovers and sandpipers, some of which migrate yearly between the Arctic and South America. Near the San Sebastián border post is the privately owned **Refugio de Vida Silvestre Dicky,** a prime wetland habitat of 1,900 hectares.

Museo Salesiano

One exception to the area's lack of historic sites is the **Museo Salesiano,** on the grounds of a mission founded by the Salesian order to catechize the Selknam but, after the aboriginals died out from unintentionally introduced diseases and intentional outright slaughter, the fathers turned their attention to educating rural youth in their boarding school. The well-preserved **Capilla**

FISHING IN TIERRA DEL FUEGO

Fishing for Atlantic salmon, brown trout, and rainbow trout is a popular activity throughout Argentine Tierra del Fuego, but the rules are a bit intricate. In the first instance, there are separate licenses for Parque Nacional Tierra del Fuego and for the rest of the island, and fees differ for residents of the province, nonresidents of the province, and foreigners.

For fishing within the park, licenses are available only from the APN in Ushuaia; rates are US$5 per day or US$20 per season (November to mid-April) for residents. For nonresidents or foreigners, rates are US$10 per day or US$100 per season. Children under age 13 and retired Argentine citizens pay nothing.

For fishing outside the park boundaries, daily rates are US$10 for residents, US$15 for nonresidents, and US$25 for foreigners; there is also a US$20 weekly rate for residents. Seasonal rates are US$40 for residents, US$60 for nonresidents, and US$100 for foreigners.

In Ushuaia, licenses are available at the **Asociación Caza y Pesca,** Maipú 822, tel. 02901/423168, at or **Óptica Eduardo's,** San Martín 830, tel. 02901/433252. In Río Grande, contact the **Club de Pesca John Goodall,** Ricardo Rojas 606, tel. 2964/424324.

(chapel) is a national historical monument, but the rest of the Magellanic-style structures need renovation, and the museum collections, dealing with natural history and ethnography, need organization and preservation.

About 11 km north of Río Grande on the west side of RN 3, the museum, tel. 2964/421642, is open 9 A.M.–12:30 P.M. and 3–7 P.M. daily; admission costs US$2 for adults, US$1 for children. From Río Grande, Colectivo (City Bus) B goes hourly to the mission from 7:30 A.M.–8:30 P.M.

Historic *Estancias*

Two of the region's largest and most important *estancias,* both belonging to the Sociedad Explotadora de Tierra del Fuego, are in the vicinity

of Río Grande. **Estancia María Behety** is 17 km west via Ruta Complementaria c (RC-c, a gravel road) and the site of the world's largest shearing shed.

Estancia José Menéndez, 25 km southwest of town via RN 3 and RC-b, is also one of the island's most historic ranches; RC-b continues west to an obscure summer border crossing at **Radman,** where few visitors of any kind cross the line to Lago Blanco on the Chilean side.

Lago Fagnano (Kami)

Named for the Salesian priest who headed the Salesian evangelical effort among the Selknam, this elongated body of water fills a structural depression that stretches across the Chilean border to the west. Also known by its Selknam name Kami, its shoreline is nearly 200 km long and its surface covers nearly 600 square km.

The most westerly part of the lake, along the Chilean border, belongs to Parque Nacional Tierra del Fuego but is virtually inaccessible except by boat. As might be expected, the lake is popular with fishing enthusiasts.

On the southeastern shore, about 135 km from Río Grande and 100 km from Ushuaia, **Hostería Kaikén,** tel. 2901/492208, offers ground-floor accommodations for US$25/35 s/d, breakfast included; second-floor view rooms cost US$30/35. Make reservations, especially in summer, as demand is high. Buses between Río Grande and Ushuaia will drop off and pick up passengers here.

USHUAIA (ARGENTINA)

Beneath the serrated spires of the Martial range, on the north shore of the Beagle Channel, the city of Ushuaia is both an end—virtually the terminus of the world's most southerly highway—and a beginning—the principal gateway to Antarctica. The surrounding countryside is increasingly popular with recreation-oriented visitors who enjoy hiking, mountain biking, fishing, and skiing.

After two decades-plus of economic growth and physical sprawl, the provincial capital is both declining and improving. On the one hand, the duty-free manufacturing, fishing, and tourist

PATAGONIA & TIERRA

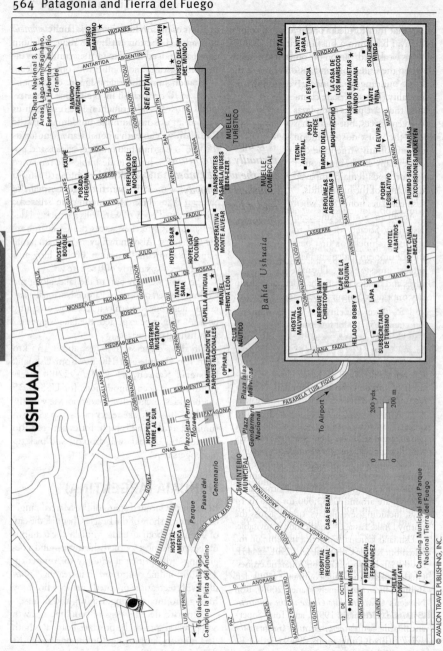

USHUAIA

To Rutas Nacional 3, Ski Areas, Lago Kami/Fagnano, Estancia Harberton, and Río Grande

MUSEO MARITIMO

YAGANES

VOLVER

ANTARTIDA

ARGENTINA

MUSEO DEL FIN DEL MUNDO

RANCHO ARGENTINO

RIVADAVIA

SEE DETAIL

GODOY

GOBERNADOR

MARTIN

MAIPU

KAUPE

ROCA

SAN

MUELLE TURISTICO

POSADA FUEGUINA

LASSERRE

EL REFUGIO DEL MOCHILERO

AVENIDA

MUELLE COMERCIAL

MAGALLANES

25 DE MAYO

TRANSPORTES PASARELA/BUSES EBEN-EZER

HOSTAL DEL BOSQUE

DE PAZ

HOTEL CÉSAR

JUANA FADUL

COOPERATIVA MONTE ALVEAR

SOLIS

9 DE JULIO

HOTEL CAP POLONIO

Bahía Ushuaia

GOBERNADOR

J.M. DE ROSAS

TANTE SARA

CAPILLA ANTIGUA

MANUEL TIENDA LEON

MONSEÑOR FAGNANO

DELOQUI

DON BOSCO

HOSTERÍA MUSTAPIC

CLUB NÁUTICO

PIEDRABUENA

GOBERNADOR

OPIPARO

MAGALLANES

GOBERNADOR CAMPOS

BELGRANO

ADMINISTRACIÓN DE PARQUES NACIONALES

Plaza Islas Malvinas

SARMIENTO

PATAGONIA

Plaza Gendarmería Nacional

HOSPEDAJE TORRE AL SUR

Plazoleta Perito Moreno

PASARELA LUIS FIQUE

ONAS

GOMEZ

Paseo del Centenario

Parque

CEMENTERIO MUNICIPAL

AVENIDA SAN MARTIN

To Airport

HOSTAL AMERICA

AVENIDA MALVINAS ARGENTINAS

DE AGOSTO

CASA BEBAN

DARWIN

LUIS VERNET

To Glaciar Martial and Camping la Pista del Andino

O. V. ANDRADE

HOSPITAL REGIONAL

RESIDENCIAL FERNÁNDEZ

PAZ

12 DE OCTUBRE

HOTEL MAITÉN

ONACHAGA

CHILEAN CONSULATE

To Camping Municipal and Parque Nacional Tierra del Fuego

SÁNCHEZ DE CABALLERO

FLORENCIA

LUGONES

JAINEN

0   200 yds
0   200 m

© AVALON TRAVEL PUBLISHING, INC.

DETAIL

TANTE SARA

RIVADAVIA

SOUTHERN WINDS

LA ESTANCIA

LA CASA DE LOS MARISCOS

GODOY

POST OFFICE

MUSEO DE MAQUETAS MUNDO YAMANA

TECNI-AUSTRAL

BARCITO IDEAL

MOUSTACCHIO

TANTE NINA

MAIPU

AEROLINEAS ARGENTINAS

SAN MARTIN

ROCA

TÍA ELVIRA

AVENIDA

LASSERRE

PODER LEGISLATIVO

RUMBO SUR/TRES MARÍAS EXCURSIONES/TOLKEYEN

DELOQUI

AVENIDA

HOTEL ALBATROS

HOSTAL MALVINAS

ALBERGUE SAINT CHRISTOPHER

CAFÉ DE LA ESQUINA

25 DE MAYO

HOTEL CANAL BEAGLE

GOBERNADOR

HELADOS BOBBY

LAPA

SUBSECRETARIA DE TURISMO

JUANA FADUL

boom that transformed a onetime penal colony and naval base into a bustling city of 45,000-plus has weakened, but on the other, it's begun to clean up the waterfront and restore some of the historic buildings that once gave the town its personality. The streets are cleaner, and there are parks and plazas and green spaces, but it still has one of the worst dust-pollution problems of any Argentine city because many streets in the outer neighborhoods remain unpaved and because of the high winds.

Ushuaia dates from 1870, when the Anglican South American Missionary Society decided to place the archipelago's first permanent European settlement here. Pioneer missionary Thomas Bridges and his descendants have left an enduring legacy in Bridges' Yahgan (Yámana) dictionary, the

The city of Ushuaia is both an end—virtually the terminus of the world's most southerly highway—and a beginning—the principal gateway to Antarctica.

memoir of his son Lucas, and the family *estancia* at nearby Harberton (sadly, the Yahgans whom Thomas Bridges hoped to save succumbed to introduced diseases and conflict with other settlers).

Not long after the establishment of Ushuaia, alarmed by the British presence, Argentina moved to establish its own authority at Ushuaia and did so with a penal settlement for its most infamous criminals and political undesirables. It remained a penal settlement until almost 1950, when the government of Juan Domingo Perón created a major naval base to help support Argentina's claim to a share of Antarctica. Only since the end of the military dictatorship of 1976–83 has it become a tourist destination, visited by many cruise ships as well as overland travelers and air passengers who come to see the world's southernmost city.

Orientation

Ushuaia is 3,220 km south of Buenos Aires, Argentina's federal capital, and 240 km southwest of Río Grande. It stretches east and west along the north shore of the Beagle Channel. Now bedecked with flower beds, the main thoroughfare is Avenida Maipú, part of RN 3, which continues west to Parque Nacional Tierra del Fuego. The parallel Avenida San Martín, one block north, is the main commercial street; the focus of Ushuaia's nightlife, it gets gridlocked on summer nights as surely as any avenue in Buenos Aires. From the shoreline, the perpendicular northbound streets rise steeply—some so steeply that they become staircases.

Westbound RN 3 actually ends at Bahía Lapataia in Parque Nacional Tierra del Fuego, 20 km from Ushuaia.

Sights

Even if it's leveled off, Ushuaia's recent economic boom provided the wherewithal to preserve and even restore some of the city's historic buildings. Two of them are now museums: the **Casa Fernández Valdés** (1903), on the waterfront at Avenida Maipú 175, houses the historical Museo del

SAILING SOUTH TO THE ICE

Since the demise of the Soviet Union, Ushuaia has become the main jumping-off point for Antarctic excursions on Russian icebreakers that, despite being chartered under American officers, sometimes still carry the shield of the hammer and sickle on their bows. For travelers with flexible schedules, it's sometimes possible to make last-minute arrangements at huge discounts—no ship wants to sail with empty berths—for as little as US$1,100. Normal rates, though, are around US$3,000 for nine to 14 days, including several days' transit across the stormy Drake Passage—medication is advisable.

Ushuaia's Oficina Antarctica Infuetur, on the waterfront Muelle Comercial, tel. 02901/424431, has the latest information on Antarctic cruises. Guidebooks to the white continent include Jeff Rubin's *Antarctica* (Lonely Planet, 2000), Ron Naveen's *Oceanites Site Guide to the Antarctic Peninsula* (Oceanites, 1997), and Tony Soper's and Dafila Scott's *Antarctica: A Guide to the Wildlife* (Bradt Publications, 2000).

PATAGONIA & TIERRA

© WAYNE BERNHARDSON

former Soviet research icebreaker, now an Antarctic cruise ship, in Ushuaia

Fin de Mundo, while the **Presidio de Ushuaia** (1896), at Yaganes and Gobernador Paz, is now the rather misleadingly named Museo Marítimo (while not insignificant, its maritime exhibits are fewer than those on the city's role as a penal colony).

Three blocks west of the Casa Fernández Valdés, at Maipú 465, the classically Magellanic **Poder Legislativo** (1894) houses the provincial legislature of Argentine Tierra del Fuego. Five blocks farther west, at the corner of Avenida Maipú and Rosas, prisoners built the recently restored **Capilla Antigua,** a chapel dating from 1898. Ushuaia's municipal tourist office now occupies the **Biblioteca Sarmiento** (1926), San Martín 674, the city's first public library. On the waterfront at the corner of Avenida Malvinas Argentinas and 12 de Octubre, is the **Casa Beban,** an elaborate reassembled pioneer residence dating from 1913; it now houses the municipal Casa de la Cultura, a cultural center.

Museo del Fin del Mundo

Steadily evolving into a more impressive facility since its exterior restoration, Ushuaia's historical museum contains improved exhibits on the Yámana, Selknam, and other Fuegian Indians, and on early European voyages to the area. There remain permanent exhibits on the presidio, the Fique family's El Primer Argentino general store, the original branch of the state-run bank Banco de la Nación (which occupied the building for more than 60 years), and run-of-the-mill taxidermy. Its celebrity artifact is one of a handful of existing copies of Thomas Bridges's Yámana-English dictionary.

On the grounds outside the building, whose block-style construction differs from traditional Magellanic design, a new open-air sector includes representations of a Yámana encampment and dwellings, plus machinery used in early agriculture and forestry projects. The museum, at Avenida Maipú 175, tel. 02901/421863, museo@tierradelfuego.org.ar, also contains a bookstore/souvenir shop and a specialized library on southernmost Argentina, the surrounding oceans, and Antarctica. Hours are 10 A.M.–1 P.M. and 3–7:30 P.M. daily in summer; admission costs US$5 for adults, US$2 for children. The rest of the year, hours are 3–8 P.M. daily except Monday.

Museo Marítimo de Ushuaia

Misleadingly named, Ushuaia's maritime museum most effectively tells the story of Ushuaia's inauspicious antecedents as a penal settlement for both civilian and military prisoners. Alarmed over the South American Missionary Society's incursions among the indigenous peoples of the Beagle Channel, Argentina reinforced its claims to the territory by building, in 1884, a military prison on Isla de los Estados (Staten Island), across the Strait of Lemaire at the southeastern tip of the Isla Grande.

Barely a decade later, in 1896, it established a civilian Cárcel de Reincidentes for repeat offenders at Ushuaia; after finally deciding, in 1902, that Isla de los Estados was a hardship post even for prisoners, the military moved its own facility to Ushuaia. Then, in 1911, the two institutions fused in this building that, over the first half of the 20th century, held some of the country's most famous political prisoners, most celebrated rogues, and most notorious psychopaths.

Divided into five two-story pavilions, with 380 cells intended for one prisoner each, the prison held as many as 600 prisoners at a time before closing in 1947. Its most famous inmates were political detainees such as immigrant Russian anarchist Simón Radowitzsky, who killed Buenos Aires police chief Ramón Falcón with a bomb in 1909, Radical politicians Ricardo Rojas, Honorio Pueyrredón, and Mario Guido (the misleadingly named Radicals are in fact a middle-class party), and Peronist politician Héctor Cámpora, who was briefly president in the 1970s.

Many if not most of the prisoners, though, were long-termers or lifers such as the diminutive strangler Santos Godino, dubbed "El Orejudo" for his oversized ears (interestingly enough, the nickname also describes a large-eared bat that is native to the island). Life-sized figures of the most infamous inmates, modified department-store dummies clad in prison stripes, occupy many of the cells. Another particularly interesting exhibit is a wide-ranging comparison with other prisons that have become museums, such as San Francisco's Alcatraz and South Africa's Robben Island.

The museum does live up to its name with an exceptional exhibit of scale models of ships that have played a role in the archipelago's history, such as Magellan's galleon *Trinidad,* the legendary *Beagle,* the South American Missionary Society's three successive sailboats known as the *Allen Gardiner,* and Antarctic explorer and conqueror Roald Amundsen's *Fram.* In addition, there are materials on the Argentine presence in Antarctica since the early 20th century, when the corvette *Uruguay* rescued the Norwegian expedition of Otto Nordenskjöld, which included the Argentine participant José María Sobral. On the grounds outdoors is a full-sized model of the Faro San Juan de Salvamento, the Isla de los Estados (Staten Island) lighthouse that figures in Jules Verne's story "The Lighthouse at the End of the World."

In addition, this exceptional museum contains a philatelic room, natural history exhibits, and admirable accounts of the region's aboriginal peoples. In fact, it has only two drawbacks: there's too much to see in a single day, and the English translations could use some polishing—to say the least.

The Museo Marítimo, whose entrance is on Yaganes at the east end of Gobernador Paz, tel. 02901/437481, museomar@satlink.com, is open 10 A.M.–8 P.M. daily. Admission costs a hefty US$7 but, on request, the staff will validate your ticket for another day; since there's so much here, splitting up sight-seeing sessions is not a bad idea. There are discounts for children (US$1), students (US$3) and senior citizens (US$5), and families (US$15 including up to four children). It has a very fine book and souvenir shop, and a good *confitería* for snacks and coffee.

Museo de Maquetas Mundo Yámana

While both the Museo del Fin del Mundo and Museo Marítimo do a creditable job on Tierra del Fuego's indigenous heritage, this small private museum consists of skillfully assembled dioramas of life along the Beagle Channel before the European presence, at a scale of 1:15. It also includes cartographic representations of Yámana, interpretations of the European impact, and panels of historical photographs.

Open 10 A.M.–8 P.M. daily, the Museo de Maquetas Mundo Yámana, Rivadavia 56, tel. 02901/422874, mundoyamana@infovia.com.ar, charges

US$3 admission for adults, US$2 for retired people, and is free for children under 13. The staff speaks fluent English.

Accommodations

Ushuaia has abundant accommodations, but it's one of the most expensive destinations in an expensive country.

US$10 or Less: Eight km west of Ushuaia on the road to Parque Nacional Tierra del Fuego, the **Camping Municipal** is free but has limited facilities (fire pits and pit toilets only). Four km west of town, the **Camping del Rugby Club Ushuaia,** tel. 02901/435796, campingpipo@tierradelfuego.org.ar, costs US$5 pp for sites with running water, bathrooms with hot showers, and fire pits with grills for barbecuing.

A stiff climb to the northwest of downtown Ushuaia, **La Pista del Andino,** Alem 2873, tel. 02901/435890 or 15/568626, pistadelandino@hotmail.com, charges US$5 pp for slightly sloping campsites at the Club Andino's ski area; the first transfer from downtown or the airport is free. It also allows those with bags to sleep in the *refugio* upstairs from its bar/restaurant which, however, is less than ideal for those who want to get to bed early.

US$10–25: Central but quiet, **Albergue Saint Christopher,** Deloqui 636, tel. 02901/430062, hostel_christopher@yahoo.com, is an independent hostel charging US$10 pp in rooms with four, six, or eight beds; there is also cable TV, Internet access, two kitchens, and a free initial pick up. Guests also get a series of discounts and specials at various services around town.

For the same price, **El Refugio del Mochilero,** 25 de Mayo 241, tel. 02901/436129, refmoch@infovia.com.ar, has almost equally good facilities but perhaps a little less ambience than it once had.

Far enough from downtown to offer reasonable quiet and high enough to offer spectacular views of the Beagle Channel, expanding **Albergue Torre al Sur,** Gobernador Paz 1437, tel. 02901/437291, fax 02901/430745, torrealsur@impsat1.com.ar, is one of Argentina's finest backpacker facilities. Rooms with two or four beds, with lockers, hot water, Internet access, and free

luggage storage cost US$10 pp with HI membership, US$12 pp without.

US$25–50: Despite continued opposition and criticism from official Ushuaia, **Hospedaje Hilda Sánchez,** Deloquí 391, tel. 02901/423622, somehow stays in business, charging US$15 pp in a friendly but somewhat disorderly environment. **Hostería Mustapic,** Piedrabuena 230, tel. 02901/421718, mustapic@sinectis.com.ar, costs US$25/40 s/d with shared bath, US$35/50 with private bath. Rates at **Hostería América,** Gobernador Paz 1665, tel. 02901/423358, fax 02901/431362, hosteriaamerica@arnet.com.ar, are US$40/50.

US$50–100: Several places charge in the US$40/55 s/d range, including **Hotel César,** Avenida San Martín 753, tel. 02901/421460, cesarhostal@infovia.com.ar; **Hotel Maitén,** 12 de Octubre 140, tel. 02901/422745, maiten@tierradelfuego.org.ar; and **Residencial Fernández,** Onachaga 72, tel. 02901/421192, which includes breakfast. For members and affiliate members, the Automóvil Club Argentino's **Hotel Canal Beagle,** Avenida Maipú 599, tel. 02901/421117, fax 02901/421120, hotelcanalb@impsat1.com.ar, charges US$40/60 s/d; nonmembers pay US$54/80.

Hostal Malvinas, Gobernador Deloqui 615, tel./fax 02901/422626, provides simple but quiet and immaculate rooms with large baths but no frills—not even TV—for US$50/60 s/d. Offering awesome views from its cul-de-sac hillside perch, **Hotel Posada Fueguina,** Lasserre 438, tel. 02901/423467, pfueguina@tierradelfuego.org.ar, charges US$79/90 s/d. Rates include breakfast, cable TV, and the like.

US$100–150: The only real drawback at the bright, new, and cheerful **Hotel Cap Polonio,** San Martín 746, tel. 02901/422140 or 02901/422131, cappolonio@tierradelfuego.org.ar, is its location on a busy street. All rooms are carpeted, with cable TV, showers and tubs in the private baths, and there's a good restaurant/*confitería.* High-season rates of US$85/105 s/d include breakfast, as do low-season rates of US$65/85. Tango shows take place Saturday at 10 P.M.

Hotel Ushuaia, Lasserre 933, tel. 02901/430671, hushuaia@tierradelfuego.org.ar, costs

US$80/110 s/d with breakfast. **Hostal del Bosque,** Magallanes 709, tel./fax 02901/430777 or 02901/421723, info@hostaldelbosque.com.ar, is an "aparthotel" whose two-room suites, with kitchenette, can sleep up to four people for US$110 with breakfast. There are large baths, with shower and tub, and cable TV; it also has its own restaurant.

The waterfront **Hotel Albatros,** Avenida Maipú 505, tel. 02901/433446, glaciar@infovia.com.ar, charges US$162 s or d with breakfast. Rates at **Hotel del Glaciar,** Luis Martial 2355 (Km 3.5 on the road to the Martial Glacier), tel. 02901/430640, fax 02901/430636, glaciar@infovia.com.ar, start at US$169/179 s/d. Each room has either a mountain or sea view.

The nearby **Hotel y Resort Las Hayas,** Luis Martial 1650 (Km 3 on the road to the glacier), tel. 02901/430710, fax 02901/430719, lashayas@overnet.com.ar, charges US$225 s or d with a buffet breakfast. It has 92 rooms and all conceivable luxuries, including a gym, Jacuzzis, and a heated indoor pool; it picks up guests with reservations at the airport and offers a regular shuttle to and from downtown Ushuaia.

Food

Dining in Ushuaia is less prohibitively expensive since devaluation of the Argentine peso, but the financially challenged may still prefer tenedor libre (literally, free fork, all-you-can-eat specials). Be particularly cautious with extras such as dessert and coffee; it's always best to ask what something costs before ordering it. Note, however, that portions are generally large—most salads, for instance, easily suffice for two.

Part of Hotel Cap Polonio, **Marcopolo,** San Martín 730, tel. 02901/430001, is a café-restaurant that serves excellent coffee, chocolate, and croissants for breakfast—try the typically Argentine *submarino,* a bar of semisweet chocolate dissolved in steamed milk, for a cold morning's pickup. **Café de la Esquina,** a favorite meeting place at Avenida San Martín 601, tel. 02901/421446, has similar offerings, as well as sandwiches for late-afternoon tea.

Open for lunch only on weekdays, but with evening hours Saturday, **Pizzería El Turco,** San Martín 1440, tel. 02901/424711, is good and moderately priced, around US$6 for a full meal. However, it lacks the variety at **Opíparo,** Avenida Maipú 1255, tel. 02901/434022, a pizzería that also serves pasta dishes; figure about US$10 for lunch or dinner. **Barcleit 1912,** Fadul 148, tel. 02901/433422, seems to have fallen a step behind some of the other pizzerias, but it also has a variety of short orders in the US$8 range.

One of Ushuaia's best new restaurants, **Tante Sara,** San Martín 137, tel./fax 02901/435005, serves outstanding pasta with a broad selection of imaginative sauces, as well as pizza, with good service in pleasant surroundings. Most entrées are in the US$8–10 range. **Tante Nina,** Gobernador Godoy 15, tel. 02901/432444, focuses on Fuegian fish and seafood, Patagonian lamb, and "homely pasta."

Barcito Ideal, Avenida San Martín 393, tel. 02901/437860, seems always to draw crowds to its US$10 *tenedor libre* buffet. **La Rueda,** San Martín 193, charges only slightly more for its own buffet *parrillada.* Nearby **La Estancia,** San Martín 253, tel. 02901/421241, has similar fare.

For US$11, **Rancho Argentino,** at Gobernador Campos and Rivadavia, tel. 02901/424247, offers a fixed-price four-course meal including grilled Fuegian lamb, but it also has a more diverse à la carte menu including beef and baked empanadas. The well-established **Moustacchio,** Avenida San Martín 298, tel. 02901/423308, has similar fare but also emphasizes seafood.

Ushuaia has a wider choice of seafood restaurants than just about any other Argentine provincial city. **La Casa de los Mariscos,** San Martín 232, tel. 02901/421928, specializes in *centolla* (king crab), but it also has many other fish and shellfish options in the US$5–16 range. Other possibilities include **Volver,** Avenida Maipú 37, tel. 02901/423977; the **Club Náutico** at Avenida Maipú and Belgrano, tel. 02901/424028, where entrées start around US$10; **Tía Elvira,** Avenida Maipú 349, tel. 02901/424725, where four-course dinners cost around US$25; and **Kaupé,** Roca 470, tel. 02901/422704, which serves an exclusively (and exclusive) à la carte menu.

PATAGONIA & TIERRA

Helados Bobby, Avenida San Martín 621, has all the conventional Argentine ice cream flavors—good enough in their own right—but also incorporates regional specialties such as *calafate* and rhubarb. **Tante Sara,** at Avenida San Martín and Don Bosco, deserves special mention for its ice cream and desserts as well.

Shopping

Boutique del Libro, San Martín 1129, tel. 02901/424750, offers an excellent selection of Spanish-language books and a smaller choice of English-language materials.

Fin del Mundo, San Martín 505, has a wide selection of kitschy souvenirs but also maps and books.

Services

Money: Several banks have ATMs, including BanSud, Avenida Maipú 781; Banca Nazionale del Lavoro, Avenida Maipú 297; and Banco de la Provincia, San Martín 396. The latter accepts traveler's checks at a 3 percent commission. Cambios Thaler, Avenida San Martín 877, also takes 3 percent on traveler's checks but keeps longer hours: 9:30 A.M.–1:30 P.M. and 4–8 P.M. week-

days, 10 A.M.–1:30 P.M. and 5:30–8 P.M. Saturday and 5:30–8 P.M. Sunday.

Postal: Correo Argentino is at Avenida San Martín and Godoy. The postal code is 9410.

Telephone and Internet: Telefónica, Avenida San Martín 957, offers long-distance telephone service. Locutorio Cabo de Hornos, at 25 de Mayo 112, provides telephone, fax, and Internet access, the latter for US$3 per hour. Try also the Instituto Fueguino de Computación, Rivadavia 165.

Ushuaia's area code is tel. 02901. Argentina's country code is 54.

Immigration: The Dirección Nacional de Migraciones is at Beauvoir 1536, tel. 02901/422334.

Laundry: Los Tres Angeles, Juan Manuel de Rosas 139, tel. 02901/422687, is quick and reliable.

Medical: The Hospital Regional is at Maipú and 12 de Octubre, tel. 02901/422950, tel. 107 for emergencies.

Information

Tourist Offices: Ushuaia's Subsecretaría Municipal de Turismo is at Avenida San Martín 674, tel. 02901/424550, toll-free 0800/333-1476 on the Argentine side of the island, muniush@tier-

mural of Yámana Indians

radelfuego.org.ar; it's open 8 A.M.–10 P.M. weekdays and 9 A.M.–8 P.M. weekends and holidays, and it normally has English-speaking personnel.

In addition, there is a subsidiary office at the Muelle Turístico, open 8 A.M.–6 P.M. daily, and another at the airport that's open for arriving flights.

The provincial Instituto Fueguino de Turismo (Infuetur) has ground-floor offices at Hotel Albatros, Avenida Maipú 505, tel. 02901/423340.

Consulate: Chile maintains a consulate at Jainén 50, tel. 02901/422177, open 9 A.M.–1 P.M. weekdays only.

Motorists: The Automóvil Club Argentino (ACA) is at Malvinas Argentinas and Onachaga, tel. 02901/421121.

National Parks: The Administración de Parques Nacionales, Avenida San Martín 1395, tel. 02901/421315, is open 9 A.M.–noon weekdays.

Antarctica: The Oficina Antarctica Infuetur, at the Muelle Comercial on the waterfront, tel. 02901/424431, antartida@tierradelfuego.org.ar, has information on Antarctic tours.

Transportation

Air: A causeway connects the city with Aeropuerto Internacional Malvinas Argentinas which, since its privatization, has the country's highest airport taxes: US$4 to Río Grande, US$13 elsewhere in Argentina, and US$20 for international flights.

Along with its subsidiary Austral, Aerolíneas Argentinas, Roca 116, tel. 02901/421218, flies twice daily to Buenos Aires (Aeroparque) except Tuesday and Wednesday, when there is only a single flight, and daily to Río Gallegos and Buenos Aires.

ARG, 25 de Mayo 64, tel. 02901/432112, flies Tuesday, Thursday, and Saturday to Río Gallegos (US$50–64) and Aeroparque (Buenos Aires). Southern Winds, Maipú 237, tel. 02901/437073, swush@arnet.com.ar, flies daily to Río Gallegos (US$49–109), Comodoro Rivadavia (US$99–159), Neuquén, and Mendoza; Wednesday and Saturday to El Calafate, Bariloche, and Aeroparque (Buenos Aires); Saturday to Puerto Madryn; and daily to Córdoba.

LADE, in the Galería Albatros at Avenida San Martín 564, tel. 02901/421123, flies Tuesday

and Thursday to Río Grande and Río Gallegos (US$30); the Thursday flight continues to Comodoro Rivadavia (US$95).

From November to March, the Chilean carrier Aerovías DAP flies 20-passenger Twin Otters Monday and Wednesday to Punta Arenas, Chile (US$100), the only scheduled international service from Ushuaia.

Bus: Lider, Gobernador Paz 921, tel. 02901/436421, goes to Tolhuín (US$8) and Ushuaia (US$15) six times daily except Sunday and holidays, when it goes only four times. Transportes Montiel, Marcos Zar 330, tel. 02901/421366, goes to Río Grande seven times daily except Sunday, when it goes four times only.

Tecni-Austral, Roca 157, tel. 02901/431612, goes daily at 7 A.M. and 6 P.M. to Río Grande (US$15, 3.5 hours); the Monday, Wednesday, and Friday buses continue to Punta Arenas, Chile. It also has Tuesday, Thursday, and Saturday buses to Río Grande and Porvenir, Chile, at 5 A.M.

Tolkeyen, Maipú 237, tel. 02901/437073, has three buses daily to Río Grande, at 8 A.M. and 2:30 and 7 P.M.; Tuesday, Thursday, and Saturday, the early bus hooks up with the 11:30 A.M. Pacheco bus from Río Grande to Punta Arenas.

Sea: The Chilean MV *Mare Australis* operates luxurious sight-seeing cruises to Puerto Williams and through the fjords of Chilean Tierra del Fuego to Punta Arenas; while not intended as simple transportation, it can serve the same purpose for those who can afford it. It's possible either to disembark in Punta Arenas (three days) or return to Ushuaia (in a week). (For more details, see the Punta Arenas entry.) These cruises are usually booked far in advance, but since the operator Cruceros Australis has added a ship, it may be possible to board more spontaneously.

Political complications between Chile and Argentina have held up regular transportation across the Beagle Channel to Puerto Williams, but in December 2001 the two countries agreed to open Puerto Navarino, at the east end of Isla Navarino, as a port of entry to Chile.

What that means for regular public transportation is not yet clear. In the meantime, ask around the Club Náutico, at Avenida Maipú and Belgrano, for private yachts that may be

PATAGONIA & TIERRA

willing to take passengers (a large enough group should be able to charter a boat at a reasonable per-person cost).

Getting Around

Bus: The bus stop for Parque Nacional Tierra del Fuego is at the corner of Avenida Maipú and 25 de Mayo. Several companies all charge US$10 round-trip; it's possible to stay in the park and return on a following day.

In summer, Transporte Pasarela, tel. 02901/ 433712, goes to the park nine times daily between 8 A.M. and 8 P.M., returning between 9 A.M. and 9 P.M. Buses Eben-Ezer, tel. 02901/ 431133, goes six times daily between 9 A.M. and 6 P.M., returning between 10 A.M. and 7:15 P.M. Bellavista goes 10 times daily between 9:30 A.M. and 6:30 P.M., returning between 10:30 A.M. and 7 P.M.

Cooperativa Monte Alvear, San Martín 132, leaves from the corner of Avenida Maipú and Juana Fadul; departures are eight times daily between 8 A.M. and 8 P.M., returning between noon and 8:30 P.M.

Car Rental: Car rentals are even costlier in Argentina than in Chile, starting around US$70 per day and ranging up to US$145 per day for a 4WD vehicle. There should be unlimited mileage within the province of Tierra del Fuego, but verify this before signing the contact.

Ushuaia rental agencies include Avis/Tagle, at San Martín and Belgrano, tel. 02901/422744; Dollar, at Maipú and Sarmiento, tel. 02901/ 432134; and Cardos, San Martín 845, tel. 02901/436388, cardosr@hotmail.com.

Bicycle: DTT Cycles Sport, Avenida San Martín 1258, rents mountain bikes.

VICINITY OF USHUAIA

Ushuaia has more than a dozen travel agencies offering varied excursions in and around Ushuaia, from conventional city tours (US$12, 1.5 hours) to Parque Nacional Tierra del Fuego (US$22–35, four to five hours) and historic Estancia Harberton (US$70–90, eight hours). They also organize activities such as hiking, climbing, horseback riding, fishing, and mountain biking.

Local operators include **All Patagonia,** Juana Fadul 26, tel. 02901/430725 or 02901/430707, allpat@satlink.com, which is the AmEx repre-

UNLEASHING THE BEAGLE

In 1978, the military dictatorships of Chile and Argentina barely avoided war over three small islands in the Beagle Channel and, though successive civilian governments have resolved the territorial dispute, freedom of movement across the channel is not yet what it could be.

According to the Chilean viewpoint, the Argentines have failed to live up to their part of the 1978 agreement, which implied reciprocal border openings at Agua Negra (in the Norte Chico east of La Serena) for Argentina and Puerto Almanza (opposite Puerto Williams) for Chile. For the Chileans, also, it's a matter of principle that, as they provide overland access to Argentine Tierra del Fuego through Chilean territory, the Argentines should supply access to Isla Navarino for the Chileans.

This sounds reasonable enough, but at the same time Argentina's federal government (unlike Chile, which is a unitary state) has to deal with elected provincial authorities still obsessed with territoriality, as well as Ushuaia business interests who astonishingly fear a loss of commerce to flyspeck Puerto Williams.

In early 2001, at the invitation of the Chilean navy, President Ricardo Lagos paid a visit to Puerto Williams in the company of Sernatur head Oscar Santelices and Argentine ambassador Daniel Olmos, so there may soon be something concrete on transportation between Williams and Puerto Almanza. The trip did not produce any definitive statement, but in December Chile declared Puerto Navarino a port of entry to permit day excursions from Ushuaia to the fjords of the southern Beagle Channel (a Chilean businessman has acquired a catamaran for this purpose). Because excursionists will have to stay in Argentina, there are hopes that this step will begin to satisfy Ushuaia interests.

© WAYNE BERNHARDSON

PATAGONIA & TIERRA

view of the Beagle Channel from Glaciar Martial

sentative; **Canal Fun & Nature,** Rivadavia 82, tel. 02901/437395, canal@satlink.com; **Rumbo Sur,** Avenida San Martín 342, tel. 02901/422441, and at the Muelle Turístico, tel. 02901/421039, rumbosur@satlink.com; **Tolkar,** 25 de Mayo 50, Local 20, tel./fax 02901/423396, tecniaustral@tierradelfuego.org.ar; **Tolkeyén,** Maipú 237, tel. 02901/423240; and **Yishka Turismo y Aventura,** Gobernador Godoy 62, tel. 15/510954, yishka@tierradelfuego.org.

Beagle Channel Boat Excursions

From the Muelle Turístico, at the foot of Lasserre, there are boat trips to Beagle Channel wildlife sites such as **Isla de los Lobos,** home to the southern sea lion *(Otaria flavescens)* and the rarer southern fur seal *(Arctocephalus australis),* and **Isla de Pájaros,** a nesting site for seabirds, mostly cormorants. These excursions cost around US$20–35 for a 2.5-hour trip on oversized catamarans such as the *Ana B, Ezequiel B,* and *Luciano Beta.* With extensions to the penguin colony at Estancia Harberton, and a visit to the *estancia* itself, the cost is about US$75.

Rumbo Sur and Tolkeyén sell tickets for these excursions from offices at the foot of the Muelle Turístico, where Héctor Monsalve's Tres Marías Excursiones, tel./fax 02901/421897, marias3@ satlink.com, operates four-hour trips on a smaller vessel (eight passengers maximum) that can get closer to Isla de Lobos than the large catamarans. They can also land on Isla Bridges, a small but interesting island with cormorant colonies, shell mounds, and even the odd penguin.

Ferrocarril Austral Fueguino

During Ushuaia's early days, prison labor built a short-line, narrow-gauge, steam-driven railroad west into what is now Parque Nacional Tierra del Fuego to haul the timber that built the city. Only a few years ago, commercial interests rehabilitated part of the roadbed to create a gentrified, antiseptic tourist version of the earlier line that pretty much ignores the unsavory aspects of its history to focus on the admittedly appealing forest scenery of the Cañadon del Toro.

The train leaves from the Estación del Fin del Mundo, tel. 02901/431600, fax 02901/437696, ush@trendelfindelmundo.com.ar, eight km west of Ushuaia at the municipal campground. From October to mid-April, there are four departures daily, while the rest of the year there are only two. The two-hour-plus excursion costs US$25 pp in tourist class, US$35 pp in first class, and US$75–100 pp with a buffet lunch or dinner.

Round-trip transportation from Ushuaia to the station costs US$14 pp with Manuel Tienda León, Avenida San Martín 995, tel. 02901/422222. Passengers can also use the buses from Ushuaia to Parque Nacional Tierra del Fuego (see the Transportation entry for Ushuaia, above).

Ski Areas

Ushuaia gets most of its visitors in summer, but it's becoming a winter sports center as well, thanks to its proximity to the mountains. Downhill skiing, snowboarding, and cross-country skiing are all possible.

The major annual ski event is the **Marcha Blanca,** which symbolically repeats Argentine liberator José de San Martín's heroic winter crossing of the Andes from Mendoza to assist his Chilean counterpart Bernardo O'Higgins against the Spaniards. Luring upward of 400 skiers, it starts from the Las Cotorras cross-country area and climbs to Paso Garibaldi, the 430-meter pass between the Sierra Alvear and the Sierra Lucas Bridges. It takes place in the second half of August, presumably on the 17th, the anniversary of San Martín's death (Argentine novelist Tomás Eloy Martínez has called his countrymen "cadaver cultists" for their apparent obsession with celebrating death rather than birth dates of their national icons).

The nearest area, only three km west of downtown, is the Club Andino's modest **Pista Andina Wolfgang Wallner,** which has a single lift, capable of carrying 300 skiers, and one 859-meter run on a 30-degree slope. For more information, contact the Club Andino Ushuaia, Juana Fadul 50, tel. 02901/422335. The principal downhill area, though, is the **Centro de Deportes Invernales Luis Martial,** tel. 02901/421423 or 02901/423340, seven km northwest of town at the end of the road, which has a single 1,130-meter run on a 23- degree slope, with a double-seat chairlift capable of carrying 224 skiers per hour.

Most of the areas east of Ushuaia, along RN 3, are for cross-country skiers: **Valle de los Huskies,** tel. 02901/431902, at Km 17; **Tierra Mayor,** tel. 02901/437454, at Km 21; **Las Cotorras,** tel. 02901/499300, at Km 26; and **Haruwen,** tel./fax 02901/424058, at Km 35. All of them rent equipment and offer transportation from Ushuaia.

The only downhill resort east of Ushuaia is the modern **Cerro Castor,** at Km 27, website: www.castor.com, castor@infovia.com.ar, which has up-to-the-minute facilities, including four lifts and 15 different runs. Lift tickets cost US$28–34 per day.

Estancia Harberton

Historic Harberton dates from 1886, when missionary pioneer Thomas Bridges resigned from the Anglican mission at Ushuaia to settle at his new *estancia* at Downeast, later renamed for the Devonshire hometown of his wife Mary Ann Varder. Thomas Bridges, of course, was the author of the famous English-Yámana dictionary, and their son Lucas continued the family literary tradition with *The Uttermost Part of the Earth,* an extraordinary memoir of a boyhood and life among the Yámana.

Harberton continues to be a family enterprise—its present manager and part owner, Tommy Goodall, is Thomas Bridges's great-grandson. While the livestock industry that spawned it has declined in recent years, the *estancia* has opened its doors to organized English- and Spanish-language tours of its grounds and outbuildings; these include the family cemetery, flower gardens, the wool shed, woodshop, boathouse, and a native botanical garden whose Yámana-style lean-tos are far more realistic than their Disneyfied counterparts along the Ferrocarril Austral Fueguino tourist train.

In addition, Tommy Goodall's wife, American biologist Rae Natalie Prosser, has also created the **Museo Acatushún de Aves y Mamíferos Marinos Australes,** website: www.acatashun.com, a bone museum emphasizing the region's marine mammals but also seabirds and a few shorebirds, open 10 A.M.–7 P.M. daily. It is also possible to visit Magellanic penguin rookeries at Isla Martillo (Yecapasela) with Piratur for US$25 pp.

© WAYNE BERNHARDSON

Estancia Harberton

Estancia Harberton, tel. 02901/434447 at Harberton proper, tel. 02901/422742, fax 02901/422743 in Ushuaia, ngoodall@tierradel-fuego.org.ar, is 85 km east of Ushuaia via paved RN.3 and gravel RC-i, but a new coastal road from Ushuaia was likely to shorten the distance soon. From mid-October to mid-April, the *estancia* and museum are open for guided tours (US$12 pp) from 10 A.M.–5 P.M. daily except Christmas, New Year's, and Easter.

Accommodations and Food: With written permission, camping is permitted at unimproved sites; the *estancia* has also remodeled the former cook house (two rooms with four to five beds each and shared bath) and shepherds' house (two rooms of three beds with private bath), but it has not yet fixed rates.

Harberton's **Casa de Té Mánacatush** serves a tasty afternoon tea for US$10 pp, and it was expanding the kitchen to serve additional meals (reservations advised).

Transportation: In summer, both Cooperativa Monte Alvear and Transportes Pasarela provide round-trip transportation from Ushuaia (US$20–30 pp), but these services change frequently. Piratur offers a US$50 package that includes transporta-

tion, the farm and museum tour, and the penguin colony.

Catamaran tours from Ushuaia are more expensive, spend less time at Harberton, and do not include the farm and museum tour fee.

PARQUE NACIONAL TIERRA DEL FUEGO

For pilgrims to the uttermost part of the earth, Parque Nacional Tierra del Fuego, where RN 3 ends at Bahía Lapataia, on the north shore of the Beagle Channel, is Mecca. Despite its size, more than 63,000 hectares, only relatively small parts of its mountainous interior, with its lakes, rivers, glaciers, and summits, are open to public access. Most visitors see only the area around the highway.

Geography and Climate

About 18 km west of Ushuaia, Parque Nacional Tierra del Fuego hugs the Chilean border as its 63,000 hectares stretch from the shores of the Beagle Channel north across Lago Fagnano (Kami). Elevations range from sea level on the channel to 1,450 meters on the summit of Monte Vinciguerra.

PATAGONIA & TIERRA

Most of the park has a maritime climate, with frequent high winds. While rainfall is moderate at about 750 millimeters per annum, humidity is fairly high, as relatively low temperatures also inhibit evapotranspiration—the summer average is only about 10°C. The record maximum temperature is 31°C, while the record minimum is a fairly mild -12°C. At sea level, snow rarely sticks for any length of time, but at higher elevations there are permanent snowfields and glaciers.

Flora and Fauna

Like southernmost Chile, the Argentine sector of Tierra del Fuego is covered by thick southern beech forests. Along the coast, the deciduous *lenga (Nothofagus pumilio)* and the Magellanic evergreen *coigüe (Nothofagus betuloides)* are the main tree species, while the stunted, deciduous *ñirre (Nothofagus antarctica)* forms nearly pure stands at higher elevations. In some low-lying areas, where cool annual temperatures do not permit complete decomposition, dead plant material compresses into *Sphagnum* peat bogs with a cover of ferns and other moisture-loving plants; the insectivorous *Drosera uniflora* swallows unsuspecting bugs.

Until recently Argentina's only protected coastal area, Parque Nacional Tierra del Fuego has a seashore protected by thick beds of kelp that serve as incubators for fish fry. Especially in the areas around Bahía Ensenada and Bahía Lapataia, the shoreline and inshore waters swarm with cormorants, grebes, gulls, kelp geese, oystercatchers, flightless and flying stèamer ducks, snowy sheathbills, and terns. The maritime black-browed albatross skims the channel waters, while the Andean condor sometimes soars overhead. Marine mammals, mostly sea lions, but also fur seals and elephant seals, cavort in the ocean. The rare sea otter *(Lutra felina)* may also exist here.

Inland parts of the park are fauna-poor, though foxes and guanacos are present in small numbers. The most conspicuous mammals are the European rabbit *(Oryctolagus cunniculus)* and the Canadian beaver *(Castor canadiensis),* both of which were introduced for their pelts but have proved to be pests.

Sights and Recreation

Within the park boundaries, but also within walking distance of Ushuaia, the **Glaciar Martial** is the best single hike in the area, offering expansive views of the Beagle Channel and across to the jagged peaks of Chile's Isla Navarino. Reached not by RN 3 but rather by the switchbacking Camino al Glaciar (also known as Luis Martial) that climbs northwest out of Ushuaia, the trailhead begins at the Aerosilla del Glaciar, the ski area's chairlift, that operates 10 A.M.–4:30 P.M. daily except Monday. The chairlift, which charges US$5 pp, reduces the two-hour climb to the foot of the glacier by half; in summer there are frequent buses to the lift (also US$5 pp) with Pasarela, Eben Ezer, Cooperativa Monte Alvear, and Bellavista from the corner of Avenida Maipú and 25 de Mayo, between 9 A.M.–9 P.M.

Where freshwater Lago Roca drains into the sea at Bahía Lapataia, the main sector of the park has several short nature trails and a handful of longer ones; most of the backcountry is off-limits to casual hikers. Slightly less than one km long, the **Senda Laguna Negra** uses a boardwalk to negotiate boggy terrain, studded with ferns, wildflowers, and other water-tolerant species. The 400-meter **Senda de los Castores** (Beaver Trail) winds among southern beeches gnawed to death to form dams and ponds where the beavers themselves occasionally peek out of their dens.

From Lago Roca, the five-km **Senda Hito XXIV** follows the lake's northeastern shore to a small obelisk that marks the Chilean border. If, someday, Argentine and Chilean authorities can get it together, this would be an ideal entry point to the wild backcountry of Estancia Yendegaia, but at present it's illegal to continue beyond the marker. From a junction about one km up the Hito XXIV trail, **Senda Cerro Guanaco** climbs four km northeast up the Arroyo Guanaco to the 970-meter summit of its namesake peak.

Accommodations and Food

Camping is the only option in the park itself, where there are free sites with little or no infrastructure at **Camping Ensenada, Camping Río Pipo, Camping Las Bandurrias, Camping La-**

guna **Verde,** and **Camping Los Cauquenes.** The only paying site, which has hot showers, a grocery, and a *confitería,* is **Camping Lago Roca,** for US$5 pp. The latter tends to be substantially cleaner than the former.

Information

At the park entrance on RN 3, the APN has a Centro de Información, where it collects a US$5 pp entry fee.

Several books have useful information on Parque Nacional Tierra del Fuego, including William Leitch's *South America's National Parks* (The Mountaineers, 1990), which is now out of print; Tim Burford's *Backpacking in Chile & Argentina* (Bradt Publications, 2001); and Clem Linden-

mayer's *Trekking in the Patagonian Andes* (Lonely Planet, 1998). The latter two are hiking guides.

Birders may want to acquire Claudio Venegas Canelo's *Aves de Patagonia y Tierra del Fuego Chileno-Argentina* Punta Arenas: Fantástico Sur Birding, 2000), Ricardo Clark's *Aves de Tierra del Fuego y Cabo de Hornos* (Buenos Aires: Literature of Latin America, 1986), or Enrique Couve's and Claudio Vidal Ojeda's bilingual *Birds of the Beagle Channel* (Punta Arenas: Fantástico Sur Birding & Nature, 2000).

Transportation

Arrange transportation to and from the park in Ushuaia (for details, see the Getting Around entry for Ushuaia).

The Chilean Pacific Islands

By quirks of geography and history, Chile possesses two of the world's most fascinating island outposts: the Juan Fernández archipelago, several hundred kilometers off the coast of Valparaíso, and Easter Island (known to its Polynesian islanders as Rapa Nui), in the subtropical vastness of the Pacific. Administratively, both belong to Region V (Valparaíso), but geographically and culturally they are worlds apart.

Rarely visited and even less appreciated by either Chileans or foreigners, the Juan Fernández archipelago has become a UNESCO World Biosphere Reserve mainly for its singular flora, but it gained global fame in the early 18th century when the Scotsman Alexander Selkirk—the *real* Robinson Crusoe—returned to Britain after spending four solitary years on what, then, was an uninhabited island. Chile annexed Easter Island, the most remote inhabited piece of land on the globe, in the late 19th century. It, in turn, is a UNESCO World Heritage Site for the stunning stone statues that have become global icons.

San Juan Bautista, Isla Robinson Crusoe

© WAYNE BERNHARDSON

view from Selkirk's lookout

The Juan Fernández Archipelago

In his classic seafaring adventure of the 1830s, *Two Years before the Mast,* Richard Henry Dana called Robinson Crusoe's island "the most romantic spot of earth that my eyes had ever seen." Dana's impression was largely thanks to novelist Daniel Defoe, who had placed fiction's most famous castaway in the Caribbean, but the real-life Crusoe was Alexander Selkirk, a Scotsman marooned more than four years on a tiny but mountainous island—then known as Isla Masatierra—in the Pacific.

In what is now almost entirely national park land, visitors to what is now called Isla Robinson Crusoe, in what is now part of Chile, can hike to Selkirk's lookout through forests of rare endemic plant species and observe endangered fur seal colonies in local launches. Air transport from Santiago is fairly frequent and there is an infrequent maritime connection with Valparaíso.

> *The real-life Robinson Crusoe was Alexander Selkirk, a Scotsman marooned more than four years on a tiny but mountainous island—then known as Isla Masatierra— in the Pacific.*

GEOGRAPHY AND CLIMATE

Almost directly west of Valparaíso, 667 km from the continent, three subterranean mountains break the surface of the Pacific to form the Archipiélago de Juan Fernández. The only permanently inhabited one is Isla Robinson Crusoe (ex-Isla Masatierra). Isla Santa Clara (known to early buccaneers as "Goat Island") is only a few kilometers off its southwesterly tip, while Isla Alejandro Selkirk (ex-Isla Masafuera) is 167 km farther west. The original Spanish names are simple geographical references—Masatierra means "closer to land" (the South American continent), Masafuera means "farther out."

All are mere dots in the vastness of the Pacific: Robinson Crusoe's area is only 93 square km, Santa Clara's only five square km, and Alejandro Selkirk's only 85 square km. All are ruggedly

CHILEAN PACIFIC

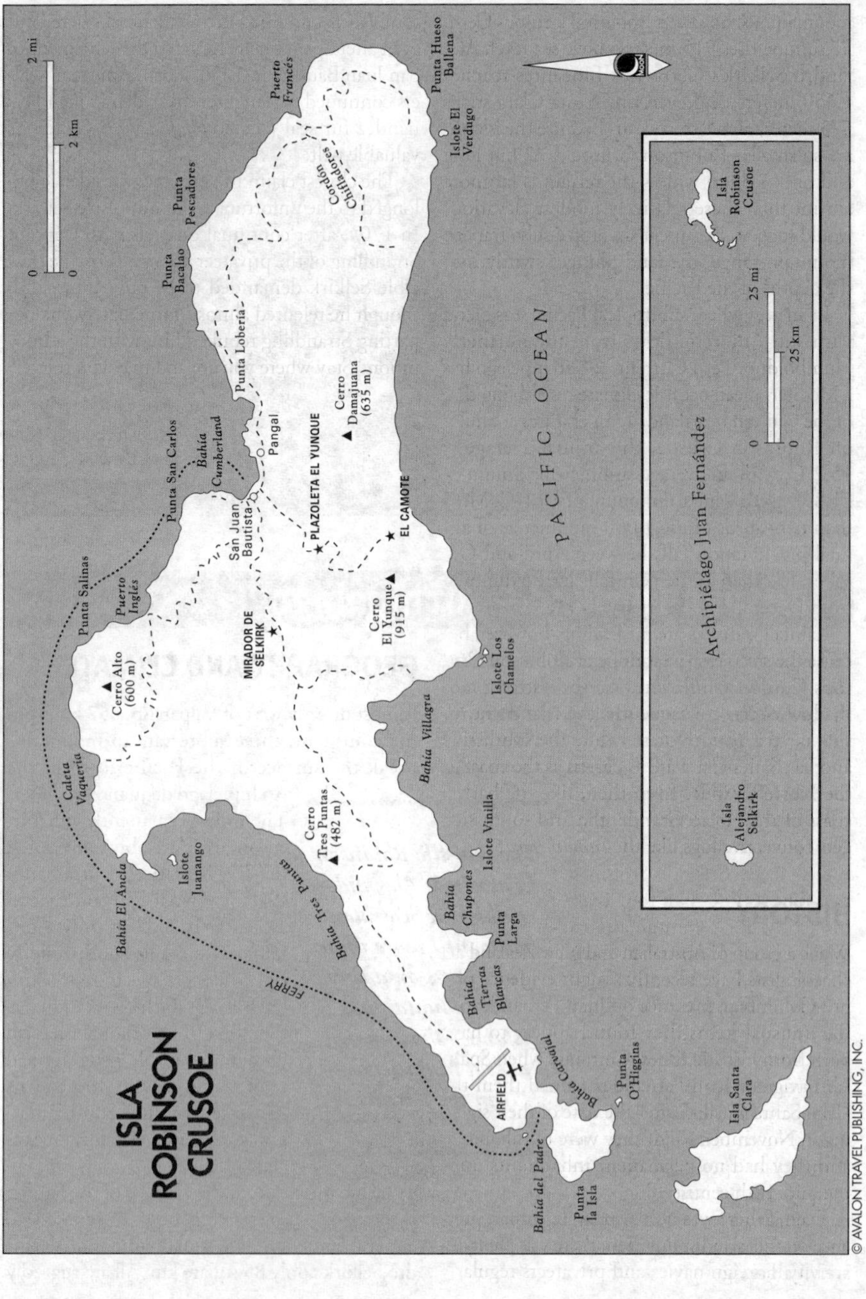

ISLA ROBINSON CRUSOE

Archipiélago Juan Fernández

PACIFIC OCEAN

Punta Hueso Ballena
Islote El Verdugo
Puerto Francés
Cordón Chifladores
Punta Pescadores
Punta Bacalao
Punta Lobería
Cerro Damajuana (635 m)
PLAZOLETA EL YUNQUE
EL CAMOTE
Pangal
Bahía Cumberland
San Juan Bautista
Punta San Carlos
Cerro El Yunque (915 m)
Puerto Inglés
Punta Salinas
MIRADOR DE SELKIRK
Cerro Alto (600 m)
Islote Los Chameleos
Bahía Villagra
Caleta Vaquería
Bahía El Ancla
Islote Juanango
Cerro Tres Puntas (482 m)
Bahía Tres Puntas
FERRY
Islote Vinilla
Bahía Chupones
Punta Larga
Bahía Tierras Blancas
AIRFIELD
Bahía Carvajal
Punta O'Higgins
Bahía del Padre
Punta la Isla
Isla Santa Clara

Isla Robinson Crusoe
Isla Alejandro Selkirk

2 mi
2 km
25 mi
25 km

© AVALON TRAVEL PUBLISHING, INC.

CHILEAN PACIFIC

mountainous, however: Robinson Crusoe's Cerro El Yunque rises 915 meters above sea level, Alejandro Selkirk's Cerro Los Inocentes reaches 1,650 meters, and even tiny Santa Clara sticks 375 meters above the ocean. Because the islands are so small—Robinson Crusoe is 22 km long and only 7.3 km wide—the terrain is far more abrupt than these relatively modest elevations would suggest. Because it sits atop a subterranean mountain range, the land plunges swiftly into the depths of the Pacific.

In an area where subtropical Pacific seas blend with sub-Antarctic flows from the northerly Humboldt or Peru Current, the archipelago has a Mediterranean oceanic climate resembling that of the Chilean heartland. Temperatures are mild: on Robinson Crusoe, the annual average is 15.2°C, with an average summer maximum of 21.8°C and a winter minimum of 10.1°C. More than two-thirds of the 1,000 millimeters of annual precipitation falls between April and October; less than 10 percent falls in the summer, from December to February.

Rainfall statistics are misleading, however, because the steep east-west ridge of Robinson Crusoe's Cordón Chifladores causes a strong rain shadow effect; consequently, the island's north side is verdant rainforest, while the south side and Isla Santa Clara are as barren as the coast of the Norte Grande. Even then, like the barren coast of the Norte Grande, the arid south side gets convective fogs like the *camanchaca*.

HISTORY

While a group of Australian and New Zealand archaeologists have recently sought evidence of a pre-Columbian presence on Juan Fernández, all the unusual items they found appear to have been from historic times. Certainly when Spanish navigator Juan Fernández named them the "Islas Santa Cecilia" after the date of their sighting in November 1574, they were uninhabited, and they had no permanent inhabitants until the mid-18th century.

Even if there was no permanent human presence on the islands until then, there was plenty of activity. Foreign navies and privateers regularly

took R&R and filled their water casks here, and even after Spain finally founded the settlement of San Juan Bautista in 1750, North American sealers continued to slaughter the endemic Juan Fernández fur seal *(Arctocephalus phillippi)* for its valuable pelt.

The closest claim to permanent residence belonged to the unfortunate but impulsive Selkirk. In 1704, after continual quarrels with Captain Strandling of the privateer *Cinque Ports,* the irascible Selkirk demanded to be put ashore and, though he relented almost immediately, the departing Strandling rebuked him with the admonition "Stay where you are and may you starve!" Overcoming his initial despair, Selkirk endured more than four years in nearly utter isolation.

Isla Masatierra was no tropical paradise but, fortunately for Selkirk, it was a temperate, partly man-made one. Wood and water were plentiful, wild cabbages abounded, and, most important, the Spaniards had introduced goats to the island. These feral beasts, while they inflicted incalculable damage on Masatierra's native flora, provided meat and clothing for the solitary exile until his rescue, in 1709, by Commander Woodes Rogers of the privateers *Duke* and *Duchess.* Rogers, whose famous pilot William Dampier had earlier gone to sea with Selkirk, left a vivid description of his first sight of the castaway:

> *Immediately our Pinnace return'd from the shore, and brought abundance of Craw-fish, with a man Cloth'd in Goat-Skins, who look'd wilder than the first Owners of them.*

Returning to Scotland, Selkirk recounted his story to journalist Richard Steele and eventually it found its way into Defoe's novel, though Defoe changed the location from the Pacific to the Caribbean.

In the decades after Selkirk's return to Scotland, figures to visit Juan Fernández included Lord George Anson, who commanded the Royal Navy's South American squadron in the course of a nearly four-year circumnavigation of the globe. Spanish concerns about foreign interlopers led to the establishment of San Juan Bautista, at Bahía Cumberland, by midcentury, but it was mainly a penal colony—in 1814, during the wars of independence, the Spaniards sent 42 prominent political prisoners here.

Even the establishment of Chilean authority in the early 19th century made little difference, as Richard Henry Dana noted that:

All the people there, except the soldiers and a few officers, were convicts sent from Valparaíso. . . . The island . . . had been used by the government as a sort of Botany Bay.

Nor did it stop the exploitation of the island's natural wealth: the valuable fur seal declined so rapidly that U.S. sealer Benjamin Morrell remarked, in an instance of either the most remarkable naïveté or transparent disingenuousness, that:

Perhaps the moral atmosphere may have been so much affected by the introduction of three hundred felons as to become unpleasant to these sagacious animals.

The islands came to world notice again in 1915 when the British navy, once again a factor in the South Pacific, forced the scuttling of the massive German cruiser *Dresden*. Two decades later, the Chilean government created the national park that, in 1977, became a UNESCO World Biosphere reserve. The only parts of the island not belonging to the national park are the airfield and the village of San Juan Bautista, which thrives on the high-value local lobster, flown daily to Santiago restaurants, and a modest but increasing tourist trade.

SAN JUAN BAUTISTA

All of Isla's Robinson Crusoe's 500 or so inhabitants live in the village of San Juan Bautista. Nearly all of them depend directly or indirectly on fishing for the so-called Juan Fernández lobster, in reality a crayfish, and from the modest but growing tourist trade. Both of these are seasonal activities, from October to April or May, though the tourist season peaks in January and February.

Though still one of Chile's most isolated settlements, San Juan Bautista has an increasingly modern infrastructure, with comfortable guest-houses and *cabañas,* a state-of-the-art phone system, satellite TV, and even roads capable of handling a handful of motor vehicles—in a town where it's impossible to work up enough speed to get out of second gear. For all of this, few islanders visit the "continent" except for education or medical emergencies; even then the Chilean air force pays literal "flying visits" to deal with routine medical and dental care.

The outstanding contemporary travel essayist Thurston Clarke describes San Juan Bautista, its people, and surroundings in the opening chapter of his *Searching for Crusoe: A Journey Among the Last Real Islands* (Ballantine, 2001).

Orientation

On Robinson Crusoe's well-watered north shore, at the foot of the precipitous Cordón Chifladores, San Juan Bautista sits on a narrow wave-cut terrace facing the sheltered Bahía Cumberland. One curving main street, Larraín Alcalde, runs most of the length of the village; toward its south end it becomes the pedestrian Costanera El Palillo. Other streets, and footpaths, rise at right angles from Larraín Alcalde.

Launches to and from the airfield at Bahía del Padre use the Embarcadero immediately east of the plaza. There is also a ramp for the Chilean navy's roll-on, roll-off cargo ferry a short distance to the south.

Sights

Best known as the site of Selkirk's solitary exile, San Juan is home to several celebrated historical landmarks, all of them only a short distance from the plaza.

In 1749, alarmed that British privateer Lord Anson had spent three months at Bahía Cumberland preparing to attack the ports of El Callao (Peru), Acapulco (Mexico), and Manila (Philippines), Spain tried to discourage incursions by sending 200 colonists to the island. Less than two years later, a tsunami destroyed the settlement, but in 1770 the Spanish Crown sent engineer José Antonio Birt to plan the fortifications of **Fuerte Santa Bárbara,** now a national monument, with mortar-covered stone walls and gun emplacements with several cannon each.

SELKIRK'S BOOKSHELF

Daniel Defoe's classic *Robinson Crusoe* gave the island its present name, even though he set his novel in the tropical Caribbean rather than the temperate Pacific. Captain Woodes Rogers of the British vessel *Duke* told the story of Selkirk's rescue in *A Cruising Voyage Round the World,* originally published in 1709 but still available as a facsimile (New York: Dover Publications, 1970). Richard Henry Dana, author of the classic sailing adventure *Two Years before the Mast,* available in many editions, also paid a brief visit to Juan Fernández.

Historian Ralph Lee Woodward of the United States published *Robinson Crusoe's Island* (Chapel Hill: University of North Carolina Press, 1969), the most comprehensive history to date despite its age. Most recently, the outstanding travel writer Thurston Clarke used the Juan Fernández group as his point of departure—or arrival—in *Searching for Crusoe: A Journey among the Last Real Islands* (New York: Ballantine, 2001).

British biographer Diana Souhami's *Selkirk's Island* (New York and London: Harcourt, 2001) is a long overdue account of the famous castaway's life, both on and after his lonely exile, but suffers from some egregious geographical errors.

Covering both the Juan Fernández group and Chile's other Pacific possessions, including Easter Island (Rapa Nui), Juan Carlos Castilla's edited collection *Islas Oceánicas Chilenas* (Santiago: Ediciones Universidad Católica, 1988) deals thematically with geography, climate, geology, and terrestrial and maritime natural history. While the articles are in Spanish, each has a concise English summary.

© WAYNE BERNHARDSON

plaques to Alexander Selkirk

CHILEAN PACIFIC

THE SCUTTLING OF THE *DRESDEN*

En route back to Europe in 1914, Captain Fritz Lüdecke of the German cruiser *Dresden* received news of the outbreak of World War I and orders to meet the German South Pacific squadron under Admiral Graf von Spee. After participating in the battle of Coronel (near Concepción) on November 1 of that year, the *Dresden* escaped a surprise British attack at the Falkland Islands on December 8, in which Von Spee died, and fled around Cape Horn to the southern Chilean fjords. After reprovisioning at Punta Arenas with help from the local German colony, it came under pursuit by the British vessels *Glasgow, Kent,* and *Orana* before eventually attempting to take refuge at Bahía Cumberland. In a hopeless situation, Captain Lüdecke scuttled the ship; the surviving crew was taken into Chilean custody and remained on Isla Quiriquina (near Concepción) until 1919.

Partially dismantled in 1817, the fortress was damaged by earthquakes in 1822 and 1835; it was reconstructed in 1974.

After Chilean nationalists suffered the so-called "Desastre de Rancagua" in 1814, Spanish commander Mariano Osorio raided the homes of 42 key figures who, transported to Valparaíso, were shipped to Masatierra aboard the corvette *Sebastiana.* Juan Egaña, Manuel de Salas, U.S. consul Matthew Arnold Hoevel, and the others spent three years in the damp grottos now known as the **Cuevas de los Patriotas,** now a national monument, before the ultimate Chilean victory freed them.

The German headstones at the village's **Cementerio San Juan Bautista,** near the lighthouse at the north end of town, recalls the odyssey of the World War I German cruiser *Dresden,* a national monument that lies beneath the offshore waters where fur seals now cavort (shells from British ships that attacked the *Dresden* are embedded in nearby headlands). Other gravestones bear mostly Spanish but also French inscriptions from the islands' colonists.

At the top of Vicente González, open for tours on request, the **Vivero Conaf** is a nursery that grows native species for reforesting the park and ecological exotics for planting near the village.

Accommodations and Food

The cheapest accommodations alternative is camping, but San Juan Bautista has a handful of decent B&B accommodations that consistently serve local lobster for dinner. Accommodations are limited, however, so reservations are a good idea in January and February.

Just above the shoreline, the municipal **Camping Los Cañones,** Vicente González s/n, has cheap sites with bathrooms and cold showers. **Hostal Charpentier,** Costanera El Palillo s/n, tel. 32/751070, fax 32/751020, rents a *cabaña* capable of lodging up to three people for US$45.

Run by a former Carabinero, directly across from the police station, **Hostal Petit Bruilh,** Vicente González s/n, tel. 32/751107 or 2/7410186 in Santiago, costs US$25 pp with breakfast, US$40 pp with half board that includes first-night lobster. The new **Pensión Farnland,** offering panoramic harbor views at La Pólvora 508, tel. 32/751066, fax 32/751098, charges US$40/64 s/d pp with half board; German, French, and Swiss food are on the menu.

Set among lush gardens, the seaside **Hospedería Cabaña Paulentz,** Costanera El Palillo s/n, tel. 32/751108, fax 32/751105, ilka-paulentz@hotmail.com, charges US$25 pp with breakfast, US$37 pp with half board, and US$58 pp with full board.

Rates at **Hostería Villa Green,** facing the plaza at Larraín Alcalde 246, tel./fax 32/751044, are US$35/60 s/d with breakfast, US$51/83 with half board, and US$60/104 with full board. Despite its rickety exterior, **Hostería Aldea Daniel Defoe,** Costanera El Palillo s/n, tel./fax 32/751075, is a good choice for US$50 pp with half board, US$67 pp with full board.

Reached by a shuttle launch from the Embarcadero or a scenic 45-minute hike that switchbacks up the slope from El Palillo before following the contour most of the rest of the way, Lassa's **Hostería El Pangal,** tel. 32/751112 or tel. 2/2734354, fax 2/2734309 in Santiago, is the classiest place around but it's also pricey at US$110 pp with half board. There are, however, more basic dorm-style rooms for US$49 pp with half board.

San Juan has few places to eat other than its accommodations and at these, it's imperative to give some notice—preferably at least a day for lobster. Directly on the plaza, **El Remo,** tel. 32/751030, is all sandwiches and soft drinks and beer. **El Nocturno,** Alcalde Larraín s/n, tel. 32/751113, serves more elaborate fresh fish dishes. **La Bahía,** Larraín Alcalde s/n, is outstanding despite its modest appearance.

Services

Money: Bring money from the continent, in small bills—San Juan has no formal exchange facilities, relatively little cash circulates, and shopkeepers have trouble making change. Hotels and *hospedajes* will accept U.S. dollars.

Postal: Correos de Chile is on the south side of the plaza; magnetic phonecards are also available here. The area code is 32, the same as Valparaíso and Viña del Mar.

Medical: For medical treatment, the only option is the government-run Posta Rural, Vicente González s/n, tel. 32/751067.

Information

Conaf's tourist kiosk, on Larraín Alcalde near the plaza, has Sernatur brochures with maps and information about the village and the national park, and it collects park admission fees. Its main office, about 500 meters uphill from the shoreline at Vicente González s/n, tel. 32/751004 or 32/751022, can provide information if the former is closed.

Transportation

For most intending visitors, air taxis from Santiago will be the only practicable means of transportation, but for those with plenty of time, or particularly good timing, sea travel from Valparaíso is conceivable.

Air: Several companies fly air taxis from Santiago's former main domestic Aeropuerto Los Cerrillos, on the southwestern outskirts of town, and from Aeródromo Tobalaba, in the southeastern suburbs. Flights are frequent in January and February, few outside the November to

March period, and windy or rainy weather can abort takeoffs and landings at any time of year. Visitors should arrange their itineraries to be able to stay a day or two extra in case of adverse weather. Round-trip fares are about US$400, but there are occasional small discounts and packages that include hotel stays and full board.

Note that San Juan Bautista is about 1.5 hours by motor launch from the passenger pier at Bahía del Padre, an ocean-flooded caldera reached by a short but precipitous dirt road from the airfield, which occupies one of few relatively level sites on the entire island. The boat transfer, usually included in the air ticket, is scenic but the seas can be rough on visitors unaccustomed to relatively small ships; consider medication.

Lassa flies out of Aeródromo Tobalaba, where it also has its offices at Avenida Larraín 7941, La Reina, Santiago, tel. 2/2735209 or 2/2731458, fax 2/2734309, lassa@terra.cl. At San Juan Bautista, it occupies a cubbyhole office behind the gymnasium, near the Embarcadero.

Several companies use Cerrillos but some have offices elsewhere. Transportes Aéreos Isla Robinson Crusoe is at Avenida Pajaritos 3030, Oficina 604, Maipú, tel. 2/5344650, fax 2/5313772, tairc@cmet.net; its San Juan representative is at La Pólvora 226, tel. 32/751099. Vic's Servicios Aéreos is at Camino Lonquén s/n, Calera de Tango, tel. 2/8553377, tel./fax 2/8553605, Parcela 12-A, serviaereo@entelchile.net; the postal address is Casilla 38, Cerrillos, Santiago.

Sea: Sailing from Valparaíso to Juan Fernández requires patience and good timing. It is, for instance, easier to get information on the quarterly naval vessels than it once was, but sailings are not any more frequent and usually require reservations a month or more in advance.

For naval vessels, contact the Comando de Transporte at the Primera Zona Naval, Plaza Sotomayor 592, Valparaíso, tel. 32/506884, whose supply ships carry civilian passengers for about US$24 pp per day; the round-trip takes five days, but if spending any time on the island you'll need to fly back from San Juan Bautista.

The private shipping company Naviera del Sur, Blanco 1041, Oficina 18, Valparaíso, tel. 32/594304, sails the small freighter *Navarino* to

San Juan Bautista early every month, but reservations are imperative for a ship that has only four passenger bunks. Rates are US$95 each way for the two-day trip.

Getting Around

Walking is the best way to get around San Juan and most of the national park, but some sights are most easily accessible by launch—ask at the Municipalidad, around the Embarcadero, or your accommodations may be able to arrange something. The Municipalidad maintains a list of prices for launch excursions around the island.

Tours: Endémica Expediciones, tel. 32/751077 or 32/751023, website: www.endemica.com, endemica@ctcinternet.cl, has an extensive offering of diving, hiking, fishing, and other excursions from San Juan. Javier Gana's Archipiélago Expediciones, tel. 32/751069, website: www.archipielagoexpediciones.cl, archipielagoexpediciones@hotmail.com, has similar offerings.

Vic's Servicios Aéreos (see Transportation/Air, above) also offers diving and other excursions around the island. Santiago-based Ecoturismo Islas del Tesoro, tel. 2/3354325, cellular 09/4388319, paralelo33jdiaz@entelchile.net, arranges excursions from the mainland and also excursions on the mainland before and after.

PARQUE NACIONAL ARCHIPIÉLAGO JUAN FERNÁNDEZ

Almost contiguous with the archipelago—excluding only the village of San Juan Bautista and the airfield at the southeast corner of the island—Parque Nacional Archipiélago Juan Fernández comprises 9,571 hectares of protected land that varies from barren desert to dense endemic forest on Isla Robinson Crusoe, Isla Santa Clara, and Isla Marinero Alejandro Selkirk. From a wildlife perspective, it may be as noteworthy for what it excludes: all the surrounding offshore areas fall under control of the Chilean navy's Gobernación Marítima.

Flora and Fauna

Having evolved in oceanic isolation, about 70 percent of the archipelago's plant species are endemic, despite broad similarities with flora from tropical Hawaii, the Andean highlands, temperate New Zealand, and sub-Antarctic Magallanes. Even at the genus level, nearly 20 percent of the flora is endemic.

There exist three principal plant communities: the evergreen rainforest, an evergreen heath, and an herbaceous steppe. In all likelihood, the lushly diverse evergreen forest once reached all the way to the shoreline, but aggressive introduced plant species, imported both intentionally and accidentally, and damage from nonnative grazers such as goats and cattle have squeezed it out of the lower elevations. On higher slopes, climbing vines cover the trunks of endemic tree species such as the *luma (Nothomyrcia fernandeziana)* and the *chonta* palm *(Juania australis),* which shade a verdant understory of tree ferns such as *Dicksonia berteroana* and *Thyrsopteris elegans.* In Selkirk's time, visiting mariners gathered forest products such as the fruits of the wild cabbage tree *Dendroseris litoralis,* which Woodes Rogers praised as "very good."

On shallow soils at higher elevations, or on nearly sheer gradients, the evergreen heath features smaller trees of the genus *Robinsonia* and tree ferns such as *Blechnum cyadifolium.* In the drier southeastern part of Isla Robinson Crusoe and on Isla Santa Clara, bunch grasses such as *Stipa fernandeziana* provide a patchy cover on the steppe.

The replacement of native flora was well under way even during colonial times, when privateers planted their own gardens. When Maria Graham visited the island with Lord Cochrane in 1823, they found apples, cherries, pears, and quinces, and mint and parsley. Barely a decade later, wrote Richard Henry Dana,

> **Ground apples, melons, grapes, strawberries of an enormous size, and cherries, abound here. The latter are said to have been planted by Lord Anson.**

Other species have been less benevolent and even invasive, such as the wild blackberry *(Rubus ulmifolius)* and the *maqui (Aristotelia chilensis),* a shrub that has displaced native forest but has an important economic use for lobster traps.

The Juan Fernández group has no native land mammals, but 60 percent of its land bird species are endemic, most notably the strikingly red male Juan Fernández hummingbird *(Sephanoides fernandensis),* which feeds on the native cabbage trees. Ground-nesting seabirds, most notably Cook's petrel *(Pterodroma cookii defilippiana),* have suffered depredations from exotic mammals such as the Norway rat, the domestic cat, and the South American coatimundi.

While Morrell and others hunted the Juan Fernández fur seal to near extinction in the 19th century, a Conaf census has counted nearly 10,000 individuals—admittedly a small fraction of hundreds of thousands that sealers killed. The near absence of a continental shelf provides little habitat for inshore fauna, but the misleadingly named Juan Fernández lobster *(Jasus frontalis)* fetches premium prices in Santiago's finest restaurants (in fact, it's a crayfish).

Sights and Recreation

Most of the park's attractions are within walking distance of San Juan Bautista, though in some cases it's a stiff hike.

El Palillo: At the south end of town, swimmers dive off the rocks at El Palillo, where Conaf has a wooded 15-site picnic ground (no camping, however) with fire pits and trash collection. From here, a trail switchbacks up the hillside before leveling out and leading to Hostería Pangal.

Mirador de Selkirk: Unquestionably the park's single most popular destination, Selkirk's lookout is a stiff hike that starts at Subida El Castillo, at the south end of San Juan's plaza. It gains 565 meters in about 2,700 meters—an average grade of nearly 21 percent through an initial badly eroded area that quickly becomes covered with blackberry vines and nonnative scrub before finally entering a dense native forest with a verdant undergrowth of ferns. This is a designated nature trail, and Conaf's inexpensive booklet *Sendero Interpretativo Mirador Alejandro Selkirk* describes the native and nonnative plants and wildlife and explains environmental damage that the area has suffered.

From a saddle on the ridge between the two sides of the island, the hiker's reward is a series of views from Bahía Cumberland and San Juan on the north to the airfield to Isla Santa Clara on the south. On the saddle itself, a pair of plaques honor Selkirk's memory. Royal Navy officers placed the first, cast by John Child & Son of Valparaíso, which says:

> *In memory of Alexander Selkirk, Mariner, a native of Largo, in the county of Fife, Scotland, who lived on this island in complete solitude for four years and four months.*
>
> *He was landed from the* **Cinque Ports** *galley, 96 tons, 16 guns,* A.D. *1704 and was taken off in the* **Duke,** *privateer, 12th Feb., 1709.*
>
> *He died lieutenant of* HMS **Weymouth,** A.D. *1723, aged 47 years.*
>
> *This tablet is erected near Selkirk's lookout, by Commodore Powell and the officers of* HMS **Topaze,** A.D. *1868.*

The second, placed nearby by a Scottish relative, reads:

> *Tablet placed here by Allan Jardine of Largo, Fife, Scotland, direct descendant of Alexander Selkirk's brother David. Remembrance 'Till a' the seas gang dry and the rocks melt in the sun.' January 1983.*

From the saddle, where wind and fog can make the weather far cooler than at sea level, the trail descends through the densely vegetated Sector Villagra before emerging onto the desert side of the island; in total, it's about 10 km farther to the airfield. The trail passes the island's principal fur seal colony at **Bahía Tierras Blancas,** where there are about 1,700 animals.

Some visitors hike to the airfield to catch their flights back to the mainland, but this requires an early departure and, if the flight is delayed for weather conditions, it might entail camping a night at the barren airfield. The only reliable water source en route is a conspicuous pipe where the trail crosses Estero El Castillo, the village's water supply, and begins to switchback toward Selkirk's lookout.

Plazoleta El Yunque: At the foot of the island's highest peak, Plazoleta El Yunque is a shorter, easier hike than Selkirk's lookout. Beginning at the village power plant and gaining only 257 meters in three km, the road becomes a footpath that leads to this placid forest clearing where Hugo Weber, who escaped the sinking of the *Dresden,* built a house whose foundations still survive. Conaf maintains a picnic area here, where one night's camping is permitted.

From Plazoleta El Yunque, Conaf permission and a guide are necessary to ascend the steep rugged route to **El Camote,** a saddle with views to equal or surpass those of Selkirk's lookout, particularly the sight of *El Verdugo,* a sheer volcanic needle that rises 157 meters out of the sea. The climb to El Camote, through thick native forest, requires as much or more arm strength than hiking ability, as it often requires pulling yourself up by tree limbs. **Cerro El Yunque** itself, a 915-meter pinnacle, is virtually unattainable.

Puerto Inglés: Only a short shot north of San Juan Bautista by launch, but two hours via a zigzag trail that climbs and descends from the ridge at the west end of Calle La Pólvora, Puerto Inglés is the site of Selkirk's replica shelter and, more recently, the seemingly futile but persistent treasure hunt of U.S. adventurer Bernard Keiser. For nonhikers, the launch to Puerto Inglés costs about US$15; in rough seas, the landing is tricky and the rocks are slippery.

Puerto Vaquería: On a small inlet on Robinson Crusoe's north shore, Puerto Vaquería features a small fur seal colony and a Conaf *refugio.* The landing is equally if not more awkward than that at Puerto Inglés.

Puerto Francés: On Robinson Crusoe's eastern shore, about half an hour by launch from San Juan Bautista, Puerto Francés is a desert area where the presence of French pirates led Spain to build a now-ruined set of ramparts overlooking the sea. From the Conaf *refugio* here, a trail climbs the **Quebrada Los Picos** through gradually thickening forest to *Cerro La Piña;* a longer trail connects Quebrada Los Picos with Pangal.

Isla Marinero Alejandro Selkirk: Rarely visited except by lobstermen, Conaf's seasonal ranger, and the odd cruise ship, the former Isla Masafuera must be one of the loneliest places on earth—even more so, in Selkirk's time, than Masatierra (Selkirk, ironically, had no connection whatsoever with the island that now bears his name). It's possible to hire a boat at San Juan Bautista, but it's not cheap; contact Julia González, tel. 32/751062, or Juanita Díaz at Ecoturismo Islas del Tesoro (see above).

Information

At its information kiosk in San Juan, Conaf now collects a US$5 park admission charge for foreigners, US$3 for Chilean nationals, and more for those who come with specific activities in mind. Senior citizens and children pay US$1 pp.

Transportation

The boat trip from Bahía del Padre to San Juan Bautista is a good introduction to Robinson Crusoe's geography—it covers nearly half the island's circumference—but hiring a launch in San Juan gives you much more flexibility and the option, if seas permit, of going ashore in otherwise inaccessible areas. Figure about US$150 for a five-hour circumnavigation of the island; expenses can be shared by as many as five or six people.

Rapa Nui (Easter Island)

More than 1,000 years ago, some of history's most truly intrepid travelers sailed east on Polynesian outriggers to the most remote outpost in the Pacific, where their descendents carved colossal *moai* from volcanic quarries, moved them over rugged terrain without the wheel and without damage, and hoisted them onto massive platforms known as *ahu*. It's still possible to reach Easter Island by boat—freighter, anyway—but almost everyone nowadays prefers the five-hour flight from Santiago in order to spend more time wandering among the world-famous monuments.

The world's most isolated inhabited place—the next closest settlement is more than 1,900 km to the west—Rapa Nui acquired its English name indirectly through Dutchman Jacob Roggeveen, the first European to see the island. Sighting land on Easter Sunday, April 5, 1772, he named it for the date after the custom of his era, and his designation spread to every European language.

Chileans commonly refer to the island as Isla de Pascua, but there is a broad consensus for using indigenous Polynesian terminology whenever possible with regard to territory, ethnology, and linguistics. Within this consensus, though, there are conflicting opinions about usage of the terms "Rapa Nui," which some consider a European invention, and "Rapanui," which is closer to other Polynesian languages. This book uses "Rapa Nui" to describe the territory, and "Rapanui" for the islanders and their language.

GEOGRAPHY AND CLIMATE

Only a few degrees south of the Tropic of Capricorn, oceanic Rapa Nui is one of a handful of islands to emerge from a submarine volcanic chain that stretches west from the Chilean mainland; the others, with no permanent inhabitants, are San Félix, San Ambrosio, and Sala y Gómez. The closest populated land is Pitcairn Island, 1,900 km to the west, beyond which are the Polynesian outposts of the Mangarevas or Gambier Islands (2,500 km to the west) and the Marquesas Islands (3,200 km to the northwest).

CHILEAN PACIFIC

© WAYNE BERNHARDSON

Rano Raraku, Rapa Nui

RAPA NUI
(EASTER ISLAND)

PACIFIC OCEAN

Cabo Norte

Playa Ovahe

Bahía de La Perouse

Playa Anakena

AHU ATURE HUKI ★
CONAF ANAKENA ■

AHU TE PITO TE KURA ★

Parque Nacional Rapa Nui

Maunga Terevaka (506 m) ▲

Motu Tautara

AHU TEPEU ★

ANA TE PAHU ★

AHU AKIVI ★

Fundo Vaitea

Rano Raraku (300m)
CONAF RANO RARAKU ■

AHU HANGA TETENGA ★

AHU AKAHANGA ★

AHU VAIHU ★

Ko te Ava o Iko

Maunga Pukatikei (370 m) ▲

Península Poike

Cabo O'Higgins

Cabo Roggeveen

Motu Marotiri ○

AHU TONGARIKI ★

PACIFIC OCEAN

PUNA PAU ✛

Hanga Roa

Maunga Orito (218 m) ▲

AEROPUERTO INTERNACIONAL MATAVERI ✈

AHU VINAPU ★

Rano Kau

Motu Iti
Motu Nui

Cabo Sur

Motu Kao Kao

ORONGO ★
CONAF ORONGO ■

2 mi
2 km

CHILE
Santiago

Archipiélago Juan Fernández

Rapa Nui

TROPIC OF CAPRICORN

PACIFIC OCEAN

© AVALON TRAVEL PUBLISHING, INC.

Even farther from the Chilean coast—about 3,700 km west of the mainland port of Caldera—Rapa Nui consists of lava flows from three distinct cones that fused to form a triangular land mass of just 171 square km, resting on a subterranean platform that plunges abruptly into the depths of the Pacific. It is nowhere longer than 24 km and nowhere wider than 12 km.

All these volcanoes are dormant but the most recent, the northerly 507-meter Maunga Tereveka, erupted as recently as 10,000 years ago. The others are much older, dating from about three million years ago: the southwesterly 410-meter crater of Rano Kau, filled with water, and the easterly 400-meter Pu A Katiki. Both are nearly three million years old, with their last eruptions more than 180,000 years ago.

In addition to these major craters, there are several smaller but significant craters and other volcanic landforms, including sprawling surface lava fields and subterranean tubes that extend for considerable distances. Much of the island's perimeter consists of rugged headlands, with no truly sheltered anchorages and only a few sandy beaches. There are no surface streams, as rainfall percolates quickly into the porous terrain, but a few areas have sufficient soil for horticulture.

ISLA DE PASCUA Y CHILE
$ 60
CORAL (Pocillopora danea)
FLORA Y FAUNA MARINA
CASA DE MONEDA DE CHILE

As a subtropical oceanic island, Rapa Nui experiences relatively minor seasonal variations—the mean summer maximum temperature is 27.3°C, the mean winter minimum 15.5°C, and the annual average 20.7°C. The average annual precipitation is 1,126 millimeters; most rain falls between late autumn and early spring, but cloudbursts can occur at any time of year.

FLORA AND FAUNA

Hundreds of years of human occupation have totally transformed Rapa Nui's flora and fauna; where native forests of *toromiro (Sophora toromiro)* and stands of palms once flourished, dense plantations of introduced eucalyptus now cover the slopes of Rano Kau crater. Grasses cover most of the hillsides.

Most remote oceanic islands are, of course, flora- and fauna-poor. Abundant when the first Polynesian settlers arrived, the sooty tern *(Sterna fuscata)* survives in reduced numbers on offshore islets. The first Polynesian immigrants brought their own domestic flora and fauna—crops such as the sweet potato and edible animals such as the chicken and Polynesian rat. Europeans brought both accidental and purposeful introductions—the Norway or brown rat that hitched a lift on oceanic voyages and the horses, cattle, and sheep that they brought as economic domesticates.

There is a good synopsis of Rapa Nui's native and introduced flora and their uses—both horticultural and medicinal—in Conaf's well-illustrated *Vegetación de Rapa Nui: Historia y Uso Tradicional* (1996), by Marcos Rauch, Patricia Ibáñez, and José Miguel Ramírez. Available from Conaf both here and in Santiago, it costs US$5.

ENVIRONMENTAL ISSUES

There is growing concern about the impact of tourism on the island' cultural resources and quality of life, and a Santiago consulting firm is conducting a study of the island's tourist "carrying capacity." While the evaluation appears to be focusing on issues of water, land, and food, water is probably the most important factor—few

BUG ALERT

It's not cause for panic, but an outbreak of dengue fever, probably arrived from French Tahiti, occurred on Easter Island in early 2002. Long-sleeved shirts and long trousers, or else appropriate applications of insect repellent, are advisable. Chilean health authorities are undertaking measures to eradicate the white-spotted mosquito vector.

CHILEAN PACIFIC

people rely on horticulture for their livelihoods, and food can be imported even if air freight becomes more expensive.

Still, the possibility exists that, in the near future, authorities may restrict access to the island, perhaps by instituting a staggered price system that would disperse business throughout the year rather than concentrate it in the summer. At the local end, relative affluence is causing problems such as the proliferation of automobiles, with their associated pollution, and the accumulation of solid waste on an island with little land to spare.

HISTORY

Rapa Nui's dramatically improbable *moai* have attracted global attention, and deservedly so—their iconic appeal is undeniable, and to contemplate how such an isolated, unknown people could create them and, without benefit of the wheel or draft animals, transport them across rugged terrain and erect them on massive platforms excites the imagination. These matters, though, often distract visitors from even bigger but ultimately related questions—the regularity and direction of cultural contacts across the vast Pacific, how and when the first immigrants arrived at this remote speck of land, and how an apparent handful of people created a society with monuments that seem far likelier in empires with millions of inhabitants.

The peopling of the Pacific is a complex topic, and its relationship to the Americas even more complex. In the remote past, as humans spread out of Africa to inhabit Europe and Asia, they eventually reached North America via a land-bridge across the Bering Strait before dispersing throughout the Caribbean and South America; by at least 12,000 years ago, when melting continental glaciers and rising seas closed the land

Rapa Nui's dramatically improbable moai *often distract visitors from even bigger but ultimately related questions—the regularity and direction of cultural contacts across the vast Pacific, how and when the first immigrants arrived at this remote speck of land, and how an apparent handful of people created a society with monuments that seem far likelier in empires with millions of inhabitants.*

bridge, humans had occupied the entire Western Hemisphere, even if their density was low. Over succeeding millennia, societies and civilizations in the Eastern and Western Hemispheres developed in geographical isolation.

Columbus's voyages across the Atlantic ended this isolation forever, but it had never been complete. Vikings had reached Greenland and Labrador around the end of the first millennium A.D., but Polynesians may have reached South America even earlier. Or vice-versa, according to speculations by the likes of Norwegian adventurer Thor Heyerdahl, who claimed pre-Columbian South Americans sailed west to Polynesia.

In this larger context, Rapa Nui fits into the long-standing academic controversy between advocates of "independent invention," who emphasize the parallel development of cultures separated by the oceans, and adherents of "diffusionism," who argue the importance of pre-Columbian contacts. As in many academic debates, there are political overtones, as diffusionists often stand accused of disparaging the ostensibly derivative achievements of New World peoples.

In 1947, on his famous voyage on the raft *Kon-Tiki,* Heyerdahl proved it possible to sail west from South America to Polynesia with the help of prevailing currents. Still, he never proved that was the way it really happened, and the pre-Columbian sailing tradition in the Americas, although it covered distances as great as those from Peru to Mexico, was primarily coastal. Still, there is material evidence of movement in both directions—key economic plants, most notably the tropical coconut and sweet potato (the latter an American domesticate), were present in both hemispheres in pre-Columbian times.

It is likelier that, with their elaborate seafaring tradition, Polynesian islanders reached Rapa Nui first (though it's conceivable they did so *after* crossing the Pacific to Peru). What seems clear is that voyages across the Pacific, in spacious double outriggers capable of carrying food, water, and domestic animals, took place on a basis of knowledge and skill. They were not fortuitous—trans-Pacific voyagers were unlikely to have survived so long a trip for which they had not planned. By observing currents, winds, clouds, and the flight patterns of birds, they could often infer the existence of land at great distances.

The Peopling of Rapa Nui

Besides the diffusionism controversy, in which Rapa Nui plays a part because of its geographical position as the most easterly inhabited point for voyages from Polynesia and the most westerly for voyages from South America, the other great issue in local history is population. While it may not be immediately obvious, it directly touches the creation and destruction of the *moai*.

According to oral tradition, Rapa Nui received two waves of immigration starting around the fifth century A.D., though the first material evidence is far more recent, about A.D. 800. Playa Anakena, the sandy beach of the north shore of the island, was the ostensible landing place of Hotu Matua, leader of the eastern *hanau eepe*, while the *hanau momoko* arrived from the west. Many accounts portray these warring groups as "Long Ears" and "Short Ears," because of the practice of earlobe elongation, but this is the result of Heyerdahl's erroneous translation of terminology that, according to Georgia Lee, would more correctly be "corpulent people" and "thin people."

In the aftermath of internal and external conflicts that nearly annihilated the island's population by the mid-19th century, oral testimony passed through a handful of survivors is, to say the least, an imprecise means of tracking local history. What seems clear, though, is that a growing population led to a remarkably complex and specialized society that produced the great monuments but which, when its limited land and sea base could support no further growth, disintegrated into a series of clan-based resource conflicts.

In its early centuries, Rapa Nui was a thinly populated island with a redistributive economy, but as the population grew its *akiri* (kings) and priests presided over a society where artisans fashioned the enormous *moai* and commoners performed the dangerously laborious process of transporting the megaliths to the imposing *ahu* (altars or platforms) on which they would stand. This consumed enormous amounts of resources, including food and forests, until shortages ignited a series of wars that, by A.D. 1600 or so, divided the island, toppled many of the *moai* that symbolically represented the lineages, and even degenerated into ritual cannibalism. In a situation that many modern scientists might interpret as a classic imbalance between population and resources, the society seen by the first Europeans was a precarious one, and things would get far worse before they got better.

The European Voyages

For more than two centuries after Magellan's circumnavigation of the globe, Rapa Nui remained unknown to Europeans. Then, on Easter Sunday of April 1722, Dutch Admiral Jacob Roggeveen's expedition became the first Europeans to sight and set foot on the island. Roggeveen's crew arrived, apparently, at a time of relative peace and prosperity; one member, Carl Behrens, published an account in which he remarked on the productive gardens, noted the *moai* and the religious ceremonies associated with them, and described the islanders' appearance in some detail. In 1770, claiming the island for Spain, the expedition of Felipe González de Haedo made similar observations, noting abundant produce and the presence of cave dwellings and *hare paenga*, the boat-shaped houses whose foundations are still common on the island today.

The most noteworthy European voyage, though, was that of the famous Englishman, Captain James Cook, in 1774. Cook's familiarity with Polynesia made him the first European to link the Rapanui explicitly to the rest of Oceania, and he was also the first to report damaged *ahu*, toppled, broken *moai*, and a ragged populace that bore the scars of conflict. He also remarked that the *moai* seemed to have lost their ritual significance, perhaps an indicator of the transition from a lineage-based tradition of ancestor worship to the Tangata Manu (birdman) cult of the creator Makemake.

THE RAPA NUI BOOKSHELF

Rapa Nui has spawned a voluminous literature that varies from the literally fantastic to the tediously scholarly and everything in between. The best example of the former is Erich von Däniken's monumentally silly and universally discredited, at least among serious readers, *Chariots of the Gods*, which linked Rapa Nui and similar sites around the world to extraterrestrials. Unfortunately, it never seems to go away completely.

For readers who can handle Spanish, the best single general source on Rapa Nui's geography and environment is Juan Carlos Castilla's *Islas Oceánicas Chilenas* (Santiago: Ediciones Universidad Católica de Chile, 1987), an edited series of essays that also covers the Juan Fernández archipelago.

Katherine Routledge, an Englishwoman who led a private research team to Rapa Nui in 1914, left her recollections in *The Mystery of Easter Island: The Story of an Expedition*, originally published in 1919 but now available in a facsimile edition (Kempton, IL: Adventures Unlimited Press, 1998). Based partly on five months' residence on the island only a few years after Routledge's visit, John MacMillan Brown's otherwise sensible *The Riddle of the Pacific* (1924) suffers from the loopy notion that Rapa Nui was related to an Atlantis-style lost continent in the Pacific; it's also available in a facsimile edition (Kempton, IL: Adventures Unlimited Press, 1995).

The well-known anthropologist Alfred Métraux published *Ethnology of Easter Island* (1940), also available as a reprint (Honolulu: Bishop Museum Press, 1971). Thor Heyerdahl's Norwegian expedition published its complete (if flawed and now largely dated) results in *Reports of the Norwegian Archaeological Expedition to Easter Island & the East Pacific. Volume 1: Archaeology of Easter Island* (London: Allen & Unwin, 1962).

Heyerdahl, of course, aroused popular audiences with *Kon-Tiki* (Chicago: Rand McNally, 1952), a chronology of the raft voyage across the Pacific, and with *Aku-Aku: The Secret of Easter Island* (London: Allen & Unwin, 1958). He expounded his audacious but largely disregarded speculations on South American colonization in *American Indians in the Pacific: The Theory behind the Kon-Tiki Expedition* (London: Allen & Unwin, 1952).

Arriving with the Métraux party in 1935, the Bavarian Capuchin priest Sebastián Englert remained on Rapa Nui until his death in 1970, publishing several books including the oral tradition history *Island at the Center of the World* (New York: Scribner's, 1970). Englert, for whom the island museum and library are named, published several other scholarly works in Spanish. His countryman Thomas Barthel attempted to translate the *rongorongo* tablets in *The Eighth Land: The Polynesian Discovery and Settlement of Easter Island* (Honolulu: University Press of Hawaii, 1978).

Several books deal with pre-Columbian contacts across the Pacific, including the collection

---

While Cook's reports contrasted with the apparent stability, harmony, and prosperity seen by the Roggeveen and González expeditions, in all likelihood neither of the earlier voyages managed a thorough assessment of conditions of the island. Later visits, by the Frenchman Jean François de Gallup, Comte de la Perouse, in 1786, and by the Russian ship *Neva* under the command of Yuri Lisiansky in the early 19th century, present contradictory visions of the island, suggesting that the fortunes of the islanders, in peace and war, went up and down. As frictions periodically intensified, *moai* were toppled and broken, and only a handful remained standing. Even before the indigenous population felt the full impact of imperialism and colonialism, the population had declined rapidly from a maximum that may have reached 20,000 (though most estimates are lower).

Contact, Conflict, and Chileanization

Rapidly expanding commercial activities—first whaling, then the systematic planting of tropical crops such as coffee, copra, rubber, and sugar—transformed the Pacific by the middle of the 19th century. While Rapa Nui, with its limited agricultural potential, did not experience this transformation immediately, the population suf-

Man across the Sea (Austin: University of Texas Press, 1971), edited by Carroll L. Riley, J. Charles Kelley, Campbell W. Pennington, and Robert L. Rands. Michael Levison, R. Gerard Ward, and John Webb used computer models to try to solve the peopling of the Pacific in *The Settlement of Polynesia: A Computer Simulation* (Canberra: Australian National University Press, 1973). See also *Easter Island in Pacific Context* (Los Osos, CA: Easter Island Foundation, 1997) by Christopher M. Stevenson, Georgia Lee, and William Morin.

New Zealand anthropologist Steven Fischer has managed to explicate the Rapanui *rongorongo* tablets, long thought indecipherable, in his popular *Glyphbreaker* (New York: Springer-Verlag, 1997) and the more scholarly *Rongorongo: The Easter Island Script: History, Traditions, Texts* (Oxford: Oxford University Press, 1997). William Liller analyzes the astronomical aspects of Rapa Nui monuments in *The Ancient Observatories of Rapa Nui: The Archaeoastronomy of Easter Island* (Los Osos, CA: Easter Island Foundation, 1993).

Petroglyph specialist Georgia Lee has published *The Rock Art of Easter Island* (Los Angeles: UCLA, 1992), as well as *An Uncommon Guide to Easter Island*, (Arroyo Grande, CA: International Resources, 1990). The latter, which can be ordered through the Easter Island Foundation (see below), comes with an annually updated information sheet on island services.

Henry Maude chronicled the Peruvian slave raid and similar "blackbirding" in *Slavers in Paradise: The Peruvian Labor Trade in Polynesia, 1862–1864* (Palo Alto: Stanford University Press, 1981). Accounts of contemporary Rapa Nui are fewer than they should be, but look for J. Douglas Porteous's *The Modernization of Easter Island* (Victoria: University of Victoria, British Columbia, 1981), and the second edition of Grant McCall's *Rapanui: Tradition and Survival on Easter Island* (Honolulu: University Press of Hawaii, 1994).

For US$30 per annum, real Rapanuiphiles can subscribe to the quarterly *Rapa Nui Journal*, c/o the Easter Island Foundation, P.O. Box 6774, Los Osos, CA 93412-6774, tel. 805/528-8558, fax 805/534-9301, rapanuibooks@worldnet.att.net. In addition to serious scholarly articles on Rapa Nui, its history, and its people, it also provides the latest island gossip, travel information, and even "*moai* sightings" around the world.

Maps

The best, most easily available map is ITM's *Easter Island*, at a scale of 1:30,000, readily found at bookstores in the United States and Canada; it can also be ordered through International Travel Maps, 530 W. Broadway, Vancouver, BC V5Z 1E9, Canada, tel. 805/879-3621, fax 805/879-4521, itmb@itmb.com.

In Chile, look for JLM Mapas' *Isla de Pascua Trekking Map*, at a scale of 1:32,000. It also includes a village map of Hanga Roa.

fered a major Peruvian slave raid and subsequent forced emigration that, when it did not kill the individuals either abducted or forced into signing one-sided labor contracts, disrupted local society and separated them from their kin. The arrival of missionaries, and of European diseases to which locals had little or no natural immunity, subjected the island to a simultaneous cultural and biological assault.

Nearly 1,000 Rapanui, many of them royalty and priests, died as a result of the 1862 Peruvian raid, which transported them to dig guano on the Islas Chinchas off the coast of Ica department. By the time Catholic missionaries settled permanently, in 1866, perhaps only a few hundred Rapanui remained on the island itself.

While the Rapanui remained politically autonomous for some years more, by 1870 commercial and ecological exploitation arrived in the person of Jean-Baptiste Dutroux-Bornier, a French sailor who took advantage of the nearly depopulated island to graze sheep at Mataveri, site of the present-day airport. Dutroux-Bornier seemingly planned to declare himself sovereign of his own minikingdom, expelling the islanders to Tahiti; the missionaries, to their credit, opposed his plans, but they were unable to prevent a violent deportation that left only about 100 residents on the island.

Dutroux-Bornier died at the hands of the remaining Rapanui in 1877 but, by 1888, naval officer Policarpo Toro had annexed the island for Chile. While Chile may have been flexing its naval muscle in the aftermath of the War of the Pacific (1879–84), it really had no clear intentions for Rapa Nui and finally leased the island to Valparaíso merchant Enrique Merlet, who continued to graze sheep for wool. Merlet in turn sold out to the Valparaíso-based Williamson, Balfour & Company, the Chilean subsidiary of a British-held company, whose Compañía Explotadora de la Isla de Pascua (Cedip) was the island's de facto sovereign from 1888 to 1952.

As the population recovered from the demographic catastrophe of the 19th century, it became, despite its Polynesian heritage, a polyglot mix of South Pacific, European, and Asian peoples dramatically different, at least in the strictest genetic sense, from its predecessors. The paternalistic Cedip regime continued until 1953, when the Chilean navy assumed control, marking the definitive incorporation of Rapa Nui into the modern state.

The Modernization of Rapa Nui

Rapa Nui was a de facto naval base into the 1960s, but an event that would change the island forever occurred in 1951, when Roberto Parragué Singer flew the *Manutara* from the Norte Chico city of La Serena to Hanga Roa in 20 hours—the first flight ever from the continent. In 1967, the new Aeropuerto Mataveri became a refueling depot on the first-ever commercial flight from Santiago to Papeete, definitively incorporating the island into the Chilean—and international—political and economic orbit.

These dramatic developments, and the navy's withdrawal from administration, addressed a variety of local issues: islanders could now travel, vote, and have a voice in local and national matters—in Rapanui (whose usage had been suppressed) as well as Spanish. The Christian Democrat administration of President Eduardo Frei Montalva (1964–70) paid greater attention than ever to islanders' concerns, including education, medical care, and infrastructure projects such as electrical power, potable water, and roads.

Even during the Pinochet dictatorship, improvements continued, but since the return to democracy islanders have become even more outspoken—and prosperous. At the same time they have argued vigorously for return of ancestral lands on an island where, for many decades, their residence was confined to a small area in and around Hanga Roa, many Rapanui have taken advantage of other opportunities. Some have traveled to the mainland and around the world for education, while others have remained to profit from the tourist trade. According to some statistics, every year upward of 20,000 tourists now visit the island, only five hours by jet from Santiago.

GOVERNMENT AND POLITICS

While Rapa Nui is administratively subject to Region V (Valparaíso), with a governor (usually a local) appointed from Santiago, it is also a separate municipality with an elected mayor.

The current local administration distrusts both the central and regional governments, resents the inability to raise revenue locally, and argues that the islanders should have autonomy within the Chilean state. Dissenters, however, argue that recognition as a separate people is a form of second-class citizenship. Land rights also continue to be a hot issue, as some oppose central government "grants" on the rationale that Chile cannot give away what it never rightfully acquired.

ECONOMY

Tourism, having grown by 20 percent over the past decade, is the backbone of the economy. While the numbers may not seem impressive by global standards, more than 20,000 tourists saw the island in 1999—more than six times the local population. Europeans, mostly French and German, account for about 40 percent of the visitors, but mainland Chileans account for nearly a third.

Tourism is making some people wealthy—the symbols of affluence, such as automobiles, color TVs, and computers are becoming abundant. Many who do not rely directly on the

© WAYNE BERNHARDSON

fisherman's shrine

tourist trade—by providing accommodations, serving meals, and renting cars, for instance—still depend on it indirectly; gardeners, for instance, grow fruit and vegetables, ranchers raise sheep and cattle, and fishermen net fish and trap lobster.

Still, many services depend on government subsidies and the island has a substantial bureaucracy. Ironically, many locals depend on central government for their employment.

POPULATION AND PEOPLE

Almost all of Rapa Nui's 3,000-plus residents live in Hanga Roa, the island's only town. More than two-thirds are of Polynesian ancestry, but many Rapanui also live in mainland Chile and overseas. At the same time, nearly 200 mainland Chileans settle on the island every year, straining its health, education, and social services.

HANGA ROA

On Rapa Nui's eastern shore, the island's only town is the base for all visitors. Most spend sev-

eral days exploring the island on foot, bicycle, horseback, or by car. The more adventurous can take their chances surfing (there are good breaks even in town despite the lack of sandy beaches) or diving.

Orientation

Sprawling Hanga Roa has street names painted on most curbs, but these fade fast in the subtropical sun. There is no numbering system for houses or any other buildings—all of them are s/n (*sin número*, without a number)—so consult the map when in doubt. Even the map can be deceptive, as most hotels, *residenciales*, and many other businesses lack identifying signs. For orientation, locals often refer to landmarks such as the airport, the church, the *Feria Municipal* (municipal market), the *Gobernación* (government offices), and the harbor at Caleta Hanga Roa.

Sights

Except for **Ahu Tautira** and **Ahu Tahai** (both of which are covered in more detail below in the entry for Parque Nacional Rapa Nui), **Ahu Vai Uri,** and **Ahu Akapu,** Hanga Roa proper has only a handful of typically tourist sights. Its vigorous village life is a very real if intangible asset, though; one of its foci is **Avenida Atamu Tekena.** At the corner of Atamu Tekena and Te Pito Te Henua, **Plaza Policarpo Toro** contains side-by-side busts of its namesake naval officer, who claimed the island for Chile in 1888, and of Atamu Tekena, who ostensibly ceded Rapanui sovereignty to the Chileans.

On a rise at the eastern end of Te Pito Te Henua, the **Iglesia Hanga Roa,** Tuukoihu s/n, is the island's Catholic church and a focus of the colorful Easter Sunday services, when the priest arrives and departs on horseback. Its airy interior is decorated with spectacular carved wooden statues, a syncretic vision of Christianity and indigenous spirituality.

At the north end of town, overlooking Bahía Cook, artificial flowers festoon headstones at **Cementerio Hanga Roa,** the mostly Polynesian cemetery. At Eastertime, the cemetery is particularly vivid with decorations.

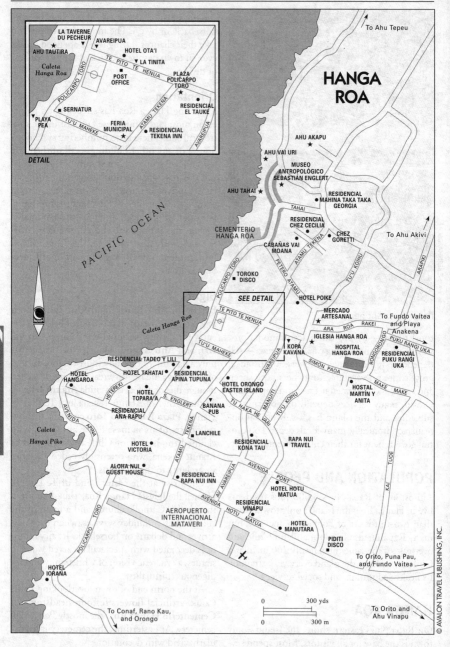

DETAIL

LA TAVERNE
DU PECHEUR
AVAREIPUA
AHU TAUTIRA
HOTEL OTA'I
Caleta
Hanga Roa
LA TINITA
POST
OFFICE
PLAZA
POLICARPO
TORO
SERNATUR
RESIDENCIAL
EL TAUKE
PLAYA
PEA
FERIA
MUNICIPAL
RESIDENCIAL
TEKENA INN

HANGA
ROA

PACIFIC OCEAN

To Ahu Tepeu

AHU AKAPU

AHU VAI URI

MUSEO
ANTROPOLÓGICO
SEBASTIÁN ENGLERT

AHU TAHAI

RESIDENCIAL
MAHINA TAKA TAKA
GEORGIA

To Ahu Akivi

RESIDENCIAL
CHEZ CECILIA

CHEZ
GORETTI

CEMENTERIO
HANGA ROA

CABAÑAS VAI
MOANA

TOROKO
DISCO

SEE DETAIL

HOTEL POIKE

Caleta Hanga Roa

TE PITO TE HENUA

MERCADO
ARTESANAL

To Fundo Vaitea
and Playa
Anakena

ARA   ROA   RAKEI

IGLESIA HANGA ROA

KOPA
KAVANA

RESIDENCIAL
PUKU RANGI
UKA

HOSPITAL
HANGA ROA

RESIDENCIAL TADEO Y LILI

HOTEL TAHATAI

RESIDENCIAL
APINA TUPUNA

HOTEL
HANGAROA

HOTEL
TOPARA'A

HOTEL ORONGO
EASTER ISLAND

HOSTAL
MARTÍN Y
ANITA

RESIDENCIAL
ANA-RAPU

BANANA
PUB

LANCHILE

RAPA NUI
TRAVEL

Caleta
Hanga Piko

HOTEL
VICTORIA

RESIDENCIAL
KONA TAU

ALOHA NUI
GUEST HOUSE

RESIDENCIAL
RAPA NUI INN

HOTEL HOTU
MATUA

RESIDENCIAL
VINAPU

AEROPUERTO
INTERNACIONAL
MATAVERI

HOTEL
MANUTARA

PIDITI
DISCO

HOTEL
IORANA

To Orito, Puna Pau,
and Fundo Vaitea

To Conaf, Rano Kau,
and Orongo

0   300 yds
0   300 m

To Orito and
Ahu Vinapu

© AVALON TRAVEL PUBLISHING, INC.

Museo Antropológico Padre Sebastián Englert: Improved in many ways, but not without shortcomings, Hanga Roa's anthropological museum sets the stage for Rapa Nui by dividing the South Pacific into "Near Oceania" (the area from Australia and New Guinea up to the Solomon Islands), settled around 40,000 years ago, and "Remote Oceania" to the northeast (Micronesia, Eastern Melanesia, and Polynesia), colonized from about 2000 B.C. to A.D. 1000.

Far more sophisticated in terms of cultural sequences than in the past, its displays provide valuable information on island geography, traditional navigation in the Pacific, immigration and population, the island's half-dozen *mata* or tribes (which later became 10), religion and the *moai,* subsistence activities (mainly fishing and horticulture), the birdman cult, body decoration (tattoos) and clothing, and rock art. There are also wood carvings, *rongorongo* tablets, weapons, and a case full of stone tools. Among the more unusual items are a female *moai,* one of only about 10 found on the island, and a *moai*'s eye made of white coral and volcanic scoria.

Its name a tribute to the Catholic priest and scholar who lived many years in Hanga Roa and who is buried just outside the church, the museum's major shortcoming is its failure to address historical or contemporary topics such as the imposition of Chilean rule, the impact of tourism, or even the demographic decline that followed the arrival of Europeans and their diseases, not to mention Peruvian slavers. On the other hand, the important Mulloy library has recently moved here from Viña del Mar's Museo Fonck.

The Museo Antropológico, midway between Ahu Tahai and Ahu Akapu, tel. 32/551020, is open Tuesday to Friday 9:30 A.M.–12:30 P.M. and 2–5:30 P.M., weekends 9:30 A.M.–12:30 P.M. only. Admission costs US$1.50 for adults, half that for children 8–18, and is free to children under eight years old.

Recreation

There are two diving operations at Caleta Hanga Roa: the **Mike Rapu Diving Center** and the

Orca Diving Center, tel. 32/100375 or 32/1-00877. Diving excursions cost in the US$45–60 range.

Caleta Hanga Roa is also the island's best surf site, busiest on weekends when local surfers line up for waves.

Accommodations

Compared with other Polynesian islands, Rapa Nui is a bargain, but price levels are higher than most of mainland Chile. The supply of accommodations is abundant for such a small place, so reservations are generally unnecessary except during the summer peak, particularly during the Tapati festival. Almost invariably, Polynesian hospitality is the rule, but some places are substantially better than others. Note that, while several hotels are near the airport, the infrequent air traffic—usually only one or two flights a day—is rarely disruptive.

For passengers lacking reservations, finding a first night's lodging is a more orderly process than it once was, since the airport arrival area now features a series of booths for each hotel or *hospedaje.* Most provide transport into town, a welcome service in surprisingly sprawling Hanga Roa. Nearly all include breakfast and private bath, and some offer additional meals, but full board is not a recommended option for anyone exploring the more distant archaeological sites—it can be a nuisance to have to return to Hanga Roa for lunch. Also, while Hanga Roa may not rival New York or Paris or even Santiago for dining, its independent restaurants are good enough to merit consideration at mealtime.

US$10 or Less: It's not in Hanga Roa proper, but Conaf's **Camping Anakena** is the national park's only authorized campground and, in fact, the only place to stay outside of Hanga Roa proper. It's free but has only basic infrastructure. A few Hanga Roa *residenciales* permit garden camping for a small charge (see the separate entries below).

US$25–50: Affable **Residencial Kona Tau,** Avareipua s/n, tel. 32/100321, konatau@entelchile.net, is the Hostelling International affiliate, charging US$20/30 s/d with breakfast in multibedded rooms, though there are also others with greater privacy. Otherwise, **Residencial Ana Rapu,** Apina Iti s/n, tel./fax 32/100540, is just about the cheapest in town at US$20/30 s/d with private bath and breakfast, even cheaper if you camp in the garden.

Residencial Tekena Inn, Atamu Tekena s/n, tel./fax 32/100289, is another economical choice at US$25/30 s/d; **Residencial Vai Kapua,** Te Pito Te Henua s/n, tel. 32/100377, fax 32/100105, costs US$20 pp with private bath and breakfast. For the same price, **Residencial Rapa Nui Inn,** Atamu Tekena s/n, tel./fax 32/1-00228, still suffers from mildew and other similar problems, but will do in a pinch.

Not bad for the price, but a bit out of the way, **Residencial Tahai,** Atamu Tekena s/n, tel. 32/10-0395, fax 32/100105, rapanui@entelchile.net, costs US$25/40 s/d with breakfast, but there are better values for only a little more money. Rates are identical at **Residencial Tahiri,** Ara Roa Rakei s/n, tel. 32/100570, fax 32/100105, and at **Residencial O Tama Te Ra'a,** Atamu Tekena s/n, tel. 32/100635, fax 32/100220. Surfers congregate at **Residencial Apina Tupuna,** Avenida Policarpo Toro s/n, tel. 32/100763, which could use some upgrading. Rates are US$25/40/45 s/d/t with breakfast and shared bath; garden camping costs US$10 per tent.

One of the best choices in the US$25 pp range is **Residencial El Tauke,** Te Pito Te Henua s/n, tel. 32/100253, fax 32/100105. **Residencial Vinapu,** Avenida Tu'u Koihu s/n, tel. 32/100393, fax 32/100105, is comparable. The newish **Residencial Puku Rangi Uka,** Puku Rangi Uka s/n, tel. 32/100405, fax 32/100105, charges US$30/50 s/d.

US$50–100: Nearby, longtime stalwart **Residencial Chez Cecilia,** Atamu Tekena s/n, tel./fax 32/100499, ccardinali@entelchile.net, charges US$30 pp with private bath and breakfast in a quiet location at the north end of town.

For the same price, a stay at the truly delightful **Residencial Mahina Taka Taka Georgia,** Atamu Tekena s/n, tel. 32/100452, fax 32/10-0105, is a real Polynesian experience, almost like being adopted into the family. The slightly out-of-town location, in a forest setting, is a bonus.

Rates at appealing **Cabañas Vai Moana,** nearby at Atamu Tekena s/n, tel./fax 32/100626, vai_moana@entelchile.net, are US$40/60 s/d with private bath and breakfast. Secluded **Hotel Poike,** Petero Atamu s/n, tel./fax 32/100283, charges the same, also with private bath and breakfast. Rates at cozy **Hotel Orongo Easter Island,** a five-room garden hotel at Atamu Tekena s/n, tel./fax 32/1-00294, are US$50/60 s/d. **Hotel Sofia Gomero,** Tu'u Koihu s/n, tel. 32/100313, hotelgomero@entelchile.net, charges US$38/65. The older and rather dark but quiet **Hotel Topara'a,** Hetereki s/n, tel. 32/100225, fax 32/100105, rapanui@lava.net, costs US$45/65 s/d.

The management seems a little brusque at **Chez Goretti,** Atamu Tekena s/n, tel./fax 32/10-0459, chezmariagoretti@entelchile.net, but its 13 rooms enjoy a quiet setting among expansive subtropical gardens, and the main building, with a central dining room and other common spaces, is a treasure. Rates are US$40/70 s/d with private bath and breakfast. **Residencial Villa Tiki,** Avenida Pont s/n, tel./fax 32/100327, costs US$45/70 s/d. The isolated *Cabañas Pikera Uri,* across from the museum near Ahu Tahai, tel. 32/100595, fax 32/100105, pantu@entelchile.net, charges US$30/70 s/d.

Near Caleta Hanga Roa, the Rapanui-French **Residencial Tadeo y Lili,** Avenida Policarpo Toro s/n, tel./fax 32/100422, charges US$50/70 s/d for *cabaña*-style accommodations with breakfast; the attractively decorated main house has a good library on island themes, though much of it is in French. The owners also offer two-, three-, or six-night packages with full board and excursions, and they can manage French, English, or Spanish.

Underrated **Hotel Victoria,** on a grassy knoll at Avenida Pont s/n, tel./fax 32/100272, enjoys fine views in all directions; rates are US$50/70 s/d for large rooms with private bath and breakfast in a quiet location. Just uphill from the church and across from the hospital, at **Hostal Martín y Anita,** Simón Paoa s/n, tel. 32/100593, hmanita@entelchile.net, rates with private bath are US$50/80 s/d with a substantial breakfast, private bath, and a/c. The owners handle English well.

In a quiet zone near the airport, **Hotel Hotu Matua,** Avenida Pont s/n, tel. 32/100242, fax

32/100445, hotu.matua@chilnet.cl, features large, comfortable rooms, a swimming pool, and sprawling subtropical gardens for US$50/80 s/d. In Santiago, contact Turismo Hotu Matua, Seminario 609, Providencia, tel. 2/6353275, fax 2/2226054.

Hostal Manavai, Te Pito Te Henua s/n, tel. 32/100670, fax 32/100658, manavai@entelchile.net, also charges US$50/80 s/d. **Hotel Chez Joseph,** Avareipua s/n, tel. 32/100373, fax 32/100281, chezjoseph@entelchile.net, costs US$45/85 s/d.

The exceptional **Aloha Nui Guest House,** Atamu Tekena s/n, tel./fax 32/100274, haumaka@entelchile.net, has sizeable rooms with private bath in a lush garden setting, for US$60/100 s/d with breakfast in high season. Hosts Ramón Edmunds and Josefina Mulloy, a granddaughter of the pioneering archaeologist William Mulloy, manage English, German, and Spanish well, and they operate a variety of excursions.

US$100–150: Hotel Manutara, across from the airport at Hotu Matua s/n, tel./fax 32/1-00297, manutarahotel@entelchile.net, ranks highly in both service and facilities, including a pool, for US$68/104 s/d.

Possibly Hanga Roa's best value, in terms of price commensurate with service, **Hotel Otai,** Te Pito Te Henua s/n, tel. 32/100250, fax 32/1-00560, otairapanui@entelchile.net, costs US$72/104 s/d with breakfast and private bath, and it has recently added a swimming pool; its biggest drawback is its exposure to sound waves from the Toroko disco. **Cabañas Taha Tai,** Apina s/n, tel. 32/100623, fax 32/100282, kiakoe@entelchile.net, charges US$90/105 s/d.

Hotel Iorana, Policarpo Toro s/n, tel./fax 32/100312, ioranahotel@entelchile.net, charging US$97/130 s/d for rooms in a relatively isolated waterfront site west of the airport, is certainly one of the best in town, but it is perhaps overpriced for the level of service.

Near Caleta Hanga Piko, the upscale **Hotel Hangaroa,** at the foot of Avenida Pont s/n, tel./fax 32/100299, reshangaroa@panamericanahoteles.cl, is a full-service hotel with a bar/restaurant with live entertainment, plus shops and a swimming pool; rates are US$120/140 s/d.

US$150–200: Rack rates at the new **Hotel Tahatai,** Avenida Policarpo Toro s/n, tel./fax 51/551192, are US$140/165 s/d with breakfast in spacious, well-lighted accommodations with private bath, breakfast, and a swimming pool.

Food

While most hotels and *residenciales* include breakfast and offer additional meals as well, travelers on a budget can buy produce and fish at the open-air Feria Municipal, on Atamu Tekena, or groceries at any of several supermarkets.

Otherwise, Hanga Roa has restaurants ranging from the utilitarian to above average to truly exceptional. Always, however, ask for the Spanish-language menu, which has prices in pesos rather than dollars and is often substantially cheaper.

Informal **Avareipua,** Policarpo Toro s/n, tel. 32/100431, serves a fresh tasty *toremo,* which holds its moisture better than tuna, plus a huge portion of garlic puree for US$6.50—about what a good fish dish would cost on the mainland. The service is enthusiastic and gracious.

The surroundings are even simpler, but **Caleta Otai,** Te Pito Te Henua s/n, tel. 32/100607, does a fine grilled tuna, well-presented with fresh vegetables, for US$8. **Kopa Kavana,** Avareipua s/n, tel. 32/100447, serves a more Polynesian-style menu with items such as *remo-remo,* which has darker meat and stronger flavor than tuna, and fried sweet potato.

At **Playa Pea,** Policarpo Toro s/n, tel. 32/100-382, try the *albacora papillón,* which features a red wine, pineapple, and mushroom sauce for US$8; the chicken and shrimp dishes are also good, and the oceanside veranda is a great place to watch the surfers.

Taverne du Pecheur, at Caleta Hanga Roa, tel. 32/100619, is the hands-down winner for the best (and most expensive) food in town, with entrées starting around US$13 and ranging up to US$40–60 for lobster, depending on the size; drinks and wine are also expensive. Still, the food is worth the price if—and it's a big if—the service is at its most attentive and responsive, even creative. If the mood of the day deteriorates, though, expect friction and even a lecture—"this is not McDonald's!"—from the chef.

Other eateries include **Iorana,** Atamu Tekena s/n near Plaza Policarpo Toro, tel. 32/100265, where fixed-price lunches or dinners cost around US$7; **La Tinita,** Te Pito Te Henua s/n, tel. 32/100813, for seafood; **Ki Tai,** Policarpo Toro s/n at Caleta Hanga Roa, tel. 32/100641; and **Pérgola Aringa Ora,** Hotu Matua s/n, tel. 32/100394.

Entertainment

Hanga Roa has a pair of discos, both of which stay open very late on weekends. You can hear the lively, youthful **Toroko,** Policarpo Toro s/n, from far off; **Piditi,** Avenida Hotu Matua s/n, draws a more mature public. The **Banana Pub,** Atamu Tekena s/n, sometimes features live music; the only other bar is **Pub Vaiace,** about a block north of the church at Tu'u Koihu s/n.

Now lighted, the soccer field at the corner of Policarpo Toro and Te Pito Te Henua is the site of spirited Sunday matches.

Shopping

The most popular souvenirs are carved replicas of *moai* (in both stone and wood), and of *moai kavakava* and *rongorongo* tablets (both in wood). The level of workmanship varies but can be remarkably high. Numerous souvenir shops line Atamu Tekena and Te Pito Te Henua, occupy the lobbies of the best hotels, and fill the departure lounge at Mataveri.

© WAYNE BERNHARDSON

cemetery at Hanga Roa

For size and variety, though, the best outlet is the **Mercado Artesanal,** across from the church at the corner of Tuukoihu and Ara Roa Rakei; the **Feria Municipal** at the corner of Atamu Tekena and Tuumaheke is a distant second. With sufficient notice, it's possible to hire a carver to create a custom stone *moai* and have it packed for shipping. The Sernatur office on Tuumaheke can put you in contact with the carvers, who are tough negotiators.

Bring film from the mainland, where it's cheaper and a wider selection is available. In a pinch, check shops along Atamu Tekena, or major hotels such as Hotel Hanga Roa and Hotel Hotu Matua.

Services

Island services are rapidly improving.
Money: Banco del Estado, Tuumaheke s/n, changes U.S. cash and traveler's checks, but rates are poor and the commission on traveler's checks is unreasonably high. It has no ATM, but it does offer cash advances on Visa only (no MasterCard). Hours are 8 A.M.–1 P.M. weekdays only.

ISLAND EVENTS

The island's biggest major annual event is **Tapati Rapa Nui,** a cultural celebration that lasts 10 days in early February and resembles the Heiva of French Polynesia. March 19's **Día de San José** commemorates the Catholic saint.

It's briefer than Tapati Rapa Nui, but **Semana Santa** (Holy Week) is crowned by Easter Sunday, when the Rapanui fill the church to overflowing to commemorate the Christian holiday that gave the island its Europeanized identity.

June 21's **Ceremonia Culto al Sol** observes the winter solstice. In late November, **Día de la Lengua Rapanui** promotes the island's Polynesian linguistic heritage.

Local merchants generally accept U.S. dollars for accommodations (Sernatur maintains a dollars-only database), meals, and many other items though they will, of course, accept Chilean pesos. Credit cards are becoming more widely accepted as well, even at some surprisingly modest accommodations, but it's still a good idea to carry some cash.

Postal: Correos de Chile is on Te Pito Te Henua, half a block east of Caleta Hanga Roa.

Telephone and Internet: Entel, Tuumaheke s/n, is directly opposite Sernatur and Banco del Estado; it's also possible to make card, collect, or credit-card calls from any of several public phones. The area code is 32, the same as Viña del Mar and Valparaíso, both of which are local calls.

M@tariki Net, Atamu Tekena s/n, is open 10 A.M.–8 P.M. weekdays, 10 A.M.–3 P.M. weekends; the restaurant Ki Tai, Policarpo Toro s/n, also offers Internet access. Rates on Rapa Nui are relatively high, however, at US$5 per hour.

Laundry: Lavandería Moana, Atamu Tekena s/n, is directly opposite the Banana Pub.

Medical: Hospital Hanga Roa, Simón Paoa s/n, tel. 32/100215, is about 500 meters southeast of the church.

Information

Sernatur, Tuumaheke s/n near Policarpo Toro, tel. 32/100255, sernatur_rapanui@entelchile.net, is open Monday to Saturday 8:30 A.M.–1:30 P.M., weekdays only 2:30–6 P.M.; there is also an airport booth that meets arriving flights. Its personnel can normally handle English and French in addition to Spanish and Rapanui.

The local tabloid *Te Rapa Nui* provides typical tourist information as well as more revealing material, such as political controversies; this ostensibly quarterly publication appears only erratically.

Transportation

Rapa Nui is easily and frequently (but not cheap-

TOURING RAPA NUI

Hanga Roa has an abundance of operators who offer tours around the island. Some have offices in Santiago where excursions can be arranged in advance, but this is more expensive and rarely necessary except for those seeking specific hotels or on a very compressed time schedule.

Partly because so many mainlanders have moved to the island and offered their services as guides, whether or not they have any formal qualifications, locals have organized an Asociación de Guías de Turismo de Isla de Pascua (Easter Island Tourist Guides Association) to regulate the industry. While it may not be quite perfect, it's a good start toward establishing and maintaining standards.

Aku Aku Tour, Hotel Manutara, Avenida Hotu Matu'a s/n, tel./fax 32/100770

Aku Aku Tour, Estado 115, Oficina 703, Santiago Centro, tel./fax 2/6328173, fax 2/6332491, aku.aku@chilenet.cl

Haumaka Tour, Aloha Nui Guest House, Atamu Tekena s/n, tel./fax 32/100274, haumaka@entelchile.net

Kia Koe Tour, Atamu Tekena s/n, tel./fax 32/100282, kiakoe@entelchile.net

Kia Koe Tour, Napoleón 3565, Oficina 201, Las Condes, Santiago, tel. 2/2037209, fax 2/2037211

Mahinatur Services, Residencial O Tama Te Ra'a, Hotu Matua s/n, tel./fax 32/100220

Manu Iti, Hotel Sofia Gomero, Av Tu'u Koihu s/n, tel./fax 32/100313, hotelgomero@entelchile.net

Martín Travel Rapa Nui, Rapa Nui Inn, Atamu Tekena s/n, tel./fax 32/100228

Ota'i Tour, Hotel Ota'i, Te Pito o Te Henua s/n, tel. 32/100250, fax 32/100105, otairapanui@entelchile.net

Rapa Nui Travel, Tu'u Koihu s/n, tel./fax 32/100548, website: www.rapanuitravel.com, rntravel@entelchile.net

Tiki Tour, Residencial Villa Tiki, Avenida Pont s/n, tel. 32/100327

Turismo Hotu Matu'a, Hotel Hotu Matu'a, Avenida Pont s/n, tel./fax 32/100242

THE ART AND ARCHITECTURE OF RAPA NUI

Famous for its towering *moai,* Rapa Nui boasts several other kinds of archaeological, artisanal, and artistic artifacts: the *ahu,* or platforms on which some *moai* stand (or stood), the *pukao,* or topknots that crowned some of the *moai,* the *hare paenga,* or elliptical houses whose scattered foundations are still common, and the petroglyphs that adorned sacred sites such as Orongo. In different circumstances, using the medium of *toromiro,* the ancestors of today's Rapanui carved the wooden *rongorongo* tablets and the *moai kavakava,* or "statues of ribs."

Unfortunately, many artifacts reside elsewhere. Only a handful of *moai* have left the island—perhaps they were even harder to get onto ships than onto their *ahu*—but mainland Chilean and overseas museums, as well as private collections, hold more portable items such as *rongorongo* tablets, stone tools and weapons, and similar artifacts.

Long after the clan wars that toppled the *moai,* local events were still hard on the island's material legacy—the Rapanui themselves recycled ancient stonework into newer, less distinguished structures. The Cedip administration, for its part, turned ruined *ahu* into boat docks at Caleta Hanga Roa and into cattle walls on the grasslands outside town.

Ahu
All around Rapa Nui's circumference, one is rarely out of sight of an *ahu;* their very density—about 350 exist—may be an indicator of how large the island's population must have been at its zenith. Very few, mostly notably Ahu Akivi on the southwestern slope of Maunga Terevaka, occupy inland sites.

The term *ahu* actually describes three distinct types of structures, sited above a plaza or similar open space. All of them share common elements, being elevated platforms of earth with a paved, level upper surface, enclosed by tightly fitted retaining walls constructed of larger stones. The most conspicuous, and most interesting to most visitors, are the elaborate *ahu moai,* on which the great stone statues stood. Some plazas contained circular ceremonial areas known as *paina;* in some cases, *apapa* or stone ramps descend from the *ahu* to the ocean.

Others were semipyramidal *ahu,* some of which were ruined *ahu moai* that were adapted into funerary structures from the 16th century on and may

have been used into the 19th; others appear to have been built specifically for this purpose. A later style, which probably appeared after Europeans saw the island, was the *ahu poe poe,* an elongated structure whose raised extremities resembled the bow and stern of a European sailing ship. Few in number, largely confined to the north coast, these were also funerary structures.

Moai
Numbering about 887, according to the best available statistics, the great stone *moai* are Rapa Nui's most emblematic achievement. Of these, 288 were erected on *moai,* 397 remain at Rano Raraku, and 92 were in transport. This leaves about 110 unaccounted for.

According to archaeologist Joanne van Tilburg, the average *moai* was 4.05 meters high and weighed 12.5 tons with a volume of 5.96 cubic meters. Mostly male, though 10 specimens or so reveal breasts and vulva, they generally range from two to 10 meters in height. Some far larger ones remained attached to the bedrock at Rano Raraku when quarry work suddenly ceased; shortages of wood to transport and raise the *moai* probably contributed to cessation of work.

In style, all *moai* have much in common. Nearly all of them begin at the torso, and nearly all their features are elongated: bodily appendages such as arms, hands, and fingers, and facial features such as noses and earlobes. Resembling statues elsewhere in Polynesia, they consist of volcanic tuff that was carved with harder basalt *toki.*

On completion, carvers separated the *moai* from its pit and, in all likelihood, laborers with ropes lowered it down the outer slopes of the crater. Once it arrived at the base—avoiding breakage or, even worse, fatalities from slippage—an even greater task remained: transporting the statue across the island and raising it onto an *ahu.*

The precise mechanism for moving the *moai* across the island has been the subject of prolonged debate, but there is no question that it required mobilizing large amounts of labor over prolonged periods—one standard for a complex society. Oral tradition says the *moai* moved by the priestly power of *mana,* but researchers from the amateur Heyerdahl to accomplished archaeologists such as William Mulloy, Vince

Lee, and Joanne van Tilburg, while disagreeing on details, have all agreed that some means of wooden transport—sledges, runners, or rollers—was responsible for getting the statues across the island. Whichever was correct, all these explanations help account for environmental deterioration that contributed to conflict on the island.

Most recently, Van Tilburg recruited robotics expert Zvi Shiller to devise a route for moving the *moai* from Rano Raraku to Ahu Akivi with a three-dimensional model, which van Tilburg corroborated with subsequent field research. According to Shiller's model, 75 to 150 people could have moved the *moai* in 4.5–9 days. In arguing for rollers as the main means of transport, Van Tilburg suggests that the *moai*'s flat backs indicate they were intended to be moved horizontally.

Once at the *ahu*, there remained the task of raising the *moai*. All sources are fairly consistent in suggesting that wooden poles or levers helped lift the heavy statues; in the course of doing so, islanders stabilized them by wedging rocks underneath until the *moai* eventually stood vertically. Most researchers have interpreted the presence of large numbers of loose stones near Ahu Akahanga and Ahu Te Pito Te Kura as evidence of this.

Pulling the statues down was no doubt easier than carving, transporting, and erecting them on *ahu*. While the islanders themselves were responsible for most damage, natural hazards—earthquakes and tsunamis—may well have contributed. The only now-standing *moai* are late 20th-century restorations.

Pukao

Quarried from the soft, easily shaped volcanic scoria at Puna Pau, the cylindrical topknots fitted atop some *moai* were apparently a late development, as fewer than 100 of them exist, not nearly enough for all the island's *moai*. Some believe they were hats, but it seems likelier that they represent a male hairstyle in fashion when Europeans first saw the island. With their hollow undersides, they were probably attached by rope to their *moai* and raised simultaneously, though they may have been rolled separately to their *ahu*. Even then, moving, tying, and raising an 11-ton *pukao* was not an easy task.

Hare Paenga

On Rapa Nui, the elliptical or boat-shaped houses known as *hare paenga* were built on basalt foundations with small, regularly spaced hollows that supported its superstructure of arched poles, all tied to a central ridge pole that also fitted into a hollow at each end. Entered by low, narrow doorways (though not so low or narrow as those at Orongo ceremonial village) at the midpoint of one side of the house, these houses belonged to families of high rank. Walled with thatch, most were 10–15 meters long and 1.5–2.5 meters wide, but some were as long as 40 meters.

Rongorongo Tablets

Still common in the mid-19th century, only a few of these original *toromiro* tablets—inscribed with minute symbols in orderly rows and shaped like elongated rectangular paddles—survive today. First described by missionary Eugene Eyraud, they ranged from 30–50 centimeters in length, but even when Eyraud took an interest in them, the Peruvian slave trade and subsequent smallpox epidemic had eliminated nearly all the islanders capable of offering clues as to their meaning.

Many of the originals are now in overseas collections, but anthropologist Steven Fischer has succeeded in bringing them alive in two recent books. Intended for the general public in both approach and price, his *Glyphbreaker* (1997) contends that surviving tablets are sacred chants whose 120 different pictograms signify a sequence of sexually explicit creation myths. His more erudite *Rongorongo, the Easter Island Script: History, Traditions, Text* (1997) appeals to an audience of academics and specialists.

The resourceful Rapanui, of course, have turned carved replica *rongorongo* tablets into one of the island's favorite souvenirs.

Moai Kavakava

Frequently found as souvenirs, the *moai kavakava* or "statues of ribs" probably date from the period when demographic pressure triggered the conflict that resulted in the destruction of the giant *moai*—certainly these emaciated wooden figures symbolize starvation. Oral tradition, though, attributes their origin to an encounter by the king Tu'u Koihu with two *aku aku* (sleeping spirits) at Puna Pau crater.

ly) reached by air, and more economically (but less easily and frequently) reached by sea.

Air: Aeropuerto Mataveri is at the south end of town, on Avenida Hotu Matua, tel. 32/100277; getting to and from the airport is not a problem, since virtually every hotel or residencial provides free transfers, but there is taxi service (see the Getting Around entry, below).

LanChile, Atamu Tekena s/n, tel. 32/100279, is at present the only commercial carrier with regular flights to and from Santiago. There are at least two international flights per week that continue to Tahiti and return to Santiago the following day; in the peak summer season, there is at least one additional domestic flight and sometimes two or even more.

Note that, for nonislanders, round-trip tickets from Santiago are expensive—up to US$900—but travelers who use LanChile for their international flights can often get major discounts to Rapa Nui.

Sea: Quarterly naval supply ships, which carry passengers for about US$24 pp per day, connect Rapa Nui with the mainland port of Valparaíso; for details, contact the Comando de Transporte at the Primera Zona Naval, Plaza Sotomayor 592, Valparaíso, tel. 32/506884; it takes about nine days to travel between the island and the mainland.

Getting Around

Car Rental: Hanga Roa has both formal rental agencies and many people who rent out their

vehicles casually—look for window signs. Be aware that there is no insurance on any vehicle on the island; you're on your own. Among the agencies are Bazar Island Rent-a-Car, Atamu Tekena s/n, tel. 32/100350; Hotu Matua Rent A Car, Atamu Tekena s/n, tel. 32/551026; Insular Rent A Car, Atamu Tekena s/n, tel. 32/100480; Kia Koe Tour, Atamu Tekena s/n, tel. 32/100282; Oceanic Rent A Car, Atamu Tekena s/n, tel. 32/100385; Rent A Car Puna Pau, Atamu Tekena s/n, tel. 32/100626; and Tekena Inn Rent A Car, Atamu Tekena s/n, tel. 32/100289.

Hanga Roa's only gas station—a seemingly out-of-place convenience store—is at the west end of Avenida Hotu Matua.

PARQUE NACIONAL RAPA NUI

Created in 1935, now under Conaf administration, Parque Nacional Rapa Nui comprises about 40 percent of the island's surface. Declared a UNESCO World Heritage Site in 1995, it protects all the island's archaeological sites as part of a *museo al aire libre* (open-air museum).

Orientation

Visiting the park entails getting around the entire island, though precise park boundaries are in flux as land is returned to the islanders. The roads, fortunately, are much improved—the highway to Anakena is smoothly paved, and the south coast road is mostly paved as far as Rano Raraku and Ahu Tongariki. Most of the remainder of the loop across the Poike isthmus and along the north coast to Ovahe and Anakena is still a bumpy dirt surface, however.

Because Rapa Nui is so compact, and the roads improved, it's possible to see a great deal in a day, but rather than hopscotching around the island it's better to explore in a systematic manner by following logical geographical routes.

The Hanga Roa Loop

Many of the island's archaeological sites are accessible from Hanga Roa—indeed, some of them are in Hanga Roa itself—via a loop that begins in town, climbs to Rano Kau crater and the Orongo ceremonial village, visits Ahu Vinapu at the

---

DEFENDING THE *MOAI*

All the monuments on Rapa Nui, from the smallest petroglyphs to the largest *moai* and *ahu*, are vulnerable enough to natural weathering without having to suffer the depredations of enthusiastic but shortsighted tourists. Even a single step, multiplied a million times over years, contributes to the deterioration of this irreplaceable heritage.

Make a special effort not to climb upon the *ahu* anywhere on the island, gently inform anyone doing so that it is inappropriate, and especially do not walk on the in situ statues in and around the quarry at Rano Raraku.

east end of the airport, detours to Puna Pau crater before continuing north to the southwestern slope of Maunga Terevaka, and then returns to Hanga Roa via the coast. It is, of course, possible to do the loop in reverse order or break it up into almost any number of segments.

Ahu Tautira: The most easily accessible *ahu,* Ahu Tautira overlooks the harbor at Caleta Hanga Roa. Two broken *moai* stand atop the platform, which was restored in 1980.

Tahai: Just north of the cemetery, restored in 1968 under the supervision of William Mulloy (whose ashes are buried nearby), Tahai was a ceremonial center with three separate *ahu,* as well as *hare paenga,* a boat ramp, and several *umu* (earth ovens). The central **Ahu Tahai** has a single *moai,* while the flanking **Ahu Ko Te Riku** sports another with its topknot in place. Nearby, five *moai* stand atop the especially large **Ahu Vai Ure.**

Rano Kau: South of Hanga Roa, a meandering road climbs the north slope of Rano Kau to the island's greatest remaining natural sight, the high crater rim that offers spectacular views, across its *totora*-lined freshwater lake, to a scattering of offshore islets and the infinite sea in the distance. From the rim, a trail drops into the steep-sided crater, where citrus trees and grapevines grow wild, and follows the muddy lakeshore.

Orongo: Suspended 400 meters above the sea, between the south rim of Rano Kau crater and a nearly vertical plunge into the ocean, Orongo was a ceremonial site for the so-called "birdman" cult that flourished on the island in the 18th and 19th centuries, long after the *moai* had been sculpted, raised, and even toppled. Superseding the ancestor worship associated with the giant *moai,* the cult venerated the creator Makemake; its annual highlight was a contest to retrieve the first sooty tern egg of the season from the offshore *motu,* or islets. The winner or his sponsor spent a year as the birdman, gaining great status but restricted to one of the ritual houses.

Orongo's 53 restored houses are among the world's most curious constructions, their walls and roofs formed by thin, overlapping horizontal wedges. Covered by earth, they were entered by doorways so small that, in the words of an English visitor in 1926:

The only method of procedure is a most undignified snake-like wiggling, which makes one appreciate the full significance of that primeval curse, "Upon thy belly shalt thou go, and dust shalt thou eat."

Today, however, visitors should refrain from attempting to enter the houses and should also avoid walking on their roofs, which are sometimes difficult to distinguish from the rest of the terrain. Do keep a eye out for the 1,700 or so petroglyphs decorating the rocks on the crater rim.

Orongo is the only site where Conaf collects an admission charge, about US$8 pp for adults, US$4 pp for children. There is a small museum here.

Motu Nui: During the years of the birdman cult, the islets of Motu Nui, Motu Iti, and Motu Kao Kao were nesting sites for the *mahohe,* or frigate bird, and the sooty tern; the former disappeared and the latter declined under human pressure for their eggs. By contracting a fisherman's launch at Caleta Hanga Roa, it's possible to visit Motu Nui, where there are cave paintings and remains of an *ahu,* but it's a tricky landing that requires a skilled boatman and calm weather.

Ahu Vinapu: Known for its finely fitted stonework, which led some overly zealous researchers to assume connections to pre-Columbian South American sites such as Tiwanaku (Bolivia) and Cuzco (Peru), Ahu Vinapu actually consists of three separate *ahu,* prosaically known as Vinapu I, II, and III. Vinapu II does outwardly resemble those Andean sites, but instead of large stone blocks it is merely a attractive facade for an otherwise rubble-filled platform.

All the *moai* at Ahu Vinapu lie broken and scattered in the immediate vicinity after being overturned during the islandwide conflicts of the 18th and 19th centuries. Some of the ruins were later used for shelters.

To get to Ahu Vinapu, follow Avenida Hotu Matua to the east end of Aeropuerto Mataveri's runway, then follow the lateral that leads south between the runway and fuel storage tanks to the beachfront parking lot.

Maunga Orito: Reached by a southbound trail about 1.4 km east of Hanga Roa on the road to Anakena, Orito was a quarry site for the glossy black obsidian that the Rapanui once used for cutting and drilling tools, and for spear points such as the *mataa*. Today, though, Rapanui artisans use the stone for souvenir jewelry.

Puna Pau: From a junction about 700 meters beyond the fork to the south coast road, a gravel road leads north toward the southern slopes of Maunga Terevaka; about 500 meters north of the junction, a dirt lateral leads west to Puna Pau, whose quarry produced the reddish scoria that forms the *moai's pukao*, or topknots.

Ahu Akivi: From the Puna Pau turnoff, the main road continues north to the southwestern base of Maunga Terevaka, where Ahu Akivi is the site of the "Seven *Moai*," restored in 1960 under the direction of William Mulloy and Chilean archaeologist Gonzalo Figueroa. Much has been made of the fact that these *moai* appear to look out to sea, rather than inland like all the island's other *moai,* but archaeologist Georgia Lee considers this a coincidence—most important, they look onto the ceremonial area. It does seem significant, though, that these seven *moai* stare straight at the setting sun on the spring and autumn equinoxes.

Ana Te Pahu: Rapa Nui's volcanic landscape features a large number of so-called "caves" that are, in fact, tubes formed as the lava from various eruptions cooled. Some are large, others small; while they served many purposes—shelter, defense, storage—one of the most interesting is Ana Te Pahu, colloquially known as the "banana cave" because its moisture and accumulated soil made it possible to cultivate tropical and subtropical crops at its sheltered subsurface entrance, despite limited sunlight. The local term for these sunken gardens is *manavai*.

Only a short distance west of Ahu Akivi, Ana Te Pahu is an inconspicuous landmark but is well-signed. The road continues northwest toward Ahu Tepeu before turning south along the coast toward Tahai and Hanga Roa.

Ahu Tepeu: About 10 km north of Hanga Roa, Ahu Tepeu has stonework that resembles that at Ahu Vinapu, but the Heyerdahl expedition of 1960 literally undermined its walls by excavating under their base. The foundation of one of the island's largest boat-shaped houses is nearby.

While there is no road north of Ahu Tepeu, it's possible to follow the coastline to Cabo Norte and then west to Playa Anakena where, though there is no regular public transportation, it's possible to ask someone for a lift back to Hanga Roa. This route is also possible on mountain bike or horseback.

Anakena and Vicinity

From Hanga Roa, a smooth paved road goes northeast to Anakena, the island's best beach and one of its major and best-restored archaeological sites. Several other points of interest dot the north coast road as it bumps eastward toward Península Poike.

Fundo Vaitea: In the approximate geographical center of the island, and roughly midway between Hanga Roa and Anakena, Fundo Vaitea contains Rapa Nui's best cultivable land. Both Dutroux-Bornier and Williamson, Balfour & Company used it for crops and livestock, but the government development agency Corfo eventually took it over.

At present, however, some of the land is being redistributed to islanders in five-hectare plots that are now being cultivated for pineapple, mango, and similar crops—transforming the island's contemporary cultural landscape. Some Rapanui, however, have objected to government "land grants," on the rationale that Chile has no right to grant lands that never belonged to it.

Playa Anakena: Legendary as the ostensible landing point for Hotu Matua (logical enough despite a lack of evidence), Playa Anakena is the island's only substantial sandy beach, a popular spot for swimming, sunbathing, and Sunday picnics. Backed by a plantation of palms, it also has the only approved campground, operated by Conaf, outside of Hanga Roa; there are also picnic tables, fire pits, and toilets.

Anakena is more notable, though, for its two substantial *ahu*. Heyerdahl's Norwegian expedition reerected the single *moai* on **Ahu Ature Huki,** while Rapanui archaeologist Sergio Rapu oversaw the 1979 restoration of **Ahu Nau Nau** and its seven *moai,* four of which sport *pukao* (two of the other three are badly damaged). In the course of restoration, the researchers found fragments of inlaid coral eyes, which they were able to reconstruct.

Playa Ovahe: A short distance east of Anakena, Playa Ovahe is the island's next-best beach, sandy with hidden caves. Though much smaller than Anakena, it gets many fewer visitors.

Ahu Te Pito Kura: On the west side of the rocky Bahía La Perouse, out of sight but indicated by a signpost, Ahu Te Pito Kura is the site of the largest *moai* (9.8 meters long, weight 82 tons, with an 11.5-ton *pukao*) ever transported and erected on an *ahu*. According to Georgia Lee, this may have been the last standing *moai,* having been toppled some time after 1838. The site takes its name from a large rounded rock that, according to legend, Hotu Matua brought from overseas (geologically it is of local origin). The term *te pito te kura* means "navel or the world" or "navel of light."

South Coastal Road

A short distance east of Hanga Roa, where the paved highway continues northeast toward Anakena, a southern fork follows the coast past a series of ruined coastal *ahu* en route to the magnificent quarry at Rano Raraku, the recently restored and almost equally impressive Ahu Tongariki, and Península Poike, the island's most easterly point.

Ahu Vaihu: On the bay of Hanga Tee, Ahu Vaihu is the site of eight fallen *moai* and their *pukao,* which were recovered from the ocean in 1986.

Ahu Akahanga: Sometimes claimed to be Hotu Matua's burial site, Ahu Akahanga is a large *ahu* that clearly has royal connections. A dozen *moai* lie fallen in the vicinity, along with many *pukao,* though William Mulloy thought the large amount of rubble in the vicinity indicated that stones were used to help raise the *moai* onto the *ahu*. Ruins of a village, primarily *hare paenga* foundations and earth ovens, are also nearby.

Rano Raraku: Just beyond the shattered **Ahu Hanga Tetenga,** where a pair of *moai* lie in ruins, a dirt track forks north to the parking lot for Rano Raraku, the crater where the ancestors of the present-day Rapanui chiseled all the mighty *ahu* before liberating them from the volcanic bedrock and transporting them to their

ahu. About 390 remain in and around the crater, in all stages of completion. Many of them stand erect, buried to their waists or shoulders in alluvium, while others patiently recline, seemingly waiting to be released from their attachment to the crater.

From the parking area on the south slope of the crater, a series of footpaths switchback up the slope to figures such as the kneeling **Moai Tukuturi,** one of few to have visible buttocks, and the reclining 21-meter Goliath, measuring four meters across, still joined to the tuff from which it was carved. Unfortunately, intentional but unattributed fires have denuded some of the slopes around the crater, potentially damaging the sites but also exposing the *moai* transport routes to view.

To the west, several parallel trails climb the contour into the crater, where *totora* reeds line the shore of the freshwater lake that fills the lower basin; in late summer, fruit from the feral guava trees still make a tasty snack. One measure of the cataclysmic warfare that hit the island is the fact that more than 300 unfinished *moai* populate the crater and its outer slopes. The crater's craggy eastern rim offers some of the best views on the entire island.

At the parking area ranger station, there are picnic tables, fire pits and toilets.

Ahu Tongariki: Its *moai* toppled in the chaos of intertribal warfare and its base destroyed by a tsunami in 1960, Ahu Tongariki underwent a major restoration when, in 1992, the Japanese Tadano company brought a crane, cash, and personnel to show how to manage it. Under the supervision of Chilean archaeologist Claudio Cristino, an island resident, about 40 Rapanui worked six-day weeks for nearly four years to finish the project. Some 15 *moai* now stand atop the *ahu*, which measures 98 meters long, six meters wide, and four meters high—the largest on the island. There are also numerous nearby petroglyphs, including a turtle, a tuna fish, a birdman, and *rongorongo* tablets.

Península Poike: Where the south coast road turns north toward Anakena, the eastern end of Rapa Nui is the site of the 400-meter Maunga Pu A Katiki, a dormant volcano almost entirely surrounded by steep volcanic cliffs except along its western isthmus, the narrowest point on the island, which parallels the north-south road. Directly across the isthmus runs the depression known as Ko te Ava o Iko (Iko's Ditch), once thought to be a defensive fortification, set afire to prevent an invasion from the west. Recent research has indicated the ditch to be a natural feature where, although there is evidence of natural fires, there is no evidence of weapons.

Information

Conaf, south of town on the road to Rano Kau, tel. 32/100236, is open 8:30 A.M.–6 P.M. weekdays only; there are also ranger posts at Orongo (which has a small museum), Anakena, and Rano Raraku.

Conaf's well-illustrated English-language brochure *Archaeological Field Guide, Rapa Nui National Park,* by Claudio Cristino, Patricia Vargas, and Roberto Izaurieta, is an outstanding summary of the park's monuments.

CHILEAN PACIFIC

Resources

Glossary

albergue juvenil: youth hostel

altiplano: high Andean steppe of the Norte Grande

anexo: telephone extension

apunamiento: altitude sickness

ascensor: literally an "elevator," but a term often applied to the funiculars of the city of Valparaíso

avenida: avenue

ayllu: an Andean moiety or kinship unit, also a geographical entity

bahía: bay

bajativo: after-dinner drink

balneario: bathing or beach resort

baño compartido: shared bath (in a hotel or other accommodations)

baño general: shared or general bath (in a hotel or other accommodations)

baño privado: private bath

barrio: neighborhood

bencina: gasoline

bodega: winery storage cellar

bofedal: marshy pasture of the altiplano, used primarily to graze alpacas; also known as *ciénaga*

boldo: the leaf of its namesake tree, *Peumus boldus;* used as herbal tea

boleadoras: round stone weights, linked by a leather strap, used for hunting by Patagonian Indians. When thrown, they would tie themselves around the legs of, say, a guanaco or rhea, immoblizing the animal; later, they would be used to capture wild cattle.

botellín: individual bottle of wine

butaca: reclining seat

cajero automático: automatic teller machine (ATM)

calafate: a shrub with dark blue berries with large seeds

calefón: hot-water heater

caliche: hardpan clay from which mineral nitrates were extracted in the Norte Grande

calle: street

callampas: "mushrooms," spontaneous squatter settlements on the periphery of Santiago and other Chilean cities

camanchaca: dense convective fog that forms on the Chilean coastline, especially in the northern desert

camioneta: pickup truck

campo minado: minefield

carretera: highway

casa de cambio: money exchange facility, often just "cambio"

casa de huéspedes: guesthouse, usually a modest family-run place

casilla: post office box

cerro: hill

chifa: Chinese restaurant, a term used mostly in the Atacama desert regions and in Peru

Chilote: in the narrowest sense, a native of the archipelago of Chiloé; in a discourteous sense, a "bumpkin"

chopp: draft beer

cobro revertido: collect or reverse-charge telephone call

cocinería: simple eatery, often in a market

colación: lunch, especially during the work day

colectivo: in Chile, a shared route taxi; in Argentina, a city bus

comedor: simple family-style restaurant

confitería: in Argentina, a restaurant/café with a menu of *minutas* (short orders)

comuna: borough, a unit of municipal government; in Chile, some of these are totally urban, while others take in huge rural areas as well

congregación: Spanish colonial policy of concentrating indigenous peoples in nucleated settlements for purposes of taxation and tribute

costanera: any road along a seashore, lakeshore, or riverside

criollo: in colonial times, a Chilean-born Spaniard; in the present, normally a descriptive term meaning "traditionally" Chilean

cueca: traditional Chilean folk dance

curanto: traditional seafood stew of Chiloé and Patagonia

desierto florido: "flowering desert" of the Norte Chico, an ephemeral explosion of wildflowers when there are substantial rains

doble tracción: four-wheel drive (4WD), also known as *cuatro por cuatro* (the latter written as "4X4")

edificio: building

encomienda: in colonial times, a grant of Indian labor and tribute within a given geographical area. The *encomendero,* or holder of the *encomienda,* incurred the reciprocal obligation to provide instruction in the Spanish language and Christian religion, though such obligations were rarely honored

estancia: cattle or sheep ranch controlling large extents of land, most often in Patagonia, often with an absentee owner, dominant manager, and resident employees

estero: estuary

ex-voto: a gift to a saint in exchange for a favor or miracle

feria: artisans' market

farmacia de turno: pharmacy remaining open all night for emergencies, on a rotating basis

ficha: token that circulated instead of cash in nitrate *oficinas*

fundo: large rural estate, nearly synonymous with hacienda

garúa: coastal fog; see also *camanchaca*

garzón: waiter

golfo: gulf

golpe de estado: coup d'etat

hacienda: large rural estate, usually assembled by Spaniards in areas where indigenous populations were low because of the devastating impact of introduced diseases

hipódromo: horserace track

hospedaje: inexpensive accommodation, usually family-run

huaso: Chilean counterpart to the Argentine gaucho

icchu: bunch grasses of the high Andes

indigenismo: exaggerated romantic appreciation of indigenous history and heritage, common in art, literature, and rhetoric

infracción: traffic violation

invierno altiplánico: "altiplano winter," in fact the summer rainy season at high altitudes in the Norte Grande; also known as *invierno boliviano* (Bolivian winter) for the direction from which the rains come

isla: island

islote: islet

istmo: isthmus

IVA: *impuesto de valor agregado,* or value added tax (VAT)

lago: lake

laguna: lagoon

latifundio: large landholding, either a *fundo* or an hacienda

liebre: small city bus, literally "hare"

local: numbered office or locale, at a given street address

lonko: traditional Mapuche leader

machi: Mapuche seer-healer

machista: male chauvinist

marisquería: fish and seafood restaurant, often on the beach or in a market

media pensión: half board, at a hotel or guesthouse

menú: menu; also, a fixed-price meal

mesero: waiter

mestizo: individual of mixed indigenous and Spanish ancestry

micro: city bus or small backroads bus

minifundio: small peasant landholding

minuta: in Argentina, a short order meal such as pasta

mirador: overlook or viewpoint

monumento nacional: national monument, usually an archaeological site or historical building

monumento natural: a category of state-protected land

municipalidad: city hall; by extension, city government

museo: museum

nevado: snow peak

oficina: nitrate mining company town in the Norte Grande

onces: afternoon tea ("elevenses")

paco: "cop," a term to be used circumspectly when discussing Carabineros, the Chilean national police force, and never to be used to their faces

pajarete: dessert wine from the Norte Chico

palafito: fisherman's house on stilts or pilings, once common in Chiloé

pampa: broad, flat desert expanse in the Norte Grande

pan amasado: kneaded bread

parada: bus stop

parque nacional: national park

pasarela: hanging bridge or walkway

paseo: pedestrian mall

peaje: toll booth

penquista: native or inhabitant of Concepción

pensión: inexpensive family-style accommodations

pensión completa: full board, at a hotel or guesthouse

peña: traditional folk music venue

picada: informal, usually family-run restaurant that often begins as a casual neighborhood phenomenon and develops into something more elaborate

pingüinera: penguin colony

pisco: potent grape brandy

playa: beach

plazuela: small plaza

Porteño: native or resident of Valparaíso

posta: clinic, usually but not always in a small town that lacks a full-service hospital

precordillera: foothills of the Andes

propina: tip, as at a restaurant

puente: bridge

puerto: port

puesto: "outside house" on a sheep or cattle *estancia;* also, a small market food stall

pukará: pre-Columbian, often Inka, fortress

Pullman: first-class bus, with reclining seats and luggage storage underneath

puna: synonym for altiplano (q.v.)

quebrada: ravine or canyon

recargo: surcharge on credit card purchases

reducción: synonym for congregación (q.v.)

repartimiento: Spanish forced-labor system

refugio: rustic or occasionally more formal shelter, usually in wild country such as a national park

requerimiento: formal Spanish obligation to offer peace to indigenous armies on condition that they accept Crown and papal authority

reserva nacional: national reserve, a category of state-protected land

río: river

rodeo: annual roundup of cattle on an *estancia;* also a festival of horsemanship

ruca: customary thatched Mapuche house

ruta: route or highway

salar: high-altitude salt lake

salón de té: European-style café, often with sidewalk seating

sendero: trail or footpath

seno: sound or fjord

soroche: altitude sickness

s/n: *sin número,* a street address without a number

tábano: aggressive horsefly of the Sur Chico

tajamares: colonial dikes built to control floods on Santiago's Río Mapocho

tejuela: shingles, common form of siding in archipelagic Chiloé; usually made of *alerce* or other native wood

tenedor libre: all-you-can-eat, literally "free fork," restaurant, more common in Argentina than in Chile

termas: hot springs

todo terreno: mountain bike

toque de queda: curfew, under military dictatorship

toqui: Mapuche war leader

totora: a sort of reed used for weaving mats

ventisquero: glacier

volcán: volcano

zona típica: "typical area," a legal designation intended to preserve a neighborhood's historic character, but lacking any financial support

Spanish Phrasebook

Spanish is Chile's official language, but the local variant, which often drops terminal and even internal consonants, can confuse those who learned Spanish elsewhere. At tourist offices, airlines, travel agencies, and upscale hotels, English is often spoken. But out on the road, it's the exception.

Visitors spending any length of time in Chile, especially students and business people, should look for John Brennan's and Alvaro Taboada's *How to Survive in the Chilean Jungle* (Santiago: Dolmen Ediciones, 1996), which has gone through multiple hilarious editions of explaining everyday Chilean expressions—some of whose usage requires *great* caution for those unaware of their every meaning.

Pronunciation Guide

Spanish pronunciation is much more regular than that of English, but there are still occasional variations in pronunciation.

Consonants

c — as 'c' in "cat," before 'a', 'o', or 'u'; like 's' before 'e' or 'i'

d — as 'd' in "dog," except between vowels, then like 'th' in "that"

g — before 'e' or 'i', like the 'ch' in Scottish "loch"; elsewhere like 'g' in "get"

h — always silent

j — like the English 'h' in "hotel," but stronger

ll — like the 'y' in "yellow"

ñ — like the 'ni' in "onion"

r — always pronounced as strong 'r'

rr — trilled 'r'

v — similar to the 'b' in "boy" (not as English 'v')

y — similar to English, but with a slight "j" sound; when standing alone, it's pronounced like the 'e' in "me"

z — like 's' in "same"

b, f, k, l, m, n, p, q, s, t, w, x as in English

Vowels

a — as in "father," but shorter

e — as in "hen"

i — as in "machine"

o — as in "phone"

u — usually as in "rule"; when it follows a 'q' the 'u' is silent; when it follows an 'h' or 'g', it's pronounced like 'w,' except when it comes between 'g' and 'e' or 'i', when it's also silent (unless it has an umlaut, when it again pronounced as English 'w'

Stress

Native English speakers frequently make errors of pronunciation by ignoring stress—all Spanish vowels—a, e, i, o, and u—may carry accents that determine which syllable of a word gets emphasis. Often, stress seems unnatural to nonnative speakers—the surname Chávez, for instance, is stressed on the first syllable—but failure to observe this rule may mean that native speakers may not understand you.

Numbers

0 — cero
1 — uno (masculine)
1 — una (feminine)
2 — dos
3 — tres
4 — cuatro
5 — cinco
6 — seis
7 — siete
8 — ocho
9 — nueve
10 — diez
11 — once
12 — doce
13 — trece
14 — catorce
15 — quince

16 — diez y seis
17 — diez y siete
18 — diez y ocho
19 — diez y nueve
20 — veinte
21 — veinte y uno
30 — treinta
40 — cuarenta
50 — cincuenta
60 — sesenta
70 — setenta
80 — ochenta
90 — noventa
100 — cien
101 — ciento y uno
200 — doscientos
1,000 — mil
10,000 — diez mil
1,000,000 — un millón

Days of the Week

Sunday — domingo
Monday — lunes
Tuesday — martes
Wednesday — miércoles
Thursday — jueves
Friday — viernes
Saturday — sábado

Time

While Chileans mostly use the 12-hour clock, in some instances, usually associated with plane or bus schedules, they may use the 24-hour military clock. Under the 24-hour clock, for example, *las nueve de la noche* (9 P.M.) would be *las 21 horas* (2100 hours).

What time is it? — ¿Qué hora es?
It's one o'clock — Es la una.
It's two o'clock — Son las dos.
It's ten to three — Son tres menos diez.
It's ten past three — Son tres y diez.
It's three fifteen — Son las tres y cuarto.
It's two forty five — Son tres menos cuarto.
It's two thirty — Son las dos y media.
It's six A.M. — Son las seis de la mañana.

It's six P.M. — Son las seis de la tarde.
It's ten P.M. — Son las diez de la noche.
Today — hoy
Tomorrow — mañana
Morning — la mañana
Tomorrow morning — mañana por la mañana
Yesterday — ayer
Week — la semana
Month — mes
Year — año
Last night — anoche
The next day — el día siguiente

Useful Words and Phrases

Chileans and other Spanish-speaking people consider formalities important. Whenever approaching anyone for information or some other reason, do not forget the appropriate salutation—good morning, good evening, etc. Standing alone, the greeting *hola* (hello) can sound brusque.

Note that most of the words listed below are fairly standard, common to all Spanish-speaking countries. Many, however, have more idiomatic Chilean equivalents; refer to the glossary for these.

Hello. — Hola.
Good morning. — Buenos días.
Good afternoon. — Buenas tardes.
Good evening. — Buenas noches.
How are you? — ¿Cómo está?
Fine. — Muy bien.
And you? — ¿Y usted?
So-so. — Más o menos.
Thank you. — Gracias.
Thank you very much. — Muchas gracias.
You're very kind. — Muy amable.
You're welcome — De nada (literally, "It's nothing.")
Yes — sí
No — no
I don't know. — No sé.
It's fine; okay — Está bien.
Good; okay — Bueno.
Please — por favor
Pleased to meet you. — Mucho gusto.

Excuse me (physical) — Perdóneme.
Excuse me (speech) — Discúlpeme.
I'm sorry. — Lo siento.
Goodbye — adiós
See you later — hasta luego (literally, "until later")
More — más
Less — menos
Better — mejor
Much, a lot — mucho
A little — un poco
Large — grande
Small — pequeño, chico
Quick, fast — rápido
Slowly — despacio
Bad — malo
Difficult — difícil
Easy — fácil
He/She/It is gone; as in "She left," "He's gone" — Ya se fue.
I don't speak Spanish well. — No hablo bien el español.
I don't understand. — No entiendo.
How do you say . . . in Spanish? — ¿Cómo se dice . . . en español?
Do you understand English? — ¿Entiende el inglés?
Is English spoken here? (Does anyone here speak English?) — ¿Se habla inglés aquí?

Terms of Address

When in doubt, use the formal *usted* (you) as a form of address. If you wish to dispense with formality and feel that the desire is mutual, you can say *Me puedes tutear* (you can call me "tu").

I — yo
You (formal) — usted
you (familiar) — tú
He/him — él
She/her — ella
We/us — nosotros
You (plural) — ustedes
They/them (all males or mixed gender) — ellos
They/them (all females) — ellas
Mr., sir — señor
Mrs., madam — señora

Miss, young lady — señorita
Wife — esposa
Husband — marido or esposo
Friend — amigo (male), amiga (female)
Sweetheart — novio (male), novia (female)
Son, daughter — hijo, hija
Brother, sister — hermano, hermana
Father, mother — padre, madre
Grandfather, grandmother — abuelo, abuela

Getting Around

Where is . . . ? — ¿Dónde está . . . ?
How far is it to . . . ? — ¿A cuanto está . . . ?
from . . . to . . . — de . . . a . . .
Highway — la carretera
Road — el camino
Street — la calle
Block — la cuadra
Kilometer — kilómetro
North — norte
South — sur
West — oeste; poniente
East — este; oriente
Straight ahead — al derecho; adelante
To the right — a la derecha
To the left — a la izquierda

Accommodations

¿Hay cuarto? — Is there a room?
May I (we) see it? — ¿Puedo (podemos) verlo?
What is the rate? — ¿Cuál es el precio?
Is that your best rate? — ¿Es su mejor precio?
Is there something cheaper? — ¿Hay algo más económico?
Single room — un sencillo
Double room — un doble
Room for a couple — matrimonial
Key — llave
With private bath — con baño
With shared bath — con baño general; con baño compartido
Hot water — agua caliente
Cold water — agua fría
Ducha — shower
Ducha eléctrica — electric shower
Towel — toalla

Soap — jabón
Toilet paper — papel higiénico
Air conditioning — aire acondicionado
Fan — ventilador
Blanket — frazada; manta
Sheets — sábanas

Public Transport

Bus stop — la parada
Bus terminal — terminal de buses
Airport — el aeropuerto
Launch — lancha
Dock — muelle
I want a ticket to . . . — Quiero un pasaje a . . .
I want to get off at . . . — Quiero bajar en . . .
Here, please. — Aquí, por favor.
Where is this bus going? — ¿Adónde va este autobús?
Round-trip — ida y vuelta
What do I owe? — ¿Cuánto le debo?

Food

Menu — la carta, el menú
Glass — taza
Fork — tenedor
Knife — cuchillo
Spoon — cuchara
Napkin — servilleta
Soft drink — agua fresca
Coffee — café
Cream — crema
Tea — té
Sugar — azúcar
Drinking water — agua pura, agua potable
Bottled carbonated water — agua mineral con gas
Bottled uncarbonated water — agua sin gas
Beer — cerveza
Wine — vino
Milk — leche
Juice — jugo
Eggs — huevos
Bread — pan
Watermelon — sandía
Banana — banano

Plantain — plátano
Apple — manzana
Orange — naranja
Meat (without) — carne (sin)
Beef — carne de res
Chicken — pollo; gallina
Fish — pescado
Shellfish — mariscos
Shrimp — camarones
Fried — frito
Roasted — asado
Barbecued — a la parrilla
Breakfast — desayuno
Lunch — almuerzo
Dinner (often eaten in late afternoon) — comida
Dinner, or a late-night snack — cena
The check, or bill — la cuenta

Making Purchases

I need . . . — Necesito . . .
I want . . . — Deseo . . . or Quiero . . .
I would like . . . (more polite) — Quisiera . . .
How much does it cost? — ¿Cuánto cuesta?
What's the exchange rate? — ¿Cuál es el tipo de cambio?
May I see . . . ? — ¿Puedo ver . . . ?
This one — ésta/ésto
Expensive — caro
Cheap — barato
Cheaper — más barato
Too much — demasiado

Health

Help me please. — Ayúdeme por favor.
I am ill. — Estoy enfermo.
Me duele. — It hurts.
Pain — dolor
Fever — fiebre
Stomach ache — dolor de estómago
Vomiting — vomitar
Diarrhea — diarrea
Drugstore — farmacia
Medicine — medicina
Pill, tablet — pastilla
Birth control pills — pastillas anticonceptivas

Suggested Reading

Archaeology, Ethnography, and Ethnohistory

Dillehay, Tom D. *Monte Verde: A Late Pleistocene Settlement in Chile,* 2 vols. Washington and London: Smithsonian Institution Press, 1989–97. Exhaustive treatment of crucially important Early Man site west of Puerto Montt, one of the continent's oldest.

Pringle, Heather. *The Mummy Congress.* New York: Hyperion, 2001. Using a congress of mummy specialists in the northern Chilean city of Arica as its starting point, this book is a lively synthesis of cultural traditions of preserving human bodies, the accidental preservation of bodies under specific environmental conditions, and their significance in the contemporary world—including the ethics of research. While Pringle's research and travels take her around the world, there is a substantial focus on the Atacama and the central Andes.

Guidebooks and Travelogues

Burford, Tim, and John Dixon. *Chile and Argentina: The Bradt Trekking Guide,* 5th ed. Guilford, CT: The Globe Pequot Press, 2001. A greatly improved hiking guide that covers much of both countries with diligence; its maps, though also improved from previous editions, could still be better and it would benefit from a sample of photographs of the spectacular scenery it covers.

Campbell, John. *In Darwin's Wake: Revisiting Beagle's South American Anchorages.* Dobbs Ferry, NY: Sheridan House, 1997. Better in concept than execution, this record of a sailboat excursion around Cape Horn and through the Beagle Channel suffers from a prosaic prose style, lack of real insight, and inadequate background—in one instance, the author mistakes the rare *huemul* for the far

more common guanaco. Still, the relatively rarity of the experience and the high quality of the photographs lend it some interest, especially for those visiting the area in their own vessels.

Chatwin, Bruce. *In Patagonia.* New York: Summit Books, 1977. One of the continent's classic travelogues, even if—but perhaps because—Chatwin blurs the line between experience and fiction.

Chatwin, Bruce. *What Am I Doing Here?* New York: Viking, 1989. This collection of Chatwin miscellanea contains an essay on the island of Chiloé and, specifically, the village of Cucao.

Clarke, Thurston. *Searching for Crusoe: A Journey among the Last Real Islands.* New York: Ballantine, 2001. One of today's most inventive travel writers explores some of the world's last island retreats, starting with the Chilean island that inspired Daniel Defoe's novel.

Crouch, Gregory. *Enduring Patagonia.* New York: Random House, 2001. Must reading for technical climbers and vicarious thrill seekers headed for southern Patagonia, though it deals primarily with Argentina's Parque Nacional Los Glaciares (an area covered in this handbook).

Darwin, Charles. *Voyage of the Beagle* (many editions). Possibly the greatest travel book ever written, Darwin's narrative of his 19th-century journey is filled with insights on the people, places, and even politics he saw while collecting the plants and animals that led to his revolutionary theories. His accounts of Tierra del Fuego, Chiloé, Concepción, Cerro La Campana, and Copiapó are so vivid that they might have been written yesterday.

Dixie, Lady Florence. *Across Patagonia.* Punta Arenas: Southern Patagonia Publications, n.d. Chronicle of an adventurous Englishwoman who, in 1879, rode across the Patagonian steppes from Punta Arenas almost to Torres del Paine. Originally published in 1881, now available in a replica edition, it shows both the strengths and the weaknesses of imperial Victorian travel literature.

Dorfman, Ariel. *Heading South, Looking North.* New York: Farrar, Strauss and Giroux, 1998. Overlapping the travel literature genre, this is primarily a memoir of reflections on the second half of the 20th century by a bilingual activist and major Chilean literary figure; one critic, though, has termed the author's self-criticism of his role in Unidad Popular as *mea minima culpa.*

Goodall, Rae Natalie Prosser. *Tierra del Fuego.* Buenos Aires and Ushuaia: Ediciones Shanamaiim, 1978. Though badly in need of an update, this bilingual guidebook is still the most informed single source about the Argentine side of the archipelago. Technically out of print, it's still available in Buenos Aires and Ushuaia.

Green, Toby. *Saddled with Darwin.* London: Phoenix, 1999. Audacious if uneven account by a young, talented writer of his attempt to retrace the tracks—not the footsteps—of Darwin's travels through Uruguay, Argentina, and Chile. Self-effacing but still serious, the author manages to compare Darwin's experience with his own, reflect on contemporary distortions of the great scientist's theories, and stay almost completely off the gringo trail.

Guevara, Ernesto. *The Motorcycle Diaries: A Journey around South America.* New York and London: Verso, 1995. Translated by Ann Wright, this is an account of an Argentine drifter's progress across the Andes and up the Chilean coast by motorcycle and, when it broke down, by any means necessary. The author is better known by his nickname "Che," a common Argentine interjection.

Leitch, William. *South America's National Parks.* Seattle: The Mountaineers, 1990. Increasingly dated in its practical information, this pioneer guidebook is still a good thematic introduction to a representative sample of the continent's protected areas, including several in Chile and Argentina.

Lindenmayer, Clem. *Trekking in the Patagonian Andes.* Melbourne: Lonely Planet, 1998. A detailed but misleadingly named hiking guide on both Argentina and Chile that includes quite a few trails not within Patagonia proper, and some not even in the Andes—on the Isla Grande de Chiloé, for example. One could argue, of course, that this additional coverage is a positive; on the negative side, no new edition is due out until at least 2003.

Sagaris, Lake. *Bone and Dream: Into the World's Driest Desert.* Toronto: Alfred A. Knopf Canada, 2000. Written by a Chile-based Canadian journalist, this literary travelogue conflates the legend of an Inka princess in the Norte Grande and the country's post-Pinochet development.

Schubert, Franz, and Malte Siebert. *Adventure Handbook Central Chile.* Santiago: Viachile Editores, 2002. This professionally produced and well-illustrated book covers recreational activities, primarily but not exclusively backcountry hikes, in the Chilean heartland between the Río Aconcagua and the Río Biobío. An excellent complement to this Moon Handbook, it also contains a great deal of useful practical and cultural information.

Sepúlveda, Luis. *Full Circle: A Latin American Journey.* Melbourne: Lonely Planet, 1996. Erratic hopscotch across the continent by a Chilean writer who spent many years in exile.

Symmes, Patrick. *Chasing Che: A Motorcycle Journey in Search of the Guevara Legend.* (New York: Vintage, 2000. Symmes follows the tire-tracks of Che's legendary trip through Argentina and Chile in the early 1950s.

Wheeler, Sarah. *Travels in a Thin Country.* New York: The Modern Library, 1999. A lively travelogue that even includes the Chilean sector of Antarctica, but the unwarranted plugs for a well-known international rental car company that underwrote part of her trip are an irritation.

History

Bauer, Arnold. *Chilean Rural Society from the Spanish Conquest to 1930.* Cambridge: Cambridge University Press, 1975. A complex, comprehensive, and systematic analysis of the continuities and discontinuities in rural history that led to upheaval in the 1960s and 1970s.

Caldera, Rafael. *Andrés Bello.* London: Allen & Unwin, 1977. Written by a former Venezuelan president at the age of 19, this translation is the first English-language biography of the Venezuelan-born 19th-century polymath who created the Chilean higher-education system.

Crow, John A. *The Epic of Latin America,* 3rd ed. Berkeley: University of California Press, 1980. A comprehensive history of the region, told more through narrative than analysis, in an immensely readable manner. Several chapters deal with Chile.

Lockhart, James, and Stuart Schwartz. *Early Latin America.* Cambridge: Cambridge University Press, 1983. A creative interpretation of colonial history that treats the region's aboriginal inhabitants as active agents rather than mere victims. There is substantial coverage of Chile, particularly the Araucanian frontier.

Loveman, Brian. *Chile: The Legacy of Hispanic Capitalism.* Oxford: Oxford University Press,

1979. Despite a title that suggests colonial origins for Chile's economic and social structure, this ostensibly general history is weak and vague until its treatment of the late 19th century, and it borders on economic determinism.

Lynch, John. *Spanish-American Revolutions, 1808–1826,* 2nd ed. New York, W. W. Norton, 1986. Comprehensive account of the independence movements in Spanish America.

Marcosson, Isaac F. *Anaconda.* New York: Dodd, Mead & Company, 1957. An authorized history of the transnational mining company that controlled the Chilean copper industry until its nationalization in 1970.

McBride, George McCutcheon. *Chile: Land and Society.* New York: American Geographical Society, 1936. Based on personal observations, this account of life on Chilean *fundos* and haciendas presents the conditions that led to agrarian discontent in the following decades, though the author may have overestimated these institutions' durability.

Mavor, Elizabeth, Ed. *The Captain's Wife: The South American Journals of Maria Graham, 1821–23.* London: Weidenfeld and Nicolson, 1993. An edited version, with commentary, of Maria Graham's lengthy account of residence in Valparaíso and travels in Chile and elsewhere in South America, and her acquaintance and friendship with historic figures such as Bernardo O'Higgins and Lord Cochrane.

Monteón, Michael. *Chile in the Nitrate Era.* Madison: University of Wisconsin Press, 1982. A scholarly account of the Norte Grande, the wealth it brought to investors and the Chilean treasury, and its impact on society.

Parry, J. H. *The Discovery of South America.* London: Paul Elek, 1979. Well-illustrated history of early voyages and overland explorations on the continent.

Slatta, Richard. *Cowboys of the Americas.* New Haven and London: Yale University Press, 1990. Spectacularly illustrated comparative account of New World horsemen, including both Argentine gauchos and Chilean *huasos.*

Souhami, Diana. *Selkirk's Island: The True and Strange Adventures of the Real Robinson Crusoe.* New York and London: Harcourt, 2001. Focusing on the real-life Crusoe, Alexander Selkirk, and his experiences on and after his four-year exile on the Juan Fernández archipelago, this award-nominated biography makes some unfortunate geographical errors.

Government and Politics

Branch, Taylor, and Eugene Propper. *Labyrinth.* New York: Penguin, 1982. Narrative of the assassination of Chilean diplomat Orlando Letelier, in Washington D.C., by agents of the Pinochet dictatorship.

Caviedes, César. *Elections in Chile: The Road to Redemocratization.* Boulder, CO: Lynne Rienner, 1991. Analysis of the elections that brought the Concertación to power.

Caviedes, César. *The Southern Cone: Realities of the Authoritarian State.* Totowa, NJ: Rowman & Allanheld, 1984. Comparative study of the military dictatorships of Chile, Argentina, Uruguay, and Brazil.

Constable, Pamela, and Arturo Valenzuela. *A Nation of Enemies: Chile under Pinochet.* New York and London: W. W. Norton, 1991. A journalistic and academic account of the Pinochet coup, its aftermath, and the transition to democracy.

Dinges, John, and Saul Landau. *Assassination on Embassy Row.* New York: Pantheon, 1980. Journalistic account of the assassination of Orlando Letelier.

Hauser, Thomas. *The Execution of Charles Horman: An American Sacrifice.* 1978. Account of the death of a young U.S. journalist during the Pinochet coup, which implicated U.S. authorities and served as the basis of Costa-Gavras' film *Missing.*

Literature

Allende, Isabel. *The House of the Spirits.* New York: Knopf, 1985. Set amidst the tumult of the agrarian reform of the author's uncle's presidency, this novel is perhaps her most political.

Allende, Isabel. *Of Love and Shadows.* New York: Knopf, 1987. Combining graphic and magical realism, Allende's second novel follows the transformation of a privileged but sheltered young woman who finally grasps the grisly truth behind the Pinochet dictatorship.

Allende, Isabel. *Daughter of Fortune.* New York: Harper Collins, 1999. Set in North and South America, Allende's 19th-century romance fashions a vivid portrait of early Valparaíso, illuminates the underappreciated role of Chileans in the California Gold Rush, and even offers an imaginative speculation on the Joaquín Murieta legend.

Blest Gana, Alberto. *Martín Rivas.* New York: Oxford University Press, 2000. Originally published in 1863, now in English translation, this early Chilean novel tells the story of a young man from the Norte Grande as he tries to make his way into Santiago society.

Donoso, José. *Curfew.* New York: Weidenfeld and Nicholson, 1988. An end-of-the-dictatorship novel from the viewpoint of a returned exile folk musician.

Dorfman, Ariel. *Hard Rain.* London: Readers International, 1990. A novel set in Allende's Chile and published shortly thereafter in Spanish but not in English until many years later.

Fuguet, Alberto. *Bad Vibes.* New York: St. Martin's Press, 1997. Tale of apolitical alienation in

Pinochet's Chile by an author whose motto is "I am not a magical realist."

Oña, Pedro de. *Arauco Tamed.* Albuquerque: University of New Mexico Press, 1948. Charles Maxwell Lancaster and Paul Thomas Manchester, eds. Epic of the 16th-century Araucanian wars by a criollo (Chilean-born Spaniard) poet.

Skármeta, Antonio. *Burning Patience.* New York: Pantheon, 1987. The fictional account of Pablo Neruda's counsel to a childishly infatuated postman, later transformed into a Oscar-winning film.

Environment and Natural History

Araya M., Braulio. *Guía de Campo de las Aves de Chile,* 4th ed. Santiago: Editorial Universitaria, 1991. A Spanish-language field guide, with English and Linnean nomenclature as well, to birds throughout the country.

Arroyo, Mary Kalin, ed. "Ecology & Biology of Mediterranean Ecosystems in Chile, California and Australia," *Ecological Studies* No. 108. New York: Springer Verlag, 1995. A comparison of Mediterranean dry-summer, wet-winter climates on three different continents.

Bahre, Conrad. *Destruction of the Natural Vegetation of North Central Chile.* Berkeley: University of California Press, 1978. A workmanlike analysis of the human impact on the environment of the Norte Chico, including mining and agriculture, but its argument is weakened by inattention to socioeconomic factors such as lopsided land tenure.

Couve Montané, Enrique, and Claudio Vidal-Ojeda. *Aves del Canal Beagle/Birds of the Beagle Channel.* Punta Arenas: Fantástico Sur Birding, 2000. A bilingual field guide, with excellent photographs, of southernmost archipelagic Chile.

Rottmann, Jürgen. *Bosques de Chile/Chile's Woodlands.* Santiago: Unisys, 1988. Written by one of Chile's leading biologists and published with assistance from the World Wide Fund for Nature (WWF), this bilingual book, embellished with appropriate photographs, provides an outstanding orientation to Chile's forests and their fauna.

Wilcox, Ken. *Chile's Native Forests.* Redway, CA: Ancient Forests International, 1996. Comprehensive survey of Chilean forests and forestry from an activist, conservation-oriented perspective.

Internet Resources

The following list does not include private tour operators, which are covered in the On the Road chapter.

Websites

AmeriSpan
www.amerispan.com
Information on language instruction throughout the Americas, including Chile

Australnet.com
www.australnet.cl
Spanish-language site with good information about outdoor activities throughout the country

Automóvil Club de Chile
www.acchi.cl
Motorist organization that also provides services to members of overseas affiliates

Auto Museum Moncopulli
www.moncopulli.cl
Private automotive museum east of Osorno

Carnegie Observatories Home Page
www.ociw.edu
Home page for Las Campanas observatory, north of La Serena; in English

Centers for Disease Control
www.cdc.gov
U.S. government page with travel health advisories

Cerro Tololo International Observatory
ctios2.ctio.noao.edu/ctio.html
Home page for Cerro Tololo observatory, east of La Serena; in English

Chile Information Project
www.chip.cl
English-language site with daily Chilean news summaries and a useful travel section

Codelco
www.codelcochile.cl
Home page for the state-run copper industry, the most important single exchange earner in the country, in Spanish and English; includes information on tourist visits to Chuquicamata and the historic company town at Sewell

Comité de la Defensa de Flora y Fauna
www.codeff.cl
Well-established group oriented toward wildlife and habitat conservation

Conaf-Tarapacá
www.chilesat.net/conaf-tarapaca
Information on national parks and other protected areas in Region I

Corporación de Promoción Turística
www.visitchile.org
Public-private Chilean site in English and Spanish.

Corporación Nacional de Desarrollo Indígena
www.conadi.cl
Official government page for indigenous affairs, in Spanish only

Corporación Nacional Forestal
www.conaf.cl
Official page of quasi-governmental agency in charge of Chile's national parks and other protected areas; in Spanish only

Currency Converter
www.oanda.com
Present and historic exchange rate
information

Defensores del Bosque Chileno
www.elbosquechileno.cl
Nongovernmental organization devoted to
native forest conservation

Department of Health
www.doh.gov.uk/traveladvice/index.htm
British government agency with country-
by-country health advice

Department of State
www.travel.state.gov
Travel information and advisories from
U.S. government; its warnings are often
exaggerated

Easter Island Home Page
www.netaxs.com/~trance/rapanui.html
Thorough, reliable information on Chile's
remote Pacific landmark, with large
collection of useful links

Eco Travels in Latin America
www.planeta.com
Ron Mader's website is a comprehensive
resource on environmentally conscious
travel throughout the Americas, both
thematically and by country; in English
and Spanish

El Mercurio
www.emol.com
Santiago's traditional daily newspaper, with
conservative editorial line; in Spanish

Escalada en Chile
www.escalando.cl
Site devoted to hiking and rock- and ice
climbing in Chile; in Spanish and English

Estrategia
www.estrategia.cl
Santiago financial daily; in Spanish

European Southern Observatory
www.eso.org
Site for astronomical observatories at La
Silla, north of La Serena, and Paranal,
south of Antofagasta; in English

Federación de Andinismo
www.feach.cl
Site devoted to climbing, including
bureaucratic obstacles in sensitive border
areas

Fundación Terram
www.terram.cl
Nonprofit promoting sustainable
development in Chile

Fundación Valparaíso
www.fundvalpo.org
Site of nonprofit organization supporting
preservation and restoration of Valparaíso's
architectural and cultural heritage

FutaFriends
www.futafriends.org
Nonprofit organization dedicated to
preserving the Río Futaleufú

Gay Chile
www.gaychile.com
Portal oriented toward gays, lesbians, and
bisexuals, including visitors to Chile; in
Spanish, English, German, and French

Hostelling International Santiago
www.hostelling.cl
Chilean affiliate of Hostelling
International, with information on hostels
and activities throughout the country

Instituto Geográfico Militar
www.igm.cl
Chilean government agency in charge of mapping, map sales, and general geographic information

La Brújula
www.brujula.cl
Index of Chilean websites

La Tercera
www.latercera.cl
Best of the Chilean tabloid dailies, serious but with a rigidly conservative editorial policy

Latin American Network Information Center—LANIC
lanic.utexas.edu
Organized by the University of Texas, this site has a huge collection of quality links to Chile and other Latin American countries

Lota Sorprendente
www.lotasorprendente.cl
Literally what it says, a guide to interesting things in a little-appreciated town south of Concepción

Museo Arqueológico San Miguel de Azapa
www.uta.cl/masma/index.html
Outstanding page from one of Chile's best museums

Museo de Bellas Artes
www.mnba.cl
Santiago's traditional fine arts museum

Museums Chile
www.elsas.demon.nl/chili.htm
Portal to a number of Chilean museums, both state-run and private

Observatorio Comunal Cerro Mamalluca
www.angelfire.com/wy/obsermamalluca
Site for teaching and tourist observatory near Vicuña, open for night-sky tours; in

English and Spanish

Parque Nacional La Campana
www.parquelacampana.cl
Exceptional site on small but interesting national park northeast of Viña del Mar; in Spanish and serviceable English

Parque Natural Pumalín
www.parquepumalin.cl
Exceptional site, in Spanish and English, for what may be the most audacious (and controversial) private conservation initiative ever

ProChile
www.chileinfo.com/ind_travel.html
Official government site with travel and tourism information

Publiguías
www.amarillas.cl
Chilean yellow pages

Renace
www.renace.cl
Alliance of Chilean environmental organizations

Ruta del Vino del Maule
www.chilewineroute.com
Alliance of wineries in the vicinity of Talca, open to tours and tasting

Sernatur
www.sernatur.cl
Chilean government tourism bureau; in Spanish and English

Viña Concha y Toro
www.conchaytoro.com
Important winery at Pirque, on the southeastern outskirts of Santiago; open for tours and tasting

Viña Cousiño Macul
www.cousinomacul.cl
> Classic winery within Santiago's city limits, open for tours and tasting

Viña Santa Rita
www.santarita.com
> Traditional winery on Santiago's southern outskirts, open for tours and tasting; also has accommodations

Usenet Discussion Groups
Soc.culture.chile
No-holds-barred discussion group that touches on many issues besides travel

Rec.travel.latin-america
Regional discussion group dealing with all Latin American countries, with a steady amount of postings on Chile

Index

National Parks and Reserves

Skiing

Acknowledgments

As does my previous *Moon Handbooks: Guatemala,* this book owes its existence in its present form to numerous individuals in North America, Chile, Argentina, and elsewhere. Once again, the highest praise to Bill Newlin and his Emeryville staff at Avalon Travel Publishing, for continuing to offer author-friendly contracts to writers even as other guidebook publishers are ruthlessly eliminating them.

In the course of more than 20 years' experience in Chile, nearly half that as a guidebook writer, I owe enormous unpayable debts to friends, acquaintances, and officials throughout the country. My apologies to anyone I may have overlooked or perhaps omitted because of an errant keystroke.

In Santiago and vicinity, thanks to Claudia Aguirre and Paulina Galeno of Patagonia Connection; customs broker Juan Alarcón Rojas for getting the doors back to Oakland; Antonio Alfonso of Holding Brokers Chile, for his efficiency in handling a complex insurance claim; Steve Anderson of the Chile Information Project; Harold Beckett of the *Guía Aérea Oficial;* Alejandra Belart of Lassa; María Fernanda Daza and Carmen Gloria Pizarro B. of the Municipalidad de Santiago; Pablo Fernández and Andrés Pivcevic of Hostelling International; Yerko Ivelic, Javier López, and the rest of the staff at Santiago's Cascada Expediciones; Mark Killinger, formerly of the Chile Information Project; Víctor Maldonado and Marisa Blásquez; Martín Montalva; Eduardo Núñez of Conaf for once again smoothing access to national parks and other reserves; Juan Luis Matassi Alonso of JLM Cartografía; Pato Ovando and Marializ Maldonado; Diana Page, formerly of the U.S. Embassy; José Manuel Rogers, formerly of the Corporación de Promoción Turística; Helen Kouyoumdjian and Joanne Ellis of the Corporación de Promoción Turística; Hernán, Carmen, Marcela, and Paula Torres; Ian Thomson, for information on railroad history; and Marco Vergara of Cruceros Australis and Navimag.

Elsewhere in the Heartland, my appreciation to Veronique Arancet Rodríguez of the Municipalidad de Valparaíso; Paola Lara of Sernatur, Viña del Mar; Todd Temkin of the Fundación Valparaíso; Tirzo González Castro of Sernatur, Rancagua; Andrea Ilabaca of Santa Cruz; Verónica Morgado Saldivia of Sernatur, Talca; Doris Sandoval Gutiérrez of Sernatur, Chillán; John and Louise Jackson of Fundo Curanilahue; and Nelson Oyarzo Barrientos of Sernatur, Concepción.

In the Norte Grande, thanks to José Gustavo Cuevas Ramírez of Sernatur, Arica; Michel Cinquin and Charlie Dekeyser of Arica; Barbara Knapton of Putre; Iván Barbaric Sciaraffia and Mario Marroquín Silva of Sernatur, Iquique; Hugo Cerda of Desértica, Antofagasta; Sergio Cortez G. of Civet Adventure, Iquique; Sergio Saavedra R. of Sernatur, Antofagasta; Alejandro Santoro of Conaf, Antofagasta; Carlos Reygadas of Calama; and Martín Beeris of Cosmo Andino, San Pedro de Atacama.

In the Norte Chico, thanks to Fernando Bascuñán of Conaf, Copiapó; Arlette Levy Arensburg and Leila Manterola of Sernatur, Copiapó; Luis Canales Leyton, now of Copiapó but formerly of Puerto Varas; Rodrigo Carvajal Robles of Pingüi Tour, Chañaral; Alicia Díaz Fraile of Sernatur, La Serena; Lucas and María Eugenia Pintz of La Serena; Rodrigo Sugg Pierry of La Serena; David González of La Serena and Cerro Tololo International Observatory; Pablo Dodds of Conaf, La Serena; and Clark Stede and Manuela Paradiser of Hacienda Los Andes, Hurtado.

In the Sur Chico, my regards to Javier Ibar Muñoz of the Municipalidad de Angol; Carolina Morgado and Gerardo Niklitschek of Alsur Expediciones, Puerto Varas; Miriam Elisa Montecinos Latorre of Sernatur, Temuco; Matthias Holzmann and Paulina Wagemann of Aqua Motion, Puerto Varas; Raúl Mauricio Manzano Molina and Richard Villegas G. of Sernatur, Puerto Montt; Moyra Holzapfel of Puerto Montt; Rony Pollak of Pucón; Béat and Claudia Zbinden of Villarrica; Patricio Yáñez Strange of Sernatur, Valdivia; Adrian Turner of Puerto Montt; Armin and Nadia Dübendorfer of Puerto Octay; Britt Lewis of Ancud, Chiloé; and Carl Grady of Chonchi, Chiloé.

In Chilean Patagonia, thanks to Nicholas La Penna of Chaitén; Chris Spelius of Expediciones Chile, Futaleufú; Patricio Guzmán, Carlos Martínez Villegas, and Peter Cado Avenali of Coyhaique; Rolando Toloza of the Ministerio de Obras Públicas, Coyhaique; Gabriela Neira Morales of Sernatur, Coyhaique; Lisette Muñoz of Turismo Yekchal; Carlos Lezama Nagel of Conaf, Coyhaique; Jonathan Leidich and Tim Langford of Puerto Bertrand; Julio Arenas Coloma and Andrea Lagunas Flores of Sernatur, Punta Arenas; British Consul John Rees Jones of Punta Arenas; Ivette Martínez of Turismo Cordillera Darwin, Punta Arenas; Miguel Angel Muñoz of Sernatur, Puerto Natales; Alfonso López Rosas and Marcelo Moreno of Path@gone, Puerto Natales; Edmundo Martínez G. of Puerto Natales; Werner and Cecilia Ruf-Chaura, of Casa Cecilia, Puerto Natales; Hernán Jofré of Concepto Indigo, Puerto Natales; Juan Santana M. of Porvenir; and Wolf Kloss of Puerto Williams.

On Juan Fernández, special mention to Juanita Díaz and Javier Gana. In Hanga Roa, Rapa Nui, thanks to Francisco Edmunds of Sernatur, Ramón Edmunds, Martín Hereveri, and especially Conny Martin.

In Argentine Patagonia and Tierra del Fuego, thanks to Julio César Lovece, Barrie O'Byrne, and Natalie Prosser de Goodall of Ushuaia, Tierra del Fuego; Mariano Besio of El Calafate; Rubén Vásquez of El Chaltén, Santa Cruz; and Alexis Simunovic and Mario Feldman of El Calafate.

Stateside, thanks to Scott Stine of California State University, Hayward, for again sharing the results of his research on the Moreno Glacier; Georgia Lee of Los Osos, CA, for once again helping out on Rapa Nui; Chilean consul Fernando Varela of San Francisco; Marisol Cabello of the Chilean Embassy in Washington, DC; Alberto Cortés and Rosana Albornoz of Lan-Chile, Miami; David Owen of PowderQuest Tours, Richmond, VA, for ski information; and Douglas Wolff of Seattle.

James Smith of Oakland made a great traveling companion in several trips, his reward for serving as ad honorem computer consultant in Oakland.

Thanks also to those whom I encountered along the way and who sent me information that has been incorporated into this book. They include Trajan Martin, Pascale Gelly of Paris (wonderful company), Ofer Matan, and Joyce Perrin of Black River Falls, WI.

And finally, thanks to my wife, María Laura Massolo; my daughter, Clio Bernhardson-Massolo; my Alaskan malamute, Gardel, who slept at my feet through most of the process of writing this up, while patiently awaiting his next walk around the neighborhood; and Gardel's adopted Akita brother, Sandro, who dozed through most of the last few months.

U.S.~Metric Conversion

1 inch	=	2.54 centimeters (cm)
1 foot	=	.304 meters (m)
1 yard	=	0.914 meters
1 mile	=	1.6093 kilometers (km)
1 km	=	.6214 miles
1 fathom	=	1.8288 m
1 chain	=	20.1168 m
1 furlong	=	201.168 m
1 acre	=	.4047 hectares
1 sq km	=	100 hectares
1 sq mile	=	2.59 square km
1 ounce	=	28.35 grams
1 pound	=	.4536 kilograms
1 short ton	=	.90718 metric ton
1 short ton	=	2000 pounds
1 long ton	=	1.016 metric tons
1 long ton	=	2240 pounds
1 metric ton	=	1000 kilograms
1 quart	=	.94635 liters
1 US gallon	=	3.7854 liters
1 Imperial gallon	=	4.5459 liters
1 nautical mile	=	1.852 km

To compute celsius temperatures, subtract 32 from Fahrenheit and divide by 1.8. To go the other way, multiply celsius by 1.8 and add 32.

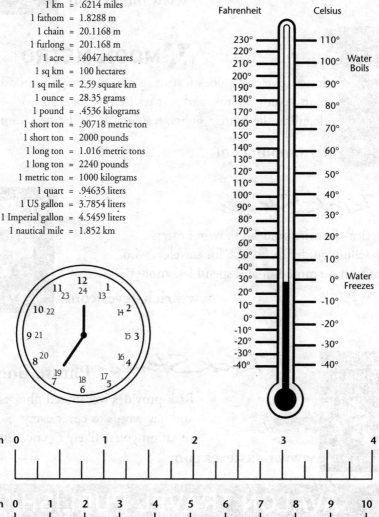

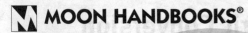

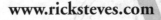